THE AMERICAN BAR ASSOCIATION

FAMILY LEGAL GUIDE

THIRD EDITION

THE AMERICAN BAR ASSOCIATION

FAMILY LEGAL GUIDE

THIRD EDITION

Everything your family needs to know about the **law** and **real estate, consumer protection, health care, retirement, home ownership, wills & estates, computers,** and much more.

RANDOM HOUSE
REFERENCE

The American Bar Association Family Legal Guide, 3rd Edition

Copyright © 2004, 1994, 1990 by the American Bar Association

All rights reserved under International and Pan-American Copyright Conventions. No part of this book may be reproduced in any form or by any means, electronic or mechanical, including photocopying, without the written permission of the publisher. All inquiries should be addressed to Random House Reference, Random House, Inc., 1745 Broadway, New York, NY, 10019. Published in the United States by Random House, Inc., New York and simultaneously in Canada by Random House of Canada Limited.

Random House is a registered trademark of Random House, Inc.

The first edition of this work was published by Times Books in 1990.
This book is available for special discounts for bulk purchases for sales promotions or premiums. Special editions, including personalized covers, excerpts of existing books, and corporate imprints, can be created in large quantities for special needs. For more information, write to Specail Markets/ Premium Sales, 1745 Broadway, MD 6-2, New York, NY, 10019 or e-mail specialmarkets@randomhouse.com.

Please address inquiries about electronic licensing of reference products, for use on a network or in software or on CD-ROM, to the Subsidiary Rights Department, Random House Reference, fax 212-572-6003.

Visit the Random House Reference Web site: *www.randomwords.com*.

Typeset and printed in the United States of America.

Library of Congress Cataloging-in-Publication Data

American Bar Association family legal guide.—3rd ed.
    p. cm.
  Rev. ed. of: Family legal guide. Rev. ed. c1994
  Includes index.
  ISBN 0-609-61042-2 (alk. paper)   —ISBN 0-375-72077-4 (trade pbk. : alk. paper)
   1. Law—United States—Popular works. 2. Law—United States—Miscellanea. I. Title: Family legal guide. II. American Bar Association. III. Family legal guide.

KF387.Y655 2004   2004041855
349.73—dc22

Third Edition
0 9 8 7 6 5 4 3 2 1

CONTENTS

CHAPTER EIGHT
Consumer Bankruptcy

CHAPTER NINE
Contracts and Consumer Law

CHAPTER TEN
Computer Law

CHAPTER ELEVEN
Automobiles

CHAPTER TWELVE

Law and the Workplace

CHAPTER THIRTEEN

Forming and Operating a Small Business

CHAPTER FOURTEEN

Personal Injury

CHAPTER FIFTEEN

Criminal Justice

CHAPTER SIXTEEN

The Rights of Older Americans

FOREWORD

Dennis Archer, *President, American Bar Association*

One out of five Americans faces a significant legal issue each year. Studies show that the legal matters that most affect us are the very stuff of everyday life. The major legal areas, in order of the frequency with which they occur, are:

- Home purchases, home rentals, and property disputes;
- Divorce, including property settlements, child custody, and child support;
- Estate planning, preparation of a will or trust, and settlement of the estate of someone who has died;
- Personal injury, encompassing damages to people or property through automobile collisions and other mishaps;
- Traffic violations.

Other fairly common legal matters that Americans face include insurance claims, credit, debt collection and bankruptcy, computer law, health law, and law in the workplace.

So the chances are very strong that you or someone in your family needs or will need practical, easy-to-understand information about these areas of everyday law.

This book covers all these topics—and more. It can be your "first response" to a very wide range of legal situations. It can give you options to consider as you try to find the best way to protect your assets or solve a problem.

Legal problems are all different—some require immediate action so that you can protect your rights, but others might be solved through negotiation, mediation, or some other means. Many legal problems can be avoided altogether by good planning.

It's important that you know and understand your rights and options. It's important that you understand the language of the law and know and respect the rights of others.

That's why public education and public service are two of the most important goals of the American Bar Association. The American Bar Association is the nation's premier source of legal information. With more than 400,000 members, representing every specialty and every type of legal practice, the ABA is uniquely able to deliver accurate, up-to-date, unbiased legal information to its members, to the media, and to the general public. The ABA website—*www.abanet.org*—is an unrivaled database in the legal field.

On this website, the ABA provides everything from suggestions on how to find and work with a lawyer to help in finding programs for persons unable to afford legal help. It also offers information for consumers on such practical topics as making a will and buying online. One part of the site—www.abalawinfo.org—gives you help in determining how the law affects such vital areas as your job, your home, and your finances. Its section on the family, for example, covers basic FAQs of family law and topics such as women and the law, children, the elderly, family health, divorce, and domestic violence. The ABA site also will help you find key information in *your* community.

This book provides you with the benefit of the ABA's network of hundreds of thousands of lawyers. It was written with the aid of ABA members from all over the country who are experts in the areas of law covered by this book, including judges and professors of law as well as lawyers who practice in these areas and cope with these issues every day. The ABA's Standing Committee on Public Education and its staff added their professional expertise.

Because of all of the lawyers who worked on this book, you can be sure that the information it includes is useful, helpful, unbiased, written in a reader-friendly style that you can understand easily, and reflective of a national picture, since ABA members practice in all jurisdictions.

Finally, we hope that this book also gives you a broader understanding of the role of law in our society. The law isn't just for lawyers, but for all Americans. Not only is the law the cornerstone of our democracy, it is also the glue that holds us together as a society. The county courthouse is a good symbol of our belief in the rule of law, because it is the place where anyone, regardless of income or social standing, can seek justice in an impartial court, under rules that assure fairness.

The law is the best way that we have devised to resolve disputes by reason instead of force. It gives us our best chance to assure justice. Preserving the rule of law, and helping people understand and appreciate the law, are central to the mission of the American Bar Association.

The ABA is the largest voluntary association in the world. Besides its commitment to public education, the ABA provides programs to assist lawyers and judges in their work, and initiatives to improve the legal system for the public, including promoting fast, affordable alternatives to lawsuits, such as mediation, arbitration, conciliation, and small-claims courts. Through ABA support for lawyer referral programs and pro bono services (where lawyers donate their time), people have been able to find the best lawyer for their particular case and have received quality legal help within their budgets.

Dennis Archer is President of the American Bar Association. He is a former justice of the Michigan Supreme Court and more recently served as mayor of Detroit.

INTRODUCTION

Alan S. Kopit, *Chair, ABA Standing Committee on Public Education*

How do you get your information? If you're like a lot of us, you often cruise the Web, flitting happily from website to website. Here's a link that looks interesting . . . that leads to this cool website . . . that takes you to one that looks even better. It's fast and fun, but does it give you the best insights and guidance? Maybe yes, maybe no. One problem with the Internet is that you don't always know who's behind a site, or when the information was updated, or if it was accurate in the first place. The Internet is a great source of information—and, unhappily, of misinformation as well.

In the work I do on television as a legal affairs commentator, I'm impressed by how much Americans want to know about the law, and by the sophistication and understanding behind many of their questions. But I'm constantly amazed at how much misunderstanding there is—about matters that are crucial to every family's well-being. That's why this book is so important. It's an authoritative reference that you can count on. It has the resources of the nation's premier legal organization—the American Bar Association—solidly behind it. The authors are experts in their fields. They range from law professors to practicing lawyers, from staff of not-for-profit organizations specializing in a particular legal area to ABA staff members and legal journalists who have a particular talent for conveying information about the law in a style that readers can easily understand.

Revising an earlier edition of the book, the authors have added hundreds of brand-new entries, and have reviewed every entry, updating them so that you'll have the latest and best information. The authors worked under the guidance of the ABA's Standing Committee on Public Education. This group, which I have the honor to chair, contains experts on reaching out to the public and explaining the law in reader-friendly

ways. Our members and our staff include teachers, university educators, law professors, writers and journalists, and others with special expertise in the challenges and opportunities of conveying clear and accurate information about the law to nonlawyers. For more than thirty years, the committee has been a national leader in helping students and the public learn about our rights and responsibilities under the law. Finally, every word in the book has been reviewed by ABA members from all over the country, who have collaborated to ensure that it contains the most accurate, up-to-date information possible. Practicing lawyers know the kinds of legal issues and problems people have—people like you. With their help, we've fashioned a book that answers the questions you're apt to have, in language you can understand.

How This Book Can Help You

This book covers the law that affects all of us every day. In nearly four thousand easy-to-understand question-and-answer entries, it will help you

- buy or rent a home;
- get a mortgage, refinance your home, or try to get the best deal possible on a credit card;
- order products online, or over the phone, or from a catalog;
- buy or lease a car;
- work at your job;
- start and operate your business;
- understand your rights to Social Security, Medicare, Medicaid, and other benefits; and
- devise an estate plan that will provide for your family, protect you if you become incapacitated, and save you as much as possible in taxes.

In this book, we provide guidance that will help you decide if you need a lawyer and, if so, how to find one that's right for you, and right for your budget. We give you tips on what to ask in your first interview, what various fee structures mean, and what your rights are as a legal client. And we give you insights into how the legal system works, how a case moves through the system, and how you can protect your rights at every stage. We also look at some specialized situations you might find yourself in, such as the need to

- recover from debt, and
- protect your rights if you're involved in an accident.

No one wants to be in such financial trouble that bankruptcy is a possibility, but this book helps by explaining what your options are, how you might get out of debt trouble without bankruptcy, how to find a lawyer specializing in bankruptcy if you decide to go that route, and what steps you need to take if you file for bankruptcy. We give you special tips on how you can preserve as many of your assets as you can, and how you might be able to save your home. We also cover personal injury law. Of course, you hope you'll never be injured and forced to seek damages, but in this book we tell you what your rights are and how to enforce them. We give you tips on finding a personal injury lawyer and provide insights into how the system works and what options you'll have. We also look at personal injury from the other side—how you can limit your personal injury liability as a driver and homeowner.

Two New Chapters: Computer Law and Health-Care Law

In the years since the first edition of the book, the world has changed greatly. Not only does this revised edition incorporate new material into every chapter included in the first edition, it adds two new chapters to give you help in areas of life that are increasingly important. Chapter 17 covers heath-care law. Health care accounts for a huge

and growing share of the national economy—and of most people's budgets. We give you help on dealing with health insurance claims and HMOs, and explain your rights to medical coverage. We explain how the law affects almost every aspect of the doctor-patient relationship, from rules guaranteeing your privacy to your rights to informed consent. And we look at how the law is dealing with such new developments as reproductive technology.

Computer law is covered in chapter 10. Ten years ago, the Internet was just getting started, and personal computers were in just a tiny fraction of the nation's homes. Now more than half the country is wired—and the law is struggling to catch up. We look at such evolving issues as online purchases and doing business online, computers on the job (how much privacy do you think *you* have?), Internet issues like spam and viruses, law enforcement and the computer, and how to protect your kids in their online activities.

Written with You in Mind

In writing this book, we worked overtime to take the mystery out of the law. We begin each section with anecdotes drawn from real life, then follow with a question-and-answer format that enables us to explain the law and your options in terms that you can easily understand. The answers aren't abstract—they try to point out how the law affects us every day, and what practical steps we can take to assure that our rights are protected. You won't find legal jargon or technicalities here—just concise, straightforward discussions of your options under the law. Within chapters, brief special sidebars alert you to important points.

- Sidebars with this icon ▶ give you practical tips that could be of benefit to you.
- Sidebars with this icon ⓘ provide key additional information.
- Sidebars with this icon ⚠ give you warnings about potential pitfalls that you can navigate with the right information and help.

- Sidebars with this icon ▤ provide clear, plain-English definitions of legal terms.

At the end of each section, a feature entitled "The World at Your Fingertips" advises you where to go for free or inexpensive materials to find more information on a topic. Most of these free resources are on the Internet—but you can be sure of them because our experts have vouched for them. Another concluding feature of each section, entitled "Remember This," highlights the most important points that section has covered. At a glance, you'll know the key information.

How to Use This Book

As the table of contents shows, each chapter covers how the law affects a major segment of everyday life. Family law, for example, covers marriage (what are the requirements for getting married, who owns what, etc.) and separation and divorce (who gets what, what support might be due, etc.). The chapter also covers how the law affects children, from adoption to the obligations of parents and child custody and support. If some material relates to information in other chapters (for example, how you hold title to your home might af-fect how it is divided at divorce), we briefly discuss the matter and refer you to other chapters for more on the topic. The book's index also will help you to research a topic by listing all of the pages where it is discussed. Frequent summaries of the important points will help you see how the material might affect your life, and frequent references to free or inexpensive sources of further information will help you delve into a matter in more detail. The information included in this book is an excellent introduction to the law in each area. It is not necessarily the final word. In some instances, you may want to pursue legal action. In those cases, you'll want to consult with a lawyer, and this book tells you how to find one through your local bar association or lawyer referral system. Armed with the knowledge and insights provided in this book, you may be confident that the legal decisions you make will be in your best interests.

Alan S. Kopit is a legal affairs commentator who has appeared on national television for more than fifteen years. He is chair of the ABA's Standing Committee on Public Education and is an attorney in private practice with the firm of Hahn Loeser & Parks, LLP, in Cleveland, Ohio.

THE AMERICAN BAR ASSOCIATION

FAMILY LEGAL GUIDE

THIRD EDITION

When and How to Use a Lawyer

The law affects almost everything you do—from making a purchase, to driving a car, to interacting with others.

There are many situations that you can handle on your own, without the assistance of a lawyer. However, when circumstances and laws are complex—for example, if you're injured, or if you might lose valuable rights—you may need a lawyer's guidance.

When do you need a lawyer? How can you find one? How do you work with one? The purpose of this chapter is to help you find the answers to these and other critical questions.

LAWYER BASICS

Sometimes it seems that lawyers are everywhere these days—in TV dramas, actual televised cases, and all sections of the newspaper, including the sports pages. But how does someone become a lawyer, and what do they do in cases that don't make news?

This section will address these questions.

What Is a Lawyer?

Q. What exactly is a lawyer?

A. A **lawyer** (also called an **attorney**, a **counsel**, or a **counselor**) is a licensed professional who advises and represents others in legal matters. Today's lawyer can be young or old, male or female. Nearly one-third of all lawyers are under thirty-five years old. Almost half of the law students today are women, and women may ultimately be as numerous in the profession as men.

Q. I come from another country, and I need to hire a lawyer. Are notary publics lawyers?

A. A "notary public," an "accountant," or a "certified public accountant" is not necessarily a lawyer. Do not assume that titles such as notary public mean the same thing as similar words in your own language. In some other countries, a lawyer is called a "barrister" or a "solicitor."

Q. What are a lawyer's main duties?

A. A lawyer has two main duties: to uphold the law and to protect a client's rights. To carry out these duties, a lawyer must know the law and be a good communicator.

Q. Is most of a lawyer's time spent arguing cases in court?

A. No. A lawyer normally spends more time in an office than in a courtroom. The practice of law most often involves researching legal developments, investigating facts, writing and preparing legal documents, giving advice, and settling disputes. Laws change constantly: new law is enacted and existing law is amended or repealed. In addition, decisions in court cases regularly alter what the law currently means, as judges interpret and apply the U.S. Constitution, state constitutions, federal or state statutes, and federal, state, and local codes and regulations. For these reasons, a lawyer must devote time to keeping current on the changes in the law, and how those changes affect his or her practice.

ⓘ UNDERSTANDING LEGAL DOCUMENTS

Many people wish that legal documents could be in language that they understand. Lawyers and others trained in the law often use legal terms as shorthand to express complicated ideas or principles. These words and phrases, many rooted in Latin, are often jokingly referred to as a foreign language—**legalese**. Although some legalese may be necessary in order to communicate certain ideas precisely, a document that is understood by very few of its readers is just plain poor communication.

Since 1978, federal regulations are required to be "written in plain English and understandable to those who must comply" with them. Many states also have laws requiring that insurance policies, leases, and consumer contracts be written in plain English. Of particular importance is the trend in law schools to discourage the use of legalese and to encourage the use of plain, comprehensible English.

Q. What are the professional requirements for becoming a lawyer?

A. To understand how laws and the legal system work together, lawyers must go through special schooling. Each state has enacted standards that must be met before a person is licensed to practice law there. Before being allowed to practice law in most states, a person must:

- Have a bachelor's degree or its equivalent.
- Complete three years at an ABA-accredited law school.
- Pass a state bar examination, which usually lasts for two or three days. The exam tests knowledge in selected areas of law and in professional ethics and responsibility.
- Pass a character and fitness review. Each applicant for a law license must be approved by a committee that investigates his or her character and background.
- Take an oath swearing to uphold the laws and the state and federal constitutions.
- Receive a license from the highest court in the state, usually the state supreme court. Some states have additional requirements, such as an internship in a law office, before a license will be granted.

Q. Once licensed in one state, is a lawyer automatically allowed to practice law in all states?

A. No. To become licensed in more than one state, a lawyer must usually comply with each state's bar admission requirements. Some states, however, permit licensed out-of-state lawyers to practice law if they have done so in another state for several years and the new state's highest court approves them. Many states also have provisions for lawyers to participate in specific cases in states where they are not licensed. The lawyer in such a case is said to be appearing **pro hac vice**, which means "for this one particular occasion."

Q. If I have a legal problem, may I hire someone other than a lawyer?

A. In some specialized situations, such as bringing a complaint before a government agency (for example, a dispute over Social Security or Medicare benefits), nonlawyers or paralegals may be qualified to represent you. (**Paralegals** are nonlawyers who have received training that enables them to assist lawyers in a number of tasks; they typically cannot represent clients in court, but they can sometimes represent clients in proceedings at a government agency.) If you are in this situation, ask the government agency involved to let you know what types of legal representatives are acceptable.

WHEN DO YOU NEED A LAWYER?

Q. Does needing a lawyer's help always mean that I have a legal dispute with someone?

A. No. In fact, lawyers very often help clients in matters that have nothing to do with disputes or legal cases. For example, people might seek their lawyer's advice on legal aspects of starting a business or engaging in a partnership, when buying or selling a home, or for information and advice on tax matters or estate planning. Often, clients receive a regular legal checkup that, like a medical checkup, is designed to prevent problems or nip them in the bud.

Q. Do I need a lawyer's help whenever I'm faced with a situation involving the law?

A. Not necessarily. There are many matters you can deal with yourself, if you know how to go about it. For example, you can represent yourself in traffic or small-claims court, or engage in negotiations and enter into contracts on your own. But if you are not sure about the consequences of your actions or are uncertain about how to proceed, getting some quick legal advice from a lawyer could be very helpful in preventing problems down the road.

▶ GET HELP EARLY

Don't just ignore those invoices or letters threatening legal action. Legal problems won't just go away. When dealing with legal issues, an ounce of prevention is worth many dollars and anxious hours of cure. Contacting a lawyer only after a legal problem has escalated to crisis proportions can lead to unnecessary anxiety, and may make the problem more difficult and expensive to solve. Lawyers should be thought of as preventers of legal problems, not just solvers.

If you call a lawyer as a last resort, it may already be too late. A lawyer may not be able to protect you after you have lost your rights.

Q. I understand that going to a lawyer may be unnecessary under certain circumstances. Are there specific cases when I should see a lawyer?

A. Yes, there are matters best handled by a lawyer. While these matters are sometimes hard to recognize, nearly everyone agrees that you should talk with a lawyer about major life events or changes, which might include:

- being arrested for a crime;
- being served with legal papers in a civil lawsuit;
- being involved in a serious accident causing personal injury or property damage;
- a change in family status such as divorce, adoption, or death; and
- a change in financial status such as obtaining or losing valuable personal property or real estate, or filing for bankruptcy.

Help from Nonlawyers

Q. If I do not use a lawyer, who else can help me?

A. There are many ways to solve a grievance without resorting to lawyers. For example, if you have trouble with a product, read the warranty to see what rights you have. Notify the merchant and see if you can negotiate a satisfactory solution. If that doesn't work, contact the manufacturer directly. If *that* doesn't work, contacting the Better Business Bureau might stir the merchant or manufacturer to resolve your complaint.

ⓘ WHEN DO PEOPLE USE LAWYERS?

You might find it helpful to look at how the American public uses lawyers. According to a recent survey of 1,000 Americans by the legal website *FindLaw*, nearly 20 percent of us faced a legal issue within the last year. The top five legal issues involved:

- real estate (buying/selling, property disputes, landlord-tenant disputes)—21 percent
- family law (divorce, child custody, etc.)—17 percent
- estate planning (wills, trusts, settling of estates, etc.)—12 percent
- personal injury—11 percent
- traffic violations—8 percent

Other fairly common matters requiring a lawyer's help include insurance claims, bankruptcy, and being a complainant or defendant in a criminal proceeding.

⚠ TIME IS RUNNING OUT

Be aware that your right to start a legal action will not last forever. Every state has a time limit within which a lawsuit must be filed. The time limits vary for different types of cases. The logic behind such limits, called **statutes of limitations**, is that most lawsuits are more easily and more fairly resolved within a short time. It is important to act as soon as you suspect that you may have a valid legal claim.

If you believe a business has cheated you, help can be obtained from a consumer protection agency run by your city, county, state, or federal government. Many businesses, stores, and utility companies have their own departments to help resolve consumer complaints. Some communities have an **ombudsman,** a government official whose job is to to mediate and resolve minor landlord/tenant, consumer, or employment issues. Local television and radio stations may have programs to resolve consumer-related disputes.

Most states also have **dispute resolution centers.** These centers, which may be known as neighborhood justice centers or citizens' dispute settlement programs, specialize in helping people who have common problems and disputes. Their services are often available for a small fee, or even at no cost.

Q. Can counseling solve some problems?

A. Yes. Sometimes problems that seem to be "legal" may be solved or prevented by other means. Many groups offer guidance and counseling for personal problems arising in marriage, child rearing, and managing finances. Private counselors or members of the clergy also may provide such help.

Q. What is a small-claims court?

A. A **small-claims court** is a streamlined forum in which people can air their dispute and have a judge decide it promptly and fairly. Most states have procedures that allow people to represent themselves in small-claims court if the total amount of their claim is under a certain dollar amount—usually under $2,500. The cost is minimal, procedures are simple, and there is usually little delay. Keep small-claims courts in mind if your problem is not very complicated and your losses are relatively small. Chapter 2, "How the

ⓘ REPRESENTING YOURSELF IN A LEGAL MATTER

People without legal training may be able to handle some simple legal matters themselves—this is called proceeding **pro se** or **pro per**. Taking on a legal matter yourself is risky, because each step may involve tax or other consequences that you may not think about. Doing it yourself also requires a lot of time and energy to learn the proper procedures and law. Moreover, a degree of objectivity is needed in most legal situations, and it may be difficult for you to stay objective when closely involved in your own case. But sometimes people feel that they can't afford legal representation or they just want to do it themselves.

A number of local courts or nonprofit organizations provide guidance to people who want to handle legal matters pro se. Court staff in or near the courthouse operate most court-based pro se assistance services. They assist people in selecting and completing court forms, in understanding court procedures and in filing a case. There are also some websites that may help you. A good starting point is the ABA's legal services website at www.findlegalhelp.org.

Legal System Works," provides guidance on how to file and proceed with a small-claims lawsuit.

Q. A friend recommended that I try a local dispute resolution center. What does this offer?

A. For the right kind of case, these centers can be a quick, low-cost (or free) alternative to formal legal proceedings. These will also be discussed in the next chapter.

Q. Can the other party and I settle a dispute without lawyers?

A. Yes, though you might want a lawyer's help in putting the agreement in writing. Always keep your mind open to possible solutions and listen to the other person's side of the story. Remember that with or without the help of lawyers, most people resolve their legal disputes out of court.

Settlement of cases is discussed in more detail in chapter 2.

Types of Lawyers

Q. Do lawyers normally work alone, or do most of them work for companies or the government?

A. About two-thirds of all lawyers are in private practice; many others work for corporations or the government. Firms of various sizes employ lawyers in private practice. Almost half of the lawyers in private practice are sole practitioners who work without any partners. Others join with one or more lawyers in partnerships. As the table shows, about a quarter of lawyers are in partnerships that have ten lawyers or fewer.

Q. What are the different areas of law?

A. Most lawyers concentrate in one or a few specific areas, such as domestic relations, criminal law, personal injury, estate planning and administration, real estate, taxation, immigration, or intellectual property law (see chart on next page).

PRIVATE PRACTITIONERS

Total practitioners: 634,475
Population/practitioner ratio: 410 to 1
Practitioners by Practice Setting and Sex

	Males		Females		Total	
	No.	%	No.	%	No.	%
Solo	225,584	45.9	72,139	50.3	297,723	46.9
2 lawyer firm	30,369	6.2	5,557	3.9	35,926	5.7
3 lawyer firm	21,706	4.4	3,775	2.6	25,481	4.0
4 lawyer firm	15,731	3.2	3,239	2.3	18,970	3.0
5 lawyer firm	12,270	2.5	2,616	1.8	14,886	2.3
6 to 10 lawyer firm	37,720	7.7	9,242	6.4	46,962	7.4
11 to 20 lawyer firm	34,249	7.0	9,007	6.3	43,256	6.8
21 to 50 lawyer firm	35,522	7.2	10,431	7.3	45,953	7.2
51 to 100 lawyer firm	21,928	4.5	6,895	4.8	28,823	4.5
101 or more lawyer firm	55,860	11.4	20,633	14.4	76,493	12.1
Total	**490,939**	**100.0**	**143,534**	**100.0**	**634,474**	**100.0**

Source: *The Lawyer Statistical Report: The U.S. Legal Population in 1995* (Chicago: American Bar Foundation, 1999)

THE WORLD AT YOUR FINGERTIPS

There are many good sources of information about everyday law that will help you understand legal matters better and give you a sense of your options. Many groups such as bar associations and consumer groups offer free or inexpensive brochures on various aspects of everyday law. There are many good practical law websites, including:

- *The ABA's Division for Public Education (www.abanet.org/publiced);*
- *The ABA's Legal Services Division, which has published a Consumer's Guide to Legal Help on the Internet (www.findlegalhelp.org); and*
- *FindLaw's public information website, which provides information on many different areas of law (www.public.findlaw.com).*
- *These websites are not the only resources you can call on, however. You can find links to many legal aid and legal services sites providing legal information in each state at www.ptla.org/links.htm.*
- *You can find useful information on consumer issues at the website of the Federal Trade Commission at www.ftc.gov, and at the website of the Better Business Bureau (www.bbb.com).*

REMEMBER THIS

- *If you have a dispute, that doesn't automatically mean you need a lawyer—keep an open mind and be aware of all your options. If you're not sure, then seek legal advice.*
- *Having said that, if your dispute is serious, if someone has commenced legal action against you, or if you're injured, you should see a lawyer without delay. Getting*

AREAS OF LEGAL PRACTICE

Business Law Advising about starting a new business (corporation, partnership, etc.), general corporate matters, business taxation, and mergers and acquisitions

Criminal Law Defending or prosecuting those accused of committing crimes

Domestic Relations Representing individuals in separation, annulment, divorce, and child custody and child support matters

Estate Planning Advising clients in drawing wills, probate, and estate planning

Immigration Representing parties in proceedings involving naturalization and citizenship

Intellectual Property Law Dealing with issues concerning trademarks, copyright regulations, and patents

Labor and Employment Law Advising and representing employers, unions, or employees on questions of union organizing, workplace safety, job protection, and compliance with government regulations

Personal Injury Representing clients injured intentionally or negligently, and those with workers' compensation claims

Real Estate Assisting clients in developing property; rezoning; and buying, selling, or renting homes or other property

Taxation Counseling business and individuals in local, state, and federal tax matters

advice early could save you time and money.

LOOKING FOR A LAWYER

You've thought about it carefully, you've spoken to friends, and you've decided that you need to contact a lawyer to discuss a legal issue. The big problem is—how to find one?

This section will give you some tips on what to look for when choosing a lawyer, and lead you through some questions you can ask a lawyer when you first meet. If you do your homework, you can hire the lawyer who has the experience and expertise to help you with your problem.

Q. What should I look for when trying to choose a lawyer?

A. The lawyer will be helping you solve your problems, so the first qualification is that you must feel comfortable enough to tell him or her, honestly and completely, all the facts necessary to resolve your problem. No one you listen to and nothing you read will be able to tell you which particular lawyer will be the best for you; you must judge that for yourself.

Q. Are there any practical considerations to keep in mind when choosing a lawyer?

A. Yes, the lawyer's area of expertise and prior experience are important. Eighteen states have specialization programs that certify lawyers as specialists in certain stated types of law. These states are Alabama, Arizona, California, Connecticut, Florida, Georgia, Idaho, Indiana, Louisiana, Maine, Minnesota, New Jersey, New Mexico, North Carolina, Pennsylvania, South Carolina, Tennessee, and Texas. To find out which types of law are certified in which states, access www.abanet.org/legalservices/specialization/source.html. In states without certification programs, you may want to ask about your lawyer's areas of specialization. You may also wish to ask about the type of cases your lawyer generally handles.

Other considerations are the convenience of the lawyer's office location, the amount of fees charged, and the length of time a case may take.

Q. Where should I start to look for a lawyer?

A. There are many ways to find a reliable lawyer. One of the best is a recommendation from a trusted friend, a relative, or a business associate. Be aware, however, that each legal case is different and that a lawyer who is right for someone else may not suit you or your legal problem.

Q. Are advertisements a good place to look for a lawyer?

A. In some ways, yes, ads are useful. However, always be careful about believing everything you read and hear—and nowhere is this truer than with advertisements. Still, newspaper, telephone directory, radio, and television ads, along with direct mail, can make you familiar with the names of lawyers who may be appropriate for your legal needs. Some ads also will help you determine a lawyer's area of expertise. Other ads will quote a fee or price range for handling a specific type of "simple" case. Keep in mind that your case may not have a simple solution. If a lawyer quotes a fee, be certain you know exactly what services and expenses the charge does and does not include.

Q. What about a local referral service?

A. Most communities have referral services to help people find lawyers. You might be able to find them under "Lawyer Referral Service" or something similar in your yellow pages. These services usually recommend a lawyer in the area to evaluate a situation. Several services offer help to groups with unique characteristics, such as the elderly, immigrants, victims of domestic violence, or persons with a disability.

Bar associations in most communities make referrals according to specific areas of law, helping you find a lawyer with the right experience and practice concentration. Many referral services also have competency requirements for lawyers who wish to have referrals in a particular area of law. You can find your local bar association in the phone book's white pages either under your community's name ("Centerville Bar Association") or under your county's name ("Cass County Bar Association"). You can also find your bar's website through your favorite search engine, or through the ABA Bar Services site (www.abanet.org/barserv/crawler.html).

Still, these services are not a surefire way to find the best lawyer or the right lawyer for you, since some services make referrals without concern for the lawyer's type or level of experience. You may want to seek out a lawyer referral service that participates in the American Bar Association-sponsored certification program, which uses a logo to identify lawyer referral programs that comply with certain quality standards developed by the ABA.

Q. My new job offers a prepaid legal services plan. What can I expect?

A. Legal services, like many other things, are often less expensive when bought in bulk. Employers, labor and credit unions, and other groups have formed "legal insurance" plans. These plans vary. Many cover most, if not all, of the cost of legal consultations, document preparation, and court representation in routine legal matters. Other programs cover only advice and consultation with a lawyer. Before joining a legal plan, make sure you are familiar with its coverage and know whether you will be required to make out-of-pocket contributions. These group plans follow the same pattern as group or cooperative medical insurance plans. Employers or unions set up a fund to pay the employees' legal fees, just as they contribute to group insurance plans to cover medical costs, with the employee sometimes contributing a small copayment. Legal group plans have become much more widespread in recent years. Some retail department stores and credit card companies even offer such plans to their customers.

Q. I want to hire a lawyer, but I do not have much money. Where can I find low-cost legal help?

A. Several legal assistance programs offer inexpensive or free legal services to those in need. Look in the yellow pages under topics such as "legal clinics," "legal aid," or "legal advice," or search online at www.lsc.gov/fundprog.htm for programs in all states funded by the Federal Legal Services Corporation. You can also access Pine Tree Legal Assistance (www.ptla.org/links.htm), which also includes programs that are not federally funded. Most legal aid programs have special guidelines for eligibility, often based on where you live, the size of your family, and your income. Some legal aid offices have their own staff lawyers, and others operate with volunteer lawyers. Note that people do not have a right to a free lawyer in civil legal matters.

Q. I have been accused of a crime, and I cannot afford a lawyer. What can I do?

A. If you are accused of a crime, the U.S. Constitution guarantees you the right to be represented by a lawyer in any case in which you could be incarcerated for six months or more. State constitutions may guarantee your right to a lawyer for lesser crimes. If you cannot afford a lawyer, either the judge hearing the case will appoint a private lawyer to represent you free of charge or the government's public defender will handle your case, also at no charge.

Q. Besides court-appointed defenders, is there any other form of government assistance available?

A. Departments and agencies of both the state and federal governments often have staff lawyers who can help the general public in limited situations, without charge. The U.S. attorney's office might be able to provide guidance about federal laws. It might also guide you to federal agencies that deal with specific concerns, such as environmental protection problems and discrimination in employment or housing.

The state attorney general also may provide

guidance to the public on state laws, without charge. Some states, for example, maintain consumer protection departments as a function of the attorney general's office.

Similarly, through their law departments, counties, cities, and townships often have government lawyers who may provide the public with guidance about local laws. Some of these local offices also offer consumer protection assistance.

To find such agencies, check the government listings in your phone book.

Questions to Ask a Lawyer

Q. Can I meet my lawyer before deciding to hire him or her?

A. A lawyer will usually meet with you briefly or talk with you by phone so the two of you can get acquainted. This meeting is a chance to talk with your prospective lawyer before making a final hiring decision. In many cases, there is no fee charged for an initial consultation. However, to be on the safe side, ask about fees before setting up your first appointment.

During this meeting, you can decide whether you want to hire that lawyer. Many people feel nervous or intimidated when meeting lawyers, but remember that you're the one doing the hiring, and what's most important is that you're satisfied with what you're getting for your money. Before you make any hiring decisions, you might want to ask certain questions to aid in your evaluation.

Q. What sort of questions should I ask a lawyer?

A. Ask about the lawyer's experience and areas of practice. How long has the lawyer and the firm been practicing law? What kinds of legal problems does the lawyer handle most often? Are most clients individuals or businesses?

Q. Is it proper to ask the lawyer if anyone else will be working on my case?

A. Since you are the one paying the bill, it is well within your rights. Ask if staff such as paralegals or law clerks will be used in researching or preparing the case. If so, will there be separate charges for their services? Who will be consulted if the lawyer is unsure about some aspects of your case? Will the lawyer recommend another lawyer or firm if he or she is unable to handle your case?

Q. I met with a lawyer who referred me to another lawyer. Should I be angry?

A. Probably not. Occasionally, a lawyer will suggest that someone else in the same firm or an outside lawyer handle your specific problem. Perhaps the original lawyer is too busy to give your case the full attention it deserves. Maybe your problem requires another's expertise. No one likes to feel that a lawyer is shifting him or her to another lawyer. However, most reassignments within firms occur for a good reason. Do not hesitate to request a meeting with the new lawyer to make sure you are comfortable with him or her.

Q. What, in particular, should I ask about fees and costs?

A. How are fees charged—by the hour, by the case, or by the amount won? About how much money will be required to handle the case from start to finish? When must you pay the bill? Can you pay it in installments? Ask for a written statement explaining how and what fees will be charged, and a monthly statement showing specific services rendered and the charge for each.

▶ **HAVE FAITH**

It is important that you trust the lawyer you hire, believing that he or she will do the best job possible in protecting your legal rights. However, remember that lawyers cannot work magic. No lawyer can be expected to win every case, and the best legal advice may turn out to be not exactly what you wanted to hear.

Q. When I first meet with my prospective lawyer, should I ask about the possible outcome of the case?

A. Certainly, but beware of any lawyer who guarantees a big settlement or assures a victory in court. Remember that there are at least two sides to every legal issue and that many factors can affect its resolution. Ask for the lawyer's opinion of your case's strengths and weaknesses. Will the lawyer most likely settle your case out of court or is it likely that the case will go to trial? What are the advantages and disadvantages of settlement? Of going to trial? What kind of experience does the lawyer have in trial work? If you lose at the trial, will the lawyer be willing to appeal the decision?

Q. Should I ask if and how I can help with my case?

A. Yes. It is often in your interests to participate actively in your case. When you hire a lawyer, you are paying for legal advice. Your lawyer should make no major decision about whether and how to go on with the case without your permission. Pay special attention to whether the lawyer seems willing and able to explain the case to you and answers your questions clearly and completely. Also ask what information will be supplied to you. How, and how often, will the lawyer keep you informed about the progress of your case? Will the lawyer send you copies of any of the documents that have to do with your case? Can you help keep fees down by gathering documents or otherwise assisting the effort?

Q. During our first meeting, should I ask what will happen if the lawyer and I disagree?

A. Yes, your first meeting is the best time to ask about resolving potential problems. Find out if the lawyer will agree to arbitration if a serious dispute arises between the two of you. (**Arbitration** is a way of settling disputes outside the courts by presenting the issue to a neutral third party; it may or may not be binding.) In some states, it is mandatory for lawyers to agree to arbitrate certain types of disputes with their clients. Most state bar associations have arbitration committees that will settle disputes that you and your lawyer may have, say over expenses.

Q. Should I interview several lawyers before settling on one?

A. Yes. Your decision will be more informed if you consider several lawyers. Even if you think that you will be satisfied with the first lawyer you interview, you will feel better about your choice if you talk to several lawyers.

THE WORLD AT YOUR FINGERTIPS

- *For your local lawyer referral program, call your local or state bar association, look in the yellow pages, or access www. abanet.org/legalservices/Iris/directory/html for a list of three hundred lawyer referral services across the country, including all those certified by the ABA.*

- *If you hire a lawyer over the Web and want to check that he or she is admitted, go to the directory of state bar admission offices: www.abanet.org/legaled/baradmissions/ barcont.html. For a listing of all state and major local bar associations with an Internet presence, access www.abanet.org/ barserv/stlobar.html.*

- *For prepaid legal services plans, check under the heading "Legal Services Plans" in your yellow pages; for a listing of prepaid legal services plans that make certain legal services available at reduced or no costs to their members, access www.aplsi. org/legal_plans/index.htm.*

- *For legal services for the poor in your area, contact your bar association or look in the yellow pages under "Legal Aid" or "Legal Services"; for a listing of legal service programs for the poor in every state, access www.abanet.org/legalservices/probono/ directory/html.*

- *If you're interested in doing some of the work yourself, some referral services will refer clients to lawyers willing to "unbundle" services; for more information, access www.findlegalhelp.org.*
- *Martindale-Hubbell, a leading source for information on lawyers practicing in the United States and abroad, offers a free website for the public. The site provides profiles of more than 400,000 lawyers and law firms, tips on selecting a lawyer, and a "Find a Lawyer" service that locates lawyers by areas of specialization and geographic location: www.lawyers.com.*

REMEMBER THIS

- *It's worth spending some time finding a lawyer who is appropriately qualified and right for you. You may have to interview more than one lawyer to find the right match.*
- *Don't be afraid to ask your prospective lawyer questions—your lawyer is there to help you!*

LEGAL FEES AND EXPENSES

Lawyers can be expensive. We all know that. But you can take a few steps to ensure that you avoid any surprises when the bill arrives in the mail. Talk to your lawyer about fees and expenses, and make sure that you understand all the information on fees and costs that your lawyer gives you. It's best to ask for it in writing before legal work starts.

Q. What billing method do most lawyers use?

A. The most common billing method is to charge a set amount for each hour or fraction of an hour the lawyer works on your case. The method for determining what is a "reasonable" hourly fee depends on several things. More experienced lawyers tend to charge more per hour

than those with less experience—but they also may take less time to do the same legal work. In addition, the same lawyer will usually charge more for time spent in the courtroom than for hours spent in the office or library.

Q. How can I be sure that my lawyer will not overcharge me?

A. The fee charged by a lawyer should be reasonable from an objective point of view. The fee should be tied to specific services rendered, time invested, the level of expertise provided, and the difficulty of the matter.

Here are some broad guidelines to help you in evaluating whether a particular fee is reasonable:

- The time and work required by the lawyer and any assistants
- The difficulty of the legal issues presented
- How much other lawyers in the area charge for similar work
- The total value of the claim or settlement and the results of the case
- Whether the lawyer has worked for that client before

▶ **TALK ABOUT FEES**

Although money is often a touchy subject in our society, fees and other charges should be discussed with your lawyer early. You can avoid future problems by having a clear understanding of the fees to be charged and getting that understanding in writing before any legal work has started. If the fee is to be charged on an hourly basis, insist on a complete itemized list and an explanation of charges each time the lawyer bills you.

Legal advice is not cheap. A bill from a lawyer for preparing a one-page legal document or providing basic advice may surprise some clients. Remember that when you hire a lawyer, you are paying for his or her expertise and time.

- The lawyer's experience, reputation, and ability
- The amount of other work the lawyer had to turn down to take on a particular case

Types of Fees

Q. Someone said that I should ask my lawyer to represent me on a "contingent fee" basis. What does this mean?

A. A **contingent fee** is a fee that is payable only if your case is successful. Lawyers and clients use this arrangement only in cases where money is being claimed—most often in cases involving personal injury or workers' compensation. Many states strictly forbid this billing method in criminal cases and in most cases involving domestic relations.

In a contingent fee arrangement, the lawyer agrees to accept a fixed percentage (often one-third) of the amount recovered. If you win the case, the lawyer's fee comes out of the money awarded to you. If you lose, neither you nor the lawyer will get any money, but you will not be required to pay your lawyer for the work done on the case.

On the other hand, win or lose, you probably will have to pay court filing charges, the costs related to deposing witnesses, and similar expenses. By entering into a contingent fee agreement, both you and your lawyer expect to collect some unknown amount of money. Because many personal injury actions involve considerable and often complicated investigation and work by a lawyer, this may be less expensive than paying an hourly rate. You should clearly understand your options before entering into a contingent fee agreement, which is a contract in itself.

Q. Are all contingent fee arrangements the same?

A. No. An important consideration is whether the lawyer deducts the costs and expenses from the amount won before or after you pay the lawyer's percentage.

ⓘ UNDERSTAND FEES AND EXPENSES

The method used to charge fees is one of the things to consider in deciding if a fee is reasonable. You should understand the different charging methods before you make any hiring decision. At your first meeting, the lawyer should estimate how much the total case will cost and inform you of the method he or she will use to charge for the work. As with any bill, you should not pay without first getting an explanation for any charges you do not understand. Remember, not all expenses can be estimated exactly because of unforeseen developments during the course of your case.

Example: Joe hires Ernie Attorney to represent him, agreeing that Ernie will receive one-third third of the final amount—in this case, $12,000. If Joe pays Ernie his fee before expenses, the fee will be calculated as follows:

$12,000	Total amount recovered in case
−4,000	One-third for Ernie Attorney
$8,000	Balance
−2,100	Payment for expenses and costs
$5,900	Amount that Joe recovers

If Joe pays Ernie after other legal expenses and costs, the fee will be calculated as follows:

$12,000	Total amount recovered in case
−2,100	Payment for expenses and costs
$9,900	Balance
−3,300	One-third for Ernie Attorney
$6,600	Amount that Joe recovers

The above figures show that Joe will collect an additional $700 if the agreement provides that Ernie Attorney collects his share after Joe pays the other legal expenses.

Many lawyers prefer to be paid before they subtract the expenses, but the point is often negotiable. Of course, these matters should be settled before you hire a lawyer. If you agree to pay a contingent fee, your lawyer should provide a written explanation of the agreement, clearly stating how he or she will deduct costs.

Q. If my lawyer and I agree to a contingent fee arrangement, should the method of settling my case affect the amount of my lawyer's fee?

A. Yes, but only if both of you agree beforehand. If the lawyer settles the case before going to trial, less legal work may be required. On the other hand, the lawyer may have to prepare for trial, with all its costs and expenses, before a settlement can be negotiated.

You can try to negotiate an agreement in which the lawyer accepts a lower percentage if he or she settles the case easily and quickly or before a lawsuit is filed in court. However, many lawyers might not agree to those terms.

Q. A friend suggested that I might want to have a lawyer "on retainer." What does this mean?

A. If you pay a small amount of money regularly to make sure that a lawyer will be available for any necessary legal service you might require, then you have a lawyer **on retainer**. Businesses and people who routinely have a lot of legal work use retainers. By paying a retainer, a client receives routine consultations and general legal advice whenever needed. If a legal matter requires courtroom time or many hours of work, the client may need to pay more than the retainer amount. Retainer agreements should always be in writing.

Prepaid legal services plans, which were discussed earlier, are similar in effect to retainer agreements: a small fee paid periodically ensures that a lawyer will be available to provide legal services at any time.

Most people do not see a lawyer regularly and do not need to have a lawyer on retainer.

Q. Is having a lawyer "on retainer" the same thing as paying a "retainer fee"?

A. No. A retainer fee is something quite different. Sometimes a lawyer will ask the client to pay

---

▶ **SOME TIPS ON KEEPING FEES DOWN**

- Be organized. Make sure you bring all relevant documents to any meeting with your lawyer, so that your lawyer's time isn't wasted.
- Be brief. If your lawyer is charging you by the hour, you don't want to waste time with irrelevant conversation or long-winded explanations.
- If your lawyer is working on something for you, don't call every time you have a minor question. Instead, save up a few questions to ask at the same time.
- Ask your lawyer if there anything you can do to help. Can you, for example, write some letters, make some phone calls, or change the title of some assets?
- Ask your lawyer to let you know if the cost of your case starts to escalate beyond the cost discussed.
- Ask for an itemized bill—that way you can see the cost or fees for each service.

some money in advance before any legal work will be done. This money is referred to as a **retainer fee**, and is in effect a down payment that will be applied toward the total fee billed.

Q. I saw an advertisement from a law firm that charges fixed fees for specific types of work. What does this involve?

A. A fixed fee is the amount that will be charged for routine legal work. In a few situations, this amount may be set by law or by the judge handling the case. Since advertising by lawyers is becoming more popular, you are likely to see ads offering "Simple Divorce—$150" or "Bankruptcy—from $250." Do not assume that these prices will be the amount of your final bill. The advertised price often does not include court costs and other expenses.

Q. Does the lawyer's billing method influence the other costs and expenses that I might have to pay?

A. No. Some costs and expenses will be charged regardless of the billing method. The court clerk's office charges a fee for filing the complaint or petition that begins a legal action. The sheriff's office charges a fee for serving a legal summons. Your lawyer must pay for postage, copying documents, telephone calls, and the advice or testimony of some types of expert witnesses, such as doctors. These expenses, often called "costs," may not be part of a legal fee, and you may have to pay them regardless of the fee arrangement you use. Your lawyer will usually pay these costs as needed, billing you at regular intervals or at the close of your case.

Q. What are referral fees?

A. If you go to Lawyer A, he or she may be unable to help, but might refer you instead to Lawyer B, at another law firm, who has more experience in handling your kind of case. In return for the referral, Lawyer A will sometimes be paid part of the total fee you pay to Lawyer B. The law may prohibit this type of fee, especially if it increases the final amount to be paid by a client. The ethics rules for lawyers in most states specify that lawyers in different firms may not divide a client's fee unless

1. the client knows about and consents to the arrangement;
2. they divide the fee in a way that reflects how much work each lawyer did, or both lawyers are fully responsible for the case; and
3. the total bill is reasonable.

If one lawyer refers you to another, you have a right to know if there will be a referral fee. If there is, then ask about the specifics of the agreement between the lawyers.

Cost-Cutting Options

Q. Is there anything I can do to reduce my legal costs?

A. Yes, there are several cost-cutting methods available to you. First, answer all your lawyer's questions fully and honestly. Not only will you feel better, but you also will save on legal fees. If you tell your lawyer all the facts as you know them, you will save time that might be spent on the case and will help your lawyer do a better job.

Remember that the ethics of the profession bind your lawyer to maintain in the strictest confidence almost anything you reveal during your private discussions. You should feel free to tell your lawyer the complete details in your case, even those that embarrass you. It is particularly important to tell your lawyer facts about your case that reflect poorly on you. These will almost certainly come out if your case goes to trial.

Q. Can I reduce my legal costs if I get more involved in my case?

A. Sometimes. Stay informed and ask for copies of important documents related to your case. Let your lawyer know if you are willing to help out, such as by picking up or delivering documents or by making a few telephone calls.

You should not interfere with your lawyer's work. However, you might be able to move your case more quickly, reduce your legal costs, and keep yourself better informed by doing some of the work yourself. Discuss this with your lawyer.

REMEMBER THIS

- *Talk to your lawyer about fees. Make sure you understand how fees are going to be charged, and get a fee agreement in writing before legal work starts.*
- *Lawyers' services can be expensive. Make sure you have a good idea of what your case is likely to cost, and be aware of ways you can reduce your fees.*

WHEN THINGS GO WRONG

When you agree to hire a lawyer and that lawyer agrees to be your legal representative, a two-way relationship begins in which you both have the same goal—to reach a satisfactory resolution to a legal matter. To this end, each

---

 WHAT IS "UNBUNDLING"?

Many lawyers are becoming receptive to opening the bundle of legal services and splitting the work with you. Maybe you'll be able to write the letter laying out your side of the case, and the lawyer will only review it (thus spending less time and costing you less money). Often lawyers will provide advice in a matter but will become heavily involved only if it goes to court.

---

of you must act responsibly toward the other. In a lawyer-client relationship, acting responsibly involves duties on both sides—and often involves some hard work.

You have a right to expect competent representation from your lawyer. However, every lawsuit has at least two sides. You cannot always blame your lawyer if your case does not turn out the way you thought it would. If you

---

▶ **SOME TIPS ON TALKING TO YOUR LAWYER**

- Before your first meeting with your lawyer, think about your legal problem, how you would like it resolved, and your ideal outcome.
- If your case involves other people, write down their names, addresses, and telephone numbers. Also jot down any specific facts or dates you think might be important and any questions you want answered. By being organized, you will save time and money.
- Bring all relevant information and documents with you to any meeting with your lawyer, including contracts, leases, or any documents with which you have been served.
- If there has been a development in your case, don't wait till your next scheduled meeting to tell your lawyer about it. Tell your lawyer immediately of any changes that might be important. It might mean that the lawyer will have to take a totally different action—or no action at all—in your case.
- Let your lawyer know if and why you are unhappy with his or her work.
- Don't wait for your lawyer to ask you about something—volunteer information that you think may be useful.

are unhappy with your lawyer, it is important to determine the reasons. If, after a realistic look, you still believe that you have a genuine complaint about your legal representation, there are several things you can do.

Q. I lost my case, and I still had to pay my lawyer's bill along with costs and expenses. I am not very happy with my lawyer. What can I do?

A. First, talk with your lawyer. A lack of communication causes many problems. If your lawyer appears to have acted improperly, or did not do something that you think he or she should have done, talk with your lawyer about it. You may be satisfied once you understand the circumstances better.

Q. I have tried to discuss my complaints with my lawyer. However, my lawyer will not discuss them. Do I have any alternatives?

A. Yes. If your lawyer is unwilling to address your complaints, consider taking your legal affairs to another lawyer. You can decide whom to hire (and fire) as your lawyer. However, remember that when you fire a lawyer, you may be charged a reasonable amount for the work already done.

Most documents held by your lawyer that relate to the case are yours—ask for them. In some states, however, a lawyer may have some rights to a file until the client pays a reasonable amount for work done on the case.

Q. What if I feel that my lawyer has acted unethically?

A. How a lawyer should act, in both professional and private life, is controlled by the rules of professional conduct in the state or states in which he or she is licensed to practice. These rules are usually administered by the state's highest court through its disciplinary board.

These rules describe generally how lawyers should strive to improve the legal profession and uphold the law. They also give more detailed rules

of conduct for specific situations. If a lawyer's conduct falls below the standards set out in the rules, he or she can be disciplined by being **censured** or **reprimanded** (publicly or privately criticized); **suspended** (having the license to practice law taken away for a certain time); or **disbarred** (having the license to practice law taken away indefinitely).

The law sets out punishments for anyone who breaks civil and criminal laws, and that includes lawyers. But because of the special position of trust and confidence involved in a lawyer-client relationship, lawyers may also be punished for things that are unethical, if not unlawful—such as telling others confidential information about a client or representing clients whose interests are in conflict.

Q. What are some specific examples of the ethical duties of lawyers?

A. Among the highest responsibilities a lawyer has is his or her obligation to a client. A number of strict rules and commonsense guidelines define these responsibilities.

Competence
Every lawyer must aim to provide high-quality work. This requires the lawyer's ability to analyze legal issues, to research and study changing laws and legal trends, and otherwise to represent the client effectively and professionally.

Following the Client's Instructions
A lawyer should advise a client of possible actions to be taken in a case and then act according to the client's choice of action—even if the lawyer might have picked a different route. One of the few exceptions occurs when a client asks for a lawyer's help in doing something illegal, such as lying in court or in a legal document. In these cases, the lawyer is required to inform the client of the legal effect of any planned wrongdoing and refuse to assist with it.

Diligence
Every lawyer must act carefully and in a timely manner in handling a client's legal prob-

lem. Unnecessary delays can often damage a case. If, because of overwork or any other reason, a lawyer is unable to spend the required time and energy on a case, the lawyer should refuse from the beginning to take the case.

Communication

A lawyer must be able to communicate effectively with a client. When a client asks for an explanation, the lawyer must provide it within a reasonable time. A lawyer must inform a client about changes in a case caused by time and circumstances.

Fees

The amount the lawyer charges for legal work must be reasonable, and the client should be told the specifics of all charges.

Confidentiality

With few exceptions, a lawyer may generally not tell anyone else what a client reveals about a case. The reason for this strict rule is to enable a client to discuss case details openly and honestly with a lawyer, even if those details reveal embarrassing, damaging, or commercially sensitive information about the client. A rule called **attorney-client privilege** helps protect confidential information from being disclosed. Ask your lawyer to explain the privilege to you.

Conflicts of Interest

A lawyer must be loyal to his or her client. This means that a lawyer cannot represent two clients who are on opposite sides in the same or related lawsuits. And, ordinarily, there can be no representation of a client whose interests would conflict with the lawyer's interests. For example, a lawyer may not be involved in writing a will for a client who leaves the lawyer substantial money or property in that will.

Keeping Clients' Property

If a lawyer is holding a client's money or property, it must be kept safely and separately from the lawyer's own funds and belongings. When a client asks for the property, the lawyer must return it immediately and in good condition. The lawyer must also keep careful records of money received for a client and, if asked, report that amount promptly and accurately.

Q. Where can I file a complaint against my lawyer?

A. If you believe you have a valid complaint about how your lawyer has handled your case, inform the organization that governs licenses to practice law in your state. Usually this is the disciplinary board of the highest court in your state.

In some states, the state bar association is responsible for disciplining lawyers. The board or the bar will either investigate the complaint or refer you to someone who can help. If your complaint concerns the amount your lawyer charged, you may be referred to a state or local bar association's fee arbitration service.

Filing a disciplinary complaint accusing your lawyer of unethical conduct is a serious matter to the lawyer. Try to resolve any differences or disputes directly with the lawyer before filing a complaint. Be aware that making a complaint of this sort may punish the lawyer for misconduct, but it will probably not help you recover any money.

If you have a case pending that your lawyer has mishandled, be sure to also protect your rights by taking steps to see that your case is now properly handled.

Q. My lawyer's incompetence meant that I lost my case. What can I do?

A. If you believe that your lawyer has been negligent in handling your case—and that negligence has ended up costing you money or injuring you or your legal rights—you may be able to bring a **malpractice** suit against your lawyer. Chapter 14, "Personal Injury," can give you more information.

Q. My lawyer settled my case out of court and refuses to pay me my share of the settlement. What can I do about it?

A. If you believe that your lawyer has taken or improperly kept money or property that belongs to you, contact the state **client security fund, client indemnity fund,** or **client assistance fund.** The state or local bar association or the state disciplinary board can tell you how to contact the fund that serves you. These funds may reimburse clients if a court has found that their lawyer has defrauded them. Lawyers pay fees to maintain such funds. Be aware, however, that most states' programs divide up the money that is available in a given period of time among all the clients who have proved cases against their lawyers. There is rarely enough money in the fund to pay 100 percent of every claim that is made.

Q. If I am having a problem with my lawyer, is there any reason that I would want to call the police?

A. Yes. If you believe that your lawyer has committed a crime such as stealing your money or property, you should report that crime to the police. This is a last resort that should be taken only when you feel certain of your position. However, if you are certain, do not feel intimidated because your complaint is against a lawyer.

THE WORLD AT YOUR FINGERTIPS

- *To complain about your lawyer, call your state bar association, which will tell you how to proceed, or access*

▶ A CLIENT'S RESPONSIBILITIES

As in any successful relationship, a good lawyer-client relationship involves cooperation on both sides. As a client, you should do all you can to make sure you get the best possible legal help. This includes:

- Being honest. Be honest in telling all the facts to your lawyer. Remind yourself of important points or questions by writing them down before talking with your lawyer.

- Notifying the lawyer of changes. Tell the lawyer promptly about any changes or new information you learn that may affect your case. And let your lawyer know if you change your address or telephone number.

- Asking for clarification. If you have any questions or are confused about something in your case, ask the lawyer for an explanation. This may go a long way toward putting your mind at ease—and will also help your lawyer do a better job of handling your case.

- Being realistic. A lawyer can only handle your legal affairs. You may need the help of another professional—a banker, a family counselor, an accountant, or a psychologist, for example—for problems that have no "legal" solution. After you have hired a lawyer you trust, do not forget about that trust. The lawyer's judgments are based on experience and training. Also, keep in mind that most legal matters cannot be resolved overnight. Give the system time to work.

- Paying. A client has the duty to promptly pay a fair and reasonable price for legal services. In fact, when a client fails to pay, in some situations the lawyer may have the right to stop working on the case. Still, the lawyer must then do whatever is reasonably possible to prevent the client's case from being harmed.

www.abanet.org/cpr/disciplinary.html *for a listing of lawyer disciplinary agencies in every state.*

- *The ABA legal services division provides information on resolving disputes with your lawyer, and links to websites on mediation, arbitration, and disciplinary action at www.findlegalhelp.org.*

REMEMBER THIS

- *If things don't turn out the way you'd hoped, discuss your concerns with your lawyer. He or she might be able to explain what happened in a way that makes sense to you.*
- *If you have serious concerns about your lawyer's conduct, don't be afraid to pursue the matter through your state disciplinary authority.*
- *Don't forget that you have responsibilities as a client, too!*

How the Legal System Works

The legal system, with its complex procedures and technical language, can be confusing and frightening to a person who does not have legal training and is caught up in it for the first time. That makes having a good grasp of the structure and function of the system particularly important. Understanding the legal system will be useful if you ever have to go to court yourself. The courts play an important part in American democracy, and understanding how they work might give you a deeper insight into our political process. And the more you know about how our legal system works, the more likely you are to respect the rights of others and demand that your own rights are respected.

Remember, federal laws and procedures differ from those in the states, and states differ among themselves. Because of the differences in the procedures each system uses, this chapter can't convey all the variations that exist in how courts operate. But focusing on the federal system should provide you with a good basic road map of the structure of the courts. If you want to pursue a lawsuit, you should talk to a lawyer about the laws that apply in your jurisdiction.

INTRODUCTION TO THE LEGAL SYSTEM

Claire suffered an injury after she slipped and fell on a greasy floor at a local restaurant. After making some preliminary investigations, her lawyer advised her to file a civil suit against the restaurant owners. What does this mean? Which court will handle the case? What happens in a trial? Will there be a jury? How can Claire be sure it will be fair?

This section is an introduction to the legal system and the difference between civil and criminal suits.

Q. What is the idea behind our legal system?

A. We have what is known as an adversarial legal system, because it is believed that the truth in a matter can best be determined by giving two sides an equal chance to make their case before an impartial judge or jury.

Our adversarial system has several essential features. Each side has a right to be represented by a lawyer, whose job it is to argue why the court should apply the law to the facts in a particular way. Each lawyer is bound by the same statutes, case law, and rules of procedure as his or her adversary. The judge is neutral and impartial, and ensures that the presentation of evidence and questioning of witnesses are carried out according to the rules of procedure. The trial procedure is based on rules, statutes, and historical precedent, modified, as necessary, by the changing needs of the justice system, and based on the experience of lawyers, judges, and litigants.

This is the basic pattern for both **criminal** cases (in which the government accuses someone of violating a criminal law and the defendant may face a fine or jail time) and **civil** cases (in which a private person or business sues another person or business, typically to seek damages for non-criminal conduct, such as a broken contract or a

personal injury). However, as noted in the next several answers, the two types of cases differ in many particulars.

Q. How does a criminal prosecution differ from a civil suit?

A. A criminal prosecution differs from a civil suit in several important ways. A criminal prosecution is brought by the government to punish an individual or corporation for committing a crime, and to deter that person and others from committing similar crimes. If there is a conviction it may result in payment of fines, restitution of property, probation, state-supervised rehabilitation, or incarceration.

Civil actions, on the other hand, provide a legal forum for persons seeking various remedies, including damages for their injuries and enforcement of contracts. Courts may, for example, provide remedies to plaintiffs who can demonstrate that a defendant has injured them while committing some legal wrong against them. Unlike a criminal case, the defendant who is found liable in a civil case cannot be sentenced to prison but, instead, may be ordered to pay compensation, or ordered to take certain steps or stop certain conduct.

Q. Are there different standards for determining liability in a civil suit and guilt in a criminal case?

A. Yes. Our system of government places a very high value on protection of the individual from state action, and because a criminal conviction can result in a prison term or even a death sentence, the **standard of proof** required in a criminal case is higher than in a civil one.

In a civil suit, the question that a trial judge or jury must address when making a decision is whether a plaintiff has proven that it was **more likely than not** that the defendant was legally responsible for the plaintiff's injury or loss. This "preponderance of the evidence" standard means that if the evidence favors the plaintiff by even the slightest bit, the plaintiff is entitled to a verdict in his or her favor. In a criminal case, on the other hand, the standard is much higher: The prosecution must prove the defendant's guilt **beyond a reasonable doubt**. Even if it is more likely than not that a criminal defendant is guilty of the crime charged, the proper verdict is not guilty if there remains a reasonable doubt about his or her guilt.

The U.S. Constitution guarantees criminal defendants many rights. It has been interpreted to guarantee a defendant the right to a jury trial when there is the possibility of a conviction resulting in a prison or jail term of six months or more, and the right to have a lawyer appointed if the defendant cannot afford to hire one where there is a possibility of a loss of liberty. State constitutions may guarantee other rights, including rights to a jury trial in less serious offenses. These will be discussed in more detail in chapter 15, "Criminal Justice." The Seventh Amendment gives defendants a right to a jury trial in civil cases in some circumstances.

REMEMBER THIS

- *The rationale for the adversarial system is that it provides the best way to find the truth of a matter. Each side has the right to a lawyer, and must argue its case before an impartial judge.*

- *Criminal cases are brought by the government, which must prove its case by a high standard of proof; civil cases are brought by people or businesses and carry a lesser standard of proof.*

THE STRUCTURE OF THE COURT SYSTEM

"Our Constitution works. Our great Republic is a Government of laws, not of men. Here the people rule."
—Gerald R. Ford

In cities and small towns across the country, the courthouse is both the symbol of the rule of law and the place in which the law is put into action. In the courthouse, criminal defendants have their day in court, as the government is put to the test of convicting them beyond a reasonable doubt. Meanwhile, private parties seek to resolve disputes in civil cases that can range from a dispute over who was responsible for damages in a car collision to multimillion-dollar lawsuits between companies. In some communities, there may also be a federal courthouse in which federal judges hear criminal and civil cases under jurisdiction granted by the Constitution and federal law.

This section will give you a broad overview of the structure of the courts, including a discussion of the meaning and significance of separation of powers and judicial independence.

State and Federal Courts

Q. Why isn't there just one court system?

A. The U.S. Constitution provides for a dual system of government, with both state and federal powers and responsibilities. A judicial system is

---

📑 WHAT'S IN A NAME?

With more than fifty jurisdictions, American law is full of courts that have different names but do almost exactly the same thing. For example, courts of general jurisdiction exist in almost every jurisdiction, but they are variously called circuit court, district court, superior court, and court of common pleas. In New York State, the court of general jurisdiction is called the supreme court. Under any name, though, these courts generally hear serious criminal and civil cases.

an essential component of both national and state governments. Article III of the U.S. Constitution calls for a **federal judiciary** operating as a coequal branch of our national government. Federal courts may only decide certain kinds of cases as provided by Congress or specified in the Constitution. Each state has a **state judiciary,** which is empowered to interpret the laws made by the state legislature. States also have their own constitutions, which can provide rights to the public in addition to those rights provided by the federal Constitution.

This dual court system is a consequence of our organization as a union of states. Such a system makes sense philosophically because it respects a state's right to establish and enforce the law with respect to its unique local problems and concerns. It also makes sense practically because, as a general rule, a state's own courts are more familiar with state and local laws. Federal courts are qualified to interpret and apply federal laws and ensure that federal laws are applied uniformly in the different states.

Q. What kinds of cases can federal courts decide?

A. Article III of the U.S. Constitution limits the kinds of cases federal courts can hear to the following:

- Cases involving issues of federal law. This so-called **federal question jurisdiction** authorizes federal district courts to decide both civil and criminal cases in which federal law must be interpreted or applied. The federal law at issue may have arisen out of a federal statute or regulation, a treaty, or a provision of the Constitution itself.
- Cases involving diversity jurisdiction over controversies:
  —between citizens of different states;
  —between two or more states; and
  —between citizens of the same state claiming lands under grants of different states.
- Cases in which the U.S. government or one of its officers is a party.

- Cases that might affect America's relations with other countries, including cases that involve ambassadors, consuls, and other public ministers.
- Cases involving the laws relating to navigable waters (the oceans, the Great Lakes, and most rivers) and commerce on those waters.

Q. What types of federal courts are there?

A. There are several specialized federal courts—Tax Court, the Court of Federal Claims, the Court of Veterans Appeals, courts of criminal appeals for each branch of the armed forces, and the Court of International Trade. Each U.S. district court also has a U.S. bankruptcy court unit, as well as one or more magistrates.

In addition, Congress has created other courts under its Article I powers to serve the people in the U.S. territories of Guam, the U.S. Virgin Islands, and the Northern Mariana Islands. These are called **legislative courts** because they are authorized by Congress to serve U. S. territories, in contrast to courts authorized under Article III of the Constitution to serve in this country. They operate much like the Article III courts, but the presiding officers of these courts do not have the constitutional protections accorded to Article III judges, such as life tenure and the prohibition against reducing judicial salaries.

⚠ TALKING ABOUT COURTS

We really have fifty-two court systems in this country—one for each state and the District of Columbia, and a federal system. Because of the differences in the procedures each system uses, this chapter can't explain all the variations that exist in how courts operate. But in focusing on the federal system and state courts in general, it should provide a good basic road map of the structure of the courts.

A party to a federal lawsuit will have an opportunity to proceed through two levels of decision: the U.S. district court or other specialized trial court and a court of appeals. In rare cases, a party may receive a third level of decision from the U.S. Supreme Court if, for example, the Court believes that the case presents an important question of constitutional law.

Q. What sorts of cases do state courts decide?

A. The state courts handle the vast majority—over 98 percent—of all litigation today. Forty-five states have two or more levels of trial courts—**special jurisdiction courts** with jurisdiction limited to specific types of cases, and **general jurisdiction courts** with jurisdiction over all other cases.

Special, or limited, jurisdiction courts have specific names that may vary from state to state, such as district, mayor's, city, justice, justice of the peace, magistrate, county, municipal, or police courts. They hear relatively minor civil and criminal disputes, and are typically dominated by traffic cases. They often have exclusive jurisdiction over juvenile cases.

Courts of general jurisdiction hear most of the serious criminal and civil cases and in addition are sometimes subdivided into subject areas such as domestic relations and state and local tax. These courts have different names in different states (see "What's in a Name"). Five states now have unified trial courts, in which all types of cases are heard.

By contrast, the Administrative Office of the U.S. Courts reports that annually the U.S. district courts receive well under half a million cases: 80 percent civil and 20 percent criminal. Among the types of civil suits filed in the federal courts are civil rights actions, patent infringement cases, prisoner petitions, and Social Security cases. The federal criminal cases filed include tax fraud, robbery, forgery and counterfeiting, and drug offenses, which are among the largest category of cases. Bankruptcy courts deal with the largest number of federal cases, with about 1.5 million cases filed each year.

The number of cases filed in federal courts is smaller, but most cases are more complex than the majority of cases filed in state court.

Q. Do I have a choice of whether to sue in state or federal court?

A. Sometimes. Although some cases are exclusively within the jurisdiction of one or the other court systems (for example, divorces are handled in state courts, and all bankruptcies are filed in federal bankruptcy courts), the state and federal courts have **concurrent jurisdiction** over many cases. This means that these cases may be filed and heard in either state or federal court. A typical example would be a case involving a state law that is being litigated by a plaintiff from one state and a defendant from another state. The state courts would have jurisdiction because of the state law issues. But, if the case involves an "amount in controversy" of more than $75,000, the federal courts would have jurisdiction as well because the parties are citizens of different

---

ⓘ THE NUMBER CRUNCH: STATE AND FEDERAL SYSTEMS

The fifty state court systems together handle the overwhelming majority of all legal disputes. According to annual reports of the Conference of State Court Administrators, the State Justice Institute, and the National Center for State Courts, about 100 million new cases are filed in state trial courts each year. Of this enormous volume of cases, about a third are civil and criminal cases, about 2 percent are juvenile cases, and the remainder—about two-thirds—are traffic cases.

states. This is known as **diversity jurisdiction** because the parties are citizens of different states. Article III of the Constitution gives federal courts concurrent jurisdiction over these cases, and plaintiffs can choose in which court they wish to file suit.

It is occasionally possible to commence an action in both the state and federal courts. For example, in the Rodney King case, in which Los Angeles police officers were accused of beating a motorist, the officers were acquitted of state criminal charges but later convicted in federal court for depriving the victim of his civil rights.

Q. How is the court system structured?

A. The courts of this country are organized as hierarchies. Higher courts have the power to review the decisions of lower courts. Basically, the courts of this country are divided into three layers:

- trial courts, where cases start;
- intermediate (appellate) courts, where most appeals are first heard; and
- courts of last resort (usually called supreme courts), which hear further appeals and have final authority in the cases they hear.

This division is generally true of both state courts and federal courts, although eleven states do not have an intermediate appellate court, and some states have more than one level of intermediate appellate review. Two states, Oklahoma and Texas, have separate courts of last resort for civil and criminal cases.

Separation of Powers

Q. What does it mean that we have a system of separation of powers?

A. Besides applying the law in individual cases, courts have an important role in the structure of American government. Just about any eighth grader can tell you that we have a system of separation of powers. But what does that mean exactly?

The framers of the Constitution created a federal government of divided power. There's an **executive branch** (the president and most government agencies), a **legislative branch** (Congress), and a **judicial branch** (the courts.) The same three branches exist in every state government.

We have this structure because the framers were deeply suspicious of unchecked executive power. They had just emerged from a revolution against a powerful king, and they wanted to ensure that the American people would never have to face a homegrown dictatorship.

Setting up three interdependent yet separate branches of government meant that there would be a **balance of powers** (each branch keeps an eye on the others) and a **separation of powers** (none can unduly influence the others, because there are some things only one branch is autho-

---

ⓘ THE NUMBER CRUNCH—JUDGES

- There are 94 U.S. district courts, as well as other specialized trial courts. Congress determines the number of authorized judgeships. There are 662 authorized judgeships in the U.S. district courts.

- There are 12 regional U.S. courts of appeals, plus the Court of Appeals for the Federal Circuit. There are 179 authorized judgeships for 13 U.S. courts of appeals.

- There is one Supreme Court, consisting of the chief justice of the United States, and eight associate justices.

rized to do.) Think of it as a three-legged stool. No one leg can stand on its own.

Q. What is judicial review?

A. The Constitution and the Bill of Rights enshrine certain rights, which cannot be abridged by our government. These rights include the right to worship freely, to speak and write freely, and to have fair and impartial trials.

When the government makes laws that are at odds with the Constitution, a court can declare that the law is unconstitutional. Under our system, it often falls to courts to enforce these constitutional rights. That sometimes means going very much against common beliefs or the clamor of the moment, and upholding positions that are unpopular.

The courts uphold the Constitution when they strike down a law that is impermissible under it. This practice of **judicial review** is often unpopular—after all, any law that got passed in the first place arguably had majority support. But judicial review is absolutely necessary if we are to live under a limited government, and if citizens are to have certain unalienable rights. A law contrary to the Constitution cannot be law. In matters of constitutional interpretation, courts have the final word—except on those very rare occa-sions when the Constitution is amended to overturn court decisions.

Q. Are there limits on the power of the courts?

A. Obviously, the ability to strike down laws contrary to the Constitution gives courts enormous power. But several things keep this branch from reigning supreme.

For one thing, judges can't strike down laws willy-nilly. Courts can rule only on the controversies that come before them. That means that—unlike the other two branches—they can't shape their own agenda. They have no power to act on their own, but only act in response to legal cases on which they are asked to rule. Courts are generally careful to use their power of judicial review sparingly. Often, judges will decide cases on narrow grounds, to avoid sweeping pronouncements. Declaring laws unconstitutional is much rarer than you might think. Since its inception, the United States Supreme Court has declared fewer than 150 federal statutes unconstitutional.

Finally, the old adage that we are a "government of laws and not of men" refers to the cornerstone of our legal system, the rule of law. This means individual judges, or juries, cannot just do what they, individually or collectively, think is

---

ⓘ THE CONSTITUTION IN ACTION

Some of the cases in which the U.S. Supreme Court struck down laws because they violated the Constitution include:

- *Brown v. Board of Education* (1954), which struck down public school segregation;
- *Baker v. Carr* (1962), which struck down state reapportionment that gave more influence to certain voters;
- *Roe v. Wade* (1973), which struck down some state laws against abortion;
- *United States v. Eichman* (1990), which struck down a federal law making it a crime to burn an American flag.
- *U.S. v. Lopez* (1995), which struck down the federal Gun-Free Schools Act on the grounds that Congress had exceeded its authority.

ⓘ JUDICIAL INDEPENDENCE

An independent judiciary makes a system of impartial, evenhanded justice possible by enabling judges to strike down actions of the legislative and executive branches without fear of reprisal.

Origins

The founders had firsthand experience of being brought before courts they felt were unfairly controlled by the English Crown, and so the Constitution created a system that guaranteed an independent federal judiciary.

Courts in the colonies were seen as instruments of oppression. Juries could be locked up until they reached the "right" decision. Judges were seen as puppets of the king. In fact, the Declaration of Independence criticized King George III for making "judges dependent upon his will alone for the tenure of their offices and the amount and payment of their salaries."

This experience convinced the founders that Americans needed independent courts to protect them from actions of overreaching government power, such as unreasonable searches and rigged trials.

Constitutional Protections

To guarantee rights such as freedom of speech and freedom of worship, and make the rule of law a reality, the founders knew that courts had to be independent of politics. Judges had to be servants of law and the Constitution, not of the political bosses, the media, or special interest groups. In the Constitution, the founders protected federal judges from political and public pressure by:

• Specifying that they hold their office "during good behaviour." This means that their appointments are for life, unless they are removed for misbehavior.

• Specifying that their salaries cannot be diminished during their tenure. This prevents Congress from retaliating against judges by cutting their pay.

• Making the removal process difficult (the only grounds are "impeachment for, and conviction of, treason, bribery, or other high crimes and misdemeanors").

In more than two hundred years, only thirteen attempts have been made to formally impeach federal judges, and only seven judges have been convicted and removed from office—for example, because of grave misconduct in office. None of the convictions were made because Congress disagreed with a judge's judicial philosophy or with a particular decision the judge rendered.

Throughout American history, the independence of the judiciary has protected individual liberties and prevented a tyranny of the majority. Examples include extending voting rights, ending segregation, and protecting the average citizen from unwarranted government intrusion.

right in a particular case. They must follow the law as enacted by the Congress or a state legislature, or as defined in case law from the U.S. Supreme Court or the highest state court. The rule of law is a discipline we have imposed on ourselves to ensure all are treated equally under the law.

Judges

Q. What is a judge's role in court?

A. Judges are like umpires in baseball or referees in football or basketball. Their role is to see that both sides follow the rules of procedure. Like the umpire, they call 'em as they see 'em, according to the facts and law—without regard to which side is popular (no home field advantage); without regard to who is "favored"; without regard for what the spectators want; and without regard to whether the judge personally agrees with the position taken by either party.

Q. How are judges selected?

A. There are important differences between the state and federal systems. All Article III judges are appointed for life by the president with the advice and approval of the U.S. Senate, and can only be removed through impeachment. Article I judges (such as bankruptcy court and magistrates court judges) do not have the constitutional protections accorded to Article III judges, since they are appointed in a different process.

The states, on the other hand, have a variety of procedures for filling judgeships. While the governor appoints some state judges for a term of a number of years, judges in many other states are required to run for election. Some state judicial elections are partisan, some are non-partisan, while others are uncontested retention elections.

Q. Which method is preferable?

A. Supporters of the electoral method believe that elected judges are more likely to be responsive to the needs of the everyday citizen, while critics argue that the appointment method gives judges the distance from politics that is necessary to ensure impartiality. Another advantage of the appointment process is that it does not require judges to raise money from lawyers or others, or to state public positions on controversial matters. The argument has been advanced that appointed judges are more likely to be unbiased and impartial, since their decisions will not be influenced by their need to stand for election in the future. In some states, judges are initially appointed, but then must win periodic retention elections in which voters simply vote yes or no to retain that particular judge.

THE WORLD AT YOUR FINGERTIPS

Federal Courts

- *The Federal Judicial Center contains many downloadable publications on recent issues in the judiciary, as well as some judicial history; visit www.fjc.gov.*
- *The Federal Judiciary Homepage (www. uscourts.gov) contains useful information on court structure and function, and links to all the federal courts. The website of the U.S. Supreme Court contains information about the Supreme Court and the full text of Supreme Court opinions; visit www.supremecourtus.gov.*
- *The Supreme Court History website provides a history of the Supreme Court, as well as a description of the decisions made by the Court; visit www. supremecourthistory.org.*

State Courts

- *The National Center for State Courts is an excellent first stop for research on state courts. The site contains information on alternative dispute resolution, criminal procedure, juries, and judges, among other topics; visit www.ncsconline.org.*
- *Your local or state bar association can be*

a good source of information. For example, bar associations often provide guides to the courts and handbooks for jurors and witnesses. You can find contact information for your local and state bar association by accessing www.abanet.org.barserv/stlobar.html.

- *Many state courts, and most courts of last resort, have established websites that contain information and history about the court, as well as schedules of oral arguments and opinions of the court. The ABA's Judicial Division website provides links to state and federal courts at www.abanet.org/jd/jdlinks.html.*

Judicial Independence

- *The Justice at Stake Campaign website provides some information on judicial independence at www.justiceatstake.org; for a state-by-state analysis of the state of judicial independence, go to www.constitutionproject.org/ci/states.html.*
- *The ABA Standing Committee on Judicial Independence site includes a resource center with links to useful sites, as well as definitions of judicial independence; visit www.abanet.org/judind/home/html.*

REMEMBER THIS

- *State and federal courts hear different kinds of cases, are differently structured, and have different names—so you should always find out which court has jurisdiction over your case, and check the law in your state!*
- *Courts have specific powers granted to them under our system of separation of powers. One of the most important is their ability to invalidate a law on the grounds that it violates the Constitution.*

THE CIVIL TRIAL: STEP BY STEP

Julie is sure she is right. When one of her suppliers failed to come through with an order, her little business lost thousands of dollars and lots of goodwilll. Negotiation has failed, and the only way to get the money is to go to court. But what will that process be like? Will it be tense? Painful? Confusing?

It is difficult to make generalizations about trials because so much depends on the facts of your case and the court in which the trial is conducted. Nonetheless, this section will give you some general information about the steps you can expect to take in a civil trial. It will lead you step by step through a civil trial. If you want to know how a jury is selected, or what happens during cross-examination of a witness, then this section will help you understand those steps in the trial. This section does not provide information on the criminal trial, which is dealt with in detail in chapter 15, "Criminal Justice."

📄 MEET THE PLAYERS

The parties in a civil case are the plaintiff and the defendant. The **plaintiff** is the party filing the lawsuit and complaining of a wrong that has been done. The word comes from the Middle French word for "complain" and the Middle English word for "grieve"—and most plaintiffs certainly feel they have a grievance. The **defendant** is just the other side of the coin—the party alleged to have caused the grievance and obliged to defend himself/herself against the charge.

Commencing Legal Proceedings and Procedures Before Trial

Q. How much time does one have to decide whether to file a civil law suit?

A. It varies depending on the nature of the suit. Each state, and the federal government, has **statutes of limitations**. These govern the amount of time you have in which to sue after the incident on which the suit is based takes place, and you have more or less time depending on the kind of suit involved. The justification for imposing these time limits is that it is unfair to require a defendant to provide a defense long after the incident occurred, when memories may no longer be fresh and evidence may no longer be available. Thus, after the time limit set forth in the applicable statute of limitations has run out, the plaintiff is barred from bringing suit—no matter how meritorious the case. Some limitation periods are very short, so you should determine early how long you have to bring your case.

📄 SERVICE

Service is the delivery of a legal document—such as a complaint, a summons, or a subpoena. The person receiving the document is said to have been **served**.

Q. What begins a lawsuit?

A. A lawsuit begins when the plaintiff files a document called a **complaint** with the court. The complaint recounts what happened to the plaintiff, what the plaintiff wants the court to do about it, and the legal reasons why the court ought to do what the plaintiff asks. The various wrongs the plaintiff claims to have suffered are listed in separate **counts** of the complaint. The complaint also sets forth the remedy the plaintiff is seeking from the court.

Q. How does a defendant find out that he or she is being sued?

A. The lawyer for the plaintiff or the clerk of the court will draft a paper called a **summons**. The summons tells the defendant that a suit has been filed against him or her, who filed it, and the time and place to appear in court. This summons, along with the complaint, must then be given to the defendant. A sheriff or marshal may deliver the documents, or a private process server may be hired, or the documents might be mailed by registered mail. You should check on the required method of service appropriate for your case. These documents provide the defendants with the first official notice that they are being sued.

Q. What are the defendant's options after being served with the complaint and summons?

A. At this point, most defendants will hire a lawyer to prepare their defense to the suit. The defendant's lawyer will determine when the defen-

---

📄 MOTION

A **motion** is a formal written or oral request that the court take some specific action. Typical pretrial motions might include a defense motion to remove some allegations from the complaint or to dismiss all or part of the complaint for specific legal reasons. If the service of the summons and complaint was improper (because, for example, the server delivered the documents to the wrong address), the defendant may file a **motion to quash** service. Or a defendant might file a **motion to dismiss** based on the complainant's failure to state a valid claim upon which relief can be granted. The parties may be required to attend a hearing on the motion to resolve the issues raised.

dant needs to respond to the complaint, discuss the details of the complaint with the defendant, and review the complaint and summons to be certain that it meets all legal requirements. If the complaint appears defective, legally or factually, the defendant may file a motion with the court.

Q. *How much information should the defendant include in the answer?*

A. Essentially, the defendant's answer must make the plaintiff and the court aware of the defendant's response to each allegation and count in the complaint, by stating whether he or she is contesting or admitting each allegation and count, or is unable to contest or admit because of insufficient information. A failure to respond can be interpreted as an admission by the defendant that the plaintiff's allegation is true. In addition, the answer may raise any affirmative defenses the defendant may have. An **affirmative defense** is a defense beyond simple denial, where the defendant attempts to counter, defeat, or remove all or a part of the contentions of the plaintiff. If a defendant raises an affirmative defense, the defendant will be required to prove it if the case goes to trial.

If the defendant has reason to believe that the court lacks jurisdiction to hear the case, the defendant should raise that issue at the earliest possible opportunity.

Q. *What if the defendant believes that the plaintiff has caused damage to the defendant?*

A. In that case, the defendant in a civil case, in addition to answering the plaintiff's complaint, may file a claim against the plaintiff. This action is known as a **counterclaim**. If a counterclaim is filed, the plaintiff becomes a defendant and will be called on to file an answer to the allegations and counts contained in the counterclaim.

Q. *What if there are other claims or parties that should be involved in the litigation?*

A. If the defendant believes that others not named as defendants in the plaintiff's suit are re-

sponsible, in whole or in part, for the plaintiff's injury or loss, he or she may seek to bring those third parties into the case as additional defendants. This is known as an **action to implead** those parties. If a person who was not named in the original suit believes he or she should be involved in order to defend his or her interests, which are affected by the lawsuit, that person may seek to join the suit as either an additional plaintiff or defendant. Such a party is said to **intervene** in the lawsuit. Finally, in suits that already involve multiple plaintiffs or defendants, parties may file **cross-claims**, which are actions by one named party against another. For example, one defendant could file a cross-claim against another defendant. These kinds of pretrial procedures are intended to encourage plaintiffs and defendants to resolve all related disputes in a single case, rather than in piecemeal litigation.

Q. *How does a court determine whether it has jurisdiction to hear the case?*

A. In federal court, the plaintiff bears the burden of proving, through citation of relevant statutes and case law, that the court has jurisdiction to hear his or her case under Article III of the U.S. Constitution. In most state courts, by contrast, it is up to the defendant to prove that the court does not have jurisdiction under applicable state jurisdictional laws.

Q. *What is a motion for change of venue?*

A. In addition to deciding whether it has jurisdiction to hear the case, a trial court may also be asked to determine whether the case should be

 VENUE

The **venue** is the county or district within a state or the United States where the lawsuit is to be tried. It is usually the place where the accident occurred, the contract was signed, or the crime was committed.

heard where it was filed or in a court in some other city, county, or state. If the court determines that it would be more convenient for the parties if the trial were held somewhere else, or if the court determines that there is so much publicity about the case in one community that it should be heard elsewhere to assure a fair trial, the court will permit the case to be heard in a different location. This is called a **change of venue**. Congress (or, in the case of state courts, the state legislature) determines the rules regarding venue, which are generally designed to ensure that neither party is prejudiced by the trial's location.

Q. What is summary judgment?

A. Summary judgment may be appropriate if the relevant facts are not in dispute and the only question is how the law should be applied to those facts. In such cases, there is no need for a jury or judge to hear witnesses or view evidence regarding what happened. All that is left for the court to do is to apply the law to the undisputed facts, without a trial.

In considering whether to grant a party's motion for summary judgment, the trial court will review the parties' **affidavits** (written statements made under oath) and discovery materials to determine whether, when viewed in the light most favorable to the opponent to the motion, there is no genuine dispute regarding an important fact.

If the court is uncertain whether a genuine factual issue exists, it will deny the summary judgment motion and the case will proceed to trial. If, on the other hand, the court is convinced that there is no such factual dispute, it will consider the parties' written arguments on the legal issues and then rule on the motion for summary judgment, disposing of the case in favor of one of the parties.

Exchange of Information

Q. Can a party in a civil action compel his or her opponent to disclose information and the names of witnesses even before the trial begins?

A. Yes. The process of finding out information from the other side before the trial begins is called **discovery**. This is a vital step in any civil litigation and a reminder that the goal of our legal system is to do justice rather than to reward the clever lawyer or secretive litigant. Surprise witnesses and secret evidence are things that happen on television or in the movies, but rarely in a real courtroom.

The exchange of information has the advantage that it becomes clear early what facts are at issue between the parties. This might result in a decrease in the amount of time that needs to be spent presenting evidence at trial, and could even help the parties resolve their dispute. It may also make summary judgment an appropriate option.

Among the pretrial discovery tools available to litigants are:

- **Depositions.** The lawyers for each side in a lawsuit may require potential witnesses to answer oral questions under oath before the trial.
- **Interrogatories.** Each party can submit a list of written questions to the other party, which again must be answered under oath.
- **Motion to produce.** Each party can ask the court to require the other to produce relevant documents or physical evidence in the other party's possession, custody, or control for the purpose of inspecting, copying, or photographing them.
- **Request to admit.** Each party can ask the other to agree that certain facts are true and thus spare both parties the trouble, expense, and delay of having to prove them at trial.

Q. What if my opponent and I agree on some but not all of the facts in my case?

A. If the parties agree on certain facts, they can **stipulate** that those facts are undisputed and thereby forgo the need to introduce evidence at trial to prove those facts. If they don't agree about some facts, then each side will have the opportunity to introduce evidence establishing those facts.

Juries

Q. Does the U.S. Constitution guarantee me a right to a jury trial in every case?

A. No, there is no right to a jury trial in every case. In civil cases, the Seventh Amendment guarantees the right to a jury trial in "suits at common law." As a general rule, suits at common law encompass only those civil suits seeking money as compensation for an asserted injury or loss—for example, breach of contract or personal injury actions. The Seventh Amendment's right to a jury trial does not apply if the plaintiff is seeking an "equitable" remedy for his or her injury or loss—for example, an order to the defendant to cease certain conduct or turn over property.

However, Congress has provided for the jury trial option in some instances where the federal Constitution does not require one. State constitutions may also guarantee greater rights to a jury trial.

Chapter 15, "Criminal Justice," provides information on jury trials in criminal cases.

Q. What is the difference between a legal and equitable claim?

A. Whether a claim is legal or equitable can generally be determined by the remedy the plaintiff is seeking. As noted above, a request for money damages is, historically, a **legal** claim, while a request that the court order a party to take or stop some action is an **equitable** claim. The question can be more complicated in cases where there are a number of different claims, some legal, some equitable, and some with both legal and equitable characteristics.

Q. Will I automatically get a jury trial if I'm constitutionally entitled to one?

A. No. Typically, a party must make a written demand for a jury trial. For tactical reasons, some parties may prefer to have their case decided by a judge alone.

Q. How does a bench trial, where a judge conducts the trial without a jury, differ from a jury trial?

A. In a jury trial, the fact-finding function belongs to the jury and the judge provides the jury with instructions on how to apply the law to those facts determined by the jury. In a **bench trial**, on the other hand, the judge must determine the facts and then apply the law to the facts.

Q. How are potential jurors selected?

A. Jurors must be representative of the community in which the trial is being conducted. Courts usually obtain the names of prospective jurors from a regularly maintained list or group of lists, such as lists of registered voters or licensed drivers. When a case is set for trial by jury, the clerk of court uses this list to provide the court with a randomly selected pool of potential jurors representing a fair cross section of the community. The jurors who will actually hear the case are then chosen in a process in which the members of the jury panel are questioned. This process is known as **voir dire**.

Q. How are the jury members selected for my particular case?

A. Potential jurors are questioned in open court by the trial judge or the parties' lawyers, depending on local statutes and court rules, in order to discover any reason to believe that they might have a potential bias or prejudice relating to the parties or to issues in the case. If a juror concedes such a bias or prejudice, or if evidence suggests he or she may have a bias, the lawyer may ask the court to **strike the juror for cause** and remove him or her from the panel of potential jurors in that case.

In addition to challenges for cause, each lawyer can make **peremptory challenges**. These challenges permit a lawyer to excuse a potential juror without stating a cause. Peremptory challenges are limited to a certain number determined by the kind of lawsuit being tried. They can't be used to remove potential jurors on the basis of race or gender.

Q. Must every civil jury have twelve jurors?

A. No. Federal civil trial juries have from six to twelve members. In state courts, there is similar variation. In many state civil cases, juries have only six or eight members.

Q. Must all jury verdicts be unanimous?

A. In the federal system, jury decisions must be unanimous. If the jury is not unanimous (if it is irrevocably divided it is called a **hung jury**), a mistrial is declared. The case may be retried later or dismissed.

There is more variation among the states. In more than a third of the states, agreement of only three-fourths or five-sixths of the jurors is needed to render a verdict in civil cases.

Q. What if I am called for jury duty?

A. If you are randomly selected to serve as a juror, you should recognize that it is an opportunity to serve your community by participating in the justice system. Remember that juries need to be representative of the community from which they are selected and that service by everyone assists in achieving that goal.

If you are called for jury service, you should inform your employer and report to the court as instructed on the jury summons. The law requires your employer to permit you to take time off from work to perform your jury duty, although you may be excused from jury service on the basis of hardship.

Jury service is becoming less burdensome than it used to be, due to an increase in the amount that jurors are paid, continuation by many employers of jurors' regular salaries for some period, and adoption in some jurisdictions of much shorter terms of jury service, known as **one day–one trial** in many states. Many jurisdictions also have provisions that provide that a juror will not be selected again for a specified number of years after serving.

Q. What if I am selected as an alternate juror?

A. At the beginning of the trial, the judge may order that more jurors be seated than are required for the verdict. These extra jurors are known as **alternate jurors**, and they are selected to guard against the possibility that some of the

jurors will become ill or otherwise be unable to complete the trial. An alternate would attend the trial along with the regular jurors, but would not be called to participate in reaching a verdict unless one of the regular jurors was unable to continue.

No matter what procedures are used, it is important for alternate jurors to always pay attention to testimony because they may be required to participate in the verdict should another juror be unable to complete his or her service.

Trials

Q. My case will be tried before a jury. What does this involve?

A. Jury trials begin with **opening statements** presented to the jury by the lawyer for each party. The opening statement serves to introduce the jurors to each side's theory of the case and outlines what each side plans to prove during the trial. For example, in a personal injury case, the plaintiff will explain that the defendant was negligent and that as a result, the plaintiff suffered a financial loss or other injury. The plaintiff will need to prove the elements of negligence: that the defendant owed the plaintiff a legal duty, that he or she breached that duty, and that the duty caused damage to the plaintiff. The defense, meanwhile, will explain why there is reason to doubt one or more of those elements of the plaintiff's case.

Q. How do parties present their case?

A. The heart of the case is the presentation of evidence. In a civil case, the plaintiff begins the presentation of a case by calling witnesses. The witnesses may testify to matters of fact. They may also be called to identify documents, pictures, or other items introduced into evidence. The defense may cross-examine the plaintiff's witnesses.

After the plaintiff has finished calling witnesses, the defense puts on its case by calling witnesses, and the plaintiff will have the opportunity to cross-examine them.

Q. How does a direct examination differ from a cross-examination?

A. Direct examination is conducted by the party calling the witness, and is intended to establish that party's case. The witnesses may be **cross-examined** by the lawyer for the opposing party, a process in which the lawyer will attempt to undermine the testimony given by the witness under direct examination by bringing forth facts favorable to the cross-examining party or discrediting that witness. Cross-examination is generally limited to questioning on matters raised in direct examination.

Q. What are the rules of evidence?

A. The rules of evidence require fact-finding judges or juries to base their decisions solely on relevant evidence that is reliable. Some evidentiary rules are fashioned to further other important policies, such as protecting civil liberties. There are several important rules of evidence.

- Witnesses generally cannot state opinions or conclusions unless they are experts or specially qualified to do so.
- Lawyers generally may not ask leading questions of their own witnesses. **Leading questions** are questions that suggest the answers desired, in effect prompting the witness. An example is: "Isn't is true that you saw John waiting across the street before his wife came home?" Lawyers may ask leading questions during cross-examination.
- There is a prohibition on hearsay. **Hearsay** is what the witness says he or she heard another person say, when the witness is trying to assert the truth of what the other person said. The witness is repeating a statement made by someone else, not what the witness actually personally saw or heard. There are complex exceptions to the rule against hearsay.

Q. How does a judge rule on objections?

A. One of your lawyer's duties is to make an appropriate **objection** to any violation of the rules of evidence by the opposing party, such as to leading questions, questions that call for an opinion or conclusion by a witness, or questions that require an answer based on hearsay.

Most courts require that a specific legal reason be stated for an objection. Usually, the judge will immediately either sustain or overrule the objection. If the objection is **sustained**, the lawyer must rephrase the question in a proper form or ask another question. If the witness has already given an answer, it is not in evidence and the jury will be instructed by the judge to disregard it. If the objection is **overruled,** the witness can answer the question, and the answer is in evidence and may be considered by the jury.

Even if the court overrules your lawyer's objection, the objection will appear in the written record of your trial and can be raised again on appeal if you should lose at trial. In many instances, a failure to object at trial means that you **waive** (give up) your right to complain about the matter later.

Judges have to rule on objections, but that doesn't mean they are not still neutral. One of the federal courts, in its handbook for jurors, points out that "a ruling by the judge does not indicate that the judge is taking sides. He or she is merely saying, in effect, that the law does, or else does not, permit that question to be asked."

Verdicts

Q. What happens after each side has presented all its evidence?

A. Each side will be given the opportunity to address the jury directly and to summarize what he or she believes was proven during the trial. At the conclusion of these arguments, called **closing statements** or **closing arguments**, the judge will consider each side's suggestions on how to instruct the jury on the law that governs the case. In some state and federal courts, judges give the jury instructions on the law prior to the closing statements to assist them in understanding the closing statements better. The judge's instructions will specify the issues the jury must decide and the law it must apply to the facts that were developed in the case. Then the jury will retire to the jury room to come to a decision. In the typical case the jury will be asked to render a **general verdict** and conclude which side won on an all-or-nothing basis. Alternatively, the judge may ask for a **special verdict**, which requires the jury to enter separate written findings on each of several issues.

Q. Is there anything to prevent the jury from deliberating on the case after each side has finished presenting its case?

A. Yes. Sometimes, before turning the case over to the jury, the judge will consider either side's **motion to direct a verdict** in its favor. A directed verdict removes the need for the jury to determine whether the defendant is liable, but such a ruling is only appropriate when the court is persuaded that a reasonable jury could decide the case in only one way. The court may grant, deny, or, more likely, **reserve** (postpone) ruling on such a motion until after the jury has rendered a verdict. If the jury rules against the party who requested the directed verdict, the judge can still overrule the jury's decision by granting a motion for **judgment notwithstanding the verdict**.

Q. What else must the verdict contain?

A. If the jury concludes that one of the parties is liable to the other, it must go on to decide what remedy is owed to the party who was wronged. In most ordinary personal injury suits, this remedy will take the form of money **damages**. If the jury makes a finding that the defendant should pay damages to the plaintiff, the court will direct the defendant to pay. The judge may decide to separate this portion of the trial from the liability portion. In appropriate cases, such a **bifurcated trial** can simplify the issues by saving the jury from having to listen to instructions and arguments about the proper damages until after it has determined whether the plaintiff is entitled to any damages at all.

Damages are supposed to put plaintiffs back in the financial position they would have been in if they hadn't been wronged in the first place. It is, of course, more difficult to calculate the proper award when the defendant's wrongful act caused more than out-of-pocket expenses: How much money does it take to compensate one for pain, suffering, loss of life's enjoyment, or damages to one's reputation?

In some circumstances, when the defendant's behavior is thought to be especially outrageous, the plaintiff may also ask the jury to find that **punitive damages** ought to be paid in addition to compensatory damages. For example, in the O. J. Simpson civil case, the jury awarded the Brown and Goldman families millions of dollars in punitive damages because they found that Simpson had caused the deaths of their family members. Punitive damages are designed to punish the defendant and to discourage others from engaging in similar conduct.

Procedures After Trial

Q. If the plaintiff wins, what happens next?

A. After the court enters judgment in favor of the plaintiff, a formal judicial order commanding the defendant to pay the compensation awarded is usually made. But winning a verdict may only be the beginning of a plaintiff's efforts to secure a remedy.

If a defendant against whom a judgment has been entered does not pay, the plaintiff will have to initiate collection proceedings. The plaintiff may have to seek orders from a judge that the defendant's property be sold, or that an amount be deducted periodically from the defendant's wages in order to satisfy the judgment.

Q. What options does the losing party have?

A. A losing party has two options. First, the losing party can ask the court to throw out the verdict and order a new trial if it can show the court that

- the verdict was contrary to the weight of the evidence; or
- serious errors or other misconduct were committed by the judge; or
- there was serious misconduct on the part of a juror, a lawyer, a witness, or a party; or
- the damages under the verdict are far out of proportion to the harm; or
- vitally important evidence that could not have been discovered before the end of the trial has only now been discovered.

Alternatively, or if these **new trial motions** do not succeed, the party may appeal the judgment to an appellate court.

Q. How does a party appeal?

A. The losing party (or a prevailing party contending that the damages were insufficient) may ask for review of the trial court's decision in an appellate court. In the federal system, the party must appeal to the court of appeals in the appropriate circuit.

In those states that have two levels of appellate courts, parties challenging trial court decisions generally must bring their appeals to the intermediate court first. However, because intermediate appellate courts often have some limited discretion to determine which civil cases they will hear, not all civil appeals will necessarily be accepted, in which case the lower court's verdict will stand.

ⓘ APPEALS

A popular misconception is that cases are always appealed. In fact, a losing party does not always have an automatic right of appeal. There must usually be a legal basis for the appeal. The fact that the losing party did not like the verdict is not sufficient.

Q. How do appeals work?

A. Appeals courts review the procedures of lower courts and ensure that the law was properly applied. As a general rule, they do not retry cases. They don't hear witnesses and weigh evidence. Instead, in an appeal, the appellant must persuade the court to reverse the trial court's judgment because of some significant legal errors that occurred during the trial, such as the improper admission or exclusion of evidence, or erroneous instructions on the law given by the judge to the jury, which are likely to have affected the result. The appellee, on the other hand, will seek to persuade the court that no error was made in the lower court or that if there was an error, it was harmless because it did not affect the outcome. A printed transcript of the trial court proceedings, together with the original papers and exhibits, may be forwarded to the court for consideration in deciding the appeal.

📄 APPELLANT AND APPELLEE

The **appellant** is the party who appeals, that is, the party who carries his case to a higher court after receiving an adverse order in the lower court. The **appellee** is the party against whom an appeal is filed, and the one who must answer allegations of the appellant in the appeal. Appellees are sometimes referred to as **respondents,** because they must respond to the appellant's case on appeal.

Q. What is oral argument?

A. An appellate court is not required to hear oral argument, but appeal cases are generally scheduled for oral argument. If the case is before an intermediate appellate court, a panel of judges will hear the argument. However, in certain important cases before an intermediate court, the oral argument will be heard **en banc,** that is, heard by all the judges of the court. Oral arguments before the U.S. Supreme Court and the highest state courts are also en banc.

Prior to oral argument, the judges who will hear the appeal read the briefs and examine the record compiled in the trial court. At oral argument the judges will listen to the arguments of the lawyers for the parties and may question the lawyers about the case and how the law should be applied to the case. Typically each side is allotted a limited period of time in which to present its case orally. However, an appellate court is free to grant more or less time, based on the significance or complexity of the case. After oral argument, each judge votes on whether to uphold or reverse the trial court's judgment, in whole or in part. The court then issues a written opinion explaining its decision. As a general rule, the parties will not know the outcome of the case until the written opinion is released.

Q. Must an appellate court reach a unanimous decision?

A. No, only a majority must agree. If a judge or judges disagree with the majority's result, they may write a **dissent** to explain their disagreement. If a judge agrees with the result reached by the majority but disagrees with its reasoning, he or she may write a separate opinion **concurring** in the judgment.

Q. What recourse is there for the party who loses at the intermediate appellate level?

A. The party can seek review in the highest court in the system. In the federal system that court is the Supreme Court of the United States. In addition to the decisions of the U.S. courts of appeal, the U.S. Supreme Court has the jurisdiction, but not the obligation, to review the final decisions of the highest state courts (or even of lower state courts if the party was unable to secure additional review within the state courts) so long as the case is the sort of case described in Article III of the U.S. Constitution and was not decided on "adequate and independent state grounds." When the U.S. Supreme Court de-

clines to hear a case, as it does in the vast majority of cases, the decision of the lower federal or state court remains the final decision.

Q. How does the U.S. Supreme Court decide whether to hear a case?

A. In the usual course, a party seeking review in the U.S. Supreme Court will file a petition asking the Court to issue a **writ of certiorari**. This is simply a request to review the case. This petition will include a copy of the lower court's opinion and a **brief**. A brief states why the Court should agree to review the decision. The other party may file a brief in opposition to the petition. The Court will then either deny the petition (its action in most cases) or grant it, and if granted, require the federal or state court to transmit the record of the case to the U.S. Supreme Court for its review. In his book *The Supreme Court: How It Was, How It Is* (New York: Morrow, 1987), Chief Justice William H. Rehnquist describes the process of selecting which petitions to grant as being influenced by the justices' views on three major factors:

1. if the decision is from one of the federal courts of appeal, whether it is in conflict with the decisions of other circuits;
2. the general importance of the case; and
3. whether the lower court's decision may be wrong in light of the U.S. Supreme Court's previous opinions.

Q. What is the effect of granting a request for review?

A. If a request for review is granted, the case will be set for briefing and oral argument in much the same way it was in the court whose judgment is being reviewed. If the Court makes a decision on the merits of the case (that is, the ultimate issues), its decision will be binding, final, and the law of the land. Sometimes, however, the Court will **remand**, or return, the case to the lower court with instructions that the court reconsider its earlier opinion in light of the Supreme Court's clarification of how the relevant constitutional or statutory provisions should be applied and interpreted.

THE WORLD AT YOUR FINGERTIPS

The Courts

- *The American Bar Association's Division for Public Education publishes three inexpensive booklets for the public about courts and their work. All are available from American Bar Association Order Fulfillment by telephone at 800-285-2221 or online at www.abanet.org/publiced/catalog.html.*
  - *Law and the Courts: Volume I—The Role of Courts provides an introduction to the courts. Product Code Number 235-002798ed.*
  - *Law and the Courts: Volume II—Court Procedures gives readers a quick look at legal cases from beginning to end. A glossary of frequently used terms is included as a ready reference. Product code 235-0041.*
  - *Law and the Courts: Volume III—Juries looks at the citizen's role in the process, both through grand juries and trial juries. Product code 235-0202.*
- *Many justice issues are explored in the ABA's Roadmaps series. These plain-language booklets cover alternative dispute resolution (ADR), judicial independence, judicial selection, changes in the American jury, funding of the courts, racial and ethnic bias in the justice system, and other issues. All titles are listed at www.abanet. org/justice/roadmaps.html. To order, contact ABA Publication Orders by telephone at 800-285-2221; or by e-mail at orders@abanet.org.*
- *The Legal Information Institute at Cornell Law School is a great starting point for more in-depth research into the substance of the law; contact www.law.cornell.edu/.*

Juries

- *An example of a handbook for trial jurors serving in the federal district courts can be found at www.nysd.uscourts.gov/ jurybook.htm. The handbook provides information on what a juror can expect and will need to know.*
- *A map leading to information about jury service in each state can be found at www. ncsc.dni.us/KMO/topics/jury/states/states/ juryusmap.htm.*

REMEMBER THIS

- *After the time limit set forth in the applicable statute of limitations has run out, the plaintiff is barred from bringing suit—no matter how meritorious the case.*
- *A lawsuit is commenced with a complaint. After being served with the complaint and the summons, the defendant may file a defense with the court. Either party may file motions or seek summary judgment. Both parties participate in discovery before the trial.*
- *There is no right to a jury trial in every case.*
- *The losing party may be able to seek review of the trial court's decision in an appellate court. Remember that there is no automatic right to an appeal—if you are unhappy with the way your case turned out, talk to your lawyer about whether an appeal is an option.*

MEDIATION AND SMALL-CLAIMS COURT

Bob gave a friend of his $3,000 to put a deposit on a boat they were buying together. The sale fell through, but Bob's friend never returned the money. Bob phoned his friend and tried to convince him to return the money, and even *visited his house to talk about the problem. Eventually his friend told him that he'd spent the money and that Bob should just forget about it. What can Bob do now?*

Not all disputes are worth the trouble and expense of a full-fledged trial, and some disputes—like those between friends and neighbors—might be better solved if the parties could work it out informally and preserve their relationship. This section will look at your options for avoiding trial altogether. This may seem a little strange after emphasizing the important role of the courts, but the fact is that the vast majority of disputes are resolved before they ever get to trial.

Resolving Your Dispute out of Court

Q. What are my options if I want to resolve my civil case without proceeding to trial?

A. You have several options.

Negotiation

The lawyers in the case can meet and negotiate a settlement. If you don't have a lawyer, you should talk to the person with whom you have a dispute. Stay calm and reasonable. You may find that if approached politely, your opponent will be willing to settle on a mutually acceptable basis. Make certain that the other person understands why you are unhappy and what you would consider a reasonable solution to the problem. Keep an open mind and listen to his or her side of the story. Making an effort to settle a dispute without

---

COURT-FACILITATED SETTLEMENTS

The courts actively encourage settlements and will often require the parties in a civil case to confer in order to give them a chance to avoid the need for a full trial.

---

a lawsuit is never a waste of time. In addition, many states require that a party first make a demand for payment or action before filing some types of lawsuits.

If you do reach a satisfactory compromise, ask your lawyer to get it in writing for both parties to sign—you will both want to make certain what you are and are not agreeing to and what, if any, issues still need to be resolved. Even if you and the other person involved are able to work out the main problem, it still may be necessary to appear before a judge if a lawsuit has been commenced. Your court appearance will be made easier if the agreement is in writing and can be submitted to the judge.

Mediation or Arbitration

If your attempts to negotiate a settlement are unsuccessful, you may want to try to resolve the dispute through mediation or arbitration.

In **mediation**, a trained mediator will help you and your opponent resolve your disagreement by identifying, defining, and discussing the things about which you disagree, in an effort to help you reach a mutual agreement. This is an informal, cooperative problem-solving process, and does not necessarily require you to know the law or to hire a lawyer, although often the parties find it useful to do so.

Arbitration, on the other hand, is a more formal proceeding in which you and your opponent will be asked to present evidence and witnesses to an arbitrator, who will issue a decision, usually in writing, to resolve the dispute. Arbitration may be binding or nonbinding. If the parties agree to a

---

ⓘ THE NUMBER CRUNCH— SETTLEMENT OF CIVIL CASES

By some estimates, more than 90 percent of all civil cases are settled before trial.

binding arbitration, it means they must accept the arbitrator's decision as final; if they agree to a nonbinding arbitration, it means the parties retain the right to go to court.

Send a Demand Letter

If negotiation and mediation have failed but you are still keen to avoid a trial, then the next step is to ask your lawyer to write a carefully thought-out letter to the person with whom you have a disagreement. This is called a **demand letter,** and should include an accurate summary of the history of the problem and a date by which you would like a response or settlement. This type of "settle-or-else" letter has many advantages. It helps you organize the facts and your thoughts logically. Your lawyer may be able to express your thoughts in a way that the other person might not have heard when you were talking to each other directly. It may be just the push needed to get the other person to settle. If the letter sets reasonable time limits, it will often help to encourage settlement.

Settlement During Trial

In the event that all of your attempts to settle before trial are unsuccessful, you may find yourself preparing for litigation. This does not mean that it is no longer possible to settle your matter. It is often the case that as parties prepare their evidence and marshal their resources for trial, they become more interested in settling. In many cases, the judge will order the parties to participate in settlement conferences, mediation, or arbitration. A party may make an offer to settle before the trial begins; during the trial; or after the trial, up until the moment that the jury returns with the verdict.

ⓘ APPEALS

In many small claims courts there is no right to appeal if you lose. However, you may be able to start **de novo,** or new, litigation in a court of general jurisdiction.

Small-Claims Court

Q. What is small-claims court?

A. All states have these special courts, most often known as **small-claims courts,** but sometimes called **magistrate court, justice of the peace court,** or **pro se court.** As suggested by their title, small-claims courts are available only

---

▤ ALTERNATIVE DISPUTE RESOLUTION

Alternative dispute resolution (ADR) is a term used to describe the methods by which parties may resolve their disputes without going to trial. These include well-known methods, such as arbitration and mediation, as well as others such as summary jury trial procedures or settlement programs. Nearly all states have established **dispute resolution centers.** These centers, which, depending on the state, may be known as neighborhood justice centers or citizens' dispute settlement programs, specialize in helping people who have common problems. For example, there are centers that specialize in resolving disputes commonly encountered by consumers, employers and employees, landlords and tenants, neighbors, and family members. Those offering assistance will work to ensure that a nontrial option is appropriate for the nature of the dispute, so that there is a maximum opportunity for successful resolution.

📑 JURISDICTION

When we say a court has **jurisdiction** to hear a case, we mean it has the legal power and authority to decide the kinds of issues raised in the case. Not every court has jurisdiction to hear every kind of case. One of the first questions to answer before filing a lawsuit is which court has jurisdiction to hear the case: Can your case be heard by a small-claims court, or does a state or federal court have jurisdiction over the case?

to resolve disputes involving small claims for money. The jurisdictional limits of small-claims courts may range from a few hundred dollars in some states to thousands of dollars in others. The popular TV program *The People's Court* is an example of the comparatively informal, quick justice provided by small-claims courts.

Q. May I represent myself?

A. Yes, you may represent yourself in small-claims court and do not necessarily need a lawyer

to accompany you. In fact, there are some states in which a lawyer is not permitted to represent a party in small-claims court.

Q. What are the advantages of filing a lawsuit in a small-claims court?

A. First, if you choose to act as your own lawyer, you may not need to pay lawyer's fees. Second, small-claims court procedures are designed to be simpler and involve less paperwork than other courts. Third, it may be possible to have a proceeding conducted after normal working hours. And finally, the case is often resolved in less time.

Q. Can I have a jury trial in small-claims court?

A. No, there is no jury; a judge will decide your case.

Q. It sounds like it won't take much work to bring my case in small-claims court. Is that true?

A. Not necessarily. You should only represent yourself in a small-claims procedure if you are willing to put some time and effort into your case. If you act as your own lawyer, you will need to do research, gather documents, and investigate factual matters to prepare and present your case. In

---

▶ SOME SUGGESTIONS

Before you decide whether you should take advantage of small-claims court, ask yourself some simple questions. Is your claim one that has only to do with money? If so, is the amount you are suing for considered a small claim in your state? Are the time and effort you will have to put in to learning your state's law and presenting your case worth what you are likely to collect?

Remember that a small-claims court is, in many respects, like any other court. You will need to be prepared on the date of the hearing—know what arguments you are going to make; have your evidence ready, with copies for the judge and opposition; and bring any witnesses who are going to give testimony. And, like other courts, small-claims courts operate according to laws and rules. Even the most careful preparation and the best presentation in court will not help if you cannot prove legally that the other person owes you the money. You must be able to prove "legal liability" in your case—in other words, that someone else's unlawful acts caused you to suffer a loss for which money damages are appropriate.

some cases, the other side may be represented by a lawyer.

THE WORLD AT YOUR FINGERTIPS

- *The National Center for Community Mediation provides information about community mediation organizations, and some links; contact www.nacfcm.org/index.cfm. Alternatively, check the listings in the yellow pages or contact your bar association or court system for information about mediation in your community.*
- *For a national list of Internet sites on mediation and arbitration, access www.abanet.org/dispute/drlinks.html.*
- *The ABA Roadmaps can give you some valuable information on representing your-self in court. Check out Litigants Without Lawyers and User-Friendly Courts. All titles are listed at www.abanet.org/justice/ roadmaps.html.*

REMEMBER THIS

- *There are many ways to resolve your dispute without going to court. You can sometimes save time and money—and end up with a better outcome—by avoiding trial.*
- *If your attempts at negotiation and mediation do fail, do some research and see whether your case could be dealt with in small-claims court. Your case might be dealt with more quickly than it would be in a state court, and you may not need a lawyer.*

Family Law

It is difficult to give simple answers to many of the legal questions that a person may have about marriage, parenthood, separation, or divorce, because the laws vary from one state to another. In addition, because so many of the issues before a court require the exercise of judicial discretion, judges applying identical laws may decide cases with similar facts in different ways.

This chapter describes some of the laws and court rulings common to most states. If you have questions or simply want to be sure you understand these basic answers about how the law would be applied to a specific factual situation or in your state, contact a lawyer in your state. You may wish to contact a specialist. Many lawyers in urban areas work only on family law matters or make it a large part of their general practice. Lawyers specializing in family law also may refer to themselves as specialists in "domestic relations" or "matrimonial law."

MARRIAGE

Tim and Sophie are young, in love, and have decided to get married. Sophie has already thought about the dress, asked her sister to be a bridesmaid, and planned a guest list. Tim's friends are planning his stag night. Looks like this marriage business could be fun.

But there's more to marriage than a dress and a party. Tim and Sophie might want to think about the legal implications of their marriage. How will it affect the property they own now, and the property they hope to acquire? Will Sophie become responsible for Tim's debts? What are the tax implications of getting married?

This section cover the legal implications of marriage. Marriages have always been about family and ceremony and celebration. It's easy to forget that the government has an interest in marriage and families too. State legislatures have passed many laws regulating marriage and divorce. Laws can also affect couples who live together without being married.

Requirements for Getting Married

Q. Legally, what is marriage?

A. Marriage is a private bond between two people, but it is also an important social institution. Most states define marriage as a civil contract between a man and a woman to become husband and wife.

The moment a man and a woman marry, their relationship acquires a legal status. Married couples have financial and personal duties to each other during marriage and after separation or divorce. State laws determine the extent of these duties. As the U.S. Supreme Court said about marriage in 1888: "The relation once formed, the law steps in and holds the parties to various obligations and liabilities."

Society recognizes marriage in several ways:

- As a way to express commitment, strengthen intimate bonds, and provide mutual emotional support.
- As a (comparatively) stable structure within which to raise children.
- As a financial partnership in which spouses may choose from a variety of roles. Both spouses may work inside or outside the home to support the family, or the husband may support the wife, or the wife may support the husband.

As our society becomes more complex, there is no longer a short answer to the question "What is marriage?" Definitions and opinions of the proper functions of marriage continue to change. The women's rights movement and gay rights movement have resulted in more equal treatment of men and women and the creation of new legal relationships, including domestic partnerships and civil unions for same-sex couples. The traditional concept of marriage remains, but it continues to evolve.

Q. What are the legal requirements for getting married?

A. The requirements are simple, although they vary from state to state. In general, a man and a woman wishing to marry must obtain a license in the state in which they wish to be married, usually from a county clerk, a city clerk, or a a clerk of court. The fee usually is low.

Parties who wish to marry must have the **capacity** to do so. This means that neither can be married to someone else, the parties must be of a certain age, and both must understand that they are being married and what it means to be married. If, because of drunkenness, mental illness, or some other problem, one of the parties lacks capacity, the marriage will not be valid.

A few states require the man and the woman to have blood tests for venereal disease before the license is issued, although most do not require a blood test. In states that require a blood test, some will not issue a license if one or both of the parties have venereal disease, while others will allow the marriage if the couple knows the disease is present.

In a few states, a couple must show proof of immunity or vaccination for certain diseases or completion of a general physical examination.

Close blood relatives cannot marry, although in some states, first cousins can marry. Of those states that allow first cousins to marry, a few states also require that one of the cousins be unable to conceive children.

Some states require a waiting period, generally three days, between the time the license is issued and the time of the marriage ceremony.

Q. At what age may people marry?

A. A man or woman may marry at age eighteen without parental consent. Most states also allow persons age sixteen and seventeen to marry with consent of their parents or a judge.

Q. When does a couple become married?

A. Most states consider a couple to be married when the ceremony ends, when the officiating person says "I now pronounce you husband and wife." Failure to have sexual relations (lack of consummation) does not affect the validity of the marriage. In all states, the proper official must record the marriage license. Recording the marriage license is proof that the marriage happened.

Q. Is a particular type of marriage ceremony required?

A. No, there is broad latitude regarding the type of ceremony required. A marriage ceremony may be religious or civil. The person or persons conducting the ceremony should indicate that the man and woman agree to be married. A religious ceremony should be conducted under the customs of the religion, or, in the case of a Native American group, the tribe. Most states require one or two witnesses to sign the marriage certificate.

Q. Are common-law marriages allowed?

A. In most states, no. In times past, particularly in the frontier days, it was common for states to consider a woman and man to be married if they lived together for a certain length of time, had sexual intercourse, and held themselves out as husband and wife, even though they never went through a marriage ceremony. Today, only nine states recognize common-law marriages. In those states, in order for there to be a legal common-law marriage, the partners must clearly represent

---

ⓘ PERSONS WHO MAY CONDUCT MARRIAGE CEREMONIES

Civil ceremonies are usually conducted by judges. In some states, county clerks or other government officials may conduct civil ceremonies. Religious ceremonies are normally conducted by religious officials, such as ministers, priests, or rabbis. Native American ceremonies may be presided over by a tribal chief or other designated official. Contrary to popular legend, no state authorizes ship captains to perform marriages.

themselves to others as being husband and wife; merely living together is not enough to create a marriage.

In states that recognize a common-law marriage, the partners have the same rights and duties as if there had been a ceremonial marriage. Most other states will accept as valid a common-law marriage that began in a state that recognizes common-law marriage.

A legal common-law marriage may end only with a formal divorce. There is no such thing as a "common-law divorce."

Q. What is a domestic partnership?

A. Some cities have passed laws providing for **domestic partnerships**, which can apply to homosexual couples, and heterosexual couples, who are living together without being married. To become domestic partners, the partners must register their relationship at a government office and declare that they are in a "committed" relationship. Domestic partnerships provide some—but not all—of the legal benefits of marriage. Some of the common benefits are the right to coverage on a family health insurance policy, the right to family leave to take care of a sick partner (to the same extent a person would be able to use family leave to care for a sick spouse), bereavement leave, vis-iting rights to hospitals and jails, and rent control benefits (to the same extent a spouse would retain reduced rent if his or her partner died.)

Q. Does a woman's last name change automatically when she gets married?

A. No. A woman's name changes only if she wants it changed. In the past, a woman would often change her last name to her husband's name when she married. Now society recognizes a woman's right to take her husband's name, keep her original name, or use both names. The general rule is that if a woman uses a chosen name consistently and honestly, then it will be recognized as her true name. The details on how to change a name can be found in the sidebar entitled "What's in a Name?" (see page 72).

Invalid Marriages

Q. What rules apply if a marriage turns out to be invalid?

A. A marriage may be invalid because it is between close relatives, underage persons, or people incapable of entering into the marriage

---

ⓘ SAME-SEX MARRIAGES

As of early 2004, no state has passed a law recognizing homosexual marriages per se. If two members of the same sex were to go through a marriage ceremony, the courts would not consider the marriage to be valid, and, in the event the parties split up, they could not seek a legal divorce. Vermont allows same-sex couples to form **civil unions,** which give same-sex couples the same benefits and protections as heterosexual couples who enter into marriages.

▤ COVENANT MARRIAGE

A few states (including Arizona, Arkansas, and Louisiana) give couples an option of obtaining what is called a **covenant marriage.** A covenant marriage requires the couple to complete premarital counseling before the marriage takes place. Covenant marriages usually limit the grounds for divorce to certain fault-based grounds, such as adultery, physical cruelty, commission of a felony, addiction to drugs or alcohol, or abandonment. If a couple chooses not to request a covenant marriage, the premarital counseling is not required and no-fault grounds are available in the event the couple seeks a divorce.

contract because of mental incompetence, or if a prior marriage exists. Sometimes people discover that their marriage is invalid only when filing for divorce.

In some states, the **putative spouse doctrine** offers some protection to the innocent party if the parties went through a ceremonial marriage. A putative (meaning "supposed") spouse may be entitled to the same benefits and rights as a legal spouse for as long as she or he reasonably believed the marriage to be valid. In states that do not accept the putative spouse doctrine, people who mistakenly believe they are married have the same status as unmarried couples who have lived together.

After a long union that both parties honestly believed was a valid marriage, a court may refuse to declare the marriage invalid and require a divorce to end the marriage.

Q. What if one person tricks the other into thinking there has been a valid marriage?

A. Sometimes the law treats an invalid marriage as valid if one person tricked the other into thinking that the couple had a valid marriage. If so, a court might not allow the deceiving partner to declare the marriage invalid. In legal terms, the court **estops** (a legal term meaning "prevents") the deceiving partner from denying that the marriage exists. In addition, a court may find that the doctrine of **laches** (or "long delay") prevents even the innocent party, who originally did not know about the invalid marriage, from having the marriage declared invalid if he or she did nothing for a long time after learning that the marriage was not valid.

Duties of Marriage

Q. Does either spouse have a duty to work outside the home?

A. No. While the husband and wife are married and living together, a court is not going to get involved in private family decisions of who works and who does not. That's left to the husband and wife to sort out. Today, more than one-half of married women—including women with preschool-age children—work outside the home. A husband or wife cannot, as a matter of law, force his or her spouse to work.

AMERICANS MARRYING LATER, OFTEN
MEDIAN AGE FOR MARRIAGE IN THE UNITED STATES

	1970	2000
Women, First Marriage:	20.8	25.1
Men, First Marriage:	23.2	26.8

Source: U.S. Census Bureau; National Center for Health Statistics

REMARRIAGE AFTER DIVORCE

	1990
Women, Remarriage After Divorce:	34.2 %
Men, Remarriage After Divorce:	37.4 %

Source: U.S. Census Bureau; National Center for Health Statistics

Q. If the wife and husband separate or divorce, can a court require them to work outside the home?

A. No, not directly. If a wife and husband separate or divorce, a court still cannot directly order one or both of them to work. The court can, however, declare that one or both parties owe a duty of financial support to the other party (alimony; also called maintenance or spousal support) or to the children (child support). If so, the court will set an amount of support that must be paid. A duty of financial support means that person who is supposed to pay support must come up with the money somehow—usually from work or from savings. If the person who is supposed to pay support does not pay the money and does not have a good excuse why the money has not been paid, that person could be held in contempt of court. The possible penalties for being held in contempt of court include payment of fines and incarceration. Payments of child support and alimony will be discussed later in this chapter.

Q. Are there legal remedies if a husband or wife refuses to have sexual relations with his or her spouse?

A. A court would not order a person to have sexual relations with his or her spouse. A spouse who forces sexual relations with a partner can be charged with rape under the state's criminal law. In some states, the refusal to have sexual rela-

tions with a spouse is a specific ground for divorce or annulment of the marriage. In other states, refusal to have sexual relations could be considered a ground for divorce because it is an "irreconcilable difference" or a "mental cruelty."

Q. May wives and husbands sue each other?

A. Yes. Husbands and wives can, of course, sue each other for a divorce. They can also sue each other in connection with financial deals in which one may have cheated the other. The vast majority of states also allow one spouse to sue the other for deliberate personal injuries, such as those suffered in a beating. Some states allow husbands and wives to sue each other in connection with an auto accident in which one of them, who was the driver, accidentally caused injury to the other, who was a passenger. In effect, the person suing may be trying to collect money from an insurance company rather from the person's spouse. Many states, fearing that this would encourage collusion, do not allow such lawsuits.

Q. Can spouses testify against each other in court?

A. Yes. Husbands and wives routinely testify against each other in divorce cases. There is an old rule that husbands and wives cannot testify about communications made between them during the marriage. Although the rule may be applied in some circumstances, it generally does not

---

📑 LOSS OF CONSORTIUM

The term **loss of consortium** refers to the loss of companionship and sexual relationship with one's spouse. The concept also can apply more broadly to the loss of companionship and affection from other family members such as a child or parent. In personal injury actions, plaintiffs may seek monetary damages from the defendant for loss of consortium in addition to payment for other losses such as medical expenses, lost wages, and physical pain and suffering. For example, if a man is injured in an auto accident caused by a negligent driver and is unable to have sexual relations with his wife because of the accident, both the husband and the wife may seek damages for that loss.

apply if the husband and wife are involved in a lawsuit against each other.

Living Together Outside of Marriage

Q. Can two people live together without being married?

A. Of course. The Census Bureau reports 3.8 million people cohabit. Two unrelated people can generally live together anywhere they want. A few states still have laws prohibiting "fornication"— sexual relations between a man and woman who are not married—but such laws are virtually never enforced.

Some states have also had laws against "sodomy," which, among other things, prohibited sexual relations between people of the same sex. Those laws have rarely been enforced if the conduct is private, consensual, and between adults. Moreover, in 2003, in *Lawrence and Garner v.* *Texas*, the U. S. Supreme Court invalidated a Texas law that criminalized oral and anal sex by consenting gay couples. This effectively declared unconstitutional all state sodomy laws as they applied to private, consensual intimacy.

Q. May two unmarried people who are living together enter into agreements about sharing expenses or acquiring property?

A. Yes. People may want to agree about who will pay what and how they will share in property that they might acquire. From a legal standpoint, it is best to make the agreements specific and in writing. An oral agreement might be enforceable, but it is more difficult to prove because the parties to the agreement often have differing views. Each party to the agreement should give some benefit to the other party, such as agreeing to pay a certain portion of expenses. If an agreement looks as

FIGURE 1. HOUSEHOLDS BY TYPE: SELECTED YEARS, 1970 TO 2000.

(Percent Distribution)

	1970	1980	1990	2000	
NONFAMILY HOUSEHOLDS					
Other nonfamily households	1.7	3.6	4.6	5.7	
Women living alone	11.5	14.5	14.9	14.8	
Men living alone	5.6	8.6	9.7	10.7	
FAMILY HOUSEHOLDS					
Other family households	10.6	12.9	14.8	16.0	
Married couples without children	30.3	29.9	29.8	28.7	
Married couples with own children	40.3	30.9	23.6	24.1	

Source: U.S. Census Bureau, Current Population Survey, March Supplements: 1970 to 2000.

ⓘ **THE NUMBER CRUNCH—
UNMARRIED PARTNERS**

In 2000, there were 3.8 million households that were classified as "unmarried-partner households." This represents 3.7 percent of all households in the United States. The Census Bureau notes, "These numbers may underrepresent the true number of cohabiting couples because . . . respondents may be reluctant to classify themselves as such in a personal interview situation and may describe themselves as roommates, housemates, or friends not related to each other."

---

though it is only creating a gift from one party to the other with the recipient giving nothing in return, the agreement might not be enforceable.

Q. Will a court enforce an agreement by which one unmarried partner agrees to keep house and the other promises financial support?

A. Probably not, but laws on this issue vary from state to state. To begin with, such agreements are rarely in writing, so they are hard to prove in court. Second, to the extent that one person is promising financial support to the other, that promise is usually contingent on a continuation of the relationship. If, for example, one partner tells the other, "I'll take care of you," the statement may be too vague to be enforceable; if it means anything, it probably means something along the lines of "I'll support you financially as long as we are living together." So, if the couple breaks up, a court would probably not find an enforceable promise for continued support.

There is a potential third problem: If a court thinks an agreement amounts to providing financial support in exchange for sexual relations, the court will not enforce it. Such an agreement is considered to be close to a contract for prostitution.

Courts are more inclined to enforce agreements that provide for tangible items, such as payment of expenses or rights to property. A promise of housekeeping services or emotional support for a partner may be sincere, but it is much more amorphous than a promise to pay half the phone bill or share the proceeds of a condominium sale.

Domestic Violence

Q. What are legal remedies for domestic violence?

A. There are several remedies. All states allow a court to issue a **protective order**, ordering the alleged abuser to stop abusing or harassing someone. In addition, the orders will often require the abuser to stay away from the spouse, the spouse's home, or the spouse's place of work. If the person continues to abuse his or her spouse (or another person protected by the order), the abuser can be charged with a criminal violation of the order in addition to being charged with other offenses, such as battery.

In many states, protection is also available for people in dating relationships that have become abusive.

⚠ **THE NUMBER CRUNCH—
DOMESTIC VIOLENCE**

In 1998, women experienced about 900,000 acts of violence from an intimate partner. In the same year, men experienced about 160,000 crimes of violence by an intimate partner. **Intimate partners** include current and former spouses, boyfriends and girlfriends. Women aged sixteen to twenty-four experienced the highest rates of intimate violence.

Source: U.S. Bureau of Justice Statistics

Q. What kinds of actions are considered domestic violence?

A. Domestic violence statutes in most states apply not only to physical attacks, but also to other types of conduct. Examples of conduct that could be considered domestic violence include creating a disturbance at a spouse's place or work, making harassing telephone calls, stalking, and threatening a spouse or family member (even though the threat may not have been carried out.)

Q. Do protective orders actually protect the victim of domestic violence?

A. Sometimes. Studies have shown that issuing a protective order or arresting a person who commits an act of domestic violence does reduce future incidents of domestic violence. When perpetrators of domestic violence see that the police and the court system will treat domestic violence seriously, many persons who commit domestic violence may be deterred from future violence. But orders of protection are not guarantees of protection or safety. Some individuals under the influence of intense anger or rage will not change their behavior regardless of whether a court order has been issued—and a court order might even add to the rage. The legal system cannot offer perfect protection, although it can reduce violence overall.

Q. Where does one turn for help in cases of domestic violence?

A. In a crisis situation, a call to 911 or the police is a good start. Many people complain that police do not take accusations of domestic violence seriously. That may be true in some circumstances, but on the whole, police treat domestic violence situations seriously, and police officers are receiving increased training on dealing with domestic violence. The local state's attorney or district attorney may also be able to offer some help. An increasing number of hospitals, crisis intervention programs, and social service agencies have programs to help victims of domestic violence. Agencies offering help in cases of domestic violence might be found in the yellow pages under "Do-mestic Violence Intervention," "Human Services Organizations," or "Crisis Intervention."

THE WORLD AT YOUR FINGERTIPS

General Information

- *The ABA Section of Family Law has a General Public Resources section that provides answers to some frequently asked questions, and has charts summarizing the laws in each state, at www.abanet.org/family/home.html.*

Marriage

- *The requirements of each state for blood tests for marriage licenses and the answers to other questions about marriage can be found at the Nolo Press website, by clicking on the "Marriage and Living Together" heading at www.nolo.com/index.cfm.*
- *Information on how to obtain records from each state regarding marriage, birth, and death records can be found at the National Center for Health Statistics at www.cdc.gov/nchs/.*

Battered Spouses

- *Many communities offer shelters for battered spouses and their children. Details on these shelters are available from the police, crisis intervention services, hospitals, churches, family or conciliation courts, local newspapers, or women's organizations. The National Coalition Against Domestic Violence is a national information and referral center. It can be contacted at P.O. Box 18749, Denver, CO 80218; by phone at 303-839-1852; by fax at 303-831-9251; or online at www.ncadv.org. You can also call the National Domestic Violence Hotline at 800-799-7233, or visit the website at www.ndvh.org.*

- *The local or state chapter of the National Organization for Women (NOW) can also provide information to help battered spouses. You can contact NOW via their website at www.now.org.*

REMEMBER THIS

- *State law determines the requirements for getting married, including the waiting period, if any, between issuance of the marriage license and the marriage ceremony.*
- *Marriage ceremonies can be religious or civil or performed under the customs of an Indian tribe.*
- *Only nine states allow common-law marriages (which are marriages that occur without a formal ceremony or marriage license).*
- *As of 2003, no state allows marriages between same-sex couples, but some governmental units and private companies do recognize "domestic partnerships" or "civil unions" that grant certain rights to the couples, such as opportunity to obtain family health insurance coverage and to take leave to care for a sick domestic partner.*

MONEY MATTERS DURING MARRIAGE

Sandy and Vic have acquired a variety of property during their marriage, including a condominium in joint tenancy; a joint checking account; a joint investment account; two cars, one in the husband's name and one in the wife's name; and individual checking accounts in each of their own names. In addition, each brought property into the marriage.

What happens to all that property if the couple divorces, or one of them dies? Sorting all that out will depend on many factors, including who has title to the property, whether it is separate property or marital property, and whether there is a premarital agreement or a will that covers the property. This section tells you about all these issues.

Premarital Agreements

Q. What is a premarital agreement?

A. A **premarital agreement**, also known as an **antenuptial agreement** or **prenuptial agreement**, is a contract entered into by a man and a woman before they marry. The agreement usually describes what each party's rights will be if they divorce or when one of them dies. Premarital agreements most commonly deal with issues of property and spousal support—who is entitled to what property and how much support, if any, will be paid in the event of divorce.

ⓘ WHY PEOPLE ENTER INTO PREMARITAL AGREEMENTS

A man or a woman who wants a future spouse to enter into a premarital agreement often has something he or she wants to protect, usually money. One or both partners may want to avoid the risk of a major loss of assets, income, or a family business in the event of a divorce. People use premarital agreements to clarify their expectations and rights for the future, and to avoid uncertainties about how a divorce court might divide property and decide spousal support if the marriage fails. For people marrying for a second or third time, there might be a desire to make sure that a majority of assets or personal belongings are passed on to the children or grandchildren of prior marriages rather than a current spouse.

Q. What does a spouse give up by signing a premarital agreement?

A. In signing an agreement, a spouse agrees to have his or her property rights and support obligations determined by the agreement rather than by the usual rules of law that a court would apply on divorce or death. An agreement can give the spouse more or less than state law allows. In most states, courts divide property as the court considers fair, and the result is less predictable: The split could be fifty-fifty or something else. If one spouse dies, courts normally follow the instructions of that person's will, but in most states the surviving spouse is entitled to one-third to one-half of the estate regardless of what the deceased spouse's will says. If the husband and wife have signed a valid premarital agreement, that agreement will supercede the usual laws for dividing property and income upon divorce or death. In many cases, the less-wealthy spouse will receive less under the premarital agreement than he or she would receive under the usual laws of divorce or wills.

ⓘ WHEN TO SIGN THE PREMARITAL AGREEMENT

Most states do not set a specific time at which a premarital agreement must be signed. Generally, it is better to negotiate and sign the agreement well before the wedding, to show that each person has considered it thoroughly and signed it voluntarily. If the wealthier person shows the agreement to the prospective spouse only one day before the wedding, a court may later find that agreement invalid because of duress. While a last-minute premarital agreement is not automatically invalid, timing may be a significant factor in determining whether the agreement is valid.

Q. Why would a spouse sign a premarital agreement if he or she would receive less under the agreement than under other laws?

A. The answer to that question depends on the individual. Some people prefer to control their fiscal relationship rather than to leave it to state regulation. They may want to avoid uncertainty about what a court might decide if the marriage ends in divorce. For some, the answer may be "love conquers all"—the less-wealthy person may just want to marry the other party and not care much about the financial details. For others, the premarital agreement may provide ample security, even if it is not as generous as a judge might be. Still others may not like the agreement, but they are willing to take their chances and hope the relationship and the financial arrangements work out for the best.

Q. What is necessary to make a valid premarital agreement?

A. In general, the premarital agreement must be in writing and signed by both parties. In most states, the parties must fully and clearly disclose in writing their income and assets to each other. This way the parties will know more about what they might be giving up. In some states, it may be possible to waive a full disclosure of income and assets, but the waiver should be done knowingly, and it is still best if each party has a general idea of the other's net worth.

The premarital agreement must not be the result of fraud or duress. An agreement is likely to be invalid on the basis of fraud if one person (particularly the wealthier one) deliberately misstates his or her financial condition. For example, if a man hides assets from his future wife so that she will agree to a low level of support in case of divorce, a court probably would declare the agreement invalid. Similarly, if one person exerts excessive emotional pressure on the other to sign the agreement, a court might declare the agreement to be invalid because of duress.

Q. Must the parties to a premarital agreement be represented by lawyers?

A. No, but it is a good idea. Lawyers can help make sure that the agreement is drafted properly and that both parties are making informed decisions. The lawyer for the wealthier party usually prepares the initial draft of the agreement. The less-wealthy party should also have a lawyer to review the agreement, even if only on a minimal-cost consultation basis. Although you do not need to have a lawyer in order to have a valid agreement, the agreement is more likely to be enforceable if each person's interests are represented and significant back-and-forth negotiations have taken place. The agreement is more likely to be challenged if one of the parties does not have an independently chosen lawyer.

Q. Do premarital agreements need to provide for a certain amount of support?

A. No, the law does not set a specific amount. In some cases, though rare, a court may decide that an agreement is enforceable even if it leaves one spouse with no property and no support from the other party. In determining whether a premarital agreement is enforceable as drafted, courts will examine circumstances that may have changed since the time of the marriage—such as the birth of a child, a career given up, or an unforeseen illness.

Some states will enforce an agreement to provide no spousal support, so long as waiver of support does not leave the less-wealthy party so poor that she or he is eligible for welfare. Many courts will apply broader notions of fairness and require support at a level higher than subsistence. Some states provide that the support cannot be "unconscionably" low. That is a somewhat vague term that means different things to different courts.

Some lawyers think it is a good idea for premarital agreements to contain an **escalator clause** or a **phase-in provision** that will increase the amount of assets or support given to the less-wealthy spouse based on the length of the marriage or an increase in the wealthier party's assets or income after the agreement is made.

Q. May premarital agreements decide future issues of custody and child support?

A. No. A court may consider a premarital agreement the parties have reached regarding child custody or support, but the court is not bound by it. Broadly speaking, parties cannot bargain away rights of children, particularly before children are even born. A later section in this chapter will discuss child support guidelines and custody.

Ownership of Property

Q. Which spouse owns what property in a marriage?

A. Most property that is acquired during the marriage is considered **marital** or **community property**. If one or both spouses buys a house or establishes a business during the marriage, that property will usually be considered marital property, particularly if the house or the business is purchased with the husband's and wife's earnings obtained during marriage.

Separate property is property that each spouse owned before the marriage. In most states, separate property also includes inheritances and gifts (except perhaps gifts between spouses) acquired during marriage. During the marriage (and afterward), each spouse usually keeps control of his or her separate property. Each spouse may buy, sell, and borrow money on his or her separate property. Income earned from separate property, such as interest, dividends, or rent, is generally separate property. However, in some states, these profits may become marital property.

Separate property can become marital property if it is mixed or **commingled** with marital property. If, for example, a wife owned an apartment building before the marriage and she deposited rent checks into a joint checking account, the rent money probably would become marital property, although the building is likely to remain the wife's separate property as long as she kept it in her name. If the wife changed the title on the building from her name alone to the names of both herself and her husband, that would probably convert the building into marital property. In addition, if one spouse put a great deal of work into the other spouse's separate property, that could convert the separate property into marital property, or it could give the spouse who contributed the work a right to some form of repayment for the work performed.

Q. What is the community property system?

A. Eight states—Arizona, California, Idaho, Louisiana, Nevada, New Mexico, Texas, and Washington—plus Puerto Rico have adopted a different concept of the relationship of husband and wife, which is rooted in Spanish law. Though these states may differ a good deal on the specifics of their law, in general they consider any property acquired during a marriage, except by gift or inheritance, to be **community property**. This is true even if one spouse supplied all the income. Each spouse owns half of the community property. Each may transfer his or her interest without the other's signature. But there's no right of survivorship; when one spouse dies, half of the couple's property—including half of the house—goes through probate.

A ninth state, Wisconsin, has certain community property features in its law. A tenth state, Alaska, changed its law in 1998 to allow married seniors to select community property as an alternative form of ownership of their property. A couple may voluntarily decide to enter into a written

---

ⓘ THREE FORMS OF CO-OWNERSHIP

There are three common forms of ownership for couples in the non–community property states and in some community property states.

Joint Tenancy

This is a form of ownership that exists when two or more people own property that includes a right of survivorship. Each person has the right to possess the property. If one partner dies, the survivor becomes the sole owner. Any two or more people—not just spouses—may own property as joint tenants. A creditor may claim the debtor's interest in joint tenancy property.

Tenancy by the Entirety

Allowed in less than half the states, this is a type of co-ownership of property by a husband and wife. Like joint tenancy, it includes a right of survivorship. But a creditor of one spouse may not **attach** (seize) the property for payment of debts. Each party usually must consent to the sale of the property. Divorce may result in a division of the property.

Tenancy in Common

This is a form of co-ownership that gives each person control over his or her share of the property, and the shares need not be equal. The law does not limit tenancy in common to spouses. A tenancy in common does not provide a right of survivorship; when one spouse dies, his or her share passes to that person's heirs, either by will or state laws.

For more information on the various forms of ownership, see chapter 4, "Buying and Selling a Home," and chapter 5, "Home Ownership."

community property agreement or **community property trust**, but, if they don't choose to do that, their property will not be held as community property.

Debts and Taxes

Q. Is a husband or wife responsible for debts incurred by the other?

A. That depends on the nature and timing of the debt as well as the state in which the couple live. If both husband and wife have co-signed for the debt, both will be responsible for paying it. For instance, assume the husband and wife apply together for a charge card. If both sign the application form and promise to pay the charge bills, both will be responsible for paying off the entire balance to the credit card company or store, even if only one of them made the purchases and the other disapproved of those purchases. Similarly, if a husband and wife co-sign on a mortgage for a home, both of them are liable to the mortgage company, even if one of them no longer lives in the home. In community property states, a husband and wife may be responsible for debts incurred by the other even if both parties do not co-sign on the debt.

Q. Is a husband or wife liable for the debts of the other without co-signing for the debt?

A. That again depends on the nature of the debt and where the couple live. Some states have family-expense statutes that make a husband or wife liable for expenses incurred for the benefit of the family, even if the other spouse did not sign for or approve of the expense in advance. Still other states impose this family-expense obligation by common law, without a statute. Thus, if the wife charged groceries at a local store or took the couple's child to a doctor for care, the husband could be liable because these are expenses for the benefit of the family. On the other hand, if the wife runs up bills for a personal holiday or the husband buys expensive coins for his personal coin collection, the other spouse normally would not be liable unless he or she co-signed for the debt. Again, in community property states, a husband or wife is generally responsible for the debts of the other, even in the absence of a cosignature.

Q. Is one spouse responsible for debts the other spouse brought into the marriage?

A. Not in most states. In states that do not recognize community property, such debts belong to the spouse who incurred them. But in community property states, a spouse may, under special circumstances, become liable for the other spouse's premarital debts.

Q. Do a spouse's credit rights depend on marital status or the other spouse's financial status?

A. The law forbids denying credit on the basis of marital status. See chapter 7, "Consumer Credit."

Q. Which spouse is responsible for paying taxes?

A. If names and signatures of both spouses appear on a state or federal personal income tax return, both parties are liable for all of the taxes. If a couple files jointly, the Internal Revenue Service generally holds each one responsible for the entire debt, although an innocent spouse who is not aware of income that has been concealed by the other spouse may not be responsible for unpaid taxes on the hidden income. A spouse who files as "married filing separately" is not responsible for the other's tax debt.

Q. May one spouse make a tax-free gift to the other spouse?

A. A person may give his or her spouse any amount of money without paying federal gift taxes if the spouse is a U.S. resident. However, it must be an outright gift or set up as a proper trust. Most, but not all, state laws have done away with taxes on gifts between spouses. But the same is not true with respect to gifts to other family members. Gifts to children or other relatives may be taxable if they exceed a certain amount per year.

Doing Business Together

Q. May husbands and wives go into business together?

A. Certainly. Wives and husbands can be business partners. They can set up a corporation and both be owners and employees of the corporation; they can form a partnership; or one spouse can own the business and employ the other. Wages and benefits can be paid, just as they are for any other employee. If wages and benefits are being paid to a spouse or a child, the amount usually should not be more than what is reasonable or a fair market value. If artificially high payments are made, the business could get into trouble with the Internal Revenue Service.

Q. Is a wife or husband liable for the other's business debts?

A. Usually, no—unless the husband or wife had co-signed on the debt or they reside in a community property state. It is common, however, for institutions that lend money to small businesses to want personal guarantees of payment from the owner of the business, and not just from the business itself. In the event the debt is not paid, lenders would like as many pockets to reach into as possible. If the owner of the business owns a home, the lender may want to use the home as collateral for the business loan. That means that the spouse of the business owner may be asked to sign a paper allowing use of the home as collateral. Thus, the home could be lost if the business cannot pay off its debts. As long as a spouse does not co-sign for the business debts, the spouse will not normally be liable for business debts incurred by his or her mate.

Q. May a couple file jointly for bankruptcy?

A. Yes. Bankruptcy provides relief for people who have more debts than they can pay. See chapter 8, "Consumer Bankruptcy," for more information.

Q. Must a working spouse provide a pension for a dependent spouse?

A. No. The law does not specifically require this, but most corporate pension plans provide for it. Generally, a pension from a corporation that provides benefits for a surviving spouse cannot be taken away from the surviving spouse without that spouse agreeing to it in writing. See chapter 16, "The Rights of Older Americans," for more information.

ⓘ WHEN ONE SPOUSE DIES

If the spouse left a will, his or her property should be distributed according to its provisions. But if the will makes no provision for the surviving spouse, a court may not invalidate the will, but will nevertheless permit the surviving spouse to obtain a statutory elective share of the estate, usually one-third in most states.

If there is no will, the property will be distributed according to the laws of the state, with a certain percentage to the surviving spouse, a certain percentage to surviving children, and perhaps some for surviving parents, brothers, and sisters.

THE WORLD AT YOUR FINGERTIPS

Taxes

- *The basic resource on federal income taxes is the Internal Revenue Service (IRS). You can find your regional office in the phone book under "U.S.Offices," or go to the IRS website at www.irs.gov. Free publications on family taxes available from the IRS include* **Community Property and the Federal Income Tax** (*Publication 555*), **Tax Information for Divorced or Separated Individuals** (*Publication 504*), *and* **Tax Rules for Children and Dependents** (*Publi-*

cation 929). You also may wish to contact an accountant or a tax lawyer.

REMEMBER THIS

- *Although the law varies from state to state, the following factors will make it more likely that a premarital agreement will be enforced:*
  - *Each party should fully disclose his or her assets and income before the agreement is signed.*
  - *The parties should understand what the agreement means. Representation of each party by a lawyer is helpful, but not essential.*
  - *Although a person is within his or her rights not to go through with a marriage unless a premarital agreement is signed, the party seeking the agreement should not apply undue pressure or insist on a premarital agreement for the first time only a few days before the wedding.*
  - *The agreement should provide for a reasonable amount of assets or income for the less-wealthy spouse, although the amount does not need to be as much as a divorce court would order.*
- *If a person entering a marriage has property which he or she wishes to minimize the risk of losing upon divorce, that person should keep the property in his or her own name, in a separate account, and not mix the property with assets or income earned during the marriage.*
- *Wives and husbands can own real estate together in different ways, including joint tenancy, tenancy in common, and, in some states, tenancy by the entirety. The different forms of title affect rights to the property upon death of one of the parties and the rights of creditors to obtain the property because of a debt of one of the parties.*

- *If both husband and wife sign a joint tax return, both are generally liable for any unpaid taxes. If, however, one spouse hides income and does not pay taxes on it, the other spouse may be able to avoid liability for the unpaid tax as an "innocent spouse."*

CHILDREN

Angela gave birth to a son a few weeks ago, and is rapidly adjusting her life to motherhood—the routine of endless diaper-changing and no sleep. At this time, she has very little interest in how the law is involved in child rearing. But every parent or would-be parent should know that the law affects every aspect of having children.

This section will begin with the decision to have children, consider the rights and responsibilities of parents and children, and briefly discuss adoption and paternity issues.

The Decision to Have Children

Q. Who makes the decision to become a parent?

A. The Supreme Court declared in the 1973 case of *Roe v. Wade* that the decision whether to have a child is very personal and is protected by the right to privacy under the U.S. Constitution. This means that individuals who wish to have a child cannot be barred from doing so (unless, perhaps, they are incarcerated). Individuals who do not wish to have a child have a legal right to obtain and use contraceptives.

Q. What if one spouse wants children and the other does not?

A. If one person in the marriage wants a child and the other does not, that could be a basis for a divorce. A disagreement on such a fundamental issue could be an **irreconcilable difference** under the no-fault divorce laws of most states. In states that have grounds for divorce based on someone being at fault, a disagreement on the question of whether to have children could be viewed as **mental cruelty**, and thus a basis for ending the marriage.

Beyond divorce, remedies are limited. The courts cannot force a pregnant woman to stop the pregnancy, nor does the law require a wife to have her husband's permission for an abortion.

Abortion

Q. What is the current status of abortion law?

A. As of the beginning of 2004, women still have a constitutional right to an abortion. In 1992, the U.S. Supreme Court in the case of *Planned Parenthood v. Casey* reaffirmed its decision in *Roe v. Wade* that women have a right to seek an abortion during the early stages of pregnancy. The Supreme Court also decided, however, that states have a right to regulate how abortions are performed and that states may ban abortions after the fetus is viable (able to live outside the womb)

ⓘ THE NUMBER CRUNCH— HOW OLD ARE WOMEN WHEN THEY HAVE THEIR FIRST BABY?

In 2000, the average American woman having her first baby was almost 25 years old. In 1970, the average age was 21.4 years for a first birth. The average varies by state. Massachusetts was the highest (27.8 years). Mississippi was the lowest (22.5 years). Several factors may contribute to the delay in childbearing, including more educational and career opportunities for women and changes in contraception use.

Source: National Center for Health Statistics

ⓘ THE NUMBER CRUNCH— BIRTHRATES

There were 4,025,933 babies born in the United States in 2001—a drop of 1 percent from the year before. The birthrate for twins, however, rose for 2001—accounting for 3 percent of all births. Births to unmarried women accounted for 33.5 percent of all births, although the teen birthrate has declined for ten consecutive years.

Source: National Center for Health Statistics

---

unless the mother's life or health is endangered. The scope of regulation and funding of abortions by the government varies from state to state and is often tested. States may impose a twenty-four-hour waiting period before an abortion is performed.

Q. May a girl under eighteen obtain an abortion without her parent's consent?

A. Yes. However, if a girl under eighteen seeks an abortion, state law can require that she obtain permission from a judge. In *Casey*, the Supreme Court upheld a statute that required a girl to obtain permission from either one parent or a judge, and noted that Supreme Court case law had required states to allow a "judicial bypass" as a substitute for parental consent.

Childbirth

Q. Are there any rules prohibiting parents from having their children born at home?

A. No. Generally, at-home births are an option for parents. The mother, however, should have good prenatal care, and she should make sure the health-care provider believes the delivery will not pose significant risks to the mother or the child. If the delivery is risky for the mother or the child, it is simply common sense to use a hospital. Some states allow nurse-midwives to deliver children at the parents' home or at a birthing center. Other states allow nurse-midwives to practice only at hospitals or under the direct supervision of a physician.

Q. If the delivery is at a hospital, may the father or a sibling be present?

A. Most hospitals permit the father to be present at birth. Hospitals often prefer that the father and mother go through some prenatal training before the delivery. Couples should check with their hospitals about other rules and about whether siblings are allowed in the delivery room.

Rights and Responsibilities of Parents

Q. What are the rights of parents?

A. Parents have a right to direct the care, control, and upbringing of their children for as long as they are minors. This gives them the power to make various decisions on behalf of the child, including where to live, what school to attend, what religion to follow, and what medical treatment to obtain. Normally, the state will not interfere in these decisions. Only in life-threatening or extreme situations will the courts step in to overrule the parents' decisions. For example, if a child might die without the medical care that the parents refuse to provide, a judge may make the child a ward of the state and order that the care be provided. Parents have been prosecuted for withholding medical treatment from seriously ill children. This is true even in situations where parents act out of religious belief.

There may be certain medical procedures that the law allows "mature minors" to decide upon for themselves, even if their parents disagree. For example, parents have no absolute veto power over a minor's decision to use contraceptives or to obtain an abortion. In addition, some states allow children of a certain age to seek men-

tal health treatment or treatment for venereal disease without notification of the parents.

Parents also have the legal authority to control their children's behavior and social lives. Parents may discipline or punish their children appropriately. They may not, however, use cruel methods or excessive force; that constitutes child abuse.

Q. Can parental rights be terminated?

A. A parent's rights can be terminated if a parent is unfit or has abused or abandoned the child. For example, in *In re S.R.* (Illinois Appellate Court, 2001), a father was in prison. The court said the man "could be a good father at times," but the court also said that the father had not seen his children for approximately two years, and the record did not indicate the father requested visitation while in prison. During the father's brief period of liberty, he did not provide financial support to the children, and he was unable to rear the minors due to alcohol, drug, and family problems. The court terminated the father's parental rights.

Q. What are the legal rights of children?

A. Children have a unique status under the law. The law defines children as unmarried persons

---

ⓘ MONEY EARNED OR INHERITED BY CHILDREN

Generally, parents do not have unlimited, direct control over their child's money. If a child receives money from his or her earnings, an inheritance, or a personal injury case, that money must be used for the child's benefit. Some states require the appointment of a guardian under court supervision if a child has substantial funds. Unless a court appoints someone else, parents are the guardians of their child's money. The parents are legally responsible for managing the money properly and using it for their child's needs.

under the age of majority—usually eighteen—who have not left home to support themselves. The law protects children from abuse and neglect. It also entitles them to the protection of the state. Children may be removed from their home if it is necessary to ensure them a safe, supportive environment. This removal may be temporary or permanent.

Children have a right to be supported by their parents. At minimum, this means food, shelter, clothing, medical care, and education.

The law allows children to sue. However, in most instances an adult legal representative must begin the suit. The representative is often referred to as **guardian ad litem** for the child, or as **next friend**.

Q. What are the rights of children who are accused of committing crimes?

A. Children accused of committing crimes are subject to the juvenile courts of the state in which the crime was committed, rather than the regular criminal justice system. Juvenile courts provide children with only some of the due process safeguards that adults receive. In return, juvenile courts have more freedom to deal with juveniles in an effort to rehabilitate them. In some states, children accused of serious crimes who are above a certain age—such as thirteen—may be tried in court as adults.

Q. How long do parents' legal obligations to their children continue?

A. Parents are legally responsible for their children until they reach the age of majority (usually eighteen), marry, or leave home to support themselves. In some states, divorced parents may be obliged to pay for a child's college or trade school education. In addition, a parent's duty to support a disabled child might continue for the child's entire life.

Q. Are parents financially responsible for the acts of their children?

A. The law on this varies from state to state. Some states make parents financially responsible for damage caused by their children, but the states may place limits on the amount of liability. In Illinois, for example, parents or guardians may be required to pay up to $2,500 for the "willful or malicious acts" of minor children who harm another person or property. If there is more damage than that, the child could be sued personally; if child had assets, they could be taken to satisfy the judgment.

Generally, if a child has an auto accident while driving a parent's car, the parent's auto insurance policy will cover the loss to the same extent it would if the parent had been driving the car (although parents usually have to pay higher insurance premiums to cover young drivers). In some states, the law may provide that if a parent knows or should have known that their child has a proclivity toward violent or malicious behavior, the parents may have a duty to take reasonable steps to control the child or give warning to persons the child might harm.

ⓘ THE DUTIES OF ADULT CHILDREN TO THEIR PARENTS

In most states, adult children have no responsibilities toward their parents and their parents have no duties towards them. However, there are exceptions. In some states, children must support parents who would otherwise be on welfare. Children may be able to avoid paying support if they can show that the parents did not care for them when they were underage. In some states, children may have to contribute to the support of parents in a state hospital or mental institution. In such circumstances, a child's ability to pay—not the actual cost of the care—usually determines how much he or she must pay.

Adoption

Q. How does one adopt a child?

A. Adoption laws vary from state to state. For a minor child who is not related to the adoptive parent or parents, there are generally two types of adoptions: **agency adoptions** and **private** or **independent adoptions**.

Q. What is an agency adoption?

A. As the name implies, the parents work though a state-licensed agency. The agency often supervises the care of biological mothers who are willing to have their children adopted by others, and it assists in the placement of children after birth. Agencies screen adoptive parents—often extensively—before the adoption proceeds. Some agencies have long waiting lists of parents. Some agencies specialize in placing children born in foreign countries.

Q. What is a private adoption?

A. Private adoptions bypass the use of agencies and may bypass the long waiting lists as well. The process may begin when people who seek to adopt a child contact a lawyer who specializes in adoptions. The lawyer may work with physicians who are aware of women willing to give up children for adoption. Sometimes would-be parents will place ads in newspapers seeking women who are willing to place their babies for adoption.

In most states, adoptive parents are allowed to pay a biological mother's medical expenses and certain other costs during the pregnancy. But adoptive parents are not allowed to pay the biological mother specifically to give up the child. The law treats this as a **black-market adoption**, the buying and selling of children, and it is a crime in every state.

Q. Is court approval necessary for an adoption?

A. Yes. Court approval is needed for both agency and private adoptions. Many states also require that the adoptive parents be studied and approved by a social service agency.

Q. Can a biological mother revoke her consent to adoption?

A. Yes, but there are limits on her right to revoke consent. In most states, a biological mother who initially consents to a child's adoption before birth may revoke that consent after birth. In other words, the mother's consent is usually not final or binding until a certain period of time after birth. In most states, that time period is relatively short, such as two to eight days. If a biological mother consented to adoption during the proper period of time after birth, it is much harder for her to revoke her consent. Generally, following an after-birth consent, a biological mother may revoke her consent only if she can show that there was fraud or duress. Fraud could be found if the adoption agency or lawyer lied to the biological mother about the consequences of what she was doing. Duress might exist if a person at the adoption agency threatened the biological mother with humiliation if she did not sign. A biological mother's change of heart is not normally enough by itself to revoke an after-birth adoption consent. Although a mother may feel emotionally drained and under stress after the birth of a child that she plans to give up for adoption, that type of stress is not enough to revoke an adoption unless the relevant person or agency used harsh tactics to obtain the mother's consent.

Q. Is the biological father's consent necessary?

A. Generally, yes—at least if the biological father is known and the father does not abandon his parental rights. The biological father should be notified of the birth and pending adoption so that he may consent or object. If the father is not known, the adoption may proceed without his consent (although adoptive parents can feel safer about the validity of their adoption if the biological father has been notified and agreed to it). If a biological father is not notified, he may later contest the adoption if he acts within a certain period of time after the child's birth or adoption (such as one to six months).

RELATED ADOPTION

A **related adoption** is one in which a child's relatives, such as grandparents or an aunt and uncle, formally adopt a child as their own. This might occur if the child's biological parents are deceased or are otherwise unable to care for the child.

Q. If biological parents give up a child to adoption, what rights and obligations do they retain?

A. In general, they lose all rights and have no obligations. They have no right of contact with the child, cannot obtain information about the child, and so on. And they have no obligation to support the child.

However, there is a growing movement toward "open adoptions," in which parents may, by agreement, retain some rights to contact with the child and information about the child. See the "Open Adoption" sidebar below.

Q. What is a stepparent adoption?

A. A **stepparent adoption** is one in which a child's biological parent marries someone who wishes to adopt the biological parent's child and is able to do so because the other biological parent consents or because consent is unnecessary.

If a biological parent does not consent to the adoption of a child, the child cannot be adopted by another person unless a court first finds that the biological parent is unfit. If a parent is found unfit, that person's parental rights are terminated, and the child can be adopted.

Q. What is the definition of an unfit parent?

A. Parental unfitness is determined by state law. Generally, an unfit parent is one who has failed to have regular contact with a child or to contribute to his or her support. A parent is also unfit if he or she has been abusive or has otherwise failed to provide adequate care for the child.

Q. What happens if a stepparent adopts his spouse's child and the parents later divorce?

A. A divorce does not affect the legality of the adoption. The stepparent continues to have all the rights and responsibilities of a biological parent, including a right to seek custody or visitation and a duty to support the child.

Q. Can a single person adopt a child?

A. Yes. Many states allow single persons to adopt, although some agencies strongly prefer to place a child with a married couple. Other agencies—particularly those dealing with children who might be hard to place—are willing to place

OPEN ADOPTION

An **open adoption** is one in which the adoptive parents agree to let the biological mother (and biological father) have some continued contact with the child after the adoption. This contact might be periodic visits or an exchange of pictures and other information between the adoptive family and the biological parent or parents. The nature of the contact is often specified in the adoption agreement. Open adoptions have become more common as more birth mothers have become involved with choosing which adoptive family will receive their child. But open adoptions are a relatively new phenomenon, and in many states it is not certain whether an open adoption agreement is enforceable by the birth mother.

a child with a single person. Single-parent adoptions are usually possible in private adoptions.

Q. Can lesbian or gay couples adopt a child?

A. Yes, in some states, including New York and California, gay and lesbian couples are able to adopt a child.

Q. Who has access to adoption records?

A. In most states, court adoption records are sealed and can only be opened by court order (although a few states—Oregon, Kansas, Tennessee, and Wyoming—allow all adopted children access to their adoption records). Procedures and standards for opening records vary by state. Increasingly, states require that certain nonidentifying information, such as the medical history of the biological family, be made available to the adoptive parents at the time of adoption. Some states also have registries in which parties to the adoption can agree to a later exchange of information, including names and addresses.

Q. What is the legal status of an adopted child?

A. An adopted child has exactly the same rights as a child reared by his or her biological parents. Similarly, adoptive parents have the same obligations to the child as they would to one born to them.

Paternity

Q. Do medically assisted pregnancies affect parental rights?

A. As medical science advances, there are a variety of ways in which individuals who wish to become parents can be helped to do so by medically assisted means, including artificial insemination and in vitro fertilization. These medical procedures have legal implications that vary by state. Generally, however, if both husband and wife consent to artificial insemination or in vitro fertilization, the rights and duties of the husband,

the wife, and the child will be the same as if the child had been naturally conceived.

Q. What is surrogate parenthood?

A. A woman agrees, with or without payment, to bear a child for someone else. This usually occurs when a wife cannot conceive or carry a child to term. In most cases, through artificial insemination, the husband's sperm fertilizes an egg belonging to either the wife or the surrogate mother. This makes the husband the biological father of the child. The surrogate mother agrees to give up all parental rights at birth. Then the wife of the biological father legally adopts the child. Some states permit surrogate parenting arrangements; others prohibit them.

Q. How do you determine paternity in cases that don't involve surrogacy or artificial insemination?

A. Paternity cases increasingly rely on scientific evidence. The blood tests used during much of the last century were useful only up to a certain point. They might prove that a man was not the father of a child, but could not prove that he was the father. New tests that sample the DNA (genetic material) of the child and the supposed father are nearly 100 percent accurate in proving or disproving paternity.

Q. May an unmarried mother legally force the father of her baby to support the child?

A. Yes. Both parents, married or not, have a duty to support their child. If the father admits paternity, the father often will be asked to sign an **affidavit** (a legal statement) to that effect. Then, if necessary, it will be easier to force the father to help support the child. If he does not admit to being the father, the mother may file a paternity suit against him. If this civil action succeeds, the court will require the father to provide support. Often the court will also require the father to pay the mother's pregnancy and childbirth expenses.

Q. If paternity is proved, how much will the father have to pay in support?

A. Unwed parents must support their children to the same extent as married parents. Child support guidelines, which have been enacted in all states, determine the amount of support. As with children born to married parents, the obligation of support usually lasts until the child is an adult.

Q. What happens if a father refuses to pay support?

A. If a father refuses to support his child, a court may garnish his wages, seize his property or bank accounts, revoke his driver's license or professional license, and perhaps even send him to jail.

Q. What may a husband legally do if his wife bears a child that is not his?

A. The law presumes that a married woman's child is her husband's. The husband must support the child unless he can prove in court that he is not the father. Some states presume the husband is the father and will not allow a husband to disprove paternity of a child born during the marriage. If a state does allow a husband to disprove paternity of a child born during the marriage, the law may set a certain time period after birth (such as two years) within which the husband must disprove paternity.

⚠ TAKING CHILDREN AWAY FROM THEIR PARENTS

Even if a criminal case is not brought, the state may remove children from the custody of their parents if there is reason to believe the parents are physically, sexually, or emotionally abusing one or more of the children. The state may also remove the children if the parents are unable or unwilling to provide adequate care, supervision, and support.

Q. May a father of a child whose mother is married to another person file suit to establish paternity of the child?

A. The law varies from state to state. Some states allow such suits to be filed and allow a man to file suit to prove paternity of a child born to a woman who is married to someone else. The man who filed suit then might be able to obtain visitation (or custody in unusual circumstances.) Other states prohibit such suits and automatically presume that the woman's husband is the father.

Abuse and Neglect Laws

Q. What is child neglect?

A. **Child neglect** or **child endangerment** occurs when parents or legal guardians willfully fail to meet a child's basic needs, including food, shelter, clothes, medical treatment, and supervision.

Q. What persons and what types of actions are covered by child abuse laws?

A. It is a crime for adults to abuse children in their care. The term "adult" includes parents, foster parents, legal guardians, other adults in the home, family members, and baby-sitters. Supervising adults may not go beyond reasonable physical punishment. For example, adults who beat children so severely that they require medical treatment have violated these laws. Child abuse laws involve not only physical abuse (such as beatings or starvation), but include other types of cruelty, such as subjecting a child to extreme humiliation.

A person may be guilty of child abuse that he or she did not personally commit if that person had legal responsibility for the child and failed to protect the child from the abuser.

Q. How does one report a suspected case of child abuse?

A. Many states use an 800 number for a child abuse hot line. Calls also can be made to the state or country department that handles human ser-

---

⚠ THE DUTY TO REPORT NEGLECT AND ABUSE

The law compels a wide range of people who have contact with children to report suspected child abuse or neglect. Such people include doctors, nurses, teachers, social workers, and child-care providers. A person who is required to report suspected neglect or abuse may face civil or criminal penalties for failure to do so. In addition, states often encourage the reporting of suspected abuse by others, such as neighbors and family members, through special hot lines. The laws of most states grant immunity to persons who make reports of abuse by granting them immunity from defamation suits by the accused parents if the report is made in good faith. Most states keep central lists of suspected child abuse cases. This helps identify parents who, for example, take their children to different hospitals in order to conceal the evidence that they have repeatedly abused their children.

---

vices or children's issues. If an emergency exists, you can call the police.

Q. If welfare officials or the court take children away from their parents, is the removal temporary or permanent?

A. The goal is usually to reunite the family after correcting the problems that led to the removal. This is not always possible. Among the factors a court will consider are the severity and frequency of the parents' deficiency or bad conduct, the efforts of the parents to correct the situation, and the amount of time it would take to correct the situation. For example, if the parents make little or no effort to improve the child's care or if the abuse is unusually severe, then the state may ask a court to end all parental rights. If this happens, the legal bonds between parents and children may be completely and permanently cut, and another family may adopt the child.

THE WORLD AT YOUR FINGERTIPS

Adoption

- *For information about agency adoptions, contact the Child Welfare League of America, 440 First Street NW, Suite 310, Washington, DC 20001. Its telephone number is 202-638-2952, or you can access its website at www.cwla.org. You also may wish to*

contact the National Council for Adoption at www.ncfa-usa.org/home.html.

- *For information on independent adoption, check with your state or city bar association. Ask if independent adoptions are legal in your state. Also ask if the bar association will refer you to lawyers who handle independent adoptions.*

Missing Children

- *The National Center for Missing and Exploited Children can offer help in finding and recovering missing children. You can contact the center at 2101 Wilson Boulevard, Suite 550, Arlington, VA 22201, by telephone at 800-843-5678 (toll-free), or access its website at www.missingkids.com.*

REMEMBER THIS

- *As of the beginning of 2004, women still have a right under the U.S. Constitution to terminate a pregnancy. Certain states may require a waiting period for an abortion, and the consent of a parent or a judge before a minor can undergo an abortion.*
- *Married and unmarried parents owe a duty of support to their children.*
- *In some states, parents can also be finan-*

cially liable for the "willful or malicious" acts of their children.

- *In order for a child to be adopted, the natural parent(s) must be deceased, give consent, be found unfit, or be unable to be located. Generally, a person challenging an adoption that has already taken place must file a legal action very soon after the adoption or his or her rights to challenge the adoption will be lost.*

- *It is an offense for parents and guardians to willfully fail to meet a child's basic needs.*

SEPARATION, ANNULMENT, AND DIVORCE

After several years of marriage, Ben and Emily have decided to separate, and plan to divorce in the future. They have two children, as well as a house, a car, and a lot of history. Ben's wages paid off most of the mortgage on the house, and he thinks he is entitled to keep it. He wants custody of the children. His parents are also determined to stay in regular contact with their grandchildren. Emily gave up her career as a nurse to raise the kids. She wants custody, and would like to continue to live in the house while the children are in school to provide them with a stable environment.

Sometimes marriages do not succeed. Despite the efforts of husband and wife, and perhaps the help of counselors and clergy, there is nothing to do but end the relationship. This often means that assets have to be divided and custody arrangements made. Sometimes people can work it out between themselves; sometimes, where there are competing interests and people just can't resolve them, the law steps in. Just as the state was involved in creating the marriage, so it becomes involved in dissolving it.

Separation and Separate Maintenance

Q. What is a legal separation?

A. A **legal separation** allows the husband and wife to live separately and formalize the arrangement by a court order or a written agreement. The order or agreement will specify what support, if any, one spouse will pay the other. If the husband and wife have minor children, the agreement or court order will set out arrangements regarding custody or visitation.

A legal separation is not the same as a divorce. A separation recognizes the possibility that the couple might reunite. In any case, its terms

---

▶ **"CAN THIS MARRIAGE BE SAVED?"**

To borrow a phrase from the monthly feature in *Ladies' Home Journal*, a question to be asked before stepping down the path to divorce is "Can This Marriage Be Saved?" The question deserves a long, deliberate examination (at different times and when in different moods), weighing the relationships and other aspects of life that will change as a result of divorce. To help with the decision-making process, it can be useful to consult a marriage counselor or mental health professional. (Counselors can be found through a variety of sources, including hospital crisis intervention services, family physicians, religious institutions, and the yellow pages.) Even if visits with a counselor do not save the marriage, the perspectives gained may help with the transitions in life and help the wife and husband avoid repeating similar mistakes in future relationships.

can be modified by the parties or the court when the couple divorces. Most important, people who are legally separated may not remarry. They must wait until a divorce is final before marrying again.

When a husband and wife legally separate, they no longer accumulate community or marital property. The property acquired after the legal separation will be considered each partner's separate or nonmarital property.

Q. Does a person have to be legally separated before obtaining a divorce?

A. No. In most states, a couple can proceed straight to a divorce without first seeking a legal separation. While waiting for the divorce, the couple might live separately (without a formal agreement); or, in some states, they could even live together pending the final divorce. A few states do require a period of separation before a divorce can be granted.

Q. Is there an advantage to a legal separation?

A. That depends on the needs of the parties. A legal separation offers a structure for the parties while they are waiting for a divorce (or while they are considering a divorce). If one spouse is paying support for the other spouse or for the children, the spouse receiving the support may want the terms put in writing. Similarly, one or both parties may want a fixed schedule of who will be with the children at what times. If these terms are part of a written agreement or court order, the parties know what to count on, and a party can go to court to seek enforcement if the other does not abide by the agreement or order. In addition, if one or both of the parties wish to obtain a religious divorce or annulment, a legal separation may provide useful transition while waiting for action by the religious tribunal. After the religious annulment or divorce is granted, the legal divorce may proceed. Depending on the wishes of the parties and tenets of the religion, the legal divorce could precede the religious divorce or annulment.

Most medical plans permit a legally separated spouse to continue to be covered in a family plan without additional cost. The parties may also file joint income tax returns if they so desire.

Q. Are there any tax advantages to a legal separation?

A. Yes, potentially. If one spouse is paying support for the other, the payer can deduct that money from his or her income for tax purposes. The payment will then be considered taxable income to the recipient. If the payer is in a higher tax bracket than the recipient, this will reduce the couple's combined tax liability. In any case, it will reduce the payer's taxes and raise the recipient's. To obtain such a deduction, the parties must be legally separated by written agreement or court order. The deduction is not available for those who have an informal separation.

Q. Why would a spouse who is receiving support agree to this arrangement if it results in more taxes for her or him and a tax advantage to the other spouse?

A. The tax advantage to the payer may encourage the payment of support in the first place, and it may result in a greater amount of support. Some couples and their lawyers may calculate a tentative amount of support that would be paid

---

> ### ▶ SEPARATION AGREEMENTS

A husband or wife should be careful about agreeing to terms of a separation agreement that they view as more generous than they would want to live with after the divorce. If the parties agree to terms of a separation agreement, but cannot agree to terms of a divorce, a court may order continuation of the terms of the separation agreement in the final judgment of divorce if the court thinks the terms have worked out reasonably well.

without any tax benefit to the payer. Then they calculate the tax benefit of creating a deduction for the payer and income for the recipient. They split the tax savings by increasing the level of support. The increased support usually exceeds the added taxes the recipient will pay, and the payer will have less money out of pocket for the year because of the tax savings.

Q. Are there psychological advantages to a legal separation?

A. For some people, yes. Some couples may want to separate but are not sure they want to go through a divorce. The separation might be a trial separation—relieving some immediate pressures while the husband and wife sort out what they want to do with their lives. A formal legal separation may provide some structure, security, and financial advantages during the period of separation. It also may meet the husband's or wife's religious requirements.

Annulment

Q. What is an annulment?

A. An **annulment** is a court ruling that a marriage was never valid. The most common ground for annulment is fraud or misrepresentation. For example, one person may have not disclosed to the other a prior divorce, a criminal record, an infectious disease, or an inability to engage in sex or have children. Annulment may also be granted for bigamy, incest, or marriage to an underage person.

Q. How common are annulments?

A. They are uncommon because divorces are easy to obtain and the bases for an annulment are narrower than the bases for a divorce. One party may prefer an annulment, however, in order to avoid some obligations that a court might impose in a divorce. Also, in a few states, spousal support that terminated because of the recipient's second marriage may be reinstated if the second marriage is annulled.

ⓘ THE NUMBER CRUNCH— DIVORCE

Approximately half of marriages of men and women under age forty-five end in divorce. First marriages that end in divorce last, on average, seven to eight years. Half of those who remarry after a divorce from a first marriage do so within three years. The divorce rate for college graduates is less than half the divorce rate for those whose education stops after high school.

Source: U.S. Census Bureau

Divorce

Q. What is a divorce?

A. A **divorce** or **dissolution of marriage** is a decree by a court that a valid marriage no longer exists. It leaves both parties free to remarry. The court will award custody, divide property, and order spousal and child support.

Q. Are most divorces contested?

A. No. Although divorces may be emotionally contentious, close to 95 percent of divorces do

---

ⓘ DIVORCE WITHOUT LAWYERS

Most states permit do-it-yourself divorces—sometimes referred to as **summary divorces.** The ease or difficulty of obtaining a do-it-yourself divorce depends on local laws and rules as well as the complexities of the issues in the divorce. The complexities of property division and taxes, or of custody in a contested case, may make it advisable for both parties to have expert legal and financial advice.

not end up in a contested trial. Usually, the parties negotiate and settle property division, spousal support, and child custody between themselves, often with the help of a lawyer. Sometimes parties reach an agreement by mediation, with a trained mediator who tries to help the husband and wife identify and accommodate common interests. The parties then present their negotiated or mediated agreement to a judge. Approval is virtually automatic if the agreement is fair.

If parties are unable to agree about property, support, or child custody, they may ask the court to decide one or more of those matters. One spouse may sue the other for divorce, alleging certain faults or offenses by the defendant. But this has become far less common than it once was. Most divorces now are no-fault divorces.

Q. What is a no-fault divorce?

A. A **no-fault divorce** is one in which neither person blames the other for the breakdown of the marriage. There are no accusations or need to prove "guilt" or cause of the breakdown. A common basis for a no-fault divorce is "irreconcilable differences" or "irretrievable marriage breakdown." As those terms imply, the marriage is considered to be over, but the court and the legal documents do not try to assign blame. Another common basis for no-fault divorce is the parties

living separately for a certain period of time, such as for six months or a year, with the intent that the separation be permanent.

Q. Why does the law provide for no-fault divorces?

A. No-fault divorces are considered a less abrasive and more realistic way to end a marriage. The laws of no-fault divorce recognize that human relationships are complex and that it is difficult to prove that a marriage broke down solely because of what one person did. However, some critics of no-fault divorces are concerned that an economically dependent spouse may not be adequately protected when it is comparatively easy for the other spouse to obtain a divorce.

All states have some form of no-fault divorce, but many states also retain fault-based grounds as an alternative way of obtaining a divorce. Some spouses want the emotional release of proving fault by their mates. Courts are not a very good forum for such personal issues, and the accuser is usually less satisfied than he or she expected to be.

Q. What are the grounds for obtaining a divorce based on fault?

A. States that allow fault-based divorce vary somewhat on the permissible grounds. Many states permit divorce for adultery, physical cru-

---

ⓘ WHAT'S IN A NAME?

When a woman divorces, she may resume her unmarried name or keep her married name. If she is changing her name, she should notify government agencies and private companies that have records of her name. Places to notify include the Internal Revenue Service, the Social Security Administration, the Passport Agency (within the U.S. State Department), the post office, state tax agencies, the driver's license bureau, the voter registration bureau, professional licensing agencies, professional societies, unions, the mortgage company, the landlord, banks, charge card companies, the telephone company, other utilities, magazines, newspapers, dentists, and schools and colleges that the woman attended or that her children attend. It can be useful to have the divorce decree state that the wife will resume her unmarried name, but generally it is not necessary to do so in order for a woman to make a valid name change.

elty, mental cruelty, attempted murder, desertion, habitual drunkenness, use of addictive drugs, insanity, impotence, and infection of one's spouse with venereal disease.

Q. Will use of fault grounds affect other aspects of the divorce?

A. That depends on the state. In a few states, fault may be taken into consideration in deciding property and spousal support, even if the divorce is granted on no-fault grounds. In some states, fault will be considered if it directly causes waste or dissipation of marital assets. In some states, a spouse who commits adultery may not be able to receive spousal support. In many states, the fault of a party in causing a breakdown of the marriage is not supposed to be a factor in dividing property or deciding spousal support. In custody cases, the marital fault of a party is not supposed to be considered unless that fault caused a harmful impact on the child. For example, a discreet extramarital affair would not normally be a major factor in deciding custody. But an affair or series of affairs that placed the child in stressful situations could be a factor in deciding custody.

Property

Q. In divorce cases, how often do judges decide who gets what?

A. Judges rule on major contested issues in only a relatively small number of cases. Instead, the parties—often with help from lawyers—reach an agreement between themselves that they present to a judge for approval. If the agreement is fair, approval is usually granted after a short hearing.

Q. How do judges decide disputed property issues?

A. Laws vary from state to state. As a starting point, many states allow parties to keep their **nonmarital** or **separate** property. Nonmarital property includes property that a spouse brought into the marriage and kept in his or her own name during the marriage. It also includes inher-

itances received and kept separate during the marriage. It also may include gifts received by just one spouse during the marriage. Some states permit division of separate as well as marital property when parties divorce, but the origin of the property is considered when deciding who receives the property. After allocating separate property, the court divides marital or community property.

Q. What is marital or community property?

A. Marital or **community property** is defined somewhat differently by different states, but it generally includes property and income acquired during the marriage. Wages earned during the marriage would be marital property. A home and furniture purchased during the marriage with marital earnings or property would usually be considered marital property.

Q. What if the property obtained during the marriage is in the name of one party only?

A. That, too, will usually be considered marital property if it was paid for with marital funds, such as wages. For example, if a wife buys a car during the marriage and pays for it with her wages, the car is marital property, even though it is in her name only. A pension is also usually mar-

---

ⓘ SETTLEMENTS AND THE LAW

The rules of law that a judge would use to decide a contested case influence the settlements that the parties reach. If it is predictable that a matter would be decided in a certain way by a judge, it is seldom worth taking the issue to trial. In many cases, the cost of pursuing a disputed property issue at trial will exceed the possible monetary gain of a victory in court.

ital property, even though it may have been earned by the labor of only one spouse during the marriage. A pension can be a very significant piece of property. The pension and the family home are often the most valuable assets acquired by a couple during the marriage. If a pension was completely earned before the marriage, it probably would be considered nonmarital or separate property. Marital or community property can be divided by the court between the parties.

Q. How does a husband or wife keep nonmarital property separate and thus less likely to be lost in a divorce?

A. The main way to keep nonmarital property separate is to keep it in one's own name and not mix it with marital property. For example, if a wife came into a marriage with a $20,000 money market account and wanted to keep it as nonmarital property, she should keep the account in her own name and not deposit any marital funds in the account. She should not, for instance, deposit her paychecks into the money market account, because the paychecks are marital funds and the deposit could turn the whole account into marital property.

If a husband inherits some stock from his mother during the marriage and he wants to keep it as nonmarital property, he should open his own investment account and should not use the account for any investments that he and his wife own together.

If a husband or wife decides to use some nonmarital funds for a common purpose, such as purchasing a home in joint tenancy, that money will normally become marital property. The courts of most states will view the nonmarital property as a gift to the marriage. The property distribution laws have many intricacies and variations between states; understanding them usually requires a lawyer's help.

Q. How do courts divide marital or community property?

A. Again, the answer varies from state to state. A few states, such as California, take a rather simple approach. They believe property should be divided equally because they view marriage as a joint undertaking in which both spouses are presumed to contribute equally, though often in different ways, to the acquisition and preservation of property. All marital property will be divided fifty-fifty, unless the husband and wife had a premarital agreement stating otherwise. Even in California, there may be complications in the details, such as disputes between the husband and wife regarding the value of community property and deciding what constitutes an equal division. Most states, however, apply a concept called equitable distribution.

Q. What is equitable distribution?

A. Equitable distribution means that a court divides marital property as it thinks is valid, just, and equitable. States applying principles of equitable distribution view marriage as a shared enterprise in which both spouses usually contribute significantly to the acquisition and preservation of property. The division of property could be 50-50, 60-40, 70-30, or even all for one spouse and nothing for the other (although that would be very unusual.) The percentage distribution need not be the same for all property, and the percentage entitlement may vary from one asset to another. Under equitable distribution, courts consider a variety of factors and need not weigh the factors equally. That gives more discretion to the judge and more consideration to the financial situation of both spouses after the divorce. However, it also makes the resolution of property issues less predictable. There are several factors that are considered by states applying principles of equitable distribution:

Nonmarital Property

If one spouse has much more nonmarital property than the other, that could be a basis for giving more marital property to the less wealthy spouse.

Earning Power

If one spouse has more earning power than the other, that could be a basis for giving more marital property to the spouse with less earning power.

Who Earned the Property

That can be a factor favoring the party who worked hard to acquire or maintain the property.

Services as a Homemaker

Courts recognize that keeping a home and raising children is work. In addition, those services often enable the spouse who is working outside the home to earn more money. Thus, services as a homemaker are a factor in favor of the homemaker. Some courts also apply a related concept of considering whether one spouse had impaired her or his earning capacity because of working as a homemaker. That factor would also favor the homemaker-spouse.

Waste and Dissipation

If a spouse wasted money during the marriage, it could count against him or her when it comes time to divide property. This factor is sometimes labeled **economic fault**, and may be considered even by courts that do not consider other kinds of fault.

Fault

Noneconomic fault, such as spousal abuse or marital infidelity, is considered in a few states, but most states do not consider it relevant to property division.

Duration of marriage

A longer marriage may be a factor in favor of a larger property award to the spouse with less wealth or earning power.

Age and Health of Parties

If one spouse has ill health or is significantly older than the other, that factor could favor a larger award to the sicker or older spouse.

Q. What if the parties have more debt than assets?

A. In that uncomfortable but common situation, the court (or the parties by agreement) will divide whatever property they have and then allocate the responsibility of each party to pay off particular debts.

Alimony/Maintenance

Q. What is alimony or maintenance?

A. **Alimony, maintenance,** or **spousal support** is money paid from one spouse to another for day-to-day support of the spouse with fewer financial resources. Sometimes alimony also can be used to pay back a debt.

Q. When do courts award alimony?

A. A court will order alimony on the basis of one spouse's need or entitlement and the other spouse's ability to pay. Although most alimony payments are made from men to women, it is possible that a well-off woman could be required to pay support to her economically dependent husband. Alimony is awarded less often now because there are more two-income couples and

---

ⓘ WHO GETS THE HOUSE?

The decision of who gets the house depends on the facts of each case. If the parties have minor children and can afford to keep the house, even though they will be living separately, the law usually favors giving the house to the spouse who will have custody of the children most of the time. If the parties cannot afford to keep the house, it may be sold and the proceeds divided (or perhaps given to one party). In some cases, there is a middle-ground approach: The spouse who has primary custody of the children will have a right to live in the house for a certain number of years. At the end of that time, that spouse will buy out the other spouse's interest or sell the house and divide the proceeds.

ⓘ CASE STUDY IN ALIMONY

The wife was a majority shareholder in company started by her family. She drew a salary of $58,100 but was also entitled to distributions from the company in excess of $340,000 per year, and her shares in the company were worth between $2 million and $3 million. The husband had been employed by the company as a field sales manager with a salary of about $59,000 per year, but his salary was reduced to $38,000 when he left the company to become an officer in a bank. The wife was ordered to pay alimony to husband of $1,500 per month, subject to review by the court after twenty-four months.

Source: In re Marriage of Shinn *(Illinois Appellate Court, 2000)*

ⓘ HEALTH INSURANCE AFTER DIVORCE

A federal law passed in the 1980s, known by the acronym **COBRA,** requires most employer-sponsored group health plans to offer divorced spouses of covered workers continued coverage at group rates for eighteen months. The divorced spouse of a worker must pay for the coverage, but the coverage is available. The person seeking coverage, however, must request coverage soon after the divorce is final.

fewer marriages in which one person is financially dependent on the other. A person who pays support may deduct it from his or her income for tax purposes; the one who receives it must pay taxes on it (unless the parties agree otherwise).

Q. What is rehabilitative support?

A. A common type of spousal support is rehabilitative support. It is intended to provide a chance for education or job training so that a spouse who was financially dependent or disadvantaged during marriage can become self-supporting. **Rehabilitative support** is designed to help make up for opportunities lost by a spouse who left a job (or did not pursue a career) in order to help the other spouse's career or to assume family duties. It may also be awarded to a spouse who worked outside the home during the marriage, but sacrificed his or her career development because of family priorities. Rehabilitative support is usually only awarded for a limited time, such as one to five years.

Q. What is permanent support?

A. Courts award permanent spousal support to provide money for a spouse who cannot become economically independent or maintain a lifestyle that the court considers appropriate given the resources of the parties. A common reason for ordering permanent maintenance is that the recipient, because of advanced age or chronic illness, will never be able to maintain a reasonable standard of living without the support. Some courts will order permanent support be paid to a spouse who, although working, will never have earning power at a level near the earning power of the more prosperous spouse. When deciding the amount of permanent support, courts often use the same criteria as for dividing property.

Although it is called permanent support, the level of support can change or cease if the ability of the payer or the needs of the recipient change significantly. Support generally ends if the recipient remarries, and it may end if the recipient lives with someone else.

Q. If one spouse supports the other through graduate or professional school, does the supporting spouse have a right to be compensated for increasing the earning capacity of the other spouse?

A. Some courts offer compensation for putting a spouse through school. For example, one spouse may have supported the other through graduate or professional school. The supporting spouse may have expected that both would benefit from the educated spouse's enhanced earning capacity, but the marriage ended before any material benefits were earned. In some states, the professional license of a spouse or many forms of enhanced earnings may be treated as a valuable asset if acquired during the marriage.

The supporting spouse does not need rehabilitation because that spouse has worked during the entire marriage, and there is no significant property to be distributed because marital resources went to the educational effort. In cases such as this, the courts may award compensation, usually as periodic payments, to the supporting spouse. The amount paid may be based upon the contributions of the supporting spouse to the educational expenses and general support of the spouse who leaves the marriage with an advanced degree. In some states, support also may be based upon a portion of the increased earnings of the educated spouse. The courts may change or end

such payments if the expected increased earnings do not occur, but the payments are not ended by remarriage of the recipient. This type of payment sometimes is often called **reimbursement alimony** or **alimony in gross**.

Custody

Q. What is child custody?

A. Child custody is the right and duty to care for a minor child on a day-to-day basis and to make major decisions about the child. In sole custody arrangements, one parent takes care of the child most of the time and makes major decisions about the child. In joint custody arrangements, both parents share in making major decisions, and both parents also might spend substantial amounts of time with the child.

Q. How do courts decide custody?

A. If the parents cannot agree on custody of their child, the court decides custody according to the **best interest of the child**. Determining the best interest of the child involves consideration of many factors, including the health and sex

---

ⓘ WHEN SHOULD ALIMONY BE PERMANENT?

Of course, it depends on the facts of each case. Here is how one court decided a case. A wife and husband, both fifty years old, had been married for twenty-nine years. During the first three years of the marriage, the wife worked as a high school physical education teacher. The parties then had four children, and the wife left her full-time job to take care of the home and children for twenty-five years. The husband worked continuously during the marriage, and at the time of divorce, was an administrator for a charitable organization earning $77,000 per year. The wife had resumed teaching and her salary was $30,000 per year. Her salary would have been significantly higher, and she would have had substantial retirement benefits, had she continued teaching full-time during the marriage. On these facts, the Illinois Appellate Court held that the wife was entitled to permanent maintenance (alimony) in the amount of $600 per month. The court said: "Marriage is a partnership, not only morally, but financially. Spouses are coequals, and homemaker services must be recognized as significant when the economic incidents of divorce are determined. The [wife] should not be penalized for having performed her assignment under the agreed-upon division of labor within the family."

Source: In re Marriage of Drury *(Illinois Appellate Court, 1980)*

of the child, the primary caregiver prior to the divorce, parenting skills and willingness to care for the child, the emotional ties between child and parent, willingness to facilitate visitation by the other parent, and each parent's moral fitness.

Q. Do mothers automatically receive custody?

A. No. Under the laws of almost all states, mothers and fathers have an equal right to custody. Courts are not supposed to assume that a child is automatically better off with the mother or the father. Of course, judges, like the rest of us, are products of their background and personal experience. Some judges may have a deep-seated belief that mothers can take care of children better than fathers and that fathers have little experience in parenting. Conversely, some judges may believe that fathers are automatically better at raising boys—particularly older boys. Judges with such biases may apply these views when they decide custody cases, although they are supposed to base decisions on the facts of each case and not on automatic presumptions. As a group, judges are fair and unbiased in their decisions, and the level of bias is less than it was in years past. Bias on the part of individual judges can be avoided if the parents are able to decide between themselves what the custody or parenting arrangements should be.

In a contested custody case, both the father and mother have an equal burden of proving to the court that it is in the best interest of the child that the child be in his or her custody. There are a couple of states that have laws providing that if everything else is equal, the mother may be preferred; but even in those states, many fathers have been successful in obtaining custody.

Q. How have the laws changed in deciding custody disputes between mothers and fathers?

A. The law has swung like a pendulum. From the early history of our country until the mid-1800s, fathers were favored for custody in the event of a divorce. Children were viewed as similar to property. If a husband and wife divorced, the man usually received the property—such as the farm or the family business. He also received custody of the children. Some courts viewed custody to the father as a natural extension of the father's duty to support and educate his children.

By the mid-1800s, most states switched to a strong preference for the mother under the **Tender Years Doctrine**. In a contested custody case, a mother would receive custody unless there was something very wrong with her, such as she abused the child or suffered from mental illness or alcoholism. The parenting skills of the father were not relevant. This automatic preference for mothers continued until the 1970s. Then principles of equality and co-parenting took over.

Q. What is the most important factor in deciding custody?

A. That will vary with the facts of each case. If one parent has a major problem with alcoholism or mental illness, has abused the child, or has committed domestic violence, that could be the deciding factor. If neither parent has engaged in unusually bad conduct, the most important fac-

---

ⓘ FINDING OUT WHAT A CHILD WANTS

The preference of the child, particularly an older child, is one of the factors judges consider in deciding custody. Judges may talk to the child in private—in the judge's chambers rather than in open court. In some jurisdictions, but not all, the mother and father's lawyers have a right to be present during the judge's interview of the child, although a judge may ask the lawyers to waive that right. In some cases, the judge may appoint a mental health professional, such as a psychiatrist, a psychologist, or a social worker, to talk to the child and report to the court.

tor often is which parent has been primarily responsible for taking care of the child on a day-to-day basis. Some states refer to this as the **primary caretaker factor**. If one parent can show that he or she took care of the child most of the time, that parent will usually be favored for custody. Use of this factor promotes continuity in the child's life and gives custody of the child to the more experienced parent who has shown the dedication to take care of the child's day-to-day needs. If both parents have actively cared for the child or if the child is older, the factor is less crucial, although it is still considered. Regardless of which parent has primary custody, children are usually best served when the child has continued, meaningful contact with both parents.

Q. May a child decide where he or she wants to live?

A. The wishes of a child can be an important factor in deciding custody. The weight a court gives the child's wishes will depend on the child's age, maturity, and quality of reasons. Some judges do not even listen to the preferences of a young child (for example, a child less than eight years old) and instead assume the child is too young to express an informed preference. A court is more likely to follow the preferences of an older child, although the court will want to assess the quality of the child's reasons. If a child wants to be with a parent only because that parent offers more freedom and less discipline, a judge is not likely to honor the preference. A child whose reasons are vague or whose answers seem coached may not have his or her preferences followed.

On the other hand, if a child expresses a good reason related to the child's best interest—such as genuinely feeling closer to one parent than the other—the court will probably follow the preference. Although most states treat a child's wishes as only one factor among many to be considered, a few states allow a child of twelve or fourteen the "absolute right" to choose the parent with whom the child will live, as long as the parent is fit.

Q. If a parent has a sexual relationship outside of marriage, how does that affect a court's decision on custody?

A. In most states, affairs or nonmarital sexual relations are not a factor in deciding custody unless it can be shown that the relationship has

---

ⓘ CYBERSEX

With new technology comes new legal issues. Here is how one court dealt with a case of virtual sexual contact.

A mother and father disputed custody of their three-year-old son. When the child was two years old, the mother admitted that she engaged in "highly erotic" discourse on Internet chat rooms with two different adult men. These communications occurred, in her estimate, perhaps "once a week." She explained to the court that "it was kind of enjoyable that someone was finding interest in me." The trial court found that the mother's conduct was "potentially harmful" and "appalling," but it also found there was no "demonstrable effect" on the child. The trial court also found both parents to be good, and that the mother had been the primary caregiver of the child. The trial court granted custody to the mother, and the South Dakota Supreme Court upheld the decision.

Source: Zepeda v. Zepeda *(South Dakota Supreme Court, 2001)*

harmed the child. A discreet affair during the marriage might not be a significant factor. Similarly, if, after the marriage is over, a parent lives with a person to whom he or she is not married, the live-in relationship by itself may not be a major factor in deciding custody, although the quality of the relationship between the child and the live-in partner can be an important factor in a custody dispute.

If the parent's nonmarital sexual relationship or relationships have placed the child in embarrassing situations or caused significant, provable stress to the child, then the relationship(s) would be a negative factor. In a few states, courts are more inclined to assume that a parent's nonmarital sexual relationship is harmful to the child. The issue of a parent's sexual conduct can be one in which individual judges may have personal biases that influence their decisions.

Q. If a parent is homosexual, what impact does that have on custody?

A. The impact varies dramatically from state to state. Courts in a few states seem more willing to assume harmful impact to a child from a parent's homosexual relationship than from a heterosexual relationship. Courts in other states treat homosexual and heterosexual relationships equally and will not consider the relationship to be a significant factor unless specific harm to the child is shown.

Q. If one parent is trying to undermine the child's relationship with the other parent, how does that affect custody?

A. Most states favor an ongoing, healthy relationship between the child and both parents. If one parent is trying to undermine the child's relationship with the other parent, that is a negative factor. If other factors are close to equal, a court may grant custody to the parent who is more likely to encourage an open and positive relationship with the other parent, unless that other parent has been abusive or otherwise harmed the child.

Q. If one parent is religious and the other is not, may the court favor the more religious parent?

A. Normally, no. Under the First Amendment to the U.S. Constitution, both parents have a right to practice (or not practice) religion as they see fit. A judge cannot make value judgments about whether a child is better off with or without religious training or about which religion is better. If a child has been brought up with particular religious beliefs, and religious activities are important to the child, a court might favor promoting continuity in the child's life, but the court should not favor religion per se. In some cases, a parent's unusual or nonmainstream religious activities may become an issue, especially if specific harm to the child is shown.

Q. Can custody decisions be changed?

A. Yes. A court may always change child custody to meet the changing needs of the growing child and to respond to changes in the parents' lives. Because courts favor stability for the child and do not want to encourage contentious litigation, a parent seeking to change custody must show that the conditions have changed substantially, and usually unpredictably, since the last custody order. The parent must also show that changing the custody arrangement would be better for the child. Sometimes the parent must show that not changing custody would be harmful to the child.

Q. What legal remedies are available if a parent abducts a child?

A. Abduction of a child by a parent is a crime under state laws and, under certain circumstances, may also be a federal offense. Local police, state police, and in some cases the FBI can help in locating missing children. Parents who abduct their children can also be forced to pay the expenses incurred by the other parent in trying to find and return the child. To recover such expenses, a parent would probably need the help of a private lawyer.

If a parent with custody fears that the other parent will abduct the child, he or she should immediately consult a lawyer.

Visitation/Access/Parenting Time

Q. If a parent does not receive custody, how much access or visitation is he or she likely to receive?

A. That will vary with the desires of the parents and the inclinations of a judge. A standard visitation schedule is every other weekend (Friday evening through Sunday); a weeknight (for dinner); the child's winter and spring breaks in alternating years; alternate major holidays; and several weeks in the summer. If parents live far apart and regular weekend visitation is not feasible, it is common to allocate more summer vacation and school holidays to the noncustodial parent. For parents who do not like the terms "visitation" or "custody," it is possible to draft a custody and visitation order, which leaves out those terms and just describes the times at which the child will be with each parent. Instead of "visitation" and "custody," some states use terms such as "parenting time" or "access to the child."

Q. Under what circumstances may a court deny the noncustodial parent visitation?

A. A noncustodial parent is entitled to visitation unless there is harm to the child. For example, if the noncustodial parent has molested the child, is likely to kidnap the child, has a long history of domestic violence, or is likely to use illegal drugs or excessive amounts of alcohol while caring for the child, a court will probably deny or restrict visitation. Visitation might be allowed only under supervision, such as at a social service agency or in the company of a responsible relative. A parent should not deny the other parent visitation without advance approval from the court unless a true emergency exists, such as a noncustodial parent coming to pick up the child while drunk or under the influence of drugs.

Joint Custody

Q. What is joint custody?

A. Joint custody—sometimes referred to as **shared custody** or **shared parenting**—has two parts: joint legal custody and joint physical custody. A joint custody order can have one or both parts.

Q. What is joint legal custody?

A. **Joint legal custody** means that both parents share in major decisions affecting the child. The custody order may describe the issues on which the parents must share decisions. The most common issues are school, health care, and religious training. Other issues on which the parents may make joint decisions include extracurricular activities, summer camp, age for dating or driving, and methods of discipline. Many joint custody orders specify procedures parents should follow in the event they cannot agree on an issue. The most common procedure is for the parents to consult a mediator.

Q. What is joint physical custody?

A. **Joint physical custody** refers to the time the child spends with each parent. The amount of time is flexible. It does not have to be fifty-fifty. The length of time could be relatively moderate, such as every other weekend with one parent; or the amount of time could be equally divided between the parents. Parents who opt for equal time-sharing have come up with many alternatives: alternate two-day periods; equal division of the week; alternate weeks; alternate months; alternate four-month periods; and alternate six-month periods. If the child is attending school and spends a substantial amount of time with both parents, it usually is best for the child if the parents live relatively close to each other. A few parents, on an interim basis, have kept the child in a single home while the parents rotate staying in the home with the child.

> ### ▶ THE PROS AND CONS OF JOINT PHYSICAL CUSTODY
>
> Supporters of joint physical custody stress that it is in the best interest of children to protect and improve their relationship with both parents. They believe shared custody is the only way to make sure that children do not "lose" a parent because of the divorce. Some argue that is a natural right of both parents to spend equal time with the child. Critics of joint custody fear that shared-time parenting is unworkable and worry about instability for the child and the potential for conflicts. The success of joint physical custody may depend on the personality of the child. Adaptable children who are relatively relaxed and laid back will do better than children who are tense and become easily upset by changes in routine. Because joint physical custody usually requires keeping two homes for the child, joint physical custody may cost more than sole custody.

Q. Are courts required to order joint custody if a parent asks for it?

A. No. In most states, joint custody is an option. Courts may order joint custody or sole custody according to what the judge thinks is in the best interest of the child. In eleven states, legislatures have declared a general preference for joint custody. That usually means the courts are supposed to order joint custody if a parent asks for it, unless there is a good reason for not ordering joint custody. The most common reason for not ordering joint custody is the parents' inability to cooperate. Courts are concerned that a child will be caught in the middle of a tug-of-war if joint custody is ordered for parents who do not cooperate with each other. Parents who do not cooperate also will have trouble with sole custody and visitation, but the frequency of conflicts may be less.

If a parent is opposing joint custody because the parent (without good reason) is trying to undermine the child's relationship with the other parent, that could be a factor in granting custody to the other parent.

Moving the Child out of State

Q. May the custodial parent move out of state with the child?

A. The law on this issue varies from state to state. Some states routinely allow the custodial parent to move out of state with the child if there is a good-faith reason for the move. Many states, however, examine requests to move on a case-by-case basis and decide the issue after considering several factors. Some states also impose notice requirements by which the parent who wants to move with the child must notify the other parent a certain number of days (thirty, sixty, or ninety days) before the proposed move so that the non-custodial parent has an opportunity to challenge the plans for a move.

Q. What are good-faith reasons for the move?

A. The most common good-faith reasons for a move are obtaining significantly better employment in another state, following one's new spouse to a new job in another state, and a desire to live near family members.

Q. What are the factors a court will consider when deciding whether to allow a move?

A. There are several factors:

1. The quality of the custodial parent's reason for the move. A good-faith reason and a likelihood that allowing the move will enhance the quality of life for the child and custodial parent helps the custodial parent's case. A bad-faith reason, such as a desire to undermine the child's relationship with the noncustodial parent, makes it more likely a court will deny permission to move.

2. The quality of the reasons of the parent opposing the move. A parent who has been very active in the child's life, sees the child often, and wants to preserve that relationship has a stronger case for denying permission to move. A parent who has not seen the child very much, or who often misses visitation, has a weaker case.
3. The quality of the relationship between the child and both parents.
4. The degree to which visitation can be restructured to preserve or foster a good relationship between the child and the nonmoving parent, including the issue of whether substitute visitation is affordable to the parties.

Child Support

Q. How do courts set child support?

A. Under federal law, all states have guidelines to determine child support. The guidelines are formulas that consider the income of the parties, the number of children, and perhaps some other factors. The formulas are based on studies of how much families ordinarily spend on child raising. The formulas try to approximate the proportion of parental income that would have been spent for support of the child if the family had not been divided by divorce. Courts plug numbers into the formula and come up with an amount of support that should be paid. The parties can argue that

because of special circumstances, a court should order more or less support than the guideline amount.

Q. When working with guideline formulas, how are the parents' incomes determined?

A. States vary, with some using the parents' net income, and others using the gross income. Gross income is the parents' income from all (or almost all) sources, including wages, investments, and other sources. Net income is equal to gross income minus federal and state income taxes, Social Security tax, Medicare tax, health insurance, and perhaps union dues. For self-employed persons, the determination of income may be complex. Courts will allow deductions of reasonable business expenses before determining net income. But courts may disallow unusually high business expenses and depreciation that reduce income artificially without hurting the parent's cash flow. Thus, certain expenses that are deductible for tax purposes may not be deductible from income for the purpose of setting child support.

Q. How much child support should a noncustodial parent expect to pay?

A. That question is difficult to answer precisely because guidelines vary among states and because courts may depart from the guidelines. The percentage formulas differ from state to state, but some examples can be given.

PERCENTAGE OF OBLIGOR'S INCOME GUIDELINES

Number of children	Percent of supporting party's net income	
	Illinois	**New York**
1 . . . . .20%		17%
2 . . . . .25%		25%
3 . . . . .32%		29%
4 . . . . .40%		31%
5 . . . . .45%		33% for 5 or more children
. . . . .50% for 6 or more children		

Q. What is an example of a guideline for child support based on the income of only the noncustodial parent?

A. On page 83 is a comparison chart showing the "percentage of obligor's income" guidelines that were in effect in Illinois and in New York in the year 2003:

Under this guideline, if a noncustodial parent (**supporting party**) in Illinois had a net income of $40,000, the annual level of child support would be $8,000 for one child; $10,000 for two children; $12,800 for three children; and so on.

Q. What's an example of a support formula based on the incomes of both parents?

A. Support guidelines based on the incomes of both parents often are referred to as **income shares models**. Under these guidelines, the court first adds the income of both parents. Then the court consults a long table—or a computer program—that assesses the total obligation of support as a percentage of the combined incomes and the number of children. Generally, the percentage drops as the combined incomes rise, on the assumption that financially well-off parents spend a smaller portion of their incomes on their children than parents who are less well off. The court multiplies the combined incomes by the percent figure and obtains a dollar amount. Then the responsibility to pay that support is divided between the parents in proportion to each parent's incomes.

Here is an example using Colorado's child support schedules. Assume a father and mother have two children and a combined annual gross income of $60,000—$40,000 earned by the father and $20,000 earned by the mother. The schedules put the guideline amount for support at $13,092 per year ($1,091 per month). Since the father earns two-thirds of the parties' combined income, he would pay two-thirds of the children's support ($8,728 a year) and the mother would pay one-third ($4,364). If one parent had primary custody of the children, the other probably would make a cash payment to that parent. The parent with primary custody probably would not make a cash payment as such, but would be presumed to be spending that amount on the children.

Q. What are reasons for ordering more support than the guideline amount?

A. This depends, in part, on what expenses the guidelines include. Some common reasons for giving support above the base guideline amount include childcare expenses, high medical or dental expenses of the child that are not covered by insurance, and voluntary unemployment or underemployment of the parent who is supposed to pay support. Expenses for summer camps and private schools also might be a basis for setting higher support levels, particularly if private

---

ⓘ JOINT CUSTODY AND CHILD SUPPORT

The effect of joint custody on child support depends on the nature of the joint custody arrangement. If the parents have joint legal custody (by which they share in making major decisions regarding the child), that will have little effect on child support. One parent still has primary custody of the child and handles payments of most of the child's day-to-day expenses. The custodial parent's expenses for the child have not been reduced by the joint custody arrangement. If the parents have joint physical custody and the child spends a substantial amount of time with each parent, support might be set at less than the guideline amount since both parents are likely to handle day-to-day expenses for the child. (Parents, however, will need to coordinate payments on major expenses such as camp, school, clothing, and insurance.)

schools or summer camps were part of the family's lifestyle during the marriage.

Q. What are reasons for setting support below the guideline amount?

A. Again, this varies from state to state, but common reasons for setting support below the guideline amounts include support obligations from earlier marriages and large debts related to family expenses to pay off. If the support guidelines are based on the income of only the noncustodial parent and if the custodial parent has an unusually high income, then the noncustodial parent can argue that the custodial parent's income is a reason for setting support below the guidelines. Also, if the guidelines do not have a cap or maximum level of income to which they apply, the high income of the noncustodial parent may be a basis for setting support below the guidelines. For example, using the Illinois guidelines described earlier, if a noncustodial parent has three children and an annual net income of $200,000, that parent may argue that the children do not need the $64,000 per year that the guidelines call for.

Q. Is child support paid while the child is with the noncustodial parent for summer vacation or long breaks?

A. In most cases, yes. Courts figure that many major expenses for the benefit of the child—such as rent, mortgage, utilities, clothes, and insurance—have to be paid whether the child is with the custodial parent or not. So, usually, a full support payment is due. On the other hand, the parties—with the court's approval—may agree on payments in different amounts during vacation periods when the child is with the noncustodial parent. The lower amount for vacation periods with the noncustodial parent might reflect savings to the custodial parent for food expenses or childcare.

Q. How is child support enforced if a parent does not pay?

A. The state and federal governments have a variety of techniques for enforcing payments of child support. The most common is a wage de-

---

ⓘ THE NUMBER CRUNCH— CHILD SUPPORT DEFICIT

The Census Bureau reports that only about half of the parents entitled to receive child support receive the full amount that is due. About one-quarter of parents to whom support is due receive partial payments, and the other one-quarter receives nothing at all. The Census Bureau estimates that each year, about $13 billion dollars in court-ordered child support is not paid. In addition to that, there are several million mothers who have not obtained orders of child support for their children. A high proportion of those women had children out of wedlock.

ⓘ COLLEGE EXPENSES

The obligation of divorced parents to pay for a child's college or trade school education (and related expenses) depends on the state and any agreements between the parents. Courts in some states will require parents to pay for a child's college expenses, assuming the parents can afford it and the child is a good enough student to benefit from college. Courts in other states terminate child support at eighteen, and note that married parents are not required to pay for their child's college expenses, and, therefore, divorced parents are not required to do so, either. Regardless of the state's law on compulsory payment of college expenses, the mother and father can agree as part of their divorce settlement to pay for these costs. Courts usually will enforce those agreements.

duction, by which the employer sends a portion of the parent's wages to a state agency that then sends the money to the parent who has custody of the child. A federal law requires that after 1994, all child support orders must provide for an automatic wage deduction unless the parties have agreed otherwise or unless a court waives the automatic order. The state also can intercept the federal and state tax refunds of persons who have not paid support. Liens can be placed on property, such as real estate and automobiles. A parent who has not paid support can be held in contempt of court, which may result in a fine or a jail term. In addition, a parent who has not paid support can lose his or her driver's license or professional license. Government lawyers may help with collection of child support, though their efficiency varies from state to state.

Child support enforcement is a matter of increasing federal concern. Under the Child Support Recovery Act of 1992, it is a federal crime to willfully fail to pay child support to a child who resides in another state if the past-due amount has been unpaid for over one year or exceeds $5,000. Punishments under the federal law can include fines and imprisonment. States also have criminal penalties for failure to pay child support.

A parent may not reduce child support payments without a court order: The unpaid amounts will accumulate as a debt, even if a court later decides that there was a good reason for the reduction.

Grandparents and Stepparents

Q. What are grandparents' rights to visitation?

Although all states had statutes allowing grandparents to seek visitation with their grandchildren, the U.S. Supreme Court issued a ruling in 2000 that will make it more difficult for grandparents to obtain court-ordered visits with their grandchildren. In the case of *Troxel v. Granville*, the Court found that fit parents should be given more deference on decisions regarding with whom the child will associate than was provided by the Washington State law. The Court left open the possibility that some grandparents could obtain court-ordered visitation if, for example, the grandparents can show that they had a particularly strong relationship with their grandchildren, it would harm the child not to continue the relationship, and it is in the child's best interest to continue. The burden of proof is on the grandparents.

Q. May courts award grandparents custody of their grandchildren?

A. Yes, but usually only if neither parent wants the children or if the parents are unfit. Courts examine such factors as the grandparents' age, health, and ability to care for the children. Courts will not deny grandparents custody because of their age, as long as they are healthy.

Some custody disputes between grandparents and parents arise when the grandparents have been raising their grandchildren for a considerable length of time under an informal arrangement. The grandparents may have become the "psychological parents" of the grandchildren by the time the parent or parents seek to regain custody. In this circumstance, courts in many states will allow the grandparents to retain custody, even if the parents are fit.

Q. What are a stepparent's duties and rights?

A. The responsibilities of a stepparent depend on state law. A stepparent is not usually liable for a spouse's child from another marriage, unless the stepparent has adopted the child. Until then, the child's biological parents are liable for his or her support. Some states, however, make stepparents liable for the stepchild's support as long as the stepparent and the stepchild are living together.

A stepparent who does not adopt a spouse's child may not normally claim custody of the child if the marriage ends in divorce, although some states allow a stepparent to seek visitation. A stepchild does not share in the estate of a stepparent, unless the stepparent has provided for the stepchild in a will. However, unmarried stepchildren under eighteen may receive supplemental retirement benefits or survivor's benefits under Social Security.

Mediation and Collaborative Law

Q. What is mediation?

A. **Mediation** is a process in which the parties to a divorce (or some other dispute) try to resolve their disagreements outside of court with the help of a mediator. The mediator cannot force a settlement, but tries to assist the parties to clarify their interests and work out their own solution. In divorce actions, mediators are often involved in custody and visitation disputes. They can also handle property disputes, support disputes, and other issues. If the parties resolve their disagreements through mediation, the lawyers for both

---

ⓘ COLLABORATIVE LAW

Collaborative law is a relatively new concept used by people who wish to resolve their disputes without a contested court hearing. Collaborative law can be used in divorces and in other types of disputes. Under principles of collaborative law, the parties hire lawyers with the understanding that the lawyers can be used only to help settle the dispute. The parties and their lawyers work together as a team to reach a settlement that they all think is fair, or at least a settlement they can live with. The parties agree that in the event their case does not settle, they will have to hire new lawyers to handle a trial. Collaborative law is usually a (comparatively) peaceful and less costly way to resolve a dispute. If a settlement is not reached, however, there will be added costs in hiring new lawyers and putting on a trial.

---

the parties should be involved in finalizing and approving the agreement.

Q. Is mediation mandatory in divorce actions?

A. That depends on the rules of the local court. Many courts require mediation of custody and visitation disputes—the mother and father must talk with a court-appointed mediator to try to resolve the problem before putting their case before a judge. The mediator cannot force a resolution, but the parties can be told to try mediation before coming to court.

Q. What is the professional background of divorce mediators?

A. Most mediators are either lawyers or mental health professionals. Some court-related mediators have degrees in social work or psychology. Private mediators are often lawyers, although many are mental health professionals. Mediators who are mental health professionals are not serving as therapists, and mediators who are lawyers are not serving as lawyers. Instead, they are professionals who are trying to help two (or more) people work out their differences. Mediators are generally not licensed or regulated by the state, although the ABA has adopted standards and many states do have some certification for court-mandated mediation.

Q. What are the advantages of mediation?

A. Mediation often is cheaper and quicker than taking a case before a judge. A good mediator can help the parties build their problem-solving skills, and that can help them avoid later disputes. Most people who settle their cases through mediation leave the process feeling better than they would have felt if they had gone through a bitter court fight.

Q. What are the disadvantages of mediation?

A. Mediation can be a problem if one or both parties are withholding information. For example, if the purpose of mediation is to settle financial issues and one party is hiding assets or income, the other party might be better off with a lawyer who can vigorously investigate the matter. Mediators are usually good at exploring the parties' needs, goals, and possible solutions, but mediators do not have the legal resources of a lawyer to look for hidden information.

Another problem with mediation can arise if one party is very passive and likely to be bulldozed by the other. In that situation, the mediated agreement might be lopsided in favor of the stronger party. A good mediator, however, will see to it that a weaker party's needs are expressed and protected. Mediators should refuse to proceed with mediation if it looks as though one side will take improper advantage of the other.

Some professionals think that mediation is not appropriate if the case involves domestic violence. One concern is that mediation will just provide a forum in which the abuser can harm the victim again. Another concern is that victims of physical abuse are not able to adequately express and protect their own interests. However, other professionals believe that disputes in families with a history of domestic violence can still be mediated, particularly if the abused party is not significantly intimidated by the other party.

A final potential drawback to mediation is that if mediation does not succeed, the parties may have wasted time and money on the process and still face the expenses of a trial.

THE WORLD AT YOUR FINGERTIPS

Divorce

- *For a variety of materials on divorce law and policy, visit the website of the American Academy of Matrimonial Lawyers: www.aaml.org.*

Child Support

- *Information about child support, including links to the support guidelines of each state can be found at www.supportguidelines.com.*

- *The Federal Office of Child Support Enforcement can be contacted at www.acf.hhs.gov.*
- *Every state has child support enforcement units that help custodial parents establish and enforce child support orders and locate absent parents. (These offices are sometimes called IV-D Offices because they are required by Chapter IV-D of the Social Security Act.) You can locate the offices by looking under county or state government listings in the telephone book or by asking the state government switchboard.*
- *Another resource is the Office of Child Support Enforcement Reference Center, Office of Child Support Enforcement, 6110 Executive Boulevard, Rockville, MD 20852. This office can help parents find their state's enforcement officers.*

Mediation

- *A good source of information on mediation is the Academy of Family Mediators, Lexington, MA (781-674-2663). The academy lists family mediators in every state by training and experience. Local courts (including the court clerk's office) may also have information regarding mediation services.*

REMEMBER THIS

- *All states provide no-fault grounds for divorce such as "irreconcilable difference" or "irretrievable breakdown." Most states also have fault grounds, such as adultery, physical cruelty, mental cruelty, abandonment, or addiction to drugs or alcohol. The degree to which fault is a factor in dividing property or setting support for a spouse varies from state to state.*

- *Upon divorce, in most states, wives and husbands are entitled to keep their own nonmarital or separate property. Such property can include money or investments earned before marriage and inheritances received before or after the marriage—assuming the property was kept in the wife's or the husband's own name and was not mixed with marital property.*

- *Unless there is a valid prenuptial agreement, the court has the power to divide marital or community property—which generally is property acquired during the marriage—between the husband and the wife. Marital or community property includes wages and pensions earned during the marriage, even though only one partner earned the wages or pension.*

- *A court can give alimony (also referred to as "maintenance") to the spouse with fewer financial means. The alimony can be temporary or permanent, depending on the facts of the case and the law of the state.*

- *Child custody (also referred to as "parenting time") is supposed to be decided according to the best interest of the child. It is the law in almost all states that judges should not give an automatic preference to the mother or the father based on sex of the parent. Important factors in deciding custody include which parent has been the primary caretaker of the child, the quality of the relationship between the child and each parent, and the child's preferences. Joint custody is a common option for parents, although the term does not refer to a single fixed schedule of time the child spends with each parent.*

- *Child support is set with reference to state guidelines. Courts generally set child support according to guidelines adopted by the state unless there is a good reason for doing otherwise. There are a variety of methods for enforcing child support orders, the most common of which is an automatic deduction from wages.*

- *People can seek to resolve their family law disputes through mediation. A mediator cannot impose a settlement on the parties, but the mediator can work with parties to focus on genuine needs and to resolve a dispute without the cost and stress of litigation.*

Buying and Selling a Home

A home is one of the largest purchases many people will ever make. But buying—or selling—a home is not as easy as it looks. Some of the things that will affect you when you're buying or selling a home are the laws where you live, the economy, your financial situation, the prevailing real estate market, current mortgage rates, and tax considerations. You'll need to work with a variety of people, including real estate agents, lawyers, lenders, home inspectors, surveyors, appraisers, and insurance agents.

    Practices and laws affecting real estate change over time, addressing new consumer issues, and over geographic regions, with laws and customs varying from city to city and state to state.

This chapter will give you some guidance, whether you're buying or selling a home for the first time or the tenth. You'll become familiar with some real estate terminology, become acquainted with the roles of different participants, and learn about your financing and tax options. The section entitled "The Steps of Buying and Selling a Home" will tell you what you need to know about the contract that controls the transaction.

As you read this chapter, remember that becoming familiar with both the buying and selling side of the process is useful even if you are engaging in only one side of the transaction. If you understand the interests of both parties, you will be able to anticipate issues and be better prepared to negotiate the contract.

INTRODUCTION TO BUYING AND SELLING A HOME

Imagine you've found the home of your dreams. It's in the right neighborhood, has the right kitchen, and it's at the right price. You contact the seller, put your own house on the market, and start packing in preparation for the big move.

But wait a minute. Are you sure you can afford to buy this dream home? Have you done some homework to check that it's really as good a deal as it looks? Do you know what steps you have to go through to buy a home, and how long it takes

This section will help you answer those questions.

Q. Why is the purchase or sale of a home more complicated than buying or selling some other object, such as an expensive car?

A. Items of personal property, such as cars and boats, have different characteristics from real estate. Personal property is usually movable and, in many cases, owned for a relatively short period of time. Possession of personal property also is a strong indicator of ownership. Real estate, also

known as **real property** or simply land, cannot be moved and possession does not necessarily mean ownership. For example, even if real estate is fenced in, it may be difficult to distinguish a neighbor's property from your own. And even if a person owns real estate, he or she may not have possession of it; for example, if it is being rented to someone else.

It is true that both types of transactions raise tax and financing considerations. However, because of the differences between real and personal property, the law treats transactions involving each differently. Some of those differences are that agreements regarding the sale of real estate must be in writing to be enforceable; absent consumer protection laws or special representations of the seller, real property is sold "as is"; foreclosing real property is usually more difficult than repossessing an item of personal property; and real estate is taxed differently from personal property.

Q. What is a home?

A. A home is not always a single-family dwelling built on an individual parcel of land. Town houses, condominiums, and cooperatives are also homes. Each one of these types of homes has unique features, which are discussed later in this chapter.

Q. Why should I buy a home?

A. People buy homes for different reasons. Some want to own property because it allows them to reduce their living costs. Others like the income tax benefits of ownership. In certain parts of the country, finding rental property is difficult, so ownership may be the only option. And owning property may allow some people to gain more control over their personal living environment.

A common view of prospective homebuyers is to think of a home solely, or at least primarily, as an investment. This view, however, may be misguided. There is no reason to assume that home prices will always rise. Home prices can fall, sometimes dramatically. And, depending on the home prices in a given area of the country, renting may be far more economical than buying, particularly if the tenant invests the difference between the rental payment and the amount that would have been paid under a mortgage, as well as repairs, taxes, and insurance.

The decision to buy a home is not just an investment decision, but it is wise to give it at least the same care as you would give to any major investment.

Q. What does title mean?

A. **Title** to real estate consists of ownership of and the right to use the property. That is, if you are the legal owner of record, you have **title to the property** and are the **title owner**. However, **title exceptions,** or **clouds on title**, which are possible claims of others to your title, may affect the interest of a title owner.

There are several kinds of title exceptions. For example, different people may have claims or liens against the real estate. A **lien** is a claim against the property that often represents an unpaid debt of the owner or unpaid judgment entered against the owner by a court of law. The most common form of lien against real property is a mortgage or deed of trust. If the titleholder does not pay the lien or claim, the creditor may ultimately have the right to sell the property to satisfy the debt.

Other types of title exceptions include min-

 DEED

A **deed** is a written document that contains the names of the seller and the purchaser, other personal information, certain conveyance language, and a legal description of the property. There are different kinds of deeds, but they must all contain at least this basic information. A deed is generally effective between the parties on delivery, but in most states it must be recorded in the public records to be effective against third parties.

---

eral rights, mechanic's liens, unpaid taxes, private and public utility easements, and road rights-of-way. **Covenants of record** or **restrictions of record**, which generally take the form of a written document that sets forth restrictions on the use of the property, are another important kind of title exception. For example, if a home has been built in conjunction with other homes, there may be a subdivision or common-ownership association declaration recorded that addresses architectural controls, limitations on renting the property, and restrictions on business activities at the property. Covenants written long ago may contain restrictions that are unenforceable today, such as prohibitions against selling your home to a member of certain racial, religious, or ethnic groups. You can ignore these, but you should understand covenants that are enforceable.

There may be questions about whether the seller can convey good title. A search of the public records is always done prior to the closing. A title search reveals who owns—and what title exceptions affect—the property, as a result of those parties recording a document evidencing their claim in the public record. A lawyer, an abstract company, or a title insurance company can conduct such a search. The results of this search are usually compiled in either an **abstract of title** or a **title insurance commitment** to help the buyer determine who owns the property and if there are any title exceptions that would interfere with the buyer's use of the property. There may, however, be other claims of an interest in the property not shown on the public record.

Any unacceptable title exceptions should be corrected before the closing if possible. Typically, the seller is responsible for remedying title defects.

In addition to title exceptions, government regulations, such as zoning or occupancy laws, also affect the use of real estate. The buyer should ask a lawyer to explain these restrictions before closing.

Even in areas of the country where the buyer receives a title insurance policy, buyers and sellers should seek the advice of a lawyer to gain an understanding of what affects title.

Q. What is a buyer's market?

A. A **buyer's market** occurs when home sales are slow. Here are some of the factors that might indicate that the home sales market in your area is a buyer's market:

- It is taking longer and longer to sell homes.
- Foreclosures are increasing.
- There are large reductions in home prices.
- Unemployment is increasing.
- Numerous "for sale" signs are displayed.

These factors indicate a **soft market** for home sales. A soft market tends to make sellers anxious and puts buyers in a stronger position than sellers. In a buyer's market, buyers have many homes to choose from and can demand special considerations from sellers.

Q. What is a seller's market?

A. A **seller's market** occurs when

- homes are selling fast;
- there are few homes on the market; and
- the local economy is good.

These factors all operate to move home prices upward. In a seller's market, sellers can and do demand high prices for their homes and often dictate the terms of the contract. Also, in a seller's market, sellers often receive several competing offers and are in a position to insist that the buyer close quickly.

If you are a potential seller in a seller's market, you are likely to be able to sell quickly and at your price. On the other hand, if you are a potential buyer in a seller's market, you will want to be particularly careful that you do not rush into a decision that you may later regret. The best way to avoid "buyer's remorse" is to do your homework to ensure that you know what you want to buy and what you can afford.

THE WORLD AT YOUR FINGERTIPS

- *The ABA publication* The ABA Guide to Home Ownership *offers a more detailed discussion of the issues surrounding buying and selling a home. The book can be ordered by telephone at 800-285-2221, or online at www.abanet.org/publiced/practical/books/home_ownership/home.html. It is also available in bookstores across the country.*

ⓘ DIFFERENT KINDS OF INTERESTS IN REAL ESTATE

A farmer leases land owned by a school district. The district owns the land, but the farmer owns the crops he plants on the land. The district was able to sell mineral rights to the land to another person. And if the district ever decides to sell the property, the local church has the option to buy it.

As the above example shows, being an owner of real estate can have different meanings. It can, for example, mean you own any or all of the following:

- The land and everything under it, including minerals and water
- Anything of value on the land, such as crops or timber
- The airspace over the land
- Improvements on the land such as a home, a building, a barn, or a fence

Ownership of the above elements may be individual or shared, and may also be subject to rights of other parties. In addition, although you may not be an owner, you may have a legally protected interest in property owned by someone else if you have the right to buy and/or possess the land or improvements under, for example, an option or lease.

- *There are many readily accessible publications that will give you some basic information on buying a home. A good place to start is FindLaw's website for the public. The real estate link will give you access to articles and information about home ownership. Visit public.findlaw. com/real_estate/homeownership/ articles.html.*

- *Nearly every state has federal information centers where information on federal services, programs, and regulations is available to consumers. The federal government publishes a listing of many free or low-cost pamphlets on home ownership and home buying. This listing can be obtained by writing Consumer Information Catalog, Pueblo, Colorado 81009, or by calling 888-878-3256. You can also check out the listings online at www.pueblo.gsa.gov. Many communities and financial institutions sponsor clinics to prepare people for home ownership and the mortgage loan process. The local library also can be a good source of helpful, free information. Various nonprofit agencies, such as the Better Business Bureau offices, can help you get more information on your legal rights and obligations in buying and selling a home. Look in your local telephone directory for the BBB office nearest to you or access www.bbb.org/pubpages/ homepage.asp.*

MEETING THE PLAYERS

As a first-time buyer, Sue was interested in purchasing a condominium but didn't want to work with a real estate agent. She saw a sign for an open house in a desired neighborhood. She went in, was greeted by a real estate agent, and put her name on a sign-in sheet. The agent assisted Sue in preparing an offer. Sue didn't have a lawyer, but the agent was able to recommend a lawyer specializing in real estate who had handled many matters for the agency before. The sale went through without a hitch, and Sue bought the condo. After the excitement had faded, Sue felt upset at the way the sale had gone. She hadn't realized the agent would be entitled to a commission out of the sale price, and she felt like the sale had been rushed. Sue wondered if she had received really independent advice about certain aspects of the sale, including whether she should get an inspection.

When you're buying a home, especially your first home, your agent and lawyer should be working in your best interests, and have no conflicts of interest. This chapter will introduce you to the players, and give you an idea of some of the things to keep in mind.

Q. Who is involved in a real estate transaction?

A. Although it is possible for a home to be bought and sold strictly between the buyer and seller, this rarely happens. In today's market, a homebuyer will usually want to use the services of a real **estate agent**, a **lawyer, and** a **home inspector.** To obtain financing, buyers will need to consult with a **mortgage broker** or lending institution. They may also meet with a **financial planner** or **accountant** about financing, and an **insurance broker** to obtain appropriate homeowner's insurance.

A seller may choose to sell without the services of a real estate agent in order to avoid paying a commission. However, the seller may turn to a financial planner or accountant for assistance in sorting out the tax consequences of selling. In addition, few sellers would forego the services of a **lawyer.** A knowledgeable person needs to prepare the documents required for the closing. In some parts of the country, it is customary to rely on a title insurance company to prepare these documents. However, it is important to understand that the title company is not representing either party to the transaction.

Selecting a Real Estate Agent to Sell Your Home

Q. Who does the real estate agent represent?

A. The role of a real estate agent will depend on which party the agent represents. If a seller signs a listing agreement with a particular agent, that agent is working for the seller. Representing the seller means that while the agent cannot lie or commit fraud on a buyer, the agent owes a duty of loyalty to the seller only. A seller's agent is not obligated to volunteer negative information about the property or the terms of the sale to a potential buyer.

However, if a second agent is involved (often referred to as a **cooperating, selling,** or **showing agent**), a question arises as to whether the second agent is working for the seller or the buyer. It was the general practice for many years that if a cooperating agent showed a property to a buyer, the second agent was still the seller's agent. Why? Because the second agent's authority to show the home and the compensation to be paid upon the sale stemmed from the seller's listing agreement.

Buyers often misunderstood this relationship. Although it had always been possible for a buyer to hire a separate person as a buyer's agent, most buyers thought that any agent showing them properties was their agent. As a result, over the past several years, many states have addressed the representation of the buyer as a consumer protection issue. Now, depending on the state, it may be that if an agent shows a property to a buyer, that cooperating agent is deemed to be a buyer's agent. The agent then owes a duty of loyalty to the buyer, meaning that the agent would be required to disclose negative information and negotiate the best possible terms for the buyer. This agent can be compensated from the total commission generated by the sale.

If the listing agent shows the property to a buyer, it is possible that one agent will act as both the listing agent and the buyer's agent, referred to as a **dual agent**. In such a case, there is the potential for the agent to have a conflict of interest. Therefore, such an arrangement must be disclosed to and approved by both the buyer and the seller, usually in writing, before the parties can proceed.

Because this is an area of law that is rapidly changing, it is important that the buyer understands whom the agent represents.

Q. What is a listing agreement?

A. The **listing agreement** is a contract that, once signed, is binding between the seller and the listing real estate agency. Its provisions include the length of the listing period, the commission rate, the responsibilities of the firm and its agents, and who will pay for the cost of advertising and other costs associated with the home sale. One important term to look for is when the commission must be paid. As a seller, you would want to owe a commission only if the closing has occurred.

ⓘ THE LISTING AGREEMENT

Read the listing agreement carefully. Do not hesitate to discuss any provisions you would like to change. To further protect your interests, avoid signing an agreement until your lawyer has reviewed and approved it, especially if you have requested changes that have been resisted.

One other suggestion could save you a lot of money. Before signing a listing agreement, let your friends and neighbors know you are selling. If any of them express an interest in buying, exclude them in writing from the listing agreement so that if one of them ultimately buys the property, you will not be required to pay any commission to the agent.

Q. *What is the role of the seller's agent?*

A. The role of the seller's agent is spelled out in the listing agreement. The agent who signs a listing agreement with the seller is known as the **listing agent**. The listing agent helps determine the asking price, suggests how to market the home, adds the property to a local **multiple listing service (MLS)**, schedules advertising and open houses, shows the home to prospective buyers, and otherwise facilitates the sale. Since the amount paid to an agent can be high, it may be possible to hire an agent to handle only limited aspects of the sale in exchange for a reduced commission.

Q. *Why should I list my home with a real estate agent?*

A. Experienced, reputable agents can provide invaluable assistance to sellers. They can suggest the listing price, estimate how long it may take to sell the property, offer suggestions about how to best show the home, and determine whether buyers who inquire about the property are **qualified**— that is, whether a potential buyer is in a position financially and otherwise to buy the property.

One of the most important reasons to use an agent is to have the property information listed on a MLS. This computer service allows information about the home to be made available to hundreds of other agents and buyers. Multiple listing services often have sophisticated websites that also enhance their value to the seller. You need to make sure that you select a listing agent who is a member of the MLS on which you want the property to appear.

Q. *How do I choose an agent to sell my home?*

A. Choosing an agent requires you to do some homework, both on the qualifications of the real estate firm and on the individual agent you engage. In order to find a person who is knowledgeable and interested in selling the property, you may want to interview several agents from various local firms and ask them a few questions. For example:

- Is the firm a member of the National Association of Realtors, a national voluntary professional organization whose members exchange information and hold seminars in order to enhance their skills and improve the services provided to buyers and sellers of real estate?
- What is the record for sales for the last six months or one year? How do these figures

---

📑 DIFFERENT TYPES OF LISTING AGREEMENTS

There are several types of listing agreements. The type commonly used in your area will be dictated by custom and will often be nonnegotiable. Most real estate firms prefer **exclusive right to sell** listings. This type of agreement provides that the seller will pay the listing agent a commission no matter who sells the property as long as it is sold during the period covered by the listing.

Other types of listing agreements include open listings and exclusive agency listings. An **open listing** allows anyone to sell the property, including the seller. Under an open listing, the commission is paid only to the person who finds the buyer. An **exclusive agency** gives one agent the exclusive right to sell the property as against all other agents. In the event of a sale, only the exclusive agent is owed a commission by the seller, and the agent does not have to share the commission with anyone else. However, if the seller is in an exclusive agency agreement but finds a buyer without the assistance of an agent, the agent is not entitled to the commission.

compare to the sales figures of other real estate agencies?

- How long do homes stay on the market?
- How much and where does the agency advertise?
- How close is the actual sale price to the listing price for homes sold over the past six months or year?
- Are the agent and firm familiar with the geographic location of your home? How well does the firm know the area's schools, facilities, and public transportation?

You should ask to see the Multiple Listing Book and compare the listings of various firms and agents. A large firm may offer more varied expertise, but may also have many listings. It is important to get assurance that a large firm's agents have the time and energy to devote to an additional listing. A small office with fewer listings

---

ⓘ YOUR MLS OPTIONS

There are some Internet services that will provide the listing on the MLS only and will charge less commission than a real estate agent. Some examples are given in the World at Your Fingertips section.

This may seem like a tempting option if you are trying to save money by not using an agent or by hiring an agent for limited aspects of the sale. However, if you do list your property on an MLS using Internet services, you will have to fill out all the details that will go on to the MLS—the size of each room, special features of the house, and so on—by yourself. This is a time-consuming process. More important, real estate agents are skilled at presenting this kind of information in the best possible way. If you do it yourself, you may not do your home justice and might not attract as many buyers as you could.

---

may not have the breadth of a larger firm, but may give better, more personal service. The possibilities opened up by the Internet may help smaller offices compete effectively with larger ones.

Once you settle on an agency, you should interview potential agents.

- Does the agent work full-time in residential real estate?
- What is the agent's experience?
- Ask the agent about plans to market the home. Who does he or she think are the best potential buyers, and how should they be targeted? For example, retirees and young families are usually interested in different amenities. If the property is a natural fit with a particular age group, ask each prospective agent how he or she intends to show the home's advantages to its target market. Agents are licensed by the state in which they do business; in many states, you can check the website of the state agency that licenses agents to determine if any complaints have been filed against a particular agent.

Finally, you should be comfortable and have confidence in the agent you selected. The agent should be responsive to you, communicating all expressed interest in the home and following up on the visits of potential buyers. You might want to know how many buyers have seen the home and why no offers have been made. Is the agent trying to discover why? Is the price is too high? Does the decor detract from the home? Should you make some minor repairs?

Q. What fee will I pay on the sale of my home?

A. Typically, real estate firms charge a percentage (generally from 5 to 7 percent) of the sale price. Some Internet-based firms have marketed themselves as low-commission realtors, advertising commissions as low as 2 percent. On some higher-priced homes, a firm may charge the full commission on the first $100,000 or $200,000 and a different percentage of any amount above that price. If the agency that lists the home is also the agency that sells it, the commission is usually shared by the agency and the individual agent who actually handled the sale. If the listing firm and the selling firm are different, the commission is shared by the two firms. The information listed on the MLS generally sets forth how the listing firm will share the sales commission when the property is sold.

Other less-common forms of fee payments include the flat-fee method, in which a set fee is charged regardless of the home's price, and the net method. The latter, which is not favored and is illegal in some states, allows the broker to retain any amount of the selling price higher than an agreed sale price.

Q. What terms in the listing agreement are negotiable?

A. While the general type of listing agreement may not be negotiable, the specific terms contained in the agreement can be negotiable. In addition to the amount of commission, a real estate agency should be willing to negotiate provisions on the following:

- The length of the contract. Many of the standard forms provide that the contract renews automatically. Many firms want a six-month listing. If you're in a hurry to sell your home, try to get a sixty-day or a ninety-day listing.

- When the commission is earned. For example, the seller might try to negotiate language stating that this will occur only when the seller and the buyer actually close the sale and transfer title, not when they sign the purchase agreement.

- Who will be responsible for the advertising expenses—the seller or the agency? Since the seller usually must pay these costs, even if there is no sale through the agency, you may want to limit or have approval over these costs.

- Payment for extra "processing" costs in addition to the commission.

- The length of the probation period. This is the length of time, usually thirty to ninety days after the expiration of the listing agreement, during which the real estate agent will still be due the commission under certain circumstances.

Q. What can I do if my real estate firm doesn't seem to be working very hard to sell my home?

A. The housing market, price, and condition of the home are usually the chief problems when a home is not selling. But sometimes a firm or a particular agent is at fault for one reason or another. The best way to prevent this problem is to limit the term of the listing agreement to ninety days or less. If the home does not sell in that period of time, then you are legally in a position to try another firm or agent.

You may also want to change firms if your agent does not return telephone calls, does not communicate with you about the progress of the sale, fails to schedule open houses, or generally appears uninterested in the sale. On the other hand, it is a mistake to be upset if the agent presents an offer that seems unreasonably low. The firm and its agents have an obligation to present all offers to the seller, even those that may seem insulting. Of course, you are not required to ac-

---

▶ **CHOOSING AN AGENT**

You should look at the website of a prospective agency, as well as the site for the MLS that the agency uses. See if the website is consistent with the image that you want the sales representative to convey. Check for the existence of broken links or other indications of poor quality.

Be wary of agents who want to list the home at a much higher price than other agents suggest. This may be just a device to get the listing. Within a few weeks, the agent may pressure you to reduce the price drastically.

cept any offer presented. But if the agent applies undue pressure, it may be time for a change or another reason to limit the length of a listing agreement.

Selecting a Real Estate Agent to Help You Buy a Home

Q. How does a buyer choose a real estate agent?

A. In selecting an agent, a buyer needs to consider many of the same factors as a seller. Usually, a buyer's agent is compensated out of the sale proceeds; however, it is also possible that the buyer will pay a separate fee to the agent. In interviewing the agent, the buyer should ask the agent for the names of recent buyers who used his or her services and talk to them. You should ask

- how much time the agent spent with the buyer,
- how helpful he or she was during negotiations, and
- whether each buyer was satisfied with the services the agent provided.

▶ **MAKE SURE YOUR AGENT IS WORKING FOR YOU**

An agent who is not the listing agent is called the cooperating agent. In many states, a cooperating agent who shows a property to the buyer is deemed to be the buyer's agent. However, this is not the case in every state. In some states, a cooperating agent who shows a property to a buyer is still an agent for the seller.

If you are in any doubt about whether your agent is a buyer's or a seller's agent, then you should ask the agent whose interests he or she is representing, and get an answer in writing if possible.

Also make sure that the agent has a good record of locating the types of homes specified by prospective buyers. For example, an agent who customarily has clients seeking $500,000 homes may not spend much time working for a client seeking a $100,000 home.

Most important, before you start working with an agent, try to make decisions about the type of home you want, the amount you are willing to pay, and all the other important aspects of home buying. Shop open houses to get a feel for various neighborhoods and the style and price range of homes you are seeking. The more specific you can be with the agent in terms of what you want, the more likely it will be that the agent will find that kind of property.

Q. What is the role of the buyer's agent?

A. The buyer's agent works with the buyer to find potential homes. The agent contacts the listing agent, helps the buyer view the home, assists the buyer in preparing an offer, monitors the transaction, and, perhaps, helps the buyer to obtain financing. In most cases, the seller pays the sales commission, which is shared by the seller's agent and the buyer's agent.

Q. What is the fee relationship with a buyer's agent?

A. Most buyers prefer to have their agent's fee paid by the seller to avoid additional costs. But be aware that this preference could create a conflict of interest for the buyer's agent. Of course, if the agent is being compensated by the seller only if the deal is closed, he or she might not represent the buyer's interests vigorously.

Alternatively, a buyer's agent may be hired based upon a nonrefundable fee, which will vary with the length of the home search and the extent of the services provided. If you choose this option, you will want to have a specific contract that, like all written contracts, should be reviewed and approved by your lawyer. The contract should specify the services to be provided and the fees that will be due. If possible, avoid having the fee connected to the purchase price of the home. You do not want to provide an incentive for your agent to encourage a more-expensive sale than you want.

Q. What should I tell a real estate agent about my personal situation?

A. If you have hired a buyer's agent, you may feel free to discuss all aspects of the sale. If you are working with anyone else, you may want to withhold certain information that could be useful to the seller. Remember, unless you have hired a buyer's agent, the agents you are working with may actually represent the seller and are required to disclose all relevant information you might give them to the seller.

Some people suggest that you disclose only home styles, prices, and amenities you want when working with a traditional agent. Otherwise, the agent could convey personal information, such as the fact that your lease expires in two months or that you are willing to bid a higher price on a home, to the seller and ultimately hurt you in the negotiation process. You can avoid discussing financial information that could be shared with a prospective seller by prequalifying for a loan.

▶ **SOME ADVANCE WORK BEFORE YOU BUY**

If you are a prospective buyer, postpone offers and negotiations until you get a feel for various neighborhoods and the style and price range of homes you are seeking. Shopping open houses is an excellent way to do this. You also may want to be preapproved by a lender for a mortgage before you have a specific home in mind. This will require filling out financial statements, making the necessary financial disclosures, and having your credit record checked. This will give you an idea of how much money the lender will loan you and, thus, make it easier for you to pinpoint your price range.

Buying and Selling Without an Agent

Q. Are there advantages to selling my home without an agent?

A. The advantage of selling without an agent is that you will not have to pay a sales commission. However, while this may seem like a large saving,

---

▶ **CHOOSE AN EXPERIENCED AGENT**

Most people prefer to work with experienced real estate agents. At least two years' experience is a good rule of thumb. Experience in handling closings is important as well. Obviously, if an agent has had two years' experience but has closed only two transactions during that time, the agent may be less experienced than one might like. And if you're buying a home, it's probably a good idea to choose an agent who has experience in representing buyers.

To find a buyer's broker, check the yellow pages of your telephone book or call the local real estate association for referrals. The Internet is also a handy tool. Sites such as HomeGain (www.homegain.com) offer screening services that enable you to compare brokers to help you get the best home purchase or sale help. In addition, all large brokerage firms have websites that enable you to see online profiles of brokers, their listings, and other information. There are some firms that only represent buyers.

you must prepare yourself to assume all the responsibilities and costs associated with selling your home. These include advertising your home, spending time with potential buyers, making required disclosures, and negotiating the sale.

Sellers familiar with local sales procedures and the real estate market may choose to sell their homes themselves, and there are various books that can help guide you through the process. Experts generally recommend that the seller hire both an appraiser and a lawyer at the beginning of the process. An appraiser can help you establish a price for your home, and the lawyer can help you with the legal issues and necessary documentation.

Q. Are there disadvantages to selling my home without an agent?

A. There are at least three distinct disadvantages.

First, you will lack the many resources that real estate agents have to attract buyers. For example, your home will not be listed in your local MLS, unless you use an Internet service to list it. If you do not list your home, many buyers will not know that the home is for sale. You will need to arrange and pay for all advertising.

Second, you will have to find time to show your home and talk to potential buyers. This could raise some security issues.

Third, you will be directly involved in negotiating the sales price and other contract provisions. You will also have to make all legally required disclosures. Your lawyer can prepare you for what to do with an offer.

At first glance, selling without a broker may seem easy enough. However, many sales fall through without the mediating influence of a third person who has the experience to bring the buyer and seller together on a variety of issues. A professional real estate agent is on the alert for deal breakers, the kind of petty disagreements over small items that can break up negotiations, and will also be able to help you find solutions for larger disagreements.

If you have decided to sell on your own and do not hire a lawyer to negotiate for you, remember that settling on the terms and conditions of sale, including the price, is a give-and-take process. The fact that you love your renovated kitchen will not influence a potential buyer who intends to remodel anyway. If, after some reflection, you conclude that you lack the necessary experience, it may be wise to turn to a real estate agent or your lawyer.

Q. How can I buy a foreclosed property?

A. Most often, foreclosed properties, called **REOs** (for **real estate owned by the lender**), are owned by the lending institution or government agency that backed the mortgage. For one reason or another, the owner failed to make payments on the loan and the lender **foreclosed** on the property (took possession of it). This means that the lender has taken title to the property and has become an owner seeking to sell. One drawback to buying a foreclosed property may be the condition of the property. Generally, the owner who was unable to keep up on payments to the lender (thus causing the foreclosure) was also unable to maintain the home properly.

Mortgages on all types of properties, includ-

▶ **DON'T EXPECT A BARGAIN**

The major advantage of buying a **for-sale-by-owner**, or **FSBO**, home should be a lower purchase price because the seller will not be paying a commission on the sale. The truth is, however, that many FSBOs are priced as high as they would be if they were listed with a real estate firm. If you are interested in a FSBO, make sure you check the prices of comparable homes on the market, as well as recent sales in the area.

ing single-family homes and condominiums, can be foreclosed. They are sold individually or through auctions. Some institutions advertise their foreclosed properties; others deal strictly through real estate agents. Local real estate agents usually have a current list of the foreclosed homes in their area and can provide information on these properties. There are also several websites, listed in The World at Your Fingertips at the end of this section, which have lists of foreclosed properties available for a fee.

Fannie Mae, the Federal National Mortgage Association, is a large government holder of mortgages. Information on Fannie Mae foreclosures, as well as foreclosures by other federally backed loans, can be found on the Internet. A useful site is given in The World at Your Fingertips.

The Federal Housing Administration (FHA) usually sells its foreclosed properties through an auction announced in the classified sections of local newspapers. Potential buyers submit bids on the day of the auction, accompanied by a certified check for a percentage of the bid price. The highest bidder usually gets the home.

Buying a foreclosed property can be risky if you are not familiar with the procedures involved. In such a sale, there may not be the safeguards that are present in a traditional sale, such as a lender and a title insurance company. Therefore, if you plan to buy foreclosed properties, it is important to familiarize yourself with the process and consult with a lawyer who specializes in this area.

The Fair Housing Act

Q. Can a homeowner legally refuse to sell a home to a potential buyer?

A. The Fair Housing Act, Title VIII of the Civil Rights Act of 1968, addresses housing discrimination. This law prohibits housing discrimination by real estate firms and homeowners. This means that homeowners may not refuse to lease or sell property based on race, religion, gender, color, or national origin. In some localities, special housing discrimination ordinances or laws also cover sexual orientation. This does not mean, however, that sellers must sell their home to anyone who makes an offer. Of course, sellers may accept a higher bid, or prefer a buyer who already has a mortgage loan commitment. Sellers also might legitimately prefer one buyer over another for noneconomic reasons, as when one buyer promises to preserve the character of the house. But a buyer could take legal action if the seller refuses to sell and the buyer believes that the true motivation was discrimination.

A homeowner can face serious financial penalties if found in violation of this law. The potential buyer could sue for actual monetary losses as well as lawyer's fees, court costs, and even punitive damages.

A homeowner may lawfully discriminate on economic grounds. Without too much fear of legal action, a seller could refuse the offer of a buyer with a poor credit rating or inability to obtain a loan. The homeowner's argument could be that he or she cannot be forced to remove the home from the market while waiting for a loan commitment that had little chance of materializing. Perhaps the safest thing for the seller to do if the economic viability of an offer is in question is to tell the buyer that his or her offer might be accepted once the loan commitment is obtained if no other offers were received in the interim.

Q. What is steering?

A. Real estate firms and agents also are covered by the Fair Housing Act, which prohibits them from **steering**, a practice of showing potential buyers homes located only in certain neighborhoods.

Q. How can I tell if discrimination is occurring, and what can I do about it?

A. You may suspect discrimination if

- somebody tells you that a listed home is no longer for sale, but it remains on the market;

⚠ ORAL PROMISES

Beware of making oral promises. Many kinds of contracts do not have to be in writing to be valid. For example, if a seller orally promised to update the electrical system, the buyer might be able to insist that the system be updated even if the matter does not arise in later negotiations.

- an agent avoids showing you homes in areas you have requested; and
- a seller refuses a full-price bid on a home.

The federal Department of Housing and Urban Development (HUD) investigates such complaints, and you can file a complaint with them at the address given in The World at Your Fingertips. You may also be able to contact a local civil rights organization to find out if your area has specific organizations to contact. Usually, you will have to consult a lawyer about possible legal action against the homeowner.

Working with a Lawyer

Q. When should I see a lawyer about buying or selling a home?

A. As a buyer, it probably is not necessary to consult with a lawyer when you begin your search for a home. However, you will want your lawyer to enter the process when you are ready to make an offer, and certainly before the purchase contract is finalized. Legal advice will be more helpful—and may be less expensive in the long run—before rather than after signing a contract.

In addition to giving you advice and help in negotiations, your lawyer will ensure that your interests are protected. If something goes wrong, you do not want to discover too late that you have signed away important rights, failed to include important protections, or failed to receive what you expected.

If you are a seller, you will probably want to consult a lawyer early in the process and before signing a listing agreement with a real estate agent. As in the case of a buyer, it is important to understand the terms of the offer before accepting it. In addition, a lawyer will be instrumental in helping the seller comply with the terms of the offer once accepted and preparing for the closing.

Q. How do I choose a lawyer?

A. To choose a lawyer, you will want to consider the following factors:

- Area of specialty. While it may not be necessary to engage a lawyer who specializes in real estate transactions, you will want a lawyer who is familiar with the laws and practices regarding real estate in your area. It is a good idea to select a lawyer who has had some recent experience in handling real estate matters.
- Office location. Your lawyer will need to review agreements and papers and appear at the closing. Costs can be minimized with a local lawyer. However, with the use of facsimile machines and the Internet, location may not be a factor.

⚠ DO YOU KNOW WHAT YOU'RE SIGNING?

Do not sign something assuming it is not a contract and, therefore, not important. Keep in mind that a typed or handwritten **letter of agreement** or **letter of understanding** signed by the parties will be binding if it meets the legal requirements of a contract. Even though many real estate agents use form contracts, you should have a lawyer review the form either before you sign it or within the lawyer-review contingency period. This is particularly true if your agent has added any language to the form.

- References. Friends and colleagues can be a good source of references. Ask them what they liked and did not like about the lawyers with whom they have worked.
- Comfort level. Real estate transactions can be very trying. You will want to hire a lawyer who can smooth the way, not one who will create obstacles to your purchase or sale of a home. At the same time, you want someone who will vigorously protect your interests.

Although most real estate agents can provide lawyer referrals, the better practice would be to find a lawyer through other means. If the lawyer is closely affiliated or dependent on the agent for referrals, the lawyer may feel pressured to close the transaction even if issues adverse to the represented party arise. You will want to interview the lawyer, ask about his or her approach to a real estate transaction, discuss fees, and, generally, get an idea of whether this lawyer is right for you.

Chapter 1 contains more information on how to hire a lawyer.

Q. What will I have to pay for the lawyer's services?

A. Fees for real estate closings vary depending on where you live, the complexity of the transaction, and the time required to complete it. A lawyer can usually tell you an hourly rate and estimate the price at the start of the transaction, but the actual fee will depend on the type and amount of work involved. It may be possible to agree upon a fixed fee or range, unless some extraordinary issues arise. You should not agree to a percentage fee—in fact, such fees are illegal in many states.

THE WORLD AT YOUR FINGERTIPS

- *An Internet search will produce dozens of results for services that provide MLS listings. Some of these will provide an MLS listing for a smaller-than-usual commission; for example, www.*

forsalebyowner.com. *Other sites will provide a listing on the MLS for a flat fee; for example, www.flatraterealtyusa.com and www.savemorerealty.net.*
- *If you are using the Internet to find foreclosed properties, a good starting point is www.uslandco.com/freeforeclosure.html. This site allows you to search, without charge, for foreclosed properties by state and city, and has search options for Federal National Mortgage Association (Fannie Mae) foreclosures and Federal Home Loan Mortgage Corporation (Freddie Mac) foreclosures. Other sites, including www.1stforeclosure.com and www. foreclosurefreesearch.com, may provide a free trial period, but will charge a fee for full foreclosure searches.*

Discrimination

- *If you suspect that someone has discriminated against you, you can request a complaint form by calling the federal Department of Housing and Urban Development at 800-424-8590 or visiting the agency's website at www.hud.gov/ hdiscrim.html.*

REMEMBER THIS

- *If you're selling a home and decide to use a real estate agent, take your time in choosing an agent. Make sure the agent has the time and expertise to do the best job possible.*
- *Take a few precautions before you sign a listing agreement: read it carefully; discuss any provisions you'd like to change; and ask your lawyer to review it before signing. If you're in a hurry to sell your home, or have any doubt about your agent, negotiate to limit the listing agree-*

ment to ninety days or less. That way you can try another firm or agent if things don't work out.

- *If you're buying a home and are working with an agent, make sure the agent is a buyer's agent, and has a duty to you and not to the seller. It's preferable to hire an agent who has experience working with buyers, and who will be sensitive to the issues faced by buyers.*

- *Sellers should consult a lawyer before signing a listing agreement. Buyers won't necessarily need to contact a lawyer when they start looking for a home, but a lawyer should enter the process before they make an offer, and certainly before they sign a contract to purchase.*

FINANCING A HOME PURCHASE

Jason had substantial investments, but while he was looking for a new home, he was laid off from his job. He was highly marketable and knew he would get another job, so he continued his search for a home. Jason eventually found a home he liked and entered into negotiations to purchase. He was embarrassed and upset to find that even though his investments exceeded the purchase price, he was unable to get a mortgage loan because he had insufficient income.

Applying for a mortgage can be a process full of unpleasant surprises. For that reason, it's a good idea to investigate how you might finance a purchase before you go too far down the path of buying a home. Do you know how much you'll be able to borrow, and how much home you'll be able to afford? What's the difference between being prequalified for a loan and preapproved? This section will take you through some finance basics, and give you an idea of your options.

The Basics

Q. How much home can I afford?

A. This is one of the first things to consider when buying a home. Unless you are paying cash for a home, how much you can afford depends on how much you can borrow, which depends on your income, assets, expenses, and debts (including automobile or education loans and outstanding credit card balances). How much you can afford will also vary with prevailing interest rates on mortgages, the cash, if any, needed for a down payment, and closing costs. Knowing what you can afford will narrow your range so you will not waste time by looking at homes that cost too much.

Q. Should I prequalify for a loan?

A. If you are a buyer and you are prequalified for a set amount, then you can be secure in the knowledge that the lender will make a loan in the amount that has been prequalified as long as the information supplied to the lender was accurate and the property appraises for at least the pur-

---

▶ **CAN YOU AFFORD A HOME?**

Consider the following factors to determine whether or not you can afford to purchase a home:

- How much money have you saved for a down payment?

- What is the status of your current income and expenses, such as car payments?

- Do you have a good credit history?

- What are the current interest rates on mortgages?

- What are your priorities and lifestyle?

chase price. If you are unsure about what price range is appropriate or if you are a first time purchaser, then prequalifiying for a loan can help smooth the process. You will know exactly what you can afford, and avoid the disappointment of being unable to buy a home you thought you could afford. To prequalify for a loan, buyers will need to go through most of the steps entailed in applying for the actual loan.

However, a better approach is to be preapproved. The lender will analyze and underwrite the loan, subject to the buyer finding a home and the lender obtaining a satisfactory appraisal of it, and the lender being satisfied with the condition and value of the property. Preapproval will entail the same steps as prequalification, but will generally take longer. In a seller's market, buyers that are preapproved will have an advantage over buyers that are prequalified or who have no evidence that they can obtain financing.

Q. Is there a formula for determining what I can afford?

A. The loan amount a lender will agree to provide is directly tied to your income and expenses. The prevailing rule says that a home should cost no more than 2.5 times your annual income. Typically, a lender expects you to pay no more than 28 percent of your gross income for housing, which includes the loan payment, the property

---

 DOWN PAYMENT

The term **down payment** generally refers to the approximate difference between the purchase price and the amount of money borrowed; that is, the "cash" that the buyer has to come up with in order to close. The down payment usually includes, but is not limited to, the earnest money and closing costs.

---

tax, the homeowner's insurance, any monthly dues or assessments, and estimated utility costs.

A lender looks for a solid history of income, employment, and credit. Therefore, the amount of your debt and ongoing expenses are relevant, including automobile payments, credit card debt, education loans, child support, alimony, and so on. As a general rule, your total indebtedness, including monthly housing expenses, should not exceed 36 percent of your gross income.

Q. What forms of financing are available?

A. Today, a wide variety of financing mechanisms exists to finance a purchase.

The most common form of financing is with a financial institution such as a bank or a savings and loan institution. The buyer agrees to pay interest on the money borrowed and the lender retains a lien (that is, a mortgage) on the property. Some buyers may qualify for federally insured loans that permit smaller-than-normal down payments and lower interest rates than prevailing market rates. In order to increase the amount borrowed (or reduce the down payment), it may be possible to place two mortgages on the property at the time of purchase—one that the buyer intends to pay off in the short term (generally, a home equity loan), and a second that the buyer views as more long term.

In some cases, buyers are able to obtain financing directly from the seller, which can take a variety of forms. In one type of seller financing,

---

▶ **LIFESTYLE CHOICES**

When you are calculating how much home you can afford, consider your lifestyle and priorities. If costly vacations, dining out, and entertainment are important to you, you may want to buy a less-expensive home than the lender says you can afford. Many people, however, find that they are willing to give up some luxuries or even stretch their budget for a more-expensive home.

the seller acts just like a conventional lender; the buyer pays a certain amount at closing and also pays principal and interest on the balance. The seller then places a mortgage lien on the property. In another form of seller financing, a buyer is able to assume the seller's mortgage. In such a case, the buyer pays the difference between what is owed on the existing mortgage and the purchase price and takes over the seller's payments on the mortgage. (Note that this can occur only if provisions in the mortgage state specifically that it is assumable. Most mortgages written today include a **due-on-sale** clause that prohibits assumption of a mortgage without the lender's consent.) In the event that a buyer assumes the seller's mortgage, the seller should remember that he or she remains liable to pay the mortgage unless the seller's lender specifically and in writing releases the seller from this obligation. One final form of seller financing, the land contract, provides that the seller retains title for a certain period, during which the buyer pays the seller a monthly amount. When the buyer pays the seller in full, title is conveyed to the buyer.

Q. How much do I need for a down payment?

A. In today's market, it may be possible to buy a home with little or no down payment. For example, some people may qualify for special government-insured loans offered through the Federal Housing Administration or the Veterans Administration (VA). You can learn more about these programs at www.hud.gov/faqs/faqbuying.cfm and www.homeloans.va.gov. Some private lenders also offer loans that require little or no down payment. Finally, it may be possible to minimize the down payment by structuring the loan as two loans, as discussed on pages 106–107.

Generally, however, unless you can qualify for a special loan or creatively structure the financing, you will need a down payment equal to 20 percent of the purchase price to avoid paying the extra cost of **private mortgage insurance** (**PMI**).

ⓘ THE LAND CONTRACT

A **land contract,** which is also known as a **contract for deed,** is another method of buying property, which combines the transfer of title with seller financing. The buyer generally gives the seller a down payment and agrees to make monthly payments for some period of time. Typically, the buyer takes possession of the property, but legal title is not transferred to the buyer until the entire purchase price is paid.

Be warned that in some states—for example, Ohio—the buyer's right to complete the purchase may take second place to the rights of anyone who obtains a lien against the seller after the contract is signed. These lien holders can include anyone who obtains a judgment against the seller, contractors who furnish labor or materials to improve the property, and lenders who obtain a mortgage on the property from the seller.

The terms of such an arrangement should be in writing and the contract (or a notice of the contract) should be recorded to protect the buyer's interest. In addition, a prudent buyer would require that evidence of title, such as a warranty deed, be placed with a third party (for example, a title company), which would hold the document until payment is completed. Once all payments have been made, the deed would be delivered to the buyer and recorded. In some places, if the buyer fails to make all payments, the seller must foreclose to clear title and take possession of the property.

With less than a 20 percent down payment, banking regulations require the buyer to carry PMI. This insures the lender against nonpayment of the difference between the customary down payment and the down payment actually paid. The charge for PMI may be high, although the amount may vary as the loan ages. It is a good idea to refinance any loan that requires PMI as soon as feasible to avoid these extra charges.

Q. Do I have to pay PMI for the life of the loan?

A. No. The federal Homeowner Protection Act, which went into effect in the summer of 1999, helps consumers understand when they no longer need to pay private mortgage insurance—and thus save thousands of dollars over the length of a home loan. Once you have built up at least 20 percent equity in the home—meaning that the money owed is less than 80 percent of the home's value—the lender is no longer at risk. At that point, you can ask that the insurance be canceled. Be aware that the insurer will need written support from a certified appraiser as to the value of your home. The value assessed by a municipality for real estate tax purposes is seldom considered in evaluating home equity.

Under the federal law, the lender must cancel the insurance when the mortgage balance falls below 78 percent of the home's original purchase price. However, because homes usually appreciate in value, you may be able to cancel it earlier because rising home values increases equity. Federal law now requires the lender to tell you annually that you have the right to cancel if you meet certain criteria.

Applying for a Loan

Q. How do I apply for a loan?

A. Obtaining a loan requires a lot of paperwork and sometimes a lot of fortitude. The savings and loan scandals and the large number of foreclosures in recent years have forced lenders to take a much more critical look at their lending practices. You won't be asked for your blood type, but it's a good bet that you will be asked about everything in your financial history. Loan applications vary, but most require the following information:

- Employment history, salary history, and proof of employment. This may require you to obtain a letter from your employer and recent wage stubs. You may be asked for copies of your federal tax returns for recent years or copies of your W-2 statements. While there is no law that requires you to submit this information, the lender has the right to turn down your request for a loan if you refuse to supply pertinent information. If you are using other income to qualify for the loan, such as income from property, child support, or income from investments, you will need to provide proof of these as well.
- Credit history. This includes the account numbers of all the credit cards that you currently have. You may be asked to submit year-end statements that reveal how much interest was paid on these cards during the preceding year.
- Outstanding debts. These include automobile loans, alimony, child support payments, and credit card debt.
- Assets. These include the value of any items you own, such as automobiles, rental property, stocks, bonds, cash, savings accounts, IRAs, retirement accounts, mutual funds, and so on.
- Source of your down payment. The lender will want to make sure that you are not borrowing money to make your down payment. (If you are borrowing money, this will be taken into consideration.) If you are receiving a gift from relatives for a down payment, the lender will expect proof that it is truly a gift and that the amount will be forthcoming.

Q. How long does it take to get a home loan application approved?

A. When you apply for the loan, ask the lender how long the approval process is expected to take.

It can take anywhere from twenty-four hours to three months, depending on a variety of factors. If you have included a mortgage-contingency clause in your purchase contract, be sure to inform your lender when you apply for the loan of the date the clause expires. Usually, your lender will work with you to meet the deadline or alert you that approval will take more time. At that point, you may be able to get an extension from the seller on the contingency.

Once your loan is approved, the lender will provide you with a loan commitment, which states in writing that the lender agrees to lend a specific amount of money on specific terms. You should read this carefully as it may set forth conditions you must meet before closing, such as clearing some credit issues or even selling your current home. A copy of this commitment can be provided to the seller to assure him or her that your financing is in place.

Q. What is the lender obligated to tell me about the loan?

A. Federal law requires that the lender reveal all costs of the loan, including such items as appraisal fees, escrow fees, fees for the lender's lawyer, service charges, and, of course, the interest rate on the loan. The interest rate must be presented as the annual percentage rate or APR. This is calculated by including the interest to be paid along with other fees, such as any points paid to originate the loan. **Points** are interest charges paid up front when a borrower closes a loan or fees imposed by a lender to cover certain expenses of making a real estate loan. They are usually a percentage of the amount loaned—for example, one point is 1 percent.

Under the federal Truth in Lending Act, all lenders are required to use the same methods for computing the cost of credit and disclosing credit terms. This requirement helps borrowers compare the costs and terms of home loans.

The federal Equal Credit Opportunity Act prohibits discrimination in any aspect of a home loan transaction on the basis of race, religion, age, color, national origin, receipt of public assis-

tance funds, sex, marital status, or the exercise of any right under the Consumer Credit Protection Act. If a lender rejects your loan application, you are entitled to know the specific reasons in writing.

Lenders are also prohibited from doing anything that discourages you from obtaining credit, including taking an excessively long time to process your application, being unwilling to discuss available types of loans, or failing to provide information required to apply for a loan. If you suspect that you are being discriminated against in applying for a loan, you can file a complaint. When making a complaint, be sure to include your name and address along with the name and address of the person or financial institution you are filing the complaint against, a short description of the alleged violation, and the date of the alleged violation.

Q. How do interest rates affect my choice of a home?

A. The interest you pay on your loan is part of the cost of owning a home. For example, a 1 percent increase in the interest rate on a $100,000 loan adds approximately $85 to your monthly loan payment over the life of a thirty-year loan. Obviously, the lower the interest rate, the more you can afford to borrow.

Q. How do lenders determine the interest rate?

A. Interest rates for home loans are determined by the overall market in interest rates. Home loan rates are very interest-sensitive; when rates are rising, they are among the first to go up, although when rates are declining, they are usually the last to be lowered. This is because most home loans are made at a fixed rate for a fairly long term (fifteen to thirty years), during which time interest rates may increase substantially. Thus, lenders attempt to protect themselves from making too many long-term loans at low rates by taking a slow approach to reducing interest rates. These rates can and will rise very quickly, however, if the prevailing trend changes and other interest rates begin to escalate. Present mortgage rates are easy to find on the Internet.

Q. Does it pay to shop around for an interest rate?

A. Since lenders are competitive, it pays to compare what several have to offer. Interest rates and fees charged to originate a loan may also vary among financial institutions. It may be possible to obtain a lower interest rate if the lender charges the prospective buyer a fee to obtain the loan, either as a flat fee or a percentage of the loan. As noted earlier, a **point** refers to a percentage point (one point is 1 percent of the loan amount).

One lender might offer an 8 percent, thirty-year fixed-rate loan with a flat fee of $200. A second lender might offer a 7 percent, thirty-year fixed-rate loan with two points. A third lender might offer the loan without points or other fees but at a higher interest rate. This could be advantageous for a buyer who wants to put as much as possible into the down payment. Another buyer might prefer to pay higher points in exchange for a lower interest rate because the IRS allows points to be deducted against taxable income in the year the home is purchased (although the IRS does not allow a deduction in a single year for points paid in connection with a refinancing—the deduction is spread out over the life of the loan).

Q. I want to buy a home but my credit history is poor. Is there anything I can do?

A. Yes, there are several options. First, before you attempt to buy, you will want to improve your credit record by paying your bills on time and by curtailing your borrowing.

Second, credit-reporting agencies can and do make mistakes. Major credit-reporting companies maintain computer files on your financial history. Credit-reporting agencies are authorized by law to disclose credit information to any person or organization with a legitimate business need for the information. On the other hand, the law also gives you the right to examine your own file. A summary of the report must be made available to you free of charge; however, there may be a fee if you request a full credit report.

If you believe your credit report is in error, you may challenge the report by explaining the error in writing. The information must be verified by the agency if it is kept in the report. If you discover inaccuracies and you can prove them, you can demand that the agency correct them within a reasonable period of time. If there are no errors, you have the right to include a letter of explana-

---

▶ SHOPPING FOR LOANS

There are several ways to shop for home loans. By far the easiest way to do this today is via the Internet, which is awash in interest rate information, and mortgage brokers that will compete with each other to get you the best deal. Most websites related to mortgages also feature useful mortgage and home finance calculators. Search for "mortgage" and the name of the state where you are planning to buy to find dozens these websites.

In addition, many metropolitan newspapers carry a weekly listing or sampling of rates offered in their areas. Rates can change very rapidly, which might mean that these listings may not be up to the minute. However, they can give you a general idea of the market. In addition, you can call a mortgage broker for information, although you should remember that the rate you are quoted on the phone may not be the rate you receive when you apply.

tion of up to one hundred words in your report. The agency must include your statement, or a clear and accurate summary of it, in all future reports. For example, if you were unable to pay a loan because you were out of work or suffered a severe illness, you could add this information to the report. You may want to consult your lawyer if you are unable to have your report changed as required by law. Credit-reporting agencies are allowed to retain negative information in your report for seven years and bankruptcy information for ten years. See chapter 7, "Consumer Credit," for more details.

Q. I want to buy another home, but I have not sold my present home yet. Is there a way to finance until I can sell?

A. Many lenders offer a **bridge loan** to allow a buyer to close on another home while waiting to sell his or her present home. You can usually obtain a bridge loan if you have a contract to sell your present home and you need the loan only for a specific, relatively short, period of time. It is much more difficult to obtain a bridge loan if you do not have a buyer for your home and, thus, need to pay loans on two properties for an indefinite period of time. A bridge loan usually carries a higher rate of interest than a traditional home loan.

It may also be possible to use the equity on your current home to provide the additional money to purchase a second home. The owner would need to obtain a home equity line of credit on the current home. The owner can then draw upon the line at the time of the second purchase. The line of credit would then be paid off at the time of the sale of the current property. Home equity lines of credit are generally interest-only loans.

Different Types of Loans

Q. What is a fixed-rate loan?

A. With a **fixed-rate loan**, the interest rate cannot be increased during the term of the loan, typically fifteen, twenty, or thirty years. Under a fixed-rate loan, buyers can feel more comfortable knowing the exact amount of their monthly loan payments throughout the life of the loan. Although the interest rate does not change, the way in which each payment is divided between principal and interest, the amortization schedule of the loan, changes over the loan period. (The **amortization schedule** is a table that shows how much of each payment will be applied toward principal and how much toward interest over the life of the loan, including the gradual decrease of the principal until it reaches zero.) At the beginning, most of the payment is applied to the interest owed to the lender. As the loan progresses, more money is applied to the principal, the face amount of the loan. This means that the amount of interest deductible for federal income tax purposes will decline over the life of the loan.

The major difference between a fifteen-year fixed-rate loan, on the one hand, and a thirty-year fixed-rate loan, on the other, is that the borrower will pay higher monthly payments on the shorter-term loan than on the thirty-year loan for the same amount of money. On a shorter loan, however, the buyer pays far less total interest, because he or she is using the money for a shorter period of time.

Q. What is an adjustable-rate loan?

A. Adjustable-rate loans vary, but they all share one common factor—the lender can change some aspect of the terms of the loan during the

---

📑 HOME EQUITY LINE OF CREDIT

This is a loan secured by the equity in your home (i.e., its value in excess of the amount remaining on your mortgage loan). It enables you to draw down money as you need it (the line of credit), up to the value of the loan.

life of the loan. The specific type of adjustable mortgage is tied to whether the change is in the rate of interest, the amount of payment, or the length of time for repayment.

Adjustable-rate loans include:

- **Adjustable-rate mortgages (ARMs)**. These loans typically offer a lower-than-market interest rate in the first year or first few years. The future interest rate, usually adjusted annually, is tied to an index that may move up or down but is not under the control of the lender. The index might be one-year Treasury bills (the **T-bill rate**) or some other rate that reflects the changes in interest rates.

  Note that the rate is tied to the index, but it is not the same as the index. The mortgage might specify, for example, that the future rate would be two points above the average T-bill rate. Typically, ARMs are adjusted once a year on the anniversary date of the loan. Additionally, ARMs usually have a provision for a **cap**, that is, the highest rate that could be charged. Some loans may include a minimum rate, or **floor**, as well.

- **Convertible ARMs**. These loans usually offer a conversion factor that allows the borrower to convert to a fixed-rate loan at a specified period of time. For example, a convertible ARM could allow the borrower the option to convert to a fixed-rate loan once a year over the first five years of the loan. The interest rate to be paid upon conversion might also be tied to an index.

- **Renegotiable-rate mortgage (rollover)**. These loans typically set the interest rate and monthly payments for several years and then allow both the rate and the principal payments to be changed depending on general market conditions. If the new terms are unacceptable, the borrower can pay the loan in full or refinance at prevailing interest rates.

- **Graduated payment mortgage (GPM)**. With this type of loan, typically sought by young buyers who expect their incomes to rise, the payments are low in the first couple of years and gradually rise for five to ten years.

- **Shared-appreciation mortgage**. These loans offer lower-than-market rates of interest and low payments in exchange for a lender's share in appreciation of the property. Usually, the lender will require that its share of equity be turned over when the home is sold or at a specified date set out in the loan agreement.

Q. What is a balloon loan?

A. With a **balloon loan**, the buyer is expected to pay off the unpaid balance of the loan completely within a fixed period of time, usually in three, five, or seven years, instead of making regular payments to completely pay off the loan. The interest rate can be fixed or variable, but in all cases the (usually substantial) unpaid balance is due at the time specified. Usually, the borrower must either refinance or sell the home to pay off the loan. Because most payments at the beginning of the loan go to pay off the interest rather than the principal, the balance at the time of the loan payoff will probably be nearly the same as the original loan.

ⓘ WHAT DOES THE BORROWER NEED TO SIGN?

The borrower will have to sign many documents in order to obtain a loan; however, two documents are essential. The first is a **promissory note** agreeing to repay the lender the money borrowed plus interest. The borrower may be responsible for repaying the money even if he or she later sells the home to a buyer who assumes the mortgage. The second is a **mortgage**, or **deed of trust**. The mortgage gives the lender a lien or security interest in the real estate. This means that the lender may foreclose and sell the property to recoup the amount due under the loan.

To attract buyers, builders often offer balloon loans during periods of high interest rates when home sales are sluggish. In most cases, the interest rate will be lower than prevailing institutional home loan rates. However, if interest rates are high when full payment is due, refinancing may not be possible. The balloon will burst, resulting in foreclosure or forced sale and loss of the home.

Q. How do FHA and VA loans work?

A. The Federal Housing Administration (FHA) and the Veterans Administration (VA) are loan guarantors. They offer loans made by the federal government or approved lending institutions. The fees associated with these loans vary and may paid at the closing, or monthly over a period of time. While FHA loans are not available through all lenders, in some areas they are very popular and can make the difference in obtaining a loan for some potential buyers who do not qualify for conventional financing. The VA offers government-insured loans to qualified veterans, often with no money down.

Income qualifications, required down payments, and the maximum allowable loans under these plans change periodically. For first-time homebuyers, local and state governments may also offer loan assistance to prospective buyers who meet eligibility requirements. For current information about these loan programs, consult local FHA and VA offices and your bank as well as your real estate agent.

Q. What are jumbo loans?

A. Jumbo loans are loans that exceed a stated loan amount allowed by Fannie Mae and Freddie Mac, the federal agencies that oversee the secondary market in mortgage loans. Fannie Mae and Freddie Mac are not loan guarantors; rather, they purchase loans from lenders and resell the loans to other organizations, such as insurance companies and pension funds. The maximum mortgage amount for Fannie Mae and Freddie Mac loans varies and as of January 1, 2004, stands at $333,700. Interest rates on jumbo loans are typically slightly higher than other loans, but this is not always the case. A lender who intends to keep a jumbo loan mortgage in its portfolio, rather than selling it, tends to offer more competitive interest rates.

Q. What is negative amortization?

A. In a typical home loan, the borrower pays off the interest and principal in installments. This reduction of the principal is known as **amortization**. In a **negatively amortized** loan, the installment payments do not cover all the interest due each month. This unpaid interest is added to the principal that is owed, resulting in a debt that increases, rather than decreases.

The worst problem with negative amortization occurs in a market in which home values decrease. In such an environment, the size of the debt could increase to the point where it would exceed the equity in the home. Sadly, upon the sale of the home, the owner may not be able to repay what is owed. Of course, in a down market, this could also happen with a conventional mortgage.

Most professionals advise buyers to avoid a negatively amortized loan. The risks outweigh the benefits of the lower payments. It may be better to postpone buying a home until you can make higher payments or investigate a lower-cost loan from the FHA or VA.

▶ KNOW YOUR HOME LOAN

If you are considering applying for any type of adjustable-rate loan, make sure you understand exactly how the mortgage works, including the spread between the interest rate and the index to which the rate is tied; how often the loan can be adjusted; the maximum allowable increase (or decrease) each year, as well as over the life of the loan; and the risk of negative amortization.

Key Provisions of the Loan Documents

Q. What is an assumable mortgage?

A. An **assumable mortgage** allows you to transfer your existing mortgage debt to the buyer of your home. The new owner would "assume" or take over your mortgage loan and pay you the difference between the amount you still owe and the agreed-upon sale price. Most lenders include a "due-on-sale" clause in the mortgage, which prohibits a buyer from assuming the existing mortgage. However, some sellers still have assumable mortgages. In addition, some lenders will allow a mortgage to be assumed by charging a fee or adjusting the interest rate on the assumed mortgage.

If the interest rate is attractive, a buyer should explore the possibility of assuming the existing loan. Prior to assuming a mortgage, a prospective homebuyer should obtain a written statement from the original lender stating

- the amount still owed on the loan;
- that there are currently no defaults under the loan;
- the rate of interest for the remainder of the loan;
- the length of the repayment period remaining; and
- whether the lender has the right to **call in** the loan (demand payment of the entire amount), change any of the existing terms, or prevent future assumption by another buyer.

Before the loan can be assumed, the lender may require the buyer to go through the lender's normal loan-application process so that the lender is sure the buyer is creditworthy. The particular form of loan-assumption agreement will vary depending upon your location.

Q. What is a due-on-sale clause?

A. A **due-on-sale clause** should more accurately be called a due-on-transfer clause. Most mortgages include such a clause, which requires the seller to pay off the entire mortgage loan when the property is sold or transferred in any way. Therefore, this clause would prohibit a buyer from assuming the seller's mortgage. In addition, a due-on-sale clause may be triggered if

---

ⓘ INSURING PAYMENT OF YOUR HOME LOAN UPON DEATH OR DISABILITY

Several types of insurance policies pay your home loan if you die or become disabled. This type of **mortgage insurance policy** establishes an annual premium cost for the life of your loan. Because your loan declines as you pay down the principal, the amount of insurance coverage decreases each year, although the cost stays the same. In most cases, a term life insurance policy that can be used to pay off the loan in the event of your death is preferable to a mortgage insurance policy. **Term life insurance** is less expensive and offers better protection and more flexibility. For example, it may give your spouse or other beneficiary the option of keeping the money in the bank and continuing to make payments—especially if the interest rate is low—whereas mortgage insurance must be used to pay off the loan. All insurance products are relatively complicated. You may want to consult a financial professional or a lawyer to check these policies before you buy one.

Because temporary or permanent disability can threaten your ability to pay your home loan, you may also want to consider buying a disability policy or participating in any disability insurance offered by your employer. Disability insurance can add to your peace of mind and that of your lender.

the seller leases or further mortgages the property. The rationale behind such a clause is that the lender is making the loan to a particular person and does not want to find that, without its consent, a different person owns the property or is living there. In some cases, federal and state laws preempt the terms of the mortgage and allow such transfers.

Q. What is a late-payment charge?

A. Most home loans include a **late-payment charge**. The borrower must pay a fee if the lender receives the monthly mortgage payment late. These charges can be very expensive. You will want to make sure you know when your loan payment is due and allow enough time for it to arrive by the due date if you are mailing your payment.

Q. What is a prepayment penalty?

A. Although it is illegal or limited in some states, home loans may include a **prepayment penalty**. This is a charge imposed if the borrower pays off the loan ahead of schedule. This penalty is usually 1 or 2 percent of the loan. It is possible that a home loan will include a prepayment penalty for only the first few years.

THE WORLD AT YOUR FINGERTIPS

- *Working out how much home you can afford involves a lot of number crunching. There are dozens of free loan calculators available on the Internet that can do some of the hard work for you. Loan calculators of varying complexity can be found at www.bankrate.com/gooword/rate/calc_home.asp, www.pine-grove.com/pi03000.htm, or by typing "loan calculator" into your favorite search engine.*
- *The ABA's website can provide you with some consumer information and advice about mortgages and loans, in easy-to-understand language: visit www.abanet.org/buslaw/safeborrowing.*

- *If you think you might qualify for a special government-insured loan offered through the Federal Housing Administration (FHA) or the Veterans Administration (VA), you should seek more information at www.hud.gov/hudqa.html and www.homeloans.va.gov.*
- *AARP provides some useful publications on loans and related issues at www.aarp.org/consumerprotect/articles.*

REMEMBER THIS

- *Work out how much home you can afford before you start looking for a home. Think about whether you want to make lifestyle compromises so you can afford a more expensive home.*
- *If possible, try to get preapproved for a loan before you immerse yourself in the business of buying. If you can't wait for preapproval, then being prequalified is better than nothing.*
- *Take some time to shop for an appropriate loan. Have an idea of what kind of loan you want, and compare interest rates and fees to find the best loan. The Internet is a useful tool for loan shopping.*
- *Ask your lawyer to talk you through the small print, so that you have a good idea of what your obligations are under the loan.*

THE STEPS OF BUYING AND SELLING A HOME

The owner of the house Mary wanted to buy was an old acquaintance. Mary gave her a signed piece of paper that said, "I, Mary Jones, agree to buy the property located at 151 Main Street for $150,000 on July 3, 2003. Please indicate your willingness to sell on these terms by signing below." Mary thought her lawyer could fill in the details later, including the fact that *she would need to obtain a loan for the purchase, who would pay for closing costs, and that she wanted to be sure the roof didn't leak. Mary didn't realize that once the seller signed the paper it became the entire contract between the parties. Mary had no right to make changes later.*

The contract is at the heart of the sale, and deals with the nuts and bolts of transferring the ownership of the home. Your lawyer can help you steer your way through the complex obligations and contingencies in the contract, so that when you go to closing you can be certain that all the details have been covered.

Selling: Setting a Price for the Property

Q. How do I establish the price of my home?

A. First of all, there is no "right" price. The value of your home is almost entirely dependent on what someone is willing to pay for it and how long you are willing to wait to find that person. Most sellers are not in the position to wait for the "ideal" buyer who will pay their "ideal" price. They want to find the optimum price at which their home will sell in a limited amount of time.

To do this, they typically rely on comparisons with recently sold homes in the area. A real estate agent can help you by giving you a list of homes sold through the local multiple listing service during the past year or so. You can also locate this information on the Internet at free websites such as realestate.yahoo.com/re/homevalues and www.domania.com.

Once you have some basic sales information, you will need to match the features of the homes that have been sold to your own home. For example, if your home is a three-bedroom, two-bath ranch on a typical lot, your agent can point out sales prices of similar homes to determine a listing price. Try to limit your study to homes that are very similar to yours. If Victorian homes are prized in your area, even a Victorian needing work will be priced higher than other styles of homes of similar size.

To narrow the price range further, you'll want to look at amenities sought by buyers. An attached garage, a wood-burning fireplace, an updated kitchen and baths, a large lot, and spacious rooms are among the factors that generally increase a home's price. Conversely, expect the selling price to be lower if your home does not have these or similar amenities. Location is also a factor. Most buyers want good schools, ample transportation,

---

ⓘ APPRAISALS

If, despite all your efforts, you cannot find comparable homes in your area, you may want to consult an appraiser in order to set a sales price. An **appraisal** is a professional's opinion of the fair market value of the home. The appraisal should be close to the probable selling price. However, keep in mind that the appraiser is basing the value in part on sales that have been completed. In a seller's market, a real estate agent may be in a better position to estimate value since the agent will have information regarding contracts that have not yet closed.

Lenders usually order their own appraisals, often paid for by the borrower, before approving a loan in order to ensure that the home is worth at least as much as the purchase price being paid. If you intend to sell your home on your own, without a real estate agent, an appraisal can provide valuable market information. Remember, however, that determining market value is not an exact science. A home is worth what someone will pay for it.

quiet neighborhoods, and little if any commercial activity. The presence or absence of these factors will affect the selling price of your home.

Perhaps equally important are your reasons for selling and how long you can wait. Typically, the most interest is generated in the first few weeks a home is listed. If you want to sell your home fast, you'll want to price it so that it stands out among comparable homes on the market. If you are willing to wait and to endure continuous showings, you can afford to price it above the competition. Sellers who try to hold out for the highest price, however, may find themselves reducing the price down the line. A house that has been on the market beyond the average marketing time generates little interest from buyers, even when the price is reduced dramatically. Most buyers will assume that the home has problems that they, understandably, want to avoid.

Disclosures

Q. What is the seller obligated to disclose to the buyer?

A. Disclosure is generally addressed by state law, and requirements vary among the states. Because this is an area of law that is rapidly changing, it is important to review your state's requirements before selling.

Some states require sellers to fill out a long form that explicitly asks about the seller's knowledge of various **significant** or **material defects** that might be present in the home. For example, the form might ask whether the seller is aware of any material defects in the basement, leaks in the roof, or unsafe concentrations of radon gas. Another form might specifically question the condition of various parts of the home, such as the age of the roof, and whether the home contained insulation or lead paint. In other states, sellers are not required to fill out disclosure forms, but are required to disclose any defects in equipment that should be functioning at the time of sale, such as the furnace, central air-conditioning, the hot-water heater, and so on.

As a seller, you may want to disclose known material defects that seriously affect the home's value even if your state does not mandate such disclosure. This will help avoid future legal problems involved with the sale of your home. Many of the lawsuits filed involving real estate transactions allege the seller's misrepresentation or failure to disclose. Responding honestly to the buyer's questions and either repairing material defects or disclosing them is an effective way to avoid future litigation.

Q. What are the real estate agent's obligations with respect to disclosure?

A. The Code of Ethics of the National Association of Realtors governs real estate firms and agents who are members. This code calls for disclosure of all known pertinent facts about the property. Members will also try to get all the buyer's questions answered. For example, if the buyer has noticed water damage in the basement, a member agent should ask the seller about it and tell the buyer about the cause of the problem. Some states require the broker to make additional disclosures that might affect the value or desirability of the property.

⚠ BUYER BEWARE

In states that require no disclosures, the Latin phrase **caveat emptor**—"let the buyer beware"—prevails. Unless you ask specific questions about defects, the seller is not required to disclose them, even if the seller has specific knowledge that one or more substantial defect exists. As a result, any problem you discover after the closing is your problem. To protect yourself, you should hire an inspector to look at the property. When in doubt, ask specific questions of the seller and obtain answers in writing if possible.

Making an Offer: The Purchase Contract

Q. How do I begin negotiations to buy a home?

A. Negotiations are handled in various ways in different parts of the country. Typically, transactions begin with negotiations over price, although other items such as date of possession may also be negotiated. The real estate agent will provide a formal offer form, which will convey the terms of your offer in writing to the seller. Once signed by both parties, the offer becomes a contract.

If you intend to have the home inspected, the offer should include an inspection contingency; if you intend to apply for a mortgage, it should include a mortgage-contingency clause; if your lawyer has not reviewed the form, it should include a lawyer-approval contingency. In other words, it should cover the basics. Remember, once both parties sign this document, it is legally binding.

The offer should specify that it expires if the seller has not accepted it by a specified date. This date may be upon presentation of the offer to the seller or as little as twenty-four hours from the time the seller or the seller's agent receives it. Also, the offer to purchase is usually valid only if both the buyer and the seller sign it within a certain time period. As a general rule, a deposit of perhaps $500 or $1,000, called earnest money, accompanies the offer to purchase. This is refundable if the offer is rejected; however, if the seller accepts the offer but the buyer backs out of the deal, it may be forfeited.

Often this is the start of negotiations. The offer to purchase may be passed back and forth between the buyer and seller before both accept all of the terms. Remember, however, that both parties must initial any changes agreed to during negotiations. Once you have agreed on terms, you will want to arrange for a home inspection and review the document with your lawyer if, as noted above, you included these contingencies in your offer. In most cases, you will not want to apply for a specific loan on the property until the home inspection and lawyer review are completed and satisfactory.

In some areas, the purchase contract will include all provisions of the transaction. In other areas, another document will be drawn up by the

---

📄 EARNEST MONEY

When the buyer signs the offer to purchase, the buyer customarily deposits a sum of money, known as **earnest money** with a third party, such as the seller's real estate agent or the seller's or the buyer's lawyer. In some cases, when there is no third party to hold the money, the parties can set up a joint order account at a bank or financial institution. Such an account cannot be accessed without the approval of both parties. The buyer's offer should specify that the earnest money deposit will be placed in an interest-bearing escrow account with the interest credited to the recipient of the principal.

In most states, earnest money is not the same thing as the buyer's down payment. If the sale goes through, however, the earnest money will be applied to the down payment. Earnest money symbolizes the buyer's commitment to take the necessary steps to complete the purchase, including, for example, obtaining a loan. Thus, if a prospective buyer does little or nothing to complete the sale, or if the sale cannot close for other reasons attributable to the buyer, he or she risks losing the earnest money deposit.

buyer or the seller that covers such items as conveyance of title and provision for insurance. In either case, you will want your lawyer to make sure, before you sign, that the final document covers all aspects of the sale.

Q. What is the purchase contract?

A. The purchase contract may be called a **sales contract**, a **real estate contract**, a **purchase agreement**, a **sales agreement**, or a **purchase and sale agreement**. Whatever it is called, it is a document that when signed by both parties is a legal contract that will govern the entire transaction. Before signing such a contract, you will want to review it carefully and have your lawyer review it. Remember, once signed, you are obligated to fulfill your part of the contract.

Q. What are the key provisions of the purchase contract?

A. A purchase contract, in most cases, is a standard form contract with certain riders, if necessary, attached. The contract can have many provisions, but should at least include the following items:

- The date of the contract.
- The purchase price of the home.
- The amount of the down payment, who is holding it, and the escrow terms if it is in escrow;
- all items of personal property to be included in the sale, such as wall-to-wall carpeting, window treatments, appliances, or lighting fixtures.
- Any items to be excluded from the sale, such as an heirloom chandelier.
- The date when the deed will be transferred (or the closing date).
- A **mortgage-contingency** clause if the buyer intends to apply for a loan. This states that the buyer intends to obtain a loan in a specified amount at a specified interest rate within a specified period of time. If the buyer is unable to obtain financing, the buyer may be released from her or his obligation. The seller usually allows the buyer thirty to sixty days to obtain a loan commitment.

- An **inspection contingency** clause. This allows the buyer to have the home inspected, usually within five to ten days of the date of the contract. If the inspection is unsatisfactory, the buyer can terminate the contract. However, the buyer may not be released if the contract allows the seller to make repairs and the repairs, when made, meet applicable standards of workmanship.
- A **lawyer-approval contingency** for both the buyer and the seller if either or both parties are signing the contract before it is reviewed by their respective lawyers.
- A legal description and the common address of the property.
- A provision that the seller will provide good title to the home, or what is sometimes called marketable title. Generally, the seller fulfills this obligation by providing an abstract of title, a certificate of title, or a title insurance policy. This indicates that the seller has the authority to sell the home. In some states—for example, Connecticut—the seller is required to deliver good title, which the buyer is expected to verify, at his or her own expense, by securing an abstract of title, a certificate of title, or a title insurance policy. If the buyer encounters problems in establishing title, he or she can reject the title at or before closing.
- Any restrictions or limitations that could affect title.
- A provision for paying utility bills, property taxes, and similar expenses through the closing date.
- A provision for the return of the buyer's earnest money deposit if the sale is not completed—as, for example, when the buyer has been unable to obtain financing after reasonable or good-faith efforts to do so.
- A provision for taking possession. Along with a firm date for transferring possession from the seller to the buyer, the buyer should in-

clude a provision that requires the seller to pay a specific amount of rent per day if the seller does not leave the home by the agreed date. If the buyer and the seller already know that possession will be delayed, the buyer may ask for a certain amount of money to be held in escrow to cover the rent for the expected time period, and for possible damage to the property during the seller's post-closing possession period. The agreement should also specify who is responsible for insurance, repairs, and the risk of injury between closing and the date that the seller delivers possession.

- A provision for a walk-through inspection within a specified period before the date of closing to allow the buyer to make sure conditions are as they should be according to the contract.

- A provision for who is responsible for maintaining insurance until the closing. The Uniform Vendor-Purchaser Risk of Loss Act applies in some states, which means that the seller assumes the risk of loss until either the transfer of title or possession. In some states, the common law requires the seller to assume this risk.

- The allocation of closing costs, and apportionment of taxes, fuel oil, homeowner's association dues, common charges, and any other items prepaid by the seller that will benefit the buyer.

- Disclosures required by state or federal law.

- Signatures of the parties.

Q. What does an inspection contingency provide?

A. The right to inspect is a very important safeguard for the buyer. There are several types of contingencies used, either as part of the printed offer or added as a rider. Most often the form falls within one of two categories. One form gives the buyer the right to have the property inspected by a professional home inspector of the buyer's choice and at the buyer's expense. If the inspector finds defects, the buyer has the right to cancel

the contract within a specified time. This type of contingency raises some of the same issues as an unrestricted lawyer-approval contingency, since inspectors will almost always find some problems with the property. Thus, it can give buyers a few extra days to decide whether they want to follow through with the purchase, although it should not be used primarily for that purpose.

The second type of inspection contingency also gives the buyer the right to have an inspection done, but then gives the seller time to either repair any problems uncovered by the inspection or agree to reduce the selling price contained in the contract by the cost of repairs. If a seller opts to do nothing, he or she must inform the buyer. Unless the parties can come to terms based on the buyer's inspection report, the buyer can cancel the contract and seek return of any earnest money previously paid.

Other forms of inspection contingencies exist, usually incorporating some or all components of the two forms described above. Some people prefer the simplest form of contingency with the hope that simplicity generates fewer back-and-forth discussions between the parties. Others may prefer a more tailored version based on some concern of the buyer about the property being sold. Generally, if the seller wants to sell, the parties can make a deal, even if there is a serious problem.

Q. What is a lawyer-approval contingency?

A. One common paragraph in a form offer or added as a rider makes the purchase contract subject to review and approval by the buyer's and the seller's respective lawyers within a short period of time, usually five to ten days after acceptance of the offer. This contingency ensures that the contract need not bind the parties if their lawyers find an unsatisfactory provision. The lawyer-approval contingency usually provides that formal notice of disapproval must be communicated within a set time period. Without such a contingency in the contract, both the seller and the buyer are bound by the terms of the contract upon execution, and those terms may be unclear or may differ from the parties' intent.

Q. What is a mortgage-contingency clause?

A. A **mortgage-contingency clause**, which may take the form of a rider or attachment to the contract, provides critical protection to the buyer. Such a clause generally provides that the contract is contingent on the buyer obtaining approval for a loan containing certain character-istics, such as a thirty-year fixed-rate mortgage for $100,000 at no more than 8 percent interest, with no points. This common provision allows the buyer a certain period of time to obtain a firm written commitment for financing upon the described terms. The contingency usually lasts for thirty to sixty days, depending on the average time needed to obtain a loan commitment.

Although the buyer is required to act in good faith to obtain the described financing, which would include timely application for the loan, it allows the buyer to terminate the contract with-out penalty if the buyer is unable to obtain the fi-nancing within the time period and on the stated terms. Because this type of clause favors the buyer, some real estate agents insist that the buyer be preapproved by a lender, which gives the seller a degree of confidence that the buyer will not use the clause to void the contract unless some extraordinary circumstance arises.

The seller may refuse to agree to a mortgage-contingency clause. This can and does happen in a very hot seller's market, in which case there is not much the buyer can do. But the absence of a mortgage-contingency clause might mean that the buyer will be forced to finance his or her home purchase at an unfavorable interest rate. In the worst-case scenario, the buyer might be un-able to obtain a mortgage and forfeit the earnest money, and perhaps even the full down payment if that is already being held in escrow pending closing. Because of this risk, buyers should be very cautious about signing a purchase contract that does not contain this clause.

Q. May the seller refuse to accept lawyer review, inspection contingency, and mortgage-contingency clauses?

A. Sellers are not required to accept any of the buyer protections covered in these kinds of con-tingencies. In fact, sellers should be wary of con-tingencies, since, during the period of review, the property could be off the market, with no assur-ance that the sale will go through. However, un-less it is a hot seller's market, most sellers will accept these and similar clauses provided that all contingencies are limited to a certain time pe-riod, after which they expire.

With a mortgage-contingency clause, sellers should ensure that the proposed interest rate is reasonable, based on current rates, and also allow

---

ⓘ FINDING AN "OUT" FROM THE CONTRACT

Depending on the wording, a contingency may allow the buyer to get out of the contract after it is signed. As a buyer, it is important to be sure that the lawyer review language gives the lawyer the right to review *and* the right to disapprove the contract. It is also important that the lawyer act within the stated period. In some jurisdictions, if the lawyer wants to terminate the contract, the lawyer need not state specific reasons as long as he or she is acting in good faith.

As a seller, you can refuse such a contingency, forcing the buyer's lawyer to review and make changes to the offer before it is submitted. In addition, it is possible to limit the buyer's lawyer to only certain legal matters contained in the contract, such as, for example, the state of title.

a limited but reasonable time for the mortgage commitment. Similarly, with respect to an inspection contingency, sellers should make sure that this clause expires relatively quickly, say, ten days from signing. Unlike a mortgage commitment, there is no reason that an inspection cannot be done within a week or so.

Q. Should I allow the seller to remain in the home after closing?

A. The better practice is almost always for the buyer to obtain possession at closing. Generally, the buyer will be paying the mortgage as of closing and will not want to pay for two residences. In addition, the buyer runs the risk either that the seller will damage the property while moving out, or will fail to move out as promised. The buyer can be faced with the expensive and time-consuming task of having to evict the seller.

Sometimes, however, a buyer may agree to allow the seller to remain for a specified period of time. For example, the seller may be moving to another state one month after the closing or, perhaps, the seller is waiting for a builder to finish a new home. The seller may need the proceeds of the sale in order to complete his own purchase. If the buyer is renting and the end of the lease falls after the closing, it may be advantageous to the buyer to delay possession.

If you are a buyer and find yourself in this situation, do not rely on oral promises or a statement about the date on which the seller promises to vacate the premises. Make sure your purchase contract or a separate document (such as a **lease** or **use and occupancy agreement**) states how long the seller may occupy the home after closing and specifies the rent owed to you for that period. The document should also specify any penalties in the event the seller does not move, does not pay rent after closing, or does any damage prior to vacating the premises. Most contracts provide that a certain amount of the seller's proceeds will be withheld in escrow from the closing to ensure that the seller vacates as promised. Finally, be sure to clarify whose homeowner's insurance applies during this interim period.

Q. Can a buyer sue a seller for backing out of the contract?

A. Depending on the terms of the contract, it is possible that if the seller violates the terms of the contract or refuses to close the sale, the buyer can sue to force the seller to complete the transaction, or recover the earnest money and cancel the contract. It is also possible for the buyer to sue for damages. For example, a buyer who had incurred costs in obtaining a mortgage or costs

---

⚠ DELETE WITH CAUTION

Some buyers make the mistake of deleting the mortgage-contingency clause if they have been preapproved. But you should keep in mind that even if you've been preapproved, the loan is still subject to your purchase of the particular property, and the lender will still need to appraise the property and review the condition of title. It's a good idea to err on the side of caution and leave the clause in; or, if you do take the clause out, to insert a clause saying that the purchase is subject to the lender obtaining a satisfactory appraisal.

ⓘ EARNEST MONEY REFUND

Generally, if the seller defaults, the purchase contract allows the buyer to get back the earnest money and any interest earned on it, unless the buyer has in some way violated the contract. If the seller refuses to return the earnest money, the buyer may have to sue the seller for it. If the buyer causes the default, however, it is very possible that the earnest money will be forfeited.

for renting temporary housing because the closing did not occur would have a case for damages.

Q. What is title insurance?

A. A **title insurance policy** serves at least two purposes: First, it provides a search of the legal records of the property and discloses who is authorized to sell the property and what title exceptions exist; second, in the case of the owner's title insurance policy, it is an agreement that the title insurance company will defend against and pay losses involved in any claim covered by the policy's terms, as long as the buyer or the buyer's heirs own an interest in the property, up to the amount of the policy.

Title insurance is available from title companies and, in some states, from lawyers' groups. Title insurance varies in price in different parts of the country. The extent of the protection is only as broad as the language of the policy itself. The buyer's lawyer can help gauge whether the policy is adequate.

Lenders usually require buyers to obtain title insurance that protects only the lender. This is known as a lender's or mortgage title policy. The buyer may have to pay for this additional title insurance or negotiate with the seller to purchase such a policy. For more on title insurance, see chapter 5, "Home Ownership."

Q. What is a survey, and what is the purpose of a survey?

A. A **survey** is an accurate depiction of the property being conveyed. There are different types of surveys, each showing a varying amount of detail about the property. All surveys show the boundaries of the property and the location of any improvements (for example, buildings and fences). Some surveys contain a legal description of the real estate. The legal description can be used on the deed conveying title. The survey is an essential element of the closing in that it is the link between what the buyer thinks he or she is purchasing (as shown on the survey) and what is legally being conveyed. For example, a survey may reveal that the actual property you are buying

ends a fair distance short of the tree line that you thought was the boundary of the backyard.

Home Inspections

Q. What is involved in a home inspection?

A. A professional home inspection can vary among localities, but generally the aim is to discover any problems with the home that might not be readily apparent to an untrained person. Most inspectors check to make sure there are no material defects or problems with such items as the electrical, plumbing, heating, and air-conditioning systems. The inspector also may check for termites; the age of the roof and when it might need replacement; condition of the basic structure, including the foundation; evidence of basement seepage; and other problems. Some inspectors check for radon concentrations, lead paint, mold, or other environmental hazards, and may also test the well water and the functioning of the septic system.

Most buyers do not want to pay for an inspection until they have settled on other terms with the seller. To do this, the buyer often uses an inspection contingency to provide that the contract is contingent on a favorable inspection of the home. The inspection should be done within a short time after the contract is signed. Inspection fees vary, depending on such factors as the size and type of building inspected. As a general rule, buyers should anticipate a fee somewhere between $250 and $500.

Q. What should the buyer do if the inspection uncovers material and costly defects?

A. There are several options. Although the inspection contingency may simply allow the buyer to walk away from the purchase, this may not be desirable, especially if the home has other qualities the buyer wants. One alternative is to negotiate with the seller to lower the previously agreed-upon price. For example, if the seller was unaware that the furnace was corroded and in need of replacement or that there was rotting timber that needed replacement, the seller may be amenable to reducing the purchase price by the estimated cost of repairs. However, if this option is chosen, the buyer should be aware of the fact that it may affect the amount of the mortgage that may be obtained from a mortgage lender. Many lenders will take such a repair credit into account in determining the amount of financing which is available to the buyer. For example if the agreed-upon purchase price was $300,000 subject to a repair credit of $20,000, the buyer may find that the lender will not lend 80 percent of $300,000, but will only lend 80 percent of $280,000, so the buyer will have to find extra funds to make the repairs.

Alternatively, the price could remain the same with the seller repairing the problems at his or her expense. The buyer's risk if this alternative is pursued is that the seller will not complete the job to the buyer's satisfaction. Whatever the outcome, the result should be evidenced in writing as part of the contract.

While some buyers use an inspection to extract further concessions from the seller, it is un-

likely that a seller is going to agree to substantially reduce the cost of a home to reflect the cost of correcting minor problems such as a repairing a porcelain chip or replacing peeling wallpaper or worn carpeting. A seller facing a long list of minor repairs may want to end negotiations unless the seller has no other alternative than selling the home to this particular buyer.

Q. What can the seller do if he or she disagrees with an inspection report?

A. Your response as a seller to a negative inspection report will depend on the buyer. Sometimes, such a report will scare away the buyer. If you strongly disagree with the inspection, you may want to obtain your own written inspection, copies of which you can provide to prospective buyers.

One response to a negative inspection report is negotiating a resolution to the problems discovered by the inspector. For example, if the inspector discovers that your home has inadequate or outdated electrical wiring, the seller may offer to have the wiring updated or to reduce the price by an agreed-upon sum to cover the buyer's costs of updating the wiring.

As a seller, you should be aware that some home buyers will take any problems and turn them into major roadblocks, hoping to force an anxious seller to reduce the selling price. If you find yourself dealing with such a buyer, you may be better off to simply refuse further negotiations, let the offer expire, return the buyer's deposit, and place the home back on the market. Even if you believe that the buyer's complaints are without merit, it could be time-consuming and costly to insist on compliance with the contract if there is an inspection contingency.

Q. Should a seller get a home inspection?

A. If you are worried about possible problems in your home, you could pay for an inspection before you put your house up for sale. The inspection would allow you to take a look at your home from a buyer's perspective and allow you time to fix any problems or reduce your asking price. The

---

▶ **DON'T PANIC!**

A professional inspector should not be an alarmist. The idea is to point out problems without exaggerating defects. It is a good idea for the buyer to accompany the inspector during the inspection. In this way, the buyer is able to ask questions and to get an idea of the cost of any repairs that are necessary or advisable. Further, the inspector may suggest ways to better insulate the home or offer maintenance suggestions that can prolong the life of operating systems such as heating and air-conditioning.

problem with doing this, though, is that inspectors vary greatly from one individual to the next. The inspector you hire may not raise the same issues as your buyer's inspector.

Most buyers will probably want to pay for their own inspections. If you do share your pre-sale inspection report with a buyer, be sure to provide the entire report; otherwise, a court might find that you intentionally withheld negative information.

Q. Are there any special considerations when you are buying new construction?

A. A buyer purchasing a new home from a developer may or may not work through an agent. If you are not working with an agent, you may want to consult your lawyer to ensure that the purchase contract with the builder contains no surprises. In addition, you may want to consider having the finished structure inspected notwithstanding that it is new. Remember, it is the quality of the construction, not its newness, that is important. An independent inspection can give you this assurance.

If you are contracting with a builder on a home that is not built or finished, you will want to make sure you will get what you think you are buying. For example, model homes typically include optional upgrades, rather than standard features. Along with superior windows and siding, these could include better-quality kitchen cabinets, higher-grade carpeting, and more expensive lighting fixtures. Make sure that the builder provides you with a complete list of standard and optional features. If you are choosing options, make sure the purchase contract includes the specific cost of all options.

You will want to know other facts as well, such as the type and extent of any landscaping to be provided by the builder, known plans for the development of surrounding property, and the exact provisions of any warranty from the builder. If possible, you will want a warranty that is insured by an insurance company, rather than a warranty guaranteed only by the builder. Finally, the builder should provide you with evidence that there are no mechanic or construction lien claims. The seller's contractors, subcontractors, and material suppliers can file such liens in the event the builder does not pay them for their work.

The purchase contract should address certain issues unique to newly constructed homes. For example, specific dates for completion and occupancy should be included if the home is not yet built. Although it is difficult to negotiate, the buyer can try to provide for a penalty or for the right to cancel the contract if the builder exceeds these dates. In addition, the contract should cover the method of prorating real estate taxes. It is also very important to visit the site frequently. The only person in the entire project concerned with your best interests is you. Errors, delays, and other issues are much more easily dealt with and corrected if caught early.

Buying in a Multiunit Building or Development

Q. What is the difference between a condominium and a co-op?

A. A **condominium** is a common-interest community in which individual units are separately owned but the unit owners also own an individual interest in the common areas of the building, such as hallways, roofs, exteriors, and any land surrounding the building. With a **cooperative**, or **co-op**, buyers generally purchase shares of stock in a corporation that owns a building and then enter into a lease to occupy a particular apartment. A condominium owner has title to his or her unit; a co-op owner receives stock in the corporation that owns the building based on the unit's proportion of the building, and the right to lease a particular apartment in the building.

For the purposes of income tax laws and other laws regarding real estate, condominiums and cooperative units are treated the same as a single-family home. But an association or corporation has the right to impose maintenance fees, demand escrow payments for large repair bills, and manage the overall operation of the entire building. Owners of both types of property must abide by the rules; otherwise, they may ultimately be evicted or sued.

See the section titled "Shared Ownership: Condos and Condominiums" in chapter 5, "Home Ownership," for more on living in this kind of property.

Q. Are there differences between common-interest home ownership and single-family home ownership?

A. In single-family home ownership, the control, decisions, and expenses are the responsibility of the owner, subject to zoning restrictions established by local law and any restrictions contained in the declaration of the builder who originally developed the property and the rules of any homeowner's association. As a general rule, multiunit ownership is subject to more extensive regulation than single-family ownership. For example, there are generally more statutes, rules, and regulations governing what you may and may not do with your condominium, co-op, or other multiunit dwelling.

Before finalizing an offer to purchase, it is important for the buyer to obtain and review all the restrictions affecting the property. Buyers should ask to see the bylaws, operating budgets, management agreements, and other regulating documents. Many states require disclosures to the purchasers of units in a common-interest community. Some states have a central agency that licenses and regulates the development and sale of common-interest community units.

With multiunit real estate, the cost of the unit is not the limit of your financial obligation. There will be monthly assessments to cover maintenance and related expenses for operating the common areas. These assessments are usually in proportion to the percentage of the total complex you own, but may also take into account the floor and view of the unit. For example, if an apartment has a 10 percent ownership stake, this generally means that the owner will pay 10 percent of the building's assessments.

Assessments and other common area charges may increase over time. In addition, unit owners are subject to special assessments above and beyond the regular monthly assessment, to pay for unforeseen improvements or repairs and major capital improvements. Always ask about pending projects and their approximate cost, as well as capital reserves for the projected work. You also should be sure that there is enough liability and fire insurance coverage for the entire development.

🗎 COMMON-INTEREST COMMUNITIES

A **common-interest community** is real estate in which ownership of a particular property carries an obligation to pay money to another person, usually an association, for maintenance, taxes, upkeep, and insurance of property other than the individually owned portion of the property. Common-interest communities can come in many forms. There are condominiums, cooperatives, planned-unit developments, and private-easement communities. In most of these common-interest communities involving residences, there is a homeowner's association charged with providing common services and maintaining the common areas. The homeowner's association may also have jurisdiction over use and occupancy within the individual units.

Almost all common interest communities are described in a **declaration,** a **master deed,** or a **declaration of covenants, conditions, and restrictions** that are recorded as public documents.

Q. What criteria should I consider when buying a condominium or a co-op?

A. First, read all of the governing documents and review minutes of recent board of directors' and owners' meetings. Another source of information about a condominium association, a cooperative corporation, or other common-interest property is to talk to owners or shareholders. Ask them what they like best about where they live and what their complaints are. Along with all the things one would consider about a single-family home, such as neighborhood, prospective common-interest buyers should consider the following:

- Percentage of owner-occupants and renters. A high percentage of renters could indicate poor sales and/or absentee landlords who are less interested in maintaining the building. Because of these risks, it is often difficult for prospective buyers to obtain loans for units in buildings with a high percentage of renters.
- Monthly maintenance fees, special assessments, and the history of such items. You will also want to ask whether the association or corporation is involved in any lawsuits brought by builders, neighbors, or former owners.
- Financial condition of the association or corporation. You will want to get a copy of the most recent financial statements and budgets.
- Quality of construction. Hire an inspector and make certain that he or she checks the soundproofing, the condition of shared common areas, such as the roof and patios, and the electrical, heating, and plumbing systems.
- Bylaws and/or covenants. If these are too restrictive, you may have trouble obtaining a loan or selling your unit or share in the corporation. Covenants will also dictate whether you can lease and other uses of the property, including whether pets are allowed.

Chapter 5, "Home Ownership," also contains detailed information about shared ownership.

ⓘ OBTAINING A MORTGAGE ON A CO-OP

Since a mortgage, by definition, is a lien on real estate, the owner of shares in a corporation cannot obtain a mortgage unless the owner places a lien against the entire building. It is unlikely that any one owner in a co-op would be permitted to lien the entire building. Because of this, it was formerly not easy to get a loan to buy a co-op, and for that reason prices on co-ops were usually much lower than condominium prices.

Now, however, the owner of a co-op may be able to obtain other forms of financing similar to a mortgage, provided that the building's cooperative association permits it. This is because the federal government amended the law to allow the Federal National Mortgage Association (Fannie Mae) to buy co-op loans, making it much easier for prospective co-op buyers to obtain loans. Generally, as a condition to obtaining a loan on a co-op, the lender will hold the stock to the cooperative as collateral.

Today, it is only slightly more difficult to obtain a loan for a co-op than for a condominium. You may have to put down more money than if you were buying real estate and the rates may be slightly higher. Prices of cooperative units generally remain lower because of the extra restrictions placed on co-op owners.

The Closing

Q. What happens at the closing?

A. The real estate **closing** (sometimes called the **settlement**) is the final stage in the process of buying a home. The closing is a meeting at which the buyer and the seller, usually accompanied by their respective lawyers and real estate agents, complete the sale. At this meeting, the buyer usually signs the promissory note and mortgage and obtains the lender's proceeds. The buyer is then able to make all the required payments due to the seller. The seller produces all documents necessary for the transfer of good title and delivers a deed that transfers the title to the buyer.

Before the closing, the parties and their lawyers will review all documents to see that everyone is fulfilling all conditions and promises of the contract. A closing statement or settlement sheet is prepared, fully listing the financial aspects of the closing. The **Real Estate Settlement Procedures Act** (**RESPA**) will apply in any transaction in which a buyer is obtaining a federally insured mortgage from a financial institution. This requires use of a settlement sheet developed by the Department of Housing and Urban Development that sets forth all credits and payments made at closing. In other closings in which the buyer is not obtaining a mortgage, another form of settlement sheet may be used.

Both buyers and sellers should expect to sign a lot of papers at the closing.

Buyers should expect to sign or provide the following:

- A promissory note promising to pay in full the loan and interest
- The mortgage document, which secures the promissory note by giving the lender an interest in the property and the right to take and sell the property—that is, foreclose—if the mortgage payments are not made
- A Truth in Lending form, which requires the lender to tell you in advance the approximate annual percentage rate of the loan over the loan's term
- A typed loan application form
- A payment letter telling the buyer the amount of the first payment and when it is due
- A survey form stating that the buyer has seen

▶ **THE WALK-THROUGH**

As a buyer, you would be wise to inspect the property just before closing to ensure that

- the property is in the same condition as it was when you signed the contract, ordinary wear and tear excepted;
- all repairs that the seller agreed to make have been completed in a good and workmanlike manner;
- all personal property that is to be included in the sale is at the property; and
- the seller has vacated the property and caused no damage in moving out.

If any of the foregoing are not the case, the buyer should quickly notify his or her lawyer or real estate agent. The problem needs to be addressed prior to closing: If something is missing, the buyer needs to see if the item will be returned before closing. If the condition of the property is not right, repairs should be made. If agreeable to both parties, the buyer and the seller may decide to reach a financial compromise to address any deficiency.

and understands the survey of the property and that it fairly depicts the property
- A private mortgage insurance application or disclosure, usually required on loans with a down payment of less than 10 percent
- A termite inspection or other inspection form, indicating that the buyer has seen a report of any inspections that were made
- A homeowner's insurance policy (in the case of a single-family home)
- An affidavit from the buyer stating that the buyer has the legal right to mortgage the property and that there are no liens or encumbrances (judgments, mortgages, or taxes owed) on the property
- If the buyer has used more than one name, an affidavit stating that the various names all refer to the same person
- An agreement to cooperate with the lender to correct any errors or omissions in the loan documents

The seller can expect to sign or provide the following documents:

- The deed transferring title in the real estate from the seller to the buyer
- A bill of sale transferring ownership of any personal property that may be included in the sale of the real estate
- An affidavit of title in which the seller states that he or she has the legal right to sell the real estate and that there are no liens or encumbrances (judgments, mortgages, or taxes owed) on the property
- An affidavit as to mechanic's liens and possession indicating that the seller has not had any work done on the property that would give rise to a mechanic's lien and that there are no parties other than the seller entitled to possess the property
- An occupancy certificate indicating that a new home complies with the local housing code
- A 1099-S reporting certificate verifying the terms of the sale and the seller's tax identification numbers for IRS reporting purposes

Both buyer and seller will have to sign the following:

- An affidavit specifying the purchase price and indicating the source of the purchase price. This affidavit assures the lender that the buyer has not received any undisclosed loans from the seller that could negatively affect the buyer's ability to repay the lender's loan;
- A RESPA form developed by the federal Department of Housing and Urban Development and sometimes a separate closing statement, specifying all costs associated with the transaction.
- Transfer declarations as required by state or local authorities.

Q. What are some financial aspects of the closing?

A. At the time of closing, the seller and the buyer will total up various credits in order to determine how much money the buyer must pay. The allocation of such expenses will depend on the terms of the purchase contract as well as the law and customs in the area where the property is located. The real estate agent or lawyer should advise the buyer before closing how much money will be needed at the time of closing. Typically, the buyer will be required to have a certified or cashier's check or wired funds in the amount required to meet these expenses.

The seller will usually receive credits for such items as fuel on hand (such as oil in the home heating tank), unused insurance premiums (if insurance is being assigned), prepaid taxes, and public utility charges such as water and sewer fees. These credits will also include any other items prepaid by the seller that will benefit the buyer.

The buyer will usually receive credits for such items as the earnest money deposited and taxes or special assessments that the seller has not paid but which, when they become due, will include the period that the seller owned the property. The settlement sheet will also specify who is responsible for the payment of various expenses. These will include the sales commissions and the costs of the title search, inspections, recording fees, transaction taxes, and the like.

The list of fees presented below by no means exhausts the types of fees that might be charged at closing. Other common fees include a loan origination fee to cover the lender's administrative costs in processing the loan; a credit report fee; a lender's appraisal fee; a mortgage insurance application fee; a mortgage insurance premium; the lender's lawyer's fees; and hazard insurance premium. The buyer may also have to put money into escrow with his or her lender to assure future payment of such recurring items as real estate taxes and insurance. This can, when added to the adjustments due to the seller, add up to a surprisingly large total. Also, there are often separate lender document fees that cover the preparation of final legal papers, such as the promissory note and mortgage or deed of trust.

Closing Costs

Q. How much will I need for closing costs?

A. In addition to the down payment, the buyer will need to pay for **closing costs**. These costs vary depending on local custom and the specific terms of the purchase agreement. If you are obtaining a loan, the law requires the lender to provide an estimate of these costs as part of the loan application process.

Closing costs usually include all or most of the following:

Appraisal fee

This is the fee paid for an appraisal of the property. It is required by the lender and is often paid for by the borrower. The Federal Housing Administration and the Veterans Administration establish the appraisal fees for mortgages that they guarantee.

Lawyer's fee

Buyers and sellers pay the fees for their own lawyers. In some states, buyers are required to pay for the lender's lawyer. This fee may be a certain percentage of the mortgage or a fixed fee.

Survey fee

The contract should specify whether the seller is obligated to provide a survey. If the seller is not, the buyer may need to obtain and pay for a survey, for his or her own use and to satisfy the lender. You may be able to avoid this fee if the lender agrees to accept a recent survey done for the seller, along with an affidavit by the seller stating that the property lines have not changed since the completion of the survey and that there have been no additional improvements to the property since the survey was taken. In addition, the title company may perform a visual inspection of the property to verify the seller's statements. Even then, a title insurance company may require a new survey unless the survey has been recertified recently.

Loan discount fee

This is the lender's charge to the buyer to obtain the loan, sometimes referred to as points or the **loan origination fee**. The buyer may have paid some of this fee in advance to secure the loan.

Inspection fees

These are charges for general inspections or inspections required by local laws. The buyer or the seller may be responsible for these fees, depending on the contract and local law and custom.

Title fees

These fees cover the cost of the title search.

Title insurance

The contract needs to spell out who is to pay the cost of title insurance. Often, it is divided between the seller and the buyer. In some states, the seller pays for the buyer's policy and the buyer pays for the lender's policy. In other states, the buyer pays all charges related to title insurance.

Transfer taxes

These taxes are imposed by the state, county, or city where the property is located on the transfer of the deed and, in some cases, on the mortgage.

Recording fees

The costs of recording the deed in order to change ownership and recording the buyer's mortgage are paid by the buyer. The cost of recording the release of the seller's mortgage by the seller's lender and recording the release of any other liens found in the record of title are paid by the seller.

Q. Is the seller responsible for any closing costs?

A. The parties can negotiate who will pay the various costs at closing. These obligations should be set forth in the contract. Generally, the seller is responsible for paying the real estate agent's commission on the sale, the seller's lawyer's fees, real estate taxes on the property to the date of closing, certain transfer taxes, and any liens that may be outstanding on the property, including any money due the current lender. Depending on local custom, the seller may also be required to pay the cost of a title insurance policy for the buyer that insures the buyer against any defects in the title to the property. In other states, the buyer customarily pays for title insurance. In either event, this obligation can be negotiated in the contract. On occasion, the seller may pay some of the costs of the buyer's loan, in order to induce the buyer to go through with the sale.

Ownership Options

Q. What form of ownership is best for a home?

A. If more than one person is buying the home, ownership must be declared in one of several ways. Generally, married couples or other co-owners with equal interests in the property prefer to hold title as **joint tenants with right of sur-**vivorship. This form of ownership enables one person to own the entire property in the event of the other person's death. At the time of a subsequent sale, the surviving person will need to present a death certificate to the closing agent. Some states also permit married couples to own as **tenants by the entirety** provided that the home is their principal residence. This form of ownership also provides a right of survivorship, and in addition provides some protection to the parties against losing the home to a creditor of one spouse.

Married or unrelated people may also own property with separate and equal or unequal interests as **tenants in common** or as a business type of entity (such as a limited liability company or partnership). There may be other forms of ownership depending on where you live, such as land trusts. The option that is best for you will depend on a variety of factors, such as your estate tax situation and provisions you may want to make for children, stepchildren, or other relatives. The deed creates the form of ownership, so buyers will want to make this decision before closing. Chapter 5, "Home Ownership," provides more detailed information on these and other ownership options. Be sure to consult a lawyer about the various advantages and disadvantages of different types of ownership so that you can make an informed decision about the form of ownership that is best for you.

THE WORLD AT YOUR FINGERTIPS

- *There are some great websites that can help you set a price for your property by providing you with a list of homes sold through the local multiple listing service within the last year. Try realestate.yahoo. com/re/homevalues and www. domania.com.*

REMEMBER THIS

- *Once you sign a contract, you're committed to buying (or selling) a home. Consult with your lawyer before you sign, don't rush into things, and make sure the contingencies you need are in the contract so that you have some options if, for example, your financing falls through.*

- *If you're a buyer, it's a good idea to get a home inspection to make sure that the home you're about to buy has no substantial defects.*

- *You might find the closing intimidating—there are so many papers to sign and so much to understand—but your lawyer should be able to lead you through the process smoothly.*

- *Consider how you and your spouse want to hold title to the property—your decision could affect your estate planning or might be important should you and your spouse divorce.*

ⓘ OWNERSHIP IN A COMMUNITY PROPERTY STATE

Community property states include Arizona, California, Idaho, Louisiana, Nevada, New Mexico, Texas, Washington, and to an extent Wisconsin. If you live in a community property state, the property you buy while married belongs to both members of the couple equally, no matter whose money actually paid for it and regardless of whose name is on the title.

This provision of state law generally applies to property acquired during the marriage, rather than property owned before the marriage or property that is inherited during the marriage. But state laws vary, so you would be wise to discover how community property laws in your state apply to any real estate purchase.

TAX CONSIDERATIONS

When Emily was negotiating to buy a home, she asked the seller how much property tax he paid. He told her he paid $3,000 a year. After the sale, Emily was shocked to discover that the property tax payable on the home had tripled.

You can't afford to forget about taxes when you are buying or selling a home. You may have to pay transfer taxes, real estate taxes, or a capital gains tax, depending on whether you are buying or selling. Talk to your lawyer about tax issues, so you don't get a nasty shock when the bills arrive. Your lawyer may even be able to tell you about ways you can minimize or deduct the tax.

Tax Considerations when Buying Your Home

Q. What is a transfer tax?

A. A **transfer tax** is a tax paid for the privilege of transferring ownership of real property. Depending on the laws in your area, there are probably state or local transfer taxes due on the amount paid to purchase a home. If the home is financed, there may also be a **documentary tax** on the note or mortgage. The documentary tax is often applied to the recording of the promissory note or mortgage by the county clerk, and is often in the form of stamps that have to be purchased and affixed to the documents before they can be recorded. There may also be an **intangible tax** on the loan, another kind of fee for recording the mortgage. Generally, the seller pays the cost of the transfer tax, but in most cases it is negotiable. The buyer generally pays the cost of the documentary tax on the note or mortgage and the tax on the loan.

Q. What are real estate taxes?

A. Most homeowners have to pay taxes on the real estate they own. This is a yearly tax based on the assessed value of the property, usually paid to the local community. As a general rule, the tax is divided among the municipality (city and town), the county, school districts (including the local school district and community colleges), and other governmental units. Currently, these taxes are deductible against taxable income on your federal tax return if you itemize.

Depending on your state's laws, the amount you pay in property tax also may be deductible on your state income tax return.

Q. How can I find out the current real estate taxes on a home?

A. The seller should be willing to disclose the amount of property taxes paid on the home over the last few years. If not, you or your lawyer can obtain this information from the local tax collector's office. If a title commitment is issued in connection with the sale, the amount of taxes will also be disclosed on the commitment.

Q. Will my purchase of a home affect the real estate taxes?

A. Depending on how your state assesses property, a purchase can affect the amount of property taxes to be paid. For example, in some states, property tax increases occur only when a home changes ownership. The tax assessor reassesses the home using the price paid as its new value; in some cases, the taxes may skyrocket. Alternatively, many states reassess property every three or four years. If you are buying the home at the end of that cycle, you may see a large increase in property taxes at the start of the new cycle. While the amount of tax may not be the deciding factor in your decision to buy, you will want to take it into account in determining your total monthly housing costs.

Q. How are real estate taxes determined?

A. The most common way of determining real estate taxes consists of two steps. The taxing body determines the total value of all real estate within its borders (assessments). It then takes the budgets (spending plans) of the various governmental units for which it collects taxes and adds them up. The ratio of budgets to assessments creates a tax rate, which is then multiplied by your own assessment.

Q. Is there anything I can do if my home is assessed at a higher value than I paid for it?

A. You may be able to appeal the assessment, based on your purchase price. Once you have purchased the home at fair market value, you can appeal to the assessor's board or office. You must prove, however, that the sale was an "arm's-length transaction." In other words, you cannot purchase the home from a relative at a below-market cost and expect that your appeal will be successful. If the assessor grants your appeal and reduces the assessment, future taxes to be paid would be lowered. See chapter 5, "Home Ownership," for more on this topic and on how to lower your property taxes.

 ASSESSED VALUE VERSUS APPRAISED VALUE

The **assessed value** of a home, determined by the tax assessor, is usually only one part of an equation that determines the total tax bill. The assessed value may or may not reflect the market value, that is, the price at which the home would be expected to sell. Be aware that not all states assess homes at their full market value.

The **appraised value,** on the other hand, is an estimate of the property's market value, usually made by a trained appraiser. A lender will normally require an appraisal to determine that the selling price does not exceed the property's market value or fall below the lender's mortgage. It is common for a lender's appraisal to equal the purchase price contained in the contract.

Q. *What items involving home ownership are deductible against federal income tax?*

A. Both property tax and interest on loans of up to $1 million in principal are deductible against your taxable income when you file your federal income tax form. Federal law also permits you to borrow up to $100,000 through a home equity loan and deduct the interest, as long as the total debt on the home (including the first mortgage) does not exceed the fair market value of the home. Remember, however, that you must itemize to claim these deductions; they are not available to taxpayers who claim a standard deduction. New buyers may deduct any loan fees or points paid to obtain a mortgage in the tax year in which the points were paid, but only if the points were paid by funds other than the mortgage funds borrowed by the buyer. (A point is equal to 1 percent of the amount borrowed.) Loan fees or points paid to refinance a mortgage cannot be claimed in a single year; they must be spread out over the life of the loan.

Be aware that transfer taxes, lawyer fees, recording charges, and other lender charges, such as for the appraisal and the credit report, are not deductible. See chapter 5, "Home Ownership," for more on possible federal tax breaks.

Tax Considerations When Selling Your Home

Q. *Do I have to pay federal capital gains taxes on the sale of my home?*

A. You have to pay federal capital gains taxes on the sale your home only if you have lived there for less than two years, or if the profit on the sale is more than $250,000 ($500,000 for a couple.)

Q. *How do I determine my profit?*

A. You can calculate your profit by subtracting the adjusted cost basis of your home from its adjusted sales price. You can compute the adjusted cost basis by subtracting certain items such as the sales commission, lawyer's fees, and fix-up expenses from the price of your home when you bought it.

To calculate the adjusted sales price, start with the selling price. Then subtract the cost of capital improvements made while you owned the home and closing costs not deducted when you bought it. Note that you may not subtract the cost of repairs. The IRS is very strict about what it considers improvements. For example, repairing a water heater is not considered an improvement, but adding a dishwasher is one. Also, you may deduct the labor costs paid to a tradesperson (such as a carpenter), but not any costs for your own labor. The IRS requires home sellers to complete a form in the year of the sale that includes these calculations. You also will want to keep all receipts for any costs you are deducting from the sale. Without such written proof, the IRS is not likely to allow your deductions.

Q. *Now I have figured my profits. What about figuring my taxes?*

A. First, remember that if there is no profit, you do not have to worry about paying taxes; however, the IRS does not allow you to deduct any loss on a primary residence.

Until May 7, 1997, homeowners who sold their house could defer payment of capital gains tax by rolling the proceeds of the sale into a new house—but only if the new house cost more than the old one did. Then, after age fifty-five, when the homeowners were probably in a lower tax bracket and ready for a smaller home or retirement community, each person was entitled to exclude up to $125,000 in profit—but only once. Because of these rules, many families bought bigger, more-expensive houses than they needed, especially if they moved to an area with lower real estate values.

All this changed in 1997 with a new tax law. Now you do not have to pay capital gains on the sale of any residence you have lived in for at least two of the last five years, unless the profit is more than $250,000 per person or $500,000 per couple. You have to count not only the profit on this house but on any other houses you sheltered by rollover prior to 1997. If special circumstances meant you had to move before living there two years, you can exclude part of the profit—for instance, half the profit if you lived there only one year, up to your $250,000 limit.

This change means that most people won't have to pay capital gains taxes at all on their home, unless they have enjoyed a very substantial profit. And you can exclude this capital gain on the sale of your residence as many times as you sell another primary residence meeting the two-year test. Note that this door does not swing both ways. If you lose money on the sale of your home, you cannot deduct the loss and pay less in taxes or carry the loss forward.

The capital gains exclusion does not apply to investment properties and vacation homes. However, people with more than one home can avoid tax on each of them with enough planning. For instance, if you have a condo in New York City and a house in Florida, you could live in the New York home as your primary residence for two years before selling it, then live in the one in Florida as your primary residence for two years before selling it. For a house to count as your primary residence, you have to live there for at least 183 days each year.

Win or lose, whenever you sell a home you have to file Form 2119, reporting the sale date, the price, and how much profit is subject to immediate taxation, if any. This one-page form takes you through the calculations required to determine gain on sale, adjusted sales price, and taxable gain. If you die without selling the home, all capital gains taxes are wiped off the slate. Your beneficiaries will inherit it at a new, stepped-up basis, and they will not have to pay any tax on capital gains accumulated on the sale of your home or homes over the years.

What if you own a duplex, live in one unit, and rent out the other? In that case, you can only avoid capital gain on the half you use as your res-

idence. The other is a business property, not subject to this tax break.

For details on IRS regulations in this area, see Publication 523, "Selling Your Home."

Q. Will I owe state and local taxes on my profits?

A. You may live in a state or a city that will require you to pay state or local taxes on the profits of a home. Some states or local communities also charge a **transfer tax** on the sale of property. This tax is usually levied as a percentage of the sales price.

Q. What is a gift annuity and how does it work?

A. A homeowner interested in converting home equity into income may want to consider a **gift annuity** in which he or she donates the home to a qualified charitable institution and is eligible for a tax deduction against taxable income in the year in which the donation is made. In return, the institution provides an annuity to the donor and grants the donor a life estate in the home. This means that the donor may remain in the home for his or her lifetime and is responsible for all taxes and maintenance on the home. At the donor's death, the property becomes the possession of the charitable institution.

This arrangement offers several tax advantages, particularly for homeowners who do not have heirs or who want to reduce the size of their taxable estate. Again, you should consult a finan-

---

ⓘ SAVE YOUR RECEIPTS

If you are making improvements to your home, you should save your receipts, because eventually your house might just gain enough in value that you will want to prove that your basis has increased and therefore the profit is not as great as it appears.

cial professional or tax lawyer for more information.

THE WORLD AT YOUR FINGERTIPS

- *The IRS website (www.irs.gov) is an excellent resource, and has many comprehensive publications and information sheets that can help you in your tax planning or answer your questions about taxes. The publications can be downloaded directly from the IRS website.*

REMEMBER THIS

- *Do some investigation into the amount of property tax you can expect to pay on the home you're buying. It might not be the deciding factor in your decision to buy, but you will want to take it into account.*
- *It's a good habit to save all receipts for any work or improvements to your house. They may come in useful for the purposes of capital gains tax if you sell your home.*

Home Ownership

Your own home! It's your little starter house, your grand Victorian, your mountain hideaway, your suburban town house. After years of renting and saving and dreaming, you've bought a home and it's yours.

Now what do you need to know to make sure you can keep on enjoying your home? Well, if you don't already know how to start a reluctant lawn mower, change a faucet washer, and cope with rising water in the basement, you'd better be prepared to learn.

There are also some legal matters you'll want to understand to make sure your ownership means what you think it does.

This chapter offers an introduction to the law of home ownership, including rights and restrictions, insurance, and the financial side of owning a home. Note that the laws of each state are different, and what follows are basic legal principles that create a framework for state laws.

PROPERTY RIGHTS AND RESTRICTIONS

You may own your home, but that doesn't give you license to do anything you want with your property. For example, you probably won't be able to turn your garage into an all-night roller disco, because your neighbors have rights, too, and there are probably zoning regulations restricting the use of your property. And when you say you own your own home, think about what exactly you mean. Do you own it outright, in fee simple? Do you own it as a joint tenant or a tenant in common? No matter how you own it, you'll want to think about protecting your title by buying title insurance.

This section will help you think about your property rights and how to safeguard them; it will also consider the rights of others, including your neighbors and the government.

Your Property Rights

Q. What are my rights as a homeowner?

A. Generally, what you do with the home you own is up to you. You have a right to maintain or neglect, preserve or remodel, keep, sell, or give away, and enjoy your home as you see fit.

However, these rights are not absolute. They are limited by federal, state, and local laws, because the people who live around you also have rights. For example, under the federal Fair Housing Act, you may not discriminate when renting your property. Under local ordinances, your home must conform to zoning and building codes. The zoning code may prevent you from adding a three-story addition. If your garage is falling down and creating a hazard, your neighbors could invoke the building inspector, or even sue you themselves, to force you to repair it or raze it.

So be mindful of such matters as zoning, building codes, easements, water rights, and local ordinances on noise, or you could find yourself in trouble.

Q. How do zoning codes affect my property rights?

A. To avoid urban mishmash, municipalities often restrict business and industry to particular designated areas. Other areas are zoned residential, including apartment buildings, or zoned

---

ⓘ RIGHTS TO NATURAL RESOURCES

You may use, sell, or restrict the use of your property's natural resources, from stands of timber on the surface to minerals lying beneath.

Water, oil, and gas are another story. Because surface water and underground water, oil, and gas move about without regard to property lines, you don't have the right to pump out as much as you want from a well on your property. Removing resources such as these is subject to state and federal regulation. For example, if there's a stream running through your land, in most states you cannot dam it up to the point where downstream neighbors get no water.

strictly for single-family homes. If your neighborhood is zoned residential, you won't have to worry about a pool hall or gas station going up next to your house. It also means there are certain restrictions on what you can do with your property.

Zoning ordinances vary among communities and can change over time. While some cities and towns mandate few if any zoning restrictions, others enforce very strict zoning, controlling such items as the maximum size of a doghouse and the height of a fence. If you are planning to build any sort of addition or new structure, check with your local building department about zoning restrictions on your property. If you are still unsure, consult a lawyer.

Q. Can zoning codes prohibit me from running a business in my home?

A. A typical residential zoning ordinance probably would not preclude you from operating a home-based business that would not alter the character of the neighborhood, such as telephone sales, freelance writing, or mail-order distribution. But if the home-based business will require signs and will lead to traffic from customers, check with the local department of building and zoning before you make an investment. Also, be sure to ask about anything you must do to license your business. Chapter 13, "Forming and Operating a Small Business," can give you more information.

Q. Is there a way to avoid zoning restrictions?

A. Most communities allow you to apply for a variance if you wish to make a minor change to your property that would violate zoning restrictions. For example, if you want to build a deck that will be close to the sidewalk and thereby violate zoning regulations, you could seek a variance; or you might seek one if you want to build a two-story extension in a one-story zone. Essentially, a **variance** is permission from the governing body to deviate from the zoning laws. The zoning department can provide materials explaining how to seek a variance. The steps may involve a public hearing, an appearance before the plan-

ning commission, and approval by the town governing board. It's up to you to show that the proposed change is required by a hardship caused by the shape, condition, or location of your property and will not change the character of the neighborhood or reduce neighboring property values.

If your plans call for a major change, you may apply for a **zoning change**. For example, if you live near the boundary of an area zoned commercial and you want to turn your nineteenth-century house into a doctor's office, you might be able to persuade the zoning authorities to extend the commercial zone boundaries a bit. Again, you would have to show that the change would not hurt property values and convince your neighbors that it would not diminish their property rights.

Q. What are covenants?

A. **Covenants**, also called **conditions**, consist of private restrictions designed to maintain quality control over a neighborhood. A builder may draw up covenants affecting a new subdivision he or she is developing—and in modern developments, these restrictions can be significant and extensive. In an older subdivision, the covenants might be recorded on the plat. A **plat** is a plan or map of a piece of land showing the location and boundaries of the land. Covenants typically restrict such things as lot size, square footage, and architectural design. They also may prohibit satellite dishes, boats and motor homes, certain types of fences, and unsightly activities such as auto repair.

Q. How do covenants affect my property rights?

A. Covenants generally **run with the land**, which means that they bind all future owners of the property unless all property owners in the affected subdivision join in releasing them or they expire after a certain term. Covenants may restrict your use of your land even if municipal zoning laws permit the proposed use. You should receive a copy of the covenants from your real estate agent or lawyer before you buy your home. Read them carefully before closing to avoid surprises.

If you don't get a copy of the the covenants from your agent or your lawyer, a copy should be available from any existing homeowner association, or they might be recorded in the public records. As with zoning codes, you may be able to negotiate a minor variance, such as building an addition slightly higher than the covenant's limit.

Note that covenants must comply with state and federal laws. Old covenants that prohibit homeowners from selling their homes to people of certain races and religions are not enforceable.

Q. What is an easement?

A. An **easement** on your property indicates that someone else may have a right to use part of your property for a specific purpose. A common example is a power company's easement to run a power line over your backyard. The developer normally establishes these types of easements when the subdivision is platted or the house is built in order to provide utilities to the development.

Neighbors also may have an easement on your property. They might have an easement to use your driveway to get to their house (a positive easement) or one that restricts you from blocking their view of the lake (a negative easement). Or they might have a **profit** (short for the French term **profit a prendre**, which means "profit to be taken"), allowing them to remove something from your property, such as raspberries, coal, or timber.

Q. How are easements created?

A. An easement or profit may be created by a deed, by a will, or by implication—such as if a previous owner divided a single lot in half and the only access to the back lot is through the front one. Or, if a neighbor has been using your property in some way for a long time, such as by driving on your private road, he or she may be able to claim a **prescriptive easement** to continue doing so whether you give permission or not.

Courts are willing to grant prescriptive easements when the neighbor has been engaging in the activity in question for a given period of years and the property owner has not physically stopped him or her, such as by erecting a locked gate. (The period varies by state, but is usually between five and twenty years.) Oddly, one of the requirements for gaining a prescriptive easement is the property owner's objections—such as the owner telling a person over and over for years not to drive on the road, without putting up a gate. The reasoning seems to be that if an owner gives someone permission to do something, that person cannot claim it as a right.

Q. What about regulations on activities in my home?

A. The general rule is that activities in the privacy of your home are your own business. There are three exceptions: when your activities are illegal; when the activities make it difficult for other people to enjoy their own homes; and when you are violating zoning codes, such as by running a prohibited business from your home. Common

---

▶ **CHECKING OUT EASEMENTS**

Easements are recorded at the county courthouse, but they may be scattered among various plats, deed books, and mortgage books. The best way to find out about them is through a professional title search, which most likely occurred if you obtained title insurance or an opinion of title before buying the house. If you discover an easement, check the wording. When a document grants an easement to a particular person, the restriction may cease when he or she dies or sells the property. But if it's granted to someone and "his heirs and assigns," it's probably in effect no matter who owns the property. Until the easement expires, your legal obligation is to refrain from interfering with that right. Conversely, the person in whose favor the easement is created may not extend the permitted use.

sense dictates that if you mow your lawn at 4:00 A.M. or blast your stereo at midnight, you should not be surprised if someone calls the police. Local noise ordinances may restrict the hours during which you can conduct certain noisy activities. Similarly, most activities that are illegal in public are also illegal in private—such as selling cocaine or serving alcohol to minors. Police generally need a search warrant to enter your home. You can find more information on search warrants in chapter 15, "Criminal Justice."

Safeguarding Property Rights: Title Insurance

Q. What is meant by the term "good title"?

A. **Good title** means you legally own your home and have the authority to sell it.

ⓘ HISTORIC HOMES

What if you own a two-hundred-year-old house with historic value? Your property rights are still extremely strong. If your home is listed on the National Register of Historic Places, no federally funded or federally licensed program may alter the building without a hearing before a federal agency. The law is only designed to protect the home from federal government activities, and does not restrict the rights of the owner—you remain free to alter, add to, convert, or even demolish the home.

Some communities have their own historic preservation ordinances that may affect what you can do to your property. In Marblehead, Massachusetts, for example, homeowners in the historic district are prohibited from carrying out exterior renovations without permission from a local committee.

Traditionally, this was determined by a study of the public record to determine the chain of ownership back to the very beginning of the property, as well as any encumbrances, such as liens on the property. This study is called an **abstract,** and some buyers, especially in rural areas, still rely on an abstract and a lawyer's opinion as to what the abstract shows for evidence of title. But metropolitan mortgage lenders generally prefer title insurance.

The chief problem with the abstract system is its lack of accountability. What happens if the abstract company or the lawyer issuing an opinion on the property fails to uncover a flaw in the title and it costs you, the new owner, a great deal of money? You could sue, but you'd have to prove that someone was negligent. With title insurance, the insurer agrees to pay covered claims whether anyone was negligent or not. Essentially, title insurance provides a thorough search of the public record, just as if you had received an abstract and an opinion, but backed by insurance. The title insurance company also assumes the obligation to defend any actions challenging title to the property.

Q. How does title insurance work?

A. Title insurance is the opposite of your home's casualty and liability insurance, which repay you in case of injury or damage occurring after the effective date of the policy. Title insurance only covers matters that occurred before the policy's effective date, but were discovered later. Instead of having to pay premiums year after year to maintain the coverage, you only have to pay once to be covered as long as you own the property. Note, however, that many lenders insist on a new policy before refinancing to make sure their new loans will have first priority. They want to know if you have taken out a second mortgage, obtained a home improvement loan, or been subject to a court judgment between the time of the original mortgage and the new one. (For more information about title insurance, see chapter 4, "Buying and Selling a Home.")

Q. What's the difference between an owner's policy and a mortgagee policy?

A. The **owner's title insurance policy** covers losses or damages you suffer if the property really belongs to someone else, if there is a defect or encumbrance on the title, if the title is unmarketable, or if there is no access to the land. The latter could occur, for example, if you would have to cross a private road to get to your house and the owner of the road refuses permission.

The lender's **mortgagee title insurance policy** includes all four of these protections. But it protects only the lender. Particularly important policy clauses for the lender are the ones that cover losses the lender would suffer if another creditor were first in line.

Owners' policies are more expensive. If the same insurer issues both, the concurrent mortgagee policy will probably cost far less—in part because the insurer doesn't have to search the records twice. The limit of the owner's policy is typically the market value of the house at the time of the purchase, while the mortgagee policy is for the amount of the mortgage. The premium is based on the amount of coverage and may vary greatly by state.

Q. What isn't covered by title insurance?

A. Title insurance policies are fairly standard. An owner's policy usually does not cover one or more of the following matters, often referred to as **standard exceptions:**

- claims of people who turn out to be living in the house, such as the prior owner's tenants or someone living there without your knowledge, if their presence there is not a matter of public record;
- boundary-line disputes;
- easements or claims of easements not shown by public records;
- unrecorded mechanic's liens (claims against the property by unpaid home improvement contractors);
- taxes or special assessments left off the public record; and
- mineral and/or water rights (especially in the western states).

In most states, you can get **extended coverage** for these standard exceptions by paying an additional premium and furnishing additional evidence to the title company, so that these exceptions from coverage can be deleted or limited. Other common exclusions from coverage include

- zoning;
- environmental protection laws;
- matters arising after the effective date of the policy;
- subdivision regulations;
- building codes and the effect of any violation of these codes;
- problems the insured caused or already knew about; and
- problems not shown in the public records and not disclosed to the insurer.

ⓘ REFINANCING

If you are refinancing, your new title insurer will probably rely on the work of the individual or company who did a title search when you bought the home. If you provide the prior owner's policy as evidence of a good title, the new insurer will simply bring it up to date by checking what you have done to affect the title, such as selling part of the property to your neighbor. If a big problem surfaces that the original title insurer should have caught, the second insurer may go after the first to cover the claim. Likewise, if you have an abstract, the insurer may bring it up to date and base the policy on that. Contact a lawyer if you have questions about your title policy.

Exclusions need to be removed by special endorsements and probably will result in additional premiums. (In some states, exclusions for problems not shown in the public record cannot be removed.) Even in a policy "without exceptions," title insurers will also list as a special exception matters of record, such as subdivision restrictions, or anything they find that might turn into a claim, whether it is this year's property taxes or the power company's easement across the property. Check your current policy to see what's on the list, in case there's anything you should be concerned about.

Ownership Options

Q. How does the deed affect property ownership?

A. The ownership description on the deed has long-term significance—both in the duration of the title and whether you are free to transfer your interest to someone else. Today, the most common form of ownership is **fee simple**. The term "fee simple" comes from feudal England, where a noble landholder would grant an estate, called a fee, to a faithful subject in exchange for service or money. If the lord intended for the tenant to be able to keep the estate in the tenant's family after he died, the lord would include the phrase "and his heirs" in the legal document. That phrase may appear on your deed, indicating fee simple ownership. Some states, though, have dispensed with it.

Fee simple is the most complete form of ownership, because, in theory, title in fee simple is valid forever. People who own property in fee simple may sell it, rent it out, transfer it to their beneficiaries, and to some extent limit its use in the future. Under some of the other forms of ownership, such as an **estate for years**, the title reverts to the former owner at some specified time.

While it is still possible to transfer a life estate in property, it is rarely done because it severely restricts the new owner's ability to sell the property.

Q. Should both my name and my spouse's appear on the deed?

A. The way in which your deed states ownership has critical long-term implications, including who can transfer interests to someone else, how much of the property is available to one owner's creditors, whether the property goes through probate when one co-owner dies, and whether the surviving owner faces a tax on any capital gain when it is time to sell.

It's important to think about what you want the deed to accomplish because, depending on your state law, at least three ownership options may be available—sole ownership, joint tenancy with right of survivorship, and tenancy in common. In some states, married couples also may opt for owning the property as tenants by the entirety. (For more on these topics, see chapter 18, "Estate Planning.")

Q. What is the most common form of joint co-ownership?

A. For couples, whether or not married, the most common form of ownership in most states is **joint tenancy with right of survivorship**. In this form, each person owns an undivided interest in the real estate. At the death of one joint tenant, the interest of the decedent is automatically transferred to the surviving owner, who becomes the sole owner of the property. When property is held in joint tenancy with right of survivorship, the beneficiaries of a deceased joint tenant have no claim to the property, even if the deceased mistakenly tried to leave the property to them in a will. Most couples choose this form of ownership to avoid having their home involved in probate after the first spouse dies.

But couples who have children from previous marriages may want their home equity transferred to their children at death rather than to their spouses in which case this form of ownership is not suitable.

Tenancy by the entirety operates similarly but requires that the tenants be spouses. This form of ownership is not recognized by some states. Consult a lawyer to determine the form of ownership most advantageous to you.

Q. What is a tenancy in common?

A. Tenancy in common gives each owner separate legal title to an undivided interest in the property. This allows the owners the right to sell, mortgage, or give away their own undivided interests in the property. When one owner dies, the deceased owner's interest in the property does not go to the other owners. Instead, it transfers to the decedent's estate. This might be an appropriate form of ownership for those who want their beneficiaries, rather than the other owners, to inherit their interest in the property.

Q. What's the difference between joint tenants with survivorship and tenants in common?

A. They have many similarities: two or more people who own a home as joint tenants with survivorship or as tenants in common are each considered the owner of an undivided interest in the whole property. That is, if there are two owners, each is presumed to own half (unless specified otherwise in the deed), but not a specific half such as the north half. If there is a court judgment against one owner, the creditor may wind up owning that person's interest in the house. In some states, an owner may sell his or her interest to someone else, whether the other owner approves or not. Such a sale ends a joint tenancy, so the new owner becomes a tenant in common with the remaining original owner(s). (The arrangement is complex if, say, A, B, and C own a house as joint tenants and A sells her interest to D; in that case, B and C are still joint tenants with respect to two-thirds of the property, but tenants in common with respect to D's third.)

The chief difference between joint tenants and tenants in common is the **right of survivorship.** If one joint tenant dies, the property automatically belongs to the other owner or owners, avoiding probate. If three people own it and one dies, the two surviving owners each become owners of an undivided one-half interest. But if the

> ### ▶ DOES OWNING A HOME AFFECT YOUR ESTATE?
>
> Ownership of property could very well affect your estate, depending on the type of ownership you have in the home. For example, if you are a joint tenant, your home will pass directly to the other joint tenant and will not be a part of your estate.
>
> As you acquire equity in your home, your estate could be vulnerable to federal estate tax or state inheritance tax, if the equity along with your other assets exceeds certain statutorily established sums. If you do not have a will, you should consider preparing one now that you own a home. (For more details, see chapter 18, "Estate Planning.")

owners are tenants in common, the other owners have no rights of survivorship—they would receive the deceased's interest in the property only if it was specified in his or her will or by inheritance.

Q. How do you stipulate that you are joint tenants?

A. The deed must specify that the property is held in a joint tenancy arrangement. The usual language for this is "Mary Smith and Amy Smith, as joint tenants with right of survivorship and not as tenants in common." That way, if there is a question—say from Mary Smith's children, who think they should inherit her half interest in the property—the intent of the owners will be clear.

It's especially important to specify joint tenancy on the deed. Otherwise the law assumes that the owners are tenants in common (except in some states, where their ownership constitutes tenancy by the entirety if they are married to each other, as explained below).

Q. What is tenancy by the entirety?

A. If the co-owners are married to each other, at least one other option may be available, depending on the law of the state where the property (land) is located. This form is for married couples to share ownership as a **tenancy by the entirety**. Its roots lie in the common-law concept that a husband and wife are one legal entity. As with a joint tenancy, this form bears a right of survivorship; if one spouse dies, the surviving spouse continues to own the whole property.

In most states that still recognize this form, a husband and wife who purchase property together are considered tenants by the entirety unless the deed very specifically states that they are tenants in common (or joint tenants) and not tenants by the entirety. Otherwise, a deed saying "to John Smith and Mary Smith, his wife," creates a tenancy by the entirety.

Q. What if one spouse wants to transfer a half interest to someone else during the marriage?

A. The ability to do so depends on where the couple lives. In most states that recognize tenancy by the entirety, one spouse's interest may be transferred, whether by sale or gift, only if both spouses sign the deed. However, in some states, either spouse may transfer his or her interest—including the right to survivorship. Therefore, it is important to know what law applies in your state.

Q. In what states are these various options available?

A. Sole ownership, joint tenancy, and tenancy in common are available in all states, though certain specific details of ownership may vary by state. Tenancy by the entirety is available in about 40 percent of the states, most of them in the eastern half of the country.

Q. Are there any special considerations if you live in a community property state?

A. There are eight community property states—Arizona, California, Idaho, Louisiana, Nevada, New Mexico, Texas, and Washington—plus Puerto Rico. A ninth state, Wisconsin, has certain community property features in its law. A tenth state, Alaska, changed its law in 1998 to allow married seniors to select community property as an alternative form of ownership of their property.

If you live in a community property state, the law may assume that the house that you acquired during the marriage by the efforts of either spouse is community property unless you specifically say otherwise in the deed. Both husband and wife probably must sign to transfer the property to someone else. Chapter 3, "Family Law," contains more information on community property.

Q. Which form of ownership is best?

A. That depends on your circumstances. You or your spouse may want to be able to bequeath half of your house to someone else. For example, if you are in a second marriage with children from the first, you may want to avoid joint tenancy with your spouse because your children could not inherit your interest if you died first. But if you don't want the house included in the estate after one of you dies, joint tenancy might be a good idea. If you are married and have reason to expect creditors to come after your house, you may want the protection offered by a tenancy by the entirety, if available in your state, because property owned by both of you in that form generally isn't subject to a judgment against one spouse.

If you live in a community property state, be aware of two significant tax advantages of holding the house as community property rather than as a joint tenancy. The first advantage has to do with tax on capital gain, which is the difference between the selling price and the house's **basis**, its cost when you took title (plus allowable adjustments). If you hold the property as community property, when the surviving spouse inherits the whole, the property receives a new tax basis (called a **stepped-up basis**) that reflects its current value. The practical effect of this is to minimize capital gains taxes if the survivor sells it soon thereafter. Unless your profit on the sale is more than $250,000 this may be irrelevant, because since 1997 tax law has allowed people to exclude the gain from the sale of their primary residence, up to $250,000 per person or $500,000 per couple, as many times as they wish as long as they've lived in the house at least two years of the five years prior to the sale.

Let's say the property was purchased initially for $250,000 and is now worth $600,000. Without the stepped-up basis, you could owe capital gains taxes on $100,000, which is the profit on the house less the surviving spouse's $250,000 exclusion. If you hold the house as community property, then with the stepped-up basis you would owe nothing if it sold for $600,000. But if you hold it as joint tenants, only half an interest changes hands when one spouse dies, which means that only half the property gets a stepped-up basis.

The other tax advantage to community property involves estate taxes. In 2004, subject to reductions in some cases for predeath transfers, every American may bequeath up to $1.5 million without paying federal estate taxes; in 2006, the amount rises to $2 million. (In some states, you still may be liable for state inheritance tax on lower amounts.) If you and your husband do not live in a community property state and hold all your property as joint tenants, none of the jointly-held property will be part of your husband's estate when he dies first. You will then own all the jointly held property free of federal estate taxes, since property can generally pass between husband and wife without tax consequences. But if your estate exceeds the exemption amount at your death, it will be subject to federal estate taxes when you die. If you live in a community property state, however, your husband's one-half share of your community property, along with whatever property he might have had separately, is his estate, and it will not be taxed unless it exceeds the exemption amount. Some or all of it could be passed to your children, tax free. Because of his death, your estate might not grow beyond the exemption amount, and thus would not be subject to tax upon your death.

Q. Should a married couple ever title their house in only one name?

A. In addition to estate tax planning considerations, one of the chief concerns when deciding whether property should be owned in a single name is liability for court judgments. For example, take the case of a house in the husband's name alone. Let's say he loses a lawsuit over a car accident and his insurance won't cover the judgment. Because the property is solely his, he might be forced to sell it to cover the judgment. (In twenty-two states, some protection is offered through a homestead exemption, which allows people to keep a small house to live in.)

Some people might want to title the house in only one name precisely to avoid such judgments. For example, a doctor without malpractice insurance might want to deed the house to her husband. But consult a lawyer about all the aspects of your situation, including tax and possible fraud implications, before making such a decision.

▶ **CHANGING THE FORM OF OWNERSHIP**

It's fairly simple to take care of the paperwork of changing the form of ownership. Basically, you sign a new deed and file it with the local recorder of deeds. But using the wrong type of deed or the wrong wording can have serious consequences. Consult an experienced property lawyer to make sure you consider all the aspects of your situation and get it done correctly. In some jurisdictions, a straightforward change may have a minimal cost; but elsewhere, transfer fees/taxes and recording fees could add up to a fair amount.

Q. How does the form of ownership affect the property settlement in a divorce?

A. In about 90 percent of all divorces, the parties divide the property up themselves in out-of-court settlements, often with the help of lawyers and mediators. The husband and wife decide what is fair and reasonable in a process of give and take. In contested divorces, it's up to the judge to decide who gets what.

Years ago, courts in most states had no authority to redistribute property in a divorce, so their job was to sort out the legal titles. Only jointly held property was subject to judicial division. But today courts are more concerned with what's fair than with whose name is on a deed. They consider a wide range of factors, from the length of the marriage to the needs of each party.

So who gets the house? If there are minor children, usually the home goes to the custodial parent. If there are other assets to divide, the noncustodial parent may get a bigger share of them to balance out loss of the home. If not, courts typically award possession of the house to the custodial parent until the children grow up. Then the house is to be sold and the proceeds divided between the parties. If neither party can afford to maintain the home, the court may order it sold promptly and the equity split. Chapter 3, "Family Law," contains more information on the division of property in a divorce.

Handling Property Constraints

Q. What is a lien?

A. A **lien**, which dates back to English common law, is a claim to property for the satisfaction of a debt. If you refuse to pay the debt, whoever files the lien may ask a court to raise the money by foreclosing on your property and selling it, leaving you with the difference between the selling price and the amount of the lien. (Your mortgage lender, though, is ordinarily first in line for payment.) It's possible to lose a $200,000 house over a $5,000 lien, although someone with a

$200,000 house would probably be able to figure out some other way to satisfy the lien.

There are several types of liens, any of which creates a cloud on your title. For example, a **mechanic's lien** or **construction lien** can occur if contractors or subcontractors who worked on your house (or suppliers who have delivered materials) have not been paid. They may file a lien at the local recording office against your property. If the lien is not removed, it can lead to foreclosure or inhibit your ability to sell your home. Liens often are filed in connection with divorce decrees. If two homeowners divorce, the court often will grant one of them the right to remain in the house. When that owner sells it, however, the former spouse may be entitled to half the equity. The divorce decree would probably grant that spouse a lien on the property for that amount. If everything goes as it should, the former spouses will get the full payment of their respective shares at the closing. Sometimes a lien created by a divorce decree is not registered, so if a purchaser is buying a house that may be subject to a divorce decree, a lawyer should examine all relevant documents to ascertain whether a lien exists. Title insurers should also be on notice to check the divorce decree.

Likewise, if you bought a home with your spouse but later divorced, your own divorce decree might give your former spouse a lien on the home for half the proceeds. That lien can hinder your ability to sell the home if your former spouse refuses to release the lien. A divorce lawyer may try to build a release mechanism—such as an escrow containing the deed and release—into the divorce decree.

Q. Can a lien be filed for unpaid child support?

A. Many states impose a lien on the property of divorced parents who fail to pay child support. That lien would have to be paid off before the property could be sold.

Q. What is adverse possession?

A. Although you have a right to keep trespassers off your land, under the law it's possible for someone who occupies the property for many years to actually become the owner. This entitlement is called **adverse possession**. It's very unlikely to occur in urban or suburban areas, where lots are plotted and homeowners know when someone else has been using their property continuously. But if you own an unvisited beach house or hunting cabin, you might not know that someone has been living there continually for years.

Adverse possession is similar to a prescriptive easement, in which, for example, a court declares that your neighbor has a right to keep his or her hedge on a strip of your land because it has been there for forty years. The difference is that while prescriptive easements concern use of the land, adverse possession ripens into actual ownership. For a claim of adverse possession to succeed, the person occupying the property must show that his or her occupation of your property was open and hostile, which means without permission. As with prescriptive easements, granting the person permission to use the property avoids a claim to ownership by adverse possession. The occupation must also have continued for a certain number of years—generally ten to twenty, but sometimes fewer, depending on the state. And in many states, the occupier must have paid local property taxes on the land.

▶ **REMOVING A LIEN**

If you discover a lien on your property, see a lawyer to determine the best course of action. If the lien is valid and for an affordable amount, the advice might be to pay it and clear the title. However, just paying it off is not enough. Have the payee sign a release-of-lien form, and file it at the county recording (or "land title") office to clear the recorded title. If the amount of the lien is major and you believe it's not your debt, consult with your lawyer about what action to take.

This last requirement provides a way to avert loss of a property through adverse possession. If you suspect that someone has been living in your hunting cabin, check the property tax records for that county to see whether anyone has made tax payments on it.

A bit of vigilance will prevent problems in this area. You should post "no trespassing" signs to warn people that this is private property. Erect gates at entry points and keep them locked. Ask trespassers to leave, and call the police if they refuse. If you suspect that someone will keep on using your property (such as for a road to obtain lake access) despite your efforts, consider granting written permission to keep on doing so, especially if the use doesn't interfere with your use. This will bar adverse possession, which requires that permission not have been granted. To make the arrangement clear, ask for a written acknowledgment, and, if reasonable, a fee or payment.

Q. What is an encroachment?

A. An **encroachment** occurs when your neighbor's house, garage, swimming pool, or other permanent fixture stands partially on your property or hangs over it.

In the case of a neighbor's roof overhanging your property, or a fence being two feet on your side of the line, your rights might be tied to the prominence of the encroachment and how long it's been in place. If it was open, visible, and permanent when you bought your home, you may have taken your property subject to that encroachment. The neighbor may have an **implied easement** on your property to continue using it in that manner. If the encroachment is less obvious, you may only discover it when you have a survey conducted for some other purpose. In that case, you might have a better chance of removing the encroachment.

A house addition could create an encroachment if it starts twenty-three feet back from the sidewalk and the local setback ordinance requires twenty-five feet. The neighbors could band together and sue you, hoping you would be forced to raze your addition. Or you might have to live with your neighbors' disapproval, perhaps after paying a fine to the city for the violation.

It's even possible to encroach on an easement—for example, by locating the apron of your swimming pool on the telephone company's easement across your property for underground cables. In that case, the company would have a right to dig up the concrete and charge you for it. If you plant bushes on the easement, the company could dig them up and not have to replace them.

Q. What can you do about an encroachment?

A. First, you could demand that the neighbors remove the encroachment. If they refuse, you could file a quiet title lawsuit or ejectment lawsuit and obtain a court order. In a **quiet title lawsuit,** you would ask a judge declare your title to the property, and clear the property of any other interests or claims. You could seek similar orders in an **ejectment action,** which is a legal action you can bring to determine who has superior title to the property.

Of course, this isn't the best course if you wish to maintain neighborly feelings, especially if the fixture in question is merely the cornice of your neighbor's house. Further, if prior owners of the neighboring property have used that bit of your land for quite a few years, your current neighbor could ask a court to declare a prescriptive easement to maintain the status quo.

Second, you could sell the strip of land to your neighbors. Perhaps you didn't know quite where the boundary line was anyway, so you might agree on a new one on your side of the encroachment and file it with the county recording office. Caution: If you or your neighbor has a mortgage, you will need to obtain the consent of the lender before either of you can transfer any land.

Third, you could grant written permission to use your land in that way. This maneuver can actually ward off a claim for prescriptive easement or adverse possession, because perfecting either of these claims requires showing that the use was open and hostile (without permission). If you like this neighbor but may not like those who follow, you might grant permission only as long as that neighbor owns the property. Your lawyer could draw up a document granting permission and file it for you.

The primary question when someone has encroached slightly onto your property is how important it is to you. Typically, disputes over encroachments arise when there's discord among neighbors. If everyone is getting along fine, chances are you can live quite happily even though your neighbors' fence does creep onto your land. Note, though, that the encroachment needs to be disclosed when you put your house on the market. An encroachment could derail a sale. Remember that when you go to sell your property, you will want to make certain that the buyer agrees to the encroachment in the contract of purchase, so it doesn't become a title issue at closing.

Government Rights to Property

Q. Can the government force me to sell my property?

A. Since ancient times, governments have had the right to obtain private property for governmental purposes such as building roads and public buildings. This principle is called **eminent domain.** In the United States, it's limited by the Bill of Rights, which grants a right to due process of law and fair compensation when the government takes a person's property. Federal and state governments may delegate their condemnation power to municipalities, highway authorities, forest preserve districts, public utilities, and other agencies. A public purpose can include anything from building a new freeway ramp to declaring your soggy back acres a protected wetland.

Q. What should I do if the government wants to take my land?

A. If the government wants your land, chances are you'll hear about it informally ahead of time.

The best approach at this time may be to rally the neighbors in hopes of influencing the authorities' plans. For example, the town might be persuaded to narrow the proposed road that would eat up some of your yard. Your first official notice will be a letter indicating interest in acquiring your property (or a portion of it) for a certain purpose. That's when informal negotiations should kick into high gear. With or without your consent, the government then has your property appraised and makes you an offer, called the **pro tanto award**, which you may accept or refuse. If you accept it, the government may ask you to sign a document waiving your right to sue for more money. Some governmental units offer a bonus to entice people into accepting the pro tanto award, because it's cheaper than going to court. In a typical project, about 75 percent of the property owners accept the government's initial offer. The rest sue for more, but three-quarters of them settle the case before trial.

If you think the offer is too low, retain a lawyer experienced in eminent domain cases to negotiate for you and prepare your case for possible trial. If the case does go to trial, it's a battle of experts who testify to the value of the property, which is ultimately decided by the jury.

Q. Can the government seize my property without paying me?

A. If you've been convicted of a crime, the federal government can seize any property used in the crime, including your house. The property may then be sold and the proceeds used to further the government's crime-fighting efforts. So if you own a crack house, your arrest and conviction may lead not only to jail time but also to permanent loss of the house and your equity in it.

For those of us who steer clear of crime, the good news is that recent changes in federal law make it far less likely that the government will seize our property. From 1970 to early 2000, police who even suspected you of committing a crime such as drug dealing or terrorism could seize any property that might have been involved, whether it was a car, an airplane, a boat, or a house. So if the tenant in your rental house was suspected of growing marijuana in the basement, the police could seize the house and sell it. It would be up to you to prove that your property should be returned. That law cost innocent property owners enormous litigation fees just to get their property back.

After a seven-year legislative battle over these **civil forfeitures**, Congress amended the law. Signed into law in May 2000, the **Civil Asset Forfeiture Reform Act** prohibits the government from confiscating property unless it can show "by a preponderance of the evidence" that the property is substantially connected to the crime. This is a much higher standard of proof than "probable cause." Property owners no longer have to post a bond in order to challenge a civil forfeiture, and they have more time to file the challenge. If a property owner successfully challenges the seizure in court, the government has to pay legal fees. And if the confiscation causes substantial hardship to the owner, the government just may release the property.

Under the new law, as long as you're staying away from crime, one thing you almost certainly don't have to worry about is the government seiz-

---

ⓘ FEES FOR EMINENT DOMAIN CASES

Sometimes the government authority condemning the land pays the lawyers' fees for the property owner. In other cases, some lawyers who specialize in eminent domain cases work on a contingency basis. Their fee is a given percentage of the difference between the initial offer and the ultimate settlement. You might want to set up a fee arrangement in which you pay a flat fee or an hourly rate for initial review, negotiation, and counteroffer, then switch to a contingent fee if the matter turns into a lawsuit.

ing your property and selling it. To be on the safe side, avoid the appearance of criminal activity in your house and vehicles. And if your property should be seized, retain a knowledgeable, assertive lawyer as fast as you can.

THE WORLD AT YOUR FINGERTIPS

- *You can learn more about the federal Fair Housing Act at the Department of Housing website at www.hud.gov/offices/fheo/FHLaws.*
- *Consumer information on what to expect when closing a home purchase is available from the American Land Title Association. Its website includes links to state land title associations; visit www.alta.org/cnsrinfo/closeproc/index.htm.*
- *You can find more information on community property states and what this form of ownership means at www.fairmark.com/spousal/comprop.htm.*

REMEMBER THIS

- *In general, owning property means you can do with it what you wish. However, because other people have rights, too, your property rights may be restricted by state and federal laws, zoning and noise ordinances, and restrictive covenants.*
- *Your title insurance policy pays you and your lender if there turns out to be problems with the title to the property.*
- *The way your deed creates title—sole ownership, joint tenancy with right of survivorship, tenancy in common, and so on—matters in cases of divorce, sale of the property, liability, and death of an owner. Make sure your deed says what you intend it to.*
- *Your property might be subject to adverse claims such as liens or encroachments. Depending on how major they are, you*

might want to consult a lawyer on how to handle them.
- *Government entities have a right to take your land for public purposes, but they have to pay a fair price. If you start talking to the agency early, you may be able to influence the project so it doesn't take as much of your property. If not, a lawyer experienced in the law of eminent domain can help you negotiate a fair price.*

PROPERTY INSURANCE AND OTHER PROTECTIONS

What if you wax the floor to impress your dinner guest, but she skids across it, falls, and breaks her leg? What if the excavation for the dream house you're building causes your neighbor's basement wall to cave in? Or what if your new pet Doberman takes a chunk out of the mailman's backside?

In any of these cases, you could be liable for thousands of dollars in damages. Any time someone gets hurt on your property because of your carelessness, you may be legally responsible. The same applies when you or your children do things that damage someone else's property. One of the major functions of property insurance is providing coverage for your liability. The other major function is helping you repair or replace your property when it's stolen, damaged, or destroyed. Theft, fire, tornado—if it happens to you, you'll be glad to have a good homeowner's policy in place. But it's important to know what your policy won't cover, such as damage from slow leaks. It's also important to know how to protect your property from preventable perils, from lead poisoning to burglary.

This section begins with a discussion of liability issues, including when you're responsible and how to reduce the chance that someone will get hurt. Then it moves to protecting your home and health from a wide range of perils. It includes suggestions on reducing your risk and making sure you'll have enough money to start over should the next sad story on the evening news tell what happened to your house.

Floor Wax and Dog Attacks: Liability Issues

Q. Am I responsible if someone has an accident in my home or on my property?

A. The question of legal responsibility hinges on whether your **negligence** (that is, carelessness) contributed to an accident or injury. Homeowners are **liable**, meaning legally responsible, only if a court finds them in some way negligent. Of course, many cases settle out of court before this point if the homeowner or her or his insurer believes that a court would find the owner negligent.

For example, in some states, a homeowner might be considered responsible if someone slips and falls on the icy sidewalk outside the front of the house. Other common injuries and negligence suits involve power lawn mowers, swimming pools, boats, and other recreational vehicles. Most homeowners carry insurance, and the insurance company generally handles any claims against the homeowner. It's only when the insurer believes the claim is unreasonable that the matter is likely to land in court. Even then, the insurer will provide the lawyer and pay any damages awarded (up to the limit of the policy), along with court costs.

Still, facing a lawsuit and going to court is no fun. Lawsuits involve months of depositions, motions, and counter motions before the trial even gets started. Even after a verdict is rendered, a party may appeal, and the battle could go on for years. As a homeowner, you are far better off both preventing injuries on your property in the first place and protecting yourself with a comprehensive insurance policy in the event the unavoidable and unexpected does occur.

Q. Am I responsible for anyone who enters my property?

A. Historically, the law identified various categories of people who might be injured on your property, from people you invite onto the property to trespassers. The category of the injured party dictated the homeowner's duty of care. Although in a few jurisdictions a trespasser is still categorized separately from "lawful" visitors, the courts in most states hold property owners to the same standard with respect to everyone: a duty to employ reasonable care in maintaining your property and to warn people of hazards. This means, for example, that if you permit someone to pick gooseberries on your property, you are obliged to warn the berry picker that the local gun club is holding target practice nearby.

Generally, courts hold homeowners responsible only if they are in some way negligent. The law does not expect the homeowner to guarantee that someone visiting his or her house will not get

---

ⓘ LIABILITY RISKS

Negligence is usually the basis of a liability suit. Take steps to avoid the conditions that would prove carelessness. Here are some examples of cases in which a court might find you negligent:

- Failure to maintain your property, or creation of a condition that may result in injury or damage to someone else's property

- Knowledge of a hazard and lack of intent to eliminate the hazard, erect barriers, or warn people who enter your property

- Lack of care in maintaining the property or creating hazards that might attract children

- Actions or inaction that might cause damage to your neighbors' property

hurt. But it is the homeowner's responsibility to take reasonable care to protect people from known hazards.

Q. What happens if someone is injured on my property and we are both at fault?

A. While your best defense to any charge of negligence is that you exercised due care, there are several other defenses available. In some cases, a jury may decide that although a homeowner was partially responsible for what happened, the person injured was also partially responsible. This is called **comparative** or **contributory negligence.** For example, if you forget to tell your houseguest that you have just dug a pit in your backyard for the new septic system, and the guest decides to get a breath of fresh air and wander around in the backyard in total darkness, a jury might find both of you partly responsible for your guest's broken leg. In that case, the jury might reduce the amount of the damage award you might otherwise have to pay.

In other cases, the jury might decide to absolve you of any responsibility because of what the law calls **assumption of risk.** For example, when a Georgia homeowner and his neighbor were trying to get rid of a nest of wasps, the neighbor climbed a ladder and sprayed the nest with insecticide. The wasps swarmed out, and the frightened neighbor fell off the ladder. When he sued the homeowner for the resulting injuries, the court ruled that the neighbor knew perfectly well that wasps tend to swarm, yet he assumed the risk. In that case, the homeowner was not liable.

Q. What is the difference between natural and artificial hazards?

A. Generally, courts do not hold homeowners liable for injuries stemming from natural hazards such as lakes and streams, even if a child is hurt, unless some other negligence is involved. Homeowners are more likely to be responsible if the hazard was created artificially. For example, a man who was pushing a child on a tree swing while attending a barbecue in New York stepped back onto a rotted plywood board covering a sewer trap,

which gave way under his weight. A court found the homeowners liable because they knew about the danger and made it worse by hanging the swing where anyone pushing a child on it would have inevitably stepped on the rotted cover.

On the other hand, take the case of a Nebraska man who just finished shoveling snow off his driveway in the freezing mist. While he was inside getting some salt to finish the job, the mail carrier slipped and fell on the driveway. The mail carrier sued, but the court ruled the homeowner was blameless because he did not create the hazard and was doing his best to eliminate it.

Q. What about liability in regard to children?

A. The law concerning a property owner's responsibility for children, even when they are trespassing, has changed over the years. In 1901, when a five-year-old drowned after falling into an uncovered excavation that had filled with water, the court ruled that because the child was a trespasser and the property owners didn't know there were children around the pit, they weren't liable. Even then, however, another legal doctrine was evolving, stemming from injuries caused to children playing on railroad turntables left unsecured in areas frequented by the public. In a series of late-nineteenth-century cases involving such injuries, the courts found the railroads negligent. The courts ruled that some dangerous places look like such fun that landowners should expect children to come play.

The law calls such places **attractive nuisances.** Even though an uninvited child wandering into your yard to inspect the swimming pool might well be a trespasser, the law says you have a special duty to erect barriers to protect children from harm's way. That's why the Supreme Court of Georgia refused to dismiss a case against the owners of a swimming pool in which a two-year-old drowned. The swimming pool was in the side yard of their home on a corner lot, three blocks from an elementary school. The yard and swimming pool were not fenced in, and the pool had both a diving board and a slide.

Another case involved a Michigan family that stopped at a private home to buy raspberries. While the adults were talking, two preschool boys wandered into the garage, where they found a loaded gun. One boy shot the other. The court ruled that although homeowners cannot be expected to make their homes childproof, those who have reason to expect children to come around—such as the couple who sold raspberries from their home—should expect children to act on childish impulses and should take steps to protect them.

The message is clear: If there is a way in, a child may find it and may get injured, and you may be liable. That's why precautions such as fences, locked gates, and swimming pool covers—and good liability insurance—are so important.

Q. Am I responsible for damage caused by my children?

A. As a rule, parents are liable for injury and damage caused by their minor children (eighteen years of age and younger). Usually, such damage caused by children thirteen or under will be covered by your homeowner's policy. In many homeowner's policies, damage and injury are not covered if the children are older than thirteen and intentionally cause the damage or injury. The best way to avoid liability is to teach your children to respect other people and their property.

Q. If I host a party in my house, am I liable for my guests' actions?

A. Some courts have ruled that a host is not responsible for the conduct of guests, unless your parties routinely turn into brawls. Likewise, if one of your guests is horsing around and hurts himself, you probably will not be liable. But you might be liable if you let your guest drink too much, then put him into his car and send him out on the highway. That's what happened in a landmark New Jersey case, in which the homeowners had been drinking whiskey for a couple of hours with one of the husband's subcontractors. They walked him to his car, saw him off, and called shortly to see if he'd made it home. He hadn't.

Thoroughly drunk, he was in a head-on collision in which a woman was seriously hurt. The case went to the state supreme court, which held the hosts liable. It's a lesson worth remembering. You can buy an insurance policy to cover host liquor liability, but it's far better to keep the drunks off the road.

Q. What about liability concerning my pets?

A. The law holds people responsible for the actions of their pets. Most states have so-called **dog-bite statutes**, holding owners legally liable for injuries inflicted by their animals. If your state has no such statute, you may still be found liable under the common-law rule that owners are legally responsible if they knew the animal was likely to cause that kind of injury. In California, a couple was convicted of criminal negligence after the pit bull they kept in their apartment attacked and killed a woman in the hall.

Many states and municipalities also have enacted **vicious dog statutes**, which enable an animal control officer or a judge to declare a particular dog or specific breed of dog vicious and require the owner to confine the dog securely or

---

ⓘ RECREATIONAL USE OF PROPERTY

If you own a lot of land and allow someone to use it free of charge for hunting, fishing, skiing, or some other recreational activity, you are probably not liable if the person gets hurt. In the 1970s, virtually all states enacted **recreational use statutes,** designed to encourage people to open their land for recreational use without fear of liability. The statutes do not protect you if you charge a fee or if you're malicious in your failure to warn of hazards. For more information about such statutes in your area, contact a local lawyer.

muzzle it in public. Some states make it illegal even to own a breed of dog that has been declared vicious. Some cities have imposed an outright ban on all pit bulls, which they consider inherently vicious. Many jurisdictions ban wild animals such as wolves, bears, and dangerous snakes from being kept as pets.

If you own a dog or another animal that might injure someone, call your local animal control office to find out the laws in your area. Know your pet's temperament and keep it out of the path of strangers. Keep vaccinations current, and post warning signs if you think your pet might injure someone. These signs should be prominent and straightforward, such as "Beware of Dog," so people are clearly informed of the danger involved. However, the signs may not absolve you from liability if a child climbs into the yard or the dog gets out.

Q. Can I be held liable if my tree falls on my neighbor's house?

A. Traditionally, property owners were not responsible for damage caused by falling tree limbs and other natural occurrences on their property. However, they were responsible for damage caused by artificial conditions—for example, if a high wind blew a loose board from your lumber pile through your neighbor's plateglass window. The current trend suggests the courts are applying an ordinary standard of care to measure negligence in both cases. This means that maintaining your property in good condition is an important protection against a negligence suit.

For example, if your trees have visible rot, you should cut them down or trim rotted limbs before they can fall on your neighbor's property. Trees should be maintained well enough that short of a tornado or hurricane, the wind won't blow limbs from your place over to your neighbor's.

Q. What is my liability for excavations and other changes on my property that may affect my neighbor's property?

A. If you excavate near the property line and cause your neighbors' land to sink, you may be liable whether their house is affected or not. Check with a civil or geological engineer if you think you have reason to be concerned. Your builder or contractor will know of one, or you can find one yourself through the yellow pages.

Similarly, if changes you make to the contours of your land cause excess rainwater to pour onto your neighbor's property and result in damage, you may be liable. If you are planning to change the contours of your land, ask a lawyer or your local building inspector about your state law.

Q. What other kinds of problems should I be concerned about?

A. Basically, if you're acting reasonably and responsibly, maintaining your property and carrying homeowner's insurance, you shouldn't fret about liability. If you're planning any changes to your property, however, you should investigate local laws to ensure that any changes will not violate them. The following areas can hold special concern:

- *Waterfront areas.* If you live along a river or stream, state and local laws designed to protect wildlife habitats may preclude your clearing brush or changing the lay of the land. Don't make these changes without checking with your department of conservation, natural resources, or wildlife, usually located in the state capital.
- *Pollution.* You could be liable for the cost of cleaning up pollution stemming from underground oil tanks or old dump sites on your property, whether or not some other party caused the problem in the first place. Look into this before you buy a piece of property, because there's not much you can do about it afterward. Ask the seller if there are any such problems, and have your lawyer include a clause in your purchase agreement that covers you in the event such problems arise. If there's special concern because of the unique nature of the property, you might even consider hiring an environmental consultant.
- *Wetlands.* Federal laws govern the draining and filling of wetlands. If you have places on

your property that are boggy even part of the year, avoid serious legal trouble by finding out what your responsibilities are before making changes. You might start with your state's department of environmental protection, probably located in the state capital. The federal Office of Wetlands Protection in Washington, D.C., also might be able to help.

- *Utility lines.* As a rule, you are not liable for maintenance of utility lines crossing your property. To be safe, don't do anything to cause potential damage to utility lines, such as planting fast-growing trees under them.

Q. *What should I do if someone is injured on my property?*

A. First and foremost, do all you can to help. Express concern, ask what injuries might have been suffered, make the victim as comfortable as possible, call for medical assistance, and so on.But don't say anything to suggest or admit guilt or negligence. While it's natural to empathize with the injured party and to want to soothe any pain and suffering, as well as your own feelings of guilt, it's not a good idea to complicate your potential liability with such statements. Rather, leave it up to the law to decide who was responsible.

ⓘ A CHECKLIST FOR A SAFE HOME

- Repair steps and railings.
- Cover holes.
- Fix uneven walkways.
- Install adequate lighting.
- Clear walkways of ice and snow as soon as possible.
- Be sure children don't leave toys on steps and sidewalks.
- Replace throw rugs that slip or bunch up.
- Reroute extension cords that stretch across traffic lanes.
- Repair frayed electrical cords.
- Keep poisons and other hazards out of the reach of children, even if you don't have children.
- Warn guests about icy conditions and other hazards.
- Restrain your pet.
- Erect barriers to your swimming pool, an automatic pool cover or a tall fence with a good lock that you lock, and an alarm on any door leading to the pool.
- Remove all guns or keep them securely locked and out of sight, where children cannot see them or gain access to them.
- Remove nails from stored lumber and secure any lumber piles.
- Don't leave ladders standing against the side of the house or the garage.
- Don't let children stand nearby when you mow the lawn.
- Don't let your guests drink and drive, or drive under the influence of drugs.

Notify your insurer in writing (and speak to your lawyer) as soon as possible. Don't talk with the other party or his or her lawyer about liability until you've taken these steps. You may well decide later to offer to defray some medical bills of the injured party, but do this after you have had the chance to review the situation with a clearer head and the appropriate parties.

There's one other situation in which the law requires you to act. If someone has been hurt on your property or is in danger, you may have a legal duty to offer humanitarian aid even though you had nothing at all to do with the injury. For example, a Minnesota cattle buyer became severely ill while inspecting a farmer's cattle. A court later ruled that the farmer had a duty not to send the man, who was helpless and fainting, out on the road alone on a cold winter night.

Liability Insurance

Q. What is liability insurance?

A. The liability portion of your homeowner's policy is designed to cover unintentional injuries on the premises and unintentional damage to other people's property. In other words, injuries caused by your negligence are covered; those you inflict on purpose are not covered. Given your potential liability as a homeowner, you're asking for trouble if you don't carry adequate liability insurance. It takes only one person who is seriously injured by your negligence to generate a huge liability award and deplete your financial nest egg, not to mention your psychological well-being.

Q. What kind of liability coverage is provided by a typical homeowner's policy?

A. A typical homeowner's policy includes $100,000 of liability insurance, which won't go far if someone is severely injured. For a slight increase in premium, you can raise that to $300,000 or $500,000. Some companies offer coverage of $1 million or more. Typically, coverage includes harm caused by your children and pets, except inten-

tional harm if the child is over thirteen. (If your pet attacks people routinely, the insurer may cancel your policy or refuse to renew it.)

Most standard homeowner's policies do not cover

- employees and clients of your home-based business, including the children in your home-based day care if you take in more than three children and have no special endorsement;
- claims by one member of the household against another; and
- any disease you pass on to someone.

Q. What is an umbrella liability policy?

A. An **umbrella liability policy,** also called a **personal excess liability policy,** is designed to

---

ⓘ WORKERS' COMPENSATION

If you have a home-based business that involves people coming to your house, be sure to obtain a separate business rider. Also, if you have a swimming pool or other special hazard, check the policy provisions to make sure you're covered.

If you have domestic employees, even part-time help such as a nanny, you may be required to carry workers' compensation insurance, which costs a little more than $100 per year. Workers' compensation sets limits on awards. If you don't have it, you could have to pay far larger damages, and there may be civil and criminal penalties if you don't carry it. Contractors working on your house should already have workers' compensation for their employees. You should ask to see proof of such coverage, and don't hire them if they don't produce sufficient verification or don't have adequate coverage.

protect you in case of a big judgment that would quickly eat up your regular policy coverage. These policies are relatively inexpensive because the insurers are betting you'll never need to file a claim. Their coverage takes up where your home and auto policies leave off; thus, you will need to have certain levels of basic home and auto liability insurance before you can qualify for an umbrella policy. Generally, these would be $100,000 in liability coverage on your homeowner's policy and $250,000/$500,000 on your auto ($250,000 per person, $500,000 per accident; or sometimes $300,000 in single-limit coverage).

You also have to meet certain eligibility requirements, such as owning no more than four cars. If you've been convicted for driving under the influence of alcohol in the past three years, you're not likely to get approved for coverage.

Some umbrella policies pay the deductible amount that isn't covered by basic policies. Others impose a deductible, called a **retained limit,** in certain circumstances. For example, if your homeowner's policy doesn't cover slander or libel (most don't without a special endorsement), an umbrella policy with a retained limit might require you to pay the first $250 of a judgment for slander. The other kind would pay from dollar one. Note that most umbrella policies don't cover injuries you cause with your motorcycle and certain watercraft, such as high-powered speedboats.

Your premium for the umbrella policy will be determined based on the number of houses, rental units, and vehicles you own. If you have one house and two cars, a typical premium costs $100 to $150 for $1 million in coverage. You will get $2 million in coverage for only about $50 to $100 more in premium costs.

Homeowner's Insurance

Q. What kind of homeowner's insurance do I need?

A. Broadly speaking, a homeowner's policy is a package deal designed to pay for the repair or replacement of your house and belongings, plus extra living expenses if, for example, you and your family have to stay in a motel for several months while your home is being rebuilt. It also covers claims and legal judgments against you for injuries people suffer in your home or damage you cause. How much the insurer pays depends, of course, on the limits of your policy, which in turn depends on how much you've paid in premiums.

Although details of insurance policies vary among companies, the general forms of coverage are fairly standard. Many homeowners opt for an inexpensive **basic policy,** called HO-1 or HO-A, which pays actual cash value of your home and contents in case of loss due to specific causes, such as fire. This minimal type of policy usually satisfies lenders, because they are interested only in your ability to repay the mortgage, not rebuild your house.

Many financial professionals recommend policies that provide at least 80 percent **replacement value,** rather than actual cash value, of your home in the event of damage from specific causes, such as fire and theft. These are called **broad policies,** or HO-2 or HO-B. In most cases, you're better off with replacement value, because

---

ⓘ WHO NEEDS AN UMBRELLA POLICY?

People usually determine their need for umbrella liability coverage not so much by how many hazards they have on their property as by the assets they have to protect. After all, the wealthier you are, the more you have to lose if someone is injured on your property. Some people buy $5 million in coverage, and some even take out umbrellas over their umbrellas. Consult your insurance agent to help decide what type and amount of coverage is best for you.

it usually costs more to replace the house than its "market" or "cash" value. Note that "replacement cost" is estimated by the insurance agent, and, for an additional small fee, guaranteed replacement cost coverage will protect you if your agent has underestimated the cost of replacing your home. Another way to guard against underinsurance is with an **inflation guard clause,** which increases the face value of the policy either according to the annual increase in local construction costs or by a given percentage every three months. This rider can reduce the chances of your being underinsured, but it doesn't guarantee replacement cost.

For the best protection, a **comprehensive** or **all-risk policy** covers any kind of damage except specific exclusions, such as floods and earthquakes. Even with this type of policy, however, insurance for luxury items, jewelry, art, and antiques may require separate riders. If you live in a condo or a cooperative, an HO-6 policy gives you coverage similar to the HO-2. A few companies do offer all-risk coverage for condo and co-op owners. As with any other type of significant purchase, it pays to shop around.

Q. What isn't covered by a homeowner's insurance policy?

A. Most policies specifically exclude damage caused by floods and earthquakes, and some policies will exclude or limit theft in high-crime areas. This doesn't mean that you can't purchase insurance for these threats; it simply means that you must pay for riders on your policy. Homeowner's policies also provide little if any coverage for home businesses. If you're operating a home business, check with your agent to see whether your business is adequately protected.

Q. Does homeowner's insurance cover natural disasters?

A. Not necessarily, because the differing nature of these perils is treated differently by the insurance industry. Consumers are often confused about what their homeowners' policy covers and what it doesn't. The following guide shows what coverage is available for specific types of disasters and how you get it:

- *Floods.* Flooding can come from many sources—rivers, lakes, the ocean, and so on. In some states, sinkholes are a big issue. Homeowner's policies absolutely exclude damage from flooding, except for a narrow range of cases such as a pipe or a water tank bursting. You can't get an endorsement to cover it at any price; however, if your community is in a flood-prone area, you can probably buy a special policy as part of the National Flood Insurance Program, administered by private insurers and backed by the federal government. Any insurance agent can sell flood policies. The cost depends on what measures your community has taken to reduce the risk of flood damage. Until your community meets the standards of the federal flood-control program, only limited coverage is available: up to $35,000 for a single-family house and $10,000 for its contents, for a cost of about $250 per year. Once the community meets the standards, you can get up to $185,000 for a single-family house and $60,000 for its contents. The premiums depend on the structure of the house and how close it is to the water, but in a moderately flood-prone area, $60,000 of coverage on a house and its contents might cost about $150.

- *Earthquakes.* The state of California requires insurance carriers to offer earthquake coverage to anyone in the state who carries one of their homeowner's policies. Usually it's an endorsement to the regular policy, expanding the coverage for a fee. But if a California policyholder decides not to buy or renew the endorsement, the carrier isn't obligated to give him or her a second chance. Of course, given the risk, earthquake endorsements in that part of the country don't come cheap. The annual premium on a $100,000 house could be anywhere from $150 to $1,200, depending on the location of the house and the materials used in its construction. Brick houses, for example, would be at the high end of the spectrum. Deductibles on earthquake endorsements are usually 10 percent of the coverage for the structure and its contents, figured separately. In other parts of the country, you can get earthquake endorsements, often for next to nothing—but most people don't because they don't expect to need them.

- *Tornadoes and hurricanes.* Although standard homeowner's policies cover windstorms, you may need extra protection if you live in an area such as Florida or Texas that is especially prone to hurricanes or tornadoes. In these areas, standard coverage may not be available; you have to buy a special policy, such as the beach and windstorm insurance plans available in seven Atlantic and Gulf Coast states. As with flood insurance, any licensed agent or broker in those states can sell it.

- *Volcanoes.* Volcanoes are specifically listed as a covered peril in standard homeowner's policies.

Q. How much does homeowner's insurance cost?

A. The cost of homeowner's insurance varies greatly with the policy coverage and the age, location, and replacement cost of your home. It pays to shop around for the cost of insurance premiums, but be sure that you are comparing similar, if not identical, coverage. Another way to reduce costs substantially is to opt for a high deductible, such as $500 or $1,000, if you can afford to pay such an amount yourself in case of damage. You also may qualify for a discount if

---

▶ **SHOPPING FOR INSURANCE**

Whether you're buying your first policy or shopping for better price and coverage, begin by listing your possessions and estimates of their value. Get your house appraised, either by an insurance representative or an independent appraiser, to figure out what it would cost to rebuild at current prices. Note valuables that might require special coverage. Then take the following steps:

- Talk with several different agents about your insurance needs. Ask them to quote premium costs with higher and lower deductibles. Compare costs and coverage. Check the reputation of the companies you're considering. Rating services study companies' financial stability and ability to pay claims. These include A. M. Best, Moody's Investor Services, Standard & Poor's, and Duff & Phelps. (For websites, see "The World at Your Fingertips" on page 167.) Your insurance agent should have the latest ratings for the companies he or she works with.

- Ask your agent to help you interpret the ratings scales, which vary between the services and can be confusing. You want to be reasonably sure your insurer will be able to pay your claim.

- Watch out for policies that limit recovery on personal possessions to "four times the actual cash value." This could mean you would get less than you need to replace your old furniture and drapes.

- Avoid policies that limit reimbursements to what the insurance company would be able to pay for a given item, because the company could probably buy it wholesale.

- Keep your agent informed of additions to your house and major purchases that might affect the level of coverage you need.

- Periodically review your coverage to make sure you're adequately insured.

you've taken particular safety precautions, such as installing deadbolt locks or cabling your mobile home to the ground. Ask your insurance agent what discounts are available and what you would need to do to qualify.

Q. What should I do if I need to file a claim?

A. The claims process for theft or damage to your home or its contents is fairly basic, but it will go more smoothly if you have taken inventory of your possessions and their worth ahead of time. In case of theft, first call the police. Then call your agent or company immediately. Ask whether you are covered for the situation, whether the claim exceeds your deductible, how long it will take to process the claim, and whether you will need estimates for repairs. Follow up your call with a written explanation of what happened. If you need to make temporary repairs to secure your home or protect it from the elements, keep track of expenses, but don't make permanent repairs until the adjuster has inspected the damage.

Don't do business with someone who comes to your door after a loss, claiming to be an adjuster. There are scam artists out there eager to take advantage of your misfortune.

Q. What can you do if you have a problem with your insurance company?

A. If you're dissatisfied with the way your adjuster handles your claim, first talk to your agent. If that doesn't help, call the company's consumer affairs department. Then try the National Insurance Consumer Helpline , which might be able to suggest a course of action. Finally, you could call your state's insurance department to complain and ask for help.

If these approaches do not bring a satisfactory settlement, consider hiring your own independent adjuster for an independent appraisal of your damage. You'll have to pay a fee of 10 to 15 percent of your final settlement. Check with your state insurance department, though, to find out whether public adjusters have to be licensed in your state.

Another option may be arbitration of the dispute with your insurance carrier. If both parties agree to arbitration, or if it is required by your contract with the insurance company, an inde-

---

▶ **TAKING INVENTORY**

Although you don't need a detailed inventory to buy insurance, and you can eventually get a sizable check from the insurance company without one, the claims adjusting process goes a lot more smoothly if you have clear, accurate records. The time-honored method is to fill in a **household inventory booklet** available from your agent, recording purchase dates of furniture, equipment, and valuables and estimating replacement costs. It helps to attach bills of sale, canceled checks, or appraisal records. The more detail you can include, the better.

Another option is to use a computer software package designed to categorize records of personal possessions and make it easy to update them. Some of these programs can print out the records room by room, in case of partial damage to your house.

For a visual record, consider either photographs or a videotaped tour of your house, complete with commentary. Include the insides of closets and cabinets, and take close-ups of computers, jewelry, and other valuables.

Be sure to have a backup copy of your inventory in a safe place away from your home. Send a copy to your lawyer, store it in a safe-deposit box, or leave it with a friend.

pendent arbitrator (perhaps selected by the lawyers for both sides) will hear the arguments and decide what compensation you're entitled to. For disputes involving just a few thousand dollars, it's probably cheaper to present your own case in small-claims court.

Security Issues

Q. What should I do if there's an intruder in the house?

A. Everyone's afraid of finding someone in the house at night. If it happens, avoid a confrontation—your life is more important than your possessions. If possible, run away and call the police. If you can't get yourself and your family out of the house, lock yourselves in a room. If you're face-to-face with an intruder, stay calm and be cooperative.

Q. May I shoot the intruder?

A. You do have a legal right to protect yourself and your property, but recognize that you may end up in court if you shoot an intruder or whack him over the head with an iron pipe. You would have to argue that you really did act in self-defense or in defense of your property, and it would be up to the jury to decide whether to believe you.

Basically, the law says that you can use reasonable force to defend yourself if you're being attacked or if you have a reasonable belief that you will be attacked. That is, you don't have to wait until the intruder is actually coming at you with a knife. The key word here is "reasonable"; the jury would have to decide whether a reasonable person would have thought that a toy gun was real or that a hand going into the pocket was reaching for a weapon.

Q. What is considered "reasonable force"?

A. States vary widely on what they consider **reasonable force**. In general, if you use force against an intruder, use no more than appears necessary. That is, if a shout sends the burglar running, don't pull a gun and shoot him in the back. If a single blow stops a burglar in his tracks, don't beat him to a pulp. If the intruder isn't threatening bodily harm to someone in the house, you're on shaky ground if you use deadly force. Some courts have held that a homeowner who could retreat safely isn't justified in beating or killing the intruder. Likewise, courts have held that a homeowner isn't justified in attacking a burglar if it appears that a shout or warning would be enough.

What about booby-trapping your home to keep burglars out? People have gotten into serious legal trouble for this sort of thing. Even if you're fed up with repeated break-ins, you can't set up a gun rigged to shoot anyone who comes through the window. First, it's not up to you to impose a death sentence on someone who might try to break in, and second, the next person through the window might be a firefighter trying to save you.

Q. Does the law prohibit me from killing wild animals on my property?

A. It depends on the animal. Many states allow the killing of gophers, rattlesnakes, and coyotes without a permit, but most states impose hefty fines for killing other wild animals without a permit. Your state department of fish and wildlife has jurisdiction over wild animals, and a call to the nearest office will probably get you some advice. In some cases, it's not difficult to deter an invading animal. An eight-foot-high fence will stop most deer. Dried blood or a commercial mixture should repel rabbits. Storing trash so that it's not accessible to raccoons quickly forces these very smart (and often rabid) animals to find new territory.

Some animals are difficult to deter. Farmers lose thousands of dollars of crops to deer, pronghorns, and other graceful neighbors. In the West, ranchers cope with marauding bears and coyotes. Many states assist farmers with reducing the damage, and some reimburse farmers and ranchers for wildlife damage. Note that in most cases reimbursement programs, which are funded by hunting license fees, aren't open to farmers who bar hunters from their land.

Environmental Hazards

Q. *What kinds of environmental hazards should I be concerned about?*

A. A home can look and smell fine, yet have deadly lead dust in the air, cancer-causing radon in the basement, or an underground oil tank leaching oil into the water table. Although toxic waste regulations apply to homeowners in much the same way as they apply to businesses, no laws require asbestos, lead, and other contaminants to be removed from owner-occupied residences. It's a matter of health and safety for you and your family.

Q. *How do I determine if there's an environmental problem in my home?*

A. In some cases, you may find out about a problem accidentally, such as when a painter points out lead-based paint on your woodwork or a re-

---

ⓘ A CHECKLIST ON HOME SECURITY

How easy would it be for a crook to get into your home? Experts advise homeowners to begin by looking at their home as a burglar might. Identify the easiest place to get in and make it harder.

- Are there exterior lights at the front and back of the house?

- Are there shrubs around your doors and windows that a burglar could use for cover? Better trim them. Do you have a privacy fence that could provide burglars with too much privacy?

- Do you have deadbolt locks on your doors? Do you keep them locked, even if you're out working in the yard?

- Are your doors solid, at least 1 1/4 inches thick, and do they fit snugly in the frame?

- Have you put in a specially designed lock for your sliding-glass door?

- Could a burglar slide a window open from the outside and climb in? If you have double-hung windows, a removable nail pinning the upper and lower halves together is quite effective.

- Should you consider grates for your street-level windows? (Be aware that they can trap you inside in case of fire.)

- Would an alarm go off if an intruder stepped inside? Burglars hate noise.

- Is there a sticker on your window declaring you have an alarm system? That may be enough to scare off some would-be intruders, whether you actually have an alarm system or not. Another tip: The sticker might help experienced burglars, who might know how to disable the alarm system of a particular company; you can counteract that by displaying the sticker of one company but using the system of another company.

- Do you ever leave your house keys with your car keys when you have your car parked? Do you carry house keys on a key ring with a name-and-address tag? Do you hide a key in a secret place outside your home? Burglars know where to look.

- When you go on vacation, could strangers tell that you're gone? Don't let mail and newspapers pile up outside, and make sure your lawn stays mowed and your walks stay shoveled. Use automatic timers for lights and a radio, and leave your blinds open in their usual position.

modeling contractor finds asbestos around the furnace and won't proceed until it's removed. You might learn about lead the hard way when your children can't think straight, or about contaminated water when the whole family gets sick. Health problems from asbestos or radon, however, wouldn't show up for another thirty years. The only way to discover and correct the problem may be to hire an expert to conduct the right tests.

Federal rules exist that require sellers to disclose information about lead-based paint; and in a growing number of states, sellers are also required by law to inform potential buyers when they know about other hazards in the house, like asbestos or radon. Then it's up to the buyer and seller to work out who's responsible for dealing with it. The seller might lower the price to compensate the buyer for having to cope with the problem. In other states, the general rule is caveat emptor, or "let the buyer beware." In these states, a seller can't set out to misrepresent or hide the condition or lie if asked, but there's no obligation to disclose the problem. These days, though, homebuyers often make the offer contingent on a satisfactory result of testing. Regular home inspectors aren't usually qualified to test for lead or radon, so getting an accurate test would require hiring a qualified specialist.

If you intend to test for radon, asbestos, lead, or other household toxins, be careful about whom you hire to test and deal with it. For example, people claiming to be asbestos consultants and contractors may find asbestos and try to convince you that it must be removed right away, even though the proper treatment for asbestos in many cases is to leave it in place. Then they'll remove it unnecessarily, which is a waste of money, and do so improperly, which can increase the health risk. To avoid such scams, do some research on the nature of each home toxin, and find out what services are available and what procedures and precautions the job involves to be done correctly. For names of licensed professionals in your area, check state or local health depart-

ments or Environmental Protection Agency (EPA) regional offices. As with any home improvements contractor, ask for references from previous clients, make sure the contractor has done similar projects, and get estimates from more than one. (See "Remodeling" on page 177 for information on hiring contractors.)

Q. What is asbestos?

A. **Asbestos** is a fibrous material found in rocks and soil worldwide. Until the early 1970s, it was widely used in flooring, walls, shingles, ceiling tiles, and as insulation or fire retardant for furnaces and wiring. When the material crumbles or flakes, tiny asbestos flakes escape into the air. You breathe the fibers, they persist in your lungs, and with repeated long-term exposure you're likely to develop lung or stomach cancer.

Q. What should I do about asbestos in my home?

A. If the asbestos-containing material is in good shape—not flaking or peeling—and not likely to be disturbed, the best thing to do is leave it in place. But if it's going to be scraped, hammered, sawed, or otherwise disturbed in a remodeling project, a trained professional should be contacted to find a way to minimize the dissemination of the material.

Since total removal is expensive and difficult, intermediate options include applying a sealant or covering it with a protective wrap or jacket. It's tricky business, and even the cleanup needs to be done with a special vacuum cleaner to avoid scattering asbestos fibers. Don't try any of this yourself. Make sure the contractors you hire don't track it through the house or break the old material into small pieces.

To avoid conflict of interest, anyone you hire to survey your house for asbestos shouldn't be connected to an asbestos correction firm. The federal government, as well as some state and local governments, offers training courses for asbestos consultants and contractors. Ask to see documentation proving that everyone working with asbestos in your home has completed state or federal training.

Q. Why is lead dangerous?

A. Lead is a soft, metallic element occurring naturally in rocks and soil all over the world. Until fairly recently, it was commonly used in pipes, plumbing solder, paint, and gasoline. If you breathe particles of lead dust or drink lead-contaminated water, it accumulates in your blood, bones, or soft tissue. High concentrations of lead can cause permanent damage to the brain, central nervous system, kidneys, and red blood cells. Lead is especially dangerous for infants, children, pregnant women, and the unborn because growing bodies absorb lead more easily and their tissues are more sensitive to it. Also, a given concentration of lead is worse on a child's smaller body than an adult's. In residential buildings, lead paint and lead in drinking water pose the major dangers.

Q. What can you do about lead in drinking water?

A. Lead-based solder has been banned since 1988, but homes built before then often have lead solder that corrodes into drinking water. You can't tell whether pipes leach lead by looking at them, but a simple chemical test can identify it. If you want to have your water tested, ask your local, county, or state health or environment department about qualified testing laboratories. If you're having plumbing work done in an older home, check for lead pipes. Even new faucets and fixtures can put some lead into the water. One way to reduce the risk is to run the faucet for one minute before using water for drinking or cooking. Never use hot water from the tap for drinking, cooking, or especially for making baby formula. Heat increases the leaching of lead into water.

If you do have lead in your water, several devices are available to reduce corrosion, including calcite filters, distillation units, and reverse-osmosis devices. Be aware that water softeners and carbon, sand, and cartridge filters are not effec-

tive for removing lead. Get qualified advice before buying or leasing a device, as their effectiveness varies.

Q. What should be done about lead paint?

A. Lead-based paint was applied to about two-thirds of the houses built before 1940 and a third of those built between 1940 and 1960, according to the EPA. Lead paint tastes sweet, so children have been poisoned from chewing on flakes of paint. There is also a potential danger from lead dust that is stirred up when lead-based paint on woodwork is scraped, sanded, or heated with an open flame stripper. Then it settles in fibers and fabric and gets stirred up again by normal cleaning.

The only accurate way to tell whether your house has lead-based paint is to remove a sample and have it tested in a qualified laboratory. Contact a local, county, or state health or environmental department about where to find one.

If lead-based paint is in good condition and there is no possibility that it will be nibbled on by children, it's best to leave it alone. Otherwise, you can cover it with wallpaper or some other building material or completely replace the woodwork. Removing lead paint properly and safely is a time-consuming and expensive process that requires everyone else to leave the house during removal and cleanup.

If the house was painted on the outside before 1950, the surrounding soil is probably contaminated with lead. Don't leave patches of bare soil, and clean your floors and windowsills regularly with wet rags and mops. Make sure everyone in the family washes their hands frequently.

Q. Are there any laws regulating disclosure of lead paint hazards?

A. Federal lead-based paint disclosure rules were enacted in 1996, and require sellers or landlords to disclose any information about lead-based paint hazards when selling or leasing to any purchaser or tenant of residential housing built before 1978. The rule also requires disclosure by brokers and real estate agents. In addition, the seller or the landlord must provide the purchaser or the tenant with an EPA-approved lead pamphlet, and copies of any record or inspection report concerning lead-based paint. The purchaser must also be given the opportunity to perform a lead inspection within ten days of signing the purchase agreement, unless the purchaser waives its right of inspection. If lead is found in the house, the rule does not require the seller to pay for a lead inspection or to remove the lead. Finally, the parties must sign a lead disclosure form, stating that the purchaser received a pamphlet and any records or reports relating to the lead-based paint.

The EPA conducts inspections of lease and purchase agreements at realty firms in order to check compliance with the rule. A person who leased or purchased a home from a seller who did not comply with the rule can bring a civil action against the seller for treble damages.

Also note that some states have stricter laws regarding lead paint and rental units. In Massachusetts, for example, few landlords would rent their units to people with children under age six unless the unit had been deleaded. That's because landlords can be held liable for any lead-induced illnesses that later develop in these children if the unit had not been deleaded.

Q. What is radon?

A. **Radon** is a colorless, odorless, tasteless gas resulting from the natural decay of uranium in the earth. It comes into your house through small cracks, floor drains, wall/floor joints, and the pores in hollow block walls, and tends to accumulate in the lowest level of the home. It can also get trapped in groundwater, so homes with wells are more likely to have a radon problem. Radon particles get trapped in your lungs, where they break down and release bursts of radiation that can damage lung tissue and cause cancer.

Q. How do you test for radon?

A. Testing for radon in well water requires sending a sample to a laboratory for analysis. Inexpensive test kits for radon in the air are available at hardware stores, but be sure they have been approved by a federal or state health, environmental, or consumer protection agency. Long-term testing over a year is most accurate, but short-term testing can let you know if you have a potential problem.

Most homes contain from one to two picocuries of radon per liter of air (pCi/L). If rooms in your home have more than four picocuries of radon per liter of air, it should be reduced. This normally isn't a do-it-yourself project, but professional radon-reduction contractors can determine the source of the gas, seal leaks, and install fans, pumps, or other equipment to keep it out. Special filter systems can remove radon from your water supply. Depending on the number of sources, the amount of radon and the construction of the home, installing radon-reduction equipment costs anywhere from several hundred to several thousand dollars but in most cases is less expensive than deleading.

Q. What is considered toxic waste?

A. Toxic waste is usually associated with chemical companies or nuclear reactors. But a residential property also can harbor toxic wastes that are potentially dangerous to the homeowner and neighbors. For example, many family farms have a ravine or a back lot that's long been a handy place to dump old tires and empty pesticide containers. Or a private home may have a leaky heating-oil tank buried under the backyard, either one still in use or an abandoned one that was never emptied when the heating system was converted to natural gas or electric heat. Oil, pesticides, or other toxic substances from these sources can seep fumes into a neighbor's basement, contaminate nearby wells, or migrate through the water table until there's an oil slick on the nearest creek.

Q. Who is responsible for cleaning up toxic wastes?

A. The law may hold homeowners responsible for the cost of cleaning up toxic waste sites even if they had nothing to do with creating the problem. Responsible parties are jointly and severally liable, including the current homeowner, the owner of the property when the pollution was caused, and the person or company who caused it (which could be another party altogether). **Jointly and severally** means that any one of them can be forced to pay the entire cost. That may be the current homeowner, who is probably the easiest one to find. Then it's up to the homeowner to find the others and sue to recover the cost.

When someone discovers the problem and contacts the city or county health department, an inspector will come out to conduct tests and determine the source of the pollution. The cost of investigation alone can be expensive. Then the department will clean up the site according to state regulations. The cleanup process might involve ordering the homeowner to hire a consultant and a remediation crew. If it's an emergency or an immediate threat to water quality, the agency may send someone in to clean it up, then sue the homeowner for reimbursement. But that is a difficult process; usually agencies first try to get the homeowner to take care of a problem.

The cleanup process may involve judgment calls and negotiation. Oil in the soil from a leaking tank, for example, will eventually degrade. Instead of hauling all the old soil out and replacing it, it might be less expensive to drill new wells for those affected. If your property has a toxic waste problem, hire a lawyer experienced with environmental matters to help you through the process. It might involve obtaining an analysis to estimate how long before the waste would degrade and how far and fast it's likely to migrate until then. In some cases, the negotiations turn into a battle of experts.

What if you don't think you should have to pay for the cleanup because you didn't have anything to do with causing the pollution? Your best hope is the **innocent landowner defense**, under the **Superfund Amendments and Reauthorization Act of 1986**, which limits the liability of a landowner who made **all appropriate inquiry**

into the environmental condition of the property before buying it. That means the only way you would be off the hook is if you had the foresight to have an environmental survey done before buying the property to see if hazardous substances contaminated it. That would include a visual inspection of the property and compilation of a history of past owners and their waste-disposal practices, contaminant releases and violations, and other information. Chances are you didn't do that. It's the sort of thing lenders sometimes require for commercial loans because lenders also can be on the hook for toxic waste sites.

In 2002, Congress revised old laws to release new owners of property with toxic waste on it from liability for environmental damage they didn't cause, if they comply with state or federal cleanup guidelines. This makes it far less likely that you'll be caught in a morass of litigation.

To prevent future problems, check with your local health authority to find out how to meet state regulations for disposal of motor oil, paint, antifreeze, and other toxic substances.

THE WORLD AT YOUR FINGERTIPS

- *You can find some useful, simple tips for making your home safer at a website operated by the Northern Illinois University Libraries: www.lib.niu.edu/ipo/ic020814. html.*
- *The MSN Money site explains the basics on umbrella insurance policies: moneycentral.msn.com/articles/insure/ home/1427.asp.*
- *You can use Internet tools to help you figure how much it would take to replace your home. The MSN Money site recommends some fast and cheap options: moneycentral.msn.com/articles/insure/ home/5726.asp.*
- *Rating services study insurance companies' financial stability and ability to pay*

claims. You can find out more about your insurance company at A. M. Best (www.ambest.com); at Moody's Investor Services (www.moodys.com); or at Standard & Poor's (www.standardandpoors. com). If you're dissatisfied with the way your insurance company handles your claim, you can call the National Insurance Consumer Helpline (telephone: 800-942-4242; fax: 212-791-1807), which might be able to suggest a course of action.

- *You can find more information about arbitration at the website of the American Arbitration Association at www.adr.org. For the name of an arbitration organization near you, contact Arbitration Forums, 3350 Buschwood Park Drive, Suite 295, Tampa, FL 33618 (telephone: 888-272-3453; fax: 813-931-4618), or the American Arbitration Association, 335 Madison Avenue, Floor 10, New York, NY 10017-4605 (telephone: 212-716-5800; fax: 212-716-5905; Customer Service: 800-778-7879).*
- *You can find more information about the lead-based paint disclosure rule, and sample disclosure forms, at the Housing and Urban Development site: www.hud.gov/offices/lead/disclosurerule.*

REMEMBER THIS

- *If someone is injured on your property because of your negligence, you're legally responsible. It pays to be careful, warn people of hazards, and carry plenty of liability insurance.*
- *Your homeowner's policy also covers property damage. That includes damage to your own property from a variety of perils and accidental damage to your neighbor's property caused by your family, your animals, your trees, or your personal property.*

Make sure the limits are high enough so you can start over in case of fire, tornado, or other calamity.

- *Standard homeowners' policies typically exclude coverage for floods, but if you're in a flood-prone area you can get a special government flood policy.*
- *It's better to prevent harm than to collect insurance for it. Take steps to protect your property and your health.*

MANAGING NEIGHBORHOOD PROBLEMS

An Illinois homeowner decided to add a second story to his modest ranch house. Then he set his sight on further expansion. Over the years he added on the house bit by bit until it looked like a 3,300-square-foot Taj Mahal, and he had plans to expand it still further to 5,700 square feet. For fifteen years his neighbors put up with noisy construction equipment, piles of lumber, stacks of clay roofing tile, and giant sewer pipes, with constant dust and debris. Fed up, the neighbors joined forces with the village to try to get the man to complete his project. The case festered in court for years, with no end in sight.

What your neighbors do with their homes may well affect you, whether because of the high fence blocking your view, the overgrown yard bringing down your property values, or the din of the teenage rock band practicing at full volume in the garage. This chapter addresses what you can do to cope with problem neighbors.

Handling Disputes

Q. What's the best way to handle a dispute with a neighbor?

A. Unless you intend to move, resolving a problem amicably is in your best interest. Neighborhood spats typically originate from minor disputes over boundary lines, fences, junk cars, noise, pets, and trees. If the problem cannot be solved between the two of you, different disputes call for different remedies.

In all cases, you'll want to know how the law, as well as municipal and subdivision regulations, can be put to use if you are unable to resolve things informally.

Q. How can I tell if my neighbor is violating a zoning ordinance?

A. City or county zoning regulations may limit the height of fences, the use of property for commercial purposes, or the decibels of noise allowed at night. In some cases, city officials notice a violation and issue a citation, but usually it's up to the neighbors to complain. If you suspect a zoning violation is causing the problem—such as the transformation of your vegetable garden into a shade garden thanks to your neighbor's new twelve-foot fence—check with your city hall or town council to see if there's a regulation on the books. Either the town hall or the local library should have copies of municipal ordinances.

Q. What can I do if my neighbor is violating a zoning ordinance?

▶ **SAMPLE WARNING LETTER**

Dear Neighbor,

Just as you enjoy playing your stereo, I enjoy a quiet environment in my home. It's impossible for me to do so when your stereo is played at such a loud volume.

Please read the enclosed municipal noise ordinance. You will see that the law requires that you comply and keep your stereo to a reasonable volume.

I trust that we can resolve this matter amicably, so that I will not have to contact the authorities. Thank you for your anticipated cooperation.

Sincerely,

A. Notifying the neighbors that they are violating an ordinance may take care of the problem. To file a complaint, you may have to contact the city attorney or the controlling agency, such as the local zoning board. If the city takes up the

---

▶ **STEP-BY-STEP GUIDE FOR RESOLVING NEIGHBOR PROBLEMS**

Step 1: Discuss the problem with the neighbor, who may not be aware that the late-night parties bother you or that Fifi is digging up your flowerbed.

Step 2: If things don't change, warn the neighbor. Obtain a copy of the applicable local ordinance (look in the **municipal code,** which should be found in your local library or in city hall, or contact your local council representative). Mail it with a letter of warning alerting your neighbor of a violation of the law. Be sure you keep a copy of the letter. Wait a reasonable time to see if the problem is resolved.

Step 3: Suggest mediation. Try to work out the problem with an impartial mediator to resolve the dispute informally.

Step 4: Contact the authorities. If all else fails, call the police and/or file a civil lawsuit against the neighbor.

▶ **HANDLING DISPUTES IN COMMON-INTEREST COMMUNITIES**

A common-interest community is real estate in which owners of a unit have an obligation to pay money to another person, usually an association, for maintenance, taxes, upkeep, and insurance of property other than the individually owned property. Condominiums and cooperatives are both types of a common-interest community.

If you are embroiled in a dispute in a common-interest community, check the bylaws and regulations of your development to see whether there is a rule against the activity in question. Your homeowners' association can be a powerful ally. After all, if a neighbor's actions are bothering you, they may be equally troublesome to other residents of the development. If your neighbor refuses to comply with your initial requests, consider asking other neighbors if the situation bothers them, too. They may be willing to sign a petition or a joint letter to the homeowners' association, which is more likely to draw the attention of the board than a complaint from an individual.

The association will investigate the complaint, ask for input from the offending neighbor, and then take a vote as to whether official action is warranted. If the board feels your neighbor has violated its governing rules, it will likely begin by issuing a formal warning letter. In extreme cases of noncompliance, homeowners' associations have referred the matter to the city attorney or have filed their own lawsuit against the offending resident.

---

cause for you, it will require less effort and expense on your part than filing a lawsuit. You won't receive money, but your neighbor will either be ordered to comply with the zoning rules, pay a fine to the city, or both.

Q. What constitutes a nuisance?

A. A **nuisance** is the legal term for a person's unreasonable action that interferes with your enjoyment of your property. Anything from noxious gases to annoying wind chimes may constitute a nuisance. The law of nuisance involves a balancing test, weighing the social value of the activity against the social value of your use and enjoyment of your property. Accordingly, authorities that have to deal with nuisance complaints expect them to be reasonable. For example, your distaste for your neighbor's cooking odors may not be enough to sustain a nuisance complaint.

Q. What can you do about a nuisance problem?

A. If your local ordinances make a nuisance a crime (usually a misdemeanor), the offender might be given a citation to appear in court at a given date, or he or she might even be arrested, held until posting bond, and ordered to appear in court. If convicted, the offender may be fined and/or jailed. If your local ordinances make nuisance a civil violation, he or she would face civil charges in court. The penalty for a civil violation is a fine.

Whether the alleged nuisance violates a civil or criminal city ordinance, the city carries the burden of prosecuting the case. Your role as the complaining neighbor is limited to testifying if the case goes to trial. Again, any money collected will be in the form of fines paid to the city, not to you.

The other option is to file a lawsuit yourself. Here you would bear the expense of bringing the case to trial, including filing fees and legal counsel, but if you won you could collect monetary damages from the neighbor, or obtain a judgment

⚠ WATCH THOSE BOUNDARIES

Before you erect a fence or other structure on your land, make sure that it is indeed your land. If you innocently, but mistakenly, erect a fence on your neighbor's property, you may be liable for trespassing on your neighbor's land. Your neighbor could ask the court for an injunction to make you tear down the fence, as well as money for any damage you may have caused to his or her property. Or, if your neighbors build a fence that encroaches on your land, your neighbor could get rights over your land, right up to the fence.

If your neighbors start building on land you believe is rightfully yours, notify them immediately. If you allow the construction to continue and wait too long to complain, you may be giving up your right to that strip of land. After many years of uncontested use, courts sometimes grant the party that has used the land a prescriptive easement allowing them to continue doing so.

How far over the boundary is enough to complain about? The reasonableness of the circumstances may dictate whether a court will support you. For example, a judge may not be too sympathetic to your request that a neighbor relocate a building that's an inch over your property line. The court may just reset the boundary line, with or without payment of damages. However, if that building is flush with your windows and blocking your sunlight and air, or twenty feet over the boundary line, the court may decide differently.

---

requiring him or her to cease or remedy the problem. Another approach that may be available in your area is to file in small-claims court, which would cost less and probably be faster. Either way, to prevail against your neighbor in court you will have to show the following elements:

- The neighbor is doing something that seriously bothers you. It helps to show a copy of a letter you wrote asking the neighbor to stop or modify his or her behavior.
- The neighbor's actions have reduced your ability to use and enjoy your property.
- The neighbor is responsible for his or her actions.
- In some states, the neighbor's conduct must also be unreasonable or unlawful.
- A request for a specific amount of money or an injunction directing the neighbor to do or to refrain from doing something would adequately deal with the annoyance.

Q. How can I handle disputes over boundary lines?

A. Disputes about boundary lines are less common than other neighbor-related problems, in part because of modern surveying techniques. Boundary lines may be set forth in the property description in your deed. Sometimes, though, if the property description was created decades or even centuries ago, that description may be a bit difficult to trace on the ground. If the neighborhood is platted, your legal description refers to a lot, and you will need to review the recorded plat for the dimensions of the lot.

If you and your neighbor are unsure where the boundaries lie, there are a number of alternatives:

- Spend a few hundred dollars to hire a surveyor.
- File a quiet title lawsuit asking a judge to determine the location of the boundary line. This is even more expensive because you will have court filing fees, lawyer fees, and possibly a survey if the court so requires.
- Agree with your neighbor that a certain imag-

inary line or a physical object, such as a fence or a large tree, will serve as the boundary. Have a lawyer draw up **quitclaim deeds** for both parties to sign, each granting to the other neighbor ownership to any land on the other's side of the line. Be sure to record the deed by filing it in the county records office (often called the **registry of deeds**). This may require the mortgage holder's approval.

Q. What can I do about noise?

A. In densely populated areas, noise is one of the most common sources of neighborhood tension. Some municipal ordinances limit noise to a given number of decibels. If the police have a decibel machine, you can ask them to measure the noise your neighbor is creating. This provides useful documentation should you need to proceed against your neighbor in court.

Timing is critical, though. Accordingly, many municipalities regulate noise levels during certain "quiet times" when most people sleep. They typically begin between 10:00 P.M. and midnight and last until 7:00 or 8:00 A.M. on weekdays; on weekends, they often extend to 9:00 or 10:00 A.M. But some noises may be unreasonable at any time, such as playing an electric guitar so loudly that it makes a neighbor's walls shake.

As with any nuisance, start by asking the neighbor to turn down the volume, and explain why. Keep a log of the noise—when it occurred, how loud it was, and how it affected your household. If the neighbor doesn't respond to a letter, consult with your town council about local ordinances that might need enforcement. Consider a lawsuit only as a last resort.

Q. My neighbor is letting his property fall apart. Is there anything I can do?

A. Blighted property decreases the value of surrounding homes and will frequently incur the wrath of surrounding neighbors. However, unless homeowners are governed by subdivision rules on exterior maintenance, they are generally free to choose how their property looks. The exception

occurs when a place is so neglected that it becomes a neighborhood eyesore, such as a yard overgrown with weeds or filled with trash, or a safety hazard, such as a dangerous structure.

If deterioration is a matter of the offenders' financial problems, perhaps you and other neighbors could pitch in for a "cleanup" day. If it's simply a matter of sloth, ask the offenders to clean up or repair what is broken. If they refuse your request that they clean up their property to a reasonable standard, you may be able to get the city to force them do it, provided it has an ordinance declaring blighted property to be a nuisance. If so requested by a resident—or if a city official observes the nuisance—the city may issue repeated notices to the offenders. In about 95 percent of the cases, homeowners clean up their property after the first notice. About 1 percent of the cases are actually prosecuted in court.

And if you are the one at fault, you may want to clean up your act. A California man was jailed twice after the city prosecuted him on misdemeanor charges over the piles of trash and junk cars on his property. While he was in jail, the city undertook the cleanup of his property—then placed a $15,000 lien on his home to recover the cleanup costs.

Q. What can I do if my neighbor is engaging in illegal activities?

A. First, if the problem is with tenants, contact the property owner, who may or may not know that the tenants are doing something illegal, such as selling illegal drugs. Some cities require such tenants to be evicted, or will fine landlords who allow such a nuisance to continue. In some cases, state and federal laws provide for the government to seize property that is being used for illegal financial gain. The threat of forfeiting the house to the government is likely to persuade the homeowner to evict the undesirable tenants. Another approach is for you and your neighbors to pursue a private lawsuit against a neighborhood nuisance. Neighbors can be a powerful, unifying force in these situations.

Pets

Q. What can I do if my neighbor's animals are creating a problem?

A. Some neighbors get along like cats and dogs—and in some cases, the problem is real cats and dogs. Consider the situation of two southern California neighbors whose yards were separated by a thick concrete wall. On one side was a litter of normally well-behaved Chinese chow dogs; on the other, two mellow cats. No problem—until the cats learned how to climb the wall, perch atop it, and glare down at the dogs. The dogs took to barking and yapping whenever anything stirred on the other side of the wall.

The entire neighborhood was unhappy. The cat owner blamed the dogs for the noise; the dog owner blamed the cats for teasing the dogs. Even more infuriated was a third neighbor, who worked nights and was trying to sleep when the "dog alarm clock" went off every morning. The trouble escalated when the dog owner started hurling shoes, balls, and other objects at the cats to chase them off the wall. One unidentified flying object sailing over the wall smacked the cat owner's child on the head. By that point, everyone was threatening to sue everyone else. The solution? The cat owner suggested a truce: The cats would go out in the mornings and the dogs in the afternoons. By late afternoon, all the animals could go out because the third neighbor would already be at work. The dog owner agreed to stop pitching things at the cats; the cat owner agreed to pluck the cats off the wall whenever she found them tormenting the dogs. The animal war ended as quickly as it had begun.

If you have a problem with a neighbor's pet, knowing your local laws can add clout to your efforts to resolve it. Your town probably has one or more applicable ordinances indexed under "Dogs" or "Animal Control" that can be enforced in court. Such laws often limit the number of animals per household, the length of time a dog may bark, or the frequency of barking allowed. Leash laws require that dogs not run at large, and pooper-scooper laws require owners to clean up after their pets. If polite requests to your neighbor don't work, call your local animal control service, which is likely to be more receptive to your problem than the police or other city officials. Unless the animal control authorities consider your complaint unreasonable, they will probably call the offending animal's owner with a warning, followed by a citation if the problem persists.

A citation is similar to a traffic ticket; it requires the offender either to pay a fine or to challenge the citation in court. After being punished in the pocketbook, many people will change their animals' behavior to conform to the law. If a person continues to allow his or her animal to annoy you, he or she can be fined repeatedly if you continue to complain.

If the problem persists, you may need to bring a civil lawsuit for nuisance to get a court order. The offender is likely to obey, because people who disobey a court order may find themselves in contempt of court. That can mean time in jail or at the bank, withdrawing hefty sums to pay a fine.

For animal problems, call the police only as a last resort. Police are generally not very interested in problem dogs, as they have more serious mat-

---

ⓘ CREATURE COURT

When fur flies between pet owners and their neighbors in Ventura County, California, the confrontation can end up in "animal court," a voluntary program and an alternative to formal court proceedings. There, the county's "poundmaster" presides over about a hundred cases each year, which have included a cat that bit a woman, a rooster that rudely awakened the neighborhood, and a variety of disputes over dogs that bit, barked, or intimidated children.

ters to worry about. Bringing the police into the equation also may sever any further relations with your neighbor.

Trees

Q. What's the law regarding trees?

A. Trees can cause as much contention between neighbors as yapping dogs, whether they block people's view, crack their foundation, or drop debris on their driveway. The general rule is that a tree whose trunk stands entirely on the land of one person belongs to that person; if the trunk stands partly on the land of two or more people, it usually belongs to all the property owners.

Someone who cuts down, removes, or harms a tree without permission owes the tree's owner money for compensation.

Q. Is there any way I can be prevented from cutting down the trees on my own property?

A. In most cases, the answer would be no, but trees are not strictly private property like barbecue grills. In some instances, neither the tree owner nor the neighbor has unlimited control over the fate of a tree. In some jurisdictions, the municipality has ordinances limiting a tree owner's right to cut the tree down. Or there may be a restrictive covenant in the deeds bearing homage to trees, as there is in one subdivision overlooking scenic Farmington Valley in Connecticut: Homeowners cannot cut them down, even on their own land. They can, however, trim diseased limbs or branches that block their view of the valley below. It is now also quite common for communities to have ordinances barring the cutting down of trees.

Subdivision rules such as this are designed to restrict the use of each lot in a tract for the benefit of all who reside there. One lot owner can enforce the restriction against another. If you are considering buying property in a subdivision, ask about any such restrictions in the general building plan.

Q. Can I trim the overhanging limbs of my neighbor's tree?

A. You may trim the branches of a neighbor's tree that hang over your property, with certain restrictions:

- You may trim up to the boundary line only.
- You need permission to enter the tree-owner's property (unless the tree poses **imminent and grave harm** to you or your property).
- You may not cut down the entire tree.
- Your trimming may not destroy the tree.

It's always best to notify the tree owner before starting any trimming, pruning, or cutting. If the owner objects to the trimming, offer reassurance that the job will be done professionally and responsibly, respecting the mutual rights of both parties involved.

Q. Am I liable for the encroachment of my trees or shrubbery on a neighbor's property?

A. The law varies from state to state, but generally it depends on the extent of damage done. It's best to avoid a confrontation—legal or otherwise. Tree roots are a more serious (and potentially costly) problem. You will save money in the long run by hiring a landscaper or "tree surgeon" to take whatever steps are necessary to prevent root damage to your neighbor's home or wall.

Views

Q. What are my rights regarding the view from my property?

A. Generally there is no absolute right to a view, air, or light, unless granted in writing by a law or subdivision rule. Such provisions are more common in coastal areas or other scenic-view locations. If a view is important to you or to the value of the property you are thinking of buying, be sure to investigate your legal rights to protect that view before closing the deal.

Q. Can my neighbor legally block my view?

A. What can you do if come home from work and find a new fence on your neighbor's land blocking your view of the mountains? That depends in part on where you live. The best way to protect a view is to purchase an easement from your neighbor, guaranteeing that no obstruction of your view will be built on the land described in the easement. (See page 140.) You may cringe at the thought of paying for a view that is already there, but in the long run it is likely to be less costly—and more scenic—to buy an easement now than to bring a lawsuit in the future.

For example, a Los Angeles Superior Court judge ordered singer Madonna to trim her driveway hedges to eight feet in height and to trim a pine tree down to her roof level—and to pay the legal fees of the neighbor who brought the lawsuit against her. The neighbor contended that the untrimmed foliage blocked his Hollywood Hills view of the city lights below and reduced the value of his property. He was able to prevail because he had a long-standing written agreement with her regarding his view, so he simply went to court to enforce that contract.

Unless you live in a community that has a view ordinance, you are unlikely to get relief in the courts without such a contract. But even given a view ordinance, the mayor won't necessarily jump in and order your neighbor to tear down the obstruction. If the city does not feel your complaint has merit, you will have to initiate a lawsuit and wait until your day in court to request an order requiring your neighbor to restore your view. Depending upon the backlog in your local courts, that wait could be months. And, of course, your neighbor might appeal the decision, causing another lengthy delay. In the interests of time and sanity, it may be advisable to forego the legal wrangling and negotiate with your neighbor.

If your city does not have a view ordinance, you can still ask a court to have the offending fence or tree removed if you can show that by erecting or planting it, your neighbor was **deliberately and maliciously** trying to block your view. This would fall under the category of "spite fences," discussed in the next section.

Fences

Q. What constitutes a fence?

A. The word "fence" is not limited to a picket or stockade-type barrier. Fence ordinances generally cover anything that serves as an enclosure or par-

---

ⓘ THE FRUITS OF YOUR NEIGHBOR'S LABOR

Fruit-bearing trees that overhang a neighbor's property pose a tasty dilemma. When apples drop onto the neighbor's property, is the fruit considered manna from heaven? According to a long-standing common law doctrine, no. The fruit belongs to the owner of the tree—and so it has been since the 1800s, when a man named Hale scooped up twenty bushels of pears from the orchard trees of his neighbor. A court ordered Mr. Hale to return his booty to the orchard owner, even though Hale had been standing on his own land when he plucked the fruit.

What if your neighbor's fruit is a problem for you? If rotting fruit habitually falls from a neighbor's tree into your yard, notify your neighbor, and ask him or her to clean the fruit from your yard and to trim the tree to avoid such droppings in the future. If he ignores your request or refuses to comply, your neighbor may be liable for any damages the errant fruit causes to your grass or garden. (The same thing goes for the fruit of a neighboring tree that may cause physical injury to you, such as a coconut that falls from a high tree and smacks you on the head.)

tition, including trees or hedges. Many zoning regulations restrict the height of fences, whether they are made of cut timber or living trees.

Q. Who owns a boundary fence?

A. A fence that sits directly on the property line of two neighbors is known as a **boundary fence**. The legal rights and responsibilities depend on a number of factors, including who "uses" the fence. Generally, boundary fences are somewhat like trees that straddle a property line—they belong to both property owners, both are responsible for the upkeep of the fence, and neither may remove or alter the fence without the other's permission. Of course, the owners are free to agree otherwise. One may wish to "buy" the fence from the other and have it recorded in the deed for posterity. Or one neighbor may be willing to give up his or her "share" of the fence if the other agrees to pay for the maintenance.

Q. What can you do about a "spite fence"?

A. A **spite fence** is one that is excessively high, has no reasonable use to your neighbor, and was clearly constructed to annoy you. For example, suppose you live atop a canyon with a view and you've been feuding with your neighbors, who live further down the slope. The neighbors suddenly erect a twenty-foot-high stockade fence near the property line. Unless your neighbors can demonstrate a reasonable need for such a high fence, such as extra privacy concerns, you can sue them under the doctrine of private nuisance. The case may be difficult to win, however, because most fences or other structures have some arguable utility to the owner.

Your remedies, depending on the law of the state where you reside, may include an **injunction** (court order) to have the fence removed (or at least lowered to a less offensive height) or **compensatory damages** (a financial payment to you). Factors the court will consider in determining the appropriate amount of compensation include the diminished value of your property and

---

ⓘ HOG-TIED BY A FENCE LAW

If you live in a historic part of the country, beware of obscure fence laws that may still be on the books. In Maryland, a Howard County landowner was subjected to an anachronistic county law that not only required him to share the cost of a fence on the property line with his neighbor, but also required the fence to be "hog-tight"—low enough so that a hog could not squeeze under it. And no, neither of the neighbors had any hogs on his property.

---

any annoyance caused by the erection and maintenance of the fence.

Most spite fences spring from a history of bad feelings in the neighborhood, which deteriorate into anger and spite. That's why it pays to be neighborly in the first place.

ⓘ MEDIATION

Mediators are trained to listen to both sides in a dispute, identify problems, and suggest compromises and equitable solutions. They provide an impartial and unbiased forum for neighbors to talk. The key to mediation, unlike a lawsuit, is that it's not an adversarial process. No judge makes a decision for either party. The outcome of the dispute is in the hands of both parties. Until both agree, there is no resolution. The parties are more likely to comply with the agreement, since both have consented to it. Chapter 1, "When and How to Use A Lawyer," and chapter 2, "How the Legal System Works," provide information on how to find a dispute resolution service.

THE WORLD AT YOUR FINGERTIPS

- *Nolo.com has much free information on neighbor law and pet law (www.nolo.com). You can also purchase books on each of these topics online.*

REMEMBER THIS

- *If you have a dispute with a neighbor, start by trying to work it out informally, then move to putting your request in writing. Suggest mediation if needed, and bring in the authorities as a last resort.*
- *Your town or city may have zoning, noise, or other ordinances that address the problem. Referring to the ordinance may give you some leverage with your neighbor.*
- *Trees, hedges, and fences that follow the property line belong to the neighbors on both sides, and both neighbors should share the responsibility for maintenance.*
- *You may trim branches from your neighbor's tree that hang over your property, but it's best to talk with the neighbor about it first. The fruit of the tree belongs to the owner of the tree, whether it's good to eat or rotting in your grass.*

REMODELING

The urge to improve your home is just about as irresistible as the urge to improve your spouse. But home improvement is both more likely to succeed and better protected by law. The legal protections are a good thing, given what can go wrong. Consider the possibilities:

- The contractor you hire to add a second story to your living room takes your deposit, tears off the roof, but is too busy with other jobs to make further progress.
- The kitchen remodeler brings in three subcontractors to do the work, then takes your check and skips town without paying them.

- The new swimming pool leaks. The contractor blames the plumber, and neither is willing to foot the bill for digging out the pipes.

A major remodeling brings enough headaches without trouble from an unreliable contractor. To make sure the project goes as smoothly as possible, take time to choose a reputable contractor and make sure you have a complete contract. This chapter will explain your legal rights, what to put in the contract, and what to do if something goes wrong.

Legal Protections

Q. Which federal laws are applicable to remodeling projects?

A. Federal Trade Commission (FTC) rules address the problem of false advertising. It's illegal for a vendor to advertise any product or service for less than it really costs or to engage in the old bait-and-switch tactic. This happens when you are **baited** by an ad for a product or service, then told that it isn't available and **switched** to another, more-expensive version. The law requires vendors to offer a rain check whenever demand for an advertised bargain exceeds supply, unless the limited supply is clearly stated in the ad.

The federal Truth in Lending Act protects consumers who obtain financing for their projects. Whether you finance your home improvement through a bank, a credit union, or the contractor, the lender must prominently state the **annual percentage rate (APR)** of interest and the loan costs you will be charged.

Note that even if the terms appear reasonable, it can be a bad idea to have the contractor secure financing for your project, and in some areas it may also be illegal. Even though the contractor may approve you as a credit risk on what look like favorable terms, you'd be better off with a home equity loan from a bank or credit union. If you qualify for a loan from a bank, take it; if you don't qualify, then you should think carefully about whether you can really afford to remodel.

These laws help keep most contractors honest, but they can't keep the bad apples off the streets. Even if you report violations to the Federal Trade Commission in Washington or one of its ten regional offices, the FTC is not likely to prosecute a small contractor. Federal enforcement tends to concentrate on major violations or patterns.

Q. What protection do I have once I sign a contract?

A. Given the number of scam artists working the streets, your best federal protection may be the cooling-off period mandated by the Truth in Lending Act. Called a **right of rescission**, the law gives you three business days to cancel any contract that was signed in your home (or any location other than the seller's place of business) that involves any financial claim to your home. This occurs, for example, when the contract gives the contractor the right to file a lien against your home to enforce payment. This law also applies to any contract that involves the borrower making four or more payments, such as when the contractor finances a project by using your home as collateral for a second mortgage.

If circumstances entitle you to a cooling-off period, the contractor must give you two copies of the Notice of Right of Rescission at the time you sign the contract. It must be separate from the contract—not buried in fine print—and a copy must be given to each owner, because any one owner may cancel. The notice must identify the transaction, disclose the security interest, inform you of your right to rescind, tell you how to exercise that right, and give you the date the rescission period expires.

Q. What kind of state and local laws apply to contractors?

A. State laws often are modeled after federal laws, and states and local agencies are much more apt to pursue a small contractor who may have violated the law. If you suspect that a contractor is breaking the law, get in touch with your state attorney general's office or local department of consumer affairs.

Some state laws specifically target dishonest contractors. For example, Illinois's **Home Repair/Fraud Act**, amended in 2000, makes it a crime to misrepresent the terms of a home repair contract, deceive people into signing one, damage someone's property to drum up home repair business, or charge an unconscionable fee for home repair services. A contractor who preys on disabled people or those older than sixty may be committing aggravated home repair fraud, a felony punishable by three to seven years in jail and a fine of up to $10,000.

Localities also can impose tough laws against unscrupulous contractors. A local law in Putnam County, New York, provides such punishments as suspension or revocation of the contractor's license, both criminal and civil penalties, and punitive damages against the contractor.

For information about legal protections and enforcement options in your state, contact your state or local consumer protection agency or the consumer fraud division of the local prosecutor's office.

Q. What's the best way to guard against swindlers?

A. Despite all the statutes, if you have to rely on the law to get your money back from a shoddy contractor, you will have to wait a long time. The best idea is not to engage contractors in the first place without a careful check of their reputation ahead of time. Be wary of contractors who:

- Claim to work for a government agency. Check it out.
- Offer free gifts. Ask the following questions: What exactly are the gifts? When will you receive them? Can you get a price reduction instead?
- Engage in door-to-door sales or try to get your business by telephone solicitations. Be especially wary if the sales pitch demands an immediate decision to take advantage of prices that won't be available tomorrow. Most rep-

utable contractors don't engage in such tactics.

- Offer an unsolicited free inspection of your furnace or basement. Rip-off artists use this ruse to get into a home and either fake a problem or damage a sound furnace and good pipes.
- Claim your house is dangerous and needs immediate repair unless you already know it does.
- Have a company name, address, and telephone number and other credentials that can't be verified. Fly-by-night operators often use a post office box and an answering service while hunting for victims.
- Promise a lower price for allowing your home to be used as a model or to advertise their work. (Has the price really been lowered? What does the "use of your home" entail?)
- Engage in bait-and-switch tactics. After luring you with an ad that offers an unbeatable deal on a job, such contractors tell you the materials aren't available for that job, but that they can give you a bargain on another, more-expensive job.
- Leave delivery and installation costs out of their estimates.
- Offer to give you a rebate or referral fee if any of your friends use the same contractor.
- Insist on starting work before you sign a contract.

Hiring a Contractor

Q. How do I find a reputable contractor?

A. After thinking through what you want and what you can afford, ask for recommendations from people who have had similar work done and talk to building inspectors, bankers, and trade association representatives—people who should know firsthand the work and reputation of contractors in your community.

For a large job, interview and solicit bids from two or three contractors from your list, but make sure they are bidding on exactly the same job to allow comparisons. The lowest bid is not necessarily the best, because a contractor with a reputation for excellent workmanship and for standing behind the work might charge more. Even if the job is small enough to warrant only one bid, take time to check out your contractor's reputation and credentials.

Make sure a contractor's references had similar work done. For a kitchen remodeling, for example, ask for former clients who have had kitchens done by the contractor. And don't just ask for references—actually call them. Most people won't mind at all chatting with you about their job. Chances are any such references provided by the contractor will be happy clients, so try to go a step or so beyond "He's a great guy" and "No problems at all."

- Ask exactly what the contractor did, and how this person found out about the contractor.
- Jot down any more names that are mentioned, with addresses and telephone numbers.
- Was the client comfortable with the way things were left at the end of a day as well as at the end of the project?
- What do the clients wish they had done differently to make the job go even more smoothly?
- What did the client's spouse (or roommate, neighbors, or children) think about the work and the construction process?
- What is the next project this person wants to hire the contractor to do?

Q. What kinds of certification should the contractor provide?

A. If you are satisfied with a contractor's reputation, check his or her credentials before signing the contract. Find out if the contractor is licensed and bonded. Although not all states require licensing for home contractors, those that do have at least a record of each contractor's name and address, compliance with insurance laws, and agreement to operate within the law. If the company is a corporation, the state has a record of the individual responsible. While some states only require contractors to register their names and addresses, quite a few require them to have some experience and pass an exam.

A state license doesn't ensure that the contractor will do a good job, but it's an indication that he or she has made an effort to comply with the law. Check with the state contractors licensing board to see if the license is current. Some states will also tell you if there have been complaints against a given contractor and whether they proved to be valid. Otherwise you can get that information from the local office of the Better Business Bureau or the office of consumer affairs.

Q. Why are bonds important?

A. Dealing with a contractor who's bonded provides important protections for you. Be aware that there are two kinds of bonds involved in construction. The phrase **fully insured and bonded** generally means the contractor's insurance coverage protects against employee theft, vandalism, or negligence. Especially if you have valuables to consider, ask to see a certificate or letter certifying such a policy.

The other kind is a performance bond, an insurance company's assurance that the contractor can finish the job as stated in the contract. If the contractor defaults, the insurance company will pay another contractor to complete the work. Contractors must take out a separate bond for each job, so bonds are usually limited to jobs of $25,000 or more, and contractors pass on the cost to the owner. It is an expensive proposition, up to 10 percent of the contract price for a residential swimming pool; but a contractor who has been approved by a bonding company is a very good risk. You're the one who decides whether to require (and pay for) a bond.

Be aware that in some areas it is so expensive and difficult for contractors to purchase a performance bond that it may be impossible to find a contractor who has one.

Q. What else should I ask about?

A. Ask your contractor about the following points:

- Whether he or she carries workers' compensation insurance, to cover injuries that workers might sustain on the job. Your homeowner's insurance probably doesn't cover workers' compensation, so if the contractor doesn't carry it, you could be responsible for some hefty bills. In addition, the contractor should carry a **builder's risk policy** to cover any damage caused during construction.
- Whether he or she belongs to a trade association. Many associations require a contractor to have been in business a certain length of time, to have passed a credit check, and to meet all legal requirements of their state. It wouldn't hurt to call the association to make sure the contractor's membership is current and inquire about complaints.
- Whether the contractor offers a warranty on work and materials. If so, what is the time limit on the warranty? Make sure any warranty is included in the contract. (Even if there is no specific warranty, most jurisdictions recognize an **implied warranty of good workmanship** that gives you some protection.) For an additional fee, some contractors offer an extended warranty such as the five-year policies available through the Home Owners Warranty Corporation. Some states have statutory warranties in addition to the contractual ones.

You should also check whether or not any civil judgments or lawsuits are pending against the contractor, by calling the local clerk of court. If someone sued the contractor over something like poor workmanship, consider it a warning. Likewise, you might want to check with the nearest federal bankruptcy court to see whether the contractor has recently filed for bankruptcy—a possible indication of financial instability.

Q. What should the contract include?

A. A home improvement contract should address several specific issues, outlined below. This list contains things you may not require in every contract. For example, a kitchen remodeling in your home that is one hundred feet from the nearest neighbor probably doesn't need an anti-noise provision.

- *Preamble.* A preamble is an introduction that states names, addresses, phone numbers, and the date the contract is executed. It should specify whether the contractor's business is a sole proprietorship, a partnership, or a corporation. (If it is a partnership or a corporation, make sure the person who signs is an authorized representative.) The preamble should also state that the remodeler is an independent contractor, not your employee. Otherwise, you might be responsible if the builder injures someone. You should also add the contractor's Federal Employer Identification Number. The contract price should state the total dollar amount, including sales tax, to be paid by the homeowner for services agreed to in the contract.

- *Starting and completion dates.* No contractor is likely to begin until after your right to rescission has safely passed. Specify an end date, stating exceptions such as weather, strikes, and so on. You may want to add a bonus-penalty clause if the date is critical. Specify a daily starting time if that matters to you. Consider interim completion dates for key phases of big jobs.

- *Scope of work.* Contractors may shy away from a clause as broad as "all labor, materials, and services necessary to complete the project." But be cautious of being so specific in the tasks and materials listed that anything else becomes an "extra" or a "change order," which may be billed separately.

- *Description of materials.* See that complete descriptions of agreed-to products are listed, including brand names and order numbers. Plans and specifications, bids, estimates, and all other documents relating to the project are part of the scope of work. Make sure that copies of these are attached to all copies of the contract before you sign it.

- *Permits, licenses, and zoning.* Specify that the contractor will obtain all necessary licenses and permits and satisfy all zoning regulations and building codes, and indemnify the homeowner in case the contractor fails to do so.

- *Cleanup policy.* Will the contractor clean up daily? After each subproject? Only at the end? Where is refuse to be placed?

- *Storage.* Specify where materials and equipment will be kept. You are probably liable for damage to materials and equipment from fire or accidents, so be sure to check your homeowner's policy and make sure these are covered.

- *Parking.* If parking is a problem, have the contract deal with parking arrangements for the contractor's vehicle as well as the subcontractors'.

▶ THE IMPORTANCE OF A WRITTEN CONTRACT

Don't allow any work to begin until there is a signed contract that protects you. (Some people might take a chance on very small jobs under $1,500, but it is a chance.) Oral agreements can be enforced in court, but it is difficult to prove who said what if you don't get it on paper. Ask to see an insurance certificate to make sure the contractor is covered for liability and workers' compensation in case a subcontractor is injured on your property. If the contractor gives you a standard contract to sign, take it home and study it carefully at your leisure. Strike out clauses you think are unreasonable and have both parties initial the change. If you are uncertain about the meaning of provisions and/or if it is a major, expensive job, make sure your lawyer checks the contract.

- *Noise.* Some is inevitable, but place limits on time and volume, according to local laws and neighborhood needs. You may wish to set specific times when work may begin and when it must end each day. That way you won't have the contractor disturbing the neighborhood every evening.

- *Theft.* Building materials are often stolen. The contract can make either the contractor or the owner responsible.

- *Damage.* What if the retaining wall collapses when they're digging for the new swimming pool? You'll want the contract to state that the contractor is responsible for damage to your property. If the contractor or a subcontractor will be doing any blasting to remove something from your property, the contract should state that the contractor is also responsible for damage to your neighbor's property. You don't want to have to pay for your neighbor's cracked foundation.

- *Change orders.* Very few jobs go exactly as planned, which requires that the contract have a provision that enables it to be amended simply and easily. The contract should provide that change orders can be written up, signed by both parties, and attached to the contract as plans change or delays occur. See the sample on this page for specific wording of this contract clause.

- *Warranties.* The contract should assure that the materials are new, and that you will receive all warranties from manufacturers for appliances and other materials used on the job.

- *Progress payments.* Contractors don't expect to be paid entirely in advance, but they also don't expect to wait until all work has been done. It is customary to pay one-third upon signing a contract to allow the contractor to buy supplies and get started. In smaller projects, two payments may suffice. In larger ones, plan to make payments after completion and approval of major phases of the work. In all cases, make your final payment as large as possible, usually at least 10 percent, payable only after the entire job is completed.

- *Financing contingency.* If your ability to proceed with the project depends on securing outside financing, include a contingency clause stating that the contract is not binding if you are unable to secure the needed funds on acceptable terms.

- *Suppliers and subcontractors.* Ask for a list of subcontractors and suppliers and attach it to the contract with their addresses, telephone numbers, and Social Security numbers. Although you are not their boss, they probably have a right to place a lien on your home if the contractor does not pay them in full. It's only fair that you know who they are, should legal action become necessary. If you prefer, arrange to pay suppliers and subcontractors directly.

- *Lawyer's fees.* You should also consider including a provision in the contract that if the contractor breaches (violates) the terms of the contract, you are entitled to recover a reasonable lawyer's fee, in addition to damages. In many states, unless the contract contains such a provision, you will be unable to recover your legal fees from the contractor even if you win in court.

ⓘ CHANGE-ORDER CLAUSE

The following wording can be used to provide for a change/order clause in the original contract:

Without invalidating this contract, the owner may order changes in the work, including additions, modifications, or deletions. Price and time will be adjusted accordingly. All such changes in the work shall be in writing, and signed by the contractor and owner and attached to this document.

Troubleshooting the Project

Q. Who should obtain building permits and when should they do it?

A. To find out whether you will need building permits, contact your local building department. Some municipalities require permits for just about anything; others require permits for only major remodeling projects. The person who takes out the permit is considered liable for the work, so follow the usual custom of having the architect or the contractor obtain it. As a homeowner, you don't want to be responsible if the work doesn't conform to standards or codes, but you need to know which permits are required and make sure they are obtained.

Q. What's the point of getting a permit, besides giving the town money?

A. First of all, the point is to abide by the law. Second, the inspector who checks your house can assure you that the work you are paying for is safe. For example, altered fire-escape routes, often caused by a door or a doorway that was renovated without permit and inspection, can be dangerous; plumbing and electrical inspectors can ensure that the work is done according to code.

Also, if you have followed proper procedures, your house will be free of encumbrances when you want to sell it.

If you live in a condominium or a cooperative apartment, or other common-interest property, your rights to renovate and remodel differ from those of single-family homeowners. Check your condominium declaration—or check with your board—to see if your renovation will be permitted.

Q. What should I watch out for when the job begins?

A. Be sure to keep a handle on the documents that can help you avoid problems later. In consultation with your contractor, draw up a schedule of what will be done when, and make sure this is followed. If you don't have the wiring inspected before the drywall goes up, for example, the inspector may require you to tear out the drywall.

Contractors report that their biggest problems with homeowners arise because owners request additional work along the way, then object when they see the bill. The best way to avoid misunderstanding is with a specific written **change order**. This document, signed by both parties and added to the original contract, specifies the additional work to be done, the materials, and any change in the schedule. For a large project, print or duplicate blank change-order forms to fill out as you need them.

Remember that if you want to make a change in what a subcontractor does, you should not ask the subcontractor directly to make the change. Your contract is with the contractor. Again, any changes should be written into a change order.

Q. What happens if someone is hurt on the job?

A. If you are dealing with an independent contractor, his or her insurance should cover expenses; but if you hired someone down the street to paint your house, someone who doesn't maintain a separate business and who relied on you for tools and supervision, that person is your employee, and any injuries he or she might suffer are your responsibility.

If someone gets hurt later because, for example, the new basement steps were not nailed down, your insurance company may pay the injured party but then go after the contractor responsible.

Q. What can I do if the contractor violates the contract?

A. If you believe there has been a contract violation, first bring the matter to the attention of the contractor with a telephone call or a conversation. For example, if you came home from work one day and found that the new picture window was in the wrong place, call the contractor immediately. To protect yourself, make a note of the conversation, summarizing your concerns and any agreements, and send it to the contractor. Keep a copy yourself. Next, if the contractor doesn't remedy the problem within a reasonable time, ask your lawyer to write a letter stating your concerns and asking for the correction.

If that doesn't work, check to see if your contract specifies alternative dispute resolution (ADR)—that is, mediation or arbitration. That means you and the contractor will have agreed to call in a mutually acceptable third party to resolve the dispute without going to court. If your contract does not specify ADR, your initial letter and the lawyer's letter will provide you with a basis for further action with a consumer protection agency or a lawsuit, possibly in small claims court.

Either way, your options are to push for **specific performance** of the contract, which means forcing the remodeler to do the work as agreed, or to have the remodeler pay any extra costs you incur by having someone else correct or complete the work.

Q. What is a mechanic's lien?

A. A mechanic's lien is a lien created by law for the purpose of securing payment for work performed or materials furnished in construction. A mechanic's lien is subordinate to any prior mortgage on your house, but the contractor may use it to enforce payment by threatening a foreclosure action on your house. In some states, contractors and subcontractors must notify a homeowner if they intend to take out a lien. In others, you only learn about it after it is filed at the local recording office. If you find out someone has filed a lien, call your lawyer immediately.

Q. How can I prevent a mechanic's lien from being filed?

A. It is possible to add a clause to the contract stating that the contractor agrees to give up his or her lien rights, but the contractor may not agree to such a clause, and in some states it is not valid. Moreover, even with a contractor's waiver, any subcontractor or supplier who is not paid for work or materials by your contractor can file a

lien against your home. Unless your job is covered by a performance bond, or your state has some sort of fund to protect homeowners from paying twice when the contractor doesn't pay subcontractors or laborers, your chief protection against a lien is holding back final payment until all work has been properly completed to your satisfaction and your contractor supplies proof in writing that everyone who worked on your job has been paid. A **release-of-lien form** is useful, because it provides places for all the subcontractors to sign. (This is one reason to have all subcontractors and suppliers named up front in your contract, so you can make sure everyone has signed off on the release-of-lien form.)

THE WORLD AT YOUR FINGERTIPS

- *You can find a summary of the federal Truth in Lending Act at www.smartagreements.com/bltopics/ Bltop41.html.*
- *The National Association of the Remodeling Industry (NARI) website includes a national directory of remodeling contractors; visit www.nari.org.*

REMEMBER THIS

- *The law protects homeowners from unscrupulous contractors. You have a right of rescission, which means you have three business days to cancel any contract*

▶ **WHEN THE JOB IS DONE**

Do not make final payment until

- all work is completed, inspected, and approved;
- subcontractors are paid;
- any liens are canceled; and
- warranties are in the proper hands.

signed in your home or any other location besides the contractor's place of business.

- *Carefully check the reputation of contractors before they start repairing or remodeling your home.*
- *Make sure you have a complete written contract before work begins.*
- *Make sure all needed permits and inspections are taken care of.*
- *Don't give the final payment until you're sure the work is finished, all subcontractors have been paid, any liens are canceled, and you have any warranties in hand.*

SHARED OWNERSHIP: CONDOS AND CONDOMINIUMS

Wouldn't it be nice to live in a spacious home in a beautiful neighborhood, but without having to do all that yard work? Wouldn't it be nice to have neighbors who shared your idea of what the neighborhood should look like? And while you're at it, wouldn't it be nice to have a swimming pool handy, and maybe a tennis court and weight room?

That's why 32 million people now live in common-interest communities. Whether it's an expensive brownstone cooperative in New York City, a high-rise beachfront condominium in Miami, or a cluster of town houses in Des Moines, a common-interest community brings together people who share a certain vision of good living. And unlike rental units, they allow people to build equity in their homes.

The key to the success of these forms is also one of the biggest bugbears: strict restrictions on what owners can do with their property. The reason a spacious planned-unit development is such an attractive place to live is that community regulators prohibit any given owner from painting her house purple or blasting a stereo from the window. But those restrictions also cause more tension and litiga-

tion than any other aspect of common-interest community living: whether Mrs. Taylor can keep her beloved Afghan hound or Mr. Smith can land his helicopter on the roof. And because everyone is a part owner of the buildings and amenities, when it's time to replace the windows or landscape the grounds, everyone has to pay.

This section will explain the various forms of common-interest community, how they're governed, and the role of the association.

Q. What is a common-interest community?

A. Thanks to creative developers, we have **common-interest communities** in a variety of configurations, with a confusing array of names and forms of ownership. Still, certain characteristics are shared—they are designed specifically for a certain type of community living by a single developer (or in the case of existing buildings, a single converter). They are created by a specific set of documents, usually drawn up by the developer and subject to change by the membership. And when the developer or converter departs, the community's affairs are governed by an association of all unit owners through its elected board.

The board has the authority to enforce the restrictions and collect assessments to pay for maintenance and improvements. This is the essential characteristic of a common-interest community—the obligation to pay for the insurance, maintenance taxes, and upkeep of property other than the individually owned portion of the community. It is a financial relationship, and most of the relevant laws regulate the fairness and power to exercise that relationship.

There are some communities that are subject to covenants for architectural control or for the restriction of uses of open space without the obligation to contribute money. Strictly speaking, these are not common-interest communities.

Q. What are the basic types?

A. Because state governing laws differ, the terminology for these ownership forms can be confusing. Whatever the general description, there are three distinct types of common-interest communities with three distinct types of ownership: the cooperative, the condominium, and the planned community or planned unit development (PUD). You can't tell which is which by looking at the architectural form of the buildings. For example, in some states, "site condominiums" look just like single-family detached homes, but the land—not the home—is part of the condominium. However, the form of ownership has significant legal implications. Be sure you understand the type specified in the community's declaration, which is essentially its constitution.

Q. What's the difference between a cooperative and a condominium?

A. In a **cooperative**, the members are stockholders in a corporation that owns the entire building, including the residential units and all common elements such as corridors, elevators, and tennis courts. Stockholders don't actually own any real estate. The corporation owns it all. Instead, stockholders lease their individual units from the corporation. Each stockholder pays a monthly **maintenance charge**, which is a proportionate share of the corporation's cash requirements for mortgage payments, operation, maintenance, repair, taxes, and reserves. The corporation, governed by an elected board of direc-

tors, may veto a proposed transfer of stock with its lease, so it has considerable control over potential buyers.

Condominium ownership provides you exclusive title to your own unit, from the interior walls in, and ownership of an individual interest in the common elements of the condominium. With limitations, you are free to mortgage your unit or sell it. As in a cooperative, all unit owners must pay their share of the assessment for operation, maintenance, repair, and reserves. The association is responsible for enforcing the rules and managing the common elements, but it doesn't actually own anything.

Q. How does a planned community work?

A. A **planned community** is a hybrid subdivision combining certain aspects of cooperatives and condominiums. In these developments, each owner holds title to a unit—in many cases, a single-family, detached house. But all common areas, such as parks and playgrounds, belong to the incorporated **homeowners' association**, which all owners are required to join. The association is responsible for maintaining common areas and, in some cases, house exteriors. Homeowners pay a periodic assessment for common area expenses and reserves.

Some planned communities include sections organized as condominiums or cooperatives. Oth-

---

ⓘ BY ANY OTHER NAME

Common-interest community is the term preferred by the National Conference of Commissioners on Uniform State Laws, a group devoted to drafting model laws for adoption by state legislatures. But the Community Association Institute (CAI), a national trade group for anyone connected with this type of development, prefers the term **community association.** Other terms in use are **common-interest realty association, common-interest development, residential community association, common property subdivision** and **interdependent covenanted subdivision.** Depending on who's talking, the association might be a **community association,** a **homeowners' association,** or a **property owners' association.** If you're talking about these developments with someone from another area, make sure you're talking about the same thing.

ers include commercial or even industrial areas, designed to allow people to live within walking distance of stores and work. Some of these developments are huge—such as Reston, Virginia, a planned community of nineteen thousand units. Further, several adjoining community associations may belong to a **master association**, which charges an additional assessment to pay for certain community-wide services. The master association may also be known as an **umbrella association**, a **master planned community**, or a **mixed-use association**.

Q. What kind of restrictions can be imposed in common-interest communities?

A. The extent of restrictions imposed on owners varies. In a planned community of freestanding houses, rules may be limited to preserving the quality and cohesiveness of the development by requiring approval of any architectural or other exterior changes. Condominiums and cooperatives tend to have much more extensive rules and regulations, because generally people are living much closer together and often in the same building.

Mid-rise and high-rise condominiums rely on the concept of the **airspace block**. The title to a single-family house or town house often includes the land underneath it and the air above it, but if you own a high-rise apartment, there are other owners above and below. So you hold title, in effect, to a block of airspace—within four walls, a ceiling, and a floor.

Within that airspace block, you may alter or remove nonsupporting walls, replace the light fixtures, change the carpet however you wish, and make other changes that don't infringe on your neighbors' property rights. On the other hand, you are responsible for the maintenance and repair of paint, wallpaper, fixtures, and appliances, except for wires and pipes running through your walls that serve other units. Sometimes people accustomed to rental apartments are surprised to learn that their condominium building manager isn't responsible for fixing their hot-water heater or a blocked toilet.

Legal Rights and Restrictions

Q. What federal laws apply to common-interest communities?

A. Few federal laws directly affect the organization and operation of common-interest communities. However, under the Fair Housing Amendments Act, effective since 1989, developments may no longer discriminate against families with children unless the development meets the act's strict qualifications for senior citizen developments. Otherwise, it is no longer legal to advertise a development as being for adults only or to steer would-be buyers elsewhere because their children wouldn't be welcome.

The Fair Housing Amendments Act also prohibits discrimination against disabled persons. Developments must permit construction of facilities for disabled residents, although the disabled resident may be required to remove the construction upon leaving. Further, all new multifamily buildings must provide access for the disabled in every unit on the ground floor or access by elevator. Under HUD regulations, this includes wide doors, free passage for wheelchairs through units, bathroom walls strong enough for grab bars, and access to at least a representative portion of the amenities.

The Federal Communications Commission requires that unit owners in common-interest communities be able to place certain forms of dish antennae (not exceeding one meter in diameter) on privately allocated spaces in common-interest communities without restriction.

Q. How do state laws apply to common-interest communities?

A. Most of the substantive law—and confusion—lies in an ever-changing patchwork of state statutes. The governance of cooperatives falls under state statutes governing corporations and nonprofit corporations, because residents of a cooperative own stock in the corporation that owns their building. The same corporation statutes apply to the associations governing planned communities, which likewise own the common areas.

In most states, condominiums don't have a corporation responsible for liabilities, taxes, and governance. That is why each state has a special set of laws detailing how condominiums must be organized and operated. These laws require each condominium to file a declaration and by-laws, with specific requirements regarding the rights and duties of the association. (In states like Florida where condominium associations are incorporated, the association must file articles of incorporation.) Planned communities require no specific statute, but some states include them in a law governing all common-interest communities.

Condominium statutes vary considerably, from state to state, and many lack protections for consumers. While some states provide only the barest framework for creating a condominium, others are incredibly complex and detailed.

Q. What else governs a common-interest community?

A. Federal and state laws govern common interest communities. In addition, each individual community is governed by its own declaration and articles of incorporation, a set of bylaws, and various rules, regulations, and decisions promulgated by the association board. Finally, given the extensive litigation over the authority of particular associations, various courts have interpreted statutes, rules, and regulations, often based on common-law (nonstatutory) principles.

A community association gains its authority from the legal documents that created it: the declaration, the articles of incorporation, and the bylaws. State statutes often back up that authority, whether in the statutes governing nonprofit corporations or the specific condominium or common-interest community act, or both. Broadly speaking, a community association may hold property, sue and be sued, receive gifts and bequests, make charitable contributions, make contracts, borrow or invest money, and assess unit owners for their share of the expense of maintaining and operating the community. Some state statutes grant even more far-reaching powers.

Q. Why are there so many documents?

A. By law, each common-interest community must file a set of master regulations, plus subsidiary documents called articles, plus a set of bylaws. For planned communities, the master regulations are called the **covenants, conditions, and restrictions,** or the **declaration of covenants** or **master deed.** The same document for a condominium is called a **declaration of condominium, declaration,** or a **master deed.**

A **condominium declaration** describes the land, building, and other improvements; the location of each unit; percentage of ownership; the common elements; and the intended use of each unit. Basically, the declaration depicts the physical arrangement, including a floor plan with tax-lot numbers for the various units. But under the

---

ⓘ UNIFORM CONDOMINIUM ACT

In hopes of bringing some uniformity to the law, the National Conference of Commissioners on Uniform State Laws has proposed model laws in the area, which twelve states have adopted or adapted, and numerous others are considering. The Uniform Condominium Act (UCA) allows flexibility for developers while offering protection to consumers, such as requiring extensive disclosure before sale. It covers such matters as insurance, tort, and contract liability. The Uniform Common Interest Ownership Act (UCIOA) extends the same provisions to cooperatives and planned communities. So far, only a handful of states have adopted UCIOA.

laws of many states, it need not contain much in the way of operational detail.

Generally declarations may only be amended by a supermajority vote of the unit owners, often two-thirds or three-quarters. Some amendments, such as changing unit boundaries or assessment ratios, may require even more of a vote, sometimes unanimity. Most amendment provisions require the consent of a certain number of the mortgage lenders as well.

The **articles of incorporation**, called **articles of association** in nonincorporated associations, involve the legal establishment of the association, including the name, address, and purpose of the association; the aggregate number of shares permitted; whether cumulative voting or other special voting or assessment rights are provided; and, in general, the power of the board to make, alter, and repeal reasonable bylaws.

Q. What do the bylaws regulate?

A. **Bylaws** dictate how the managing board will be elected and define their duties and powers. Bylaws cover such matters as whether the board will manage the property or engage a management firm; rules critical to settling disputes that might arise; how assessments and reserves are to be determined; what restrictions apply to the lease and sale of units; and to what extent board decisions bind unit owners. Basically, bylaws cover the internal corporate operating standards. In some older condominium statutes, the bylaws may include restrictions on use and insurance provisions as well.

Although bylaws in most corporations may be altered freely by the board or by a simple majority of the members, many condominium statutes require a two-thirds or even three-quarters majority to change them. States that have adopted the Uniform Condominium Act allow a bit more flexibility, to reduce the chance that a condominium will be unable to adapt to changing conditions.

ⓘ CHALLENGING ASSOCIATION RULES

In the course of operating the association, boards periodically enact other rules and regulations regarding the details of community life, such as how parking spaces are allocated. These are subject to judicial review if a unit owner believes that the board overstepped its authority in adopting a given regulation. In reviewing regulations, courts tend to consider four questions:

- Is the rule consistent with the declaration and other superior documents?
- Was the rule adopted in a good-faith effort to serve a purpose of the community?
- Are the means adopted to serve the purpose reasonable?
- Is the rule consistent with public policy?

If a court rules that the answer to one of these questions is no, it might set aside the rule in question. In general, however, the decisions of the board are protected from second-guessing by the membership by the **business judgment rule,** which states that if the decision was arrived at honestly and with no fraudulent intent, the board's decision will be upheld even if it was stupid or reasonable persons may disagree with it. It has been called the **pure heart but weak mind rule.** In a democracy the voters have to put up with the decisions of the legislators they elected, until those legislators can be made accountable at the ballot box.

The Board of Directors

Q. How is the board of directors established?

A. The board of directors or managers is elected by the membership to carry out day-to-day operations and oversee enforcement of the rules. A typical board has five to seven members who are elected on a rotating basis. The board in turn elects officers, such as a chairman or a president, a secretary, and a treasurer.

Q. What is the role of the board of directors?

A. Typically, the board has broad powers under state law. The board may raise or lower assessments and impose special assessments to cover specific repairs or improvements. It also may insist that unit owners obey the policies of the association.

Many associations grant the board of directors a right of first refusal to buy or lease a unit on behalf of the association. The way this generally works in practice is that the owner must offer to sell the unit to the board at a price that matches the good-faith price offered by an outside purchaser before agreeing to sell it to anyone else. Although this power is mostly used to keep out an undesirable purchaser, it can be used to acquire a management office or superintendent's apartment. Some cooperatives require a right of approval of any purchaser before a sale can be consummated.

Q. How does the board enforce the association's rules?

A. When a unit owner ignores the rules, the board usually levies fines against the owner. If the fines pile up and the owner refuses to pay, the board may exercise its right to enforce its lien against the owner's unit and, if necessary, foreclose on it to get the money. Some declarations permit the suspension of privileges of a unit owner while an assessment remains unpaid or another covenant remains in breach, such as the right to use recreational facilities, or even the right to vote. Another approach is for the association to sue the violator, seeking an injunctive order to stop the practice in question. A violator who refuses to follow the court order could be found in contempt of court.

The uniform acts and many other statutes require that the unit owner who is alleged to have breached a covenant receive a right to notice and a hearing before fines or other sanctions may be levied.

In theory, any unit owner may sign a complaint against a neighbor to initiate a process that could lead to fines. In practice, though, most unit owners are hesitant to sign formal complaints against people next door, even though they voice their concerns loudly to the board. If the community hires a management company—standard practice in larger communities—the company's routine maintenance inspections include checking for violations of the rules. The employee who discovers the infraction then serves as a complaining witness to the board, which more than likely will start by sending someone to talk to the violator. Most board members try to be evenhanded in their enforcement, because they don't want to be criticized for punishing one violator and showing leniency towards another.

If the board decides to resort to the courts, it must do so promptly or risk losing the authority to enforce the rule. If the rules say you cannot build a toolshed and you do it anyway, board members cannot walk past it every day for years and then sue to have you remove it.

Q. How does the board handle assessments?

A. One of the most onerous tasks of an association board is raising the monthly assessment that pays for maintenance and various services, from trash collection to snow removal. Some state statutes mandate certain levels of reserves to guard the community's financial stability and prepare for inevitable capital expenditures. Even without a mandate, a board is wise to build up a substantial reserve to avoid having to require a massive special assessment when the furnace needs to be replaced.

In two states, California and Illinois, associations may not raise the assessment higher than a set amount without membership approval. In Illinois, for example, condominium boards must hold a referendum of unit owners if the budget increase rises above 15 percent. Many condominium declarations set similar dollar caps on increases in assessments without owner approval.

Q. What can the board do if I can't pay the assessment?

A. When unit owners are doing well, they may grouse about the assessment but chances are they'll pay it. But what if a unit owner is in serious financial trouble, with several thousand dollars worth of assessments unpaid? If the owner goes bankrupt, creditors line up for their share of what's left—and the community association is normally far down the line, well behind the bank that holds the mortgage. If the association cannot obtain payment of the bankrupt owner's assessment, all the other property owners in the community will have to cover it.

One provision of the Uniform Common Interest Ownership Act, in effect in Connecticut, Alaska, and several other states, gives community associations a **super-priority lien**, putting them first in line ahead of the mortgage lenders for the bankrupt unit owner's share of the past six months' assessments. Numerous states are considering this provision, although in a few states the banking lobby opposes it. The Federal National Mortgage Association, the Federal Home Loan Mortgage Corporation, the VA, and the FHA have all endorsed the concept as it strengthens the association's ability to pay its bills and strengthens the whole community.

Q. What can I do if the board isn't doing its job?

A. Most problems arise if a board neglects the enforcement of rules or misuses the funds entrusted to it. If you suspect financial problems, you are entitled to review the association's finan-

cial documents, including its budget, financial report, bank loan documents, and record of reserves. Together with other concerned unit owners, you may hire an independent accountant for an audit even if the board refuses to do so.

If you believe the board has become autocratic and tyrannical, review the minutes of the board meetings to see whether decisions were made in accordance with the association's bylaws, rules, and regulations. Was there proper notice of meetings? Were all procedures proper? If not, some of the board's actions may be void.

When the board has seriously mismanaged its responsibilities, you have two basic options. The first and best option is to run for a position on the board yourself and convince some suitably qualified neighbors to do the same. If the board has clearly exceeded its authority or even undertaken activities with which a majority of the unit owners disagree, the unit owners, by petition, may order a **recall** of some or all of the board members, by an election in which new board members can be elected. Another option, which should be a distant second only undertaken with great care, is to litigate the issue. Be aware, though, that the board has a right to assess the unit owners to pay for its own defense, so you will be paying for the legal representation of both sides. Under the uniform acts, the loser will also have to pay the winner's fees. And remember that the business judgment rule described above can protect the decision of the board as long as it has been arrived at honestly. Arbitration or mediation may be a less costly approach. In fact, your bylaws might require it.

Handling Problems

Q. Can an owner obtain a variance from the association rules?

A. Under the rules of most community associations, you cannot make changes to the exterior of your home without the consent of the board. Normally, the board delegates the review of plans to an architectural control committee, which sets standards and uses them to rule on whether you can add a skylight or put on a screen door. As a homeowner, you submit your plans to the committee and cross your fingers. Be aware, though, that courts have found that covenant committees do not have the authority to approve major violations of the restrictive covenants.

If the board denies your request, you will either have to change your plans or steel yourself for a major battle. One New Jersey homeowner sued his association after its board denied him permission to build a deck. The case was in and out of court for years, with neither side willing to budge.

Q. What can I do if my neighbor is a problem?

A. The first step is to check the bylaws and regulations governing the association to see whether the practice in question is a violation. Then talk about it, first to the neighbor posing the problem and then to one of the members of the board, which often acts as a mediator to help unit owners informally work things out.

If the neighbor is clearly violating the rules, the board may ask you to sign a formal complaint to begin a proceeding that could lead to fines against your neighbor or even a court injunction to stop the behavior. If the problem isn't addressed in the documents and a polite request doesn't help, one option is to try alternative dispute resolution. Again, it is important to act promptly if a neighbor's behavior makes life unpleasant for you. If you have put up with it without comment for ten years, you may have trouble prevailing.

Q. What can you do if the community has too many rental tenants?

A. Owner-occupants often object to renters, who are perceived as not caring about the property enough to maintain it properly. Likewise, absentee owners generally want to keep up the rental value but don't want to pay for extras. And although restrictions apply to tenants as well as

to owner-occupants, they are more difficult to enforce.

But if the board slaps a lien on a unit owner because of the tenant's behavior, the owner may well terminate the tenant. If a majority of the unit owners believe the number of renters is a problem, they may be able to band together and convince the board to call for a vote on a change to the bylaws that would restrict leases.

Q. What can I do if I have a problem with the developer of a condominium?

A. In an increasing number of cases, condominium associations have sued their developers over shoddy construction, breach of contract, negligence, or fraud. These lawsuits are complex, time-consuming, and expensive, often involving hundreds of people and millions of dollars. But the law expects a developer who cuts corners on construction or breaks promises to the unit owners to make up for the damage.

If only your unit is involved in the problem, it's up to you to engage a lawyer and try to settle the matter out of court, if possible. But if the problem involves common areas or common funds, the association may assess all unit owners to pay its legal fees in pursuing the developer. In some cases, the developer may agree to arbitration to save the time and expense of a lawsuit. The important thing, though, is to act quickly, because the longer you wait, the harder it is to find witnesses or collect a judgment. In many states there is a limited time, sometimes as little as one to three years, to bring a lawsuit against the developer for breach of its warranties.

THE WORLD AT YOUR FINGERTIPS

- *The New York State Attorney General's Office has a Cooperative & Condo Conversion Handbook on its website (www.oag. state.ny.us/realestate/conversion.html). It is designed to help people understand the law on condominium and cooperative conversion in New York. Even though it*

⚠ IS YOUR ASSOCIATION ADEQUATELY INSURED?

Condominium associations typically carry several insurance policies to cover damage to building exteriors and common elements, as well as liability for injuries on the premises. In a common-interest community containing attached dwellings or dwellings within a single building, most lenders and enabling statutes require a single policy of property insurance covering the entire building, or all of the buildings in the project. This policy should not name the unit owners as the insured party, but should name the association or a trustee as insured for the benefit of unit owners and their mortgage lenders.

In such a community, you would only have to purchase property insurance on your unit's interior and contents, including paint, wallpaper, decorative items, furniture, and probably appliances; and on flooring, interior walls, carpeting, and the customized built-in portions of the unit. Your unit owner's insurance should also include a small amount, from $1,000 to $2,500, to cover uninsured losses to the overall community. This coverage may pick up your share of large deductibles in the community association insurance, or it may cover losses that are not covered by the association's insurance.

The issue of "dovetailing" insurance in this way between the association's policy and the unit owner's policy has become very complex, particularly in circumstances where there are construction disputes or damage from the elements. The insurance agent will need to review the condominium declaration carefully to ensure there is no gap in coverage between the policies.

In an attached-unit project, liability insurance should be maintained by the association to cover the entire project. Once again, this liability insurance should not name each unit owner individually as insured, but should name the association as the insured for the benefit of the unit owners. The association policy will cover your liability for association activities on the common areas and within the community, and for association activities that occur outside of the community.

Your individual policy should cover your liability for injuries that occur outside the community, or that you cause on the premises that were not the responsibility of the association.

In a common-interest community that consists of detached dwellings on their own lots, often the common insurance only covers the common areas or those areas that are the responsibility of the association. In these communities, the association insurance should cover the liability of the homeowners for the association's activities, as well as the property of the association.

In addition, associations usually carry liability policies on directors and officers in case the board members are sued over their decisions, and an umbrella liability policy to cover catastrophic judgments. Unit owners pay the premiums on all their association insurance as part of their regular assessments.

You have a right to see the association's master policy, which the association generally must supply within thirty days of your request. For a quicker response, ask the insurance company directly for a copy of the building policy. With that and a copy of the association's declaration and bylaws in hand, your insurance agent can help you determine how much homeowner's insurance you need.

While you are looking at the master insurance policy, ask your agent if the association is adequately insured. Full replacement cost is important, as the victims of hurricanes have learned. And if someone is seriously injured on the property and the association's liability policy doesn't cover the judgment, each unit owner could be assessed for a portion of the cost. Your own homeowner's policy, if broad enough, should protect you against these and other emergency assessments resulting from a casualty or liability loss. Without your own coverage, however, you could be subject to a catastrophic assessment.

---

is state specific, it does provide some useful general information.

- *An article from South Coast Today, a Massachusetts newspaper, points out some of the mistakes you should avoid when buying a condominium; visit www.s-t.com/daily/03-02/03-09-02/t10ho138.htm.*

REMEMBER THIS

- *Make sure you understand what type of common-interest community you live in, and which documents govern it.*
- *Before making changes to your unit, check the bylaws to make sure they are permitted.*
- *If a problem arises, take it to your association. If the association is the problem, work with your neighbors to elect new members.*
- *If you have a major problem with the developer or remodeler, see a lawyer promptly to assess your options.*

THE FINANCIAL SIDE OF HOME OWNERSHIP

So you've finally bought your own home . . . now you can lie back and relax in the sun.

Or can you? When you bought your home, you probably saved up for a down payment and got a mortgage that you'll be paying off for the next twenty years. So, even though the long

business of actually buying a home may be over, you can't forget all about the dollars and cents. You'll want to keep an eye on your lender or mortgage service company to make sure you're not the victim of costly accounting errors. You'll want to make sure your family would have enough money to make mortgage payments if something happened to you. If interest rates are low, you may want to consider refinancing. If you run into financial problems, you'll want to know your legal rights and responsibilities, and what your lender can do to protect its interests. And when the glorious day arrives when you have enough money, you'll want to know how to pay off your mortgage so you'll own that home free and clear.

Understanding Your Mortgage

Q. Who owns the mortgage on my house?

A. Traditionally, banks and savings and loan institutions owned most residential mortgages. Today, it's much more common for the original lender to sell the mortgage to an investor, such as a mutual fund or an insurance company. This means that borrowers are usually dealing with a mortgage servicer, rather than the actual person or institution that owns the mortgage.

Q. What happens when your mortgage is transferred?

A. Most mortgages are sold soon after the loan is closed. This means that you'll probably deal with at least two and possibly more mortgage servicing agents during the life of the mortgage. The mortgage servicer is responsible for collecting monthly payments and handling the escrow account, such as paying property taxes. The **National Affordable Housing Act**, passed in 1990, addresses the responsibilities of a mortgage servicer and consumer protection in this area. Under this act, lenders are required to do the following:

- Notify you at least fifteen days before the effective date of the transfer of your loan servicing. (The servicer has up to thirty days after the transfer to notify you if you have defaulted on the loan, the original servicer filed for bankruptcy, or the servicer's functions are being taken over by a federal agency.)

- Include the following in the notice: the name and address of the new servicer; the date the current servicer will stop accepting mortgage payments and the date the new servicer will accept them; and a free or collect-call telephone number for both servicers if you have questions about the transfer.

- Adhere to the contracted terms of the mortgage. The new servicer may not change any terms or conditions, and this must be disclosed to the borrower. For example, if your former lender did not require that property taxes or homeowner's insurance be paid from an escrow account, the new servicer cannot demand that such an account be established.

- Provide a sixty-day grace period, during which a late fee cannot be charged if you mistakenly send your mortgage payment to your former servicer. Moreover, the new servicer cannot report late payments to a credit bureau.

Q. What can I do if I have a problem with a mortgage servicer?

A. Contact your servicer in writing if you believe you shouldn't have been assessed a late penalty or for any other problem. Include your account number and explain why you think there was an error in your account.

The servicer must acknowledge your inquiry in writing within twenty business days, and it has sixty business days to either correct your account or explain why it is accurate. While you're waiting, don't withhold any disputed amount of mortgage payment, because that could count as a default on the mortgage.

Q. What is an escrow account?

A. An **escrow account** is the account a lender establishes to set aside part of your monthly mortgage payments to cover property tax, homeowner's insurance, and similar expenses.

Q. How do I determine how much equity I have in my home?

A. **Equity** is the value of your unencumbered interest in your home. It's determined by subtracting the unpaid mortgage balance and any other home debts, such as a second mortgage or home equity loan, from the home's fair market value. For example, if your mortgage is $50,000 and your home is worth about $100,000, you would have $50,000 in equity, or 50 percent equity, in your home. On the other hand, if the value of your home has fallen, you may have less equity than when you bought the home.

Q. What can I do if falling home prices have eliminated my equity?

A. Homeowners can find themselves in this situation if they bought when housing prices were soaring and the home market later collapsed.

This is a difficult problem if you're trying to sell or refinance. If you sell, you may owe the lender more money than you receive from the sale, because the sale price is lower than the remaining mortgage. If you're trying to refinance, a lender will want to know that you have at least 20 percent equity in the home, but an appraisal may not bear this out. Don't accept the first appraisal. You may find that another appraiser will give your home a higher value.

Unfortunately, if your equity has fallen below what you owe on your mortgage, there's little you can do. If you must sell, you'll have to take a loss on your home and perhaps pay the bank the remaining balance (to retain a good credit rating.) If you're trying to refinance, you may be able to talk to your lender and renegotiate more favorable rates on your outstanding mortgage. The one exception is for homeowners who have FHA and VA loans—they can apply for a special refinancing without an appraisal. (See "Refinancing FHA and VA Loans," page 200.)

Q. Is there anything I can do if I can't pay my mortgage?

A. When people get behind on their mortgage payments, it's usually because of job loss, divorce, illness, or medical bills. The first thing to do if you're having trouble making your mortgage payments is to take the matter seriously. Many peo-

---

ⓘ IS YOUR ESCROW TOO BIG?

The Real Estate Settlement Procedures Act limits the amount of money that can be held in an escrow account. The calculation is rather complex. Let's say the expenses paid by your escrow account add up to $3,600 per year, or $300 a month. The law requires that at least once a year, the escrow account be no more than twice the monthly payment required, or $600. The practical reason for this is that taxes are usually collected once or twice a year. Between collections, the account may have a sizable balance, but immediately after the collection it should have no more than $600.

If you notice on your monthly statement that your escrow is larger than that, you have the right to question the lender. This happens more frequently than one might imagine, so take the time to figure out if your lender is following escrow regulations. Otherwise, you're paying more in monthly payments than you should be.

---

ple refuse to face the fact that their home is on the line and delay doing anything until it's too late.

Lenders don't like to foreclose on property because they may not retrieve the full amount of their loan. In most cases, the homeowners would sell and repay the mortgage if they could. Typically, the bank ends up with a property that's not worth the outstanding amount on the mortgage. A lender will recover all its money only if it is foreclosing on a home that has much more equity than what's owed on the mortgage. There may be ways to work with the lender to reduce your monthly payments or at least delay foreclosure until you can sell your house.

Q. What is foreclosure?

A. **Foreclosure** is a legal action in which a lender takes ownership of the property used to secure the loan because the owner failed to make mortgage payments. Foreclosure terminates the homeowner's ownership interest. A **foreclosure decree** orders the sale of mortgaged real estate so the proceeds can satisfy the debt.

Q. What happens when a lender forecloses on the mortgage?

A. The law varies by state, and these differences have a critical impact on the homeowner's rights. That's why it's important to consult a lawyer in your state as soon as you can. In general, if the lender forecloses, all your rights to your home will end immediately or soon thereafter. This may be in no more than six months, though some states have a more lengthy process, including rights of redemption.

State laws do provide homeowners with certain protections. In Illinois, for example, when a foreclosure suit is filed, the homeowner has ninety days to make up the back payments to reinstate the mortgage. After that date, the lender can legally require that the mortgage be paid in full within seven months of the original foreclosure notice. The important thing to remember is that you must act immediately to protect your home if your lender intends to foreclose.

ⓘ WHAT TO DO WHEN YOU CAN'T PAY YOUR MORTGAGE

- Take the problem seriously. You could lose your home.
- *Contact your lender as soon as possible.* Call or write to explain your problem, and be sure to include your account number to speed the process.
- Ask if you could defer paying principal for a few months.
- Ask if you could refinance the loan at a lower rate to help make your payments affordable.
- If that won't work, ask for time to sell the home yourself. If you're actively trying to sell your home, your lender may cooperate by reducing monthly payments.
- Contact the nearest housing counseling agency, which offers advice and services to help you ward off foreclosure. If your loan is insured by HUD, for example, a HUD-approved agency can help you apply for federal mortgage-relief programs that may provide temporary aid. If you have a VA-insured loan, contact a local VA office for assistance.
- Consider filing for bankruptcy, which in some states may ward off immediate foreclosure. But be sure to talk with a lawyer before beginning any bankruptcy proceedings.

Q. Should I pay off my mortgage?

A. If you have enough money, should you pay your mortgage down sooner than scheduled or even pay off the loan completely? That depends on your circumstances. It's usually considered a good idea to make extra payments on your principal when you can, because that can reduce the term of the loan by several years and save you a bundle in interest.

Don't pay your mortgage off if it'll leave you strapped for cash. You may need a cushion later. But if you can manage it without sacrificing other things you need, paying off your mortgage can be an excellent investment.

When you make the final payment, get a **Certificate of Satisfaction of Mortgage** (sometimes called a **Deed of Reconveyance** or a **Release of Deed**). This document states that the loan has been paid in full. Have it signed by the lender, **acknowledged** (notarized), and entered in the public records.

This document is especially important if you've been paying a previous owner rather than a bank. In that case, ask your lawyer to draw up the certificate, then send it with a return envelope. If the previous owner balks, ask your lawyer to apply more pressure because it's extremely important to have that document filed.

If the bank offers to file the document for you, wait a few months and then check with the county register of deeds to make sure it's been done. Florida and some other states have laws requiring that the satisfaction of mortgage be filed sixty days after demand. If the lender was holding the abstract for your property, you should get it back now. And if you were paying into an escrow account for tax and insurance bills, ask to see what's left in your account and get a refund.

Refinancing and Home Loans

Q. How can you figure out whether it makes sense to refinance your mortgage?

A. This is an easy question for some homeowners—if you have a double-digit interest rate on your mortgage when rates have dropped to below 8 percent, there's no question that you'll save money by refinancing. Even if you refinanced two years ago, refinancing again may make sense if interest rates have fallen a point or two.

Or you may need cash to pay college tuition. Borrowing the money on your home equity and deducting the interest is almost always going to be cheaper than taking out an unsecured loan.

For other homeowners, the question is more difficult. You may want to do the following:

- Compare interest rates to figure out how much you would save on your monthly payments, based on the life term of the mortgage. For example, on a $100,000 mortgage, a mortgage interest rate of 7 percent versus 8 1/2 percent results in a savings of about $100

ⓘ WHEN A BUYER ASSUMES YOUR LOAN—AND DEFAULTS

Suppose that when you sell your house, you arrange for the buyer to assume your mortgage. Then the buyer runs into financial trouble and defaults on the mortgage. Are you liable for the loan?

That depends on when and how your mortgage originated. Some assumable mortgages dictate your responsibilities in case of an assumption.

- On most assumable conventional loans, you remain liable for the life of the loan.

- The same is true for loans insured by the FHA before December 15, 1989.

- On FHA mortgages originated after that date, you would share liability with the new owner for five years.

If this happens to you, talk to your lawyer right away to figure out what to do. The law of such liability is very complicated, and all may not be lost.

---

a month, or $1,200 a year on a thirty-year loan. To more precisely calculate the difference, you will want to get an amortization chart from a banker or real estate agent. Compare what you're currently paying each month in principal and interest with what you would be paying on the new loan.

- Include the costs of points, closing costs, title insurance, and other expenses for the new mortgage. Some lenders offer **no-fee mortgages** with rates maybe a quarter point higher but with virtually no up-front fees, closing costs, or points. This makes sense if you expect to sell or refinance within a few years, but not if you'll be paying those higher rates year after year.

- Calculate the difference between your current payment's after-tax cost versus your future payment's after-tax cost. Because Uncle Sam gives you a tax break on mortgage interest (15 to 31 cents per every dollar of interest paid, depending on your tax bracket), it's important to figure the tax break into your calculations, especially if you are (or expect to be) in the top tax bracket. Multiply the annual interest you pay currently by .15 or .31, depending on your tax bracket, to figure out your current tax savings. Then multiply your annual interest paid on the new loan by the same number. For example, if you're currently paying $7,800 in mortgage interest annually ($650 per month) and you're in a 31 percent bracket, you currently have an annual tax savings of $2,418 ($7,800 multiplied by .31).

- Compare rates and charges between several lenders, including your current mortgage servicer.

- Consider switching from a thirty-year to a fifteen-year mortgage. You may be able to pay off your loan in half the time without increasing your monthly payment by much.

Note that the amount remaining on the loan must be less than your home is now worth. Mortgage lenders are bound by strict state and federal guidelines spelling out the percentage of current value they can lend. Generally speaking, you can refinance if your home is worth 10 percent more than the loan amount.

Q. Are there times when it doesn't make sense to refinance?

A. In almost all cases, you won't recover the closing costs for a few years, so if you are planning to sell your home in the near future, it makes little sense to refinance unless you can obtain a no-points adjustable-rate mortgage at a low "teaser" rate.

Q. What's the difference between a home equity loan and a second mortgage?

A. They are similar in that the interest on both is tax deductible (up to $1 million of loans secured by the same property), and the home serves as collateral for both types of loans. They differ because a second mortgage usually consists of a fixed sum for a fixed period of time, while a home equity loan usually works as a line of credit on which you may draw over time. Typically, a home equity loan carries an adjustable interest rate, while a second mortgage carries a fixed rate, although this is not always the case in today's market.

Q. Which is better?

A. If you need a lump sum of cash, you are probably better off with a second mortgage because you will get a better interest rate on the loan. If you need money over a longer period of time, such as to pay college tuition or to pay for renovations planned over the next few years, it may be better to obtain a home equity loan. That way, you won't be paying interest on the money until you actually withdraw it as you need it. You can refinance at the end.

Q. Do the same rules apply to original mortgages and refinancing?

A. When you refinance, you pay off the original mortgage and replace it with a new one. State and federal laws protect consumers in both obtaining a mortgage loan and refinancing, but you will want to go through the same steps as you would in obtaining a first mortgage. (See chapter 4, "Buying and Selling a Home," for advice on shopping for mortgage interest rates and mortgages.)

▶ RENEGOTIATING YOUR MORTGAGE

Instead of refinancing, you may be able to get the savings you want by modifying your existing loan. Refinancing involves paying off the first loan and replacing it with a new one. But if your mortgage is fairly recent, you may be able to go back to the lender and renegotiate the terms to bring the existing loan in line with the market. This won't work if your original lender sold the loan to a mortgage service company.

Savings and loans and small-town banks, which often keep mortgage loans in their portfolios rather than selling them, are often willing to do this rather than lose your business. The new rate might be slightly higher than if you refinanced, but the costs could be significantly lower because there is likely to be less paperwork.

For loans originated within the past few years, some lenders require only a one-page loan modification form and a modest onetime fee. Ask your lender if a loan modification is feasible for you.

ⓘ REFINANCING FHA AND VA LOANS

Homeowners who have an FHA or VA loan may be able to qualify for a special program, called FHA Streamline Refinancing, which does not require a home appraisal, employment verification, or qualifying ratios as long as the mortgage is current. If you want to refinance an FHA or VA loan, call your local HUD office for information.

Q. Can I deduct the points I paid to refinance my mortgage on my federal tax return?

A. With one exception, points paid on a refinancing must be amortized over the life of the loan, while points paid to obtain an initial mortgage may be deducted in the year the home was purchased. For example, if you paid two points to refinance a new thirty-year mortgage, you would be allowed to deduct one-thirtieth of the points paid each year over the next thirty years. If you pay off the loan before it is due, however, you may deduct any remaining amount in the year the loan was paid in full.

The exception to this rule is if you pay the points yourself and use part of the proceeds of the refinancing to pay for home improvements. Then you are allowed to deduct a portion of the points in the year of the refinancing. For example, if you paid $2,000, or two points, to refinance a $100,000, fifteen-year mortgage and you used $25,000 to renovate your kitchen, you would be able to deduct 25 percent of the $2,000, or $500, in the year that you refinanced; the other $1,500 would have to be divided over fifteen years, allowing a $100 annual deduction.

Tax Considerations

Q. What tax breaks are available to home-owners?

A. On your federal tax return, both your local property tax and mortgage interest paid on your home loan (up to $1 million) are deductible against other income as long as you itemize and do not use a standard deduction. **Deductibility** simply means that you don't have to pay federal taxes on the income you spend on mortgage interest and state and local taxes. In the early years of a home loan, for example, when most of your payment goes toward interest, you might shelter as much as a quarter to a third of your income. You can deduct mortgage interest on a vacation home, too, as long as it's not used principally as a rental property.

Federal tax law also allows you to deduct interest paid on up to $100,000 of a home equity loan as long as the total debt on the home (in-

---

▶ REFINANCING TIPS

- Get a copy of your credit report before you apply and correct any errors.

- Make sure you have minimum 20 percent equity in your home; otherwise, you'll be expected to put down more money or be forced to pay private mortgage insurance (PMI).

- Make sure you understand the fee you will be charged or the increase in the loan interest rate if you use a mortgage broker.

- Consider shortening the term of the loan, perhaps from thirty years to fifteen years; you will pay more each month but save a lot in interest payments over the life of the loan.

- Be prepared to wait. Refinancing can take three months or more because when mortgage interest rates decline, many homeowners jump at the chance to refinance.

cluding the first mortgage) does not exceed the fair market value of the home.

You also may be eligible for a deduction of property tax paid on your home on your state income tax return, but this is not the case in all states.

Q. Is there any way to lower the property taxes on my house?

A. To lower property taxes, you need to lower the assessed value of your property, which is the basis for calculating your taxes. By providing evidence that the assessed value of your home or business property is too high, you should succeed in lowering the assessment and consequently your property taxes.

In most states, an assessor or a board of assessors places a value on your property for tax purposes. If the property has recently been sold, its sale price will be an important factor in setting the value. If there has been no recent sale, they will estimate its market value using other evidence. This assessment may be done annually or on some other schedule, such as every four years. In most cases, then, the assessor uses a complicated schedule to get from appraised value to dollar amount of taxes owed. For example, in many states, the value is reduced by a certain percentage, then multiplied by the local property tax, or millage, rate to establish the amount of taxes you will actually pay.

Your role in the process should begin when you get a notice indicating the assessed value placed on your property. If you think it is too high, you will want to file an appeal as soon as possible. To challenge the assessment, first look for obvious mistakes in the notice. Make sure the address and description of your property is correct. It may be necessary to look up the information about your home at the assessor's office. Check to make sure the number of rooms, the number of bathrooms, the square footage, and other details are accurate, and make a note of any discrepancies.

Next, check to see if you qualify for a special tax break. Some jurisdictions provide tax breaks to certain categories of property owners. For example, tax waivers of 10 percent or more may be available to owner-occupied homes, owners age sixty-five and older, disabled veterans, and persons with certain disabilities. Finally, make sure the assessor has any information about damage to the property, such as flood or fire damage. If any of these conditions apply, ask your local assessor's office how to file an appeal and note any of these problems in your appeal.

Even if none of these special conditions apply, investigate whether the market value determined by the assessor is higher than the true market value of your property. Local real estate agents or the county registrar of deeds should be able to provide recent sales figures of comparable or similar properties in your area. Also, check the assessed value of similar neighboring properties; this is public information in most places. Remember, however, that the assessed value is based on the market value of your home on a certain date the previous year, not its current value.

Once you have the information you need to protest your assessment, you will either be required to fill out a form or make an appointment with the assessment board. Be prepared to bring facts and figures. If your appeal fails, you may appeal that decision to a special board of equalization, a board of appeals, a state court, or a special tax tribunal (depending upon the state in which you live). State laws vary as to how and when property is assessed and appeal procedures. For specific information, consult your local government officials or your lawyer. Just remember, if your inquiries result in a visit by a tax assessor who didn't realize you have added a swimming pool, you could end up with a larger assessment.

Q. How can I qualify for a tax deduction on a home office?

A. If you run a business from your home, your office expenses are probably deductible. Depending on the size of your home and how much of it is designated as your office, the deduction can be significant enough to justify the extra effort needed to qualify. If your office meets the stan-

---

ⓘ FILING AN ASSESSMENT APPEAL

Most municipalities allow a limited time for assessment appeals. Don't wait until you get your tax bill, when it is too late to appeal. In most states, the procedures for tax appeals are relatively simple, and homeowners may be able to represent themselves. If the case is complex or involves a large amount of money, you may want to consult a lawyer or real estate appraiser.

---

dards spelled out by the IRS, you can deduct the cost of repairs, furniture, computers and office equipment, extra telephone lines, and other business-related expenses. You can also deduct a proportional share of your home's **depreciation** (ordinary wear and tear), utility bills, and insurance. Although you can no longer deduct the entire cost of a desk or computer the first year, you may claim **accelerated depreciation** if you use the item more than 50 percent of the time for your job. This allows you to claim most of the deduction the first two years.

Be aware, though, that you can deduct no more than your business actually generated. Also, the deduction lowers the home's **basis,** the figure used to calculate capital gains. This would be a problem, under current tax law, only if you generated a profit of at least $250,000 on the sale, so taking a home office deduction may not cause tax problems for most people.

THE WORLD AT YOUR FINGERTIPS

- *If you think you might qualify for a special government-insured loan offered through the Federal Housing Administration (FHA), you should seek more information*

▶ DEDUCTING YOUR HOME OFFICE

The IRS has liberalized its standards for determining if a home office (or studio or workshop) qualifies as a business deduction. To qualify, your office must be

- a part of your home that you use regularly and exclusively for your business; and
- your principal place of business, which isn't necessarily where you generate most of your income, but where you perform such administrative tasks as billing customers, setting up appointments, keeping records, and so on.

Even if your home is not your principal place of business, you will qualify if

- you use it regularly to meet with clients, patients, or customers; or
- it is a separate structure not attached to the home.

To increase the chances that your home office will qualify, especially if you do some of your work away from the home office, it's a good idea to

- install a separate phone line for the business;
- keep records of visits by clients, patients, or customers to your home office;
- have all business-related correspondence sent to the home office; and
- keep records of the time you spend working in the office.

FAMILY LEGAL GUIDE**THE FINANCIAL SIDE OF HOME OWNERSHIP**203

at the Department of Housing and Urban Development (HUD) website at www.hud.gov/hudqa.html. Some more good, basic information on FHA loans is available at www.mortgagebyreferral.com/fhaloans.htm.

- *You can find more information about Veterans Administration (VA) home loan basics at www.homeloans.va.gov. More information is available at www. militaryfinance.net.*

REMEMBER THIS

- *If you can't make your mortgage payments, contact your lender immediately to work something out. Don't just hope the problem will go away.*
- *Find out if refinancing your home or renegotiating your mortgage can save you money.*
- *If you think your property tax is too high, you might be able to find an error in the assessment or make your case before the assessment board.*
- *If you have a home office, you can deduct the expenses of running your business, including a portion of your home's depreciation.*

Renting Residential Property

Renting an apartment—or any living space—is an important decision. As a tenant, you will probably spend more of your income on rent than on any other monthly expense. As a landlord, you will depend upon the tenant to pay the expenses of running the building as well as provide you with an income. You should make the decision to rent carefully, and not act in haste. This chapter will help you to make a good decision that you will not regret.

    This chapter will also give you some suggestions on how to handle problems that arise after moving in, and talk about your options, whether you're a landlord or a tenant, if problems continue after moving out.

RENTING BASICS

The landlord and tenant relationship is created when the landlord and the tenant choose each other. The tenant has to want to rent from the landlord, and the landlord must consent to accept the tenant applying for the apartment. How well each of them makes that decision will probably affect the success of the relationship more than any other single factor.

If you are a tenant, you should try not to be so desperate for a place to live that you accept whatever the landlord is offering at whatever price and condition. If you are a landlord, you should try not to be so desperate for the income from the rent that you accept whoever walks into your office with cash in his hand. Bad decisions are often the result of hasty decision making. This section will cover topics that apply to both tenants and landlords.

Choosing a Landlord

Q. How can tenants choose a good landlord?

A. The first thing to do is check out the apartment. Look in every room and closet, open every door, drawer, and window, operate every appliance provided, and take your time. It is better to find problems now than after you move in. You should ask for repairs or improvements as a condition of moving in. Good landlords will put their promises in writing.

The second thing to do is read the lease. Most tenants never read a lease before signing it. There is no such thing as a standard lease. Landlords can and do write their own unique leases. You should ask for changes before you sign. Especially, you should ask for lower rent, more services, and better terms. Negotiating does not mean accepting whatever is offered.

The third thing to do is to check out the landlord. This is not as hard as it may seem. Much of the landlord's history is a public record. Has the city cited the landlord for code violations? Have other tenants sued the landlord? Is the landlord known by tenants' unions, consumer services organizations, or other regulatory bodies? Prospective tenants can also learn a lot about a landlord by asking other tenants in the building about how they are treated.

Q. Does the negotiation process give the prospective tenant some indications of whether the landlord will keep his or her promises?

A. Yes. Look for landlords who will put their promises in writing. There are winners and losers in the landlord derby. In first place are landlords who mean what they say and will back it up. They will agree to put promises in writing. They will agree to make repairs and specify when they will make them. They are clearly landlords acting in good faith.

▶ **THE MAILBOX TEST**

There is an easy way to judge how well the landlord maintains the building. Look at the mailboxes and doorbells.

Are the tenants' names on the labels all uniform, such as those made on a label maker? If so, the landlord at least cares about how his building appears to others.

Is the writing of the names all different, as if the tenants put up their own names? If so, the landlord is at best indifferent to the way the building looks.

Are the tenant's names written with a felt marker or etched into the metal? Are the mailboxes broken or unlocked? This suggests that nobody cares at all about appearances. If you do care, you should look elsewhere for an apartment.

In second place are the landlords who make oral promises to get you to rent from them, but won't put the promises in writing.

In last place are the landlords who will not even make any promises to get you to rent. They have no word to trust. You should rent elsewhere.

Q. What information can I find about my landlord on the public record?

A. The Internet has made more information available more easily than ever before. A skillful surfer may discover

- whether the landlord actually owns the building;
- whether the landlord has ever been taken to court by the city, other tenants, or workmen the landlord has hired; and
- if there is a record of complaints against the landlord.

The regulatory consumer agencies in your area may maintain websites that record complaints and evaluate customer satisfaction. Also, newspapers frequently carry stories about landlords and tenants; those articles can be discovered on the Web. Some websites list bad landlords. Check these sites out by typing "bad landlords" into your favorite browser.

For years, landlords have checked out tenants by using computerized credit reports. Now the tenant can check out the landlord.

▶ **GET IT FIXED BEFORE YOU MOVE IN!**

If you see things that are broken or need repair when you inspect an apartment, make sure repairs are satisfactorily completed before you sign a lease or hand over a security deposit. After you've signed the lease, the landlord no longer has any incentive to do the repairs quickly.

Choosing a Tenant

Q. How can landlords choose a good tenant?

A. The very first thing to know when renting an apartment is that you are not selecting a friend. Renting is a commercial relationship. You should approach selecting a tenant the same way you would select a building to buy. Ask yourself: Will I get the rent I want from the tenant without too many hassles?

Require the tenant to fill out a written application. Forms can be purchased from stationery stores and real estate offices. Ask for current and former employers. Ask for current and former landlords. Go back five years, if possible.

Make phone calls to verify the information. If the prospective tenant has worked for the same employer and rented at the same place for a few years, you probably have a good tenant.

Good tenants will appreciate that you check them out. If they are good tenants, they will want

---

ⓘ **LOCAL LAW IS IMPORTANT**

More than many other areas of law, landlord-tenant law is apt to be local. Many laws and legal rules that affect the landlord and tenant relationship are unique to the community in which you live. Don't assume that you know what's in your community's laws. For specific answers to your questions, consult your local government, a tenants' union, a landlords' association, or a lawyer who practices in the landlord and tenant field.

One other note: The discussion in this chapter assumes that both the landlord and the tenant are private parties. If a government agency is involved, that will very likely bring an additional set of laws and rules into play.

to know that you've checked out your other tenants and that they're good neighbors.

Q. How else can landlords evaluate prospective tenants?

A. They can hire companies that specialize in checking prospective tenants out. Landlords who only rent a few units may not possess all of the skills necessary to investigate prospects effectively. These companies charge a fee but earn it if they screen out undesirable tenants.

A check by a credit bureau will tell you about judgments against the tenant, bankruptcies, and slow payments to or adverse information from other creditors.

Q. Is a landlord allowed to discriminate in the selection of tenants?

A. Yes. The landlord can use legal criteria to select tenants, such as their past history of tenancy, the amount of income they have with which to pay the rent, their credit history, and their past criminal record. The landlord may also use personal criteria in selecting tenants, such as purple hair or nose rings. In some places, a landlord may even refuse to rent to certain people because of their occupation.

Q. Can I get in legal trouble by rejecting a prospective tenant?

A. Federal, state, and city laws prohibit discrimination. (For further discussion of the Fair Housing Act, see page 229.) Of course, discrimination means refusing to rent to people because of their race, color, or national origin. But other distinctions that a landlord might want to make between applicants are no longer legal. Other categories protected against discrimination include sex, family status, and handicaps or disabilities. States and municipalities have often added additional categories. You should know the law in your city and state. The best way to avoid problems is to treat all prospective tenants in the same way.

 WHAT IS A LEASE?

When the landlord has decided to rent to the tenant and the tenant has chosen to rent from the landlord, they will enter into a lease or rental agreement. **Leases** or **rental agreements** are contracts, written or oral, in which the landlord grants to the tenant exclusive possession of the property in exchange for rent for a period of time.

Leases

Q. What is the difference between an oral and a written lease?

A. When a lease is oral, it means that there is no written agreement setting out the conditions of the lease. Most standard lease forms are written by lawyers who work for landlords and the real estate industry, so the slant of the lease is usually in favor of the landlords. However, well-written and well-negotiated leases are preferable for both the landlord and the tenant, because they provide indisputable evidence of the terms of the agreement.

Q. What is the difference between a month-by-month lease and a fixed-term lease?

A. A month-by-month lease can be written or oral. Rent is payable monthly, and the lease can

---

▶ **THINK OF THE LONG HAUL**

The landlord and the tenant will have to deal with each other until the tenant moves out or the landlord turns over the property to someone else, and that could mean years. A "problem" tenant or a "problem" landlord usually does not improve over time. Both the landlord and the tenant should do all they can to make sure of a good match.

be changed or ended by either the landlord or the tenant after giving some notice. Usually, notice must be given thirty days in advance. In the notice, the landlord could ask the tenant to leave or pay more rent, or the tenant could inform the landlord of a move. The advantage of a month-by-month lease to tenants is that they can give notice, move, and stop paying rent. Since about 20 percent of all tenants move each year, the ease of mobility can be important. The disadvantage to tenants is that the landlord can raise the rent or otherwise change the rental conditions, such as refusing to allow pets in the future, on short notice. The landlord does not usually have to state any reason for the decision to end the lease or to make changes.

When the lease is for a fixed term, neither the landlord nor the tenant can end or modify the lease before the end of the term without the permission of the other. Fixed-term leases protect landlords from the vagaries of tenants' decisions to move (so long as the lease is supplemented by adequate security deposits) and protect tenants from rent increases during the term of the lease. But month-to-month agreements are better for parties who want flexibility.

Q. What are the most important lease clauses from the point of view of landlords?

A. The most important clause to landlords is the duty of the tenant to pay the rent in full and on time. This includes the right to charge a late payment fee. Other important clauses grant the landlord the right to enforce the rules and regulations written into the lease.

Q. What are the most important lease clauses for tenants?

A. It's important that the lease state the duty of the landlord to maintain the physical condition of the premises. Also of importance is the handling of the tenant's security deposit and the timing and mechanism for getting it back.

It is possible that the contract may contain clauses that give the tenant the right to terminate the lease if the landlord fails to make needed repairs, and give the tenant the right to hire workers to correct defects in the premises and to charge the landlord for the cost or deduct it from the rent. However, these clauses are rare because landlords draft contracts weighted in their favor. This is the reason why courts have implied remedies for tenants.

Q. How should the tenant or the landlord change the lease if either doesn't like it?

A. If either one can persuade the other to remove a particular provision, that provision should be marked out in ink on all copies. Both the landlord and the tenant should then initial the marked-out sections.

Many preprinted forms contain large blank spaces for the landlord and tenant to write additional agreements, which become part of the lease. Both landlord and tenant should initial these inserted paragraphs. If the spaces are absent or are too small, the additional terms should be written on a separate sheet of paper and signed and dated by both the landlord and tenant.

Q. Does the law regulate the provisions in a lease?

A. Yes. Courts have restricted what provisions can be enforced in a lease. Some of the most ob-

---

ⓘ NEGOTIATING THE LEASE

A lease is not written in stone, even though it may seem that way. A residential lease is just a form of contract and subject to most of the same laws as all contracts. The most important part of any contract is that the two parties negotiate terms that they can live by. Usually, prospective tenants do not try to negotiate, but they should always try to delete clauses they do not like and add clauses that they would like before they sign the lease.

jectionable clauses in leases are now illegal. For example, most state courts have struck down lease clauses that provide that the tenant accepts the apartment in "as is" condition and that the tenant must pay the rent regardless of whether the landlord maintains the property. So, if a landlord sues to evict for nonpayment of rent, tenants can defend themselves by arguing that the premises were not worth the full contract rent because of the deteriorated condition. This legal concept is called the *implied warranty of habitability* (for a further discussion, see page 213). It prevents the landlord from evading the responsibility to maintain the premises even if the tenant signed a lease waiving the right to maintenance.

Many states and municipalities have enacted laws that prohibit some clauses from residential leases. An example of a commonly prohibited clause is **confession of judgment**. Such a clause would permit the landlord's lawyer to go into any court and to represent the tenant without any prior notice, service or process. The lawyer, on the tenant's behalf, would waive a jury trial, confess judgment to whatever the landlord sues for without any defense, waive all errors or omissions made by the landlord in making the complaint,

and authorize an immediate eviction or wage deduction.

Lease Clauses to Consider

Q. *Can the tenants own pets?*

A. With an oral lease, tenants would probably have the right to own a pet unless the landlord specifies otherwise.

Written leases usually have a clause prohibiting pets on the premises or requiring tenants to get written permission for them from the landlord. A tenant who violated this clause could be evicted if the pet remained after the landlord asked for its removal.

Q. *Is the lease canceled if the landlord sells the building or the tenant dies?*

A. Most preprinted standard lease forms contain a paragraph on heirs and successors. This paragraph provides that the lease does not expire upon the sale of the building or the death of the tenant. If the tenant dies during the term of the lease, the tenant's estate will continue to owe the rent until legally released; it will also have the right to occupy the premises. If there is no provi-

---

ⓘ **MAY I COME IN?**

Normally, a landlord has no right to enter a tenant's apartment unless the tenant gives consent. Under the general tenets of landlord-tenant law, the landlord has surrendered possession of the premises entirely to the tenant for the term of the lease.

But a written lease will almost always give the landlord the right to enter to show the premises to prospective buyers or prospective tenants and to make necessary or agreed-upon repairs. A lease may require the landlord to give advance notice before entry (twenty-four or forty-eight hours), but some leases do not require any prior notice or restrict the time or frequency of entry.

State and local laws may also give landlords the right of access. Usually, these ordinances require landlords to give reasonable advance notice and to enter only at reasonable times and not so often as to be harassing.

Even if the landlord has the right to unlimited access, the police will normally ask a landlord to leave an apartment if the tenant requests it.

sion in the written lease, or if the lease is oral, then the death of either party terminates the lease.

Most written leases also include a clause specifying that the lease does not expire on the sale of the building. Unless otherwise provided, an oral lease will also continue in effect under the new landlord without any changes.

Q. Does the tenant owe the landlord a late fee if the rent is not paid on the date specified in the lease?

A. Not unless a late fee is specified in the written lease. Some municipal ordinances restrict the amount of late fees that a landlord may charge. State courts have also ruled that such a fee may be charged as **liquidated damages** (a sum specified in advance) but cannot be so large as to constitute punishment. Only the government has the right to punish or penalize someone for misconduct.

Q. Is the landlord liable for the damages incurred by a tenant who was injured because of inadequate maintenance of the property?

A. Many leases contain clauses, called **exculpatory clauses**, in which the tenant automatically excuses the landlord from any liability for damages from any cause whatsoever. Only about half of the states prohibit such clauses in residential leases.

Courts in other states have interpreted exculpatory clauses narrowly or have refused to enforce them because they are against public policy. If a tenant is injured it will be up to a court to decide whether the injury resulted from some negligent act by the landlord.

Some courts have held that if the tenant's injury resulted from the landlord's violation of the housing code, the landlord is plainly negligent and liable. Other courts have required the tenant to prove negligence. That is, there must be evidence that the landlord knew or should have known of the defective condition before the ten-

ant's injury. Furthermore, the landlord must have failed to make repairs within a reasonable time or in a careful manner.

The legal concept is called **premises liability.** A tenant who is injured on their rented property should consult a lawyer who has experience litigating these issues, because the laws vary greatly.

Possible landlord liability for injuries is discussed at greater length in chapter 14, "Personal Injury."

Q. If the landlord loses the building to the bank by foreclosure for failure to pay the mortgage, is the tenant's lease still valid?

A. Most leases provide that the lease is subordinate to any mortgage. This means that if the landlord fails to make payments to the mortgage holder, the landlord can lose the property through a lawsuit, called a foreclosure. Since the lease is subordinate to the mortgage, the bank can disregard it and evict the tenant. However, the bank must usually go to court and get permission to evict the tenant.

Some leases do provide **subordination, nondisturbance,** or **attornment** language, which explicitly provides that the lease remains in effect upon a foreclosure, provided that both the tenant and the landlord are honoring the lease terms.

Q. If the property burns down, does the tenant still owe rent under the lease?

A. In most cases, no. But a few state laws still on the books call for continued payment.

Q. If the local government condemns the property and decides to tear it down, is the tenant's lease still valid?

A. No. Most leases state that the landlord or the government may terminate the tenant's lease if the government condemns the property. The right of the government to condemn private property is called eminent domain. The government must compensate landlords for taking their property. The lease may provide that the tenants are not entitled to any of this money, but in some areas the law may entitle them to a portion of the settlement.

If the building is condemned, the tenant will have to leave. However, the local government must still get the permission of the court to evict the tenant.

Q. Can the tenant, with the landlord's consent, operate a business out of the rented premises?

A. Maybe. It depends on the lease and on local law. Most leases provide that the tenant must use the premises solely for residential purposes, but the landlord might waive this if the business seemed unlikely to disrupt other tenants or damage the property.

However, some business uses would be illegal under zoning laws even if the landlord allowed them. Local **zoning ordinances** govern how residential property may be used legally. In residential areas, some ordinances permit white-collar work, such as accounting, word processing, tu-toring, and counseling, but forbid any commercial, retail, industrial, or manufacturing use.

Likewise, local zoning laws may prohibit people from living in a commercial, retail, industrial, or manufacturing building. Therefore, if the landlord rents manufacturing space to a residential tenant in violation of the zoning ordinance, the lease is unenforceable because it is for an illegal purpose.

Q. If the landlord provides laundry facilities in the building at the time that the tenant signs the lease but later discontinues this service, does this violate the lease?

A. Maybe. Most leases provide that the tenant's use of any facility in the building outside of the apartment is a license and not a lease. These facilities include laundry in the building, storage areas, garages and parking spaces, bike rooms, swimming pools, workout rooms, and party and recreational areas. A **license** conveys permission to exercise a privilege in the use of the property and can be revoked by the landlord.

ⓘ WHOSE CHANDELIER IS IT?

Disputes often arise when tenants install more or less permanent fixtures, such as chandeliers or ceiling fans, in their apartments. A **fixture** is an object that is bolted or otherwise attached to the property.

Can a tenant install these kinds of fixtures? Under the general concept of landlord-tenant law, tenants may do anything they wish as long as they do not damage the property. But most leases do not allow a tenant to install such fixtures without the landlord's approval.

Can a tenant remove fixtures they installed when they move out? In the absence of a lease provision, fixtures belong to a landlord. Some leases permit removal of the fixtures if the wall or ceiling is restored to its original condition. Some states and cities have passed laws making it legal for tenants to remove fixtures that they purchased and installed from the premises when they move. It might be easier for the tenant to avoid a potential problem by specifying in a separate attachment to the lease those items that will be attached, and inserting a clause entitling the tenant to remove them at the end of the lease.

But state statutes or municipal ordinances may define the term "premises," which are rented to the tenant, to include the common areas of the property. In that case, the landlord cannot discontinue such services. If the landlord discontinues services that are included in the premises, the tenant probably would be entitled to a reduction in rent.

Q. What can the tenant do if other tenants in the building make noise and interfere with the tenant's "right of quiet enjoyment" of the premises?

A. Traditionally, the **right of quiet enjoyment** referred to the ability of a tenant to live somewhere without being disturbed by the landlord giving another person a right to the property. Today, the concept has been broadened to include the right to live somewhere without being disturbed by the noise from other tenants. The reasoning is that if the landlord imposes the duty to be quiet upon his tenants, then those tenants have the right to force the landlord to enforce that lease clause so they will not be disturbed by the noise from other tenants.

Q. If there is a legal dispute between the landlord and the tenant, does the tenant have to pay the landlord's lawyer's fees?

A. Most leases make the tenant responsible for the payment of all lawyers' fees incurred by the landlord in the enforcement of the provisions of the lease. But some state or local laws restrict that provision to situations where the landlord wins a lawsuit and the court awards fees.

THE WORLD AT YOUR FINGERTIPS

- *A good source of general landlord-tenant information, with many links, is provided on the website of Cornell Law School's Legal Information Institute,* www.secure.law.cornell.edu/topics/landlord_tenant.html.
- *Many states and localities have good sites that give the tenants an understanding of their rights. For example, Know Your Rental Rights is a useful guide for tenants in Cleveland, Ohio at* little.nhlink.net/nhlink/housing/cto/know/kyrr.htm.
- *Landlords can check the credit records of prospective tenants at various credit bureaus, including* www.accuratecredit.com *and* firstcreditbureau.com/landlord.htm.

REMEMBER THIS

- *Prospective landlords and tenants should take advantage of the many ways to get information about one another.*
- *A lease is a contract, and, like all contracts, is negotiable. Both landlords and tenants have every right to propose changes in the draft lease they are considering, but the other party does not have to accept the changes.*

⚠ CONDOS ARE SPECIAL

A tenant who rents a condominium has obligations to the condo unit's owner, to the condo association, and of course to the other residents of the condo.

The condo owner is the landlord. But the association sets the rules and regulations for the building and controls the common areas. Depending on local law, the association may have the right to seek eviction of a condo tenant who violates the rules. It may also have the right to seek the tenant's eviction if the condo owner fails to pay the regular association assessments.

All states and many municipalities have passed special condo laws, although in some cases they do not apply to buildings with only a few units. If you rent a condo, you must check the local law.

- *Besides the lease, local and state law may have a lot to say about the rights and responsibilities of both parties, and in fact may make certain lease clauses illegal, even if both parties have agreed to them.*

MAINTAINING RENTAL PROPERTY

A major source of conflict between landlords and tenants concerns maintaining and repairing rental property. Regardless of how high or low the rent is, there is an inherent tension between the desire of landlords to make money and the desire of tenants to have money spent on the property. This section covers the responsibilities of both the landlord and the tenant.

Q. Does the landlord have the obligation to maintain the premises and to make repairs if defects occur?

A. Yes. Both court rulings and state and local laws impose the duty to maintain rental property on the landlord. If a government agency is enforcing a housing maintenance code, the agency will cite the landlord for a defective condition regardless of who actually caused the defective condition to exist. (The landlord might have legal recourse against the tenant if the tenant damaged the property, but the landlord must still repair the property.)

Q. Does the tenant have any obligation to the landlord regarding the maintenance of the premises?

A. Traditionally, the tenant has the duty not to **commit waste**. That means the tenant may not cause unreasonable and permanent damage to the property.

Landlord-tenant laws have modified this concept. The tenant must comply with the sections of housing codes concerning keeping the premises clean and disposing of trash in a reasonable manner and in the facilities that the landlord supplies. The tenant must not damage the property negligently or deliberately. When moving out, the tenant must return the property to the landlord in clean and repaired condition, except for reasonable wear and tear. (See "Security Deposits" on page 225.)

Some leases still place some of the burden of maintaining the apartment on the tenant. Some leases require the tenant to return the apartment to the landlord upon moving out in perfect condition, without any wear and tear. Some of these lease clauses may be legal in some places, but even so, a landlord probably could not enforce such requirements on a tenant.

Q. What is an express warranty of habitability?

A. An **express warranty of habitability** is a written provision in a lease in which the landlord promises to make a specified repair or maintain a specified condition.

When the tenant signs a lease, he or she should make sure it lists all repairs that are needed now and contains a clause by which the landlord agrees to make future repairs when needed. Then, if the landlord fails to maintain the premises up to the express standard written into the lease, the landlord would be breaching the contract in not making repairs. The tenant could then sue the landlord for **specific performance** (a court order compelling the landlord to make the repairs) or for money damages for the breach.

Q. What is the implied warranty of habitability?

A. The **implied warranty of habitability** is an unwritten promise that the landlord will maintain the apartment in the condition required by the housing code and will make the repairs necessary to keep the apartment in that condition. The unwritten promise exists because the courts have ruled that all landlords have made that implied promise to their tenants.

Since the late 1960s, courts in nearly all states have ruled that the lease of every residential tenant contains an implied (that is, unwritten but understood) warranty that the property was in good condition and the landlord would keep it that way. Lease clauses in which the tenant waives the right to maintenance have been declared illegal and unenforceable in almost all the states. By passing laws requiring the landlord to maintain the property, state legislatures and municipalities have also created the standard of maintenance required by the implied warranty.

The implied warranty of habitability requires **substantial compliance** by the landlord. Thus, the landlord does not have to correct every building code violation to satisfy the warranty.

If the landlord breaches the implied warranty of habitability, the tenant will probably have the right to withhold from the regular contract rent an amount that reasonably reflects the reduction in value of the apartment by the presence of the code violations. The landlord's breach will also give the tenant the right to sue the landlord for the overpayment of rent if the tenant paid the full contract rent in spite of the presence of code violations. And the landlord's breach will give the tenant a defense against an attempt by the landlord to evict the tenant if the tenant does not pay the full contract rent.

Q. What is a housing code?

A. A **housing code** is a municipal ordinance (sometimes a state statute) that sets standards for the construction, rehabilitation, and maintenance of buildings. To qualify for funding from the federal urban renewal program, about five

thousand municipalities passed these codes between 1954 and 1965. They also hired inspectors to enforce the codes.

Housing codes govern new construction, energy conservation, fire regulations, fuel gas controls, private sewage disposal, mechanical equipment, plumbing, electrical, zoning, and general property maintenance.

Property owners must comply with these standards when constructing a new building, rehabbing or upgrading one, and making repairs as defects arise. A standard provision in these codes prohibits a landlord from renting a property that does not meet the code standards. The tenant will benefit by having decent housing if the landlord complies.

Q. What kind of standards do housing codes require landlords to maintain?

A. Tenants should know what the local housing code requires because they have the right to demand these conditions of the landlord. Landlords should know the requirements because the municipality expects them to maintain these conditions in the property.

The following areas are typically covered in detail in local housing codes:

- The building outside the apartment, such as garbage and refuse removal, stairs, porches, railings and handrails, windows and doors, screens, storm windows, walls and siding, roofs, chimneys, foundations, basements, signs, awnings, and other decorative features
- The interior of the apartment, such as walls, floors, and ceilings without holes, cracks, mold, or water damage; no lead-based paint; waterproof bathroom and kitchen floors; and no rodent or insect infestation
- Light, ventilation, and space, such as minimum lighting for halls and stairways, window or mechanical ventilation, and minimum adequate space for occupants
- Plumbing facilities and fixtures, such as running water, adequate hot water, sufficient water flow, no leaks, and working fixtures

---

▶ **WHAT YOU'RE ENTITLED TO**

Remember the difference between repairs and improvements. A tenant is entitled to have things in good working order. A tenant may not be entitled to a new refrigerator if the old one is still working.

- Mechanical systems, such as hot-water tanks, furnaces, air-conditioning, cooking equipment, and fireplaces
- Electrical systems, such as elevators, sufficient circuits and capacity, working fixtures, switches, and receptacles
- Fire safety, such as smoke detectors, fire extinguishers, automatic sprinkler systems, adequate exits, and control over storage of flammable materials
- Physical security, such as locks on windows and doors, peepholes in doors, and shatterproof glass on windows

Q. Does the implied warranty of habitability apply only to tenants living in slum buildings?

A. No. It applies to all tenants. The original lawsuits that led to the courts creating the implied warranty were brought by legal services' lawyers on behalf of poor tenants. However, the courts did not create a legal distinction between tenants based on their income level. The standard of maintenance required applies to all residential buildings, all landlords, and all tenants.

Tenants at all income levels sometimes have problems with landlords providing inadequate maintenance. There is always a tension between a tenant wanting service and a landlord wanting revenue. It is not rare for an expensive apartment to have a faulty furnace, corroded plumbing, and even an infestation of roaches or rodents.

Q. How do housing codes relate to the implied warranty of habitability?

A. Housing codes require **strict** compliance with their standards. The implied warranty of habitability only requires **substantial** compliance.

Some municipalities have adopted ordinances that give the tenant the right to hold the landlord to strict compliance for maintenance. Some of the following sections explain how the tenant's right to strict compliance works.

Q. Can the tenant do anything if the landlord refuses to make repairs?

A. Yes. The tenant has a number of options, though not all are available in all states. The tenant might

- complain to the municipal code enforcement agency,
- take the landlord to court,
- repair the defect and deduct the cost from the rent,
- reduce the rent payment, or
- terminate the lease.

Municipal Code Enforcement

Q. Can the municipal government force the landlord to maintain the property and make repairs?

A. Yes. If the municipality has adopted a housing code, it will probably have also adopted a mechanism for enforcing that code against violators. The tenant can report the landlord to the municipal department responsible for enforcing the code. The municipality hires employees to inspect properties for code violations. Small towns and small suburbs usually don't have staff to enforce property maintenance standards against landlords.

Q. How does municipal code enforcement work?

A. Municipalities make two basic types of inspections: inspections upon complaint from residents, and inspections upon a preset plan.

Some landlords have contested the right of municipal inspectors to enter their property; they call it trespassing. The municipality may have to go to court to get a warrant if the landlord refuses to let an inspector enter. The municipality does not need a warrant, however, if tenants invite the inspector onto the property.

Some courts have restricted the right of the municipality to enter apartments in a building as part of a preset plan. A municipality's plan is simply a schedule of inspections. It may call for inspection of the common areas of every rental building every year, or inspections of all buildings with more than three stories every two years, or every building in a certain neighborhood every three years, or any variation of that timetable.

If a local inspector finds any violations of the housing code, a citation can be issued against the landlord. Besides stating the violations, the citation may give the landlord a specified number of days to comply with the law.

If the landlord does not make the required repairs, the next stage of enforcement will probably be an administrative hearing. If the landlord fails to correct the code violations after a hearing, the municipality can take the landlord to court.

Q. Is municipal code enforcement effective?

A. It certainly can be. A municipality has police power to enforce the public welfare. If the landlord refuses to make repairs, the city can fine the landlord. If the landlord does not pay the fine, the city can place a lien on the property. The city can also foreclose on the lien. The city can have another person, called a receiver, appointed to manage the building, collect the rents, and make repairs until the code violations are corrected. The city can even condemn the building and have it demolished at the landlord's expense. In other words, the landlord can lose his building if the city vigorously enforces its housing codes.

If a municipality is committed to code enforcement, this is probably the most effective way to maintain the physical quality of housing in a community.

If a municipality does not make code enforcement a priority, then compliance by landlords with the codes will to some degree be voluntary, and there is the risk that some landlords will only comply minimally.

Q. What can the tenant do if the landlord refuses to maintain the premises?

A. If tenants take the landlord to court for failure to maintain the premises and make repairs, the tenant can pursue three possible legal paths:

- A tenant might argue the concept of the implied warranty of habitability, which was established by tenants attempting to force landlords' substantial compliance with local housing codes in court.
- Many local landlord-tenant ordinances permit the tenant to seek a court order if the landlord fails to maintain the premises. The legal standard for the landlord to obey may be strict compliance with the city codes. These ordinances may also require the landlord to pay the tenant's lawyer's fees.
- A number of state statutes on consumer fraud include the landlord-tenant relationship. Under these laws, it is fraud for a landlord to rent premises in defective condition. The legal premise behind fraud is that the city prohibits the landlord from renting substandard units but the landlord is doing it anyway. The statutes often provide for punitive damages and for the landlord to pay the tenant's lawyer's fees.

Repair and Deduct

Q. What is repair and deduct?

A. **Repair and deduct** is a law that permits the tenant to hire someone to make repairs and then to deduct the cost from the rent. State or local law may only cover repairs that are required to keep the premises habitable, such as the repair of a broken furnace or a leaking plumbing pipe.

Q. How does a tenant use repair and deduct?

A. The tenant must serve a written notice on the landlord. This notice must list specifically what repairs the tenant needs, provide a period of time for the landlord to comply, and state that if the landlord fails to do so, the tenant will hire someone to make the repairs and will deduct that cost from the rent.

Q. Are there any limitations on the use of repair and deduct?

A. Local laws may place a maximum dollar amount that the tenant can spend on repairs. For example, a Chicago ordinance limits a tenant's repairs to $500. Some laws limit repair costs to one month's rent.

However, in jurisdictions that have no explicit repair and deduct legislation and rely on the implied warranty of habitability, the right to use repair and deduct is limited only by the reasonableness of the repairs. Therefore, under the right circumstances, a tenant may even be able to buy a new furnace and deduct the cost from the rent.

Reduced Rent

Q. What is reduced rent?

A. In some states, when the premises do not comply with the standards of the local housing code, the tenant can pay the landlord a rent reduced from the full contract amount, which reflects the reduced value of the premises.

Q. How does a tenant go about paying reduced rent?

A. The tenant must serve a written notice on the landlord. This notice must list specifically what repairs the tenant needs, provide a period of time for the landlord to comply, and state that the tenant will pay a reduced rent unless the landlord makes the repairs within the time specified.

Q. May the tenant withhold all the rent?

A. A tenant might do that, especially to get the landlord's attention. But the landlord could reply with a notice to pay up or get out. And if the premises remained habitable at least to some extent, some rent would be owed. The tenant should pay some rent to the landlord as long as the tenant is still living there. (It would be up to a court to decide how much of a reduction is justified.)

Withholding rent is very risky for a tenant. If the tenant fails to prove a breach of the implied warranty of habitability, the tenant might be evicted. It is safer to pay the rent and sue for damages from the breach.

Q. Must the tenant put the withheld rent money in an escrow account?

A. It might be required by a local ordinance or the court might order it for the duration of a trial.

▶ **SHOULD YOU GO TO COURT?**

If the state courts are responsive to municipalities' lawsuits for code enforcement, they will be responsive to tenants' lawsuits as well. In those cases, suing will be quite effective.

The major problem is that the complexity of the court system really requires tenants to be represented by a lawyer. Poor tenants may have access to free or low-cost legal services, but most tenants are not eligible for such assistance. Middle-income tenants may not want to pay legal fees up front and may prefer to find a lawyer willing to represent them on a contingency fee basis (that is, paid upon winning the case). Thus, suing the landlord is not easy. However, some lawsuits in California have resulted in judgments against landlords for millions of dollars, including payment of the fees of the tenants' lawyers.

On the other hand, if the courts are not responsive to municipal code enforcement, then the tenants will not do well in court. The ability to sue successfully, particularly under the consumer fraud law, often depends upon the sensitivity of the courts.

For small problems that have not resulted in the loss of a large amount of money, it may be appropriate for a tenant or a landlord to pursue a remedy in small-claims court. Chapter 2, "How the Legal System Works," provides more information on how small-claims courts work.

But, whether required or not, it is a good idea to put the rent in escrow so that the money would be readily available if needed.

Q. What is a rent strike?

A. A rent strike is usually a collective action by a number of the tenants in the same building. They may withhold all of the rent or perhaps only a portion. It is a good idea to place the rent money in escrow in a rent strike so that all tenants know that their neighbors are participating; this also protects the money and limits each individual tenant's liability. Some localities allow tenants to withhold all of the rent money in a dispute about repairs. Provided they have the money to pay the landlord back for any rent that the court finds to be owed, they will not be evicted.

Q. How do the courts calculate rent reductions?

A. There are several standards, and they are not consistent across the country. Some courts have permitted reductions based on the reduction in the fair market rental value of the premises based on code violations. This means that the rent is reduced from the contract amount to the value the court considers fair with the defects. Other courts have adopted a standard for a reduction in the value of the apartment based upon how much and what parts of the apartment are adversely affected by the code violations. This **proportional use standard** means the reduction is determined by how much the defects reduce the use of the premises. If the use is reduced by 40 percent, for example, the rent may be reduced by 40 percent.

Q. If the tenant paid full rent but the premises were defective, can the tenant seek a rent reduction for past months?

A. Maybe, but the tenant would have to sue the landlord to collect. This concept is called **retroactive rent abatement**.

Both the implied warranty of habitability and local ordinances provide that the tenant has the right to recover damages from the landlord for failure to maintain the premises.

For example, suppose that the lease called for rent of $800 a month and the tenant paid that amount for ten months, $8,000 in all. And suppose that the court later determines that the value of the premises was only $500 a month, or $5,000 in all. The court could order the landlord to refund the $3,000 overpayment to the tenant.

Lease Termination for Code Violations

Q. Can the tenant terminate the lease if the landlord fails to maintain the premises?

A. Yes. Three different legal theories justify such an action. They are called illegal lease, constructive eviction, and material noncompliance.

Q. What is an illegal lease?

A. If the landlord has been cited by the municipality for serious violations of the housing code, the tenant can argue the **illegal lease** concept—basically, that the lease is illegal because the code makes it against the law for the landlord to rent the premises in defective condition. This theory holds that the landlord should not benefit economically from the illegal act.

Q. What is constructive eviction?

A. **Constructive eviction** means the property is in such poor condition that the tenant really cannot live there. For example, there is no water, no electricity, no heat, or a seriously leaking roof in danger of collapse.

The tenant has to serve notice on the landlord of the conditions, but there is usually not a minimum time period before the tenant can vacate. The tenant must actually move out in order to argue constructive eviction. If constructive eviction applies, the tenant will not be responsible for paying the rent.

Q. What is material noncompliance?

A. **Material noncompliance** means substantial noncompliance with the housing code. In other words, the premises don't meet the standards of the local or state housing code.

To terminate the lease on these grounds, the tenant would have to serve written notice on the landlord, specify the conditions that represent material noncompliance, demand the correction of the conditions within a specified period of time, and inform the landlord of the date that the lease will terminate if the conditions are not corrected.

THE WORLD AT YOUR FINGERTIPS

- *Information on local housing codes is available from the local code enforcement department—such as the building inspectors' office, the health department, or the fire department.*
- *Established in 1994, the International Code Council has developed a set of eleven comprehensive national model housing codes. These codes create standards for new construction, rehabilitation work, and property maintenance. See the council's website at www.iccsafe.org/index.html.*
- *The three regional organizations that compose the International Code Council provide technical, educational, and informational products and services to the public, professionals in the field, and their members. They can be contacted at www.bocai.org, www.icbo.org, and www.sbcci.org.*

REMEMBER THIS

- *The law imposes duties on both landlords and tenants, but ultimately it is the landlord's responsibility to maintain the property.*
- *A lease might give a tenant an explicit warranty about the condition of the property; if it doesn't, local law will impose an implied warranty about the condition of the property.*
- *Housing codes exist almost everywhere and give landlords a standard to meet.*
- *Tenants have many remedies for substandard housing, including complaining to*

housing authorities, suing the landlord, reducing the rent, doing the repairs and deducting the cost from the rent, and terminating the lease.

ENDING THE LANDLORD-TENANT RELATIONSHIP

Venus was having problems with the heating in her apartment. She complained to her landlord, who promised to fix it, but three weeks later he still hadn't made repairs. Venus decided to stop paying rent until her landlord repaired the problem. Five weeks later, Venus went on holiday for a few days. When she returned, she found all of her possessions piled on the sidewalk outside her apartment, and the locks on her apartment had been changed. This was the first notice she'd had that she faced eviction for nonpayment of rent. Venus probably shouldn't have stopped paying rent, but her landlord should have taken some steps to notify her before he could legally evict her.

This section will give you some important information on lease termination and eviction.

Lease Termination by Landlords

Q. Does the landlord need a reason to terminate the lease at the expiration of the term?

A. No. The landlord does not need a reason to terminate the lease unless the lease requires a written notice or provides for automatic renewal. However, a security of tenure law or a retaliatory conduct law may govern the nonrenewal of the lease. Security of tenure is discussed in the sidebar on page 227.

Q. How does the landlord terminate the lease at the expiration of the term?

A. It depends upon the type of lease.

If there is an oral or written lease with month-to-month tenancy, the landlord ends it by serving a written notice. The notice must give the tenant thirty days to vacate if rent is paid monthly, and seven days if it is paid weekly, although some states have different rules. Most cities or states require that this notice be delivered personally to the tenant, although some permit delivery by mail.

If there is a written lease with a specific duration or term, the lease automatically ends on the last day of the term. However, some municipal ordinances require a thirty-day written notice to the tenant before the end of the term. Without such a notice, the tenant does not know whether the landlord wants to renew the lease or not. It is always a good idea for the landlord and the tenant to discuss the matter well before the term ends.

Q. Can the landlord terminate the lease because the tenant is paying reduced rent?

A. It depends on the reason. If the tenant is paying reduced rent because of the landlord's breach of the implied warranty of habitability or violation of the housing code, the landlord may not have the right to terminate the lease. A retaliatory conduct law may prohibit such a termination.

ⓘ EVICTING A TENANT

A landlord can terminate the lease and evict the tenant for good cause. The most common causes are nonpayment of rent, damage to the premises, and violation of the rules and regulations of the lease. The most common rule violations are disturbing the neighboring tenants with noise, possession of pets, and occupancy by persons who are not named on the lease. Often the landlord must give the tenant a short period in which to correct the problem before eviction action begins.

Q. What kinds of actions by the tenant are protected from the termination of the lease by the landlord?

A. The landlord may not retaliate by terminating a tenancy if the tenant exercises any right or remedy under the law. These rights include complaining to the government agency responsible for code enforcement, complaining to the landlord about code violations and the failure to make repairs, and organizing or joining a tenants union.

Q. What kinds of conduct by the landlord does the law consider retaliatory?

A. Landlord-tenant laws define four actions as retaliatory:

- filing an eviction action or the threat of filing an eviction,
- nonrenewal of the lease,
- increasing the rent, and
- decreasing the services.

Q. How does the tenant prove that the landlord's conduct was retaliatory?

A. The tenant has to prove that the landlord knew about the tenant's conduct, such as complaining to the city department in charge of code enforcement. The tenant also needs to prove that the defects complained of were code violations.

The tenant might not have to prove that the conduct was retaliatory. Sometimes, the law assumes that the conduct was retaliatory if the tenant engaged in a protected activity within a specified period of time, sometimes as long as twelve months. The landlord would then have the burden to prove some other valid motive in terminating the lease or increasing the rent. The tenant can further assure legal protection by keeping a log of events and communications pertaining to the landlord's conduct.

Q. How does the landlord terminate the lease for cause?

A. For nonpayment of rent, the landlord can serve a written notice threatening to terminate the lease unless the tenant pays the past due rent within a certain number of days (depending upon the area, from three to ten days). If the rent is paid within the period specified by the notice, the tenant may remain. The landlord must accept the rent.

For violation of the rules and regulations of the lease or damage to the premises, the landlord can serve a written notice terminating the tenancy after a certain number of days (from ten to thirty days, depending upon the area). Some localities, but not all, provide that the tenant may remain if the violation ends—for example, by getting rid of a forbidden pet or repairing the damage to the premises.

Q. What does all this emphasis on written notices mean to the landlord?

A. In every jurisdiction the law imposes specific statutory obligations on the landlord as to the method of termination of leases. If the landlord fails to give the written notice where required or if the notice is not properly written or not properly served on the tenant, the landlord will not have the right to terminate the tenancy. When the landlord goes to court, it is already too late to correct any deficiencies in the written notice.

Besides hiring a lawyer to advise on the entire procedure, the landlord can get standardized termination forms from stationery stores, the local apartment association, or the Board of Realtors. Landlords should use these forms and fill in every blank space accurately to be sure that they follow the law.

Q. What can the landlord do if the tenant doesn't move after the lease is terminated?

A. The landlord must take the tenant to eviction court. The landlord cannot just decide to evict the tenant and carry it out unilaterally. For an eviction to be legal, there must be a court order signed by a judge. Also, the sheriff or some other governmental agent must actually carry out the physical removal of the tenant from the apartment.

Q. Why would the landlord sue the tenant? Isn't it easier to ask the tenant to leave?

A. Of course, the landlord can ask the tenant to leave. But the landlord must sue the tenant if the tenant does not move after being asked. That lawsuit is for eviction, which is referred to legally as **forcible entry and detainer** or **unlawful detainer**.

Q. What does the landlord need to do to evict the tenant?

A. If the tenant will not voluntarily leave the property, the landlord must take three steps in order to successfully evict the tenant.

First, the landlord must serve the tenant a piece of paper called a **termination of tenancy notice**. This notice must be properly filled out and properly served upon the tenant. Each state has different but quite specific procedures to follow. Although the landlord may sue the tenant without a lawyer, a lawyer will probably protect the landlord from making the kind of legal errors that result in the eviction lawsuit being dismissed by the court.

Second, the landlord must file a complaint with the local court and have a summons served

---

⚠ CHANGING THE LOCKS

Most people have heard stories of landlords changing the locks or shutting off the water or electricity to force a tenant out. That sort of conduct is illegal.

In fact, some jurisdictions consider such action a criminal offense. If the tenant is not allowed back in, the landlord could be arrested. The law might also provide a process by which the tenant could sue the landlord for monetary damages and lawyer's fees for an unlawful interruption of the occupancy.

upon the tenant by a process server. The landlord may have to pay a filing fee. Service of the summons must comply with strict legal procedures or the court will not have jurisdiction to hear the case. If the process server cannot obtain service on the tenant, there is probably a procedure for an alternative method of service. Once again, hiring a lawyer will help the landlord work through the legal procedures.

Third, the landlord must win the trial. Each state has different but specific rules about the conduct of trials. Trials for eviction often have different rules from the trial of other kinds of cases. For example, some states allow the tenant to file for a jury trial. To conduct a jury trial without a lawyer is nearly impossible.

Q. How long does the eviction process take?

A. After the notice period expires, the landlord may file a lawsuit alleging forcible entry and unlawful detainer. The court will assign the case for trial as a **summary proceeding** (meaning an expedited, quick process). The trial may be scheduled as soon as two weeks after the suit is filed. Assuming proper service of the summons and complaint on the tenant, the court will render judgment after a **default proceeding** (if the tenant does not show up) or a trial (if the tenant does contest the suit).

In some states, the judge can order eviction immediately at the end of the trial. But the court customarily gives the tenant time to move out, usually one to four weeks. If the tenant remains after that period, the landlord has to hire the sheriff or marshal to carry out a forcible eviction. That will take several weeks more. Further delays are possible if the tenant files a motion for more time or objects to the court determination. Eviction may take longer if the tenant is being evicted during the winter months. Some municipalities prohibit eviction if the temperature falls below a certain level.

Thus, the eviction process from the end of the notice period can take from five weeks to three months. And that assumes there are no delays.

Q. What can delay the judgment?

A. There are several factors that can delay the judgment. First, the landlord must hire the sheriff, a licensed process server, or a lawyer to serve the summons and the complaint on the tenant. If that agent is unable to serve the papers properly, the trial cannot go forward on the scheduled date, and the landlord has to try again. In some jurisdictions, the landlord's agent may **nail and mail** the summons and complaint (that is, post the papers on the tenant's front door and then mail copies to the tenant). In some other areas, the landlord has to employ an agent to serve the papers the first time but may nail and mail the second time.

The trial may be delayed by procedural matters, such as problems with the landlord's termination notice or problems with the method of service of that notice or of the court summons and complaint. Or the tenant may request certain procedural rights, such as pretrial investigation of the facts or a jury trial.

Action may also be delayed if the tenant has substantive defenses against the eviction, such as the landlord's violation of the implied warranty of habitability, discrimination, or retaliation.

Q. What happens if the tenant does not show up in court?

A. As noted earlier, if the tenant does not respond properly to the lawsuit or show up in court, the judge will issue a default judgment in favor of the landlord. This is what happens in most eviction suits.

Q. What kind of judgment may the court enter in an eviction case?

A. If the court rules in favor of the landlord, it may require the tenant simply to vacate the premises or to vacate and pay back rent, damages, court costs, and, in some places, the landlord's lawyer's fees.

Q. Can the landlord take the tenant's possessions or physically throw the tenant out after the court allows eviction?

A. No. The landlord must have the sheriff or other proper authority carry out the physical eviction. Only the court can evict a tenant, and the purpose of the court proceedings is to prevent the landlord from undertaking "self-help" evictions. If the court issues a judgment for unpaid rent, the landlord must use the normal debt-collection procedures, which may include wage garnishment and attachment of bank accounts.

Q. Is any of the tenant's property protected from seizure if the tenant owes money to the landlord?

A. Yes. All jurisdictions exempt some property from seizure by creditors, but they vary greatly in specifying which property is exempt. States may exempt used cars of low value, household furnishings, clothing, tools or equipment used in the tenant's business, and most of the tenant's wages. Chapter 8, "Consumer Bankruptcy," provides more detailed information on this area of the law.

Q. Does the tenant owe rent after the termination of the lease and eviction?

A. The landlord and the court may terminate the right of the tenant to occupy the premises. In many areas, however, the tenant can still be held liable for the payment of rent if the lease provides for it. But it is unusual for the landlord to sue the tenant a second time if the reason for the first lawsuit was nonpayment of rent. Debt collection against a tenant who was evicted for nonpayment of rent is usually a waste of time because the tenant who did not have the money to pay the rent does not have the money to pay a judgment.

Lease Termination by Tenants

Q. If the tenant moves out before the expiration of the lease, is the lease terminated?

A. No. The lease does not terminate just because the tenant moves out. The lease is a contract in which the tenant promises to pay the landlord for the right to possess the premises whether the tenant actually lives there or not.

Q. How can the tenant terminate the legal obligation of the lease?

A. There are three ways for the tenant to get out of the rental obligation:

1. Termination for legal misconduct by the landlord
2. Replacement in the premises by a new tenant
3. Agreement between the landlord and the tenant

Failure to maintain the premises may constitute legal misconduct. Local laws may provide for termination of the lease if the landlord violates other provisions of the law, such as by abusing access to the premises or failing to disclose code violations cited by the municipality.

If another tenant replaces the existing tenant, the first tenant can avoid the rental obligation. The landlord cannot legally collect from the original tenant if the replacement tenant pays the full rent.

Obviously, the landlord and the tenant can end the tenancy by mutual agreement. This simple approach is often overlooked, but should always be attempted first.

ⓘ **DON'T FORGET OTHER OPTIONS**

In addition to the lease-ending options for tenants discussed here, leases can be canceled under various legal theories when the housing is substandard. We cover this earlier in discussing code violations.

Q. How is one tenant replaced by another?

A. Under the common law, if there is no written lease, the tenant has the unrestricted right to transfer the leasehold to anyone else. A written lease will undoubtedly contain a provision giving the landlord the right of approval over prospective replacement tenants. Whether the landlord is acting reasonably in approving or disapproving of the replacement tenant can be an issue.

Q. Does the landlord have the duty to mitigate the rental obligation of the tenant who moves out?

A. In many places, the landlord is obligated to make a good-faith effort to find a new tenant promptly so that the old tenant can discontinue paying rent. The first tenant can also help find a new tenant.

Q. What is the difference between subleasing and reletting?

A. In **reletting,** the landlord signs a completely new lease with the replacement tenant and releases the original tenant from the obligation to pay rent.

In **subleasing** or **subletting,** the first tenant rents to another one. Although the subtenant now has the obligation to pay rent, the original one still remains responsible for the remainder of the lease term. Therefore, if the subtenant fails to pay, the landlord may sue the original tenant for the rent even though that tenant is no longer using the premises.

The original tenant may also be liable for damages if the subtenant breaches the lease or destroys the property.

Q. Can the tenant stay after the expiration of the lease?

A. A tenant who stays after the expiration of the lease is called a **tenant at sufferance** or **holdover tenant.** The landlord can sue for eviction or can choose to continue accepting rent,

---

ⓘ SUBLEASING

For many tenants, the commitment to a six- or twelve-month lease is inconvenient. For example, if you're a student, you might only need to live in an apartment for nine months before you take off for the summer; or perhaps your plans or your job might change, and you'll want to move earlier than you expected. When you have to leave your rented property and you don't want to break the lease, subleasing can be an appealing option.

How does the landlord fit into all of this? It's a good idea to inform your landlord of the proposed sublet well in advance, and seek the landlord's consent. Most of the time, there won't be a problem—after all, you'll be responsible for any damage your sublessor causes, as well as any rent they don't pay. Moreover, in most states, landlords may not unreasonably deny consent to a proposed subtenant. A landlord cannot withhold consent based on his or her personal taste, convenience, religious beliefs, sensibility, or desire to charge a higher rent. If a landlord denies consent for such reasons, the landlord may be deemed by some courts to have acted in bad faith, and the tenant might assign the lease without the landlord's consent, or even terminate the lease.

Rent-controlled apartments are the exception in some states. Generally, if a tenant of a rent-controlled apartment does not have an existing lease (and many tenants don't), then the tenant cannot sublet the apartment without the owner's written consent.

thus renewing the lease. The renewal will be on a month-to-month basis or for another year, depending on the terms of the lease and the provisions of the law. Moreover, a provision of the lease or a statute may give the landlord the right to charge double the current rent during the holding over period.

Since the landlord has the choice of eviction or renewal, the tenant who needs to stay past the expiration of the lease should try to negotiate an agreement with the landlord and get it in writing.

Security Deposits

Q. What is a security deposit?

A. It is money to protect the landlord in case the tenant damages the property or fails to pay rent. Usually, the tenant pays the security deposit before moving in. The landlord may ask for any amount, but some local laws restrict the deposit to the equivalent of one or two months' rent.

Q. What does the lease say about security deposits?

A. A preprinted standard lease form will probably contain a paragraph explaining that the tenant has made the deposit to assure compliance with all the terms of the lease. The lease will also set forth the conditions under which the landlord will return the deposit to the tenant. Most leases allow the landlord to keep all or part of the deposit if the tenant owes rent upon moving out or has caused property damage beyond normal wear and tear. Some of it may also be kept to pay for cleaning the premises for the next tenant.

Q. Are deposits for cleaning, pets, parking, or garage door openers considered security deposits and, thus, refundable?

A. Yes. If the tenant complies with all the terms of the lease agreement and leaves the place in good condition, the tenant should get most, if not all, of the money back, whether the lease calls it a security deposit or by some other name. In some states, however, the landlord may charge the tenant a nonrefundable fee for anticipated damage to the apartment. This is used most commonly for pets.

Q. Must landlords hold security deposits in a separate bank account apart from other assets?

A. In some states, the law imposes a requirement on landlords to keep the security deposit in a separate account from their own money—this makes sense because, legally speaking, the money does not belong to the landlord. A security deposit belongs to the tenant until it is later refunded or applied to cover unpaid rent or damage beyond normal wear and tear.

Q. Under what conditions does the landlord owe a refund of the security deposit?

A. The landlord will owe the tenant a refund if the rent was paid in full and the cost of repairs is not beyond normal wear and tear. The tenant should insist on accompanying the landlord during the final inspection to verify the items claimed by the landlord to be "deducts," and dispute the charges or explain why the damage is normal wear and tear.

ⓘ INTEREST ON DEPOSITS

Some states have statutes requiring the landlord to pay interest on the security deposit. In those states, the landlord cannot avoid paying interest simply because a lease says the deposit does not earn interest.

If the landlord fails to pay interest on the security deposit, the law may provide for the tenant to recover damages from the landlord for that failure. The law may also provide that the landlord has to pay the lawyer's fees of the tenant who sues to collect the interest.

Q. What should the tenant do if the land-lord does not refund the deposit or does not refund all of the deposit?

A. The tenant should first try to negotiate with the landlord, perhaps with the help of a mediator. If that fails, the tenant should take the landlord to small-claims court. Many states have a special small-claims court in which people can sue to collect money owed to them without the need to hire a lawyer. These courts are sometimes called **pro se courts** (pro se is Latin for "for oneself") because the tenant, who will be the plaintiff in the lawsuit, is often required to appear without a lawyer. (In some states, the landlord may still hire a lawyer.) This type of court is not as intimidating as regular court because the judge does not expect legal sophistication from the tenant.

THE WORLD AT YOUR FINGERTIPS

- *Tenants may seek the assistance of the National Housing Institute, which provides information and referral to local tenant organizations. NHI is located at 439 Main Street, Suite 311, Orange, NJ 07050. You can also reach NHI by telephone at 973-678-9060, by fax at 973-678-8437, or online at www.nhi.org.*
- *Landlords may seek the assistance of local real estate or building management organizations. A good website, www.landlord.com, provides legal information, downloadable forms, and much more.*
- *State and local bar associations may provide referrals to local lawyers who are familiar with landlord-tenant law, consumer protection law, or fair housing law in the community.*

REMEMBER THIS

- *Landlords can cancel a lease for such causes as nonpayment of rent and violation of rules, but if tenants do not move out willingly, landlords have to go to court to* seek an eviction order. Tenants can defend against the eviction attempt in court.
- *If tenants want to leave rental property early, they will usually still owe rent unless they have negotiated a settlement with the landlord or found a replacement tenant acceptable to the landlord.*
- *The landlord has a right to ask for a security deposit, but the law in many jurisdictions may govern how much can be requested, whether the deposit gathers interest, and the terms under which the deposit may be returned.*

OTHER ISSUES

Renting property may look pretty simple—all you need is some property and a lease. But there are other issues that may be important to you, whether you're a landlord or a tenant. This section will address some issues—including condominium conversion and political signage—that don't apply to every rental property, but might be of interest to you, now or in the future.

Q. What is the Uniform Residential Land-lord and Tenant Act?

A. In response to the civil rights movement of the 1960s, the federal government funded a legal services project to draft a model residential landlord-tenant code. From this model code the National Conference of Commissioners on Uniform State Laws drafted the Uniform Residential Landlord and Tenant Act (URLTA) in 1972. The American Bar Association approved this act in 1974. Subsequently, many states and municipalities have passed statutes or ordinances based upon this act.

Q. Does the URLTA favor tenants over landlords?

A. No. URLTA provides obligations and remedies for both landlords and tenants.

Q. Are there tenants' rights not covered in URLTA?

A. Yes. URLTA does not provide for security of tenure; control over rent increases; payment of reduced rent for reduced services; freedom of speech in the relationship with a landlord; appointment of a receiver to manage the building if the landlord fails to do so; payment of interest on the security deposit; separate handling of the deposit and the rent money; or condominium conversion protection for tenants.

Q. What is condominium conversion protection for tenants?

A. During the late 1970s, thousands of rental buildings were converted to condominium ownership by real estate developers. The tenants had to buy the apartments if they wanted to stay in the buildings. This was financially impossible for many tenants, and they had to move out.

Protests by tenants led to the passage of laws in many communities controlling the method of the conversion, and in some cases even the right of developers to convert buildings at all. These

---

⚠ **VOTE FOR . . .**

A landlord may be able to force you to remove a political sign from your window.

The First Amendment to the Constitution provides that the government may not abridge any citizen's right to freedom of speech, and that means political expression of any kind. But the amendment does not cover private relations, such as between a landlord and a tenant. It is common for a lease to contain a clause that forbids the tenant to exhibit any sign, political or otherwise, in the window or elsewhere in the apartment without the approval of the landlord.

---

laws' most common restriction required the developer to bring the building fully up to the standard of the local housing code. The restriction most desired by tenants was the requirement that a certain percentage of the existing tenants had to buy in order for the conversion to go forward. Sometimes the existing tenants who did not buy had the right to continue to rent in the building even if the conversion occurred. In no area, however, has legislation stopped conversions entirely. In fact, condo conversions accelerated in the 1990s with the lowering of interest rates and the general failure of tenant power to stop conversions.

Rent Control

Q. What is rent control?

A. Rent control laws or regulations limit the amount of rent or rental increase that landlords can charge.

Q. Has there ever been nationwide rent control in the United States?

A. Nationwide rent controls existed during World War II. President Nixon also imposed rent

---

ⓘ **SECURITY OF TENURE**

Security of tenure means that the tenant has the legal right to continue the tenancy indefinitely unless the tenant violates certain rules or regulations or the landlord has a compelling reason to reclaim possession of the premises. This provision is a major departure from the traditional concept that the landlord had the arbitrary right to terminate the lease at the end of any term. The right of the landlord to raise rent is the major area of conflict in the enforcement of security of tenure. All municipalities with rent control have security of tenure laws. New Jersey has the only statewide security of tenure law.

controls in 1971 during the initial phase of the effort to control inflation.

All public housing has rent control by definition, because the government sets the rent level for each tenant. Privately owned rental housing in which the government gives some special subsidy to the developer or landlord has rent control because the landlord must secure the approval of the government before raising rents. Most privately owned rental housing is subject to rent control only if the local or state government has passed a rent control ordinance or statute.

Q. What areas of the country have rent control?

A. The District of Columbia and some municipalities in New York, New Jersey, and California have passed rent control ordinances. Most state legislatures have outlawed local rent control ordinances. Some form of rent control covers less than 10 percent of the tenants in the country.

Q. What kinds of rent control laws are there?

A. New York City was the only municipality in the country to retain rent control after the end of World War II. The law there did not permit rent increases without specific permission from an administrative board. Rents could be raised based upon a pass-through of certain expense increases, such as the cost of fuel. Only a few apartments in New York are still governed by rent control. The current ordinance "stabilizes" rents.

From the late 1960s through 1978, other communities adopted rent control. Most of these laws allow automatic but limited rent increases without any requirement on the part of the landlord to show expense increases. Landlords are allowed to petition for larger increases on the basis of major repairs or extraordinarily large expenses that the normal rent increase would not cover. These so-called second-generation rent control laws have prevented some of the large rent increases experienced by tenants in other cities.

Q. How does rent control regulate the amount of rent?

A. Usually, the mayor of the city with rent control appoints a board to administer the law. That board determines how much the annual rent increases will be and whether individual landlords get extra rent increases. Some communities elect the rent control board members directly. Some observers think the elected boards are more independent from landlords.

Q. Are there state laws against rent control?

A. Yes. Legislatures in more than half of the states have forbidden municipalities to enact rent control ordinances.

Q. What is vacancy decontrol?

A. **Vacancy decontrol** is a provision of a rent control law that allows landlords to charge whatever rent they can collect from a new tenant who moves in to fill a vacancy. This is really an anti–rent control provision. Within a few years, new tenants in the same building can be paying twice as much as old tenants.

Fair Housing

Q. What is fair housing?

A. **Fair housing** is a legal term applied to federal, state, and municipal laws that prohibit land-

---

ⓘ ABILITY TO PAY NOT A FACTOR

Rent control does not consider a tenant's ability to pay. It is not a social welfare program providing subsidies to the tenant. Even in communities with rent control, there are tenants spending a large percentage of their incomes on rent. Rent control does not make housing affordable for everyone.

lords from refusing to rent property because the prospective tenant falls into one or more certain protected classes.

The Fair Housing Act (Chapter 42 of the U.S. Code, beginning at Section 3601) forbids landlords to discriminate in choosing tenants because of their race, religion, ethnic origin, color, sex, physical or mental handicap, or family status. Landlords cannot refuse to rent to a family with children. It is also illegal under the Fair Housing Act for landlords to harass, intimidate, threaten, interfere with, or evict a tenant because of the same factors. Furthermore, the same law prohibits the landlord from attempting to evict a tenant for filing a complaint or lawsuit charging the landlord with discrimination.

The Civil Rights Act of 1866 (Chapter 42 of the U.S. Code, Section 1982) prohibits discrimination because of the race, ethnic origin, or color of the tenants. This federal law applies to all landlords without any exceptions.

All the states and many cities have enacted fair housing laws as well. Some of these laws are not as strict as the federal law, but some are stricter because they protect additional classes of persons.

Some states and municipalities forbid rental discrimination based on marital status, age (especially over forty), less than honorable discharge from the military, sexual orientation, or source of income (welfare, Social Security, alimony, or child support).

Q. What can a prospective tenant do against a landlord who discriminates illegally?

A. The fair housing laws provide for two remedies. A prospective tenant can file an administrative complaint with the agency enforcing the law or can sue the landlord in court.

The U.S. Department of Housing and Urban Development (HUD) is responsible for enforcing the federal fair housing laws. The complaint must be filed within one year of the date of the discriminatory conduct. States and many cities have human rights agencies that accept complaints.

HUD has the authority to award monetary damages to the person discriminated against; the agency of the state or municipality may have similar authority.

The prospective tenant may also file a lawsuit in federal court to enforce the Fair Housing Act or the Civil Rights Act. The person may file an administrative complaint with HUD and sue in court at the same time. The prospective tenant may file a lawsuit in state court to enforce the state or local law.

Q. How can the prospective tenant prove that the landlord has illegally discriminated?

A. The prospective tenant has the burden of proving that the landlord's conduct was discriminatory. The person can establish a case against the landlord by proving four things:

- that the plaintiff is a member of a protected group;
- that the plaintiff applied for and was qualified to rent a certain property;
- that the plaintiff was rejected by the landlord; and
- that the property remained unrented thereafter.

Q. What are the possible outcomes for a prospective tenant who files a complaint or a lawsuit for discrimination?

A. If the prospective tenant wins, the landlord can be ordered to rent the premises to the prospective tenant and perhaps to pay actual and punitive monetary damages as well. The landlord can also be assessed the lawyer's fees incurred by the prospective tenant. The landlord may also have to submit to periodic review of documents and practices by the enforcing authority for a certain number of years.

THE WORLD AT YOUR FINGERTIPS

- *Many states and cities have departments of housing, departments of fair housing, departments of consumer affairs, or de-*

partments of human relations. Employees there can usually answer questions and accept complaints. Check government listings in the local telephone directory.

- The U.S. Department of Housing and Urban Development (HUD) has offices in many large cities and is involved in many landlord-tenant issues. HUD has regulations governing public housing, publicly subsidized housing, and fair housing. HUD can answer questions and accept complaints of housing discrimination. You can visit its website at www.hud.gov.

- The National Fair Housing Center (www.fairhousing.com) offers a terrific website, with recent developments, a legal research section, and many links.

- You can find the entire text of the Uniform Residential Landlord and Tenant Act (URLTA), with annotations, at www.lectlaw.com/files/lat03.htm.

- A site that opposes rent control, the National Multi Housing Council (www.nmhc.org/Content/BrowseContent.cfm?IssueID=66) offers a state-by-state breakdown on rent control, as well as many articles. Typing "rent control" into your favorite search engine will lead you to many additional sites.

REMEMBER THIS

- The Uniform Residential Landlord and Tenant Act (URLTA) favors neither landlords nor tenants; it is the basis of state laws in a number of jurisdictions.

- Rent control exists in relatively few communities, but in those communities it is highly important.

- Federal fair housing laws seek to outlaw discrimination on the grounds of race and a number of other factors. State and local laws may provide further protections.

Consumer Credit

Credit can work well for consumers, but there is a potential downside. Many people have overextended themselves by using credit to buy products now and pay for them later. They consume rather than save, and become mired in staggering credit card debt with high interest rates. They struggle to make minimum payments and find themselves with limited options.

This chapter will explain credit and its costs, break down the credit application process, discuss the major consumer credit protection statutes, explain the credit reporting process, and delve into fair debt collection practices.

CREDIT BASICS

Imagine that you apply for a new credit card with a high credit limit. You have other cards with high balances and need some more credit to buy stuff that you want. You believe that this card will be the magic key that enables you to buy products and pay for them later. You fill out the credit application and start dreaming about that new car stereo, entertainment set, and jet skis. But a week later a rejection letter arrives saying that you do not qualify for the high-balance credit card. Suddenly, you stop and think. Is my credit really that bad? How will I be able to get a loan to buy a new car or new home if I can't get a credit card? What exactly is credit, anyway?

This section will help answer your questions about credit – what it is and how to get it.

Q. What exactly is credit?

A. Your **credit** refers to your ability to make payments when they are due. Credit also refers to the sale of money for a certain price. An individual uses credit to obtain money to make a purchase. Credit allows you to buy and use goods and services now and pay for them later. For example, credit lets you own and use a car or a washing machine before you have fully paid for them. You pay for them as you use them. Of course, you could save now to buy the car in the future, but you may want or need the car now, not three years from now. Similarly, you may buy a pair of shoes or a dinner on your credit card now and pay for them later.

Q. What are the basic forms of consumer credit?

A. There are three basic forms of consumer credit: **noninstallment credit** (sometimes called **thirty-day** or **charge-account credit**); **installment credit** or **closed-end credit,** which is legally defined as credit that is scheduled to be repaid on multiple installments for a fixed period of time; and **revolving** or **open-end credit.** In addition, some lease arrangements operate like consumer credit and may be subject to similar laws, so these are discussed briefly in this chapter. However, credit secured by real property—your home, for example—is discussed in chapter 4, "Buying and

TYPES OF CREDIT AND BASIC OPERATION

Charge account or thirty-day credit Balances owed on such accounts usually require payment in full within thirty days. Such arrangements are not considered to be installment credit, since the debt is not scheduled to be repaid in two or more installments. Travel and entertainment cards, such as American Express and Diners Club, operate this way, as do most charge accounts with local businesses, especially service providers like doctors and plumbers.

Installment or closed-end credit A consumer agrees to repay the amount owed in two or more equal installments over a definite period of time. Automobile loans and personal loans are examples of this type of consumer credit.

Revolving or open-end credit In this more flexible method, the consumer has options of drawing on a preapproved open-end credit line from time to time and then paying off the entire outstanding balance, only a specified minimum, or something in between. With this type of credit, the consumer may use the credit, make a payment, and use the credit again. Credit cards such as Discover, MasterCard, and Visa, and those issued by major retail establishments, are examples of revolving credit.

Selling a Home," and chapter 5, "Home Owner-ship."

Q. Why does credit cost money?

A. To buy now and pay later, you must usually pay a finance charge. This is because the supplier who waits for payment, or the lender who lent you the money to pay a supplier, could have invested the money instead and earned interest. Thus the finance charge you pay compensates them for that lost interest, as well as covering the costs and risk involved in extending your credit.

FEDERAL LAWS THAT AFFECT CONSUMER CREDIT

There are many federal laws that provide certain protections and rights to consumers. Here is a brief description of some of the major consumer credit protection statutes.

Consumer Credit Protection Act of 1968 (CCPA) This law is the major federal consumer protection statute. Many other commonly known consumer credit laws are actually parts, or titles, of this law. For instance, the Truth in Lending Act is Title I of the CCPA, while the Fair Credit Reporting Act is Title VI of the CCPA.

The Consumer Leasing Act (CLA) This requires disclosure of information that helps you compare the cost and terms of one lease with another. It also orders firms that offer leases to reveal facts that help you compare the cost and terms of leasing with those for buying on credit or with cash.

Truth in Lending Act (TILA) This is the popular name for Title I of the CCPA. It requires creditors to disclose the costs and conditions of credit to consumers.

Fair Credit and Charge Card Disclosure Act This law amended the Truth in Lending Act, to require creditors to disclose the costs of credit when a creditor solicits a consumer for a credit card.

Fair Credit Reporting Act (FCRA) This law amended the Consumer Credit Protection Act and became Title VI of the CCPA. This law provides that credit bureaus maintain accurate information about consumers in so-called consumer reports. In 1996, the law was amended to impose some requirements on businesses that furnish information to the credit reporting bureaus.

Electronic Fund Transfer Act This law provides protection to consumers with respect to the electronic transfer of monies to pay creditors.

Equal Credit Opportunity Act This law prohibits creditors from discriminating against consumers with respect to credit on the basis of race, color, religion, national origin, sex, marital status, age, welfare assistance, or the fact that the applicant has in good faith exercised any right under the Consumer Protection Act.

Fair Credit Billing Act (FCBA) This law explains how a credit card holder can resolve disputes with the credit card companies.

Fair Debt Collection Practices Act (FDCPA) This law regulates the conduct of debt collectors during the collection of consumer debt.

Identity Theft and Assumption Deterrence Act of 1998 (Identity Theft Act) This law criminalizes the use of another person's identity or personal identifiable information to commit fraud or theft.

Links to the text of these laws can be obtained from the Federal Trade Commission's website at www.ftc.gov/bcp/menu-credit.htm.

The supplier may be a car dealer, an appliance dealer, a shoe store, or a restaurant. The lender may be a bank, a credit union, or a finance company. Only you can decide whether it is worth the cost of the finance charge to have a car or other goods and services now, rather than later.

Many states regulate by law how much finance charge you can agree to pay, and provide penalties if the supplier or lender charges too much. (You can find out whether your state caps these charges by contacting a state or local consumer protection agency.) However, some states allow competition among credit extenders to determine what you pay. You should shop for credit much as you shop for the best deal on a car or television set. The federal Truth in Lending Act and similar state laws allow you to do that.

Q. I keep seeing references to the Truth in Lending Act. What is it?

A. The Truth in Lending Act (TILA) is a federal law that requires creditors to disclose the cost of credit in consumer transactions. Creditors include banks, department stores, credit card issuers, finance companies, and so on. The Truth in Lending Act is part of a larger federal law known as the Consumer Credit Protection Act.

Under TILA, before you sign an installment contract, creditors must show you in writing the amount being financed, the monthly payment, the number of monthly payments, the dollar amount of the finance charge, and—very important—the **annual percentage rate** (APR.) The APR is an annual rate that relates the total finance charge to (l) the amount of credit that you receive and (2) the length of time you have to repay it. Think of the APR as a price per pound, like 20 cents per pound for potatoes. You may buy five pounds for $1 or ten pounds for $2. In either case, the rate is 20 cents per pound. However, the total cost in dollars depends on the amount of potatoes you buy. When you buy credit instead of potatoes, you buy a certain amount of credit for a given number of months. The total dollar amount of your finance charge will depend upon how many dollars worth of credit you obtain initially and how many months you use those dollars.

TILA also regulates credit advertising. For example, if an automobile ad emphasizes the low monthly payment (giving a dollar figure), it must also tell you other pertinent information, like the APR.

The APR can help you in shopping for a credit card and other forms of open-end credit.

Q. How do I select the best way to finance the purchase of, for example, a car?

A. Let's see how you can use the information required by TILA to get the best deal for you in financing a used car that has a cash price of $5,000. You have $1,000 in savings to make a down payment on the car and need to borrow the remaining $4,000. Suppose that by shopping around you find the four possible credit arrangements shown on page 235.

Let's begin with an easy decision. Notice that the four-year loan of Creditor B is a better deal than the four-year loan of Creditor C. Since their lengths are equal, we know that an 11 percent loan is cheaper than a 12 percent loan for the same amount of money. Forget about Creditor C.

However, look what happens when the lengths of the loans vary. Even though Creditors

---

▶ **CAREFULLY EVALUATE YOUR OPTIONS**

The example on these pages illustrates the importance of checking all financing options before making a decision. Fortunately, the law allows you to obtain the information that you need to shop comparatively. You should use this information, and factor it in with your own situation and needs to determine which loan or credit arrangement is best for you.

A and B charge an APR of 11 percent, the total dollar finance charge is a good deal greater on the four-year loan from Creditor B than on the three-year loan from Creditor A. Of course, the difference makes sense, since with Creditor B you would have another year to use the lender's money. You have to decide whether you would like to have the lower monthly payment that is available on the longer loan. Note that it doesn't help to look just at the total finance charge, which is lowest on the loan from Creditor D. But that creditor charges 12 percent rather than the 11 percent available from Creditors A and B. The only reason the total finance charge is the lowest of the four is that you would have the use of the creditor's money for only two years. You might choose Creditor D if you wanted to be indebted for a shorter amount of time.

If your chief concern were the best deal in money terms without regard to length, your choice would narrow to either Creditor A or Creditor B. Your choice would depend on how easy it will be to meet the monthly payments. A big decision is whether having a car today, rather than later, is worth the monthly payments at the 11 percent financing rate.

Q. Does this mean that I should look only at the APRs when shopping for credit?

A. No, when buying on credit, you will not be shopping wisely if you merely compare APRs. For example, in the scenario in the previous question,

you have to decide how long you want to owe a creditor. If you want to minimize that time period, Creditor D might be a good choice. Even better, you might consider asking Creditor A if it would make an 11 percent loan for two years.

Q. Are there any other points to consider when using installment credit?

A. Yes, consider whether the interest that you pay for the credit is deductible when calculating your federal income taxes. Almost all homeowners may still deduct their entire mortgage interest for tax purposes. However, the interest that you pay on credit card debt, auto loans, and other debts, which was deductible on your federal taxes until 1991, has now been completely phased out.

If you itemize deductions in preparing your taxes, you might consider financing major credit purchases through a home equity loan. This type of loan is discussed in the chapter on owning a home. However, remember that if you use a home equity loan, you are placing your home at risk. And if the items that you are permitted to deduct for tax purposes are less than your standard deduction, you will find that the interest on home equity credit will not help you cut your tax bill.

There is another factor to consider. What if you pay the loan off early? You need to check how the rebate of unearned finance charges will be calculated.

POSSIBLE CREDIT ARRANGEMENTS

	APR	Length of Loan	Monthly Payment	Total Finance Charge
Creditor A 11%		3 years	$131	$714
Creditor B 11%		4 years	$103	$962
Creditor C 12%		4 years	$105	$1,056
Creditor D 12%		2 years	$188	$519

(Note that the figures for total finance charge are correct, even though not precisely equal to the sum of the payments less the amount financed [$4,000]. Creditors often round off monthly payments to the nearest dollar, and adjust the final payment to make up the difference.)

THE WORLD AT YOUR FINGERTIPS

General information

- You can find the addresses and telephone numbers for consumer protection offices in your local telephone directory. You also can find them in the Consumers Resource Handbook, available free by writing to Handbook, Consumer Information Center-N, P.O. Box 100, Pueblo, CO 81002; telephoning 719-948-3334; or accessing www.pueblo.gsa.gov.

- The Federal Reserve has many publications related to credit available on its website at www.federalreserve.gov/consumers.htm. These can also be obtained without charge by writing to Board of Governors of the Federal Reserve System, Publications Services, Mail Stop 127, Washington, DC 20551. Among its many publications are:

  Consumer Handbook on Adjustable Rate Mortgages
  Consumer Handbook to Credit Protection Laws
  A Consumer's Guide to Mortgage Refinancings
  How to File a Consumer Complaint about a Bank
  SHOP: The Card You Pick Can Save You Money
  When Your Home is on the Line: What You Should Know About Home Equity Lines of Credit
  Keys to Vehicle Leasing

- The Federal Trade Commission has a Consumer Protection website on credit with a long list of publications, from 66 Ways to Save Money to Utility Credit. This site also has links to the major legislation: www.ftc.gov/bcp/menu-credit.htm. All FTC publications are available by writing to Public Reference, Federal Trade Commission, 6th and Pennsylvania Avenue, NW, Washington, DC 20580.

- The Legal Information Institute gives a brief overview of consumer credit, and provides links to relevant legislation and to other consumer credit sites; visit www.law.cornell.edu/topics/consumer_credit.html.

- MsMoney.com has a section on credit, which provides some good practical information, at www.msmoney.com/mm/banking/credit/crupdown_intro.htm.

- The National Consumer Law Center has online information and a variety of publications dealing with consumer credit at www.nclc.org/publications.

REMEMBER THIS

- Not all credit costs the same. Federal law (the Truth in Lending Act) requires creditors to disclose the cost of credit to you, the consumer, before you sign the contract. Use this to your advantage.

- There are several forms of credit: noninstallment credit; installment or closed-end credit; and revolving or open-end credit. You should understand the credit arrangement that you are entering into, including the amount of finance charges; the amount of monthly payments; the length of time you must make such payments; interest charges; and whether interest charges are deductible.

- You should look at several aspects of a credit arrangement beyond the annual percentage rate (APR). You must evaluate other factors, such as finance charges, interest charges, and length of debt obligation. Remember that shopping for credit is like shopping for other products. You must compare and contrast to make the best deal for yourself.

CHOOSING A CREDIT CARD

A credit card company sends you an attractive mailing. They say you are a select customer preapproved for a gold or platinum card. They offer enticing cash advances, balance transfers with little or no transaction fees, and no annual fee. It sounds nice and easy, but there may be more than meets the eye. You must look beyond the cover letter and examine all the information. Remember to keep reading after the asterisks at the bottom of the first page. Many cards have high APRs (annual percentage rates), charge high penalties if you miss consecutive payments, and charge even higher rates for cash advances. Cards with low rates may increase those rates if you miss a payment or fail to pay another creditor.

In this section, we will examine terms that are typically offered to consumers by banks and other issuers of credit cards. We'll use examples from actual solicitations and explain how they might affect whether a card offered to you is a good "fit" for your own credit needs.

Q. Who provides revolving credit?

A. Revolving or open-end credit is becoming increasingly popular in this country, as more people have credit cards than ever before. Discover, MasterCard, Optima, and Visa are examples of the many credit cards issued by banks, savings and loans, and credit unions. In shopping for a credit card, you need to recognize that credit cards with the Visa and MasterCard logos are issued by thousands of different banks, savings and loans, and credit unions. Hence, if you do not like the terms on one Visa card, you can always check with other issuers to see if their terms are preferable. Major retailers issue their own credit cards, and oil companies also have their own cards, although many of the oil companies do not offer revolving credit, only thirty-day credit (except on purchases of tires, batteries, and accessories).

Q. What legal protections help consumers select the best card for their purposes?

A. Because there are many card issuers, you have a wide choice among cards, and the law gives you some tools that will help you rank cards. First of all, it is illegal for card issuers to send you a credit card unless you have asked for it or unless it replaces a card you previously asked for. Furthermore, under TILA, every solicitation for a credit card must contain a brief disclosure statement. More extensive disclosures are due before you use a credit card you have applied for, and specific disclosures about finance and other charges and transactions are required with your periodic statement, which is usually monthly.

Q. How should I judge the APR shown in the solicitation?

A. The law requires credit grantors to quote the APR and to tell you the balance calculation method they use to work out the finance charge you pay. Since credit grantors use many different methods to compute the balance to which the APR is applied, credit grantors who quote identical APRs may charge you very different dollar finance charges each month. It depends on how you use the account and how they calculate the unpaid balance for assessing the charge.

▶ **ONLINE HELP IN CHOOSING CARDS**

There are several places online where consumers can get information that will help them choose a credit card. These include:

    Cardweb – www.cardweb.com

    Bankrate – www.bankrate.com

    CreditCardSearchEngine – www.creditcardsearchengine.com

Q. How do credit grantors figure an account's balance?

A. The most common system used by card issuers is to apply the APR to the average daily balance in your account over the billing period. A typical offering of a credit card states:

> *Method of Computing the Balances for Purchases:*
> Average Daily Balance (including new purchases)

Occasionally, retailers compute the balance by subtracting payments made or credits given during the billing period from the total amount you owe. They refer to this as the **adjusted balance method**. A few credit grantors do not subtract from the balance any payments made during the billing period. This **previous balance method** can cost you more than the other two methods, depending on how you use your account. Other methods also are employed, but these three methods can be used to illustrate the differences.

As you can see from the examples below, finance charges may vary greatly depending on how the credit grantor calculates them. In the first example, the average daily balance of $300 determines the amount of finance charge owed. The average daily balance is the average of the $500 owed for half a month and the $100 ($500 minus $400) owed for the other half. You owe the $500 and the $100 each for half a month because you paid the $400 in the middle of the month.

In the adjusted balance method, which is used by relatively few creditors, you owe a finance charge only on the amount owed at the end of the period. Since you paid $400, and thus only owe $100, you pay a finance charge only on the $100.

In the previous balance method, you owe a finance charge on the amount owed at the beginning of the pay period—the entire $500.

Q. Can I avoid paying a finance charge?

A. Many credit cards offer a grace period for prepayments, which is the time between the end of the billing cycle and the date that you must pay the entire bill to avoid paying a finance charge. It is usually between twenty and twenty-five days. The grace period is shown on the disclosure statement in the following manner:

> *Grace period for repayment of the balance for purchases*
> No finance charges are assessed on current purchases if the balance is paid in full each month within 25 days after billing.

Note that the grace period starts on the billing date. By the time you receive the bill, you may have only two weeks to make your payment. You must be careful to ensure that your payment is received by the due date. Be aware that the full balance must be paid each month to avoid finance charges and that the grace period applies only to purchases. If you obtain a cash advance on your bank credit card, you will almost always pay finance charges from the date of the advance and probably a cash advance fee as well.

	Average Daily Balance	Adjusted Balance	Previous Balance
Monthly interest rate	1.5%	1.5%	1.5%
Previous balance	$500	$500	$500
Payment on 15th day	$400	$400	$400
Finance charge	$4.50	$1.50	$7.50
Calculation of finance charge	$300 × 1.5%	$100 × 1.5%	$500 × 1.5%

The credit grantor may adjust the grace period under another method of assessing monthly charges on your bill called the retroactive or two-cycle balance method. Under this system, if the opening balance on your bill was zero, and then you made credit purchases but did not pay your entire bill, your next monthly bill will include a finance charge for these purchases from the dates that they were posted to your account.

For example, assume that you used a credit

⚠ IDENTITY THEFT

Consumers should be aware of the growing problem (some have called it an epidemic) of **identify theft,** or **ID theft.** The Identity Theft Resource Center (www.idtheftcenter.org) refers to it as the "nation's fastest growing crime." It occurs when a person takes another's personal information to commit fraud or theft. A common example is when someone uses another's identity to open up a new credit card account. The identity thief then makes purchases and ruins the victim's credit by not paying the bills. This conduct violates a federal law known as the Identify Theft and Assumption Deterrence Act of 1998. This law provides that someone commits a crime when he or she "knowingly transfers or uses, without lawful authority, a means of identification of another person with the intent to commit, or to aid or abet, any unlawful activity that constitutes a violation of federal law, or that constitutes a felony under any applicable state or local law." There are steps you can take to minimize exposure to identity thieves:

- Be careful to whom you reveal personally identifiable information. Do not give out this kind of information over the phone or online unless you know with whom you are dealing.

- Use passwords for your bank and credit card accounts. Do not use easily obtainable passwords, such as your mother's maiden name or the name of your spouse.

- When you are writing checks to pay on your credit card accounts, don't put the complete account number on the check. The last four digits are sufficient, and that way your full account number will not be exposed.

- When your wallet is lost or missing, call the three national credit reporting organizations immediately to place a fraud alert on your name and Social Security number. (Their numbers are given in "The World at Your Fingertips" on page 250.) The alert means any company that checks your credit knows your information was stolen.

- If you do not receive a bill from a regular creditor, contact your creditor to make sure that they still have your current address. An identity thief may have changed your billing address.

- If your credit card has been out of your hands (for example, taken by a waiter), the individual may run it through a small device that can read and store the magnetic stripes on the back of credit cards. These devices are readily available, and sell for around $100. The "skimmer" can then load the data onto another credit card to use at will. You will become aware of the theft when charges that you never made show up on your bill. Notify the card issuer immediately and call the Federal Trade Commission's Identify Theft Hotline toll-free at 877-IDTHEFT.

- Many states have passed ID theft laws. You can contact a local consumer protection agency or attorney general's office to learn more about applicable laws in your jurisdiction.

card on an account with no outstanding balance to buy a $500 item that the credit grantor posted to your account on March 15. Say that the credit grantor bills you on April 1, and you must pay in full by April 20 to avoid a finance charge. However, assume further that you make a payment of only $200, which the credit grantor credits to your account on April 18. Then your next bill (say May 1) will include a finance charge composed of two parts. One portion of the finance charge will be for the use of $500 for the period from March 15 to March 31. The other charge will be for the period from April 1 through April 30. You must read the disclosure statement or cardholder agreement very carefully to determine whether the card issuer uses this retroactive method.

Q. Does the APR on a credit card always stay the same?

A. Not if there is a **variable-rate provision**. More and more credit card issuers set APRs that vary with some interest-rate index, such as the market rates on three-year U.S. Treasury bills (T-bills) or the prime rate charged by banks on short-term business loans. These issuers must disclose in their solicitation to you that the rate may vary and how the rate is determined. This may be done by showing the index and the spread. The latter is the percentage points added to the index to determine the rate you will pay. An example of a disclosure on a variable-rate credit card offering is shown below:

> *Variable Rate Information*
> Your Annual Percentage Rate may vary quarterly. The rate will be the Prime Rate as published in *The Wall Street Journal* plus 9%. The rate will not go below 15.0% or exceed 19.9%.

The issuers of fixed-rate cards can also change the rate from time to time in accordance with the cardholder agreement and state and federal law.

Q. Is there a charge each year for the right to use a credit card?

A. Whereas few, if any, credit cards issued by retailers have annual fees, some credit cards issued by financial institutions have annual fees. These may range from $15 to $25, and perhaps $35 to $60 for "premium cards" that provide a higher line of credit. Charge accounts, such as American Express or Diners Club, have annual fees that probably exceed annual fees charged for bank cards. If you usually pay your credit card accounts in full each month and do not expect to pay a finance charge, you should shop for a credit card with no annual fee or one that is low. However, if you often don't pay the balance in full each month, then a low APR may be better for you than a low annual fee. A credit card solicitation must disclose any annual or other periodic fee, and certain other fees such as transaction, cash advance, and late fees if they are imposed.

Q. What other fees and charges should I look for on the disclosure statement?

A. In your disclosure statement, you will find a statement something like the following (assuming these fees are part of the plan):

> *Transaction fee for cash advances, and fees for paying late or exceeding the credit limit*
> Transaction fee for Cash Advances: 2% of the amount of the advance ($1.00 minimum; $10.00 maximum.)
> Late payment fee: $15.00, if the amount due is $2 or more. Over-the-limit fee: $15.00.

Note there may be other fees as well, such as replacement card fees, copy fees, wire transfer fees, and insufficient funds fees.

▶ **PAY AS MUCH AS YOU CAN AFFORD**

If you cannot pay off the entire balance on your credit card, you should pay as much as you can afford. If you only pay the minimum amount shown on the bill every month, it may take you more than ten years to pay off the debt, even if you never use the card again.

Unless you expect to be late in your payments, your choice of a card should not be heavily influenced by the size of the late fee. An over-the-limit fee may be more troublesome. Most credit card issuers set a limit on the amount of credit that they are willing to provide you at any one time. To encourage you not to exceed this limit, some banks may charge an over-the-limit fee. Unless you keep careful track of your charge slips, it is difficult for you to know how much you owe in relation to the credit limit. If you believe that you might be close to your credit limit from time to time, you might want to shop for a bank credit card that does not have an over-the-limit fee, or has a very low charge.

Q. What if I can't get a credit card from a financial institution—either because of a bad credit record or because I have not established a credit record?

A. You may want to consider applying for a **secured credit card**. This is a credit card issued by a bank or other financial institution that is secured by a savings account that you have deposited with the bank or other financial institution. You need to shop carefully for the best terms. Generally, you should be able to avoid an application fee. In the past, these have been quite high. Your line of credit will typically be limited to 90 percent or 100 percent of your savings account. In shopping for a secured card, compare the rates paid on savings accounts, the APR charged, and the annual fees. The APR is important, since you are not likely to be repaying your account in full each month. Also important are the late fee and any over-the-limit fee. These are sometimes quite high on secured credit cards.

Having a secured card is something like using training wheels on a bicycle. Once you have shown you can handle a revolving credit account, you should ask the institution that issued you the secured credit card to offer you the opportunity to switch to an unsecured card with more favorable terms. If the offer is not made, even after you have established a good credit record, apply for a regular credit card from another financial institution.

Protections for the Consumer

Q. How does the Truth in Lending Act affect me?

A. The federal Truth in Lending Act (TILA) helps you to choose credit wisely by requiring credit grantors to give you plenty of information before you make a choice. However, the law alone cannot protect you fully. You have to make it work by being an informed consumer.

▶ ## CHOOSING THE *RIGHT* CREDIT CARD

A credit card must fit your financial habits. If you often do not pay your account in full each month, you will pay more attention to the annual percentage rate than someone who never pays a finance charge. That person will be more concerned with an annual fee that would be levied.

Just knowing the APR is not enough, since there are different ways of calculating the balances against which the APR is applied. If you don't think that your income will rise if interest rates go up, you might prefer a credit card with a fixed APR, rather than one with a variable rate.

If you expect to use the credit card to obtain cash advances, the cash advance fee is important to consider. If you have a hard time keeping track of charges on your credit cards, a high over-the-limit fee may be worth avoiding. And if late fees promise to be a major problem, perhaps you should not take on another credit card.

TILA does not set finance charges, nor does it tell you what rates are fair or unfair. In some states, laws exist to prevent you from paying finance charges that are thought by legislators to be too high, but in most cases it is competition that serves to keep credit card rates in line, and they have been declining in recent years. But for competition to be effective in controlling rates, you must use the information provided by the credit grantor to select the credit card that best fits your needs.

Q. How can I limit the amount of finance charges that I pay for credit?

A. Your shopping for credit plays a key role in limiting and minimizing the finance charges that you must pay. It does not matter whether you are looking for closed-end credit (installment credit) or open-end credit (revolving credit.) And even though most states impose rate ceilings on various credit grantors or types of credit—for example, state law usually limits the rates that finance companies may charge—your shopping can still save you money.

In shopping for the best terms for you, check the *Wall Street Journal* and other newspapers that frequently publish shopping guides to credit cards from financial institutions that cover all of the relevant terms discussed above. You can easily shop for credit cards and compare terms by logging on to www.cardweb.com/cardtrak/ and other sites that provide information on credit cards. The Federal Reserve Board also gathers credit card rate terms for publication.

Q. In shopping for a credit card, I found that one credit card issuer charges a higher rate than that allowed by my state law. How can that be?

A. Many states impose rate ceilings on retail or bank credit cards. However, these limits do not always apply across the board. For example, under federal law, national banks may **export** their finance charge rates on credit cards. (State-chartered, federally insured institutions generally have the same exportation rights.) Thus, a na-

tional bank may issue cards from an office in South Dakota, a state that has no rate ceiling on bank cards, so the bank may charge cardholders in Iowa any rate the agreement specifies. While most retailers selling to Iowa consumers may not charge rates on their credit cards higher than Iowa law permits, some major retailers have established credit card banks and issue cards from those banks. In those instances, they abide by the laws of the state in which the bank is located. Of course, competition forces national banks and retailers to keep their rates in line with those charged by state-chartered banks, other financial institutions, and retailers. In this example, the pressures of the marketplace—the choices made by informed consumers—set the rates. The law does not set them.

Nonetheless, if you believe that the rate being charged violates state law, you should report the case to the state office of consumer protection (or similar office), your state's attorney general, or the federal authorities for national banks or federal credit unions. Competition and enforcement activities usually prevent such violations; but if there is a violation, you may be able to recover all of your finance charges plus a penalty, depending upon your state's law.

Q. What if a credit grantor fails to obey TILA?

A. Violations include failing to disclose timely information as required under the Truth in Lending Act or giving you inaccurate information. You should inform the proper federal enforcement agency. To enforce your rights, you may bring a lawsuit for actual damages (any money loss you suffer.) You may also sue for the greater of twice the finance charge or $100. However, the most you can recover, even if the finance charge is high, is $1,000. If you win the lawsuit, the law also entitles you to court costs and lawyer's fees.

Under some state laws, a violation of TILA is an unfair or deceptive act or practice, or is a violation of other state law, and other remedies may be available.

▶ ## PROTECT YOUR CREDIT CARDS AND KNOW YOUR RIGHTS

1. Sign new credit cards as soon as they arrive. Cut up and throw away expired credit cards. Destroy all unused preapproved credit applications.

2. Keep a list of your credit card numbers, expiration dates, and the toll-free telephone number of each card issuer in a safe place, so that you can report missing or stolen credit cards and possible billing errors (see discussion on page 254).

3. Don't lay your credit card down on a counter or table. Hand it directly to the clerk or waiter. Keep an eye on your card after you give it to a clerk. Take your card back promptly after the clerk is finished with it, and make sure that it is yours.

4. Never leave your credit card or car rental agreement in the glove compartment of a car. Never leave your credit card in an unlocked desk drawer, grocery cart, or hotel room.

5. Never sign a blank credit card receipt. Draw a line through any blank spaces above the total when you sign receipts.

6. Open credit card bills promptly, and compare them with your receipts to check for unauthorized charges and billing errors.

7. Write or telephone the card issuer promptly to report any questionable charges. As a practical matter, most consumers would prefer to call the card issuer's 800 number for billing questions, and most disputes can be settled in this way. (You can find the correct 800 number on your billing statement.) However, written inquiries will leave a paper trail that might be helpful in certain situations. Written inquiries will better preserve your legal rights because the Fair Credit Billing Act only protects written—not telephone—inquiries. These inquiries should not be included with your payment. Instead, check the billing statement for the correct address for billing questions. Either a written or a telephone inquiry must be made within sixty days of the statement date to guarantee your rights under the federal Fair Credit Billing Act.

8. Never give your credit card or checking account number over the telephone unless you make the call. Never put your credit card number on a postcard or on the outside of an envelope.

9. Do not write your credit card number on your check, and do not allow the merchant who takes your check to do so either.

10. If any of your credit cards is missing or stolen, report the loss as soon as possible to the card issuer. Follow up your telephone calls with a letter to each card issuer. Send each letter by certified mail and keep a copy. The letter should contain your credit card number, the date the card went missing, and the date you called in to report the loss.

11. If you report the loss before a credit card is used, the issuer cannot hold you responsible for any subsequent unauthorized charges under federal law. If a thief uses your card before you report it missing, the most that you will owe for unauthorized charges on each card is $50, though if you lose a number of cards you could be out hundreds of dollars.

Protections for Consumers Who Lease Products

Q. *What is the Consumer Leasing Act?*

A. The federal **Consumer Leasing Act**, which is part of the Truth in Lending Act, applies to any lease of consumer goods for more than four months in which the total contractual obligation does not exceed $25,000. (It does not apply to leases of real estate.) This law requires the lessor (the owner of the auto you lease, for example) to disclose information before you sign the lease. Among the most important items are

- the capitalized cost—that is, the cost of the goods being leased (the capitalized cost is negotiable to the same extent that the price of goods is negotiable if you were buying them instead of leasing them);
- the total amount of any initial payment you are required to pay;
- the number and amounts of monthly payments;
- the total amount for fees, such as license fees and taxes;
- any penalty for default or late payments;
- the annual mileage allowance and the extra charges involved if you exceed that allowance;
- whether you can end the lease early, and the method of computing the charge if you do so;
- whether you can purchase the auto at the end of the lease and for what price;
- any liability that you may have for the difference between the estimated value of the auto and its market value at the time you end the lease; and
- any extra payment that you must make at the end of the lease.

You can report apparent violations of the Consumer Leasing Act to the same agencies that enforce TILA.

THE WORLD AT YOUR FINGERTIPS

Choosing a Credit Card

- *The Federal Reserve Board website contains useful information about choosing a credit card in "Shop: The Credit Card You Pick Can Save You Money," at www.federalreserve.gov/pubs/SHOP/default.htm.*
- *The Federal Trade Commission provides a fact sheet for consumers called "Choosing and Using Credit Cards." This is another useful source of information. You can download it from www.ftc.gov/bcp/conline/pubs/credit/choose.htm.*
- *Cardtrak is a resource that contains information—APRs, annual fees, and so on—about different credit cards, and is a useful tool when shopping for a credit card; it can accessed by visiting www.cardweb.com/cardtrak. Other websites like www.kiplinger.com provide similar information. In addition, many large banks offer information on their websites about the cards they offer.*

Leasing

- *The Consumer Justice Center provides more information about leasing and the Consumer Leasing Act at www.consumerjusticecenter.com/consumer/lease.htm.*

ID Theft

- *If you believe an identity thief has victimized you, call the Federal Trade Commission's Identity Theft Hotline toll-free number, 877-IDTHEFT (877-438-4338). The FTC has also developed a so-called ID Theft Affidavit, which is a form you can fill out to track where an ID thief has struck.*
- *For more information on identity theft, read the Federal Trade Commission's publication ID Theft: When Bad Things*

Happen to Your Good Name. *This report is available online at www.ftc.gov/bcp/conline/pubs/credit/idtheft.pdf.*

- *Further information about identity theft can be obtained by visiting the website of the Identity Theft Resource Center at www.idtheftcenter.org.*

REMEMBER THIS

- *All credit cards are different. Selecting one is a decision that should be made carefully. You want and need a good fit.*
- *Remember that federal law requires credit card companies to disclose the cost of credit to you, the consumer. They must tell you the APR, how it's computed, finance charges, and a host of other financial information.*
- *However, bear in mind that the Truth in Lending Act (TILA) is primarily a disclosure statute. It does not set limits on the interest rates that credit card companies may charge.*
- *Some cards do not offer fixed APRs. Many cards have variable rates, usually tied to the prime rate. If you plan to use your card for cash advances, then carefully consider the cash advance fee.*
- *Credit card companies use different methods to calculate the balance upon which you pay finance charges. Pay attention to this when you receive a credit card advertisement.*
- *The Federal Consumer Leasing Act applies to any lease of consumer goods for more than four months and under $25,000. This law requires lessors to disclose information to you, the lessee-consumer.*

APPLYING FOR CREDIT

A number of African-Americans apply for retail installment credit to purchase motor vehicles. The applicants find out that they were charged higher credit charges than similarly situated white persons. The African-American plaintiffs sue the dealership and its finance company, claiming that the finance company allowed the dealership and its employees to subjectively raise its risk-based finance charge rates on the basis of race.

A federal law known as the Equal Credit Opportunity Act prohibits discrimination against credit applicants on the basis of race, color, religion, national origin, sex, marital status, age, welfare assistance, or the fact that the applicant has in good faith exercised any right under the Consumer Protection Act. This section will explain how.

The Credit Score

Q. How do creditors decide whether to issue you credit?

A. Many employ scoring systems that weigh different factors deemed relevant to your creditworthiness. A **credit scoring system** attempts to determine how likely it is that a consumer will pay her or his debts.

The company Fair, Isaac developed a scoring system called the FICO score. But not all credit-scoring systems are alike. They attach different weights to different factors. For this reason, a consumer may have varying credit scores with the credit bureaus. The following factors are generally relevant:

- Payment history—have you paid your bills on time? (35 percent)
- Amount of debt—how much debt do you currently have? How much debt do you have as compared to your current credit limits? (30 percent)
- Length of your credit history—how long have your accounts been open? (15 percent)

- Recent applications for credit—have you recently applied for several new accounts? If your applications were denied, this can negatively affect your credit score. (10 percent)

Under current law, creditors do not have to tell consumers their credit scores. Some lawmakers want to change this. They have introduced bills that would require consumer-reporting agencies to disclose credit scores when a consumer applies for an extension of credit by using their dwelling as security. As of early 2004, none of these bills had become law.

Even though credit bureaus are not required by law to reveal the scores, Equifax and Experian, two of the three major credit bureaus, offer credit scores to consumers for a fee.

The Equal Credit Opportunity Act

Q. When I apply for credit, are there factors that credit grantors must consider in a fair manner?

A. The federal Equal Credit Opportunity Act (ECOA) says that credit grantors may not use certain factors to discriminate against you in a credit deal. A credit grantor may not use age (pro-viding that you are old enough to enter into a legally binding contract), race, color, national origin, sex, marital status, religion, receipt of public aid, or the exercise of rights under the Consumer Credit Protection Act to

- discourage or prevent you from applying for credit;
- refuse you credit if you otherwise qualify;
- extend you credit on terms different from those granted to someone with similar risk (as determined by such factors as ability to repay, credit history, stability, and assets); or
- give you less credit than you asked for, if someone with similar risk would have received that amount or more.

The Equal Credit Opportunity Act does not, however, guarantee that you will receive credit. You must still meet the credit grantor's standards of whether you are worthy of receiving credit.

Q. When I apply for credit, may a credit grantor ask my age?

A. Yes, but if you are old enough to sign and be liable for a contract (usually eighteen, depending on state law), a credit grantor may not

---

DETERMINING CREDITWORTHINESS

Credit grantors may use any of the following factors to decide whether to extend credit to you. If your credit history is bad, they will usually not give you credit, or will charge you a high finance charge for the risk they accept in giving you credit.

Ability to repay This depends on the stability of your current job or income source, how much you earn, and the length of time you have worked or will receive that income. Credit grantors may also consider your basic expenses, such as payments on rent, mortgage loans or other debts, utilities, college expenses, and taxes.

Credit history This shows how much money you owe and whether you have large, unused lines of open-end credit. Some very important considerations are whether you have paid your bills on time, and whether you have filed for bankruptcy or had judgments issued against you.

Stability Your stability is indicated by how long you have lived at your current or former address and the length of time you have been with your current or former employer. Another consideration is whether you own your home or rent.

Assets Assets such as a car or a home may be useful as collateral for a loan. Credit grantors also look at what else you may use for collateral, such as savings accounts or securities.

- refuse to give you credit or decrease the amount of credit just because of your age;
- refuse to consider your retirement income in rating your credit application if the creditor considers income in evaluating creditworthiness;
- cancel your credit account or require you to reapply for credit just because you are a certain age or have retired; or
- refuse you credit or cancel your account because you cannot get credit life (or related) insurance due to your age.

The law does allow a credit grantor to consider certain age-related facts. These include how long your income will continue or how long it will be until you reach retirement age. Consider, for example, a loan that will take a long time to pay back. If an older applicant does not provide adequate security, he or she may not be a good credit risk.

Q. May a credit grantor deny credit if I receive public assistance?

A. No, a credit grantor may not deny you credit for that reason alone. However, credit grantors may ask the age of your dependents, since you may lose federal benefits when they reach a certain age. A credit grantor may also consider whether you will continue to meet residency requirements for receiving benefits and whether the creditor can reach the benefits by legal process if you do not pay.

Q. Does my gender or marital status affect whether I am worthy of credit?

A. No, the law protects both men and women from discrimination based on gender and marital status. In general, a credit grantor may not deny you credit or take any adverse action, such as lowering your credit limits or raising your APR, just because of your gender or because you are married, single, widowed, divorced, or separated. There are some specific prohibitions:

- A credit grantor usually may not ask your gender when you apply for credit. One excep-

tion would occur if you applied for loan to buy or build a home, or to repair, rehabilitate, or remodel a home. In those cases, asking your gender helps the federal government look for housing discrimination by determining whether equally qualified females and males are able to obtain residential mortgage loans. However, you may refuse to answer this question.

- Normally, you do not have to use a gender title (Mr., Miss, Mrs., or Ms.) when applying for credit. Sometimes credit grantors may ask whether you are married, unmarried, or separated if your marital status relates to their right to obtain repayment. Such a request would most likely be made in a state with community property laws or if the credit will be secured.
- A credit grantor may not ask women if they use birth control or whether they plan to have children.
- You do not have to reveal child support or alimony payments to a credit grantor unless you wish the credit grantor to consider it as income.

Q. May married people open credit accounts that are not also in their spouses' names?

A. Married people may open credit accounts that are not also in their spouses' names. People do not have to open joint accounts or take out loans with their spouses. Moreover, even if you have a joint account with your spouse, when a creditor sends information about your account to a credit bureau, it must report the information in each of your names, so you will not lose your separate identity for credit purposes. The credit bureau will maintain a separate file on you, so that a creditor may be able to access your personal credit history and rely on it when making a credit decision. Under the law, a credit grantor may not do the following:

- Refuse to open a separate credit account just because of your gender or marital status.

- Require your spouse to co-sign your account, unless you live in a community property state where spouses are liable for each other's debts.
- Ask about your spouse or ex-spouse when you apply for credit based on your own income. However, a credit grantor may seek this information if a community property state is involved or if you are relying in part on your income from alimony, child support, or maintenance payments from your ex-spouse for the purpose of obtaining credit.

Q. If my marital status changes, may a credit grantor force me to reapply for credit?

A. No, a credit grantor may not require you to reapply for credit just because you marry or divorce, or because your spouse has died.

In addition, a credit grantor may not close your account or change its terms for these reasons alone. There must be a change in how worthy of credit you are, such as a decrease in your income. For example, if your spouse dies or you get a divorce, and you had used your spouse's income to get credit, a credit grantor may have you reapply. The credit grantor must allow you to use the account while considering your new application.

Denial of a Credit Application

Q. What happens if a credit grantor denies credit to me?

A. Under the Equal Credit Opportunity Act, a credit grantor must notify you whether it has approved or denied your credit application within thirty days after you have completed your credit application. If the credit grantor denies credit to you, the notice must be written and list the reasons for denying credit or tell you how to request an explanation. Another law, the Fair Credit Reporting Act, affects credit denials as well. It requires that the notice tell you if the credit grantor used a credit report to deny you credit and, if so, the name and address of the credit bureau that

provided the report. You are then entitled to ask for a free copy of your report. These rights also apply if a credit grantor takes any adverse action, such as closing an existing credit account or reducing an open line of credit.

Q. What may I do if a credit grantor will not say why it has taken an adverse action against me?

A. First, ask the credit grantor to supply a written explanation as required by law. If you think the credit grantor has discriminated against you, tell the credit grantor why you think this, then try to resolve the issue through negotiation. If the credit grantor continues the adverse action and has not given a satisfactory explanation, you may complain to the appropriate federal enforcement agency (the Federal Trade Commission or your local consumer protection agency may be able to refer you to the right federal agency). You might have to enter a mandatory arbitration process or have the option to sue (see below.)

Q. Can I sue if a credit grantor has discriminated against me?

A. Under the Equal Credit Opportunity Act, you may sue for actual damages (the actual losses you suffered), plus punitive damages of up to $10,000. The amount of punitive damages awarded depends on whether the credit grantor should have known it was violating the law and other factors like the number of violations. Punitive damages penalize the credit grantor because it has violated the law.

Credit Insurance

Q. What is credit insurance?

A. There are many different types of credit insurance. **Credit life insurance** will pay off the balance owed should you die. **Credit accident and health insurance** will make the monthly payments on the covered debt for the period of time that you cannot work as a result of an accident or illness. The coverage may not become available until after you have been disabled for a specified number of days. Occasionally, you may be offered **unemployment insurance**, which would provide for payments on the covered debt during the period that you become unemployed. Again, there may be a waiting period.

Q. What requirements must creditors follow when they offer credit insurance?

A. There are certain basic requirements that creditors must observe in offering you any of these forms of credit insurance:

- The creditor should disclose to you in writing that your decision whether to accept the insurance will normally not be a factor in the approval of your loan. However, if the credit insurance is required, the premiums for the insurance must be included in the annual percentage rate that is disclosed to you.
- The cost of any credit insurance offered must be disclosed to you in writing.
- You must give affirmative, written indication of your desire to have such insurance. Usually this means that you must check the "yes" box on the loan form and sign that you want the insurance.

Q. Do I have to have credit insurance?

A. No. If possible, you should decide ahead of time whether you want credit insurance. Once you are at the point of sale, you may be pressured to accept it, just as you maybe pressured to buy a more expensive TV set or more options on a car. Buying a car can be pretty exciting, but be sure that your decision prevails when it comes to the credit insurance. Tell the salesperson whether you want the insurance. If you are told to "sign here, here, and here," be sure to study the loan agreement to see that your wishes on credit insurance have been observed. When you are at the final closing, check again. If you have made arrangements over the phone for a loan, and specified "no credit insurance," check the loan document when you are at the lender's office to

get the loan. If you had stated that you did not want credit insurance but find that it is provided on the loan agreement, don't sign it, even if the lender moans that the form will have to be completely redone.

Q. Is credit insurance a good idea?

A. Whether you should buy any credit insurance is a personal decision. Surveys of consumers who have purchased credit insurance indicate that they have done so because they did not have much other life insurance and did not wish to leave their family with the obligation to pay off the debt. The cost per $100 of credit insurance is definitely higher than the cost per $100 of a decreasing term life insurance policy. However, if the credit life insurance covers a $5,000 auto loan, the comparison is not very meaningful, since most consumers cannot buy $5,000 decreasing term life policies. The minimum amount purchasable is usually $50,000 or $100,000, depending on the insurer. Thus, you should expect to pay more per $100 of coverage for credit life insurance than for a $50,000 decreasing term life insurance policy—just as you expect to pay more per ounce for a glass of milk in a restaurant than for a gallon of milk at the supermarket.

As for credit insurance for credit cards, remember that it makes only the minimum payment each month, even though you may have been paying a larger amount before the disability or unemployment that triggered the benefit.

If you think credit insurance makes sense, and especially if you are trying to protect your beneficiaries from having to pay off the mortgage, you should investigate purchasing decreasing term life insurance. Though you may have to purchase a minimum amount, you would protect your family better, and get more for your money.

THE WORLD AT YOUR FINGERTIPS

- *The Federal Trade Commission provides more information on the Equal Credit Opportunity Act at www.ftc.gov/bcp/ conline/pubs/credit/ecoa.htm.*

- To learn more about your own credit and credit score, you can contact a credit reporting agency such as these:
  - Equifax:
    800-685-1111, or www.equifax.com
  - Experian:
    888-397-3742, or www.experian.com
  - TransUnion:
    800-916-8800, or
    www.transunion.com/index.jsp.

REMEMBER THIS

- *The Equal Credit Opportunity Act prohibits discrimination against any applicant for credit or any part of a credit transaction based on race, color, religion, national origin, sex, marital status, age, welfare assistance, or the fact that the applicant has in good faith exercised any right under the Consumer Protection Act.*
- *If you believe that you have been discriminated against based on one of the above-mentioned criteria, you should consult with a lawyer.*
- *Under the Equal Credit Opportunity Act, a successful plaintiff who proves discrimination can recover actual and sometimes even punitive damages.*
- *You should decide whether to purchase credit insurance based on an evaluation of your personal needs. For instance, if you have already purchased a term life insurance policy, you may not need credit insurance.*

CREDIT RECORDS

Wilkins Micawber is denied credit based on a bad credit history. The creditor relied on a negative consumer report on him from a major credit bureau, or credit reporting agency. He requests a copy of the credit report from the credit bureau. Much to his dismay, the report contains items from another individual by the same name, includes information more than ten years old, and contains other inaccurate information. What can Mr. Micawber do to correct these mistakes on his credit report?

Fortunately, a federal law known as the **Fair Credit Reporting Act is designed to protect consumers from inaccurate information in consumer reports. This section will reveal how.**

Establishing a Credit Record

Q. How can I get credit if I've never had it before?

A. First-time borrowers soon realize that in order to get credit they must have a credit history. There are several ways to start building a good, solid credit history. For example:

- You may open a checking or savings account. When credit grantors see such accounts, they can judge whether you have adequate money and know how to manage it.
- You can apply for limited credit from a large, local department store, and use it. If you want to build a credit history, remember that some small local retailers, travel-and-entertainment cards, credit unions, and gasoline card companies do not report your credit performance to a credit bureau.
- You could obtain a secured credit card (discussed on page 241) or deposit money in a bank, a savings and loan association, or a savings bank, and then borrow against it.
- You might have someone co-sign the loan with you; that person must have a favorable credit record and will be liable for the debt if you cannot pay. With your first loan based on someone else's credit, it will be easier to get credit on your own after you pay back the loan. If you are asked to co-sign for another person's loan, be very careful—if that person fails to pay, the debt will be your responsibility.

Q. Should I get credit in my own name, even though I am married?

A. Yes, if you have your own sources of income, you should establish a credit history in your own name in case you become divorced or your spouse dies. This is also important if your spouse has a poor credit record and you do not want your credit records tarnished with his or her payment performance. However, many divorced or widowed persons do not have credit histories separate from their former spouses. In these cases, credit grantors will look at the credit history of any accounts held jointly with the former spouses. The nonearning spouse may be able to obtain credit by using checks, receipts, or other records to show that he or she is worthy of credit. If their former spouses had poor credit records, nonearning spouses may show that the records do not reflect whether they deserve credit by producing previous explanatory letters sent to credit grantors, copies of contracts signed only by the spouse, receipts, or other evidence.

Credit and Divorce

Divorce can negatively affect people's credit for many reasons. It is important for people who are getting divorced to realize whether their various accounts are individual or joint accounts. If an account is an individual account, then only the individual is responsible for the debts of that account. However, if the account is joint, both persons listed on the account are responsible. This can prove costly when a spouse or ex-spouse refuses to act responsibly or does not pay his or her bills. In some states, called community property states (Arizona, California, Idaho, Louisiana, Nevada, New Mexico, Texas, Washington, and Wisconsin), both spouses may be responsible for all debts incurred during the marriage, even under individual accounts. Just as couples who are getting divorced usually negotiate a settlement in which they agree to divide their property, so dividing responsibility for debts is usually negotiated. If the couple can't agree on a settlement, the court will divide the assets and debts. The Federal Trade Commission has a short report entitled *Credit and Divorce* that is available online at www.ftc.gov/bcp/conline/pubs/credit/divorce.htm.

Q. What is a credit bureau?

A. **Credit bureaus** (sometimes called **credit reporting agencies** or **consumer reporting agencies**) maintain computer files of your financial payment histories, public record data, and personal identifying data. Your credit record does not contain information on your medical history. There are several competing major credit reporting systems: Experian, Equifax, and TransUnion. You can find the bureaus serving your area by looking for credit reporting companies in the yellow pages of your phone book. Activities of credit bureaus are governed by a federal law: the **Fair Credit Reporting Act** (**FCRA**). Several states have enacted similar laws.

Credit bureaus do not make credit decisions. Instead, they provide data to credit grantors for use in making credit decisions. How does this work? Credit grantors provide information on their customers' debts and payment habits to credit bureaus, usually on a monthly basis. The data is then made available, sometimes on an online basis, to other credit grantors to whom you apply for credit. For this reason, a good credit record is very important to your ability to obtain credit to purchase goods and services, to rent an apartment, or to buy a home. Credit reports may also be used when you apply for insurance or for employment. The law punishes unauthorized people who lie to obtain a credit report, or credit bureau employees who supply a credit report to unauthorized people. These people may receive fines of up to $5,000 or prison terms of one year, or both, if they are proven guilty. In addition, they may also face civil liability, in the form of money damages a court may impose on them.

Since your credit record is critical to obtaining credit, it is very important that you check to make sure that each item in your credit record really reflects your credit history and not that of another person. Whenever you apply for credit, you should use the same name. Thus, if you are James R. Jones Jr., always append the "Jr.," and do not sometimes use J. Randall Jones and other times J. R. Jones. Finally, you will typically be asked for your Social Security number on a credit application. If so, provide it. The request is not to invade in your privacy but to assure that your credit records do not get mixed in with those of some other James Jones.

Checking Your Credit Record

Q. May I look at my credit record?

A. Yes, you have the right to know the content of credit files that contain information on you, and many consumer credit experts suggest that you examine these credit files about once a year. A periodic checkup will enable you to find out what the credit bureaus will report to those businesses with a legitimate reason to check your credit record. Whenever you ask to learn the contents of your file, you will need to provide adequate identification to the credit bureau so you will receive your report and not that of someone with a similar name.

The FCRA allows you to review your file at any time, and it is particularly important for you to do so if you plan to apply to rent an apartment or apply for a job or a home mortgage loan or other major loan or credit purchase. Under the FCRA, the credit bureau is permitted to charge you a reasonable fee for providing this service, unless your inquiry is after adverse credit action has been taken against you. Currently, credit bureaus that are members of the industry's trade association, Associated Credit Bureaus (ACB), charge no more than $9 for a single report. Some members offer consumers one free report each year upon request.

As noted earlier, a creditor may turn you down or take other adverse credit action because of a report from a credit bureau. If so, the law requires that the credit grantor give you the bureau's name and address. You are allowed to request information about the data from the

credit bureau by phone, mail, or in person. If a credit grantor has denied you credit within the past sixty days because of data supplied by a credit bureau, the bureau may not charge you for the information. The FCRA requires the credit reporting agencies to "make all disclosures pursuant to section 609 once during any 12-month period without charge to the consumer" if the consumer makes a request for the information.

The FCRA requires the credit bureau to tell you the names of the creditors who provided the data and the name of everyone who has received a report on you in the last six months (or within the past two years for employment reports). The credit bureau must also help you interpret the data.

Q. What does a credit report look like?

A. The basic format used by members of the ACB contains these major types of information:

ⓘ UNDERSTANDING YOUR CREDIT REPORT

Contrary to popular belief, a credit bureau neither tracks all aspects of your personal life nor explicitly evaluates credit applications, though the **risk score summary** that credit grantors can ask for does suggest the probability of bankruptcy or serious delinquency in the future. Credit bureaus are simply organizations that collect and transmit four principal types of information: identification and employment data; payment histories; credit-related inquiries; and public record information.

A good credit report is vital to your access to credit. Therefore, it is important for you to understand and find out what your credit report contains, how to improve your credit report, and how to deal with credit problems.

- Identification and employment data: your name, birth date, Social Security number, addresses (present and former), and employment history.
- Public record information: Events that are a matter of public information related to your creditworthiness, such as bankruptcies, foreclosures, or tax liens, will appear in your credit report. An example would be record of a dispute between the consumer and an appliance dealer that was settled in a small-claims court.
- Payment history: your account record with different credit grantors, showing how much credit has been extended and how you have repaid it.
- Inquiries: Credit bureaus maintain a record of all credit grantors who have checked your credit record within the past six months. Credit bureaus typically do not include credit prescreeening inquiries in credit reports, but will provide them to consumers as a part of disclosure. Prescreening occurs when, for example, credit bureaus enable issuers of credit cards to develop mailing lists to make preapproved offers of their credit cards.

Q. What does the law allow me to do if the credit bureau will not cooperate?

A. Under the Fair Credit Reporting Act, you may bring a lawsuit against any credit bureau or credit grantor who violates any provisions of the act. This includes any credit reporting agency that fails to observe the restrictions about who may access your credit file and any credit bureau that does not properly reinvestigate and correct inaccurate data in your file that you have disputed. However, if the agency has followed reasonable procedures, it has obeyed the law. If you win the lawsuit, you deserve to receive actual damages (which might include damages for emotional distress or lost wages for a job you did not get), as well as punitive damages if you prove the violation was intentional. If you are successful, you also will receive court costs and a reasonable amount for lawyer's fees.

Maintaining a Good Credit Record

Q. What may I do if I believe the credit bureau has incorrect information in my file?

A. If you find that information in the credit report is inaccurate, incomplete, or outdated, you may challenge its accuracy or completeness by notifying the credit bureau. (See "World at Your Fingertips" on page 250 for contact information.)

Unless it believes that your request is "frivolous or irrelevant," the credit bureau must either verify the facts within thirty days or delete the information from its files. The "frivolous-or-irrelevant" provision is there in part to deal with some credit repair clinics who challenge all negative information, whether there is a basis for the challenge or not. If your complaint is justified, the credit bureau will automatically notify the other bureaus of the change and, if you request it, notify any creditor that has checked your file in the past six months (two years for employment reports).

If reinvestigation of disputed information by a credit bureau does not resolve the matter, you may file your version of the story in a statement of up to one hundred words. The credit bureau must include your statement, or a clear and accurate summary of it, in all future credit reports containing the disputed item. This right is of limited value because credit grantors rarely pay any attention to a consumer's statement. You also may ask the credit bureau to mail copies of your statement to anyone who received a report containing the disputed item during the last six months. This time period is two years for employment reports. If you are correct that the information is not accurate and the creditor continues to report the incorrect information to the reporting agency, then you can sue the creditor. If you win, you can obtain damages and lawyer's fees.

Q. How does the passage of time affect my credit report?

A. Under the FCRA, most negative information (such as late payments, accounts charged off) may only be maintained on your credit record for seven years, unless the information is used when you apply for $50,000 or more in credit, for a life insurance policy with a face amount of $50,000 or more, or for a job paying at least $20,000 a year. Records of bankruptcies may be reported for ten years (and up to twelve years for certain forms of bankruptcy). The fact that negative information remains on your credit report for such a long time emphasizes the importance of maintaining a good credit record.

Q. What is the story behind companies that advertise their abilities to repair faulty credit histories? They sound too good to be true.

A. These **credit repair clinics** can help you review and update your credit record and report. However, their fees could be as high as $1,000, whereas you can deal directly with a credit bureau on your own. If your credit report has an error, you may correct it yourself for free or at very little cost. If the information in your credit report is accurate, only better management of your debts can offset the negative record, and only the passage of time can remove it. Be very suspicious and careful if a credit repair clinic promises that it can remove accurate records of bankruptcy and bad debts from your credit record or if it promises to get you credit. Credit repair organizations are regulated by federal and by some state laws, and federal law prevents a credit repair company from receiving any money from you before it has completed its services. If a credit program sounds too good to be true, it probably is.

Correcting Credit Mistakes

Q. Will my credit rating suffer if my bill contains an obvious error?

A. No, if you pay despite the error. Yes, if you don't pay and don't bring the error to the attention of the creditor. The Fair Credit Billing Act requires credit grantors to correct errors promptly.

Q. What exactly is a billing error?

A. The law defines a **billing error** as a charge

- for something that you didn't buy, or for a purchase made by someone not authorized to use your account;
- that is not properly identified on your monthly statement, or that is for an amount different from the actual purchase price; or
- for something that you refused to accept on delivery because it was unsatisfactory, or that the supplier did not deliver according to your agreement.

Billing errors may also include

- errors in arithmetic;
- failure to reflect a payment that you made or another credit to your account;
- failure to mail the billing statement to your current address (if the credit grantor received notice of that address at least twenty days before the end of the billing period); and

---

▶ **KEEP YOUR SALES RECEIPT**

Even when you buy an item on credit, it's a good idea to keep the receipt. One reason is so that you may return the item in case it is defective or damaged or the wrong size or color. Another reason to keep sales slips is to correct billing errors. Most creditors do not provide a sales slip with the monthly statement. Under this billing procedure, the statement usually gives only the date and amount of purchase and the store and department from which you bought the item. Therefore, you need to keep all sales slips, at least until you have checked them against the monthly billing statements. This also enables you to determine whether some unauthorized person is charging purchases to your account.

- extension of credit about which you request additional clarification.

Q. What should I do if my bill seems wrong?

A. If you think your bill is incorrect, or if you simply want more details about it, take the following steps:

1. Technically, you should notify your creditor of the potential billing error in writing in order to preserve your legal rights. However, most creditors readily handle billing complaints over the phone, and it is a lot faster and easier than writing a letter. Be prepared to provide your name, your address, your account number, and a description of the error. If you aren't satisfied with the results of your phone call, note the name of the person that you talked to and send a letter to the address your credit grantor has supplied for this purpose so that it receives the notice within sixty days after it mailed the bill. If you don't do this, you may lose your rights under the Fair Credit Billing Act. The sixty-day period is very important.

2. The letter should contain your name, address, and account number. State that you believe your bill contains an error, specify the error, and explain why you believe it is wrong, and include the date and the suspected amount of the error.

Q. What happens after I notify the credit grantor about the possible billing error?

A. The law requires the credit grantor to acknowledge your letter within thirty days. (This does not apply if the credit grantor can fix the billing error in less time.) The credit grantor must correct your account within two billing periods. It should never take longer than ninety days from the time the credit grantor receives notice of your dispute. If the credit grantor does not correct the error, it must tell you why it believes the bill is not wrong.

If the credit grantor does not find an error, it must promptly send you a statement showing what you owe. The credit grantor may include any finance charges that accumulated and any minimum payments you missed while questioning the bill.

Q. Must I pay finance charges on the contested amount?

A. There are two possible outcomes. If the bill is not correct, you do not have to pay the finance charges on the amount in dispute or the amount that was improperly billed to your account. If you have already paid these amounts, the credit grantor should refund them. If the bill is correct, you must pay the amounts owed, including finance charges.

Q. While I am trying to solve a billing problem, may a credit grantor threaten my credit rating?

A. Not because you fail to pay the disputed amount or related finance or other charges while you're trying to resolve a billing dispute. Once you have taken the steps described above by writing down your question and sending it to the credit grantor, the law prohibits your credit grantor from reporting the account as delinquent because of the disputed amount or related finance or other charges. Until the credit grantor answers your complaint, the law forbids it from taking any action to collect the amount in dispute. You must, however, continue paying any undisputed amounts.

Q. What happens after the credit grantor has explained that my bill is correct?

A. The credit grantor may then take action to collect if you do not pay and may report you to the credit bureau as overdue on the amount in question.

Q. What if I still disagree with the credit grantor?

A. Notify the credit grantor of your views in writing. The credit grantor must then report to the credit bureau that you have challenged the bill and give you written notice of the name and address of each person who has received information about your account after the dispute arose. When you settle the dispute, that outcome must be reported to each person who has received information about your account. If you are unable to settle the dispute to your satisfaction, you may want to consult a lawyer.

Q. What happens if the credit grantor does not follow all the rules within the proper time limits?

A. The law does not permit the credit grantor to collect the disputed amount or related finance charges up to $50. This is true even if it is money you truly owed. In addition, the creditor is subject to remedies available for violating the Truth in Lending Act.

Defective Goods or Services

Q. May the law help me if I bought a product on credit that is defective or not provided, or if there is a billing error or if the merchant has breached a contract with me?

A. Yes, if you use a store credit card to purchase shoddy or damaged goods or poor quality services, the Fair Credit Billing Act may help. If you have not already paid off the balance, it allows you to withhold payment that is still due for the disputed transaction when you first notify the card issuer or merchant of your claim or defense, as long as you have made a real attempt to solve the problem with the merchant. A real attempt could be demonstrated by a letter or by notes from a phone call to the complaint department of the retailer—a note made by you on the date of the call and the name of the person with whom you spoke.

You have this right even if you bought the goods or services with a bank card such as Visa or MasterCard, or a travel or entertainment card. Thus, if you purchase a tour or an air travel ticket

using your bank credit card, you may be in a good position to recover the cost from the bank that provided the credit for your purchase if the tour or airline goes bankrupt. However, when you use your bank credit card, the law limits your right to withhold the payment to purchases totaling more than $50 that took place in your home state or within one hundred miles of your home address. Banks will often shift this charge back to the merchant. These restrictions do not apply to store credit cards.

If you refuse to pay because the goods or services were defective, the creditor might sue you for payment. If the court finds the goods or services to be truly defective, you probably won't have to pay. Also, during the dispute period, the card issuer cannot report the amount as delinquent to a credit bureau.

Lost or Stolen Credit Cards

Q. Am I liable for all the bills that may arise if I lose my credit card or someone steals it?

A. No, the Truth in Lending Act limits your liability on lost or stolen credit cards. However, it is very important that you notify the credit card company as soon as you notice the loss or theft of your card or cards. You do not have to pay any unauthorized charge made after you notify the company of the loss or theft of the card. Under TILA, the most you will have to pay for any unauthorized charges made before that time is $50 on each card.

Q. How may I prepare for the possibility of losing a credit card or having it stolen?

A. As noted in "Protect Your Credit Cards and Know Your Rights" on page 243, it is a good idea to keep a list of all your credit cards showing their account numbers and how to notify the credit card issuers of theft or loss. Since you may lose credit cards when traveling, always take a copy of the list with you and keep the list separate from your credit cards. And be sure to keep the list itself in a safe place, since someone with the numbers may be able to make purchases on your account. Also, it is advisable to keep your Social Security number separate from your credit cards, since some issuers of credit cards use that to check the identity of a card user.

THE WORLD AT YOUR FINGERTIPS

- *For information on credit scoring, access the Federal Trade Commission (FTC) website at www.ftc.gov/bcp/conline/pubs/ credit/scoring.htm, or the Credit Info Center site at www.creditinfocenter.com/ creditreports/scoring.*

- *The Fair Credit Reporting Act can be found at www.fair-credit-reportingact.com/ index.htm.*

- *The Federal Trade Commission publishes a useful summary of your rights under the Fair Credit Reporting Act, which includes information on who to contact in the event of a complaint, at www.ftc.gov/bcp/ conline/edcams/fcra/summary.htm.*

- *The Federal Reserve Board has a section on credit histories and records in its Consumer Handbook to Credit Protection Laws, which is available at www.federalreserve. gov/pubs/consumerhdbk/histories.htm. The same handbook contains other relevant information in the chapter "Other Aspects of Using Credit"; you can access it at www. federalreserve.gov/pubs/consumerhdbk/ aspects.htm.*

- *The Federal Trade Commission also gives information on the Fair Credit Billing Act, and includes a sample letter that could be copied and sent to a creditor at www.ftc. gov/bcp/conline/pubs/credit/fcb.htm.*

- *Two other useful publications about credit bureaus are "The Credit Reporting Dispute Resolution Process" and "Credit Reports, Credit Reporting Agencies, and the FCRA".*

These two publications are also available in Spanish and can be obtained from:
Associated Credit Bureaus
1000 Vermont Ave., NW, Suite 200
Washington, DC 20005-4905

REMEMBER THIS

- *The Fair Credit Reporting Act (FCRA) provides a private right of action to consumers to ensure that their credit reports contain accurate information.*

- *Many would-be creditors obtain information on consumers from major credit bureaus or credit reporting agencies. These credit bureaus contain files of your financial payment history, data from public records, and personal identification data. Your credit history should not contain any medical information.*

- *You are entitled to a free copy of your credit report when a creditor denies you credit based on a report generated by a credit bureau. The FCRA enables you to review your credit files upon request to a credit bureau. The credit bureau is entitled to charge you a reasonable fee unless there has been an adverse credit action against you. The fees are generally no more than $9 for an individual report.*

- *The FCRA imposes duties upon credit bureaus and reporting creditors to submit and maintain accurate information on consumers. If you dispute items on your credit report, the credit bureau must either verify the facts within a reasonable time or remove the information from its files.*

- *Negative information cannot stay on your credit report for life. Much information must be removed after seven years. Records of bankruptcies can be reported for ten years (and up to twelve years for some forms of bankruptcy).*

- *Creditors make mistakes. The Fair Credit Billing Act (FCBA) requires credit grantors to correct errors promptly. If you believe that a billing charge is incorrect, dispute the item. Notify the credit grantor of your concerns in writing. Don't delay if you have a meritorious dispute. There are time limits built into the FCBA.*

DEBT, DEBT COLLECTION, AND CREDIT REPAIR

Stacy has become overwhelmed with credit card debt. Debt collectors are calling her at home and at work. Some debt collectors contact her late at night when she is trying to sleep. Is there anything she can do to relieve the mounting pressure and to prevent harassment by creditors and collection agencies?

There are many agencies, both nonprofit and for-profit, that offer ways to help people manage their debt and start the process of rebuilding credit. This section will discuss these issues of debt, debt collection, and credit repair.

Much Debt Can You Handle?

Q. What are the costs to me or my family of becoming overindebted?

A. First, as we have learned from the section on credit reports, your creditors will report your delinquencies to the credit bureaus. As a result, you will have difficulty in obtaining more credit or keeping the lines of credit that you now have on your credit cards. Some may be canceled or not renewed on their renewal dates. If you are already overindebted, that result may not be entirely bad. But when you really need a good credit record to rent an apartment, to get a home mortgage loan, or to get a new job, having a bad or even a weak credit report can hurt.

Also, as you will see in the next section, "Debt Collection and the Law," you will be the target of vigorous collection efforts, both from your creditors and ultimately from professional collection agencies. These people want to recover the money that you owe and will write and telephone you frequently.

Finally, there is the ultimate possibility of bankruptcy, which is discussed in the next chapter. Regardless of what you might be told by others, that is not a pleasant experience. Moreover, the fact that you filed for bankruptcy stays on your credit record for ten years or sometimes more, and can handicap your access to various forms of credit for much of that period of time.

Q. What guidelines are there for how much debt I can handle?

A. As a rough guideline, one long-standing rule is that if your monthly payments on debts, excluding your home mortgage payment, exceed 20 percent of your after-tax or take-home pay, you have most likely reached your debt limit. Or, to put it another way, a roughly equivalent debt limit for those same credit payments is 30 percent of your pretax income. Since less than 3 percent of American families find themselves with payments at 30 percent or more of their gross income, you can see that relatively few families permit their debt burdens to reach or exceed that limit.

Q. Are there danger signs that I am heading for debt troubles?

A. Aside from the percentage of payments to take-home pay or gross income, there are some very reliable danger signs:

- You are making only minimum monthly payments on your credit card accounts.
- You have to use credit for expenditures that you once paid cash for.
- You have used a series of consolidation loans, home equity loans, or other types of loans to pay overdue bills.
- You are borrowing from one lender to pay another. For example, you take a cash advance on your bank card to pay amounts owed to other banks or retailers.

- You begin to run a few days late on critical payments, such as your rent or mortgage payment, or you are consistently late with all your bill payments so that late fees are piling up.
- You dip into savings for normal living expenses.

Q. So what do I do when I see one or more of these danger signs?

A. The first step is to slow down on the use of credit. If you are going shopping, take only the one credit card that you will need, or try using cash instead of credit cards. Cut up excess credit cards and return them to the creditor, asking that the credit bureaus be notified that you have closed the account. It is important that your credit report reflect that the account was closed at your request rather than at the creditor's demand.

Next, find out where your money is going by keeping track of family purchases for just two weeks. If you start out the day with $30 in cash and end with $5, where did $25 go? Do this every day, and add any credit card slips from credit purchases during the two weeks. Then have a family conference to discuss how those outflows can be reduced. Now is the time to begin financial training for teenagers and even younger children.

See where you can cut spending, so that you can free more money to meet your monthly bills. Adopt the industry approach of **zero-based budgeting**. Show a real need for any expenditure above zero. In addition to cutting cash outflows, you may be able to improve cash inflows. For example, a spouse or teenager might take a part-time job.

Once you have a good understanding of where the money is going, you may find it useful for the family to prepare a cash budget that will show the highest monthly payments you can afford on your debts.

Q. What do I do if I can't meet my monthly credit card payments?

A. If you are not able to meet your monthly payments, you may want to approach one or more of your creditors and try to reduce or defer monthly payments without having to pay a penalty. Simply be honest in explaining your cash flow problem and ask the creditors if they can help you get back on your feet. While there is no guarantee that creditors will agree to this arrangement, the worst thing that you can do is to try to avoid them or to make promises to pay that you don't keep. If these self-help efforts don't do the job, you may want to contact a consumer credit counseling service that can help you set up a new budget. (These are discussed on page 262.)

Debt Collection and the Law

Q. What can happen to me when I don't pay a debt?

A. As noted earlier, creditors are very likely to report your delinquencies to one or more credit bureaus, thus harming your credit record. In many states, they may seek a judgment and a court order to garnish your wages; that is, an order to your employer to pay some portion of your wages directly to the credit grantor. Federal law sets a limit on what portion may be taken, and many state laws are even more protective. But if you have a good income, the probability is that some of it is subject to garnishment.

You will always have a chance to appear in court to defend yourself before the garnishment is approved. If the garnishment is approved, the creditor will then notify your employer to subtract a given amount from your paycheck each payday and pay that amount to the creditor until the debt is satisfied.

For a car, truck, home appliance, or other durable good purchased on credit, your creditor probably has a lien on the item that you purchased. Having a lien means that if you fail to pay as agreed, the creditor may recover (repossess) the item that you purchased with credit. Many state laws require that the creditor notify you, say two weeks in advance, of its intent to repossess so that you may have a last chance to pay your outstanding debt on the item. The creditor may not breach the peace when repossessing your car. For example, he may not seize it by force if you refuse to surrender it or break into your garage to seize the car.

Remember, most agreements specify that when you are in default, the entire debt, not just the monthly payment, is immediately due. Nor does repossession of your car, for example, end your obligation to the creditor. If your unpaid balance and accumulated, unpaid finance charges, plus the creditor's costs of repossessing the car, are more than the net amount that the creditor obtains from the sale of the car, you are still legally liable to the creditor for the shortage. If the creditor thinks that you may be able to pay something toward the shortage, the creditor can ask a court to assess a deficiency judgment against you for the shortage. Laws in a few states prevent deficiency judgments in some cases.

If you are sued on a debt and believe you shouldn't have to pay, consult a lawyer. Failure to do so could lead to the court accepting the creditor's version of events.

Q. Who is a debt collector?

A. Under the federal **Fair Debt Collection Practices Act (FDCPA)**, a **debt collector** is someone, other than a creditor, who regularly collects debts on behalf of others. This federal law does not cover creditors, although your state laws in many cases may govern them. Thus, a retailer who attempts to collect unpaid debts owed to it would not be covered by the FDCPA, but

---

⚠ YOUR JOB MAY BE AT STAKE

Don't take garnishment lightly—it can even cost you your job. Your employer cannot fire you because of garnishment by one creditor, but may be able to if another creditor also garnishes your wages.

---

may be covered by the laws of the state where the delinquent consumer resides. These laws are usually similar to the federal Fair Debt Collection Practices Act.

Q. How may a debt collector contact me?

A. Under the FDCPA, a debt collector may contact you by mail, in person, or by telephone or telegram during convenient hours. Unless you agree in writing (or a court specifically grants permission), a collector may not contact you at inconvenient or unusual times or places. Examples of poorly chosen times are before 8:00 A.M. or after 9:00 P.M. Also, a debt collector is not permitted to contact you at work if the collector knows or has reason to know that your employer forbids employees from being contacted by collectors at the workplace. You can tell the debt collector what times and places are inconvenient for you to receive calls.

Also, a debt collector is forbidden from contacting you if he or she knows that you are represented by a lawyer.

Q. How can I stop a debt collector from contacting me?

A. By notifying a debt collector by mail not to contact you. After that, the attempts at contact must stop. There are two exceptions to this. The debt collector may tell you that there will be no more contact, and that some specific legal or other action may be or will be taken. However, debt collectors may state this only if they actually plan to take such action.

Debt collectors must also stop trying to contact you if you notify them, by mail within thirty days after they first contact you, that you dispute all or part of the debt or that you are requesting the name and address of the original creditor. However, debt collectors are permitted to begin collection activities again if they send you proof of the debt, such as a copy of the bill, or the information you requested about the original creditor.

Q. What does the law require the debt collector to tell me about my debt?

A. Within five days of your first contact, a debt collector must send you a written notice stating

- the name of the credit grantor to whom you owe the money;
- the amount of money you owe;
- that the debt collector will assume the debt is genuine unless you challenge all or part of it within thirty days, and what to do if you believe you do not owe the money;
- that if you ask for it, the debt collector will tell you the name and address of the original creditor, if different from the current creditor.

Q. Whom may a collector contact about my debt?

A. A debt collector may contact any person to locate you. However, in doing so, the collector usually may not talk to anyone more than once or refer to the debt when talking to that person. If debt collectors use the mail to contact you or another person, they may not send letters in envelopes identifying themselves as bill collectors. They may not send a postcard. Once collectors know that you have hired a lawyer, they may communicate only with your lawyer.

Q. What types of debt collection practices does the law prohibit?

A. A debt collector may not harass, oppress, or abuse any person. For example, a debt collector may not

- use threats of violence to harm you, your property, or reputation;
- use obscene or profane language;
- repeatedly use the telephone to annoy you;
- make you accept collect calls or pay for telegrams; or
- publish a "shame list" or other roster of individuals who allegedly refuse to pay their debts (though the debt collector can still report you to a credit bureau).

A debt collector may not use false statements when trying to collect a debt. For example, a debt collector may not

- misrepresent the amount of the debt;
- falsely imply that the debt collector is a lawyer;
- tell you that your property or wages will be seized, garnished, attached, or sold, unless the debt collector or the credit grantor intends to do so and it is legal;
- threaten any action unless the action is lawful and the debt collector (or creditor) intends to take that action.

Q. What may I do if the debt collector breaks the law?

A. If a credit grantor (for example, a retailer or a bank) is making the collection effort, check with the consumer protection office of your state attorney general's office and write that office a letter detailing your complaint (with a copy to the offending credit grantor). If the collection effort is from an independent debt collector, write to the nearest office of the Federal Trade Commission or the office in Washington, D.C. (The addresses can be found at the FTC website: www.ftc.gov.) The FTC has been active in pursuing violators and may fine them heavily or even put them out of business.

In addition, if debt collectors violate the Fair Debt Collection Practices Act, you may sue them in a state or federal court. However, you may do so only within one year from the date they violated the law. You may recover money for the actual damage you suffered. In addition, the court may award up to $1,000 for each violation. You may also recover court costs and your lawyer's fees.

Q. Where can I file a complaint about debt collection agencies?

A. You should file complaints about consumer credit reporting agencies or debt collection agencies with the Federal Trade Commission. The same goes for complaints about violations of the Truth in Lending Act and other federal laws involving credit issued by retail stores, department stores, and small loan and finance companies and for credit-related complaints about oil companies, public utility companies, state credit unions, or travel and entertainment credit card companies.

Credit Counseling

Q. Are all financial counseling services the same?

A. No, there are nonprofit and for-profit financial counseling centers. The National Foundation for Consumer Credit provides leadership for about 1,470 nonprofit **consumer credit counseling services** (**CCCS**) throughout the United States. CCCS offices get most of their fees from credit grantors, but will typically charge consumers a small fee for setting up a budget plan. Hence, the costs to you may be lower than those of for-profit centers, which must cover all their costs from charges to consumers who use the center's services. However, it is possible that because of the source of their funding, nonprofit centers may favor arrangements that benefit creditors the most.

While many for-profit financial counseling centers provide worthwhile services, some may exaggerate the benefits that they promise. For-

---

ⓘ WHERE TO GET CREDIT COUNSELING

You can get credit counseling from several sources. These include credit unions, lawyers, and university-sponsored programs. The personnel offices of some firms also offer the service, as do those of some of the armed forces. Nonprofit and for-profit specialized financial counseling services are also available. The major problem is not so much finding a source of credit counseling services, but being willing to admit that there is a problem and share the problem with a stranger.

---

profit centers receive all of their compensation from you. For this reason, they tend to be more expensive than CCCS-affiliated nonprofit services.

Counseling services seldom recommend bankruptcy, even that is the best option for you. It might be wise to consult a lawyer before calling a credit counselor.

Q. What kinds of services can I get from a credit counseling center?

A. Most specialized counseling offices provide two types of services. First, they can help you set up a realistic budget so that you can manage your debts better. Second, if you still have trouble paying your debts on time, the center will contact your creditors and arrange a repayment plan based on your budget. You will make a single payment each month to the center, which will then distribute the payment among your creditors until it pays all your debts in full. Most creditors prefer this type of plan (since they will eventually get most of their money) rather than "straight" bankruptcy. While many credit grantors agree to such arrangements with CCCS offices, some will not work with for-profit counseling offices.

Under a repayment plan through a CCCS, you may still have to pay finance charges on your debts. However, many creditors will **waive** (not require payment of) finance charges and delinquency fees after you have agreed to repay your debts through a CCCS.

Q. How can I find a CCCS or a for-profit counseling center?

A. Check the yellow pages of your phone book for "Credit & Debt Counseling Services" or call this toll-free number: 800-388-2227. Or find a CCCS on the web at www.nfcc.org or write and send a self-addressed, stamped envelope to:

National Foundation for Credit Counseling
8611 Second Avenue, Suite 100
Silver Springs, MD 20910

When looking in the phone book or newspaper, be sure to check if the credit counseling service is affiliated with the National Foundation for Credit Counseling (NFCC).

THE WORLD AT YOUR FINGERTIPS

- *The Federal Trade Commission provides simple information on the Federal Debt Collection Practices Act, and what debt collectors can and cannot do, at www.ftc. gov/bcp/conline/pubs/credit/fdc.htm.*
- *Online, nonprofit credit counseling services can be accessed at www.cccsintl.org.*
- *If you have a complaint about a debt collector or a consumer credit reporting agency, you can mail it to the Federal Trade Commission, Consumer Response Center, 6th Street and Pennsylvania Avenue NW, Washington, DC 20580. Alternatively, you can call the FTC's toll-free number, 877-FTC-HELP (877-382-4357); or you can use the online complaint form on the FTC website at www.ftc.gov/ftc/ consumer/htm.*

REMEMBER THIS

- *If you can only afford to make minimum payments on your credit card, you are heading for debt problems.*
- *If you are having debt problems, slow down on the use of credit if possible. Keep track of your money flow and try to budget.*

ⓘ WHERE TO RESOLVE DISPUTES AND GET MORE INFORMATION

What if you believe that a credit grantor has treated you improperly? Resolving the problem involves a sequence of four possible steps—each one more aggressive than the other. Disputes can almost always be settled long before the third and fourth steps.

1. Check to be sure that you have the correct information regarding your rights under the law and the credit grantor's obligation to you under the law.

2. If you are reasonably confident that your complaint is well founded, contact the creditor by phone or, if the matter is quite serious, by letter. Be sure to provide your name, address, and account number, and a statement of your concern. If your initial contact is by telephone, get the name of the person with whom you talked. To compete effectively, most credit grantors wish to keep good customers by settling complaints fairly and quickly. Nonetheless, create a "paper trail" by keeping a written record or log of all of your contacts with the creditor.

3. If you are not satisfied with the settlement offered by the creditor, based on your study of your rights under the law, the next step is to contact any state or federal agency that regulates your creditor. It is best to write to the appropriate agency and supply a copy of the written record that you have maintained. By sending a copy of the letter to your creditor, you may focus attention on your complaint. While the regulatory agency may require some time to get to your problem, it will often be able to arrange a solution that will be satisfactory to you.

   To find these agencies, the FTC or your consumer protection office may be able to help. For the number of your consumer protection office, look in your local telephone directory under the listings for your local or state government.

4. If the regulatory agency fails to satisfy you, you can consult with a lawyer about pursuing the matter. Check to see if the lawyer will handle the case on a contingency-fee basis. Under that fee arrangement, you pay your lawyer only if you recover monies from the lawsuit.

- *Debt collectors will contact you at home or at work by mail, in person, or by telephone after 8:00 A.M. or before 9:00 P.M. If a debt collector is contacting you at other times, they are violating Section 805(a)(1) of the Fair Debt Collection Practices Act (FDCPA).*
- *You may notify a debt collector by mail to stop contacting you. You may also inform a debt collector to stop calling you at work.*
- *Debt collectors may not harass, oppress, or abuse you. They may not repeatedly call you on the telephone to annoy you. The federal law known as the Fair Debt Collections Practices Act regulates the conduct of debt collectors. Read this law and become familiar with it if you are in debt.*
- *If you need credit counseling, try to find a consumer credit counseling service (CCCS) affiliated with the National Foundation for Consumer Credit.*

Consumer Bankruptcy

Many Americans find themselves in serious debt. The creditors keep calling, but the debt just keeps growing. Historically, debtors were sent to prison. But in America, we have a system of bankruptcy law that provides relief and a fresh start to those who are in financial trouble.

Bankruptcy is one of the alternatives for financial distress. You need to examine the options available to you for dealing with your financial problems and decide which course of action is best for you.

Some people in financial trouble can improve their situation by negotiating directly with creditors. Others get help from a local financial counseling program or a consumer credit counseling service with experience in negotiating with creditors and in formulating and establishing repayment plans. For some people, some form of bankruptcy may be the only realistic alternative.

The choice of a remedy is not always easy. As a first step, consider the pros and cons of filing for bankruptcy and selecting one of the two basic types of consumer bankruptcy: **Chapter 7** ("straight bankruptcy") or **Chapter 13** (sometimes called "wage earner's bankruptcy"). Each of these types of bankruptcy is a section of the federal **Bankruptcy Code**, under which bankruptcies are filed all over the country.

The purpose of this chapter is to provide you with information that will help you make informed choices and to provide references to other sources of information. Also, see chapter 3, "Family Law," for topics regarding bankruptcy and marriage, and chapter 7, "Consumer Credit," for bankruptcy-related discussions.

If, after you have reviewed this material, you decide to seek protection in bankruptcy, you should select a lawyer who is familiar with bankruptcy law.

INTRODUCTION TO BANKRUPTCY

Jason has been spending out of control for months. Most of his income is spent paying credit card bills, and he needs to borrow more just to pay the rent. Jason's debts keep growing, and he is falling behind on some payments. Jason thinks he may have to declare bankruptcy, but he is worried that it will have implications if he wants to get a loan in the future.

Bankruptcy is a serious legal procedure with long-term consequences. Before he takes that step, Jason should learn more about bankruptcy and how it works, and explore his other options with a credit counselor.

Alternatives to Bankruptcy

Q. Right now, I cannot pay my debts. Besides bankruptcy, do I have any options?

A. Yes, there are alternatives that you may use to take care of debts that you cannot pay. Creditors might be willing to settle their claim for a smaller cash payment, or they might be willing to stretch out the term of the loan and reduce the size of the payments. This would allow you to pay off the debt by making smaller payments over a longer period of time. The creditor would eventually receive the full economic benefit of its bargain.

You may also find you are **judgment proof** and do not need to file for bankruptcy to protect your property and wages. Judgment proof simply means that you have so little money and property that you couldn't pay a court judgment against you. Under state exemption laws, creditors are not allowed to seize certain income, such as Social Security or wages below certain levels, and

personal property. If there's no point in creditors going after you in court, there may be less reason for you to declare bankruptcy.

Discuss this option with your credit counselor. However, remember that if you don't declare bankruptcy, the creditors can continue their collection efforts and will be able to enforce court judgments against you if your financial situation improves.

Q. Is there anybody in particular I should contact about these options?

A. Yes. If you are behind on your payments, the collectors for each of your creditors may already be calling or writing you. You might be more successful if you phone each creditor, ask for the collection department, ask and note the name of the person you talk to, and explain your intent to repay the account and your need to stretch out the number of monthly payments and reduce the dollar amount of each payment. You might offer to come to the collection department office to discuss your situation. Ask each creditor to agree to a voluntary plan for the repayment of your debts.

In dealing with creditors, ask them to reduce late fees and interest. Get all agreements in writing before making payment. If you reach a settlement for a single payment, when the payment is made be sure to include language on the face and back of the check indicating that the payment is "in full, final, and complete satisfaction of ac-

---

⚠ **KEEPING CURRENT**

The information in this chapter is current as of early 2004, but at that time Congress was considering major changes in many parts of the Bankruptcy Code. For more recent legal developments, if any, consult your lawyer and the American Bankruptcy Institute (ABI) website at *www.abiworld.org.*

count no. 000x." Never give creditors information that would enable them to directly access your checking account. Maintain control over the payment.

Q. I owe money to many creditors. What should I do?

A. The problem of dealing with many creditors is that some of them might not want to give you more time to pay without knowing what the other creditors are willing to do. Unless your debts are very large, it will be difficult for you to arrange for a meeting of your creditors and negotiate a reduction in your monthly payments or the amount of your debt. You can seek the help of a lawyer to negotiate an arrangement with your creditors. Some universities, local courts, military bases, credit unions, and housing authorities have credit counseling programs, but they may not have the ability or experience to negotiate with your creditors to gain their consent to reduce your monthly payments.

Your best bet may be to seek the help of a nonprofit consumer credit counseling service (CCCS). As noted in chapter 7, "Consumer Credit," you can find the nearest CCCS by calling 800-388-2227 or going online at www.nfcc.org. Some of these centers charge a small monthly service fee. However, you should be aware that creditors provide most of the support for financial counseling services. Some observers think that as a result, they may tend to downplay bankruptcy as an option.

⚠ A WORD OF WARNING

Be cautious when seeking out a for-profit counseling service. If you choose a for-profit service, be sure you understand its fees. Investigate the service and its credentials carefully. Consider calling the local Better Business Bureau for information on the service.

The repayment plans arranged through credit counseling centers enable you to make monthly payments that are then distributed by the program among creditors until all your debts are paid in full. Creditors usually prefer this kind of plan, since they will eventually get more of their money with this approach than they will under Chapter 7 bankruptcy.

Under a repayment plan through a financial counseling service, you still might have to pay interest charges on your debts. However, many creditors will waive or reduce interest charges and delinquency fees.

Q. Should I consolidate my debt?

A. Occasionally, you may buy time by consolidating your debts. That is, you can take out a big loan to pay off your smaller debts. The primary danger of this is that it is very easy to go out and use your credit cards to borrow even more. In that case, you end up with an even bigger total debt, and no additional income to meet the monthly payments. Indeed, if you have taken out a second mortgage on your home to get the consolidation loan, you might lose your home as well. You should also analyze the interest rate thoroughly. Make sure your consolidation loan's interest rate is lower than your credit cards' rate.

Bankruptcy Defined

Q. What exactly is bankruptcy?

A. **Bankruptcy** is a legal process through which people and businesses can obtain a fresh financial start when they are in such financial difficulty that they cannot repay their debts as agreed. The fresh start is achieved by eliminating all or a portion of existing debts and/or by stretching out the monthly payments under the protection and supervision of a court. The process is also designed to protect creditors, because general unsecured creditors share equally in whatever payments the debtor can afford to make.

During your bankruptcy case, most creditors cannot try to collect their debts from you directly.

Nor can they try to collect from you after the conclusion of the case for any and all discharged debts—that is, debts that the court has excused you from paying.).

Q. What is the process of filing for bankruptcy?

A. Filing for bankruptcy is a very personal, very serious decision. Most people file when they have made a good-faith effort to repay their debts, but see no way out other than to file for bankruptcy. Such people and businesses may declare bankruptcy by filing a petition with the U.S. Bankruptcy Court—that is, a request that the court provide protection and relief under the Bankruptcy Code. In addition to that request, the debtor must provide information about his or her assets, liabilities, income, and expenditures. Complete disclosure, candor, and honesty are required. Often, debtors have a lawyer prepare and file the petition and other information for them, but some debtors represent themselves.

Q. What are the advantages of filing for bankruptcy?

A. There are several advantages to filing for bankruptcy.

ⓘ SECURED AND UNSECURED DEBTS

A **secured debt** is one that the creditor is entitled to collect by seizing and selling certain assets of the debtor if payments are missed, such as a home mortgage or a car loan. With those two major exceptions, most consumer debts are **unsecured,** and creditors are not allowed to seize your assets if you miss payments.

By far the most important advantage is that debtors may obtain a fresh financial start. As we shall see below, consumers who file for Chapter 7 may be **discharged from** (forgiven from paying) most *un*secured debts. You may be able to **exempt** (that is, keep) many of your assets, although state laws vary widely in defining which assets you may keep.

Another big advantage is that collection efforts must stop. As soon as your petition is filed, there is by law an **automatic stay,** which prohibits most collection activity. If a creditor con-

---

⚠ USE BANKRUPTCY WITH CAUTION

Bankruptcy may be the best, or only, solution for extreme financial hardship. However, it should be used only as a last resort, since it always has long-lasting consequences. The record of a Chapter 13 bankruptcy can remain in your credit files in credit bureaus for as long as twelve years, which is a long time in today's economic system, in which so much depends on having good credit. Moreover, there are limits on how often you can fully benefit from certain forms of bankruptcy. If you have equity in your home or car, you may lose the asset, since that equity may be realized for the benefit of your creditors. (Most of this depends on state law exemptions.)

Study the pros and cons carefully before resorting to bankruptcy as a means of solving your economic troubles and be sure you understand the types of bankruptcy cases you can file. Do not wait until the last minute to seek help—the day before a foreclosure or court date may be too late to get good advice or to take advantage of nonbankruptcy options. Get advice when you find you cannot pay your monthly expenses in full for more than three months, or if you face a sudden large debt, such as a medical bill, for which you cannot make payment arrangements.

tinues to try to collect the debt, the creditor may be cited for contempt of court or ordered to pay damages. The stay applies even to the loan that you may have obtained to buy your car. If you continue to make payments, it is unlikely that your creditor will do anything. If you miss payments, however, your creditor will probably petition to have the stay terminated in order either to repossess the car or to renegotiate the loan.

Federal law protects your right to file for bankruptcy. For example, you cannot be fired from your job solely because you filed for bankruptcy.

Q. Is there more than one type of bankruptcy?

A. Yes, there are several types, each provided for in a separate chapter of the federal Bankruptcy Code.

Proceedings under **Chapter 7** (straight bankruptcy) involve surrendering most of the borrower's assets. A bankruptcy trustee is appointed in every Chapter 7 case to administer the assets (if any) and distribute either the assets themselves or the proceeds from **liquidating** (selling) them among the creditors. Some assets are exempt under Chapter 7, and cannot be sold to satisfy debts. The assets that are exempt depend on specific federal laws and on state laws that vary significantly around the country.

Proceedings under **Chapter 13** (wage earner's bankruptcy) require the debtor to propose a plan for repaying all or a portion of the debt in installments from the debtor's income. Plans can extend as long as three to five years, but some plans are much shorter.

Chapter 11 of the code generally covers businesses that are restructuring while continuing operations. While an individual may file for Chapter 11 bankruptcy under some circumstances, such proceedings are more expensive and complex, and consumer debtors normally use Chapter 7 or Chapter 13.

Under any chapter, once the bankruptcy case ends, most borrowers are **discharged from** (no longer liable for) most of the debts they incurred before filing their bankruptcy petition, called **pre-petition debts**. This means the court has excused the borrower from having to pay most debts. The borrower then starts over again with a clean financial slate, except that the record of the bankruptcy will remain on the borrower's credit record for up to twelve years.

ⓘ GETTING CREDIT AFTER BANKRUPTCY

A study by the Credit Research Center at Purdue University found that about one-third of consumers who filed for bankruptcy had obtained lines of credit within three years of filing. One-half had obtained them within five years. However, the new credit itself may reflect the record of bankruptcy. For example, if you might have been eligible for a bank card with a 14 percent rate before bankruptcy, the best card that you can get after bankruptcy might carry a rate of 20 percent—or you might have to rely on a card secured by a deposit that you make with the credit card issuer. Use your cards only when necessary, and pay them off each month.

ⓘ WHEN ARE DEBTS DISCHARGED?

The bankruptcy court enters a discharge order relatively early in a Chapter 7 case. In Chapter 13 cases, the borrower makes full or partial payment to creditors under a court-confirmed plan over a period of at least three years and up to five years, and then receives a discharge.

It should be noted, however, that in a Chapter 7 case, the discharge does not wipe out a secured creditor's lien, student loans, or support payments to children; these are still due and payable, along with, perhaps, certain other, specifically nondischarged debts. In some cases, a discharge may be denied altogether.

Q. A bankruptcy filing could remain on my credit record for up to twelve years. How will that affect my future finances?

A. Twelve years is the outer limit for all types of bankruptcy. In a Chapter 13 bankruptcy, the bankruptcy could be entered on your credit report when you filed for bankruptcy, and, if you were not discharged from the bankruptcy until five years had elapsed, would not come off until seven years after the discharge, adding up to twelve years in all. But even if it's "only" ten years, the consequences could be severe. Creditors may deny you credit in the future or charge you significantly higher interest rates. So long as your credit record has unfavorable information, you may have credit problems. This means that you may have trouble renting an apartment, getting a loan to buy a car, or obtaining a mortgage for a house.

In one respect, bankruptcy may improve your records. Because Chapter 7 provides for a discharge of debts no more than once every six years, lenders know that a credit applicant who has just emerged from Chapter 7 cannot soon repeat the process.

Working with a Lawyer

Q. How would I find a lawyer to represent me in a bankruptcy action?

A. There are a number of ways.

- The American Board of Certification has certified some 1,000 lawyers specializing in bankruptcy. You can get their names and locations from the ABI website at www.abiworld.org.
- In addition, some states certify lawyers as bankruptcy specialists when they have had significant experience in the field. Access an ABA webpage, www.abanet.org/legalservices/specialization/source.html, for a list of state certification programs, some of which encompass bankruptcy law.
- You could also ask a lawyer who you know well to recommend a specialist.
- Suggestions from a friend, a relative, a neighbor, or an associate who has had a good experience with a particular lawyer also may help.
- Bar associations and groups operated for people with special needs, such as the elderly or persons with disabilities, often provide referral services. For a list of bar association referral programs, access the ABA webpage www.abanet.org/legalservices/lris/directory.html.
- You might also find a lawyer by looking in the yellow pages of your telephone directory and advertisements in your local newspaper. If you hire from the phone book or a direct mail solicitation, be sure to check the references

---

▶ **IF YOU'RE SELF-EMPLOYED**

Chapter 13 bankruptcy can be an effective tool for a self-employed individual; the business income and debts could be included in the payment plan and schedules.

▶ **DO IT YOURSELF?**

Of course, it is legal and proper to file your own bankruptcy petition, though the more complicated your debt situation, the more risky it is to represent yourself. It is not advisable to hire a nonlawyer to help you file bankruptcy.

of the lawyer. Remember that phone book ads and direct solicitation ads do not ensure you will receive good service.

Chapter 1, "When and How to Use a Lawyer," contains more information about finding and hiring a lawyer.

Q. How would I evaluate lawyers who might represent me in a bankruptcy action?

A. Be careful in your selection and make sure that your lawyer is familiar with bankruptcy law and procedures, and has a good reputation. When you have an initial talk with a prospective lawyer, does he or she seem to understand your problems and have solutions, or are you in a "factory" that merely processes paper?

Q. How can I learn about fees?

A. You can, and should, discuss your lawyer's fees in advance and understand what procedures are included in the fees. This will give you as clear an idea as possible of what the bankruptcy procedure will cost. For more details, see chapter 1, "When and How to Use a Lawyer."

Discuss whether a lawyer will charge additional fees if there are proceedings other than filing the case. The basic case will include preparing and filing the petitions and additional schedules and attending the creditors' meeting. In some states, it may also include preparing and filing a homestead deed. In a Chapter 7 bankruptcy, there may be reaffirmation agreements to negotiate and sign, objections to exemptions, or objections to the discharge of some or all of your debts. In a Chapter 13 case, there may be objections to your repayment plan or the way you value your assets. In either chapter, creditors may file **motions for relief from the automatic stay,** seeking court approval to repossess property or foreclose on real estate.

Under some Chapter 13 cases, you can pay the lawyer from the assets of your estate, which is administered by the court in the bankruptcy case. Depending upon the complexity of your case,

your legal fees might range from $400 to $5,000. Generally, Chapter 13 is more expensive than Chapter 7, though it helps that the costs may be included in your repayment plan.

THE WORLD AT YOUR FINGERTIPS

- *Myvesta.org, formerly known as Debt Counselors of America, offers an interactive website focusing on nonbankruptcy remedies such as debt consolidation; access www.myvesta.org.*
- *Debt Advice is a major nonprofit site, affiliated with the National Foundation for Credit Counseling and offering much information for consumers; access www.debtadvice.org/index.html.*
- *Another nonprofit site is American Consumer Credit Counseling; visit www.consumercredit.com.*
- *DebtReliefUSA.net is a for-profit site that can help you reduce your debt; visit www.debtreliefusa.net.*
- *To find a certified bankruptcy lawyer, access the American Board of Certification website at www.abcworld.org/abchome.html.*
- *To understand more about bankruptcy, access the U.S. Bankruptcy Code and bankruptcy rules at www.thebankruptcysite.com/bankruptcy_law.htm.*
- *For bankruptcy basics and forms, access the site of the U.S. Bankruptcy Courts: www.uscourts.gov/bankruptcycourts.html.*

REMEMBER THIS

- *You may try negotiating directly with creditors to obtain some financial relief. The creditors may reduce their interest rates or allow a longer payment plan.*
- *You may seek help from a local financial counseling program or a consumer credit counseling service. They may be able to*

help you consolidate (and reduce) your debt.

- *Remember that not all for-profit and non-profit credit counseling services are equal. Some are better than others. Contact the Better Business Bureau before dealing with such a service.*
- *Bankruptcy is a legal process through which people and businesses can obtain a fresh financial start. It is for people who are not in a financial position to repay their debts.*
- *Select a bankruptcy lawyer with care. Do not rely solely on advertisements. Contact your local bar association or refer to the American Board of Certification. Do not hire a nonlawyer to file your bankruptcy.*
- *During bankruptcy, creditors cannot call you to collect debts. Once a bankruptcy petition is filed, an automatic stay prohibits most collection activities.*
- *Bankruptcy cases begin with the filing of a petition to U.S. Bankruptcy Court.*
- *Use bankruptcy with caution; it remains in your credit files for as long as twelve years.*
- *There are different types of bankruptcy. Two major types for consumers are Chapter 7 (straight/liquidation bankruptcies) and Chapter 13 (wage-earner bankruptcies).*
- *Most consumer debts are unsecured. Some creditors are called secured creditors because they have the right to seize and sell the collateral for a loan, such as a car or your home, if payments are missed. Secured creditors have more protection in a bankruptcy than unsecured creditors.*

STRAIGHT BANKRUPTCY: CHAPTER 7

Mr. Smith makes a modest income and has few significant assets. He rents an apartment. He is struggling to pay his rent because of his mounting credit card bills and other debt. He defaults on payments to many creditors. He receives phone calls every day at home and on the job from creditors. He has consulted with a credit counseling service. They have told him his best option is to file bankruptcy. What type should he file?

Bankruptcy law, like much of the legal system, can be quite complicated. It is intimidating to the average consumer, who simply knows he cannot pay his bills. You hear lawyers talk in legal jargon about Chapter 7, Chapter 11, and Chapter 13. What do they mean? This section explains the most common type of bankruptcy for the average consumer—Chapter 7. It is the type of bankruptcy for a person with few assets and comparatively high debt.

Q. What is Chapter 7 bankruptcy?

A. Straight bankruptcy under Chapter 7 is available if less drastic methods will not solve your financial problems. It allows you to discharge (eliminate) most debts. About 70 percent of all consumer bankruptcy filings nationwide are Chapter 7 cases.

Q. May I use bankruptcy to get rid of all my debts?

A. No, bankruptcy does not discharge all types of debt. If a debt is excepted from discharge, you remain legally responsible for it. Exceptions include

- tax claims,
- alimony,
- child support (including past-due support),
- many property settlement obligations from a divorce or separation,
- most student loans,
- fraudulent debts (there is a presumption of fraud in last-minute credit card binges involving more than $1,150 in either cash advances or luxury purchases within sixty days before a bankruptcy filing),

- criminal obligations such as fines, and
- a court-ordered judgment from a drunk-driving incident.

Chapter 7 bankruptcy also will not release you from damages for "willful and malicious" acts such as assaulting another person.

Q. How does a Chapter 7 bankruptcy case begin?

A. It starts when you file a petition with the U.S. Bankruptcy Court asking it to relieve you (or, if you both file, you and your spouse) from your debts. As of the date you file the petition, your assets will be under the protection of the court. In addition, the law imposes an **automatic stay**, which prohibits most collection efforts against you. However, if someone has co-signed a loan for you, the automatic stay does not stop creditors from seeking payment from your cosigner.

When you file the petition, you also must file a **statement of financial affairs** and **schedules** that, among other things, describe your financial history and list your income, all of your debts, and all of your assets. If you are self-employed, your business affairs must be included. These schedules are quite detailed, and the information you provide must be complete and accurate.

Q. What is included in the liabilities portion of your schedules?

A. Typically, liabilities include

- your priority debts (such as taxes and past-due support payments);
- your secured creditors (auto and furniture dealers, home mortgages, and so on); and
- your unsecured creditors (department store credit cards, medical bills, and the like).

Be sure that you list all your creditors and their correct names and addresses. Even if you are current on your bills, if you omit some, or provide incorrect addresses, you might not be discharged from those debts. It may be very helpful to access your credit report before filing in order to discover what debts are outstanding (chapter 7, "Consumer Credit," explains how to do that). Also, make sure to give your lawyer copies of all your bills and collection letters.

Q. What should be listed in the assets portion?

A. You would generally include

- all your real estate, including any you own with your spouse or other persons;
- all your personal property (such as household goods, clothing, cash, retirement funds, accrued net wages, and tax refunds to which you may be entitled);
- any lawsuits in which you are a plaintiff or a potential plaintiff (e.g., workers' compensation claims and/or personal injury claims).

From the above, you will designate the real or personal property you want to exempt from creditors. Note that your post-petition earnings are not part of the bankruptcy estate.

ⓘ ENCUMBERED ASSETS

Assets pledged as collateral on a loan are known as **encumbered assets**. When you have borrowed money to buy a car, a boat, household furniture, an appliance, or other durable items, the lender commonly has a lien (legal claim) on that property to secure the debt until the loan is fully repaid. You may also have given a lien on property you already owned to obtain a new loan, such as a second mortgage to finance home improvements. Some creditors may obtain liens without the debtor's agreement, either because they have won a lawsuit against the debtor or because the law automatically provides a lien for certain claims, such as for duly assessed taxes or purchases that haven't been paid for in full.

Q. Will I lose some of my assets if I file for Chapter 7?

A. Under Chapter 7, you might well have to turn over many, if not all, of your nonexempt assets to the trustee who is appointed to supervise your case. What happens depends upon the classification, or value, of the asset and state or federal law exemptions.

Q. What happens to encumbered assets during a bankruptcy?

A. In bankruptcy, a claim is secured to the extent that it is backed up by collateral. Often the collateral is worth less than the amount of the debt it secures, such as a $1,200 car securing a loan balance of $3,000. In that case, the lender is **undersecured** and is treated as holding two claims: a $1,200 secured claim and an $1,800 unsecured claim. On the other hand, sometimes a debt is secured by collateral having a value that exceeds the loan balance at the time of bankruptcy, such as a $65,000 home subject to a $30,000 mortgage. In that case, the lender is **oversecured.** The lender is entitled to no more than the $30,000 it is owed. The excess value of $35,000 is referred to as the debtor's equity.

If you cannot make the required payments on a secured claim (and also catch up on any back payments), the creditor has a right to take back the collateral after having the automatic stay lifted or after the discharge. However, you may be able to keep your car, boat, or other encumbered item by redeeming it or reaffirming your debt (as explained on page 276), or by continuing to make payments (allowed in some jurisdictions).

Generally, the value of an asset is its **liquidation value.** This refers to what the asset would bring at an auction, yard sale, or pawnshop.

Q. What is the situation with unencumbered assets?

A. **Unencumbered assets** include (1) assets on which there is no lien at all and (2) the debtor's equity in assets that are collateral for oversecured claims. The debtor retains unencumbered assets to the extent that they are exempt; otherwise they must be surrendered for distribution among those creditors holding unsecured claims, or the equivalent value must be paid to the trustee. However, if your unencumbered assets are worth less than a certain amount, or would be difficult to sell, the trustee might abandon them, if he or she decides it would not be cost effective to sell those assets and distribute the money to the creditors.

Q. What are exempt assets?

A. **Exempt assets** are assets that you must list on your schedules (specifically Schedule C) and that you may shield from your unsecured creditors. Federal and state laws define the assets that you may protect in this way.

Q. Do the exemptions vary much by state?

A. Yes, they vary widely. For example, under the federal statute a person can exempt up to $17,450 of the equity in a home. A couple filing jointly may exempt twice this much—a total of $34,900—in equity in their home. This is called their **homestead exemption.** Thus, if the home is worth $65,000 and has a $25,000 mortgage, creditors can claim only $5,100 (the difference between the equity of $40,000 and the $34,900 exemption). As a matter of practice, the couple would probably keep their home—perhaps at the cost of paying that $5,100 in nonexempt equity to the trustee—rather than have it sold for the benefit of the creditors. The couple may also be able to exempt the equity under another category.

Florida, along with six other states, has no dollar cap on homestead exemptions. Florida al-

---

ⓘ WHICH LAW APPLIES?

In about ten states, you may elect to exempt assets under either federal or state law. In most states, however, you may use only the state exemptions.

lows a homestead exemption that protects from creditors a debtor's home and property so long as it does not exceed half an acre in a municipality or 160 acres elsewhere. So investment bankers and Hollywood stars who file for bankruptcy could retain beachfront homes valued in the millions. A number of other states have high caps on homesteads, in effect enabling debtors to shield a considerable amount of money from creditors under the right circumstances. In Georgia, in contrast, the homestead exemption is limited to $5,000.

Similar variations among the states are found concerning a broad array of other exempt assets such as cars, jewelry, household furnishings, books, and tools of the debtor's trade.

Q. How do the exemptions work if you're married?

A. In cases involving an individual married debtor or joint debtors, several specific points about exemptions are worth noting.

- First, in joint cases, each spouse must claim exemptions under the same law, either both relying on state law or both relying on federal law. If they each want to claim exemptions under different law, they need to file separate cases.
- Second, when married debtors elect to apply federal exemptions (and often as well when state law applies), each spouse can claim the full exempt amount on his or her own behalf, in effect doubling the amount of exemptions that a single person would be entitled to.
- Third, in some cases, such as when one spouse has debts and the other is debt free and has assets, it might be preferable for only the one with debts to file. In about a third of the states, creditors of only one spouse are barred either completely or in large part from reaching real and/or personal property owned by the debtor with a nondebtor spouse as joint tenants or tenants by the entirety. Those bars generally apply in any bankruptcy case in which state law exemptions govern. The way your property is titled may determine the exemption. Give your lawyer copies of your deeds, bank account statements, and car titles to find out which exemption applies.

Q. How do the exemptions apply if the lender has a security interest in the property?

A. As mentioned above, exempt assets are beyond the reach of *unsecured* creditors. However, exemptions do not ordinarily affect the rights of creditors to assets over which they have liens. For example, homestead exemptions generally do not affect the rights of a mortgage lender to foreclose on the debtor's home. Furniture bought on store credit may be subject to a **purchase money security interest,** and some credit cards attempt to

---

⚠ CHANGES ON THE WAY?

Congress has recently been considering proposals to introduce greater nationwide uniformity in exemptions, including a dollar cap on the most generous state homestead provisions. Be sure you understand the current laws when evaluating your situation. Remember that both federal and state laws can and do change.

ⓘ WHAT THE TRUSTEE CAN LIQUIDATE

The Bankruptcy Code requires that you give all nonexempt unencumbered assets to the bankruptcy trustee—that is, all the assets that aren't exempted by the law and aren't secured as collateral to a loan. Unless it would be too costly, the trustee will then liquidate (sell off) these nonexempt assets to pay your creditors.

create liens. Under some specific circumstances, the Bankruptcy Code may permit the debtor to undo a lien and then assert exemption rights. This is a matter about which it is probably best to consult a lawyer.

In actual practice, over 85 percent of Chapter 7 filings are "no-asset filings"—that is, there are no assets with value left for unsecured creditors after the exempt assets have been claimed and the secured assets returned to the creditors.

Chapter 7 in Action

Q. How may I keep certain possessions that I do not want the trustee to sell?

A. If you are required to surrender some nonexempt property that you wish to keep—for example, a car—you may under certain circumstances arrange to **redeem it** (buy it back) for a price no greater than its current wholesale value. For example, if you owe $3,000 on your car, but its wholesale value is only $1,200, you can recover the car by paying $1,200 to the creditor who has a lien on it.

In the real world, of course, it may be very hard to come up with $1,200, which must be paid from the debtor's personal assets, not property that has been set aside for the distribution to creditors. Possible sources of funds would include the debtor's post-petition salary, proceeds from the voluntary sale of exempt assets, or loans from relatives or friends. Sometimes you can negotiate a short payment plan, but it is up to the creditor to allow this.

Q. Is redeeming the property the only way to keep it?

A. No. You may **reaffirm** some debts, if the creditor is willing. By reaffirming debts, you promise to pay them (usually, but not always, in full), and you may keep the property involved, so long as you keep your promise. But if you later default, the creditor can repossess the property and the remaining balance is not discharged.

You have the right to cancel a reaffirmation agreement within sixty days after it is filed with the court or prior to the discharge, whichever occurs later. Reaffirmation is not always in the best interest of the debtor, especially when the reaffirmed debt relates to property worth far less than the debt being reaffirmed. Most reaffirmations relate to mortgage loans and personal property especially valued by the debtor—for example, a car or a boat.

If you can, it is a good idea to take reaffirmation negotiations as an opportunity to renegotiate the loan, especially on personal property that has **depreciated** (i.e., decreased in value). If there are items that are worth less than the secured debt against them and the debtor wishes to retain them, a Chapter 13 reorganization may make more sense.

After discharge, it is too late to reaffirm, and the creditor may repossess the property, but cannot collect the balance due.

Q. Is there any other way to keep property?

A. Yes. For personal property securing a loan (for example, if you are paying off a loan for a computer or furniture), you may simply be able to continue to make payments and keep the item. The law in this area is not particularly clear and varies from state to state, but as a practical matter lenders will often not take action if they con-

---

ⓘ YOUR INTENTIONS

Within fifteen days of filing, and usually as part of the papers you file, you must advise your secured creditors on a court form whether you intend to surrender or redeem any collateral, or reaffirm any debt. You can address the issue of reaffirmation at the creditor's meeting.

tinue to receive full payment and if your payments were up to date when the case was filed.

If you just keep making the payments and do not reaffirm the debt, and then you default, the creditor can repossess the property, but the creditor cannot collect the balance of the debt (i.e., the amount owed that exceeds the value of the item). Again, if there are a number of assets in this category you wish to keep that are worth less than the debt, a Chapter 13 bankruptcy may be more useful.

Q. Can I protect some assets, such as a vacation home, by transferring title to relatives prior to filing for bankruptcy?

A. Not if you just transfer them in return for nothing, or in return for an insufficient amount of money. You will be asked whether you have transferred property within a year prior to filing. If you have transferred property without getting enough in return, the trustee can cancel the transfer and recover the property for your bankruptcy estate. Moreover, if the trustee discovers that you made the transfer with the intention of defrauding any creditor, you may be denied discharge and face federal criminal charges of committing a fraudulent transfer.

The bottom line is that you cannot keep any debts or assets out of bankruptcy, and if you do not disclose everything you may face criminal charges or loss of your discharge, even after liquidation.

The greater the period of time between the transfer and the bankruptcy filing, the less likely it is that the transfer will be perceived as fraudulent.

Q. What happens after I submit all the required financial information to the court?

A. The bankruptcy court clerk will notify your creditors that you have filed a bankruptcy petition. Creditors must immediately stop most efforts to collect the debts you owe. A trustee will be appointed, usually a local private lawyer approved by the court who does this kind of work in

the normal course of practicing law. Your bankruptcy case is a federal court action.

Q. What will I have to do?

A. The procedures may vary greatly by state, but you might be required to take the following steps:

- In some states, you may have to file your homestead deed for exempt property in the appropriate state court; there are deadlines for this that must be met. A **homestead deed** is a document intended to protect the property from your creditors. Generally, it describes the property and assigns an approximate value to it. The document may also have to be recorded in the appropriate office (such as a land record office) in the county in which you live. (In some states, you may be required to take this step *before* you file for bankruptcy.)

- You probably will be required to appear at a first meeting of creditors, where the trustee will examine you under oath about your petition, statement of financial affairs, and schedules. Creditors can also question you about your debts and assets, and often attend this meeting to discuss reaffirmation, surrender of property, and related issues. Later the trustee will determine whether to challenge any of your claimed exemptions or your right to a discharge.

- If you disagree with the trustee's decision, you may protest to the court, which will make the final decision.

Q. The trustee is obviously a key person. What are some of the options that the trustee has?

A. The trustee might "abandon"—that is, return to the debtor—property that would bring no value to the unsecured creditors. This will include nonexempt assets and those with minimal resale value.

Also, encumbered assets with no equity will be returned to the secured creditor, because there would be no value from the sale to help pay off the unsecured creditors.

Q. How does the trustee go about wrapping up the bankruptcy?

A. After determining your exemptions, the trustee will assemble, liquidate, and distribute the value of your nonexempt assets (if there are any). The trustee will first distribute to secured creditors the value of their collateral, or the collateral itself. Next, the trustee will pay unsecured priority claims, such as most taxes and past-due support, such as alimony and child support. If any funds are left, the trustee will make a distribution among your general unsecured creditors on a pro rata (proportionate) basis.

Say, for example, that after the payment of secured and priority claims, the proceeds from the sale by the trustee of your nonexempt assets equal 20 percent of your remaining debts. Then the trustee will pay each general creditor 20 percent of what you owe. In return, the court will discharge you from paying any remaining balance on your general unsecured debts.

The trustee will also pay the administrative claims, such as his or her commission (ranging between 3 percent and 25 percent, depending on the value the trustee recovers), and professionals, such as lawyers and accountants.

THE WORLD AT YOUR FINGERTIPS

- *To obtain the the statement of financial affairs form, access www.uscourts.gov/rules/comment2002/b7.pdf.*
- *For a list of exemptions in different states, visit BankruptcySite.com at www.thebankruptcysite.com/what_do_i_keep.htm.*
- *The Nolo website has information on states with large homestead exemptions. Go to www.nolo.com/lawcenter/index.cfm, and search "Keeping Your Home During Tough Times."*
- *For a Q & A on bankruptcy debts, access www.debtwipeout.com.*
- *For a discussion of reaffirmation of debt in bankruptcy case, access www.mauilaw.com/article5.htm.*
- *You can download the official bankruptcy forms for all types of bankruptcy from the U.S. Courts website at www.uscourts.gov/bankruptcycourts.html. The forms are long and detailed, and you may need a lawyer to help you complete them.*

REMEMBER THIS

- *Chapter 7 allows debtors to discharge most of their debts. It is the most common form of bankruptcy by individual consumers. In a Chapter 7 bankruptcy case, a trustee is appointed to supervise your case.*
- *When you file a Chapter 7 bankruptcy, you must file schedules and a statement of*

ⓘ SHOULD HUSBANDS AND WIVES FILE JOINTLY FOR BANKRUPTCY?

Spouses are permitted to file jointly for bankruptcy, but whether it is to their advantage depends on many factors, such as how closely entwined their finances are and whether they live in a community property or separate property state (see chapter 3, "Family Law"). Spouses are best advised to seek the counsel of a bankruptcy lawyer well versed in the law of their state. If both spouses file for bankruptcy at the same time, only one case-filing fee with required charges (in all, about $200) will have to be paid to the court in a Chapter 7 or 13 case. State law may require separate homestead deeds. You should be wary of a joint filing if there are already marital problems that appear to be leading to divorce court.

financial affairs. This includes your financial history, income, debts, and assets.

- *On your schedules, list all your debts, including priority debts, secured creditors, and unsecured creditors.*

- *Some of your assets may be exempt from creditors during bankruptcy under either federal and/or state law. States have different exemptions. Exempt assets are beyond the reach of unsecured creditors.*

- *The Bankruptcy Code requires that debtors give all nonexempt, unencumbered assets to the trustee. If these assets have sufficient value to make a sale worthwhile, the trustee will then liquidate them to pay creditors.*

- *Debtors may be able to reaffirm some debts—that is, promise to pay them—in order to keep certain assets.*

- *You cannot avoid the reach of creditors during bankruptcy by transferring title of property you own in the twelve months before you file for bankruptcy. Generally, the period for transfers is within one year of the filing, but, depending on the circumstances and state law, transfers more than a year before the bankruptcy may also be undone.*

- *You cannot keep any debts or assets out of the bankruptcy, and if you do not disclose everything you may face criminal charges or loss of your discharge, even after liquidation.*

- *Depending on state law, you may be required to file your homestead deed in the appropriate state court (this is a document that shields certain assets from creditors).*

- *You must attend a creditors' meeting, during which creditors can question you about your debts and assets.*

- *Bankruptcy does not discharge all debts. You are still liable for tax claims, alimony,*

child support, fraudulent debts, student loans, and criminal obligations.

- *Husbands and wives, depending on state law and the status of joint debt, may want to file jointly for bankruptcy.*

CHAPTER 13

Mr. and Mrs. Jones make an excellent combined salary. Unfortunately, they underestimated the effect of the declining stock market, the cost of college for their children, extreme and unexpected medical costs, and other expenses. They have substantial assets that they don't wish to see swallowed up by creditors. They want to discharge some of their debt but can still afford to make payments. They just need some relief in the form of reduced payment plans.

The Joneses might find that a Chapter 13 bankruptcy suits them better than a Chapter 7 filing. Chapter 13 allows individuals with regular incomes to pay a portion of their debts under a court-approved payment plan.

The following section explains the basic features of a Chapter 13 bankruptcy plan.

Q. What is Chapter 13 bankruptcy?

A. Chapter 13 allows individuals who have steady incomes to pay all or a portion of their debts under the protection and supervision of the court. Under Chapter 13, you file a bankruptcy petition and a proposed payment plan with the U.S. Bankruptcy Court. The law requires that the payments have a value at least equal to what would have been distributed in a Chapter 7 liquidation case. An important feature of Chapter 13 bankruptcy is that you will be permitted to keep all your assets while the plan is in effect and after you have successfully completed it.

Q. Who is eligible for Chapter 13 bankruptcy?

A. Chapter 13 is available to almost everyone who has a regular income. The only other requirement is that debtors have less than $290,525 in unsecured debts (such as credit cards) and less than $871,550 in secured debts (such as mortgages and car loans). These figures are subject to periodic adjustments. Anyone with greater debts usually must declare bankruptcy under Chapters 7 or 11 of the Bankruptcy Code. In a joint Chapter 13 case, those limits are not doubled, but instead are applied to the total amount owed by the debtors.

Q. How does Chapter 13 differ from Chapter 7?

A. The major difference is that in Chapter 7 you pay debts out of your *assets*; in Chapter 13, you pay debts out of your *income*. So a repayment plan under Chapter 13 normally extends your time for paying debts and usually involves your paying off more of your debts. The permitted repayment period is usually three years or, with special permission of the court, up to five years.

Typically, the amount that you repay under a Chapter 13 plan is determined by the total of your planned monthly payments over three years, given your good-faith effort to do the best that you can. Your payments represent either (1) full satisfaction of your debts or (2) all of your disposable income for a three-year period. **Disposable income** consists of whatever is left over from your total income after you have paid for taxes and necessary living expenses (determined on a monthly basis). The plan must also pay secured creditors the value of their lien, over time, and cannot change the terms of the loans secured by your home.

A Chapter 13 repayment plan often results in your repaying less than you owe. If you are unable to pay a secured creditor the value of its collateral, it can choose to obtain relief from the automatic stay to repossess the collateral.

Chapter 13 in Action

Q. What are the mechanics of a Chapter 13 filing?

A. You submit your plan to the court and a Chapter 13 trustee is appointed to handle your case. The trustee will verify the accuracy and reasonableness of your plan. The plan will then be distributed to the creditors. They will have the opportunity at a hearing to challenge your proposal if they believe that it doesn't meet specific requirements of the Bankruptcy Code.

With that in mind, the trustee will want to be sure that your plan provides enough for you to live on, but will also challenge expenses that are unreasonably high. The issue is whether you are making a good-faith effort to repay your debts, even if it means a reduction in your living standards, such as cutting your entertainment expenses down from $500 per month. Since the trustee's recommendation will carry considerable weight with the court, it pays to be honest and open with the information that you provide.

Q. How is secured collateral valued for the purposes of a bankruptcy?

A. Secured creditors will have the chance to object to the value you place on the collateral and the rate of interest you propose. In some jurisdictions, you should use the *Blue Book* retail value for cars, unless you show something that would affect value, such as damage. The interest rate does not have to be as high as in the contract, but you will prompt objections if you go too low.

Q. What is this proposed payment plan?

A. If there is no objection to your proposed plan, it may be somewhat flexible. The plan that you prepare for review by your lawyer should take into

---

▶ **IF YOU'RE SELF-EMPLOYED**

If you are self-employed and filing under Chapter 13, you will show your average monthly business expenses and income. You would also include incidental income, such as part-time wages for baby-sitting, alimony/support income, and rental income.

account your income from all sources and your reasonable necessary expenses. Your plan should anticipate any known future changes in your income or expenses, such as retirement or a rent increase. What is left from your income after paying living expenses will be available for disbursement to your creditors.

Your plan must provide for payment in full of all **priority claims**. These are certain taxes, fraudulently incurred credit card debt, family support obligations (including overdue child support and alimony), and most student loans. You can arrange to pay such overdue debts over the life of the plan.

Q. What if there is an objection to the plan?

A. Under Chapter 13, a creditor or the trustee might object to your plan. If this happens, you must redraft your plan to address the objection.

Q. What happens once the plan is approved?

A. Once the court holds a hearing and approves your payment plan, you make regular monthly payments to the trustee. These payments begin within a month of the filing. The trustee distributes the money among your creditors according to the plan. A Chapter 13 discharge is granted after completion of the payments in the plan (this is three to five years later). If the payments are not completed, there are some circumstances under which a more limited discharge may be granted, or the case may be dismissed or converted to Chapter 7, particularly if there is significant equity in nonexempt assets.

Q. What happens if I can't keep up the payments under my Chapter 13 plan?

A. There are several possibilities, depending on the circumstances. For example, if you have an accident that causes you to lose time from work temporarily, you may be able to arrange a **moratorium,** which means that you can miss a payment and catch up later. Further, if there is a major permanent reduction in your income—for example, from lost hours due to a chronic ill-

ness—your trustee may support a **modification** in the plan if you meet certain legal requirements. This might involve either stretching payments out over a longer period and accordingly reducing the amount of each payment, or perhaps giving up some asset for which you had planned to make payments. If you complete performance of your modified plan, you are entitled to a full Chapter 13–type discharge, described in the next section of this chapter.

Q. What is the hardship discharge from Chapter 13?

A. If there is no modification of your plan but the default on your plan payments has resulted from circumstances for which you "should not justly be held accountable," and if the unsecured creditors have already received as much as they would have received under Chapter 7, you may qualify for a **hardship discharge**. This is a Chapter 7–type discharge.

Q. Are Chapter 13 bankruptcies ever converted to Chapter 7 bankruptcies?

A. Yes. If there is neither a modification nor a hardship discharge, you may instead choose to convert your case to Chapter 7. Following conversion, you would presumably receive a Chapter 7 discharge unless you have received one within the preceding six years. (Of course, in a Chapter

---

ⓘ CHAPTER 13 TRUSTEE

The role of Chapter 13 trustees varies among judicial districts. Some trustees work with debtors to help them learn to manage their finances, and may arrange for (or require) automatic payroll deductions of the monthly payments to be credited directly to the trustee's account for disbursement to the various creditors. A small part of the monthly payments goes to the trustee for these services.

7 case, you are obliged to surrender your nonexempt unencumbered assets.)

Q. What happens if I can't keep up with my Chapter 13 plan but just don't do anything?

A. Bad things happen. If you fail to take the initiative in dealing with defaults under your Chapter 13 plan—whether by modification, hardship discharge, or conversion—a creditor or the trustee may seek to have your case either converted to Chapter 7 or dismissed outright. If the case is dismissed, the collection calls will begin again, and you may have your car repossessed or your home foreclosed upon as if there had been no bankruptcy.

THE WORLD AT YOUR FINGERTIPS

- *The forms for Chapter 13 bankruptcies are available at www.uscourts.gov/ bankruptcycourts.html.*
- *You can find more information and FAQs at the Nolo website (www.nolo.com). Just click on bankruptcy and follow the links for more information on Chapter 13.*

REMEMBER THIS

- *Chapter 13 allows individuals with steady incomes to pay all or a portion of their debts under protection and supervision of a court. Under Chapter 13, you file a bankruptcy petition and a proposed three-to-five-year payment plan with the U.S. Bankruptcy Court.*
- *The bankruptcy trustee or court clerk will take your proposed payment plan and distribute it to your creditors. Creditors will have a chance to challenge your proposals. Once the payment plan is approved, you make monthly payments to the trustee, who then disperses the money among the creditors.*

- *If you cannot make payments under a Chapter 13 plan, you may be able to convert your case to a Chapter 7.*

CHAPTER 13 OR CHAPTER 7?

Choosing the best form of bankruptcy for a particular situation is often difficult. This section compares Chapters 7 and 13, and gives specific information on the factors you may wish to consider if you want to save your home.

Q. Compared with Chapter 7 (straight bankruptcy), what advantages may there be to filing for Chapter 13?

A. There may be several advantages. The most important, probably, is that you will be able to retain and use all your assets as long as you make payments to the trustee as agreed in your Chapter 13 plan.

Q. I've heard about "cram down" as an advantage of Chapter 13, but I don't understand it. What is it and why might it be good?

A. **Cram down** might save you thousands of dollars in certain debts. For example, say that you have an unpaid balance on your car loan of $8,000, but that the car is worth only $5,000. In that case, the court will approve the "cram down" of the loan to $5,000 as the secured claim, with your monthly payments reduced to reflect that lower balance. You can alter the number of months you pay. In most cases, the law requires that little or nothing be paid on the car lender's $3,000 unsecured claim. (If you cannot make the required monthly payments on your car, you must return it, unless the creditor agrees otherwise.) Proposed legislation would prohibit cram downs on most car loans.

Q. Can I cram down the loan on my home?

A. It depends on where you live. There is an important difference between the treatment under

Chapter 13 of two types of your secured creditors: those who have a lien on your home (as, for example, to secure your home mortgage), and those who have a lien on some other asset. Even if the market value of your home has fallen below the unpaid balance on your first or only mortgage, the court generally cannot cram down the amount you owe on your mortgage to the market value of your home. However, depending on the bankruptcy court where you live, you may be able to strip off any mortgage not secured by any value in a home—that is, a second or third mortgage—if there is absolutely no equity to support the debt.

Q. Can you discharge more debts under Chapter 13 than under Chapter 7?

A. Yes. The discharge of debts under Chapter 13 is broader than it is under Chapter 7. Once you successfully complete a repayment plan under Chapter 13, individual creditors cannot require you to pay them in full, even if you gave them false financial information when you applied for the credit, or used some other fraudulent means to get credit. You can discharge debt arising from embezzlement or intentional injury to others or their property, as well as debts for cash advances or luxury purchases made shortly before bankruptcy.

The story is different if you file for straight Chapter 7 bankruptcy. In Chapter 7, any creditor to whom you gave false or fraudulent information may object to discharging you from repaying the debt you owe.

Another large distinction is that divorce-related *property* settlements may be nondischargeable in a Chapter 7 but may be discharged in a Chapter 13. Divorce-related *support* payments are nondischargeable in either chapter.

Q. What is the situation with cosigners under Chapter 13?

A. Better than under Chapter 7. Under Chapter 13, if you had people co-sign any of your loans or other credit representing consumer debts, and you have the collateral, your creditors cannot collect from these cosigners until it is clear that the Chapter 13 plan will not pay the entire amount owed to the creditors. In contrast, if you file a straight bankruptcy (Chapter 7) petition, your creditors have the right to demand payment from your cosigners immediately.

Q. Can I use Chapter 13 more often than Chapter 7?

A. Yes. This is another advantage of Chapter 13. You may discharge debts under Chapter 13 more often than under Chapter 7. The law forbids you from receiving a discharge under Chapter 7 more than once every six years. However, Chapter 13 allows you to file repeatedly, although each filing will appear on your credit record. You should also remember that all Chapter 13 plans have to be filed in good faith.

▶ **KEEP THOSE PAYMENTS UP**

What happens to your home and home loan in Chapter 13? To avoid losing your home, you must make your regular monthly payments to the Chapter 13 trustee *and* make your monthly future mortgage payments on your home as they become due after the filing. If you've skipped some mortgage payments before you filed your Chapter 13 bankruptcy, you can put the delinquent mortgage payments (with interest to account for your delay) under the Chapter 13 plan. In other words, you can spread them out. However, to be sure of keeping your house, you must also make the *future* monthly payments on your home mortgage loan as they come due. If you don't, you may have to turn your home over to the lender.

Note, however, that after you have been discharged under Chapter 13, you must wait six years before you are eligible for Chapter 7 discharge. That six-year rule does not apply if your Chapter 13 case paid your unsecured creditors at least 70 percent of their allowed claims and your plan was proposed by you in good faith and was your best effort.

Q. *I see the advantage of Chapter 13, but why might some debtors fare better in Chapter 7?*

A. There are several circumstances in which straight bankruptcy may be preferable.

First, there are many debtors for whom the advantages of Chapter 13 do not matter: debtors with no nonexempt assets they particularly wish to keep, no debts excepted from discharge in Chapter 7, no history of receiving any bankruptcy discharge within the last six years, and no cosigners on their consumer debt loans.

Second, the benefits of Chapter 13 may come at the price of committing the debtor's disposable income to creditors for as long as three or even five years. In Chapter 7, the debtor can keep post-petition earnings free and clear from discharged prebankruptcy debts.

Third, some debtors are legally ineligible for Chapter 13, either because their income is not sufficiently regular to fund payments under a plan or because the amount of their debt exceeds the limits mentioned above.

Fourth, the bankruptcy may be off of your credit report sooner with a Chapter 7 case than a Chapter 13 case. This is because, in a filing under either chapter, the bankruptcy is noted when the case is filed, but the time for when it comes off differs because the bankruptcy does not come off your credit report until discharge. So even though the seven-year clock (time on the credit report) for Chapter 13 cases is far shorter than the ten-year clock for Chapter 7 cases, the clock runs from discharge, and that can be three to five years *later* for a Chapter 13 case than for a Chapter 7 case. This makes the outer limit that a Chapter 13 bankruptcy can be on your credit re-

port twelve years, while the outer limit of a Chapter 7 case is ten years.

Q. *If debtors are legally eligible for either Chapter 7 or Chapter 13, may they choose between them solely on the basis of their own interests?*

A. The choice between chapters is generally left to any eligible debtor. However, courts have on grounds of **substantial abuse** dismissed some consumer Chapter 7 cases filed by debtors with significant incomes but minimal unencumbered assets. The reason for those dismissals is primarily that such debtors should be committing some of their income to unsecured creditors, rather than leaving them with a minimal Chapter 7 distribution based solely on the debtor's heavily mortgaged assets. This effectively requires the debtor to choose Chapter 13 instead.

The courts disagree over the meaning of "substantial abuse" and the issue has come up relatively infrequently, perhaps because it can be raised only by the court itself or a public officer

---

ⓘ **CHANGES IN THE WIND?**

For several years, Congress has come close to passing more stringent restrictions on the use of Chapter 7 by debtors whose incomes would fund a significant payment to creditors (based on actual income less set expenses available under IRS workout guidelines). The proposed legislation may require some Chapter 7 cases to be converted to Chapter 13 cases, if the debtor's income is high (above the state's "mean") and the debts could be paid in significant proportion. This is called "means testing." There would be a complicated formula used to determine if a debtor must file Chapter 13. Your lawyer should be able to tell you whether these changes in the Bankruptcy Code have occurred.

known as the U.S. trustee and cannot be raised by creditors.

Saving Your Home

Q. It is very important that we keep our home. What steps can we take?

A. First, under either Chapter 7 or Chapter 13, you will be able to keep your home only if you continue to make the required monthly payments on your mortgages.

If you've fallen behind under Chapter 7, you must make arrangements acceptable to your mortgage lender to catch up on any delinquent payments, and it's up to the mortgage company to decide whether to work with you. Under Chapter 13, you may be able to include the delinquent payments in the payment plan and pay those off over, for example, three years, while maintaining ongoing monthly mortgage payments. So you must have sufficient cash flow to cover the payments to the Chapter 13 bankruptcy trustee and the regular ongoing mortgage payments.

As will be seen in the next set of questions and answers, a willingness to make monthly payments on the mortgage will not ensure that you can keep your home. But *not* making monthly payments in the future will make it likely that you will *not* keep your home.

Q. We think we'll have to file under Chapter 7—what will become of our house?

A. Even if you're willing to continue making the agreed monthly payments, you can still lose your home if you file for Chapter 7.

Under a Chapter 7 filing, if you have no equity and are in default, the creditor can foreclose, even if your unsecured debts are discharged.

But if you have equity, your unsecured creditors may also have an interest in your home, especially if it is worth more than the total of the mortgage debt and any applicable homestead exemption. In that case, the trustee may take possession of your home and sell it for the benefit of the unsecured creditors; that is, it may become part of the collection of your assets taken by the trustee.

Q. Under what circumstances would the trustee take our home?

A. Whether the trustee will actually take your home will depend upon two basic factors: how much equity is in the home and how much of the home's value is sheltered by law from creditors.

The homestead exemption is the amount of your home's value that the law puts out of the reach of creditors. In general, the lower the exemption and the higher the equity, the better the chance that the trustee will take your home.

Q. Can you give an example?

A. Assume that the market value of your home is $90,000, and you have a mortgage of $55,000. Your equity is the difference between those two figures, or $35,000. If your homestead exemption were $30,000 (as in Colorado), the creditors could seek to claim the $5,000 left over from your exemption. As a practical matter, the trustee would probably not go to the expense and trouble of taking over the property and selling it for the benefit of the unsecured creditors, but you could be called upon to pay the $5,000 to the trustee.

Of course, if the homestead exemption were $10,000, then $25,000 might be realized through a sale, which would make selling the home a more attractive option for the trustee.

Q. What's an example of a case in which taking the home could pay a great deal to the unsecured creditors?

A. The greater the difference between the market value of your home and your mortgage debt, the more likely is it that the trustee will find it worthwhile to take over your home and sell it for the benefit of creditors. Take the example of the house in Colorado given above, but assume that the market value is $190,000, not $90,000. Now, if the house is taken over by the trustee and sold for the benefit of the bankruptcy estate, the funds available for unsecured creditors would amount to $105,000.

$190,000	Selling Price
–$55,000	Mortgage Loan
$135,000	Value of Your Equity
–$30,000	Homestead Exemption
$105,000	Available for Unsecured Creditors

In some jurisdictions, to determine equity, you would also deduct the costs of sale, such as a typical realtor's fee. Alternatively, the value may be determined by typical foreclosure results (such as 80 percent of retail), or by reference to tax assessed value.

Q. Are there any states that shield all of a home's value from creditors?

A. In a few states, such as Florida, there is no dollar limit on the homestead exemption, only a limit on the acreage that can be shielded from creditors. In Texas, unsecured creditors cannot seek payment from a homestead, so long as it is not more than one acre in a city or 200 acres elsewhere, *regardless of the value of the property.*

However, the homestead owner will still have to make the required monthly payments to the bank that is financing his $2 million town house in downtown Dallas or his home in Palm Beach.

⚠ WHAT IF THE FORECLOSURE ISN'T ENOUGH?

A lender who recovers less from the sale of the house than the amount that you owe will have an unsecured claim for the difference, which may be asserted and usually discharged in your bankruptcy case. In some states, a confirmation action in state court is required to verify the foreclosing mortgage company's entitlement to such a deficiency claim.

ⓘ IF ONE SPOUSE OWES A LOT . . .

Another factor in whether you'll keep your home is whether you own the property with your spouse. Let's say you have plenty of debt, but your spouse has little or none. Many states completely block or seriously limit your unsecured creditors from reaching property that you own together with your nondebtor spouse. Much may depend on how you hold the home (i.e., in what form of joint ownership).

Q. How can we preserve our home if we file under Chapter 13?

A. Under a Chapter 13 plan, your basic choice is either

- to agree to continue your lender's lien on your home and to make the required ongoing monthly payments, in addition to agreeing to pay any skipped payments (defaults) through your payment plan; or
- to turn the property over to the lender.

It is possible that if housing values are greatly depressed, a lender might be willing to lower the monthly payments in order to gain some income and keep the house occupied. But don't count on it.

THE WORLD AT YOUR FINGERTIPS

- *Good overall information on bankruptcy can be found at the American Bankruptcy Institute website, which has particularly useful areas such as the Consumer's Corner, links to lists of lawyers who are certified bankruptcy specialists, and highlights of recent legislative developments; access www.abiworld.org.*
- *In print, consider Surviving Debt: A Guide for Consumers (2002), by the National*

Consumer Law Center (NCLC). It is available for approximately $19 at bookstores or directly from the NCLC, 18 Tremont Street, Boston, MA 02108-2336. You can also order it online at www.consumerlaw.org/publications/guides/surviving_debt.shtml. The website has some samples from the book.

REMEMBER THIS

- *There may be several advantages to filing under Chapter 13 instead of Chapter 7. A main advantage is that under Chapter 13 you will be able to retain and use all of your assets as long as you make the promised payments. The discharge of debts is broader under Chapter 13 than Chapter 7.*

- *There may also be advantages to a Chapter 7 bankruptcy. For instance, Chapter 13 debtors have to keep making payments for at least three to five years. In Chapter 7, a debtor can keep post-petition earnings free and clear from discharged prebankruptcy debts.*

- *Debtors can choose whether to file for bankruptcy under Chapter 7 or Chapter 13.*

- *Under either Chapter 7 or Chapter 13, you will not be able to keep your home if you don't make the required monthly payments on your mortgage after the filing.*

- *Often, there is a homestead exemption with a dollar amount that is shielded from creditors, but don't assume that you will be able to keep your home simply because you file for bankruptcy.*

ⓘ AN ALTERNATIVE FOR FARMERS: CHAPTER 12

Family farmers have the option of a special type of bankruptcy under Chapter 12 of the Bankruptcy Code. It is one of a series of special farm-aid provisions enacted to help farmers survive periodic economic slumps.

Chapter 12 allows family farmers with regular income to avoid foreclosure on their farms by pledging part of the profits from their future crops to pay off the debts, particularly those secured by the farm.

Only farmers acting in good faith have the right to adjust their debts under Chapter 12. In order for a petition to proceed quickly, as in other chapter filings, the debtor must submit to the bankruptcy court a list of creditors, a list of assets and liabilities, and a statement of financial affairs. The farmer-debtor usually will require legal help. The process is similar to a Chapter 13 case, but the discharge that is issued is that granted in a Chapter 7 case (subject to the same exceptions).

The Bankruptcy Code specifically defines who can qualify as a "family farmer" under Chapter 12, and you must meet this definition. Further, Chapter 12 has expired in the past and may or may not be available at the time you need it.

Contracts and Consumer Law

Recognizing what constitutes a contract is key to understanding many legal questions. Very often a dispute centers not on whether someone has violated a contract, but whether a contract existed in the first place. Other disputes center on whether a change in circumstances has made a contract unenforceable.

This chapter will explain what contracts are and how they are created. It focuses on contracts common in daily life such as leases and warranties and highlights issues of interest to consumers. It will also provide information on consumer protections in such areas as advertising, door-to-door sales, telemarketing, and travel.

Lastly, it will explain what you can do when things go wrong, whether the problem is breach of a term of a contract, or a company liquidating before sending you goods for which you've paid. A final section includes information on how courts resolve contract disputes.

These sections merely scratch the surface of this highly complex area of law. The chapter will not deal in detail with the millions of contracts made every day between merchants and other businesses, or investment-related contractual relationships. While many common contracts don't require the services of a lawyer, be aware of when legal assistance may help you to avoid serious problems in the future.

INTRODUCTION TO CONTRACTS

Consumers enter into and complete many contracts every day without even realizing it. Certainly, people know they have entered into a contract when they agree to buy big-ticket items like a house or a car and the agent tells them "Sign this, initial that" and "Hand over the check, please." But most people do not take into account that they have completed contracts when they pay for that tank of gas, purchase that train ticket, or buy that cup of coffee on the way to work.

Unfortunately, contract disputes are not uncommon between sellers and consumers. Small-claims courts are filled with cases brought by customers saying a store did not deliver the item ordered. However, stores also bring many cases saying the customer failed to make good on his or her agreement to pay for an item. Hence, it is just as important for you to know when you are not bound by a contract as it is for you to know when you are. This first section outlines what contracts are and how people form them. It goes on to consider those cases in which the necessary parts of a contract are missing and discuss your defenses against other people's claims that they have a contract with you.

A Contract Defined

Q. What is a contract?

A. Normally, a **contract** consists of voluntary promises between competent parties to do, or not to do, something, which the law will enforce. These are binding promises, which often can be oral but are almost always more enforceable if written. Depending on the situation, a contract could obligate someone even if he or she wants to call the deal off before receiving anything from the other side. The details of the contract (who, how, what, how much, how many, when, and so on) are called its **provisions** or **terms**.

For a promise to qualify as generally enforceable, it must be supported by something of value bargained for between the participants or parties. This something, known as a **consideration**, is most often money but can be some other bargained-for benefit or detriment. The final qualification for a contract is that the subject of the promise (including the consideration) may not be illegal.

Suppose a friend agrees to buy your car for $1,000. Your promise to sell and your friend's promise to buy are the promises. You benefit by getting the cash. Your friend benefits by getting the car. Because it is your car, the sale is legal, and you and your friend have a contract.

It is common for the word "contract" to be used as a verb meaning "to enter into a contract." We also speak of contractual relationships to refer to the whole of sometimes complex relationships, which may comprise one or many contracts.

Q. May anyone enter into a contract?

A. No. To make an enforceable contact, people must be able to understand what they're doing. That requires both maturity and mental capacity. Without both, one party could be at a disadvantage in the bargaining process.

Q. What determines enough maturity to make a contract?

A. **Maturity** is defined as being at a certain age—regardless of whether a person is in fact "mature." State laws permit people to make contracts if they have reached the **age of majority** (the end of being a minor), which is usually age eighteen.

Q. Does that mean minors may not make a contract?

A. No, minors may make contracts. But courts may choose not to enforce some of them. The law presumes that minors must be protected from their lack of maturity, and won't allow, for example, a Porsche salesman to exploit a minor's naiveté by enforcing a signed sales contract whose real implications a young person is unlikely to have comprehended. Sometimes this results in minors receiving benefits (such as goods or services) and not having to pay for them, though they would have to return any goods still in their possession. This would apply even to minors who are **emancipated**—living entirely on their own—who get involved in contractual relationships, as well as to a minor who lives at home but is unsupervised long enough to get into a contractual fix.

However, a court may require a minor or the minor's parents to pay the fair market value (not necessarily the contract price) for what courts call **necessaries** (what you would likely call "necessities"). The definition of a necessary depends entirely on the person and the situation. It probably will always include food and probably will never include CDs, Nintendo cartridges, or Porsches. Minors who reach full age and do not disavow their contracts may then have to comply with all their terms. In some states, courts may require a minor to pay the fair value of goods or services purchased under a contract that minor has disavowed.

Q. When does mental capacity invalidate a contract?

A. While the age for legal maturity is easy to determine, the standards for determining mental capacity are remarkably complex and differ widely from one state to another. One common test is whether people have the capacity to understand what they were doing and to appreciate its effects when they made the deal. Another approach is evaluating whether people can control themselves regardless of their understanding.

Q. May an intoxicated person get out of a contract?

A. At times, someone "under the influence" can get out of a contract. The courts don't like to let a voluntarily intoxicated person revoke a contract with innocent parties this way—but if someone acts like a drunk, the other party probably wasn't so innocent.

On the other hand, if someone doesn't appear to be intoxicated, he or she probably will have to abide by the contract. The key in this area may be a person's medical history. Someone who can show a history of alcohol abuse or blackouts may

---

ⓘ CAPACITY

We've discussed the fundamental requirements for competence to make a contract—maturity and mental capacity. Of course, it should go without saying that there's an even more fundamental requirement: that both parties be people. (However, in modern contracting, that might include a so-called electronic agent that is programmed to make inquiries and responses.)

In the case of a corporation or other legal entity, which the law considers a "person," the requirement that the parties be people could be an issue. A problem in the formation or status of the entity could cause it to cease existing legally, thus making it impossible to enter into a contract. In that case, however, the individuals who signed the contract on behalf of the legally nonexistent entity could be personally liable for fulfilling the contract.

Historically, the law has had other criteria for capacity. Slaves, married women, and convicts were at one time not considered capable of entering into contracts in most states. Even today, certain American Indians are regarded as wards of the U.S. government for many purposes, and their contract-law status is similar to that of minors.

be able to void the contract, regardless of his or her appearance when the contract is made. This is true especially if the other party involved knows about the medical history.

Q. Do I need a lawyer to make a contract?

A. If you satisfy the maturity and mental capacity requirements, you don't need professional advice. But it is clearly a good idea to see a lawyer before you sign complex contracts, such as business deals, or contracts involving large amounts of money.

Q. Must contracts be in writing?

A. Technically, most types of contracts don't have to be written to be enforceable. An example is purchasing an item in a store. You pay money in exchange for an item that the store warrants (by implication) will perform a certain function. Your receipt may be proof of the contract. In fact, with some important exceptions (discussed below), virtually any transaction agreed to orally *could* be enforceable—if you could prove that it existed and what its terms were.

Courts will only enforce a contract that has been proven to exist. But an oral contract can be very hard to prove—you seldom have it on video. An oral contract is usually proved by showing that outside circumstances would lead a reasonable observer to conclude that a contract most likely existed, such as payment for the delivery of goods. Even then, there is always the problem of what the terms of the oral contract were. Also, even in written contracts the courts typically look only to unrefuted testimony to help them fill in the blanks, and are hesitant to add words or terms to any written document.

Q. Are there any advantages to putting a contract in writing?

A. Although most states recognize and enforce oral contracts, the safest practice is to put any substantial agreement in writing. Get any promise from a salesperson or an agent in writing, especially if there already is a written con-

tract—even if it is only an order form, a printed receipt, or a handwritten letter of agreement or understanding—covering any part of the same deal. Otherwise, that order form or other paper may be regarded as a complete statement of all understandings between the parties. Anything not in that written contract would be deemed not to be part of the deal. Writing down the terms of a good-faith agreement is the best way to ensure that all parties know their rights and duties.

Q. Which contracts must be in writing?

A. Under state laws known as **statutes of frauds,** as modified by other state law or the federal E-SIGN Act (see "E-Signature Bill Faciliates E-Commerce" on page 292), courts will enforce certain promises only if they are in writing or in other "record" form, such as displayed on a computer screen and downloadable, and signed manually or electronically by the parties who are going to be obligated to fulfill them. In most states, these include

- any promise to be responsible for someone else's debts—often called a surety contract or a guaranty (an example would be an agreement by parents to guarantee payment of a loan made by a bank to their child);
- any promise that the parties cannot possibly fulfill within one year from when they made the promise;
- any promise involving the change of ownership of land or interests in land, such as leases;
- any promise for the sale of goods worth more than $500 or the lease of goods worth more than $1,000;
- any promise to bequeath property (give it after death); and
- any promise to sell stocks and bonds or to make a loan or other extension of credit.

Some states have additional requirements for written contracts. These statutes are designed to prevent fraudulent claims in areas where it is uniquely difficult to prove that oral contracts have been made, or where important policies are at stake, such as the dependability of real estate ownership rights.

The last few years have seen a trend in many states away from the concrete list given above and toward allowing lawsuits containing claims that traditionally had to be based on written contracts to be pursued even when based on contracts not in writing. So if you are facing a serious financial issue and fear that the statutes of frauds could prevent you from recovering, a lawyer may be able to help you.

Q. What are the rules regarding signatures?

A. A signature can be handwritten, but a stamped, photocopied, or engraved signature is often valid as well, as are signatures written by electronic pens. Even a simple mark or other indication of a name may be enough.

Furthermore, if there is sufficient evidence of trustworthiness, many states now permit e-mail from a specific account to be regarded as signed. Other states have set out specific requirements for electronic mail signatures, and a worldwide standard may eventually be established.

What matters is whether the signature is authorized and intended to authenticate a writing, that is, indicate the signer's **execution** (completion and acceptance) of it. That means that you can authorize someone else to sign for you as well. This someone else, called an agent or representative, can even be a computer program or electronic agent. But the least risky and most persuasive evidence of assent is your own signature.

Q. Must contracts be notarized?

A. In general, no. Notary publics (or notaries), once important officials specially authorized to draw up contracts and transcribe official proceedings, act now mostly to administer oaths and to authenticate documents by attesting or certifying that a signature is genuine. Many commercial contracts, such as promissory notes or loan contracts, are routinely notarized with the notary's signature and seal to ensure they are authentic, even where this is not strictly required. Many

---

ⓘ E-SIGNATURE BILL FACILITATES E-COMMERCE

A recent federal law—Electronic Signatures in Global and National Commerce Act (E-SIGN), which was passed in 2000—gives online signatures the same legal validity as a signature in pen and ink for most—but not all—purposes. The law, which is expected to further e-commerce, permits consumers to sign a mortgage or an insurance contract online, as well as perform other tasks, such as opening a brokerage account. A similar law enacted in some states is the Uniform Electronic Transactions Act.

The law assures that a contract will not be denied legal status simply because the signature on it is electronic. However, the law does not give legal status to all electronic contracts. As a safeguard against fraud, most contracts and documents must be capable of being reproduced for later reference if they are to be enforceable.

Under these laws, no one is *obligated* to accept electronic signatures, and certain kinds of documents are typically exempted from these laws, including wills, codicils, and testamentary trusts; adoption papers; divorce papers or other documents relating to family law matters; notices of foreclosures or evictions from one's primary residence; and cancellation of health or life insurance benefits.

technical documents required by law, such as certificates of incorporation, must be notarized if they are going to be recorded in a local or state filing office.

Q. What is an offer?

A. For a contract to exist, the parties must assent to the transaction. Assent usually takes the form of offer and acceptance. Offer and acceptance are the fundamental parts of a contract, once capacity is established. An **offer** is a communication by an **offerer** of a present intention to enter a contract. It is not simply an invitation to bargain or negotiate. For the communication to be effective, the **offeree** (the person to whom the offer is made) must receive it.

Q. What makes a contract valid?

A. In a contract to buy and sell, for an offer to be valid, all of the following must be clear:

- Who is the offeree?
- What is the subject matter of the offer?
- How many of the subject matter does the offer involve (quantity)?
- How much (price)?

Let's say you told your friend, "I'll sell you my mauve-colored Yugo for $1,000." Your friend is the offeree, and the car is the subject matter. Describing the car as a mauve Yugo makes your friend reasonably sure that both of you are talking about the same car (and only one car). Finally, the price is $1,000. It's a perfectly good offer.

Q. Is an advertisement an offer?

A. No. Courts usually consider advertisements something short of an offer. They are an "expression of intent to sell" or an invitation to bargain.

Q. Does an offer stay open indefinitely?

A. Not unless the offeree has an option, an irrevocable offer for which the offeree bargains (discussed on page 295). Otherwise, an offer ends when

- the time to accept is up—either a "reasonable" amount of time or the deadline stated in the offer;
- the offeror cancels the offer;
- the offeree rejects the offer; or
- the offeree dies or is incapacitated.

An offer is also closed, even if the offeree has an option, if

- a change in the law makes the contract illegal; or
- something destroys the subject matter of the contract.

Q. Must both sides give consideration?

A. In general, yes. There's a crucial principle in contract law called **mutuality of obligation**. Both sides must be committed to giving up something. If either party reserves an unqualified right

---

ⓘ IN CONSIDERATION

The doctrine that consideration is in most cases a central element of a contract is of relatively recent origin. Until the last few centuries, elaborate formality rather than consideration was the chief requirement to form a contract. The necessary formalities were a sufficient signed writing, a seal or other attestation of authenticity, and delivery to whomever would have the rights under the contract. A seal could be an impression on wax or some other surface, bearing the mark of a notary public or other official. The vestiges of the seal remain in some contracts, where the initials L.S. (for the Latin term *locus sigilli*, "place of the seal"), or simply the word "seal," is printed to represent symbolically the authentication of the contract's execution. Even today, traditional Jewish wedding contracts are made on these formal bases: a written record, an attestation by witnesses, and delivery.

to bail out, the other person's promise is not enforceable.

Q. How much consideration, or payment, must there be for a contract to be valid?

A. There is no minimum amount. A price is only how people agree to value something, so there's no absolute standard of whether a price is fair or reasonable. The courts presume that people will only make deals that they consider worthwhile. So if you want to sell your car to your friend for $1 instead of $1,000, you can do it. An exception may be found if the consideration given is so out of line with what is being received that it would "shock the conscience of the court." The idea of unconscionability will be discussed on page 304.

Q. Does consideration have to be money?

A. No. Consideration is any promise, act or promise not to act, or transfer of value that one is not already bound to give or perform that induces a party to enter a contract. Consideration is a bargained-for benefit or advantage, or a bargained-for detriment or disadvantage. A benefit might be receiving $10. First dibs on Super Bowl tickets might be an advantage. A disadvantage may involve promising not to do something, such as a promise not to sue someone. For these purposes, even quitting smoking, done with the reasonable expectation of some reward or benefit from someone else, is a detriment: Even though it's good for your health, it took effort that you otherwise would not have made.

For example, you could agree to give your car to your friend in exchange for his promise that he'll stop letting his schnauzer out late at night. Your friend is giving up what is presumably his right to let his dog out any time he wants. In return, you are giving up your car.

Consideration cannot be merely illusory, or it is no promise at all.

Q. Must the consideration be a new obligation?

A. Yes, because someone already obligated to do something hasn't suffered any detriment. Suppose you agree to have a contractor paint your house this Thursday for $500. Before starting, though, his workers strike for higher wages. He tells you on Wednesday night that he settled the strike, but the job will now cost $650. You need the house painted before you leave for the North Pole on Friday, and there's no time to hire another contractor, so you agree to the new price. But absent other circumstances the new agreement is not enforceable by him. He already had agreed to paint your house for $500. He should have figured the possible increased costs into the original price. You didn't get anything of benefit from the modified contract, since you already had his promise to paint the house. Therefore, you only owe $500.

Q. Does that mean I can't renegotiate a contract?

A. No, it only means that no one can force you to renegotiate by taking advantage of an existing agreement. You could, of course, decide that the other party deserves more, or want to renegotiate so that you can use the other party on other jobs, or feel that the other party does the best job at any price. Considerations like these allow many sports stars to renegotiate their contracts.

Keep in mind that whenever you get involved in a deal, you are taking a risk that it might be less beneficial for you than you planned when you agreed to the contract terms. The other party doesn't have to ensure your profit, unless the two of you included that in your bargain.

Q. Is a promise to make a gift a contract?

A. Not if it truly is only a promise to make a gift, because a gift lacks the two-sided obligation discussed earlier. But if the person promising the gift is asking for anything in return, even by implication, a contract may be formed. The key, again, is consideration.

Q. What if someone makes a promise without consideration, but I rely on it?

A. Remember that consideration may be a disadvantage to one party. From that idea, the law has developed the concept of **promissory reliance**—that a contract may be formed if one party reasonably relies on the other's promise. That means that he or she does more than get his or her heart set on it. The party has to do something he or she wouldn't have done, or fail to do something he or she would have done, but for the promise. If that reliance causes some loss, he or she may have an enforceable contract.

Suppose that rich Uncle Murray loves your kids. On previous occasions, he has asked you to buy them expensive presents and has reimbursed you for them. This past summer, Uncle Murray told you he would like you to build a swimming pool for the kids and send him the bill. You did so, but moody Uncle Murray changed his mind. Now he refuses to pay for the pool, and claims you can't enforce a promise to make a gift. The pool, however, is no longer considered a gift. You acted to your detriment in reasonable reliance on his promise, by paying for a swimming pool you would not normally have built. Uncle Murray has to pay if you can prove that he induced you to build the pool, especially if this understanding was consistent with many previous gifts. Remember, however, that you still have to live with your Uncle Murray.

Q. What is an option contract?

A. An **option** is an agreement, usually unenforceable unless made for consideration, to keep an offer open for a certain period. For example, in return for a $50 deposit today, you might agree to give your friend until next Friday to accept your offer to sell her your Yugo for $1,000. Now you have an option contract, and you may not sell the car to someone else—even for $1,200—without breaching that contract. Selling an option puts a limit on your ability to revoke an offer, a limit that the **optionee** (the option holder) bargains for with you.

Q. What constitutes the acceptance of an offer?

A. Acceptance is the offeree's voluntary, communicated agreement or assent to the terms and conditions of the offer. **Assent** is some act or promise of agreement. A simple example of an assent might be your friend saying, "I agree to buy your mauve Yugo for $1,000."

Generally, a valid acceptance requires that every term agreed to be the same as in the offer, although for sales and leases of goods some flexibility is allowed if the intent to accept is clear. However, significant deviation will not suffice; an offer to sell 100 units of some item cannot be accepted by an agreement to buy 25 or 200 of that same item. You must communicate your acceptance by some reasonable means (by telephone, mail, or facsimile). On the other hand, an assent that is not quite so specific but is crystal-clear would also suffice—such as, in the Yugo example, saying, "It's a deal. I'll pick it up tomorrow." Once again, the standard is whether a reasonable observer would think there was assent.

Q. Can silence signal acceptance?

A. In most cases, the answer is no. It isn't fair to allow someone to impose a contract on someone else. Yet there are circumstances in which failure to respond may have a contractual effect. Past dealings between the parties, for example, can create a situation in which silence constitutes acceptance. Suppose a fire-insurance company, according to past practice to which you have assented, sends you a renewal policy (which is in effect a new contract for insurance) and bills you for the premium. If you kept the policy but later refused to pay the premium, you would be liable for the premium. This works to everyone's benefit: If your house burned down after the original insurance policy had expired but before you had paid the renewal premium, you obviously would want the policy still to be effective. And the insurer is protected from your deciding not to pay the premium only after you know what claims you might have.

Q. Can acts qualify as acceptance?

A. Yes. Any conduct that would lead a reasonable observer to believe that the offeree had accepted the offer qualifies as an acceptance. Suppose you say, "John, I will pay you $50 to clean my house on Sunday at 9:00 A.M." If John shows up at 9:00 A.M. on Sunday and begins cleaning, he adequately shows acceptance (assuming you're home or you otherwise would know he showed up).

To take another example, you don't normally have to pay for goods shipped to you that you didn't order. But if you were a retailer and put them on display in your store and sold them, you would have accepted the offer to buy them from the wholesaler and would be obligated to pay the invoice price. Sometimes this is called an implied contract.

Q. When is the acceptance effective?

A. The contract usually is in effect as soon as the offeree transmits or communicates the acceptance—unless the offerer has specified that the acceptance must be received before it is effective, or before an option expires. In these situations, there's no contract until the offerer receives the answer, and in the way specified.

ⓘ THE REASONABLE PERSON

Throughout this and any other law book, the word "reasonable" will appear many times. Very often you'll see references to the "reasonable man" or the "reasonable person." Why is the law so preoccupied with this mythical being?

The answer is that no contract can possibly predict the infinite number of disputes that might arise under it. Similarly, no set of laws regulating liability for personal or property injury can possibly foresee the countless ways human beings and their property can harm other people or property. Since the law can't provide for every possibility, the standard of the "reasonable person" has evolved to furnish some uniform standards and to guide the courts.

Through the fiction of the "reasonable person," the law creates a standard that the judge or jury may apply to each set of circumstances. It is a standard that reflects community values, rather than the judgment of the people involved in the actual case. Thus a court might determine whether an oral contract was formed by asking whether a "reasonable person" would conclude from the circumstances that one did exist. Or the court might decide an automobile accident case by asking what a "reasonable person" might have done in a particular traffic or hazard situation.

There are two principles that extend that fictional person's capacities into the realm of contracts. One is the concept of the "reasonable observer," a reasonable person who sets the standard of whether an action or a statement would reasonably suggest, for example, an offer or acceptance of a contract, or a repudiation of one. This person is not an eagle-eyed expert, but stands for common sense.

Closely related is the concept of "knew or should have known." If parties to a contract are considered to know, or be "on notice," of something—say, that their offer has been accepted—it is not enough to ask whether they actually knew it. If it were, we would have only their word as really reliable evidence that they knew or didn't know. The law will not allow parties who should have known something through the reasonable exercise of their senses and intelligence to fail the use them. Thus, it isn't enough to say, "I didn't know the Yugo I sold you had no engine." That's something that someone selling a car reasonably should know.

At times, the point at which the contract is made is not easy to determine. This is not necessarily fatal. Also, if the parties understand that the terms to be delivered with the product are to be a part of the deal, those later terms may be included as part of the contract.

Q. Is an "agreement to agree" a contract?

A. Generally not, because it suggests that important terms are still missing. Rarely will a court supply those terms itself.

Q. Can a joke be the basis for a contract?

A. It depends on whether a reasonable observer would know it's a joke, and on whether the acceptance was adequate. In our Yugo example, you probably couldn't get out of the contract by saying, "How could you think I'd sell this for $1,000? I meant it as a joke!" On the other hand, if someone sued you because you backed out on your promise to sell her France for $15, the joke would be on her—no one reasonably could have thought you were serious.

Q. What is a condition?

A. People often use the word "condition" to mean a term of a contract. A more precise definition is that a **condition** is an event that must occur if the contract is to be performed. For example, in an auto sale contract, the sale might be made conditional by language such as this: "The existence of this contract is conditional on our (the dealer's) ability to obtain financing for you on the terms specified in this order." Similarly, the sale of real estate is often conditional on the buyer's obtaining financing on specified terms.

Neither party is required to agree to a condition that comes up during the bargaining process, and the one who wants the condition may have to pay extra for it. When a condition is put into negotiations, you must decide whether insisting on or agreeing to the condition is worthwhile to you, considering the risks and costs of not having the condition. In this respect, a condition is the same as any other term, such as price or quantity.

The most common conditions include those in real estate sales contracts requiring that the sale be conditional on the buyers obtaining financing or selling their current home, or on an acceptable home-inspection report.

Q. May someone else make a contract on my behalf?

A. Yes, but only with your permission. The law refers to such an arrangement as **agency.** We couldn't do business without it. All sorts of people in our economy are agents, from the person who staffs the movie box office to the clerk who sells you clothes. They are agents, someone with the authority to bind someone else—in these cases, the movie theater or the store—by contract. (In these simple examples, the contracts are that in return for your money the theater will show you the movie you selected and the store will sell you the clothes you have chosen.)

The **principal** is the person or company for whom the agent acts. Today, agents can be so-called electronic agents (computer programs). Within their programs, they can bind either principal. But if you, for example, impose a condition beyond their programming, and you should know that limitation, the condition may negate the agreement.

As long as agents do not exceed the authority granted them by their principals, the contracts they make bind their principals just as if the principals had made the contracts themselves. If something went wrong with the contract, you would sue the principal—not the agent—if you couldn't resolve the dispute in a friendly manner. An agent normally does not have any personal obligation.

While acting on behalf of principals, agents are required to put their own interests after those of the principal. Therefore, they may not personally profit beyond what the principal and the agent have agreed to in their agency contract. That means the agent cannot take advantage of any opportunity that, under the terms of the agency, is meant to be exploited by the principal.

Q. What happens when an agent exceeds the authority granted by a principal?

A. That depends on the circumstances. Suppose an agent exceeds her authority, but the person she's dealing with reasonably doesn't understand that she's exceeding it. If the principal knew (or reasonably should have known) that the agent has exceeded her authority in similar circumstances, but has done nothing about it, the principal may be bound by the contract negotiated by the agent. On the other hand, if the principal is not aware of the agent's actions that exceed her authority, the contract will only be enforceable against the principal if it was reasonable for the other person to believe the agent was acting within her authority.

For example, suppose the teenage boy wearing a service station uniform who fills your gas tank—and who appears to be an agent, to some limited degree, of the service station—offers to sell you the whole service station in trade for the Yugo you are driving. It's not reasonable for you to assume he has that power when common sense tells you he can only sell you his boss's gasoline for a fixed price.

In contrast, if an insurance agent wrote you an insurance policy from his company that exceeded the policy amount he was authorized to write, but the insurer never told you this, you would be acting reasonably to assume he was authorized, and you probably could collect on a claim above his limit. Or if an automobile salesperson signs a contract on behalf of a car dealer that, without the dealer's authority, gives the customer a warranty for forty thousand extra miles, the dealer might very well be bound by the contract.

Q. May I transfer my duties under a contract?

A. Yes, unless the contract prohibits such a transfer or the transfer might materially impair the other party's expectation. The law refers to a transfer of duties or responsibilities as a **delegation.** If, however, someone contracts with you because of a special skill or talent only you have, you may not be able to transfer your duty. Such cases are quite rare. There are arguably no car mechanics that are so good at tuning an engine that they may not delegate someone else to do it for them, unless they specifically promise to do it themselves. On the other hand, if you hire well-known entertainers to perform at your wedding, they may not send other entertainers as substitutes without your permission.

Q. May I assign my rights?

A. A delegation or transfer of rights, called an **assignment,** is more flexible than a transfer of duties. For example, you may wish to transfer the right to receive money from a buyer for something you have sold. Generally, a contract right is yours to do with as you wish, as long as you didn't agree in the contract not to assign the right. You can sell it or give it away, though most states require you to put an assignment in writing, especially if it is a gift. If the assignment is the grant of a security interest, in many cases a contractual and even a statutory restriction may be ignored.

There are exceptions to the rule that assignments may be made freely. If an assignment would substantially increase the risk, or materially change the duty of the other party to the contract, the contract may not be assignable, even if its terms contain no explicit agreement to the contrary. Such an assignment would be regarded as unfairly upsetting the expectations the other party had when he or she entered the contract.

For example, suppose you made a contract for fire insurance on a garage for your Yugo. Then a notorious convicted arsonist and insurance cheat contacted you upon release from prison and asked you to sell the garage and assign your rights under the garage's fire insurance policy to the arsonist. You would probably be in for a disappointment, even if the insurance policy didn't prohibit assignment. Since the insurer made its decision to insure in part based on your solid citizenship, insuring the arsonist would greatly increase its burden by taking on a risk it never anticipated.

Limits to a Contract

Q. May someone make a contract to do or sell something illegal?

A. No. The courts will not help someone collect an illegal gambling debt, or payment for illegal drugs or prostitution. The law treats these contracts as if they never existed; they are unenforceable or void. This is the contract defense of **illegality**.

Similarly, some contracts that are not specifically outlawed will also not be enforced if a court determines enforcement would violate public policy. An example would be a contract to become a slave, which may not be prohibited by any specific statute but offends the law's view of what kinds of contracts society will permit.

Q. What if the contract became unenforceable because something made it illegal after the people agreed to it?

A. Generally speaking, the Constitution forbids lawmakers from passing laws that would impair the rights people bargain for in contracts. Therefore, courts usually consider a contract in light of the law that applied at the time the contract was made—unless the change in the law involves a compelling public policy.

⚠ MONEY ON THE LINE

What if it is illegal to gamble in your state, but you go online and gamble over the Internet using your credit card? Chances are you will still have to pay your losses. The website operator may be in violation of local law, and you may be also. But your credit card agreement probably requires you to pay your gambling debts regardless, and until this area is regulated and controlled you must assume that when you put your money on the line, online, that you may never see it again—exactly the bargain you make whenever you gamble.

For example, a contract between a railroad and a property owner who leased a right-of-way to the railroad stated that the railroad would not be responsible for any fire damage to the property caused by locomotives. Later, the state legislature made it illegal to fail to keep certain precautions against fire damaging an adjoining property. The court, however, would uphold the contract because the law that would have made the contract illegal (since it didn't include the newly required precautions) was passed after the deal was struck.

Typically, however, courts say that because of a change in *public policy* as a result of the change in the law, they will not enforce the old contract. Obviously, a contract to sell someone a slave could not be enforced after slavery became illegal; neither could you enforce a contract to purchase a banned assault rifle that was made before the ban went into effect. This works both ways: A contract that was illegal when made usually will not be enforced, even though it would be legal if entered into today. One case involved a contract that violated wartime price controls. One of the parties wanted it enforced after the war. The court ruled that a contract that was so damaging to the public good when made should never be enforced. To do so would provide an incentive to enter into illegal contracts in the hope that they will someday be enforceable—a bad prescription for effective public policy.

Q. Does the same hold true for a contract to do something immoral?

A. The courts will only enforce a moral code that the law (or "public policy") already reflects, such as laws against prostitution or stealing. You may feel that X-rated movies or fur coats are immoral, but as long as they're legal, they can be the subjects of enforceable contracts.

Q. May a contract that I am a party to that was made against my will be enforced against me?

A. No. A contract that someone agrees to under duress is void. **Duress** is a threat or an act that overcomes someone's free will. The classic case of duress is a contract signed by someone "with a gun to his head." Because this kind of duress is very rare—and often very hard to prove—the defense of duress is rarely successful.

Duress goes beyond persuasion or hard selling. Persuasion in bargaining is perfectly legal. It also isn't duress when you say, "I would never pay that much for a Yugo if I had a choice." You do have a choice—to buy a nice Taurus instead. But if you want that mauve Yugo, you have to pay what the owner demands. In contrast, duress involves actual coercion, such as a threat of violence or imprisonment.

Q. Are there other kinds of duress besides physical threats?

A. Duress is a suspension of your free will. There may be duress in some circumstances in which there is no threat of physical violence—for example, if a person makes threats to abuse the court system to coerce your agreement.

There is also economic duress. That was alluded to in the example on page 294, when the contractor demanded more money after his workers went on strike and you needed your house painted before you left the country. This isn't the same as driving a hard bargain. Rather, the contractor had already made a deal. When the contractor threatened to withhold his part of the deal, he left you with no practical choice but to agree. The classic case is when the supplier of a necessary ingredient or material threatens, on short notice and at a critical time, not to deliver it—in violation of an existing contract—unless he or she gets more favorable terms. Courts have set aside contracts made under such economic duress.

Q. What should I do if someone forces me to sign a contract under duress?

A. Once you get out of danger, see a lawyer who can tell you how to protect yourself. The lawyer can help you determine whether you have assumed any obligation, and what legal rights you might have besides disavowing the contract. It's important to act quickly. Courts are especially

---

ⓘ IS IT OR ISN'T IT A CONTRACT?

The principles discussed will go a long way toward determining if people have formed a contract. You now know that a contract has to be made between willing, competent parties. Also, the contract must concern a legal subject matter. The preceding section also discussed many aspects of consideration.

Applying these principles isn't always easy. Sometimes special protections in the law complicate matters. If successfully invoked, only one of these may be needed to provide a complete defense against someone claiming you owe him or her money or something else you supposedly promised. It would prompt a court to resolve the dispute as if there never were a contract. Since the contract is **void,** neither party may enforce its terms in court against the other.

Other contracts are **voidable,** but not automatically void. What's the difference? A contract produced by fraud is not automatically void. People who are victimized by fraud have the option of asking a court to declare that contract void, or to **reform** (rewrite) it. On the other hand, if they went along with the contract for a substantial period of time, they could lose their right to get out of it. This is called **ratification,** and is based on the idea that they have, by their actions, made it clear that they are able to live with the terms. A checklist of contract defenses appears on page 304.

skeptical of a claim of duress made long after the danger has passed.

Q. Are there other uses of unfair pressure, less severe than duress, that void a contract?

A. There is a contract defense called **undue influence,** which doesn't involve a threat. Rather, it's the unfair use of a relationship of trust to pressure someone into an unbalanced contract. Undue influence cases usually involve someone who starts out at a disadvantage, perhaps due to illness, age, or emotional vulnerability. The other person often has some duty to look out for the weaker one's interests.

An example would be a court-appointed guardian who persuades his twelve-year-old charge to lend him $25,000 from his trust fund, free of interest. The loan contract would be unenforceable because of undue influence, regardless of whether the minor otherwise had the capacity to make a contract.

Q. What is fraud?

A. A court can cancel a contract because of fraud if one person knowingly made a material misrepresentation. A **material misrepresentation** is an important untruth, made with the intent to deceive, that the other person reasonably relied on, to his or her disadvantage.

Consider our earlier example involving a car sale. You offered to sell your Yugo to a friend. Suppose you knew it had a defective transmission, and you knew she wanted it for the usual purpose of driving it. You told her it was working fine, and she relied on your statement. Therefore, the contract you made may be set aside on the grounds of fraud.

Here, there is no issue of the statement being merely the seller's opinion, or exaggerated sales talk puffery that people know not to believe literally. You didn't merely say it was a great car when really it was mediocre. Saying it's great is just an opinion, while fraud requires an outright lie, or, in many cases, a substantial failure to state a material fact about an important part of the contract.

Some common examples of fraud occur in used car transactions and sale-by-owner real estate deals. Used car dealers may lie about the repair history, odometer readings, and prior use of their cars. Homeowners may find it too tempting to fail to disclose serious defects, like drainage problems.

Q. If I enter into the contract under a mistaken impression, does that affect the contract's validity?

A. Probably not, if the other party didn't know about your mistake. This defense, **unilateral mistake,** is almost impossible to prove, even if the mistake is about the most important terms of the contract. If allowed liberally, it would lead to a lot of abuse. People would claim they made a mistake to get out of a contract they didn't like, even though they had no valid legal defense. Therefore, courts hardly ever permit such a defense—and even then, only in specialized business cases.

Q. When is unilateral mistake ever a defense?

A. Courts have permitted a mistake defense most commonly if there has been an honest error in calculations and the other party knew or should have known of the mistake. The calcula-

---

ⓘ WHEN SOMEONE FORCES YOU TO SIGN

Between the defenses of duress and undue influence, you should never have to fear a court holding you liable for a contract that someone forces you to sign. Both concepts are hard to define, though, and people often use them interchangeably. Also, their limits vary from one state to another. If you think either might apply to an agreement you want to get out of, see a lawyer.

tions must be material to the contract, and the overall effect must be to make the contract **unconscionable**, that is, unfairly burdensome. Such mistakes often happen when a government agency puts public work out for bid. If a contractor mistakenly bids $5 million to construct a bridge and a road, when the true cost to build the bridge alone was $5 million, and the government should have known that the bid was far too low, the contractor might be able to raise this defense. But say that the government didn't realize the bid was too low. Several months have now elapsed, and the government has materially relied on the mistaken figures (for example, by taking steps to move the process forward) before the mistake was discovered. It would then be unfair to the government to cancel the deal, and the defense would probably fail.

Of course, if you explicitly state your mistaken idea, the other party has a duty to correct you. Then the issue is no longer one of mistake, but of fraud. In our car-sale example, suppose the car's heater worked, but not too well, and you, the seller, knew that. Under contract law, if you and your friend hadn't discussed it, you probably wouldn't have to tell your friend about it. But suppose your friend told you, "The best thing about this car is that it's so hard to find a Yugo with a perfect heater." Then you would be obliged to tell your friend that the heater was faulty. If you didn't, many states would permit your friend to set aside the contract, or would allow your friend to collect damages for repairs required on the heater.

Having said this, the best defense is a good offense. Don't assume anything important or questionable. Ask the questions now—before you sign.

Q. What if both sides make a mistake?

A. Then you don't have the mutual assent to the contract discussed earlier. To avoid injustice, the court will often set aside the contract, under the theory of a **mutual mistake**.

The classic case of mutual mistake occurred when someone sold a supposedly infertile cow for $80. It turned out soon afterward that the cow was pregnant, which made her worth $800. The court ruled that since both parties thought they were dealing with a barren cow, the contract could be set aside.

Q. Does that mean contracts always have a built-in guarantee against mistakes?

A. No. As you can imagine, this is a very tricky and unpredictable area. For example, a poor prediction is not a mistake, nor is the case in which both parties acknowledge they do not know the value, and one is disappointed. Moreover, many people make purchases on the understanding that the object is worth more to one person than to the other. You wouldn't pay $80 for a cow if she were not worth at least $80.01 to you. That is, you figure you're somewhat better off with the cow than with the $80. (Economists call this amount the "marginal benefit.") Similarly, the seller would not sell her if she were worth more than $79.99 to the seller. Both people have to be getting some benefit to agree to the sale. In the case of the cow, both buyer and seller understood clearly—but mistakenly—that the cow could not get pregnant. It's as if they made the contract for a subject that turned out not to exist.

Various courts draw the line between $80.01 and $800 at different places, if they are willing to draw it at all. Get competent legal advice about the law in your state if you are considering voiding a contract because of a mistake.

Q. What are statutes of limitations?

A. These are laws setting time limits during which a lawsuit can be brought. The typical deadline for bringing a contract action is six years from the time the breach occurs. The idea of this policy is that everyone is entitled, at some point, to close the book on a transaction. It encourages people to move on and reduces the uncertainty that businesses, for example, would face if they could be sued for breaching contracts that no one in the organization remembers.

Changing Situations

Q. What if it becomes physically impossible to perform a contract?

A. Suppose you hire a contractor to paint your house on Thursday, and it burns down Wednesday night through no fault of your own. Then the contract will be set aside, unless there was an agreement allocating such risk to one party, because there's no way to perform it. You won't have to pay the painter, under the doctrine of **impossibility of performance.** Both of you are out of luck. The same is true if the contract covers a specific kind of product, and it becomes unavailable because of an act of God, such as an earthquake or a blizzard. Courts usually will not enforce such a contract.

For example, suppose you contract to deliver one hundred barrels of a specific grade of oil from a specific Arabian oil field by a certain date. Then an earthquake devastates the oil field, making recovery of the oil impossible. You're probably off the hook under these circumstances.

This doctrine is also known as **impracticability of performance,** which reflects the fact that it may apply even if performance is not literally impossible, but is seriously impractical.

Q. What if changing circumstances make it much more costly to fulfill the contract, but it's still possible to do what the contract promised?

A. The courts probably would enforce the contract, on the grounds that the new circumstances were foreseeable, and that the possibility of increased costs was or could have been built into the contract. For instance, suppose again that you contract to deliver one hundred barrels of Arabian oil. This time, fighting breaks out in the Persian Gulf, interrupting shipping and greatly increasing the cost of the oil. When a court considers these facts, it's likely to say that you should have foreseen the possibility of fighting and built that risk into the price. The contract will stand.

Q. What if the contract can be performed, but to do so would be pointless?

A. Sometimes a change in conditions doesn't make performance impossible or impractical, but it does make performance meaningless. The legal term for this is **frustration of purpose.** One famous case involved a person who rented a London apartment to view the processions to be held in connection with the coronation of the king of England. Because of the king's illness, the coro-

---

ⓘ SHOULD THE BUYER STILL BEWARE?

The well-known Latin maxim **caveat emptor**—"let the buyer beware"—is a strict rule placing the risk in a transaction with the buyer. Under this rule, each party protects itself only by inspecting and analyzing a potential transaction, because there is no remedy if there is a hidden problem.

In fact, this "ancient" law really predominated only in the nineteenth and early twentieth centuries, when the idea of the sanctity of the contract reigned. More common are the principles of just prices and fair dealing in transactions. These are part of religious law, medieval law, and, more recently, statutory law—particularly the statutes governing warranties and the consumer fraud acts prohibiting unfair or deceptive acts and practices.

Having said that, every buyer should recognize that the first line of defense is common sense, and not depend on a sympathetic judge to save him or her from a bad deal.

nation was postponed. The court excused the renter from paying for the room. Through no fault of his own, the whole purpose of renting it—which the people who owned the room knew—had disappeared. Such cases, though, are rare. More typically, you take your chances when you make a contract in expectation of some third party's or outside force's action; many contracts have a term to that effect built in.

There are three important criteria for a contract to be set aside for frustration of purpose.

1. The frustration must be substantial—nearly total, and with almost no chance at improved benefit.
2. The change in circumstances must not be reasonably foreseeable.
3. The frustration must not have been your fault.

Q. May someone have a contract set aside because it simply isn't fair?

A. It is possible, but not likely. Courts have a powerful weapon called unconscionability at their disposal. **Unconscionability** means that the bargaining process or the contract's provisions "shock the conscience of the court." For example, selling $10,000 worth of rumba lessons to a ninety-five-year-old widow living on Social Security would probably be held unconscionable. An unconscionable contract is grossly unfair. Its terms suggest that one party took unfair advantage of the other during negotiations. The courts are reluctant to use this weapon, but consumers have a better chance with it than anyone else, especially in installment contracts. You might ask, why would anyone sign such a contract? The answer is that unfairness is usually accompanied by procedural problems, like obscure language, or lack of choice.

Though courts sometimes will void contracts on these grounds, unconscionability is uncommon. Make the effort to understand all the terms of a contract.

ⓘ GETTING OUT OF A CONTRACT

A contract may be set aside if competent parties have not made it voluntarily. It also may be set aside if there was grossly insufficient consideration. In addition, certain contracts must be in writing, or they are unenforceable. Here is a list of other contract defenses:

- Illegality
- Duress
- Undue influence
- Fraud
- Mistake
- Unconscionability
- Impossibility of performance
- Frustration of purpose

If you can prove any of these, the contract will probably be deemed void or voidable. In either case, it is practically as if there never was a contract. If either party paid money, it would have to be returned.

For more details, see "Remedies for Breach of Contract" on page 326.

THE WORLD AT YOUR FINGERTIPS

- *Cornell University Law School provides an overview of contract law on its website at www.law.cornell.edu/topics/contracts.html.*
- *To investigate whether a company has a record for not living up to its end of a contract, contact the Better Business Bureau at www.bbb.org.*
- *The Federal Trade Commission provides tips for consumers on its website; to access, visit www.ftc.gov.*

REMEMBER THIS

- *A contract requires an offer by one party and acceptance by the other. Without both, there is no deal.*
- *Each side must be surrendering something (such as an item, money, or the freedom to do nothing) for a contract to be valid.*
- *A promise may go from being just hot air to a binding contract if the other party reasonably relies on those words and sacrifices something of value (such as money or a good) in expectation that the pledge will be kept.*
- *You cannot be contractually bound to perform an illegal act.*
- *You should understand the distinction between fact and opinion. A seller commits fraud when he or she lies about what a product actually contains, rendering a contract void. However, salesmanship allows a seller to opine that a product is the best he or she has ever seen.*
- *Contract claims come with time limits. Consumers have a limited time in which to sue after they realize the seller has not satisfied his or her end of the bargain.*

TYPES OF CONTRACTS

Consumers generally do not ask to see a sales contract; the contract is thrust upon them by the seller, most commonly at a car dealership, real estate agency, or apartment manager's office. The contract terms are generally set out in a form with numerous blanks on it, which can be filled in with the names of the parties, the financial terms, and so on. You'll probably be expected to sign without asking any questions, and the other side probably won't be sympathetic if you ask for time to read the contract from start to finish.

This section will help you understand what you can do to protect yourself, and what to look for in various contracts.

Practical Contracts

Q. Are form contracts worth reading?

A. Believe it or not, it pays to read form contracts. Failure to read a contract is virtually never a valid legal defense. In most states, the courts have held that people are bound by all the terms in a contract, even if they didn't read the contract before signing it (unless the other party engaged in fraud or unconscionable conduct). Don't trust the other party to tell you what it means; even with good intentions, the party could be mistaken. Also, be suspicious if the salesperson urges you to "never mind, it's not important." (Ask the salesperson, "If it's not important, is it okay to cross out the whole paragraph?") When a substantial amount of money is at stake, take the time to sit down with the form and underline parts you do not understand. Then find out what they mean from someone you trust.

At the same time, you must be realistic about exercising your right to read a form contract. At the car rental counter at the airport, you probably don't have time to read the contract and get an explanation of the terms you don't understand. Even if you did take the time, with whom would you negotiate? The sales clerk almost certainly doesn't have the authority to change the contract.

Similarly, when agreeing to the license terms of a commercially sold software program, no negotiation is possible. If you want the program, you have to agree. However, the contract forms and terms are usually available to examine while you are considering a transaction and before you are actually ready to enter into a deal.

Q. What if all the time I take to protect my legal rights results in my losing a great bargain?

A. Rarely will a truly great bargain not be there tomorrow. For all the great deals that work out fine, the one you will remember is the one that went sour—where the seller socked you with the fine print you didn't bother to read.

Q. What is a rider?

A. A **rider** is a sheet of paper (or several pages) reflecting an addition or **amendment** (change) to the main body of a contract. Often it's simpler to put changes in a rider, which supersedes any con- tradictory parts of the main contract, than to try to incorporate the changes on the original form.

Q. What can be so dangerous in fine print?

A. Very often the fine print contains terms that could greatly affect your personal finances beyond what the actual deal would lead you to believe. It may contain details about credit terms, your right to sue, and your right to a jury in a lawsuit.

Q. What should I do about the fine print?

A. First, try to read it. If you sit down and examine the fine print sentence by sentence, you'll often find that you can understand a lot more than you expect, especially in states that have passed "plain-English" laws requiring that consumer contracts use nontechnical, easy-to-understand words. You will at least, by expending the effort, identify which terms raise questions for you. The trick is not to be intimidated by the salesperson or the fine print in the contract.

⚠ FILL IN THE BLANKS

There are two main points to be aware of regarding form contracts, which can be purchased at stationery stores.

First, while they may be standardized, there's no such thing as a standard contract. Many innocuous-looking forms are available in several different versions. One might be a "landlord's" contract, in which the preprinted terms are more favorable to the landlord, while a nearly identical one is a "tenant's" contract. In any event, don't let anyone tell you it's "standard." If it is feasible, insist on crossing out or changing any term you don't like. If the other party refuses to accept changes that are important to you, don't sign the contract. In today's economy, there is usually more than one source for the product or service you want, and the market will tend to establish reasonable terms.

Second, fill in all the blanks! A contract with your original signature but containing blank spaces can be like a blank check if altered unscrupulously. Be sure all blanks are filled, either with specific terms or straight lines to indicate that nothing goes there. And insist on your own copy with the other side's original signature.

Q. *If I understand it but don't like it, must I accept the contract?*

A. No. You never have to accept a contract. Every part of a contract is open for negotiation, at least in theory. Just because the salesperson gave you a form contract doesn't mean that you have to stick to the form. You can cross out parts you don't like. You can write in terms that the contract doesn't include, such as oral promises by a salesperson. (Make sure that all changes to the form appear on all copies that will have your signature; initial altered but unsigned pages and have the other party do the same.)

That doesn't mean the other side has to agree to your changes. You have no more power to dictate terms than they do. But if you get a lot of resistance on what seem to be reasonable issues, take a hard look at with whom you are dealing—especially if they resist your request to put oral promises in writing.

Q. *What if I come across legalese that I just can't figure out?*

A. Until you understand every important term in a substantial contract, don't sign it. Legalese most often occurs in contracts that include some type of credit terms, such as when you buy something that requires installment payments. Chapter 7, "Consumer Credit," and chapter 11, "Automobiles," explain many of these terms. If you still have questions, ask someone you trust (not the salespeople) to explain the terms to you. That could be someone experienced with the kind of contract you are considering, a state or local consumer agency, or a lawyer.

Q. *Are there any laws that protect consumers against the use of confusing language?*

A. Yes. Many states now require plain English in some or most consumer contracts, with potentially confusing sections or clauses in precise, standard terms that nearly anyone can understand. Federal and state truth-in-lending laws require providers of credit to furnish specific information about credit contracts in clearly understandable form. Finally, legal doctrines regulating contracts of adhesion may protect you.

Q. *What are contracts of adhesion?*

A. **Contracts of adhesion** are contracts that give you little or no power to change the preprinted terms, as often is the case in many of the form contracts discussed above, such as loan documents, insurance contracts, and automobile leases. These are called contracts of adhesion because, if you want the deal, you have to "adhere," or stick, to the terms. "Click box" contracts for software or other computer-related merchandise, or access to websites, are also contracts of adhesion.

⚠ GET IT IN WRITING

When dealing with a written contract, a court will almost always treat the contract's terms as the final, complete contract. The court usually will not even consider oral promises that are not in the contract. The main exception to this is when oral promises are used fraudulently to induce one party into signing the contract in the first place. That is, the party is persuaded by the fraudulent oral promise to enter into a contract he or she otherwise would have avoided. The general rule prohibiting evidence of oral promises in all other cases protects both parties, since they each know that once they sign the contract, they have clearly and finally set the terms.

Don't be swayed if the salesperson orally promises you an extended warranty or a full refund if you're not completely satisfied. Get it in writing.

Since there is no case-by-case negotiation, form contracts are cost-efficient. But they can also be abusive.

The consumer has some protection, however. Courts generally assume that such contracts have been drafted to provide maximum benefit to the lender, the lessor, or the insurance company. So when a dispute arises over terms or language, the courts usually interpret contracts in the way most favorable to the consumer.

In one case, for example, a woman tried to collect on an airline trip insurance policy she had purchased. The insurance company insisted that the policy applied only to a trip on a "scheduled airline" and that "technically" under some obscure regulations the woman's flight was not scheduled, even though she had every reason to believe it was. The court held in favor of the woman, saying that the ordinary insurance buyer's understanding should apply.

This doesn't mean the consumer gets the benefit of the doubt on any question about any terms of an adhesion contract; it only applies to confusing or unclear clauses. To some extent, though, even contracts that are not contracts of adhesion are interpreted to favor the party who didn't draft them.

Like the doctrines of unconscionability and fraud, this rule isn't something to depend on before signing a contract. Rather, it's a strategy that you and your lawyer may choose if a problem arises.

Leases and Surety Contracts

Q. What is a lease?

A. A **lease** is a type of contract. It has all the elements of a contract explained earlier: It involves something someone lets you use for a specified time, for a specified fee. There are two main kinds of leases. The first involves real estate, such as a lease for an apartment. The second includes all other kinds of property, such as leases for office equipment and vehicles.

Q. Why would I lease something instead of buying it?

A. Leasing may not require you to invest as much of your money up front as buying because you are not paying for ownership of the item. You must return the item to the owner at the end of the lease period. A lease also cushions you from the risk of owning a piece of equipment that may become obsolete in a few years.

The drawback is that your payments never add up to **equity** (an ownership interest) in the property. Also, because leases involve calculations that are not required to be disclosed—unlike the cost of credit in a sale—it may be difficult to ascertain the true cost of a lease.

Leases may come with service contracts of some sort. We'll discuss this type of contract on pages 309 and 312.

Q. What should I look for in a lease for equipment or a vehicle?

A. These leases, usually on preprinted forms with very few blanks, often offer little room for bargaining. Hence, it is very important that you understand the terms and are sure you'll be able to meet them, especially where there's an option to buy. Make sure that the lease states the price at which you'll be able to buy the item. The lease may specify the price as a dollar figure or as a percentage of some amount that you should be able to figure out easily. Obviously, be sure that at least from where you stand now, it's a price worth paying. If you have no intention of buying, of course, then there's no problem—but you should be able to get a less-expensive deal by not including an option to buy in the contract.

Q. Are there laws designed to protect renters under residential leases?

A. Yes. Most states have laws that protect people who lease their homes. Chapter 6, "Renting Residential Property," discusses them fully. Many states also have laws that require special disclosures and other protection for people who enter into other types of consumer leases. These laws may even cancel out what the contract states.

Q. What are surety contracts?

A. A **surety contract** is an agreement in which one party, called the **surety,** accepts the responsibility for someone else's contractual obligations. For example, you might agree to pay back your son's bank loan if he does not. Usually, a surety is bound with the other person (the **principal**) on the same promise, often on the same document; under such an arrangement, the surety is sometimes called a cosigner.

A **guaranty contract** is similar, but with a guaranty the person who's vouching for the principal—called the **guarantor**—makes a separate promise and is liable only if the principal breaches and it is impossible to collect from him or her. In many cases, the terms "surety" and "guaranty" are used interchangeably, because their practical effects are nearly identical.

Warranties

Q. What are warranties?

A. Warranties are obligations taken on by the provider or imposed on the provider by law. Some warranties deal with the quality of the goods: Will they do a specific job or meet certain specifications? Are they reasonably fit for their intended purpose? Other warranties might deal with the ownership of the goods: Does the seller have good title or ownership rights that may be lawfully transferred to the buyer?

Q. Does the law regulate warranties?

A. Yes. A federal law, the Magnuson-Moss Warranty Act, covers written warranties for consumer goods costing more than a few dollars. It does not require that merchants make written warranties. If they do make such a warranty, however, it must meet certain standards. The warranty must be available for you to read before you buy. It must be written in plain language and include the following information:

- The name and address of the company making the warranty
- The product or parts covered
- Whether the warranty promises replacement, repair, or refund, and if there are any expenses (such as shipping or labor) you would have to pay
- How long the warranty lasts
- The damages that the warranty does not cover
- The action you should take if something goes wrong
- Whether the company providing the warranty requires you to use any specific informal (out-of-court) methods to settle a dispute
- A brief description of your legal rights

Many states have warranty laws that provide consumers who purchase new automobiles with greater protection than the Magnuson-Moss federal warranty law. These are commonly called "lemon laws." Some require disclosure and many regulate deceptive practices. Chapter 11, "Automobiles," contains more information.

Q. How can I make the best use of warranties?

A. Consider all warranty terms when you shop. The terms of a warranty are seldom negotiable, especially the length of the warranty, whether it covers only parts or certain problems, and what you must do to use your rights. But some elements, such as the price of an extended warranty, may be negotiable. Many companies offer such extended warranties (sometimes called service contracts) for varying lengths of time and for varying amounts of money. Often the cost to the retailer is less than half the price the retailer asks the consumer to pay. This is an area where careful, aggressive negotiation by the consumer can result in substantial savings.

Q. What is the difference between a full warranty and a limited warranty?

A. Magnuson-Moss requires all written warranties for consumer products costing more than a few dollars to be designated as either a full warranty or a limited warranty. A **full warranty** is a promise that the product will be repaired or replaced free during the warranty period. State and federal laws require that if the **warrantor** (the company making the warranty) will repair the item, it must be fixed within a reasonable time and it must be reasonably convenient to get the item to and from the repair site. Many stores will offer a short full warranty of their own (thirty to ninety days), above what the manufacturer offers, and some premium credit cards will double a warranty for up to a year for products purchased with the card. Repairs or replacement during the extended warranty period become the responsibility of the card issuer after the manufacturer's warranty expires.

A **limited warranty** is much more common. Not surprisingly, it covers less. It may cover only parts and not labor. Or the dealer warranty on a used car may provide that the cost of repairs be split fifty-fifty for the first thirty days.

Q. What are express and implied warranties?

A. Express warranties are any promises to back up the product or about the product that the warrantor expresses either in writing or orally. Suppose your friend bought your Yugo and you said, "I guarantee you'll get another ten thousand miles out of this transmission." That's an express warranty. It isn't an opinion about quality or value, such as "This Yugo is the best mauve used car for sale in town." Rather, it's a specific statement of fact or a promise.

A warrantor does not state **implied warranties** at all—they're automatic in certain kinds of transactions. There are two main types of implied warranties: the implied warranty of merchantability and the implied warranty of fitness for a particular purpose.

Q. What is the implied warranty of merchantability?

A. When someone is in the business of selling or leasing a specific kind of product, the law requires that the item be adequate for the purpose for which it is purchased or leased. This is the **implied warranty of merchantability.** This general rule of fairness means that what looks like a carton of milk in the supermarket dairy case really is drinkable milk and not sour or unusable. In many states, the implied warranty of merchantability cannot be disclaimed in a consumer transaction with respect to new and unused consumer goods.

So, to take a car-sale example, if the buyer's purpose is only the ordinary one of general transportation, the implied warranty of merchantability is what assures the buyer or the lessee that the product will work. And that warranty applies if the product does not work, even if great care was taken in its manufacture. For this reason, only a merchant makes this implied warranty. The implied warranty of merchantability doesn't apply to

---

> ▶ **WARRANTY SENSE**

The best-made products usually have the best warranties, because they're less likely to need them. Thus, the manufacturer can guarantee a long period with little risk.

A warranty is a statement about the maker's confidence in its products. Because it involves the manufacturer's pocketbook, it's a statement you should take seriously. Try to figure the value of a warranty into the price of a product and make it part of your formula.

Extended warranties really are service contracts, not warranties, and their price is negotiable. Also remember that the dealer that sells you the merchandise is not the only source of service contracts—you can search online and elsewhere for companies that may offer you a better deal.

sellers or lessors of cars unless they are in the business of selling or leasing cars.

Q. What is the implied warranty of fitness for a particular purpose?

A. The **implied warranty of fitness for a particular purpose** means that any seller or lessor (even a nonprofessional) is presumed to guarantee that an item will be fit for the particular purpose for which the buyer is getting it, as long as the seller has reason to know that the buyer is relying on the seller to supply a suitable item. For example, if your friend tells you she needs a car that could tow a trailer full of granite up steep mountains in the snow, and you sell her the Yugo as a suitable vehicle, then she relies on your skill and judgment about the Yugo. When you sell her the Yugo knowing that she intends to use it for a specific purpose, you make an implied warranty that it can do that. If the car fails in that purpose, your warranty will have been breached.

On the other hand, if your friend tells you she's buying your car only because she needs spare Yugo parts, you can sell your Yugo to her—even if it's sitting out back on cinder blocks—without breaching a warranty of fitness for the intended purpose.

⚠ SOFTWARE WARRANTIES

Computer software transactions also may come with warranties, although not the same warranties that come with sales or leases of goods. Contracts for services normally only involve an obligation of reasonable care, unless there is an express warranty.

Of course, courts may impose a warranty in some cases, and some legislation may impose warranties. For example, the Uniform Computer Information Transactions Act imposes warranties in some sales and leases.

Q. How long do warranties last?

A. It depends on the type of transaction and warranty involved, and the applicable law. In most states, you have up to four years to enforce an implied warranty after the start of the transaction. In cases involving written warranties, the period may be shorter or longer. A written warranty will disclose how long it lasts. It may be as short as ninety days for a portable radio. A warranty on a new car, on the other hand, may last several years or many thousand miles.

Q. May a merchant disclaim a warranty?

A. Not after you've made the deal. But before you buy, unwritten express warranties and (in most states) implied warranties of merchantability or fitness may be excluded or disclaimed if the contract or disclaimer is in writing and the relevant language is obvious. The word "merchantability" may have to appear for a disclaimer of an implied warranty to be valid, or it may have to state that a product is delivered "as is." In contrast, a less communicative written statement may disclaim the implied warranty of fitness for a particular purpose. In any event, a person may not disclaim an express warranty that's written in the contract.

Q. Is disclaiming a warranty common?

A. It cannot be done on a consumer product that carries a written warranty. If there is not such a warranty, a disclaimer is common. In many cases of consumer products, a warranty will be stated and the contract you sign will state a specific remedy if the product fails. This means that the buyer gets a warranty, and the seller or the lessor is protected to some extent. For example, the contract may provide that the seller will repair or replace the merchandise, if necessary, but that the customer has no right to get money back. This protects the seller against the worst-case scenario (having to give your money back) while still protecting the buyer.

Q. Does the law ever overrule the guarantees contained in a warranty?

A. Yes. Lemon laws provide a good example. Most states have these laws, which provide extra guarantees to people who have been unlucky enough to buy new cars (and in some cases other products) so bad that they fit the statutory definition of a "lemon." (Chapter 11, "Automobiles," has more on these laws.)

Q. Most warranty limitations exclude some forms of consequential damages. What are consequential damages?

A. Consequential damages are losses caused by the product's defect, including your lost time and expense that result from the defect and repair costs. If, for example, your new computer crashes and destroys weeks of work, you may get a new computer. But under the terms of the wording in the warranty that came with the computer (as well as the disks), the warrantor will almost certainly not reimburse you for the lost time, work, or software—much less a lost job or client. At some point, the law expects you to protect yourself, in this case by backing up your computer files. However, you usually may recover damages in cases of personal injury that result from a product's defect.

Q. What about extended warranties or service contracts?

A. Both of these will cost you extra. Take a hard look and ask if the benefits are worth the cost. Consider how the extended warranty or service contract enhances your regular warranty. Find out where you'll have to send the product for repairs. Also check, especially in service contracts, whether there's a deductible amount. For example, the contract might not cover repairs costing less than $50. The deductible amount, or a per-repair flat fee that you agree to pay, can add up to erase all the expected savings. Sometimes it pays to wait until the warranty has expired before deciding to buy a service contract, if you can. By then, you should have a sense of a product's reliability.

Be sure to take a good look at who is backing up the contract or warranty. Is it a well-known manufacturer? The store where you got it? Or a company you have never heard of with only a post office box or a website for an address? You don't have to buy an extended warranty from the dealer, by the way. Just search online under "warranties" and you will see a wealth of alternatives. They can at least provide you with useful comparative shopping information.

Ultimately, don't be pressured by a salesperson into taking one of those contracts. They're frequently a major source of profit on the transaction. Ask the salesperson why you should be so concerned about insuring yourself for repair costs if the product is well made.

▶ **READ WARRANTIES BEFORE YOU BUY**

Don't wait until a product needs repair to find out what's covered in any written warranty you get. Compare the terms and conditions of the warranty before you buy and look for the warranty that best meets your needs.

There are several points to consider. How long is the warranty, and when does it start and end? Will the warranty pay 100 percent of repair costs? Does it cover parts but not labor? What kinds of problems are covered? What do you have to do to enforce your warranty rights? And when do you have to do it? Are regular inspections or maintenance required? Do you have to ship the product to the repair center? If so, who pays for shipping? What about a loaner? Who offers the warranty—the manufacturer or the retailer? How reliable is each?

Q. How can I protect my warranty rights?

A. First, keep your receipts through the warranty period. They are your proof of when the warranty period starts and ends, and are more important than the warranty return card. (That card often is just a marketing device to learn more about you.)

Also remember that any violation of the manufacturer's operating and service instructions probably will void the warranty.

If a problem arises, try the store where you got the item. It may be able to go around the warranty process, especially if it's very soon after your acquisition. If you end up contacting the manufacturer, do so only as instructed in the warranty. Keep a list of the people with whom you have spoken or letters you have written. It's a good idea to contact the manufacturer in writing, keeping copies of all correspondence, at the address specified in the warranty. That's especially true if you aren't getting quick responses. Your correspondence file will protect your warranty rights near the end of the coverage period.

SPECIAL CONSUMER PROTECTIONS

Advertising

Q. Store advertisements are not usually offers. Are there any exceptions to this?

A. Yes. Suppose a store advertises that it will give a free gift or a special discount to "the first 100 customers" or to a person who has made some other special effort. If so, the store has made an offer. You can accept it by making the special effort successfully. (In fact, a few years ago a major department store got into hot water by carelessly advertising: "Be among the first 1,000 shoppers at our store tomorrow to win a $1,000 shopping spree." The wording suggests that all 1,000 would win.)

Q. What is false advertising?

A. **False advertising** is an unfair method of competition forbidden under federal law and state consumer-fraud statutes. The advertiser's intent isn't important. The overall impression conveyed is what counts.

False advertising misleads about a product's place of origin, nature or quality, or maker. An example of misleading about a product's origin is putting French labels on sweaters made in Arkansas. Promising first-quality socks and delivering irregulars or seconds is misleading about an item's nature or quality. Claiming a Yugo is a Lexus is misleading about a product's maker. As for services, false advertising would mislead you into thinking that someone has qualifications (such as being a master carpenter) that he or she actually does not have.

Q. How exact must advertisements be?

A. They must be accurate about material aspects of the product or service in the offer. It's no crime to sell a dress that looks better on the fashion model in the ad than on a normal person. It also is legal to prepare a food product in a special way to make it look more tempting on television than it will be at home. If an advertisement led you to expect green spark plugs and you got gray ones, the ad did not materially mislead you. But if the ad said the plugs would last a long time and they failed early on, you probably were misled.

Q. What about contests and investment schemes?

A. The rule is this: Any contest or get-rich-quick scheme that requires you to part with money probably is a losing proposition. Often these are pyramid schemes. Someone may contact you by mail or over the phone, promising you some huge return on your money and telling you of real people who made a bundle. That part is true, actually. Some did get a lot of money. But they did it illegally—by inducing people like you to pony up. The only way you could do the same is to con a large number of people to make the same mistake you did. The courts have held these scams—and any promotion that promises an unrealistic return—to be false advertising. If they involve mail, they are postal violations. Some cases might involve violations of securities laws. One good rule of thumb is that no legitimate speculative investment will ever promise or even strongly suggest a specific return to you.

If you are contacted by mail regarding what seems like a fraudulent scheme, contact the office of the U.S. Postal Service Inspector General. Otherwise, report such a pitch to your state or city consumer protection office or state attorney general and the Federal Trade Commission (FTC). Virtually all states now provide a way for shutting down these scams and recovering victims' money, but the process may be long and may not always be successful.

Q. What is bait and switch?

A. The bait is an advertisement luring you with the promise of an unbeatable deal on a product. The switch occurs when you walk into the store

⚠ BEWARE OF INTERNET SCAMS

Exercise the most care when participating in contests or the like over the Internet. It is difficult and often impossible to tell whom you are dealing with on the Web, and virtually impossible for a private citizen to get satisfaction after being swindled by someone online who may not even be in this hemisphere. Common scams are those in which an e-mailer asks for assistance in recovering millions of dollars. All the consumer need do is provide the number of her bank account so the e-mailer can send the millions. Instead of filling up your bank account, the e-mailer will empty it out—before the victim is even aware of it. Don't fall for it.

▶ COMPLAIN, COMPLAIN, COMPLAIN

One of the best pieces of advice for consumers it to understand the role of filing complaints with the offices of state attorneys general or other state consumer officials. The more people who complain about a particular problem, the more likely it is that a state will undertake an inquiry that could lead to a claim for restitution. The key website is www.naag.org, because it can lead you to the attorney general in your state.

and the salesperson tells you the advertised model isn't available but a more expensive model is. The salesperson has "switched" you from the one you wanted to buy. This practice is illegal in most states if the advertised model was never available in reasonable quantities or is falsely disparaged to discourage its sale. It also is illegal if the store never intended to sell the item but advertised it just to get you into the store so that it could try to sell you a more expensive item.

You have a right to see the model that appeared in the newspaper ad. If the store is "fresh out of them," it also may be guilty of false advertising. You're allowed to be persuaded, but keep up your guard, and don't let someone talk you into buying a model you can't afford. If insisting on your rights gets you nowhere, keep the ad, get the salesperson's name (and that of anyone else you spoke to), and report the matter to the state or local consumer-protection office.

Telemarketing

Q. Should I ever buy a product or a service over the phone?

A. Imagine you're sitting down for dinner after a busy day. Suddenly, the telephone rings. You seriously consider not answering, but you have family and friends who might be trying to contact you. So you pick up the receiver—and your worst fear is realized: It's a telemarketer.

So you listen to the sales pitch and, much to your surprise, you want to buy what he or she is selling. Should you close the deal over the phone?

The simple answer is: absolutely not. You know nothing about this person or the company he or she ostensibly represents other than the fact that the individual has no compunction about disturbing your supper. Request that he or she send you written information about the product or service being sold, as well as a written contract with all terms and warranties for your perusal. Do not trust yourself to understand—or the marketer to explain fully—the terms of the sale, especially when you're tired and hungry. If the marketer is legitimate, he or she can certainly send you the information in writing. After all, he or she is most likely reading from a script.

Q. I've had it with telemarketers and wish they'd stop calling. What can I do?

A. You are not alone. Many states have established do-not-call lists that compile the names and telephone numbers of residents who do not want to be contacted by telemarketers, who in turn must honor these requests. If you put yourself on your state's list, and telemarketers victimize you anyway, you may be able to get help from your state's authorities.

In addition, the federal Do-Not-Call Implementation Act authorizes the Federal Trade Commission to compile a list of people who do not wish to receive telemarketing calls. Though the constitutionality of the law has been challenged, unless it is overturned all you have to do is contact the FTC either online (www.donotcall.gov) or by a toll-free number (888-382-1222 [TTY: 866-290-4236]) and tell the agency that you want to be added to the list. Placing your number on the National Do Not Call Registry will stop most telemarketing calls, including those from overseas. However, you may still receive calls from political organizations, charities, people tak-

ing surveys by telephone, or companies with which you have an existing business relationship.

Or you can contact the Direct Marketing Association, which represents the telemarketing industry, and request to be put on its do-not-call list. The DMA's website is at www.the-dma.org/consumers/offtelephonelist.html.

Door-to-Door Sales

Q. What are the problems in door-to-door sales?

A. Most people feel secure in their homes. Ironically, that feeling makes them especially vulnerable to door-to-door salespeople. That's particularly true of homebound people, such as the elderly. You have few facts by which to judge a door-to-door salesperson. There is no manager, no showroom, and no immediate way to assess the company that the salesperson represents (if there is one.)

Q. Do any laws protect purchases made as a result of door-to-door sales?

A. Federal law requires a three-day cooling-off period for door-to-door sales. During that time, you can cancel purchases you make from someone who both solicits and closes the sale at your home.

You don't have to give any reason for changing your mind, and the three days don't start until you receive formal notice of your right to cancel. You can cancel almost any sale not made at a fixed place of business, such as sales made at your home, someone else's home, or a hotel. Federal law extends this cooling-off period to both credit and noncredit sales. It also forbids the company to charge you any cancellation fee.

The federal law applies to most such cases, and many states have similar laws.

Q. What if I do buy from a door-to-door salesperson?

A. Federal and state laws usually require such salespeople to provide you with the following details on your receipt:

- The seller's name and place of business
- A description of the goods and services sold
- The amount of money you paid, or the value of any goods delivered to you
- Your cooling-off period rights (see above)

Some of these laws also require that if the salesperson makes the sale in Spanish or another language, the seller must give you all the above details in that language.

Q. What happens if I cancel my order during the cooling-off period?

A. State law usually will require the salesperson to refund your money, return any trade-in you made, and cancel and return the contract. The salesperson has ten business days to do this under federal law. You must make the goods available to be picked up during that period. Under federal law, if the salesperson waits longer than twenty calendar days, you may be allowed to keep the goods free.

Q. What about door-to-door home repair sales?

A. Tell anyone who supposedly has some left-over asphalt, shingles, or other material from a nearby job, and offers you a sweet deal to fix your driveway, roof, or whatever, to go somewhere else. Make your home repairs when you're ready, and only with contractors you know. (See "Home and Home Appliance Repair and Improvements" on page 319 for more on home repairs.)

Buying by Mail

Q. How long does a mail-order company have to deliver goods that I ordered?

A. Under federal law, the goods must be in the mail within thirty days of your order. If they aren't, you must at least have received a letter informing you of the delay and when to expect delivery. The seller also must offer you a refund within one week if you don't want to wait any longer. The exception is goods that you understand not to be available until a certain time, such as magazines or flower seeds. Many states have laws that protect you even further than the federal law.

Q. May the company send substitute goods to me?

A. Yes, but you don't have to accept them. You can send them back and ask for a refund. If you keep them, though, you have to pay their usual price, unless the company offers them for less. Pick up a pen or the telephone and try to negotiate. Since mail-order firms depend on goodwill more than other companies do, a reputable company should be able to strike an acceptable deal with you.

⚠ PROTECTING YOURSELF IN CATALOG PURCHASES

Shopping via catalogs, whether printed or online, has grown tremendously in the last few years. It has been a blessing for consumers with little time to browse in stores. But there are occasionally some drawbacks, including delays in receiving orders, uneven customer service, and inconvenience if repair or replacement is necessary. In addition, there is a possibility of fraud, since it's hard to assess the company without seeing a showroom or salespeople.

Try to find established merchants that have been in business for at least a few years. Placing an order for an inexpensive item is a good way to check a company's performance before investing in more costly merchandise. Payment by credit card also is highly recommended—it usually makes it easier to resolve disputes.

Q. What about unordered merchandise I receive in the mail?

A. Federal law requires the sender of an unordered item sent through the mail to mark the package "Free Sample." (The law permits charities to send you Easter Seals, Hanukkah candles, and the like, and ask for a contribution.) Consumers who receive unordered merchandise in the mail should consider it a gift. They have no obligation to pay for the merchandise, and they may keep it. Sending you a bill for such merchandise may be mail fraud, which is a federal crime. Report such practices, or any harassment or threats to force you to pay the bill, to the U.S. Postal Service and your state consumer protection bureau. But first make sure you, or a family member, didn't actually order the item.

Q. Does the same rule about unordered goods apply to merchants?

A. A merchant who receives unordered merchandise from a supplier doesn't have to pay for it, but the sender must be allowed to arrange for its return. If, however, the merchant does something that shows that he or she is willing to buy the merchandise, such as selling or displaying it, then the merchant must pay for it.

Time-Shares

Q. What are time-shares?

A. Time-shares are a period of time, maybe a week or so per year, that you can buy for a specific property (usually a residence at a resort), during which the right to use the property belongs to you. The idea is that you benefit by prepaying for a vacation place rather than renting it, as you otherwise might do. The profit that would have gone to the owner supposedly stays in your pocket.

Q. What problems should I be aware of when buying a time-share?

A. One problem is that expenses often offset the savings. If, like most people, you finance your time-share purchase over time, the interest costs alone may eat away that supposed profit. Even if you pay cash, you lose the interest you could otherwise have earned on that money.

And unlike renters, who have the option of coming or not coming from season to season as a resort becomes more or less desirable, time-share owners are generally locked in. In some cases, they may be able to exchange their property, but that involves a formal exchange program and costs money. They usually cannot sell the property except at a substantial loss.

Furthermore, your time-share contract will make you responsible to pay any increases in taxes, maintenance, or repairs. If you think any of these amounts are going to decrease, you're in for a big surprise.

Q. Don't time-shares eventually break even?

A. Time-share sellers will often point out that notwithstanding these problems, once you pay off

---

⚠ ONLINE SHOPPING

Much of what has been said above regarding mail and catalog sales applies to shopping for merchandise over the Internet—only more so. It is remarkably easy to put up a slick website that has nothing real, or nothing legitimate, behind it. Do not assume that because a merchant displays an authentic trademark or accepts credit cards that it is what it seems to be. Nothing could be easier than copying these marks or arranging for a third party to act as a credit card clearinghouse with little or no accountability. Avoid buying luxury goods over the Internet except from established merchants you know from the "real world." Chances are that luxury goods from unknown merchants are counterfeits.

the time-share you will have "free" vacationing, so at some point you will break even with the cost of renting and eventually be in the black. But that break-even point, which takes into account all of your costs, including interest, may not come for ten to twenty years. Ask yourself whether you are prepared to vacation in the same place every year for the next decade so you can eventually save on your vacation expenses.

Q. If I don't like the time-share deal, though, can't I just sell it?

A. In theory, yes. Practically speaking, though, many people who bought time-shares in the 1980s or 1990s—when any investment involving real estate looked like a winner—are finding themselves with white elephants on their hands. You may have to unload the time-share for much less than you paid, if you can find a buyer at all. You may be stuck making an agreement with the sponsors that they will take back the time-share during the payment period and let you off the hook for the rest of the term. You would get nothing back for what you've already paid in (which might be several times what you would have paid in rent), but you would have no further obligations.

Pets

Q. What may I ask about a pet before I buy it?

A. You may ask anything. You have a right to know about the pet's health, family history or pedigree, training, and medical care, both normal and unusual.

Q. Do states have pet laws that cover an owner's rights when purchasing an animal?

A. Many states do have such laws. Some require pet stores to make detailed disclosures to buyers on such topics as the animal's health, age, and history (for example, immunization records and other health information). Some

even have lemon laws that make it easier for buyers to get their money back if they have purchased a sick animal. If your state doesn't have such laws, then general warranty laws apply.

Q. What should I do if I am dissatisfied with my pet purchase?

A. Immediately notify the seller in writing, keeping a copy for yourself. Keep all contracts and papers—even the original advertisement, if there was one. If you have not received a replacement or refund within thirty days, consider filing a small-claims lawsuit. Don't worry about becoming an expert on pet law. The judge will probably base a decision on the fairness of the case, not on technicalities.

▶ **DO PETS COME WITH GUARANTEES?**

Suppose you buy a pet and it turns out to be sick or injured. Legally, what can you do? The answer may depend on whether you bought the pet from a pet shop or a private owner. It also may depend on whether you had a written contract, and what express and implied warranties exist under your state's laws. It also matters whether you bought this pet for a specific purpose, such as breeding it for competition. In general, it's best for you and the seller to sign a written agreement about your pet that will clarify most of a new owner's questions.

Another way of avoiding problems is to ask the seller for the name of the pet's veterinarian. Ask the vet for an opinion on the pet's health, which may alert you to potential problems before you complete the purchase.

Home and Home Appliance Repair and Improvements

Q. Are there laws that specifically protect consumers against shoddy workmanship and fraud in home repair contracts?

A. Roofs leak. Pipes burst. Dishwashers go on the fritz. Often homeowners have to call repair personnel to fix an immediate and serious problem. The owner goes to the yellow pages, finds a name, and dials—but what can owners do to protect themselves from getting ripped off?

Luckily, there are laws that specifically protect consumers in these situations. Many states have registration requirements for companies offering home repair services, and may even set up guaranty funds to help you recover your money. They also may set up three-day cooling-off periods, letting you get out of a deal within three days without paying a penalty.

The Federal Trade Commission and federal truth-in-lending laws also police this area.

Q. What should I watch out for?

A. Generally, as in any other contract, home repair contractors may not mislead you in any way to get the job. Be aware of these tricks:

- Promising a lower price for allowing your home to be used as a model or to advertise their work
- Promising better quality materials than they will use (beware of bait and switch here as well)
- Providing "free gifts"—find out when you will receive them, or try to get a price reduction instead
- Not including delivery and installation costs in the price
- Starting work before you sign a contract, to intimidate you
- Claiming that your house is dangerous and needs repair
- Claiming that the contractor works for a government agency

- Offering you a rebate or a referral fee if any of your friends agree to use the same contractor

Q. How may I protect myself?

A. Get several written estimates. Check into a contractor's track record with the Better Business Bureau and other customers before you sign a contract. Don't pay the full price in advance, and certainly not in cash. Don't sign a completion certificate or receipt until the contractor finishes the work to your satisfaction—including cleanup.

Q. Are there special things to look for in a home-improvement contract?

A. Yes. Be sure the contract has all the details in writing. Too often a contract of this type will read "work as per agreement." Instead, it should specify who will do the work, and include a detailed description of the work, the materials to be used, and the dates of starting and completion. It also should contain all charges, including any finance charges if you are paying over a period of time. If the financing is to be provided by a third party, do not sign the repair contract before you sign the financing contract. In addition, the contract should include the hourly rate on which the total cost is to be based. Be sure any guarantee is in writing.

Be especially wary of any mortgage or security interest the contractor takes in your home, which means that you may lose your home if you don't meet the payments for the work. If the contractor takes a mortgage or security interest, federal law gives you three days to change your mind and cancel.

Consider having a lawyer look at the contract, especially if there's a security agreement. If problems do arise that threaten your rights to own your home, see a lawyer immediately.

Q. What about appliance repairs?

A. You can best protect your rights by getting a written estimate. At least make sure you get an oral estimate before work begins, and find out how the repair shop will figure the total charge, including parts and labor. Also, tell the repair shop to get your approval before beginning work. It will then be able to give you a better idea of how much the repair will cost.

Buying Clubs

Q. What is a buying club?

A. There are several different types of buying clubs. One of the more popular kinds is a compact disc (CD) club. It offers five or ten CDs to you for an initial nominal price. You might pay only a nickel or a dollar, plus postage and handling, which can often exceed $10. In return, you agree to buy a certain number of CDs at the "regular club price" over a period of time. The "regular club price" is much higher than the initial price and higher than normal retail store prices, especially with postage and handling. In fact, though, the average price, including the introductory deal, usually works out to your benefit.

The problem with these clubs is that they automatically send you a CD every month or so. Before shipping the item, the club sends you a notice of the upcoming shipment. The only way

to prevent the automatic shipment is to return the notice before the date it specifies. Book clubs operate on a similar basis. Other clubs, such as those that sell children's books or science books, don't send you any notice—they assume you want the whole "library".

Q. So should I avoid these clubs?

A. Not necessarily. You may want to meet your additional obligation quickly and then resign your membership. Also, the clubs do offer many incentives to try to keep you as a member, which may be worthwhile to you. But if you forget to return the monthly notice, you will receive unwanted CDs and be obligated to pay for them or to return them, sometimes at your own expense.

Q. What about merchandise clubs?

A. The idea behind merchandise clubs is that you pay a fee to qualify for discounts. The club presumably obtains these discounts because of its volume buying power. Before joining one of these, take a good look at what it promises. Will it limit you to certain manufacturers? Are catalogs easily accessible? Shady clubs often appear on

---

⚠ THE TOP FIVE CONSUMER PROBLEMS

New Jersey's Office of Consumer Protection published a list of five of the most troublesome consumer problems in that state. Unfortunately, these exist nationwide.

- Fly-by-night home repair contractors (see page 319).

- Telephone solicitations. Always ask the caller to send written information. Also, determine your total obligation before agreeing to anything. Don't give credit card or checking account information to strangers over the telephone.

- Furniture delivery delays. Do not take ASAP (as soon as possible) as a delivery date in a sales contract. Get an exact date. If the merchandise doesn't show up by that date, you would then have the right to cancel.

- Free vacation offers. An example is the postcard telling you about a "free vacation" you have won: just call a toll-free number and "confirm" your credit card number. Later, you find out that the vacation is not as free as you thought. Play it safe—book your travel arrangements through a reliable agent or directly with travel carriers.

- Bait and switch tactics. (See the suggested countermeasures on page 314).

lists put out by the offices of state attorneys general and consumer protection agencies. Check with them first.

Funeral Homes

Q. What is the Funeral Rule?

A. When a loved one dies, bereaved survivors are in no mental state to negotiate a contract. Exploiting this vulnerability, some unsavory funeral homes used to charge exorbitant fees for burial services. To protect consumers, the Federal Trade Commission adopted the **Funeral Rule**, which requires mortuaries or funeral homes to quote you prices and other information you request over the telephone. The intention is to prevent corrupt operators from requiring you to come to their showrooms, where they can take advantage of your weak emotional state.

Q. Does the Funeral Rule require anything else?

A. If you visit a funeral home, it must give you a written list with all the prices and services offered—including the least expensive. You can keep this list. You have the right to choose any service offered, as long as it does not violate state law. The funeral home must give you a copy of that state law. The funeral home must reveal any fees charged for outside items, such as flowers, and may not charge a handling fee for purchases of caskets from third parties. The home may not falsely state that embalming is required by state law, and must give general information about embalming options. The Funeral Rule also entitles you to an itemized list of all charges you incur. The general idea of the Funeral Rule is that the funeral home must inform you of your options every step of the way.

⚠ BE WARY OF THIS LIST

What are the worst industries for consumer complaints? Every year the National Association of Consumer Agency Administrators and the Consumer Federation of America come up with a list based on surveys of consumer protection agencies. In a recent year, the following industries were the ones about which the most complaints were made, with the most complained about listed first:

- Home improvement (companies going out of business and reopening under another name; companies accepting payment but not completing work; shoddy work; inflated costs)
- Household goods (appliances, furniture, computers, etc. were often reported defective; there were also complaints of deceptive advertising and failure to honor warranties or provide refunds)
- Auto sales (complaints about financing deals, inability to get title)
- Auto repair
- Credit/lending
- Telecommunications
- Collections
- Pyramid schemes and business opportunities
- Recreation and vacations

Travel

Q. Is overbooking by hotels a violation of my contract?

A. It is if you have paid in advance. Otherwise, the reservation is just a courtesy. Therefore, it is often worthwhile to pay for a hotel reservation by credit card when you make it. If you cancel within a couple of days before the reservation date, you probably will get a complete credit, depending on the credit card company's arrangement with the hotel. Also, many premium credit card companies guarantee their cardholders' hotel rooms through the evening if the rooms are reserved with the card. (Contact the credit card company if the hotel doesn't honor your reservation.)

If your room is unavailable even after you speak to the manager, you could have a contract claim. But it probably won't be worthwhile to pursue it legally because of the cost. Perhaps the best advice is to request firmly that the hotel arrange suitable alternative accommodations for you.

Q. What about an airline bumping me off my flight?

A. Generally, even if you have paid in advance, you do not have a contract to go at a certain time. You only have a contract for a ticket for transport (or carriage) to a certain city. You do, however, have certain rights if you check in on time and have a confirmed ticket. Federal regulations require that if you get bumped against your wishes, the airline must give you a written statement describing your rights and explaining how the airline decides who gets on an oversold flight and who does not.

Travelers who don't get on the flight are often entitled to an on-the-spot payment as compensation. The amount depends on the price of their ticket and the length of the delay. There's no compensation if the airline can arrange to get you on another flight that is scheduled to arrive at your destination within one hour of your originally scheduled arrival time. If, however, the substitute transportation is scheduled to arrive more than one hour but less than two hours after your original time of arrival, the airline must pay you an amount equal to the one-way fare to your final destination, up to $200. You're entitled to up to $400 if your substitute transportation will not arrive within two hours (four hours for international flights.)

If you're just delayed, not bumped, ask the airline staff what services it will provide. Ask about meals, telephone calls, and overnight accommodations.

ⓘ LAW EVOLVES TO MEET E-COMMERCE DEMANDS

Many airline tickets and hotel rooms are bought online these days. Most consumer protection laws apply to these online merchants as well as to catalog and "brick-and-mortar" merchants. In addition, these laws are often supplemented in the states by laws aimed specifically at Web merchants. These often require the Web merchant to prominently post the legal name of the business, its return and refund policy, and the street address where it conducts business. Sometimes procedures for resolving complaints must be included as well.

Other laws deal with protection of privacy online, including the collection and use of personal information for marketing purposes. Special guidelines apply to selling stock over the Web.

Any company maintaining a website would be well advised to check with its lawyers about the rules and laws that apply—and to be aware that the legal framework is highly likely to continue to evolve.

You can complain to the U.S. Department of Transportation if you think an airline has abused you. But contact the airline first. In these competitive times for the travel industry, airlines often are responsive to consumer complaints.

Q. How can I protect myself when paying for charter tours?

A. Your money often takes a twisting route to the tour operator. This leaves you vulnerable at the many different stops that exist in between. The best approach is to pay by credit card, and receive the protections of the Fair Credit Billing Act. If you pay by check, the tour operator's brochure usually will specify the name of an escrow bank account in which all payments eventually go. Make out your check to that account. Also, if possible, put the destination, dates, and other details on the face of the check, which should guarantee that the payment goes where it should. That may help you get your money back if the tour is canceled or if the tour operator or travel agent goes out of business. Your contract is with the tour operator.

U.S. Department of Transportation regulations require that you be shown and sign an operator/participant contract, which describes your rights, before your payment is accepted. Demand it if it is not offered to you.

Some operators carry bonds to reassure their customers, rather than using escrow accounts. If an operator doesn't have an escrow account, ask whether it is bonded and how you would be reimbursed in case of default.

Often, the travel agent will insist that the check be made out to the travel agency, because it is the policy of some agents to write a single check to the tour operator themselves. That's fine, but insist on a written guarantee from the tour operator and the agency, and make sure that the agency's check is made payable to the tour operator's escrow account. Reputable agents and operators should be willing to stand behind the tour.

You also can protect yourself by getting trip insurance. This guards you if you have to cancel the trip because of your illness or an illness in the immediate family. Various types of trip insurance, as well as message relaying and referrals to overseas legal and medical help, are also provided free by many premium credit cards.

THE WORLD AT YOUR FINGERTIPS

- *The most comprehensive government website on the topic of consumer protection is www.consumer.gov. This site is a project of numerous federal agencies and is updated on a regular basis.*
- *The U.S. Department of Transportation's Aviation Consumer Protection Division provides travel tips, rules, and guidelines. The website is at airconsumer.ost.dot.gov.*
- *A private website with extensive information about lemon laws, including a state-by-state listing of such laws, can be found at www.autopedia.com/html/HotLinks_ Lemon.html.*
- *The Electronic Privacy Information Center has a website explaining how consumers can block, or at least reduce, telemarketing calls; access www.epic.org/privacy/ telemarketing/#reduce.*

REMEMBER THIS

- *Form contracts are written on paper, not etched in stone. Do not be afraid to question terms you do not understand or do not like.*
- *If the seller won't budge on terms you do not understand or do not like, walk away.*
- *Beware of the salesperson who says, "It's just a standard contract."*
- *Beware of scams.*
- *Take the time to read contracts, even when you feel rushed (such as when the pipes burst) or upset (like after a loved one dies).*
- *Protect yourself when you can by paying with a credit card and, in some cases, by purchasing insurance.*

WHEN THINGS GO WRONG

Now you know how contracts should work, and how to avoid the more troublesome kinds of contracts. But what happens when something goes wrong? A significant violation of a contract is a breach. A remedy is how you can go about repairing a breach, or getting compensated for the loss it causes. You might also find yourself out of pocket if the company you're dealing with goes out of business, or is merged with another company. If you act fast, you may be able to collect your layaway goods. And if you're worried about your warranty, you may still have some options.

This final section discusses the last resort when things go wrong: the different kinds of contract relief you can seek from a court. Remember, whenever one side can prove one of the contract defenses discussed in the second section, there's no breach, because there's no enforceable contract. Then the party that does not or cannot perform merely has to pay back any money or return any goods transferred in the agreement.

Breach of Contract

Q. What is a breach of contract?

A. A breach of contract—also called a **default**—is one party's failure, without a legally valid excuse, to live up to any of his or her responsibilities under a contract. A breach can occur by

- the failure to perform as promised;
- making it impossible for the other party to perform; and
- the repudiation of the contract (announcing an intent not to perform).

Q. What qualifies as a failure to perform?

A. One party must not have performed a material part of the contract by a reasonable (or stated) deadline. Suppose your friend promised to buy your Yugo for $1,000, and to pay you "sometime early next week." It would be a material breach for your friend never to pay you, or to pay you six months later. If your friend paid you on Thursday of next week, however, it probably would not be a breach. You did not explicitly make time an essential part of the contract—the source of the phrase "time is of the essence."

Q. How is a contract breached by making performance impossible?

A. Suppose you hire a cleaning service to clean your house on Sunday at a rate of $90 for the day. Early Sunday morning you go out for the day, neglecting to make arrangements to let the cleaning people into the house. You've breached by making performance impossible, and would owe the money since the cleaning service was ready and able to clean your house and presumably turned down requests to clean for other clients.

Q. What if someone partially breaches a contract?

A. That happens when the breach does not go to the heart of the matter, like failing to pay a bill by

---

▶ **SHOULD YOU BREACH A CONTRACT?**

Sometimes, someone will breach a contract with you. Or you'll find yourself in a position where you have to breach a contract. Breaching a contract isn't always a bad thing to do, as long as you're ready to take your lumps. Sometimes the price you pay through a remedy for breach is less damaging than performing a contract that has just become a big mistake.

Remember, though, that a contract is your pledge. If you want to be known for keeping your word, you'll take your contract commitments seriously—even if you don't profit each time.

the precise date specified. It also may happen when the contract has several parts, each of which can be treated as a separate contract. If one of those parts is breached, you could sue for damages even though there isn't a total breach. An example of this would be a landowner hiring a contractor to perform a construction project within certain deadlines. These deadlines have already been missed, but overall the project is going well. As long as the delay (the breach) is not material, the owner can continue the contractual relationship but sue for whatever damages were suffered as a result of the delay (for example, canceled leases). On the other hand, if the delay is material—so damaging to the project that it seriously undermines its value—the breach strikes at the heart of the contract and is total. The owner may terminate it and pursue remedies against the builder while hiring someone else to finish the job.

Q. What is a breach by repudiation?

A. **Repudiation** is a clear statement made by one party before performance is due that the party cannot or will not perform a material part of that party's contract obligations. Suppose that on the day before your friend was to pick up the Yugo that you promised to sell to her, you sent her a message that you decided to sell the car to someone else. That would be a repudiation. There can also be repudiation by act, such as actually selling your Yugo to another party.

It's not repudiation if one party will not perform because of an honest disagreement over the contract's terms.

Remedies for Breach of Contract

Q. What are the main types of remedies for a breach?

A. When someone commits a material breach of a contract, the other party is no longer obligated to keep its end of the bargain, and may proceed in several ways:

- The injured party may urge the breaching party to reconsider the breach.

- If the contract is with a merchant, the injured party may get help from local, state, or federal consumer agencies.
- The injured party may bring the breaching party to an agency for alternative dispute resolution.
- The injured party may sue the breaching party for damages or other remedies.

Q. What's the point of asking the breaching party to reconsider?

A. One advantage is that it's cheap. Often, the only cost is the price of a telephone call and a little pride. The breaching party may have breached the contract because of a misunderstanding. Perhaps the breaching party just needs a little more time. Or maybe you could renegotiate. That would almost certainly leave both of you better off than if you went to court. If you do hire a lawyer, the first thing that lawyer is likely to do is try to persuade the breaching party to perform.

Q. Should I keep records of my communications with a breaching party?

A. Yes. Once you see you're in for a struggle, make a file. Keep copies of any letters you send and move all receipts, serial numbers, warranty cards, and the like to this file.

Q. Assuming the breaching party does not budge, what else can I do?

A. If the dispute is between you and a merchant, you might want to contact the manufacturer of the product. If it involves a large chain of stores, contact the management of the chain. This goes for services, too.

If that doesn't help, contact a consumer protection agency, either in your city or state. The Federal Trade Commission is less likely to get involved in small disputes. If, however, the FTC believes that what happened to you has occurred to many people nationwide, it might be interested. The FTC's involvement carries a lot of weight. The same goes with your state attorney general or local consumer agency. Another resource is your local post office, where you can report any shady business practices that took place through the mail.

Q. If these methods don't work, what else can I do short of filing a lawsuit?

A. Other chapters in this book discuss many different types of alternative dispute resolution systems, such as mediation. Note that the contract itself may include a specific type of alternative dispute resolution that you must use. You may have already agreed not to go to court to resolve disputes. Sometimes, however, these agreements are not enforceable, and there is a burgeoning body of law refusing to enforce arbitration agreements in adhesion contracts. Consult a lawyer if you've signed such an agreement—do not assume that you have given up your right to a day in court.

Stopping Payment

Q. What if I want to cancel a contract or void a purchase that I made, but I already paid with a check?

A. First, you should call the seller and ask for a cancellation of your contract and the return of your check. If the seller won't do this, you may call your bank and stop payment on that check. Remember, you're still liable for the purchase price, and the seller may sue you for its amount, unless you have a legal excuse not to pay, such as that the seller is in breach. But if the seller's breach is small, a refusal to pay could put you in breach and make you liable for damages.

Also be aware that when you stop payment, you raise the stakes and diminish the chance of a settlement. Merchants don't take kindly to this technique.

Q. Isn't stopping payment on a check a criminal act?

A. No. It's not the same as having insufficient funds to cover the check, which may carry criminal penalties (see the sidebar, "Passing Bad Checks" on the next page). Stopping payment on a check is your legal right.

Q. How do I stop payment on a check?

A. Call your bank and provide the relevant information about the check. The bank will then send you a form to confirm your instructions in writing, which you must return within a certain number of days for the bank to honor your original

---

ⓘ WHEN IN ROME . . .

Why are there so many foreign legal terms? Many legal concepts trace their roots to Roman legal principles, though the classical Anglo-American judge-oriented legal system—the common law—has less in common with Roman law than the European "code" system. (The code system is also used in Louisiana, where the Napoleonic code took hold before the territory became part of the United States.) Also, much of the infamous redundant language of the law—such as "cease and desist," "open and notorious"—is a result of the introduction of Norman French terms alongside Anglo-Saxon ones in legal procedure after the Norman conquest of England in 1066. (English legal proceedings were carried on in the French language until the late fourteenth century.) Numerous French terms are still in common use, such as petit and grand juries.

With the decreased knowledge of classical languages and the trend away from elitism, fewer and fewer non-English terms have remained in use over the years. Any lawyer who tries to impress you with his proficiency in Latin legalisms should be taken with what the great Roman advocate and orator Cicero would have called *cum grano salis*—with a grain of salt.

request. If you don't provide all the information your bank requires, your stop-payment order might not be good. The bank's charge for this service will usually be $10 to $30 or even more.

Don't try to avoid the fee by reducing your bank balance so the check won't clear. The bank can't read your mind, so other checks you've written may not be paid, or the bank might even pay the check you don't want paid, in an attempt to accommodate you. More important, you will have gone from exercising a legal right (stopping payment) to committing a legal wrong (passing a bad check).

Q. Is there anything else that I should do after I place the order to stop payment?

A. You could inform the seller of your action, but you don't have to.

Q. What if the seller has already deposited the check in a bank account?

A. If the check has not cleared your account, your bank may still put through the stop-payment order. If your bank has paid the check, you'll have to try to void the contract and get your money back in other ways discussed in this chapter.

⚠ PASSING BAD CHECKS

If you give someone a check for which you do not have sufficient funds, you may face criminal charges. Passing a bad check is a misdemeanor is many states and can result in a hefty fine and even a months-long jail term. However, a single infraction rarely results in a criminal conviction. Many states have diversion programs that do not impose penalties but rather attempt to educate offenders so that they don't repeat the offense.

Q. What if I'm dissatisfied with goods or services that I've paid for with a credit card?

A. Then the Fair Credit Billing Act may protect you. Under the act, products you refuse to accept on delivery or that aren't delivered according to an agreement are regarded as billing errors that the card issuer must investigate and may correct by granting you a credit. So long as the consumer has not accepted the goods, the appearance of a charge on the bill is a billing error. If the seller does not press the matter, the consumer will get a credit. If the seller protests, then the card issuer may or may not issue a credit, depending on the issuer's agreement and practices with merchants.

The law may also give you protection against having to pay for shoddy or damaged goods. These are not billing errors, but another section of the FCBA, Section 170, may give you rights against the card issuer. See chapter 7, "Consumer Credit," for more details.

If you have a right not to pay under state law, you may be able to assert that right against the credit card issuer as well, under certain circumstances. You also have billing error rights if you've used a debit card for a purchase.

Dealing with Failing or Failed Companies

Q. If I have a contract for services or goods with a company that goes out of business, what can I do?

A. You've just ordered and paid for an expensive item. The next day, you read in the newspaper that the company has gone out of business. You are afraid that your money has disappeared as well.

If another firm bought the company, as in a corporate merger, usually the new company must take responsibility for the contract obligations of the old company.

If the company has ceased doing business, or is under the protection of the bankruptcy laws, your chances of recovering anything of value are small. If the company went through the bankruptcy process, your contract could legally be disavowed, though any debt owed to you might not be. If the company is in bankruptcy, the bankruptcy court may contact you, or you may need a lawyer's help to put in your claim. If your claim isn't substantial, though, it's usually not worth the trouble.

If you have a contract that still is in force with a troubled company, you may have to get the rest of your contract needs filled by another company if the one you have a contract with can't come through. Then you may have a damages claim against the first company

Q. My supplier went bankrupt, and so I need to buy goods from another company. What can I do about the money the first company owes me under the contract?

A. If the company is in bankruptcy, you can file a claim against it through the bankruptcy court. You'll have to stand in line with the other creditors, and you may get only a small percentage of what the company owes you, if you recover anything at all. If the business is a corporation that's dissolving under state law, you can file a claim against the corporation through the state agency (usually the secretary of state) for any losses you have accumulated. Whatever assets remain will be divided according to the number of claims filed and their amounts.

Q. If the financially troubled company is holding goods for me on layaway, can I still get my goods?

A. Most companies that go out of business will notify people they are closing; often, they want you to come in and finish the purchase because they need the cash. If they've tried to contact you and you haven't responded, they may sell those goods, and you'll have no way to recover the merchandise, although the law still entitles you to any money you paid toward the purchase.

Q. If the merchandise is gone and I've paid money, how can I recover that money?

A. If the store is still open, it probably will pay you when you present your receipt for payments made toward the purchase price. If the store has closed, you might need to file a claim in the bankruptcy court or with the proper state agency, as described above.

Q. What can I do about merchandise that was under warranty? Who'll cover it now that the seller has gone out of business?

A. If you've purchased a national brand of goods, there probably will be a service center or a licensed warranty center in your area. It may not be as convenient for you as the seller's store. Almost all manufacturers will stand behind their products regardless of where you purchased them. The only drawback is that you may need to present an original receipt to show that the manufacturer's warranty still covers the product.

Q. I also purchased an additional retailer's warranty when I bought the goods that extended the manufacturer's warranty. What will this extra retailer's warranty cover?

A. Retailers usually offer this warranty for extended parts and labor for a much longer period of time than the manufacturer offers. Unfortunately, the retailer's warranty is useless if the place that made the promise is now out of business, unless its obligations have been taken over by another company.

Lawsuits as Remedies

Q. What's the most common legal remedy for a breach of contract?

A. The usual legal remedy is cancellation of the contract, followed by a suit for damages, usually **compensatory damages**. This is the amount of money it would take to put you in as good a position as if there had been no breach of contract. The idea is to give you "the benefit of the bargain."

In some cases, you may not cancel, but only may recover damages for the breach.

For example, if the seller has failed to deliver an item costing $10,000 and you buy it from another source for $12,000, your damages are $2,000. You may have to sue to obtain that. Of course, the cost of lawyer's fees is often a practical bar to a lawsuit. Instead, you might consider a small-claims action in which you can represent yourself. Chapters 1 and 2 can give you more information on procedures in small-claims courts. Another method, if you know of a lot of people who are in your position, is a so-called class action, in which the cost of the lawsuit is spread among many. If the violation of a consumer protection law is involved and established, the law may require the other side to pay your lawyer's fees, and you may be entitled to a minimum recovery without proof of actual damage. Also, if many people are involved, the state agency charged with consumer protection, such as the attorney general, may be persuaded to bring suit on behalf of all the consumers affected.

Q. What's an example of compensatory damages?

A. Suppose you hired a contractor to paint your house for $500. This job could cost as much as $650, but you're a good negotiator. Now the contractor regrets agreeing to the $500 price and breaches. If you can prove that you had a contract that was breached and that it will cost you more to have the job done as a result, you can recover $150, or whatever the difference is between $500 and what it ultimately cost you to have your house painted.

Q. What other kinds of damages are there?

A. There are several common types of damages:

- **Nominal damages,** which are awarded when you win your case but have not proved much

of a loss. The court may award you a small amount as a matter of course.

- **Liquidated damages**, which are an amount that is built into the contract. Although one or both parties have effectively breached the contract, this term will stand, as long as it fairly estimates the damages. In contrast, the courts will not enforce a **penalty clause,** an amount of liquidated damages that is way out of line with the actual loss.

- **Consequential damages,** which were discussed in the section on warranties (see page 312). These are rarely available in a contract suit if there is a formal contract. In formal contracts, the document typically excludes consequential damages. In informal contracts, however, including most retail cash purchases, there typically is no exclusion of them, and they may be recoverable. Further, in the warranty context, if the repair-or-replace remedy fails of its essential purpose, then consequential damages typically are available.

- **Punitive damages,** which are available if the breaching party's behavior was offensive to the court. Punitive damages are virtually never recovered in a suit for breach of contract, but it may be possible to get punitive damages or some form of **statutory damages** (legal penalties) under a consumer fraud law or in a suit for fraud.

Q. Are there other remedies in a contract suit besides damages?

A. Yes. The most obvious remedy is a court order requiring the breaching party to perform as promised in the contract. This is known as **specific performance.** Courts are reluctant to award this because they presume that the proper remedy for breach of a contract is the monetary equivalence of full performance and because specific performance is awkward to enforce. They will impose specific performance only if there is no other remedy available because of the contract's unique subject matter, such as real estate or a unique piece of personal property.

Q. *What else can a court do?*

A. A court may **rescind**, or cancel, a contract that one party has breached. The court may then order the breaching party to pay the other side any expenses incurred; it could also order the return of goods sold. Or, the court could **reform** the contract. That involves rewriting the contract according to what the court concludes, based on evidence at trial, the parties actually intended. These are often used under the provisions of many states' consumer fraud laws. Such laws also may provide for minimum damages or a multiple of actual damages.

Q. *What are consumer protection or consumer fraud acts?*

A. Laws prohibiting unfair or deceptive trade practices in consumer transactions have been enacted in every state. They apply to almost all consumer transactions and are extremely flexible and very potent—often providing for treble (triple) damages where a violation is found. Generally requiring lower legal hurdles than traditional fraud remedies—for example, intent to deceive is usually not a requirement—these laws usually provide for state action and recovery by private lawsuits. These laws are the ultimate legal reaction to "let the buyer beware." Their use involves numerous technicalities, though, and competent legal advice is absolutely necessary to take advantage of them.

THE WORLD AT YOUR FINGERTIPS

- *The Federal Trade Commission explains the Fair Credit Billing Act on its website at www.ftc.gov/bcp/conline/pubs/credit/fcb.htm.*
- *The federal government publishes helpful handbooks for consumers, which are available for little or no charge from the Federal Citizen Information Center, Pueblo,*
Colorado 81009, 800-FED-INFO, or access www.pueblo.gsa.gov.
- *State and local bar associations often publish free pamphlets and handbooks on legal problems, and can provide lists of lawyers who handle consumer cases. These bar associations are easily located on the Internet by searching for "bar association" along with the name of the state or locality you are searching for. Or you can access www.abanet.org/barserv/stlobar.html for a list of bar groups.*

REMEMBER THIS

- *Pay by credit card rather than check. The Fair Credit Billing Act allows you to withhold payment if goods are not delivered or are sent in shoddy condition.*
- *Keep copies of all correspondence with the seller. These documents will be important if you need to prove he or she breached the contract.*
- *Stopping payment on a check without telling the seller decreases the chance for an out-of-court settlement.*
- *You will probably receive your goods if another company bought the company from which you made the purchase.*
- *You will have to wait in line behind creditors if the company is in bankruptcy.*
- *You are out of luck if the company has been liquidated.*
- *Compensatory damages are the usual remedy for breach.*
- *Punitive damages are rare in cases of breach.*
- *Specific performance is also an unusual remedy, generally ordered only in cases when the performer has a special talent.*

Computer Law

Computers are everywhere, and they are changing the way we shop, work, and correspond.

At the click of a mouse, we can purchase goods and have them delivered to our homes. With the use of a modem, our home computers can connect us to our employers, in many cases eliminating the need to go to the office. Electronic mail enables us to communicate across long distances at less than the cost of a local phone call.

But with this technology come potential dangers. Just how secure are those online purchases? Can my employer eavesdrop on my Internet and e-mail use at the office? Is there any way to stem the mounting tide of unwanted e-mail I receive from advertisers? How can I safeguard the important messages and documents on my computer from viruses and hackers? Can I legally download anything available over the Internet, including music? Could I unwittingly enter into a contract online? Can I write anything I want on my personal website? What's to stop my kids from accessing sites I would rather they not visit? Is Big Brother watching?

This chapter examines how the law is responding, often slowly, to these issues and provides helpful hints to protect computer users from potential harm.

ONLINE PURCHASES

More and more of us are buying products online, whether through the websites of established vendors who also have brick-and-mortar stores or from folks whose whole business is on the Internet. Online auctions are particularly popular. E-shopping can be safe—if you follow some precautions and are aware of legal protections. This is a fluid, rapidly changing area of law. If you are a consumer encountering a problem with an online purchase—or a businessperson selling over the Internet—you should consult your lawyer to determine your rights and responsibilities under state and federal law.

This section covers all forms of E-shopping, from auctions to airline tickets to personal finances.

Q. How do I shop safely online?

A. Common sense will prevent many potential problems in cyberspace.

When shopping online, you lack many of the telltale signs of a company's reliability that you witness firsthand when shopping in person. Over the Internet, you cannot readily judge how well products are maintained, how well stocked or stable the company is, or how knowledgeable the salespeople are. Therefore, for safety's sake, it might be best to shop online with companies you know and trust. Also, there are a number of seal of approval programs, such as the Better Business Bureau's site (www.bbbonline.org), that allow you to assess an online company.

Q. What else can I do to protect myself in shopping online?

A. Investigate thoroughly and decide what you want before buying. If the vendor tries to talk you into a different model than you planned on getting and the recommended model sounds really good to you, don't buy anything just yet. Check out the new model and decide if it serves your needs better than your first choice (sometimes you will find that it does). If so, check comparative pricing and then, depending on pricing, go back to the vendor that recommended it, or choose another. Impulse buying can get you burned badly.

Before buying any consumer electronics goods online, you should find a local brick-and-mortar store that sells the item and go look at it. Check it out thoroughly to ensure that it has the features that you want and works as you expect. Be sure that you want that particular model before buying it online to reduce the risks and problems you might encounter if you make the purchase online and it proves unsatisfactory.

If you buy online, check your order carefully and thoroughly when it arrives. Verify that the item and the model you received matches the one

---

▶ **USE THE WEB TO CHECK WEB MERCHANTS**

You can reduce your exposure by doing some online investigation before you buy. Several website services provide information about vendors. These sites often include customer ratings and evaluations of the vendors, their policies, and their performances. You can access such information—and pricing data, too—at www.CNET.com. For prices, check out www.shopper.com, www.pricegrabber.com, and www.pricescan.com.

that you ordered in every respect. Check to verify that you received the manufacturer's U.S. warranty registration card, if you required one as a part of your order.

You should also trust your instincts. If you do not feel comfortable buying an item over the Internet, or if you feel pressured to place your order immediately, maybe you should not complete the purchase.

Q. On balance, is online shopping worth the risk?

A. Understand that the risks of buying online do not differ significantly in type from risks associated with buying from a brick-and-mortar store. But it may be more difficult to protect yourself if you buy online, and the level of risk may be somewhat higher than if you deal with an established local vendor. If you take reasonable precautions and act carefully, you can often achieve substantial savings by purchasing online.

Q. Is it safe to pay online by credit card?

A. A major concern of online shoppers is whether the credit card information they provide is truly protected from the prying eyes of thieves and computer hackers. Some credit card associations offer zero-liability policies for use of credit cards and branded debit cards. Under such policies, cardholders are not responsible for any amount of unauthorized purchases.

Another way to protect yourself is make sure you use a recent version of one of the standard browser systems, which will encrypt or scramble the information you send and thus increase the security of the transaction. Most computers come with such a browser already installed, or else you can upgrade for no charge. Software programs are also available. A 128-bit secure browser is generally better, since a 40 bit can be broken.

In addition, many online companies—aware of consumer concerns—use Secure Sockets Layer (SSL) technology to **encrypt** (encode for the purposes of security) the credit card information you send over the Internet and give you assurances

of the identity of the website. These sites usually inform you they are using this technology. For example, some sites use a padlock icon in the bottom right-hand corner to indicate an encrypted transmission. Or check if the Web address on the page that asks for your credit card information begins with "https:" instead of "http:"— if so, this technology is in place.

With these security mechanisms in place, it is safer to pay by credit card than by check, money order, wire transfer, or cash. Once the vendor negotiates your check or receives the wire transfer, the money is in their possession and control and it may take considerable effort to recover it if there is a problem. If you pay with a credit card and a problem arises, the federal Fair Credit Billing Act protects the transaction. This law gives you the right to dispute charges and temporarily withhold payment while the charges are being investigated.

You can further protect yourself by keeping good and up-to-date records of your online transactions. Print copies of your online communications with the company and your purchase order and confirmation number. Keep these documents on file. And keep in mind that reputable online merchants will provide all of this information to you in an easy-to-print format, because they want you to be a repeat customer. It makes sense to them to make your experience with them pleasant and agreeable throughout. Also, review your bank and credit card statements for billing errors or unauthorized purchases, which might have been made by someone who illegally accessed your information.

You can further limit your exposure by acquiring a low-limit credit card and using that card to pay for your online purchases. The lower limit reduces potential exposure if the number is misappropriated.

Many online vendors have policies limiting shipping to the billing address of the credit card used to pay for your purchase. If you want to have your purchases delivered to your office instead of your house, you will find that it is much easier to accomplish that goal if you use the office address for billing purposes on one of your credit cards.

Q. Are there other online payment methods?

A. Yes. Many websites accept payment by check. There is no need for you to write a real check; all you need to do is fill out your account details, and payment is automatically deducted from your checking account and will show up on your next bank statement.

The PayPal system used by eBay and other services works in a similar way. The payer and payee must both be registered with PayPal. If the payer wants to send money to the payee, the payer simply enters the payee's e-mail address and specifies the amount he wants to send. The transaction goes through the PayPal database, and money is electronically transferred from the payer's account to the payee's account. The lucky payee receives an e-mail telling him that cash has been deposited in his bank account.

It is also possible to make some kinds of payments directly from your bank account if you use online banking. More and more of us are paying bills online, often at the urging of service companies, such as utilities. You simply need to give your bank the relevant information—the number of your utility account, the amount you wish to pay, and that date on which you would like to pay.

⚠ VALUABLE INFORMATION— ABOUT YOU

Be advised that online merchants will track your online purchases and buying habits. This information can prove valuable to marketing companies that might then send you unsolicited e-mails advertising products in which you have shown an interest or in which they believe you might have an interest. Be sure to check the privacy polices of all entities with whom you deal.

Q. What are debit card payments?

A. Some companies offering online payment use a debit card payment system, under which you authorize them to debit your account with them electronically after each transaction. Debit cards can also be cards branded with credit card association marks and processed using the credit card networks, or they might be cards from your bank processed through the ATM networks.

The federal Electronic Funds Transfer Act (EFTA) gives you many of the same protections for debit payments as you have for credit card payments. Within various time limits, you can point out mistakes on your statements, and the financial institution must investigate the mistakes, tell you the result of its investigation, and correct the problems after determining that errors have in fact occurred. Debit cards not issued by financial institutions may offer you fewer protections, though some, like Visa and MasterCard, protect you through their zero-liability policies.

Q. I never signed anything; is the online company still under contract to send me my goods?

A. Yes, so long as it is clear through your correspondence with the company that you have agreed to pay a specific price for a specific product. This clarity and specificity requirement prevents confusion and misunderstandings that can arise later, particularly in cyberspace, if the company fails to send you the items you ordered.

On the flip side, it is just as important to state clearly in your online correspondence with the company when you do *not* want to make a purchase. These messages should make it clear to the company that you do not wish to buy, that it should not send you the merchandise, and that you should not be charged for the items, their shipping, or their handling.

Q. How do you "sign" a contract electronically?

A. These days, an increasing number of businesses are engaging in electronic commerce to enable them to reach more consumers while cutting down on their paperwork and advertising costs. These companies are striking deals with consumers and other businesses via the Internet or online services. That usually means no face-to-face contact, no paper contract, no ink or "wet" or handwritten signature. And it might also mean confusion down the line about whether a contract has actually been made and what exactly has been agreed to. The general trend is to use technology to verify the identities of the parties and permit them to decide on acceptable electronic signing technologies. This is an evolving area of law, and your lawyer can help guide you through the shoals.

A federal law, the Electronic Signatures in Global and National Commerce Act (E-SIGN) of 2000, gives electronic signatures the same legal validity that handwritten signatures on paper would have. The law permits consumers to sign a mortgage or insurance contract online, as well as perform other tasks, such as opening a brokerage account.

The law ensures that a contract or signature will not be denied legal status simply because it is electronic. A provision of the E-SIGN law specifies that retaining an electronic copy that can be printed or otherwise accessed is sufficient to meet legal requirements.

ⓘ CLICK HERE

Another way to "sign" a contract electronically is the "click-through" contract. Most courts will enforce the provisions of a click-through contract if the vendor can prove that the purchaser clicked on a button labeled "I accept" above a clear notice that referenced the online contract terms. To protect yourself in such contracts, make sure you read the online terms before you click—they can significantly affect your rights to a warranty or customer service.

Q. Are there any other laws on electronic transactions?

A. In addition to the federal law, many states have adopted the Uniform Electronic Transactions Act, a model statute that gives legal validity to electronic signatures and contracts.

The federal and state laws in this area may exempt certain kinds of documents, which has the effect that electronic signatures may not be sufficient for wills, codicils, and testamentary trusts; adoptions, divorces or other family-law matters; notices of foreclosures or evictions from one's primary residence; and cancellation of health or life insurance benefits.

Furthermore, two states (Maryland and Virginia) have enacted the Uniform Computer Information Transactions Act (UCITA). This law covers, among other things, electronic transactions involving software and provides certain protections for consumers. However, it also allows software companies to disclaim most warranties.

Q. How can I protect my privacy when shopping online?

A. You can visit so many websites so quickly that you might forget to take some basic precautions to protect personal information when shopping online. First of all, you should check each site's privacy policy to discover how the information that you provide will be used, and whether it will be forwarded to other companies or individuals. Make sure to read these policy statements thoroughly, as the most important details are often in the fine print.

Also, be aware that Internet commerce sites often leave **cookies,** small bits of information that track your Web usage, on your hard drive. Cookies aren't all bad, and in fact serve many useful purposes. They store your preferences for certain websites, allowing the websites to recognize you as a returning customer and to pick up where you left off (and not have to enter all your information all over again). However, if you don't like the idea of outsiders tracking at least some of your Web use, most Web browsers permit you to block cookies from being left without your approval. This blocking technology can slow down your browsing if you set it to warn you, but if you frequently check into uncharted territory on the Web, you may want this sort of control over who is leaving their cookies on your computer. Cookies can also be manually deleted.

To assuage the concerns of computer users, the nonprofit groups TRUSTe and BBB*OnLine* have created a "trustmark," a logo appearing on websites intended to serve as a seal of approval for online companies that have made good on their pledges to ensure their customer's privacy. The TRUSTe website is *www.truste.org.*

Q. How can I protect my password(s)?

A. The best way to protect a password and your privacy is to have multiple passwords, thus making it more complicated for thieves and computer hackers to access your account. For example, if you use a password to log on to your network or computer, use a different password for placing orders online. You may also want to create a special password for particularly sensitive webpages, such as your home-banking site. (Of course, the more passwords you have the more likely you are to have to write them down—in which case, it may be better to use one password that you can remember, and maintain its confidentiality.)

ⓘ COOKIES

Cookies are small data files written to your hard drive by some websites when you view them in your browser. These data files contain information the site can use to track such things as passwords, lists of pages you have visited, and the date when you last looked at a certain page. Note that these files remain on your hard drive even after you log off the Internet and until you specifically delete them.

Source: CNET Networks.

Other password protection principles:

- While you should try to use easily remembered passwords, you should not use easily guessed passwords, such as your birth date or children's names.
- Do not write down any password near your computer where someone could see it. If you do record it somewhere, either encrypt it via a software vault or lock it. If you don't do that, at the very lease scramble the order of the characters. That way, someone finding it won't have discovered your true password.
- You should never respond to an e-mail, phone call, fax, or letter from anyone who asks for your password(s), Social Security number, birth date, bank account, credit card number, mother's maiden name, or other personal information. To verify that the person contacting you really does work for the seller, call the company and request to speak to that person directly. Except for your password, credit card number, and the billing address for your credit card, you should never have to give any personal information to place an order online.
- You should only give your password and credit card number in a secure connection on a website, not in an ordinary e-mail. Ordinary e-mail is not encrypted. Identity theft, in which someone gets access to your bank account or gets credit cards or loans in your name, is one of the fastest-growing crimes.

Q. What can I do if I don't get what I ordered?

A. You should take steps to protect your consumer rights even before you place an order. You can safeguard these rights by doing the following:

- Review the company's return, refund, and shipping and handling policies. Look under the company's online contract agreement for "legal terms" or "disclaimers." If you cannot find the contract, ask the seller through an e-mail or telephone call to indicate where it is on the site or to provide it to you in writing.

- Print and save all company correspondence. You should print out and date a copy of the company's terms, conditions, warranties, item description, and confirming e-mails, and save them with the records of your purchase.

When your purchase arrives, examine the item carefully as soon as you receive it. Contact the seller as soon as possible if you discover a problem with it. Tell the seller in writing about any problem that you are concerned with, ask for a repair or refund, and again keep a copy of your correspondence in case you have to take the company to court.

Q. What if my order never arrives?

A. Under federal regulations, companies that take orders by Internet have up to thirty days to deliver the merchandise. Consumers who have not received their goods within thirty days may demand a refund under the federal Mail or Telephone Order Rule. Companies that cannot make delivery within thirty days must tell the consumer and inform the customer of his or her right to cancel the order with a full refund.

Q. Are there special concerns when buying from foreign companies?

A. The online marketplace has made all stores appear local. But do not be lulled into assuming that the same rules apply both in the United States and abroad, even on the Internet.

Before ordering from a foreign company, the Federal Trade Commission advises you to get the seller to answer the following questions:

- Are the prices posted in U.S. dollars or some other currency? If in another currency, the date of conversion to dollars may also be important.
- Does the company ship internationally?
- How long will it take for an order to be delivered?
- Will unexpected taxes or duties be added to the price?
- If a dispute arises, where will it be resolved?

The answer to the last question might be a deal breaker. Merchants, except in very rare cases, will want you to agree to have all disputes resolved in their local courts and under their

---

▶ IDENTITY THEFT

If you believe you are the victim of identity theft, the Federal Trade Commission advises you to take three steps:

1. Contact the fraud departments of each of the three major credit bureaus: Equifax, Experian, and TransUnion. Tell them you are a victim of identify theft and request that a fraud alert be placed in your file, as well as a statement requesting that creditors call you before any accounts are opened or changed in your name.
    - Equifax's website is www.equifax.com.
    - Experian's website is www.experian.com.
    - TransUnion's website is www.transunion.com.
2. Close all accounts that you know or suspect have been tampered with or opened fraudulently.
3. File a report with your local law enforcement or the police department where the identity theft occurred. The report might not help catch the thief, but it will help you if creditors need proof of the crime.

local law as a condition of completing the sale. For example, if you are an Illinois resident upset that a French company has not sent you the wine you ordered, your only recourse might be to litigate the dispute in Paris rather than Chicago. Much as you might want an excuse to go to Paris, the expense of pursuing a case in a distant court is considerable, so think twice about ordering from an out-of-state or foreign company, especially for high-value goods.

Q. Are there any scams I should watch out for when buying online?

A. Internet and telephone vendors use a variety of techniques to try to take advantage of the unwary customer. You can protect yourself by taking these steps:

- *Understand gray-market goods.* Sometimes vendors will sell goods that were not manufactured or intended for sale in the United States. These products, sometimes called **gray-market goods,** have found their way to the United States through a circuitous route. Gray-market vendors will happily sell them to you at an often substantial discount. Many of the so-called gray-market goods are made by well-known manufacturers, arrive in excellent condition, and work perfectly fine. On the other hand, gray-market goods may also arrive without a set of instructions in English. More important, they will almost definitely arrive without a U.S. warranty. The absence of a U.S. warranty means that if something fails, you have to find a repair center and pay to repair or replace it. Buying gray-market goods is a bit like rolling the dice in Las Vegas.
- *Beware of the "U.S. warranty" scam.* Some vendors, particularly in the consumer electronics area, anticipating that a customer will know enough to ask for a U.S. warranty, sell gray-market goods with a third-party warranty contract provided by a U.S.-based repair or warranty service. Since the third-party warranty comes from a United States firm, the

vendor will, "truthfully," tell you that they will sell the item to you with a U.S. warranty. These third-party warranties often do not match the breadth of coverage of the manufacturer's warranty. Unless you feel like gambling when you order, be clear that you want goods with the manufacturer's U.S. warranty, not gray-market goods.

- *Watch out for the shipping charges scam.* Some discount vendors will quote you a very favorable price for the item of your choice. While you are congratulating yourself on the great deal you just made, the vendor will then recover some of the profit discounted out by adding an excessive amount for shipping and handling—say $60 or $75 when the true cost should be $20 or $30. Consider the cost of shipping a part of the acquisition cost when comparing prices among vendors.
- *Turn down service contracts.* Often, you will have the opportunity to purchase a vendor or third-party extended-service contract for consumer electronics items to supplement the manufacturer's warranty. Distinguish these from extended warranties from the manufacturer. They are either a store arrangement or a third-party warranty package. Generally, the service contract or extended warranty costs 10 to 30 percent of the cost of the item, depending upon its scope and term and which vendor offers it. The primary purpose of these contracts appears to be creating an opportunity for the vendor to make a few extra dollars. These extended warranty packages often do not represent a good value, and you probably should forgo the "opportunity."

If you detect any scam, report it to the Internet service provider (ISP), in the hope that the scammer's e-mail account will be closed.

Q. Are there any other online scams I should watch out for?

A. Internet scams are so common the Federal Trade Commission has a term for them: "Dot Cons."

Among the most common scams are Internet sites that appeal to computer users' prurient interests by promising them they can visit adult webpages for free simply by giving credit card information to confirm they are at least eighteen years old. But the next thing these computer users see is not what they expected; rather, they see unfamiliar charges on their credit card bills. To protect yourself from this and similar scams, the FTC advises you to share your credit card information only with companies you trust.

Another notorious online con is the Nigerian scam, which has many variations. In its original form, a person claiming to be a government official from Nigeria sends an e-mail promising the recipient a percentage of the millions of dollars he is trying to transfer out of his country. But first, the message states, the recipient must send the name of his or her bank, account numbers, and other identifying information, ostensibly so the Nigerian can transfer the funds. Once he receives that information, the con artist has all the personal data he needs to pass himself off as the e-mail recipient and can easily draw funds from the person's account. The FBI notes that people have lost their entire savings after falling for this scam.

To avoid being a victim, recipients of this type of e-mail promising riches should simply delete it. They might also forward it to the FBI or U.S. Secret Service. If you know someone who is falling for the scam, the FBI says you should encourage him or her to contact the agency or the Secret Service. In any event, the FBI says you should always be skeptical of anyone who says he or she is from a foreign government or other authority and needs your help in handling large sums of money. Scammers claim to be from a variety of other countries besides Nigeria.

Cyberspace Auctions

Q. How should I protect myself, and how should I pay for the product?

A. With online auctions, the age-old rule "Let the buyer beware" certainly applies. If yours was the highest bid, you will generally deal directly with the seller (not the auction house) to complete the deal.

ⓘ COMPETITION MAY PROTECT PRIVACY

Many Internet service providers are shying away from providing information about their customers to other companies because of public criticism of spam and personal questions on ISP questionnaires, aimed at helping marketers target their e-mails. Increased competition within the industry, especially from companies that pledge not to share subscriber information, has also limited the practice of ISPs sending data to other companies.

Nevertheless, the best advice is to examine ISP agreements carefully before signing up. Peruse the privacy policy to find out what information the seller is gathering from you, how the information will be used, and how you can stop it from being shared with marketers. If a provider's site does not have a privacy policy posted, you may not want to do business with that company. If the ISP does have a privacy policy, there will probably be a link to it from the company's home page, or it might be included with the legal terms.

Note also that privacy policies can change, and typically you agree to be bound by the privacy policy as is and as amended. If you don't like the privacy policy once it changes, find out how you can opt out.

Hence, it is essential for you to be knowledgeable about Web-based auctions. You should take special care to familiarize yourself not only with the rules and policies of the auction site itself but with the legal terms (warranties, refund policy, etc.) of the seller's items on which you wish to bid. Also, if you are buying from an individual, some online auction sites offer feedback areas where customers discuss their experiences with a particular person auctioning off goods. Before submitting a bid on an item, check the remarks made about the seller. Additionally, some sites offer some insurance protection for your purchases.

Other precautions include verifying the seller's identity and asking about return policies. You should also find out what the seller will charge for shipping and handling. It is risky to pay by certified check or money order. If you pay by credit card, you can challenge the charge with the credit card company if the merchandise does not come or is not what you thought you had bought. You can also protect yourself by paying upon delivery. Another alternative is to restrict your shopping to cyberspace auctioneers that provide fraud resolution, fraud protection, or similar services to ensure the privacy and integrity of online transactions.

Internet Service Providers (ISPs)

Q. What should I look for in an ISP?

A. With telephone and cable companies offering high-speed Internet access, consumers have become inundated with options and sales pitches. Make your selection carefully. As with any service contract, you are well advised to try to get the best service for the lowest price and beware of scams. If the ISP is a telephone company or a common carrier, it is regulated by such agencies as the state public utilities commission or the FCC.

Q. What about those "free" Internet offers?

A. A popular marketing tool among ISPs is to give would-be customers free Internet service for a limited time, such as for one month or five hundred hours, to see if they like it and want to subscribe. But beware. Many service providers will sign these customers up for service at the end of the trial period if they have not heard otherwise from them. A bill will follow, or, even worse, the customer's card will simply be charged.

Hence, before opting for this free service, you should check the provider's information about what you must do, and when, to cancel if you choose not to continue beyond the trial period, or simply ask the provider what you'll have to do. Also, you will want to find out whether the month of free service begins when you sign up for it or days later, when the service is actually established. A difference of only a few days can leave you liable to pay for a period of service if you miscalculate and use the service beyond the trial period. Finally, be aware that the number of free hours might be difficult or impossible to use within the free period.

Q. How do I protect my privacy?

A. A first step is to read the privacy statements, agreements, and disclosures of Internet service providers. They can often be long, tedious, and written by people (usually lawyers) who apparently were never admonished for run-on sentences. But it is critically important for consumers to read through the privacy terms of Internet service providers. In these sometimes cumbersome, dry agreements lies the critical information regarding what the company plans to do with the information you provide. Look for clauses alerting you to the fact that the site will share your information with related companies. Beware of any provisions that say that the site will forward, or sell, your e-mail address and other personal information to marketing companies—or you may receive unsolicited e-mails, mail, and phone calls. If you don't like what you see there, you can try to find a company whose policies are more to your liking.

Professional Services Online

Q. How do I know that what the professional says online is true?

A. The truth is that often you cannot be sure that a professional's webpage contains the unvarnished truth. A webpage, like any advertisement, is subject to potential embellishment of the facts.

Common sense again plays a crucial part. Just as you should not hire a doctor, a lawyer, or other professional without doing diligent research (i.e., inquiring about references or board certification), you should not retain professional services based solely on an Internet advertisement. Also, because of the Internet's global reach, you must confirm that the professional is in fact licensed to practice in your state (assuming that such a license is required).

To assuage client and patient concerns, several professional organizations have begun establishing "seals of approval" to award to websites of practitioners who adhere to standards of privacy and quality. For example, Hi-Ethics has begun

such a program for health-related websites. For more information, visit www.hiethics.org.

Another safeguard may come through domain registration. For example, RegistryPro (www.registrypro.com) is developing a service by which domain names are issued to accounting, medical, or legal professionals only after confirmation that they are currently licensed and are who they claim to be. Domain name registration companies (**registrars**) working to register names ending in ".pro" will register names for these professionals. While authenticated domain names do not guarantee that everything said on a professional's website is true, at least there will be assurances of identity and licensure status.

Airline Tickets

Q. Should I buy an airline ticket online?

A. Buying a ticket online could save you money, albeit you may have to fly at odd hours and endure a bunch of layovers on your way to your destination. But be careful: Many of these great rates are nonrefundable, and many are posted without the approval of the airline. Also, travelers who book their flights online may not necessarily be informed when the airline changes or cancels the scheduled departure. Always print out your reservation details, and phone the airline to confirm the flight the day before you are scheduled to leave.

Q. Last time I bought an airline ticket from an travel website I was stranded at the airport because my plane was overbooked. Are there any steps I can take to prevent this from happening again?

A. Read the policy statement of the airline or the agency that is operating the website. Often, airlines contract out their online reservations to an agency whose policies differ from those of the airline. These statements cover the company's obligations in the event the flight is canceled or rescheduled.

⚠ ISP DOT CONS

The Federal Trade Commission is warning consumer users of a scam in which con artists send e-mails that appear to be from your ISP but are well-disguised efforts to get your credit card data. These messages state that your "account information needs to be updated" or that "the credit card you signed up with is invalid or expired and the information needs to be reentered to keep your account active." The FTC advises that you should not provide any information without speaking first to your ISP and confirming that the provider in fact sent the e-mail. In most cases, the update of the account is via the Web and only after you sign in with your user name and password.

Generally, the onus is on you to confirm your reservations, even if the website gives you a message thanking you for making your reservations after you provide your credit card information. You should also confirm that your flight is still scheduled to leave on time.

Q. What recourse do I have when I get to the airport with my bags but no flight?

A. Do you remember the old days when you got bumped from a flight? The airline would try to find you a seat on the next available flight, often with a first-class upgrade. Well, the same still generally holds true, so long as you can show that you had booked a seat. There should be an electronic ticket that provides proof of purchase. To be extra careful, you might want to arrive at the airport with a printout of a confirming e-mail from the site or a printout or your reservation from the website as additional proof.

Online Banking

Q. How safe are online money transfers?

A. The federal government has taken steps in recent years to make online banking quite safe. The Electronic Funds Transfer Act (EFTA) and related federal regulations are designed to protect consumers when making banking transactions from their computer, such as transferring money between accounts or transferring money from their account to pay bills.

Under the law, banks that permit online transfers must inform consumers of the institutions' and customers' liability for unauthorized transfers and provide the telephone number and address of the bank employee to be told if you think an unauthorized transfer has been made. The bank must also tell the customer the fees it charges for transfers and any limits on the frequency and dollar amounts of the transfers. Customers must also be told of their right to receive documentation of all transfers, and their right to stop payment on transfers. In addition, the bank must tell the customer under what circumstances

it will tell third parties, such as governmental agencies, about the account.

Under the law, customers have sixty days from the time they receive a bank statement containing a potential error to alert the financial institution. The Federal Trade Commission advises customers to alert the bank by a certified letter, return receipt requested, so the customer can prove that the institution received the letter within the sixty days. Customers should keep a copy of the letter for their records.

Failure to notify the bank within sixty days lets the institution off the hook for prompt investigation of a claim. Under the law, the bank is under no obligation to investigate the alleged error within specific time limits if the deadline is missed, although it must still make any required refunds to a consumer for an unauthorized transfer.

Q. Under the law, how must the bank investigate and make corrections?

A. Once it has received your letter complaining about an error, the bank has ten business days to investigate. The bank must tell you the results within three business days of completing its investigation. If the bank discovers it has made an error, it has one business day to make the correction. If the bank needs more time to investigate, it may take up to forty-five days. However, it must return the disputed money to your account. If, after the forty-five days, the bank can find no error, it can take the money back and send you a written explanation.

Stock and Securities

Q. How do I protect myself from falling into a trading trap in which the website operators promise big returns?

A. Trading stocks online or off line can be akin to gambling. Be careful of any site promising a sure thing. The Federal Trade Commission recommends that investors on the Internet check out the stock promoter with state and federal securities regulators and talk to people who have invested through the website.

The U.S. Securities and Exchange Commission (SEC), which oversees publicly traded companies, also warns computer users of the dangers of investing online. In particular, the SEC says online investors should beware of "pump-and-dump" stock scams in which unsavory individuals tout a company on a website, in an online investment newsletter, or via e-mail with the sole purpose of creating high demand for the stock and pumping up its price. The perpetrators of the scam then sell their stock when the price is at its peak, resulting in a quick and sharp fall in the stock price. The unwitting investors then usually lose their money.

"Some online newsletters falsely claim to independently research the stocks they profile," the SEC states on its website. "Others spread false information or promote worthless stocks. The most notorious sometimes 'scalp' the stocks they hype, driving up the price of the stock with their baseless recommendations and then selling their own holdings at high prices and high profits."

Q. The investment newsletters seem so thorough—what should I watch out for?

A. Some of those sleek online documents, which often read like unbiased reviews, are actually paid for by companies to trumpet their stocks, the Securities and Exchange Commission reports. Such publications are not illegal, so long as the newsletters disclose who paid for them and how much and how they paid. Nevertheless, the SEC says that many newsletters fail to disclose this information.

"Never, ever, make an investment based solely on what you read in an online newsletter or bulletin-board posting, especially if the investment involves a small, thinly traded company that isn't well known," the SEC says on its website. "And don't even think about investing on your own in small companies that don't file regular reports with the SEC, unless you are willing to in-

vestigate each company thoroughly and to check the truth of every statement about the company."

Q. Commentators on investment bulletin boards sound so knowledgeable—should I heed their advice?

A. Not unless you know the commentators and trust their advice. The Securities and Exchange Commission says many messages on these Internet sites are "bogus—or even scams." These scams often involve lies stating that they have "inside" information, the agency says.

"People claiming to be unbiased observers who've carefully researched the company may actually be company insiders, large shareholders or paid promoters," the SEC states on its website. "A single person can easily create the illusion of widespread interest in a small, thinly traded stock by posting a series of messages under various aliases."

Online Pharmacies

Q. What are some potential problems with online pharmacies?

A. There may be advantages in using online pharmacies, such as saving money, trouble, and embarrassment, but remember that you need a prescription to get a drug. And, with hundreds of drug-dispensing sites in business, don't just assume that a site is legitimate.

Q. How can consumers protect themselves?

A. The FDA website—www.fda.gov—has a number of good cautions, including the following:

- Purchasing a medication from an illegal website puts you at risk. You may receive a contaminated or counterfeit product, the wrong product, an incorrect dose, or no product at all.
- Taking an unsafe or inappropriate medication puts you at risk for dangerous drug interactions and other serious health consequences.
- Before buying, check with the National Association of Boards of Pharmacy (www.nabp.net;

847-698-6227) to determine whether a website is a licensed pharmacy in good standing.

- Don't buy from sites that offer to prescribe a prescription drug for the first time without a physical exam, sell a prescription drug without a prescription, or sell drugs not approved by the FDA.
- Don't do business with sites that have no access to a registered pharmacist to answer questions.
- Avoid sites that do not identify with whom you are dealing and do not provide a U.S. address and phone number to contact if there's a problem.
- Steer clear of sites that include undocumented case histories claiming amazing results.
- Consumers who suspect that a site is illegal can report it to the FDA at www.fda.gov/oc/buyonline/buyonlineform.htm.

THE WORLD AT YOUR FINGERTIPS

- *You can check an online company's reputation by contacting the Better Business Bureau at www.bbb.org, or the attorney general's office in your state or the state where the seller is located. The attorney general can be found through the website of the National Association of Attorneys General (www.naag.org).*
- *The Federal Trade Commission offers consumers tips on avoiding what the agency calls "Dot Cons." The FTC's website is at www.ftc.gov/bcp/conline/pubs/online/dotcons.htm.*
- *The Securities and Exchange Commission provides investors with tips on avoiding fraud. Its website is at www.sec.gov/investor/pubs/cyberfraud.htm.*
- *The American Bar Association offers assistance for finding lawyers online. Its website is at www.abanet.org/legalservices/findlegalhelp/hirelawyer.html. Chapter 1,*

"When and How to Use a Lawyer," can give you more information about finding and hiring a lawyer.
- *Many of the recommendations in this section are adapted from a site developed by the American Bar Association's Section of Business Law. You can visit the site at www.safeshopping.org.*
- *More information about the Uniform Electronic Transactions Act is available at www.uetaonline.com.*
- *For information on a wide variety of Internet issues, access Nolo's legal encyclopedia (www.nolo.com/lawcenter/ency/index.cfm) and scroll down to "Internet law."*

REMEMBER THIS

- *Use some common sense when you're shopping online. People generally feel safer dealing with companies they already know and trust. If you are not familiar with the name and reputation of a company, find out more before you buy.*
- *Use the safest way to pay on the Internet: Pay for your order using a credit card.*
- *Keep a copy of all correspondence between you and the company regarding the purchase. Just because you can now purchase goods electronically does not mean you can forget the old adage "Get it in writing." Keep a copy on paper or on your system electronically so that you can retrieve it later.*
- *If you're booking travel online, print out your booking information and bring it with you to the airport, and be sure to confirm your flight twenty-four hours before you're due to fly.*
- *Online banking is pretty safe these days. Check your records for unauthorized*

transactions, and notify your bank quickly if there's anything amiss.

- *Take care with online trading—don't assume that online newsletters are giving impartial advice, and investigate companies thoroughly before investing.*

COMPUTERS ON THE JOB

Warning: Your employer may monitor the office computer you are using. So be careful what websites you visit, what e-mails you send and receive, what games you play, and how long you spend online. And if you think returning to the home page and deleting e-mails will cover your wayward computer use, you are sadly mistaken. Cookies and other memory caches enable employers to see your files even after you have "deleted" them.

This section covers all the ways in which employers may monitor what you do on your office computer.

Q. May employers really monitor my activity like that?

A. The overwhelming majority of legal commentators, as well as courts that have decided such cases, say yes. The office computer, they note, is no different than the telephone on your work desk, the use of which employers have traditionally and quite legally limited to work-related communications (such as by prohibiting personal calls on company time).

In fact, many employers now have written policies saying they can and will monitor office computer use. These policies are often contained in the reams of documents given to new employees. These employees are often instructed to sign a piece of paper confirming that they have received the policy document.

Companies defend their examinations of employee e-mails and website visits as necessary to protect proprietary information from being downloaded and e-mailed, to discourage harassment in the workplace, to reduce waste, fraud, and abuse of the company's resources, and to ensure that office computers are being used for company business.

Q. What if my company has pledged not to conduct e-mail and Internet searches?

A. You must still be careful.

Companies are often the targets of lawsuits, either from customers or clients alleging negligence, or from former employees claiming discrimination. During litigation, the parties suing seek and generally receive the court's permission to examine a wide range of documents and e-mail communications pertaining to the alleged negligence or discrimination. As part of this **discovery process,** lawyers for those suing can gain access to company's computers and the sites visited and people contacted by employees. This information, though not sought by your employer, could come to the attention of your company in the discovery process. It will need to gather relevant information to turn over to the other side in response to their request for records and will likely review the records before disclosing them to find out what the other side's lawyers will see. Your company might end up winning the lawsuit, but you might end up losing your job for having visited certain websites or having sent personal e-mail on the company's equipment and time.

Q. May I use my work computer for personal e-mail and online shopping?

A. The official answer is only if your employer lets you. Such overt permission is very rare, but informally employers often don't object as long as the use is minimal, does not interfere with doing your job, and is perhaps subject to other restrictions (very few if any companies want you visiting porno sites on one of their computers).

All in all, it's best to be cautious. Before sending that e-mail or visiting that website, ask yourself if your company lets you make personal phone calls or shop on company time. Now ask yourself if you mind having your employer see the content of your e-mail or discover when and where you shop. Even if your employer allows these practices, it's best to use your work computer sparingly for personal business.

Q. If my employer does not want me to play games, why is solitaire on my computer?

A. Games such as solitaire come with many computer programs, including those destined for companies. The company does not install them. That a company computer contains games should not be interpreted as the employer's tacit approval of employees playing them. Employers may still prohibit employees from playing computer games on company equipment, particularly on company time.

Q. What if I am working from home on my own computer?

A. The computer age, as never before, has enabled employees to work from home. Thanks to the marvels of technology, workers can use their home computers and be fully networked into their employers' office computer systems.

Those working at home, however, should know that while the employees are connected to the company's computer network, the employer can access records of the websites that its employee visit, just as if they were working in the office. Employers remain concerned about protecting proprietary information, preventing harassment, and ensuring that company time is devoted to company work. Breaching any of these employment policies remains cause for disciplinary action even if you are working from the comfort of your home office.

Q. Must I return all the nifty software my employer allowed me to put on my home computer?

A. Yes. The software belongs to your employer, or is licensed from another company by your employer, who lets you install it or download it to your computer for the very limited purpose of doing the company's work. Once that employment ends, the law or perhaps an agreement with your employer may require that you return the employer's goods to the company.

The law is not settled, however, on the issue of whether companies can require ex-employees to surrender their home computers for the former employer's inspection. Employers, having lent their software to the employees, might want to ensure that no company-owned programs or proprietary information has been downloaded to the personal computer. Companies, especially those that have licensed their own software, are especially concerned in the Internet age with protecting their products and confidential data. A lot of companies provide in their employee nondisclosure agreements that they have the right to inspect any computer that you may use in order to ensure that confidentiality is maintained.

Q. Do these rules also apply to freelancers and contractors?

A. Yes, unless the contract between the company and freelancer states otherwise. It would be a rare company that would cede any equipment to someone who is not an employee.

In this highly computer-connected world, an increasing number of people are opening home consulting businesses in which they perform outside work for many companies. Their home computers become a smorgasbord of software programs from the companies they serve. These workers are called contractors for a reason: They are governed by a contract with each company.

The contract will generally spell out the terms under which a company allows a consultant to use its software and related equipment. This permitted use is often very limited so as not to blur any legal lines between a contractor, who relies predominantly on his or her own materials, and an employee, who has freer rein on the company's equipment.

Even in the absence of a written contract, one hallmark of a freelance relationship is that you use your own equipment. Anything given to you by the company is for a limited purpose and must be returned. And consultants, freelancers, and contractors often are required to sign nondisclosure agreements that allow for the inspection of their computers if there is reason to determine compliance with the company's policy.

REMEMBER THIS

- *Be careful how you use your computer at the office. A great safety rule is to imagine that your employer is looking over your shoulder whenever you access websites or send or receive e-mail.*
- *Be aware that many employers have termination policies in place for employees who visit certain offensive websites.*
- *Exercise the same caution when you are working from home on the company's computer network that you would if you were working in the office.*
- *Your company's software belongs to the company even though it is on your personal computer. When the company wants it back, return it.*

INTERNET ISSUES

Junk mail is as old as the Pony Express of the nineteenth century. So it is no surprise that the electronic-mail world of the twenty-first century has its own version of unsolicited, unwanted messages advertising everything from get-rich-quick schemes to magazines you don't need. In the old days, junk mail was largely a minor nuisance that quickly wound up in the garbage can. Now, these messages—called "spam"—are often a major distraction, forcing people to wade through a river of junk before getting to their important e-mail or, worse, containing a virus that wipes out an entire hard drive. Viruses are computer programs, often sent via e-mail, that can wipe out your computer information—including important documents and records—in less than a second. They are so named because they can spread as fast as the most virulent contagion, forwarded innocently by computer users who do not know the message they are sending contains the virus.

Spam

Q. Can the law regulate spam?

A. Only the spammers like spam, but is massive disapproval enough to do it in? As of 2003, legislators in about half of the states had passed antispam laws, but many have low penalties. Moreover, the fact that states have boundaries but the Internet does not may make enforcement difficult because of jurisdictional problems.

One of the latest laws, in Virginia, imposes harsh felony penalties for sending spam by deceptive means, such as forging the return address line of an e-mail message or hacking a computer to send spam. Those found guilty of sending more than ten thousand deceptive messages in one day could serve prison terms and forfeit profits and assets. Since Virginia is the home of AOL and other major Internet providers, half of all Internet traffic flows through the state, lessening jurisdictional problems.

Doubting that state laws would do the trick, in late 2003 Congress passed a law to address the problem nationally. The law, which took effect the first day of 2004, bans sending bulk commercial e-mail using false identities and misleading subject lines. All commercial e-mail messages now have to include valid postal address and give recipients opportunity to opt out of receiving more messages.

Q. How do I prevent spam from reaching my in-box?

A. As with death, taxes, and junk mail, there are no foolproof ways to prevent spam. However, you can make it more difficult for the e-mail marketers who rely on spam to discover your address.

For example, you can be very circumspect about to whom you give your e-mail address. When purchasing items online, you can choose to do business only with companies that promise not to give your address to others. That, however, can be cumbersome, as it will require you to examine the often tedious and wordy privacy policies, agreements, or disclosures of each company. Another very common way to get bombarded with spam is to have your e-mail address on a website, which is picked up by a spammer. Some people try to avoid this by spelling out the @ symbol, making their address more difficult to search.

You can also purchase software or utilize an online service that screens out spam by refusing to accept any e-mail from a sender whose name the program does not recognize. However, spam software can have the unwelcome result of also screening out mail from new acquaintances or potential new clients if you rely on e-mail for your business. With a service, however, suspected span or e-mail containing viruses is trapped and stored for review by the recipient.

The race between the spammers and anti-spammers goes on and on. For the latest in anti-spam technology and tactics, type "anti-spam" or "stop-spam" into your favorite search engine and see what's out there.

One last tip. Any answer to a spam message is a big mistake. Even if you're just responding to an offer to take your name off the spammer's list, don't do it. The spammer will then know that you're a live address and that you've read the message. You'll find yourself on even more mailing lists.

Q. What can I do if spam reaches my inbox?

A. You can send a copy of the spam to your Internet service provider's "abuse" desk. This lets the ISP know that a spam problem exists on its service. In addition, you can complain to the sender's ISP. Internet providers generally do not like companies and individuals abusing their service.

You might also tell the Federal Trade Commission. The agency stores information on spam to pursue possible legal action against companies and individuals who send unfair or deceptive e-mail solicitations. Though they might not take action against spam that is merely unwanted, it might be worthwhile to send a copy of the e-mail to the FTC at uce@ftc.gov.

▶ **DODGING SPAM**

An increasingly popular method of spam avoidance is the creation of separate e-mail addresses—or "aliases"—that you use for your online purchases and other business transactions. That way, if marketers gain access to that address, their spam will end up in a separate account from the one you use for personal e-mail.

⚠ **CHAIN E-MAILS**

One especially pernicious form of spam is the chain e-mail letter in which the recipient is promised money in return for sending the letter on to several friends. The friends who receive the letter are in turn instructed to send it on to several friends, hence creating a chain. The transmission of chain letters, either electronically or through the post office, is a federal offense. And to make matters worse, those sending chain letters very rarely receive the promised money. If you receive a chain e-mail letter, the Federal Trade Commission advises you to tell your Internet service provider and forward the e-mail to the FTC at uce@ftc.gov.

Viruses

Q. How much of a problem are viruses?

A. The speed and danger of viruses is perhaps best illustrated by this quote from a U.S. Justice Department press release (December 9, 1999) announcing the guily plea of the perpetrator of of an infamous virus:

"The Melissa virus appeared on thousands of email systems on March 26, 1999, disguised as an important message from a colleague or friend. The virus was designed to send an infected email to the first 50 email addresses on the users' mailing lists. Such emails would only be sent if the computers used Microsoft Outlook for email.

"Because each infected computer could infect 50 additional computers, which in turn could infect another 50 computers, the virus proliferated rapidly and exponentially, resulting in substantial interruption or impairment of public communications or services. According to reports from business and government following the spread of the virus, its rapid distribution disrupted computer networks by overloading email servers, resulting in the shutdown of networks and significant costs to repair or cleanse computer systems."

The Melissa virus caused more than $80 million in damage by disrupting personal computers and computer networks in business and government.

Q. What was the lure that caused users to open the infected mail?

A. David L. Smith, who pled guilty to creating and distributing the virus, described in state and federal court how, using a stolen America Online account and his own account with a local Internet service provider, he posted an infected document on the Internet newsgroup Alt.Sex. The posting contained a message enticing readers to download and open the document with the hope of finding pass codes to adult-content websites.

Opening and downloading the message caused the Melissa virus to infect victim computers. The virus altered Microsoft word-processing programs such that any document created using the programs would then be infected with the Melissa virus. The virus then proliferated via the Microsoft Outlook program, causing computers to send infected electronic mail.

Smith acknowledged that each new e-mail greeted new users with an enticing message to open and, thus, spread the virus further. The message read: "Here is that document you asked for . . . don't show anyone else;-)."

Q. What was the legal resolution of the Melissa case?

A. Judge Joseph A. Greenaway Jr. of the U.S. District Court for New Jersey sentenced Smith to twenty months in federal prison to be followed by one hundred hours of community service. Smith was also fined $5,000 and ordered not to be involved with computer networks, the Internet, or Internet bulletin boards during three years of supervised release unless authorized by the court.

Q. How do I protect my computer against viruses?

A. Don't open .EXE files or download files that you are not expecting to receive. Protect your computer with antivirus software. Many computers come with antivirus software installed. The software can also be purchased from a store or an online merchant. Many brands of antivirus software invite you to register with the company, which then may send you e-mails alerting you to downloadable updates from their websites or may simply send you regular updates that enable you to upgrade the software online to thwart the latest viruses, which are always becoming more sophisticated. Be sure to purchase good antivirus software, install it, and regularly check the publisher's website for updates and new virus definitions. Keep the software current, as it may not protect against newer viruses if you do not update it regularly.

In addition, services to screen e-mail for viruses are also available.

Q. What else can I do?

A. In addition to relying on technology, you should use your own wits to protect your computer. First of all, make sure you don't fall for a "fibbing" e-mail, as the Federal Trade Commission warns. Remember that the people who got burned by the Melissa virus yielded to an enticing message that they subsequently regretted opening. People sending viruses have also used other tempting subject lines to encourage people to access the danger-filled e-mail messages, including "FWD: Funny Text" and "As Per Your Request."

In addition, you should not open any e-mail messages warning of a new virus. These seemingly well-intentioned e-mails are a favorite tactic of those who wish to spread viruses, the FTC says. Instead, try to educate yourself about new viruses. There are many good sites to check for up-to-date information on viruses, including Symantec (www.symantec.com) and McAfee (www.mcafee.com). Urban Legends (www.snopes.com) also contains useful information regarding chain e-mails and other Internet and computer

---

> ⚠ **BEWARE OF ATTACHMENTS**
>
> If you don't trust your antivirus software entirely, you should also be very careful about opening attachments to e-mails, because the virus often exists not in the message itself but on the attached files. This caution against opening attachments extends to messages that appear to have been sent by friends and coworkers, so do not open the attachments unless you are expecting the message or know what the attached file contains.

hoaxes. Your Internet service provider can also inform you about new viruses that are infecting computers.

In any event, you should always play it safe and be sure to back up important files by copying them onto a backup medium (such as a floppy disk or CD), a different machine, or printing them out.

Q. What do I do if my computer has become infected?

> ⚠ **NEITHER A BORROWER NOR A LENDER BE**
>
> Some computer users may be tempted to get the cheapest antivirus protection available. Savvy computer users will resist this temptation, however, and obtain an appropriate form of protection from a reputable software or solution provider. The high demand and cost of antivirus software make the borrowing of these programs from friends especially inviting. But avoid such practices. Companies that provide antivirus software prohibit its transfer between customers if both customers retain a copy. If you want the software, you will have to pay for a copy yourself or receive it as a bona fide gift from someone who has not opened the box, downloaded it beforehand, and kept it on his or her system.
>
> Moreover, the value of antivirus software is also in the online updates that are available to subscribers to the service. These keep the user's system protected from the most recently diagnosed viruses out there. An antivirus software program that is no more recent than two or three months back may be woefully out of date and leave the user exposed to hundreds and perhaps thousands of viruses created or released since the last update.

A. The Federal Trade Commission advises that you should disconnect from the Internet immediately and scan your computer with up-to-date antivirus software. You should also try to figure out how your computer became infected and take steps to avoid a recurrence. For example, did you open an e-mail attachment or rely on out-of-date software? If you discover the source, you should notify the person who sent you the virus.

In addition, you should report the incident to your Internet service provider as well as the sender's provider, if you know who it is.

Q. Can I get into trouble for inadvertently spreading viruses?

A. The police will not come after you if you mistakenly spread a virus you did not know existed. However, people who receive the virus from you might be none too happy and sue you for any damage caused by it. In court, it's conceivable that you could be found liable if you negligently passed on the virus. You might be negligent, for example, if you helped spread a virus by opening up an e-mail at work that you had no business accessing, such as the adult-oriented message that contained the Melissa virus. You may also be negligent for failing to take reasonable care to prevent viruses by obtaining and using antivirus software.

THE WORLD AT YOUR FINGERTIPS

- *Emailabuse.org, an ad hoc group, provides advice on combating spam. The group's website is www.emailabuse.org.*
- *The Federal Trade Commission stores information on spam to pursue possible legal action against companies and individuals who send unfair or deceptive e-mail solicitations. Though they might not take action against spam that is merely unwanted, it might be worthwhile to send a copy of the e-mail to the FTC at uce@ftc.gov.*
- *MSNBC provides news on antivirus efforts on its website at www.msnbc.com/news/TECHCRIMES_Front.asp.*

REMEMBER THIS

- *You cannot stop spam, but you can contain it by doing the following:*
  - *Opt out of receiving commercial solicitations by using the "opt out" functions contained in most privacy policies.*
  - *Limit the number of companies that know your e-mail address.*
  - *Read privacy agreements before buying items online.*
  - *Install software that screens out unwanted e-mail messages.*
  - *Create a separate address for your online purchases*
- *Viruses are generally spread by e-mail. Therefore, it is incumbent upon computer users to exercise caution when opening and forwarding e-mail.*
- *Make sure your computer has up-to-date antivirus software.*
- *Do not open e-mails when you cannot identify the sender.*
- *Do not open attachments unless you know or have contacted the sender.*
- *Do not forward e-mails unless you know who sent you the message.*

COMPUTER COPYRIGHT AND TRADEMARK ISSUES

Federal copyright law protects everything from books by bestselling authors to drawings by your four-year-old child that you put on your refrigerator. So it should be no mystery that the law also protects words and pictures put on Internet sites. Therefore, you could be putting yourself at legal risk if you cut and paste words and pictures from an Internet site to include on your personal website or in a document you are producing. Breaking federal copyright law will not likely land you in prison—though the criminal penalties for copyright law violations are increasingly being applied—but it could lead to a lawsuit from the person or company that owns the copyright.

Copying software and downloading music and videos from the Internet is as easy as double-clicking a mouse. Ease, however, does not make these activities legal. Users must beware that the software, music, and videos are often licensed or copyrighted to companies willing to go to court to protect what they own. Just ask Napster. The now-defunct Internet company provided a peer-to-peer file-sharing network that allowed users to download copies of musical works. Recording companies, however, held the copyright to that music. Of even greater concern to individuals are cases such as the one where a federal court required Verizon to turn over the identity of an individual who downloaded six hundred copyrighted songs in one day.

This section covers copyright and trademark issues. Copyright is one of several legal issues you'll face if you have your own personal website. If you use your webpages to express strongly held political views, your statements will be protected by the First Amendment—up to a point. For example, website messages that call for immediate violence would not necessarily be protected, especially with federal and state law enforcement personnel on guard against potential terrorism.

But even before you get your first visitor, or "hit," your personal website is fraught with legal peril. The selection of a domain name for the site can get you in trouble for trademark infringement if, for example, it too closely resembles a product or a company name.

Copying Words and Pictures from the Internet

Q. When is it OK to copy words and pictures?

A. It is safe to copy information from the Internet when you have the permission of the copyright holder. Please note that permission from the author of the written material or from the artist of the picture is not always valid because often the creator is not the one who owns the copyright. For example, it may be that the publishing company and not the author of the book has the copyright. In most cases, even if the author holds the copyright, requests to produce artwork or extensive text passages not covered by fair use would be made to the publisher and not directly to the author or artist.

You also may copy material that is copyright protected if your purpose is a "fair use" under the law. Specifically, you may be able to copy protected material if you are using it as part of a criticism, a comment, a news report, or a valid educational or research tool—for example, you can copy an image of an artwork for an article that discusses or criticizes the work, but you can't copy the same artwork to make a poster.

The copyright law specifies that fair use shall be determined on a case-by-case basis, weighing the following four factors:

1. The purpose and character of the use, including whether such use is of a commercial nature or is for nonprofit educational purposes
2. The nature of the copyrighted work
3. The amount and substantiality of the portion used in relation to the copyrighted work as a whole
4. The effect of the use upon the potential market for or value of the copyrighted work

In general, teachers may be permitted to make copies of small portions of otherwise copyright-protected material if it is intended solely for classroom use, but in many cases they should seek copyright permission first, especially when the amount of the work being copied is large and many copies are being made.

Finally, it is acceptable to copy material that you know (correctly!) is in the public domain.

Q. May I print or e-mail articles from online newspapers or magazines?

A. Newspapers and magazines are copyrighted, and reproducing them, with some narrow exceptions such as for educational purposes, would normally be illegal. However, in recent years, many of these publications have openly encouraged computer users to print or e-mail the articles by providing printer-friendly versions of articles and inviting users to "e-mail this article to a friend." Some online **zines** (self-published magazines) permit the forwarding of entire articles only.

Q. May I copy and print reports and information from government websites?

A. Yes. Copyright protection does not extend to reports and other documents generated by government agencies.

But beware of copying information from private sites to which the government site might refer you. Generally, information on private sites, though linked to the government site, is copyright protected.

Copying Software and Downloading Entertainment

Q. Why is software copyrighted?

A. Software is a product that costs money to produce, just like literary works (such as books, poems, and articles), movies, records, and TV shows. The producers of this **intellectual prop-** erty are just as entitled to payment as the producers of cars, food, and shelter. The fact that there is no direct cost to the producer if someone makes an illegal copy of the software does not change this legal and moral fact. (There are indirect costs to unauthorized copying, starting with the lost revenue to the developer or owner.) The fact that "everyone does it," of course, is also of no moral or legal consequence.

Q. What can I tell my kids about the (im)morality and (il)legality of copying software?

A. Illegally copying software is no more legitimate than copying videotapes, books, or musical recordings. For that matter, it is no more legitimate than stealing an apple—a costly apple—from the front of the grocer's store simply because you can, or cashing someone else's paycheck. Software piracy deprives the producer of the fruit of the producer's labor, something that any working person or anyone who owns property should understand. You should be no more ready to steal software than to steal anything else.

Q. How is copyright protected on the Internet?

A. The basic copyright laws providing protection for intellectual property apply to products on the Internet. In addition to traditional laws governing copyright, the federal 1998 Digital Millennium Copyright Act addresses some issues specific to the Internet, such as circumvention of copyright protection systems, digital fair use, and ISP liability when subscribers post copyrighted content illegally. For example, in one case a court found that the law permits companies that suspect their copyright has been infringed to seek a court order that Internet service providers divulge the name of the subscriber suspected of infringing on the copyright. The case is now on appeal, and this area of law is not yet settled. Information about the law can be found at www.educause.edu/issues/dmca.html.

Many companies have also turned to technol-

ⓘ THE PUBLIC DOMAIN

Material in the public domain is material that is not subject to copyright protection, or any other kind of intellectual property protection. This material can be copied, without limitation, and without payment of a fee.

ogy to protect the copyright of the audio and video images they put on the Internet. A technology known as digital watermarking lets companies put hidden marks on their computer data that travel with the images when they are copied, enabling the company to trace the distribution of their words and pictures.

Even without watermarking, some companies are able to trace copyrighted materials as they are copied and posted on the Internet.

Q. How can software be legally used?

A. Software is protected by copyright and is only legally usable by people or businesses that purchase a **license,** which is simply permission to use the software. Most software that you buy in the store, and much of what comes with your computer (such as software on compact discs) comes with a shrink-wrap license. Under this license system, the manufacturer regards you as having agreed to the terms of its licensing agreement contained inside the package once you open the plastic shrink-wrap of the package.

The software already loaded onto your computer is covered by licenses arranged with the company that preloaded it, and to which you agree under a principle analogous to the shrink-wrap license.

Increasingly, you are also required to navigate a click box that comes up on the first screen you see during installation, during which time you click "YES" to the terms of the license agreement if you want to proceed—and "NO" if you want to return the merchandise and seek a refund. This device is also used for licenses that allow you access to certain websites and other online resources.

You should, therefore, beware of friends bearing gifts. For example, suppose your friend has just sent you an e-mail stating he has bought and downloaded the most amazing software. It can do everything but pour coffee. He says he would like to give you a copy of his software as a gift.

Q. What should you tell him?

A. Thanks, but no thanks. By downloading the software, your friend has agreed to the conditions of the software manufacturer, who retains intellectual property rights to the product. As a result, the manufacturer has imposed conditions on the use of the software, including that it not be transferred, given, or sold to another person once it has been downloaded, including to a friend.

You, in turn, will be unable to claim that you are merely an innocent recipient. Software companies are savvy enough to include the terms of the software's use on the programs themselves so that the warning against unauthorized downloading, use, or copying is clearly displayed on your computer screen before you even start to download or use the software.

ⓘ SHAREWARE AND FREEWARE

Besides software that you purchase, there are two legitimate sources of sophisticated programming that can be copied with the company's permission.

Shareware is protected by copyright, but the copyright holder permits free copying and distribution. The new user is usually requested, on the honor system, to remit a relatively small payment for costs and to register as a user.

Freeware is what it sounds like: free as the air. Programmers make it available through online bulletin boards and user groups. You may not have the right to copy it for others, however, because the programmer might want it to keep tabs on where it goes.

You can search for shareware and freeware at many websites, including www.shareware.com, www.nonags.com, and www.tucows.com.

Your friend, however, remains free to buy another edition of the software and give you that one as a gift.

Q. May I copy software from my desktop to my laptop computer and vice versa?

A. That depends. Some lawyers specializing in this field maintain that you are entitled to use software that you buy on both the computer you keep at your desk and on your laptop. Presumably you are not using both of these at the same time, though it gets muddier if one is for your use and one is for the use of your high schooler or spouse.

Other legal experts—many of whom represent software developers—disagree, and say each software license is for use on one machine, period. It would not hurt to read the license to see what rights the license actually does grant you, as some licenses authorize use of the software on both a home and a work computer, provided that it is not used at the same time in both places.

Q. May I copy software as a backup to protect myself in case my computer crashes?

A. Yes. Even though your software comes on a disk, most lawyers in this field agree, as do many software manufacturers, that you are entitled to make a backup copy of the software for protection in case the original disk is damaged or defective. In fact, in most software licenses you are authorized to make a backup copy. And a specific section of the copyright law allows you to create a single copy of a computer program for archival purposes. The copy on your computer's hard drive is always vulnerable to a crash or other system disaster, and software companies recognize this as well as anyone—especially since their software often causes the problem! The use of zip drives and other backup media, as well as affordable Internet-based automatic backup solutions, may also be an intelligent way to protect yourself.

Q. May I download music and videos from the Internet?

A. Be very careful. Just as a software company retains intellectual property rights to its computer programs, entertainment companies hold copyright protection for their music and videos and will safeguard these works from unauthorized reproduction. A good rule of thumb is that if you are downloading or copying something from the Internet as a way to avoid paying retail price, you are probably doing something you should not.

Q. What if I use peer-to-peer services to share music with my friends?

A. If the music being shared is protected by federal copyright (which it very likely is), you might be running afoul of the Digital Millennium Copyright Act. Remember that Napster was a peer-to-peer sharing service.

In addition, the federal 1997 No Electronic Theft Act makes it a crime to exchange copyrighted materials for money or other copyrighted materials. Punishments range from up to one year in prison, for exchanging a copyrighted work worth more than $1,000, to up to six years in prison for the second offense of distributing ten

---

▶ **GETTING HELP AS A SOFTWARE CONSUMER**

Software may come on a CD or an online download, but it can present as many performance problems and threats to your well being as any large appliance. It's best to have software that includes at least some degree of free telephone support, at least for a limited period. However, this is increasingly rare these days, with most companies offering support through webpage FAQs or e-mail. The developer's confidence in his product is ultimately reflected in the extent to which the developer stands behind it.

copies of a copyrighted work worth $2,500 or more.

Legal Issues and Your Personal Website

Q. What is a domain name?

A. A domain name is the your unique Web address, which is used by the Internet's infrastructure to allow other computers to find you on the Internet.

Q. How can I make sure that the domain name I want to register has not already been taken?

A. When using your browser, you can try to place the name in your browser and see if a website using that name already exists or if it "cannot be found." If you want a more definitive word of whether a domain name is registered, you can check the "Whois" database of registered names by using a search service such as www.whois.net or www.geektools.com, or checking with one of the domain name registrars (listed, for example at betterwhois.com).

Q. How do I register my domain name?

A. Check with your Internet service provider. Many ISPs provide registration services or can refer you to a domain registration service.

Q. Am I safe once my name is registered?

A. That depends on whether your name infringes on a trademark. If it does, your going online might be the most risky moment in the process.

Domain name registration companies generally only check to determine whether a name has been used for a Web address, not whether another company or individual has trademarked the name. To determine whether a name has been trademarked, you should check with the U.S. Patent and Trademark Office at www.uspto.gov or have a lawyer perform the check for you.

Many companies aggressively protect their trademarks and are willing to take alleged infringers to court after the failure of more peaceful efforts at resolution, such as a letter requesting that the offending party change its name. For example, Mattel, maker of the Barbie doll, sued Adventure Apparel, saying that its

---

⚠ DODGE THIS NAME GAME

You should beware of scam artists who have been offering computer users the chance to preregister domain names under new "dots" that will soon be made available by the Internet Corporation for Assigned Names and Numbers (ICANN), a nonprofit corporation responsible for the allocation of Internet addresses and domain name management. These dots—which will be added to the familiar .gov, .com, .edu, and .org.—are .aero, .biz, .coop, .info, .museum, .name, and .pro.

The scam involves fax and e-mail invitations for people to register their names using these new dots as soon as they become available. Do not be fooled.

The FTC warns computer uses to avoid any preregistration service promising preferential treatment in the assignment of domain names. In fact, the FTC tells consumers to avoid doing business with anyone who sends unsolicited faxes, which the agency says is illegal.

Note, however, that legitimate registries are offering "sunrise" periods in which owners of existing trademarks can register their domains before the domains are opened up for anyone to register.

BarbiesBeachWear.com and BarbiesClothing.com sites infringed on the toy company's trademark in violation of the 1999 Anticybersquatting Consumer Protection Act. The U.S. District Court for Southern New York ruled for Mattel in September 2001, saying the use of Barbie's name diluted the value of the trademark. The court awarded the company $2,000 in damages.

Under the law, a person can have a domain name that would otherwise infringe on a trademark if the name is designed to be a parody, is not meant to be used as part of a commercial site, and does not dilute the value of the company's trademark. These are all legal questions, which are often left to the courts. Consult a lawyer if, after checking with the U.S. Patent and Trademark Office, you believe you still have cause for concern but nevertheless want to use the name.

Q. How do domain registrars sort out conflicts over names?

A. The URL www.icann.org/udrp/udrp.htm has complete details, but the short answer is that all registrars in the .biz, .com, .info, .name, .net, and .org top-level domains follow the **Uniform Domain-Name Dispute-Resolution Policy (UDRP)**. This policy provides that before a registrar will cancel, suspend, or transfer domain names, the disputes over domain names and transfers must be resolved by agreement, court action, or arbitration. If it's a question of alleged cybersquatting (see sidebar), the trademark holder can file a complaint with an "approved dispute-resolution service provider" and receive an expedited hearing.

Q. May I set my webpage to music?

A. Yes, provided it is in the pubic domain or you do not infringe on the copyright of the recording company or artist. For example, downloading the music from a website without authorization from the recording company or artist could be illegal. Purchasing and downloading the music from a website owned by the company would also probably not be enough to put you on the right side of the law. When music is purchased (such as on a CD), it does not usually come with a right of public performance You'll need to get a license from the copyright holder for the public performance of the music, not just buy a copy.

Of course, you should not use your website to resell or e-mail music without explicit authorization from the copyright holder.

Q. May I post names and addresses of people?

A. Yes, if you get their consent. If they don't want you to, it is a courtesy not to post it. Moreover, if the posting of this information is likely to spur violence, the postings might be illegal. For example, radical groups opposed to abortion have come under investigation for listing the names and addresses of doctors who perform this controversial procedure. There are other privacy issues here as well—it's best to be cautious.

Q. May I post pictures on the Internet?

A. You generally may post pictures on your website with the consent of their owners, unless the photographs are illegal, such as if they depict obscene child pornography, or infringe on the privacy rights of the person in the picture. In addition, you can generally post pictures you took of people in public places where they had no rea-

---

📄 CYBERSQUATTING

Cybersquatting is illegally attempting to profit by reserving a domain name that is or contains a trademark and then attempting to resell or license the domain names to the trademark owner. An example would be a person who registers coke.com and then tries to get money from the Coca-Cola Company for the name. People who engage in these efforts are called cybersquatters. These activities are outlawed under the 1999 Anticybersquatting Consumer Protection Act.

sonable expectation of privacy, such as in a mall or at a stadium. You also may reprint the pictures if they are in the public domain.

But unless it's fair use, reprinting pictures from a website, a book, a newspaper, or a magazine or other copyrighted material is generally forbidden. You must have the permission of the copyright holder before reprinting the pictures.

Q. May I write whatever I like on my site?

A. No. The laws against libel apply to the Internet. You may not recklessly disregard the truth or knowingly write falsehoods about public figures or make negligent statements about private citizens. Private threats do not have First Amendment protection, and could subject you to prosecution.

Q. What can I do if someone copies what I write or draw on my site?

A. You own the copyright to the original work you put on your site and can enforce that right in court against anyone who copies your work without your permission. A copyright exists once something is written or drawn. Unlike a trademark or a patent, a copyright need not be registered with the federal government. However, before you can sue for copyright infringement, you must register or at least be in the process of

copyright registration in the U.S. Copyright Office. Consult a lawyer before deciding to wait to obtain a copyright registration, because certain recoveries against an infringer are precluded by registration after infringement has begun.

If you don't want to register, it is a good idea to put others on notice that you have the copyright and thereby discourage them from copying. This notification can be accomplished by simply putting the familiar circled letter "c" (©) on your website followed by the year and your name, or by spelling out the word "copyright" followed by the year and your name.

THE WORLD AT YOUR FINGERTIPS

- *Doug Isenberg's book, The GigaLaw Guide to Internet Law (New York: Random House, 2002), is touted as a "one stop legal resource for conducting business online." The book shouldn't replace the services of a good lawyer, but it is certainly a useful resource that covers many issues you should be aware of if you're starting up your own website or Web-based business.*

- *For a good overview of trademarks and copyright, access Nolo's legal encyclopedia (www.nolo.com/lawcenter/ency/index.cfm) and scroll down to trademarks and copyright.*

- *Nova Southeastern University law professor Samuel Lewis has created a website dedicated to intellectual property and the Internet. The site can be accessed is at www.complaw.com.*

- *The San Francisco-based Electronic Frontier Foundation, which promotes "digital rights," opposes a number of the new laws protecting intellectual property. Its website is at www.eff.org.*

- *For more information on domain names and the new dots, visit the Internet Corporation for Assigned Names and Numbers' website at www.icann.org.*

⚠ BEWARE OF SPINNING

If you have a website, you should educate yourself on what you have to do to be sure your domain registration is kept up. Domain registrations aren't forever, and some registration companies "spin" customers by approaching them to register the name again before their time is up. In general, you are not locked into the company that registered your domain in the first place. You can transfer any time, with or without a fee for the transfer.

- *If you are involved in a dispute over a domain name, the Uniform Domain-Name Dispute-Resolution Policy (UDRP) will probably apply to you, and you must attempt to resolve the dispute by agreement, court action, or arbitration. Visit www.icann.org/udrp/udrp.htm for more details.*

REMEMBER THIS

- *If you are trying to avoid infringing on a copyright, your best protection is to have the permission of the copyright holder.*
- *You may copy otherwise protected material if it falls under the fair-use exception.*
- *Fair use is open to interpretation; a lot*

depends on the facts of each case, and it's risky to assume that copying is fair use.
- *Information from government websites can generally be copied at will.*
- *Software companies require you to buy their software and get very upset when you copy a friend's version. A good rule to follow is to buy the software in a store or download it over the Internet.*
- *Be careful when downloading music or videos from a website not operated, approved, or sponsored by a recording company or artist.*
- *You should feel free to post your résumé, family photos, and opinions on your personal website. But exercise caution when*

ⓘ CAN YOU GET IN TROUBLE FOR LINKING TO PROTECTED MATERIAL?

On your website, you can easily create links to other sites. Easy, yes, but does it create possible legal hassles? Let's look at copyright issues first. You can take visitors of your site to the websites of others with just the click of a mouse, thanks to "hot links," or Web addresses contained on your pages. In fact, you can do the same thing for recipients of your e-mail by copying a URL from a website into your message.

This may well not be a copyright violation. There is no copying, for one thing—you are merely directing people to material on the Web that the copyright holder put up there. Moreover, the copyright holder presumably wants people to notice this material—that's why it was posted in the first place. The copyright holder might hope to generate revenue by providing samples on its site.

However, such links may be a *trademark* violation if they create a confusion of sponsorship or an association in the mind of users between the trademark and your site. For example, several legal cases have found that certain metatags can impermissibly compromise someone else's trademark. **Metatags** are programming codes that Web creators use. You can't see them, but they're crucial to the success of a website because they help search engines find them. In one case, a Web operator used "playboy" and "playmate" as metatags, but a court found that Playboy Enterprises had the trademark on these words and that their use on a non-Playboy site constituted trademark infringement and unfair competition. In effect, it's like luring customers into a store by posting a sign with another company's trademark on it. Possibly a simple link might similarly confuse Web surfers and attract the attention of the trademark holder's lawyers.

putting someone else's résumé, photos, and musings on your website.

• *Be careful what you write regarding the activities of others, or you may run the risk of a libel action.*

LAW ENFORCEMENT AND THE COMPUTER

While police continue to seek warrants to wiretap phone lines, now they also seek judicial permission to gain access to e-mail messages. These searches have become a potent tool of law enforcement because e-mail communications, unlike an unrecorded telephone call, contain a written record of the conversation long after it has ended.

Whereas law enforcement officials in the past have sought phone-company records, the police now seek information from the computer banks of Internet service providers. As a result, police—with probable cause to suspect illegal activity—can get search warrants to access past e-mail messages not from home computers but from ISPs.

Civil rights groups have voiced concerns that in the post–September 11 world of increased domestic security, innocent computer users might get snared in a police e-mail investigation simply because they inadvertently visited a website or received junk e-mail or spam from a group that law enforcement suspects might be linked to terrorism.

This section covers basic questions on how laws affect you and how you can protect yourself.

Q. *What about the Fourth Amendment?*

A. This constitutional safeguard against unreasonable police searches and seizures is based in large part on an individual's "reasonable expectation of privacy." For example, a person's expectation of privacy is great when one is in his or her own home or on a private telephone call, so the police need to make an extra-strong showing to convince a neutral magistrate to issue a search warrant.

But courts are undecided on how much Fourth Amendment protection people have with regard to their e-mail conversations. A major sticking point is whether people communicating by e-mail have a reasonable expectation of privacy, considering that these messages are collected and held by service providers. In at least one case, the U.S. court of appeals upheld a lower court order allowing the police to seize an individual's e-mail records to search for evidence of a crime.

Q. *How do federal antiterrorism laws affect my Internet privacy?*

A. The USA Patriot Act, enacted just six weeks after the September 11 terrorist attacks, gives the U.S. Justice Department authority to install its DCS1000 Internet tracking device (formerly known as "Carnivore") at an Internet service provider if the government has probable cause to suspect cyberspace is being used to further terrorism. This state-of-the-art equipment can track all Internet activity, including e-mails, traveling through the ISP. The government says that with the use of filters law enforcement authorities can limit e-mail searches only to those communications permitted under a valid search warrant. However, civil rights groups and other opponents of the law say that the filtering software is not precise enough to limit surveillance to only those limited e-mails and that innocent cyberspace conversations are bound to be collected as an unintended result of the government's increased surveillance.

To illustrate the increased vigilance of the authorities, one need only look at the full name of the USA Patriot Act: the Uniting and Strengthening America by Providing Appropriate Tools Required to Intercept and Obstruct Terrorism Act. In addition, the Homeland Security Act of 2002 gives the federal government broad tracking and surveillance capabilities to thwart future acts of terrorism.

Q. How do I protect myself from suspect spam?

A. If you receive spam from a suspicious group, do not engage in conversation. Contact the Federal Trade Commission or tell the police about the communication immediately.

As discussed on page 348, you can avoid spam by being circumspect when it comes to giving out your e-mail address.

Q. I'm not a hacker, but what if I accidentally find myself on a computer site I have no business being on?

A. It is a federal crime to hack into, or illegally access, a computer system belonging to another person, company, or governmental agency. Federal, state, and local law enforcement have been cracking down on hackers in the aftermath of the September 11 attacks.

Agencies, companies, and individuals have turned to high-tech software to protect their computers against hackers. These software programs have been dubbed "firewalls" to illustrate the strength of their protection. Nevertheless, computer-savvy individuals have in many cases been able to stay one step ahead of these programs and have hacked into websites and computers of utilities and agencies.

It remains possible, though highly unlikely, for computer dabblers to find themselves inadvertently in areas of websites and on computers they have no business being on. If this blind luck should happen to you, one option is just to leave, perhaps by hitting the "back" button on your browser. Another is not to touch your computer but to contact a lawyer to help safeguard your rights as you attempt to inform the appropriate people (the operator of the site, law enforcement officials, etc.) of what occurred.

THE WORLD AT YOUR FINGERTIPS

- *The U.S. Justice Department has a website devoted to the discussion of Internet crime at www.usdoj.gov/criminal/cybercrime.*
- *The Computer Law Association helps link*

Internet users with legal experts. The CLA's site is at www.cla.org.

REMEMBER THIS

- *The law is unclear as to whether people have an expectation of privacy with regard to their e-mails. It's probably safest to assume that you have no privacy and act accordingly.*
- *Police are becoming more vigilant in their cyberspace investigations since the September 11 terrorist attacks.*
- *In the unlikely event that you accidentally hack into a secure website, exit the site immediately.*

CHILD PROTECTION AND THE INTERNET

The Internet has quickly become a valuable educational and research tool. At the click of a mouse, students can access information in seconds that it would have taken hours to find in a library just a generation ago. Young minds can let their imaginations soar as they visit websites covering virtually every subject.

The ease of Internet use, however, contains an enticing pitfall for young students. The ability to cut and paste information with ease can lead to plagiarism as youngsters find shortcuts to completing their homework and reports.

The technology also contains even greater dangers in the view of parents, caregivers, and lawmakers. Many websites concern subjects and contain images that are inappropriate for youngsters, such as pornography, violence, and gambling. To protect children, many parents and libraries have installed blocking software on their computers to prevent users from accessing these sites.

Online chat rooms that provide a forum for children to communicate with each other about common interests have proven to be fertile ground for pedophiles seeking to meet youngsters, according to law enforcement officials. The Federal Bureau of Investigation urges parents to be careful what sites their children visit, and what they say and receive online.

This section covers what every parent should know about protecting their children on the Internet.

Q. What is the legal situation regarding protecting young people who use the Internet?

A. Congress has taken steps over the past decade to protect children by outlawing the transmission of obscene, indecent, or offensive messages to anyone under age eighteen. Lawmakers have also denied federal funding to libraries that fail to install blocking software.

While the law clearly allows parents and caregivers to restrict Internet access to their children, the First Amendment right of free speech puts some constraints on the ability of Congress and public libraries to similarly safeguard children.

Q. How have courts ruled?

A. In the battle between Congress and the Constitution, the First Amendment has won some battles, but Congress has won the most recent one.

The Supreme Court in 1997 struck down provisions of the federal Communications Decency Act designed to protect children. These provisions outlawed the "knowing" transmission of "obscene or indecent" messages to recipients under age eighteen and knowingly sending or displaying a message "that, in context, depicts or describes, in terms patently offensive as measured by contemporary community standards, sexual or excretory activities or organs."

The Court ruled that the law's restrictions were too broad, and encroached on the constitutional rights of computer users.

"The general, undefined terms 'indecent' and 'patently offensive' cover large amounts of non-pornographic material with serious educational or other value," the Court said in *Reno v. American Civil Liberties Union.* "It [the law] may also extend to discussions about prison rape or safe sexual practices, artistic images that include nude subjects, and arguably the card catalogue of the Carnegie Library."

However, in a 2003 case, *United States v. American Library Association,* the Court ruled that the Children's Internet Protection Act, which provides that public libraries that receive federal assistance to provide Internet access must install software to block images that constitute obscenity or child pornography, does not induce public libraries to violate patrons' First Amendment rights and is a valid exercise of Congress's spending power. The Court held that Congress has wide latitude to attach conditions to the receipt of federal assistance to further its policy objectives.

According to the majority opinion, "a public library does not acquire Internet terminals in order to create a public forum for Web publishers to express themselves, any more than it collects books in order to provide a public forum for the authors of books to speak. It provides Internet access . . . for the same reasons it offers other library resources: to facilitate research, learning, and recreational pursuits by furnishing materials of requisite and appropriate quality."

Q. What can a parent do?

A. Concerned parents and caregivers should closely monitor what sites their children are accessing and consider the installation of blocking software. Parents can refuse to give their children their own Internet account, thereby making it more difficult for them to disguise what sites and chat rooms they have visited.

However, the FBI warns parents that children can access an online chat room even if they have no account at home. Children can get online at a friend's house or the library. In addition, most computers are preloaded with online software, and sex offenders can provide children with an online account to facilitate e-mail communication.

Parents should, therefore, speak with their child about the dangers of communicating with strangers online and spend time with their child while he or she is on the computer. In addition, computers should be kept in a common area of the house, where a parent can monitor use, and not in the sanctity of the child's bedroom.

Q. Are there stronger steps parents can take?

A. Most ISPs, such as MSN.com and AOL.com, have parental permission restrictions if you want to set them up, as do some browsers, such as Internet Explorer.

If more aggressive monitoring is in order, the FBI recommends that parents should maintain access to their child's online account and randomly check his or her e-mail. In addition, parents should ask what safeguards are being used on computers at the public library and at friends' homes.

Parents have warned their children for generations to "Beware of strangers," and this should be extended to people that children encounter online. Parents should instruct their children never to meet with a person they have met online or to post pictures of themselves on the Internet or in an online message to people they do not know. Children also should be told never to disclose their name, address, or telephone number online or respond to suggestive, obscene, belligerent, or harassing online messages.

Parental oversight will be difficult to enforce outside the home. However, parents have been waging the same battle for years with regard to their children's television viewing at friends' houses.

Q. What signs of trouble should parents look for?

A. Parents should become suspicious if their child spends a lot of time online, particularly at night. While pedophiles are online all the time, many have day jobs that keep them from their computers until the evening and early-morning hours.

Parents also should be alarmed if they find pornographic pictures on their child's computer. The FBI says that pedophiles will often send graphic images as a way to broach the subject of sex with children. You can run a search of the most common file formats for all pictures in your computer, such as .jpg and .gif, and list them as thumbnails to see what's there. You can also look in the history of visited sites (the **cache**) to find out which sites the child has visited most recently.

Children may also exhibit certain behavior when they are engaging in inappropriate conversations online. For example, they will turn the computer off or quickly change websites when a parent enters the room.

Q. What should a suspicious parent do?

A. The FBI recommends that parents warn their children of the dangers of sex offenders who use the Internet and, if appropriate, talk candidly about their suspicions. Parents should also review and monitor what sites their child is visiting and with whom he or she has communicated.

Q. What should a parent do if a child has received obscene photos or a sexual solicitation via e-mail?

A. The FBI advises parents to turn off the computer to preserve any evidence for law enforcement and then call the police, the FBI, and the National Center for Missing and Exploited Children. The center's website is at www.missingkids.com.

Q. How can a parent protect a Web-surfing child's privacy?

A. Federal law places restrictions on operators of websites and online services directed at children under thirteen. Under regulations issued by the Federal Trade Commission, the Children's Online Privacy Protection Rule, these operators must post clear and comprehensive privacy policies on their websites describing what they plan to do with information provided by children. The

FTC issued the rule under the Children's Online Privacy Protection Act.

Under the regulations, the operators also must provide notice to parents and obtain parental consent before collecting personal information from children. In addition, the regulations also require operators to provide parents access to their child's personal information and have it deleted if they wish. The regulations also bar operators from prohibiting a child's participation on the site unless he or she provides personal information beyond that reasonably necessary to allow the child to participate.

Q. On the subject of homework, how can a parent prevent children from plagiarizing?

A. Tell them that plagiarism is a form of stealing and, again, monitor the websites they visit.

Today's parents can remember being told in school that they should not simply copy what they read in the encyclopedia. Likewise, today's students must be told not to just cut and paste what they read during their online research.

But the advent of the Internet means that it has become much easier to plagiarize and correspondingly more inviting. Whereas parents would have had to actually retype what was printed on a page to plagiarize, their children can simply cut and paste the page electronically. In addition, prewritten (and well-written) reports are available for sale—and even for free—on many Internet sites, making academic theft and cheating accessible to children without even having to leave their desks.

Q. As for gambling, don't those websites check to make sure the gambler is of age?

A. Gambling websites are open twenty-four hours per day every day. Federal Trade Commission visits to more than one hundred gambling websites recently concluded that children could easily access them. Agency staff said that about 20 percent of the sites displayed no warning that underage gambling is illegal nationwide. On many other sites, the warnings were hard to find, the FTC said. In addition, the sites had no effective mechanism to block children from entering, the agency added.

To access these sites, often the only thing a child needs is a credit or debit card. Therefore, parents and caregivers trying to prevent their children from accessing these sites should sharply restrict their access to these cards. Parents should also warn their children about the hazards of gambling, including the fact that the odds are always with the house (or, in this case, the website) and they can lose their money, become addicted, and mess up their credit rating.

Q. Should parents also warn their kids against hacking?

A. Yes. It may be hard for many adults to accept, but children often have greater expertise than they do in using computers. Many children have displayed sufficient computer savvy to tap into computers that are not theirs.

In the 1990s, Boston teenagers hacked into a telephone company computer and shut it down, cutting off telephone service for about six hundred customers. The U.S. Secret Service investigated and found the culprits. The teenager who masterminded the hacking was ordered to pay the phone company $5,000, serve 250 hours of community service, surrender his computer, and

---

ⓘ USING TECHNOLOGY TO FIGHT PLAGIARISM

Schools from college level down have become wise to the ways of plagiarism-friendly Internet sites and have investigated and caught students who have bought reports rather than written their own. One website, Turnitin.com, enables educators to catch plagiarism in papers by comparing student submissions to billions of pages of content on the Internet.

serve two years' probation, during which time he was barred from using a computer with a modem.

The U.S. Justice Department urges parents and teachers to warn children that hacking is a federal offense that will be prosecuted.

THE WORLD AT YOUR FINGERTIPS

- *The Federal Bureau of Investigation has made its publication "A Parent's Guide to Internet Safety" available online at www. fbi.gov/publications/pguide/pguide.htm.*
- *The U.S. Department of Justice has a website devoted to teaching children how to act ethically online; you can access it at www.usdoj.gov/criminal/cybercrime/rules/ kidinternet.htm.*
- *To learn more about online plagiarism, visit the website run by the creators of Turnitin.com at www.plagiarism.org/ plagiarism.html.*
- *You can find out more about the Children's*

Online Privacy Act at www.ftc.gov/bcp/ conline/pubs/buspubs/coppa.htm.

REMEMBER THIS

- *The Internet is this generation's television.*
- *Responsibility for your children's online habits begins at home. If you give no structure there, expect them to create their own structure for the online world—perhaps one not in compliance with the laws of the land and social decorum.*
- *Parents can monitor their children's Internet use in the home and install blocking software to prevent them from accessing pornographic, violent, racist, and gambling sites.*
- *Parents have significantly less control outside the home.*
- *Several pieces of legislation designed to prevent children from accessing sites have been struck down by courts as violating the First Amendment.*

Automobiles

Every driver should have at least a basic knowledge of the implications of buying or leasing and operating a motor vehicle. This chapter covers everything about the law and automobiles—the initial contract, consumer protection, maintenance and inspection, traffic law, and insurance.

BUYING, RENTING, AND LEASING A CAR

So, you need a car. If you are going to buy a new or used car, you are about to make a major purchase and part with a substantial amount of hard-earned dollars. Even if you're leasing instead of buying, you're still looking at spending thousands of dollars. With all this money on the line, you'd better pay attention to the legal implications. Virtually all car sales are going to be governed by a contract you'll sign, as will all leases.

This section highlights the many laws that protect you in buying or leasing a car and gives guidance on the confusing world of vehicle financing.

Buying a New Car

Q. What information should an automobile advertisement include?

A. This is an area largely regulated by state laws, which vary from state to state. In some states, the ad must state the number available of that type of vehicle. Other items that may be required include price, dealer- and factory-installed options, and warranty terms. In addition, if the vehicle is "on sale," the ad should state the date on which the sale ends.

Q. What if the advertisement omits details?

A. If the dealer knows important facts about the vehicle, but fails to reveal them, the law may consider that a deceptive act. You may be able to cancel the deal and even recover damages in court. Clearing up the missing facts later does not erase the dealer's deceitful act. (For more information, see "Lemon Laws" on page 377.)

Q. Must a car contract be in writing?

A. Yes, for all but very inexpensive cars, according to the Statute of Frauds of the Uniform Commercial Code (UCC). The UCC, which is in effect in some form or another in every state but Louisiana, regulates sales of goods and securities; it governs many kinds of commercial transactions. This means that the UCC governs almost all auto transactions in the country. The UCC says any sale of goods of $500 or more must be in writing and signed by the party against whom enforcement is sought. If the contract is challenged, the courts will not be permitted to enforce it unless it is in writing.

⚠ BAIT-AND-SWITCH ADS

Bait-and-switch advertising is advertising for a vehicle that the dealer does not intend to sell. Usually, this is done to lure the unsuspecting customer toward buying an unadvertised, often higher-priced vehicle. The ad draws the customer into the showroom, but the advertised car is not available at that time or at the stated price.

If you suspect that you have been the victim of such advertising, contact the consumer protection division of your state attorney general's office. If state officials have received a number of reports about this kind of advertising, they may file a claim against the dealer on behalf of all of the duped customers. If they find that yours is an isolated incident, they may still help you pursue an individual claim. In either case, it may be possible to hold the dealer to providing the vehicle at the publicized price. See chapter 9, "Contracts and Consumer Law," for more on legal remedies for bait and switch.

Q. Who signs the contract?

A. Besides you, either an authorized salesperson or a supervisor or a manager signs it. Before you sign, make sure you understand and accept all the contract terms, because you'll probably have to abide by a contract you have signed, even if you have not read it. Read the contract carefully. Ask questions. Cross out blank spaces to avoid any additions after you sign. Make sure that all the dealer's promises appear in the contract. If the dealer makes a promise orally but doesn't put it in the contract, it's extremely unlikely you'll be able to enforce that promise. Do not sign until the contract satisfies you. The contract you sign binds you, and escaping from the contract is both difficult and expensive. You can find more information about contracts in chapter 9, "Contracts and Consumer Law."

Q. May I change a seller's preprinted contract?

A. If you do change terms, cross out the unwanted language, and write or type in the substitute terms. Both you and an authorized dealer representative should initial the changes. Handwritten or typed changes to both copies of a printed contract overrule printed terms.

Q. May I cancel the contract even after I sign it?

A. Read your contract carefully *before you sign* to review the cancellation provisions and to make sure that you understand what the contract means. If you cancel for no reason, you risk losing your deposit. The dealer also might file a lawsuit to recover lost profits, for time spent with you and on your car, and other damages.

You may be able to cancel the contract in some circumstances. For example, your state may have special provisions regarding contracts entered into by minors, and may give minors greater ability to cancel a contract. Most car dealers are aware that special rules may apply to car contracts involving minors, and they insist that the car be bought by, or in the name of, a financially responsible adult. Or if the car you buy is not what the dealer promised, the dealer may have breached its warranty. (See "Warranties and the

---

▶ **TERMS THE CONTRACT SHOULD INCLUDE**

The sales contract should describe the car and include the **vehicle identification number (VIN)**. You can find the VIN on the driver's side of the dashboard near the windshield. Make sure the contract also states

- whether the car is new, used, or has had a previous life as a demonstration vehicle, rental car, or taxicab;
- price terms consistent with your oral agreement;
- details on any trade-in you will supply, including mileage and the dollar amount credited;
- warranty terms (see "Warranties and the Uniform Commercial Code" on page 378 of this chapter); and
- financing terms, including price, deposit, trade-in allowance, annual percentage rate of interest (APR), and length of term.

In addition, you should insist on a cancellation provision that enables you to get your deposit back if you're the buyer.

Uniform Commercial Code" on page 378 in this chapter.) If so, then you might attempt to cancel the contract because of the breach.

Q. If I wind up in court in a contract dispute, may I offer information in addition to the contract?

A. Generally, under the **parol evidence rule**, courts look at the actual contract rather than at any information outside of that agreement that does not appear in that document. Courts typically focus on what are called the "four corners" of the document. The court generally assumes that both parties read and understood the contract before signing it, and will not consider evidence of any terms that were discussed before the contract was signed that vary or contradict the contract. However, you may be able to present evidence of an oral agreement made after the written agreement.

If you have legal problems over a contract, or if you are sued over a car contract, you should consult a lawyer.

Q. What if I want to add something after I sign the contract?

A. Ask the dealer to write a contract **addendum** (a supplement), or write it yourself. Both parties should sign it. Make sure that whoever signs for the seller has the legal power to do so. Mention the original contract in the addendum, state that everyone should consider the adden-

---

⚠ LOSING YOUR DEPOSIT

If you decide to cancel the contract, you could lose your deposit. Your state may allow you to get a refund of your deposit in limited circumstances—for example, if you cancel the contract before a dealer representative signed the contract. In some states, you may be able to get a refund if you cannot get financing to buy the car.

---

dum an inseparable part of the original contract, and state that the addendum overrides any inconsistent terms in the two documents. This will help you avoid the parol evidence rule discussed above.

Q. What if I do not have enough cash to buy my new car, even after my trade-in?

A. Then you need financing. Banks, credit unions, loan companies, and car dealers are all potential funding sources. Interest rates will vary among these options. Shop around for the best deal by comparing the various loan terms and annual percentage rates (APRs). The APR determines the actual interest you will have to pay on the unpaid balance of the loan, and may depend partially on your credit history. For more information on comparing terms and APRs, see chapter 7, "Consumer Credit."

Q. What information must the creditor give me?

A. The **creditor** (the person or institution to whom you will owe money) must tell you

1. the APR (this must be conspicuous—for example, printed in red or in much larger type than the rest of the document);
2. the method by which the creditor sets the finance charge;
3. the balance on which the creditor computes the finance charge;
4. the dollar amount of the finance charge (this must also be conspicuous);
5. the amount to be financed (the loan);
6. the total dollar amount that will be paid (loan plus finance charge); and
7. the number, amount, and due dates of payments.

Q. What if the creditor does not comply with Truth in Lending Act?

A. If a creditor fails to disclose timely information as required under Truth in Lending Act (TILA), gives you inaccurate information, or breaches the

TILA in some other way, you should inform the proper federal enforcement agency. You may also bring a lawsuit for actual damages (any money loss you suffer). You may also sue for the greater of twice the finance charge or $100. However, the most you can recover, even if the finance charge is high, is $1,000. If you win the lawsuit, the law also entitles you to court costs and lawyer's fees.

Under some state laws, a violation of TILA is an unfair or deceptive act or practice, and other remedies may be available. Chapter 7, "Consumer Credit," provides detailed information on TILA.

Q. What happens if I can't pay my finance payments?

A. You may lose your car if you finance the purchase and you do not make your car payments when they become due. The creditor is then permitted to repossess your car.

ⓘ MAKING SURE A CREDITOR TREATS YOU RIGHT

The Truth in Lending Act (TILA) is a federal law that requires creditors to disclose to consumers the costs and conditions of credit. Congress passed it in 1969 to ensure that consumers get enough facts to enable them to make an informed decision about financing. TILA applies to consumers who seek credit for money, property, or personal, family, or household purposes. (TILA does not cover business, commercial, and agricultural credit.)

Creditors—both people and organizations—who regularly extend consumer credit that requires more than four installment payments are subject to the act, as are creditors who require (or may require) a finance charge.

Q. So if I don't pay, can the secured creditor just come and take my car away?

A. Afraid so. The only limitation on automobile repossessions is that the repossessor must do it without breaching the peace. In many states, the creditor does not even have to sue you or tell you about the default before reclaiming the vehicle.

Q. What is a breach of the peace?

A. A **breach of the peace** generally is any act likely to produce disorder or violence, such as an unauthorized entry into your home.

Q. What happens after the repossession?

A. If this happens to you, you should consult a lawyer in your state to advise you of your rights under the law. As a general rule, the creditor (the entity that financed the car in exchange for a legal interest in the car) can resell the car. However, before that happens, you may have the right of **redemption,** or, in other words, the right to buy back the car (in legal terms, **redeem the collateral**).

Q. How does redemption work?

A. As a general rule, you (the debtor) must pay the entire balance due, plus any repossession costs and other reasonable charges. Watch out

---

⚠ THE RIGHT TO REPOSSESSION

When you buy a car on credit, you may have to give the creditor rights in your property (the car) that have priority over the rights of your other creditors. When you are loaned the money, you sign a **security agreement,** which gives the creditor a **security interest** in your car (the **collateral**). You are agreeing to give the creditor a lien on the car. If you don't pay, the creditor may try to get the car back and sell it to satisfy your debt.

for consumer credit contracts containing acceleration clauses. These force you to pay the entire outstanding debt, not just the amount of overdue payments. If default and repossession have already occurred, you probably don't have enough money to pay the entire balance. Redemption rarely takes place.

Q. How does the sale take place?

A. The creditor can sell the car to satisfy the debt. The sale has to be **commercially reasonable,** and different states may give that term different meanings. Some states may require the creditor to get a court's permission before holding a sale. The rules may vary from state to state, but you should have notice of the time, place, and manner of the sale. If the sale is public, you have the right to participate by putting in a bid on the car.

If the sale does not bring in enough money to pay off the car debt and related expenses, you can be held responsible for the rest of the debt. If the sale brings in more money than the debt owed and permitted expenses, the creditor selling the car should give the extra money to you.

Q. What else can the creditor do with the car?

A. The creditor may keep the car to satisfy the debt fully. The law refers to this as **strict foreclo-**sure. There is no duty to return excess money in a strict foreclosure. Creditors seldom use it, because dealers want to sell, not keep, cars.

Buying a Used Car

Q. Should I buy from a dealer or a private seller?

A. Go with the seller who gives you the best deal and with whom you are most comfortable. Some experts believe you may be better off buying from a private seller. They think a private seller will give you a more accurate description of the car's faults based on personal knowledge, and a lower price. Private sellers, however, seldom give warranties, which dealers sometimes offer. (See "Warranties and the Uniform Commercial Code" on page 378 in this chapter.) Also, some states have regulations governing used car sales that may apply only to dealers.

Q. Do I need a written contract if I buy from a private seller?

A. It is a good idea to put any car-buying agreement in writing. As a general rule, you should have a written contract if the price is more than $500. Depending on the law of your state and the amount of money at stake, the court might not be able to enforce a contract that is not in writing.

⚠ THE RISK OF LOSS

After you have signed the contract to buy the car, you should be very clear about whether the vehicle is insured and when your insurance covers the car. Under the Uniform Commercial Code (UCC), if the seller is a merchant (for example, a car dealer), the risk of loss passes to buyers when they receive the car. A merchant seller who keeps physical possession may bear the risk of loss long after the title has passed and after the dealer has received payment. If the seller is not a merchant, as in a private sale of a used car, the risk passes to the buyer on tender of delivery. **Tender of delivery** usually occurs when the seller actually tries to deliver the car, or makes the vehicle available for pickup.

A sales contract that specifies when the risk of loss passes will override the standard UCC provision. That is another reason why you need to read the contracts concerning your car purchase carefully, and be sure that you understand what any contract says before you sign it.

WHAT IS A USED VEHICLE?

A used vehicle is a vehicle that was driven farther than the distance necessary to deliver a new car to the dealer or to test-drive it.

Q. Do I need to get anything else in writing?

A. You should have a **bill of sale**. Many states require you to present a bill of sale to register your car. A bill of sale also may serve as a receipt. The bill of sale should contain the following:

- The date of the sale
- The year, make, and model of the car
- The vehicle identification number (VIN)
- The odometer reading
- The amount paid for the car, and the form in which it was made (cash, check, etc.)
- The buyer's and seller's names, addresses, and phone numbers

The seller should sign and date the bill of sale, and both you and the seller should get a copy.

ⓘ SPECIAL RULES FOR USED CAR DEALERS

The Federal Trade Commission has issued a **Used Car Rule** for dealers. Under the rule, **dealers** are those who sell six or more used cars in a twelve-month period. The rule forbids used car dealers from misrepresenting the mechanical condition of a used car or any warranty terms. Used car dealers must also provide you with the terms of any written warranty they provide, and must post a Buyer's Guide on the side window of the car.

Q. How much information should the seller give to the buyer?

A. If possible, the seller should provide the buyer with the car's complete service records and other accurate information. No seller—whether a dealer or not—should lie about the car. If the buyer is disappointed because it is not as described or does not perform as it was supposed to, the buyer may have a breach of warranty action against a deceptive seller.

Q. Does the seller have to tell the buyer the car's mileage?

A. Yes, federal law entitles the buyer of a used car to receive a mileage disclosure statement from the seller, even if the seller is not a dealer. On request, the seller must give a signed written statement to the buyer that provides the odometer reading at the time of transfer. The statement

▶ WHAT THE BUYER'S GUIDE HAS TO SAY

The Buyer's Guide contains the following information about the car:

- Whether the car comes with a warranty. If there is a warranty, the specific coverage must be outlined.
- Whether the vehicle comes with implied warranties only, or is sold as is, that is, with no warranties at all.
- A statement that you should request an inspection by an independent mechanic before you buy.
- A statement that you should get all promises in writing.
- A list of some of the major problems that may occur in any car.

If you do buy a used car from a dealer, you are entitled to receive a copy of the actual Buyer's Guide that was posted in your car.

> ### ⚠ INSPECT BEFORE YOU BUY
>
> You should take the car to a mechanic for an inspection before you buy it. If the seller, whether a dealer or a private party, will not allow your mechanic to inspect the car, do not buy it unless it is such a good deal that you will not mind paying for car repairs later.

also should certify the odometer's accuracy, to the seller's knowledge. If the seller knows the odometer is incorrect, the seller must admit it. Refusal to provide such a statement, or illegally tampering with the odometer, exposes the seller to stiff penalties.

Q. Are there other ways to find out about a car's history?

A. Yes. Websites such as www.autocheck.com and www.carfax.com make it easy to find services that will provide you with detailed repair, odometer, and histories for many used cars on the market. The car's vehicle identification number (VIN) is the key to getting details about a car's history, and search services will ask for this number to do a search.

You should confront the seller if the vehicle history report does not match what the seller told you about the car.

Q. May I get out of a contract to sell my used car?

A. The same contract laws that govern a new car purchase also cover a used car purchase. Again, whether you can get out of a contract to sell your car depends on the laws of your state, the terms of the contract, and how far along the contract process has progressed.

Q. May a court force me to sell my car to a buyer after I have decided I do not want to sell?

A. It depends on the circumstances. Courts try to "leave the parties as they find them," and usu-

ally will not force a buyer to make a purchase or a seller to sell an item. However, depending on the situation, a court might order the seller to go through with the contract. This is called specific performance of the contract.

Car Leasing and Renting

Q. What do I need to rent or to lease a car?

A. You must have a valid driver's license. You may be required to show a good driving record. In several states, major car rental companies have electronic links to government computers and obtain driver records (motor vehicle reports) when someone wants to rent a car. They may refuse a rental contract if a person has accidents or too many violations on his or her record.

Some major rental and leasing companies require that customers have a major credit card and be at least eighteen years old; some consider only credit card holders age twenty-five or older. The company may waive the age requirement if you have an account number in your name through a motor club or other association, or if you have a rental account through your business. You must sign a contract when you rent or lease a car.

Q. How does leasing differ from renting?

A. A lease is essentially a long-term rental. Leases usually have a one-year minimum. You may rent a car for shorter periods, just a day or a week.

> ### ⚠ READ THE FINE PRINT
>
> A car leasing or rental contract is a legal contract. As with any other contract, make sure that you read and understand the terms of the contract before you sign the papers.

Q. Is it better to lease a car or buy a car?

A. Whether it is better to lease or buy a car depends on many factors, such as the following:

- A car lease should mean lower monthly payments. Your installment payment for a leased car depends on the purchase price minus the car's estimated value at the end of the lease term. If you're buying a car, on the other hand, your installment payment will depend on the full value of the car.
- Leasing usually avoids a down payment and sales tax. There also may be tax advantages if you lease mainly for business use.
- On the other hand, a leased car does not give you any equity. Buying a car on credit does.
- When your lease is up, you must return the car.

Q. What is a "closed-end" lease?

A. Under the **closed-end lease contract,** sometimes called a **walkaway lease,** the car's value when you return it does not matter unless you have put extreme wear on the car. You return the car at the end of the term and walk away. Payments are higher than under an open-end lease because the **lessor** (the person or company leasing the car to you) takes the risk on the car's future worth.

Q. What is an "open-end" lease?

A. An **open-end lease** involves lower payments. However, you gamble that the car will be worth a stated price, the **estimated residual value,** at the end of the lease. If the car's appraised value at the end of the term equals or exceeds the specified residual value, you owe nothing. You may receive a refund of any excess value, if your contract provides for a refund. The downside: If the car is worth less at the end of the term, you pay some or all of the difference, often called an **end-of-lease payment**.

Q. How much does a lease cost?

A. The cost of a lease depends upon the specific terms of the contract. Make sure that you understand the terms of your contract, and what the contract says about your responsibilities and the responsibilities of the lessor, including who pays for things like taxes, fees, repairs, and insurance.

You probably will have to pay a security deposit and lease fee for the first month and perhaps the last month as well. You may have to pay an initial **capitalized cost reduction.** This is similar to a down payment when you buy a car. By paying a large amount up front, you could, in effect, reduce your monthly payments. But by doing this, you lose one of the advantages of leasing: lower up-front costs. Other expenses may include sales tax and title and license fees, though the lessor may pay them. A lease may include insurance. If not, you must provide your own. You might have to pay for repairs and maintenance after any warranty period expires, unless the lessor agrees to pay in your contract. At the end of the lease term, you may have to pay an excess mileage cost if you have a closed-end lease. (Under an open-end lease, the final appraised value of the car will reflect any excess mileage.) Excessive wear and tear also may cost you.

Q. May I renew or extend my lease at the end of the term?

A. Yes, if your lease contained this option or you negotiated for it. Such an option may reduce your initial costs.

Q. May I get out of my lease early?

A. You have signed a binding contract that obligates you to make payments for a stated term. However, your contract may contain an early termination clause. This usually requires a minimum number of monthly payments before you may cancel, and may require you to pay a penalty.

Q. What is a purchase option?

A. A purchase option allows you to buy the car when your lease term ends. The lessor must state the purchase price or the basis for setting this price in the initial lease contract. Purchase options are more common in open-end leases than in closed-end leases.

Q. What should my car rental contract include?

A. As an absolute minimum, it should list the base rate for the rental car, any extra fees, and the length of the rental period.

Q. What extra fees could there be?

A. The rental company might offer you the collision damage waiver (CDW) option. The rental company covers damage to your rented car if you accept the CDW. However, coverage does not include personal injuries or personal property damage. Before accepting this expensive option, make sure your own automobile, medical, and homeowner's insurance policies do not already protect you in an accident involving a rented car. If traveling on business, your company's insurance policy might cover you. Check with your credit card company to see if using the card to rent a car comes with any insurance benefits, and find out what they are.

Other additional fees might include drop-off fees, if you pick up and return the car in different locations. There may also be fuel charges, extra mileage fees, and fees for renting equipment like child safety seats or ski racks.

THE WORLD AT YOUR FINGERTIPS

- *Many state government websites provide consumer information about buying a car. You can access your state government website, and various agencies and departments, at www.statelocalgov.net.*
- *The Federal Trade Commission is a useful resource for information about buying, financing, or selling a car. You can find a consumer guide with information about buying a new or used car at www.ftc.gov/ bcp/conline/edcams/automobiles/index.html.*
- *The National Automobile Dealers Association provides consumers with purchase information on a wide variety of vehicles at www.nadaguides.com.*

- *The State of California Department of Consumer Affairs has a helpful website for consumers who want to understand more about vehicle leases at www.dca.ca.gov/ legal/l-6.html.*
- *You can find more information for consumers on vehicle leases at www.leaseguide. com.*

REMEMBER THIS

- *State laws and some federal laws protect you when buying a car. Remember that state laws vary from state to state.*
- *If you are buying a used car, you should give the car a good going-over or pay for a professional inspection before you open your wallet. It may save you money or help you negotiate a contract if you detect problems that can be repaired before purchase.*
- *Contracts are extremely important. Be sure that you read and understand any contract before you sign on the dotted line. This goes for the contract that covers the purchase of the car as well as any contract that deals with how you pay for the car, and any contract that deals with insurance for the car.*
- *If you default on your finance payments, your car may be repossessed. You can find more information about the repossession process in chapter 7, "Consumer Credit."*
- *It's important to understand the differences between open-end and closed-end leases, as well as to understand the many provisions of car-leasing contracts, such as the terms on termination, option to renew, and purchase option. The time to negotiate is before you sign.*

CONSUMER PROTECTIONS

You have a right to know what you're buying, and unfair and deceptive practices laws exist in every state to protect consumers when they're making a purchase. If a seller makes misleading statements about a car and you buy the car because of those statements, you may have a case if something goes wrong.

This section covers all the ways in which you can protect yourself when you purchase a motor vehicle. Lemon laws exist to protect consumers who purchase new cars for personal, family, or household use. Depending on the law in your state, you might be able to get a replacement car or a refund if your new car is so defective that it is beyond satisfactory repair by the dealer. You must, however, give the dealer a reasonable opportunity to repair the car. Another important protection is the car warranty, which dealers offer with the purchase of many new and used cars. Buying a car is a pretty big investment, so it's a huge benefit to have a car warranty in case something goes wrong. Even if you don't have a warranty from the seller, state law may protect you if something goes wrong with your car. Car recalls may also protect you against auto defects and provide a way to correct problems.

Unfair and Deceptive Acts and Practices

Q. The dealer told me the car was "a great little runabout." It's had to have several repairs in the months since I bought it, so can I sue the seller for making a misleading statement?

A. The seller is, obviously, trying to sell you a car, so it is inevitable that he or she is going to attempt to talk up the car. Many general statements that the seller makes are mere puffery or bluster, and you should take everything the seller says with a pinch of salt. Sales talk probably doesn't amount to misleading or deceptive conduct.

Q. Must an unfair or deceptive act be intentional?

A. No. In most states, the seller does not even have to know about the deception. Rather, the court considers the effect that the seller's conduct might possibly have on the general public or on the people to whom the seller advertised the product.

Q. What must I do in order to use an unfair and deceptive practices statute?

A. If you think that you are the victim of an unfair or deceptive act or practice, you should consult a lawyer who can advise you of your rights under the law. There are time limits that apply when taking action to protect your rights, includ-

---

▶ **HOW TO SPOT UNFAIR OR DECEPTIVE BEHAVIOR**

Each state's unfair or deceptive practices act has different definitions of unfair and deceptive practices. The most common violations include

- hiding dangerous defects;
- not revealing that the dealer advertised the car at a lower price;
- odometer tampering;
- failing to reveal that the dealer is charging excessive preparation costs; and
- withholding facts about the car's previous use—for example, as a racing car.

Generally, a dealer's failure to disclose any important facts about the car, or an attempt to make such facts hard to see, is illegal.

ing the filing of a lawsuit, so you should not delay in seeking help with your legal problem.

Your state may require that you make a written demand for relief before you sue, and the law may allow the seller one last chance to make good.

If you have to sue, many states require proof of injury before you may recover. Loss of money or property is enough to prove this. You should also be able to show that the seller's actions actually caused the injury by showing that you bought the car because of the seller's unfair or deceptive act.

Q. What happens if I win?

A. Many states permit you to recover double or triple damages, as well as lawyer's fees, in unfair and deceptive practices cases. The purpose of these harsh penalties is to discourage sellers from committing unfair or deceptive acts in the future.

Lemon Laws

Q. What's a lemon?

A. States vary in how they define a lemon. As a general rule, a lemon is a car that continues to have a defect that substantially restricts its use, safety, or value, even after reasonable efforts to repair it. There may be specific legal rules concerning how many repair attempts you must make over a period of time for the car to qualify as a lemon.

Q. What must I do to make lemon laws work for me?

A. First, you must notify the manufacturer and, in some states, the dealer about the defect. Keep a copy of every repair receipt or service receipt. These receipts record that the required number of repair attempts has been made, and can be especially important if your car's defect had to be repaired at another garage or in another city because it was physically impossible to drive the car back to the seller's repair location.

Most states require that you go through an arbitration procedure before you can get a replacement or refund. Some states sponsor arbitration programs, which may be more objective than those run by manufacturers. Arbitration is usually free, and results often are binding only on the manufacturer; if you don't like the result, you can probably still take the manufacturer to court, depending on the rules that apply to the arbitration proceeding.

Some states require arbitration only if the manufacturer refuses to give you a satisfactory replacement or a refund. You also may have the option of bypassing arbitration and going directly to court.

If you successfully pursue a lemon law claim, you may get a refund of what you paid for the car, as well as reimbursement for things like taxes, registration fees, and finance charges. If you choose, you may get a replacement car. Be sure that it is of comparable value to the lemon it is replacing, and that it satisfies you completely.

Q. Do lemon laws cover used cars?

A. That depends on the state law that applies to your car purchase. A growing number of states apply lemon laws to used cars, and in some states lemon laws may apply to car sales by both dealers and private sellers. Sometimes a state's lemon laws are related to state law regarding safety inspection stickers. (See "Inspections" on page 383.)

Q. What if the used car I just bought fails inspection?

A. Depending on the state safety inspection sticker law that applies to the used car you buy, you may have certain legal rights if the used car you just bought fails the inspection. These safety sticker laws usually protect you if two conditions are met. First, the car must fail inspection within a certain period from the date of sale. Second, the repair costs must exceed a stated percentage of the purchase price. Then you may have the right to cancel the deal within a certain period. You will probably have to notify the seller in writing of your intention to cancel, including your reasons. You must return the car to the place of sale, even if it requires towing. If the seller offers to make repairs, you can decide whether to accept the seller's offer or get your money back. Again, all of these details may vary, depending on the state law that covers your used car deal.

Q. What if the car passes the safety inspection but still turns out to be a lemon (by requiring costly repairs or repeated repair attempts for the same problem)?

A. A car might pass the safety inspection and still be a lemon. Some state laws define "lemon" for used cars the same way they do for new cars: by using a formula of repair attempts/time spent in the shop. These laws protect buyers of used lemons in much the same way as they protect buyers of new lemons.

Q. May I drive the car while we are deciding whether it is a lemon?

A. Yes, you may drive the car (if it is drivable), but be aware that if the car does indeed turn out to be a lemon, the law usually allows the seller to deduct a certain amount from your refund based on the miles you have driven. This applies to both new and used car sales.

Warranties and the Uniform Commercial Code

Q. What is a warranty?

A. A warranty is a guarantee of the product's quality and performance. A warranty may be written or oral. The Uniform Commercial Code (UCC) provides for three kinds of warranties given by a car seller: an express warranty, an implied warranty of merchantability, and an implied warranty of fitness for a particular purpose. A seller may also sell a car "as is," which means it is not covered by any warranties.

Q. What creates an express warranty?

A. Whenever a seller gives any description, makes any declaration of fact, or makes any promise on which the buyer relies when deciding to make the purchase, the seller creates an express warranty. A seller may create an express warranty orally, in writing, or through an advertisement.

▶ OTHER LAWS THAT PROTECT CAR BUYERS

A number of statutes besides lemon laws protect car buyers, including:

- The federal Anti-Tampering Odometer Law, which prohibits acts that falsify odometer mileage readings.
- The federal Used Car Law, which requires that dealers post Buyer's Guides on used cars.
- The federal Automobile Information Disclosure Act, which requires manufacturers and importers of new cars to affix a sticker, called the Monroney label, on the windshield or side window of the car. The Monroney label lists the base price of the car; the options installed by the manufacturer, along with their suggested retail prices; how much the manufacturer has charged for transportation; and the car's fuel economy (miles per gallon). Only the buyer is allowed to remove the Monroney label.

Every state has enacted laws against unfair and deceptive acts and practices, which are a strong source of protection for buyers of new or used cars.

Q. What about the seller's personal opinion of the car?

A. An opinion or recommendation does not form an express warranty. Sales talk—for example, "This car runs like a dream"—will not create an express warranty. However, statements such as "This car needs no repairs," or "This car has a V-8 engine," will create an express warranty.

Q. What creates an implied warranty of merchantability?

A. An implied warranty of merchantability applies automatically if the seller is a merchant, such as a car dealer. The implied warranty of merchantability is a representation that the car will do what it is supposed to do. The **quality guaranty** means that the car should possess that level of quality needed to pass without objection in the trade; and the **fitness guaranty** means that the car should serve the buyer's ordinary purposes.

Most people agree that the implied warranty of merchantability is part of a new car purchase. All states impose implied warranties for used cars bought from dealers, unless the warranty is disclaimed specifically, in writing, by words like "as is" or "with all faults."

Note that implied warranties may have only limited duration.

Q. How is the implied warranty of fitness for a particular purpose created?

A. Suppose that you tell the seller that you need the vehicle for a special purpose, such as towing a trailer, and the seller recommends a specific vehicle. You buy it, relying on the seller's skill or judgment. This creates an implied warranty of fitness for a particular purpose that the vehicle can do what you told the dealer you needed it to do.

Q. What is the difference between a limited warranty and a full warranty?

A. A full warranty provides for a refund or free replacement part, including installation, if the dealer cannot fix a car or a part after a reasonable number of attempts. A dealer must replace the car or the part within a reasonable time. A full warranty applies to anyone who owns the car during the warranty period.

A limited warranty is any kind of warranty that is not a full warranty. At least one of the above promises is missing. Most car dealers do not give full warranties on the entire car, but may do so on a specific part, such as the battery. Most used car warranties are limited.

Q. What if I bought my car as is?

A. If you bought a car as is, it means that you accepted it with all its faults. Any post-sale defects are your problem. A car may be sold as is through a dealer or a private person. The implied warranty of merchantability does not automatically arise in as-is purchases.

Some states do not permit as-is sales for used cars.

Q. Do sellers have to offer a warranty with every car they sell?

A. Not necessarily. A seller may disclaim or change warranties. Obvious language that mentions merchantability may exclude or modify the implied warranty of merchantability. And an obvious disclaimer in writing may exclude the implied warranty of fitness for a particular purpose. Language such as "sold as is" cancels implied warranties. If the seller has given you an express warranty, however, courts will not uphold any attempted disclaimer that is inconsistent with or which cancels the express warranty.

⚠ AS-IS SALES OF USED CARS

When buying a used car, you should look out for whether the sale is as is or not. All states provide for implied warranties for used cars bought from dealers, unless the warranty is disclaimed specifically, in writing, by the words "sold as is" or "sold with all faults."

Q. *What if the seller gives me express and implied warranties that are inconsistent?*

A. According to the Uniform Commercial Code, the parties' "mutual intention" decides which warranty takes priority. If there is no way to decide this, the following rules determine priority:

1. Specific or technical language usually wins over descriptive language that is inconsistent and general.
2. Express warranties override inconsistent implied warranties of merchantability.
3. Implied warranties of fitness for a particular purpose survive other inconsistent warranties.

Q. *What are my options if the seller will not honor its warranties?*

A. If you discover the defect within a short period of time after the purchase (one or two weeks), you may be able to **reject the car.** You must give the seller specific information about what is wrong. You need only show that the car does not conform to the contract; the defect need not be major. If you want to reject the car, you should behave as if you are no longer the owner and not drive it, except to return it. You may hold the car for the seller to reclaim, or you may return it yourself. The advantage of rejecting the car is that you are in effect canceling the deal—you no longer have to worry about it or its warranties, though in practical terms you might have to wait a while to get back any deposit you may have made.

Unfortunately, sometimes the law regards just driving the car off the dealer's lot as acceptance, as long as you had a chance to inspect the car—even if you do not discover the defect for some time. Acceptance may also occur if you take possession of the car despite knowing about its defects. Acceptance does not mean that the seller no longer has to honor its warranties, but rather that you'll have to try to enforce them through negotiation, threat of suit, or actually filing suit.

Q. *What may I do if I have accepted a car that proves to be defective?*

A. Once you have accepted the car, you must continue to make your car payments; for the time being, at least, you are considered the car's owner and are responsible for its costs. (You may be able to get your money back later.) You may not reject a car that you've already accepted, unless you accepted it on the assumption that the seller would repair the defect within a reasonable period.

ⓘ YOUR WARRANTY RIGHTS: THE MAGNUSON-MOSS WARRANTY ACT

The Magnuson-Moss Warranty Act is a federal law that applies to all cars manufactured after 1975. If you are buying the car from a dealer and the warranty is in writing, the law gives you the right to see the car's warranty before you buy. The warranty information is more detailed than the Buyer's Guide, and includes an explanation of how to obtain warranty service. Any written warranty must have a conspicuous label saying whether the warranty is limited or full. In addition, if a written warranty is given, then implied warranties may not be disclaimed. The law also creates remedies for breach of warranty, including the right to sue for breach of express warranties, implied warranties, or a service contract. If you win, you can recover your lawyer's fees and your court costs.

Careful—this law does not apply to as-is sales, or to cars bought from private sellers.

However, you may be able to revoke your acceptance. You must give the seller notice of the defect, and show that it substantially impairs the value of the car to you. **Revocation** involves a higher standard than rejection. Generally, the defect will have to be major to allow revocation. After revoking acceptance, you must act as if you have rejected the car. Leave the car in your driveway until the seller reclaims it, or return it yourself.

Q. May I get my money back if I reject the car or revoke acceptance?

A. You should be able to recover your money. If your written demand for a refund is denied, you will have to sue the seller. The seller has the right to deduct an amount per mile driven from your refund. If your rejection is found to be wrongful, the seller may recover damages against you.

Q. May I simply use lemon laws and consumer protection statutes instead of warranties?

A. You may use any of these options. But note that there are differences among these laws, and that they may provide for different kinds of remedies. If you are in the position of taking legal action against a seller, consult a lawyer about what options you have under federal and state law.

If you can prove that the seller engaged in fraud or deception, you may be able to take advantage of your state's laws concerning unfair or deceptive acts and practices. If the car truly is a lemon, you may have options under your state's lemon law. Keep all of your papers concerning the car, including records and receipts.

Recalls

Q. What is the purpose of the recall system?

A. The recall system is designed to notify car owners about automobile defects.

Q. What defects does the recall process include?

A. Generally, recalls concern defects that affect the car's safety, cause the car to fall below federal safety standards, or both, and are common to a particular type of car or equipment. The defect can be in performance, construction, components, or materials found in the car or in related equipment, such as child safety seats.

⚠ WATCH OUT FOR SECRET WARRANTIES

A **secret warranty** develops when a manufacturer knows that many cars have the same problem and tells dealers to charge customers to repair the problem unless the customer complains. A secret warranty is not really a warranty at all—it is more like a deceptive practice in that it represents a manufacturer's unpublicized policy about making repairs to problem cars. Unlike a recall (see the discussion beginning above), the manufacturer is not required to notify owners of the problem. A secret warranty hides what the manufacturer knows about the defect and allows the manufacturer to make money from unsuspecting consumers who do not complain.

If you suspect that a warranty should have covered your car repair or that the defect is widespread, complain to the dealer. Perhaps the dealer will fix your car without charging you. Follow up with a complaint to the consumer protection division of your state attorney general's office. If government officials find that a secret warranty exists, the manufacturer may be required to notify owners, to pay for repairs, and to reimburse those owners who have already paid to fix the problem.

Q. How does the recall process begin?

A. A manufacturer may issue a recall in response to owner complaints. The National Highway Traffic Safety Administration (NHTSA) influences the recall process, and orders many recalls. The NHTSA fields safety-related complaints through letters and its toll-free telephone hot line. When the NHTSA registers enough complaints, NHTSA engineers perform an engineering analysis. Then the NHTSA engineers contact the automobile's manufacturer. The manufacturer must either remedy the defect or launch its own defect investigation.

Q. How does the automobile's manufacturer conduct a defect investigation?

A. The investigation begins with a press release, then the manufacturer creates a public file to collect comments and information. If the information confirms the defect and the manufacturer declines to recall the vehicle voluntarily, engineers then recommend an initial determination of a safety defect to the NHTSA administrator. If approved, there is a public hearing and the manufacturer receives notice of the basis for the agency's finding. Then the NHTSA decides if a final defect determination and recall is proper. Occasionally, the NHTSA administrator seeks the transportation secretary's approval before ordering a recall.

Q. What happens if the NHTSA orders a recall?

A. Once the recall campaign begins, the NHTSA assigns a campaign number and file. During the campaign's first six quarters (year and a half), the manufacturer must report its completion rate based on the number of vehicles actually repaired. The NHTSA may verify these figures.

The manufacturer may challenge the recall in court, but if its case fails, it faces a huge fine.

Q. How effective are recall campaigns?

A. Usually about 60 percent of the vehicles targeted by the recall receive repairs.

Q. Who pays for the recall—the automobile's manufacturer or the owners?

A. If the first buyer bought the car less than eight years ago, then the manufacturer must remedy the defect for free.

Q. What must the manufacturer do?

A. The manufacturer has the option of repairing the defect, replacing the car, or refunding the purchase price. If the manufacturer chooses to repair the defect, it must do so within a reasonable time. If the manufacturer does not opt to repair the defect, the manufacturer may choose to replace the vehicle or refund the purchase price. When refunding the purchase price, a manufacturer may deduct a certain amount for depreciation (loss in value).

THE WORLD AT YOUR FINGERTIPS

- *The Better Business Bureau offers great information about automobile-related complaints, particularly regarding warranties, at www.bbb.org.*

- *The Consumer Federation of America has online and printed material dealing with auto safety, consumer protection for motorists, and insurance. Contact them at www.consumerfed.org.*

- *FindLaw provides links to several different sources of information on lemon laws, car repair, and what to expect when making a claim at public.findlaw.com/lemon.*

- *You can find a private website with extensive information about lemon laws, including a state-by-state listing of such laws, at www.autopedia.com/html/HotLinks_ Lemon.html.*

- *If your state's department of motor vehicles sponsors a website, this might be an excellent resource for more information about warranties, repairs, odometer disclosure, lemon laws, and other topics. The Califor-*

nia DMV website is a good example; check it out at www.dmv.ca.gov.

- *The National Highway Traffic Safety Administration (NHTSA) provides much useful online and printed information on auto safety, car recalls, and defect investigations. You also can report safety-related defects. The home page also has a link to a search engine for vehicles subject to recalls at www.nhtsa.dot.gov.*

- *Ralph Nader's consumer protection organization is the Center for Auto Safety. Its website, www.autosafety.org, provides online information on automobile defects for various models of cars, warranties, secret warranties, and many other topics.*

- *For information about particular used cars you are thinking of buying, access www.autotrader.com or www.carfax.com; for general tips, offices of consumer protection often have good information posted online. A good example from New York City can be found at www.nyc.gov/html/dca/html/used_car.html.*

REMEMBER THIS

- *State protections against unfair and deceptive acts and practices may provide a remedy if you think that a car dealer has illegally crossed the line between bluster and misrepresentation.*

- *Lemon laws may offer you protection if your new car does not run despite repeated efforts at repair.*

- *Your car may be covered by an express warranty or by implied warranties, depending on the circumstances surrounding the purchase and the applicable law. If you bought the car "as is" or "with all faults," the usual implied warranties do not apply.*

- *If the seller will not honor its warranties,*

you can try to reject the car or revoke your acceptance of it.

- *If a recall is issued on your vehicle, you should be able to get your car repaired or replaced within a reasonable time.*

INSPECTIONS AND REPAIRS

One way that states try to see that vehicles meet minimum safety standards is by imposing an inspection sticker requirement. Safety sticker requirements and inspection requirements vary from state to state. One thing you can be certain of is that at some stage you will need to make repairs on your car. You will need to decide whether to take your car to a dealer or to a local mechanic, or you might even want to make repairs yourself.

This section reveals how to protect yourself against fraudulent practices, incompetence, and overcharging. Many states have enacted statutes specifically governing car repairs, or have included car repairs in their unfair and deceptive practices statutes.

Inspections

Q. What exactly does the state inspect?

A. Inspection standards vary from state to state. Most states check the car's lights, brakes, windshield wipers, and horn. Some states also inspect the tires, the windows, the body, and the seat belts. Many states also test the emission levels, taking into account the automobile's make, model, and age.

Q. What if I am buying the car?

A. A new car should pass inspection easily. Someone other than the seller should inspect a used car. In many states, a used car sale is not final until the car passes inspection. In other states, failing inspection cancels the sale at the buyer's option. Contact your state department of motor vehicles for further information.

Q. Where do I get my car inspected?

A. States often authorize certain private repair shops and car dealers to make inspections. A few states have government-operated inspection stations.

Q. What will happen if my car does not pass the state's safety inspection?

A. The rules vary from state to state. You may get a "failed" sticker attached to your windshield. You may have a grace period that allows you to make repairs or to get your car off the road. If you fail to comply, you could face fines and other penalties.

Repairs

Q. Where should I take my car for repairs?

A. You can take your car to a dealer, which may be required under the terms of the warranty. Or you could take it to an independent garage or a franchise operation specializing in specific repairs. You could even try to repair it yourself. Each option has its advantages and disadvantages.

Q. Isn't it always best to take my car to a dealer?

A. Dealers may charge more. Yet a dealer may be more familiar with your car model and make than other repair shops, and may have new and better equipment to service your car. Manufacturers want to ensure that dealerships run quality repair operations, so they invest in training mechanics.

Q. Should I bring my car to a service station?

A. This is a good option for nonwarranty work if the mechanics have adequate training and test equipment. Parts might cost more, but labor might be less expensive than dealer repairs. If you regularly use a particular service station, the mechanics get to know your car, and they might spot potential problems early.

Q. What about highly advertised repair chains?

A. Specialty shops may repair one part of a car, such as brakes or mufflers. Some repair franchises advertise complete car care services. Sheer size and volume means lower costs than dealers and independent mechanics. If you know what repairs your car needs, franchise shops can be a good deal.

Q. Must I receive a cost estimate for the repairs before work actually begins?

A. Getting a cost estimate is always a good idea, and it may be required in some states. Some states may provide that the final cost of repairs cannot exceed a certain percentage or dollar value of the original estimate, unless the customer consents. Repair shops generally have the right to charge for making estimates, but you must receive advance notice of any such charge.

Q. What if I do not pay for the repairs?

A. In most states, if you refuse to pay for completed repairs, the shop may keep your car. For example, if you have authorized extensive work, but decide that the car isn't worth that much after the shop completes the work and refuse to pay, the shop obtains a mechanic's lien on your

---

▶ **MECHANIC QUALIFICATIONS**

To help determine whether a mechanic is qualified, ask if the National Institute for Automotive Service Excellence (ASE) has certified the mechanic. A certified mechanic has taken one or more written tests in areas such as engine repair and electrical systems. The ASE certifies a mechanic who passes all the tested areas as a General Automobile Mechanic.

Of course, certification is not everything. Often, you can discover the best mechanics from friends' recommendations and word of mouth.

▶ REPAIR CONTRACT CHECKLIST

The **repair contract,** often called the **repair order,** is essential to getting a satisfactory repair job done on your car. The repair order describes the work to be done and, once signed, creates a contract authorizing the mechanic to make the described repairs.

The repair order should contain

- the make, model, and year of your car;
- the repair date;
- the car's mileage;
- an accurate description of the problem;
- a list of parts to be used and their cost;
- the amount of labor estimated to be needed (time to be spent fixing your car);
- the rate to be charged, either per hour or the flat rate to do the work; and
- your name, address, and telephone number.

The mileage and repair date are important, because they help to verify warranty terms and simplify service records. Make sure the shop has your telephone number, so that the mechanic can contact you if an unexpected problem arises. If the mechanic cannot reach you, the mechanic has to decide whether to proceed, and you may have to live with the results of that decision. In some states, you might not be responsible for repair charges if the mechanic fails to get your signature on the repair order.

car. The car's actual value, and the actual cost of the repairs, does not matter. If you abandon your car in this manner, the mechanic may ultimately sell your car so that it can recover as much of the cost of repairs as possible. In states that require written estimates and repair authorization, the shop does not obtain a mechanic's lien if it does not comply with these requirements. Of course, if you do pay for the repairs, the repair shop must return your car.

▶ WARRANTIES AND REPAIRS

If your car is under warranty, make sure that you understand the terms of the warranty when taking the car in for repairs. Some warranties include language requiring that a car dealer make repairs. If you take the car to another mechanic or try and make repairs yourself, you may invalidate the warranty.

In lieu of a manufacturer's warranties, you may have warranties from the shop that did repairs on your car. These depend on your circumstances and the applicable state law. If the repair shop makes an express warranty, you are protected as long as you abide by the terms of the warranty. Some state courts have held that the implied warranty of merchantability covers car repairs.

Q. How do the state unfair and deceptive practices statutes protect me from a repair shop rip-off?

A. The unfair and deceptive practices statutes usually require price estimates and repair orders. Many states give you the right to keep or examine replaced parts, and require repair shops to prepare a detailed invoice, which must state the labor and parts supplied, warranty work done, guarantees, and installation of any used or rebuilt parts. In some states, you may have the right to same-day repairs, unless you agree to a longer period or the delay is beyond the shop's control. Shoddy repair work must be corrected at no charge, especially in states where the implied warranty of merchantability has been extended to repair work. Finally, many states require repair shops to post price lists conspicuously. If you think a repair shop has intentionally cheated you, you should notify your state attorney general's office and call your lawyer to discuss your options.

Q. What can I do if the automobile mechanic makes unauthorized repairs?

A. First, you may wish to complain to your state attorney general's office, or the local branch of the Better Business Bureau, or even to the Chamber of Commerce. For many mechanics, their business depends on a good reputation, and they will take care to maintain that reputation. If you do not get satisfaction, you may wish to sue—if, for example, the shop made unnecessary repairs or reinstalled the original part rather than a replacement. If the shop tried its best to correct a fault by fixing something that was broken, even though it was not the problem's ultimate cause, you should pay the shop. After all, the repair shop did fix one of your car's problems.

Service Contracts

Q. What is a service contract?

A. A **service contract** is a contract for the provision of car repair services and maintenance for a set period of time. Manufacturers, contract companies, insurance companies, and car dealers offer service contracts.

Like all contracts, you should read a service contract carefully and understand what it says before you sign.

Q. Should I purchase a service contract on my automobile right away?

A. If you buy one at all, you should consider waiting until your warranty period expires. After all, why pay extra for duplicate coverage? Be sure to look out for exclusions and exceptions in the service contract, and be sure to understand what the contract really covers.

THE WORLD AT YOUR FINGERTIPS

- *Your state government website will be able to give you more information about inspections in your state. You can access your state government website, and various agencies and departments at www. statelocalgov.net.*
- *For online information about using certified car technicians for repairs, contact the National Institute for Automotive Service Excellence at www.asecert.org.*
- *The Federal Trade Commission has a Webpage devoted to service contracts; visit*

⚠ **UNCONDITIONAL GUARANTEES**

Beware of "unconditional" guarantees offered by many franchise repair shops. There are always some limitations on written guarantees. As with any contract or document, be sure to read the fine print. The warranty may include special procedures that you are required to follow in order to obtain the benefits of the warranty.

www.ftc.gov/bcp/conline/pubs/autos/
autoserv.htm.

REMEMBER THIS

- *If your car needs repairs, think carefully about your options. You may invalidate a warranty if you do not take the car to the dealer for repairs; however, if the warranty is not an issue, you might save money by taking the car to a trusted mechanic.*

- *Be sure to get a written repair order that contains all of the key information. Get an estimate in advance.*

- *If you will not or cannot pay your mechanics, they have a right to hold your car until you pay, or sell it to recover their costs after a given time period.*

- *Remember that a warranty and a service contract are two different things.*

▶ ## SERVICE CONTRACTS VERSUS WARRANTIES

Unlike a warranty, a service contract may not come from the manufacturer. Service contracts are optional and expensive, and the coverage often overlaps with warranty protection. A service contract often contains more limitations and exclusions than a warranty, may require you to pay a deductible fee, and might not cover all parts and labor or routine maintenance. If a service contract is available on a used car, the appropriate box must be checked on the Buyer's Guide. Finally, if you believe that your service contract has been breached, in addition to any state remedies available to you, you may be able to sue under the Magnuson-Moss Warranty Act, and recover your lawyer's fees and court costs, as well as your damages.

- *Read the fine print on any service contract, and be wary of exclusions.*

YOUR AUTOMOBILE AND THE POLICE

No one likes to think about the prospect of being pulled over by a police officer. The law in this area changes all the time, so if you have a serious legal issue you should consult a lawyer without delay.

This section covers a few basic things that may be helpful to keep in mind if you and your car have an encounter with the police.

The Stop

Q. An officer is signaling me to pull over. What should I do?

A. Pull over to the side of the road as quickly and safely as possible. Remain in your vehicle until the officer otherwise directs you. Get ready to produce your license, registration, and proof of insurance, because you may be asked to do so. Sit quietly and keep your hands in view, so the officer does not think that you may be reaching for a weapon.

Q. The officer is at my window. Now what?

A. Stay composed and politely ask why you were stopped. If you have any doubt that you were stopped by a real police officer—if, for example, you were pulled over by an unmarked vehicle— politely ask to see the officer's photo identification, not just his or her badge.

The Search

Q. Suppose the officer wants to search my car?

A. Ask why the officer wants to conduct a search. If you have absolutely nothing to hide, you could save time and effort if you simply let the search proceed. If you don't want the search to proceed, you should state clearly that you do not consent. Denying a search is not an admission of guilt. Ask courteously whether the officer has a search warrant or if you are under arrest. If the officer replies that you are under arrest, ask for an explanation.

Usually, the officer is permitted to conduct the search only if

- you consent; or
- the officer has probable cause to believe that the vehicle contains incriminating evidence; or
- the officer reasonably believes that he must search the vehicle for his or her own protection.

Q. What if the officer insists on searching my car?

A. Don't interfere. You can always challenge the legitimacy of the search later in court.

Q. Can the police legitimately search my vehicle without a warrant?

A. That depends on the circumstances. A key factor is whether you've been arrested. For example, the police usually would not have the right to search your automobile when you are stopped only for a minor traffic offense such as speeding. However, if the violation requires that you be taken into custody (for example, a driving under the influence (DUI) arrest or driving with a suspended license), the search generally would be permitted.

🗐 PROBABLE CAUSE

Probable cause, in the context of vehicle searches, is a reasonable basis for the officer to believe that the vehicle contains incriminating evidence. An officer is legally justified in searching your car if he or she has probable cause.

Even when an arrest is not involved, the police have more latitude to search a vehicle than to search a home. The U.S. Supreme Court recognizes an automobile exception to the Fourth Amendment's protection against warrantless searches. The rationale for permitting warrantless searches of cars is that the mobility of automobiles would allow drivers to escape with incriminating evidence in the time it would take police to secure a search warrant. The Court has held that a person expects less privacy in an automobile than at home. No one ever said, "A man's Chevy is his castle."

Q. May the officer search in my glove compartment without a warrant?

A. The law is constantly changing the legal contours of searches. Generally, the police officer may search the immediate area at the driver's command, that is, under and around the front seat and in the glove compartment. Sometimes state constitutions offer greater protection against searches than the U.S. Constitution. If you have questions about a search the police have made of your vehicle, it is best to consult a lawyer in your state.

Q. May the officer search a closed container inside my car without a warrant?

A. The Supreme Court has ruled that the police do not need a warrant to search closed containers found in the passenger compartment of an automobile whose occupant is under arrest.

The police may search a closed container even if you are not under arrest if the container might reasonably contain evidence of a crime for which the officer had probable cause to search the vehicle in the first place.

Q. May the police search my car without a warrant after they have impounded it?

A. The police do not need a warrant to undertake a routine inventory of an impounded vehicle. The reason is that such an inventory protects the driver's possessions against theft, and also protects the police against claims of lost or stolen property. Such an inventory also protects the holding facility from dangerous materials that may be in the impounded vehicle, and may aid in the identification of the arrested person.

Q. Suppose the officer sees a packet of marijuana on the backseat?

A. Again, the law is always changing; if you find yourself in this situation, you should contact a lawyer without delay. When the police can see evidence readily from a place in which they have a right to be, the law generally does not consider it a search. Rather, it is a plain-view seizure. As long as the officer has a legitimate reason to be standing by the car and easily sees what the officer has probable cause to believe is evidence of a crime, the officer can make the seizure. Then the officer could probably conduct a warrantless search of the rest of the passenger compartment of the ve-

hicle and possibly the trunk (if probable cause exists to believe the trunk may contain evidence).

Roadblocks

Q. What are the constitutional constraints on roadblocks?

A. The U.S. Supreme Court has ruled that a search or seizure (such as at a checkpoint on the road) is unreasonable under the Fourth Amendment unless there is individualized suspicion of wrongdoing—that is, unless the police have a particular reason to pull a particular driver over—but there are a limited number of exceptions. For example, the Court has upheld brief, suspicionless seizures at a fixed checkpoint designed to intercept illegal aliens, and at a sobriety checkpoint aimed at removing drunk drivers from the road. The Court has also suggested that a similar roadblock to verify driver's licenses and registrations

---

ⓘ A SAMPLER OF SUPREME COURT RULINGS INVOLVING AUTOMOBILES AND THE POLICE

The law relating to automobile stops and searches is an area that changes rapidly, as the list of cases below reflects.

Maryland v. Dyson (1999) In this case, the Supreme Court declared that police do not need to obtain a search warrant to search a vehicle when they have probable cause to believe the vehicle contains contraband. Contraband includes controlled or banned substances and weapons.

Wyoming v. Houghton (1999) The Supreme Court declared that police officers who have probable cause to search a car may also inspect passengers' belongings when those belongings could contain the object of the search. Passengers, like drivers, enjoy a reduced expectation of privacy regarding possessions they transport in cars.

Florida v. White (1999) The court held that police may seize an automobile from a public place when they have probable cause to believe the vehicle is stolen and subject to forfeiture under the law.

City of Indianapolis v. Edmond (2000) The Supreme Court struck down road checkpoints that have the primary purpose of intercepting narcotics. The Court held that without some individual suspicion, such stops violate the Constitution, and in this instance they did not serve some other main aim, such as maintaining road safety.

would be permissible to serve a highway safety interest.

Q. So the police can pull me over in a roadblock and demand to check my license and registration?

A. Yes, under certain circumstances. The U.S. Supreme Court has said that such roadblocks do not constitute an unreasonable search as long as police stop all the cars passing through the roadblock or follow some neutral policy, such as stopping every fourth car. The police can't single out your car unless they have a suspicion that you don't have your driver's license, that your vehicle is unregistered, or that you or your car may be seized for violating the law.

Q. And is it legal to design a roadblock to catch drunk drivers?

A. Yes, provided the selection of vehicles to be stopped is not arbitrary and the inconvenience to drivers is minimized. Courts have upheld such roadblocks as constitutional. In some states, the prosecution must show that a roadblock is the least intrusive way to enforce drunk-driving laws. Some states require that the ranking police officer who supervised a roadblock testify at the offender's trial.

Q. Then what would constitute an unconstitutional roadblock?

A. In a 2000 case entitled *City of Indianapolis* v. *Edmond,* the U. S. Supreme Court struck down vehicle checkpoints set up to intercept unlawful drugs. The Court explained that because the checkpoint program's primary purpose was indistinguishable from the general interest in crime control, the checkpoints violated the Fourth Amendment. The checkpoint program was unlike the roadblocks the Court previously had approved, "which were designed to serve purposes closely related to the problems of policing the border or the necessity of ensuring roadway safety." The Court went on to say that its holding "does not alter the constitutional status of searches in airports and government buildings,

where the need for such measures to ensure public safety can be particularly acute. Nor does it impair police officers' ability to act appropriately upon information that they properly learn during a checkpoint stop justified by a lawful primary purpose."

📄 DRUNK DRIVING UNDER OTHER NAMES

Different states call the offense of drunk driving different names. These include **driving under the influence (DUI), operating under the influence (OUI),** and **driving while intoxicated (DWI).**

Drunk Driving

Q. Does it really matter what the police call it?

A. Yes—each one is a slightly different offense. For example, the offense of OUI does not require that the vehicle be in motion. In most states, a person may be charged with OUI if he or she is in **actual physical control.** Actual physical control may be shown when the person is seated in the driver's seat, in possession of the ignition key, and capable of starting the motor.

Q. What does "drunk driving" mean?

A. The elements of the basic offense vary from one state to another. However, the Uniform Vehicle Code says proof is necessary that the person is under the influence of alcohol or drugs. Depending on the controlling law, "being under the influence" could refer to any substance that impairs your ability to drive.

Most states agree that a person is **under the influence** if he or she has a diminished ability, either physically or mentally, to exercise clear judgment and to operate a vehicle with safety. The person must be driving or in actual physical control of a vehicle. Some states' legislations require prosecutors to prove that the person was driving "on a public highway" or was drinking "intoxicating liquor."

Q. How does the prosecution prove that a person was drunk driving?

A. The prosecution relies heavily, sometimes solely, on the arresting officer's testimony about the defendant's operation of the vehicle and the defendant's behavior (observations of the defendant's appearance, speech, and an odor of alcohol). The prosecution also relies on the results of field sobriety tests and chemical tests (breath, blood, or urine). For example, the arresting officer might give evidence that "the car was weaving over the center line of the highway," or that "the driver had slurred speech, heavy odor of alcohol, glassy bloodshot eyes, and could not walk straight."

Q. What are field sobriety tests?

A. If the police observe you driving strangely or violating the rules of the road, they are permitted to stop your vehicle. If the police then smell alcohol on your breath or have other reason to believe you are driving while under the influence of alcohol or drugs, they have the right to ask you to take certain tests. The law refers to these as field sobriety tests. Every police department has its own preferred tests. Police may ask you to stand on one foot for a specified time or walk in a straight line. The police also may ask you to touch your nose with your index finger with your eyes closed and head back, and have you stare at a flashlight or a pen so that the officer can see how your eyes respond.

If you do not perform these field sobriety tests satisfactorily, the police will ask you to submit to a scientific test that shows how much (if any) alcohol is in your body. Many states will offer you one of three choices—give a blood sample, give a urine sample, or take a Breathalyzer test. The Breathalyzer test involves blowing into a balloon attached to a machine that measures the percentage of alcohol in your breath.

Q. Do I have to take field sobriety tests if the police ask me to?

A. In most states, the police are not allowed to force you to take these tests. However, depending on the law in your state, they might use your refusal as evidence against you in court. Also, in many states, refusal to submit to such tests will result in automatic suspension or revocation of your driver's license.

Q. Suppose I fail the tests?

A. It is not like school. You cannot promise to study harder next time. A skilled lawyer, however, may argue that the police administered the tests improperly, or that the tests were inaccurate for some reason. In addition, a lawyer may present qualifying evidence. For instance, a chronic knee injury may prevent you from supporting your weight on one foot.

Q. How does a breath-testing device work?

A. The person blows into a small machine, which measures the percentage of alcohol in the person's blood. The law fixes a standard measure, over which a person is deemed to be intoxicated. This measure might be 0.10 (one-tenth of 1 percent blood-alcohol concentration) or 0.08, depending on the state. The law often entitles the defendant to two breath tests that must measure within 0.02 (or some other percentage) of each other.

Q. If my test result is under 0.08 or 0.10, will the charge against me be dismissed?

A. Not necessarily. Even if you have a blood-alcohol level less than the prohibited level of 0.08 or 0.10, you may still be impaired. The prosecutor may decide to proceed to trial, in which event the officer's testimony as to impairment will be given as evidence, in addition to the breath test results.

Q. If the breath-testing device hits 0.10, am I in serious trouble?

A. Probably, but a lawyer may be able to show that the machine's operator received inadequate training, the operator's certification had lapsed, or the operator did not maintain the machine well. Other factors may also affect the breath-testing device's reading and may be established through an expert witness. Diabetics, for example, have high levels of ketone (a naturally occurring chemical), which could yield false results when they are tested. In most cases, however, the result of a breath test will be allowed into evidence.

Q. Should I take a blood test or a Breathalyzer test if I am asked?

A. There is no hard-and-fast answer to that question. The law varies by state and is always subject to change. If you find yourself in this situation, you should consult a lawyer if you are allowed to call one.

Unless you are certain that you have had less than three or four drinks in the past hour, or less than five drinks in the past several hours, common wisdom holds that it is a good idea to refuse the tests. It generally is more difficult to convict a driver of drunk driving if no chemical tests are taken.

On the other hand, if you refuse to take a blood test or a Breathalyzer test, your driver's license will probably be suspended automatically for a long period of time. In some states, for example, it will be suspended for six months if you refuse to take a test, but only three months if you take and fail the test (if you are a first offender). In other states, the suspension period might be the same, but you will have to do several days of jail time if you refuse to take the test.

Q. May I change my mind after declining to take a blood or breath test?

A. You have no right to change your mind once you have refused a blood test. Even if you subsequently have a change of heart and agree to a test, your license can still be suspended on the basis that you initially refused the test. It is a good idea to call a lawyer while you are thinking over a decision, if the police allow you to do so.

However, in most states you will have to decide whether to submit to the test fairly soon after being asked to do so.

Q. What kind of penalty am I likely to get for drunk driving?

A. Consult a lawyer in your state because penalties vary widely and depend on several factors, such as whether you are a repeat offender. A number of states require minimum penalties for a first-time offender, which might involve enrollment in an alcohol treatment program and a license suspension of a month or several months. A second-time offender might suffer a two-year license suspension or revocation of license. Some states impound the license plates or vehicles of habitual drunk drivers, and others revoke the licenses of habitual offenders.

This is an extremely volatile area of the law. Jail terms for first offenders are more common than they used to be. Community service and enrollment in mandatory alcohol programs, as well as heavy fines, are regularly doled out by courts in various combinations as a result of changing public perceptions about drunk driving.

License Suspension and Revocation

Q. Suppose the police stop me and I've left my license at home?

A. Driving a motor vehicle on a public street or highway without a license is an offense in most states. Often, a person accused of driving without a license might be able to avoid conviction if able to produce a license in court that was valid at the time of the police stop.

Q. What conduct could lead to license suspension?

A. Grounds for suspension vary by state. A local lawyer will be able to give you details about your state laws. Refusal to submit to a field sobriety or Breathalyzer test will probably result in suspension.

ⓘ THE NATIONWIDE CRACKDOWN ON DRUNK DRIVING

Statistics indicate that at least one-third of all drivers involved in fatal accidents were alcohol-impaired at the time. The ranks of groups such as Mothers Against Drunk Driving (MADD) and Students Against Destructive Decisions (SADD) continue to swell. State legislatures have responded by introducing harsh new drunk-driving laws at a dizzying clip. Society is no longer satisfied with giving offenders a slap on the wrist when it comes to drunk driving.

The majority of states have enacted so-called **per se laws,** which prohibit a person from driving an automobile if the person has a blood-alcohol reading of a certain amount or more. When the per se law is used, the prosecution need not show that the person is under the influence by presenting evidence of his behavior. Instead, the prosecution need only prove that the person was driving and showing a blood-alcohol reading of the certain amount or more at the time. These laws make it easier to convict drunk drivers. A blood-alcohol reading of 0.10 remains the legal presumptive level of intoxication in some states, but a growing number of states have lowered their per se limit to 0.08.

Another trend among legislatures is to pass laws that create harsher penalties for higher breath-testing device results. Some states provide for enhanced penalties for blood-alcohol readings of 0.20 and higher. Other states have created lesser offenses, such as **driving impaired,** when the blood-alcohol level is 0.07 or less.

In some states, there is zero tolerance for those under twenty-one who drive with any measurable alcohol in their body. In Maine, for example, your license will be suspended for a year under these circumstances, and for eighteen months if you refuse a test.

In civil courts throughout the country, "dramshop" cases and "social host" cases are gaining wider acceptance, and expanding the liability for negligence. These cases hold taverns and restaurants legally responsible for providing alcohol to intoxicated persons if they have knowledge that the person is likely to drive and the driver goes on to have an accident.

🗐 THE DIFFERENCE BETWEEN LICENSE SUSPENSION, CANCELLATION, AND REVOCATION

Suspension involves the temporary withdrawal of your privilege to drive. The state may restore your driving privileges after a designated time period and payment of a fee. You may also be required to remedy the cause of the suspension; for example, by purchasing auto insurance.

License **cancellation** involves voluntarily giving up your driving privilege without penalty. Cancellation allows you to reapply for a license immediately.

Revocation aims both to discipline the driver and protect the public. Revocation involuntarily ends your driving privilege. Revocation of your license applies for a minimum period set by law, until you become eligible to apply for a new license. The state may conduct a reinstatement hearing. You may have to retake a driver's license examination.

Q. What conduct could lead to license revocation?

A. Grounds for revocation also vary from state to state. Your license may be revoked for violating specific laws, such as those pertaining to habitual reckless driving, drunken driving, nonpayment of your motor vehicle excise tax, using a motor vehicle to commit a felony, or fleeing from or eluding the police.

Q. Am I entitled to notice and a hearing before the state revokes my license?

A. Barring an emergency, due process under the Fourteenth Amendment generally requires notice and a chance to be heard before the state ends a person's license privileges. However, for certain serious offenses, the state may simply rely on the court conviction to revoke the person's license without the need for any hearing.

Q. What if the state charges me with an offense that requires a license suspension?

A. Unless another law says otherwise, no notice is necessary before a state may suspend your license under the mandatory provisions of a law. As a driver, you are presumed to know the law.

Q. If the state does notify me, what should the notice say?

A. The time, place, and purpose of the hearing should appear on the notice of a hearing to suspend or revoke your license.

Q. Does the law entitle me to a jury?

A. No. A suspension/revocation hearing is an administrative, not a judicial, proceeding. You are entitled, however, to confront and cross-examine witnesses against you at such a hearing. It is a good idea to have a lawyer to represent you at the hearing.

Q. State A suspended/revoked my license, but I have a valid license in State B. Can I drive in State A?

A. Consult your lawyer if you find yourself in this situation. Under the law of some states, a valid driver's license from another jurisdiction does not enable you to drive on the highways of a state that has cancelled, suspended, or revoked your license. However, other states have held that a license properly issued by a foreign state under the Driver's License Compact ends the suspension or revocation of a motorist's original license.

License Renewal

Q. Must I take another examination to renew my license?

A. You should check with your state division of motor vehicles. Some states permit renewal by

---

⚠ **THE PERILS OF DRIVING WITH A SUSPENDED OR REVOKED LICENSE**

If you are stopped while driving with a suspended or revoked license, you are likely to be arrested. The state usually has to show that your license or privilege to drive was revoked or suspended on the occasion in question, and that you were driving a motor vehicle on a public highway at the time of the offense.

At a minimum, the offense is usually a serious misdemeanor that carries with it a stiff fine and possibly some time in the local jail. Some states consider the crime a felony that lands the offender in state prison or with a significant amount of community service to work off, particularly if the suspension or revocation was based upon a DUI.

mail. Most states require a vision test, and, in some instances, a new photograph for renewal. A few require a written test. Prerequisites for license renewal could include as much as a vision test, a written test, a thumbprint, a signature, and a photograph. Some states impose additional requirements if a driver has amassed a number of traffic convictions or if the driver is of a certain age or has certain physical problems. Some states require a road test for "elderly" drivers (those over a specific age that is set by state law) prior to renewal.

Q. May a physical or mental affliction prevent me from driving legally?

A. Yes. A few states require doctors to report physical and mental disorders of patients that could affect driver safety.

Seat Belt Laws

Q. My kids hate wearing seat belts. Must they wear them?

A. All fifty states and the District of Columbia require children to be restrained while riding in motor vehicles. State laws vary, however, concerning the age of the child subject to the child restraint law.

Q. Do I have to wear a seat belt?

A. It depends where you live and perhaps where you sit in the car. Depending on the law in your state, you may only be required to wear belts if you are in the front seat. The Insurance Institute for Highway Safety website has a complete listing of state laws. You can access it at www.hwysafety. org/safety_facts/state_laws/restrain3.htm.

Q. May I still recover payment for my injuries if I am in an accident and not wearing my seat belt?

A. Most states reject the so-called seat belt defense, and will not accept evidence that plaintiffs did not buckle up as proof that they were negligent in a way that contributed to the injuries. In some jurisdictions, however, evidence of the plaintiff's failure to use a seat belt may reduce the amount of damages awarded to the plaintiff.

Speeding and Other Offenses

Q. I got stuck in a speed trap. What can I do about it?

A. If the speed limit was clearly marked and you were exceeding it, you should grit your teeth and pay the fine. If you think you've been unfairly prosecuted, you might report the trap to your auto club or state authorities to spare other drivers the same expense.

Q. I was stopped for speeding by a radar gun. Do those things work?

A. Courts today regularly accept the ability of radar to measure vehicular speeds accurately. That doesn't mean that you can't try to prove that the particular radar gun in your case was poorly maintained or that its operator misread the results or was inadequately trained to use the device, but you may face an uphill fight.

Q. Aren't radar detector devices the best way to avoid speed traps and radar guns?

A. Radar detector devices alert the driver to police radar and to speed guns, allowing the driver to slow down before he or she is detected exceeding the speed limit. A few states have declared radar detectors illegal for all vehicles, but in general the laws single out "commercial" vehicles over ten thousand pounds (i.e., trucks). Some states use radar detector detectors to stop drivers who have radar detectors installed. Access www. afn.org/~afn09444/scanlaws to get a complete state-by-state list of the laws.

Q. What are the elements of a speeding charge?

A. It depends on whether your state bases its speeding laws on **absolute** or **fixed maximum limits,** or **prima facie limits**. It is a violation to exceed a fixed maximum limit regardless of the circumstances at any time. On the other hand, prima facie limits allow drivers to justify the speed at which they were driving by considering traffic and road conditions and visibility.

Q. Does the type of speed limit change the nature of the complaint against me?

A. Yes. The complaint and notice or summons to appear for a fixed maximum violation will specify both your alleged speed and the maximum speed allowable within the locality. In contrast, in prima facie jurisdictions, driving above the posted speed limit is not the offense. The police must charge you with driving above a speed that was reasonable and proper given the existing conditions. One example might be driving fifty miles per hour in a school zone.

Speeding laws vary greatly from state to state. Therefore, it is a good idea, for legal and safety reasons, to get into the habit of reducing your driving speed whenever you approach a railway crossing or intersection, drive around a curve, or encounter special hazards, such as severe weather.

Q. Are there any excuses I can offer that might prevent a police officer from writing up a speeding ticket?

A. If you are taking a pregnant or sick person to the hospital, you might be spared a speeding citation, and you might even get a police escort to the hospital. Sometimes a court emergency (be sure to display the court papers to the officer) or a broken speedometer (be prepared to give the officer a test ride) may succeed.

Q. What kind of information is included on a traffic ticket?

A. The color, model, and registration of your vehicle, and the date, time, and place of the alleged offense are provided on the ticket. You will probably also find the specific violation with which you have been charged (if it's a parking meter offense, the meter number as well), the officer's name and badge number, the fine schedule, and a notice of your ability to have a hearing to contest the ticket. Each jurisdiction has its own form. If the officer includes incorrect information in writing the ticket, such mistakes may provide you with a defense against the citation.

Q. What is "reckless driving"?

A. The language varies from jurisdiction to jurisdiction, but increasingly, states are following the Uniform Vehicle Code, which defines **reckless driving** as "willful or wanton disregard for the safety of persons or property." Essentially, the prosecution must show that the driver was indifferent to the probable harmful results of his or her driving, and that the driver should have realized that such driving posed a hazard.

THE WORLD AT YOUR FINGERTIPS

- *Mothers Against Drunk Driving (MADD) is the definitive source for information on drunk driving. There are many local chapters, which can easily be located at the MADD website at www.madd.org.*
- *Nolo sponsors several Web pages with information about the police and your car. The link called "Cars & Tickets" contains FAQs regarding traffic accidents, police stops, and drunk driving. You can access the website at www.nolo.com.*
- *For driver's license requirements in all states, including special provisions for older and younger drivers, access the Insurance Information Institute site at www.iii.org/individuals/auto/a/stateautolaws.*

REMEMBER THIS

- *License renewal laws vary greatly by state, and the requirements may be different depending on your age, driving record, and other factors. Contact your state department of motor vehicles to see what you have to do.*
- *Criminal and traffic laws affecting motorists vary from state to state, but a little common sense goes a long way. Using care*

and keeping a wary eye on the speedometer will help you avoid trouble.

- *Drunk driving is very serious business, and you should consult a lawyer if you face charges on this score.*
- *Driving on a suspended or revoked license is likely to get you arrested.*

ACCIDENTS AND INSURANCE

Using skill, care, and common sense to avoid accidents is always the best policy. If an accident happens, there are some basic things to keep in mind that may help you to avoid unnecessary trouble.

This section is a guide to the major issues concerning accidents and insurance. The possibility that you will have an accident is one reason why insurance is so important. But most drivers would rather drive cross-country nonstop than attempt to decipher the mysteries of automobile insurance. Virtually every state has its own insurance regulations, yet not every state has mandatory insurance. As with every topic in this chapter, the law varies from place to place, so you should consult a lawyer if you need to understand the legal repercussions of any serious matter.

Accidents

Q. If I am in an accident, do I have to worry about civil law? Criminal law? Both? Neither?

A. The annoying answer is "It depends." In some accidents, especially fender benders, no one will get a ticket or face any other criminal problem. If insurance handles any property damage and no lawsuit is filed, then you won't have to worry about civil law, either.

But let's say the accident is more serious and the police charge at least one of the drivers with an offense. That criminal charge could mean a fine or jail time for the offender. But in the same

case, a personal injury lawsuit for negligent driving could be filed, and this civil lawsuit could lead to money damages being paid by one driver to the other (or others).

Chapter 14, "Personal Injury," discusses the civil law on automobile collisions (including personal injury lawsuits arising from auto collisions) in more detail.

Q. According to the law, how safely must I drive?

A. You have to use reasonable care under the circumstances. **Negligence**—the failure to exercise reasonable care—is the most common basis for liability. Ordinary negligence is not a crime.

However, if your driving is really bad, to the extent that it is willful or wanton, then you may be guilty of reckless driving, which is a crime.

Q. Do I need to exercise more care toward pedestrians and passengers?

A. No, the same standard applies to pedestrians, passengers, and other drivers. Motorists must exercise reasonable care under the circumstances toward pedestrians. In practical terms, this means keeping a careful lookout for pedestrians, and maintaining control over your vehicle to avoid injuring them. You must also sound your horn to warn of your approach when you believe that a pedestrian is unaware of danger. In some states, you must stop if you see a pedestrian anywhere in a crosswalk. The law does not, however, expect you to anticipate a pedestrian darting out into the roadway.

You must also exercise reasonable care under the circumstances toward passengers, although this may change based on your passengers' relationship to you. You will not be liable if a passenger sustains injury through no fault of your own.

Q. To what standard of care will I be held if someone else is driving my car, and I am a passenger?

A. The law in some states will assume you still have "control" over the vehicle. Other states require the owner to take steps to stop the negligent driving as soon as the owner becomes aware of it. In other words, if you are the owner of a car, you can be liable for the way in which another person drives it.

Q. Am I legally responsible even if I am not in the car if an accident occurs?

A. Possibly. You still might be liable for property damage, injuries, and even death if you permit someone else to operate your defective vehicle, or if you allow an inexperienced, habitually intoxicated, or otherwise incompetent person to drive your car. The law refers to this conduct as **negligent entrustment.**

Q. What if my child is driving my car and an accident occurs?

A. Some jurisdictions recognize the **family purpose doctrine,** under which the "head" of the family who maintains a car for general family use may be held liable for the negligent driving of a family member who was authorized to use the vehicle.

Q. Should I contact a lawyer after an accident? What should I tell the lawyer?

A. If you are filing a lawsuit against another driver, you will need to hire your own lawyer. If the other driver is suing you, your insurance company may provide a lawyer for you.

If you do file suit, you will need to supply information to your lawyer about

- your family status and employment situation;
- the accident, including witnesses' names and addresses;
- your injuries; and
- your out-of-pocket expenses, such as doctors' bills, ambulance and hospital costs, automobile repairs, rental car costs, and any lost income.

Chapter 1, "When and How to Use a Lawyer," provides more detailed information about hiring a lawyer.

Q. What might happen if I believe an accident is at least partly my fault?

A. You may not be in the best position to determine how an accident happened. Defective equipment in your vehicle, a malfunctioning traffic signal, or another driver's intoxication are among the many possible causes of the accident. If you accept blame and apologize to the other driver, your statements may be used as evidence against you at trial. Leave it to the judge or the jury to decide who is at fault.

Q. If the accident is partly my fault, may I still receive payment for my injuries?

A. The answer depends on whether you live in a contributory negligence, comparative negligence, or no-fault jurisdiction. These legal standards set out varying rules for determining fault in a collision.

Q. What is contributory negligence?

A. Essentially, **contributory negligence** bars you from recovering money for your injuries if your own negligence in any way contributed to the accident's occurrence. The other driver must prove that you were negligent. Only a few states still accept the concept of contributory negligence, which once was widely supported.

Q. What is comparative negligence?

A. Adhered to in the vast majority of states, **comparative negligence** divides the damages among the drivers involved in an accident based on their degree of fault. In "pure" comparative negligence states, you can receive payment for your injuries regardless of how much of the blame you carry for the accident, as long as the other driver is at fault to some degree. In "modified" comparative fault states, you may recover payment only if your own fault is below a certain threshold, such as 50 percent. See chapter 14, "Personal Injury," for more information about comparative negligence.

Q. What is the status of negligence in no-fault states?

A. Many states have enacted no-fault laws. Negligence law for auto collisions exists in no-fault states, but it is limited in its application.

No-fault laws essentially provide (1) that you must purchase a minimum amount of no-fault insurance in order to drive and (2) that if you are injured you will be compensated by your own insurance carrier for your economic losses up to a specified level, regardless of who was at fault for the accident. In other words, the state law regarding negligence in auto collision cases is modified in most instances, though lawsuits alleging negligence might be filed in certain circumstances, such as in the case of economic losses beyond a certain level, injuries that included some specified serious conditions such as permanent disfigurement, and property damage to your vehicle.

Q. What does "leaving the scene of an accident" mean?

A. Consult a lawyer about your state's criminal law for this offense. Generally, drivers of vehicles involved in an accident in which personal injury or property damage occurs must stop and identify themselves and their vehicles. Drivers must also notify police, and help any injured persons. Even if the driver has a reason for leaving the scene of the accident or doesn't own the vehicle, he or she can still be liable.

Q. What are the defenses to such a charge?

A. Again, it is a good idea to consult a lawyer about the law that applies to your situation. As a rule, it is a complete defense if no personal injury or property damage resulted from the accident, or if you had no knowledge that an accident had occurred. On the other hand, claiming that you left intending to drive directly to the police station to report the accident probably would not be a good defense.

Q. If I collide with a parked car, am I required to do anything?

A. The law requires you to try to find the owner. Alternatively, you are permitted to attach a written note to the parked car identifying yourself and your vehicle. You also should notify the police.

Q. Must I tell the police if I am in an accident?

A. Alert the police immediately if someone is hurt or killed. Generally, if the accident involves a death, personal injury, or property damage above a specific amount that varies among states, you must notify the police and file a written accident report immediately or within a short time span, usually five to ten days. Often, states require you to file the report with the bureau of motor vehicles or similar state authority. Some states do not require you to report an accident if no one is injured or if property damage is less than a certain dollar amount. Other jurisdictions require a report only if no police officer responded to the accident scene.

Failure to file a written report is a misdemeanor in most states. Some states may suspend your driver's license until you file the report. Remember, by completing an accident report, you are verifying that the report contains a recital of all important facts known to you. Providing false information in a written report is illegal.

Insurance

Q. What is auto insurance?

A. Like all insurance, auto coverage is designed to protect you against risk. Auto insurance protects you against financial loss in the event of an accident. Coverages vary by policy, but typically protect you against property damage to your vehicle, liability for injuries you cause to other people and property, and medical expenses you or your passengers may incur.

Q. Does state law require me to have insurance?

A. It probably does. Almost all states require you to buy insurance, though the states vary in the minimum level of coverage set by law for liability insurance. Some states require you to show proof of financial responsibility if you choose not to purchase insurance.

Q. What are "compulsory insurance" statutes?

A. Compulsory insurance statutes mandate that drivers file proof of insurance as a condition of receiving their vehicle registration. Many states require drivers to purchase certain insurance options, such as **collision,** which pays you for damage to your car irrespective of who was at fault, and **comprehensive,** which pays you for damage done to your car caused by theft, fire, and vandalism.

Q. Does the lender who lent me money to buy a car have a say in the amount of insurance I buy?

A. Possibly. Many states allow such lenders to protect their collateral by requiring you to purchase insurance options such as collision and comprehensive.

Q. What happens if I don't have insurance?

A. You may be asked to show proof of insurance any time police stop you on the road, and be sent to court if you don't have it. Some states have minimum fines that judges must assess, and you'll have to pay court costs, too. The court will then mandate that you get the insurance you should have had in the first place. If you're a repeat offender, the fine will be higher and you may face the loss of your car and a long suspension of your driver's license.

But the worst consequence, by far, is that

▶ WHAT YOU SHOULD DO IF YOU HAVE AN ACCIDENT

If you are involved in an accident, try to park on the shoulder of the road and do not obstruct traffic. Use your car's flashers or flares to warn approaching motorists of the accident. Most important, you should help any persons who are injured.

If asked, give the other driver your

- name,
- address,
- vehicle registration certificate, and
- proof of insurance.

Get the same information from the other driver.

You should identify yourself to any police officers who respond to the scene, and show your license and proof of insurance coverage if asked. Write down the names and addresses of all passengers and possible witnesses. Also, get the names and badge numbers of the police officers. If you have a camera handy, photograph the damaged cars, skid marks, and the accident scene. Draw a diagram of the accident and make notes about the weather, the lighting conditions, and the road conditions.

Do not make any statements about who was at fault. Do not admit blame to the other parties or witnesses. As soon as possible after the accident, notify your insurance company. If you sustained any personal injury, seek medical attention promptly. Consult a lawyer if you intend to file suit.

you'll have no coverage if you're in an accident and cause damages. You could lose everything you've worked for, including your house.

Q. May my insurance agent force me to pay my premium in a lump sum?

A. Check your particular state's law. Some states limit the amount an agent may demand before renewing your insurance to a certain percentage of the premium. If you have not paid your premium payments in the recent past, however, an insurance agent may legally ask you to pay your entire premium before renewing your policy.

Q. May my insurance agent charge me a service fee for issuing or renewing a policy?

A. Consult your state's law. Some states forbid agents from charging service fees for issuing or renewing auto insurance policies, and do not require you to pay for services that your agent performs without your consent.

Q. How are insurance rates determined?

A. A classification system based on objective criteria helps actuaries to determine the risk of an accident and thereby set the varying rates that drivers pay. Criteria include your age, sex, marital status, and geographic location; the age, make, and model of the car; and the car's primary use (cars used for recreation are statistically less likely to be involved in an accident

than a vehicle used for commuting). In some states, the insurance rates are set by the state's insurance commission, which regulates insurance companies.

If you have been involved in several accidents over a short period of time, you are a high risk, so insurance companies would add a surcharge to the basic premium you pay. On the other hand, insurance carriers might offer safety discounts if your vehicle is equipped with automatic safety belts, antilock brakes, or air bags. Insurance companies will offer other types of discounts as well, such as for being a senior citizen or a good student, joining a car pool, or insuring multiple vehicles with the same carrier.

Q. My teenage son's insurance premium is much higher than mine. Is it unconstitutional to discriminate based on age?

A. No. Actuaries cite research that persons under age twenty-one, especially males, have the highest rate of car accidents. This is the justification for the disparity in rates between adults and minors.

Q. Will my insurance premium automatically increase if I have an accident?

A. Not necessarily. If the insurance carrier has to dole out $300 to $500 or more in claims, you are likely to see a premium increase. If you have been accident free for the previous three years, the surcharge, if any, might still be less than your costs to pay for the repairs out of pocket. If you are on your third accident and just getting warmed up, prepare yourself for a 20 to 50 percent premium hike.

Q. Do I have to buy uninsured motorist coverage?

A. It depends where you live. Some states now require drivers to purchase such coverage, which enables you to collect from your insurer if you are injured in an accident caused by an uninsured driver. The insurance carrier, in turn, receives **subrogation rights** against the uninsured wrong-

---

WHAT IS A DEDUCTIBLE?

A **deductible** is the amount that you agree to pay in the event that you make a claim. The higher the deductible you choose, the lower your annual insurance premium. But if you select a high deductible, you'll need more cash on hand if you have an accident. Typical deductibles are $50, $100, $250, and $500.

doer; that is, the carrier takes your place (and your rights) as the legal claimant against the uninsured driver. Skyrocketing hospital costs, combined with a tight economy that causes many people to underinsure (or fail to insure) their vehicles, make this coverage a good idea.

Q. How do I collect on my uninsured motorist coverage?

A. Generally, you must prove that the other driver was both at fault and without liability insurance to compensate you. An uninsured motorist actually may have no coverage, or may be de facto uninsured if underage, unlicensed, or otherwise ineligible for protection under the policy covering the vehicle that caused the accident, as, for example, when the driver at fault used the vehicle without the owner's permission. Practically speaking, if the insurance carrier of the driver at fault denies coverage, you are dealing with an uninsured motorist.

Q. How much can I recover on an uninsured motorist claim?

A. Check your state's law. Some states, for example, prohibit adding together the liability limits for two policies to determine how much coverage is available to injured persons.

Q. How does underinsured motorist coverage work?

A. Underinsured motorist coverage, which exists in a majority of states, will cover the shortfall if an injured person suffers more damage than can be covered by the driver's insurance. If, for example, the driver who injured you has only $50,000 in bodily injury coverage, but you have $70,000 in damages, you can look to your own insurer to cover the $20,000 shortfall after you have recovered damages from the other driver's carrier.

Q. Do underinsured motorist policies differ?

A. Yes. A minority of those states that recognize this insurance option weigh the insured accident victim's damages against the driver at fault's liability coverage, compensating the injured person only if the driver at fault's liability coverage is less than the damages the victim suffered or was entitled to receive. Other states examine the injured person's uninsured motorist coverage and the driver at fault's liability insurance, with the insurance carrier paying out only when the driver at fault's liability insurance limit is less than the victim's underinsured motorist coverage. Most policies enable the insurer to deduct ("set off") the amount the victim receives from the driver at fault from the sum it pays to the victim carrying the underinsured motorist protection.

Q. What is no-fault insurance?

A. Under **no-fault insurance,** which is usually compulsory, insurance carriers compensate their own policyholders for medical and other costs associated with automobile accidents. This type of insurance is designed to protect you, any passengers in your car, and any pedestrian you may injure, without having to enter a court of law to determine who is at fault for the accident. Most no-fault statutes apply only to bodily injury claims, and do not encompass property damage claims.

Q. What are the pros and cons of no-fault laws?

A. The purported advantage of no-fault laws is that the injured party is reimbursed relatively promptly by his or her insurance company, saving the party from a protracted court case. On the debit side, no-fault laws restrict the injured person's right to sue the other driver for general damages. No fault insurance has also been criticized for

- not providing an incentive to drive safely, because both the careless driver and the innocent victim are entitled to the same compensation, and
- not resulting in reduced insurance premiums, as promised by insurance companies.

THE WORLD AT YOUR FINGERTIPS

- *Several online legal advice pages have information about the law relating to auto accidents. Check out accident-law. freeadvice.com/auto, and www.lawguru. com/faq/1.html. Remember that online legal information, even if it seems appropriate to your own circumstances, is no replacement for the advice of a lawyer.*
- *You can find more information about insurance at the Autopedia website at autopedia.com/html/Insure.html.*
- *You can find detailed information designed to help you understand state laws and auto insurance at the website of the Insurance Information Institute; visit www.iii.org.*

REMEMBER THIS

- *In an accident, try to keep your head and to be civil and cooperative with the police and the other parties. When the police ask, be ready to provide identification and proof of insurance.*
- *Be careful not to admit fault or guilt, or even apologize to the other party—let the courts determine who is responsible for the accident.*
- *Try to gather as much information as you can about the scene of the accident and ask for the contact details of any witnesses.*
- *When shopping for insurance, make sure you understand the requirements in your state.*
- *Even if your state does not require it, you may want to look into uninsured (or under-insured) motorist coverage, in the event that you are involved in an accident with a driver with little or no coverage.*

Law and the Workplace

The law affects just about every aspect of work. Federal and state laws regulate the hiring process, the terms and conditions of employment, and the circumstances under which employees can be terminated.

The law helps shape the relationship between employer and employee. The law does not address every issue that can arise on the job, but a basic understanding of what the law does require can help both the employer and the employee anticipate problems and avoid trouble.

Understanding your legal rights does not mean that you can only enforce them through a lawsuit. A lawsuit should be a last resort, not the starting point. Lawsuits are costly and time-consuming. Rather, employers and employees should first try to discuss their differences. Such discussions are easier and more productive when both sides understand how the law affects the situation. Many employers try to anticipate problems before they occur, and solve problems when they do arise.

This chapter helps both employees and employers understand how the law affects their rights and obligations at work. It explains the laws and suggests places to turn for further details. While this chapter discusses both federal and state laws, it does not go into detail on the laws of each specific state. We'll refer to state law and generally discuss how state law can affect the work relationship. However, no two states' laws are exactly alike, so we won't provide guidance as to how a specific state's laws affect the workplace. Each section in this chapter answers commonly asked questions about a specific area of law.

INTRODUCTION TO LAW AND THE WORKPLACE

Q. What is the law of the workplace?

A. There is no single "law of the workplace." Today's workplace law consists of federal and state laws, civil service rules, collective bargaining agreements, contracts, company personnel handbooks, and employer practices.

Q. Will this chapter answer specific questions for the employee or employer?

A. No, this chapter cannot cover every situation or offer advice on your specific problem. Instead, you should view it as a basic road map.

This chapter will help employees determine if the law provides help for a problem they encounter at work. It will help employers determine if their policies or practices are consistent with the law. It will tell you where to find more information, and which government agencies can provide assistance in dealing with certain workplace issues. After reading this chapter, you will be in a better position to decide whether to seek legal advice for a particular problem.

Q. Does it matter if a person works for the federal or a state government, instead of a private employer?

A. Yes, it makes a big difference. Generally, labor contracts and federal and state laws regulate the relationship between private employees and employers, such as a retail business or a manufacturer. The government, however, is a public employer and is subject not only to any labor contracts and the laws but also to the restrictions imposed by federal and state constitutions. For example, the First Amendment restricts government interference with free speech and prohibits the government from disciplining one of its workers who speaks out on issues of public concern. The First Amendment, however, generally does not apply to a private employer and thus does not prohibit a private employer from firing such an employee. In addition, most governmental employment is also regulated by civil service rules.

Q. What is the legal significance of a union contract?

A. When employees select a union as their bargaining representative, the union negotiates a **collective bargaining agreement** (contract) with the employer. This contract contains the terms and conditions of employment for the employees in the bargaining unit. The terms of the contract are legally binding on both the employer and the employees, providing a source of enforceable employment rights. Individual employees cannot usually negotiate separate deals with the employer, but collective bargaining agreements in fields such as professional sports and the entertainment industry often permit union members to negotiate separately.

If there is no union contract, the employee deals directly with the employer and negotiates his or her own terms of employment. Generally, that employee does not have the protections of a written contract.

Q. Does this chapter cover independent contractors?

A. No. Workplace law regulates the relationship between employers and employees. As a matter of law, independent contractors are not employees. Generally, if an employer controls, directs, and supervises you in performing your work, you are considered to be an employee. Courts also would consider you an employee if you're paid on a salary or wage basis rather than a per project basis and if the employer furnishes the equipment you use in the performance of the work.

But if the employer merely specifies the result to be achieved, and you use personal judgment and discretion in achieving that result, then you may be considered an **independent contractor.**

For example, ABC Company hires Jill to construct a fence around its property, and agrees to pay her $1,000. ABC does not supervise Jill's work; it does not tell her how to build the fence or what time to report to work. The company cares only about getting the fence built. Jill's income is based on the profits she makes on the job after subtracting the cost of buying the fencing materials. Her relationship with ABC ends when she finishes the job. Jill is an independent contractor, not the employee of ABC.

FEDERAL LAWS REGULATING THE WORKPLACE

Throughout this chapter, we'll often refer to federal law. Many of these laws affect not just one aspect of the employment relationship, but the entire spectrum of rights and responsibilities within the workplace.

In this section we'll introduce some of the most frequently encountered laws and other federal laws that we'll discuss in more depth in subsequent sections of this chapter.

▶ **GETTING LEGAL HELP**

The law of the workplace is complex, and it's often worthwhile to consult with a lawyer trained to deal with these matters. Contact your state or local bar association to find lawyers in your area. Many of these organizations have a lawyer referral service. Chapter 1, "When and How to Use a Lawyer," can help you find a lawyer.

Q. What is Title VII of the Civil Rights Act?

A. Title VII is a federal law that prohibits discrimination in employment based on race, color, religion, sex, and national origin.

Q. What types of employers are regulated under Title VII?

A. This federal law covers both public (government) and private employers that employ at least fifteen people. Title VII also covers unions and employment agencies. Remember, however, that state or local law prohibiting employment discrimination may cover employers with fewer than fifteen employees.

Q. Is there a federal agency responsible for enforcement of Title VII?

A. Yes. The Equal Employment Opportunity Commission (EEOC) enforces Title VII.

Q. What is 42 U.S.C. Section 1981?

A. Section 1981, as it is commonly known, is a federal law that prohibits employment discrimination based on race or ethnicity.

Q. What types of employers are regulated under Section 1981?

A. This law covers all public and private employers, regardless of size.

Q. Is there a federal agency responsible for enforcement of Section 1981?

A. No. This statute is enforced solely by individual people filing lawsuits.

Q. What is the Age Discrimination in Employment Act?

A. The Age Discrimination in Employment Act (ADEA) prohibits employment discrimination based on age. For purposes of this statute, age is defined as forty years of age or older. Thus, under the ADEA, an employer could refuse to hire you because you are twenty-five years old. However, some state laws prohibiting age discrimination have a broader definition of the protected class. For example, Oregon prohibits age discrimination against anyone eighteen years of age or older, while Michigan has no specific age limits.

Q. What types of employers are regulated under the ADEA?

A. This federal law covers public and private employers employing at least twenty employees. It also covers unions and employment agencies. Remember, however, that state or local laws prohibiting age discrimination may cover employers with fewer than twenty employees.

Q. Is there a federal agency responsible for enforcing the ADEA?

A. Yes, the EEOC enforces the ADEA.

Q. What is the Americans with Disabilities Act?

A. The Americans with Disabilities Act (ADA) prohibits discrimination in employment against persons with disabilities, both physical and mental.

Q. What types of employers are regulated under the ADA?

A. The ADA covers public and private employers employing at least fifteen employees. It also covers unions and employment agencies. Remember, however, that state or local laws prohibiting disability discrimination may cover employers not covered under the ADA.

Q. Is there a federal agency responsible for enforcing the ADA?

A. Yes, the EEOC enforces the ADA.

Q. What is the Rehabilitation Act?

A. The Rehabilitation Act, or Rehab Act, prohibits discrimination in employment against persons with disabilities, both physical and mental.

Q. How is the Rehabilitation Act different from the Americans with Disabilities Act?

A. The main difference is the type of employers covered by each statute. Whereas the ADA covers employers who employ at least fifteen employees,

the Rehabilitation Act applies to employers who are contractors or subcontractors of the federal government, and to employers who receive federal funds.

Q. I work for a state government agency. Can I sue my employer for violating an employment law?

A. It depends on what law you are claiming the state has violated. If it is a state law (and the law applies to state employers), then you can file suit against the state agency. However, if it is a federal law, you may not be able to file a lawsuit. The Eleventh Amendment to the Constitution provides that state governments have immunity from federal lawsuits filed by individuals. The Supreme Court has held that Congress can abrogate state immunity only under very specific circumstances. Both Title VII and the Family Medical Leave Act have been held to overcome state immunity validly; therefore, individual employees can sue state employers under these two federal statutes. However, the ADA, the ADEA, and the Fair Labor Standards Act (FLSA) do not abrogate state immunity, and individual employees cannot sue state employers for violating these federal laws.

This immunity doesn't mean that the states do not have to comply with these laws. If states fail to comply, the federal government (through the EEOC with respect to the ADEA and the ADA, and the Department of Labor [DOL] with respect to the FLSA) can initiate lawsuits against the state to enforce compliance. Moreover, some states, such as Minnesota, have waived their immunity, allowing employees to file a lawsuit against their state employer.

Finally, immunity does not apply to local government employers, which can be sued by their employees for violating any federal law.

Q. Is there a federal agency responsible for enforcing the Rehabilitation Act?

A. Yes. The Office of Federal Contract Compliance, in the Department of Labor, enforces the Rehabilitation Act.

Q. What is the National Labor Relations Act?

A. The National Labor Relations Act (NLRA) deals with the role of unions as the bargaining representative of employees and prohibits discrimination in employment based on union activity or other protected concerted activity.

Q. What types of employers are covered under the NLRA?

A. The NLRA covers only private employers that have an impact on interstate commerce. It specifically excludes public employers, railway and airline employers, and people who are employed as agricultural laborers. Generally, the dollar volume of business the company generates determines whether it affects interstate commerce. For example, the law covers a retail or service establishment with annual gross receipts of at least $500,000. It also covers manufacturing companies that ship at least $50,000 worth of goods across state lines, or that purchase at least $50,000 worth of goods from out of state. The NLRA also covers labor unions. Remember, however, that state labor relations acts might cover an employer not covered by the NLRA.

Q. Is there a federal agency responsible for enforcing the NLRA?

🗐 THE MEANING OF "DISABILITY"

Both the ADA and the Rehabilitation Act protect individuals with disabilities. The definition of the term **disability** is the same for both laws. A qualified individual with a disability is one who

- has a physical or mental impairment that substantially limits a major life activity; or
- has a record of having such a physical or mental impairment; or
- is regarded as having such an impairment.

This broad definition includes any physiologically based impairment or any mental or psychological impairment, but it does not include mere physical characteristics or cultural, economic, or environmental impairment. For example, a person with dyslexia may have a disability, but a person who is illiterate does not; a person who is a dwarf may have a disability, but a person who is short does not.

The impairment must cause a substantial limitation to a major life activity. Major life activities include walking, seeing, hearing, or being able to care for oneself. Temporary conditions, such as a broken leg or a cold, would not be considered substantial limitations. Whether an impairment causes a substantial limitation is determined on a case-by-case basis, taking into account how the impairment affects the particular person involved. Thus, for some people, epilepsy will cause a substantial limitation, while for others it will not.

The second meaning of the term includes people who no longer have a disability but have a record of a disability, such as a person who successfully recovered from a disabling disease.

The third meaning of the term includes people who have a condition that does not substantially limit a major life activity but are faced with an employer who believes it does cause such a limitation. For example, this definition would include a worker who has asymptomatic HIV/AIDS and is not hired because the prospective employer mistakenly believes that the worker is unable to care for himself and therefore would cause disruption in the workplace.

A. Yes, the National Labor Relations Board (NLRB) enforces the NLRA.

Q. *What is the Fair Labor Standards Act?*

A. The Fair Labor Standards Act (FLSA) establishes minimum wage and overtime standards for employees, and regulates child labor.

Q. *Is there a federal agency responsible for enforcing the FLSA?*

A. Yes, the Wage and Hour Division of the Department of Labor enforces and administers the FLSA.

Q. *What types of employers are covered under the FLSA?*

A. The FLSA generally covers a private employer if at least two employees are engaged in interstate commerce activities and if the annual volume of business is at least $500,000. It also covers hospitals, educational institutions, and state and federal public employers. Moreover, it covers individual employees who are engaged in interstate commerce activities even if their employer does not gross $500,000 a year. Remember that state laws regulating minimum wages, overtime, and child labor may cover employers not covered by federal law.

ⓘ **BY ANY OTHER NAME . . .**

The NLRA is referred to by several different names. It is also called the Wagner Act, and is part of the Labor-Management Relations Act (also called the Taft-Hartley Act).

ⓘ **DETERMINING WHEN INDIVIDUAL EMPLOYEES ARE ENGAGED IN INTERSTATE COMMERCE**

The Wage and Hour Division of the Department of Labor has identified five categories of employees that it considers engaged in interstate commerce and therefore covered by the FLSA.

- Employees participating in the actual movement of commerce—for example, employees employed in the telephone, telegraph, television, transportation, banking, and insurance industries

- Employees doing work related to the instrumentalities of commerce—for example, employees who maintain and repair roads, bridges, or telephone lines; or employees who work at warehouses, airports, or bus stations

- Employees who regularly cross state lines in the performance of their duties—for example, traveling salespersons or traveling service technicians

- Employees who produce or work on goods for commerce—for example, assembly workers in an auto plant, coal miners, shipping department employees, or clerical and administrative workers who do the support work necessary to produce goods for commerce

- Employees who are employed in a closely related process or occupation essential to producing goods for commerce—for example, employees who build tool and die machines used by auto plants

As you can see, FLSA coverage is extremely broad.

Q. What is Executive Order 11246?

A. Executive Order 11246 imposes obligations on employers with a federal contract or subcontract. If a contract is worth at least $10,000, the employer can't lawfully discriminate based on race, color, religion, sex, or national origin. The nondiscrimination requirement is essentially the same as that imposed under Title VII. If a contract is worth at least $50,000 and the contractor employs at least fifty employees, the employer must also develop and use an affirmative action plan.

The Rehabilitation Act prohibits federal contractors and subcontractors who have contracts in excess of $2,500 from discriminating against people with disabilities. It also requires them to take affirmative action to employ people with disabilities.

Developing affirmative action plans and putting them into action will be discussed on page 425.

THE WORLD AT YOUR FINGERTIPS

- *The Legal Information Institute at Cornell University maintains a website on topics relating to many aspects of workplace law. You can access the list of topics at www.law.cornell.edu/topics/topic2.html# employment%20law. The LII website also contains the full text of all the legislation referred to in this section. Some of the*

▶ A CHECKLIST OF OTHER FEDERAL LAWS REGULATING EMPLOYMENT

Besides those laws listed in the accompanying questions and answers, other federal laws affect employment. Here is an introductory checklist of these laws; we'll discuss them in more detail later in this chapter.

Unions The Railway Labor Act regulates union activity in the workplace and prohibits employment discrimination based on union activity. It only covers airlines and railways.

Wages and Hours The Davis-Bacon Act, the Service Contract Act, and the Walsh-Healy Public Contracts Act require employers with certain types of federal government contracts to pay their employees a minimum wage as determined by the secretary of labor.

Equal Pay The Equal Pay Act requires employers to pay equal wages to male and female employees who are performing substantially equivalent work.

Workplace Safety The Occupational Safety and Health Act (OSH Act) requires employers to furnish a workplace free from hazards likely to cause death or serious injury and to comply with safety and health standards promulgated under the law.

Mine Safety The Mine Safety and Health Act requires mine operators to comply with safety and health standards promulgated under the law.

Pensions and Welfare Benefit Plans The Employee Retirement Income Security Act (ERISA) establishes eligibility and vesting rights for employees in company pension plans, and establishes administrative, fiduciary, funding, and termination requirements for pension plans. This law also regulates, to a lesser degree, other types of employee benefit plans, such as medical insurance or legal services.

Immigrant Workers The **Immigration Reform and Control Act (IRCA)** prohibits employers from hiring illegal aliens, requires employers to verify the work eligibility status of applicants, and protects lawfully admitted aliens by prohibiting discrimination in employment based on citizenship status.

Other Terms of Employment The **Uniformed Services Employment and Reemployment Rights Act (USERRA)** requires employers to reinstate employees who have served in the armed forces to their former jobs upon completion of their military duty and prohibits employment discrimination because of an employee's past, current, or future military obligations.

The **Worker Adjustment and Retraining Notification Act (WARN Act)** requires employers to give sixty days' advance notice of plant closings or mass layoffs to workers, unions, and state and local governments.

The **Employee Polygraph Protection Act (EPPA)** prohibits employers from requiring employees or applicants to submit to polygraph examinations.

The **Family and Medical Leave Act (FMLA)** requires employers to grant employees up to twelve weeks of unpaid leave during any twelve-month period because of the birth or adoption of a child, because the employee has a serious health condition, or because the employee has to care for a parent, spouse, or child with a serious health condition.

The **Jury System Improvements Act** prohibits disciplining or discharging an employee because of federal court jury duty.

The **Drug-Free Workplace Act** requires federal government contractors and grantees to establish a drug-free awareness program for their employees.

---

topic headings that you will find are collective bargaining; employment discrimination; employment law; labor law; pension law; unemployment compensation; workers' compensation; and workplace safety. By clicking on the relevant topic, you can access information providing a general overview of that topic and links to source materials and other references discussing the issue.

REMEMBER THIS

- *The law of the workplace consists of federal law, state law, contracts such as collective bargaining agreements, employee manuals, and much more.*
- *Workplace laws apply to employees, but independent contractors are not considered employees.*

- *Because they work for a unit of government, public employees have certain constitutional rights that private employees lack.*

THE HIRING PROCESS

Several stages are involved in hiring employees: soliciting and reviewing applications, interviewing candidates, and selecting a candidate for hire. As you will see in this section, the law affects each of these stages.

Q. How do the formal laws against discrimination apply?

A. Federal antidiscrimination laws prohibit discrimination in employment, including in the hiring process, based on race, color, religion, national origin, sex, age, disability, and union affiliation.

Most states have laws duplicating the prohibitions contained in federal law. Moreover, many state laws forbid discrimination based on other types of classifications as well. For example, Wisconsin prohibits discrimination based on arrest and conviction records, sexual orientation, and marital status.

Q. Are there laws specifically on hiring?

A. Yes. Some federal and state laws regulate the use of certain types of tests and screening devices in the hiring process. Also, a state's common law

of torts may impose a duty on employers not to invade employees' privacy unnecessarily.

Q. Do public employers face additional restrictions on hiring?

A. Yes. The U.S. Constitution and civil service laws come into play. Because of the constitutional guarantee of freedom of association, government employers cannot discriminate in hiring based on political affiliation (unless party affiliation is a necessary requirement for effective performance of the job, as would be the case, for example, with

---

ⓘ EMPLOYING DOMESTIC WORKERS

Thinking of getting some work done around the house? Are your workers going to be employees or independent contractors? (See the question discussing the differences between employees and independent contractors on page 406.) For example, if you contract with a landscaping company to mow your lawn and maintain the flower beds, the employees the company sends out to perform the work are not *your* employees. If, however, you employ a cook/housekeeper whose work you control, then the worker is your employee.

Employment laws don't govern the relationship between you and an independent contractor. However, if a domestic worker is your employee, then certain federal employment laws regulate that relationship. Examples of domestic workers who may be considered employees are in-home child care workers, cooks, housekeepers, and baby-sitters.

You must make quarterly Social Security payments to the IRS for every domestic employee at least eighteen years of age who earns more than $1,200 per calendar year. You must also pay federal unemployment taxes for every domestic employee who earns more than $1,000 per calendar quarter. Consult your accountant for rules regarding withholding taxes from an employee's pay.

Here's how wage and hour laws affect domestic workers. The Fair Labor Standards Act (FLSA) covers baby-sitters if they work more than twenty hours per week. The FLSA applies to other domestic employees who earn more than $50 during a calendar quarter and work for one or more employers for more than eight hours in any workweek. Any employee who meets this definition must be paid the federal minimum wage and overtime for hours worked in excess of forty during any one workweek for a single employer.

If a domestic employee resides in your house, then the overtime provisions of the FLSA do not apply, but the minimum wage requirements do. Later in this section, we discuss federal laws governing the employment of aliens (see page 421).

Finally, you may want to buy workers' compensation insurance for your domestic employee—it's a wise precaution.

a governor's speechwriter). Civil service laws generally provide that hiring decisions should be based on the "merit" of the applicant, which is usually determined by administering competitive examinations.

Q. What are the elements of a good job advertisement?

A. The main idea is to avoid discrimination while at the same time targeting qualified candidates. Ads should avoid words suggesting a preferred race, sex, religion, national origin, or age. For example, using "recent college grad," instead of "college degree required," could indicate a preference for young people and discourage older qualified applicants from applying. Using the term "salesman" instead of "salesperson" suggests that only men should apply. The phrase "An Equal Opportunity Employer" in an ad means the employer will judge all applicants based on their qualifications for the job, without regard to race, sex, religion, national origin, age, or disability.

Q. Can employers set basic job requirements and work standards?

A. Yes, as long as they do not discriminate based on a protected classification. Qualifications listed for a job should be necessary for the performance of the job. Even neutral job requirements can cause discrimination. For example, requiring a college degree for a job on a factory assembly line could disproportionately screen out minority applicants vis-à-vis white applicants, since disproportionately fewer minority students attend college. The minority applicants would be screened out based not on their ability to do the job but based on a factor (college education) unrelated to being a good assembly line worker.

Q. What are some other examples of neutral job requirements that can cause discrimination?

A. Refusing to hire single custodial parents may discriminate against women, since women are more likely to have physical custody of their children. Requiring applicants to speak fluent English

for a job that does not require communication skills may discriminate against applicants whose nation of origin is not the United States. Height and weight standards can discriminate based on sex and national origin.

Whenever seemingly neutral requirements have a discriminatory effect, the employer must be able to show that the requirements are related to job performance. Thus, requirements for job-related experience and specific job-related skills are usually valid.

Q. How does the ADA (Americans with Disabilities Act) affect an employer's ability to establish basic job requirements and work standards?

A. Job requirements and work standards that would screen out a person based on his or her disability must be job-related and consistent with business necessity. Under the ADA, in order to be job related, a job requirement must be related to the essential functions of the job and not merely an incidental aspect of job performance. For example, a job description for a receptionist position states that typing skills are required; however, the employer has never required the receptionist to type. This requirement, therefore, is not an essential function of the job, and requiring typing skills could have the effect of screening

---

⚠ YOU NEED A LICENSE FOR THESE JOBS

State rules limit some jobs to people who have licenses. Depending on the state, these might include cosmetologists, barbers, electricians, heating/air-conditioning technicians, engineers, nurses, builders, lawyers, accountants, dental hygienists, and physicians. If you're considering such a career, contact your state licensing authorities to see what requirements apply.

out a person with only one arm or a person who is a paraplegic.

Q. How can an employer identify the essential functions of a job?

A. The EEOC regulations list several factors that help determine the essential functions of a job:

- The extent to which the position exists to perform the function—for example, a secretarial position that exists to type letters and documents.
- The number of other employees available to perform the function—for example, even though the receptionist's main duty is not typing, the company has only one other secretarial employee, and when that employee is sick or on vacation the receptionist fills in.
- The amount of time spent performing the function—for example, the secretary spends 75 percent of his or her time typing documents.
- The effect of not requiring the person in this job to be able to perform the function—for example, a firefighter may be called upon to carry a heavy person from a burning building only rarely, but failing to perform this function could cost a life.
- The work experience of employees who have previously performed the job.

Q. If a person with a disability cannot perform an essential function of the job, can the employer refuse to hire him or her?

A. Not necessarily. The question is whether the inability to perform the essential function of the job is due to lack of qualifications or due to the disability. If the employer is hiring for secretarial positions and an applicant cannot type, then the employer could refuse to hire him or her even if the applicant suffered from a disabling disease. (For more on this point, see the discussion in "The Protected Class Under the ADA.")

If, however, the applicant does possess typing skills, then the question becomes whether, with a reasonable accommodation, he or she would be able to perform the essential function of the job. For example, an applicant for a secretarial position who is blind may be unable to use the word processor. However, if the applicant is provided with a Braille keyboard, the applicant can use the word processor and would thus be able to perform the essential function of the job.

Q. How does an employer know if an applicant or employee needs a "reasonable accommodation" to be able to perform the essential functions of the job?

A. The applicant or employee should inform the employer of the need for an accommodation. The ADA does not require the employer to provide an accommodation if it is unaware of the need for one.

Also, the employer may ask for documentation of the need for an accommodation when the disability is not an obvious one.

Q. Is an employer's obligation to provide an accommodation unlimited?

A. No. The ADA only requires the employer to provide reasonable accommodations that do not

---

📑 THE PROTECTED CLASS UNDER THE ADA

The ADA protects "qualified individuals with a disability" from discrimination in employment. An individual with a disability is **qualified** if he or she has "the requisite skill, experience, education and other job-related requirements" for the job. For example, in deciding whether someone with epilepsy is qualified to teach, you'd ask if he or she had a teaching certificate or a college degree in education. If not, then the person is not qualified and is not a member of the protected class under the ADA.

cause undue hardship. The law specifically lists what factors should be considered in determining **undue hardship:**

- The nature and cost of the accommodation needed
- The overall financial resources of the facility involved, including the number of persons employed at the facility, the effect on expenses and resources of the facility, and the impact on the operation of the facility
- The overall financial resources of the employer as a whole, including the overall size of the business
- The type of operation of the employer, including the composition, structure, and function of the workforce and the relationship of the facility in question to the employer as a whole

Whether an accommodation causes an undue hardship is determined on a case-by-case basis. An accommodation that would violate a bona fide seniority system is not "reasonable."

Q. Is it ever appropriate to indicate a preference for applicants of a specific sex or age?

A. Rarely. Antidiscrimination laws require employers to consider applicants as individuals and not make decisions based on stereotypical assumptions. If a factory job requires a worker regularly to lift forty pounds, an employer cannot express a preference for young male applicants based on the stereotyped notion that men are strong and older people and women are weak. Some women and older people can lift forty pounds, just as some young men cannot. Rather, the employer's job ad should state that the job requires "regularly lifting forty pounds."

In some rare circumstances, however, it is an objective fact that people who are members of a protected class cannot perform the job in question. For example, a filmmaker may hire only men for male roles, or a kosher deli may hire only Jewish people as butchers. In both of these examples, sex and religion are **bona fide occupational qualifications (BFOQ).** Both Title VII and the ADEA allow employers to limit a job to applicants of a specific group when the employer can prove that sex, religion, national origin, or age is a BFOQ for the job in question. Race, color, and disability, however, can never qualify as a BFOQ.

ⓘ EXAMPLES OF REASONABLE ACCOMMODATIONS

The following are examples of the actions an employer may be required to take to provide a reasonable accommodation:

- Making existing facilities readily accessible
- Restructuring the job
- Modifying work schedules or making a job part-time
- Modifying equipment
- Providing readers or interpreters

Employers are not required to provide equipment or devices primarily for personal use, such as corrective glasses, hearing aids, or wheelchairs. Whether a particular employer is required to provide a specific accommodation will depend on whether providing it will cause undue hardship.

Q. Some employers find applicants through word of mouth, by talking to their current employees. Is anything wrong with this?

A. That depends on the makeup of the workforce. Using the old-boy network generally results in applications mainly from other old boys. If the workers are mainly nonminorities, news about the job vacancy will be limited to their circle of acquaintances, who may be mostly Caucasian non-Hispanic people as well. This has the effect of closing out minority applicants. An employer can avoid problems by disseminating news of job openings as widely as possible to reach a broad pool of applicants. Placing ads in newspapers and magazines with a widespread circulation base, and using employment agencies, can help in reaching a variety of qualified applicants.

Q. What should employers be aware of when conducting job interviews?

A. By their very nature, job interviews are subjective. Employers cannot help but form an assortment of impressions in judging an applicant's

---

ⓘ RELIGIOUS INSTITUTIONS CAN EXPRESS A PREFERENCE FOR EMPLOYEES OF A PARTICULAR RELIGION

Title VII expressly allows religious corporations and sectarian educational institutions to hire applicants of a particular religion. For example, a Catholic grade school could decide to hire a teacher because the teacher is a Catholic rather than hire an applicant who is a Protestant. This exemption applies only to religion, however, and the school may not discriminate in hiring teachers based on race, color, sex, national origin, age, or disability.

---

ambition, motivation, creativity, dependability, and responsibility. Realizing the inherently subjective nature of the process, employers should try to make an interview as objective (fact-based) as possible. Concentrating on objective information helps to avoid decisions made based on conscious or subconscious prejudice and focuses the hiring process on an applicant's qualifications and employment experience.

Employers should also try to make job interviews as uniform as possible. They should ask the same set of questions of all applicants for the same position. This allows for a better basis for comparison among applicants. It can also prevent discrimination in the content of a job interview. For example, asking an applicant "Do you type?" but not asking another applicant the same question could indicate discriminatory stereotyping if the applicant who is asked the question is a woman.

Q. Does federal law prohibit any specific questions?

A. Yes. The ADA prohibits an employer from asking an applicant whether he or she has a disability or inquiring into the nature or severity of a disability (though the employer may ask questions about the applicant's ability to do the job). The National Labor Relations Act (NLRA) prohibits employers from questioning employees about union membership or activities. Neither Title VII nor the Age Discrimination in Employment Act (ADEA) prohibits any specific questions. An employer, however, should not ask questions that may imply discrimination. Moreover, some state laws, such as those in West Virginia, expressly prohibit certain types of preemployment questions, such as questions about marital status or number of dependents.

Q. What types of questions may imply discrimination?

A. Direct questions relating to an applicant's age, family background, or religious affiliation may indicate discrimination. Questions or comments based on stereotyped notions may also imply discrimination.

Interview questions should relate to the requirements of the job and the applicant's qualifications, work experience, and history. Even when the information sought is related to the job, the interviewer must be careful that the way the question is asked does not imply discrimination. For example, an employer trying to determine whether a female applicant is going to stay with the company for the next few years should not ask, "Do you plan to get married?" or "Do you plan to have children?" or "What kind of birth control do you use?" More direct, job-related questions, such as the following, permit an employer to obtain the desired information without being discriminatory:

- We are looking for employees who will make a commitment to the company. Is there any reason you might not stay with us for the next few years?
- What are your career objectives?

- Where do you see yourself in five years?

Similarly, suppose an employer is trying to determine a female job candidate's commitment to living in a particular area of the country. It is better to ask, "Do you intend to stay in the area?" rather than "Is your husband's employer likely to transfer him?"

If attendance is the issue, questions such as "Does your husband expect you to be home to cook dinner?" or "What will you do if your children get sick?" are indirect and inefficient. It is more direct to ask, "How was your attendance record with your prior employer?"

Q. What is "need-to-know," and how does it apply to job interviews?

A. The key is whether there is an objective, job-related reason why an employer wants applicants to answer a question. Questions that do not violate the antidiscrimination laws may still create

---

📄 BONA FIDE OCCUPATIONAL QUALIFICATIONS

Title VII allows an employer to make a hiring decision based on sex, religion, or national origin if the employer can prove that a particular sex, religion, or national origin is a bona fide occupational qualification (BFOQ) for the job in question. The ADEA also allows the employer to make a hiring decision based on age if the employer can prove age is a BFOQ.

The employer must prove that his or her hiring decision falls within the very narrow limits allowed by the BFOQ defense. The employer must show both that

- all persons of the excluded class would be unable to perform the requirements of the job, and
- the requirements of the job directly relate to the essence of the employer's business.

The evidence that the employer presents must be objective and not based on stereotyped beliefs about persons in the protected class.

Years ago some airlines tried to defend their decision not to hire men as flight attendants on the basis that males were unable to provide reassurance to anxious passengers or give courteous, personalized service. The court held that even if this were true, the ability to reassure and give courteous service did not relate to the essence of the employer's business, which was the safe transport of passengers.

The BFOQ defense applies in very limited circumstances, such as for actors or fashion models.

problems. The tort law in some states protects people from unwarranted invasions of personal privacy. An employer that makes offensive inquiries into an applicant's personal life, unrelated to the requirements of the job, may be liable for invasion of privacy.

Sometimes employers clearly must have certain information. For example, whether an applicant has ever been convicted of a crime may substantially affect the applicant's fitness for a specific job. And employers do need to make their job offers dependent on candidates' production of proper documentation of their citizenship or work authorization. (However, asking about national origin may be viewed as discriminatory.)

A good general rule—don't ask about something in an interview unless there is a legitimate business reason for the question.

Q. What should an applicant do if the interviewer does ask questions that seem inappropriate or discriminatory?

A. The tactful applicant might avoid answering the discriminatory question directly, and in that way alert the interviewer to the fact that the question was inappropriate. For example, if the interviewer asks an applicant if he or she has children,

the applicant could respond, "Oh—you're wondering whether I'll be able to work long hours. I can assure you that I will. My current boss can confirm that."

If the interviewer continues to ask inappropriate or discriminatory questions, the applicant should make a written record of all those questions as soon as the interview is over. If the applicant does not get the job, the applicant may need a record of the discriminatory questions to file a charge with the EEOC.

Q. May an employer use a lie detector to find out if a job applicant or an employee is honest?

A. The Employee Polygraph Protection Act (EPPA) prohibits employers from requiring employees or applicants to take a polygraph test. This federal law covers all private employers with at least two employees engaged in interstate commerce activities and an annual volume of business of at least $500,000. It does not apply to any public employer. The law provides an exception to the use of a polygraph in two situations:

- An employer can use a polygraph in connection with an ongoing investigation into theft (see the sidebar "Polygraphs and Theft Investigations").

▶ **HOW EMPLOYERS CAN HIRE WITHOUT DISCRIMINATION**

It helps to use a standard application form that avoids irrelevant questions. Avoid asking about age, height, weight, marital status, and education or arrest record unless they relate to the job. For example, questions about height and weight may discriminate against women or members of some ethnic groups. Asking about marital status may suggest sex discrimination. Asking about disabilities is against the law.

Employers and prospective employees both benefit when job openings are clearly defined. Ideally, employers should prepare a detailed job description for each position, specifying what the work is and what qualifications the employer requires. During the interview, the employer should use a checklist based on the job description to rate applicants in an organized and consistent manner predicated on their respective qualifications for the job. If both sides come to the interview with a clear idea of what the job involves, the interview is more likely to focus on the qualifications essential for doing the job.

- Employers that provide security services can administer a polygraph to certain applicants, as can employers engaged in the manufacture of controlled substances.

Most states also have state laws that either prohibit or regulate the use of polygraph tests in employment. A few states, such as Massachusetts and Minnesota, prohibit all tests and devices purporting to determine honesty.

Q. May an employer run a background check on an applicant?

A. Background checks may be necessary for certain jobs. These include jobs involving security or trade secrets. Moreover, background checks help if the employer should later face a negligent hiring suit, and they should be done for any employee who interacts with the public, has access to homes, or has responsibility for the aged, the infirm, or children.

Checks should be made fairly and without bias and should comply with the FCRA (see next

---

ⓘ POLYGRAPHS AND THEFT INVESTIGATIONS

Under the law, employers can't normally use polygraphs in the hiring process. The law also severely limits how they're used on the job.

An employer is allowed to request that an employee take a lie detector test if the test is administered in connection with an ongoing investigation involving economic loss or injury to the employer's business. The employer may only make this request of employees who had access to the missing property or whom the employer reasonably suspects were involved in the incident. An employee is free to refuse to take the test, and the employer cannot take action against the employee based on the refusal.

---

answer). They should concern only issues relating to performance of the specific job. An employer that unnecessarily pries into private information or uses unreasonable methods to get data could be sued for invasion of privacy.

Q. May an employer run a credit check on an applicant?

A. Yes. They are very helpful when the information is necessary for a job-related purpose. This might include anyone who handles credit cards, or has access to merchandise, which is most of the retail service industry. It also encompasses a number of individuals in the wholesale sector, such as warehouse workers, shippers, and so on.

However, it's wise not to use credit checks indiscriminately. Court cases under Title VII have held that requiring people to have good credit before they can be hired can have a discriminatory result, since nonwhites are more likely than whites to live below the poverty level. Even if a credit check is necessary for the job in question, the Fair Credit Reporting Act (a federal law discussed in chapter 7, "Consumer Credit") requires employers to notify applicants if they intend to obtain credit information from a consumer reporting agency and to get written authorization from the applicant. If an employer decides not to hire applicants based in whole or in part on a credit report, the employer must inform the applicant, provide a copy of the report, and tell the applicant about his or her rights under the Fair Credit Reporting Act.

Q. May an employer require applicants to undergo a physical examination?

A. Generally speaking, no. The ADA prohibits employers from requiring preemployment physical examinations. After offering an applicant a job, however, an employer may require the applicant successfully to undergo a physical exam before starting the job under certain conditions:

- All employees in the same job category must be required to take a physical exam.

- Information obtained from the exam must be maintained in a separate medical file and kept confidential.
- The employer cannot use the information to discriminate against the employee because of a disability.

Q. May an employer require applicants or employees to undergo drug-screening tests?

A. Federal law does not prohibit drug-screening tests. Several states, however, have placed restrictions on them. Iowa and Rhode Island, for example, require employers to have probable cause before they can test employees. Other states, such as Minnesota and North Carolina, have established guidelines that must be followed in administering drug tests. In a workplace where employees are represented by a union, an employer must bargain with the union before it can begin testing employees for drugs.

Moreover, the method used by an employer in administering a drug test (such as direct observation of urination) could be considered outrageous and make the employer liable under tort law for invasion of privacy or intentional infliction of emotional distress.

Q. Can government employees be subject to random drug testing?

A. The Fourth Amendment of the U.S. Constitution prohibits the government from engaging in unreasonable searches and seizures. This restriction acts as a limit on a public employer's ability to use a drug test on its employees. Courts have generally been reluctant to allow public employers to engage in random drug tests. Instead, they usually require the employer to show some reasonable suspicion of drug use, or some compelling evidence that public safety would be jeopardized if the employee used drugs. Drug testing has been upheld for customs officers who are directly involved in drug interdiction, and for employees who are required to carry firearms.

Q. May an employer use other types of tests (such as a skills test or an intelligence test) to screen applicants?

A. Yes, but they should be job related. A test may have an illegal discriminatory result on a protected class, even if it seems fair. This may cause an employer to deny jobs to an unusually high number of minorities. For example, a test of English-language skills might disqualify an unusual number of persons for whom English is a second language. Unless the job requires English proficiency, the test may be illegal.

Extensive federal regulations govern the use of employment tests. A test has a discriminatory impact if the pass rate for a protected class is less than 80 percent of the pass rate for white men. If 50 percent of the white males pass the test, then 40 percent or more of black males must pass. If

---

ⓘ DRUG-TESTING REQUIREMENTS FOR CERTAIN OCCUPATIONS

U.S. Department of Transportation (DOT) regulations require drug testing of railroad workers and employees who operate commercial motor vehicles in interstate commerce. Testing occurs before employment, and then periodically or for reasonable cause. The U.S. Federal Aviation Administration (FAA) has also issued drug-testing regulations, similar to those issued by the DOT, covering airline flight personnel.

The Drug-Free Workplace Act, while not requiring drug testing, does require all federal contractors with contracts worth at least $25,000 or more to establish a drug-free awareness program and communicate the program to all their employees. Some states also impose drug-testing requirements for certain jobs, mainly in the transportation industry.

the pass rate is less than 80 percent of the pass rate for white males, the test is considered discriminatory under Title VII unless the employer can prove that the test is directly related in a significant way to successful job performance. If the test is job related, then the employer is allowed to use it.

Q. Are there laws that govern hiring workers under eighteen years of age?

A. Yes. The Fair Labor Standards Act (FLSA) regulates the employment of minors. With few exceptions (such as newspaper delivery), children under fourteen years of age may not be employed. Children under the age of sixteen may only work in nonhazardous jobs, and their hours of work are limited. During the school term, work hours are limited to a maximum of three hours a day and eighteen hours a week. Outside the school term, children under sixteen may work up to eight hours a day and forty hours a week. In either case, children under sixteen years old may work only from 7:00 A.M. to 7:00 P.M. (9:00 P.M. in the summer). Workers who are sixteen and seventeen years old are not limited in the number of hours they may work, but are prohibited from working in hazardous jobs.

Many states have their own rules for youth employment. An employer must follow these if they are more restrictive than federal law. For example, many states require all minors to get work permits from school authorities.

Q. Are there laws that govern the hiring of alien workers?

A. Yes. The Immigration Reform and Control Act (IRCA) prohibits all employers from hiring unauthorized alien workers. As part of the hiring process, employers must complete an eligibility form (Form I-9) for each new employee. This form ensures that the employer has verified the identity and legal eligibility of the applicant to be employed in this country. Employers who hire unauthorized aliens may be fined and imprisoned.

The employment-related provisions of the Immigration Reform and Control Act are aimed solely at steps an employer must take to ensure that it hires only people eligible to work in the United States. These provisions do not affect the immigration status of the applicant.

Q. Must an employer verify the employment status of current workers?

A. The Immigration Reform and Control Act applies only to employees hired after November 6, 1986. An employer doesn't have to verify the employment eligibility of any workers hired before that date. However, if the employer has reason to believe that a worker hired before November 6, 1986, is an unauthorized alien, then the employer would face penalties under the law if it did not verify the worker's status and, if the employee was not authorized to work, fire that worker.

▶ THE ADA AND ADMINISTERING EMPLOYMENT TESTS

Under the Americans with Disabilities Act (ADA) employers must be careful how they give employment tests. This is to ensure that the way the test is administered does not screen out applicants based on a disability. Tests should be administered in a way that accurately reflects the applicant's job-related skills rather than reflecting an applicant's disability. For example, an applicant with dyslexia or with a visual disability might fail a written test because he or she could not properly see the material and not because of a lack of knowledge. In such a circumstance, the employer may be required to provide a reader to help the applicant read the test instructions and materials. Similarly, oral tests may screen out applicants with a hearing disability. Usually, it is the responsibility of applicants to tell the employer that they need an alternative method for administering the test.

THE WORLD AT YOUR FINGERTIPS

- *For more information about workplace discrimination and equal opportunity in hiring and in all aspects of employment, contact the Equal Employment Opportunity Commission (EEOC) at 1801 L Street NW, Washington, DC 20507. You can also contact the EEOC by phone at 202-663-4900 or 800-669-3362 for publications. The website is at www.eeoc.gov.*
- *Your state may also have its own civil rights agency that handles employment discrimination. The EEOC has information on state agencies.*
- *If you work for, or are, a federal contractor, you can receive information about additional legal requirements imposed on contractors and about affirmative action programs from the Employment Standards Administration (ESA) at the Office of Federal Contract Compliance Programs,*

200 Constitution Avenue NW, Washington, DC 20210. You can contact the ESA by phone at 202-693-0023. The website is at www.dol.gov/esa/ofccp/index.htm.
- *You can find some general information on the FLSA on the DOL website at www.dol.gov/esa/regs/compliance/whd/mwposter.htm. The site provides links to the law, the regulations, and useful fact sheets.*
- *Regarding the IRCA, a good source of information is the home page of the Office of Special Counsel for Immigration-Related Unfair Employment Practices (www.usdoj.gov/crt/osc/) and the FAQ page of this same agency (www.usdoj.gov/crt/osc/htm/facts.htm).*

HOW TO VERIFY THE IDENTITY AND EMPLOYMENT ELIGIBILITY OF AN APPLICANT

The following documents are considered acceptable verification under IRCA: a U.S. passport; a birth certificate showing birth in the U.S.; a naturalization certificate; a valid foreign passport with an endorsement authorizing employment in the United States; a resident alien card with photograph and authorization for employment in the United States; or a Social Security card and a driver's license with photograph. So long as an applicant has documents that properly verify his or her identity and eligibility, an employer cannot require a particular or different document.

REMEMBER THIS

- *Many federal antidiscrimination laws affect the hiring process. These laws protect you from discrimination on the basis of race, color, religion, national origin, sex, age, disability, and union affiliation.*
- *State and local laws may give you extra protection; for example, some protect against discrimination based on marital status, sexual orientation, or arrest record.*
- *Employers can set job standards and requirements, but they can't lawfully discriminate against members of protected groups, even indirectly.*
- *Employers should make job openings known widely in the community, and should have interview procedures that encourage questions that focus closely on the requirements of the job; they should especially avoid any questions based on stereotypes.*
- *Certain federal laws regulate aspects of the hiring process; for example, employers usually can't give lie detector tests, are regulated in hiring children, and have to*

verify the eligibility of new hires to work in the United States.

ON THE JOB

The law affects almost everything a worker does when on the job. This section provides the rundown on the laws on unlawful discrimination, sexual harassment, job safety, and privacy, as well as unions and wages and hours.

Discrimination in the Workplace

Q. Besides hiring, what other aspects of the employment relationship are regulated by antidiscrimination laws?

A. Antidiscrimination laws regulate all aspects of work, including hiring, firing, promotions, job duties, wages, benefits, and reviews. Generally speaking, the laws do not require an employer to provide specific benefits or to institute job review procedures or to draw up job descriptions. Rather, the employer is allowed to establish its own policies so long as they are applied to all employees in a nondiscriminatory manner and so long as the policies do not have the effect of discriminating against a protected class.

Q. What are the major federal antidiscrimination laws?

A. Title VII prohibits discrimination based on race, sex, color, national origin, or religion. The ADEA prohibits discrimination based on age (if forty or over). Title I of the ADA prohibits discrimination based on disability. The NLRA prohibits discrimination based on an employee's union activity or concerted activity.

Almost every state has antidiscrimination laws that mirror the protections found under federal law. Some state statutes and local ordinances also have more expansive protection than federal law. For example, some prohibit discrimination based on marital status, sexual orientation, or weight.

Q. How do I know if an action is discriminatory in violation of the law?

A. First, the law does not forbid all discriminatory actions. The law only prohibits discrimination when it is based on a person's protected status under federal law—race, color, religion, national origin, sex, age, disability, or union activity.

Thus, if an employer makes a decision because of an employee's race, that employer has engaged in prohibited discrimination. Paying a worker lower wages than other employees because that worker is an African-American violates Title VII. But paying a worker lower wages than other employees because that worker is performing different kinds of job duties does not violate Title VII. The question is whether the reason for the difference in treatment is based on the employee's protected status. Different treatment based on protected status is called **intentional discrimination** or **disparate treatment**.

Title VII also prohibits conduct that has the effect of discriminating against people in a protected class even if the employer's reason for the different treatment is not based on protected class. For example, an employer may decide to hire only applicants who do not have custody of preschool-age children. On its face, the reason for the employer's hiring decision is not a protected class reason. However, the effect of this

DEFINING "SEX DISCRIMINATION"

The term "sex discrimination" as used in Title VII refers to gender and does not include discrimination based on sexual orientation. Some states, such as California, Hawaii, and Wisconsin, and some cities, such as Chicago, have enacted antidiscrimination laws that prohibit discrimination based on sexual orientation.

policy is disproportionately to screen out female applicants as compared with male applicants because more women are custodial parents. This policy, therefore, would have a **discriminatory effect,** also called **disparate impact**. Title VII also prohibits disparate impact discrimination, unless the employer can prove that the policy is required by business necessity and is significantly related to the requirements of the job.

The ADA defines discrimination not only in terms of disparate treatment and disparate impact but also in terms of a refusal to provide reasonable accommodation to an otherwise qualified individual with a disability. (The previous section of this chapter, "The Hiring Process," discusses this in more detail.)

Q. What should I do if I think I have been discriminated against in violation of the law?

A. It is usually a good idea to bring your complaint directly to the attention of the employer and attempt to resolve the problem informally. The employer may not be aware that people within the organization are discriminating, or the employer may want to address your complaint and fix the problem.

If, however, you want to pursue a legal remedy, you should get expert advice and act relatively quickly. Antidiscrimination laws have strict time limits for making a claim. The federal laws require employees to file a complaint first with the EEOC before filing a lawsuit in court. In some circumstances, an employee is also required to file a complaint with the state agency charged with enforcing the state's antidiscrimination laws. For claims arising under the NLRA, employees are required to file a charge with the NLRB.

Lastly, if you are fired or not hired for discriminatory reasons, you should look for another job. Do so even if it seems that you are entitled to the former job. If you do not actively seek other work, it appears as though you are not seriously interested in employment. This can weaken your claim and may limit any award of back pay.

Q. Am I protected if I complain about discrimination to my employer, or if I file a charge with the EEOC or the NLRB?

A. Federal law makes it illegal for an employer to retaliate against an employee because the employee has participated in enforcement procedures. This protection applies not only to current employees but also to former employees and applicants. Thus, it is illegal for an employer to give a former employee a negative job reference because the employee filed an EEOC or NLRB charge.

You are protected if you file a charge, testify at a hearing, or assist the government in the investigation. Moreover, Title VII, the ADA, and the ADEA also protect you if you have opposed discrimination. For example, an employee who complains to the employer about sexual harassment at work is engaged in protected opposition activity. However, the employee must have a reasonable and good-faith belief that the conduct complained of violates the law. Parallel antiretaliation protections may also exist under state law.

ⓘ SENIORITY SYSTEMS AND ANTIDISCRIMINATION LAWS

Bona fide seniority systems are immune from attack under Title VII and the ADEA. A seniority system is bona fide so long as it was not established for the purpose of discriminating against a protected class and is applied equally to all employees covered by the system.

A bona fide seniority system may have unfortunate effects. For example, decisions as to who is laid off during a downturn in business that are based on who has the least seniority are legal, even if all the most recent hires (and therefore all the employees laid off) are female.

Q. Do the antidiscrimination laws protect only women and minorities?

A. No. The antidiscrimination laws protect all workers from employment decisions based on protected status. Thus, if an employer pays a female worker better wages than a male worker performing the same job, that employer may have discriminated against the male worker based on his sex in violation of Title VII. Similarly, if an Asian-American worker who misses three days of work is suspended but a Caucasian worker who misses three days of work is fired, then the Caucasian worker may have been discriminated against on the basis of race.

Q. What is an affirmative action plan?

A. An **affirmative action plan (AAP)** establishes guidelines for recruiting, hiring, and promoting women and minorities in order to eliminate the present effects of past employment discrimination. An employer analyzes its current employment practices and the makeup of its workforce for any indications that women and minorities are excluded or disadvantaged. If the employer identifies some problems, it then devises new or different policies and practices aimed at solving the problems. Lastly, the employer develops goals by which it can measure its progress in correcting the problems.

Q. Are employers required to have affirmative action plans?

A. Title VII, the ADEA, and the ADA do not require affirmative action plans. Employers who have contracts with federal, state, and local governments, however, are often required to develop AAPs. Executive Order 11246 requires federal contractors with contracts exceeding $50,000

▶ **TIME LIMITS UNDER TITLE VII AND THE ADA**

If you have been discriminated against and want to proceed under federal laws, you must file a charge with the EEOC within 180 days from the date of the discriminatory act. The EEOC has regional offices in most major cities in the United States.

There is an exception to this time limit if the discrimination occurred in a state that has a state law prohibiting discrimination. In most instances, work-sharing agreements between the EEOC and the state agencies mean that you can file with the EEOC and it will be immediately cross-filed with the state agency, thus allowing virtually all persons making a complaint the opportunity to file in the three-hundred-day filing period.

However, in the absence of such coordination between the EEOC and a state agency, you must first file a charge with the state agency responsible for enforcing the state law. The state agency has at least sixty days to investigate your complaint. After sixty days, the EEOC can investigate your complaint, but your complaint must be filed with the EEOC within thee hundred days from the date the discrimination occurred or within thirty days after the state agency terminates its proceedings, whichever occurs first.

When the EEOC completes its investigation of the charge, it sends you a letter stating whether the EEOC found reasonable cause to believe the law was violated and informing you that you have ninety days within which to file a lawsuit in court. This letter is called a **right to sue** letter. A lawsuit under either Title VII or the ADA must be filed within ninety days of receipt of the right to sue letter. You may file a lawsuit even if the EEOC has not found reasonable cause.

and that employ at least fifty employees to develop an AAP. Many states, such as Iowa, California, and Pennsylvania, require employers who have state contracts to implement AAPs. Governors, mayors, and other public officials may require public employers to adopt AAPs. In addition, some employers voluntarily adopt AAPs.

Q. If an employer gives preferential treatment to a woman or minority employee under an AAP, isn't this reverse discrimination in violation of Title VII?

A. Not necessarily. The U.S. Supreme Court has held that voluntary AAPs remedying discoverable past discrimination are lawful. Evidence of such past discrimination might include obvious racial or sex imbalances in traditionally segregated job categories.

The question involves balancing the interest of minority employees in being free from the effect of unlawful discrimination with the employment interests of nonminority employees.

Q. What factors do the courts consider in deciding the validity of an AAP?

ⓘ DISCRIMINATION BASED ON RACE

Federal law forbids job discrimination because of race. Executive Order 11246 also requires that employers doing business with the federal government not discriminate because of race and take affirmative steps to hire and promote racial minorities. Most states and many local governments have laws prohibiting racial discrimination in employment. These laws protect all races, including African-Americans, Hispanics, Asians, Native Americans, and Caucasians.

A. The law is still developing in this area, but the courts tend to focus on four factors.

First, the AAP should be designed to eliminate obvious racial or sex-based imbalances in the workforce.

Second, the plan cannot "unnecessarily trammel the interests" of nonminority (white or male) workers. It should not exclude nonminority employees from consideration for the job in question automatically. The minority employee favored by the AAP should be qualified for the job; employers should avoid favoring unqualified workers.

Third, the AAP should not adopt strict quotas. It should strive toward realistic goals, taking into account turnover, layoffs, lateral transfers, new job openings, and retirements. These goals should also take into account the number of qualified minorities in the area workforce. Moreover, goals should be temporary, designed to achieve, not maintain, racial balance.

Fourth, courts are more likely to validate AAPs that focus on recruiting, hiring, and promotion practices, rather than plans that give special treatment in the event of a layoff. The courts are more willing to protect incumbent employees' interests in their current jobs than any speculative expectations employees might have about a job that they don't currently hold.

Q. Is an employer required to pay workers the same wage when they are performing substantially the same job?

A. No. The law prohibits differences in wages only when the reason for the difference is the race, color, religion, national origin, sex, age, or disability of the worker. An employer is allowed to pay workers different wages based on seniority, merit, piece rate, location, or another nondiscriminatory factor.

Q. Some benefits cost more to provide based on an employee's age. Must an employer provide all employees with exactly the same benefits even if it has to pay more for some of the employees?

A. Generally speaking, the employer cannot discriminate in providing benefits based on age. However, the ADEA recognizes that age affects the cost of providing some benefits. For example, the cost of providing life insurance for a sixty-year-old employee may be more than the cost of buying the same insurance for a twenty-year-old employee. So long as the employer pays the same amount in premiums for both the sixty-year-old and the twenty-year-old, it will not violate the ADEA even though the effect of paying the same premium is that the sixty-year-old will have less coverage than the twenty-year-old. However, where age does not affect the cost of the benefit, the employer cannot discriminate based on age. For example, an employer could not grant three weeks vacation to all employees under fifty but only give two weeks vacation to all employees over fifty.

Q. If an employer provides health insurance for its employees, must it offer coverage to employees with disabilities?

A. Yes. Under the ADA, an employer cannot deny employees with disabilities equal access to health insurance coverage.

Q. Must health insurance cover all medical expenses of an employee with a disability?

A. Not necessarily. Many insurance policies have **preexisting condition clauses** that disallow coverage for medical conditions that someone had before being employed by his or her current employer. Such clauses are lawful so long as they are not used as a subterfuge to evade the purposes of the ADA. Many health insurance policies also limit coverage for certain procedures or treatments to a specific number per year. For example, some provide reimbursement for only twelve psychiatric treatment sessions per year. Such limitations are generally allowed. It is not clear, however, whether an employer could offer a health insurance policy that puts a cap on the amount of reimbursement for a specific disease—for example, a $5,000 reimbursement limit for cancer—as opposed to a cap on the amount of

---

ⓘ EQUAL WAGES AND THE EQUAL PAY ACT

The Equal Pay Act (EPA) prohibits an employer from discriminating in wages on the basis of sex if the employees are performing substantially equivalent work. This same type of discrimination is also prohibited under Title VII. Both statutes are enforced by the EEOC, but there are some differences between the two.

The EPA applies to all employers covered by the FLSA (at least two workers engaged in interstate commerce and $500,000 annual volume of business), whereas Title VII covers employers with fifteen or more employees.

The EPA prohibits wage discrimination based only on sex, whereas Title VII prohibits wage discrimination based on race, color, religion, national origin, and sex.

An employee who brings a lawsuit under the EPA may be entitled to recover twice the amount of lost wages, whereas under Title VII the employee may recover lost wages, as well as compensatory damages if there is intentional discrimination and punitive damages if there is malice or recklessness. In some circumstances, the total amount of damages awarded may be greater under Title VII.

reimbursement that is available for any type of medical condition—for example, a $1 million lifetime limit.

Discrimination Based on Gender

Q. Must an employer provide health insurance coverage for pregnancy?

A. The answer depends on whether the employer provides any health insurance coverage at all. The antidiscrimination laws do not require an employer to provide any benefits, including health insurance coverage. However, if an employer does provide such benefits, they must be available to all employees without regard to sex, race, color, religion, national origin, age, or disability. Thus, if an employer provides health insurance, it must include coverage for pregnancy and pregnancy-related conditions.

Q. Must the employer's health insurance pay for abortions?

A. No. The Pregnancy Discrimination Act expressly provides that employers do not have to pay health insurance benefits for abortion, "except where the life of the mother would be endangered if the fetus were carried to term, or except where medical complications have arisen from an abortion."

Q. May employers provide health-care coverage for dependents to married male workers but deny it to married female workers?

A. No. Title VII prohibits all discrimination in benefits based on sex. Employers don't have to offer health insurance at all, to employees or their spouses, but if they do they can't discriminate. Thus, if the employer provides health insurance benefits to the spouses of male workers, it must provide the same coverage to the spouses of female workers. Moreover, the extent of the coverage provided for dependents must be equal. For example, if all medical expenses of female workers' spouses are covered, then all medical expenses of male workers' spouses must be covered.

Q. Is there any exception under Title VII that allows the employer to take sex into account in providing fringe benefits?

A. No.

ⓘ PREEXISTING MEDICAL CONDITIONS

The Health Insurance Portability and Accountability Act of 1996 (HIPAA) limits the effect of preexisting condition clauses in health insurance contracts. Individuals with a preexisting medical condition that was diagnosed, or for which treatment was received, within six months before enrolling in a new health insurance plan are not covered for that condition for the first twelve months. Thereafter, the condition is covered for as long as the employee keeps the insurance. A preexisting condition clause can never be applied to pregnancy, newborns, or adopted children.

The employee's new health plan must give "credit for time served"—that is, the amount of time you were enrolled in your previous plan—and deduct it from the exclusion period. Thus, if you've had twelve or more months of continuous group coverage, you'll have no preexisting-condition waiting period. And if you had prior coverage for ten months, you can be subject to only a two-month exclusion period when you switch jobs. In order to make sure that coverage is "continuous", you cannot let it lapse for more than sixty-two days.

Q. May an employer refuse to hire an applicant because she is pregnant, or fire a worker who becomes pregnant?

A. No. The Pregnancy Discrimination Act prohibits employment discrimination based on pregnancy.

Q. May an employer require a worker to take leave when she becomes pregnant?

A. No.

Q. When an employee takes time off to give birth to a child, will she get her old job back?

A. Title VII does not require the employer to provide either paid or unpaid leaves of absence with rights of reinstatement for pregnancy. What Title VII does require is that the employer treat absences due to pregnancy the same as it treats absences due to any other medical condition. For example, if an employer's leave policy provides for time off when employees are unable to work due to medical conditions, a worker unable to work due to pregnancy has the same right to time off as a worker unable to work due to a broken leg. The duration of any leave time also depends on the employer's policy. Thus, if the employer provides two weeks of medical leave per year, a pregnant employee would be entitled to her job back so long as her leave did not exceed two weeks. This basic principle of equal treatment applies to other decisions regarding the pregnant worker. If disabled workers are paid while on disability leave, the pregnant employee must be paid. If an employer requires that all employees submit a doctor's statement regarding their inability to work in order to be eligible for leave, then the employer may require the pregnant worker to submit such a statement.

Of course, if the employer meets the coverage requirements for the Family and Medical Leave Act (FMLA), then the employer must provide twelve weeks of unpaid leave per year for serious medical conditions, including pregnancy and childbirth. The FMLA also entitles a worker to her old job or to a substantially equivalent job after her maternity leave, regardless of how an employer treats other workers who are absent from work for other causes (see the discussion of the FMLA on page 430).

Q. Is an employer required to give workers maternity/paternity leave?

A. If an employer is covered under the terms of the Family and Medical Leave Act, it is required to give workers maternity and paternity leave.

Title VII requires employers who grant leaves of absence for other types of personal nondisability reasons to grant maternity/paternity leave on the same terms. If there is a medical reason for an extended leave after childbirth, then the employer must treat the leave in the same way as it would treat any other request for medical or disability leave.

Some states, such as Washington and Minnesota, have laws requiring employers to grant parental leave to employees.

Q. May employers fire female workers who get married?

A. Title VII does not protect workers based on their marital status. However, if the employer

---

ⓘ **DISCRIMINATION BASED ON PREGNANCY**

In 1978, Congress passed the **Pregnancy Discrimination Act,** amending Title VII so that the prohibition against sex discrimination includes discrimination because of pregnancy, childbirth, and related medical conditions. Thus, an employer cannot base employment decisions on the fact that a worker is pregnant. Moreover, the employer must treat pregnancy in the same way as it would treat any other non-work-related employee medical condition.

fires only female workers who get married but not male workers, the employer has violated Title VII by engaging in disparate treatment sex discrimination—because it has applied an employment policy only to women.

Some states, however, such as Wisconsin, Oregon, and Illinois, have laws that expressly prohibit employment discrimination based on marital status. In those states, firing married workers would violate the law, even if the employer applied its policy to both sexes.

Q. Since actuary tables show that women live longer than men, can employers provide different retirement and pension plans for each sex?

A. No. The U.S. Supreme Court has held specifically that pension plans cannot discriminate based on sex. Thus, in defined contribution plans, an employer must contribute the same amount for both males and females. In defined benefit plans, both males and females must receive the same benefits.

ⓘ THE FAMILY AND MEDICAL LEAVE ACT

The Family and Medical Leave Act (FMLA) is a federal law requiring employers to grant up to twelve weeks of unpaid leave with right to reinstatement to employees under certain conditions. The law applies to private employers who employ at least fifty employees and to all public employers. Employees are eligible for leave if they have worked for their employer for at least a year, if they have performed at least 1,250 hours of service for their employer in the previous twelve months, and if there are at least fifty employees at the employees' work site or at least fifty employees within seventy-five miles of that worksite.

The law requires employers to grant employees up to twelve weeks of unpaid leave during any twelve-month period for any one of the following reasons:

- Because of the birth of a child and in order to care for the child
- Because of adoption or foster care placement of a child and in order to care for the child
- Because of a serious health condition that makes the employee unable to perform his or her duties
- In order to care for a spouse, a child, or a parent with a serious medical condition

If the employer provides health insurance coverage for its employees, it must continue that coverage during the leave of absence with no additional charge to the employee. At the end of the leave period, the employer is required to reinstate the employee to his or her previous position or to an equivalent position.

Employees can enforce their entitlement to the rights granted under the FMLA by filing a lawsuit. A few states have enacted leave laws that apply to smaller employers or that allow for more than twelve weeks of unpaid leave for childbirth or serious health conditions. At least one state, California, has enacted legislation providing for six weeks of *paid* leave for reasons relating to childbirth, adoption, or serious health conditions.

Other Protections for Workers

Q. Employees who are in the army reserve must attend training camp every year. Is the employer required to give the reservist time off?

A. Yes. The Uniformed Services Employment and Reemployment Rights Act (USERRA) requires all employers to grant employees who are in military service unpaid leaves of absence to perform their military obligation. Upon completion of their military duties, employees are entitled to their previous job with such seniority, status, pay, and vacation as if they had not been absent. The reemployment rights granted by this law apply to all types of military service—active or reserve armed forces and National Guard—whether the employee is drafted or enlisted.

Q. Can an employer lay off an employee because he or she has been called for jury duty?

A. No. The Jury System Improvements Act is a federal law that prohibits an employer from disciplining or discharging an employee because he or she has been called to serve on a federal jury. Additionally, more than thirty-five states prohibit employers from firing a worker who is called to perform jury service in the state court system.

Q. Can an employer fire an employee for refusing to work on Saturdays if his or her religion requires attendance at services on Saturdays?

A. Title VII requires employers to accommodate the religious beliefs of their employees unless the accommodation would cause an undue hardship for the business. If other employees are willing to work the shift on Saturdays, and the employer would not have to pay them more, the employer may be required to accommodate the employee. However, if the accommodation would cost the employer additional money, or would cause a disruption in the business or violate the provisions of

a collective bargaining agreement, accommodation would probably be considered unreasonable. There are many types of relatively cost-free accommodations that an employer may make, such as

- allowing employees to wear religiously significant garments, such as a yarmulke or a hijab;
- allowing an employee to leave work early in order to attend a religious service, where the employee could make up the missed work by coming in early or staying late on another day; and
- permitting an employee to take a short prayer break that does not disrupt other employees' work.

Sexual Harassment

Q. Is sexual harassment illegal?

A. Yes. The U.S. Supreme Court has held that Title VII's prohibition against sex discrimination

---

ⓘ **TIME TO VOTE**

Approximately thirty states, including New York, Ohio, and Maryland, have state laws requiring employers to grant employees time off from work to vote in elections. The purpose of the laws is to ensure that those employees whose work hours do not allow sufficient time to vote can take time off from work to vote. Thus, if an employee's work shift were from 3:00 P.M. until 11:00 P.M., the employer would not have to give the employee time off to vote. But if the employee worked from 8:00 A.M. until 6:00 P.M., the employer may be required to grant time off. Most of the laws apply to all elections, whether federal, state, or local, although a few are limited to particular types of elections. Most of the laws do not allow the employer to deduct wages for the time off.

includes sexual harassment as a type of illegal sex discrimination. Moreover some states, such as Illinois, Michigan, and North Dakota, have laws expressly prohibiting sexual harassment. Most other states interpret their laws prohibiting sex discrimination to include sexual harassment.

Q. How is sexual harassment defined?

A. The EEOC defines **sexual harassment** as "unwelcome sexual advances, requests for sexual favors, and other verbal or physical conduct of a sexual nature . . . when . . . submission to or rejection of such conduct is used as the basis for employment decisions . . . or such conduct has the purpose or effect of . . . creating an intimidating, hostile or offensive working environment."

Thus, sexual harassment consists of two types of prohibited conduct:

- quid pro quo—where submission to harassment is used as the basis for employment decisions; and
- hostile environment—where harassment creates an offensive working environment.

Sexual harassment is harassment of an individual because of his or her sex. Sometimes, this harassment is sexual in character, as in the case of sexual propositions, sexual groping, or lewd remarks. But sexual harassment can also occur when severe or pervasive harassing conduct, not necessarily sexual in nature, is targeted at a person because of his or her sex. In these kinds of cases, it can be more difficult to show that the harassing conduct is because of sex—that is, to show that

the reason the victim is being singled out for the comments is because she is a woman.

Both men and women can be victims of sexual harassment, and harassment because of sex (as distinguished from harassment because of sexual orientation) is illegal under federal law whether the harasser is the same sex or the opposite sex. Harassment on the basis of sexual orientation is not illegal under federal law, but is illegal under some state and local laws.

An employee who is a victim of sexual harassment can file a claim with the EEOC. If the state in which the employee lives prohibits this type of harassment, the worker should also contact the proper state agency.

Q. What is quid pro quo harassment?

A. **Quid pro quo harassment** occurs when a job benefit is tied directly to an employee submitting to unwelcome sexual advances. For example, a supervisor promises an employee a raise if she will go out on a date with him, or tells an employee she will be fired if she doesn't engage in intimate conduct with him.

Only people with supervisory authority over a worker can engage in quid pro quo harassment, since it requires the harasser to have the authority to grant or withhold job benefits.

Courts look to whether the harassment results in a tangible employment action—that is, whether there was a significant change in employment status, such as firing, failure to promote, or a change in wage rate.

ⓘ HARASSMENT THAT'S NOT SEXUAL

Title VII also forbids words and conduct that vilify and denigrate people based on their race, religion, or national origin. Severe and pervasive racial, religious, and ethnic slurs can create a hostile work environment. This concept—**discriminatory harassment**—is very similar to the concept of sexual harassment caused by a hostile work environment, and the employer's liability for this conduct is based on similar principles.

The ADEA and the ADA also prohibit comments related to age or disability that create a hostile work environment.

Q. If a worker "voluntarily" has sex with a supervisor, does this mean that she has not been sexually harassed?

A. Not necessarily. In order to constitute harassment, sexual advances must be "unwelcome." If an employee by her conduct shows that sexual advances are unwelcome, it does not matter that she eventually "voluntarily" succumbs to the harassment. In deciding whether the sexual advances are unwelcome, the courts often will allow evidence concerning the employee's dress, behavior, and language, as indications of whether the employee welcomed the advances.

Moreover, sexual advances that initially may have been welcomed subsequently may become unwelcome. Thus, an employee who engages in a welcomed office romance with a supervisor, but later decides to end it, may become the victim of quid pro quo harassment if the supervisor demotes the employee because she refuses to continue the romance.

Q. Is an employer liable for quid pro quo harassment engaged in by its supervisors?

A. In general, an employer is held to be strictly liable—meaning the employer is liable even if it did not know about the harassment—when a supervisor engages in quid pro quo harassment that results in a tangible adverse employment action.

Q. What is hostile environment harassment?

A. Hostile environment harassment occurs when employees are regularly subjected to comments of a sexual nature, offensive sexual materials, unwelcome physical contact, or derogatory and insulting comments aimed at an individual because of the individual's sex, race, religion, national origin, age, or disability. Generally speaking, a single isolated incident will not be considered hostile environment harassment unless it is extremely outrageous and egregious conduct. The courts look to see whether the conduct is both serious and frequent.

Supervisors, managers, coworkers, and even customers can be responsible for creating a hostile environment.

Q. Is an employer liable for hostile environment harassment?

A. It depends on who has created the hostile environment. The employer is liable when supervisors or managers are responsible for the hostile environment, unless the employer can prove that it exercised reasonable care to prevent and

---

▶ **WHAT CAN VICTIMS OF SEXUAL OR DISCRIMINATORY HARASSMENT DO?**

Employees subjected to sexual or discriminatory harassment should immediately notify their supervisors. If the supervisor is the harasser, the worker should go to the supervisor's superiors or to the company's human resources department. Employers cannot solve the problem if they do not know about it. If there is a grievance procedure, employees should use it. If the employer has an established antiharassment policy containing a complaint procedure, employees must utilize this procedure.

Victims should keep a written record of all incidents of harassment, detailing the place, time, people involved, and any witnesses. Victims can also express their disapproval of the conduct to the perpetrator and tell him or her to stop. Victims should also keep a written record of how, when, and to whom they have reported any harassment, and the results of such reports.

ⓘ EXAMPLES OF SEXUAL HARASSMENT

Sexual harassment can take many forms. It can consist of vulgar or lewd comments, or forcing workers to wear sexually revealing uniforms. It can involve unwanted physical touching or fondling, or suggestions to engage in sexual conduct. Even obscene, or sexually suggestive, cartoons and posters can be sexual harassment. Occasional inappropriate touching, off-color jokes, or repeated sexual references can be sexual harassment. It depends on the circumstances. Courts consider the nature, severity, and frequency of the conduct, as well as the conditions under which the conduct occurred.

promptly correct harassing behavior and that the employee unreasonably failed to take advantage of any preventive or corrective opportunities provided by the employer.

When coworkers and/or customers create the harassment, the employer is liable if it is negligent in addressing the problem. Thus, if the employer knew or reasonably should have known of the harassment and failed to take prompt and effective remedial action to end the harassment, it may be liable.

Remedial action usually requires a prompt investigation and corrective action. The action taken by the employer should be in proportion to the severity of the offense. Employers are not required to terminate alleged harassers in all situations. Employers must address employee harassment complaints and are not excused from

▶ HOW EMPLOYERS CAN PREVENT SEXUAL AND DISCRIMINATORY HARASSMENT

Employers can take several measures to prevent sexual and discriminatory harassment in the workplace.

- They can develop a written policy dealing with harassment, indicating that sexual harassment is against the law and also violates company policy. The employer can contact the EEOC in Washington, D.C., for its guidelines on sexual harassment. These will help the employer formulate its policy.

- They can develop an effective complaint procedure for workers subjected to harassment.

- They can provide a mechanism for employees to bypass their supervisor when the supervisor participates in the harassment or fails to take proper action. The complaint procedure should encourage a prompt solution to the problem.

- They can promptly and effectively respond to harassment complaints.

- They can undertake a complete and confidential investigation of any allegations of harassment and impose appropriate disciplinary action.

- They can prevent harassment before it occurs. Employers should circulate or post the company antiharassment policy and the EEOC rules on sexual harassment, express strong disapproval of sexual harassment, and tell employees of their right to be free from harassment.

- They can protect employees from retaliation based on complaints of harassment. Any written harassment policy should contain a clear statement that retaliation will not be tolerated.

acting on the basis that the complaint was uncorroborated and/or was denied by the harasser.

Age Discrimination

Q. Can employers force workers to retire?

A. Generally speaking, no. The ADEA prohibits mandatory retirement based on age. If an employee can no longer perform his or her job duties, however, the employer is allowed to discharge that person based on nonperformance.

There are some exceptions to the general rules against forced retirement. Executives or high-level policy makers can be forced to retire at age sixty-five if they are entitled to receive retirement benefits of at least $44,000 a year, exclusive of Social Security. Firefighters, police officers, and prison guards employed by state and local governments can also be forced to retire if required to do so by state or local law and pursuant to a bona fide retirement plan.

Q. Can employers offer voluntary retirement incentives?

A. Yes, so long as they are truly voluntary, and the decision whether to accept the incentives and retire is up to the employee.

Privacy in the Workplace

Q. Are there any federal laws that protect the confidentiality of workplace records?

A. The ADA requires employers to keep any medical records regarding employees confidential and separate from employee personnel files. The law states that the only people who may be informed about an employee's medical conditions are

- first aid or safety personnel if the medical condition may require emergency treatment, and
- government officials investigating compliance with the ADA.

The employer may also inform supervisors and managers about restrictions on work duties or necessary accommodations required by a disability.

The Privacy Act forbids federal government employers from disclosing any information contained in employee files without the written consent of the employee in question.

Q. Do state laws protect the confidentiality of workplace records?

A. Some states have statutes prohibiting the disclosure of certain employee information. Several

---

▶ HOW TO FILE A CHARGE UNDER THE ADEA

If you believe you have been the victim of age discrimination, you may file a charge with the EEOC. There are regional offices of the EEOC in most major cities in the United States. If you are in a state that has a state law prohibiting age discrimination, you may also file a complaint with the state agency charged with enforcing the state law. Before you can bring a lawsuit, you must first file a charge with the EEOC and with the state agency, if there is one.

The time limit for filing a charge with the EEOC is 180 days after the discrimination happened; or, if you are in a state with a state age law, 300 days after the discrimination occurred, or 30 days after the state agency terminates proceedings, whichever happens first.

When the EEOC completes its investigation it issues a right to sue letter. You must file any lawsuit within ninety days of receipt of the right to sue letter.

states, including California, Florida, and Pennsylvania, prohibit disclosure of employee medical records. At least one state, Connecticut, prohibits disclosure of any employee personnel information without the written consent of the employee in question.

Unnecessary disclosure of information in which the employee has a reasonable expectation of privacy may result in employer liability in tort for invasion of privacy or intentional infliction of emotional distress.

Q. Do employees have a right of access to their personnel files?

A. The Privacy Act allows federal government employees to have access to their records and to make a copy of any portion of the documents. It also provides for a procedure by which federal employees can challenge the information contained in their files.

Several other laws apply to the private sector. The Occupational Safety and Health Administration (OSHA) requires private employers to give employees access to medical records that the law requires employers to maintain when employees are exposed to potentially toxic materials at work.

The National Labor Relations Act (NLRA) imposes a duty on the private employer to disclose to unions information that is necessary and relevant for collective bargaining purposes, which can include access to employee personnel files. There is, however, no duty to disclose such information directly to the employee.

Approximately fifteen states, including California, Massachusetts, Michigan, and Wisconsin, grant employees access to their personnel files. Some of the statutes also provide for procedures by which employees can challenge information in their files.

Q. Can employers listen to employee telephone calls?

A. The Omnibus Crime Control and Safe Streets Act prohibits employers from eavesdropping on, or wiretapping, telephone calls. There is a large exception allowing employers to listen in on an extension telephone used in the ordinary course of business. A second big exception allows employers to monitor telephone calls where employees have been notified expressly that their telephone conversations will be monitored. Some courts have indicated, however, that once the private nature of a telephone conversation is determined, any continued eavesdropping would not be in the ordinary course of business and may subject the employer to liability. An employer violating the law can be sued for money damages.

Some states have enacted laws that place more restrictions on telephone monitoring—for example, requiring the consent of all parties to the conversation or requiring that employees be notified that their calls may be monitored.

Q. Can employers use video cameras to monitor workers?

A. In general, yes, if the monitoring is for security or antitheft purposes and employees are advised of the surveillance. The NLRA, however, prohibits employer surveillance of employee union activity, discussions about unions, or union meetings. In addition, if a union represents employees, an employer is required to bargain with the union before instituting workplace surveillance.

Some state laws regulate the extent to which an employer can monitor workers. For example, Connecticut prohibits surveillance or monitoring "in areas designed for the health or personal comfort of the employees or for the safeguarding of their possessions, such as rest rooms, locker rooms or lounges." Moreover, state tort law may protect employees against highly offensive intrusions upon privacy in a place where a person has a reasonable expectation of privacy. For example, monitoring an employee bathroom may be considered an invasion of privacy.

If the video camera also records audio, laws that regulate the interception of oral communication will also apply. The federal wiretap law prohibits the recording of oral communication, as do many state laws.

Q. Can the employer monitor employee use of the computer at work?

A. Yes. There is currently no federal or state law prohibiting employers from monitoring their own computer system.

Q. Can the employer read employee e-mail?

A. Although the law is still developing in this area, employers can monitor e-mails sent or received over employer-provided computer equipment. Currently, neither federal nor state law prohibits a private employer's access to e-mails stored in the company computer system. If the employer intercepts e-mail as it is being sent from or to computer equipment owned by the employer, there may be a violation of the federal **Electronic Communications Privacy Act** unless the employer notifies employees that their e-mail may be intercepted. See chapter 10, "Computer Law," for more about e-mail on the job.

Q. Can employers search workers or their possessions?

A. Yes, generally, if workers have been told in advance that the employer can do so. Within limits, the law usually allows such searches. However, a collective bargaining agreement might restrict or prohibit such conduct. (For a discussion of the constitutional restrictions on public employers, see "Special Rights of Public Employees" on page 438.)

It is extremely important, however, that employers are careful about the manner in which they conduct searches so as to avoid tort liability for assault, battery, false arrest, and intentional infliction of emotional harm or invasion of privacy.

First, employers should have a work-related reason for the search, although they do not have to prove probable cause to conduct a search. Second, any search should be conducted by the least intrusive means possible. Third, employers should inform employees that searches might be conducted. Fourth, employers should not physically harm employees in the course of the search

or threaten employees with physical harm. Fifth, the employer should not attempt to prevent employees from leaving the premises by threat of harm or other coercive means, although they are usually allowed to tell employees that they will be disciplined or discharged if they leave.

Q. Can employers impose dress and grooming codes?

A. Generally speaking, the law allows employers to impose dress and grooming policies. A few instances, however, may run afoul of Title VII. Some employers, for example, impose a dress code on female employees but not male employees. This could be a violation of Title VII for disparate treatment based on sex. Or a grooming code may have a more severe effect on members of a particular protected class, thus having an adverse impact under Title VII. For example, a rule requiring employees to be clean-shaven may particularly affect members of certain religious groups. In that case, the employer would have to show a business necessity in order to enforce the policy.

Q. Can employers require employees to speak only English while at work?

A. The EEOC has interpreted Title VII to prohibit the promulgation of an English-only rule unless it can be justified by business necessity. Requiring employees to speak only English may have an adverse impact on persons of certain ethnic or national origin. Thus, an employer may be able to justify an English-only rule when its employees are dealing with customers but could not enforce such a rule in the employee lunchroom.

Q. Can employers prohibit smoking in the workplace?

A. Yes, but if the employees have a union, the employer must bargain with the union about implementing such a policy.

Q. Can employers base employment decisions on employees' off-duty conduct?

A. It depends. Several states—such as Illinois, Minnesota, Montana, and Nevada—prohibit an employer from taking adverse action against an employee because that employee uses lawful products off employer premises during nonworking time. Thus, in those states an employer could not refuse to hire, or fire, a worker who smokes off duty or drinks alcohol. Moreover, most states prohibit employers from refusing to hire, or firing, employees because they use tobacco products off employer premises during nonworking time.

A collective bargaining agreement may require the employer to justify employment decisions based on **just cause.** As a general rule, in order to satisfy a just cause requirement, the employer would have to show that the employee's off-duty conduct somehow implicated the employer's legitimate business interests.

Q. What are the legal implications of providing employee references to prospective employers?

A. Approximately twenty states prohibit employers from engaging in blacklisting. Blacklisting consists of intentionally taking action aimed at preventing someone from obtaining employment. Truthful statements concerning an individual's ability to perform the job in question are not considered to be blacklisting.

The manner in which a reference is made and its content can give rise to employer liability under state tort law relating to defamation, intentional interference with a prospective employment contract, intentional infliction of emotional distress, or negligent misrepresentation. (See chapter 14, "Personal Injury," for more on tort law.)

Defamation occurs when one person's false statement injures the reputation of another person. However, most states recognize that giving references to prospective employers in good faith is a defense against defamation charges.

Providing false information to a prospective employer with the intent of causing an applicant to lose the job constitutes **intentional interference with a prospective employment contract.**

Disclosure of private personal matters unrelated to work can result in an **invasion of privacy** or **intentional infliction of emotional distress** claim.

Last, a false statement that causes a loss of money can be grounds for **negligent misrepresentation.**

To be safe, an employer should limit the number of people authorized to provide references on its behalf. Second, statements based on hearsay or gossip should be avoided. Third, only items that have a direct bearing on an individual's work performance should be disclosed. Finally, obtaining a release from the former employee before providing any information to third parties can help to limit any liability.

Q. Must an employer provide an employee with a reference?

A. Generally speaking, no. However, at least four states—Indiana, Missouri, Texas, and Washington—require an employer to provide, upon request, a service letter to the employee. A service letter contains the nature of the employee's job while employed by the employer, the duration of the employment, and the reason for the separation.

Special Rights of Public Employees

Most of the antidiscrimination laws that have been discussed in this chapter apply to public employers as well as private workers. Moreover, even though the National Labor Relations Act expressly excludes public employers, the federal government and most states have collective bargaining laws patterned after the NLRA that give public employees the right to be represented by labor unions and negotiate collective bargaining agreements.

Public workers have additional protections not normally available to private employees. These protections, found in the civil service laws and the federal and state constitutions, apply only to government employers.

Q. What are civil service laws?

A. Civil service laws establish employment policies for public employees based on the merit principle. The purpose behind establishing civil service laws was to eliminate political considerations in the employment process. The elements of a civil service system generally include guidelines for recruiting applicants, testing programs for screening applicants, impartial hiring criteria, job classifications based on duties and responsibilities, and protection against arbitrary discipline and discharge. A commission is usually established to ensure that the public employer is following the civil service rules. The particulars of civil service laws and the role and operation of the commission vary from state to state.

Q. What type of protection does the U.S. Constitution afford public employees?

A. The most important protections afforded by the U.S. Constitution (that are not duplicated by antidiscrimination laws already discussed) are

- freedom of association,
- freedom of speech,
- freedom from unreasonable searches and seizures, and
- due process protections in the event of discharge from a job.

Q. How does freedom of association protect a public employee?

A. Basically, a public employer cannot base employment decisions on the fact that someone belongs to certain types of clubs or associates with particular people. Thus, a public employer can't refuse to hire applicants just because they are Republicans, or belong to a motorcycle club, or are members of the American Civil Liberties Union.

Q. How does freedom of speech protect a public employee?

A. When public employees speak out on issues of public concern, their employer cannot discipline or discharge them for their comments. For example, if a schoolteacher writes a letter to the newspaper criticizing the curriculum developed by the school board, the school board could not discharge that teacher for the criticism. However,

if the comments of the employee relate to matters of purely private concern, such as the teacher complaining that he or she did not get a requested day off, the principle of freedom of speech would not protect the teacher in the employment arena.

Q. How does freedom from unreasonable search and seizure protect a public employee?

A. An employee may have a reasonable expectation of privacy in certain places at work, such as a desk or a filing cabinet that is not shared with other workers. In those areas where the employee has such a reasonable expectation of privacy, an employer may conduct a work-related noninvestigatory search, as well as an investigatory search for work-related misconduct, only if there are "reasonable grounds for suspecting the search will turn up evidence that the employee is guilty of work-related misconduct, or that the search is necessary for a noninvestigatory work-related purpose such as to retrieve a needed file."

Although the law on this point is unsettled, public employers would likely need probable cause to suspect workplace misconduct before they could search personal items such as a briefcase, luggage, or a purse that an employee brings into the workplace.

As for searches relating to drug testing, see the question on Drug Testing and the Constitution in the section of this chapter entitled "The Hiring Process."

Q. How does due process protect a public employee?

A. The Fifth Amendment to the U.S. Constitution provides that no person shall be "deprived of life, liberty, or property, without due process of law." This means that people accused of crimes have certain protections under the law, as do those whose property the government seeks, as when the government needs a homeowner's property to widen a road. But when is a job "property"?

The courts have held that an employee has a **property interest in a job** if there is a written or implied contract granting the employee a property interest in the job; if past practice of the employer shows that the employee has a property interest in the job; or if a statute gives the employee a property interest in the job. For example, a teacher with tenure is considered to have a property interest in his or her job, because there is the express or implied understanding that a teacher cannot lose that job without just cause.

If a public employee has a property interest in a job, he or she cannot be discharged without due process. Due process requires that the employee be given notice of the reason for being discharged and a fair hearing at which to contest the decision.

Unions in the Workplace

Unions represent employees. They deal with employers concerning workplace issues. Instead of each worker negotiating separately with the employer regarding wages, health insurance coverage, and other employment issues, the union bargains with the employer on behalf of the workers in the bargaining unit.

The National Labor Relations Act (NLRA), which regulates union-employer relations at work, is premised on the notion that individual employees have very little leverage in bargaining with their employer, and that in practice the employer unilaterally sets wage and benefit levels without any discussion with the workers. If the workers pool their individual bargaining power, however, and negotiate collectively through a union, the result more likely will be a product of true give-and-take, and the workers will have an effective voice concerning workplace issues.

Q. What kinds of employees are covered by the NLRA?

A. The NLRA covers private employers engaged in interstate commerce, but excludes railroad, airline, and public employers. (For more information, see "Federal Laws Regulating the Workplace" on page 406.)

However, even if you work for a covered employer, you may not be protected. Certain categories of workers fall outside of the statute: domestic employees of a family, farmworkers, persons employed by a parent or a spouse, independent contractors, supervisors, and managers.

Q. Who is a supervisor or manager?

A. Supervisors are defined as people who have the authority to hire, fire, discipline, promote, or adjust the grievances of other employees or effectively to recommend such action. Managers are generally high-level employees who use independent judgment in formulating company policies and carrying them into effect.

Q. How does the NLRA regulate the union-employer relationship?

A. First, the NLRA gives employees certain rights and prohibits employers and unions from interfering with those rights. Second, the NLRA sets up a mechanism by which employees can vote by secret ballot on whether they want a union to represent them in the workplace. Third, it requires employers and unions to engage in collective bargaining, and regulates the type of employer and union tactics that may occur during the course of collective bargaining.

Q. What rights do employees have under the NLRA?

A. The NLRA gives employees the right to
• join unions;

ⓘ **UNION-MANAGEMENT RELATIONS IN THE AIRLINE AND RAILWAY INDUSTRIES**

The Railway Labor Act regulates union-management relations in the airline and railway industries. It is similar to the NLRA regarding the types of employee activities protected and the types of employer conduct regulated.

- engage in conduct aimed at promoting or helping unions;
- choose a union to represent them in collective bargaining with their employer; and
- engage in group conduct that has as its purpose collective bargaining or helping each other regarding workplace issues (this includes the right to strike).

The law also says that employees have the right not to do these things if that is their desire.

Q. What are some examples of how employees might use these rights?

A. Employees might utilize these rights by attending union meetings, talking to co-employees about unions or other workplace issues, passing out union literature, wearing union buttons, campaigning for union office, circulating petitions advocating workplace improvements, or engaging in a work stoppage or picketing.

Q. Must there be a union in the workplace in order for employees to be able to use their rights?

A. No. Employees have these rights regardless of whether a union represents them in the workplace. For example, a group of workers in a nonunion workplace who circulates a petition asking the employer for a wage increase is engaged in a "protected concerted activity" that is covered by the NLRA.

Q. Can an employer fire workers because they exercise their rights under the NLRA?

A. No. The NLRA prohibits an employer from discharging, disciplining, or otherwise discriminating against employees who exercise their rights under the NLRA. Prohibited discrimination includes demotion, layoff, wage cut, and denial of a promotion.

Q. What other types of restrictions does the NLRA place on employer conduct?

A. The NLRA prohibits an employer from interfering, restraining, or coercing employees in the exercise of their rights. Employers cannot threaten employees with discipline or other adverse actions because they have exercised their rights. For example, an employer who tells employees that they will lose their jobs or have their wages reduced if they vote for a union has violated the NLRA.

Neither can an employer promise employees benefits in order to get them to vote against a union, such as promising a wage increase if the employees reject the union.

As a general rule, employers cannot question employees about their union activities, ask them

---

ⓘ UNION-MANAGEMENT RELATIONS IN THE PUBLIC SECTOR

Although the NLRA does not apply to public employees, other federal and state laws regulate the role of unions in government employment. Title VII of the **Civil Service Reform Act** (5 U.S.C. Sections 7101–7135) grants federal employees the right to be represented by a union for purposes of collective bargaining and prohibits discrimination in employment based on union activity. This statute also establishes the Federal Labor Relations Authority and the Federal Services Impasse Panel to enforce the rights and duties contained in the law.

As of early 2004, twenty-seven states had comprehensive legislation covering union representation and collective bargaining for all state and municipal employees. An additional thirteen states authorized collective bargaining for certain categories of employees, including firefighters, police, and schoolteachers. Ten states prohibit collective bargaining for public sector workers.

ⓘ UNION ACTIVITY ON COMPANY PROPERTY

While employees have the right to discuss work issues and union issues with their co-employees and to distribute leaflets and pamphlets addressing union issues, these rights can be limited when the employees are on company property.

As a general rule, employers can prohibit discussions and the distribution of literature during working time, that is, during those periods of the workday when employees are required to work. Thus, an employer could prohibit discussions while employees are working at their machines, but could not prohibit discussions while both parties to the conversation are on breaks; an employer could prohibit passing out literature on an assembly line but not passing out literature in nonwork areas.

ⓘ EXAMPLES OF EMPLOYER CONDUCT PROHIBITED BY THE NLRA

If a group of employees asks the employer for a raise and the employer fires them for asking, the employer has violated the NLRA—the employees were engaged in a protected concerted activity. An employer who refuses to promote an employee because that employee had spoken with her coworkers about union representation has also violated the NLRA. Similarly, an employer who suspends a worker for handing out union leaflets in the locker room during lunch has violated the NLRA.

whether other employees support a union, or ask them what happened at a union meeting.

Q. How does a union represent a group of workers?

A. A union organizing campaign can start either because the employees in the workplace have

contacted the union or because the union on its own seeks to organize the workers.

The first step in an organizing campaign is to determine whether the employees have any interest in having a union represent them. The union asks the employees to show their interest by signing authorization cards. This card indicates that the employee is interested in union representation. If at least 30 percent of the workers sign cards, then the union can ask the NLRB to hold a secret ballot election.

Before the election is held, there is usually

⚠ EMPLOYEE ACTIVITIES THAT ARE NOT PROTECTED BY THE NLRA

Even if employees are exercising a right under the NLRA, their conduct may remove them from the protection of the law. The law does not protect slowdowns, violence, sabotage, or vandalism of company property.

Also, the NLRA generally protects an activity only if it involves more than one employee. For example, one worker asking the employer to institute health insurance coverage is not engaged in protected conduct. However, if the worker was acting as a spokesperson for other employees, or if the employees went as a group to ask the employer for health insurance coverage, then the law would protect that group. A single employee attempting to organize colleagues would also be protected.

time for both the union and the employer to campaign among the workers, discussing the pros and cons of union representation. The election itself usually is held at the employer's place of business so that it is easy for the workers to vote. The NLRB conducts the secret ballot election.

If the union wins the election, it becomes the bargaining agent for the employees and negotiates a collective bargaining agreement with the employer. The employer must negotiate with the union. If the union loses the election, the status quo prevails.

The key point is that it is up to the employees to decide whether they want a union; it is their choice to make.

Q. If the union wins the election, which workers does the union represent?

A. If a union is voted in to represent the workers, it doesn't necessarily represent every worker employed by the company. The union election is held among those employees who are considered to have a "community of interest" at the workplace. These employees form a **bargaining unit,** which is the group of workers voting in the election who will be represented by the union in the event the union wins the election.

Employees have a community of interest if they share similar working conditions, jobs, hours of work, and supervision. For example, employees who work on an assembly line probably do not have a community of interest with office workers, whereas salespeople in a department store would probably share a community of interest even though they work in different departments and sell different types of goods.

Q. If a worker votes against the union in the election and the union wins, does the union represent that worker?

A. Yes. The law requires the union to represent all employees in the bargaining unit, fairly and nondiscriminatorily, regardless of whether they supported the union.

Q. If a union wins the election, must the workers join the union?

A. No. Just as the NLRA gives employees the right to join unions, it also gives employees the right to refuse to join a union. The NLRA prohibits both employers and unions from forcing employees to join a union.

However, employees can be forced to pay for the work that the union performs on their behalf, even if they do not want to join the union. Most collective bargaining agreements contain a **union security clause.** In effect, this clause requires

---

ⓘ FILING A CHARGE UNDER THE NLRA

If workers believe their rights under the NLRA have been violated, they can file an unfair labor practice charge with the National Labor Relations Board (NLRB). There are regional offices of the NLRB in most major cities in the United States. The time limit for filing a charge is six months from the date of the unlawful action. The regional office will investigate the charge and decide whether the law has been violated. If it decides there was no violation, it will dismiss the charge. A worker whose charge has been dismissed may appeal the decision to the NLRB in Washington, D.C., but does not have the right to file a lawsuit in court.

If the regional office decides the charge has merit, it will issue a complaint and set a hearing before an administrative law judge, at which evidence is taken and arguments are made. The administrative law judge will then decide whether the law was violated. The decision of the administrative law judge can be appealed to the NLRB in Washington, D.C. The decision of the NLRB can be appealed to the federal circuit courts of appeal.

workers to pay the dues and fees that union members are required to pay. If a worker refuses to pay dues, he or she can be fired.

Because the law requires the union to represent all the workers in the bargaining unit, regardless of whether they are members of the union, the law allows the union to "tax" the workers for the benefits they receive from union representation. Some states prohibit union security clauses.

Q. What is a collective bargaining agreement?

A. A collective bargaining agreement is the contract that the employer and the union negotiate. When a union wins a NLRB election, the law requires the employer to sit down and bargain in good faith with the union about the terms of a contract. This contract will cover the wages, hours, and other terms and conditions of employment for the employees in the bargaining unit. While this contract is in effect (usually a term of three years) the employer, the union, and the employees must comply with its terms. Generally, an employer cannot make any changes in working conditions unless the union agrees to those changes.

Q. What is covered in a collective bargaining agreement?

A. Most collective bargaining agreements cover the basic terms and conditions of employment. These include rates of pay, hours of work, health insurance, pension benefits, vacations, seniority rights, job assignments, work rules, and procedures for promotions, layoffs, recalls, and transfers. Most contracts also contain a provision allowing the employer to discipline or discharge employees only if there is "just cause" and a provision in which the employer deducts union dues directly from the employees' paychecks and sends them to the union.

Q. What happens if the employer fails to live up to the terms of the collective bargaining agreement?

A. Most union contracts contain grievance procedures. If the union believes that the employer has violated the contract, then the union can file a complaint through the grievance procedure. This procedure has several steps, during which the union and the employer attempt to settle the dispute themselves. If they are unsuccessful, the complaint may be submitted to an arbitrator for an impartial decision. At a hearing, the arbitrator

---

ⓘ RELIGIOUS AND OTHER OBJECTIONS TO UNIONS

If your religion prohibits you from supporting a labor union, you're exempt from paying dues and fees to a union under a union security clause. But the law permits an alternative requirement to be imposed on you—you must pay an amount equivalent to union fees and dues to a nonreligious, nonlabor charitable organization. Both the NLRA and Title VII require that such an accommodation be made to your religious beliefs.

If your *personal* views conflict with those of the union, you can object to paying dues or fees used for purposes unrelated to collective bargaining. You are entitled to have the financial obligation imposed by the union security clause reduced. For example, if 20 percent of union dues money is spent on activities unrelated to collective bargaining and representing workers, then you only have to pay 80 percent of your dues. The burden is on you to notify the union of your objection.

will listen to evidence and arguments from both sides and decide whether the contract was violated. In most instances, the decision of the arbitrator is final.

Q. What is the union's responsibility in representing the workers?

A. The union has two major duties toward the employees in the bargaining unit:

- The union is required to represent the workers in bargaining with the employer.
- The union has a duty to represent fairly all workers in its dealings with the employer.

Q. What does the duty to represent the workers fairly entail?

A. In carrying out its responsibilities, the union has to make many decisions. It has to decide whether to ask the employer for better wages or better pension benefits. It has to decide whether an employer's decision to discharge a worker violated the contract or was based on just cause. The basis on which the union makes its decision on these and other issues affecting the workers cannot be arbitrary, discriminatory, or in bad faith.

For example, a worker is discharged for tardiness and complains to the union. The union has to decide whether it should file a complaint under the contract's grievance procedure to protest the discharge or whether the employer was within its rights to discharge the worker. If the union decides not to file a grievance because the worker is not a union member, or because the worker is African-American, it has violated its duty to represent the worker fairly. That decision is based on a discriminatory reason. If, however, the union decides not to file the grievance because the worker was tardy for fourteen days in a row and this violated a known company rule, then the union has not violated its duty to represent the worker fairly.

Unions are allowed considerable discretion in making such judgments. Mere negligence is not a violation of the duty of fair representation. But if a union decision is based on arbitrary, discrimina-

tory, or bad-faith reasons, the concerned worker can file a charge with the NLRB alleging a breach of the duty of fair representation. In some circumstances, such a claim can also be the basis for a lawsuit in federal court.

Q. What are the legal consequences of engaging in a strike?

A. That depends on what caused the strike. If the reason for the strike is to protest workplace conditions or to support union bargaining demands, it is called an **economic strike.** The employer can permanently replace the strikers. If the employer replaces them, it's like being laid off. When the strike ends, if the replacement worker is still employed, the striker is not entitled to be reinstated to his or her job. However, as soon as a vacancy occurs, the striking employees may have the right to be reinstated to their jobs.

If the reason for the strike is to protest the fact that the employer has violated the NLRA, it is called an **unfair labor practice strike.** Unfair labor practice strikers cannot be permanently replaced, and they have the right to be immediately reinstated to their jobs when the strike ends.

In neither event is an employer allowed to discharge, discipline, or otherwise discriminate in terms or conditions of employment because an employee engaged in a strike.

Q. Are all strikes legal?

A. No. Although the NLRA grants employees the right to strike, not all strikes are protected. If a collective bargaining agreement contains a **no-strike clause** (the union agrees not to go on strike while the contract is in effect), a strike during the life of the contract would not be protected. The strikers could be fired.

The NLRA requires health-care workers to give ten days notice before they go on strike. If these workers strike without giving notice, then they are not protected and can be fired.

Sit-down strikes and intermittent strikes are also unprotected. An example of an intermittent strike is when employees engage in a five-hour work stoppage one day, then two days later engage in another five-hour work stoppage, and then two days later do it again.

Wages and Hours

Q. What is the major law governing wages and hours?

A. The Fair Labor Standards Act (FLSA) sets the minimum wage that an employer may pay its workers. It also establishes overtime payment requirements. The act only applies to some employers, as explained in "Federal Laws Regulating the Workplace" (see page 406). However, even if the employer itself is not covered by the act (because, for example, it does not gross $500,000 annually) it will still be required to pay the minimum wage and overtime if its employees are engaged in interstate commerce.

Even if an employer and its employees are not covered by the FLSA, many states also have minimum wage and overtime laws that will apply to all employers doing business within the state.

Q. Does the FLSA require employers to offer benefits?

A. No. It deals solely with wage-related issues. It does not require employers to provide any other type of employment benefit, such as health or life insurance or vacation or holiday pay.

Q. What is the minimum wage?

A. The minimum wage under the FLSA is $5.15 an hour. The majority of states that have minimum wage laws peg their minimum wage to the federal minimum. A few states, such as New Mexico and Kansas, have set their state minimum wage below the federal limit. About ten states have set minimum wage rates that are higher than the federal rate. For example, Oregon's minimum wage is $6.50, and Hawaii's is $5.75. A few states have no minimum wage laws.

In states having a minimum wage above the federal rate, all employers, even those covered by the FLSA, must pay the higher state rate. In states where the state minimum rate is below the federal level, those employers covered by the FLSA must pay the higher federal rate.

Q. How is an employee's minimum wage rate determined?

A. The minimum wage is paid for every hour worked in any workweek. Thus, an employee covered under the federal minimum wage of $5.15 who works twenty hours a week must be paid at least $103 for that week's work.

Q. What does the law consider as an "hour worked"?

A. Generally speaking, hours worked include all the time spent by employees performing their job duties during the workday. When a worker's job requires travel during the workday, such as a ser-

---

ⓘ GOVERNMENT CONTRACTORS AND FEDERAL WAGE LAWS

The Walsh-Healy Public Contracts Act covers employers performing contracts of at least $10,000 for the federal government. These contracts must involve the manufacture or furnishing of materials, supplies, articles, or equipment. This law requires that the employer pay all employees the prevailing minimum rate for similar work performed in the locality. The secretary of labor determines the prevailing minimum rate. Employers are also required to pay all employees who work in excess of forty hours per week time-and-a-half pay for overtime.

The Davis-Bacon Act requires that federal contractors performing work valued in excess of $2,000 on federal construction projects pay their employees the prevailing area wage and fringe benefit rates. The secretary of labor determines the prevailing area wage.

vice technician who repairs furnaces at customers' homes, the time spent traveling is considered "hours worked." Preparatory time spent prior to the start of the workday that is required in order to perform the job is considered hours worked. For example, workers who have to sharpen their knives at a meat-processing plant, or workers who are required to wear special protective clothing at a chemical plant, would have to be compensated for the time spent sharpening their knives or changing their clothes. Mandatory attendance at lectures, meetings, and training programs is considered hours worked. Also included in hours worked are rest periods and coffee breaks shorter than twenty minutes.

The following activities are generally not considered hours worked for purposes of minimum wage compensation:

- Commuting time to work
- Lunch or dinner breaks of at least thirty minutes
- Changing clothes when done for the benefit of the employee
- On-call time away from the employer's premises that the employee can use for his or her own purposes
- Holidays or vacations

Q. Must the minimum wage be paid in money, rather than benefits?

A. Yes, but an employer is allowed to take a credit for the cost of providing certain noncash benefits to employees from the minimum wage owed.

Q. What types of credits is an employer allowed to take against the wage owed?

A. The employer can credit the reasonable cost of board, lodging, and other facilities customarily provided to employees. In order to credit the cost of such noncash benefits, they must be furnished for the worker's convenience and must be voluntarily accepted by the worker. Examples of noncash items whose fair value can be credited to the minimum wage owed are

- meals furnished at the company cafeteria,
- housing furnished by the company for residential purposes, and
- fuel or electricity used by the employee for nonbusiness purposes.

Employers who have a policy of requiring workers to pay for breakage or cash shortages cannot take such amounts as credit toward the minimum wage owed. Nor are employee discounts allowed as credits toward minimum wage.

Q. Can the employer withhold money from an employee's paycheck?

A. The employer is required to withhold taxes and amounts that have been garnished from an employee's paycheck. (See "Garnishment of Wages" on page 450.)

An employer is allowed to withhold certain items from an employee's paycheck if the employee has authorized the withholding. Examples of such withheld items are union dues, charitable contributions, or insurance premiums. These withholdings are allowed even if the amount received falls below the minimum wage.

ⓘ EMPLOYER RECORD-KEEPING REQUIREMENTS UNDER THE FLSA

Employers are required to maintain and preserve certain wage records in order to show their compliance with the FLSA. Employers must keep employee payroll records containing such information as employee names, hours worked each workday and workweek, wages paid, deductions from wages, and straight-time wages and overtime paid for three years. The employer must also keep documents supporting the payroll records, such as time cards, work schedules, and order and billing records for at least two years.

Certain types of items cannot be deducted from employee paychecks if the deduction would cause the pay to fall below the minimum wage. Examples of such items are the cost of uniforms used for work, the cost of cleaning uniforms used for work, or employee breakage or cash shortage debts.

Some states limit the reasons for which an employer can make deductions from wages in other ways, or require an employer to follow certain procedures before making deductions.

Q. When is a worker eligible for overtime pay?

A. The general rule is that employees must be paid overtime for all hours worked over forty hours in any workweek.

Q. Are all employees entitled to overtime pay?

A. No. There are several categories of workers who are exempt from the overtime requirements. The most common employee exemptions are

- certain executive, administrative, and professional employees;
- outside salespeople;
- retail commission salespeople whose regular rate of pay is more than one and a half times the minimum rate and more than half of whose wages come from commissions;
- taxicab drivers; and
- computer system analysts, computer programmers, or software engineers who are paid at least $27.63 an hour.

Q. What is the overtime pay rate?

A. The FLSA requires employers to pay employees one and a half times (150 percent) their reg-

---

ⓘ TIPPED EMPLOYEES AND THE FLSA

Under certain circumstances, the FLSA allows employers to credit tips received by tipped employees against the minimum wage owed to those employees. In order to qualify for the credit, the tipped employee must be engaged in an occupation in which he or she customarily receives more than $30.00 per month in tips—for example, a waiter or a beautician. The employer must pay a tipped employee at least $2.13 an hour. The employer is then allowed to credit all tips received by the employee for the amount of minimum wage owed above $2.13 an hour. Some states, however, do not allow a tip credit under their minimum wage laws or have different cash-payment levels when a tip credit is allowed.

Of course, the employer can credit only that amount the employee actually receives in tips. Thus, if the employee receives only $2.00 an hour in tips, the employer would be required to pay the additional amount necessary to ensure the employee received the minimum wage. The employee must always receive at least the minimum wage when wages and tips are combined.

For example, a waitress works 40 hours in a week, during which time she earned $80.00 in tips, which is $2.00 per hour in tips. The employer is allowed to take $2.00 per hour as credit against the $5.15 minimum wage. Thus, the employer is required to pay the waitress at least $126.00 for that week's work ($5.15 - $2.00 tip credit = $3.15 x 40 hours).

Employers may not take the tip credit unless the employer informs the workers about it. Employers must also be able to prove that the employee actually receives tips equal to the tip credit taken by the employer.

ular rate of pay for each hour, or fraction of an hour, over forty hours in any workweek.

Q. How is the overtime pay rate computed?

A. The main issue is to determine the regular rate for the employee in question. When an employee is paid an hourly rate, the employee's regular rate and hourly rate are the same. For example, an employee who is paid $6.00 an hour and who worked 43 hours in the last work week, would be owed $27.00 in overtime pay ($6.00 regular rate x 1.5 = $9.00 overtime rate; $9.00 x 3 [hours worked in excess of 40] = $27.00). The employee's earnings for that week would be $267.00 ($6.00 x 40 hours = $240.00 + $27.00 [overtime] = $267.00).

When an employee is paid a salary or a commission, the employee's compensation must be converted to an hourly rate. Let's say an employee is paid a fixed salary for a regular workweek of 40 hours. This conversion to an hourly rate is accomplished by dividing the employee's compensation for the week by 40 hours. For example, an employee who was paid $240 a week would be paid $6 an hour. If that employee worked 45 hours, he or she would be owed as additional compensation one and one half times the regular

rate (5 hours overtime x $6 an hour = $30 x 1.5 = $45). The employee's earnings for that week would be $285 ($240 + $45).

Workplace Safety

Q. What is the Occupational Safety and Health Act?

A. The Occupational Safety and Health Act (OSH Act) is a federal law whose purpose is to

---

> ### HOW TO ENFORCE YOUR RIGHTS UNDER THE FLSA

Employees who believe they are not being paid in accordance with the requirements of the FLSA can file a complaint with the Wage and Hour Division of the U.S. Department of Labor. There are regional offices of the Wage and Hour Division in most major cities in the United States. The division will investigate to determine whether the FLSA has been violated.

Employees can also sue in state or federal court to collect double the back wages and overtime pay owed.

GARNISHMENT OF WAGES

A **garnishment** is an order issued by a court. It requires that the earnings of a worker be withheld from the worker's paycheck and paid to a third party to whom the worker owes a debt. Employers should take garnishment notices seriously. If they ignore them, they risk being liable for the amount that should have been garnished.

The Consumer Credit Protection Act is a federal law that limits the amount of money that may be garnished. The general rule is that the maximum amount that can be garnished from a paycheck is the lesser of 25 percent of an employee's take-home pay or that part of take-home pay exceeding thirty times the federal minimum wage. The law permits a larger amount to be deducted when the debt owed is for child support payments, bankruptcy, or back taxes.

The Consumer Credit Protection Act also prohibits an employer from discharging an employee because his or her wages have been garnished once.

"assure so far as possible every working man and woman . . . safe and healthful working conditions." The statute is administered and enforced by the Occupational Safety and Health Administration (OSHA).

The OSH Act applies to all private employers engaged in a business affecting commerce. The courts have broadly interpreted the phrase "affecting commerce," such that almost every business in the country with at least one employee is covered by the act. The OSH Act does not apply to public employers.

States may also regulate workplace health and safety in two ways. First, they may have regulations covering workplace conditions that are not dealt with by OSHA standards. Second, they may adopt a state safety and health plan that duplicates the requirements of the OSH Act; if approved by OSHA, the state then would be responsible for enforcing safety and health regulations within its borders. In the absence of approval by OSHA, however, a state may not regulate any safety and health issue that is already regulated by the OSH Act.

Q. What obligations are imposed on employers under the OSH Act?

A. The act imposes three obligations on employers:

- Employers are required to furnish a workplace "free from recognized hazards that are causing or are likely to cause death or serious physical harm" to employees.
- Employers are required to comply with the safety and health standards promulgated by OSHA.
- Employers are required to keep records of employee injuries, illnesses, deaths, and exposures to toxic substances, and to preserve employee medical records.

There are some exemptions from some requirements under the OSH Act for employers with ten or fewer employees. These small companies do not have to maintain certain types of records, and they are exempt from certain types of penalties and enforcement activities; however, they are still required to provide a safe workplace and comply with OSHA standards.

Q. What types of workplace conditions do the health and safety standards address?

A. The standards regulate such issues as

- the safety of working areas such as ladders, scaffolding, stairs, and floors;
- provision of sufficient entryways and exits;
- exposure to noise, carcinogens, radiation, and other types of harmful substances;
- fire protection systems for the workplace;
- safety devices for machines and equipment used in the workplace; and
- provision of medical and first-aid services.

There are literally hundreds of standards covering all aspects of the workplace.

Q. What should an employee do if he or she thinks there is a safety or health hazard at work?

A. There are two methods of addressing safety and health problems: The employee can notify his or her supervisor or company safety director and discuss the problem; and an employee can also contact OSHA and request a safety inspection.

Q. How does an employee initiate a request for an OSHA inspection?

A. OSHA has regional and area offices in cities throughout the United States. An employee either can make an oral complaint to OSHA or file a formal written complaint. In either case, the employee should indicate what workplace conditions he or she believes constitute a safety or health hazard. OSHA will decide, based on the information received, whether there are reasonable grounds for believing a violation of the law exists. OSHA then either will send the employer a letter regarding the alleged violation and informing the employer how to correct the problem, or will send an inspector to the workplace to conduct an on-site safety inspection.

Q. What happens during an OSHA inspection?

A. The OSHA inspector will meet with the employer and explain the nature of the inspection and review employer documents pertaining to workplace injuries and hazards. Then the inspector will conduct a "walkaround" of the plant, and physically inspect the workplace. The employer and a representative of the employees are allowed to accompany the inspector on the walkaround. The inspector will also talk with employees and ask them questions. At the end of the inspection, the inspector will tell the employer informally of any possible violations that may have been uncovered during the inspection.

Q. What are the penalties for violating the OSH Act?

A. First, an employer is required to correct any hazards that violate the law. The employer can also be fined a monetary penalty, the amount of which is determined by the seriousness of the vi-

olation. An employer also faces criminal liability and imprisonment for willfully violating an OSHA standard that results in an employee's death.

Workers' Compensation

Q. What are workers' compensation laws?

A. **Workers' compensation laws** provide money to pay for medical expenses and to replace income lost as a result of injuries or illnesses that arise out of employment. The employee is not required to prove that the injuries were caused by some negligence of the employer in order to recover under the workers' compensation laws. Employees receive compensation even though their own negligence or that of a coworker caused the injury. These laws impose strict liability on employers for injuries suffered at the workplace. (For more on strict liability, see chapter 14, "Personal Injury.")

Each state has its own law providing workers' compensation benefits. While the dollar amounts recoverable and certain procedural or coverage

---

⚠ WORKING WITH HAZARDOUS CHEMICALS

OSHA requires that employees who work with hazardous chemicals be informed of the types of chemicals they are working with and be trained in their handling. Chemical manufacturers and distributors are required to label containers identifying any hazardous chemicals and give appropriate hazard warnings.

Employers who use such hazardous chemicals in the workplace are required to develop a written hazard communication program for their employees. As part of this program, the employer must compile a list of all hazardous chemicals used in the workplace; identify the physical and health hazards associated with these chemicals; state precautions to be used in handling the chemicals; and indicate emergency and first-aid procedures to be used in the event of a problem. This information must be made available to the employees.

Employees must also receive training in detecting the presence of chemicals in the workplace and protecting themselves from hazards.

details vary among the states, the general requirements of the laws are similar. There are separate federal workers' compensation laws covering federal government employees and employees of the railroad and maritime industries.

Q. Who pays for workers' compensation?

A. The cost of providing workers' compensation is borne solely by the employer, usually through the purchase of a workers' compensation insurance policy from an insurance company. The cost of providing this insurance cannot be deducted from the employees' wages.

Q. Are all employees covered by workers' compensation?

A. Most employees are covered. Some state laws exempt certain categories of workers, such as ca-

sual employees, agricultural employees, domestic employees, and independent contractors. Moreover, a few states require coverage only if an employer has a minimum number of employees. For example, in Alabama, coverage is compulsory only if an employer has at least three employees.

Q. What types of injuries are compensable under workers' compensation?

A. Injuries and illnesses that "arise out of and in the course of employment" are compensable. This means that there must be some connection between an employment requirement and the cause of the injury. Injuries arising from an automobile accident that occurs on public streets during the commute to work is not compensable, but the injuries of a traveling salesperson who is in an accident while on her way to a sales call

---

ⓘ YOUR PROTECTION FOR EXERCISING RIGHTS UNDER THE OSH ACT

The law expressly protects employees from discharge or discipline in two ways.

First, the employer cannot discriminate against an employee because the employee has filed a complaint with OSHA, asked OSHA to inspect the workplace, talked to the OSHA inspector during the walkaround, or otherwise assisted OSHA in the investigation.

Second, the law protects a worker who refuses to perform a job that is likely to cause death or serious injury. As a general rule, employees do not have a right to refuse to perform work, and normally the employer could discipline or discharge an employee for such a refusal. However, an employee cannot be discharged or disciplined for refusing to perform a job if all the following circumstances apply:

- The reason for the refusal is a good-faith belief that there is a real danger of death or serious injury.
- A reasonable person in the employee's position would conclude there is a real danger of death or serious injury.
- There is insufficient time to eliminate the danger through the regular OSHA channels.
- The employee has asked the employer unsuccessfully to fix the problem.

In addition, employees acting together concerning safety-related matters are generally engaged in protected concerted activity under the National Labor Relations Act and cannot be disciplined or discharged because they have acted together. In addition, a refusal to work in good faith because of abnormally dangerous conditions is not a strike under federal law.

would be compensable. (Injuries incurred by an employee in an auto accident in the employer's parking lot might also be compensable.) Some examples of compensable injuries are injuries caused by defective machinery, fires or explosions at work, repeated lifting of heavy equipment, or slipping on an oily floor surface at work.

Illnesses that are caused by working conditions, where the job presents a risk of contracting the illness that is greater than the normal risks of everyday life, are also compensable. So a coal miner who contracts black lung disease would be eligible for compensation. However, if a clerical worker who works in an office with coworkers who smoke contracts emphysema from second-hand smoke, her illness probably would not be compensable. The reasoning is that there is nothing peculiar about her job that increased the risk of contracting emphysema.

Q. If a workplace injury causes death, is compensation provided to the worker's survivors?

A. Yes, death benefits generally are provided to the spouse until remarriage, and to the children until they reach the age of majority (usually eighteen). Death benefits consist of a burial allowance and a percentage of the deceased worker's weekly wage. There also may be a maximum cap on benefits receivable.

Q. How much compensation is paid for an injury or illness?

A. Workers receive a fixed weekly benefit based on their regular salary. The percentage of regular salary received varies from state to state but is generally in the 50 to 66 percent range. This wage payment is made for the period during which the employee is temporarily unable to work due to the injury.

Workers' compensation also pays for all medical expenses associated with the injury or illness. Most state laws also provide some compensation for the costs associated with medical and vocational rehabilitation.

Employees who suffer a permanent disability,

whether partial or total, are also eligible for a payment to compensate for the decrease in earnings attributable to the permanent nature of the disability. The amount payable may be determined by a **schedule** (a list that specifies wage loss for specific disabilities; for example, $8,910 for loss of an index finger), or by percentage of the weekly wage.

Q. For a straight medical claim (assuming no disability), is filing a workers' compensation claim preferable to filing a medical insurance claim?

A. Yes. Generally, the employer will pay 100 percent of the medical bills incurred in a workers' compensation claim, while the employee frequently must pay a percentage of the medical bills if no workers' compensation claim is filed and the claim is treated as covered by a medical insurance plan.

Q. What must a worker do to obtain compensation for a work-related injury?

A. If you are an employee injured at work, the first thing you should do is notify the employer as soon as possible after an injury occurs. Usually, the employer will have claim forms available for you to fill out. The employer then submits the documents to the insurance company and the state workers' compensation agency. If your employer does not have claim forms available, you should contact the state workers' compensation agency.

If the employer does not challenge a claim, the insurance company will pay your medical bills and wages. If the employer contests a claim, a hearing is scheduled and evidence relating to the circumstances of the injury and the extent of the injury is presented. The resulting decision as to whether, and how much, compensation is owed can be appealed by either the employer or the employee.

As a general rule, the only way you can be compensated by your employer for workplace injuries or illnesses is by filing a claim under workers' compensation. There are a few exceptions to the exclusivity rule, such as when an employer intentionally injures an employee. In that situation, you may sue in court to collect damages for the injuries suffered if you can prove that the employer was guilty of intentional wrongdoing. If you or your employer are not covered by the workers' compensation law, you can file a lawsuit to collect damages if you can prove that the injury was caused by the employer's negligence.

Social Security Disability Insurance

Q. How does Social Security Disability Insurance differ from workers' comp?

A. The Social Security Disability Insurance system differs from workers' compensation in that the cause of the injury is irrelevant for purposes of Social Security. To get money under workers' comp, the employee's injury must arise out of employment. But under Social Security, the main issue is whether the injury prevents the employee from being able to work, regardless of the cause of the injury. So, if you're injured in an automobile accident on the commute to work, you probably won't be able to get workers' comp, but you may be eligible for Social Security benefits if your injuries prevent you from earning a living.

Q. What are the requirements for an injured worker to receive Social Security benefits?

A. An employee has to be in a job covered by Social Security, and the injury or illness has to be considered "disabling."

Q. What types of injuries are considered "disabling"?

A. A **disabling medical condition** is one that can be expected to last at least twelve months and causes the employee to be unable to work anywhere in the country. The Social Security Administration has published a list of impairments that are considered disabling, such as severe epilepsy and loss of vision or hearing. A medical condition that does not appear on the list still may be considered disabling if the worker can show that the condition is the medical equivalent of a listed impairment—that it is equal in severity and duration to a listed impairment.

Q. What if a worker does not suffer from a medical equivalent of a listed impairment?

A. Then the worker would be eligible for benefits only if he or she could prove a disabling medical condition by another means. The employee would have to show that the condition or disease is so severe that it prevented him or her from doing his or her former job or other similar work. It is not easy to prove this.

Q. Can a disabled worker's spouse and children receive Social Security benefits for a worker's disability?

A. If the spouse and children meet the requirements for the worker's Social Security retirement benefits, they should qualify for disability benefits.

Q. Where can workers apply for Social Security disability benefits?

A. If you are an employee who needs to apply for Social Security disability benefits, you should file a claim at the local Social Security Administration office. There are offices in most large cities in the United States. Submit the following documents with the application:

- Your medical history, along with a detailed statement from a doctor concerning the cause of the disability
- Your detailed work history
- Information concerning your educational background

These documents help the Social Security Administration decide whether the condition is disabling. You can also submit statements from family and friends.

Q. What happens if the Social Security Administration rejects my application for benefits?

A. There is an appeals process for rejected applications. This process is explained in the section on Social Security retirement benefits in chapter 16, "The Rights of Older Americans."

THE WORLD AT YOUR FINGERTIPS

- *Agencies of the federal government are a good source of information about your rights and duties on the job. We list the main office addresses in Washington, D.C., below, but most agencies also have regional offices located in major cities throughout the United States. To find a federal agency, look in your local phone directory under "United States Government."*

- *Contact your local U.S. Department of Labor office for information concerning the Family and Medical Leave Act (FMLA). The main office can be contacted at Employment Standards Administration, U.S. Department of Labor, 200 Constitution Avenue NW, Washington, DC 20210. The Department of Labor can be contacted by phone at 202-693-0023, and also maintains a toll-free number for providing information on the FMLA at 800-959-FMLA. Information on the FMLA can be found on the DOL website at www.dol.gov/dol/topic/benefits-leave/fmla.htm.*

- *You can find information regarding your rights and responsibilities under the National Labor Relations Act (NLRA); contact the National Labor Relations Board, 1099 Fourteenth Street NW, Washington, DC 20570. You can phone the NLRB at 202-273-1991, or access its website at www.nlrb.gov.*

- *The Wage and Hour Division of your local U.S. Department of Labor office can give you details on laws affecting wages and working conditions. The Wage and Hour Division also offers many publications. The main office is located at Wage and Hour Division, U.S. Department of Labor, Room S-1302, 200 Constitution Avenue NW, Washington, DC 20210. You can contact the Wage and Hour Division by phone at 202-693-4650, or access its website at www.dol.gov/esa/whd.*

- *You can direct inquiries concerning job-related safety issues to the Occupational Safety and Health Administration (OSHA). The staff can answer your questions and send literature about the OSH Act. You can contact them at U.S. Department of Labor (OSHA), Office of Public Affairs, Room N-3649, 200 Constitution Avenue NW, Washington, DC, 20210. You can also contact OSHA by phone at 202-693-1999, or access its website at www.osha.gov/index.html.*

- *For specific workers' compensation information in your state, write to your state department of labor.*

- *The Legal Information Institute at Cornell University maintains a website at www.law.cornell.edu/topics/workers_compensation.html that provides an overview of workers' compensation and has links to source materials and references discussing workers' compensation issues.*

- *Your local Social Security Administration office can provide details and literature about your Social Security Disability Insurance benefits. The main office for the Social Security Administration is located at Social Security Administration, Office of Public Inquiries, Windsor Park Building, 6401 Security Blvd., Baltimore, MD 21235. The Social Security Administration can be contacted by phone at 800-772-1213, or you can access its website at www.ssa.gov.*

- *For more general information, it is worth researching federal government publications. The federal government publishes hundreds of books, booklets, and pamphlets about employment. These range from how-to books for teenagers looking for jobs to statistics on the number of OSHA claims in a specific year. To find out if there is a publication about your specific problem, check the government bibliographies, which are available without charge from the Superintendent of Documents, U.S. Government Printing Office, 732 N. Capitol Street NW, Washington, DC 20402. The telephone number is 202-512-1119, and you can access the website at bookstore.gpo.gov. Sales Product Catalog 44 (Employment and Occupations) is a good place to start.*
- *The federal government's Citizen Information Center also distributes free or inexpensive booklets. For a free listing of available publications, write to Consumer Information Catalog, Pueblo, CO 81009, or call the toll-free number, 888-878-3256. You can access its website at www.pueblo.gsa.gov.*

REMEMBER THIS

- *Many laws prohibit discrimination in the workplace. They cover hiring, firing, promotions, job duties, wages, benefits, and reviews. Federal laws prohibit discrimination based on age, disability, race, sex, color, national origin, religion, and union activity. State laws may provide greater protections.*
- *Antidiscrimination laws don't only protect women and minorities. Everyone is protected from discriminatory decisions based on race, color, national origin, or gender.*

- *The laws prohibit both overt discrimination and policies that don't discriminate directly but have a discriminatory effect.*
- *Sexual harassment is against the law. It can be either quid pro quo, in which job benefits are tied to sexual favors, or hostile environment, in which harassment creates an offensive working environment. Both genders are protected from sexual harassment.*
- *A number of state and federal laws protect privacy in the workplace, but there are many exceptions.*
- *Public sector employees (i.e., government workers) have certain legal and constitutional rights on the job that aren't usually available to private employees.*
- *The federal government and many states have laws that govern unions and union-management relations; employees' right to organize is protected.*
- *Federal and state laws govern wages and hours, workplace safety, and workplace injuries.*

LEAVING A JOB

All good things come to an end, they say, and that's surely true with jobs, whether they're good or not. The law can affect many of these terminations—for example, if you are fired or laid off, or if you choose to retire. This section will reveal the legal implications of leaving a job.

Being Fired

Q. Can employers fire employees without worrying about legal consequences?

A. It depends. In the United States, most employees are considered **employees at will.** This means that they have no written contract that governs the length of their employment or the reasons for which they may be fired. The employer is free to lay off or fire such employees with no notice and for no reason.

Not all employees, however, are employees at will. Unionized employees covered by a collective bargaining agreement usually cannot be fired "at will." Their contracts normally provide that they can be terminated only for just cause (that is, for a cause that a person of ordinary intelligence would consider a fair and reasonable justification for dismissal). Moreover, the grievance mechanism contained in most collective bargaining agreements provides a process by which union employees can challenge their firing. (For a fuller discussion of union protections, see page 440, "Unions in the Workplace.")

Q. What about government workers?

A. Civil service laws protect public workers. These normally require the employer to have just cause to fire the worker. Civil Service Commissions provide a mechanism by which public employees can appeal any decision to discharge them. (For further discussion of civil service laws, see page 438, "Special Rights of Public Employees.")

Q. Are there any laws that affect an employer's ability to fire employees at will?

A. Yes, the NLRA, Title VII, the ADEA, and the ADA all prohibit an employer from firing an employee if the reason for the decision to fire is based on the employee's union activity or membership in a protected class—race, sex, religion, national origin, color, age, or disability. Most federal laws regulating the workplace also prohibit employers from retaliating against workers who assert their rights under federal law. (See the "Whistle-blowers" sidebar.)

Moreover, many state antidiscrimination laws protect a broader class of workers from discrimination in firing. For example, Wisconsin prohibits firing based on weight, height, or sexual orienta-

tion. (For further discussion of the antidiscrimination laws, see page 423, "Discrimination in the Workplace.")

One state, Montana, expressly requires an employer to have good cause in order to terminate or lay off a worker.

Finally, several states, such as New Jersey and California, have passed laws to protect "whistle-blowers" from being fired.

Q. Have the courts recognized any exceptions to an employer's ability to fire at-will employees at will?

A. Yes. In approximately forty states, including Oregon, California, Illinois, Wisconsin, and Michigan, the courts have held that an employer cannot fire a worker for reasons that conflict with, or undermine, a state's public policy. This is known as the **public policy exception** to employment at will.

Q. How does firing a worker conflict with a state's public policy?

A. Generally speaking, the public policy of a state can be found in the state's statutes and constitution. Courts have determined that four categories of discharge undermine public policy.

- Firing workers because they refuse to perform an act that state law prohibits. For example, an employer tells workers to dump toxic waste into the city sewer system. The workers refuse and are fired.
- Firing workers for reporting a violation of the law. For example, workers report to the state agriculture department that an employer is selling contaminated meat, and the employer fires them.
- Firing workers for engaging in acts that public policy encourages. For example, employees report to jury duty and the employer fires them for missing work.
- Firing workers for exercising a statutory right. For example, injured workers file a claim under the state workers' compensation law and the employer fires them.

Q. I have no written contract, but my employer told me that as long as I perform my work well I'll have a job. Can my employer fire me even if I'm performing my job well?

A. It depends. Many state courts, such as those in Michigan, will enforce an oral promise by the employer under certain circumstances. Generally speaking there must be

- clear, unequivocal evidence that a promise was made; and
- evidence that the employer and employee specifically discussed the issue of job security and reasons for termination.

It also may be helpful to the employee's case if he or she can show

- evidence of the employer's past practice that it fires employees only for cause; and
- evidence that the employee turned down other job offers or left a job in reliance on the promise made.

Other courts, however, will not enforce such an oral promise.

Q. If the employer's handbook states that employees will be fired only for just cause, can the employer still fire someone at will?

A. It depends. Over thirty states, such as Wisconsin, Michigan, and California, will enforce specific terms contained in an employment handbook or personnel manual under certain conditions. The handbook or manual must have been given to the employee.

The language of the manual must be specific. For example, "all employees will be treated fairly" would be considered too vague to be enforced, whereas "employees will be fired only for just cause" is specific enforceable language.

However, not all handbooks or manuals create enforceable contracts. For example, if the manual has clear and express disclaimers informing employees that the information is not meant to create a contract and can be changed or re-

---

🗐 WHISTLE-BLOWERS

A whistle-blower is an employee who reports to a government agency possible violations of state or federal law occurring in the workplace. The whistle-blower statutes prohibit employers from firing a worker who makes reports with reasonable cause to believe that there is a violation. The laws also prohibit employers from firing employees who take part in government investigations and hearings relating to violations of law at the workplace.

Enforcement of employment laws relies heavily on information and help provided by employees. After all, employees are in the best position to know whether their rights have been violated. To stop complaints, employers might try to pressure employees not to make complaints; for example, by threatening layoffs or firings. Because of this potential problem, almost all federal employment laws expressly prohibit employers from taking adverse actions against employees because they have filed a complaint to enforce their rights or cooperated in an investigation conducted by a federal agency enforcing the law.

The Sarbanes-Oxley Act, for example, passed in the wake of the Enron scandals, protects employees of publicly traded companies against firing and other adverse actions if they have provided information about certain types of corporate wrongdoing or cooperated in investigations of corporate fraud.

voked at any time, courts probably will rule that it does not create an enforceable contract.

Q. Must an employer provide notice to an employee prior to discharge?

A. If the employee has a written contract requiring notice, or if there is a collective bargaining agreement with a notice requirement, then the employer must provide notice. But generally no notice is required, except in cases where there is a mass layoff or a plant closure.

Q. Is an employer required to pay severance pay when it fires a worker?

A. There is no law requiring employers to pay severance pay. If the employee has a written contract guaranteeing severance pay, or if there is a collective bargaining agreement providing for severance pay, then the employer will be required to pay severance. Otherwise, the employer is under no obligation to pay it.

Q. An employer offers severance pay only if the employee agrees to sign a waiver of rights to sue the company. What is the legal effect of signing such a waiver?

A. Generally, a **knowing and voluntary waiver** is enforceable and would prevent employees from being able to sue the employer for anything that occurred while they were employed. Whether a waiver is knowing and voluntary depends on the

circumstances. The courts usually consider several factors in deciding if it is knowing and voluntary.

- Is the waiver written in a manner that the employee can understand?
- Did the employee receive benefit in exchange for the waiver that he or she was not already entitled to receive?
- Did the employee have a reasonable time to consider the offer?

The ADEA contains a list of specific requirements that must be met in order for a waiver of employee rights under the ADEA to be effective. Included among those requirements is that the employee be advised in writing to consult with a lawyer before signing the waiver and that the employee be given at least twenty-one days to consider the waiver before signing.

The courts will not enforce a waiver of any claims that arise under the FLSA.

Q. How are employee disputes involving termination commonly resolved?

A. Recently, employers have been turning to arbitration as the forum for resolving employment disputes, especially those involving termination. **Arbitration** is a quasi-judicial procedure in which a neutral third party presides over a hearing. At the hearing, the disputing parties present their claims, the evidence in support of their claims, and their arguments. The arbitrator then

---

ⓘ PLANT CLOSING AND MASS LAYOFFS

The Worker Adjustment and Retraining Notification Act (WARN) is a federal law requiring employers to provide workers, their unions, and state and local government officials sixty days advance notice of any plant closing or mass layoff. The law applies to private employers with one hundred or more employees. A **mass layoff** is defined as a reduction in force that results in the layoff at a single site of employment of at least 33 percent of the workforce and at least fifty employees, or at least five hundred employees. Failure to give the sixty-day notice subjects an employer to liability for back pay and benefits under an employee benefit plan for each day that the notice was not given. Employees can enforce the law by filing a lawsuit in federal court.

issues a final and binding decision that resolves the dispute. Many employers believe the process is faster, cheaper, and eliminates the risks associated with a jury deciding a case. Accordingly, some employers are requiring employees to sign arbitration agreements before they are hired, or as a condition of continued employment. By signing an agreement to arbitrate, employees are waiving their right to file a lawsuit in court, and agreeing instead that they will submit the dispute to arbitration. For example, employees who have signed a valid arbitration agreement, and subsequently believe they were fired because of their race, would not be able to pursue their claim by filing a lawsuit under Title VII in federal court. Instead, they would be required to present their claim to the arbitrator, and the arbitrator would decide if Title VII had been violated.

ⓘ LOSING YOUR JOB DOESN'T MEAN LOSING YOUR HEALTH INSURANCE

The Consolidated Omnibus Budget Reconciliation Act (COBRA) provides that workers who lose their jobs will not lose their health insurance coverage automatically. This federal law requires companies with at least twenty employees carrying group health insurance to offer terminated employees the opportunity to continue participating in the company's health insurance plan for up to eighteen months. The employee may be required to pay no more than 102 percent of the cost of the premium. Usually, 102 percent of the premium cost at the group rate will be less than the premium for an individually purchased policy.

There may be state COBRA laws that apply to smaller employers.

As a general rule, the courts will enforce an agreement to arbitrate if certain conditions are met:

- The arbitrator hearing the case is a neutral and impartial third party
- The conduct of the hearing is fair, allowing for the opportunity to be heard, to present evidence, and to cross-examine witnesses
- The remedies available from the arbitrator are the same as those available in court
- The cost of the arbitration process is not unduly burdensome to the employee

Even a valid arbitration agreement cannot, however, prevent an employee from filing a charge with a government agency alleging a violation of the law. Thus, an employee who signed an agreement to arbitrate could still file a charge with the NLRB or the EEOC, though he or she might be precluded from filing a lawsuit.

Unemployment Insurance

The states administer the **unemployment insurance (UI)** system to provide workers and their families with weekly income during periods of unemployment. When unemployed due to plant closures, layoffs, natural disaster, or other acts or circumstances that are not caused by the worker's fault or misconduct, an employee may receive UI benefits.

The system is funded by state and federal taxes that employers pay. Within certain federal guidelines, each state determines the scope, coverage, and eligibility requirements for UI benefits.

Q. What workers are covered under the UI system?

A. Most workers are covered, but there are some exceptions. Generally excluded from coverage are self-employed people, independent contractors, casual employees, and agricultural workers.

Q. If workers are covered under UI, are they automatically entitled to receive benefits if unemployed?

A. No. In order to receive benefits, they must meet the eligibility requirements and not be otherwise disqualified from receiving benefits.

Q. What are the eligibility requirements for UI?

A. The eligibility requirements vary from state to state but most states look at four criteria, all of which have to be met:

- The applicant earned a minimum amount of wages within a specified period and/or worked for a minimum period in the recent past (for example, the applicant worked at least twenty weeks at an average weekly wage of at least $20)
- The applicant registered for work with the state unemployment office
- The applicant is available for work
- The applicant is actively seeking employment

Q. What will disqualify a worker from receiving UI benefits?

A. As a general rule, workers are disqualified if they voluntarily quit without good cause or were fired for misconduct. In some states, even if workers' conduct disqualifies them, the disqualification will last only for a specific length of time, after which they will be eligible to receive UI benefits.

The meaning of **good cause** varies greatly among the states. Some states consider certain types of personal reasons as good cause, such as having to care for a sick relative or following a spouse who has found work in another state. Most states, however, require that good cause be due to the employer's actions. For example, working conditions that are so bad that they would cause a reasonable person to quit would be considered good cause in some states. The "reasonable person" perspective is very important to determining good cause. It is not enough that a situation is intolerable to a specific worker; the conditions must be such that a reasonable person, in the same position as the employee, would feel compelled to quit.

The meaning of **misconduct** also varies by state, but incompetence alone generally is not considered misconduct. Violations of known company rules and insubordination are examples of employee behavior normally deemed to be misconduct.

Q. Can a worker refuse a job offer and still collect UI benefits?

A. It depends on why the worker refused the job offer. If the job is not suitable work, then the refusal is allowable. A job is not suitable if the worker has no experience in it, if it is more hazardous than the worker's previous job, or if the physical condition of the worker prevents him or her from accepting it. States also consider travel costs and time, bad working hours, community wage levels, and compelling personal problems in deciding if a job may be rejected. Finally, workers usually cannot lose benefits for refusing a job that is available because the current workforce is on strike.

If the wages and conditions of a new job are below those of the worker's previous employment, he or she may not have to accept it. For example, a skilled craftsperson is permitted to refuse a job as a janitor. After a certain period of time, however, most states require the worker to "lower his sights" and accept a lesser job.

Q. Are workers who are on strike entitled to collect UI benefits?

A. It depends on the specific state law. A few states allow workers to collect UI if the strike is caused by an employer's violation of the NLRA or an employer's breach of the collective bargaining agreement. Some states allow workers to collect UI if the employer has locked out the workers.

Most states, however, do not permit workers on strike to collect UI benefits. The period of disqualification varies by state—in some states, the disqualification lasts for the duration of the strike; in other states, the disqualification lasts for a fixed period of time. If a striker is permanently replaced, however, the worker then may be eligible for UI benefits.

Q. How does a worker apply for UI benefits?

A. Employees file claims for UI benefits at their local state unemployment office. The claim should be filed as soon as possible after unemployment begins, since benefits will not be paid until all the paperwork is processed and eligibility for benefits is verified.

Employees should take the following documents with them to the unemployment office to help verify their eligibility: Social Security card, recent pay stubs, and any documentation relating to the reason for the job loss.

After filing the initial claim, employees are usually required to report on a regular basis to the unemployment office to verify their continued eligibility for benefits. Failure to report when required can result in a loss of benefits.

Q. How is the amount of UI benefits determined?

A. While the amount varies by state, the general formula is 50 percent of the employee's weekly wage, not to exceed a statutory cap on amount paid. The cap is based on a percentage of the state's average weekly wages for all workers. Because of the cap on maximum benefits, most workers receive much less than 50 percent of their weekly wage.

Q. How long are UI benefits paid?

A. The usual duration for UI benefits is twenty-six weeks. In times of extended high unemployment, however, benefits may be paid for an additional thirteen weeks and sometimes longer.

Q. Can an unemployed worker receive other benefits or earn extra money while collecting UI benefits?

A. Some states ignore small amounts of money earned. Usually, however, income received is deducted from UI benefits. Most states reduce or stop UI benefits for weeks in which an unemployed worker received disability benefits, severance pay, and other types of income.

Pension Plans

Q. Does the law require employers to provide pensions?

A. No, but if an employer does offer a pension plan, the federal Employee Retirement Income Security Act (ERISA) probably covers it. ERISA applies to private employers whose plans are "qualified" under the federal tax laws. The tax laws provide important advantages to companies whose plans qualify, so most pension plans are regulated by ERISA. (For further information on pensions, see chapter 16, "The Rights of Older Americans," chapter 18, "Estate Planning," and chapter 3, "Family Law.")

Q. What are the participation provisions of pension plans?

A. ERISA provides that where an employer offers a pension plan, most workers must be allowed to participate if they are at least twenty-one years of age and have completed one year of service to the company. ERISA defines one year of service as a twelve-month period dur-

---

▶ **MOVING OUT OF STATE AND COLLECTING UNEMPLOYMENT**

If workers move to another state to look for work, they can still collect UI benefits, because all states belong to the Interstate Reciprocal Benefit Payment Plan. This plan allows workers to register for work and file for UI benefits in a state different from the one in which they previously worked. The law of the state in which the employee previously worked, however, is the applicable law for determining eligibility for benefits. The workers must satisfy that state's requirements in order to receive UI benefits in the new state.

ing which an employee has worked one thousand hours or more.

Q. How does a worker accrue benefits under a pension plan?

A. Benefit accrual is the process of building up benefits once an employee qualifies for the pension plan. Normally, employees start accumulating benefits as soon as they begin participating in the plan. How benefits accrue depends on the type of pension plan.

A **defined contribution plan** establishes a separate retirement account for each participant. The employer (and sometimes the employee) makes a contribution to the account. The benefit due to the worker upon retirement depends on the amount of money in the account, the investment returns on contributions, and the payout method selected. Benefits accrue based on a predetermined amount that the employer at least annually pays into the account.

A **defined benefit plan** promises a worker a specific level of benefit payment upon retirement. The benefit is financed by the employer's contributions and investment gains on those contributions. Benefits are paid to the worker based on total years of participation in the plan and usually his or her final salary or his or her average salary for the last several years of his or her employment.

One significant difference between a defined contribution plan and a defined benefit plan is that in a defined contribution plan the ultimate return depends on the investment return on the contributions, while in a defined benefit plan the level of benefits is predetermined and the employer must make additional contributions if there is a poor return on the plan's investments.

Q. When do benefits vest in the worker?

A. Vesting refers to the point after which the employee's accrued benefits cannot be taken away—they must be paid to the worker upon retirement. If a worker leaves his job before his pension vests, he loses any pension benefits that he accrued. Once the benefits vest, however, a worker is entitled to a retirement benefit even if he subsequently quits that job.

ERISA provides two different methods for vesting. One method requires that after five years of service employees are eligible for 100 percent of their retirement benefit. A second method provides for a graduated system of vesting: after three years of service, employees are eligible for 20 percent of their pension benefit; after four years, 40 percent; after five years, 60 percent; after six years, 80 percent; and after seven years, 100 percent.

ⓘ THE PURPOSE OF ERISA

ERISA protects workers who participate in pension and benefit plans. It also covers the beneficiaries of such workers. This federal law preempts almost all state laws covering pensions and other types of benefit plans.

ERISA deals with the following aspects of pension plans: (1) participation; (2) benefit accrual, vesting, and breaks in service; (3) funding; (4) administration of funds; (5) reporting and disclosure; (6) joint and survivor provisions; and (7) plan termination.

ERISA sets legal minimums that a pension plan must provide. However, an employer may provide more liberal terms in its pension plan.

Q. What happens if there is a break in service before pension benefits become vested?

A. A **break in service** occurs when employment is interrupted. If a break in service occurs before benefits become vested, the worker loses any entitlement to those benefits. When an employee works less than five hundred hours in a year for the employer, a break in service has occurred.

Q. What are ERISA's funding requirements?

A. Generally, the law requires that the employer contribute enough money to cover pension payments when they become due under a defined benefit plan, as determined actuarially. Funding provisions are designed to strengthen pension funds and prevent abuses. The employer and the fund's administrators are obligated to ensure that the funding requirements are met.

Q. How does ERISA prevent misuse of pension funds?

A. Those who manage pension funds are considered to be **fiduciaries** and are obligated to act with "care, skill, prudence, and diligence" in conducting the affairs of the pension plan. This means that the assets of the pension plan must be diversified among a group of investments so as to minimize the risk of large losses. Plan administrators are prohibited from using pension assets to invest in funds or property in which they have

a financial interest. ERISA prohibits a plan administrator from borrowing money from the fund for personal use or making loans with pension money to the employer. It also gives pension plan participants the right to sue administrators who breach their duty and violate ERISA.

Q. How does an employee file a claim for benefits?

A. Each pension plan specifies the claims procedure. Generally, a vested participant is eligible for payments from a pension fund when he or she reaches the age of sixty-five (or the normal retirement age specified in the plan) or upon leaving the company. Most pension plans require the participant to file a written claim in order for payments to begin. Within 90 days (which can be extended to 180 days), the plan administrators must either begin payment to the participant or notify the participant in writing that the claim is denied.

If a claim is denied, the participant can appeal that decision. Some plans provide for arbi-

---

ⓘ **FIRING WORKERS TO AVOID PAYING PENSIONS**

Employers may not fire employees to avoid making benefit payments or to prevent benefits from vesting. Neither may employers force workers to quit for these reasons. However, a worker can lose nonvested benefits if fired for other reasons, or if he or she voluntarily quits.

▶ **HOW CHANGING JOBS BEFORE RETIREMENT AFFECTS PENSIONS**

If you change jobs before retiring, ERISA provides that you are entitled to all your vested benefits. Any benefits that are not vested at the time of the job change are forfeited. Vested funds may be put into an individual retirement account (IRA) or may be transferred to your new employer's pension plan. You can also take the vested funds as a lump-sum payment. However, if you do this, the money most likely will be taxed as income. You can avoid the tax consequences if you **roll over** (quickly transfer) the vested pension funds into an individual retirement account or another qualified pension plan.

tration as a means of appeal. When arbitration is required, the participant must use the mechanism. The denial of a claim eventually can be challenged in court by filing a lawsuit under ERISA.

Q. If a plan participant dies, can the surviving spouse still collect the pension?

A. Under ERISA, a qualified pension plan must pay vested pension benefits to the spouse if a plan participant dies before retirement. This is known as the **survivor's benefit.** The survivor's benefit is automatic unless the spouse consents in writing to waive it.

ERISA also provides that a qualified plan must continue to pay retirement benefits to a spouse when a plan participant dies after he or she begins to receive retirement benefits. This is called the **qualified joint and survivor annuity benefit.** It is automatically provided under the terms of the pension plan unless the spouse consents in writing to waive the benefit.

Q. If a plan participant gets divorced, is the ex-spouse entitled to a share of the pension?

A. This depends on state law. Most states consider a pension to belong jointly to a participant and the participant's spouse. If a state court issues an order (called a **qualified domestic relations order,** or **QDRO)** that part of a participant's vested benefits must be paid to an ex-spouse or child, ERISA requires the plan administrator to honor the court order.

Q. How can I find out about the specific terms of my pension plan?

A. ERISA requires the plan administrator to give a **summary plan description (SPD)** and a summary of the annual financial report to every participant in the pension plan. The SPD is a nontechnical explanation of how the plan works and how benefits are paid out. It explains the benefit accrual rules, vesting requirements, and procedures for filing a claim for benefits. The summary of the annual financial report is a non-

technical explanation of the financial data relevant to the operation of the plan contained in the annual report. ERISA also requires that the employer make available to the plan participants, upon request, copies of the plan itself and the annual report.

Q. Does an employer have the right to terminate a pension plan?

A. If an employee's union negotiated for the inclusion of a pension plan in the collective bargaining agreement, then the employer cannot terminate the plan without bargaining with the union over the issue. ERISA itself does not prohibit an employer from terminating a pension plan.

ERISA does, however, provide some protection if a plan is eliminated, by establishing the **Pension Benefit Guaranty Corporation (PBGC).** ERISA requires defined benefit pension plans to pay insurance to the PBGC. In return, the PBGC guarantees the vested benefits of participants in the fund, up to a certain limit.

The PBGC provides this protection only for certain benefits in specific types of plans. Thus, the PBGC may not protect your benefits if you do not participate in a qualified defined benefit plan, if your benefits have not vested, or if your plan provides medical and disability benefits.

THE WORLD AT YOUR FINGERTIPS

- *For information about unemployment compensation, contact the local office of your state's employment security or unemployment department or the state job service.*
- *The Legal Information Institute at Cornell University maintains a website at www.law. cornell.edu/topics/unemployment_ compensation.html that provides an overview of unemployment compensation and has links to source materials and references discussing unemployment compensation issues.*

- *For information about ERISA and your rights under a pension plan, contact the Employee Benefits Security Administration (EBSA)—formerly known as the Pension and Welfare Benefits Administration—at the U.S. Department of Labor, 200 Constitution Avenue NW, Washington, DC 20210. You can phone EBSA at 202- 219-8776 or 800-998-7542 (to order publications toll free), or access its website at www.dol.gov/ebsa.*

REMEMBER THIS

- *Most nonunion workers in this country are "employees at will," who may be fired with no notice for any reason.*
- *Workers protected by a collective bargaining agreement, as well as government workers, may have more protections.*
- *Antidiscrimination laws apply to firing or laying off workers. Antiretaliation laws also apply.*
- *Unemployment compensation provides some income to workers who are laid off or fired for reasons other than misconduct.*
- *Federal law protects most pension plans, and workers have rights under the law to information about their plan and to appeal if benefits are denied.*
- *A deceased worker's spouse is guaranteed a benefit under a qualified pension plan unless the spouse has waived the right to the benefit.*

Forming and Operating a Small Business

So you've decided to take the plunge. No more wage slavery! You're starting your own business.

Of course, you want to get started on becoming the national standard in your industry immediately. But first, take some time to look at how the law will affect your business—a little planning now might save plenty of time, money, and heartache down the line. This chapter deals with the legal and other issues that have to be resolved when forming and operating a small business. Whether you're manufacturing lawn furniture, selling stuffed animals, or offering high-tech computer consulting, you'll have to face certain basic issues, all of which have legal dimensions. What will you call your business? Will you need permits or licenses? What form of business structure is most suitable for your business? This chapter also will answer some of the questions you might have if you're thinking of buying a franchise or an established business. The final section will consider some issues that may become important once your business is up and running, including some information on the last resort of the failing business, bankruptcy.

Some of the important legal issues affecting small businesses are covered in more detail in other chapters of this book. Chapter 12, "Law and the Workplace," gives you some information on your obligations to employees, and their rights; chapter 9, "Contracts and Consumer Law," provides you with information on two areas that are crucial to the small business owner; and more information on liability issues can be found in chapter 14, "Personal Injury."

STARTING A BUSINESS

Thea is a florist, and she's keen to start her own floristry business. She thinks there's a market for floral displays in her neighborhood, but she has no idea how to get financing, or even how much money she'll need. But she's already thought of a name: Fleurtation.

Thea needs to sit down and do some homework. She should undertake market research, prepare a business plan and a financial forecast, and explore her financing options. What kinds of licenses and permits will she need? Where can she set up shop? She'll need to register her business name (if it isn't already being used by someone else) and think about getting a domain name if she wants to do any Internet business.

Starting a small business is a high-risk exercise that requires a huge amount of hard work. This section will give you some information on the first steps you need to take when starting out, but you should work with a team of advisers, consisting of a business lawyer, an accountant, and an insurance broker, at a minimum.

Q. I have an idea for a business. What is the first thing I should do?

A. You should take four preliminary steps:

- Make sure your manufacturing process, or your service, or your business idea, will work in the way you want it to work.
- Conduct market research.
- Prepare a business plan, covering projected sales, employees needed, and so on.
- Prepare a financial forecast, so you'll know what the business is going to cost.
- Determine where the money you'll need for start-up and day-to-day costs will come from.

For the most part, these preliminary steps have relatively minor legal considerations, but they merit a brief discussion because they're so fundamental.

Q. What does market research involve?

A. The failure rate for new businesses is high. Before you commit yourself and your hard-earned money, determine whether a market exists for your service or product. Have similar businesses in this area failed? Can you determine why? If a market does exist for what you're thinking of offering, what's the best way to exploit it?

Use the resources of your library and the Internet to find out as much at you can about the industry/service you're interested in. Be especially concerned with actual and potential competitors—who are they, what are their strong points/weaknesses, do you feel you have an edge on them?

One important issue is the location of the business. Obviously, you don't want to open up a greeting card shop across the street from another greeting card shop in a small town. But two greeting card stores located in different parts of a major shopping center might both be successful. A legal issue is whether there are any legal restrictions (for example, exclusivity provisions in the shopping center leases) that might limit your location.

In addition, if your market is specialized or has particular needs, market research will help you to understand what your buyers want and how to communicate that your new business can meet that need.

Q. How do I develop a business plan?

A. Lots of new businesses fail for a very simple reason: they fail to establish a sound business and financial plan or forecast, which leads to inadequate or unwise financing. The financial requirements of businesses vary greatly. Fortunately, there are many resources to help you figure out what your particular business will need financially.

- Trade associations are often a good source of information about the capital needs of a particular business.
- The local office of the federal Small Business Administration (SBA) and equivalent state business development offices also can assist with business and financial planning for a new business.
- An accountant, financial planner, or business lawyer who has experience with start-up businesses can be invaluable.
- A business banker will have useful information and may provide professionals to help in developing a business plan.
- If you're purchasing a business, look at prior financial statements and information on taxes paid, including sales taxes and payroll returns as well as the overall return. These should give you bases for forecasting costs.
- If the business is going to be run as a franchise operation, the franchisor is required to provide information about many aspects of the business, which will help you determine the financial resources you will need.
- Finally, software can be really helpful—there are good budgeting programs and overall business planning programs that can take you through some key steps.

Once you have gathered this information, you are in a position to develop a business and financial plan.

Financing a Business

Q. How do I go about financing my business?

A. There are usually several potential sources of capital for a new business:

- Contributions made by you
- Loans from family and friends
- Loans from banks and other financial institutions
- Loans underwritten by a government agency
- Investments made by others who will be actively involved in the management of the business
- Investments from other individuals and institutions who won't be actively involved in the business and are looking just at the profit potential

How the funds are raised and where they come from have many significant legal considerations.

Q. Can I just finance the business myself?

A. It may be possible for you to finance the business yourself. There are a number of alternatives for personal contributions:

Savings

This source is obviously very simple and easy, since it's your money, but how many of us have enough salted away to open much more than a lemonade stand? And if you do have substantial savings, the question is whether all your savings should be invested. Remember, you may have other personal or family needs requiring your savings.

Paid-up Life Insurance

The **surrender** or **cash value** of a life insurance policy is the equity you've built up over the years through the premiums you pay. This is what the insurance company would pay you if you canceled the policy. You could do that and use the proceeds for your business, but then you'd have no life insurance, perhaps at a time when your family is relying more than ever on you. A better option is to borrow against this amount from the company. Rates are low, and the loan is easy to arrange (after all, it's your money). Repayment plans can also be flexible. This is a good option.

Borrowing Against Your Retirement Plan

This is an option only if you continue to work for your employer while starting up your business, and only if you've built up equity (in retirementese, **vested benefits**) in your 401(k) or similar plan. If you have, borrowing against this equity is relatively easy (once again, it's your money), rates are low, and the repayment period can be as long as five years. Best of all, you're repaying yourself. Depending on the terms of your plan, however, you may face another problem: The money can't be two places at once. While you're using it for your business, it may not be growing in your retirement plan, and you may be shortchanging your sunset years. Your benefits person at work can explain how such a loan operates under your plan, and he or she can tell you how such a loan can be arranged.

Home Equity Loans

This is a third way to borrow against your own money. A home equity loan is, in essence, a second mortgage. Rates are usually higher than first mortgages, since there is greater risk for the lender. You usually can deduct the interest you pay on your federal income tax returns. The downside is that you have to go through most of the paperwork and much of the expense and delay of a first mortgage, including paying mortgage-recording taxes in some states, and your home is at risk if you can't pay the loan back. You can find more information on this kind of loan in chapter 5, "Home Ownership."

Borrowing Against the Value of Your Stocks and Bonds

If you're fortunate enough to have such investments, this is one more way of borrowing against your own money. Instead of selling stocks or bonds and incurring taxes (and maybe missing out on some big gains), you can use them as collateral for a loan from your brokerage firm. As with home equity loans, you can't get the full amount of their current value (too much risk), but once again, rates are low and repayment flexible. This is an alternative worth considering, but remember that if the stocks fall in value you could be in for a rude shock, since you will be obligated to deposit additional funds with the broker or pay back part of the loan to keep the loan-to-value ratio appropriate.

Credit Card Debt

Every once in a while you read about a now-successful entrepreneur who rolled the dice and maxed out her credit card to get the business going. That can happen, but all in all this is not as attractive a route as the other alternatives we've listed. Credit card rates are often very high, so you'll pay a lot in interest if you can't pay off the balance quickly.

Q. What do I need to consider if I want to get a loan from family and friends?

A. The next best thing to using your own money (either directly or as collateral for a loan) may be a loan from family and friends. The pluses are that you won't have to go through a lengthy application process, repayment terms could be more liberal than you'd get from a bank, and rates could be lower, maybe even nonexistent. The minuses are that you'll strain your relationship with family and friends if the business fails.

If you do get a loan from this source, it probably will be at least as much because of personal relationships as because of the potential of your business. But that doesn't mean that it should be just a handshake deal. It's almost always best to put the terms in writing by signing a **promissory note.** Loans that go sour are probably right up there with martini abuse as a source of family eruptions. At least with the agreement in writing, you won't have two (or more!) widely different memories of who promised when and what. And if you are unable to repay, Aunt Carol is in a far better position with a promissory note to convince tax authorities that her loan to you should be a tax write-off and not a gift. (She might be in an even better position to get a tax write-off in case of loss if she had an ownership interest, either as a partner or a stockholder; see page 492, "Types of Business Organizations.")

A promissory note is a legally binding document in which you set out the terms of the loan: how much you got, the interest rate, how long you have to repay, the rate of repayment. You can get forms for promissory notes in stationery stores; some personal finance computer programs have them, too. The forms are just the template—you add the terms for your particular agreement by filling in the blanks.

Q. I think I can get a loan from my bank. What do I need to consider?

A. Commercial banks and other commercial lenders are a possibility for additional working capital, though they know very well the high failure rates of new businesses and probably will take a lot of persuading to part with some of their money for your start-up. Expect to go through a lengthy application process. It could mean lots of time and paperwork.

If you do decide to borrow capital, the business must have collateral to secure the loan—something tangible the bank can take to recover its losses if you can't pay the debt. Most start-up businesses don't have a building or a fleet of trucks that can be pledged as collateral, nor do they have a big stock of inventory or accounts receivable that could be pledged. As a result, banks will generally require personal guaranties and collateral from the owners of the business. This means that you will have to back up the loan with your home or other valuable property to get funding—and that you could lose this property if you fail and default on the loan.

You've also got to consider the long-term effect of paying off the debt. Most rates of profit are under 10 percent, making the assumption of an interest-paying burden of even just 10 percent a severe strain on a business.

Q. Are there any government programs that will help me?

A. The Small Business Administration has loan and lease guaranty programs that are designed to

---

▶ **MANY WAYS TO REPAY**

Especially with family and friends, you may be able to tailor the repayment schedule to your needs. If you anticipate not showing much income in the early stages, you can put the periodic payments closer to the end of the loan, or maybe have it all come due at the end. Or you can pay the interest periodically and repay the entire principal at the end. Or you can set low periodic payments at the beginning, gradually becoming larger as the term of the loan nears. It's up to you and your financial angels.

⚠ **GOING AFTER YOUR SPOUSE**

Banks always want as many places as possible to turn to in case the debt isn't repaid. That's why they often insist on a **cosigner,** someone who pledges to make good the repayment if you can't. If your spouse co-signs, he or she puts at risk any separate property he or she may have, as well as the property that you own jointly. And if you live in a community property state, a spouse generally will be liable for your debts even without his or her signature. In any case, to avoid problems and promote marital bliss, be sure to keep your spouse informed about your plans and your business.

encourage banks and other financial institutions to lend money to small businesses. The SBA doesn't make loans itself, but by guarantying most of the amount lent it encourages banks to make loans they might not normally make.

Q. I've heard that my state offers special loan programs. What are they, and how can I find out more about them?

A. Many states have special loan or guaranty programs or financial assistance packages and tax relief plans for small businesses. In Texas, for example, low-cost loans are available to childcare providers, small businesses located in enterprise zones, and historically underutilized businesses. There are special provisions designed to promote growth in rural areas, and a statewide loan fund provides opportunities for small businesses across the state. You can get information about such programs from the local SBA office or the office of your equivalent state or local agency. You can get state information over the Internet by accessing www.state.[two-letter abbreviation of your state]. us. Texas, for example, is *www.state.tx.us.*

You can find out about the many SBA loan programs by checking out its website (*www.sba. gov*) or by calling the SBA at 800-827-5722. Through the website, you can also get information about the SBA office closest to you.

SBA loans can be used for most business purposes, including purchasing real estate; construction and renovation; acquiring furniture, fixtures, and equipment; acquiring working capital; and purchase of inventory. Franchises are eligible, too. The SBA imposes a limit on the size of the businesses it will help (your start-up should have no trouble meeting that requirement!) and it requires business owners to put some of their own money, including personal assets, into the business.

The SBA has several loan programs.

- The 7(a) **Loan Guaranty Program,** a basic lending program that could enable you to borrow as much as $1 million at rates only a few points above the prime rate; you can have as long as seven years to repay a loan for working capital, twenty-five years to repay a loan for real estate and equipment
- Short-term loans and revolving lines of credit
- **LowDoc** loans that streamline the process of SBA approval for loans of under $150,000
- **SBAExpress** loans that permit certain lenders to make an SBA guarantied loan of up to $250,000 without first getting SBA approval
- **MicroLoans** that range from $100 to $35,000 and are processed quickly

Finally, don't forget that cities also may have loan or guaranty programs. You can check with your local government's business development office to see if yours has programs that might be helpful to you.

Q. I think an investor may be interested. What do I need to consider?

A. If you're borrowing money, you're retaining full ownership of the company. Once the loans are repaid, you have no further obligations to the

---

ⓘ HELP FOR WOMEN AND MINORITIES

The SBA has programs that help small business development centers counsel minority and women borrowers on how to develop viable loan application packages. If the SBA approves a package, it will guarantee up to 80 percent of loans of up to $250,000.

The SBA also licenses Specialized Small Business Investment Companies to make loans to socially or economically disadvantaged individuals. A number of private loan programs also encourage business development by minorities, women, and people with disabilities.

lenders. If you have investors, on the other hand, you're giving them a slice of the pie. You don't have to repay what they put into the business, but you'll have to share the profits with them.

Under the law, investors who are actively involved in the business (**active investors**) generally have a different status from investors who are putting up money but not taking part in how the business is run on a day-to-day basis (**passive investors**). The section of this chapter entitled "Types of Business Organizations" will provide you with more information about how to structure your business according to whether you have active or passive investors.

Naming Your Business

Q. What do I need to consider when coming up with a name for my business?

A. Of course, you want your business name to be catchy and compelling, hard to ignore and impossible to forget. We can't help you there, but we can suggest a few steps that will help you avoid hard-hitting "cease and desist" letters from somebody else's lawyer—the basic first step in dealing with infringement issues—that can result in your being forced to trash signs and stationery you can no longer use.

Do Some Research

There's no point in launching a business and finding out too late that someone nearby is using the same name, or one that's very similar. The best way to avoid this is to do an informal search. Look in telephone books in your area and business directories, and on the Internet by using *www.google.com* or another search service. Another very useful starting place is the U.S. Patent and Trademark Office website, *www.uspto.gov*, where you can check, for free, whether anybody has registered the trademark you want to use for your business. You can also check with the county or city clerk in your area, or your state's secretary of state. These officials maintain a list of business names that have been filed.

Register Your Name

If you plan to do business under your name—and your full, legal name—then you *may* not need to register your business name with the authorities. This applies also if you form a separate entity—that is, a limited liability company or corporation—and use that entity's actual name as the name of your business. As long as you use the full, legal name of the entity as the business name—Smokey Joe's Smokin' Ribs, Inc.—you may not have to register the name. But if Smokey Joe's is owned by Ozark Lakes Restaurants, Inc., then you'd have to register the name of the business.

So if you plan to use a business name that has no part of your name or your business entity's name ("Comet Café") or only a part of it ("Cory's Creations") then you need to file what's known as a **fictitious business name, assumed business name,** or **doing business as (DBA) name** with the clerk in your county or city and your state's secretary of state.

This filing—sometimes coupled with the requirement that you publish the fact that you are doing business under this name in a newspaper in your area—puts the world on notice that Cory's Creations is your business name. Filing gives you the right to conduct business under that name—like advertising under that name, or using it when filing for permits, billing customers, paying taxes, and so on. In legal terms, it's your **trade name.**

But that doesn't mean you're totally off the hook. Even if your name really is Wendy, and there are no restaurants with "Wendy" in their name in your area, and you register "Wendy's Burgers" with the county clerk, you're still going to draw the attention of Wendy's International, Inc. That's because they own the **trademark** "Wendy's" and very probably can force you to change your business name. (See "Trademarks" on page 504 for a further discussion of this issue.)

Sometimes registration is good for only a set number of years, after which you must renew the registration. In some states, you could potentially face criminal charges for not filing your business name.

Rules, Regulations, Licenses, and Permits

Q. What rules and regulations do I have to comply with?

A. It's impossible to know exactly what regulations might apply to your particular business. Regulations vary by state and locality. And they vary depending on the type of business. Some businesses—for example, those that are involved in health care or food service—face complex regulation by many federal, state, and local agencies.

Many types of business might have to be concerned with **environmental regulations,** including rules on air and water pollution, disposal of toxic materials, or use of certain products (for example, the gas freon, used in air-conditioning systems). For more information, check out the website of the U.S. Environmental Protection Agency (www.epa.gov/smallbusiness/).

Q. Does the size of the business affect how it is regulated?

A. It can. The size of the business often affects the extent of the regulations. The laws of many states, for example, exempt businesses with fewer than four or five employees from having to carry workers' compensation insurance covering injuries to employees. (Even if your business is exempt, however, you might still decide to carry workers' compensation insurance because of the protection it will give both you and your employees in the event one of your employees is injured while working in the business.) A number of other workplace laws kick in once you employ a certain number of workers.

Q. Are there regulations that affect all businesses?

A. Some kinds of regulations affect—or potentially affect—all businesses:

- Businesses open to the public must comply with the Americans with Disabilities Act (ADA). You may be able to get information about it through your city or state's economic development office.
- **Building codes** set certain standards that construction must meet; they also may require you to get a permit if you do renovations. You can get information from your locality's department of building or department of safety.
- **Zoning ordinances** regulate which types of business are permitted in certain areas.

Q. What kind of licenses and permits do I need?

A. What licenses and permits are required depends on the type and location of the business.

Licenses

All states have statutes and regulations that require tests, proof of financial responsibility, and compliance with other requirements to obtain a license to engage in certain businesses or professions. A state license to operate a day-care center is one example. Doctors, lawyers, architects, and structural engineers have to be licensed by the state before they can practice their profession. In some states, even barbers, bill collectors, funeral directors, and an assortment of other businesspeople have to be licensed. The type of businesses subject to these licensing requirements varies from state to state. Your state should be able to tell you what's required.

Most cities and many counties also require businesses located in their jurisdiction to have a business license. In reality, this is a tax based generally on the gross receipts of the business rather than a regulatory license designed to protect the public against shoddy work and incompetence. Avoiding this tax can be an important factor in choosing the location of a business.

Permits

Some businesses exempt from state licensing regulations are required to obtain a license or permit from a county or city to perform certain operations. Building contractors, for example, have to get a city or county building permit to build or remodel a house or commercial building.

Commercial Leases

Q. What are the advantages of renting space instead of buying?

A. One of your first decisions will be whether to own your space or rent it. A lot of start-up businesses won't have the capital to buy existing space or build their own new space, so that won't even be an option. If you're one of the lucky ones who does have that much capital, consider the changes you're anticipating for your business, such as future growth and other financial needs. Is buying or building better than leasing for your particular business? If the building is mortgaged, the term of the mortgage frequently will be longer than the lease term of a similar space, so you're making more of a commitment. You can try to have the best of both worlds by negotiating for a lease with an option to purchase or a right of first refusal if the owner decides to sell.

Q. What information does a commercial lease contain? How should I approach it?

A. The saying "Don't sweat the small stuff" does not apply to commercial leases. Leases are binding legal contracts. What you agree to today will affect you and your business where it counts most—the bottom line—for years.

First, read the lease. All of it. Even the small print. Especially the small print. Now is the time to be picky. Be clear on exactly what is included in the lease. Is parking included? Who is responsible for keeping the sidewalk and parking lot cleared of ice and snow? If the phones go down, who is responsible for getting them fixed? Who pays for the cleaning crew? Elevator repairs? Security? Minor repairs? Bathroom supplies? Garbage removal? Double check the obvious: square footage, the name of the company, and the length of the lease.

Most landlords will provide you with their standard lease form. This is probably a "one size fits all" type of lease that may be inappropriate for your business. Remember, the landlord's lawyers drafted this lease for the benefit of the landlord. Just because they call it "standard" doesn't mean it's fair or that you can't negotiate the terms.

How much leverage you'll have in the negotiations depends on the market you're considering.

⚠ YOU FACE MORE REGULATION IF . . .

In general, certain types of businesses face more regulation than others. A lot of this is common sense, with fields that have the capacity to do more harm facing more scrutiny. Besides health care and anything involving food preparation, a partial list of these fields includes

- construction (even home repair in some places);
- anything to do with alcohol;
- anything having to do with dangerous materials (chemicals and the like);
- transportation (of freight and passengers), and
- anything to do with firearms.

Some are regulated by the state; some by the federal government; some by both. Consult a trade association that covers your industry. They should be able to fill you in on the regulations that apply to you.

If there is a shortage of commercial real estate, you may have to do more compromising than if there is an abundance of space available.

Second, if it isn't in the lease, it doesn't exist. Forget what the landlord promises you as you're negotiating the lease. If it isn't in writing, it isn't yours. For example, the building is patrolled by security guards hired by the landlord. If your lease does not include language that the landlord will provide security for the customers and the tenants, the landlord has the right to stop providing security, and there's nothing you can do about it. On the other hand, if your lease states that the landlord will provide a certain number of security guards to patrol the building during business hours, the landlord must do so.

Q. What are the most important clauses in a basic commercial lease?

A. A basic lease will require you, the tenant, to pay the landlord a sum of money for the privilege of operating your business in the landlord's building. This will generally be referred to as base rent. **Base rent** is calculated by taking the square footage of the space and multiplying it by a set dollar amount (i.e., 5,000 square feet x $2.25 per square foot = base rent for the year). The square

---

▶ **LEGAL HELP PAYS HERE**

Whatever you decide is right for your business, you can be sure it will involve several long and complex documents, as well as a big outlay of money. With so much at stake, this is one of those times when legal help is strongly recommended, if not absolutely necessary. Have your lawyer review all documents involved in purchasing, building, leasing, or remodeling a building or other space. Your lawyer might even do the negotiating, though a good broker may be more familiar with the going lease rates and building costs.

---

footage used in the lease is not the same as the "usable" square footage, as the usable footage is always less than what you pay rent on. The rent per foot, and the way the square footage is figured, may or may not be negotiable, depending on supply and demand.

Q. Does the monthly rent have to be the same throughout the year?

A. No. If your business is highly seasonal—for example, a restaurant that is open full-time during the summer in a tourist area but closed or only partly open in the winter season—you may wish to determine if the landlord will agree to a rental schedule where your business pays more during the summer months and less during the winter months.

Q. Are there any additional expenses or hidden costs in addition to the rent?

A. Here comes the tricky part. The base rent is only part of what you have to pay the landlord. Be aware that there will be another clause to cover **additional rent.** This section is negotiable, and you should pay extra attention to every word. This clause can be a blank check for the landlord's benefit if you're not careful.

Have the landlord define, in great detail, "additional rent." Find out whether the base rent includes taxes, insurance on the building, and utilities, or whether these are part of the additional rent. The landlord may charge you for **excess use** under the additional rent clause, for such items as after-hours heating, ventilation, and air-conditioning (HVAC). The landlord might even charge you for improvements made to the building that may not benefit you. These items can quickly add up to several hundred dollars per month, especially if the building is large. Find out if the common area costs are shared among all the tenants in the building. In some cases, the landlord may try to collect the full cost from each tenant. Try to negotiate the right to challenge the landlord's calculation of additional rent and operating expenses (see the following sidebar), and try to add a provision requiring the landlord to submit details of its charges.

Q. What are operating expenses?

A. Another clause that can cost you a bundle perains to **operating expenses.** A standard landlord lease will require you to pay for all costs of owning, managing, maintaining, and operating the complex. This usually will include the key phrase "without limitation." Experienced commercial landlords do not expect you to agree to this clause, although they will be quite happy if you do.

At the very least, you will want to exclude the following from operating costs:

- Capital costs for the building
- The costs of any debt financing
- Construction costs for improvements to the space of other tenants
- Costs covered by the landlord's insurance
- Costs covered by warranties under the landlord's construction or equipment contracts

Sophisticated tenants won't stop there, however. You will also want to exclude

- costs of disputes between the landlord and other tenants,

▶ **BE REALISTIC**

It pays to read the lease carefully, and to try to negotiate the best terms you can, but at the same time, don't be unrealistic in your expectations or demands. A lease is a document that gives you, the tenant, rights to use someone else's property, generally for a long time. It must contain many provisions that to you may make it seem one-sided. However, these are "fences" around your rights to use the property belonging to the landlord, and will be found in virtually all well-drafted commercial leases.

- costs connected to concessions operated by the landlord, and
- costs of obtaining and installing art or decor for the complex.

Find out how the common area charges are calculated. If the cost is shared, find out whether it is calculated on a pro rata basis. In most shopping complexes, large retailers, often called "anchors," are given cost reductions to encourage them to lease space in the center. One concession is that the large retailer will pay a flat rate, rather than a pro rata share, toward common area costs or operating expenses. The landlord deducts this amount from the overall operating expenses and than divides up the remaining operating costs on a pro rata basis among the smaller tenants.

Q. How do you determine the length of the lease?

A. In many cases, a new business owner attempts to obtain an initial term of several years at a fixed rental rate. Although this may be advantageous to an existing business owner, it can be disastrous for the new business owner. As mentioned elsewhere, the failure rate for new businesses is very high. If, for whatever reason, the business fails within the first year, for example, and you have an initial term of five years, you are still obligated to pay the rent for the remaining four years. This is true even though you may not be using the rental space.

Consequently, if you decide you want to enter into an initial term for more than one year, you want to make certain you have the right to sublet the premises or, as an alternative, the right to assign the lease to another. Your lawyer should negotiate lease provisions concerning subletting and assignment with the landlord. Your lawyer can also advise you as to what rights you have as a tenant under state law in addition to any rights that may be contained in the lease.

For the new business owner, an alternative may be to lease for one year with an option to renew (discussed in the following sidebar) for a longer period of time.

Remember, businesses can fail for many reasons other than poor business judgment. A poor economy or the death or disability of a key employee or owner can have disastrous consequences when a small business is involved.

Q. What is an option to renew?

A. An **option to renew** is a clause in the lease, which you bargain for, that enables you to renew the lease at the end of the lease term for an additional term. Without an option to renew, you may be forced to move or to pay an extraordinarily high rent to remain where you are just at the time the business is becoming very profitable. To provide maximum protection, the rent, or at least a formula for determining the rent during the renewed period, should be specified.

ⓘ IMPORTANT CLAUSES IN A COMMERCIAL LEASE

The lease should state the full name and legal address of the building, its owners, and the management company. It should give the exact size of both the building and the space to be rented, in square footage. Find out how the space is measured to prevent surprises later on. Or ask the landlord to make an "exhibit"—a diagram of the space showing dimensions—part of the lease. The lease should state the term of the lease both by months and by date. The lease might also clarify who the brokers represent. Many tenants are surprised to learn that their broker actually represents the landlord. You should try to include the following specific clauses in your lease:

- Insurance
- Parking
- Competition—a provision, if you can get it, prohibiting the landlord from leasing space to a competitor
- An option to renew the lease
- An option to expand by leasing additional space
- A termination clause, if you can get it, permitting cancellation of the lease if the business suffers a significant decline
- Security deposit
- The proposed use of the premises
- Date of occupancy (the date you can move your furniture in), and date of commencement (the date you start paying rent)
- Tenant improvements—what is permitted, and who pays
- Building services provided by the landlord
- Whether the lease complies with the Americans with Disabilities Act
- Signage
- Relocation (whether the landlord will permit—or force—you to move to another location during your lease term)
- Subleasing
- Rebuilding in the event of a casualty loss

Q. *What is an option for additional space?*

A. An **option to lease additional space** allows the new business to lease only the amount of space it needs, with the protection of being able to increase the amount of space when and if it is needed. The advantage of an option is that you are not obligated to rent the additional space unless you want to. An added protection is a clause specifying the rent (or at least the maximum rent) for the additional space.

Q. *Can the lease protect my business from competitors?*

A. Yes. In some types of businesses, it is important to try to negotiate a provision prohibiting the landlord from leasing space to a competitor. If the landlord will not agree to this, try to get a provision stating that space leased to any competitor must be located on a different floor or in a different wing of a shopping center.

Working from Home

Q. *Can I work from home?*

A. Obviously, starting a business at home has lots of pluses. You are probably comfortable there, the price is right, you can dress as casually as you like. But just because it's your PC in your den, you don't necessarily have the right to do whatever you want. There are a few legal hurdles to clear if you're starting a home-based business, as well as tax and insurance considerations that you should be aware of. As usual, it's better to deal with these early rather than late. Shuffling them off to the back of your mind or the bottom of the to-do pile might lead to trouble and hassles later on.

Q. *I've heard that zoning can be an issue for home-based businesses. What is zoning, and how does it affect me?*

A. Zoning is a way of keeping neighborhoods from getting cluttered. Property values in your nice suburb would plummet if your next-door neighbor opened a combination mink farm and roller rink in the backyard. That's why your town or city probably has zones for heavy industry, commercial space, and residential space, as well as some for mixed use.

If you want to run a business from your home, you may face a problem if your neighborhood is strictly zoned for residential use only. You can find out by tracking down your local zoning office (it might not be easy to find), and asking some questions based loosely on the business you're thinking of starting. The quieter and less obtrusive it is, the more likely that you're okay with the law. Red flags are apt to be raised by

- visibility (don't try to repair cars in the front yard),
- noise (no printing press in your condo's extra bedroom),
- smell (a tannery in the garage just won't make it),
- signs (maybe the law will mandate none, or specify a maximum size),
- traffic (perhaps caused by plenty of clients visiting the business and taking up parking spaces, or a steady stream of deliveries and messengers), and
- employees (the zoning laws might limit you to a certain number; again, controlling the number of people in the neighborhood is the primary concern).

Q. *Are there any private regulations that could prevent me from running a business from home?*

A. Even if the zoning folks don't raise any problems, you might run afoul of other regulations. If you live in a condo or co-op, there is certainly a governing document (the **declaration** or **master deed** for a condo, or the **proprietary lease** for a co-op) that spells out the rules and regulations of living there. If you rent, there's probably a lease that tells you what you can and can't do. Sometimes residential developments have **declarations of covenants and restrictions** put in by the builder, to assure buyers that the quality of living there won't deteriorate.

All of these probably include some standard language designed to deter (or at least limit) the business use of the property. You may be able to gain permission to use your home for business purposes by explaining that it will be unobtrusive, not increase traffic in the area, and not lower the value of other units or homes in a development. It's important to be willing to negotiate and compromise.

Q. What are the tax implications of running a business from home?

A. The good news first. You can deduct many of the expenses of your home office if you satisfy Internal Revenue Service (IRS) requirements. (And you can deduct other business expenses such as business supplies and equipment just as if you had a business not based in the home.)

The bad news? Satisfying the IRS is not easy. After all, almost everyone has a home, and it is tempting to create a little home business (at least on your tax forms) that would enable you to save on taxes. You might want to consult a lawyer or an accountant before deciding to operate your business from your home to be sure that you will meet all the requirements and the deduction will be upheld, even if challenged by the IRS.

Q. If I'm running a business from home, does my ordinary homeowner's insurance cover my business equipment?

A. Not necessarily. You'll have to read your policy to be sure. Often, the policies exclude business use. You can probably upgrade yours to cover the increased risks caused by the business. You'll pay a little more for a business rider, but the peace of mind will be worth it.

Certain home businesses—for example, those that store a pricey inventory or attract a lot of people coming and going through the premises—might have to get a special policy. Some companies offer a **homework policy** that combines homeowner's insurance with business protection. If that's not available, work through your insurance agent to get your business protection through the same company as your home-

owner's or tenant's policy. That should enable you to tailor the business policy to cover only the increased risks caused by the business, so you won't have to pay double for the same protection.

Insurance

Q. How do I go about finding the right level of insurance for my business?

A. You'd probably do best to buy all of your business insurance from one source, so you don't duplicate coverage. Ask other business owners which insurance agents or brokers they'd recommend. It's best to work with an insurance agent who represents a number of insurance companies. Because of this independence, he or she is not tied to a particular company and is in a position to select advantageous coverage for you from a wide range of vendors. If your business has special insurance needs, your business association or an owner of a similar kind of business might be able to suggest agents with experience in insuring businesses such as yours. Usually, it's a good idea to discuss your needs with several agents. Not only will you be able to compare quotes, but from each you will get a perspective on which types of insurance your business needs.

Q. Is there a standard kind of insurance that will cover most businesses?

A. One big part of insurance won't be new to you. You probably have homeowner's insurance to protect your home from fire and other hazards, and to protect you from lawsuits if someone's injured on your property. You can get a **business owner's policy** (**BOP**) to cover similar risks to your business, as well as some others that are unique to the business situation. The insurance industry has come up with standard packages for certain kinds of businesses (stores, contractors, etc.), and they're a good place to start. Make sure, however, that your agent truly understands your business—it may be that the standard policy the agent so quickly whipped out really doesn't fit what you're doing.

ⓘ A TAX BY ANOTHER NAME

You've probably heard of **unemployment insurance.** It's actually not insurance at all, but a tax based on the payroll of a business used to pay benefits to all long-term unemployed workers in a state. You can't save money by shopping for it, and you can't simply not have it. It's a tax, and you have to pay it.

Q. What kind of coverage does my business need?

A. Not all BOPs cover the same risks. You'll want to look at coverages carefully to make sure you're getting what you need. Here are a few general tips:

- **Coverage for property loss** should include the basic perils that can destroy your property (fire, theft, etc.) as well as any special perils that you're aware of. (Are you in an earthquake-prone area, a floodplain, a high-locust zone?) In assessing the risk of natural disasters like earthquakes and floods, you'll have to weigh the likelihood of their happening (does the river rise every five years? every fifty?) against the extra cost of the insurance. Also, depending on your situation, it may be important that the policy cover some other perils, such as damage from a burst pipe or smoke damage from a malfunctioning furnace.
- As in homeowner's insurance, there are general levels of coverage built in to policies, with the more expensive covering the broadest range of hazards to your property. **Specific form** policies are the most comprehensive, and don't cost that much more.
- If you own your property, you'll want coverage for everything you own, including the business property on the premises. You can try to negotiate to have the policy broadly written to cover some kinds of equipment and other property that you don't have now but might have in the future. Also, make sure the policy covers leased equipment, if the risk of its loss would fall on you. (Your lease might require you to insure it.)
- Get a policy that gives you **replacement cost coverage.** That way, you'll get what you need to buy new property to replace the old.
- **Protection from liability** covers you if someone does a swan dive in aisle three or steps in a hole in your parking lot. As in your homeowner's policy, the insurance company will defend you in court and pay damages up to the amount of insurance purchased.

⚠ GOING BARE

The Insurance Information Institute— www.iii.org—estimates that 40 percent of small business owners have no insurance. Think carefully before assuming this risk.

▶ ANOTHER CHEAP FORM OF "INSURANCE"

From your perspective as the owner of the business, you should consider whether you need personal protection from business liabilities. While not strictly a form of insurance, a limited liability entity (i.e., a corporation or a limited liability company) will shield you from most personal liabilities of a sole proprietorship or general partnership business. You might lose the business in a disaster, whether of Mother Nature's making or as a result of a difficult market or your own management shortcomings, but saving your home and personal assets from that disaster might leave you in a better frame of mind.

Q. Are there any specific types of insurance I should consider to cover specific losses?

A. You may want to insure against several eventualities that generally are not covered by BOP policies:

- **Business interruption insurance** (often referred to as **business continuation insurance**) will offset losses if the business is forced to shut down for a substantial period because of a fire, a flood, or some other catastrophe.

- **Product liability insurance** protects you against damage claims filed by third parties injured by a product produced by your business. If you sell food or any product that you make, you'd better have it.

- **Workers' compensation insurance** is of great benefit to businesspeople. It protects you against damages that arise under your state's workers' compensation system. All states have such a system. It requires that workers be paid for injuries they suffer on the job, no matter what the cause. Even if the employee is clearly at fault, you'll have to pay, though under state law the benefits are set according to a preexisting schedule and are relatively low. You're well advised to carry insurance against this risk.

- **Disability** (or **loss of income**) insurance pays a portion of your gross income if you have a long-term disability and cannot work.

- **Life insurance** will provide a death benefit to your family. If you have co-owners, you can take out a policy that names them as beneficiaries and provides funds to compensate the business for your loss and funds to purchase your interest in the company. This **key person** insurance thus benefits your family and keeps the business going.

Tax Requirements

Q. What are the tax issues I'll need to consider if I'm starting a small business?

A. Your accountant can assist you with the following federal and state tax requirements:

Federal Tax Identification Number

All businesses must obtain an **Employer Identification Number (EIN),** also known as a federal tax identification number, before beginning to operate. Each state also requires tax registration by a new business. In most cases, the state will use the Employer Identification Number.

You get your EIN by filing an IRS Form SS-4. You can get one from any office that has IRS forms, or online through the IRS website, www.irs.gov. If you mail the form, you'll get your EIN in four to six weeks. You can also fax the SS-4 to 816-926-7988 and the EIN number will be issued within twenty-four hours, or you can call direct (816-926-5999) and receive the EIN number verbally. If you phone, you must place the

---

▶ **MONEY-SAVING TIPS**

- Consider taking high deductibles. Yes, you'll be forced to pay more of the share of each claim, but your premiums will go way down. Unless you're constantly filing small claims, you will probably save money overall.

- Take steps to make your business safer for all concerned. Limit the hazards that might lead to lawsuits: install sprinklers, fire extinguishers, and a fire alarm system (which will lessen the risk of fire and lower premiums); also install high-quality locks and antitheft devices. Preventive steps like this make your business a better risk, so you're a candidate to save on insurance.

> ### ► YOUR NUMBER ONE TASK
>
> Getting your Employer Identification Number (EIN) number should be a very, very high priority. You'll need it to open bank accounts, apply for loans, apply for licenses, hire employees—just about everything you need to do to get your business up and running. Get it now.

number on the SS-4 and mail it to the IRS for processing.

State Sales Tax Registration

All states that have sales taxes also require any business not exempt from the tax to register with the appropriate state agency. You'll be required to collect the tax and remit it to the state regularly (monthly or more frequently). To avoid paying taxes on the materials you buy from wholesalers, you should get a **resale tax certificate** from the state tax authorities. As long as you sell the product to the public, and collect the tax at that time, you shouldn't have to pay taxes to get the product in the first place.

Withholding Requirements

If you have employees (including yourself, if your business is a corporation), you'll be required to withhold federal and state income taxes and FICA (Social Security and Medicare) taxes from their wages. You have to remit these funds regularly to the IRS (in the case of federal and FICA taxes) and the applicable state tax agency. The state requirements may or may not be the same as the federal deposit requirements. All this is very confusing, but it's important to know the requirements and follow them, since there may be heavy penalties for late payment. Remember that the principal officers of the company may be personally liable for payroll taxes that are not paid to the IRS. You may find that it pays to use a payroll

tax service for this job. And any business, no matter its size, should have a tax adviser.

Unemployment Insurance Tax

Most states require your business to register or at least periodically file with the state agency that administers the state unemployment insurance tax. This tax is based on the business's payroll. Periodically, a business also must pay the federal unemployment insurance tax, which is based on its total payroll.

Federal and State Income Tax Returns

As if all this weren't enough, all businesses must file annual federal and state income tax returns. The applicable forms vary with the type of business. Partnerships, S corporations, limited liability companies, and other businesses that as a general rule pass the tax consequences of their operations to their owners file a different type of return from that of businesses that are operated as C corporations.

THE WORLD AT YOUR FINGERTIPS

General Information

- *Quicken, at www.quicken.com, has a good small business site that includes much useful information, including small business forums where you can ask questions and exchange ideas.*
- *The website for the Service Corps of Retired Executives at www.score.org gives you the opportunity to obtain free, confidential advice via e-mail. You can also seek business counseling face-to-face at one of their local chapters.*
- *You can access www.sba.gov/sbdc for a state-by-state list of over nine hundred Small Business Development Centers.*

Legal Requirements

- *Your state government's website is a great place to research what's required legally.*

Access it through www.state.[your state's two-letter abbreviation].us.

- *Your local Chamber of Commerce probably has a package containing all the information and forms you'll need to get started in your community.*

Tax Information

- *The IRS website, www.irs.gov, is an excellent place for getting information on all the federal tax issues that affect a business.*
- *State and Local Governments on the Net (www.statelocalgov.net/index.cfm) is a site that will lead you to the department of revenue in your state, as well as to a host of other departments, agencies, and boards.*

REMEMBER THIS

- *Find the business that's right for you—that uses your particular talents and interests.*

- *Do as thorough a financial plan as you can; anticipate how much money you'll need, when you'll need it, and for how long.*
- *Be creative in looking for funding. Look to your personal circle, the commercial world, and the resources of government.*
- *You'll very probably have to register your business name.*
- *You'll also probably need some licenses and permits.*
- *A lot of the problems associated with running a business out of your home can be solved by being flexible, using a little common sense, and negotiating with neighbors or the authorities.*
- *Uncle Sam and the state make you start going through tax hoops right away, but there are usually packets of information that will guide you.*
- *The steps you need to take to start a business are not terribly burdensome. They may take some time, but you can do them.*

ⓘ WHAT YOU'LL NEED, TAXWISE

The Internal Revenue Service publishes a packet of forms and publications entitled "Your Business Tax Kit," which is available at any IRS office, as well as on the IRS website (www.irs.gov). It's a good idea to get one when you apply for your EIN. It contains a great deal of helpful information on the various federal taxes that apply to a business. Many state tax commissions have similar publications describing the state taxes that apply to a business. Both types of publications contain samples of the tax registration and other forms that must be filed.

FRANCHISING AND BUYING A BUSINESS

Starting a business can be scary. There are so many unknowns, from how to market, to where to locate, to how to work out (and control) costs. Buying a franchise or an established business means you're not starting from scratch, but rather building on the expertise of other people.

This section will reveal that there are advantages to buying a franchise or a business, but there are also pitfalls. You should engage an experienced lawyer to help you understand and negotiate the franchise agreement or the contract. The provisions of the contract or agreement can have a huge effect on whether your venture turns out to be a success.

Buying a Franchise

Q. How does a franchise work?

A. A franchise is a way of doing business. The franchisor, be it McDonald's, the Ford Motor Company, or Motel 6, grants you, the franchisee, the rights to sell the company's products or services. No matter what you're selling, though, the franchisor will license you to use its established trademark or trade name or both.

Why are big companies eager to let little old you have a slice of the pie? From their standpoint, the logic behind franchising is simple: It costs them lots less money to distribute goods and services by using franchises than by operating company-owned units. And they get extra money from licensing trademarks and trade names and from other services they provide to franchise holders.

What do you get? You always get the goodwill of the franchisor's trademarks and trade name, and you usually get expert guidance in such matters as site selection, training of employees, bookkeeping, and other managerial services. This help is particularly valuable to businesspeople with little or no prior experience.

Q. How much does it cost to buy a franchise, and what am I paying for?

A. Usually, you pay an up-front franchise fee for the right to use the trademarks, trade names, and trade secrets of the franchisor and for managerial services involved in getting the franchise established. Frequently, you'll also be required to purchase all of the franchise's initial equipment,

including signs and trade fixtures, from the franchisor. You also may be required to purchase many of your supplies from the franchisor or from franchisor-approved sources.

And that's not all. You'll normally pay the franchisor a royalty based on a percentage of your gross receipts. It's usually about 5 percent, but the percentage can vary widely. The royalty covers advertising and continuing managerial services, as well as a licensing fee for use of the franchisor's trademark and trade names. If the franchisor owns the franchised location, you'll obviously have to pay rent to the franchisor.

Q. What are the advantages of running a franchise?

A. There are many advantages to a franchise:

- You can reap the benefits of the franchisor's knowledge and experience. If you're a rookie in the business, you'll especially need the franchisor's help with training and consultation.
- Because the franchisor is promoting its business, usually vigorously, your business will often receive a boost from the franchisor's advertising.
- As a franchisee, you do not need years to establish a reputation for quality goods or services, because the franchisor has provided you with a proven, recognized product.
- Because some franchisors offer the products, supplies, services, and equipment used in your business for sale at a reduced rate, your operating costs could be reduced.
- Both federal and state laws regulate the offer of franchises, which means that you will have some level of protection in dealing with the franchisor.

Q. What are the disadvantages?

A. There are also disadvantages that you should consider before investing in a franchise:

- You lose control. The franchisor sets the rules. You must follow standardized procedures and offer certain products.

▶ **BEST FRANCHISE OPPORTUNITIES**

Every year, the January issue of *Entrepreneur* magazine lists its Franchise 500, the best franchise opportunities. Check it out at www.entrepreneurmag.com.

- The franchise agreement is prepared by the franchisor, and naturally favors the franchisor. If you're buying from a well-established franchisor, you have unequal bargaining power and sometimes little room to negotiate the terms.
- The royalty fees you pay are based on a percentage of annual gross sales, not profits. You must pay them even if you're losing money.
- The standard franchise agreement may restrict your transfer of ownership, preventing you from selling the business to the highest bidder or bequeathing it to your spouse without the franchisor's prior approval.
- The termination clause in your contract may let the franchisor terminate the relationship by canceling the contract or not renewing it. This can punish franchisees who don't toe the line.
- Because you're buying into a name, you're also getting any problems associated with that name. If there's bad publicity about the national company, or even if your customers get lousy service from another franchisee, you'll be socked with guilt by association.
- The franchise agreement may be only for a period of five or ten years. After that, you may not be able to continue your business.
- Finally, you must file annual reports with the franchisor, which involves voluminous, cumbersome paperwork.

Q. How do I work out whether a franchise is a good deal?

A. The Federal Trade Commission (FTC) has a **Franchise and Business Opportunity Rule**, also known as the **FTC Franchise Rule**. It requires franchisors to give you information that will enable you to decide whether the deal is one you should accept or run away from. A number of state laws require somewhat more stringent disclosures, and usually franchisors meet both requirements at once with a **Uniform Franchise Offering Circular.**

Under FTC rules, the franchisor is required to give this document to you at your first face-to-face meeting with the franchisor, or least ten working days before you legally commit yourself to the purchase or pay any money. The offering is a detailed disclosure statement. It's not fun reading, and neither is the proposed **franchise agreement** (contract) that has to accompany it. But if your life savings are on the line, you have plenty of incentive to check this opportunity out. Remember, the government doesn't vouch for the accuracy of these documents. It's up to you to verify the information and use it wisely. The FTC offers a wealth of information on franchising on its website at www.ftc.gov.

Q. What is the franchise agreement?

A. The franchise agreement is simply the contract that governs the franchise. From the franchisee's perspective, franchise agreements are rarely friendly. The franchisor and its lawyers draft them, and they're intended to protect the franchisor's interests. They are typically very lengthy (over thirty pages) and very detailed when spelling out the franchisor's rights and your obligations, but sketchy as to what are your rights and their obligations. Your lawyer can guide you through the complexities and pitfalls of a franchise agreement.

Depending on the state of the market and the type of franchise, it may be possible to negotiate some terms of the franchise agreement. It's certainly worth trying.

Q. What steps should I take to increase the probability that I'll get a good franchise deal?

A. You should retain the services of a lawyer who concentrates on business start-ups or franchises. He or she can help in almost every step of the process. But you should do some legwork, too. It'll save you in legal fees, and you'll get a better sense of the business. You also should consult an accountant, who can help you assess the financial disclosures in the franchise offering circular.

Contact Other Franchise Owners

They can help you match disclosure statement information with their own experiences. Spend some time with them during the workday, to see the operation in action.

Ask what help they got from the company, and how it followed up on its promises. Did it give them the tools they needed to get the business up and running? Are they getting enough advertising and support for their royalty payments?

Ask about problems. Ask if they'd make the same investment again.

Be Skeptical of the Franchisor's Sales Presentation

A franchisor who has a legitimate offer does not need to use high-pressure tactics such as "Better hurry, another buyer wants this deal" or "Do this today because who knows how much it will cost tomorrow." Such language should raise a red flag. Remember, the FTC rule requires that the franchisor must wait ten days after giving you the required documents before you have to pay any money or sign any agreement. And while

---

ⓘ STRUCTURING A FRANCHISE

If you purchase a franchise, does the fact that it's a franchise affect whether it should be a sole proprietorship, a partnership, a corporation, or a limited liability company? (We discuss the pros and cons of these forms of business organization in the next section.) Just because the business is a franchise doesn't mean that you have to rule out any option. Being a franchise does not really affect how the business should be structured. Key factors are the size and financial success of the business, tax considerations, and your potential exposure to liabilities from operating the business. If you set up a corporation or limited liability company to be the franchisee, however, it is likely that the franchisor will ask you to sign personal guaranties of your obligations to the franchisor.

---

you're being skeptical, also disregard any franchisor's claims that the job will be easy. Success requires hard work.

Buying a Business

Q. I'm thinking about buying a business. Should I buy the whole business, or is it a better bet to buy only the assets?

A. To the layperson, this seems like a no-brainer. When you buy a business, you buy it lock, stock, and barrel. But often it's best to buy just part of the business—the part with the most potential benefit and least potential risk.

Let's look at your choices. When you buy from a corporation, you could either buy a controlling interest through buying enough of its stock, or you could buy the *assets* of the corporation but leave the corporate shell behind, kind of like a crab in molting season.

What assets are we talking about? That varies with the business, of course, but it could be

- tangible property, such as manufacturing or office equipment; trucks, cars, and other vehicles; and inventory; and
- intangible property, such as patents and trademarks, goodwill, or the seller's noncompetition agreement.

One advantage of just getting the assets is that you have less chance of picking up the corporation's existing or future liabilities, including

- lawsuits by customers, employees, or suppliers, some of which might not even be filed for months, if not years;
- violations of government regulations; and
- long-term contracts that you want no part of.

Another advantage of buying the assets only is that you may well get significant tax breaks, including the opportunity to depreciate anew some assets that already may have been depreciated by the corporation. This enables you essentially to show a "paper" cost—and thus show fewer earnings and possibly pay less in taxes. You'll also start off with a higher tax basis for the assets—and thus pay less in capital gains when you eventually sell them.

On the other hand, if the corporation benefited strongly from existing contracts, you might want to buy the corporation as such and continue the contracts.

Because of considerations such as these, most small business sales are of assets rather than the entire business.

Q. What is the selling prospectus?

A. If you are working with a business broker, your first detailed look at a business for sale will be something called a **selling prospectus.** You may not learn the name of the business in this document—sellers often want to maintain confidentiality, so that their customers and business contacts don't know the business is for sale. However, you will find out about

- the basic story of the business, including its history and current status, location, assets, operations, competition, and profit-and-loss picture;
- the role of the owner, including the part the owner plays in day-to-day operations and his/her role in making the operation successful;
- the owner's reasons for selling;
- at least a summary of the business's finances; and
- the asking price and terms.

Q. What's the next step?

A. If the prospectus interests you, you'll want to have a personal interview with the owner and review detailed accounting information. The interview should include a disclosure of more difficult information and an immediate review of the accounting in place. The owner may require you to sign a confidentiality agreement.

You'll have to make a determination with respect to the accuracy and validity of the accounting. You'll very likely want to have expert advice at this stage, and you should look at the following documents:

- The company's "books"—its profit-and-loss statements and balance sheets for not just the most recent year, but several previous years as well.
- Tax returns going back at least several years.
- Other important documents, if you're going to acquire the whole business. These might include loan documents, contracts, pending lawsuits, regulatory tangles, and the like.
- All accountants' documents.

Q. What is the statement/letter of intent?

A. It is generally difficult for the parties to determine if the deal can be done without discussing the major terms of the transaction, including overall structure and price. Whether the discussion is detailed or general, you and the seller will want to document the status of your evolving understanding, before you get to the point of negotiating an actual contract.

This desire often will result in a statement of intent document. The **statement** (or **letter**) **of intent** is by definition an agreement to agree, and may not be enforceable as a contract. It is important that this fact be repeated in the language of the document and that you and the seller fully understand the limitations of the document. You also may need a lawyer to advise you on how to make sure that the document is not enforceable.

As long as you and the seller understand that the statement of intent is just designed to clarify your thinking and points of agreement during the negotiation process, it can be very helpful in drafting the contract for purchase and sale of a business.

Q. What is in the contract?

A. The contract for purchase or sale of a business is absolutely central to the transaction. Like a contract to sell a home, it will determine the basis upon which the business is sold.

What, Exactly, Are You Buying?

The structure of the contract will depend upon whether you're purchasing specific assets of the business or the entity conducting the business. If you're buying assets, they should be specified, along with any liabilities of the business you've agreed to pick up. If it's an entity purchase, the contract should specify that you will not assume any undisclosed liabilities. This is usually accomplished by a warranty from the seller to the buyer, which essentially gives you the legal right to come after the seller should an undisclosed claim against the business surface.

Defining what is actually being purchased is frequently accomplished by attaching detailed schedules to the contract that specifically identify the assets and liabilities, or specifically define the balance sheet of the entity, so that the exact nature of what constitutes the business and what is being transferred can be identified, item by item.

Contingencies

If you haven't been able to investigate the purchase fully before preparing the contract, the contract might provide that it is contingent on certain factors (i.e., that facts about the business as asserted by the seller can be verified). That way, you can have an additional period to investigate without irreversibly committing yourself.

Access to the Business

If there will be a period between the execution of the contract and the closing (**interim period**), the contract can specify that you will be allowed to come onto the business premises, access business records, and otherwise be informed about the nature of the business.

Cash

Generally, don't look to get an infusion of cash from the sale. Cash normally is not transferred. In an entity purchase, cash accounts usually will have minimal balances. In an asset purchase, cash accounts normally will not be transferred. Accounts receivable usually will be treated similarly to cash except where collection of an account receivable is linked to future performance.

Noncompete Agreements

The last thing you want is to buy a business and have the old owner pop up a few months later as a competitor. That's why you'll want the seller to provide you with an assurance that after the sale of the business, he or she will not compete or remove personnel from the business. Sometimes these agreements are included in the sales contract (where they become part of the intangible assets you acquire), and sometimes they are handled in a separate document.

Either way, you have to make sure that the courts will enforce the agreement. In general, that means it must be reasonable both in terms of duration (how long it will last) and geographic area (what region it will cover). What is "reasonable" for such agreements? In many states, a period of two or three years is an outer time limit. Geographic restraints will, of course, vary depending on circumstances. Fifty miles might be reasonable in a very sparsely settled region, but twenty-five miles might be too many in the heart of a huge metropolitan region. Have your lawyer look into the statutes and cases in your state and any other state that may have jurisdiction to get an idea of what might be reasonable in the circumstances.

Q. What does the closing process involve?

A. Just as in a real estate transaction, the closing process involves signing the final purchase papers of the purchase and sale. Here's some of what may take place.

- Often, you won't know the final purchase price until closing, when it will be determined in accordance with procedures set forth in the contract. The actual purchase price may depend on such procedures or events identified in the contract as inventories of assets, final accounting for payments received, and identification of certain receipts after initial periods of operation under the new owner.
- At closing, the seller, and often the buyer, will be required to certify that the warranties and representations given in the contract, which will remain the basis for a legal action after

the closing, were and are true, accurate, and correct.

- You and the seller will sign the documents of transfer, and you will sign documents relating to payment and usually make a payment.
- The contract may provide for certain allocations of payments or deposits between you and the seller.

Typically, at the end of the closing process, the seller will have accomplished the transfer of the business to the buyer. You will have paid for the business and will take possession of it.

THE WORLD AT YOUR FINGERTIPS

- *The FTC provides a package of information about the FTC Franchise and Business Opportunity Rule. It's free. Call 202-326-3128, or access www.ftc.gov. The website has many resources relating to franchising, including commentary about the federal rule, state rules, and FAQs.*
- *The Small Business Administration has a pamphlet titled "Understanding the Franchise Contract." Get it from a local office or the SBA website (www.sba.gov).*
- *The Better Business Bureau has helpful information about franchises. Contact*

your local office, or access the information on the BBB website (www.bbb.com).

- *Franchise-oriented websites include Franchise Handbook Online (www.franchise1.com), BetheBoss (www.betheboss.com), the International Franchise Association (www.franchise.org), and the American Franchisee Association (www.franchisee.org). In addition, articles on franchising and small business issues are available online at www.ltbn.com.*
- *The American Express small business site has much useful information on buying a business. Access www.americanexpress.com.*
- *Quicken (www.quicken.com) has a good small business site that includes much useful information, including small business forums where you can ask questions and exchange ideas.*
- *The website for the Service Corps of Retired Executives (www.score.org) gives you the opportunity for free, confidential ad-*

▶ ### CAN THE SELLER STAY ON AS A CONSULTANT?

The flipside of noncompete agreements is provisions for the seller staying on as a member of your team—at least for a while. Your contract can include a section specifying that the seller will stay on as a consultant for a specified term, at a specified salary. You get the value of what should be very good advice—and you can deduct the cost as a business expense.

ⓘ ### KEEPING IT UNDER WRAPS

Until the purchase is finalized, the seller will not want customers, employees, vendors, creditors, and debtors of the business to know that the business is for sale. You will probably be under an agreement that you will not divulge or use information discovered but not readily available to the general public. You may be asked to sign a letter of confidentiality specifying that you will use the information gathered only in deciding whether to buy the business. The letter also might indicate that your investors and advisers will be asked to keep the information to themselves.

vice and business consultation. The website also includes articles.

REMEMBER THIS

- *Franchising has advantages, but success is not automatic.*
- *Get as much information as you can—before you commit.*
- *The franchise agreement is one of the most important documents you will ever sign. Make sure you understand it fully, and receive good legal advice, before you sign.*
- *Buying a business is a huge decision. Investigate every important aspect thoroughly, and be sure to get expert help in evaluating the opportunity, valuing the business, and negotiating.*
- *Try to buy the assets of the business; try not to buy the problems.*
- *Don't be offended if the seller needs to learn a good deal about you—communication is the key for both parties.*

TYPES OF BUSINESS ORGANIZATIONS

Willie and Billie plan to start a business offering 1950s nostalgia items: instant sock hops for your party, gold lamé suits for him and her—the works. They've got some investors and capital, and have done a marketing plan, but before they start up they need to dot the legal Is and cross the legal Ts. They've at least considered various legal forms for their business, but they're confused and uncertain, and what they really want is someone to tell them what they should do.

Sorry, Willie and Billie, there is no answer that will work for all businesses—otherwise we'd have only one form of business organization.

Yes, one choice—the sole proprietorship—will work for many start-up businesses. If there's just you, and you're willing to risk some personal liability, or have insurance to cover at least some of your liability risks, then this isn't a bad option.

But not all businesses have just one person—there may be two or three or more principals. For a variety of reasons, you may want to give other people a piece of the action. And not all are on a shoestring—some have investors or other sources of capital. Some want to operate in more than one state. Some "new" businesses may be building on the foundation of existing businesses.

Hiring an experienced business lawyer would help Willie and Billie make this critical decision. The lawyer could take some of the burden off of them by examining their particular situation, suggesting a business form and then helping them take the steps to meet all the legal requirements. Accountants or other professionals who know about their business can also get involved in these and other important issues that must be dealt with in setting up and operating a new business.

But in the final analysis, the business owner must make the decision, and often there are no clear answers, even if you do have professional help. You just can't meld all the relevant tax and non-tax factors into a neat set of guidelines. You have to look at your situation carefully—what might be the best choice in one case might not be the best choice in a similar but slightly different set of circumstances.

Q. *What type of business organization is appropriate for my business?*

A. If you're like most business owners, you want

- protection against being personally liable for judgments against the company, its debts, and so on;
- the ability to transfer ownership as you wish, especially if you want to keep it in the family

or continue the business after you or one of the other principals leaves;

- a simple, workable management structure;
- low organizational and administrative costs;
- an ability to do business without complications in more than one state (maybe not relevant now, but you can dream); and
- an ability to take advantage of tax laws and keep taxes as low as possible.

Guess what? In all these areas, your choice of how your business is organized legally makes a big difference.

This section summarizes the most important considerations you will face in choosing among the alternatives. You can get most or all of these features in most types of business organizations, but often you have to do some juggling and weigh one factor against another. You have some flexibility—it's possible to combine different features of some of the basic business structures, and your state law may give you particularly good options.

By the way, you're not stuck forever with the choice you make when you're just starting out. If the nature of your business changes, you can go from one form of organization to another, although you should check with your tax adviser on how the conversion might affect your taxes. For example, going from a corporation to a partnership can potentially have very serious tax consequences.

Q. Why is protection from personal liability so important?

A. Because you want to put as few of your *personal* assets at risk as possible. If the structure of your business does not protect you personally from lawsuits, then you might be liable for big personal injury damages if your firm is successfully sued, or you might be personally liable if your firm defaults on a loan. You might lose your home, your car, your brokerage account—everything. Some ways of organizing your business protect you from such catastrophes.

Sole Proprietorships

Q. What is a sole proprietorship?

A. If you're the sole owner of your company and don't create a corporation or some other form of business, then, know it or not, like it or not, you're a sole proprietorship. If there is more than one owner or the business is incorporated as a corporation, a process that is described later in this chapter, it cannot be a sole proprietorship.

A sole proprietorship can have employees, however. And, except for a few restrictions that vary from state to state, it can operate any type of business.

Q. What are the advantages of a sole proprietorship?

A. It is an inexpensive and informal way of conducting a small business. In fact, it's the simplest form of business organization. The only statutes that deal with its organization or operation are those that apply to all businesses. In contrast, many laws spell out the legal requirements of a corporation, a limited liability company, or a partnership. A sole proprietorship gives you an opportunity to own your own business without the formalities and expense of incorporation or the necessity of sharing control of the business with partners or shareholders in a corporation.

Q. What are the disadvantages of a sole proprietorship?

ⓘ SOLE PROPRIETORSHIPS

Sole proprietorships are the most prevalent form of business in this country. Recent statistics indicate that there are more than 14.0 million sole proprietorships compared to 3.5 million corporations and 1.6 million partnerships.

A. The biggest problem is that your business assets and obligations are not separate from your personal ones. This means you're fully liable for the debts and other liabilities of the sole proprietorship. Your home, car, personal savings, and other property could be taken away to pay a court judgment. Insurance can protect you against some of the potential exposure to personal liability. But insurance cannot protect you from the claims of creditors and some other types of liability claims. Moreover, adequate insurance coverage may be too expensive for the sole proprietor. Protection against personal liability is one reason why many entrepreneurs choose to operate as a corporation or other business format that has limited liability.

The single-ownership principle, combined with the lack of separate entity status, also creates severe problems when you die. Legally, a sole proprietorship ceases to exist at the proprietor's death. Unless the executor of your will is authorized to continue the business during the administration of the estate, a new owner is found, or the business is incorporated, the sole proprietorship will have to be liquidated. This means your family will lose the going-concern value of the business. Providing an optimum estate plan may, therefore, be more difficult for a sole proprietorship than for other forms of business organizations.

A sole proprietorship also has the least flexibility of all the business forms in raising capital. You can't sell ownership interests to other persons. Your ability to borrow money for the business depends on your net assets.

Partnerships

Q. What is a partnership?

A. The legal definition of a partnership is pretty simple. It is an association of two or more persons who

1. have not incorporated; and
2. carry on a business for profit as co-owners.

A partnership exists if these conditions are met, even though the people involved may not know it or even intend that the business be a partnership—and even if they don't actually make a profit.

Q. Are partnerships widely used?

A. Not as widely as they once were. As a way of organizing a business, they appear to be giving way to the limited liability form of business organization (see page 498). This form of organization has many of the advantages of partnerships and few of the disadvantages.

Q. What are the different kinds of partnerships?

A. There are two main types of partnerships recognized in the United States: general partnerships and limited partnerships.

In a **general partnership,** each partner has unlimited liability for the debts and obligations of the partnership. Moreover, any partner can bind the partnership contractually to third parties. For these reasons, it is important to define in a writ-

---

ⓘ ORGANIZING A SOLE PROPRIETORSHIP

It could hardly be easier to organize a sole proprietorship. Depending on the laws of your state and locality, you may have to apply for one or more business permits and licenses, but you'd have to do that no matter what business form you chose. If your business is to operate in a name other than your own, you may have to comply with a state or local assumed name statute and file a Doing Business as Certificate or Assumed Name Certificate. Again, you'd have to do that in any event. Other than that, no special written documents will be necessary for your sole proprietorship unless you are buying or leasing property or will operate a franchise.

ten agreement what decisions partners can make individually and which ones require a vote of the partners. In addition, most states require that the partnership file a certificate in the county in which it will do business.

Unlimited liability means that if you're a general partner, not only can you lose whatever money or other property you have put into the partnership, but also your house, boat, and stock portfolio might go to pay the claims of the partnership's creditors. In terms of management responsibility, general partners carry the load—they actively run the business on a day-to-day basis.

In a **limited partnership,** there must be at least one limited partner and one general partner. The advantage of being a limited partner is that if the business is unsuccessful, the limited partner may lose the amount of money invested in the partnership, but has no other financial risk. So if you are the limited partner, you'll bear the same risk of loss as a shareholder in a corporation or a member of a limited liability company. That's why limited partners are said to have **limited liability.** Limited partners also have no management responsibilities within the company, and are in fact forbidden from managing company business.

In terms of the business's stability, adding or subtracting limited partners is not potentially as disruptive as the retirement, death, or disability of a general partner. In terms of paperwork, there's more if you set up a limited partnership.

Professionals, such as accountants, lawyers, and architects, frequently use limited liability partnerships. The advantage of these partnerships is that each partner is not personally liable for the malpractice of other partners. However, they may be personally responsible for the debts and obligations of the business, so their liability is less limited than it would be in a corporation or a limited liability company.

Q. What are the advantages of partnerships?

A. There are several advantages to a partnership as opposed to a sole proprietorship or corporation.

- Partnerships can be flexible; the partners have the ability to make virtually any arrangements defining their relationship to each other that they desire. The partners can agree to split the ownership and profits in flexible ways, and losses can be allocated on a different basis from profits.
- Because you can sell **equity** interests (ownership) in a partnership, it's easier to raise capital in a partnership than in a sole proprietorship. (However, since investors are more familiar with the corporate form, a corporation may have a greater ability to raise capital than a partnership.)
- With careful advance planning, a partnership can avoid some of the problems inherent in a proprietorship when an owner dies, retires, or becomes disabled.

Q. What are the disadvantages of partnerships?

A. The major disadvantage is that in both limited and general partnerships, general partners have unlimited liability. This means that to protect their personal assets they have to take some additional (and maybe costly) steps. For example, a general partner doesn't have to be a person.

ⓘ **PARTNERS INDEED**

Fred and Ethel are husband and wife. They jointly operate a retail shoe store that they've never incorporated. Guess what? They're probably partners in business, as well as in life. Unless it is clear from their financial records that one of them is the true owner and the other is merely an employee (in which event the company would be classified as a sole proprietorship), the business will be a partnership and both Fred and Ethel will be considered partners and co-owners of the business.

Often, the general partner is a corporation or a limited liability company, and this form of business then provides liability protection for the owners. In this way, the threat to a general partner's assets often can be minimized or eliminated. Another important disadvantage is that a partnership is not as stable as a corporation. A general partnership and a limited partnership dissolve in many cases automatically when a general partner

- dies,
- files for bankruptcy,
- retires,
- resigns, or
- otherwise ceases to be a partner.

The partnership will shut down unless either a remaining general partner continues the business or all the partners (or in some states, a majority) agree to continue it. However, a corporation, under most statutes, continues forever or until some specific action is taken to dissolve it.

It may be more difficult in a partnership than in a corporation to have a hierarchy of management and to raise capital from outside sources. But creative agreements can provide for specific management arrangements and variations in capital ownership in the partnership.

Q. How are partnerships taxed?

A. Partnerships are taxed on a conduit, or flow-through, basis. This means that the partnership itself does not pay any taxes. Instead, the income and various deductions and tax credits from the partnership are passed through to the partners based on their percentage interest in the profits and losses of the partnership. Then the partners include the income and deductions in their individual tax returns.

Corporations

Q. What makes corporations different from sole proprietorships or partnerships?

A. The basic attributes of a corporation include

- limited liability of corporate directors, officers, and managers;
- perpetual existence (a life independent of the life of the directors, the officers, the management, etc.);
- free transferability of shares;
- the ability to own property in the corporation's name;
- the ability to bring suit and be sued in the corporate name; and
- status as a separate taxpayer.

All but the last of these are good things, and even status as a separate taxpayer can be a good thing in certain circumstances. This helps explain why the corporate form is popular. However, the tripartite system of corporate management—consisting of shareholders, directors, and officers—can be cumbersome, especially for a small business. That helps explain why corporations are not the best form for all businesses.

Q. How are corporations created?

A. A corporation is a legal entity that you form by filing **articles of incorporation** (in some

---

ⓘ TRUST YOUR PARTNER

If your partnership agreement doesn't limit the authority of the partners to make deals, then you need to be very sure of your partner. One partner's brainstorm to buy a lifetime supply of a product, or launch a megabucks ad campaign, commits the other partners. Even if you weren't informed, you could be liable for the debts. In the absence of an agreement to the contrary, partners act simultaneously as agents and principals in all partnership business, and therefore can bind their copartners to contracts without explicit approval of the copartners.

states, the term used in the statute is **certificate of incorporation**) with the secretary of state in the state in which you have chosen to organize the corporation, along with the required filing and license fees.

One or more persons can form a corporation. Thus, a sole proprietor can incorporate if he or she wants to. With some exceptions (doctors and lawyers are prohibited by ethical and regulatory constraints from operating in certain types of corporations), corporations can generally operate any type of business.

The people who file the articles or certificate of incorporation are called **incorporators.** The equity ownership interest in a corporation is called **stock,** and the owners of shares of stock are called **shareholders** or **stockholders.** There are two types of stock, **common stock** and **preferred stock.** Voting rights typically belong to common stock holders, but dividends generally must be paid on the preferred stock before the common stock receives dividends.

Q. How do corporations limit the liability of their owners?

A. Sole proprietors and many kinds of partners potentially face unlimited liability. Shareholders of a corporation, on the other hand, generally are at risk only for the amount of money or other property they invest in the corporation, though some state laws make shareholders of small corporations liable for unpaid wages. So if you put up $5,000 in return for stock in the company, you may lose $5,000, but creditors of the corporation can't come after you personally for more payment. Even if the business is deader than a three-day-old halibut, shareholders can lose only their investment.

This ability to shield personal assets from the creditors of a corporation is attractive to investors. Given a choice, an investor always will choose limited liability over unlimited liability.

When shareholders of a corporation guarantee its debts, co-sign its notes in their individual capacity, or pledge their own assets as security for loans to the corporation, which frequently occurs

because of creditors' demands, the shareholders waive their limited liability with respect to those debts, notes, or assets. But this is a limited waiver. The shareholders in question still have limited liability with respect to other debts or obligations of the corporation.

The following example will help to illustrate this distinction. Suppose Bill is the sole shareholder in Bill's Bakeries, Inc. He personally guarantees payment of a $20,000 bank loan that is used to purchase a new delivery truck for the corporation. Alas, people don't want Bill's buns, and the corporation ceases doing business and is liquidated. At the time of liquidation, the corporation has $50,000 in assets, and the creditors of the corporation other than the bank that made the truck loan have valid claims of $75,000. The bank can recover whatever is still owed on the truck loan directly from Bill because of the personal guaranty. The other creditors, however, can recover only $50,000 from the corporation. They cannot recover the additional $25,000 they are owed from either the corporation, because it does not have any more assets, or from the shareholder, because the shareholder's other assets are protected by the limited liability doctrine.

There are some exceptions to limited liability. For example in cases of fraud or wrong-doing, a shareholder or director of a corporation may be personally liable.

Q. What does it mean that corporations have "perpetual existence"?

A. The life of a corporation is indefinite, which means that if a shareholder leaves, there is no risk of liquidation. **Perpetual existence** gives a corporation permanence, and this in turn may make investments in a corporation somewhat safer than investments in other, less permanent business organizations.

Q. Can shareholders of all corporations, large or small, transfer their shares?

A. Being able to transfer shares freely to anyone gives an investor the right to liquidate his or her investment at any time. This right to transfer makes shares of the stock very marketable—provided, of course, there is someone who wants to buy them. The shares of all the corporations whose stock is registered with a stock exchange like the New York Stock Exchange are, for example, freely transferable.

But in a small corporation with only a few shareholders, free transferability of stock can often be a detriment. For example, imagine there are three founding shareholders of a small company and one shareholder decides to sell his shares to someone the other two intensely dislike. For the store to be successful, all three shareholders have to work there regularly without undue friction between them, so it could be a disaster.

In many states, a complete prohibition against the transferability of stock is not possible. That's why in most small corporations, the shareholders enter into what is known as a **shareholder's agreement** or a **share transfer restriction agreement**, which will impose restrictions on the sale of stock. These agreements

have to conform to your state's corporation laws, as well as precedents established by other cases. It's a good idea to get legal counsel to draft such an agreement.

Q. What actions can a corporation take under the law?

A. A corporation has the right to own and dispose of property in its own name and to sue and be sued in its own name. This makes things a lot easier for everyone doing business with the company, since it does not require action by all the shareholders.

A limited liability company, like a corporation, may own property and sue and be sued in its own name. A proprietorship, on the other hand, does not have separate entity status, but this does not cause any practical problems because there is only one person, the sole proprietor, in whose name title to property belonging to the proprietorship is taken. Moreover, suits by and against a proprietorship must be in the name of the sole proprietor, even if the proprietorship operates under a name different from that of the proprietor.

Q. How are corporations taxed?

A. Anyone thinking of setting up a corporation—or any other form of business—ought to be concerned with how their choice of business form affects the taxes they'll have to pay. For partnerships and sole proprietors, the company isn't taxed per se, but rather tax obligations are simply passed through to the owners. This results in income being taxed only once.

A corporation is a separate taxable person and faces double taxation: a tax on the earnings of the corporation as an entity and a tax paid by the shareholder on dividends paid by the corporation.

Fortunately, there's a way around this for most small corporations—if they meet the requirements of Subchapter S of the Internal Revenue Code and choose to be taxed under this section. There are two subchapters in the Internal Revenue Code that govern corporations. One is Subchapter S, which small corporations meet-

---

⚠ CORPORATE LIMITED LIABILITY IN THE REAL WORLD

Shareholders are limited in their liability, but if you invest in a small corporation you might very well have to give your creditors another way to get at your personal assets. Banks and others who lend money to small, new corporations know very well that they can't routinely get their money back if their claims are greater than the assets of the corporation. Therefore, they often require investors to obligate their personal assets by personal guaranties or by co-signing a note or other obligation in their individual capacity, which means you still could lose your car and your home if the business goes wrong.

ing certain criteria can choose; corporations that meet the requirements of this subchapter are known as **S corporations.** The other is Subchapter C, under which many corporations, including large corporations, operate; corporations meeting its criteria are known as **C corporations.**

Q. How are S corporations taxed?

A. S corporations are taxed like partnerships. Except in a limited number of circumstances, an S corporation does not itself pay any taxes. Rather, the income and the deductions generated by the S corporation are passed through to the shareholders, who report their share on their individual tax returns.

The basic eligibility requirements are that the corporation be a domestic corporation and

- not have more than one class of stock;
- not have more than seventy-five shareholders; and
- not own 80 percent or more of the stock of another corporation.

Q. How are C Corporations taxed?

A. Unless your corporation has chosen to be taxed as an S corporation, it's automatically taxed as a C corporation. This means it must pay a tax on its net taxable income, and then the shareholders must pay a second tax on any of the corporation's net earnings that are distributed as taxable dividends.

But in a small corporation, where all the shareholders work in the business, it may be possible to avoid taxation on profits by avoiding the profits! If the owner-employees pay themselves enough (while still satisfying IRS rules that the compensation be "reasonable") there would be no profit, and thus no tax on the business or on dividends.

In such a situation, a C corporation might enjoy some tax advantages over the other forms. The key is that a corporation is a separate taxable person. Shareholders who are employed by a corporation in some capacity can qualify as employees of the company. As a result, they're eligible for special life and medical insurance programs and other fringe benefits. These can result in tax deductions to the company for the cost of these business expenses. These breaks aren't available to sole proprietors, partners, and the members of a limited liability company, who are regarded as self-employed.

Limited Liability Companies

Q. What is a limited liability company?

A. A **limited liability company (LLC)** combines certain attributes of a corporation and a sole proprietorship or a partnership.

Since an LLC is not a corporation, it provides the flexibility of organization of a proprietorship or a general partnership—you don't have to have shareholders, directors, and officers, to say nothing of the mandatory meetings. And it has the same pass-through taxation that sole proprietorships and partnerships do.

But because an LLC protects against individual liability, it can give you the same protection as the shareholders of a corporation enjoy. As an owner of an LLC, you won't be at risk for more than the money you invested—creditors won't be able to come after your personal assets.

An LLC is attractive to entrepreneurs because of the combination of flexibility, limited liability, and avoidance of the two-tiered tax on C corporations.

Other features of LLCs make them attractive. First, the owners (called **members**) can have full or limited management rights, as desired. They don't have to adopt the three-tiered management structure of shareholders, directors, and officers, as do corporations, though in fact some choose to. The members of an LLC can take an active part simply and directly.

Second, as a member, you have some protection against unacceptable new members becoming involved in managing the business. Under many state LLC laws, members can transfer their financial rights in an LLC freely, but their right to

▶ CORPORATIONS AT WORK

From time to time, you'll have to do things differently because you're a corporation. Many of these activities are necessary to maintain the corporate "veil"—that is, to avoid misleading third parties as to the fact that your business is a corporation. Maintaining the veil makes sure the corporation is liable, not you personally. Here's a brief checklist of activities you should undertake as a corporation.

- Don't mingle—money, that is. Keep your personal finances separate from those of the corporation. If you dip into corporate money, don't just reach into your pocket—establish a paper trail that shows that you receive a salary or took out a loan.

- Make sure everyone who deals with your company knows that you—and the other officers—are acting in your capacity as agents of the corporation, not personally. That means using appropriate titles—president, secretary, treasurer—when signing everything from checks and contracts to ordinary correspondence. Document that all major activities were taken by the corporation, and not by you personally.

- Be sure to use the correct, full corporate name—on your letterhead, ads, contracts, and the like.

- Maintain the appropriate corporate records—including your bylaws, resolutions, and minutes of meetings. Issue share certificates.

- Hold the meetings required by law—usually you'll have to hold annual meetings of shareholders, at which you'll appoint or reappoint directors, and of directors, who appoint officers.

participate in the governance may not be transferred without the consent of the remaining members. (Of course, the flip side is that this restriction may make it harder to dispose of your ownership interest in an LLC than your shares of stock in a corporation.)

Third, you and the other members can be creative in how you agree to divide profits and losses. There's no requirement that these be divided according to the percentage of ownership, but there is such a rule for corporations.

Want some more advantages? There are no re-

ⓘ THE COST OF YOUR BUSINESS STRUCTURE

If you're on a budget (and what start-up isn't?), you'll have to keep an eye on organizational and administrative costs. Proprietorships and general partnerships cost the least. They require no written documents or public filings, except possibly to comply with an assumed name statute. (However, you're certainly well advised to have a written agreement or general partnership agreement defining the rights and obligations of the partners.)

Also, proprietorships and partnerships generally pay no annual fees (other than business license fees and the like), but you'll have to contend with written documents and various filing and annual fees for all the other business forms. These expenses can mount up. And neither proprietorships nor general partnerships offer limited liability.

CHART COMPARING CHARACTERISTICS OF BUSINESS FORMS

Characteristics	Proprietorship	General Partnership	Limited Liability Partnership	Limited Partnership
Limited Liability	No	No	Yes	No, general partners; Yes, limited partners
Management Rights of Owners	All rights belong to sole proprietor	Yes, partners vote on a per capita basis unless agreed otherwise	Same as general partnership	Yes, general partners; No, limited partners, who can, however, have voting and other rights so long as no control
Transferability of Ownership Interests	Freely transferable - but very limited market	Financial rights are transferable but transferee does not become partner without the consent of all remaining partners	Same as general partnership	Same as general partnership unless agreement provides otherwise
Business Continuity on Dissociation of Owner	No	No - withdrawal of a partner generally results in a dissolution and liquidation unless all the partners agree that the business can continue	Same as general partnership	No - withdrawal of a general partner results in dissolution unless business continued by agreement of the remaining partners; withdrawal of a limited partner generally has no effect on continuity
Taxation	Single tax - owner taxed directly	Single tax - partners include their pro rata share of income and deductions on their individual tax returns	Same as general partnership	Same as general partnership
Distinctive Features	There is no legal distinction between the sole proprietor as an individual and the business	(1) Unlimited liability of the partners; (2) lack of continuity because of danger of liquidation when a partner leaves	All partners have limited liability to some degree but existing statutes differ in the amount of limited liability protection; some only protect the partners against vicarious liability for tort and some types of contract claims while others provide corporate-style limited liability	(1) Unlimited liability of the general partners but limited liability of the limited partners; (2) the inability of the limited partners to take part in the control of the business

Regular Corporation	S Corporation	Close Corporation	Professional Corporation	Limited Liability Company
Yes	Yes	Yes	Yes as to liabilities other than shareholders' own malpractice	Yes
Holders of majority of voting shares elect directors who in turn select officers and other agents	Same as regular corporation	Same as regular corporation, but right to vary by agreement	Same as regular corporation, but right to vary by agreement	Yes - same as general partnership but most statutes specify that the members vote in accordance with % ownership of capital
Shares freely transferable and no distinction between financial and management rights as in partnerships and limited liability companies	Shares freely transferable but as a general rule transfers are restricted by share transfer restriction agreements to protect the remaining shareholders against unacceptable transferees	Same as S corporation	Same as S corporation, but only licensed professionals of the same profession can be transferees	Same as general partnership
Perpetual existence	Perpetual existence	Perpetual existence	Perpetual existence	Essentially the same as a limited partnership
Double tax - income initially taxed at corporate level; shareholders pay additional tax on dividends and other distributions from the corporation	Except in limited circumstances, single tax at the shareholder level basically similar to partnerships	Will be taxed as either a regular corporation or an S corporation	Same as close corporation	Same as partnership
(1) Limited liability of the shareholders; (2) the three-tiered management scheme of shareholders, directors, and officers	1) Limited liability of shareholders; (2) lack of flexibility because of restrictions on number and types of shareholders (individuals and some trusts)	(1) Limited liability; (2) ability to modify the management and free transferability characteristics of a regular corporation	(1) Exclusion of shareholder's own malpractice from limited liability; (2) only useful for those professionals who cannot have corporate limited liability because of ethical or statutory restrictions	Combination of the same limited liability as a corporation and the tax and nontax flexibility of a partnership

strictions on the number or type of people who can be members of an LLC, or on the types of ownership interests. That means LLCs can be used in far more situations than S corporations, which can have no more than seventy-five shareholders, all of whom, with the exception of certain types of trusts and estates, must be U.S. citizens or resident aliens. Your LLC, for example, can have a nonresident alien, a corporation, a partnership, or another limited liability company as a member.

Q. Are there any disadvantages?

A. Surprisingly few. In some states, filing and publication requirements may make it somewhat more expensive to organize an LLC than a corporation. For example, in some states, the official filing costs and the cost of publishing a notice of the formation of the LLC can exceed $2,000.

If you plan someday to finance the company through a private placement or eventual public offering, an LLC would not be appropriate. However, you can always convert the LLC to a corporation at a later date.

Q. Are LLCs a newcomer to the business scene?

A. LLCs are a pretty new form of business entity in the United States. The first LLC statute in this country was enacted in 1977 by Wyoming. Florida adopted a similar act in 1982. Very few LLCs were formed, however, until after a benefi-

cial tax ruling in 1988. Within a decade, all states had enacted LLC statutes.

Q. What is a single-member LLC?

A. In some states, an LLC can have a single member. The single-member LLC, or SLLC, is a very attractive form of doing business for several reasons.

First, for the sole proprietor who is seeking liability protection, he or she will enjoy as the sole member of a SLLC the same liability protection as that of a corporate shareholder.

Second, the IRS will not regard the SLLC as a separate *taxable* entity from its member. This means that a single member will report profits or losses on Schedule C of his or her federal income tax return, under his or her own Social Security number. The SLLC does not file its own tax return. In the event your state has an income tax, you should consult a lawyer or accountant in your jurisdiction to determine if a separate return has to be filed for any state income tax.

Third, the fact that a SLLC is a separate legal entity allows the member to transfer all or part of his or her interest in the SLLC to another, which would be impossible for a sole proprietor.

Finally, you may not need to file for an EIN (which was discussed on pages 482-3) if you are operating a SLLC and have no employees. However, if you hire employees, then you will need to obtain an EIN. If your business is already established as a sole proprietorship with employees and you are converting the business to a SLLC, you will want to refer to IRS Notice 99-6. That notice discusses when a SLLC should apply for its own EIN and when you should continue reporting under your preexisting EIN. Consult your accountant or lawyer if you have any questions concerning the EIN requirements.

ⓘ PUTTING THE WORLD ON NOTICE

LLCs have to announce—or at least whisper—their status. They're required to put after their company name the words "limited liability company," or the abbreviation "LLC." Like "Inc.," which indicates that a business is incorporated, this lets suppliers and customers know the type of entity they're dealing with.

THE WORLD AT YOUR FINGERTIPS

- *The website www.bizmove.com discusses some points to consider when entering into a partnership. The site also has other useful information for the businessperson.*

- *The Business Owner's Toolkit is a very useful site for small businesses. It contains much useful information on starting corporations and other practical legal matters. Access the material on corporations at www.toolkit.cch.com/text/P01_4770.asp.*
- *The IRS is a good source of information on the taxing question of S Corporations versus C Corporations. See in particular Publication 542, Corporations; Publication 17, Your Federal Income Tax; Publication 535, Business Expenses; Publication 533, Self-Employment Tax, Self-Employment Income; and Publication 550, Investment Income and Expenses. The IRS website—www.irs.gov—has all of these online, as well as much more.*

REMEMBER THIS

- *A sole proprietorship has no red tape—it's simple and cheap.*
- *Everything you own could be at risk if you are a sole proprietor and something bad happens to the business; you might find it hard to raise capital; and your death may cause real trouble for the business.*
- *Partnerships can be a very effective way for two or more people to be in business together.*
- *Partners should agree in advance about how the company will be run, how the profits will be split, and so on. A written partnership agreement will help make everyone clearer on what's been agreed to.*
- *A limited partnership permits limited partners—those who invest in a company but do not take part in its day-to-day management—to protect themselves from unlimited liability; generally, they can only lose what they invested in the business.*
- *Corporations have a separate legal status, apart from you and any other investors.*

- *Investors can buy and sell shares freely, and are shielded from personal liability, yet can control the business.*
- *The corporation can own property, sue or be sued, and go on indefinitely, no matter if investors come and go.*
- *Limited liability companies have many of the benefits of corporations, but, depending on state law, may require fewer legal formalities.*
- *LLCs provide both protection against personal liability and a good tax status.*

INTELLECTUAL PROPERTY

You've dealt with the paperwork, you've set up a nice office, and it looks like your good idea is turning into a money-spinner. But now that your business is up on its feet, there are even more things for you to think about. Do you need intellectual property protection for your trademark or your products?

Running a business is a complex job. This section will give you some useful general information, and your lawyer can give you more detailed advice tailored to your circumstances.

Q. Why do I need to know about intellectual property if I'm starting a small business?

A. A surprising number of small businesses have a stake in what is called **intellectual property.** Intellectual property is an intangible asset that consists of human knowledge or ideas. It might be just your logo or slogan. Maybe it is an audiovisual work or an original writing or some other creation for which a copyright is possible. Maybe it is a trade secret, such as a secret formula, or even a design that can be patented. Just like physical property—a building or a car—intellectual property can have value, and you should take steps to protect it.

Trademarks

Q. *What is a trademark?*

A. A trademark is any

- word or words,
- name,
- symbol or picture, or
- device

that a company or business uses to distinguish its goods from someone else's. A trademark can be any combination of the above and can even be a saying or slogan, such as Coke's "It's the Real Thing." The Nike "swoosh" is a trademark, as is the Gap logo and thousands of other familiar symbols and logos. Trademarks that have been registered with the U.S. Patent and Trademark Office can be identified easily by the ® after the mark on the product or its packaging. Before the mark is registered, the owner can assert common-law trademark rights by using this mark ™ after the mark's first use in each document, advertisement, or other visual medium.

Q. *How are trademarks protected?*

A. Common-law protection of a trademark occurs automatically as soon as you begin to use your mark—such as on signs, your letterhead, your products, or your ads. Common-law protection of a mark simply means that the first entity using a particular name or slogan has a certain right to the use of that name. If you are just starting your business, or if your business is local and will likely remain local, you may find that common-law protection of your trademark or service mark is sufficient.

Q. *What are my alternatives if I want to register my trademark?*

A. State trademark registration is a relatively simple and inexpensive option that a small business may wish to consider. State-level registration provides trademark protection beyond common-law protection, but only in the state in which it is registered. For a company with only a local focus, this may be the optimum level of protection.

State trademark registration is generally quicker and less expensive than federal trademark registration, but it only prohibits others in that state from using the mark and can be superseded by a federal trademark. If you think your trademark is valuable and you want it to be protected in all the states, indefinitely, it may be worth the cost and the paperwork to undertake federal trademark registration. In fact, most businesses either apply for federal registration or rely on common-law trademark rights rather than seek state trademark registration.

Q. *What is a trade name?*

A. A **trade name** generally is defined as a name a business uses for advertising and sales purposes that is different from the name in its articles of incorporation or other officially filed documents or its official name. An example of a trade name is the use of the name "Tom's Burger Shack" by a company whose official, registered name is Smith's Restaurants Services, LLP. A sole proprietor also may do business under a trade name. Most states authorize the protection of a trade name by filing certain documents with county clerks of court or other appropriate officials in the state. Although a company name or a trade name may sometimes also be a trademark, a trade name is not, in itself, a form of intellectual property.

Q. *I'm concerned about the legal side of choosing an Internet name or Internet slogan. Can I automatically use my trade name as a domain name?*

A. You can use almost anything as an Internet name. Your name on the Internet will be your **domain name**—the unique address used by the Internet's infrastructure to allow other computers to find you on the Internet. Your domain name is a word or phrase ending in one of the now ubiquitous **top-level domain extensions** such as ".com" or ".org" or ".net". Your preferred domain name might be the name of your business followed by the popular .com extension—"yourbusiness.com"—or or you might use a phrase or slogan, such as "worldsgreatestwidgets.com." The ".com" top-level domain extension was originally intended to refer to a commercial enterprise, while ".org" refers to a not-for-profit enterprise and ".net" signifies that the domain name is held by an Internet-related organization.

Once you have selected a domain name you would like to use, you need to find out whether it is available. You might want to do a Web search before you select your trademark or trade name. Someone else may have registered the domain name even if they are not claiming trademark rights in the name or mark. If a company has already registered a domain name as its own, then you are too late. But even if a domain name is available, it may not be a wise choice. Other businesses may be using the same word or phrase, or an almost identical word or phrase, as a trademark or a trade name.

These businesses may choose not to register their trademarks as domain names. But they might still be very interested in protecting their trademarks. They may have the money to go to court to try to prevent you from using your chosen domain name on the grounds that it infringes their trademark. A trademark owner might obtain a court order preventing you from using your chosen domain name if the trademark owner shows either that consumers will be confused about who is behind your domain name or that your business will attract consumers unfairly because their trademark is well known and consumers will seek

---

📑 TRADE SECRETS

A **trade secret** is sometimes referred to as "know-how." It is data or information—not generally known in a particular industry—that gives a business an advantage over its competitors. Common examples of know-how are

- formulas (and not just chemical ones—trade secrets include recipes and directions for making everything from lipstick to soft drinks to succotash),

- manufacturing techniques and processes (how to do something better, faster, cheaper),

- customer lists (you have them—and the competition would kill to get them),

- computer software (not the stuff users can see on their screen, but the source codes that make it all work).

Other possible trade secrets are designs, patterns, programs, systems, forecasts, specifications, and other technical data. A trade secret is not patentable, nor can it be registered as a trademark. However, trade secrets *are* recognized legally as a form of property, and you can turn to the courts to protect against their unauthorized use.

How do you get the most protection possible for your secret? The key is to take steps to protect it from disclosure and maintain its confidentiality. Reveal nothing to most outsiders, and as little as possible to a trusted few among your suppliers, consultants, employees, and others. Require employees and selected outsiders who have access to trade secrets to sign confidentiality agreements, by which they acknowledge that the information is a secret and agree not to reveal it.

The Trade Secrets Home Page has a huge amount of helpful information. Access it at www.rmarkhalligan.com.

it out on the Internet. In some cases, a trademark owner can also initiate a domain name arbitration under the Internet Corporation for Assigned Names and Numbers (ICANN) Uniform Domain-Name Dispute-Resolution Policy to prevent others from using domain names that are similar to their trademarks. You can learn about this type of arbitration at www.icann.org.

Patents

Q. What is a patent?

A. A **patent** gives you an exclusive and potentially valuable right, within the United States, to make, use, and sell your invention for a period of years. Not every invention is patentable—there are all kinds of tests that an invention must pass in order to be patented. For example, the invention must not be obvious, must have some utility, must not be frivolous or immoral, and must be more than just an idea or a scientific principle.

If your application for a patent is successful, you become the **grantee** of the patent. That gives you the nonrenewable exclusive monopoly in the United States to use or assign rights to use a utility patent for twenty years from the date the patent application is filed. Maintenance fees are required about every four years to keep a patent in force. These fees can be as high as $3,000.

All this effort is worthwhile because you can then prevent anyone from selling or using your invention without your permission. However, there are no patent police to do this for you—you must file (and finance) a lawsuit against the infringers, and that might take years of litigation and a great deal of money.

Q. How do I apply for a patent?

A. You apply for a patent by filing an application with the U.S. Patent and Trademark Office. This is a highly technical and lengthy process that may take up to several years to complete. Patent registration can cost several thousand dollars in filing fees, legal fees, costs of drawings, and costs of patent searches.

Just as with trademarks and trade names, part of getting a patent is demonstrating that you have come up with something new—which means you have to do a search of what has already been done. You can do a preliminary search up front to determine if it is worth your time to go ahead with a patent application, or you can hire a lawyer to do a search for you.

Q. What is a provisional patent?

A. According to the U.S. patent office, "Since June 8, 1995, the Patent Office has offered inventors the option of filing a provisional application for patent which was designed to provide a lower-cost first patent filing in the United States and to give U.S. applicants parity with foreign applicants." It only lasts for twelve months, and you must apply for a full patent within that time. However, it does allow you to talk freely with investors, strategic partners, and other potentially interested parties about your patentable concept, without fear of making the concept unpatentable.

Copyright

Q. What is copyright?

A. **Copyright law** protects creative works, giving the copyright owner the exclusive right to reproduce the work, prepare derivative works, distribute copies, and in some cases perform or display the work. A **copyright** allows you to prevent anyone else from appropriating your creations—that is, copying or manufacturing them—without your permission.

Under the law, seven types of works can be copyrighted:

- Literary works
- Musical works
- Dramatic works
- Pantomimes and choreographic works
- Pictorial, graphic, and sculptural works, including fabric designs
- Motion pictures and other audiovisual works
- Sound recordings

These categories are broad enough to cover all sorts of media, old (books, plays, records) and new (CDs, CD-ROMs, DVDs, video games, software, etc.). They also cover advertising materials, trade publications, label designs, operations manuals, photographs, and databases. But your "work" cannot be just an idea (the notion of superheroes that can transform to fight evil) to qualify for copyright protection. It must be realized in a "fixed form"—a book, a computer disk, a website, or an actual TV series about transforming superheroes. And it has to be original, and be the result of at least some creativity.

Copyright lasts the lifetime of the creator plus 70 years if the creator is an individual, and between 95 and 125 years if the copyright is held by a business. Copyright gives you the right to sell the whole bundle of rights, or to unbundle the rights and sell or license them in a variety of ways. In book publishing, for example, you could license the right to reproduce the work to publishers abroad and to a paperback publisher in this country, as well as the right to prepare derivative works (a movie, a play, a TV show, etc.) based on the original work.

Q. How do I get copyright protection?

A. Getting copyright protection is easier than getting a patent or a trademark. You have basic, common-law copyright protection automatically whenever you put your idea into a fixed form (write an article, record a song, make a videotape, store your software on disk).

You can get better copyright protection—that is, protection that's more apt to stand up in a legal fight—by placing the symbol © the year of first publication, and the name of the copyright holder prominently on every publication of the material. It also helps to file a copyright application for the artistic work with the Federal Copyright Office. The copyright office's website, at *www.copyright.gov/*, has application forms you can download, a database of registered copyrights and other records, and electronic versions of many of its publications, such as *Copyright Basics*.

THE WORLD AT YOUR FINGERTIPS

- *For more on intellectual property generally, the Intellectual Property Owners Association (IPO) might be able to help. The IPO is a membership association that represents intellectual property owners. The IPO can be contacted at www.ipo.org.*

- *For trademarks, check out the U.S. Patent and Trademark Office, a division of the U.S. Department of Commerce, Crystal Park, Arlington, VA 22202 (telephone: 800-786-9199; website: www.uspto.gov). The website has much helpful information, including links to related websites and a searchable database of trademarks that are pending or already registered.*

- *For more on patents, contact the U.S. Patent Office (see previous listing for address and website; call 800-786-9199 for the free handbook "Basic Facts About Patents"). You can also obtain information from the National Association of Patent Practitioners website www.napp.org. A law firm website—www.patents.com—contains much useful information and links about patents and other forms of intellectual property.*

- *For copyrights, the Copyright Office located at the Library of Congress, Washington, DC 20559-6000—provides plenty of information on protecting creative material. You can access its website at www.lcweb.loc.gov/copyright.*

- *Another source of copyright information is the Copyright Society of the U.S.A, 1133 Avenue of the Americas, New York, NY 10036. Its website—www.csusa.org—has a legal research center that provides hundred of links to related websites.*

REMEMBER THIS

- *The law often gives you extensive rights in the intellectual property you create. For example, copyright lasts the lifetime of the creator plus 70 years if the creator is an individual, and between 95 and 125 years if the copyright is held by a business. It's an asset that you can hand down to your grandchildren and even great-grandchildren.*

- *Just like it's up to you to lock up shop at night to keep intruders out, it is up to you to protect your intellectual property. This time, though, your weapons include getting good legal help, showing that you own the property (often by registering it), informing infringers in writing that they must stop their unauthorized use of your property, and (usually) filing suit against those that don't comply.*

- *It may not be entirely clear what branch of intellectual property law offers the best protection—your design might be copyrighted, patented, or even registered as a trademark. If there's some doubt, you'll probably need legal help to figure out what is best for your particular situation.*

- *This is a plugged-in area of law—you can get basic information and conduct searches on the Internet, and even file electronically to register your intellectual property. By the same token, the ubiquitous computer is making it easier for people to snag images, designs, and secrets and wing them halfway around the world. Be on the alert for major changes as the law strives to keep up.*

BUSINESS PROBLEMS

By their very nature, businesses have problems. Some are caused by competitors, some by government regulators, some by employees—but almost all of them have a legal dimension. This section gives you some tips about some of the problems you might encounter. Are you on the lookout for con artists who might seek to take advantage of your lack of experience? What kinds of things can go wrong as your business grows, and what precautions should you take to ensure that your business keeps running smoothly?

Small Business Scams

Q. I've been warned about small business scams. How do con artists take advantage of small businesses?

A. Small businesses are frequent targets for con artists looking to profit from people's inattention to detail. Usually, small businesses have no centralized accounting department or security department. It's up to the owner to take care of dozens of details—and examining every invoice may be far down the list of priorities. Too often, the same company gets fleeced more than once by the same scam, as the supplier puts the company on an automatic shipment program in hopes of the invoice being paid by the accounting department as a matter of routine.

Q. What are some of the more common scams?

A. There are dozens of common scams. One of the most common involves a caller offering cut-price photocopying paper or toner. When the shipment arrives, it's normally of mediocre to low quality. The invoice doesn't come for another five or six weeks—typically long enough for someone to have opened the boxes and started using the supplies. It usually goes to someone other than the person who ordered the product and noticed the poor quality. The accounts payable department may not notice that not only is the base price grossly inflated, but there's a "shipping and handling" charge that adds another 10 to 17 percent to the "discounted" price. After the company pays the bill, the supplier may put your company on an automatic reorder program, sending even larger shipments from time to time until someone catches on. To add insult to injury, if you figure out what's going on and return a shipment, the supplier may charge you for shipping costs, plus a sizable "restocking fee."

This scam can be particularly damaging because the shoddy office supplies—say, remanufactured toner cartridges—can void the warranty on your equipment. That can blot out any savings you'd have had if the discount were on the level.

Some con artists exploit the same inattention to detail of some small businesses and don't even send merchandise—just an invoice demanding payment for goods that were neither ordered nor delivered.

Advertising scams generally start with a high-pressure pitch over the phone, asking you to order key chains, mugs, and other merchandise with your company logo on them, with an incentive like a VCR or a microwave oven.

When the stuff arrives, chances are it's of such poor quality that you wouldn't want to use it to represent your company. It'll sit in your storeroom for years, an embarrassing reminder of the time you thought you could get something that was too good to be true. One business owner thought he had a deal when he ordered promotional mugs that came with a motorboat as an incentive to the owner to buy them. The mugs turned out to be ugly tan plastic, not ceramic, and the company logo was just painted on. The motorboat turned out to be inflatable, with a tiny angler's motor.

Other scams may be as simple as an unfamiliar repairman who promises a special deal, but then does a shoddy repair job or swaps your good equipment for something inferior. Or a caller claiming to represent a charity who will squirrel your donations into his or her own pocket.

⚠ START-UP SCAMS

Sadly, scamming business start-ups is a growth industry. With more and more people looking to begin a small business, often at home, there's no shortage of potential victims who lack savvy in the wiles of the world. Here are some common "biz op" scams targeting the self-employed.

- Work-at-home opportunities, in which you make crafts, stuff envelopes, or do something else that promises you a big return without ever leaving home. Pitfalls include having to buy a big inventory to get started, and no guaranteed markets or volume of business.

- Pyramid schemes, in which the core of the business is the new distributors that you bring in. If the business itself is not profitable, selling new people on investing is a risky way to make a living. The history of pyramids is that the first few people do well, but everyone else loses when the pyramid collapses.

As always, your best defense is to resist high-pressure tactics and go slow. Ask for documentation. What percentage of people do well at this business? Who are they? Can you contact them (and not just the ones the promoter steers you toward)? Ask for a written statement verifying their earnings claim. Check the company out with the Better Business Bureau and your state and local department of consumer affairs. Get all promises in writing, and in the contract you sign. Make sure you have advice from people on your side—a lawyer, an accountant, or an experienced businessperson.

Q. What steps can I take to avoid being scammed?

A. The Better Business Bureau offers numerous advisory publications on scams against businesses on its website, www.bbb.org. American Express's Small Business Service also offers warnings against scams, especially for start-up/home-based businesses. Check out its website at www.americanexpress.com/smallbusiness. Here are a few tips that might help you avoid getting fleeced.

- Don't make commitments to people you don't know—especially over the telephone.
- Do conduct business with individuals and organizations you know.
- Do insist that all sales pitches, charitable appeals, and advertising propositions be sent in writing.
- Don't agree to advertise in a publication without verifiable circulation figures, sample copies, publication dates, and the name of the publisher.
- Do keep an approved list of publications in which your advertisements appear, so employees won't fall for the claim that your company has advertised in the salesperson's publication before.
- Don't pay invoices that can't be matched with a purchase order.
- Do centralize authority for supply and repair orders.
- Don't contribute to charities without the full name, address, and purpose of the charity, along with the latest financial statements indicating that most of the money collected actually goes to the work of the charity.
- Do issue charitable contribution checks to the charity itself, rather than an individual solicitor.
- Don't order supplies from an unknown supplier without first comparing prices and quality with known suppliers.

Operational Problems

Q. What legal problems does a business typically encounter after it is organized and operational?

A. There are four general types of legal issues that a new business might encounter:

1. Major transactions such as a bank loan, or a purchase or lease of equipment or real estate that involves the drafting or review of various legal documents and the preparation of minutes authorizing the transaction
2. Changes in statutes and regulations that necessitate changes in the company's contractual documents and internal manuals
3. Ongoing regulatory compliance—for example, timely filing of corporate annual reports and assumed name refilings
4. The necessity of periodically reviewing and updating the company's legal structure

Q. Must a business have a lawyer involved in all these transactions?

A. At the very least, a business should consult a lawyer regularly about major transactions and compliance problems. Even if the law firm representing a bank prepares the loan documents and

---

ⓘ TIMING YOUR ANNUAL LEGAL AUDIT

If you decide you need an annual legal audit, the best time is a month or so before the end of the company's taxable year. This enables the audit to include year-end tax-planning issues. Frequently, you can save significant amounts of taxes by either completing a transaction this tax year or deferring the transaction until the next taxable year.

the borrower has to pay for this work, which is customary, the borrower's lawyer should review all of the documents before they are signed.

To provide adequate legal protection for a business, the company's lawyer should be involved whenever a major change occurs in the business. Some companies may wish for the additional security of having the company's legal documents reviewed on a regular basis, preferably at least once a year. This annual legal audit might uncover omissions, such as the absence of corporate minutes and changes in documents necessitated by changes in statutes and regulations. The review of the annual audit with the client could also provide the lawyer with the opportunity to discuss with the client recent legal changes so that the executives and employees will be alerted to potential problems and will be better able to comply with the changes. As part of this process, the lawyer may uncover potentially serious legal problems at a time when they can be resolved in an efficient, cost-effective fashion.

Q. What kinds of issues and documents should be reviewed by the company lawyer?

A. From time to time, it's a good idea to look at

- basic constituent documents (for example, articles of incorporation, bylaws, and stock transfer records of a corporation; the articles of organization and operating agreement of a limited liability company; the partnership agreement; and, in a limited partnership, the certificate of limited partnership);
- employment agreements;
- all leases, licensing agreements, and other contracts with third parties, with particular emphasis on termination dates, renewal options, and the like;
- insurance policies, with an emphasis on policy limits;
- all standardized contract forms used by the business—for example, purchase order forms, warranties, brochures, and the like;

- internal policy and procedural manuals—for example, the employee policy and procedures manual, or the antitrust compliance handbook;
- transactions that require additional documentation, such as official minutes;
- regulatory compliance—for example, environmental regulations, ERISA problems, and Securities and Exchange Commission requirements;
- structural changes in the business organization—for example, conversion to another business form, or the adoption of a retirement plan or a fringe benefit plan;
- tax-planning issues—for example, S Corporation status, legal audit, or alternative minimum tax review;
- the filing of tax returns, licenses, and reports;
- pending and potential litigation involving the company; and
- recent legal developments affecting the business.

Bankruptcy

Q. What is bankruptcy?

A. Businesses and individuals typically explore the option of bankruptcy when they are having trouble paying debts when the debts become due. When this happens to a person or a business (known as the **debtor**), that person or business then may be entitled to file for bankruptcy under the bankruptcy laws, also known as the Bankruptcy Code. The parties to whom the debtor owes money are known as the **creditors.**

Q. What are my bankruptcy options if my business is in trouble?

A. There are three main types of bankruptcy that apply to business owners: Chapters 7, 11, and 13. All are available to individuals (and thus to sole proprietors), and the first two are also available to business entities (e.g., corporations). Chapter 8, "Consumer Bankruptcy," provides some useful information on Chapter 7 bankruptcy and Chapter 13 bankruptcy. Sometimes, a business will file for one form of bankruptcy and later have it converted to another form.

Chapter 7

A previous chapter of this book looks at Chapter 7 bankruptcy as it applies to individuals and couples, but it's important to remember that it is available to "persons," which includes business entities themselves—that is, corporations, LLCs, and the like. This form of bankruptcy is also available to individuals who own businesses as sole proprietors. In the case of a sole proprietor who files under Chapter 7, the bankruptcy will involve all of the person's assets and debts, both business and personal. In other words, the business itself can't file bankruptcy separately, but it can be in bankruptcy as part of the overall bankruptcy of the owner.

Chapter 7 (sometimes called **straight bankruptcy**) enables you to **discharge** your debts (not pay them); but within limits set by law, your property could be sold and the proceeds split among your creditors (this is called **liquidation**).

Chapter 11

Chapter 11 is open to all forms of business entities, including sole proprietorships. A Chapter 11 bankruptcy is used to reorganize a business. Chapter 11 allows a business to continue operating while it repays creditors through a plan approved by the bankruptcy court. It gives breathing room to businesses that are having financial problems, but that can generate a steady income and meet payroll. The goal is to give the business a chance to get back on its financial feet.

Under Chapter 11, management usually is allowed to continue to run the business on a day-to-day basis, though a trustee might take over if fraud or gross mismanagement were established. The bankruptcy court, however, must approve significant business decisions. The time it takes

to get approval could mean the debtor will lose business.

At least one committee will be appointed to represent the interests of the creditors. The committee will work with the company to develop a plan of reorganization to get the business out of debt. This plan must be accepted by the creditors and approved by the court. If the creditors reject the plan, the court still may approve it if the court finds it to be fair.

The irony of Chapter 11 is that it pulls management in different directions. The need to comply with requirements imposed by the bankruptcy court and the law demands a lot of the debtor's attention just when the debtor needs to spend more time focusing on the business's financial health.

The assets of the business (debtor) will be used to pay at least some of the costs associated with a Chapter 11 restructuring. For example, the expenses of the committee of creditors may come out of the assets. However, each creditor will pay for the services of the professionals (lawyers, accountants, etc.) working for them.

This type of bankruptcy is costly and time consuming. The courts (and lawyers) are extensively involved. Some Chapter 11 bankruptcies end up being converted to Chapter 7 bankruptcies if the business can't meet its obligations under its plan.

Chapter 13

Chapter 13 also provides for debt reorganization. It is not available to businesses per se, but, because there may be no legal distinction between the sole proprietor and his or her business, a sole proprietor filing under Chapter 13 may include business debts that he or she is personally liable for. Unlike Chapter 11, it has stringent limits on the amount of debt involved in the bankruptcy—no more than $290,525 in unsecured debt and $871,550 in secured debt. The advantage of Chapter 13 is that it costs much less and is much easier than Chapter 11. The fees for filing under Chapter 13 are much less than those for Chapter 11, but the biggest cost difference is in professional fees. A Chapter 11 bankruptcy involves more lawyers and accountants, is more complicated, and takes longer than Chapter 13. The more hours put in by those lawyers and accountants, the bigger your bills.

Q. Is there any way my business can file for Chapter 13 bankruptcy? We are a limited liability company, but there are only three members.

A. Although Chapter 13 is reserved for individuals and sole proprietors, there is a way you can file under that chapter. You and your members can transfer all the assets to one individual as a sole proprietor. Then the sole proprietor can file under Chapter 13. This is known as "rolling up" the company. Keep in mind that bankruptcy will show up on the new sole proprietor's credit report.

Q. How much does it cost to go bankrupt?

A. Each form of bankruptcy will cost you money out of pocket. As a general rule, Chapter 7 is the least expensive, followed by Chapter 13 and Chapter 11. Workouts, discussed on page 514, are less expensive than Chapter 13 and Chapter 11 bankruptcies.

Q. What are the advantages of declaring bankruptcy as soon as I think my business is in financial trouble?

A. The timing of the bankruptcy filing can be very important because the filing of the proceeding results in an automatic stay of all legal actions against the debtor business. This means that no further action in the pending lawsuit can take place without the permission of the bankruptcy court. The ability to get the stay is often the primary reason for filing a petition, even in circumstances where the company currently is not unable to meet its ordinary debts as they become due.

Q. Is bankruptcy my only option if I can't pay my debts when they fall due?

A. No. Frequently, it is possible for the business to work out accommodations with its creditors on a voluntary basis that will enable the business to survive through a rough period. Banks and mortgage companies, for example, are often willing to refinance indebtedness, especially if they can be convinced that the business's financial difficulties are temporary. Trade creditors are also amenable to stretching out payments for the same reason. After all, the last thing a creditor wants is to foreclose on property securing a debt or reduce a debt to judgment. Everyone loses in that situation.

A slightly more formal option is an out-of-court restructuring, or **workout,** in which the financially distressed business and its major creditors, such as lenders or suppliers, agree to adjust the business's obligations. That means that your creditors will cancel some of the debt you owe them. This can be a slow process. Creditors will want to bring in accountants and lawyers—at your expense—to understand and negotiate the restructuring. While you may believe that your initial restructuring plan is the fairest to your creditors, the creditors will most likely consider it your "first offer" and begin negotiating from that point.

A workout may be draining, but it is usually faster than a Chapter 11 restructuring. In addition, it is almost always a better deal for your business than bankruptcy. An out-of-court restructuring doesn't carry the stigma associated with bankruptcy. Third parties may decide that if the business's creditors are willing to do a workout, the creditors must feel the business can regain sound financial footing. Thus, other parties will have more confidence in doing business with you when you're in a workout than when you're in bankruptcy. Unlike Chapter 11, a workout allows the business to choose those creditors it believes are necessary to the restructuring. The business gets to decide how to approach those creditors, and has more flexibility in negotiating the plan.

Another advantage of workouts is that they are less obtrusive. In a Chapter 11 bankruptcy, the financially strapped company's executives are required to appear at a meeting of the company's creditors. At this meeting, the creditors get to question the executives, who are under oath. The creditors also can get court orders to make the executives available for questioning at other times, and to force the company to hand over copies of documents that deal with the company's business affairs.

A workout, on the other hand, gives the company more control. A workout allows the company to limit the release of its financial records to those creditors the company considers essential. The company also can require that this information be kept confidential.

The biggest problem is getting the creditors to agree to the plan. Each creditor will have to decide whether a workout is more beneficial than the outcome of a bankruptcy. Creditors may distrust the business's management. They may not have confidence in the restructuring plan. They may believe they would be better off if the company went through a Chapter 11 reorganization or was liquidated. Creditors will have less say, however, if the business goes into bankruptcy court. Thus, the threat of bankruptcy may convince creditors to agree to the plan.

THE WORLD AT YOUR FINGERTIPS

Business Scams

- *To find out more about a business proposition or report a suspected con artist, call your local Better Business Bureau. In addition, the Better Business Bureau offers many advisory publications on scams against businesses on its website, www.bbb.org.*

- *The Federal Trade Commission has started a crackdown on get-rich-quick self-employment schemes. Download information from www.ftc.gov.*

- *The National Fraud Information Center has much information on small business scams at www.fraud.org.*

- *American Express Company's Small Business Services offers warnings against scams, especially for start-up/home-based businesses. Access www.americanexpress.com/smallbusiness.*

Bankruptcy

- *Go to www.about.com and click on "Small Business" and then on "Bankruptcy" to bring you to a comprehensive list of valuable bankruptcy resources on the Web. This is a good starting point when you're considering your options.*

- *For more in-depth information, the IRS site is at www.irs.ustreas.gov. Use the search function to find forms and publications on bankruptcy.*

- *Check out www.bankrupt.com for the "Internet Bankruptcy Library," largely intended for bankruptcy professionals but of interest to businesspeople seeking information about various alternatives.*

REMEMBER THIS

- *Educate yourself and your employees about scams. By knowing what to expect, you could save your business thousands of dollars. Be skeptical of pitches, get everything in writing, and watch for red flags. It's not hard to avoid these scams if you're vigilant.*

- *Check out any suspicious company with the Better Business Bureau or the authorities in your state or the state the company is headquartered in.*

- *If you've been the victim of a scam, complain to the attorney general's office in your community or the consumer protection bureau. If the mails have been used in the scam, contact the U.S. Postal Service.*

- *If you're struggling with bankruptcy, you should seek legal help at the first sign of financial difficulties. The earlier the intervention, the better. Talk to your lawyer about your options.*
- *A workout is quicker than a Chapter 11 bankruptcy, and almost always a better deal for your business. There are some instances, though, when a workout will not be feasible.*
- *Some business owners can file a Chapter 13 bankruptcy, although that is generally only an option for individuals.*

Personal Injury

Personal injury law, also known as tort law, is designed to protect you if you or your property are injured or harmed because of someone else's act or failure to act. A personal injury or tort lawsuit is a civil (not criminal) cause of action. The wrongdoer compensates the victim with money. There are three different classifications of torts: negligence, strict liability, and intentional torts. The remedy in most tort suits is the same: payment of money by the defendant to the plaintiff. Sometimes the remedy is an injunction rather than monetary damages (for example, if your neighbor plays loud music, you can file a nuisance action seeking an injunction to stop him). Every tort claim, regardless of its basis, whether negligence, strict liability, or intentional, has two basic issues — liability and damages. Was the defendant liable for the damages you sustained, and, if so, what is the nature and extent of your damages? If you can prove liability and damages, our system of justice will award you compensation for your loss. Even if liability is established, the parties in a lawsuit may argue strenuously over the proper amount of damages. Some types of damages, such as lost wages and medical bills, are easy to calculate. But reasonable minds can differ on other kinds of damages, like a person's expected future earnings and how to quantify "pain and suffering."

THE BASICS OF PERSONAL INJURY LAW

John was driving to work. He was in moving traffic when he felt the urge to sneeze. He sneezed, involuntarily closed his eyes, and the car swerved into another lane. John panicked, accidentally pressed the accelerator instead of the brake, and caused a major pileup. Noreen was waiting for the bus with her brother when she witnessed the accident. John's car ran up onto the sidewalk and Noreen's brother was killed instantly. Noreen has become a nervous wreck. She is in therapy, has nightmares and flashbacks, and has had to leave her job. A local newspaper covered the accident. The cover story stated that John (who was not injured) was drunk when he caused the accident.

Several people may have a personal injury case arising from the scenario above. Certainly, the people injured in the accident might be able to bring a case against John, but Noreen also might be able to bring a case against John for the injuries she suffered as a result of witnessing her brother's death. John himself might have a case against the newspaper for defamation.

Q. How do I know if I have a personal injury case?

A. First, you must have suffered a legally recognized injury to your person or property. Second, your injury must be the result of someone else's fault. Your injury need not be physical to bring a personal injury lawsuit. Suits may be based on a variety of nonphysical losses and harms to your reputation or psyche. In the intentional tort of assault, for example, you do not need to show that a person's action caused you actual physical harm, but only that it caused an expectation that some harm would come to you. (Assault is de-

---

ⓘ INVASION OF PRIVACY

In recent years, society has become more aware of privacy rights. The tort of invasion of privacy actually consists of four separate and distinct torts.

- Intrusion upon seclusion—intruding upon a plaintiff in a way that would be highly offensive to a reasonable person. For example, secretly photographing employees and customers in a rest room is an intrusion upon seclusion, as is a reporter gathering news about a person in a place where the person has a reasonable right to expect privacy.

- Misappropriation of name or likeness—using the plaintiff's name or picture for financial gain without permission or without compensating the plaintiff. For example, using pictures of an athlete in a magazine without her permission or paying her is misappropriation of a likeness, as is taking secret video footage of a neighbor and posting it on the Internet for profit.

- False light—portraying a plaintiff in a false light in a way that would be highly offensive to a reasonable person. For example, running a news story about streetwalking prostitutes and including introductory footage of a woman walking the street who is not actually a prostitute is portraying a person in a false light.

- Public disclosure of private facts—publicizing the private facts of a plaintiff in a manner that would be highly offensive to a reasonable person. For example, revealing the personal sexual history and life of a private person to the public is a public disclosure of a private fact.

scribed in more detail on page 546.) You also may have an action if someone publicly has attacked your reputation (the tort of **defamation**), invaded your privacy, or negligently or intentionally subjected you to emotional distress.

Q. *If I have suffered a personal injury and think I have a case, how do I go about finding a personal injury lawyer?*

A. Contact a local bar association for referrals to lawyers who handle personal injury cases, talk with lawyers you know, or ask your friends about lawyers they know or have used. You can find the telephone number of the local bar association in your telephone directory. Most lawyers offer free consultations, so you are able to meet with as many as you like. Choose a lawyer you feel most confident about—and comfortable with—to handle your case. Chapter 1, "When and How to Use a Lawyer," gives you more guidance on finding the right lawyer for your case.

Many personal injury lawyers advertise in a wide variety of media, including radio, television, yellow pages, billboards, and newspapers. But remember that the selection of a lawyer is an extremely important step and one that should not be taken lightly.

Keep in mind that the law of torts is constantly evolving. Many areas of tort law are complex and require a lawyer with expertise in that particular area. Particularly if you believe that you have a medical malpractice, product liability, or toxic tort case, use care in selecting counsel.

If a case is outside a lawyer's usual practice area, the lawyer has an ethical obligation to tell you and may refer you to someone who can better represent your interests.

Q. *Should I bring any documents with me to the consultation?*

A. Yes, you should supply any documents that might be potentially relevant to your case. Police reports, for example, contain eyewitness accounts and details about conditions surrounding auto accidents, fires, assaults, and the like. Copies of medical reports from doctors and hos-

pitals will describe your injuries. Information about the insurer of the person who caused the injury is extremely helpful, as are any photographs you have of the accident or of your injury. The more information you are able to give your lawyer, the easier it will be for him or her to determine if your claim will be successful. If you haven't collected any documents at the time of your first meeting, don't worry. Your lawyer will be able to help you obtain them.

Q. *What kind of legal fees should I expect in a personal injury case?*

A. Personal injury lawyers generally charge their clients on a **contingency fee** basis. That means you pay your lawyer only if you win. Your lawyer is paid a percentage of the total amount recovered. You'll sign a retainer or fee agreement with the lawyer you choose to represent you, clarifying all fees and charges. Remember that whether you win or lose the case, you are likely to have to pay the expenses of investigating and litigating your case, such as court filing fees and payments to investigators, court reporters, and medical experts, as well as the expenses of securing medical records and reports.

Q. *What can I expect after the first consultation?*

A. If a lawyer believes your claim is insurable and one you can recover on, then, after you have

---

ⓘ INFORM YOUR INSURERS

If you are looking for a lawyer to defend you against a tort case, you should let your auto or homeowner's insurer know that you are being sued. Under most policies, they have a duty to defend you. Let them know even if you think the case has no merit or is not included under your policy. If you need your own lawyer to defend you, then you should expect to pay an hourly rate for these services.

signed the retainer, he or she will proceed to gather information about your claim. In order to arrive at a figure for damages, your lawyer will need to determine the extent of your injuries, including pain and suffering, disability and disfigurement, the cost of medical treatment, and lost wages. Your lawyer will then provide your damages figure to the insurer of the person who injured you. If the insurer considers it a valid claim, the case is likely to be resolved early on and won't have to be tried in court.

Q. What does it mean to settle a case?

A. Settling a case means that you agree to accept money in return for voluntarily dismissing your action against the person who injured you. You'll actually sign a release absolving the other side of any further liability.

Most cases are settled before trial, so don't be surprised if your case never goes to trial. After all, the purpose of most tort suits is to recover money from the person who caused the harm. Often, it benefits both sides from an economic and a personal standpoint to resolve the legal dispute without a trial.

The sidebar "Should You Settle Your Case?" discusses some of the general factors that go into deciding whether an offer to settle a case should be accepted. Your lawyer will be able to provide a realistic assessment of whether a lawsuit based

---

▶ SHOULD YOU SETTLE YOUR CASE?

Most lawsuits are settled, or resolved. The settlement process results in plaintiffs—the people filing a lawsuit—agreeing to drop their lawsuit against the defendant in exchange for a specific sum of money. Sometimes, the settlement negotiations require that the settlement amount be kept confidential.

If you are a plaintiff, the rules of legal ethics require your lawyer to tell you the terms of every settlement offer. It is you, not the lawyer, who has the ultimate power to accept or reject a settlement.

A settlement can help you receive needed monies much quicker than the often lengthy trial process. On the other hand, you might accept less money than you should in order to resolve the matter quickly.

An experienced trial lawyer will have expert knowledge on how much a case is "worth." Some factors important in determining the value of your case are

- the severity and permanence of injury;

- the age of the victim (younger people generally have more future medical expenses);

- the duration of needed treatment and the size of medical bills;

- pain and suffering; and

- loss of wages, including the loss of future economic opportunities.

Courts encourage settlements. They hold status conferences to help the judge manage the timeline of a case, and settlement discussions are often part of these conferences. Many court systems will have a judge hold a settlement conference between the parties to determine the chances of settling the case. In other jurisdictions, disputes may be referred to arbitration, mediation, or another form of alternative dispute resolution.

on your claim will be successful, but the decision to accept a settlement offer is yours, not the lawyer's. Remember also that settlement can take place at any point in a lawsuit once it is filed, including before trial or even after a case has been tried but before a jury reaches a verdict.

Q. What happens if I file a lawsuit?

A. You become the plaintiff in the case, and the person who you sue becomes the defendant. Lawyers for each side typically begin gathering facts through exchange of documents, written questions (**interrogatories**) or **depositions** (questions that are asked in person and answered under oath). This process is called discovery.

After discovery, most cases are settled before trial. Of the cases that do go to trial, most plaintiffs ask for a jury to hear their case, but judges can decide personal injury cases as well. That is known as a bench trial, as opposed to a jury trial.

Q. What if more than one person has caused my injury?

A. You must bring an action against every person who caused your injury. The negligence of two drivers, for example, may have produced a collision in which you were injured as you walked across a street. According to traditional legal principles, each driver could be held 100 percent liable to you. In a more recent legal trend, however, many jurisdictions have abolished such **joint and several liability** and each defendant, known legally as a **joint tortfeasor**, becomes responsible for only that proportion of the harm he or she caused. This is the rule of comparative negligence, which exists in most states, and is discussed more fully on page 525 and in chapter 11, "Automobiles."

Q. What will I get if I win my case?

A. If you win, a judge or jury awards you money, known as damages, for your injuries. Damages may include compensation for such expenses as medical bills and lost wages, as well as compensation for future wage losses. It also may compensate you for medical expenses and for pain and suffering. In addition, you may receive damages for any physical disfigurement or disability that resulted from your injury.

The amount awarded is intended to compensate you for your loss, is not considered as income, and is not taxable as income by the federal government or the states.

In some states, the judge may change the amount awarded if the award is excessive or inadequate.

Q. Will I have to take any extra steps to get my money?

A. Maybe. An award of damages does not necessarily translate into hard cash, especially if the person who caused your injury does not carry insurance or is underinsured. You may have to take further legal steps actually to collect the money. For example, if a defendant against whom you have won a judgment does not pay it, you may have to initiate collection proceedings. If the defendant owns property, you may be able to foreclose on it. Another option would be to garnish the defendant's wages. Your lawyer will be able to help you in this regard.

Q. Will the government punish the person who caused my injury?

A. No. Governmental punishment comes from criminal cases, not civil cases. Defendants in civil

---

📄 WHAT IS A TORTFEASOR?

"Personal injury" is the more common way to refer to this body of law these days, but in the old days it was known as tort law. "Tort" comes from the French word "tortus," which means "twisted," and you can see how this became applied to civil wrongs. "Feasor" comes from Old French, and means "doer" or "maker." In the arcane language of the law, someone who commits a tort is a "tortfeasor."

actions for personal injury do not receive jail terms or stiff fines as punishment. Those are criminal sentences, and personal injury cases are civil disputes.

However, there is a form of punishment under personal injury law. In certain rare kinds of cases, juries and courts can award punitive damages. The civil justice system uses punitive damages to punish defendants who have behaved maliciously, intentionally, or recklessly. Courts also hope that ordering the payment of punitive damages will deter defendants from engaging in the same kind of harmful behavior in the future. Note that unlike fines, which go to the government, punitive damages are paid to the plaintiff.

Q. Does a personal injury lawsuit have to be filed within a certain amount of time?

A. Every state has certain time limits, called statutes of limitations, which govern the period during which you must file a personal injury lawsuit. In some states, you may have as little as one year to file a lawsuit from the date the accident oc-

---

ⓘ WHEN IS A PUNITIVE DAMAGE AWARD TOO HIGH? THE CASE OF THE REPAINTED BMW

Judges and juries also have the power to punish defendants with punitive damages awards. On rare occasions, juries will send a message with a high award, often to wealthy corporate defendants, that the defendant's conduct is terrible and should be changed. Defense lawyers argue that some of these awards are excessive and bear no rational relationship to the harm actually committed. Often, defendants challenge these awards by appealing to a higher court.

The U.S. Supreme Court considered such a case in 1996 in *BMW of North America, Inc. v. Gore*.

Facts: Dr. Ira Gore Jr. purchased a black BMW sports sedan for more than $40,000 from a BMW dealer in Birmingham, Alabama. Nine months later, he took his vehicle to a car detailing business. The detailing business discovered evidence that the car had been repainted. Dr. Gore sued BMW, claiming that its failure to disclose to him that the car was repainted was fraudulent. Dr. Gore put forth evidence that BMW had engaged in similar conduct with respect to 983 cars nationwide. An Alabama jury awarded Gore a little more than $4,000 in actual (compensatory) damages and $4 million in punitive damages. The Alabama Supreme Court reduced the punitive award to $2 million. BMW appealed all the way to the U.S. Supreme Court.

Supreme Court Ruling: The U.S. Supreme Court determined that the punitive damage award of $2 million was so excessive as to violate the Constitution. The Constitution provides that a defendant gets notice of the severity of a penalty that a state may impose. In this case, the majority of the Supreme Court determined that the award was excessive because it punished BMW for conduct that may be lawful under other states' laws. The Court also determined that BMW's conduct was not reprehensible enough to justify such a high award. Finally, the Court determined that the ratio between compensatory and punitive damages (in this case 500 to 1) was too high.

Quotable: "Elementary notions of fairness enshrined in our constitutional jurisprudence dictate that a person receive fair notice not only of the conduct that will subject him to punishment but also of the severity of the penalty." (Justice John Paul Stevens)

curred. If you miss the statutory deadline for filing a case, your case is thrown out of court. (As explained on page 535, limitations in medical malpractice cases are often calculated differently.) For this reason, it is important to talk with a lawyer as soon as you receive or discover an injury.

Q. What if a person dies before bringing a personal injury lawsuit?

A. It depends on whether a person dies as a result of the injuries or from unrelated causes. If a person injured in an accident subsequently dies because of those injuries, that person's heirs may recover money through a lawsuit. Every state has some law permitting an action when someone causes the wrongful death of another. And if a person with a claim dies from unrelated causes, the tort claim survives in most cases and may be brought by the executor or the personal representative of the deceased person's estate or heirs, although the amount that can be recovered may change.

Q. Do I have any other options aside from a lawsuit?

A. You are permitted to negotiate with the other party or his or her insurance company without a lawyer. However, it is likely that such negotiation is beyond your skills, and you will have a much better chance of a positive outcome if you have a lawyer.

In addition to, or perhaps instead of, making a tort claim, you might want to pursue other methods of complaint. Consumer protection agencies can be found in every state. State attorney generals' offices offer information and accept complaints. You also can contact state boards that regulate the conduct of lawyers, doctors, veterinarians, and even barbers. Check the government listings in your telephone directory for the numbers of these agencies.

THE WORLD AT YOUR FINGERTIPS

- *Tort law covers a broad spectrum of potential injuries to persons and property, but nearly all the cases involve insurable interests—your life, your health, your home, your property, and your car. For that reason, qualified insurance representatives might be the best place to start to get information about the insurance you would need to protect you if a claim were brought against you. Should a claim on your own behalf arise, you probably will need to contact a qualified personal injury lawyer, following some of the suggestions set out earlier in this chapter. Chapter 1, "When and How to Use a Lawyer," also gives you advice on how to find and hire a lawyer.*

- *For more information on privacy torts, see www.privacilla.org/releases/Torts_Report. html.*

- *You will find information from the U.S. government on alternative dispute resolution by accessing the website of the Office of Personnel Management: www.opm.gov/ er/adrguide/toc.asp.*

REMEMBER THIS

- *If another person caused you to suffer injury, you may be able to recover money damages from that person in a personal injury lawsuit.*

- *Take time when selecting a personal injury lawyer. Contact the lawyer referral program of your local bar association.*

- *When you meet a lawyer at an initial consultation, bring supporting documents with you. Such documents may include police reports, medical reports, insurance policies, and documentation of lost wages.*

- *Most personal injury lawyers will represent you on a contingency fee basis. Read the retainer or fee agreement carefully. Win or lose, you will be responsible for litigation expenses, which include court filing costs and payments to investigators.*

- *Many cases settle before ever reaching trial. You have the ultimate decision on whether to accept a settlement.*
- *Personal injury lawsuits must be filed within a specified period of time, called a statute of limitations. Many such limitations periods are only one year.*

NEGLIGENCE

You are driving down the road at an excessive speed. Suddenly, a bicycle rider veers into your path without looking behind him. You strike the cyclist, and he is injured. The cyclist and his lawyer claim you were negligent, or at fault, for driving above the speed limit. They allege that your speeding prevented you from avoiding him in the road. You and your insurance company claim that the cyclist was at fault, for veering into the roadway and into the path of your car. What is the cause of the accident: your speeding, or the cyclist's failure to observe your car?

Now imagine another scenario: your Uncle Herb, always the life of the party, slips and falls while showing off a tricky salsa step at a party at your house. Could you be liable for his injuries?

This section will shed some light on the answers.

Q. How does the law define negligence with respect to personal injury cases?

A. The most common type of tort case is based on negligence. If someone is **negligent,** he or she is at fault and has acted unreasonably under the circumstances in a way that causes harm to another. Much of tort law is designed to compensate those who have been harmed by socially unreasonable conduct. Unlike someone who commits an intentional tort, a negligent tortfeasor does not intend to cause harm or bring about a certain result. The person simply did not use reasonable care.

For instance, let's say that Jill is driving her car down the road when her cell phone rings. She picks up the phone and inadvertently swerves into another lane, striking another car. Jill did not commit an intentional tort because she did not intend to strike the other car. But Jill was negligent because she failed to act with reasonable care while operating her vehicle.

Q. How would a legal case determine negligence?

A. There are generally four basic elements of a negligence action:

1. Duty
2. Breach of duty
3. Causation
4. Damages

In the above example, Jill had a duty to drive her car safely. When she swerved into the other lane, she breached that duty. Her actions in not paying attention to the road caused the harm. She caused damages to be suffered by the other driver. If a legal case filed by the other driver found these four elements, Jill's negligence would be established and she would be liable (legally responsible) and probably would be required to pay money to the other driver.

Q. Is negligence the basis of many suits?

A. Yes. Negligence reaches far beyond claims stemming from car accidents. It is the basis for liability in most personal injury lawsuits, including slip-and-fall cases and acts of professional negligence, such as medical and legal malpractice.

Q. If I am hurt because someone failed to act, might that person be found negligent and therefore be liable?

A. Yes. Negligence stems from careless or thoughtless conduct or a failure to act when a reasonable person would have acted. Conduct becomes negligent when it falls below a legally recognized standard of taking reasonable care under the circumstances to protect others from harm.

Q. Negligence law seems so confusing. It uses words such as duty and causation. What do they mean?

A. Negligence law can be complex and confusing even for people who are familiar with it. To understand it better, forget all the legal jargon and go back to the car accident example. A driver has a duty to use reasonable care to avoid injuring anyone he or she meets on the road. If a driver fails to use reasonable care and as a result of that failure injures you, then the driver is responsible (liable) to you for those injuries.

Q. Who determines whether a defendant has acted reasonably?

A. After your lawyer presents the evidence, a judge or a jury will decide what a reasonable person would have done in similar circumstances. In the example of an automobile accident, a judge or a jury is likely to find a driver negligent if his or her conduct departed from what an ordinary or reasonable person would have done in similar circumstances. An example would be failing to stop at a stoplight or stop sign. But remember, you

must suffer damages to have a valid personal injury lawsuit. In other words, you could not sue another driver if he or she ran a red light and did not hit your car.

Automobile Collisions

Q. Is negligence the basis of auto collision cases?

A. In general, yes. Automobile collisions, the area in which many personal injury actions arise, provide a good example of how the concept of negligence works in our tort system. Tort law with respect to auto accidents works differently depending upon the state in which you live. That is because some states are "fault" states and others are "no-fault" states.

In a fault state, you have a negligence claim if you are injured by a driver who failed to exercise reasonable care, because drivers have a duty to exercise such reasonable care anytime they are on the road. When they breach that duty and your injury results, personal injury law says you can recoup your losses.

In a no-fault state, the insured person's insurance carrier pays for the insured's damages, no matter which driver was at fault.

Q. I was in a car accident, but it was partly my fault and partly the other driver's fault. Will this make a difference with regard to what damages ultimately are awarded?

A. Yes. In the past, the rule was that if you could prove the other driver contributed in any way to the accident, he or she could be totally barred from recovering anything from you. But now, most states have rejected such harsh results and instead look at the comparative fault of the drivers. If a jury finds that you were negligent and that your negligence, proportionally, contributed 25 percent to cause your injury and that the defendant was 75 percent at fault, the defendant would be responsible for only 75 percent of your damages, or $75,000 if your damages totaled

---

📄 **NEGLIGENCE LAW JARGON**

A **duty of care** is a legal duty to take reasonable care in the circumstances. **Reasonable care** is, naturally, the level of care that would be exercised by a reasonable person—that is, a person with an ordinary degree of reason, prudence, care, and foresight. The reasonable person is a legal fiction that is used to provide an objective standard of reasonable, ordinary behavior to guide the courts. When a person fails to take reasonable care, the person breaches that duty. There must be an **element of causation,** which simply means that the breach of duty must cause the accident. And the accident must cause damages, which is simply some kind of loss or harm.

$100,000. In some states, a plaintiff may recover even if he or she were more negligent than the defendant—that is, negligent in the amount of 51 percent or more. (See the sidebar on "Comparative and Contributory Negligence" below and chapter 11, "Automobiles," for more on standards of negligence for car accidents.)

Q. A neighbor who rides with me to work was injured when I got into a car accident. Do I have to pay her medical bills?

A. In many states today (about half), no-fault automobile insurance would protect you—and often passengers in your car—by compensating

---

ⓘ COMPARATIVE AND CONTRIBUTORY NEGLIGENCE

There are different systems of negligence law in American jurisprudence. The traditional system used to be contributory negligence. Under contributory negligence, a plaintiff could not recover any damages if he or she contributed to his or her injuries (was contributorily negligent). Although there were some common-law doctrines that lessened the impact of this doctrine, this doctrine was seen as providing a harsh all-or-nothing outcome. It was all-or-nothing, because a plaintiff could recover all the damages (if considered not negligent) or no damages at all (if determined contributorily negligent).

The vast majority of states have switched to a system of comparative negligence to avoid the all-or-nothing rule of contributory negligence. Most states did so legislatively. In other words, the state legislature passed a law saying that comparative negligence is the law of the land. But, in a minority of states, the state's highest court (usually called the supreme court) made the change. Under a system of comparative negligence, a jury compares the actions of the parties and then allocates fault between the plaintiff and the defendant. A defendant is obligated to pay only the amount of damages caused by his or her own negligence. So if you're the plaintiff and the jury finds that your own negligence caused 20 percent of the damage, then the defendant would only be responsible for 80 percent of it. To put it another way, your recovery is reduced by your own percentage of negligence.

Most states switched from contributory to comparative negligence between 1969 and 1992. Tennessee became the forty-sixth state to adopt comparative negligence in 1992. Four states (Alabama, Maryland, North Carolina, and Virginia) still use contributory negligence.

There are different types of comparative negligence. Under a "pure" form of comparative negligence, a plaintiff can recover no matter how negligent he or she was. In other words, if a plaintiff suffered $10,000 in damages and was 80 percent at fault in a pure comparative negligence system, he or she still could recover $2,000 ($10,000 − $10,000(.80) = $2,000).

Under a "modified" or "50 percent" system, a plaintiff must be either equal to or less than 50 percent at fault in order to recover. In some states, the plaintiff's negligence must be less than 50 percent. In other states, the plaintiff's negligence must be 50 percent or less in order to recover.

For more on contributory and comparative negligence, access the website of a North Carolina law firm, Glenn, Mills, and Fisher, P.A.: www.gmf-law.com/publications/publications_comparative_negligence.pdf.

those injured up to a specified level, regardless of who was at fault in the accident.

A few states still have **automobile guest statutes,** although there is a strong trend away from them. Many of these statutes have been repealed by legislatures or ruled unconstitutional by courts. These statutes make drivers liable for injuries to nonpaying or guest passengers only if the drivers were "grossly negligent" by failing to use even slight care in their driving. In jurisdictions that still have such laws, the parties often litigate over whether the passenger was a guest. A neighbor also may be able to recover from you under ordinary negligence principles if she can prove that she was not a guest passenger by showing that both of you agreed to share expenses.

Courts also have held a driver liable for the negligent operation of a car and for harm caused by known defects, but not for injuries caused by defects in the vehicle about which the driver had no knowledge.

Q. I sustained an injury when the bus I ride to work was involved in an accident. Is the bus company at fault?

A. Most likely. **Common carriers**—bus lines, airlines, and railroads (even elevators and escalators in some states)—owe their passengers "the highest degree of care" and are held to have a special responsibility to their passengers. Common carriers must exercise extra caution in protecting their riders and do everything they can to keep them safe.

Whether you win your case will depend on the circumstances of the accident. Did the driver pull out in front of a car and have to slam on the brakes? What were the road conditions? A jury will have to consider those factual circumstances to determine if your driver acted negligently. But as an employee of a common carrier, the driver must provide you with a high degree of care. (If the bus were hit by another car, the other driver also may be liable for your injuries.)

Q. My car sustained damage when it hit a pothole on a city street. Can I recover from the city?

A. Some cities have pothole ordinances, a form of immunity that releases them from any liability for pothole accidents, except where they had prior notice. Whether you can recover will depend on your city's law controlling liability and its immunities against suits. For instance, some states have **governmental tort liability acts,** which sharply limit suits against governmental bodies.

Q. I was in a car accident during my pregnancy and my baby was born with a deformity as a result of injuries from the accident. Does my child have any legal recourse?

A. Many states today will permit a lawsuit by a child for the consequences of such prenatal (before birth) injuries. In states with no-fault automobile insurance, your right to sue often is limited. Most courts also will allow a wrongful death action if the baby dies from the injuries after birth.

Q. Someone recently stole my car and then wrecked it, injuring passengers in another vehicle. Now those passengers are trying to sue me. Can they win? Am I responsible?

A. Probably not, since the thief did not have your permission to use the car, although a lot would depend upon the law in your state. Suppose you left your car unlocked with the keys in it, making it easy for the thief to steal. This could be negligence. Even then, most courts generally will not hold you liable if the thief later injures someone by negligent driving. That is because courts hold that you could not foresee that your actions ultimately would result in such injuries.

In a few cases, though, courts have looked at whether your actions caused an unreasonable risk of harm to someone else. If you left your car parked with the engine running, for example, you might be liable if the car thief then injures children playing nearby. In a no-fault state, on the other hand, it might be difficult—if not impossible—for the passengers to sue you.

Q. I was hit by a car that was driven by a drunk driver who was going home after a night out. What can I do, in addition to suing the drunk driver?

A. You may be able to collect from your own uninsured motorist or underinsured motorist coverage for damages you suffered from the drunk driver. In other words, if the drunk driver does not have automobile liability insurance, your uninsured or underinsured coverage from your own policy may provide you some relief.

If you live in a state that has a **Dramshop Act,** you may be able to recover damages from the owner of the tavern where the drunk driver was served the liquor. Such acts usually come into play when intoxicated people served by a bar later injure somebody while driving. Some of those laws also make tavern owners liable when drunken customers injure others on or off the premises. But some courts say that a tavern owner will not be liable unless the sale of the liquor itself was illegal.

Q. My wife was injured when her car was hit by one being driven by some kids who had been drinking at the home of our neighbor. May I take any action against the neighbor, who supplied the liquor to the youths?

A. Possibly. Courts have imposed liability against such neighbors or parents when they have served liquor to minors. Parents can be liable for **negligent supervision** of their children. But as a general rule, courts have said that social hosts are not responsible for the conduct of their guests, unless the hosts routinely allow guests to drink too much or take illegal drugs—and then put them into their cars and send them out on the highway.

Q. I was injured when my automobile collided with a truck driven by a delivery person. Can I recover damages from the driver or the employer?

A. You may be able to recover from both. Under a form of strict liability known as **vicarious lia-**bility, you probably can recover from the delivery person's employer. Under the law, employers may be held liable to third parties for acts committed by employees within the scope of their jobs. Although the employer was not negligent, it becomes indirectly liable for the negligence of its employee. Was the employee making a delivery when the accident occurred? If so, the employer is liable, since making deliveries clearly is part of the driver's job. But if the employee first stopped at a restaurant for drinks and dinner with friends, the employer may be able to escape liability. **Respondeat superior** is a type of vicarious liability used in the employer-employee context. Literally, it means "Let the superior respond." In practice, it means that if you are injured by an employee, you usually can sue the employer.

Q. What is the rationale for vicarious liability?

A. Vicarious means "taking the place of another." In the case of the delivery person, it means that the employer will be liable for the actions of its driver *if* the injury occurred in the course of business and *if* there is a connection between the conduct and what the driver was employed to do. Yes, in theory the driver might be a defendant also, but since the employer presumably has far greater resources than the driver, the employer is the more attractive target of the suit and will face the primary liability.

Many may feel that this concept is unfair to employers, which have to insure against this liability. However, the concept is often justified because it helps secure fair compensation for victims, and gives companies every incentive to deter harmful conduct by maintaining high standards and having rigorous training programs and procedures to guard against these risks.

Q. Is an automobile leasing company vicariously liable when the drivers of leased vehicles get into collisions?

A. Sometimes. In some states, car rental companies are liable for property damage or personal injury caused by operators of leased vehicles under state law. One state supreme court explained the rationale: " . . . to protect the safety of traffic upon highways by providing an incentive to him who rents motor vehicles to rent them to competent and careful operators by making him liable for damages resulting from the [negligent] operation of the rented vehicle." In these states, car rental companies must purchase liability insurance, and pass the cost of that insurance on to the consumer.

In other states, the car rental company is not liable for the renter's negligence. The car renter is primarily liable for damages, and must carry appropriate insurance as a condition of renting the car.

Q. Are there other instances in which a party not directly involved in causing a personal injury might be liable?

A. Yes. Besides vicarious liability per se, there are many other cases in which someone besides the direct perpetrator of the injury *may* be liable to the victim. In these cases, the question is whether the negligence of the third party may have been a fundamental cause of the injury.

Examples include whether a mall owner is liable for attacks in the mall (**premises liability,** discussed on page 537) and whether tavern owners and social hosts are liable for the drunken driving of those to whom they have served alcohol.

Q. A car ran over my dog. Can I recover from the driver?

A. Yes, you might win a lawsuit. A dog is property, and you have suffered property damage. You will have to show that the driver was negligent.

Injuries at Your Home and on Your Property

Q. A furniture delivery person was injured when he tripped over an electrical extension cord in my living room. Can he recover damages from me?

A. He could sue, though it is not certain that he would win. As noted in the sidebar "Different

---

ⓘ A CASE FOR TORT REFORM?

You may have heard of *Liebeck v. McDonald's,* the "spilled hot coffee" case against McDonald's in which it was widely reported that a woman recovered millions of dollars. The case came to be seen as the poster case for tort reform, as the ultimate example of a tort system run amok. But was there more there than met the eye? Or, rather, were there relevant facts that the media failed to report?

An older woman named Stella Liebeck ordered a cup of coffee from a drive-through window at McDonald's. She was sitting in a car driven by her grandson. Ms. Liebeck opened her cup to add sugar and cream when the car was stopped. She spilled the coffee because it was so hot. McDonald's served the coffee twenty degrees higher than industry standard even though they had received more than seven hundred complaints about the temperature of the coffee from customers.

McDonald's refused to pay Liebeck's initial medical expenses of $11,000. She suffered third-degree burns requiring skin grafts over much of her inner thighs. A jury awarded her $200,000 in damages though it found her 20 percent at fault, lowering her recovery to $160,000. The jury also levied $2.7 million in punitive damages. A judge later reduced the award to less than $500,000.

Strokes for Different Folks?" (see page 530), until recently, your liability for someone's personal injuries while at your home hinged on why he or she was there. If people were doing work for you, the law held that you had a special duty to make your home reasonably safe. In those situations, a court would have asked if the cord was dangerous to anyone who came into your living room, or was it only dangerous if someone moved your furniture? Did you warn the delivery person to watch out for the cord? Courts would need the answers to such questions to decide if you are liable to the delivery person. A growing trend would make you liable for the injury only if you failed to exercise a general duty of care.

Q. A door-to-door salesperson tripped on our front steps, injuring himself. May he hold me responsible?

A. Perhaps. A door-to-door salesperson may expect that you will warn him about dangerous conditions on your property that may not be obvious. If your steps were in perfect condition and he merely lost his footing, a court would not hold you responsible. However, if he tripped because one of the stairs was wobbly and you knew about it, you should have repaired it or posted a warning sign.

Q. What if a salesperson, or another passerby, falls on an icy sidewalk in front of my house?

A. In some places, ordinances say that landowners whose property is next to a public sidewalk are responsible for keeping the sidewalk in repair and clear of ice and snow. You might be fined in such a locality if you don't keep the sidewalk clear, but that doesn't necessarily mean that you would be found liable in a personal injury lawsuit.

Elsewhere, owners have no duty to remove natural accumulations of ice and snow that have collected on adjacent public sidewalks. However, they might be found liable for negligence if they attempt to clear the ice and snow and in fact create a more dangerous condition—as when a property owner uses hot water to melt the snow and the water later freezes into a sheet of ice. So the issue isn't so much local law as it is general principles of negligence law.

Q. What about other dangerous conditions on a sidewalk?

A. If landowners fail to take reasonable action to correct other dangerous conditions on sidewalks adjacent to their property, they might be held liable. For example, if there is a dangerous condition on the sidewalk (other than ice and snow) that the landowners knew or should have known about, and they do nothing about the condition, they may be liable in negligence if a person slips and injures himself or herself.

Q. Would I be liable if a trespasser were injured on my property?

A. You generally are not liable for any injury to a trespasser on your property. Suppose, however, that you know certain people continually trespass on your property, perhaps using it as a shortcut. Then a court might find that you should have notified these regular trespassers about any hidden artificial conditions of which you were aware that could seriously injure them.

Q. A group of eight-year-old children has been playing in a vacant lot that I own. Could I be liable if one of them gets injured?

A. Yes, the law generally places a greater burden on landowners when injuries involve children. The reason is that children are too young to understand or appreciate danger in certain situations. Under a legal theory known as the **attractive nuisance doctrine,** owners who know or should know about potentially dangerous artificial conditions on their lot must warn children who are playing there, or must take reasonable precautions to protect them. If, for example, there is machinery or other equipment on your vacant lot that could present an unreasonable risk to children, you should remove it. If you don't, you very well could be liable to the children for any injuries they suffer, even if they were trespassing. In some jurisdictions, the attractive nuisance doctrine is being replaced by a duty of reasonable care under the circumstances.

Q. Our children's friends often come to swim in our backyard pool, even though we are not always able to be there. What if one of them gets hurt?

A. You probably will be liable because you have a legal duty to protect children who are actual or implied invitees from possible harm should they decide to play around a dangerous place on your property. You should make sure an adult is present when children are swimming, though this will not necessarily help you avoid liability. And warning the children that they should not swim without an adult present may not be enough to help you avoid liability if one of them gets injured. Also check with your state or city to find out its requirements for residential swimming pools. Under them, you may have a legal duty to erect barriers or other protective features, such as an automatic pool cover, a tall fence with a good lock that you keep locked, or an alarm on the sliding-glass door from your home to the pool.

Injuries on Others' Property

Q. What if I get injured while at the home of my neighbor, who invited me there for a party?

A. As a social guest, you might be able to recover from your neighbor, depending on how your injuries happened. Homeowners must tell their guests about—or make safe—any dangerous conditions that the guests are unlikely to recognize. Suppose, for example, that your injury was caused when you tripped on a throw rug. You may be able to recover if you can prove that your neighbor knew other people had tripped over it and you were unlikely to realize its danger. Your neighbor probably should have warned you about it, removed it during the party, or secured it to the floor with tape or tacks.

Q. I was walking on a public sidewalk next to a construction site when I tripped and fell on a brick from the site, spraining my ankle. May I recover damages from the construction company?

DIFFERENT STROKES FOR DIFFERENT FOLKS?

Does it matter why the people suing you for injuries that happened on your property were on your property? It used to. Under traditional legal principles, your liability to people injured on your property changed according to the reason they came onto your property. Were they there to visit, to sell, to solicit, to fix something, or to trespass?

The general categories of those injured on another's property were **trespassers, licensees, and invitees.** A landowner owed a higher duty of care to an invitee—someone invited to a home for a business purpose—than to either a licensee or a trespasser. The legal difference was that a landowner had a duty to inspect his or her property for hidden dangers with respect to invitees.

A more recent trend, however, holds landowners or property owners to a general duty of care to prevent injury to anyone coming onto their property, unless the dangerous condition was open and obvious. In other words, some courts today will apply a reasonable person standard of care with respect to landowners.

A. In some circumstances, you will be able to recover damages from the construction company, which has a duty to take reasonable steps to keep sidewalks near its construction sites free from bricks and other debris. If the company fails to remove such obstructions and you trip and fall, the company may be liable for your injuries.

Construction companies also should warn pedestrians that they could be injured if they stray from the sidewalk. But posting a sign is not enough. If a company fails to place barriers or warning lamps by a building pit, for example, it may be responsible if anyone falls into it and gets injured.

Q. I fell on a broken piece of a city sidewalk and injured my ankle. Do I have a case against the city?

A. In many states, municipal immunity statutes prohibit recovery in many kinds of cases against a city or a town. If there is not such a statute or or-

---

ⓘ IF YOU GET INJURED IN A STORE . . .

Suppose you tripped on a spilled can of paint and fell in a hardware store where you were shopping, injuring your foot. Can you recover damages from the store? It depends on the facts of the case. Store-owners must keep their premises reasonably safe for customers, inspecting and discovering any dangerous conditions. They also must keep all aisles clear and properly maintained. A judge or a jury will look at whether the owner was aware that the paint can was in the aisle and how long it had been there. But a judge or a jury also might find that you discovered the spilled paint and proceeded to walk right through it. Then the judge or the jury might deny your damages claim or find you're comparatively at fault, thus reducing your recovery.

---

dinance, however, you may have a case. Municipalities have a duty to keep streets and sidewalks in good repair. You might have a successful case against the city if you can show that it failed to maintain the sidewalk properly or knew of the dangerous condition and had the opportunity to fix it but failed to do so.

Q. My son received an injury during basic training in the U.S. Army. May he recover damages from the federal government?

A. No. People in the armed services who receive injuries during the course of their duties are not permitted to recover for their injuries. The Federal Tort Claims Act (FTCA) allows people to sue the United States for certain tortious acts committed by its employees. However, the U.S. Supreme Court has stated that there is a broad exception for those serving in the military. The Court explained in a 1950 case that "the Government is not liable under the Federal Tort Claims Act for injuries to servicemen where the injuries arise out of or are in the course of activity incident to service."

For other kinds of claims, the Federal Tort Claims Act provides that the federal government can be sued in tort "in the same manner and to the same extent as a private individual under the circumstances." People injured by federal governmental employees who act within the scope of their office may bring suit in a federal district court against the government for negligent acts. A high proportion of such claims arise out of automobile accidents. Before suing in federal district court, the aggrieved person first files a claim with the appropriate administrative agency that allegedly caused the harm. If the agency fails to respond to or rejects the claim within six months, the person can sue in federal court. The federal courts must follow the law of the state in which the tort allegedly occurred. The federal judge serves as the judge and jury (fact finder) in these cases. There are many exceptions under the FTCA. A person injured by a federal governmental employee should consult a lawyer who is well versed in this area of the law.

Q. My daughter and her friends went snowmobiling on a nearby farm. When the vehicle ran into a fence, one of them got hurt. The farmer now says he is not liable. Is that true?

A. If landowners know that others are using their land for snowmobiling, most states say they must warn snowmobilers about hidden dangerous conditions or remove them. Was the fence visible? Did the farmer recently build it? A few states, such as Michigan, have laws specifically dealing with liability when someone uses property for recreational purposes without permission. In those states, the farmer probably would not be liable if he did not authorize the group to be on his land and had not acted recklessly. You might want to ask a lawyer about your state's law.

Q. I was injured on a ski lift. May I recover against the ski resort?

A. Possibly. Can you prove that the resort was negligent? Remember that some states have laws limiting the liability of resorts, saying that there are certain risks that a person assumes when skiing. However, some states hold that ski lifts are common carriers, like buses. They have higher duties than others, so in one of these states you might have an excellent case.

Medical Malpractice

Q. What is medical malpractice?

A. Medical malpractice is negligence committed by a professional health-care provider—a doctor, a nurse, a dentist, a technician, or a hospital or nursing facility—whose performance of duties departs from a standard of practice of those with similar training and experience, resulting in harm to a patient. Most medical malpractice actions are filed against doctors and hospitals.

▶ AVOIDING LIABILITY IF YOU'RE A LANDLORD

In recent years, many states have required landlords to maintain residential property in "habitable" condition by imposing a warranty of habitability. If you're a landlord, a violation of that warranty could result in your being sued for failing to maintain the property and thus violating the warranty. But negligence claims are also possible. If guests are injured when a back porch that is part of a unit collapses during a party, the landlord probably would be held liable, especially if he or she had been warned that the porch was sagging or was infested with termites but had not repaired it. Of course, the landlord may be able to argue that the porch collapsed because there were too many people on it.

Landlords also must maintain any common area of the building—including stairs, corridors, and walkways—for both tenants and guests of the building. If a guest is injured when she trips over some loose carpeting in a corridor, for example, the landlord generally would be liable.

If you are a landlord, there are ways to reduce your chances of liability. Consider having your insurance company inspect the premises and then promptly repair any safety problems the inspector uncovers. If you inspect the premises yourself, look for unsafe wiring, loose railings, poor lighting, or similar flaws. You might also write tenants a letter each year asking them to point out hazards or needed repairs they may have noticed. If a tenant who lives in the building every day fails to notice a hazard, it is hard to argue that the landlord should know about it. However, that still may not protect you in a suit by someone who is injured while visiting.

The profession itself sets the standard for malpractice by its own custom and practice.

Q. Hasn't there been talk about changing the way that malpractice cases are handled?

A. Yes. Starting in the 1980s and continuing into the twenty-first century, doctors and members of the insurance industry have said there was a "malpractice crisis," with spiraling insurance premiums and unreasonably high jury verdicts. In response, some states passed laws capping damage awards, limiting lawyers' fees, and shortening the time period in which plaintiffs could bring malpractice suits. Some states instituted no-fault liability for malpractice claims, or developed arbitration panels to hear medical malpractice claims before they could be filed in court to be determined by a judge or jury. California limited recovery for pain and suffering in malpractice lawsuits.

Q. What do I do if I think I have a medical malpractice claim?

A. Talk to a lawyer who specializes in such work. Tell the lawyer exactly what happened to you, from the first time you visited your doctor through your last contact with him or her. Gather all your medical records from all your doctors and hospitals. They have to provide you with copies if you ask for them. (They may charge you copying costs.)

What were the circumstances surrounding your illness or injury? How did your doctor treat it? What did your doctor tell you about your treatment? Did you follow your doctor's instructions? What happened to you? Answers to these and other relevant questions become important if you think your doctor may have committed malpractice. Your lawyer will look at all this information and may have it reviewed by a doctor. Your lawyer might tell you that the care you received was proper or that a suit is warranted.

Q. How does a jury determine if a doctor's actions were within the standards of good medical practice?

A. A jury will consider testimony by experts—usually other doctors—who will testify whether they believe your physician's actions followed standard medical practice or fell below the accepted standard of care. In fact, many states require a plaintiff in a medical malpractice case to have expert testimony supporting the plaintiff's position. In deciding whether your heart surgeon was negligent, for example, a jury will be told to rely on expert testimony to determine what a competent heart surgeon would have done under the same or similar circumstances. A specialist, like a heart surgeon, is held to a higher standard of care than that expected of a nonspecialist.

Q. I signed a consent form before my doctor performed surgery. What did it really mean?

A. It is standard practice in hospitals for patients to sign a form giving the doctor their consent, or approval, to perform surgery. In the form, the patient usually consents to the specific surgery as well as to any other procedures that might become necessary. Before you sign it, your doctor should give you a full description of the surgery and the risks involved, as well as the ramifications of forgoing such treatment.

If you can prove that your physician misrepresented the facts or failed adequately to inform you of the risks and benefits before surgery, your consent may be invalid. The only time the law excuses doctors from providing such information is in emergencies or when it would be harmful to a patient. But even if your doctor should have secured your consent and did not, you still may not automatically recover damages. You may still have to prove that if adequately informed, a reasonable person would not have consented to the surgery.

Q. If the consent form is considered valid, can I recover any damages in a malpractice action against my doctor?

A. Yes, you still may be able to recover damages. A consent form does not release a physician from liability who did not perform the operation following established procedures or who was otherwise negligent. You may also have a claim that the surgery performed went beyond the consent you gave. In such a case, the doctor might even be liable for battery.

Q. What if I'm just not satisfied with the results of my surgery? Do I have a malpractice case?

A. In general, there are no guarantees of favorable medical results. In order to prevail in a medical malpractice case, you would have to show an injury or damages that resulted from the doctor's deviation from the appropriate standard of care for your condition.

Q. I became pregnant even though my husband had a vasectomy. Can we recover damages?

A. Yes, you may be able to win such a case. A number of negligence cases have been permitted against physicians for performing unsuccessful vasectomies or other methods of sterilization that resulted in unwanted children. Courts increasingly allow a suit to be filed by the parents of a child born as a result of wrongful conception or wrongful pregnancy. Damages generally are lim-

---

⚠ AS TIME GOES BY

Assuming that you have a claim that supports a lawsuit, a malpractice suit may take anywhere from two to seven years. If the judgment or verdict is appealed for some reason, it will take even longer. The time frame for your case will depend on how complicated your claim is, as well as the number of cases that were scheduled for trial before yours. It's because of factors like these, and the uncertainties of litigation, that most malpractice cases are settled before trial.

---

ited to those associated with the pregnancy and birth and do not extend to support of the child.

Q. I don't think it was necessary for me to have a cesarean section when I delivered my daughter. Is there anything I can do about it?

A. Although most malpractice cases involving cesarean sections are brought against doctors

---

ⓘ SHOULD YOU STOP AND HELP SOMEONE IN AN EMERGENCY?

Generally, you do not have a duty to stop and help someone in an emergency. The law says that if you did not cause the problem and if you and the victim have no special relationship you need not try to rescue a person. (Of course, you always are free to go voluntarily to the aid of someone in trouble.)

To encourage people to help, many states have passed so-called **Good Samaritan laws** that excuse doctors—and sometimes other helpers—from liability for negligence for coming to the aid of someone in an emergency. Some states' Good Samaritan laws will protect a rescuer from ordinary negligence, but still allow them to be sued for so-called gross (extreme) negligence.

In some states, if you injure someone while driving, you must help that injured person, regardless of who was at fault. Some courts look at the circumstances of the rescue. They say that if you know someone is in extreme danger that could be avoided with little inconvenience on your part, you must provide reasonable care to the victim. But if you abandon your rescue efforts after starting them, you may be liable if you leave a victim in worse condition than you found him or her.

who did not perform them when they should have, with resulting injuries to the mother or child, it is possible for a woman to win damages against her doctors for unnecessarily delivering her child by cesarean section. It still would be necessary for an expert to state that in doing the cesarean section, the delivering doctor deviated from the appropriate standard of care.

Q. My aunt discovered that a sponge left in her during an operation years ago was the source of stomach trouble. May she still sue?

A. Like other personal injury cases, medical malpractice lawsuits are subject to specific statutes of limitations (discussed on page 521). Until recently, your aunt's suit may have been thrown out of court. In many statutes, time limits on filing began when the injury occurred—on the day of the operation. To alleviate such a harsh and final result, many states today have altered their laws, and the clock for filing a case does not begin to tick until people discover that they have suffered an injury, or should have discovered it.

Q. How much can I win?

A. Forget about those huge sums you read about in the newspaper. It may seem that people are walking out of courtrooms with wheelbarrows full of money, but in reality, those cases are few and far between. In the majority of malpractice cases, the doctor wins. Moreover, many states put a limit, known as a **damages cap**, on the amount of punitive damages that may be awarded and on noneconomic damages such as pain and suffering. Others states have damages caps for medical malpractice cases generally. The health-care lobby has argued that there must be a limit on damages in order to prevent the rise of malpractice insurance and health-care costs that are passed on to patients/consumers.

The dollar amounts of these caps vary, though they are often in the hundreds of thousands of dollars. While that still may sound like a lot of money, remember that you will have to pay large lawyer's fees, or perhaps a percentage of your award in a contingency arrangement. There is a good chance that you will get less than the amount of the cap. The doctor may appeal if you win, or the judge may reduce the amount of your award. Do not think of medical malpractice as a way to hit the jackpot. Think of it as a way to provide minimum compensation for your injuries.

Q. What exactly is a damages cap?

A. A damages cap limits the amount of money a jury may award to you in a malpractice case. The damages cap varies by state. Some states do not cap damages at all, claiming that to do so would violate that state's constitution. Indiana caps damages at $500,000, while California caps damages at $250,000. States may put a limit on

---

ⓘ DUTY OF CARE FOR THE ELDERLY

With Americans living longer and longer, the nursing-home population is growing rapidly. Care for the elderly, in nursing homes or elsewhere, can give rise to personal injury claims. Let's say a ninety-five-year-old woman has Alzheimer's and lives in a nursing home. She wanders off unsupervised and is hit by a car. She is not competent to testify or to begin a lawsuit, but nonetheless her rights can be protected.

Incompetent adults can have a guardian or conservator appointed to protect them and sue on their behalf. Several states have enacted special statutes to protect the frail and elderly from abuse by those hired to protect them. A lawyer skilled in representing the elderly can help evaluate these claims.

punitive damages only, or on both punitive damages and any money that compensates you for your injury alone. Putting caps on damages is a hot topic in legal and political circles. The type of cap may vary from state to state, but look for more states to put a cap on damages in the coming years.

Q. Why would a state put a cap on damages?

A. A cap on damages discourages people from bringing lawsuits simply because they think they can win a lot of money. When there are fewer lawsuits, the cost of your health care goes down (theoretically) because doctors are not passing on the insurance costs to you.

Q. Can the jury get around the damages cap?

A. Usually. For that reason, some states do not allow lawyers or judges to tell the jurors that there is a damages cap. That way, the jurors will not be tempted to change their decision about other compensation for the victim. The point is to keep the legal process fair for both you and the doctor. For instance, let's say you live in a state where the cap is $100,000. The jury knows about the cap and decides that you suffered a minor injury. The jury may start with the $100,000 and decide that you deserve a quarter of that because your injury was minor. That leaves you with $25,000. If the jury had not known about the cap, they might have started

with a figure of $500,000 and awarded you a quarter of that, which is $125,000. Because of the cap, you would only receive $100,000 of that award, but that would still be much more than the $25,000 you would have gotten if the jury knew of the cap.

On the other hand, it is not fair for the jury to award you a million dollars simply because they think the doctor's insurance will cover it, regardless of whether the doctor actually caused your injury. A sympathetic jury is not always a fair jury. The damages cap may protect the doctor from a jury that is disproportionately sympathetic toward you.

Some Special Situations

Q. What about malpractice actions against professionals such as lawyers? I recently hired a lawyer who seemed inexperienced, and I was unhappy with the outcome of the case.

A. Like doctors, lawyers and other professionals must possess and apply the knowledge and the skills of other reasonably qualified professionals. Not only must they exercise reasonable care in handling your case, they also must possess a minimum degree of special knowledge and ability. That means that they will be liable to you if their skills do not meet the accepted standard of practice. You also must prove that the case your lawyer mishandled was likely to succeed. Lawyer malpractice usually results in money damages only. You cannot recover for the emotional distress of hiring a negligent lawyer.

In your case, you may have a malpractice action against the lawyer if he or she was negligent in representing you. You'll have to show more than dissatisfaction with the outcome of the case. Did he or she fail to meet a deadline for filing for a court proceeding? Were all the crucial legal elements of the case fully explored? If you are unsure about a basis for a malpractice case, check with the state agency that regulates lawyers in your state. Your state bar association will be able to tell you the name of the agency.

> ▶ **NOT A GET-RICH-QUICK PROPOSITION**
>
> Doctors win most malpractice lawsuits. Very few patients receive large sums of money. Media attention in those cases, however, may make it seem as though winning a malpractice claim is as easy as hitting the jackpot. It's not.

Q. *My daughter, who plays on the local park's basketball team, brought home a note asking us to sign a form saying we won't hold the park district responsible for injuries. What is that?*

A. You are talking about a **waiver of liability** that is intended contractually to release the organization from any liability should an injury occur. If you are worried about the safety of the activity, you should check out the facility and the coach before you sign the form.

If you must either sign such a form or deprive your child of the chance to participate in the activity, a court may hold that your waiver is not really voluntary and thus not valid. Furthermore, even in those states that recognize waivers, signing the waiver might not mean that you are giving up your right to sue entirely. If an injury results because of intentional or reckless behavior, you probably will be able to seek damages. Some states allow volunteer coaches immunity from actions in negligence if they complete a safety training class.

Q. *I was staying at a motel when there was a fire, but there was no water sprinkler system and no escape route posted in the room. Isn't the motel required to have those safety precautions?*

A. The motel management probably should have exercised reasonable care in maintaining the fire alarms and fire escapes, and they should have helped you escape. As in the case of the common carrier (see page 526), the law generally says that innkeepers, who have a special relationship with their guests, have a higher duty of care.

Q. *Someone attacked my daughter on the campus of the college she attends. May she hold the school responsible for this attack?*

A. Your daughter may have a negligence action against the college. In a developing area of law known as **premises liability,** some courts have found such entities as universities, motels, convenience stores, and shopping malls liable for attacks because they did not exercise reasonable care in preventing victims from being harmed. However, courts are divided on this issue, and plaintiffs bear a heavy burden of proof in showing that the crime was foreseeable. The most important factor is whether there had been similar crimes in the location. A court would also consider what security precautions the college had taken.

Q. *I was attacked after withdrawing money from an automated teller machine (ATM). What can I do?*

A. Under the tort theory of premises liability discussed above, customers have sued banks for failing to protect them from assault at ATMs. While

---

ⓘ LIABILITY AT SPORTING EVENTS

Suppose you went to a baseball game, and a ball that a player hit into the stands injured you. What can you do? Spectators at a baseball game know they may be injured by a flying foul ball. That is why courts generally say that spectators assume the risk of being hurt by a ball. The same usually holds true if a golf ball hits you while you are watching a golf match. Likewise, if you are struck by a wheel from a car in an automobile race that flies into the stands, the courts will hold that you assumed the risk of getting hurt. The legal term for this doctrine is **assumption of the risk.** It means that you agreed to face a known danger. But if there is a hole in a screen intended to protect spectators at the baseball park, you then probably could argue that it was negligence not to have it repaired.

there used to be no common-law duty to provide security against such crimes, some courts today have recognized such a duty.

A key question would be whether the crime was a reasonably foreseeable danger. The business owner will argue that third-party criminal attacks are inherently unforeseeable, and that the act of the third party, the criminal, is an intervening, superseding act that breaks the chain of causation. In other words, they will argue that the true cause of the harm is the act of the third party.

You may be able to overcome these arguments if you can show that the business owner knew or should have known about prior incidents of crime at or near the location. In such a case, a judge or jury would determine if there were past occurrences and if a likelihood of a crime was foreseeable. If so, they may hold that the bank had a duty to protect people using that machine and that the bank was liable.

Recently, the banking industry has been successful in limiting banks' liability if they comply with security and lighting requirements.

Q. Is there anything else crime victims may do?

A. Yes. Most states have laws compensating victims of violent crimes for lost wages, counseling, and medical expenses. Many states also have victim assistance programs. Check with your local prosecutor's office (possibly called the office of the state's attorney or district attorney).

Q. We recently got a call from the hospital where someone had taken my mother. The hospital told us that she had died of a heart attack. In fact, she had not died or suffered a heart attack, and the hospital was simply mistaken. The hospital's false report devastated us. What can we do?

A. The circumstances you describe are rare. Nonetheless, you may be able to recover from the hospital for the **negligent infliction of emotional distress**. That is, you may be able to sue the hospital for negligently causing you to endure emotional pain. Courts generally have maintained that a person must have physical injuries to recover in such cases, but courts in some states have allowed recovery when there are no physical injuries. Other successful emotional distress suits have involved bystanders. For example, a court allowed a mother who saw her child fatally hit by a car to recover money damages against the driver of the car.

Q. The store where I bought my wedding gown failed to deliver it in time for the ceremony. What can I do?

A. Although you no doubt suffered some distress, it is unlikely that you have a personal injury case. The store was negligent in failing to get your dress to you on time. Although it may have been traumatic for you, you generally would have to show a physical manifestation of the mental anguish. You may, however, have a case for breach of contract. You can find more information about what to do in this kind of situation in chapter 9, "Contracts and Consumer Law."

THE WORLD AT YOUR FINGERTIPS

- *General information on auto accident law can be found at accident-law.freeadvice. com/auto.*
- *The website LawGuru has a frequently asked questions (FAQs) section on auto accident law at www.lawguru.com/faq/1. html.*
- *For FAQs on slip-and-fall cases, see accident-law.freeadvice.com/slips_falls.*
- *Nolo.com has FAQs on landlord liability for tenant injuries under the heading "Landlords and Tenants" at www.nolo.com/ index.cfm.*
- *MedMalUSA is a website that has discussions on several major areas of medical practice and malpractice; access it at www.medmalusa.us.*

- *The Lectric Law Library on Medical Malpractice offers much practical litigation information; visit the website at www. lectlaw.com/tmed.html.*

REMEMBER THIS

- *Negligence refers to unreasonable conduct that injures another person. To be negligent, a person must have acted unreasonably, or below the general standard of care of a reasonable person. A judge or jury usually determines what is reasonable.*

- *Common carriers owe their passengers a high degree of care.*
- *Landowners owe a duty of care to those who come onto their property. In some cases, even a trespasser can recover in tort from a landowner, if the landowner is aware of a dangerous condition that is not obvious to third parties upon reasonable inspection.*
- *Landowners should be particularly careful if their land contains what is known as an attractive nuisance—an object (for exam-*

ⓘ IF YOU GET INJURED AT WORK

Workers' compensation laws, currently in place in all fifty states and the District of Columbia, cover most workers injured on the job. Under these laws, employers compensate you for your injuries, including medical expenses, lost wages, and permanent or temporary disability, regardless of who was at fault. All you have to do is give notice to your employer and file a claim with the state's workers' compensation commission or board. (See chapter 12, "Law and the Workplace," for more details.)

Legislatures created the laws because they thought that liability for workplace accidents should be placed on the one most able to bear the loss—the employer. Before the advent of workers' compensation laws, employees were required to sue their employers in tort actions. These suits were often unsuccessful because of several defenses available to employers, such as contributory negligence, assumption of the risk, or the **fellow-servant rule,** which held that an employer was not liable for an injury caused to an employee by the negligence of a co-worker. These defenses made it hard for employees to recover any monies. Thus, legislatures passed workers' compensation laws in the early part of the twentieth century. The statutes fall under strict liability principles discussed later in this chapter (see page 540), so no employer or employee negligence or fault need be shown. In fact, the statutes prohibit employees from filing tort claims against their employers for conditions covered by the law. Instead, an employee gets paid according to a fixed schedule of benefits, regardless of who was at fault.

In the unlikely event that you are not covered by such a law, you may be able to recover from your employer on a negligence claim. To do so, you must show that your employer failed to exercise reasonable care in providing you with safe working conditions or that your employer failed to warn you of unsafe conditions that you were unlikely to discover. Other possible suits against your employer might include an action alleging an intentional injury or an intentional disregard of your safety. Or your spouse might sue for loss of consortium. (See chapter 3, "Family Law," for more details.)

ple, a swimming pool) that is likely to attract trespassing children.

- *If you slip and fall in a store and injure yourself, you may have a claim against the storeowner. Storeowners must keep their premises reasonably safe for their customers.*

- *Spectators generally cannot sue for injuries suffered at a sporting event because many courts will hold that the spectator assumed the risk, for instance, that they may be struck by a foul ball at a baseball game.*

- *If you are injured on the job, your remedy generally will be limited to a workers' compensation claim, rather than a personal injury tort action. Every state's workers' compensation law is different. You may need to consult a lawyer who specializes in workers' compensation law to ensure that you are treated fairly.*

- *Medical malpractice is a form of professional negligence. Physicians and other health-care providers can be liable if they do not adhere to the necessary standard of care.*

- *Medical malpractice actions, like other tort actions, are subject to statutes of limitations. States provide for an exception in that a plaintiff generally has one year after he or she reasonably discovered the alleged malpractice to commence a lawsuit.*

STRICT LIABILITY

A truck is driving down the road carrying ultrahazardous chemicals. The driver of the truck is traveling within the speed limit. Suddenly, a bicycle pulls in front of the truck. The driver swerves violently to avoid crushing the cyclist. The driver succeeds in avoiding the cyclist but flips the truck. The truck then ex-plodes into flames, causing extensive injuries to several bystanders.

This section covers issues related to strict liability. In the example above, may the bystanders sue the company in tort even though the driver was not at fault and certainly did not intend to harm anyone? In other words, can the victims pursue a claim of strict liability? Can the company be held strictly liable for carrying the hazardous materials?

Q. Is there any other basis for liability besides negligence?

A. Courts hold some people or companies **strictly liable** for certain activities that harm others, even when they have not acted negligently or with wrongful intent.

For example, people or companies engaged in blasting, storing dangerous, toxic substances, or keeping dangerous animals can be strictly liable for harm caused to others. Strict liability standards also apply in other areas of personal injury, such as workplace accidents. The most prominent example of strict liability is in product liability cases—holding manufacturers liable for injuries their products cause. (For more information on product liability, see page 542.)

Q. What is the rationale behind "strict liability"?

A. The theory behind imposing strict liability on those conducting inherently dangerous activities is that these activities pose an undue risk of harm to members of the community. Thus, anyone who conducts such an activity does so at his own risk and is liable when something goes wrong—even innocently—and someone is harmed. The people who posed the risk are in the best position to pay for it.

Q. We live near a site where a gasoline company stores its flammable liquids. Would we be able to recover damages if an accident were to occur?

A. Probably. Courts have found such storage to be an inherently dangerous activity. This means that the act is hazardous by its very nature, whether it is done well or poorly. Courts normally are likely to impose strict liability against the company for injuries that an accident may cause.

Courts still might look at the location of the storage, however. If storage in the middle of a large city poses unusual and unacceptable risks, then courts might impose strict liability. The same holds true when a factory emits smoke, dust, or noxious gases in the middle of a town. But a company may not be held strictly liable if it conducts such activities in a remote rural area and is not doing the activity in any unusual manner.

Q. What if one of my animals escapes from our fenced-in yard and goes onto our neighbor's property?

A. In most jurisdictions, keepers of all animals, including domesticated ones, are strictly liable for damages resulting from the trespass of their animals on another person's property. But courts make exceptions for the owners of dogs and cats, saying they are not strictly liable for trespasses unless the owner is negligent or where strict liability is imposed by statute or ordinance for certain breeds of dogs with aggressive traits (pit bulls, for example).

Q. Am I automatically liable if my dog, normally a friendly and playful pet, turns on my neighbor and bites her?

A. It may depend on where you live. A number of jurisdictions have enacted dog-bite statutes, which hold owners strictly liable for injuries inflicted by their animals. If there is no such law in your town, you still can be found liable under a common-law negligence claim if you knew the animal was likely to cause that kind of injury and failed to exercise due care in controlling the pet. If, on the other hand, you did not know or have any reason to suspect that your dog had such a dangerous trait, courts have said that owners generally are not liable. It is important that you contact your local animal control department to find out about any regulations in your area.

ⓘ TOXIC TORT CASES

Toxic torts are cases of mass torts that involve many plaintiffs suing multiple defendants for the damages resulting from harmful exposure to various harmful (toxic) substances. Toxic tort cases can be difficult to prove. There is often a big legal dispute as to the cause of the plaintiffs' harm in these cases. Were their damages caused by long-term exposure to the toxins, or were their damages caused by factors peculiar to their individual environments (relative of a smoker, proclivity to a certain health condition, etc.)?

Examples of toxic torts include asbestos litigation, breast implant litigation, lead exposure litigation, litigation involving radiation spills, litigation over long-term exposure to chemical solvents, and the classic Agent Orange litigation from Vietnam. The cases become class-action lawsuits because a number of people allegedly were injured by exposure to a certain toxin or pollutant. Many cases like these are settled for millions of dollars paid by the defendant, but since there are so many plaintiffs, each person may receive only a few thousand dollars.

Several websites offer further perspectives on toxic torts.

- There is a forum about toxic tort law at www.toxlaw.com.
- A law review article from the Washburn University School of Law on toxic tort litigation is available at washburnlaw.edu/wlj/41-3/articles/kann.pdf.

Q. Our neighbors have a vicious watch-dog. We are scared to death that the dog will bite one of our children, who often wander into the neighbor's yard. What can we do?

A. The situation you describe is a common one and, as in the example above, is precisely the reason a number of municipalities regulate dog ownership, especially of vicious dogs, through ordinances. A great deal would depend on the ordinance that applies where you live. Unless your neighbor posts adequate warnings, he may be strictly liable for injuries caused by a vicious watchdog. (And even if he does post warnings, they may not be sufficient if a child is injured, since children may not be able to read or fully comprehend what they can read.) Even if the dog never bit before, such liability is imposed because of the mere fact that the breed of dog is known to be vicious—or has certain dangerous traits.

Product Liability

Q. How does strict liability apply to product liability cases?

A. Strict product liability, now the law in nearly every state, allows an action against a manufacturer that sells any defective product that causes an injury to a buyer or anyone who uses it. A product can be defective in design, manufacture, or labeling.

ⓘ VISITING A ZOO

Zoos go to great extremes to protect visitors from the risks posed by their animals. Generally, they restrain or confine the animals. For that reason, courts usually do not impose strict liability when a visitor to a zoo gets injured. Instead, the visitor must show that the zoo was somehow negligent in how it kept the animal.

Strict liability holds designers and manufacturers strictly liable for injuries from defective products. If you are injured by a defective product, you do not have to establish negligence of the manufacturer. Rather, you need to show that the product was defective—designed or manufactured in a manner that made it unreasonably dangerous when used as intended.

Q. I was opening a jar of pickles when it exploded in my face and flying glass cut me. Was somebody at fault?

A. Yes, someone was at fault, since jars ordinarily do not explode in a person's face. Courts often decide such cases under principles of strict liability, meaning that instead of having to prove that someone was negligent, a plaintiff would only have to prove that the jar exploded and that he or she was injured by it.

Some courts continue to decide such cases under negligence principles, however. If the manufacturer sealed the jar and it was handled carefully between the time it left the manufacturer's possession and the time of the explosion, some courts assume—or consider it circumstantial evidence—that the manufacturer was negligent.

Q. Our brand-new power mower back-fired and injured me. From whom may I recover damages?

A. This is a typical product liability case. Not only can you sue the mower's manufacturer, but you can also sue the distributor and the retailer. You may also have a claim against the assembler of a specific part of a product. If the manufacturer hired a design consultant, a quality-control engineer, or a technical writer to help with the instructions, these individuals could also be liable.

Q. A disclaimer that came with the lawn mower said the manufacturer did not warranty it in any way. Will that defeat our claim?

A. While limited warranties are sometimes enforced by courts, full disclaimers often are not. Courts find such warranties invalid because you, as the consumer, are not in an equal bargaining position. They also rule that such clauses are **unconscionable** (grossly unfair) and contrary to public policy. (See the discussion of contracts of adhesion and unconscionability in chapter 9, "Contracts and Consumer Law.") Most courts limit the effect of limited warranties to repairs. A limited warranty is not a waiver of liability for injuries.

Q. A toy my grandson was playing with came apart, and he put one of the pieces in his mouth and started choking. Do we have any redress against the toy manufacturer?

A. The federal **Consumer Product Safety Commission (CPSC)** closely monitors such products. Like others that put products into commerce, toy manufacturers have a duty to consider any foreseeable misuse of their products.

You do not have any redress if all your grandson did was gag and spit out the part, with no damage caused. If, on the other hand, he choked and stopped breathing, causing brain damage, then you probably would have an action against the manufacturer. As in any strict liability action, several questions would need to be answered to determine the manufacturer's culpability. Did it have a duty to warn of the danger of the toy falling apart? If so, what was the likelihood that it would break into small parts that could be dangerous to a small child? Was anyone supervising your grandson while he was playing?

Because toy manufacturers outside the United States can be difficult to sue, you also might want to consider suing other parties in the toy's chain of distribution—the toy store, for example, or perhaps a fast-food chain that distributed the toy as part of a promotion. Such retailers also can be liable for injuries.

Q. I suffered a severe allergic reaction to some cosmetics I used and needed medical treatment. May I recover money from the manufacturer?

A. Perhaps. Did the manufacturer warn you that the cosmetic could cause such a reaction? Some

courts normally will not hold the manufacturer liable for failing to warn you of the risk of an adverse reaction unless you can prove that an ingredient in the product would give a number of people an adverse reaction. You also must prove that the manufacturer knew or should have known this and that your reaction was because you were in that group of sensitive people, and not because you are hypersensitive. In addition, courts will determine whether you used the product according to the directions provided with it. Misuse is a defense recognized in strict liability. If the court does not find strict liability, you still might recover on a negligence claim.

Q. I got hepatitis from a blood transfusion. Is someone liable?

A. In many states, laws protect suppliers against strict liability when people who receive blood transfusions contract an illness from contaminated blood. However, you may recover if you can show negligence by the supplier.

Q. My father's job exposed him to asbestos. Now he has lung disease. Is it too late to file a claim?

A. It may not be too late. Many people who suffered injuries from toxic substances such as asbestos did not know at the time of exposure that the compounds were harmful. As a result, some states have enacted laws allowing people to file lawsuits for a certain amount of time from the date when the lung impairment or cancer begins, rather than from the date of exposure. A lawyer can tell you whether your father still has time within the statutes of limitations applicable in your state.

Q. I was injured because of a brake defect in a used car I bought. May I recover from the dealer?

A. At least one used car dealer has been subject to a negligence action for failing to inspect or discover such defects. But courts are split on whether dealers in used goods should be subject to strict liability. Holding them strictly liable appears to be a minority position.

ⓘ BREAST IMPLANT LITIGATION

There have been thousands of lawsuits filed by women who have undergone breast implantation and now allege that the implants contributed to a wide array of health problems, ranging from cancer and autoimmune diseases to joint pains and interference with cancer detection. In addition to saying that both silicone breast implants and other artificial implants were responsible for adverse health effects in them, women have alleged that the implants caused miscarriage and harmful effects in their children, some of them because they were breast-fed. The suits generally say that the manufacturers were negligent and that they knew the product was defective.

Many states have provided special extended statutes of limitations for breast implant and asbestos cases. For example, while a typical statute of limitations in an auto accident is one year, some states provide that in breast implant or asbestos cases the period can be as long as twenty or twenty-five years.

MegaLaw provides many links to pages on breast implant litigation and related areas at www.megalaw.com/top/breast.php.

THE WORLD AT YOUR FINGERTIPS

- *There are several agencies that have helpful background material on their websites. The federal Consumer Product Safety Commission (CPSC)—www.cpsc.gov—for example, regulates many products put into commerce, including toys, and could be helpful if you believe a product is defective. The federal Food and Drug Administration (FDA)—www.fda.gov—regulates drugs and other items, like breast implants, that have been subject to recent litigation.*

- *Cornell Law School, as part of its Legal Information Institute, offers a product liability overview and links to the applicable legislation at www.law.cornell.edu/topics/products_liability.html.*

▶ WHAT YOU SHOULD DO IF YOU ARE INJURED BY A PRODUCT

- Keep the evidence. If a heating fixture ruptures and injures someone in your family, keep as many pieces of the equipment as you can find and disturb the site as little as possible.
- Make note of the name of the manufacturer, the model, and the serial number.
- Keep any packaging or instructions.
- Keep any receipts showing when and where the product was purchased.
- Take pictures of the site and of the injury.
- Make a record of exactly when the incident occurred and under what circumstances.
- Be sure you have accurate names and addresses for all doctors and hospitals treating the injury.

- ProductsLaw.com has a great deal of information on products liability lawsuits; see the website at www.productslaw.com.

REMEMBER THIS

- Even though negligence is the most common standard or theory of tort law, strict liability applies in certain circumstances, including injuries resulting from abnormally dangerous activities, injuries caused by wild or trespassing animals, and certain product liability cases.
- Some jurisdictions will hold dog owners strictly liable for injuries caused by their dogs. Other jurisdictions will hold the owners liable only if they knew of their dog's vicious tendencies.
- There are different types of product liability actions. The three most common are manufacturing defects, design defects, and failure to warn cases.
- If you are injured by a product, keep the evidence. Keep all receipts showing when the product was purchased. Make detailed records of when the incident occurred and what happened.

INTENTIONAL WRONGS

A woman with a large, baggy purse enters a store. She kneels down and begins examining various products. The store has just hired a security guard because of a recent rash of shoplifting incidents. The guard believes that the woman is stealing. The guard tells the store manager, who confronts the woman. The woman denies taking any items.

Undeterred, the manager and the guard take the woman to the back of the store and call the police. They prevent the woman from leaving until they question her. A female police officer then comes and strip-searches the woman. No items are found. The police and

the store manager then apologize profusely to the distraught woman.

Can the woman sue the store, the store manager, and the police for false imprisonment? Can the shop argue that it has a privilege to detain persons suspected of shoplifting for a reasonable period of time?

Q. What are intentional torts?

A. **Intentional torts** are those in which the wrongdoer intends to act in a certain way. For example, let's say Jack picks up a golf club, swings it at Jill, and hits her in the shoulder. Jack has committed the intentional torts of assault and battery. He intended to strike Jill, causing harm.

Q. But isn't hitting someone a crime?

A. It can be. Conduct that forms the basis for an intentional tort can lead to both criminal and civil proceedings. In the above example, Jack can be criminally charged by the state and sued by Jill in a tort action. The state's action is criminal law, while Jill's action is a civil tort action.

Q. What are some typical intentional torts?

A. There are intentional torts against a person and property. Some common intentional torts against a person include assault, battery, defamation, false imprisonment, and intentional infliction of emotional distress.

There are also intentional torts against property. These include trespass to land, trespass to **chattel** (personal property), and **conversion** (converting someone else's property into your own).

Q. Is a civil lawsuit based on liability for an intentional tort different from a lawsuit based on negligence or strict liability?

A. Not really. You may claim the same types of damages, but you must prove different things. A person who is found liable for an intentional tort does more than just act carelessly. The person committing the intentional tort knows the consequences of his or her action. If you pick up a realistic model of an AK-47 and point it at another person out of the window of your car, you are going to scare that person. Under the law of intentional torts, you may be liable for an assault.

You do not have to intend to harm that person to be liable for an intentional tort, either; you even may be attempting to help that person. In one reported case, for example, a defendant was found liable for an intentional tort when he proceeded to set the broken arm of a woman who had fallen, despite her protests. Unlike a negligence action, a plaintiff alleging an intentional tort does not need to show actual damages to recover.

Q. I got a black eye in a fistfight with a man whose car accidentally bumped into mine while we sat at a red light. I would love to get even with him. Can I recover if I sue him?

A. Normally, you could recover damages in a civil battery case against someone who hits you. But a court might hold that two people who get into a fistfight in effect agree to being hit by one another. If so, a battery case probably would fail. A lot would depend on the facts of the case. Who started the fight? Were you simply trying to defend yourself from his aggression? Were there witnesses? What would their testimony be?

Q. Isn't battery a crime?

A. Yes, battery can be a crime, but as a personal injury action it is a civil claim, as are all tort actions. The law considers torts to be wrongs against an individual, allowing the individual to sue for money damages. (For more on criminal assaults and batteries see the "Criminal Justice" chapter.)

As a tort, a **battery** is a harmful or offensive touching of one person by another. Anyone who touches you or comes into contact with some part of you—even your purse—when you do not agree to it may be liable to you for battery. The law does not require any harm or damage. You do not even have to know a battery is occurring at the time in order to bring a battery claim.

The person committing the battery may have meant no hatred or ill will. In one case, for example, a plaintiff successfully recovered damages for an unwanted kiss. Also, a court found a battery when a person forcibly removed a woman's hat. However, damages for technical batteries are small. After all, you were not actually hurt, so how much should you get?

Q. What is the tort of assault?

A. An **assault** is a reasonable apprehension (expectation) of some harm that may come to you. Unlike a battery, you must know that an assault is occurring at the time it takes place. A court will look at what happened. A great deal will depend on the reasonableness of your own feelings when threatened. The court will consider whether the closeness of the physical threat subjectively should have upset, frightened, or humiliated you. Words alone usually are not enough to bring a case for assault.

Q. My neighbor fired his shotgun to scare a solicitor whom he did not want coming to his door. One of the pellets grazed a passerby. Will my neighbor be liable?

A. Under a legal doctrine known as **transferred intent,** your neighbor could be liable for a battery to the passerby. This is true even though the passerby was an unexpected victim whom your neighbor did not intend to harm. The solicitor also is likely to win an assault case against your neighbor. The firing of the gun placed the solicitor in reasonable apprehension of a battery, which is the legal definition of an assault.

Q. A security guard in a store suspected me of shoplifting and detained me. I have heard about something called false imprisonment. Do I have an action for that?

A. If the security guard was acting in good faith, most courts will allow the guard to detain you briefly on the store premises. A number of states by law have given shopkeepers a limited privilege to stop suspected shoplifters for a reasonable amount of time to investigate. Nonetheless, you may be able to recover damages for false imprisonment. Suppose the security guard genuinely restrained you against your will, intending to confine you. Damages for such an action generally include compensation for loss of time and any inconvenience, physical discomfort, or injuries. If the guard acted maliciously, you also may be able to receive punitive damages.

Q. Someone broke into my house in the middle of the night and attacked me. I chased and knocked down the culprit running down the street. Will I be liable to him?

A. If you reasonably believe someone broke into your house and attacked you, you have the right to defend yourself by injuring him. If you believe someone is about to inflict bodily harm, you may use nondeadly force to defend yourself. In situations in which you believe an intruder is about to inflict death or serious bodily harm, courts allow you to use deadly force. The question then becomes whether the force you used was reasonable under the circumstances.

In this particular case, if the culprit was already running down the street, courts may say that there was no longer danger to you or your property. Then, outrageous as it sounds, you might well be liable for the injuries you caused to the culprit.

Q. We got behind on our bills and a bill collector has been stopping by and calling us day and night. The bill collector intimidates us, calls us names, and threatens to destroy our credit record. We are nervous wrecks. What may we do?

A. You may be able to make a case that the collector's conduct is a tort, the **intentional infliction of mental distress**. Courts recently have begun to recognize such actions as extreme and outrageous conduct that someone else intentionally inflicts on you. For you to recover damages,

you must show more than hurt feelings. Without aggravating (intensifying) circumstances, most courts have not allowed recovery if the collector was merely profane, obscene, abusive, threatening, or insulting. The collector would need to have used outrageous and extreme high-pressure methods for a period of time.

If the collector touched you offensively without your consent, you might even want to consider adding claims for two other intentional torts—assault and battery.

You also might want to consider a case against the collector's employer. Just as employers are vicariously (indirectly) liable for the negligent acts of an employee, employers can be liable for the intentional acts of an employee. A court would need to determine whether the collector's particular conduct fell within the scope of his or her job. (See chapter 7, "Consumer Credit," for more information about debt collection and your rights.)

Q. What about someone hurting our reputation? Is that a tort?

A. Yes. The tort of **defamation** involves your reputation. If something is said or shown to a third person and is understood by that person to lower your reputation, or keep others from associating with you, you may have a defamation claim. **Libel and slander** are two types of defamation.

To recover for defamation, you have to prove that the information is false and defamatory. (If something is false, but doesn't damage reputation, there isn't a claim.) The defendants can raise truth as a defense. That is, if they can prove that what they said or wrote about you was true, then there is no slander or libel. Your consent to the publication of defamatory matter concerning yourself is a complete defense as well.

Defamation generally is easier to prove if you are a private person. Courts treat public officials and figures differently from private persons in deciding whether someone has defamed them. Public figures must show that the speaker or publisher either knew the words were false or made the statement with reckless disregard for the truth. Courts have established certain constitutional protections for statements about public officials. That is why they must show that the speaker or the publisher made the statement knowing it was false—or seriously doubting its truth. Private individuals must show only that the defendant was negligent in that he or she failed to act with reasonable care in the situation.

For more information on defamation law, see the Media Law Resource Center (formerly known as the Libel Defense Resource Center) website, www.ldrc.com.

Q. What is the difference between slander and libel?

A. A defamation action for slander rests on an oral communication made to another that is understood to lower your reputation or keep others from associating with you. Libel generally is considered written or printed defamation that does the same thing. Radio and television broadcasts of defamatory material today are nearly universally considered libel.

Q. My late grandfather, who owned a textile factory, was called "unfair to labor" in a recent book about the industry. Is that libelous?

A. While it can be libelous to write that someone is unfair to labor—or is a crook, a drunk, or an anarchist—no defamation action can be brought for someone who is deceased. If your family still owns the factory and the same accusation made against your grandfather was made against your living family or your business, a defamation action could be brought.

Q. I have a tax-return preparation business, and a neighbor recently told a potential client that I did not know a thing about tax law. Isn't that slander?

A. You might have a case if the statement is untrue. If someone says something falsely that affects you in your business, trade, or profession, you can recover in a slander action even without

showing actual harm to your reputation or other damages. You can do the same in three other situations—if someone says that you committed a crime, that you have a loathsome disease, or that a specific female is unchaste (impure).

Of course, you can recover in other slander cases, but in those you must show that you actually were damaged.

Q. Are there defenses to defamation?

A. There are several defenses that will defeat a defamation claim. As mentioned above, consent is one; truth is another. And certain persons and proceedings (such as a judge in his or her courtroom, witnesses testifying about a relevant issue in a case, and certain communications by legislators) are said to be privileged. They are protected from defamation claims.

Many states have so-called **retraction statutes,** which enable media defendants to retract, or take back, defamatory statements. Many retraction statutes merely limit a defendant's liability. Some statutes, for example, prevent a plaintiff from recovering punitive damages if the defendant properly retracts the statement. Sometimes, defendants can put forth a libel-proof-plaintiff defense. This defense revolves around a plaintiff who has no claim to a good reputation.

THE WORLD AT YOUR FINGERTIPS

- *For an overview of the false imprisonment tort, access or.essortment.com/ falseimprisonme_rmol.htm.*
- *For discussions of defamation or intentional torts, search on those terms on the Nolo site (www.nolo.com) or the FindLaw site (public.findlaw.com).*

REMEMBER THIS

- *An intentional wrongdoer (tortfeasor) knows the consequences of his or her actions.*

- *The major intentional torts against a person are defamation, assault, battery, false imprisonment, and intentional infliction of emotional distress.*
- *A major difference between assault and battery is that assault does not require actual contact, while battery requires a harmful or offensive touching. Conduct that constitutes the torts of assault and battery can also form the basis for a criminal action.*

- *False imprisonment is the intentional confinement of someone against his or her will. Shopkeepers often have a limited privilege to detain those whom they reasonably suspect of shoplifting.*
- *Intentional infliction of emotional distress requires that the wrongdoer engage in extreme and outrageous conduct. Such conduct must go beyond the pale of social decency.*

Criminal Justice

Our system of justice was designed carefully to prevent people from being unfairly convicted by guaranteeing many legal rights to anyone charged with a crime. For example, you have a right to have a lawyer present during police questioning. You have the right to remain silent to avoid incriminating yourself, which means that you do not have to answer any questions asked by police, and do not have to give evidence at trial. Just being aware of these rights will help you if you ever become involved in the criminal justice system. This chapter discusses those rights, provides you with a basic understanding of the steps in the criminal justice system, and suggests where you can look for more help. It also provides information on the role of other people involved in the criminal justice system—victims, witnesses, and the jury.

It is important to be informed about the criminal law in your jurisdiction. Most crimes are punishable under state, rather than federal, laws. Some, like drugs and weapons offenses, may be punishable under both. Although all states must comply with certain federal constitutional minimums, there are considerable variations from one state to another. For example, some state constitutions provide a higher degree of personal and procedural rights to the criminally accused than others. Therefore, the information in this chapter generally will be true in most states, but may not be true in all.

THE BASICS OF CRIMINAL LAW

Kevin was charged with assault after a bar brawl. He was arrested and taken to the police station, where he answered police questions and informed them that someone else started the fight by throwing a punch at him. He told his lawyer the same story.

At trial, Kevin agreed to give evidence, saying he had nothing to hide. The first question the prosecutor asked him was whether he had any other convictions. To his lawyer's surprise, Kevin said he had two other convictions for assault.

This section provides an introduction to issues related to the criminal justice system.

Q. How do civil and criminal law differ?

A. Civil matters are private matters, which involve the plaintiff suing the defendant for a money award, often in combination with other orders of the court, like an injunction to make a party stop a course of action.

A crime is considered a wrong against the public. Although a criminal defendant may have injured only one victim directly, any violation of the criminal laws harms society. Criminal cases are always initiated by the government, which has a monopoly on bringing charges. The defendant in criminal cases is usually a person and very rarely a corporation. While victims of crime may be consulted, they have no power to make the prosecutor bring charges or to prevent the prosecutor from dropping charges. A convicted defendant may be ordered to pay a fine, given probation, given community service, or sentenced to jail or prison, or even death.

Q. Are there different standards for determining liability in a civil suit and guilt in a criminal case?

A. Yes. The Bill of Rights—the first ten amendments to the U.S. Constitution—together with state constitutional provisions, treats a criminal conviction (and the possibility of a prison term or death sentence) as more serious than a finding of civil liability. Accordingly, it is more difficult to convict someone of a crime than it is to obtain a civil judgment against a defendant.

In a civil suit, the question that a trial judge or jury will ask when making a decision is whether a plaintiff has proven that it was more likely than not that the defendant was legally responsible for the plaintiff's injury or loss. This preponderance-of-the-evidence standard means that if the evidence favors the plaintiff by even the slightest bit, the plaintiff is entitled to a verdict in his or her favor. In a criminal case, on the other hand, the standard is much higher: The prosecution must prove the defendant's guilt beyond a reasonable doubt. Even if it is more likely than not that a criminal defendant is guilty of the crime charged, the proper verdict is not guilty if there remains a reasonable doubt about his or her guilt.

The United States Constitution guarantees criminal defendants many other rights, including the right to a jury trial when there is the possibility of a conviction resulting in a prison term of six months or more, the right to have a lawyer appointed if the defendant cannot afford to hire one where there is a possibility of a loss of liberty, the right to confront one's accusers, and the right to a swift and public trial. State constitutions may guarantee other rights, including rights to a jury trial in lesser offenses.

Q. How does the criminal justice system work?

A. It is useful to think of the criminal justice system as being made up of three main components:

- Law enforcement: the police
- Courts/adjudication: after arrest, the defendant is charged and brought into the court system to have his or her case heard
- Corrections: if a defendant is convicted, he or she may go into the corrections system—jail or prison

Q. What distinguishes a misdemeanor from a felony?

A. Each state has a body of criminal law that categorizes certain offenses as felonies and others as misdemeanors.

The federal government and most states classify a **felony** as a crime that carries a minimum sentence of more than one year. A **misdemeanor** is an offense punishable by a sentence of one year or less. Some states draw the line based on the place of possible confinement. If incarceration is in the state prison, the offense is a felony. If the offense is punishable by a term in a county jail or a state facility other than a prison or a reformatory, it is a misdemeanor.

Felonies are more serious crimes than misdemeanors. Robbery, kidnapping, sexual assault, and murder are examples of felonies. Public drunkenness, resisting arrest, and simple battery are misdemeanors. Depending on the degree of the offense, however, the same offense might be either a misdemeanor or a felony. Petty larceny (stealing an item worth less than the dollar amount specified in the relevant state legislation) is a misdemeanor. Over that amount, the offense is grand theft (a felony). Similarly, the first offense of driving under the influence of drugs or alcohol may be a misdemeanor. After a certain number of convictions for that same offense, the state may prosecute the next violation as a felony.

Q. How do juvenile proceedings differ from adult criminal proceedings?

A. The jurisdiction of juvenile court varies by state. Juvenile courts usually hear cases involving persons between the ages of ten and eighteen. Not all states agree that the maximum age is eighteen; in New York, the age limit is sixteen, and in many other states it is sixteen. In some circumstances, even juveniles under the applicable age limit may be transferred to adult court. If the prosecution charges an older juvenile with a particularly serious or violent offense, the district attorney or prosecutor may request that an adult court try the juvenile as an adult. In some states, juveniles fourteen or older who are charged with serious acts like murder, rape, or armed robbery must, under the relevant statute, be dealt with in adult courts unless the judge transfers them to juvenile court.

Because juveniles do not have a constitutional right to a jury trial unless tried as an adult, judges hear most juvenile cases. Juveniles also do not have a right to a public trial or to bail. However,

---

ⓘ THE REQUIREMENTS OF A CRIME

Most crime requires both a criminal act **(actus reus)** and a criminal intent **(mens rea).** Even if you committed a criminal act (injuring someone, for example), you might not have had the required mental state, or wrongful purpose, for it to be a crime.

Both criminal act and criminal intent must be proved beyond a reasonable doubt if a person is to be convicted of a crime. If the facts in your case show that you did not have a criminal intent, then all the elements of the case have not been proved, and you may not be convicted of a crime.

You can be convicted even if you did not intend to commit a crime in some circumstances. A person who kills another unintentionally commits a crime if his or her actions were reckless or sufficiently negligent. For example, if an accident occurs while you are driving one hundred miles per hour on a city street and a pedestrian is killed, you have committed a crime even though there was no conscious intention to injure that person or anyone else.

the fundamental elements of due process apply in a juvenile proceeding as they do in the criminal trial of an adult. For example, a child charged in a juvenile proceeding is entitled to notice of charges given in advance of any adjudication of delinquency; a lawyer, including one paid for by the state if the family cannot afford one; the right to confront and cross-examine witnesses; the right to pretrial release unless the child is a danger to himself or others; and the right to assert the Fifth Amendment privilege against self-incrimination. Finally, the state is required to prove its charges beyond a reasonable doubt, just as in the trial of any adult on a criminal charge.

Under most state laws, juvenile offenders do not commit "crimes." They commit **delinquent acts,** which are acts that would constitute crimes if committed by an adult. The trial phase of a juvenile case is referred to as an **adjudication hearing.** This means that the judge hears the evidence and determines whether the child is delinquent. The court then may take whatever action it deems to be in the child's best interest. The purpose is to rehabilitate, not punish.

THE CHARACTERISTICS OF SOME SERIOUS CRIMES

Crimes are defined by law and found in a state's criminal or penal code. They also may be found in a state's vehicle or health and safety code. Crimes can be as serious as murder or as minor as jaywalking. There are many categories of crimes, including drug offenses, weapons offenses, child and spousal abuse, child endangerment, welfare fraud, and driving under the influence. The following table describes only a few of the most serious crimes.

Crimes Against the Person

Homicide A person is guilty of criminal homicide if he or she purposely, knowingly, recklessly, or negligently causes the death of another human being, without legal justification or excuse.

Sexual Assault Sexual assault consists of forced sexual conduct or penetration without the victim's consent or when the victim is underage. These crimes often are called rape, sexual assault, sexual conduct, or sexual battery, and may include special designations when the victim is a child.

Robbery Robbery is the unlawful taking or attempted taking of property that is in the immediate possession of another, by force or threat of force.

Assault Simple assault is the unlawful intentional infliction of bodily injury on another. Aggravated assault is the unlawful intentional infliction of serious bodily injury, or the unlawful threat or attempt to inflict bodily injury or death by means of a deadly or dangerous weapon, with or without actual infliction of injury. Many states have separate categories of assault for assaults committed on people to whom the law gives special status, like children and the elderly.

Crimes Against Property

Burglary Burglary consists of entry into, or remaining in, any residence, building, or vehicle without consent, with the intent to commit a felony or a larceny within.

Larceny (Theft) Larceny or theft is the unlawful taking or attempted taking of property from the possession of another, without force and without deceit, with intent permanently to deprive the owner of the property.

Arson Arson is the intentional damaging or destroying of property or attempted damaging or destroying of property by means of fire or explosion, without the consent of the owner, or of one's own property, with or without the intent to defraud.

THE WORLD AT YOUR FINGERTIPS

- *The ABA's Criminal Justice Section has a page of links that lists some good criminal justice websites at www.abanet.org/ crimjust/infosvcs/home.html.*
- *The American Civil Liberties Union website has information on recent criminal justice issues, and links to relevant legal documents and legislation at www.aclu. org/CriminalJustice/CriminalJusticeMain. cfm.*
- *A good starting point to find more information on criminal law is FindLaw's website at public.findlaw.com/criminal.*
- *Nolo provides some excellent information for the public on various aspects of criminal law and procedure. Click on "criminal laws" at www.nolo.com.*
- *The website of Florida State University's School of Criminology and Criminal Justice provides links to state organizations that can provide information on crime in your state at www.criminology.fsu.edu. Click on "Links and Resources".*
- *More information on criminal law relating to juveniles can be found, in question-and-answer format, at criminal-law.freeadvice. com/juvenile_law/.*

REMEMBER THIS

- *In criminal cases, the government is always the prosecuting party. The prosecution must prove its case "beyond a reasonable doubt."*
- *Defendants have rights guaranteed by the U.S. Constitution, which help to ensure that they have a fair trial. State law and state constitutions may protect other rights.*
- *If the crime is serious, juveniles may be tried as adults in some states.*

THE POLICE AND YOUR RIGHTS

A police officer observed Terry and two of his friends in front of a store acting suspiciously. The officer watched the men standing on a street corner, and then taking turns walking down the street to a store, peering in, and returning to the corner. This occurred a number of times over a ten-minute period. The officer

---

⚠ THE IMMIGRATION CONSEQUENCES OF CONVICTION

Noncitizens should be aware that there are often tremendous immigration consequences to a criminal conviction. For instance, the Immigration and Naturalization Service (INS) can deport a noncitizen convicted of a crime—even when the crime is classified as a misdemeanor or even if the defendant is not sent to prison in punishment. In addition, if the noncitizen defendant pleads guilty to a criminal offense, a judge rarely will be required to explain these associated immigration consequences at the time that the defendant enters his or her guilty plea. For these reasons, it's very important that if you are a noncitizen facing criminal charges, you explain your immigration status to your lawyer so that he or she can advise you correctly as to what your legal remedies are. Even if you are not residing in this country legally, you should tell your lawyer about your immigration status. This information is protected by the attorney-client privilege, and your lawyer is required to protect it from third parties.

was in plain clothes, had thirty-nine years of experience, and, based on his training and experience, believed that they were about to rob the store. He thought that they might have a gun. He approached them, identified himself, and asked their names. When they mumbled something, the officer grabbed Terry and spun him around so they both were facing the other two, with Terry between the officer and the others. The officer patted down the outside of Terry's clothes and felt a gun in his breast pocket. He took off Terry's coat and took the gun from the pocket. During a pat-down of the other two, he discovered a gun in another man's pocket as well. The officer took that gun and arrested the two men for carrying concealed weapons.

Imagine you were looking in a store window and were suddenly grabbed by a police officer and frisked for weapons. Could the police do this to you lawfully? Or would the police have to arrest you? What would happen if you were arrested? Do you have to answer any questions the police might ask you?

It's a good idea to know what to expect in case you ever have to deal with police, whether you're a victim reporting a crime, a witness, or a suspect. This section will give you information on your rights when dealing with police, your rights to a lawyer, and some information on the process of being charged.

Q. How do the police investigate crimes?

A. When the police receive a report of a crime (such as a home burglary in progress), they send investigating officers to the scene as soon as they can. If the officers arrest a suspect, they will transport that person to the police station or the jail for booking. The officer will write an arrest report, detailing when and why the officer went to the scene, along with any observations, and why the officer arrested the suspect. The officer also will fill out a property report, detailing what items (for example, drugs or cash) the police found on the suspect during booking. The officer also will list any items of evidence found at the scene,

such as tools the suspect might have used to gain access to the home.

If the crime is complex or serious, the police then assign an investigating officer (usually a detective) to the case. That officer will make a return visit to the crime scene, look for more evidence, and interview any other witnesses. If the police have not arrested anyone, the detective will analyze the evidence and try to narrow down the list of suspects. The detective will question suspects and sometimes will obtain a confession.

Q. How long may police hold suspects before charges must be filed?

A. If the police have probable cause to believe a person has committed a crime but the prosecutor has not yet brought formal charges, the police may detain the suspect in custody for a short period of time (generally twenty-four to forty-eight hours). **Probable cause** is defined as facts sufficient to support a reasonable belief that criminal activity is probably taking place or knowledge of circumstances indicating a fair probability that evidence of crime will be found. It requires more than a mere hunch, but less than proof beyond a reasonable doubt.

After this short period of detention, the police must release the person, or bring formal charges and take the suspect before a judge. If released, the person may be rearrested at a later date if the police obtain sufficient evidence.

Q. Do the police have the right to tap my telephone?

A. Yes, if they can show the court that they have probable cause to believe that intercepting your telephone conversations is necessary to help solve certain crimes (such as treason, terrorism, drug trafficking, wire fraud, and money laundering).

The law considers wiretapping to be very intrusive. Therefore, it is closely regulated by federal and state law. A court will permit wiretapping only for a limited period. The authorities that listen to your telephone calls must make efforts to minimize this intrusion by limiting the number of intercepted calls to those involving the investigation. An example of this would be tapping a bookie's telephone only during the hours when it is likely that bets will be placed. After the wiretap period has ended, the authorities must inventory the calls and reveal to the court the content of the conversations they intercepted.

Less-intrusive forms of electronic surveillance are the pen register and the trap and trace. A pen register device records every number dialed from your telephone. A trap and trace records every number dialed from an outside line to your telephone. These devices do not enable anyone to listen to your conversations, as they simply list telephone numbers.

You should assume that any conversation from a jail or visitor's phone is being tapped. Do not discuss any aspect of your case with anyone in jail, except your lawyer.

It is also technologically possible for the police to tap a cellular telephone. In order to do so, they also would need a warrant. Similarly, police generally need a warrant in order to search e-mail records.

Q. Has the law regarding telephone taps and other surveillance changed since the terrorist attacks of September 11, 2001?

A. Yes. The USA Patriot Act has made sweeping changes to a wide variety of laws, in an attempt to strengthen the hand of law enforcement and deter future terrorist attacks. The law was introduced a week after the terrorist attacks of September 11, 2001, and was enacted by Congress a little over a month later. For example, in the area of surveillance and searches, the law amends the following:

- Wiretap Statute (Title III)
- Pen Register and Trap and Trace Statute
- Electronic Communications Privacy Act
- Computer Fraud and Abuse Act
- Foreign Intelligence Surveillance Act
- Bank Secrecy Act
- Right to Financial Privacy Act

It also amends a wide variety of other laws, including the following:

- Family Education Rights and Privacy Act
- Immigration and Nationality Act
- Money Laundering Control Act
- Fair Credit Reporting Act

As this list shows, the law reaches into computer law, search and seizure law, the law regulating financial transactions and reporting, and immigration law. Some commentators have argued that

---

▶ **HOW TO REPORT A CRIME**

Call the police and say that you wish to report a crime. If you have observed a crime or know that a crime took place, the law considers you a witness. If somebody has committed a crime against you, the law regards you as a victim. In either case, the police will want to talk to you to determine what you know about the incident so they can decide whether to investigate further.

If you were in any way involved in the crime, the law might consider you a suspect. In this instance, you should call a lawyer immediately, before you talk to the police. A lawyer will be permitted to accompany you to the police station and be present to protect your interests during police questioning. Many people believe that what they say to the police is not admissible unless written down, recorded on tape, or said to a prosecutor or judge. That is not true. To be on the safe side, you should assume that anything you say to anybody but your lawyer could be used against you at trial.

the law is too sweeping and lacks the checks and balances and other safeguards that are a traditional part of our system of criminal law. Others have pointed out that the act includes **judicial safeguards** in several areas (meaning that a judge has to approve certain activities), and that many of the wiretapping and foreign intelligence amendments are to go out of existence on December 31, 2005, unless Congress extends them. Also, Congress has considered bills to modify some of the act's more controversial provisions.

Q. Has the constitutionality of the Patriot Act been challenged?

A. Yes. For example, in the summer of 2003, the ACLU filed suit in federal court on behalf of six Arab-American and Muslim groups. The ACLU challenged provisions dealing with the government's expanded search powers in such areas as Internet records from public library computers. The ACLU claimed that the challenged provisions violated the Fourth Amendment by permitting unreasonable searches not based on probable cause.

ADMISSIBLE AND INADMISSIBLE EVIDENCE

What does it mean if evidence is "admissible" or "inadmissible"? If evidence is said to be **admissible,** it simply means that it can be "admitted into evidence" and relied on in court. If there is some problem with the evidence—it was procured unlawfully, or it is likely to be unreliable for some reason (see the discussion on hearsay on page 573)—then a judge can rule that it is **inadmissible.** This means that it cannot be relied on in court when the case is being argued. For example, if the police seize drugs, but they seize them by means of an unlawful search, the drugs are inadmissible as evidence.

Q. May the police search me without a warrant?

A. That depends on whether you are under arrest. If the police have lawfully arrested you, they are permitted to search you. They also are allowed to search the area under your immediate control (also known as your wingspan, or where you can reach). This may include, for example, the glove box of your car.

If you are not under arrest, the police generally are not permitted to search you. There are a number of important exceptions to this rule. The police may search you if you consent, but doing so limits the range of your defense in later proceedings. Your consent, for example, will make it difficult to challenge the legality of the search at a pretrial suppression hearing. Many people feel they should consent in order to show the police they have nothing to hide—but what you consider insignificant, such as a piece of paper with a telephone number, may be incriminating if it links you to a crime.

The police also can search you for weapons if a police officer reasonably feels in danger.

Q. Does the law permit the police to search my home or items in it?

A. You have greater rights in your home than you do in your car. (See chapter 11, "Automobiles," for information on car searches.) That is because the courts have decided that the law entitles people to greater privacy rights in their homes. Therefore, the police normally cannot search your home unless they have a warrant. The warrant must specify what the police are looking for and the specific areas of the house they are allowed to search. The police may search outside those specified areas in some circumstances—for example, to prevent the destruction of evidence or to ensure the safety of the police.

If the police do search without a warrant, the search is presumed invalid, so you have the right to challenge it in court. If the judge finds there was a valid exception to the warrant requirement, he or she will rule the evidence admissible. On the other hand, if there was no such exception, the **exclusionary rule**—which prevents illegally obtained evidence from being introduced at the trial—may prevent the evidence from being used against you.

One exception to the warrant requirement is that the police do not need a warrant to search your home if you agree to the search. Consent must be voluntary and must be given by someone who has the legal right to be in the home. Obviously, you can give consent to search your home or apartment. But you are not the only person whose consent would be valid. Your spouse could consent, as could an adult child living in your home. It is important to note that in seeking your consent, the police are not required to explain the consequences. For example, they need not tell you that any item in plain view or found during a search, if it is somehow connected to a crime, can be used against you or any other member of your household. Consenting to a search may have unexpected consequences—the police may recover evidence you did not know was in your home or was linked to a crime.

Even if you do not agree to a search, the police are permitted to search your home without a warrant if there are sufficiently exigent circumstances—that is, if there is an emergency situation in which the police have reason to believe someone's life is in danger, a suspect is about to escape, or you might destroy the evidence (flush illegal drugs down the toilet, for example) if they do not conduct the search immediately. In cases such as these, when there is no time to get a warrant from the court, the police can search your home without permission.

ⓘ STOPPING AND FRISKING SUSPECTS

The police always can seek to question you in a public place, but you are free to refuse to answer and leave. If police have observed unusual activity suggesting that a crime is going on and you are involved, then they can stop and briefly detain and question you. The Supreme Court has determined, for example, that people in high crime areas may be pursued and stopped for merely running away at the sight of police. Once you have been stopped by a police officer, you do not have the right to walk away. Remember, you do not have to answer any questions they may ask you. In these brief detentions, police do not have to give Miranda warnings (see "The Miranda Rule" on page 560).

Do the police have a right to frisk you? That depends on the circumstances. On the one hand, the Supreme Court has ruled that an anonymous tip that a person is carrying a gun is not, without more evidence, sufficient to justify a police officer's frisking that person. On the other hand, suppose the police reasonably suspect that you are engaging in a criminal activity and that you may be armed and dangerous. Then they may stop you and frisk you for weapons. The one and only purpose of a frisk is to dispel suspicions of danger (to the officer and other persons; i.e., to ensure that this person isn't armed and dangerous). For example, assume that the police observe you walking back and forth in front of a store after dark. They observe you looking around nervously and apparently casing the place to break into it. The police are permitted, under these circumstances, to stop you, and to conduct an outer clothing pat-down (also known as a frisk) for weapons if they believe you are armed. If the officer who frisks you has good reason to believe that you committed a crime, or are hiding an illegal item—a gun or drugs, for example—he or she then may search you more extensively.

Q. May the police use information from a confidential informant against me?

A. Confidential informants are people who supply information to the police without having their identities disclosed. The law allows police to use such information if it is reliable. The police often use such information to obtain search warrants. For example, an informant might tell the police where someone has hidden evidence of a crime. The police will provide this and other information (such as the informant's prior reliability, how the informant obtained the information, and evidence obtained from other sources that confirms the informant's story) to a judge or **magistrate** (a type of court official). If the judge or magistrate determines there is probable cause to believe that this evidence will be found at the location specified, the judge or magistrate will issue a search warrant. The prosecutor must not reveal the confidential informant's identity unless he or she is ordered to do so by the court. In addition, the prosecutor can ask the judge for a protective order sealing the warrant and the supporting affidavit to keep the identity of the informant secret.

Q. What procedures must the police follow while making an arrest?

A. The police do not have to tell you the crime for which they are arresting you, though they probably will. They are not permitted to use excessive force or brutality when arresting you. If you resist arrest or act violently, the police are allowed to use reasonable force to make the arrest or keep you from injuring yourself. It may be a separate crime to resist the arrest.

While the police are arresting you, they probably will read you your Miranda rights. They do not have to read you these rights if they do not intend to ask you questions.

Q. When am I in custody?

A. The most obvious example of being in custody, of course, is when the police say, "You are under arrest." But you might be in custody even if the police do not say, "You are under arrest." Generally, the law considers you in custody when you have been arrested or otherwise deprived of your freedom of movement in a significant way. This may occur when an officer is holding you at gunpoint or when several officers are surrounding you. Other examples are when you are in handcuffs or when the police have locked you in the backseat of a police car. There are no absolute rules on when a person is in custody—the test is whether a reasonable person in the circumstances would have felt free to leave the scene, and a court will consider all the circumstances.

⚠ WHEN MUST POLICE KNOCK BEFORE ENTERING?

The police must execute a search warrant promptly after the court has issued it. This requirement prevents a warrant from becoming "stale" and ensures that police will not conduct a search when there is no longer reason to believe that evidence of the crime is still present. Some jurisdictions have a knock-notice requirement. This means that the police must knock on the door and announce their presence and purpose before entering the premises to search for items in the warrant.

If there are sufficiently exigent circumstances, however, the police have a right to force entry without knocking to execute the warrant. For instance, the police may not need to knock if they have evidence that doing so would place them in danger. Also, some states are beginning to pass no-knock laws for particular searches, like drug raids.

Q. After arresting me, may the police make me provide fingerprints, a handwriting sample, or a voice example?

A. Generally, the police are permitted to force you to supply these. They will take your fingerprints during the booking procedure at the police station. The law considers handwriting samples and voice examples evidence of physical characteristics. Therefore, you may not claim that the police are forcing you to incriminate yourself through these identification procedures. The police may use these samples as evidence against you in court if they help prove that you committed a crime. For example, your handwriting may be compared to the signature on a forged check or to the writing on a note handed to a teller in a bank robbery.

Q. What are my rights if the police put me in a lineup?

A. In a lineup, several people who look somewhat similar will be shown to victims or witnesses who observed the crime. The police will ask the witnesses if they can identify anyone in the lineup as the person who committed the crime.

If formal charges have been filed against you and the police put you in a lineup, you have a right to have a lawyer present to protect your rights. A lineup is not supposed to be unfairly suggestive—that is, if the victim said her assailant was approximately six feet tall with a red beard, the lineup cannot include five short, clean-shaven, dark-haired men and only one tall, bearded redhead.

Similarly, the police are not permitted to suggest to the victim that a certain person in the lineup is their main suspect—for example, they may not point to one person and ask, "Could that be the man who stole your purse?"

Neither are police permitted to make such a suggestion during photographic identifications, when a witness is asked to pick the suspected or accused criminal from six similar photographs on

---

ⓘ THE MIRANDA RULE

In 1966, the U.S. Supreme Court ruled in *Miranda v. Arizona* that when law enforcement officers question people taken into custody, the evidence collected in their interview cannot be used against them unless they have been informed of their constitutional rights to counsel and to remain silent. When a person is taken into custody, before he or she is questioned, some version of the Miranda rights, such as the following, must be given to the individual before questioning: "You have the right to remain silent. If you give up the right to remain silent, anything you say can and will be used against you in a court of law. You have the right to a lawyer. If you desire a lawyer and cannot afford one, a lawyer will be obtained for you before police questioning."

The Miranda rule was developed to protect the individual's Fifth Amendment right against self-incrimination. Many people feel obligated to respond to police questioning. The Miranda warning ensures that people in custody realize they do not have to talk to the police and that they have the right to the presence of a lawyer.

If the Miranda warning is not given before questioning, or if police continue to question a suspect after he or she indicates a desire to consult with a lawyer before speaking, statements by the suspect generally are inadmissible. However, it may be difficult for your lawyer to suppress your statements from being used against you in all circumstances.

The best rule is to remain silent until you can consult with a lawyer. You have the right to a lawyer. Insist on it.

a card. The suspect does not have a right to have a lawyer present during a photographic identification. The suspect is not present at photo IDs.

When you are in a lineup, the police have the right to ask you to speak if the witnesses feel they can identify you by your voice. The law permits the police to have you speak the words used during the crime. They might ask you to say, for example, "Give me your money."

Q. What is an interrogation?

A. An interrogation might be explicit questioning, such as the police asking you, "Did you kill John Doe?" Interrogation also might be less obvious, such as comments made by the police that they know are likely to elicit incriminating information from you. It is legal for the police to lie to you about what they know or suspect or what other people have said about you. The police may try to trick you into talking. This is one reason why it is so important to have a lawyer present during your interrogation.

Q. How do the police recommend that criminal charges be filed against someone?

A. Criminal cases go through a screening process before a defendant faces charges in court. This is a two-step process that begins with the police inquiry. The investigating officer (or another officer superior to the arresting officer) will review the arrest report. That officer will determine whether there is enough evidence to recommend filing charges against the arrested person. If the officer decides not to recommend filing charges, then the police will release the arrested person.

If the officer decides to recommend that a charge be filed, a prosecutor from the district attorney's office will review the officer's recommen-

---

ⓘ WHERE POLICE ARE PERMITTED TO MAKE ARRESTS

Where the police are allowed to arrest you may depend on whether the police have a warrant for your arrest. The police make most arrests without a warrant. If you commit a misdemeanor in the officer's presence, that officer is permitted to arrest you without a warrant. If the officer has probable cause (the minimum level of evidence needed to make a lawful arrest) to believe that you committed a felony, the officer is allowed to arrest you without a warrant, even if he or she did not see you commit the crime. The law permits warrantless arrests in public places, such as a street or a restaurant.

But to arrest you in your home, the police must have a warrant or your consent unless there are exigent circumstances. There are two types of warrants: an **arrest warrant** and a **search warrant.** To arrest you in your own home, the police must have an arrest warrant. If they lack a warrant but have probable cause for a warrantless arrest, they are permitted to put your home under surveillance. They then will wait until you leave your home and arrest you in a public place. When the police arrest you without a warrant, the law entitles you to a prompt hearing to determine whether there was probable cause for the arrest.

If the police arrest you in someone else's home where you are an overnight guest, the same rules apply. If you are briefly in another's home, the police can arrest you without a warrant. If they have a search warrant, the police can use any evidence they find against either you or the owner of the home; without a search warrant, evidence seized is inadmissible against the owner of the home.

ⓘ WHO EXERCISES DISCRETION

Police have discretion on whether or how to

- enforce specific laws;
- investigate specific crimes;
- search people or areas;
- question people; and
- arrest or detain people.

Prosecutors have discretion on whether or how to

- file charges or petitions for adjudication;
- seek indictments or file **informations** (alternatives to indictments, filed by prosecutors rather than grand juries);
- reduce charges; and
- try cases.

Judges or magistrates have discretion on whether or how to

- issue warrants;
- set bail or conditions for release;
- accept pleas;
- determine criminal guilt (or delinquency in the case of juveniles);
- dismiss charges;
- impose sentences; and
- revoke probation.

Correctional officials have discretion to

- assign convicted people to correctional facilities;
- award privileges; and
- punish prisoners for disciplinary infractions.

The paroling authority has discretion to

- determine the date and conditions of parole; and
- revoke parole.

dation. Based on the arrest report and any follow-up investigation, the prosecutor's office will decide whether to file charges and what criminal offenses to allege.

Lawyers and Criminal Law

Q. When do I have a right to a lawyer—before or during police interrogation?

A. You have a constitutional **right to counsel**—the right to have a lawyer's advice—before and during police interrogation. If the police are asking you questions and you think they may think you are involved in a crime, tell them that you do not want to answer questions and that you want a lawyer, regardless of whether you have been given Miranda warnings. Police frequently obtain damaging admissions before you are in custody, and prior to providing Miranda warnings. Do not answer any questions until your lawyer arrives. If the police place you in a lineup, the law entitles you to have a lawyer present if you have been formally charged. You also have a right to a lawyer at all your court appearances.

Q. If the police arrest a friend or a relative, may I send a lawyer to the jail to offer help?

A. Yes, but the right to counsel is personal to the accused. This means that the person who is under arrest must tell the police that he or she wants a lawyer. In some states, if your friend waives the right to counsel and agrees to talk to the police, the police do not have to tell your friend that you are sending a lawyer. Or, in some states, if your friend has not requested a lawyer, the police are even permitted to turn away the lawyer upon arrival at the station without telling your friend. If a friend telephones you, the best thing you can do is to say that a lawyer is on the way to offer help. Your friend should tell the police that he or she does not want to answer questions until he or she has had the opportunity to talk to a lawyer.

Q. How do I find a lawyer?

A. If you have a family lawyer, call him or her immediately. If your family lawyer does not do criminal work, he or she may be able to recommend another lawyer who does. If you cannot afford a lawyer, tell the police you wish to have a lawyer appointed on your behalf. A counsel for the defense—whether private, a public defender, or assigned—will be appointed on your behalf.

Q. What should I tell my lawyer?

A. You should tell your lawyer the truth. Your lawyer has to know exactly what happened in order to defend you effectively. Tell your lawyer as many details as you can remember. Anything you tell your lawyer is confidential and will be kept secret, unless it applies to any continuing or future crime. The law refers to this as the attorney-client privilege. Your lawyer has ethical obligations to you as the client.

A lawyer also has an ethical obligation to the court. A lawyer may not lie to the court for you or knowingly offer a false defense. In practical terms, that means that if you tell your lawyer you did not commit the crime but were present when it happened, your lawyer cannot bring in alibi witnesses who will testify falsely that you were with them in another state when the crime took place. If you tell your lawyer that you did commit the crime, he or she is limited in the way he or she can present the case.

Q. May I represent myself without a lawyer?

A. You have a right to represent yourself before the trial, and the court may even allow you to act as a lawyer in your own defense at trial. The law refers to self-representation as **pro se** representation. If you request to proceed pro se, the judge must allow you to represent yourself if he or she determines that you are mentally and/or physically able to represent yourself, that you are making an informed and voluntary decision to give up your constitutional right to counsel, and that you are aware of the dangers and disadvantages of self-representation.

Q. Is it better to represent myself than to rely on a court-appointed defender?

A. No. It is not a good idea for untrained people to try to represent themselves in criminal cases. The opponent will be a skilled prosecutor who has conducted many trials. The rules of evidence at trial are complicated, and an untrained person may miss many opportunities to present his or her strongest case. The judge or jury will not necessarily be sympathetic toward you simply because you decided to go it alone.

Some defendants choose to represent themselves because they feel they can do a better job than a public defender or a lawyer whom the court has appointed to represent them free of charge. This simply is not true. First, any lawyer is sure to know more than you do about the legal system. Lawyers must complete a three- or four-year program in law school and pass a rigorous bar examination. Second, do not assume that the public defender is an inadequate lawyer who could not get a "real job" in a law firm. Many top law students choose public-interest work because they want to help people. Public defenders have substantial experience defending people in criminal cases.

In addition, most people charged with a crime are too close emotionally to their own problems. Therefore, they cannot maintain the clear, cool-headed thinking that is necessary in court. Even lawyers charged with a crime usually hire another lawyer to represent them. Those lawyers are being guided by the old saying, "A lawyer who represents himself has a fool for a client."

ⓘ CONFESSIONS

A lot of people believe that only written, signed confessions are admissible as evidence. This is not true. Oral and unsigned written confessions are also admissible.

Whether a confession that you made before a lawyer arrived is admissible depends on whether you gave up your right to a lawyer and your right not to talk. If you voluntarily talked to the police after they read you your Miranda rights, you might have waived (given up) your right to counsel and protection against self-incrimination. The prosecution probably could use the confession against you in court. This is true even if the police lied to you or tricked you in order to get you to talk. Once you agree to talk to the police, you do so at your own risk.

If the police continued to question you after you told them you wanted a lawyer, your confession probably would not be admissible in court, because your lawyer probably would be able to persuade the judge to exclude the confession as evidence.

Remember that you are permitted to change your mind about wanting a lawyer. If you voluntarily begin to talk to the police, but then tell them that you want a lawyer present, the questioning must stop immediately. Or if you have talked to the police once, you may refuse to talk to them a second time until a lawyer arrives.

Miranda rights must be read only when an individual is in police custody and is under interrogation, so if you made a confession when you were not in custody or when you were not being interrogated, then it may be admissible even if you did not have a lawyer. If, for example, the police stop you to give you a traffic ticket, and you start explaining to them that you were speeding because you were drunk, you cannot later protest that your confession (of drunk driving) is inadmissible because you were not read your Miranda rights.

By representing yourself, you are giving up a very important constitutional right: the right to counsel. If you represent yourself and are convicted, you cannot claim that your incompetence as a lawyer denied you effective assistance of counsel.

For these reasons, self-representation is a risk that most criminal defendants should not take. Remember that you have the right to dismiss your lawyer for good cause (although if you do not have a good reason for wanting to dismiss your lawyer, the judge may fail to find good cause and refuse to replace the appointed counsel). You can change lawyers or reconsider representing yourself, if the court will allow it (though the court may require you to proceed immediately with the case, without extra time for you or your new lawyer to prepare).

Once you have experienced the complexities of the legal process, you probably will realize that you need a professional at all times to protect your interests.

Criminal Charges

Q. How are criminal charges brought against someone?

A. There are basically three ways in which formal charges may be brought: information, indictment, or citation. An **information** is a written document filed by a prosecutor alleging that the defendant committed a crime. The information may be based upon a criminal complaint, which is a petition to the prosecutor requesting that criminal charges be initiated.

An **indictment** is a formal charge imposed by the **grand jury,** which is a group of citizens convened by the court. Its function is to determine whether there is sufficient evidence to charge a person with a crime and to bring him or her to trial. The grand jury conducts its proceedings in secret and has broad investigative powers. The federal system and about half of the states use grand juries in felony cases. The majority of defendants are not charged by a grand jury, but through some other mechanism.

A **citation** is issued by a police officer, most often for a misdemeanor or other minor criminal matter such as jaywalking, littering, or a minor traffic offense.

None of these mechanisms determines the guilt or innocence of defendants. Rather, they indicate that the issuing authority has determined that there is sufficient evidence to bring a person to trial.

Q. What is a citation?

A. A citation is the charging document issued for the least serious offenses. The normal penalty is a fine, which may range from under $20 to several hundred dollars. In some municipalities, a citation for an offense could result in a short jail sentence. Police typically give citations for such offenses as minor traffic violations (for example, speeding, parking in a no-parking zone, or jaywalking). If the police cite you for such an offense, they will issue you a ticket. You usually will have the option of not contesting the citation by mailing in the ticket with the specified payment. Or if you feel the police have given you a ticket wrongly, you have the right to contest the citation at a hearing.

Q. What is the grand jury's role in charging individuals with crimes?

A. In about half the states, grand juries must be used to bring charges for felonies. In the other states, they may or may not be used to bring charges for felonies—prosecutors have discretion to use them or bring charges on their own.

Grand juries also have a second role in many states: investigating public corruption or undertaking such tasks as monitoring conditions in the jail.

Q. What's the difference between a grand jury and a trial jury?

A. The purpose of the grand jury is not to decide guilt or innocence—that's the role of the jury at the trial. It is, instead, to determine whether there is sufficient evidence to bring a person to trial.

In general, grand jurors answer this question: "Is there sufficient information to believe that a suspect should be held accountable for a crime?" If people are indicted, they have the opportunity to defend themselves at the ensuing trial. The judge or the jury at the trial will determine whether a person is guilty of the charges.

Q. Why is it called the "grand" jury?

A. Because it's usually bigger than the trial jury. The grand jury is a body of citizens that varies in size depending on the jurisdiction, but often includes as many as twenty-three jurors and usually more than twelve (which is why juries at trial—twelve persons or fewer—are sometimes called "petit," the French word for "small").

Q. How does a grand jury work?

A. The jurors are summoned by the court to serve for a certain period of time, often many months, though they may be called into session only a few days a month. They may consider a number of cases during their term of service. They do not have to agree unanimously to issue an indictment, though state law often requires a vote of two-thirds or three-quarters of the jurors to indict. Typically, the prosecutor works very closely with the grand jury. Using the grand jury's broad investigative power to compel witnesses to appear and answer questions or submit documents, records, and other evidence, the prosecutor and jurors weigh the evidence and try to decide whether it is sufficient to issue an indictment against one or more persons.

Unlike trials, grand jury proceedings are secret. In many states, it is a crime to reveal information about a grand jury's proceedings. The public, the news media, and the person being investigated have no right to be present. The secrecy of the proceedings is intended to encourage witnesses to speak freely without fear of retaliation, such as threats from someone who does not like their testimony. It also protects the persons being investigated in the event that the evidence is deemed insufficient and an indictment isn't issued.

In most jurisdictions, people called to testify before a grand jury are not allowed to have their lawyers present in the grand jury room. In fact, the lawyers for the persons under investigation rarely play any role in grand jury proceedings, meaning that the grand jury makes its findings without hearing both sides of the case. Nor is a judge usually present during grand jury sessions, since normal rules of evidence don't apply in grand jury proceedings, making the role of the prosecutor all the more important.

Q. Once I'm charged with an offense, does it mean that I'll definitely have to go to court?

A. Not necessarily. Police may place you on **diversion,** also called supervision. The result of successful completion of a diversionary program is that the charge is dismissed and the person charged has no criminal record. Diversion programs usually are run by the prosecutor's office. A guilty plea may be required as a condition of being placed on diversion in some states. Diversion ordinarily involves your participation in a service program designed to rehabilitate you. For example, some states allow a first-time drug offender to attend a program such as Cocaine Anonymous instead of being tried. In many jurisdictions, diversion is only available for some crimes, such as nonfelonies.

Q. What does it mean if I have been charged with an "attempt"?

A. An **attempt** means that you had the intent to commit the crime, you took some step toward committing the crime, but for some reason you did not complete it. Suppose you went into a bank and demanded money from a teller at gunpoint. Then an alarm rang, so you ran out of the bank before you could get the money. The prosecutor probably would bring charges of attempted robbery. Conviction for an attempted crime usually carries a sentence somewhat less than for the crime, although in some states the sentence is identical.

Q. What is a conspiracy?

A. A **conspiracy** is an agreement between two or more people to commit a crime followed by any activity to carry out the agreement. The conspiracy itself is a separate crime. Therefore, the prosecutor can bring charges of conspiracy even if you did not complete the crime you intended to commit. Because conspiracy charges carry separate penalties, you can be convicted of both conspiracy and a crime that you or your fellow conspirators accomplished during the conspiracy (the "substantive" count). If you are convicted of both the crime and the conspiracy to commit the crime, then you will receive a sentence that covers both convictions.

Q. What is complicity or accomplice liability?

A. Complicity, also known as aiding and abetting, is the act of being an **accomplice.** An accomplice is someone who helps in, or in some states merely encourages, the commission of a crime. Courts sometimes refer to such a person as an aider or an abettor. This person did not commit the crime, but his or her actions helped enable someone else to do so. Examples of complicity include supplying weapons or supplies, acting as a lookout, or driving the getaway car. Other examples are bringing the victim to the scene of the crime or signaling the victim's approach. Accomplice liability means that anyone who helps in the commission of a crime is as guilty as the person who committed the crime and could be punished as severely if convicted.

THE WORLD AT YOUR FINGERTIPS

- *FindLaw's website for the public contains some practical information on your rights and dealing with police at public.findlaw. com/criminal.*
- *A huge amount of information on warrants, searches, and arrests can be found at criminal-law.freeadvice.com/arrests_ and_searches.*

- *The National Association of Criminal Defense Lawyers can put you in touch with associations of criminal justice lawyers in your state and also provides links to state information on public defenders at www. nacdl.org/public.nsf/freeform/Links? OpenDocument.*

REMEMBER THIS

- *The police have some rights to search you or your home even if you're not under arrest and they do not have a warrant. Remember, if you consent to a search, you may limit the range of your defense in later proceedings. If the police search you or your home unlawfully, then anything they find may be inadmissible at trial.*
- *If you are being arrested, the police must tell you your Miranda rights if they intend to ask you questions.*
- *If the police are asking you questions and you think they may think you are involved in a crime, you should tell them that you do not want to answer questions until you see a lawyer, even if they have not yet read you your Miranda rights. You have a right to a lawyer. Insist on it.*

COURT PROCEDURES

Tom was buying a newspaper one morning when two men with guns came into the store. They emptied the cash register, and then held Tom and another customer at gunpoint while they took their wallets. Later, Tom gave his name and address to the police. The police were able to arrest two suspects, and the store clerk was able to identify them.

Months later, Tom received a subpoena to appear in court as a witness. He still felt traumatized by the incident and didn't want to get involved. He was also nervous about having to go to court. He wanted to know whether he could get out of it somehow. Surely he couldn't be compelled to appear as a witness against his will?

Going to court can be intimidating, whether you're a suspect, a witness, or a victim. But one day you may be forced to get involved. In this section you'll learn how the system works and what to expect, just in case.

Initial Criminal Court Proceedings

Q. How does a defendant appear in court?

A. The first step is an initial appearance (often referred to as a **first appearance**), before a judge of a lower court or a magistrate. If the defendant is in custody, jail officers will bring him or her to court. The police may not hold a defendant for more than a reasonable period of time without an initial or first appearance. In some jurisdictions, this may be twenty-four or forty-eight hours; in others, it may be seventy-two hours. A defendant on pretrial release must come to court as ordered. If a defendant fails to appear, the judge issues a bench warrant. A police officer locates the suspect and places him or her under formal arrest.

The purpose of the first judicial appearance is to ensure that the defendant is informed of the charges and made aware of his or her rights. It is also an opportunity for the defendant to end the proceedings quickly with a guilty plea. If the defendant was arrested without a warrant, as is common, this is the time at which the judge will determine probable cause to arrest.

The procedure for a first appearance for a misdemeanor and a felony is outlined below.

Misdemeanors

- The charge or charges are read to the defendant, and penalties are explained.
- The judge or magistrate advises the defendant of his or her right to trial, and right to trial by jury if applicable.
- The right to counsel (legal representation) is explained, and the judge or magistrate appoints a lawyer if the defendant requests one and is found to be **indigent** (too poor to afford a private lawyer).
- The defendant enters a plea. If counsel has been requested and appointed, or if the defendant indicates that private counsel will be retained, a plea of not guilty is entered. If the defendant enters a not guilty plea, a trial date will be set.
- If the defendant pleads guilty, either a date will be set for sentencing or the magistrate or judge will impose probation, fines, or other sentences immediately. In some jurisdictions, in some cases, the judge or magistrate may allow a defendant to plead **nolo contendere,** or no contest. In many jurisdictions, a plea of no contest is equivalent to a guilty plea, except that the defendant does not directly admit guilt.
- Assuming the defendant has pled not guilty, the judge or magistrate sets the amount of bail (see page 569).

Felonies

- The process is quite similar here, except that there is the additional step of the **preliminary hearing,** as a safeguard warranted by the more serious nature of the charges. The charge or charges are read to the defendant, and the penalties are explained.
- The defendant is advised of his or her right to a preliminary hearing and the purpose of that procedure, as well as his or her right to trial, and right to trial by jury in trial court.
- The right to counsel (legal representation) is explained, and the judge or magistrate appoints a lawyer if the defendant requests one and is found to be indigent.
- In most jurisdictions, the defendant does not enter a plea.
- The matter is set for preliminary hearing. This is a hearing to establish if a crime has been committed and if there is probable cause to believe that the defendant committed the offense(s) alleged in complaint.

- The judge or magistrate sets the amount of bail.

Q. What is involved in a preliminary hearing?

A. The preliminary hearing differs from a first appearance in several regards.

- The government must demonstrate to a judge or magistrate that there is sufficient evidence, or probable cause, to believe the suspect committed the crime with which he or she is charged. Defendants usually must be present at this hearing, although they do not commonly offer evidence in their defense. Victims seldom appear at preliminary hearings. Often, there is just one witness, the police officer who investigated the crime or who arrested the defendant. This procedure has a similar function to grand jury proceedings, in that it is a safeguard against unfettered government action.
- If the court finds there is no probable cause, the matter is dismissed (this would be the equivalent of a grand jury declining to press charges). If this happens, defendants are released.
- If the court finds there is probable cause, as is usually the case, the matter is transferred to trial court. Many courts use the term **bound over,** as in "the defendant is bound over to the district or circuit court for trial."
- Bail is continued or reset at a different amount because of evidence that came out in the preliminary hearing.

Note that in the federal system, the government can prosecute for felonies only by obtaining an indictment voted upon by a grand jury. If you are indicted by a grand jury, you have no right to a preliminary hearing because the grand jury has already determined that there is probable cause to believe you committed the offense you're charged with.

Q. Am I likely to be released before my trial?

A. You are not guaranteed the right to be released before trial. The judge will consider whether you are likely to flee or pose a danger to the community if the court releases you before trial, or pending disposition of your case. Points in your favor include strong family ties in the area, longtime local residence, and current local employment.

Release on recognizance (or **own recognizance** or **personal recognizance,** often abbreviated ROR, OR or PR) is common for most offenses. This does not involve posting bail money, but you will have to make a binding promise to return to court on a date specified by the judge. Some types of release do not involve posting a money bail, but do have a money liability attached in case of failure to appear. Attachment of a financial condition that does not have to be posted is usually referred to as an **unsecured bond.**

If the court grants you OR status or releases you on bail, you must reappear in court as agreed. If you do not appear, the judge could revoke your bail or OR status. Failure to appear also may be a separate criminal act. The judge also could issue

---

📄 BAIL

Bail is money or property that you provide to ensure that you will appear in court for trial. Bail is not a fine. It is not supposed to be used as punishment. The purpose of bail is simply to ensure that you will appear for all trial and pretrial hearings for which you must be present. If you fail to appear, you forfeit the bail. If you do not have the money or property to post bail, a relative or friend can post bail on your behalf (or you can go to a bail bondsman, described in the sidebar on page 570). After the trial ends, the court will refund the bail money, usually keeping a percentage for administrative costs.

a bench warrant for your arrest. The police then will find you, take you into custody, and place you in jail.

If the judge decides that it is appropriate to set a financial bail, the issue then becomes the amount that you must post for your release. Your bail may not be excessive (unreasonably high). Some states have bail schedules that set out the charges and the bail that would apply to each charge. The judge also may condition release on bail upon a hearing at which you must satisfy the court that the source of money and collateral for the bail is legitimate.

Q. What is the difference between a plea of guilty and a plea of nolo contendere?

A. The vast majority of criminal cases eventually result in pleas of guilty or nolo contendere. Under either plea, you are guilty of the crime originally charged or of a lesser offense agreed to by the parties. On the other hand, a guilty plea is a specific admission of guilt. The practical effect of a nolo plea in some states is that it avoids automatic civil liability. Let us say a nursing home operator is accused of the crime of abusing patients. If the operator pleads guilty, anyone who sues him or her for civil damages will not have to prove that the abuse occurred. If the operator pleads nolo contendere, then the civil court will have to decide whether the acts alleged took place.

In a few jurisdictions, a defendant may elect to **stand mute** instead of making a plea. When the judge asks for a plea, the defense lawyer states, "My client stands mute." The court will enter a plea of not guilty. By standing mute, the accused avoids admitting to the correctness of the proceedings against him or her until that point. By standing mute, the accused preserves his or her right to attack the validity of the proceedings on appeal.

Q. Must the judge accept my plea?

A. A plea of not guilty must be accepted. A judge cannot accept a guilty plea unless he or she ensures that you understand the rights you are giving up and that you are doing so of your own will (free from coercion or threats). In many states, the judge also must determine that there is a factual basis for your plea; in other words, that you actually are guilty of the offense. If you assert that you are innocent, but want to make a guilty plea for the sake of expediency, you are entitled to do so as long as the judge finds a factual basis for

---

ⓘ THE ROLE OF A BAIL BONDSMAN

Many defendants cannot raise the entire amount of their bail. In some states, defendants may arrange for their release through a bail bondsman, who guarantees to pay the bail amount to the court if the defendant fails to appear for trial.

There are inherent problems with commercial bail bonding. First, the defendant will pay a nonrefundable premium, usually 10 percent of the bail amount set. Second, the defendant or a party acting on behalf of the defendant must put down collateral for the entire bond. Third, should the defendant abscond, a bail bondsman is likely to hire a bounty hunter who has powers exceeding those of police officers in terms of crossing jurisdictional borders and in the use of force.

The ABA has called for the abolition of commercial bail bonding and universal use of court deposit systems, in which the defendant provides a deposit of 10 percent of the bail to the court, which is returned after the trial (less a small administrative fee).

the plea, and finds that you are competent to enter a guilty plea.

Q. What are plea bargains?

A. **Plea bargains** are legal transactions in which a defendant pleads guilty to a lesser charge or pleads guilty to the original charge in exchange for some other form of leniency, such as the imposition of the minimum sentence or dismissal of more serious charges in a multiple dismissal case. The rationale is based on the notion of judicial economy—plea bargains avoid the time and expense of a trial, freeing up the courts to hear other cases. The benefit to defendants is that the process is completed much sooner than it would be if they went to trial. Further, defendants are afforded a sense of certainty; they know what the outcome of their case will be, rather than taking their chances at trial.

Generally, such offers are more generous in the early stages of prosecution as an incentive to the defendant to bring the case to an early conclusion. An early disposition of the case tends to be favored by the prosecution and the judge because it eliminates several additional court appearances that would have been required had the case continued to trial.

In most cases, the defense would be better off waiting to investigate the case thoroughly and consider a later offer or possible dismissal of the charges. For example, consider the case of a person charged with attempted murder because he allegedly uttered a death threat when he shot someone in the leg. An early offer might be to plead guilty to assault with a deadly weapon, which is a serious felony carrying a sentence of several years. However, if the victim testifies inconsistently at a preliminary hearing, the prosecutor might realize that he or she would not be a credible witness at trial. Rather than risk an acquittal at trial, the prosecutor may offer to plead the case down to a misdemeanor, such as negligent discharge of a weapon.

If you do not accept the offer when the prosecution first makes it, the prosecutor is allowed to reduce or withdraw the offer.

You do not have a right to have the prosecutor negotiate a plea with you or your lawyer, but prosecutors usually will offer a plea bargain to reduce their heavy caseloads. In most jurisdictions, the court has no obligation to adhere to the bargain the prosecution offers, but in many cases the judge will accept the plea if a legal basis for it is established in court (see the question below regarding the judge's role in plea negotiations).

The plea bargaining process is not without its critics. Some victims' rights groups feel it is immoral for criminals to serve less time through plea bargaining than they would if convicted of actual crimes committed. In response to citizen pressure, some states, such as California, have passed laws severely restricting or even prohibiting plea bargaining in certain serious or violent crimes.

Q. What role does the judge play in plea negotiations?

A. The judge is under no obligation to accept all terms of the plea bargain. Most often, however, the judge will honor the plea bargain reached between the parties unless he or she feels it is unfair. Before accepting your guilty plea, the judge will explain the maximum time to which you may be sentenced and the maximum fine, if any, that may be imposed. That time may exceed the sentencing recommendation of the prosecution, or the judge could impose a shorter term in the interests of justice. If you do not accept at that point, your guilty or nolo contendere plea will not be entered and you will go to trial.

ⓘ **PLEA BARGAINING**

Over 90 percent of convictions in felony cases in state courts are the result of a guilty plea. Not all of those who plead guilty do so as part of a plea bargain.

Source: Bureau of Justice Statistics

Q. Can the charges against me be dropped?

A. Yes, this can occur for several reasons. For example, charges may be dropped if there is insufficient evidence, which means the police either could not find enough evidence to link you to a crime or found evidence pointing to your innocence. Witness problems also prompt prosecutors to drop charges—for example, when those who observed a crime fail to appear, are reluctant to testify, or testify inconsistently. Sometimes, cases are dropped **in the interests of justice,** a broad category that means the prosecutor does not feel the case is significant enough to pursue, such as minor property damage.

Evidence in Criminal Cases

Q. How may I recognize and preserve evidence to help me at my trial?

A. Physical evidence—such as a gun or a piece of clothing—can be very important in helping a judge or a jury piece together what actually happened. These people were not there when the alleged crime took place. The physical evidence can provide a way to show that your version of the facts is correct.

You should preserve any items that might be useful as evidence, whether you think the evidence will help or harm your case. It is against the law to destroy evidence. In any event, let your lawyer determine whether the evidence is harmful. For example, you might believe that the prosecution will use a gun with your fingerprints as evidence against you in a shooting. But if your lawyer can show that the gun was too big or the trigger too hard to pull for someone of your size to have fired it, then the evidence will help your case. The only logical explanation then would be

---

ⓘ TYPES OF IMMUNITY

If you refuse to testify by asserting your Fifth Amendment right against self-incrimination, the prosecutor can compel you to testify by providing you with immunity. There are two types of immunity that can be provided to a witness: use immunity and transactional immunity.

The different types of immunity give different protections. **Use immunity** means the prosecutor is not permitted to use what you say or evidence derived from what you say to help prosecute you later. **Transactional immunity** gives far greater protection. It means the prosecution will never prosecute you for the crime, even based on evidence independent of your testimony.

▶ OVERLOOKED EVIDENCE

Some evidence is far less obvious than a gun. At a crime scene, tiny items such as rug fibers, hair, cigarette ashes, matches, and even DNA samples may become important evidence in your defense. Therefore, if you are at the scene of a crime before the police arrive, you should leave everything undisturbed. Do not vacuum, move items, or touch anything. The police will secure the area and record everything to maintain what the law calls "crime scene integrity." Once evidence gets misplaced or damaged, a crucial link in winning your case may be lost. In addition, the judge or the jury might view tampering with the evidence as an indication of your guilt.

The nature of the offense will determine the evidence to preserve. For instance, if the prosecution charges you with an economic crime such as fraud, you must preserve any important documents.

that you picked up the gun after the shooting. This may cause the jury to have a reasonable doubt about your guilt.

Q. What kind of evidence may the prosecution use against me at the trial?

A. The prosecution may use almost any type of legally admissible evidence that will help establish your guilt. This includes physical evidence, such as a murder weapon or items stolen during a burglary. Testimonial evidence is likely to be used as well. That involves **testimony** (oral statements) from a person on the witness stand. For example, the owner of a stolen car might testify that no permission was given to anyone to take the car on the day the crime occurred. The prosecution also may introduce circumstantial evidence of a crime, such as the fact that the defendant hurriedly packed and moved out of state within hours after the crime, circumstantially indicating a consciousness of guilt—or that a man charged with killing his wife took out a $100,000 life insurance policy the day before she was slain, circumstantially indicating motive.

If a lawyer asks a witness to testify about statements that someone else made outside the courtroom, the opposing lawyer may object to the admissibility of the testimony because it is **hearsay.** The problem with hearsay is that the person who made the statement is not a witness and is unavailable for cross-examination.

To decide whether the testimony would be hearsay, the court must decide why the witness is being asked the question. If the witness's testimony about someone else's out-of-court statement is being introduced to prove the truth of the out-of-court statement, it is hearsay. If it is only being introduced to prove that the out-of-court statement was made, it is not hearsay.

For example, assume Jane testifies, "John told me my husband was having an affair." If John's out-of-court statement ("Your husband is having an affair") were being introduced to prove that Jane's husband was in fact having an affair, it would be hearsay. If, on the other hand, Jane is only testifying about what John said in order to

explain why she slapped him in the face, her testimony would not be hearsay. Here the only issue is whether John made the statement, not whether the statement was true.

There are many exceptions to the rule against hearsay, so do not be surprised to hear such statements allowed during the trial.

Witnesses

Q. Who are witnesses? What makes a good witness?

A. The prosecution and the defense may both present witnesses. Witnesses might be victims or defendants who are testifying voluntarily on their own behalf, or people who are compelled to testify through the use of a subpoena. Or a witness might be someone testifying as an impartial eyewitness to a crime, or someone with information about it.

Q. What do I do if I'm called to be a witness at a trial?

A. The most important thing is to be honest. When you are on the witness stand, the law requires you to tell the truth. Answer the questions as completely as possible, but stick to the point. Do not add details that are not necessary to answer the question. If you do not understand the question, politely ask the lawyer to rephrase it. Do not answer any questions if you are unsure of the answer. If you do not know the answer, your answer should be "I don't know." If you hear a lawyer say, "Objection," after a question is asked, do not answer the question. Wait until the judge rules on the objection. The judge then will tell you whether you may answer the question.

Testifying can be tiring and frustrating. Try to remain relaxed and keep a pleasant attitude. The worst thing you can do is to appear angry, lose your temper, or argue with the lawyer who is asking the questions. If the judge and the jury disapprove of your behavior or attitude, they might not believe your testimony.

CIRCUMSTANTIAL EVIDENCE

Circumstantial evidence is best explained by saying what it is not—it is not direct evidence from a witness who saw or heard something. Circumstantial evidence is indirect evidence, that is, it is proof of one or more facts from which one can find another fact. For example, X has been murdered, and Z is a suspect. Z's fingerprints are found on a book in X's bedroom. A judge or jury may infer that Z was in the bedroom. The fingerprints are circumstantial evidence of Z's presence in the bedroom. Circumstantial evidence is usually not as good as direct evidence (an eyewitness saw Z in the bedroom) because it is possible to make the wrong inference—Z may have loaned X the book and X then may have carried it to the bedroom herself; or Z may have been in the bedroom, but not on the day of the murder. Circumstantial evidence is generally admissible in court unless the connection between the fact and the inference is too weak to be of help in deciding the case. Juries must consider both direct and circumstantial evidence. The law permits juries to give equal weight to both, but it is for the jury to decide how much weight to give to any evidence. Many convictions for various crimes have rested largely on circumstantial evidence

---

Q. What should I do if I receive a subpoena?

A. A **subpoena** or **summons** is a legal process compelling you to appear or to produce certain evidence before a court or a grand jury. As soon as you receive a subpoena, you should take certain steps to protect your interests. First, be sure to preserve all related documents so that you will not risk being charged with obstruction of justice.

Find a lawyer and speak only to him or her about the subpoena. Do not confide in friends or contact others who may be in the same situation, since they may be cooperating with the authorities and could end up testifying in court against you.

If you receive a subpoena ordering you to appear in court or before a grand jury at a certain date and time, you must obey or risk being held in contempt of court and receiving a fine or a jail

---

 EXPERT WITNESSES

Expert witnesses are specialists in certain fields, such as narcotics, psychology, medicine, or engineering. The prosecution or the defense may call them to testify at a trial. Their testimony is another form of evidence that the judge or the jury will consider. Usually, the experts' role is to offer an opinion of what they think the evidence means when laypeople are unlikely to understand that evidence without help. For example, a narcotics expert might testify that the quantity of drugs seized and the way the defendant packaged them indicate a commercial drug operation. A fingerprint expert may compare the prints lifted from a crime scene to a fingerprint sample taken from the defendant and then give a professional opinion of whether the prints match.

The U.S. Supreme Court has ruled that in federal cases the trial judge must act as a "gatekeeper" and rule upon the admissibility of expert testimony before it is offered. The judge will weigh the qualifications of the expert and the opinion he or she is offering, using such factors as the reliability of the principles and methods used by the expert to arrive at his or her opinion.

sentence. A contempt finding also could mean that you have to pay certain court costs for time lost because the case could not proceed.

The subpoena may compel you to produce an item you possess, instead of or in addition to your testimony. This **subpoena duces tecum (SDT)** compels you to produce certain evidence, usually in the form of documents. Before you obey this type of subpoena, call a lawyer. Depending on the content of the documents, you might be able to fight the subpoena as forced self-incrimination. Or, based upon the items listed in the subpoena, your lawyer may be able to offer your cooperation to the authorities in an effort to show that no crime has been committed or that you were not part of it.

In some cases, your lawyer may be able to negotiate a deal in which you are granted immunity in return for producing the documents. The Supreme Court has determined that if you respond to a government subpoena seeking discovery of sources of potentially incriminating documents in exchange for being granted immunity, the government cannot use the fact that you produced the documents against you.

Do not deal with the authorities yourself. Your lawyer will need to ensure that your cooperation will not be used against you at a later date.

Q. May the court force me to testify?

A. If you are a defendant, no. The Fifth Amendment of the U.S. Constitution gives you the right against self-incrimination.

If you are a witness or the victim of a crime, a subpoena compels you to testify, even if you don't want to get involved. You may refuse to answer a question on the witness stand if you feel the answers might incriminate you, unless the district attorney or prosecutor has granted you immunity in exchange for your testimony—in that case, you must answer (see the sidebar "Types of Immunity" on page 572). A witness should rely on the advice of his or her lawyer regarding whether to refuse to answer questions. The lawyer should be a person who has no role in the proceedings other than to advise the witness.

Sometimes a crime victim gets cold feet and changes his or her mind about testifying. This is especially true if the victim knows the defendant personally or is afraid of revenge. If you are the victim and no longer want to go forward with the charge, you should make your wishes known to the prosecutor. However, even if you reported the crime and later decide you want the charges dropped, the prosecutor might not agree. The prosecutor often considers a victim's wishes, but technically the injured person is only a witness. The "victims" are the people of the state where the criminal committed the crime. Therefore, it is up to the district attorney or prosecutor to decide whether to proceed with the case and whether to subpoena a witness to testify.

Q. Should I take the stand in my own defense?

A. You should listen to your lawyer's advice, but the final decision regarding whether to testify is yours. Many defendants do not testify. The judge will instruct the jury not to hold it against you if you do not testify because the Fifth Amendment gives you the right not to incriminate yourself.

Many defendants feel that they should testify because they are innocent and have nothing to hide. A defendant should bear in mind that he or she will be subject to tough cross-examination from the prosecutor. For instance, if you take the stand, the prosecutor may ask you whether you have had any prior felony convictions. You must answer truthfully. If you do not take the stand, no one will reveal such information to the jury.

Q. Should I talk to the police if they want to question me about a criminal investigation?

A. If you are a witness to a crime, you should share your knowledge with the police. Without information from witnesses, police would be unable to solve crimes and prosecutors would be unable to convict guilty defendants in court. If, on the other hand, you played a role in the crime, or you think the police want to question you as a possible suspect, you have a right to refuse to talk to the police. You also have the right to consult with a lawyer regarding whether you should talk to the police. It is generally sound advice to consult with a lawyer before you agree to talk to the police.

Defenses Against Criminal Charges

Q. What are my possible defenses?

A. In arguing an **affirmative defense,** a defendant accepts that the elements of the crime have been shown, but argues that the acts were justified or excuse the crime. A person accused of a violent crime will not be found guilty if he establishes that he was justified in using the force involved; this is generally referred to as self-defense, but it might involve defense of another or defense of property. Another defense is that the defendant was forced by another to commit the crime and had no alternative but to do the acts involved. There are other defenses, which are rarely successful, such as asserting that the defendant was insane at the time of the crime, or that the defendant improperly was induced by the government to commit the crime (**entrapment**), or that natural forces outside of the defendant's control forced him to commit the crime in order to prevent greater injury (**necessity**).

A defendant may provide evidence showing that the state has failed to prove the elements of the crime. This is not strictly a defense. A defendant also may present alibi evidence showing that he was not at the scene of the crime when he is alleged to have committed it.

Q. How does a defendant's mental health affect the legal process?

A. Under our system, it is unconstitutional to make anyone who is mentally **incompetent** stand trial. This means defendants must be able to comprehend the nature of the charges against them and to assist properly in their own defenses (such as explaining to a lawyer what happened and which witnesses may be able to substantiate their accounts). When a defense lawyer has reason to question a client's competency, he or she will ask the judge to order a psychiatric evaluation. A defendant who is found not competent may be committed to a psychiatric facility for treatment, where he or she will stay until he or she is competent to stand trial. In some states, the psychiatric patient must be released after a certain period.

Q. Is incompetence the same as an insanity defense?

ⓘ WITNESS ASSISTANCE

Most district attorney's or prosecutor's offices have witness assistance departments that provide a number of services to simplify the process for prosecution witnesses. They will give you directions to court and even arrange transportation for you if necessary. If you must travel a distance to testify, these departments may provide you a per diem (daily allowance) for food and lodging. Witness assistance coordinators can help you with other necessary arrangements (such as child care) so you can testify.

If testifying puts you in danger, witness protection programs are available. The police will escort you between your home and court if necessary. If you are a confidential informant in fear for your life, steps will be taken to hide your identity.

The defense does not have all of the resources that the government possesses. It may not be able to pay you a daily allowance. Despite this, if you have been subpoenaed, you must appear.

A. Being incompetent for trial differs from being insane at the time of the offense. **Insanity** is a defense to certain crimes that require proof of intent. For example, it could be argued that one who is insane cannot commit first-degree murder because his or her mind is incapable of premeditating and deliberating (planning the crime).

A few states have abolished the insanity defense but allow psychiatric evidence at trial on the issue of intent. For example, a defendant in a drug case could not have formed the intent to sell an illegal substance if he was delusional and believed that he was a doctor dispensing medication.

Most states require formal notice of plans to raise the insanity defense. Such defendants enter a plea of not guilty and proceed to trial. If convicted, such an individual may be found guilty, not guilty by reason of insanity, or, in a few states, guilty but mentally ill. Defendants found not guilty by reason of insanity are placed in a mental health facility until their mental condition improves so that they are no longer a threat to themselves or the community.

Pretrial Procedures

Q. Does discovery take place in criminal cases as in civil cases?

A. Discovery is a process that allows the parties (state and criminal defendant in criminal cases; and plaintiff and defendant in civil cases) to learn the strengths and weaknesses of each other's case—for example, by obtaining the names and statements of witnesses the other side intends to call at trial. Because the defendant in a criminal case has certain constitutional safeguards (such as the right against self-incrimination), discovery in criminal cases is far more limited than in the civil context.

It is common for discovery rules or laws to require both parties to provide in advance of trial lists of names of witnesses and physical evidence that may be introduced at trial. The state usually has to hand over any statement made by the defendant that it intends to introduce at trial and to indicate criminal record histories of defendants

and witnesses as well as any benefits (such as reduced charges) offered or provided to witnesses. Defendants are entitled to receive the same kinds of discovery material as are made available to the state. It is common for defendants to have to tell the prosecution about their intention of relying on certain defenses, such as insanity, in advance of trial. The prosecution is required as a matter of federal constitutional law to hand over to the defense all evidence favorable to the defendant that concerns either factual guilt or sentencing issues.

Q. Do criminal cases involve interrogatories and depositions?

A. Interrogatories are written questions about the facts and background of the case, which the opposing party must answer in writing. Depositions involve the same types of questions, but are oral examinations conducted in a conference room without a judge present. These common civil discovery procedures are rare in criminal cases, although some states such as Florida do permit the taking of depositions in criminal cases. In addition, a rule of federal criminal procedure permits the taking of a witness's deposition where the prosecution or defense can show that it is necessary to preserve his or her testimony because the witness's testimony is material and he or she will be unavailable for trial.

In a civil case, the parties must participate in depositions if requested by the opposing side; in a criminal case, because of the guarantees of the Fifth Amendment, it would be unconstitutional to force the accused to answer questions about the case (unless he or she elects to testify at trial). Criminal defendants must be present at depositions in their cases (or waive that right) because of the Sixth Amendment right to be present and to confront witnesses.

Trial

Q. What happens at trial?

A. First, the jury is selected (unless the defendant elects and the prosecution agrees to have a trial by judge, commonly referred to as a bench trial). Once the jury has been **impaneled** (seated for the duration of the trial), the proceedings begin. Defendants have a constitutional right to a public trial.

Opening statements then follow. The prosecutor addresses the jury first, explaining the nature of the case and what he or she intends to prove happened. Then the defense lawyer may offer an opening statement, or may reserve the opening statement until after the prosecution has finished its case.

Next, the prosecution puts on its case in chief, which usually involves direct testimony by witnesses and the introduction of any physical evidence against the defendant, such as a gun or other implements of the alleged crime. Defense lawyers may cross-examine the prosecution witnesses by asking questions designed to raise doubt about the government's case. After all prosecution witnesses have testified, the process repeats itself in reverse: the defense puts on any witnesses it may have, and the prosecution cross-examines them.

Because the prosecution bears the burden of proving the defendant's guilt beyond a reasonable doubt, the defense is not required to offer any witnesses, nor are defendants required to testify unless they so choose upon the advice of their lawyers.

When the defense has rested, the prosecutor will give a closing argument, summing up the evidence presented against the defendant. The defense lawyers then will make their own closing argument. The prosecutor has one last chance for a rebuttal argument, addressing the points made by the defense in closing. Note that the order of the closing arguments may vary in some states. When the closing arguments have concluded, the judge instructs the jury on the law to apply in deciding the case.

Q. How many jurors sit on a federal criminal jury?

A. A federal criminal trial jury usually has twelve members, unless the defendant and prosecutor agree to fewer. In some states, there may be fewer than twelve jurors in criminal misdemeanor cases, in which the maximum punishment is usually no more than a year's imprisonment. In more serious felony cases, in which the punishment may be more than a year of imprisonment in the penitentiary, twelve jurors are often required.

Q. What is the role of a jury in a criminal case?

A. The jury weighs the evidence and finds the defendant guilty or not guilty. (Juries are discussed more fully in chapter 2, "How the Legal System Works.") It is important to understand that you have certain rights. First, you have a right to a jury trial in serious criminal cases (for example, for crimes punishable by more than six months' imprisonment). Second, you have a right to a jury that is chosen from a fair cross section of the community and is not biased against you. Both the state and the defense may seek to remove potential jurors who would not be fair and, in addition, both sides usually are allowed to remove a set number of jury members without showing cause; however, it is unconstitutional to use these peremptory challenges to remove jurors on the basis of race or gender.

Q. What are jury deliberations?

A. After closing arguments, the judge will **charge** the jury (give them instructions on how to

---

ⓘ YOUR RIGHT TO A JURY

In criminal cases, the right under the federal Constitution extends to defendants facing a possibility of being sentenced to a prison term of six months or more. Congress has provided for the jury trial option in some instances where the federal Constitution does not require one. State constitutions also may guarantee greater rights to a jury trial.

apply the law to the evidence they have observed at trial). The jury then retires to a private room for deliberations, which involve discussion among the jurors as they review the evidence and attempt to reach a unanimous verdict. Deliberations are carried out in complete secrecy, to ensure fairness to the person on trial. If the jurors have questions, they may send a note to the judge, who usually will respond in writing to clear up any legal questions.

In the federal system, jury decisions in criminal cases must be unanimous. If the jury is not unanimous (if it is irrevocably divided it is called a **hung jury**), a mistrial is declared. The case may be retried later or dismissed.

There is more variation among the states. In felony prosecutions, juries in almost all states must reach guilty verdicts unanimously. In more than a third of the states, agreement of only three-fourths or five-sixths of the jurors is needed to render a verdict in misdemeanor cases.

Q. Will the court protect jurors against danger of threats or violence?

A. The law entitles jurors to such protection. Very occasionally, the court **sequesters** the jury (houses it in a hotel to isolate it from outside influences) throughout the trial. It is more common to sequester a jury during its deliberations. Police officers or court officials escort the jury to and from court. After the trial, the police will continue as best they can to ensure the safety of

---

ⓘ FEW CASES COME TO TRIAL

The overwhelming majority of criminal cases are resolved by dismissal or a plea bargain—only about 5 percent of cases ever make it to a trial.

---

discharged jurors, at least for a time. On rare occasions the court can even empanel an anonymous jury.

Sentencing of Convicted Criminals

Q. If a judge or a jury convicts me, how and when will the court sentence me?

A. In felony cases, sentencing is a separate procedure from the trial, and usually is held several weeks or even months after a conviction. After the verdict is read, the court will order a presentencing report from the probation department, which contains, among other things, the offender's criminal record and a sentence recommendation.

In misdemeanor cases, on the other hand, sentencing usually immediately follows a finding of guilt, and presentencing investigations are not conducted.

In most states the judge has some discretion in choosing your sentence. For misdemeanors,

---

ⓘ TRIAL BY JURY OR JUDGE

Should you exercise your right to a jury trial, or waive it in favor of a bench trial, which is a trial before a judge? This is a decision that you and your lawyer must make. In nonpetty criminal cases punishable by more than six months' imprisonment, you generally have the right to be tried by a jury of your peers (fellow citizens). Your chances might be better with a jury, because the prosecutor must convince each juror that you are guilty. On the other hand, you should bear in mind that juries are unpredictable. In some rare cases, you might stand a better chance of acquittal with a judge. Listen to your lawyer's advice, but remember that in most jurisdictions, you cannot waive trial by jury without the consent of the prosecutor.

the judge usually chooses between a fine, probation, a suspended sentence, or a jail term (or a combination of these). For felonies, the choice is often between imprisonment and probation, depending on the crime.

For state offenses, the criminal code often specifies the minimum and maximum sentences for each specific crime. Often, these are designated as a range, such as three to five years. You may not receive more than the statutory maximum sentence. Any factor that would increase the maximum would need to have been submitted to the judge at trial. For federal offenses, the court follows the strict federal sentencing guidelines. Similar strict guidelines have been adopted by some states, including Florida, Minnesota, and Michigan.

The federal guidelines involve a complex formula that calculates an offense level based on several factors, such as the nature and complexity of the crime, any injuries to victims, and the defendant's criminal history. It then results in a certain number of points, which gives a range of incarceration (prison) time. In some very limited instances, a federal judge might be able to sentence you to a term that varies slightly from the required guidelines. If, for example, the judge finds that your criminal history score significantly underrepresents or overrepresents the seriousness of your actions, he or she can adjust your score upward or downward, affecting the length of time you would spend in prison.

Repeat offender laws have been enacted in some states to deter and punish people who commit crimes repeatedly. Under repeat offender legislation, judges are required to sentence people who commit crimes within a certain time period after their release from prison to the statutory maximum sentences on conviction. Offenders must then serve 100 percent of their sentence.

Q. Is the judge the only person who may decide the sentence?

A. In most states and in federal courts, the judge alone determines the sentence. The exception in some states is those cases in which the defendant may receive the death penalty, in which case the jury, not the judge, must determine whether the death penalty should be imposed. In capital cases, the penalty phase becomes a minitrial of its own, with witnesses commonly testifying about the defendant's character and family upbringing, in an effort to show why he or she should be sentenced in a certain way.

Q. What determines the sentence I will receive?

A. The primary factors are the sentencing range provided in the penal code and your prior convictions, if any. The judge also may consider any aggravating or mitigating factors. **Aggravating factors,** such as the violent nature of a crime or a high degree of sophistication in planning it, suggest a tougher sentence. **Mitigating factors** may be a good family history, a stable employment record, or any benefits you have bestowed on the community, such as volunteer work.

In addition, before imposing your sentence, the judge must allow you to make a statement. You should discuss this with your lawyer in advance. Sometimes, a plea for mercy or a promise to improve your behavior will be effective at this point—it depends on the judge and on whether the judge believes you.

Q. Are there any alternatives to jail or prison sentences?

A. Yes. For crimes not covered by mandatory sentences of incarceration, judges may impose what are called **alternative sentences.** Some involve the offender making some sort of payment; others involve being supervised; and others involve enrollment in a residential program or attendance in a day program.

One such option is monetary. The judge may order you to pay a fine as punishment, or to make **restitution** (repayment to a victim who lost money because of your crime.) Another possibility is **probation.** When you are on probation, the court releases you into the community. During probation, you must obey the conditions set forth by the court, which may include periodic drug testing, acquiring a GED, job training, abstinence from alcohol and drugs, and staying away from the victim. If you violate these conditions, the court can revoke your probation and resentence you. Some crimes have mandatory minimum sentences, during which probation is not an option.

These alternatives frequently are combined. For example, a person on probation also may be required, as a term of release, to make restitution to the victim.

A less restrictive sentence involves **community service.** The court could require you to spend a certain number of hours (usually hundreds or thousands) doing service work at a community center.

If the court requires you to remain in custody, you may be eligible for a residential program, such as a halfway house or a "boot camp." In a halfway house, you may be allowed to leave during the day to work at a job or go to school, but you must return to the building every evening. There are also day-reporting programs, which run in reverse to the halfway house: you are required to attend the program during the day but can return home at night.

In a boot camp, you are housed at a prison facility and may not leave at all. You are segregated from the general prison population and are housed with "soft-core" criminals, usually first-time offenders under the age of thirty-five. Your experience will be similar to a boot camp in the military—early morning rising and demanding physical labor during the day. You also will be allowed to attend educational or job-training classes and may receive counseling. Boot camp programs are notoriously difficult to complete. Failure to complete the program successfully usually results in the participant's immediate incarceration.

Appeals of Criminal Cases

Q. May I appeal my conviction?

A. A person convicted at a trial has the right to appeal the conviction at least once. Appeal is not a right under the federal Constitution, but all jurisdictions permit all those who are convicted to make one appeal. Also, the federal Constitution has been interpreted by the U.S. Supreme Court to guarantee counsel for all indigent persons for that appeal.

On appeal, the defendant can raise claims that mistakes were made in applying and interpreting the law during the trial. For example, the defendant might claim that the judge erroneously admitted hearsay testimony, gave improper jury instructions, should not have permitted the prosecution to use evidence obtained in violation of the defendant's constitutional rights, or permitted the prosecution to make improper closing arguments. There are very few grounds for appeal if the defendant pleaded guilty. If the appellate court agrees that there were significant errors in the trial, the defendant will get a new trial.

There is one ground of reversal that leads to the defendant being freed and bars retrial; that occurs if the court finds that at the trial, the government failed to prove all of the elements of the offense beyond a reasonable doubt.

ⓘ **THE RIGHTS OF PRISONERS**

The law entitles prisoners to fair treatment as human beings. This means that jailers may not subject prisoners to brutality and that prisoners are entitled to food, water, medical attention, and access to the legal system. Such access includes a library in which to do legal research and typewriters.

If your state laws provide for a right to **parole** (early release from prison), you can apply for parole when you become eligible. If the parole board denies your request for parole, you must be told why, and you must be given an opportunity to be heard. Parole is not available in the federal system.

Q. What if the law changes after a court convicts me?

A. If a court convicted you for something that is no longer a crime, you might be able to have your conviction overturned. This also might be possible if a trial court denied you a right that the U.S. Supreme Court later rules is guaranteed by the U.S. Constitution. Your rights will depend on whether the new rule or law is retroactive, that is, applied to past court decisions. As a general rule, a change in the law would be retroactive to your criminal case if the case has been appealed but not resolved at the time the law is changed. If, on the other hand, your case on appeal has been resolved, the change in the law would not be retroactive to your case, unless the change is one that directly enhances the accurate determination of your guilt or innocence.

Q. Will the same lawyer who represented me at trial also handle my appeal?

A. Because trial and appellate (appeals) work are two different types of legal practice, the lawyer who represented you at the trial will not file or handle your appeal automatically. You must ask your lawyer to do so, or find another one who will. If you want to appeal your conviction, be sure to inform your lawyer specifically and clearly of that fact—the U.S. Supreme Court has determined that a lawyer's failure to file a notice of appeal does not necessarily constitute ineffective assistance of counsel so long as the defendant did not convey clearly his wishes on the subject. In many states, the state or county public defender (or another assigned counsel) generally will handle the appeal for those unable to pay.

Trials require the skills of a lawyer who has experience in the courtroom and working before juries. Appeals involve a large amount of writing and legal research, as well as the ability to argue legal doctrines before a judge. It is recommended that you obtain a lawyer for your appeal.

Q. What is a habeas corpus proceeding?

A. Literally, **habeas corpus** means "you may have the body." A habeas corpus proceeding challenges a conviction based upon the grounds that you are being held in prison in violation of your constitutional rights. Habeas corpus is not an appeal but a separate civil proceeding used after a direct appeal has been unsuccessful. It is a federal civil proceeding initiated in federal district court. A common constitutional challenge under habeas corpus is that defendants received "ineffective assistance of counsel" at trial, meaning that their lawyers did not do a competent job of defending them. Such a claim is difficult to prove and will require the defendant-appellant to find a different lawyer to argue the incompetence of the previous lawyer. Legal arguments in a habeas corpus case generally are made through written motions, although an evidentiary hearing may be held as needed. Many jurisdictions require that habeas corpus petitions be filed within strict time periods after a decision is rendered on final appeal.

THE WORLD AT YOUR FINGERTIPS

- *The American Bar Association's Division for Public Education publishes an inexpensive booklet for the public about courts and their work,* Law and the Courts: Volume II–Court Procedures. *The book includes a detailed step-by-step guide to a trial, both civil and criminal. It is available from American Bar Association Order Fulfillment by telephone at 800-285-2221, or by fax at 312-988-5528. The relevant sections can also be found online at www. abanet.org/publiced/courts/trialsteps.html.*

- *Many legal websites have a useful section on criminal law. Check out FindLaw's site at public.findlaw.com/criminal and Nolo's at www.nolo.com. Also visit the FreeAdvice.com site (www.freeadvice.com) for more FAQs.*

REMEMBER THIS

- *Trial procedure may be different depending on whether you have been charged with a felony or a misdemeanor.*

ⓘ THE RIGHTS OF VICTIMS

Victims are a critical component of the criminal justice process. They have a right to be treated with fairness and respect for their dignity and privacy. Yet, until about twenty years ago, victims' rights were almost unheard of. Today, more than thirty states have passed constitutional amendments protecting victims' rights and nearly thirty thousand federal and state laws protect victims' rights to notice and participation in the criminal justice system. These rights often are called the Crime Victims' Bill of Rights and also may protect certain rights of witnesses.

While laws differ in their definition of who is a victim for purposes of triggering these rights, they generally include victims of violent crimes, domestic violence, and sexual abuse. Some also include victims of identity theft or telemarketing fraud. The laws protecting victims' rights sometimes include certain witnesses. The laws may require victim and witness cooperation in the apprehension and prosecution of the offender. The laws differ in the procedures for securing victims' rights. Some provide notices and information automatically, but many require victims to request rights by calling, writing, or otherwise notifying the appropriate authorities.

One of the most basic rights is the right to notice of proceedings. This may include a general overview of the criminal justice process, as well as specific notice of dates, times, and places of the court hearings in your case. For example, most laws provide notice of the time and date of trial and sentencing. Most also require that victims be given notice of parole hearings or early release, such as release on parole. An emerging technology called automated victim notification can help victims stay informed about their case automatically. States began working on automating notices after a disturbing case a few years ago in Kentucky in which a young woman was kidnapped and raped by her ex-boyfriend. Although she was supposed to have been notified when he posted bond and secured his release, manual notification procedures were too slow. Within a week of his release, before she could be notified, he shot and killed her. Today, automated victim notification systems can provide notice immediately. These systems are called by different names in the states, but they generally allow a victim to call a computerized toll-free phone number and give a defendant's name, court case, or other identifying information to get computerized updates on the status of the case and the next court date or prison release date. In fact, anyone with a telephone instantly can find out the status of a defendant in a pending criminal case in some localities. These systems allow you to register your number so that you can be notified automatically of any change in court date or in the status of the defendant.

Another critical right of victims is the right to participate in the criminal justice process. The victim is, most often, the key eyewitness, and therefore the victim's testimony is critical. Many of the laws require a separate waiting area so that victims are not harassed or intimidated by the offender while attending court proceedings. Victim considerations in setting bond are included in many victims' rights laws. Special bond conditions may be entered to prevent the offender from contacting the victim while the case is pending. Victims also have the right to have input in sentencing through a victim impact statement. Special conditions also may be attached to a sentence to prevent the offender from contacting you on release.

Crime victims suffer personal and financial losses as a result of crime, and many laws require notice of available services and assistance to enable victims to obtain the emotional and financial support needed for their recovery. For example, free or low-cost counseling may be available to crime victims. Also, government-run crime victims' compensation programs help pay out-of-pocket costs, like medical bills or employment losses as a result of crime. Restitution is mandatory for many crimes, and offenders can be ordered to pay for the damages they caused the victim.

Police or prosecutors should be able to provide information about your rights as a crime victim or a witness. Many of these agencies have specialized crime victim advocates who can help secure the necessary information to help you participate in your case. Some states have developed ombudsman programs that oversee complaints; others have a designated statewide office that handles victims' rights information and complaints of violations of victims' rights. Government services are free of charge. Private agencies also exist in many jurisdictions and may provide free or low-cost services such as advocacy or counseling for crime victims. The U.S. Department of Justice's Office for Victims of Crime has published a bulletin on victims' rights in the United States. It is accessible at their website at *www.ojp.usdoj.gov/ovc*, or you can call the Office for Victims of Crime at 800-627-6872. The National Center for Victims of Crime is a private, not-for-profit agency that also can help you find local resources; its website is *www.ncvc.org*, and its phone number is 800-FYI-CALL.

- *You may be eligible for ROR release, bail, or other conditions that ensure appearance and protect the community from danger. Money bail typically is listed as a last resort. Talk to your lawyer, and investigate all your options before you approach a bail bondsman.*

- *If you are a victim of a crime or witness a crime, do not interfere with a crime scene. You could disturb valuable evidence.*
- *If you are a defendant and you are convicted at trial, you have the right to an appeal.*

The Rights of Older Americans

Why a chapter on the rights of older Americans? A generation ago, even a few years ago, such a chapter would have been unnecessary. Now both the law and society have changed. There's a wide array of laws directly addressing the legal needs of older people, and a growing recognition that the law is crucial to the social and health needs of older persons and their families.

The legal issues discussed in this chapter reflect three realities:

- First, we are rapidly aging as a society. Far more people are living into their seventh, eight, ninth, and tenth decades of life than ever before. Thus, the problems and opportunities of aging affect more older people and more families of older people than at any time in history.
- Second, the law permeates almost every aspect of our society, especially the programs, protections, and opportunities that benefit older people. This chapter provides a basic knowledge of the law that will help you navigate through such programs as Medicare, Medicaid, Social Security, and pension benefits.
- Third, the personal and financial autonomy of older people is at greater risk than that of the remainder of the adult population, because of the increasing risk of physical and mental impairment. This chapter responds to this risk by offering a variety of planning strategies to preserve personal autonomy and financial security.

AGE DISCRIMINATION ON THE JOB

Dennis is fifty-two, and has an executive position with a large company. Dennis has worked for the company for years, enjoys work, and always planned to continue work until he turned sixty-five. Recently, the company downsized, and Dennis was offered a retirement package. He feels like he is being discriminated against because of his age and his salary package. Is this discrimination?

In the past, most of us viewed sixty-five as the age of retirement. Today, more people are choosing to continue working full- or part-time well into their seventies or even eighties. Many even change their careers in later life. The contributions of older workers testify to their vitality.

The Age Discrimination in Employment Act (ADEA) ensures that older workers receive equal and fair treatment in the workplace. It protects most workers forty years of age and older from arbitrary age discrimination while on the job. It also seeks to support the employment of older people based on their ability rather than age. See chapter 12, "Law and the Workplace," for a detailed discussion of the ADEA.

This section covers the basics of age discrimination at the workplace, including your rights to employment and benefits, and what to do if you are discriminated against.

Q. Can I be forced to retire from my job when I reach a certain age?

A. Not if you are at least forty years old and work for either a private employer with twenty or more employees, or the federal government or local government. If you meet these criteria, you are protected by the federal Age Discrimination in Employment Act (ADEA) and cannot be forced to retire.

Although the ADEA also applies to state employees, the U.S. Supreme Court has held that the ADEA cannot be used to sue state governments for damages, but it can be used to obtain an order directing the state to end the discrimination. However, most states have statutes that are similar to the ADEA that state employees can use to obtain both damages and orders prohibiting discrimination.

Q. My employer says that I do not have to stop working at age sixty-five. However, I will have to accept a job with less responsibility and less pay. Is this legal?

A. No. The ADEA also protects you in your present job situation. Your employer may not force you to take a less responsible job or accept a lower salary.

Q. Are there exceptions to the rule that employees may not be forced to retire?

A. Yes. The ADEA does not protect two categories of employees. One such exception is for government officials who are elected or appointed to a policymaking level. This exception includes the non–civil service staff of these officials. The other is for persons in bona fide executive or high policy-making positions.

Q. Must I retire if I become ill or disabled?

A. The law protects you only from being forced to retire because you have reached a certain age. If an illness or a disability prevents you from doing your job satisfactorily, the ADEA does not prevent your employer from requiring you to retire, regardless of your age. However, other federal and state laws—including the 1990 Americans with Disabilities Act (ADA)—forbid discrimination against persons with disabilities or handicaps, including those associated with certain illnesses. So, if the ADEA does not cover you in these circumstances, you should consider whether you are being unfairly treated because of disability.

Q. Are there any circumstances in which age discrimination by an employer is allowed?

A. Yes. If the employer can prove that age is a bona fide occupational qualification (BFOQ), discrimination is allowed. One obvious example of age as a BFOQ is a part in a movie requiring a child actor. The possibility of age as a BFOQ most commonly arises in jobs directly involving public safety or public transportation personnel. However, the BFOQ exception is limited and difficult to prove, and the burden of proof is on the employer. The employer must show

- that the job qualifications are reasonably necessary to the essence of the employer's business; and
- that substantially all persons over the age limit cannot perform the job safely and efficiently, or that it is impossible or highly impractical to assess fitness on an individualized basis.

Q. If I am part of a company division or class of employees being laid off, does the ADEA protect me?

A. Yes, if the employer considered age as a factor in the layoff. Employers may make layoff decisions based on reasonable factors other than age. However, sometimes those factors merely mask age discrimination. For example, if an employer lays off only higher-paid employees, it is possible that the employer is unlawfully discriminating against older employees. Higher pay is often synonymous with higher age.

Q. Can my fringe benefits, such as employee insurance benefits, be reduced because I am older?

A. Normally no, although the law gives employers some flexibility in applying this rule. The general rule, with some exceptions, requires employers to provide all age groups the same benefit, or, alternatively, provide a benefit that costs the same for all age groups. For example, if a given life insurance benefit actually costs the employer more for older workers, then the employer may provide older workers a smaller insur-

---

ⓘ THE BREADTH OF AGE DISCRIMINATION IN EMPLOYMENT

The ADEA does not offer a concrete definition of discrimination. Instead, the act prohibits employers from doing anything that harms an older worker's status because of his or her age. This may range all the way from offensive age-related jokes to using age as a factor in hiring, firing, layoff, promotion, demotion, working conditions and hours, training opportunities, compensation, or benefits. Historically, most ADEA lawsuits have involved firings or layoffs of older workers.

ance benefit, as long as the cost of the benefit to the employer is the same as that offered to younger workers.

As to health insurance, employers must cover older workers and their spouses under the same conditions as they cover younger workers. Your benefits cannot be lowered just because you become eligible for Medicare. In fact, the employer insurance must remain the primary insurer. Medicare will cover you as a secondary insurer while you continue working.

Q. Can I be denied new training that younger workers are receiving?

A. No. Older workers must be given the same privileges of employment as younger workers. These privileges include training.

Q. What are older workers' rights to promotions?

A. Under the ADEA, older workers must be given the same chance to receive promotions as all other workers. But age does not entitle a person to a promotion; an employer may have a valid reason, apart from age, for promoting a younger person rather than an older one.

Q. Can a change in job assignments be considered a form of discrimination?

A. Yes. Employers cannot use terms or conditions of employment to discriminate against older workers. If a change in job assignments is used for this purpose, it is prohibited.

Q. What if my age is only one of the reasons I was discriminated against?

A. As long as age is a determining factor for the discrimination, you are protected by the ADEA. Age does not have to be the sole factor. Other laws cover other unlawful forms of discrimination, based on factors such as race or sex.

Q. If I work in a foreign country, does the ADEA protect me?

A. Yes, if you work for an American corporation or its subsidiaries and if the ADEA does not conflict directly with the law of the country you work in.

Q. Can an advertisement state that only younger workers are wanted for a job?

A. Not unless age is a bona fide occupational qualification. Except for this rare exception, advertisements are not allowed to exclude or discourage older workers from applying. Although courts differ as to which phrases are permissible and which are not, a general rule is that ads can-

---

ⓘ EMPLOYMENT AGENCIES AND UNIONS

The ADEA also applies to employment agencies and labor organizations. These organizations may not discriminate on the basis of age in referrals, notices, advertisements, or membership activities.

⚠ OVERQUALIFIED OR DISCRIMINATED AGAINST?

Could a prospective employer say that you are overqualified for a job? Is this legal? It depends. Sometimes, it might be reasonable to deny you a job because you have too much experience or education. For example, it is reasonable to assume that someone with a Ph.D. in education is overqualified for a teacher's aide position that requires only two years of college education. In other cases, a court might decide that calling you overqualified is just an employer's pretext to avoid hiring an older worker. Therefore, be wary if a potential employer says, "I'm sure that with your long experience, you wouldn't be interested in this entry-level position."

not imply that only certain age groups are wanted for the job.

What to Do if You Are Discriminated Against

Q. What can I do if I have been forced to retire, fired, or otherwise discriminated against because of my age?

A. You should file a **charge** of age discrimination in writing with the federal Equal Employment Opportunity Commission (EEOC). If your state has an age discrimination law and enforcement agency (not every state has one), you should consider filing the charge with both the EEOC and your state agency.

In most cases, filing a charge with either the EEOC or the state agency automatically is treated as filing with both. To be on the safe side, you should take the initiative and file with both.

If you file a charge, your name will be disclosed to the employer. If you wish to remain anonymous, you can file a **complaint** instead. A complaint may start an EEOC investigation; however, the government gives complaints lower priority than charges. In addition, even if EEOC intervention leads an employer to correct its discriminatory practices, your own past unfair treatment may not be remedied if you filed only a complaint.

Q. What is the EEOC?

A. This federal agency has the power to investigate, the duty to mediate, and the option to file lawsuits in order to end practices of age discrimination. See chapter 12, "Law and the Workplace," for more about the EEOC.

Q. Do I have to contact the EEOC with my claim, or can I file my own lawsuit?

A. You must file a charge with the EEOC first. After sixty days, if the EEOC has not filed a lawsuit, you may do so.

Q. What information should be included in my charge?

A. You should include as much relevant data as possible. Be sure to include information about how to contact you, the name and address of the discriminating party, the type of discrimination, relevant dates and witnesses, and specific facts. If pertinent, you also might include employment contracts, brochures, or similar documents that demonstrate company policy. Before you file the charge, make sure you sign it.

Q. How long do I have to file a charge with the EEOC?

A. Normally, you have 180 days from the date of the violation or reasonable notice of it (whichever occurs first). It is important to understand the time limits. If you are given notice of layoff on January 1, to take effect March 1, the time limit begins to run from the earlier date and not the date of layoff.

If your state has an age discrimination law and enforcement agency, the time limit may be extended to 300 days, but every effort should be made to act within the 180 days to be on the safe side. You may file your charge with your state's agency.

Q. What happens once I file a charge with the EEOC?

A. The EEOC is required to contact the discriminating party and attempt conciliation between the parties. The agency also has the power to investigate charges and file a lawsuit to enforce your rights. However, the EEOC files lawsuits in only a small proportion of cases. It is important to realize that the EEOC does not make findings on your charge. Only a court can do that.

Q. If the EEOC files a lawsuit on my behalf, can I still sue separately?

A. No. Once the EEOC begins a suit, private individuals are prohibited from bringing their own action.

Q. If the EEOC does not file a lawsuit, is there a limit to how long I have to sue the discriminating party?

ⓘ SPECIAL PROCEDURES FOR FEDERAL EMPLOYEES

Federal employees or applicants for employment who believe they have been discriminated against have these options:

- They may file a complaint with the EEOC or the federal agency they believe has discriminated against them.

- They may proceed directly to federal court by filing a notice of intent to sue with the EEOC within 180 days of the discriminatory action. The individual then has the right to file a lawsuit 30 days after filing the notice.

A. Yes. The statute of limitations is two years from the time you knew or should have known of the violation. If the violation was willful, you have three years to file a lawsuit.

Sometimes, it is hard to determine when a person should have known of the violation. Other times, however, the exact date is easy to pinpoint. For example, suppose you receive a letter on March 12 from your labor union stating that you are expelled, and you do not open the letter. On April 12, when your union dues are not taken out of your paycheck, you call and discover your expulsion. March 12 is the date when you should have known of the violation, and so that is when the statute of limitations began to run.

Q. Are state age discrimination laws identical to the ADEA?

A. Not necessarily, and not all states have such laws. It is important to check the applicable laws in your state. Some state statutes offer different protection or more protection against discrimination than the ADEA. If this is the case, you may be able to bring an action under a state law that you would not be able to bring under the ADEA.

Q. How do I know if my state has an enforcement agency?

A. If you are unsure whether your state has an enforcement agency, contact your state's department of labor or an EEOC office in your area.

Q. What should I consider in deciding whether to file a private lawsuit under the ADEA?

ⓘ EARLY RETIREMENT INCENTIVE PROGRAMS AND WAIVING YOUR ADEA RIGHTS

Early retirement incentive plans frequently are offered by employers to reduce their workforce. Generally, such plans are lawful if they are voluntary and otherwise comply with federal law. They often provide substantial benefits to employees willing to retire early. However, giving up employment also has great disadvantages, economically and personally. You should be given sufficient information and plenty of time to consider an early retirement offer. Review your options with a financial adviser if possible.

Some companies ask employees who accept an early retirement offer or other exit incentive to sign a waiver of their rights under the ADEA, including the right to sue the employer. Waivers are legal only if they are knowing and voluntary and the employer follows specific procedures required by the act. The required procedures involve extensive notices, disclosures of information, and time periods to ensure the employee has sufficient time to make a decision.

A. If you have suffered significant loss as a result of age discrimination and you are willing to invest substantial time and money, filing a private lawsuit may be worthwhile. The costs of such a lawsuit should be weighed realistically ahead of time. ADEA cases can involve a great deal of legal analysis, discovery, and effort. Generally, lawyers do not take ADEA cases on a contingency basis (that is, payment when and if the case is decided favorably). However, if your lawsuit is successful, the ADEA permits you to seek lawyer's fees from the discriminating party.

Q. What role will the EEOC play in my lawsuit?

A. If the EEOC files a suit either on its own or on your behalf, the commission enforces your rights and you can no longer file a private lawsuit. If the agency does not file a suit, you may do so sixty days or more after the date you file a charge with the EEOC. Unlike other areas of civil rights law, you do not have to wait for a right-to-sue notice from the EEOC. Your own lawsuit will be a private one, and you must bear the court costs and lawyer's fees. A big advantage of a suit filed by the EEOC on your behalf is that you would not be required to pay its costs.

Q. What if my employer retaliates against me because I file a charge?

A. The ADEA forbids such retaliation. If your employer nonetheless takes action you think is retaliatory, you should file another discrimination charge.

Q. If there is already a lawsuit against my employer for age discrimination, can I join it?

A. Yes. The ADEA allows class-action lawsuits. However, unlike many other class-action cases, you are not automatically part of the subject class. You must opt in by consenting in writing.

Q. What will happen if I win my case?

A. The court will order the employer to make up to you what you lost through discrimination. This might include

- the awarding of back pay for salary you did not receive while unemployed;
- the awarding of future pay, or "front pay," for a period of time;
- compensation for lost benefits, or reinstatement of lost benefits—such as seniority rights, health or insurance benefits, sick leave, savings plan benefits, expected raises, stock bonus plan benefits, and lost overtime pay;
- reinstatement in your former job, with your former salary and benefits; and
- double damages in cases of willful violations of the ADEA.

If you win your case, the company that discriminated against you may have to pay for your lawyer and other expenses, as well as for court costs.

THE WORLD AT YOUR FINGERTIPS

- *EEOC offices are listed in the telephone directory under "United States Government." You also can find the location of the office nearest you by calling 800-669-4000, or visiting the EEOC website at* www.eeoc.gov.
- *The AARP website provides some information about age discrimination at* www.aarp.org.

ⓘ YOUR RIGHT TO A JURY TRIAL

In most lawsuits, the type of relief you seek can affect whether you will receive a jury trial. The ADEA, however, grants a right to a trial by jury on any issue of fact, even if you seek only equitable (nonmonetary) relief. A party who wants a jury trial must ask for one specifically. If not requested, a jury trial is automatically waived.

REMEMBER THIS

- *The ADEA protects employees and job applicants who are at least forty years old from discrimination on account of age.*
- *The ADEA applies to private employers with twenty or more employees and to government employers, both local and federal. The ADEA provides more limited protection to state employees.*
- *The ADEA prohibits an employer from forcing you to retire because of your age, except in the case of executive and other high-level employees.*
- *Early retirement incentive plans may or may not be unlawful, depending on the circumstances.*

PENSIONS

Maria is in her fifties, and works for an employer that has a defined contribution pension plan. She is thinking about retiring, but isn't sure when she'll be able to start collecting her pension, or even how much she'll get.

When you retire, your financial security will probably depend on pension income, Social Security benefits, and personal savings. The availability of income from a private pension plan can make the critical difference between a comfortable retirement and one plagued by financial worries. This section discusses three basic kinds of employer-sponsored pension plans: traditional defined contribution and defined benefit pension plans; a simplified employee pension plan; and Section 401(k) plans. It is important to understand your legal rights regarding private pension plans, so that you can make sure the funds are prudently invested and that you receive all the benefits to which you are entitled.

Traditional Pension Plans

Q. Is my employer or union required to set up a pension plan?

A. No. The law does not obligate an employer to set up a pension plan. Less than half of American employees in the private sector are covered by traditional defined contribution and defined benefit pension plans, although many other employees are covered by employer-sponsored simplified employee pension plans and 401(k) plans. Most pensions are governed by rules of the Employee Retirement Income Security Act (ERISA), which sets minimum standards for pension plans that already exist and new pension plans that are created.

Q. Does ERISA apply to all pension plans?

A. No. It does not cover pension plans for federal, state, and local public employees, nor does it cover church employees unless their employer has elected to have ERISA apply. Most ERISA provisions apply to plan years beginning in 1976. As a result, it does not protect workers who stopped working or retired before 1976. However, the terms of an employee's pension plan, as well as state law, do offer some protection.

Q. What are the different types of traditional pension plans?

A. There are two major kinds, and they are quite different. One kind, called a defined benefit plan, guarantees you a certain amount of benefits per month upon retirement. For example, a defined benefit plan might pay you $10 a month per year of service. Under that plan, a person who retires after ten years of service would receive $100 per month in pension benefits.

Under the other kind of plan, called a defined contribution plan, the employer and/or the employee contribute a certain amount per month during the years of employment. The amount of the benefit depends on the total amount accumulated in the pension fund at the time of retirement. And that amount depends not only on how much you and your employer contributed, but also on how much that money earned when it was invested.

Typically, pension trustees invest the fund's money in stocks, real estate, and other generally safe investments. If those investments do well over the years, the fund grows and your monthly benefits may be relatively high. But if the investments do poorly, the fund may not grow much or may even shrink. In that case, your monthly benefits may be far smaller. (See the discussion later in this section of the requirement that plans make prudent investments.)

Even in the defined contribution plan, your benefit will be determined by some formula that takes into account your age, how long you worked for the employer, and how much you were paid.

The choice of defined benefit or defined contribution plan is not yours to make. The employer decides.

Q. I am fifty-five years old and I want to retire now. Can I start collecting my pension at once?

A. Maybe. All pensions set a "normal" retirement age, often 65. They usually set a minimum retirement age as well, perhaps 55, 60, or 62. Check with your pension plan administrator. You may be able to collect benefits now, or you may have to wait until you are older. Remember that benefits usually are calculated partly on the basis of your age. The younger you are when you retire, the smaller the benefits, but presumably you will get them for a longer period.

Q. When must I begin to collect my pension?

A. Each plan sets a normal retirement age. However, if you choose to retire later, you must begin collecting your pension by April 1 of the year after you turn $70\frac{1}{2}$ years old.

Q. Do I get to choose how my pension will be paid to me?

A. Yes, to some extent.

The most common type of payment is called the **joint and survivor annuity benefit.** It pays the full benefit to a married couple until one dies, then pays a fraction of the full benefit to the survivor as long as he or she lives. The fraction typically is half or two-thirds. The Retirement Equity Act of 1984 requires this kind of disbursement unless the worker's spouse signs a waiver. The waiver permits payment of a higher benefit, but only as long as the retired worker lives. When he or she dies, the benefits end and the surviving spouse gets no more.

The joint and survivor annuity may allow you some options. You might be able to have benefits guaranteed for a certain number of years. For example, if the guarantee is for fifteen years, benefits would be paid as long as one or both spouses are alive. But if both die before fifteen years has passed since retirement, benefits would continue to be paid to their beneficiary until the fifteenth year. Other guarantees might be for longer or shorter periods; the longer the guarantee, the lower the benefit.

There are some other kinds of pension disbursements as well. One pays a fixed amount for a fixed number of years, which means you could outlive your benefits and get nothing in your oldest years. Another pays all your benefits in a single lump sum when you retire, which could cost you a lot in income taxes.

Q. Will my pension benefits rise over the years?

A. Perhaps. Your union may negotiate cost-of-living increases with your employer. Or a nonunion employer may increase benefits voluntarily. But generally your benefits are frozen at the level they were at when you retired. You also probably will be collecting Social Security benefits, however, and those benefits do rise with the cost of living.

Q. What if I get sick after retiring? Will I still have health insurance?

A. Companies are not required to continue to provide health insurance after retirement. But when they have promised to do so, some courts are requiring them to keep that promise. Under a 1985 federal law known as COBRA (Consolidated Omnibus Budget Reconciliation Act), you must be notified when you retire that you may continue coverage, but your employer may require you to pay the premiums. Coverage generally lasts for eighteen months after you stop working, but may be extended up to twenty-nine months if you are found eligible for **Social Security disability** or **supplemental security income (SSI)** disability benefits. You also will be eligible for Medicare at age sixty-five or possibly earlier if you qualify for disability under Social Security or SSI.

Q. Can my company's pension plan cover some employees but not others?

A. Yes. Some companies establish pension plans only for certain kinds of workers. A plan might cover assembly line workers, for example, and not file clerks. There might or might not be a separate plan for the clerks. But a plan cannot discriminate against employees who are not officers, shareholders, or highly compensated. For example, a supermarket's plan could not include only the company's president and top executives while excluding the managers, baggers, and cashiers. The Internal Revenue Service determines whether a plan is complying with these complicated nondiscrimination rules.

Q. What rules govern when an employee can participate in a pension plan?

A. ERISA sets up two criteria for when employers must permit workers to begin earning credit toward pensions. The employer must permit the earning of credit toward a pension if the worker is at least twenty-one years old and has worked for the employer for at least one year. ERISA calculates a year of employment as one thousand or more hours of work in twelve months. Once employees satisfy these two requirements, they must be allowed to begin accruing credits that will affect the amount of their pensions.

Of course, as with all ERISA requirements, these are the minimums allowed by law. Individual pension plans can have more generous credit-earning policies. For example, they can permit employees to start earning pension credits from their first day on the job, and they can permit workers younger than twenty-one to earn pension credits.

Q. Once I become a participant, how do I know what my rights are under the plan?

A. ERISA requires that participating employees be given detailed reports and disclosures. Within either 90 days of becoming a participant or 120 days of the plan's beginning, the employee must receive a summary plan description. This gives details of the employee's rights and obligations, gives information on the trustees and the plan's administration, sets conditions for participation and forfeiture, and outlines the procedure for making a claim and the remedies available to employees who appeal claims that are denied.

A summary of the plan's annual financial report also must be distributed. If you do not receive a summary, you should ask the plan's administrators for it. Or you can obtain one by writing to the U.S. Department of Labor, Employee Benefits Security Administration, Public Disclosure Room, 200 Constitution Avenue NW, Suite N-1513, Washington, DC 20210.

Q. How are years of accrual determined?

A. After you meet the participation requirements, each year you work for an employer counts as a year of accrual time. A year is defined as one thousand or more hours of work in twelve months. You can work the thousand hours at any time during the twelve-month period; it need not be evenly distributed during the year. Days taken for sick leave or for paid vacation count toward the one-thousand-hour minimum.

It is important to note that, depending on your company's policy, the first year you work for an employer does not have to count toward your years of accrual. Thus, your years of accrual will not always equal the number of years you worked for an employer.

Q. If I stop working for an employer and later return, do I get credit for my previous years of service?

A. That depends on the length of this break in service. An employer can discount the years of your previous service if two conditions are met: first, your break lasts five or more continuous years; and second, your break is longer than the years you previously worked for the employer. If, for example, after six years of work, you took a seven-year break in service, you may be out of luck. However, an employer can have more lenient rules than the ones set out by ERISA. These rules on breaks in service are complex, so you should consult an expert if you think they apply to you.

Q. Is my right to collect my pension guaranteed?

A. You always have the right to money you contributed to the pension fund. If you leave a company after only a few years, that money should be paid back to you in a lump sum. If you work for the employer long enough, you will have a vested interest in your pension, meaning that your benefits cannot be denied even if you quit. If the total value of your pension is $3,500 or less, your plan can require that you take it as a lump-sum payment.

Q. When are my pension rights vested?

A. Amendments to ERISA in 1989 changed the vesting rules. Now, your pension rights must either vest completely after five years or vest par-tially after three years of service. Complete vesting after five years is called **cliff vesting.** If you work less than five years under cliff vesting, you are not entitled to any pension benefits, but once you hit the five-year mark you have a right to 100 percent of the benefits you have earned. Partial vesting is called **graded vesting.** Under this system, your rights become 20 percent vested after three years of service, 40 percent vested after four years, and so on up to 100 percent vested after seven years.

You do not get to choose which vesting method applies. The employer decides.

Q. I want to change jobs. May I take my pension benefits with me to my new job?

A. If you change jobs before your pension has vested, you usually lose all the benefits you built up in your old job, although your employer must refund money you put into the fund. If you change jobs after your benefits have vested, you are entitled to those benefits. You may put (or roll over) those funds into an individual retirement account (IRA) or some other type of retirement program (to avoid taxation) or transfer the funds to the new employer's pension plan if possible. It is often not possible, though some unions have reciprocal agreements that allow you to change employers and transfer your benefits. There are also some state or nationwide pension systems that allow job changes with continued participation in a unified pension program (such as Teachers Insurance and Annuity Association, known as TIAA-CREF).

Q. What if I join an employer at age sixty-two and retire at age sixty-five?

A. ERISA assures older employees that their rights will vest completely at normal retirement age, regardless of the number of years they have worked for an employer.

Also note that since 1988, employers have been required to make contributions to the plan for workers age sixty-five and over.

▤ VESTING

Your pension is said to **vest** when you have the right to all the benefits you have earned. If your pension has vested, you have a right to the benefits, even when you leave the job for another job or for any reason.

Q. If I retire and begin receiving my pension, can I still work?

A. Yes. You can retire, collect your pension, and work full- or part-time. However, if you work for the same employer that is paying your pension, you are limited to fewer than forty hours a month.

Q. Can my employer change an existing pension plan?

A. Yes. ERISA permits an employer to change the way in which future benefits are accumulated. However, the employer may not make changes that result in a reduction of benefits that you already have accrued. In addition, ERISA specifically prohibits plan amendments that alter vesting schedules to the detriment of employees.

Q. What protection does ERISA offer when my company is sold or taken over?

A. This area of law is not entirely clear. In some cases, **successor liability** is found and the company must continue the plan. If such liability is not found, your new employer is under no obligation to continue an existing pension plan. The new employer can go without a plan, set up a new plan, or continue the existing plan. If the new employer decides to continue the plan, however, ERISA requires that previous years of service be counted.

And you still have a right to all the benefits earned under the old employer. If the new employer abandons the plan, though, you will not continue to earn benefits.

Q. Do I have a right to know how my pension plan is investing money?

A. Yes. You should receive a summary of the plan's annual financial report. Each year, a report summarizing the plan's financial operations must be made to both the Internal Revenue Service and the secretary of labor.

Also, ERISA requires that the people in charge of investing your plan's money use care, skill, and prudence and invest only in the interest of participants and beneficiaries. A requirement for investment diversity minimizes the risk of losses. ERISA forbids several investment practices. For example, the pension directors cannot invest more than 10 percent of the fund in the employer's stock or real property. They cannot personally buy the fund's property or lend the fund's money to their friends.

Q. What should I do if those in charge of investing my plan's money violate ERISA?

A. First, you should contact the nearest office of the U.S. Department of Labor. Then, if needed, ERISA permits you to file a lawsuit in federal court to enforce its rules.

Q. I am worried about my pension plan going broke. Do I have any protection against such a disaster?

A. You might have some protection. ERISA established the Pension Benefit Guaranty Corporation (PBGC). If your company has a defined benefit plan, it must pay insurance premiums to the PBGC. If the plan goes broke, the PBGC will pay vested benefits up to a certain limit, but it may not pay all you are owed. If the pension plan is still functioning but in danger of going broke, the PBGC will step in and take control. It will use the plan's remaining money and the insurance

---

ⓘ PROTECTION AGAINST BEING FIRED RIGHT BEFORE YOUR PENSION VESTS

ERISA prohibits an employer from firing you or otherwise treating you unfairly in order to stop the vesting of your pension rights. However, the burden is on you to show that you were not fired for legitimate reasons but because your employer did not want to guarantee you a pension.

premiums paid by other plans to keep your benefits flowing.

Certain pension benefits are not covered, particularly for highly paid people and for those who retire before being eligible for Social Security.

If your plan is of the defined contribution type, the PBGC will not get involved. If that plan goes broke, you may be out of luck. You should keep an eye on how the administrators are handling the fund's money, because ERISA requires that plan trustees act in the best interests of participants. The secretary of labor or plan participants can sue trustees if they act improperly.

Q. Does the amount of Social Security I collect affect my pension benefits?

A. It might. Some pension plans allow a reduction of benefits, depending on how much you receive from Social Security. However, federal law places limits on the amount by which your pension can be reduced. These Social Security **integration rules** are extremely complex and are different for defined benefit and defined contribution plans. You should check with your plan's administrators to see whether your pension plan is integrated with Social Security and if so, how this will affect your benefit.

Q. If I do not agree with the decision on my claim, how do I appeal?

A. The claim and appeal processes are regulated in ERISA. The plan summary must also contain information on the plan's appeal process. All plans must give written notice of the claim decision within ninety days of receipt of the claim. If the plan notifies you within ninety days that it needs an extension, one ninety-day extension is allowed. If you do not receive a written decision by the deadline, consider your claim denied.

If your claim is denied, the decision must give specific reasons for the denial. You then have sixty days to file a written appeal. The plan must make available important documents affecting your appeal, and you must be allowed to submit written support for your claim. The plan then has 120 days to issue a written decision on the appeal.

If you are still dissatisfied after going through this process, you have the right to sue in federal court to recover unfairly denied benefits. However, you may not get the opportunity to present additional evidence in court, so be sure to submit all relevant information and documentation in your appeal to the trustees.

Q. What if I die before retiring? What are my spouse's rights to my pension?

A. If you are vested and if you have been married for at least a year, your spouse is entitled to pension benefits. Typically, he or she will receive an immediate annuity for the rest of his or her life. However, if you and your spouse have executed a written waiver of survivor benefits, your spouse will not be entitled to survivor benefits.

Q. What are a divorced person's rights to an ex-spouse's pension benefit?

A. In order to be eligible, the divorced person must have been married to the worker for at least one year. State law governs the pension rights of divorced spouses. In most states, these benefits are part of the marital property divided during the divorce. If a divorced spouse is granted a share of pension benefits either through a property settlement or a court order, he or she can collect the appropriate sum when either

- the worker has stopped working and is eligible to start collecting the pension (even if he or she hasn't yet applied for it); or

---

▶ **CLAIMING YOUR PENSION**

Each individual plan establishes the procedure for submitting pension claims. To find out about your plan's filing procedure, check the plan summary provided by your employer. To claim your pension, follow the procedure. You should then receive a decision about your claim.

- the worker has reached the earliest age for collecting benefits under the plan and is at least age fifty.

401(k) Plans and Simplified Employee Pension Plans

Q. My employer offers a Section 401(k) plan. How does this differ from a traditional retirement plan?

A. A Section 401(k) plan is another kind of defined contribution plan. In the early 1980s, federal regulations were issued that permitted the use of salary reductions as a source of plan contributions. Since then, 401(k) plans have become very popular, and many companies have elected to set up 401(k) plans rather than provide a traditional pension plan as an employee benefit.

A 401(k) plan is funded by contributions you elect to make that are deducted from your salary before taxes. A 401(k) plan is therefore also often referred to as a deferred compensation plan. In some cases, the employer may match all or part of your contributions. There are limits on the amount that may be contributed, which increase annually. In 2004, there was a $13,000 cap on the amount you could contribute on your own behalf. It goes up by $1,000 a year through 2006. Effective in 2002, only for persons age fifty and over, the law also provides an additional increase in the contribution limits — called "catch-up contributions" — applicable to 401(k) plans. For 2004, the catch-up contribution limit is $3000 and increases by $1000 per year until 2006. Additional limits may apply to the amount that may be contributed on your behalf by the employer.

Q. What happens to my contributions after I make them?

A. The contributions are placed in a fund and invested for your benefit. In some 401(k) plans, the employer controls the investment of 401(k) contributions made by both the employee and the employer. In other plans, employees are given control over the investment of their accounts.

Q. How are retirement benefits paid out of 401(k) plans?

A. Instead of a pension benefit, upon retirement employees receive distributions from their 401(k) accounts. Your plan may permit the distributions to begin as early as age 59½ without penalty, but the participant cannot defer the start of distributions any later than April 1 of the year following the year in which you reach age 70½.

Also, unlike traditional pension plans, you may be permitted access to the funds in the plan before retirement. For example, if you are an active employee, your plan may allow you to borrow from the plan. Also, your plan may permit you to make a withdrawal on account of hardship, generally from the funds you have contributed. If you make an early withdrawal that is not permitted by the plan, you will be subject to significant tax penalties.

Distributions upon retirement can take the form of periodic payments, installment payments, or even a single distribution of the entire amount in your account. Because deciding on the form of your distribution can have a great effect on both your economic security in retirement and your tax liability, it is a good idea to get professional advice before making this decision.

Q. Does ERISA apply to 401(k) plans?

A. In general, the rules that apply to traditional defined contribution plans apply to 401(k) plans. Participants in 401(k) plans have the right to receive summary plan descriptions and annual statements that tell them the amount currently in their 401(k) accounts.

Q. I have read about the retirement savings lost by employees who participated in the 401(k) plans at Enron, WorldCom, and other companies. How can I protect my retirement savings from similar losses?

A. First, you should study your summary plan description and your annual statement to see how the plan's assets are invested. If you have concerns about how the plan's funds are being invested, you should contact the nearest office of the Department of Labor.

Second, if your plan permits you to control the investment of your contributions, you should be careful not to put a large percentage of your account into your employer's stock or any other single investment.

Third, it is likely that Congress will enact legislation providing greater protection to employees covered by 401(k) plans. Proposals for changes in the law include limiting overconcentration of employer stock in 401(k) plans and traditional defined contribution pension plans; requiring that employees be given investment advice and more financial information about their particular accounts; and requiring employee representation on 401(k) boards of trustees.

Q. I work for a small company that has a simplified employee pension plan (SEP). How does a SEP differ from traditional pension plans and 401(k) plans?

A. SEPs are particularly popular with small companies because they are relatively uncomplicated retirement savings plans (self-employed workers also can participate in a SEP). A SEP allows employers to make contributions on a tax-favored basis to individual retirement accounts (IRAs) owned by the employees. SEPs are subject to minimal reporting and disclosure requirements. There are limits on the amount of contributions, and the contribution limit applicable to your plan will depend on the kind of SEP your employer has set up.

⚠ WARNING SIGNS THAT 401(K) CONTRIBUTIONS ARE BEING MISUSED

The Department of Labor's website urges employees to be alert to the following warning signs that your 401(k) contributions are being misused:

1. Your 401(k) or individual account statement is consistently late or comes at irregular intervals.
2. Your account balance does not appear to be accurate.
3. Your employer failed to transmit your contribution to the plan on a timely basis.
4. There is a significant drop in the account balance that cannot be explained by normal market ups and downs.
5. Your 401(k) or individual account statement shows that your contribution from your paycheck was not made.
6. Investments listed on your statement are not what you authorized.
7. Former employees are having trouble getting their benefits paid on time or in the correct amounts.
8. There are unusual transactions, such as a loan to the employer, a corporate officer, or one of the plan trustees.
9. There are frequent and unexplained changes in investment managers or consultants.
10. Your employer recently has experienced severe financial difficulty.

Q. Does the form of business organization limit the ability to offer a SEP?

A. No. Any employer, whether a corporation, a partnership, or a sole proprietorship, can offer this employee benefit.

Q. Can an employee have a SEP and an IRA?

A. Yes. The SEP can be an additional IRA for employees. The difference is that the employee (and perhaps the employer) makes the contributions to the IRA, while the employer alone makes them to the SEP.

Q. What is the value of a SEP from the employer's perspective?

A. It is very flexible. You don't have to make a contribution every year—you can lower the contribution in years when business is off, or even skip the contribution entirely. Record-keeping requirements are relatively minor.

Q. What is the value of a SEP from the employee's perspective?

A. The employee has access to the funds immediately, though the employee will face a penalty for early withdrawal (before age 59½). Contributions are 100 percent vested immedately, meaning that they belong to the employee as soon as they are made—the employee does not have to work a particular number of years or months.

THE WORLD AT YOUR FINGERTIPS

- *Information regarding retirement plans and your rights under ERISA can be obtained from the Pension Rights Center at 1140 Nineteenth Street NW, Washington, DC, 20036-6608 (telephone: 202-296-3776; website: www.pensionrights.org). The Pension Rights Center also has contact information for legal organizations and lawyers with expertise on legal issues relating to pension claims.*
- *Information regarding federal regulation of*

retirement plans can be obtained on the website of the Department of Labor's Employee Benefits Security Administration at www.dol.gov/ebsa, and on the website of the Pension Benefit Guaranty Corporation at www.pbgc.gov.
- *Your plan's annual financial report can be obtained by writing to the U.S. Department of Labor, Employee Benefits Security Administration, Public Disclosure Room, 200 Constitution Ave. NW, Suite N-1513, Washington, DC, 20210.*

REMEMBER THIS

- *Pension plans are governed by the rules of the Employee Retirement Income Security Act (ERISA), which provides extensive protection to employees who participate in the plans.*
- *ERISA requires that participating employees be given detailed reports and disclosures.*
- *Employees should review these reports carefully to make sure that the plan's assets are being invested prudently.*
- *Section 401(k) plans are rapidly growing in popularity. In these plans, you make a defined contribution to your account (often matched, at least in part, by your employer). You often have some investment options for your account. You can start to make withdrawals at age 59½ without penalty. It's important to keep a close eye on the investments in the plan.*
- *SEPs are very simple retirement plans— basically employer contributions to an IRA in the employee's name. They give both employee and employer much flexibility. For example, the employer does not have to make contributions to a SEP every year, and any contributions that are made vest immediately (belong to the employee).*

SOCIAL SECURITY AND SUPPLEMENTAL SECURITY INCOME

Diane retired when she was fifty, and has held a part-time job in an art gallery for three years since then. When does she become eligible for Social Security benefits? Will wages from her part-time job affect how much she receives?

For most people, Social Security is the major source of financial support during retirement. For people without significant income or assets, the federal supplemental security income program and other public benefit programs, such as veterans' benefits and federal or state housing subsidy programs, may kick in. This section covers Social Security and supplemental security, eligibility rules, and how benefits are calculated.

Q. When can I retire?

A. The normal or full retirement age is sixty-five for workers born before 1938. For workers born between 1938 and 1960, the full retirement age will increase gradually to sixty-seven. To determine your full retirement age, you can go to the retirement section of the Social Security Administration's website, www.ssa.gov/retirement, and enter your birth year. The statement you receive each year from Social Security also should contain this information.

You can collect partial benefits as early as age sixty-two if you are fully insured. The benefits are reduced, because you potentially have more years of retirement to cover. Early retirement benefits will not be raised when you turn full retirement age, except for normal cost-of-living adjustments.

If you delay retirement until you are older than your full retirement age but no older than age seventy, your benefits will be increased, because you will not have as many years of retirement in which to collect.

Of course, you can retire whenever you want or can afford to, but you will not receive Social Security retirement benefits until you are at least sixty-two.

Q. What types of Social Security benefits are available?

A. Qualified workers are eligible for old-age and disability benefits. Benefits are also available for the spouse and dependents of a retired or disabled worker. When a worker dies, members of the surviving family who qualify can collect the benefits.

Social Security is the United States' most extensive program to provide income for older and disabled Americans. It is paid for by a tax on workers and their employers. The program is complicated, and the law and the regulations change from time to time.

Q. Who is covered?

A. Over 95 percent of American workers, including household help, farmworkers, self-employed people, and employees of state and local governments and (since 1984) federal workers. Railroad workers are covered by a separate federal program, railroad retirement, which is integrated with Social Security.

Q. Will my Social Security benefits be enough for me to live on?

A. You won't get as much as when you were working, so it is important to start financial planning for retirement early. Social Security was not set up to be a complete source of retirement income, but rather to provide a floor of protection. You probably will need other sources of income, such as a pension from your employer or union, a part-time job, or income from your life savings. Social Security benefits do rise with the cost of living.

Q. Who qualifies for Social Security?

A. Individuals must meet two fundamental qualifications to collect Social Security benefits:

1. A worker must be "insured" under Social Security. The simplest rule of thumb is that ten

years of work in covered employment will insure a worker fully for life. However, there are alternative measures of insured status that enable many workers with less than ten years of covered employment to be eligible, too.

2. A worker must meet the status requirement for the particular benefit (for example, age, disability, dependency on a worker, or survivorship).

Q. Just how much money will I get when I retire?

A. That depends on how much money you have earned over your lifetime, your age at the time of retirement, and other factors.

Every year, three months before your birthday, the Social Security Administration will send you "Your Social Security Statement," which will list your annual credited earnings and the amount of your estimated retirement and disability benefits. It's a good idea to check this statement carefully, not only to see how your benefits might change, but also to make sure your employers have been depositing to the Social Security Administration your share and theirs of the Social Security tax.

Q. I want to retire, but then take a part-time job. Will this affect my benefits?

ⓘ DO I HAVE TO BE A U.S. CITIZEN TO COLLECT BENEFITS?

Noncitizens who are lawful aliens are eligible for Social Security benefits provided that they meet coverage requirements. If you are not a citizen, you will need to prove that you are a lawful resident of the United States. (The rules are different for the Supplemental Security Income [SSI] program.)

A. Yes. If you are under full retirement age and receiving benefits, you may earn only a certain amount of wages before your Social Security benefits are cut.

- **If you are between age sixty-two and the year you reach full retirement age:** For 2004 the earnings limit is $11,640. When you start getting your Social Security payments, $1 in benefits will be deducted for each $2 you earn above the annual limit. Remember, the earliest age that you can receive Social Security retirement benefits remains sixty-two even though the full retirement age is rising.

- **In the *year* you reach your full retirement age:** For 2004, the earnings limit is $31,080. Until the month you reach full retirement age, $1 in benefits will be deducted for each $3 you earn above a different limit, but only counting earnings before the month you reach full retirement age.

- **Starting with the month you reach full retirement age:** You will get your benefits with **NO** limit on your earnings. These new rules became effective January 2000.

Check with the Social Security Administration office to see what the earnings limit is when you take your new job. If you have reached the full retirement age, you may earn an unlimited amount and still receive your full retirement benefit. Note that these limits apply only to wages. Any money you earn from savings, investments, insurance, and the like will not affect your benefits.

Q. When the worker dies, who is eligible for benefits?

A. The following family members qualify for disability benefits: a spouse who is at least sixty years old; a disabled spouse who is at least fifty; children who are under eighteen (or under nineteen if attending elementary or high school full-time) or are disabled; and parents who are sixty-two or older and who received at least half of their support from the worker at the time of his or her death.

Q. When are spouses of retirees entitled to collect benefits?

A. Depending on the situation, a husband or wife may collect benefits based on the other's work record. A husband or wife need not prove that he or she was dependent on the other. In general, spouses qualify if they are at least sixty-two years old. They also qualify if they are under sixty-two but are caring for a worker's child who is either under sixteen years old or who has been disabled since before age twenty-two. The amount the spouse receives is usually one-half of what would have been paid to the worker. If the spouse is entitled to benefits based on his or her own work record, the spouse will receive the higher of the two benefits.

Q. Are divorced spouses eligible?

A. Yes. As long as the divorced spouse is sixty-two or older, was married to the worker for at least ten years, and has not remarried. Divorced spouses who have been divorced for at least two years may draw benefits at age sixty-two, as long as the former spouse is eligible for retirement benefits; the former spouse does not actually have to be drawing benefits. A divorced spouse also may be eligible for survivor benefits if the worker dies while being fully insured or while receiving benefits.

Q. Which children can receive benefits?

A. A deceased or disabled worker's unmarried children under eighteen are eligible. Children under nineteen who attend elementary or secondary school full-time also can collect. Also, a disabled child of any age can receive payments equal to approximately one-half of the worker's benefits, as long as the child became disabled before age twenty-two.

Q. When should I file my claim to collect Social Security benefits?

A. If you are retiring, you should file two or three months before your retirement date. Your first Social Security check should arrive soon after you quit working. It is important not to delay filing for either retirement or survivor benefits because you will get paid retroactive benefits only for the six months prior to the month you file your application, provided that you were eligible during those months. Retirement and survivor benefit applications take two to three months to process. Disability benefit applications, however, take longer.

Q. What documents should I bring with me to apply for benefits?

A. A worker applying for retirement or disability benefits should bring his or her Social Security card or proof of the number; a birth certificate or other proof of age; W-2 forms from the past two years or, if you are self-employed, copies of your last two federal income tax returns; and, if applicable, proof of military service, since you may be able to receive extra credit for active military duty.

Spouses applying for benefits from the worker's account also should bring a marriage certificate. Divorced spouses should have a divorce decree.

Children or their guardians seeking benefits need a birth certificate and evidence of financial dependence.

Dependent parents who want to collect benefits must bring some evidence of financial dependence.

Finally, spouses, children, or parents seeking death benefits need the worker's death certificate.

Q. If I am filing for disability benefits, what other documents should I bring with me?

A. In addition to the documents listed above, you should try to bring a list, with addresses and telephone numbers, of the doctors, hospitals, or institutions that have treated you for your disability; a summary of all the jobs you have held for the past fifteen years and the type of work you performed; and information about any other checks or payments you receive for your disability. The next section of this chapter provides more information about disability benefits.

> ▶ **WHAT TO REMEMBER WHEN DEALING WITH THE SOCIAL SECURITY OFFICE**
>
> As with any large government office, the best way to work with the Social Security Administration is to keep a full, organized account of your communications or conversations. Make a note of when you had each conversation, with whom you spoke, and what was said. When you file a claim, you are automatically assigned a SSA worker. Keep this person's name and telephone number handy in case you need to contact the SSA for any reason.
>
> Before you submit any forms or documents to the SSA, make sure you keep copies for yourself. That way, if anything is lost, you have a backup copy.
>
> Since the SSA keeps records by Social Security numbers, all forms or documents you submit should have your Social Security number on the top of each page. Then, if any page becomes separated, it will still be placed in your file.

Q. What if I check on my benefits or file my claim and discover that the Social Security Administration has made an error in the number of quarters I worked or the amount of wages I was paid? Can I fix mistakes?

A. Yes. You have approximately three years from the year the wages were earned to fix mistakes. However, mistakes caused by an employer's failure to report your earnings have no time limit.

You can fix these mistakes any time, but you will need proof. A pay stub, written statement from the employer, or form OAR-7008 (Request for Correction of Earnings Record) are all acceptable types of proof.

Disability

Q. What if I am under sixty-five and become disabled? Am I entitled to benefits from social security?

A. Yes. Social Security protects all workers under sixty-five against loss of earnings due to disability. However, you must meet certain strict requirements for the number of years employed, the age at which you became disabled, and the severity of your disability.

Q. If I become disabled, how long may I get benefits?

A. Once you qualify for disability benefits, they will continue for as long as you remain medically disabled and unable to work. Your health will be reviewed periodically to determine your ability to return to work.

Q. What about my family?

A. If you are disabled, your unmarried children under age eighteen (or nineteen, if still in school full-time) may be eligible for benefits from Social Security. In addition, unmarried children over eighteen who are disabled also will be eligible. If your spouse is caring for a child who is either under sixteen or disabled, he or she may be eligible, as is a spouse who is sixty-two or older. In some cases, the disabled widow or widower or the divorced spouse of a deceased worker may become eligible for disability benefits. Check with your local SSA for specific eligibility requirements.

Claims, Decisions, and Appeals

Q. How will I know the outcome of my application for benefits?

A. You should receive written notification informing you whether your claim has been approved or denied in sixty to ninety days. If your claim is approved, you will be told how much your benefits will be and when to expect your first check. If, however, your claim is denied, your letter should list the reasons.

Q. Can my Social Security benefits be reduced or terminated?

A. Yes. Benefits may be terminated if you leave the United States for more than six months; you are deported; you remarry; or you are convicted of certain crimes, such as treason and espionage. Convicted felons cannot receive benefits while in prison. Disability benefits can be terminated when the recipient recovers, or if the recipient refuses to accept rehabilitation efforts.

In any case, you should receive a letter notifying you of the reduction or termination before SSA takes any action.

Q. If my claim is denied, or my benefits reduced or terminated, can I appeal?

A. Yes. You have sixty days from the date on the written notification of denial to appeal. Make sure the SSA gives you a written denial; you cannot appeal an oral statement.

Q. Should I bother to appeal?

A. Since a large number of claim decisions are reversed on appeal, it is probably worth your time and effort. Also, if you do not appeal, the claim decision becomes final and you give up the chance to appeal later.

Q. Do I need a lawyer to appeal?

A. A lawyer is not required for an appeal. However, you should consider the complexity of your case and the amount of money you are seeking before deciding whether to hire one. If your appeal goes all the way to a federal court, you probably should have a lawyer to represent your interests. Lawyers who take Social Security cases usually receive up to 25 percent of your back benefits if the claim is successful. The SSA must approve the fees. An experienced advocate who is not a lawyer also can represent you.

Q. What if I just need some assistance in my appeal but do not want to hire a lawyer?

A. Check with your state or local area agency on aging. They may be able to direct you to a community group that can provide help.

Q. How do I appeal?

A. The first step in the appeal process is to file a written request for reconsideration of your claim within sixty days of the notification of denial, re-

---

🗐 DISABILITY

A **disability** is defined as the inability to engage in substantial gainful activity by reason of any medically determinable physical or mental impairment that can be expected to result in death or that has lasted or can be expected to last for a continuous period of not less than twelve months. The disability must be medically certified. Some illnesses or handicaps are so serious that the SSA automatically treats them as disabilities, such as severe epilepsy or blindness; SSA has a list of such impairments. If you believe you are disabled but your impairment is not on the list, you will have to prove that it is just as severe and disabling as the ones on the list.

ⓘ FINDING LEGAL HELP

If you cannot afford the services of a lawyer, you may be able to obtain legal representation through an organization that provides legal services to low-income or older persons. Check with your state or local area agency on aging (AAA).

duction, or termination of benefits. This reconsideration is an examination of your paperwork by an SSA employee other than the one who first decided your claim. You may add more documents to your file if you think they will help.

You should receive written notice of the reconsideration decision within thirty days. However, reconsideration of disability benefits will take longer, usually two to three months.

Q. What is the next step?

A. If you are dissatisfied with the outcome of the reconsideration, your next step is to file a written request for an administrative hearing. You have sixty days after the reconsideration decision to make such a request. Normally, however, the hearing will not take place for several months.

Q. Who acts as the judge at these administrative hearings?

A. An administrative law judge of the SSA's Office of Hearings and Appeals will preside over your case. The administrative law judge is a lawyer who works for SSA but has not been involved in your claim thus far. The hearing will be a new examination of your case, conducted by an impartial judge.

Q. What if witnesses refuse to appear on my behalf?

A. You can ask that witnesses be subpoenaed (ordered to appear before the judge). You must request subpoenas at least five days before the hearing.

Q. Will a lawyer represent the SSA at the administrative hearing?

A. No, the office does not have a lawyer presenting its side of the case.

Q. How long does it take to receive a decision from an administrative hearing?

A. You should receive a decision within two to three months after the hearing. You will receive a written decision. If your claim is approved, you

may be able to collect benefits dating back to when you filed your original claim. For disability, back benefits may date as far back as twelve months prior to the application date.

Q. Can I appeal an administrative hearing decision?

A. Yes. You have sixty days to file a written appeal with the SSA Appeals Council in Washington, D.C. The council will review the file and issue a decision. You and your representative do not appear before the Appeals Council, but you can add additional information to your file. If you wish to appeal the decision further, you must sue the SSA in federal district court.

Q. Should I file a federal lawsuit?

A. That depends. You must take into account the expense of filing a lawsuit, the amount of benefits you are claiming, and your chances of winning. And, although you are not required to have a lawyer, it is highly recommended that you do.

Q. If I do want a lawyer, how do I find one who specializes in Social Security appeals?

A. You can contact the district SSA office, or call the National Organization of Social Security Claimants' Representatives at 800-431-2804.

ⓘ PREPARING FOR YOUR ADMINISTRATIVE HEARING

Before the hearing you can, and should, examine your file to make sure it contains every document you have filed. At the hearing, you can represent yourself or be represented by a lawyer or a nonlawyer advocate. You should provide evidence, such as documents or witnesses about your medical condition and why you cannot work, and your own explanation of why the decision at the reconsideration level should be reversed.

Q. What if I receive a notice from SSA that I have been overpaid?

A. If you disagree that you were overpaid, make a written request for a reconsideration of your claim. If you cannot repay the amount, you can ask for a waiver within thirty days of notification of overpayment. You will be asked to fill out an Overpayment Recovery Questionnaire. You will need to show that the overpayment was not your fault, and that you are unable to repay the amount without hardship.

Supplemental Security Income

Q. I have virtually no money. I don't qualify for regular Social Security or disability benefits. Can Social Security help me anyway?

A. The supplemental security income (SSI) program pays benefits to persons who

1. are age sixty-five or over, or are disabled or blind; and
2. have very limited income and personal property.

The Social Security Administration runs the SSI program. However, it is supported with income tax dollars rather than Social Security taxes on workers' wages.

▶ GETTING YOUR CHECKS

Social Security checks normally are mailed on the first day of each month. However, the SSA strongly encourages you to have your check deposited directly in your bank account. This is safe and convenient. The money is available a day or two earlier than if you get a check in the mail. It's handy if you have trouble getting to the bank. And it makes it impossible for a thief to take the check out of your mailbox.

SSI benefits are not large and the eligibility requirements are strict. You must have very little income and own very little property. If you think you qualify, check with your local Social Security Administration office. One of the benefits of getting even a dollar in SSI is that in most states you become eligible for free medical care through Medicaid.

To apply you will need your Social Security number, proof of age, and a wide variety of financial information. You'll want to have a record of your mortgage and property taxes, records of your utility costs and food costs, payroll slips, income tax returns, bankbooks, and insurance policies.

If you are applying because of disability or blindness, you also will need copies of your medical records. Be sure to have the names and addresses of physicians who have treated you and hospitals where you have been a patient. You also will need information about jobs you have held in the past. If you have worked with a social service agency, give the name of a worker who knows you.

Q. What if I am not a U.S. citizen?

A. Certain noncitizens may be ineligible for SSI. The specific rules are available on the SSI website: www.social-security-disability-claims.org.

Q. I think my elderly father is eligible for SSI, but he is much too ill and confused to visit an office or complete an application. How can he receive benefits?

A. If you know someone who should be receiving SSI benefits but can't apply for him- or herself, you can do it for that person. However, you will still need to bring all the information described above. To deal with this problem, you may also want to designate a representative payee (representative payees are discussed on page 640).

Q. If I am denied SSI benefits, can I appeal?

A. Yes, the appeals process is essentially identical to appealing a Social Security claim, as described on pages 605–7.

THE WORLD AT YOUR FINGERTIPS

- *Contact your local office of the Social Security Administration (SSA) for literature about Social Security benefits or to ask specific questions about your own case. They are listed in the "United States Government" section of your telephone directory; you can also call 800-772-1213, or go to the SSA website at www.ssa.gov.*

REMEMBER THIS

- *Most American workers are covered by Social Security, and "qualified" workers are eligible for old-age and disability benefits.*
- *The age at which you can retire with full benefits is between sixty-five and sixty-seven, depending on your birth year.*
- *You have the right to appeal a decision denying a claim for benefits or reducing or terminating benefits.*
- *If you are not eligible for Social Security but have very limited income and personal property, you may be eligible for supplemental security income (SSI).*

HEALTH AND LONG-TERM CARE BENEFITS

Ben just turned sixty-five years old. He knows he's eligible to be covered under Medicare, but he does not remember signing up for it. Does he have to pay to be covered by Medicare? Will Medicare make him change doctors? What is the difference between Medicare and Medicaid?

The federal government provides a program of basic health-care insurance for older and disabled individuals called Medicare. Practically everyone who has a work history and is sixty-five or older is eligible for Medicare, even those who continue working after age sixty-five.

The federal and state governments together also provide a comprehensive medical benefits program, called Medicaid, for qualified low-income people. Medicare and Medicaid are not the same, though some older people qualify for both. Medicaid coverage rules vary from state to state, but Medicare is the same all over the United States.

The questions in this section examine Medicare and Medicaid, as well as private Medigap insurance commonly used to supplement Medicare coverage. The section then turns to long-term care benefits under public programs and under private long-term care insurance. Since Medicare and Medicaid came into being in 1965, they have been revised many times. More revisions are certain. Sources for current information are noted throughout this section and at the end of this section in "World at Your Fingertips."

Medicare

Q. What is the basic structure of the Medicare program?

A. The **Centers for Medicare and Medicaid Services (CMS,** formerly known as the Health Care Financing Administration), a branch of the U.S. Department of Health and Human Services, is the federal agency responsible for administering the Medicare program.

Original Medicare has two main parts. The hospital insurance part, or **Part A,** covers medically necessary care in a hospital, skilled nursing facility, or psychiatric hospital, home health care, and hospice care. **Part B,** the medical insurance benefits part, covers medically necessary physician's services, no matter where you receive them, outpatient hospital care, many diagnostic tests, rehabilitation services, and a variety of other medical services and supplies not covered by Part A.

The exact coverage rules and limitations are complex. The actual coverage determinations and payments to providers of care are handled by insurance companies under contract with Medicare. These insurance companies are referred to as "fiscal intermediaries" under Part A and "carriers" under Part B. They determine the appropriate fee for each service. That is why original Medicare is referred to as a "fee for service" program.

Medicare beneficiaries also have the option of joining a **managed care organization (MCO)** or care option permitted under Medicare+ Choice. Managed care organizations provide or arrange for all Medicare-covered services and generally charge a fixed monthly premium and small or no co-payments. They may also offer benefits not covered by Medicare, such as preventive care and prescription drugs. However, Medicare+Choice plans are not available in all parts of the country. Also, you may have to pay a monthly premium for the extra benefits. Because of problems with the program, changes in its structure now are being considered. You should be careful to get complete information before deciding to enroll in a Medicare+Choice program.

Q. What does Medicare cost me?

A. Part A coverage is provided free to all individuals sixty-five and older who are eligible for Social Security (even if they are still working). If you are not eligible for Social Security benefits, you can enroll in Part A after age sixty-fve, but you will have to pay a sizable monthly premium.

Part B is available to all Part A enrollees for a

▶ DENIALS OF BENEFITS

Never accept a denial of benefits without further questioning it. Incorrect denials of Medicare benefits occur with surprising frequency. Medicare beneficiaries who appeal erroneous denials have a substantial likelihood of success on appeal. Your appeal rights are explained on pages 613–14.

▶ PRESCRIPTION DRUG BENEFIT UNDER MEDICARE

In late 2003, Congress passed a major law that will provide prescription drug coverage under Medicare. However, the coverage does not go into effect until January 1, 2006, and many details of how the new program will operate have yet to be worked out. Medicare premiums will rise under the law for most people. Beginning in June 2004, Medicare beneficiaries can buy drug discount cards that may lessen the retail price of prescription drugs.

monthly premium that changes yearly. The Centers for Medicare and Medicaid Services or the Social Security Administration office can tell you the cost of the current premium. Under both Parts A and B, beneficiaries must pay certain deductibles and coinsurance payments, depending on the type of service, unless they are enrolled in a managed care organization. **Deductibles** are payments you must make before Medicare coverage begins. **Coinsurance payments** are percentages of covered expenses that you are responsible for paying.

If you meet certain income and resource tests, your state's Medicaid program will assist you in paying your share of Medicare costs. The income and resource tests are more generous than the limits for regular Medicaid eligibility, so even if you are not eligible for Medicaid, you may still be eligible for help under one of the Medicare Savings Programs. You can get information about the Medicare Savings Programs at www.medicare.gov or by contacting your local Medicaid agency. To apply, contact the local office of your state Medicaid program.

Q. I will turn sixty-five soon, but I do not plan to retire then. Am I still going to be able to receive Medicare benefits?

A. Yes, but you must file a written application. This can be done in two different ways. Your initial enrollment period begins three calendar months before your sixty-fifth birthday month and extends three months beyond your birthday month. You can enroll at any time during this seven-month period. Your benefits will begin on the first day of the month in which you turn sixty-five.

If you do not enroll during this time, you can enroll during the general enrollment period, which runs from January 1 to March 31 of each year. However, you may pay a higher monthly premium if you delay enrollment beyond your initial enrollment period.

If you are working and are covered by your employer's health insurance program, or if you are covered under your spouse's plan, Medicare is the secondary payer after the other insurance pays. If you haven't enrolled in Medicare and you lose the other insurance, you may sign up for the Medicare program during a special seven-month enrollment period that begins the month the other program no longer covers you.

To make sure you receive maximum coverage without penalty, talk to your employer's benefits office, the Centers for Medicare and Medicaid Services, or your local Social Security Administration office.

Q. Is Medicare only for older adults?

A. No. In addition to older Social Security recipients, younger persons who have received Social Security disability benefits for more than twenty-four months are eligible, as well as certain persons with kidney disease. If you are under sixty-five and receiving disability benefits, your enrollment in Medicare will begin automatically as soon as you have been receiving benefits for twenty-four months.

Q. What does Medicare Part A (hospital insurance) cover?

A. Medicare Part A helps pay for medically necessary hospital care, skilled nursing care, home health care, and hospice care as described below.

Hospitalization
This includes

- a semiprivate room and board;
- general nursing;
- the cost of special-care units, such as intensive care or coronary care units;
- drugs furnished by the hospital during your stay;
- blood transfusions;
- lab tests, X rays, and other radiology services;
- medical supplies and equipment;
- operating and recovery room costs; and
- rehabilitation services.

The coverage period for hospitalization is based upon a **benefit period.** A benefit period begins the first time you receive inpatient hospital care. It ends when you have been out of a hospital and have not received skilled nursing care for sixty days in a row. A subsequent hospitalization begins a new benefit period.

On the first day of hospitalization during a benefit period, the patient is responsible for a sizable inpatient hospital deductible—$876.00 during 2004. If you are hospitalized more than once during a benefit period, the deductible does not have to be paid for the other hospitalizations during the same benefit period. After the deductible,

---

▶ **SIGNING UP FOR MEDICARE**

Enrolling in Medicare is no problem for most people. Everyone who is turning sixty-five and applying for Social Security or railroad retirement benefits is automatically enrolled in Medicare Part A. If you are receiving these benefits before turning sixty-five, you should receive a Medicare card prior to the month you turn sixty-five. The Medicare benefits normally begin on the first of the month in which you turn sixty-five.

Part A pays for all covered services through the sixtieth day of hospitalization. Coverage continues from day sixty-one through day ninety, but the patient is responsible for a daily coinsurance payment. After day ninety, Medicare covers up to sixty extra days (called "reserve days") during the lifetime of the patient. The patient pays a sizable coinsurance payment during reserve days.

If psychiatric hospitalization is needed, Part A helps pay for a lifetime maximum of 190 days of inpatient care in a participating psychiatric hospital.

Skilled Nursing Facility Inpatient Care Following a Hospitalization of at Least Three Days

Your condition must require skilled nursing or skilled rehabilitation services on a daily basis, which, as a practical matter, can be provided only in a skilled nursing facility. You must be admitted within a short time (usually thirty days) after you leave the hospital, and the skilled care you receive must be based on a doctor's order.

Most nursing-home residents do not require the level of nursing services considered skilled by Medicare. Consequently, Medicare pays for relatively little nursing home care. In addition, not every nursing home participates in Medicare or is a skilled nursing facility. Ask the hospital discharge staff or nursing-home staff if you are unsure of the facility's status.

The coverage period for skilled nursing facility services is limited to one hundred days. In a benefit period, Medicare pays for all covered services for the first twenty days. For days twenty-one through one hundred, the patient is responsible for a sizable coinsurance payment.

Home Health Care

Medicare covers part-time or intermittent skilled nursing care; physical, occupational, and speech therapy services; medical social services; part-time care provided by a home health aide; and medical equipment for use in the home. Both Part A and Part B of Medicare cover some home health care. Medicare does not cover medications for patients living at home, nor does it cover general household services or services that are primarily custodial.

To be eligible for home health-care services you must meet four conditions, presented in simplified terms here. First, you must be under the care of a physician who determines you need home health care and sets up a plan. Second, you must be homebound, although you need not be bedridden. An individual is considered homebound if leaving home requires a considerable and taxing effort and if any absences from the home are either for medical care, to attend adult day care or religious services, or are infrequent or for periods of relatively short duration. Third, the

---

ⓘ SKILLED CARE OR CUSTODIAL CARE

Medicare helps pay only for "skilled" nursing-home care. Medicare does not pay for "custodial" care. However, the distinction is often fuzzy, and many Medicare denials based on a finding of custodial care can be appealed successfully. Generally, care is considered custodial when it is primarily for the purpose of helping the resident with daily living needs, such as eating, bathing, walking, getting in and out of bed, and taking medicine. Skilled nursing and rehabilitation services are those that require the skills of professional or skilled personnel such as registered nurses, licensed practical nurses, or therapists. Care that is generally nonskilled may nevertheless be considered skilled when, for example, medical complications require the skilled management and evaluation of a care plan, observation of a patient's changing condition, or patient education services.

care you need must include intermittent skilled nursing, physical therapy, or speech therapy. Finally, your care must be provided by a Medicare-participating home health-care agency.

The coverage period for home health care is unlimited with no deductible or coinsurance payment (except for durable medical equipment) as long as you continue to meet all four conditions.

Hospice Care

A hospice is an agency or organization that provides primarily pain relief, palliative care, symptom management, and supportive services to people with terminal illnesses. Hospice services may include physician or visiting-nurse services, individual and family psychological support, inpatient care when needed, care from a home health aide, medications, medical/social services, counseling, and respite care for family caregivers.

To be eligible for hospice care, a patient must have a doctor certify that he or she is terminally ill (defined as a life expectancy of six months or less); the patient must choose to receive hospice care instead of standard Medicare benefits; and the hospice must be a Medicare-participating program.

The coverage period for hospice care consists of two ninety-day periods, followed by a thirty-day period, and when necessary, an indefinite extension. There are certain coinsurance payments required under the hospice benefit, but no deductibles.

Q. What does Medicare Part B (medical insurance) cover?

A. Medicare Part B covers a wide range of outpatient and physician expenses regardless of where they are provided—at home, in a hospital or nursing home, or in a private office. Covered services include

- doctors' services, including some services by chiropractors, dentists, podiatrists, and optometrists;
- outpatient hospital services, such as emergency room services or outpatient clinic care,

radiology services, and ambulatory surgical services;
- diagnostic tests, including X rays and other laboratory services, as well as some mammography and Pap smear screenings;
- durable medical equipment, such as oxygen equipment, wheelchairs, and other medically necessary equipment that your doctor prescribes for use in your home;
- kidney dialysis;
- ambulance services to or from a hospital or skilled nursing facility;
- mental health services, although Medicare generally pays only 50 percent for such services;
- certain services of other practitioners who are not physicians, such as clinical psychologists or social workers; and
- many other health services, supplies, and prosthetic devices that are not covered by Medicare Part A (Part B also covers some home health services).

Medicare does not cover

- routine physical examinations;
- most routine foot care and dental care;
- examinations for prescribing or fitting eyeglasses or hearing aids;
- prescription drugs that do not require administration by a physician;

▶ **SIGNING UP FOR MEDICARE PART B**

If you are receiving Part A coverage, you automatically will be enrolled for Part B coverage as well. If you don't want Part B coverage, you must notify the Social Security Administration. Also, anyone over sixty-five can buy Part B coverage. Enrollment periods are similar to those for Part A. Your Part B premium will be deducted from your monthly Social Security check.

- most cosmetic surgery;
- immunizations except for certain persons at risk;
- personal comfort items and services; and
- any service not considered "reasonable and necessary."

Recently, Medicare Part B began covering certain preventive services under certain circumstances. These services include

- certain vaccinations such as those for flu, pneumonia, and hepatitis B;
- prostate cancer screenings;
- Pap smear and pelvic examination;
- mammograms;
- diabetes monitoring;
- colorectal cancer screening; and
- bone-mass measurements.

Q. What is my share of the cost of Medicare Part B services?

A. For Part B benefits, you must pay a $100 annual deductible. Then Medicare generally pays 80 percent of Medicare-approved amounts for covered services for the rest of the year. You pay the other 20 percent of the approved amount. There is no cap on the patient's share of the cost.

If a physician or other provider charges you more than the Medicare-approved amount, then your liability depends on whether the provider **accepts assignment.** Accepting assignment means that the provider agrees to accept the Medicare-approved amount as payment in full. This means that your liability is limited to the annual deductible and 20 percent co-payment. If the provider does not accept assignment, generally you must pay for any excess charge over the Medicare-approved amount, but only up to certain limits. If you are a Medicaid recipient, then your physician must accept assignment.

The government presently sets the limit on physician's charges at 115 percent of the Medicare-approved fee schedule. Doctors who charge more than these limits may be fined, and you should get a refund from the doctor.

Here is an example of the difference accept-

ing assignment can make. Mrs. Jones sees Dr. Brown on June 1 for medical care. She has already paid her $100 annual deductible for covered Part B medical care this year. Dr. Brown charges $230 for the visit. The Medicare-approved amount for such services is $200, and Medicare pays 80 percent, or $160.

If Dr. Brown accepts assignment, Mrs. Jones must pay

- a $40 co-payment (that is, 20 percent of the $200 approved).

If Dr. Brown does *not* accept assignment, Mrs. Jones must pay

- $40 plus the $30 excess charge. Her total payment is $70.

Note that Dr. Brown's actual charge ($230) is within 115 percent of the Medicare-approved amount ($200) and is therefore permissible.

Q. How are Medicare claims filed and paid?

A. For Part A benefits, the provider submits the claim directly to Medicare's fiscal intermediary (the insurance company). The provider will charge you for any deductible or coinsurance payment you owe. For Part B claims, doctors, suppliers and other providers are required to submit your Medicare claims to the Medicare carrier (the insurance company) in most cases, even if they do not take assignment. The provider will charge you directly for any deductible, coinsurance, or excess charge you owe. If you belong to a Medicare-participating managed care organization (MCO), there are usually no claim forms to be filed, although there may be a co-payment for any covered services.

Q. What if I disagree with a Medicare decision? How can I appeal?

A. You have the right to appeal all decisions regarding coverage of services or the amount Medicare will pay on a claim. If your claim has been denied in whole or in part, it is usually a good idea to appeal, especially if the basis of de-

> ▶ **FINDING A DOCTOR**
>
> Doctors and suppliers who agree to accept assignment under Medicare on all claims are called Medicare-participating doctors and suppliers. You can get a directory of Medicare-participating doctors and suppliers from your Medicare carrier or on the Internet at www.medicare.gov. The directory is also available for your use in Social Security Administration offices, state and area agencies on aging, and in most hospitals.

nial is unclear. A surprisingly high percentage of denials are reversed on appeal. In any case, the appeal will make clear the reason for the denial.

Medicare Parts A and B have different procedures for appealing and several steps in the appeal process. After the initial levels of review, Parts A and B both include the option of a hearing before an administrative law judge and even a review by a federal court if sufficient amounts of money are at stake.

Always be conscious of time limits for filing appeals. You may lose your rights if you wait too long. You may want to get assistance with your appeal from a legal services office or a private lawyer, particularly if large medical bills are involved. Nonlawyer volunteers and nonlawyer staff members of legal service programs help a number of people with benefit appeals without charging fees.

Medicaid

Q. What is Medicaid?

A. Medicaid is a medical assistance program for poor older or disabled persons and certain children and families whose income and assets fall below certain levels set by federal and state law. Unlike Medicare, which offers the same benefits to all enrollees regardless of income, Medicaid is managed by individual states, and the benefits and eligibility vary from state to state. The following questions address Medicaid as it applies to older and disabled adults.

Q. Is it possible to receive both Medicare and Medicaid?

A. Yes, if you qualify for both programs. Even if you do not qualify for Medicaid, the Medicaid program still may assist you in paying for all or part of the Medicare premium, deductibles, and coinsurance payments through the Medicare Savings Program, if you meet the special income and resource tests.

Q. If I qualify for Medicaid, what sorts of services do I get?

A. Medicaid covers a broad spectrum of services. Certain benefits are mandated by federal law. They include

- inpatient and outpatient hospital services;
- doctors' and nurse practitioners' services;
- inpatient nursing-home care;
- home health-care services; and
- laboratory and X-ray charges.

Other services may include services from podiatrists, optometrists, and chiropractors; mental health services; personal care in your home; dental care; physical therapy and other rehabilitation; prescription medications; dentures; eyeglasses; transportation services; and more. In all cases, you may receive these services only from a Medicaid-participating provider. As with Medi-care, providers may choose whether to participate in Medicaid, and they must meet certain standards. Some states have contracted with managed care organizations to provide comprehensive care to Medicaid-eligible individuals. In these states, you may be limited to using the designated care provider for regular care.

Q. Does owning a home disqualify me from Medicaid?

A. No. All states exempt your home as an asset as long as you or your spouse lives in it. If you must leave your home in order to receive nursing-home care or other long-term care, the state still may exempt it, but state asset exemption rules differ from state to state and can be complex. Besides your home, all states allow you to keep a very limited amount of cash and personal property.

Q. What does Medicaid cost me?

A. Medicaid does not require you to pay premiums or deductibles like Medicare. Providers may not charge Medicaid patients additional fees beyond the Medicaid reimbursement amount. However, states are permitted to impose a nominal deductible charge or other form of cost sharing for certain categories of services and prescription drugs. No Medicaid recipient may be denied services by a participating provider because of the patient's inability to pay the charge.

Individuals whose income or assets exceed the state's permissible Medicaid amount may be eligible for Medicaid only after spending down their income or assets to a poverty level by incurring medical expenses. These spend-down amounts can be very high, especially for nursing-home residents whose income far exceeds the Medicaid eligibility level but who face enormous monthly expenses for care.

▶ SOME TIPS FOR APPEALING MEDICARE DECISIONS

Denials by Any Part A Provider (Hospital, Nursing Home, Home Health-Care Agency, or Hospice)

Do not accept oral denials. You should be given a written notice of noncoverage from the provider explaining why the provider believes Medicare will not pay for the services. This is not an official Medicare determination. You should ask the provider to get an official Medicare determination. The provider must file a claim on your behalf to the Medicare fiscal intermediary if you ask for an official determination. If you still disagree, you may make use of several additional appeal steps if minimum threshold amounts of money are in dispute.

Hospital Coverage Denials

Hospital coverage decisions are normally made by **Quality Improvement Organizations (QIOs,** formerly called Peer Review Organizations). QIOs are groups of doctors and other health-care professionals under contract with the federal government to review care given to Medicare patients. When you are admitted to the hospital, you will receive a notice called "An Important Message from Medicare" that explains the role of QIOs and describes your appeal rights. If you disagree with a QIO decision, the initial review will occur very quickly, usually within three days. You cannot be required to pay for hospital care until the third day after you receive a written denial of Medicare coverage.

Part A and B Coverage Denials

The Medicare carrier will make these decisions. After your doctor, supplier, or other provider sends in a Part A or B claim, Medicare will send you a notice called "Medicare Summary Notice." The notice tells you what charges were made and the amount Medicare approved and paid. It also shows the amount of any co-payments, deductibles, or excess charges that you are responsible for paying. The notice gives the address and telephone number for contacting the carrier and an explanation of your appeal rights. You have 120 days from the date of the decision to ask the carrier to review it. If you still disagree, you may make use of several additional appeal steps if minimum threshold amounts of money are in dispute.

ⓘ **QUALIFYING FOR MEDICAID**

Medicaid programs in each state have different standards to determine whether needy individuals are eligible for assistance. All states require that adults be at least age sixty-five, or blind or disabled, and that they meet income and asset tests. In most states, persons eligible for supplemental security income (SSI) or Temporary Assistance to Needy Families (TANF) are covered automatically. Most states also cover some people whose income falls below a certain level after they "spend down" their income on medical bills. Medicaid eligibility rules are so complicated that it is advisable for older people with low incomes or with high medical expenses to talk with someone with expertise in Medicaid—such as a legal services lawyer, a paralegal, a social worker, or a private lawyer experienced in handling Medicaid issues.

Q. How do I apply for Medicaid?

A. Contact the state or local agency that handles the Medicaid program. Its name will vary from place to place. It may be called Social Services, Public Aid, Public Welfare, Human Services, or something similar. You can also call your local agency on aging or senior center for information.

Q. How are Medicaid claims filed and paid?

A. Medicaid providers always bill Medicaid directly. The state Medicaid program reimburses providers according to the state's particular reimbursement formula. Providers cannot charge you additional amounts for covered services, but states may opt to charge you small deductibles or fees for certain items such as prescriptions.

Q. If I disagree with a decision made by my Medicaid program, what can I do?

A. You have the right to appeal all decisions that affect your Medicaid eligibility or services. When a decision about your Medicaid coverage is made, you should receive prompt written notice of the decision. This will include an explanation of how you can appeal the decision. The appeal process includes a right to a fair hearing before a hearing officer. You may need a lawyer or a public benefits

---

ⓘ **THE APPLICATION PROCESS**

When you apply for Medicaid, you will have to document your financial need in detail, as well as your residency. The application form can be lengthy and complex, but the Medicaid agency can help you complete it. However, a better alternative is to obtain the help of an independent expert, such as a Legal Aid attorney or private attorney with expertise in Medicaid. If you are in a hospital or other institution, a staff social worker should be made available to help you apply. Don't let inability to get to the public agency keep you from seeking assistance. Since the start of benefits is linked to your date of application, it is important to establish an application date as soon as you need Medicaid assistance. Almost any written request with your signature may be enough to establish your application date, even if you have not yet completed the full application form. The effective date can be retroactive, up to three months from the date you submit your signed application.

specialist experienced in Medicaid law to represent you.

Medigap Insurance

Q. Do I need any other insurance coverage besides Medicare?

A. Yes. Most older people need to purchase a supplemental, or **Medigap,** insurance policy to cover some of the costs not covered by Medicare. However, there are exceptions, explained in the following answer.

In addition, if you can afford it, you may also want to consider purchasing a long-term care insurance policy, because Medicare and Medigap policies do *not* cover long-term care. Long-term care insurance is discussed in the next section, "Paying for Long-Term Care."

Q. Who doesn't need a Medigap policy?

A. While most people need Medigap coverage, you may already have enough coverage without it if you meet one of these four conditions:

1. If you are already covered by Medicaid, you do not need a Medigap policy. Medicaid covers the gaps in Medicare and more.
2. If you are not eligible for Medicaid, but your income is low and you have limited resources, you may be eligible for help in paying Medicare costs under the Medicare Savings Programs. Under the Medicare Savings Programs, states have programs that pay some or all of Medicare's premiums and may also pay Medicare deductibles and coinsurance for certain people who have Medicare and a limited income and limited assets.
3. If you have retiree health coverage through a former employer or union, you *may* not need Medigap insurance. Often, this coverage is comprehensive and has a provision about how it coordinates its coverage with Medicare. But this coverage may not provide the same benefits as Medigap insurance and may not have to meet the federal and state

rules that apply to Medigap. Examine the coverage, costs, and stability of your coverage to determine whether it is a better option than Medigap.
4. If you belong to a managed care organization, you probably do not need a Medigap policy, since MCO coverage is normally comprehensive. But do not be too quick to give up your Medigap coverage if you are just joining a Medicare MCO. If you can afford it, keep it long enough to be sure you are satisfied with the MCO.

Q. How do I find a good Medigap policy?

A. Since 1992, all Medigap insurance has had to conform to standardized benefit plans. There are ten possible standardized plans, identified as Plan A through Plan J. Plan A is a core package and is available in all states. The other nine plans have different combinations of benefits. Check with your state department of insurance for additional information. Many states provide buyer's guides.

You should purchase only one Medigap policy. Federal law prohibits the sale of duplicative policies, and multiple policies almost always will provide overlapping coverage for which you will pay twice but receive the benefit of only once. In evaluating policies, decide which features would best meet your health needs and financial situation. Prescription drug coverage, for example, may be right for you if you are on continuing maintenance medications, even though such coverage may be expensive. When you compare policies of the same type (A through J), remember that benefits are identical for plans of the same type. For example, all type G plans have essentially the same benefits. However, the premiums and potential for premium increases may differ greatly.

Q. What is a Medicare SELECT policy?

A. Medicare SELECT policies, which are available in some states, generally cost less than other Medigap plans. However, with a Medicare SELECT plan, you must use specific hospitals and, in some cases, doctors, to get full insurance benefits (except in an emergency). If you don't use a Medicare SELECT hospital or doctor, you will have to pay what the original Medicare plan does not pay. The original Medicare plan will pay its share of approved charges no matter what hospital or doctor you choose.

Q. When should I get a Medigap policy?

A. Buy a Medigap policy at or near the time your Medicare coverage begins, because during the first six months that you are sixty-five or older and enrolled in Medicare Part B, companies must accept you regardless of any health conditions you have, and they cannot charge you more than they charge others of the same age. After this period, you may be forced to pay much higher premiums for the same policy due to your health status. During this open enrollment period, companies may still exclude preexisting conditions during the first six months of the policy.

Different enrollment rules apply to people under sixty-five who are eligible for Medicare because of disability.

Q. What if I have an old Medigap policy and am considering a replacement? Is that a good idea?

A. If you have a Medigap policy that predates the standardized plans (before 1992), you may not need to switch policies, especially if you are satisfied. Some states have special regulations allowing beneficiaries to convert older policies to a standard Medigap plan. Check with your state insurance department or health insurance counseling service for details.

Beware of illegal sales practices. Both federal and state laws govern the sale of Medigap insurance. These laws prohibit high-pressure sales tactics, fraudulent or misleading statements about coverage or cost, selling a policy that is not one of the approved standard policies, or imposing new waiting periods for replacement policies. If a sales agent offers you a policy that duplicates coverage of your existing policy, the duplication must be disclosed to you in writing. If you feel you have been misled or pressured, contact your state in-

surance department, your state's health insurance counseling program, or the federal Medicare Hotline at 800-MEDICARE (800-633-4227).

Paying for Long-Term Care

Q. What federal programs will pay for long-term care in a nursing home?

A. Medicare does not pay for a significant amount of nursing-home care. Coverage of skilled nursing care, as described in the section on Medicare (see page 611), is narrowly defined and limited to twenty days of full coverage and a maximum of eighty additional days with a large coinsurance payment.

Medicaid, on the other hand, pays a substantial portion of the nation's nursing-home bill (over 40 percent). Medicaid, however, pays only when most other funds have been depleted. Medicaid will cover nursing-home expenses if your condition requires nursing-home care, the nursing home is certified by the state Medicaid agency, and you meet income and other eligibility requirements to receive this benefit.

The Department of Veterans Affairs (VA) pays for some nursing-home care for veterans in VA facilities and private facilities, but the benefit is limited to the extent that resources and facilities are available. Priority is given to veterans with medical problems related to their military service, and to very old veterans of wartime service, and very poor veterans. Contact your local VA office for more information.

Q. What if I don't want to live in a nursing home? Are home care services available under Medicare or Medicaid?

A. Yes, but to a limited extent. The home health-care benefit under Medicare focuses mainly on skilled nursing and therapeutic services needed on a part-time or intermittent basis. The benefit is described in the section on Medicare (see page 611).

Medicaid home health care is usually quite limited, too. But in addition to home health care, several state Medicaid programs also provide "personal care" services to Medicaid-eligible individuals who need help with normal activities of daily living, such as dressing, bathing, using a toilet, eating, and walking. Many states also have instituted Medicaid waiver programs that allow the state to use Medicaid dollars for home- and community-based services that normally would not be covered under Medicaid. These waiver programs usually target people who otherwise would have to live in a nursing home. Some of the services covered under Medicaid waiver programs include personal care, adult day care, housekeeping services, care coordination and management, and respite care. Respite care enables primary caregivers to take a break from their responsibilities. Check with your local office on aging or department of human services about the options available in your state.

Q. What happens if my husband needs nursing-home care but I am still able to live independently? Will all our income and assets have to be used for his support before Medicaid will help pay expenses?

A. If your spouse resides in or may be entering a nursing home, Medicaid has special rules that allow the spouse remaining in the community, the **community spouse,** to keep more income

---

ⓘ SPENDING DOWN TO ELIGIBILITY

Many persons who normally are not eligible for Medicaid become eligible after a period of time in a nursing home. This happens because the high cost of nursing-home care forces many individuals to spend down their assets and income to a level that qualifies them for Medicaid in many states. The rules and availability of this option vary from state to state.

---

and assets than permitted under the regular eligibility rules. The specifics vary from state to state, but the general structure is as follows.

The community spouse can keep all income, no matter how much, that belongs exclusively to the community spouse. Joint income is another story. The state may require all or part of joint income to help pay nursing-home expenses, depending upon the particular state's rules.

Most of the income of the nursing-home spouse is considered available to pay for nursing-home care. However, a portion of the nursing-home spouse's income may be kept by the community spouse as a "minimum monthly maintenance needs allowance" if the community spouse's income is below a spousal allowance figure set by the state. States must establish a spousal allowance of at least 150 percent of the poverty level for a two-person household. Thus, for the first half of 2004 (this figure changes every year on July 1), this calculation results in a minimum spousal allowance of at least $1515 per month that could be kept by the community spouse (Alaska and Hawaii have higher figures). States also permit the community spouse to keep a shelter allowance, if shelter costs (rent, mortgage, taxes, insurance, and utilities) exceed a specified amount.

Assets or resources are treated quite differently. The state applies a two-step rule. First, Medicaid counts all resources owned by either spouse. This inventory will exclude a few resources. The excluded resources are your home, household goods, personal effects, an automobile, and a burial fund of up to $1,500.

Second, Medicaid permits the community spouse to keep one-half of the total countable resources, as long as the one-half falls between a specified floor and ceiling amount, adjusted yearly. If the one-half falls below the floor ($18,552 in 2004), the community spouse may keep more of the couple's resources up to the floor amount. If the one-half exceeds the ceiling (about $92,760 in 2004), the excess will be considered available to pay for the cost of nursing-home care. Thus, the community spouse is permitted to keep no more than the ceiling amount even if it equals far less than half of the couple's assets. A more liberal approach in some states permits the community spouse to keep the maximum allowance ($92,760), even if this is more than one-half of countable assets. (Note: unlike the monthly spousal income allowance, which changes on July 1 of each year, the resource floor and ceiling amounts change every year on January 1.)

Another special rule applies to your home. Even though your home is an excluded resource, the state, in limited circumstances, can place a lien against your home equal to the amount of nursing-home expenses paid. The rules are complicated and vary by state; the advice of a lawyer experienced in Medicaid law is advisable. Moreover, almost all these rules have hardship exceptions in special circumstances.

Q. If I have assets that exceed my state's Medicaid eligibility requirements, can I transfer these to my children or to a trust in order to qualify? After all, these are assets I intend to leave to my children when I die.

A. The law on transferring assets before making a Medicaid application is complex. Such transfers can result in a period of ineligibility for Medicaid benefits. Several strategies are available to shelter or preserve some of your assets, but there are a number of legal, financial, ethical, and practical consequences to any such transfer of property. Anyone who may need to rely on Medicaid to pay for nursing-home care should seek advice from a lawyer experienced in Medicaid planning.

Q. Must children pay for parents in nursing homes?

A. There is no legal obligation for children to pay for their parents' care. Only a spouse may be held legally responsible to help pay for the cost of nursing-home care, and as a practical matter, the responsibility is often difficult to enforce against an unwilling spouse. If Medicaid enters the picture, the special rules for spousal responsibility described above apply.

Children sometimes feel pressured to help pay for a parent's nursing-home cost because of the shortage of nursing-home beds, especially Medicaid-covered beds. Some nursing homes give admission preference to private-pay patients over Medicaid patients because private-pay rates are often higher than the amount Medicaid pays. While admission priority for private-pay patients is permissible in some states, it is illegal in others. In all states, federal law prohibits nursing homes from requiring a private payment from families, or a period of private payment, prior to applying for Medicaid coverage. Federal law also prohibits nursing homes from requiring patients to waive their rights to Medicare and/or Medicaid.

Q. What is long-term care insurance?

A. Long-term care insurance helps pay for nursing-home care and usually home care services for a period of two or more years. Long-term care insurance is still a relatively new type of private insurance, so the features of this type of insurance continue to change frequently. For example, newer policies cover assisted-living facilities, adult day care, respite care, or other long-term care services.

Most individual policies are available for purchase only to people between the ages of fifty and eighty-four, and a medical screening of applicants is typically required. Not every older person needs or can afford a long-term care insurance policy. Policies are appropriate for those with substantial income and assets to protect, and who wish to buy this form of protection against the potential costs of long-term care.

Most long-term care policies are structured as indemnity policies. That is, they pay up to a preset cap for each day of a covered service. Other policies pay a percentage of costs up to a cap. The specific provisions should be closely examined before purchasing one, since the possible conditions and limitations on coverage can be complex.

Q. How are the costs of a long-term care policy determined?

A. The cost of the premium is determined in part by your age, the extent of coverage you purchase, and your health history. Age is clearly the single greatest factor because the risk of needing long-term care increases significantly with age. The premium for a seventy-five-year-old can be double or triple that for a sixty-five-year-old.

Q. What is the tax treatment of both the insurance premiums paid for long-term care insurance and of the benefits received under the policy?

A. The Health Insurance Portability and Accountability Act of 1996 (HIPAA) clarified the tax treatment of both premiums and benefits so as to make it the same as for major medical coverage.

Under HIPAA, benefits from a federally qualified long-term care policy—that is, a policy that meets minimum federal standards—are generally not taxable. For taxpayers who itemize their deductions, premiums for long-term care, as well as consumers' out-of-pocket costs for long-term care, can be applied toward meeting the 7.5 percent floor for medical expense deductions (that is, medical expenses are deductible only to the extent that they exceed 7.5 percent of your income). There are limits, based upon one's age, for the total amount of premiums paid for long-term care insurance that can be applied to the 7.5 percent floor, so check with a tax adviser before taking this deduction. For taxpayers who do not itemize their income tax deductions, Congress is currently considering a change in the tax law that would allow middle-income taxpayers to take a tax deduction for the cost of their long-term care insurance premiums.

Q. How do I evaluate a long-term care policy?

A. Compare several policies side by side. Your state's insurance department should have names of companies offering long-term care insurance. Many states are beginning to set minimum standards and consumer protection guidelines for these policies. Guides for evaluating long-term care insurance may be available from your state insurance department or state office on aging.

⚠ HOW MUCH HEALTH INSURANCE DO I NEED?

Some people covered by Medicare think they need several additional policies to cover Medicare gaps, specific diseases, and long-term care. That is probably not a good strategy. Chances are the policies would duplicate too many benefits to justify the cost. That is why insurance companies are no longer permitted to sell duplicate Medicare supplement policies. The consumer may purchase only one.

The best recommendation for someone on Medicare, who is not also on Medicaid, is to purchase one good Medigap policy, and possibly one long-term care insurance policy if you can comfortably afford the cost of a good policy. Lower-income people are likely to qualify for Medicaid if they need long-term care, so purchasing private long-term care insurance may be a waste of money.

THE WORLD AT YOUR FINGERTIPS

- *The Centers for Medicare and Medicaid Services maintains a website at www.cms. gov that contains comprehensive information regarding Medicare and Medicaid. The website includes features such as detailed explanations of coverage under the two programs, frequently asked questions, and a list of publications, many of which can be accessed online. The Centers for Medicare and Medicaid Services can also be contacted at 7500 Security Boule-*

vard, Baltimore, MD, 21244-1850, and by telephone at 410-786-3000 or 800-MEDICARE.

- *The free booklet, "Guide to Health Insurance for People with Medicare," can be obtained from your local Social Security Administration office. The guide is also available online at www.medicare.gov This guide explains how Medigap insurance works; explains the ten standardized plans; tells you how to shop for Medigap insurance; and lists addresses and phone numbers of state insurance departments and state agencies on aging. Most states offer free insurance counseling services.*

- *Medicare also maintains a "consumer" website at www.medicare.gov, which provides a wealth of information about Medicare, Medigap, Medicaid, and nursing homes. The website also has a Medi-*

▶ WHAT TO LOOK FOR IN A LONG-TERM CARE POLICY

- Make sure your policy will pay benefits for all levels of care in a nursing home, including custodial care.

- Buy a federally qualified long-term care policy so that you can be certain of its tax advantages.

- A good policy will pay benefits for assisted-living and home care, including in-home personal care. Personal care refers generally to help with activities of daily living, such as dressing, bathing, using a toilet, eating, and walking.

- Consider whether the amount of daily benefits will be adequate now and in the future. Many policies give you a range of daily benefit amounts to choose from. The right amount depends in part on the amount of assets you have. Make sure the policy has an "inflation adjuster" under which benefits increase by a certain percentage each year to keep pace with inflation.

- Do not assume that more years of coverage are always better. Some policies offer benefit options of six, seven, or more years. It is possible to buy too much coverage.

- Avoid policies that exclude coverage of preexisting conditions for a lengthy period. Six months is considered a reasonable exclusion period for preexisting conditions.

- Policies should allow payment of nursing-home or home health benefits without requiring a prior period of hospitalization as a condition of coverage.

- Most policies impose waiting periods that restrict the starting time of benefits after you begin receiving nursing-home care or home care—twenty to ninety days is a common waiting period. First-day coverage will increase your premium.

- Be sure your policy covers victims of Alzheimer's disease and other forms of dementia. About half the residents of nursing homes suffer some form of dementia.

- Be sure that the premium remains constant over the life of the policy and that the policy is guaranteed renewable for life.

- Buy a policy only from a company that is licensed in your state and has agents physically present in your state. Out-of-state mail-order policies often leave you powerless to remedy problems if anything goes wrong.

gap Compare feature. This is an interactive tool for Medicare beneficiaries to help find the insurance companies in each state that sell Medigap plans.

- *Information on educated health-care choices is also available at the AARP website at www.aarp.org/hcchoices.*
- *A Guide to Long-Term Care Insurance is available on the Health Insurance Association of America website at www.hiaa.org/consumer.*

REMEMBER THIS

- *Medicare Parts A and B provide nearly universal basic insurance coverage to older adults, but they have significant limitations in coverage, particularly with respect to prescription drugs and long-term care.*
- *Most, but not all, older people need to purchase a Medigap policy to cover some of the costs not covered by Medicare.*
- *Medicaid provides medical assistance, or Medicare Savings Programs, for low-income older or disabled people whose income and assets fall below certain levels.*
- *Medicare does not provide coverage for most long-term care. Possible alternative sources of coverage include Medicaid, but only when most other resources have been spent, and private long-term care insurance, which is costly.*

HOUSING AND LONG-TERM CARE OPTIONS

Dillon is eighty-two years old and lives in the home he's owned for fifty years. He is able to take care of himself for the most part, but he can no longer drive and relies on neighbors and family members to bring him groceries. It is getting more difficult for Dillon to prepare meals for himself, so now he sticks to breakfast cereal and other things he does not need to cook. His house could use some repairs. Dillon and his family agree that he is unable to keep up his house, but they do not think he needs the daily care in a nursing home. Is a nursing home Dillon's only option?

The range of housing options for older people is enormous—from staying in your own home or apartment, to home sharing, to moving to a senior housing facility or development. The questions and answers that follow begin by exploring an important financial option, home equity conversion, that may help you stay in your home, and end by describing the wide variety of housing choices that provide shelter plus some combination of recreational and social opportunities or supportive services and health care. In all these areas, older people need to be aware of the personal and financial risks and benefits involved, and, above all, their legal rights.

Home Equity Conversion

Q. I own my own home, and do not want to move, but I'm having trouble making ends meet. What can I do?

A. Home equity conversion plans can help you add to your monthly income without having to leave your home. These plans fall into two broad categories: loans and sales. Loan plans permit you to borrow against the equity in your home. They include reverse mortgages and special-purpose loans on which repayment is deferred. They should not be confused with home equity loans and home equity lines of credit, which require you to make monthly payments immediately or risk losing your house.

Q. How does a reverse mortgage work?

A. A reverse mortgage lets you borrow against the equity in your home, receiving a lump sum or monthly installments, or drawing on a line of credit. The amount of the loan you will receive is based on your age, the value of your home and your equity, the interest rate, the term of the loan, and some other factors. Except for some special-purpose state- or local-government-sponsored plans, like those designed to pay for home repairs, there are no restrictions on how you use the money.

The loan usually does not have to be repaid until you die, or sell or move from your home. When the loan does come due, the amount to be repaid cannot exceed the appraised value of the property.

Q. Who is eligible for a reverse mortgage?

A. A borrower must be at least sixty-two years of age, and own and occupy the home as a principal place of residence. The property should be free of liens or mortgages except for those that can be paid off at closing. Unlike traditional loans or home equity lines of credit, the borrower's income is not considered. Single-family residences, including some condominiums, and some manufactured homes, as well as duplexes and triplexes, are eligible. Mobile homes and cooperatives are not.

Q. Are reverse mortgages available in my area?

A. Reverse mortgages can be obtained in all fifty states (although availability is limited in Texas), the District of Columbia, and Puerto Rico. The most common products are the federally insured home equity conversion mortgage, or HECM, and the HomeKeeper Reverse Mortgage available through Fannie Mae. Other products include state-subsidized home repair plans, lender-insured plans, and reverse annuity mortgages.

Q. How will a reverse mortgage affect my other benefits?

A. The income from a reverse mortgage will not affect eligibility for Social Security, Medicare or other retirement benefits or pensions that are not based on need. However, without careful planning, the income from a reverse mortgage could affect eligibility for supplemental security income (SSI), Medicaid, food stamps, and some state benefit programs.

In general, reverse mortgage payments are considered to be a loan and will not affect benefits if the money is spent during the month in which it is received. But if the money is not spent during that month, it will be counted as a resource and may lead to termination of benefits. Be aware that payments received under the annuity mortgage plans will be considered income, even if they are spent in the month in which they are received.

Q. What about tax consequences?

A. There are two issues here. The first is whether the income from a reverse mortgage is taxed. So far, it has not been, under the assumption that it is a loan advance. Second is whether the interest can be deducted. Generally, interest cannot be deducted until it is paid. Since the interest on a reverse mortgage is not paid until the loan comes due, it cannot be deducted until that time.

Q. What other kinds of home equity conversion are available?

A. In addition to loan plans, you can generate income from the equity that you have acquired in your home through sale plans. Sale plans include

---

▶ **HOW MUCH CAN YOU BORROW?**

How much you can borrow will depend on the kind of reverse mortgage. HECM mortgages are insured by the Federal Housing Administration, which sets national limits annually according to the area of the country where the property is located. For 2004, FHA is insuring single-family home mortgages up to $160,766 in low-cost areas and up to $290,319 in high-cost areas. Fannie Mae's Homekeeper has a single national limit, which in 2004 is $333,700 (but higher in Alaska and Hawaii).

sale-leasebacks (see sidebar on this page), life estates, and charitable annuities.

Q. What if I sell my house and keep a life estate?

A. In a life estate, or sale of a remainder interest plan, you sell your home to a buyer, but keep the right to live there during your lifetime. The buyer pays you a lump sum, or monthly payments, or both. You are usually responsible for taxes and repairs while you live in the house, but you pay no rent. At your death, full ownership passes automatically to the buyer. This arrangement is most common within families, as part of an estate plan. As with a sale-leaseback, it might be difficult to find an outside investor.

There also may be a tax disadvantage to this arrangement. If you sell the house to a family member, but keep a life estate, the tax basis in the property for the family member will be the same as your basis in the house, which is the amount you paid for the house plus the cost of any improvements you made in the property—let's say $125,000. This amount typically will be considerably lower than the stepped-up basis (that is, the market value of the property at the time of inheritance—let's say $225,000) to which your heir would be entitled if he or she inherited the property upon your death. If your heir later sells the

property, he or she will have to pay a capital gains tax on the difference between your basis and the amount for which the property was sold—or $100,000, assuming the property sells for the market price at the time of your death.

Q. What about a regular home equity loan?

A. A traditional home equity loan is very different from a reverse mortgage and can be a risk for an older person on a fixed income. As with a reverse mortgage, you borrow against the equity you have built up in your home. But in a home equity loan, you must make regular monthly payments, or you may lose your home.

There may be some tax advantages, however. Since it is no longer possible to deduct interest on consumer goods such as car loans and credit card bills, many homeowners have turned to home equity loans. With such loans, you can use the money for any purpose, and deduct all the interest you pay on a loan up to $100,000. You can even deduct the interest on a home equity loan that exceeds $100,000 if you use the money for home improvements. However, if the difference between the fair market value (FMV) of your house and any preexisting debt on the house, such as a mortgage, is less than $100,000, interest on the home equity loan is deductible only for

---

ⓘ SALE-LEASEBACKS

In a sale-leaseback, you sell the equity in your home, but retain the right to continue living there, often paying a monthly rent. The buyer usually makes a substantial down payment to you. You act as a lender by granting the buyer a mortgage. You receive the buyer's mortgage payments; the buyer receives your rent payments, which are set lower than the mortgage payments, so you gain a positive net monthly income. You remain in the home, and can use the down payment and the mortgage payments as income. The buyer can deduct the mortgage interest payment from his or her income, and the buyer also will benefit if the value of the property increases.

Be aware, however, that the IRS requires that both the sale price and the rental payments be fair market rate. Before 1986, the tax laws made sale-leasebacks good investments, especially for adult children. Today, however, there are fewer tax advantages, so finding an investor may be difficult.

an amount no greater than the difference between the FMV and the preexisting debt. For example, if your house is worth $150,000 and the balance on your mortgage is $110,000, you can deduct the interest on only $40,000 of a home equity loan, although you may take out a larger loan if you wish.

Q. Is home equity conversion the only way to increase my monthly income?

A. Not necessarily. If you find that your monthly income does not meet your expenses, you may be eligible for government benefits, such as supplemental security income, food stamps, or Medicaid. (See "Social Security and Supplemental Security Income" on page 601.) Some states also have property tax credit or deferral programs for which you may be eligible. To find out more about these programs, call your local agency on aging. You should consider all of the options available to you before you make a decision. If you already are receiving public benefits, you should make sure that the home equity conversion plan you choose does not affect those benefits.

Q. I am not sure that I can continue to live in my own home, but I would like to stay in my community. What other choices do I have?

A. You have several choices, depending on your current and future health needs, your financial circumstances, and your personal preferences, although not all may be available in your community. There are home-sharing programs, in which homeowners are matched with individuals seeking housing in exchange for rent or services; accessory units that provide private living units in, or next to, single-family homes; or assisted living (described below), which combines a homelike setting with services designed to meet individual needs. These programs may be privately owned and operated, government supported, or sponsored by religious or other nonprofit organizations. For information, contact your local agency on aging.

Retirement Communities

Q. I have heard a lot about retirement communities that offer all kinds of different services and amenities. What types of retirement communities are available today?

A. In the last several years, there has been a large increase in the number of living options for older people as both the public and private sectors attempt to respond to the growing numbers of elders. The modern model of retirement community first appeared in the 1950s in the Sunbelt states as senior communities that offered independent living with a variety of social and recreational opportunities. Much has changed today. Between the extremes of independent living and nursing-home care, a variety of alternatives now offers endless combinations of shelter plus services or amenities. Physically, facilities may range from single-family-type housing, to high-rise or garden apartment buildings, to campuslike developments.

Facility definitions differ among states and sometimes even within states. For simplicity's sake, it is useful to distinguish three levels of housing based on the services provided. At one end of the continuum are **independent-living communities**. These offer little or no health and supportive services, although they may have recreational and social programs. At the opposite end are **continuing-care retirement communities** (**CCRCs**). These provide a fairly extensive range of housing options, care, and services, including nursing-home services. In between are facilities that offer a wide variety of housing and health or supportive services but not nursing-home care. Today, these are commonly referred to as **assisted-living communities,** but they include facilities variously called "housing with supportive services," "congregate care homes," "board and care homes," and "personal care homes," to list just a few.

Q. What purchase or payment arrangements do retirement communities offer?

A. Conventional independent-living communities without health services typically involve home ownership or rental arrangements that are similar to standard real estate purchases or rentals. These transactions are governed by local real estate or landlord-tenant law, and residents pay the costs of their mortgage or lease, and condominium or association fees if applicable. In facilities that promise additional services, accommodations, or health care, the payment arrangement includes some mechanism to pay for these added benefits. One may distinguish four basic types of contract, based on payment arrangement, although keep in mind that state regulations may categorize facilities differently:

1. Turnover-of-assets or total-fee-in-advance contracts without monthly fees. These types of contracts are all but extinct today. They were common in the original continuing care communities, often called life care communities, developed by religious or fraternal organizations. Many communities using this model failed, because the assets received by the sponsors were not sufficient to keep up with rising health-care expenses of residents over their lifetimes.
2. Entrance-fee-plus-monthly-fee contracts. Entrance fees, ranging from $20,000 to over $400,000, are charged by most continuing-care retirement facilities today. An entrance fee may represent a partial prepayment for future services. It normally does not buy an interest in the real estate. Increasingly, CCRCs are providing greater refundability of entrance fees, even 100 percent refundability, although this usually results in higher monthly fees. Residency rights and obligations are governed by a long-term lease or occupancy agreement. Monthly fees are subject to periodic inflation adjustments, and, possibly, adjustments when the resident's level-of-care needs change.
3. Pay-as-you-go contracts. With no entrance fee, these contracts are essentially straight rental arrangements with a defined set of services included in the fee or available when needed for an additional charge. Most assisted-living and an increasing number of continuing-care facilities offer this arrangement. This type of contract involves no initial investment, but it is subject to greater changes in monthly fees, since the resident assumes most or all of the financial risk for services.
4. Condominiums or cooperatives with continuing-care contracts. Retirement communities that offer an ownership interest to residents under a condominium or cooperative arrangement with a service package included are relatively new to the scene. These ownership/contractual arrangements are unavoidably complex and bring with them special advantages and risks.

Q. *What sorts of things do I need to consider before moving into a continuing-care community?*

A. This is a major financial investment, frequently using up most or all of an older person's financial resources, so consider it carefully and seek professional advice from a lawyer or a financial adviser before you make a commitment. You may not be able to get your money back. Be sure to visit the facility at length and talk to both staff

---

ⓘ WHO SPONSORS AND WHO REGULATES RETIREMENT COMMUNITIES?

Most retirement communities are developed privately, although many are sponsored by nonprofit groups and agencies, including churches and charitable organizations. All states regulate one or more types of assisted living, and most states regulate continuing-care communities, but the extent of regulation varies considerably among states.

and residents. The following checklist highlights key questions you should ask.

Solvency and Expertise of the Provider

1. What is the provider's background and experience? The provider is the person or entity legally and financially responsible for providing continuing care. Some facilities may advertise that they are "sponsored" by nonprofit groups or churches that in reality may have no legal control or financial responsibility. Be wary if such illusory sponsorship is trumpeted in sales literature.

2. Is the provider financially sound? Have the facility's financial, actuarial, and operating statements reviewed by a professional. Determine whether the facility has sufficient financial reserves.

3. Are all levels of care licensed or certified under applicable state statutes regulating continuing-care, assisted-living, and nursing-home care?

4. How does the facility ensure the quality of care and services provided? Is the facility accredited by any recognized private accrediting organization?

Fees

5. What is the entrance fee, and when can you get all or part of it back? The facility should provide a formula for a pro rata refund of the entrance fee, based on the resident's length of stay, regardless of whether the facility or the resident initiates the termination. Some facilities offer the option of fully refundable entrance fees.

6. What is the monthly fee? When and how much can it be increased? What happens if fee increases exceed your ability to pay? Some facilities have a program that grants financial assistance to residents whose income becomes inadequate to pay increasing monthly fees and personal expenses.

7. Will fees change when the resident's living arrangements or level-of-care needs change (for example, transfers from independent living, to assisted living, to nursing care)?

Services and Health Care

8. Exactly what services are included in the regular fees? Especially inquire about coverage, limitations, and costs of the following:

Housing/Social/Recreational

- Meal services
- Special diets/tray service
- Utilities
- Cable television
- Furnishings
- Unit maintenance
- Linens/personal laundry
- Housekeeping
- Recreational/cultural activities
- Transportation

Health and Personal Care

- Physician services
- Nursing services outside a nursing unit (for example, assistance with medications)
- Private-duty nursing
- Dental and eye care
- Personal care services (that is, assistance with eating, dressing, bathing, and using bathroom facilities
- Homemaker/companion services
- Drugs
- Medication
- Medical equipment/supplies
- Facility services

9. If the facility provides a nursing unit, what happens if a bed is not available when you need it?

10. To what extent does the facility have the right to cut back, change, or eliminate services, or change the fees?

11. Does the facility limit its responsibility for certain health conditions or preexisting conditions? When are you too sick or impaired to be cared for by the facility?

12. Can you receive Medicare and Medicaid coverage in the facility?
13. Does the facility require residents to buy private insurance or participate in a special group insurance program for residents?
14. What are the criteria and procedures for determining when a resident needs to be transferred from independent living to assisted living, or to a nursing-care unit, or to an entirely different facility? Who is involved in these decisions?

Residents' Rights

15. What does my living unit consist of, and to what extent can I change or redecorate it?
16. What happens if I marry, divorce, become widowed, or wish to have a friend or family member move into the unit?
17. What rights do residents have to participate in facility management and decision making? How are complaints handled?
18. On what grounds can residents' contracts or leases be terminated against their wishes?
19. What other rules and policies cover the day-to-day operation of the facility?
20. Does the contract release the facility from any liability for injury to a resident resulting from negligence by the facility or third parties? Such waivers should be avoided.

Nursing-Home Care

Q. What is a nursing home?

A. A **nursing home** is a facility that provides skilled nursing care and related services for residents who require medical or nursing care; rehabilitation services for injured, disabled, or sick persons; and health-related care and services, above the level of room and board, that can be made available only through institutional facilities.

Often, nursing facilities make distinctions between levels of care—skilled and custodial—for purposes of Medicare, Medicaid, or private insurance coverage. The distinction between "skilled" and "custodial" care affects Medicare and is discussed on page 611.

Only about 5 percent of people age sixty-five and older live in nursing homes at any given time, but researchers estimate that older persons overall have about a 40 percent chance of spending at least some time in nursing homes. While some older nursing-home residents stay for extended periods, the majority stay in a facility less than six months.

Q. How does living in a nursing home affect my personal rights and privileges?

A. You do not check your rights and privileges at the door when you enter a nursing home. Although institutional care, by its very nature, substantially limits one's lifestyle and scope of privacy, one should nevertheless expect high-quality, compassionate, and dignified care from nursing facilities.

The federal Nursing Home Reform Amendments of 1987, and corresponding state laws, protect residents in nearly all nursing facilities. For residents who lack decision-making capacity, the resident's agent under a power of attorney for health care or another legal surrogate recognized by state law (typically a family member) may exercise the resident's rights. Federal law requires that nursing homes meet strong basic standards for the quality of life of each resident and for the provision of services and activities. Specific rights guaranteed by federal and state law include the following:

Information Rights
Nursing homes must provide

- written information about residents' rights;
- written information about the services available under the basic rate and any extra charges for extra services;
- advance notice of changes in room assignment or roommate;
- upon request, latest facility inspection results and any plan of correction submitted to state officials;

- explanation of the resident's right to make a health-care advance directive—that is, power of attorney for health care, or living will—and facility policies on complying with advance directives (see the discussion of advance directives under "Health-Care Decision-Making Issues" on page 644); and
- information about eligibility for Medicare and Medicaid and the services covered by those programs.

Self-Determination Rights

Each resident has the right to

- participate in an individualized assessment and care-planning process that accommodates the resident's personal needs and preferences;
- choose a personal physician;
- voice complaints without fear of reprisal and receive a prompt response; and
- organize and participate in resident groups (such as a resident council) and family groups.

Personal and Privacy Rights

Residents have the right to

- participate in social, religious, and community activities as they choose;
- privacy in medical treatment, accommodations, personal visits, written and telephone communications, and meetings of resident and family groups;
- confidentiality of personal and clinical records;
- access to the long-term care ombudsman, their physician, family members, and reasonable access to other visitors, all subject to the resident's consent;
- freedom from physical or mental abuse, corporal punishment, and involuntary seclusion;
- freedom from any physical restraint or psychoactive drug used for purposes of discipline or convenience, and not required to treat the resident's medical symptoms; and

- protection of resident's funds held by the facility with a quarterly accounting.

Transfer and Discharge Rights

Residents may be transferred or discharged only if

- the health, safety, or welfare of the resident or other residents requires it;
- the resident fails to make necessary payments (nonpayment of fees);
- the resident's health improves so that he or she no longer needs nursing-home care; or
- the facility closes.

Normally, residents must receive at least thirty days' advance notice, with information about appealing the transfer and how to contact the state long-term care ombudsman program. The facility must prepare a discharge plan and orient residents to ensure safe and orderly transfer from the facility.

Protection Against Medicaid Discrimination

Nursing homes must

- have identical policies and practices regarding services to residents regardless of the source of payment (however, be aware that not all facilities participate in Medicaid);
- provide information on how to apply for Medicaid;
- explain the Medicaid "bed-hold" policy—that is, how many days Medicaid will hold the resident's bed, or ensure priority readmission, after temporary absences;
- not request, require, or encourage residents to waive their rights to Medicaid;
- not require a family member to guarantee payment as a condition of a resident's admission or continued stay; and
- not "charge, solicit, accept or receive gifts, money, donations or other considerations" as a precondition for admission or continued stay for persons eligible for Medicaid.

Q. What can I do to ensure that I will receive quality care and that my medical and personal needs will be met?

A. The key to ensuring that you receive individualized care that adequately addresses your medical and personal needs is active participation in the care-planning process. Federal law requires a resident assessment and a written plan of care that is prepared with the resident or the resident's family or legal representative. This process should occur just after admission and then yearly, or after any significant change in physical or mental condition.

Q. What can I do if I think a nursing home is not providing adequate care or respecting my rights?

A. Different problems require different responses. The following steps should help resolve most problems. The order may vary depending on the problem.

1. Keep a log of the relevant details, including dates and personnel involved.

2. Try to resolve the problem informally by talking to supervising staff.

3. Many facilities have active resident councils or family councils. Bring the problem before these groups.

4. Contact your long-term care ombudsman (see the following Q & A).

5. Contact the state regulatory agencies that license, certify, and survey nursing homes. Usually, the state department of health has this responsibility.

6. Contact a community legal assistance program, other advocacy organization, or private lawyer experienced in long-term care issues.

Q. What is the long-term care ombudsman program?

A. The federal Older Americans Act requires every state to operate a long-term care ombudsman program. The ombudsman is responsible for advocating on behalf of nursing-home residents and residents of other long-term care facilities, such as assisted-living or board-and-care facilities. The ombudsman provides education on long-term care options and residents' rights, and investigates and resolves complaints made by or on behalf of residents.

Most states operate local or regional programs with paid or volunteer ombudsmen. Residents and family members often find ombudsman staff to be helpful partners in resolving problems. Federal law requires nursing homes to allow the ombudsman access to residents and access to resident records. In addition, the ombudsman usually has special authority under state law to inspect records and take other steps necessary to respond to complaints.

ⓘ BASIC QUALITY-OF-LIFE STANDARD FOR NURSING HOMES

Federal law requires each nursing facility to "care for its residents in such a manner and in such an environment as will promote maintenance of and enhancement of the quality of life of each resident." Federal law further requires each nursing facility to "provide services and activities to attain or maintain the highest practicable physical, mental and psychosocial well-being of each resident in accordance with a written plan of care that . . . is initially prepared, with participation to the extent practicable of the resident or the resident's family or legal representative."

THE WORLD AT YOUR FINGERTIPS

- *Information on reverse mortgages can be obtained from the AARP at www.aarp.org/revmort. A consumer guide entitled "Home Made Money" is particularly useful, and a primer entitled "Exploring Reverse Mortgages" is also available. The National*

Center for Home Equity Conversion also may be able to provide information at 651-222-6775 or at www.reverse.org.

- *The FHA can be contacted at 888-466-3487 (toll-free), or at www.hud.gov.*
- *Information regarding not-for-profit retirement communities is available from the American Association of Homes and Services for the Aging and its affiliated organization, the Continuing Care Accreditation Commission, at the CCAC website, www.ccaconline.org (click on "List of Accredited Communities") or the AAHSA website, www.aahsa.org.*
- *The National Citizens' Coalition for Nursing Home Reform (NCCNHR) can provide you with information regarding the rights of nursing-home residents, including how to contact the state long-term care ombudsman. They also publish an excellent resource to help you with the care-planning process, entitled Nursing Homes: Getting Good Care There. It is available by writing to the organization at 1424 Sixteenth Street NW, Suite 202, Washington, DC 20036, or by calling 202-332-2275 or visiting its website at www.nccnhr.org.*
- *State or local agencies on aging frequently prepare directories or guides on housing options for older persons and persons with disabilities. You can find your local agency's number in your local telephone book.*

REMEMBER THIS

- *Home equity conversion plans, such as reverse mortgages, can help you add to your monthly income without having to leave your home.*
- *Continuing-care retirement communities are a major investment, so you should seek professional advice from a lawyer or a financial adviser before you sign a contract.*
- *Federal law guarantees the rights of nursing-home residents, including information rights, privacy rights, self-determination rights, and the right to a personalized care plan.*
- *Each state has a long-term care ombudsman who is responsible for investigating complaints and problems at nursing homes.*

RIGHTS OF PEOPLE WITH DISABILITIES

Margaret had a stroke in her fifties, which left her paralyzed down her left side. She is not wheelchair-bound, and is able to walk, but she needs to hold on to a bar when she goes up and down stairs. She lives on the ground floor of her apartment block, but there are four steps leading up to the front door. Her landlord won't let her install a bar next to the stairs because he thinks it is unsightly. Margaret is willing to pay. What can she do?

Many older people are unable to manage their daily activities as well as they once did. Others have disabilities that have worsened with age. Two major federal laws, the Americans with Disabilities Act and the Fair Housing Act, protect people with physical or mental disabilities from discrimination in virtually every aspect of their lives. In addition, these laws require employers and the providers of services to modify their rules and policies, as well as the physical environment, to meet the needs of persons with disabilities. A third law, Section 504 of the Rehabilitation Act of 1973, provides the same protections against discrimination by organizations that receive federal contracts.

Q. *Who do these laws protect?*

A. These laws protect people with mental or physical impairments that limit their ability to perform one or more major life activities. These activities include walking, seeing, hearing, taking care of personal or health needs, or doing everyday chores. The laws also protect people who are perceived to have a disability, or whose family members or friends are disabled.

They do not protect people who threaten the safety or health of others, or whose behavior would result in substantial damage to the property of others. Nor do they protect current users of illegal drugs.

Q. What situations does the Americans with Disabilities Act cover?

A. The Americans with Disabilities Act (ADA) protects people with disabilities against discrimination in employment, public transit, and public accommodation, such as hotels, restaurants, stores, banks, schools, and senior centers. It generally does not cover housing (but the Fair Housing Act does; see below), although it does cover some nonhousing activities that are based in a housing facility, such as meals or activity programs to which the public is invited.

Q. What laws cover housing?

A. The Fair Housing Act (FHA) applies to almost all housing transactions. Most important for the purposes of this chapter, the law prohibits landlords from refusing to rent to older people, or asking them to move, simply because they need assistance with certain activities. The law does not apply to rental buildings that contain fewer than four units, where the owner also lives in the building. Examples of prohibited discrimination include

- refusing to rent to a family because a family member has a mental illness;
- requiring applicants for senior housing to provide a doctor's letter stating that they are in good health and can live on their own;
- denying a resident who uses a wheelchair or a walker access to a communal dining room; and
- evicting a tenant because he or she is receiving homemaking help or other services.

Section 504 offers similar protections to residents of federally subsidized housing.

Q. What does "reasonable accommodation" mean?

A. Reasonable accommodations are changes in rules or procedures that are reasonable under the circumstances, and give a disabled person equal opportunity to participate in a specific activity, program, job, or housing situation. They are very individualized and often can be worked out informally by the people involved. Examples include

- giving a job or housing applicant more time to fill out an application;
- providing large-print notices, leases, or other written materials;
- waiving a no-pets rule for a tenant with a mental disability who is emotionally dependent on his or her pet, or waiving a no-guest rule for a tenant who needs a live-in aide; and
- assisting a customer who needs help with packages, or with opening and closing doors, or even with dialing a telephone.

Q. What are reasonable modifications?

A. Reasonable modifications are changes to the physical structure of a building or property, which are reasonable under the circumstances, and which give a person with disabilities equal access to the premises. Examples include

- widening doorways and installing ramps;
- replacing doorknobs with lever handles; and
- installing grab bars in bathrooms.

Q. Who pays for these alterations?

A. In an apartment or other privately owned housing, the tenant is responsible for the cost of alterations. Modifications of public facilities, hotels, public meeting rooms, rental offices, and other sites covered by the ADA are paid for by the owner of the facility. In buildings that are federally subsidized, the owner is responsible for modifications to individual apartments as well as public areas.

Q. How do I go about getting some changes made in my apartment?

A. Although many housing providers are familiar with the FHA and are working to make sure that their buildings are accessible, they may not be aware of accommodations that would make life easier for individual tenants. All you need to do is request the changes in writing; if they are related to your disability, and reasonable, they should be honored. Remember that you are responsible for the cost of physical alterations inside your own apartment. Also, you may be required to return the premises to their original condition when you move.

Q. What do I do if I believe I am being discriminated against?

A. The ADA, the FHA, and Section 504 of the Rehabilitation Act can be enforced through court action or by filing a complaint with an administrative agency.

THE WORLD AT YOUR FINGERTIPS

- *Information about the Americans with Disabilities Act can be obtained from the U.S. Department of Justice at 800-514-0301 (voice) or 800-514-0383 (TDD), or at www.ada.gov.*
- *The U.S. Department of Housing and Urban Development's website includes a Web page for persons with disabilities at www.hud.gov/groups/disabilities.cfm.*
- *The National Association of Protection and Advocacy Systems provides information, including the location of each state's disability rights agency, at its website, www.protectionandadvocacy.com.*
- *If you have been discriminated against and the discrimination involves housing, you can call the U.S. Department of Housing and Urban Development's Housing Discrimination Hotline at 800-669-9777.*
- *If you have been discriminated against and the discrimination involves employment,*

public accommodations, telecommunications, or public transit, you can contact the U.S. Department of Justice, Office on the Americans with Disabilities Act, Civil Rights Division, at 800-514-0301 (voice) or 800-514-0383 (TDD).

REMEMBER THIS

- *The Americans with Disabilities Act protects people with disabilities against discrimination in employment, public transit, and public accommodations, such as hotels, restaurants, stores, banks, schools, and senior centers.*
- *The Fair Housing Act prohibits landlords from refusing to rent to older people, or asking them to move, simply because they need assistance with certain activities.*
- *Federal law requires landlords to allow tenants to make reasonable modifications to an apartment to improve accessibility, but the tenant must pay for those changes unless the building is federally subsidized.*

A RIGHT TO CONTROL YOUR OWN AFFAIRS

Ruby is diagnosed with Alzheimer's. She knows that as the disease progresses she will become unable to make decisions about her finances, living situation, and health. She consults a lawyer to find out her options.

As we grow older, all of us face the possibility that one day we may become incapacitated mentally. The time may come when we are no longer able to make our own health-care decisions, manage our own financial affairs, or act on our own behalf.

If that happens, you and your property must be protected, and people should honor your wishes wherever possible. This section addresses the critical legal issues regarding your right to control your own affairs. How and where do you want to live? What decisions can you make? What decisions should you leave to someone else? Whom do you want to make decisions for you? Several alternative methods of advance planning can ensure that people respect your wishes whenever possible. Through planning, the decisions made on your behalf can be those you would have made yourself.

Durable Power of Attorney

Q. What may I do to make sure that people consider my wishes if I become incapacitated?

A. You should make plans now, while you have capacity, to be sure your wishes are met. Several planning tools guarantee you a voice in your future. If incapacity strikes, these tools will name the person you want to act on your behalf and/or tell other people how to care for you and your property.

There are different types of planning tools. Some—such as the **durable power of attorney,** joint property arrangements, and living trusts— cover your property and financial affairs. Others, known as advance directives for health care, address your health-care concerns, including decisions near the end of life.

The details of creating these documents vary from one state to another. However, some general principles apply.

Q. What is a power of attorney?

A. A **power of attorney** is a written document in which you (the **principal**) grant certain authority to another person (the **agent** or **attorney in fact**) to act on your behalf. A power of attorney may be very specific, authorizing a person only to sell a car for you, for example. Or it can be very broad, allowing the agent to do almost anything on your behalf. Traditionally, powers of attorney were used to authorize a trusted family member, friend, or lawyer to act on your behalf in financial matters—the sale of real estate, the making of in-

vestments, and so on. When drafted to cover all financial matters, this authorization is called a **general power of attorney.** However, you should note that the Social Security Administration will not permit your agent to cash or deposit your Social Security check. To deal with this problem, you may want to designate a representative payee (discussed on page 640).

Q. Will a power of attorney be valid if I become mentally incapacitated or incompetent?

A. In most states, a power of attorney is not valid if you become incapacitated, unless you use a durable power of attorney. A durable power of attorney clearly states that you intend the power to continue if you become disabled or incapacitated. It generally remains in effect until you deliberately revoke it or until you die. However, in some states, your durable power of attorney is terminated if a guardian is appointed for you (although appointment of a guardian is usually unnecessary because the durable power of attorney takes care of the management of your affairs).

Q. Whom should I name as my agent under a durable power of attorney? Does the person have to be a lawyer?

A. Your agent does not have to be a lawyer. In most states, it can be any adult or an institution. However, it should be someone who knows you well and whom you trust completely to manage your affairs. After all, decisions made by your agent can have tremendous consequences for you. Your agent has to carry out your wishes and should always act as you would choose or with your best interests in mind. If there is no one whom you trust with this power, it may be best not to draw up a power of attorney. Other planning tools may suit you better.

You may name multiple agents who exercise all or some of the powers jointly (that is, all must agree) or separately (that is, any one may act). But only do this with great caution because disputes among agents can become a significant obstacle. With multiple agents, some process for handling disagreements among agents should be considered. In all cases, it is a good idea to name an alternate to serve as your agent in case your first choice becomes unavailable.

Q. What if I do not want a power of attorney to take effect now, but only if I become disabled or incapacitated?

A. In general, a durable power of attorney becomes effective when you sign it. However, you may tell your agent not to act until you become incapacitated or disabled. If your agent acts prematurely, you still have the right to act on your own behalf, and you may revoke the durable power of attorney at any time while you still have capacity. It may be possible to write your durable power of attorney so that it becomes effective only if you become incapacitated. This is called a **springing power of attorney.** Many states allow you to write this type of durable power of attorney. Consult a knowledgeable lawyer to find out what is possible in your state.

Q. Do I need a lawyer to write a durable power of attorney?

A. While not required, it is advisable to contact a lawyer to draft your durable power of attorney for property. A lawyer should make sure that your document meets your state's requirements and

that the powers you wish to give your agent are actually spelled out in language that will be legally effective.

Some powers may not be presumed to be within the scope of the power of attorney unless they are specifically spelled out—for example, the power to make gifts or loans or file tax returns. Some states require a specific format or specific wording in the document. Certain states provide a do-it-yourself short-form durable power of attorney that allows you to check off the powers to be granted to the agent, with state law providing an interpretation of what each power means. Even with these simplified forms, legal consultation is advisable.

Q. My father has Alzheimer's disease. I would like him to appoint me to act for him under a durable power of attorney, since he can no longer manage on his own. May he do this now, or is it too late?

A. It is up to your father to decide if he wants to give you his power of attorney. And it may or may not be too late. Durable powers of attorney and other planning tools must be made while a person still has mental capacity. This is why advance planning is so important.

ⓘ A LEGAL TEST OF CAPACITY

There is no universal legal test of mental capacity or incapacity. Laws vary from state to state, but some general principles apply everywhere.

Incapacity is always evaluated in connection with specific tasks. The question is always "Incapacity to do what?" Different legal standards of capacity may apply to different tasks, such as capacity to make a will, to drive, to enter contracts, to manage money, or to make medical decisions. In a typical guardianship proceeding, most but not all states use a two-part test to determine incapacity (sometimes called incompetency). First, some type of disability must be verified—for example, mental illness, mental retardation, and/or Alzheimer's disease. Second, there must be a finding that the disability prevents the person from performing activities essential to take care of his or her personal needs or property. Most courts also will insist that all feasible alternatives to guardianship have been explored before appointing a guardian.

However, just because doctors diagnose someone as having a specific disease does not mean that the patient is necessarily incapacitated. Also, incapacity does not affect all functions in the same way. Thus, people in the early stages of a disease such as Alzheimer's usually have the capacity to make some decisions. They may have more capacity at certain times of the day than at others, or their capacity may be affected by medication.

Capacity must be assessed on a case-by-case basis. If your father is willing to see a lawyer about writing a durable power of attorney, the lawyer can help assess whether your father understands the purpose and consequences of the durable power. Sometimes a medical assessment will be recommended before signing legal documents.

Q. Who decides whether I'm incapacitated?

A. You can specify how you wish to have your incapacity and mental status determined if the need should arise. For example, in your durable power of attorney, you can name a doctor to make this determination, or you can say that two doctors must decide whether you have capacity. Any doctor or clinical psychologist who makes evaluations of capacity should have experience in this area. If you provide no instructions, then a court might ultimately decide the issue, guided by generally accepted standards used by other courts in making these determinations.

Living Trusts

Q. What is a "living trust"?

A. A **living trust** (also called an **inter vivos** trust) is an arrangement under which you transfer ownership of all or part of your property to the trust during your lifetime. As the person establishing the trust, you are called the **grantor** or **settlor.** You name a **trustee,** who manages the property according to the terms of your written trust document. The trustee may be an individual or an institution or yourself. The trust is for the benefit of one or more persons, including you, called the **beneficiaries.**

Frequently, a will is used to set up a trust (called a **testamentary trust**) that becomes effective after the death of the person establishing the trust. A living trust, however, is effective during the lifetime of the settlor, although it may be written to continue beyond the lifetime of the settlor. In a living trust, the settlor and/or members of his or her family are usually the beneficiaries of the trust. A living trust may be revocable or irrevocable.

Q. What is a living trust useful for?

A. Living trusts are one way of ensuring that someone (a trustee) has the legal authority to manage your estate properly if you become incapacitated or simply do not wish to manage your own estate anymore. They also may be used to avoid probate proceedings after the death of the person establishing the trust. They are especially useful when there is a substantial amount of property and professional management is de-

> ▶ **REVOKING A POWER OF ATTORNEY**
>
> If you change your mind about whom you want as your agent under a power of attorney (durable or not), you may revoke the document. In fact, while you are capable, you may revoke a power of attorney at any time for any reason. Simply notify the person you have named to act as your agent. For your protection, it is best to do this in writing. You also should destroy all copies of the power of attorney and notify any third parties with whom this person might have done business in writing. Where substantial assets are at stake, you may also want to file a document called a "Revocation of Power of Attorney" in the public records where you live or own real estate, and maybe even in the local newspaper if business interests are at stake.

sired. Like the durable power of attorney, a living trust may make it unnecessary to have a guardian or a conservator appointed to manage your financial affairs. However, a trust is generally more expensive to create and to manage than a durable power of attorney.

Q. How may I use a living trust to plan for possible incapacity?

A. You may design a living trust so it takes effect only if you become incapacitated. In this way, you keep control over your affairs until the proper person determines that you are incapacitated. As with a durable power of attorney, the process for such a determination should be spelled out in the document.

You also may write your living trust so that it is effective before you become incapacitated and continues even after you lose capacity. For example, you might name yourself as trustee and manage the trust's assets while you have capacity, but name a successor trustee who will take over for you if you become incapacitated. Again, you should designate in the trust document how that determination of incapacity should be made.

To make the trust effective, you must transfer money or property into the trust. The trust will only control the assets and property that have actually been transferred into the trust.

Q. I thought a trust simply paid an allowance to someone. If I need a trust because I cannot manage my own finances, how would this help me?

A. Some trust arrangements do just pay a sum to the beneficiary periodically. However, you may design a living trust in which the trustee handles many of the daily tasks of managing the estate, including paying bills and taxes. You may state in the trust agreement exactly what you want the trustee to do, how you want your assets managed, and how much discretion you want to give your trustee.

Q. Is a living trust just for someone who is incapacitated?

A. No. While it's an excellent way for someone to plan and avoid the need for a guardian or a conservator of the estate, a living trust also is useful for someone who wishes to turn over financial management of his or her affairs to another person.

To find out more about living trusts, contact an estate-planning lawyer in your state. He or she will be able to give you particulars about how your state's laws affect such trusts and about the consequences of making a trust.

Q. My father has a lot of money in his estate, but he is becoming increasingly forgetful every week. May he still write a living trust?

A. Like the durable power of attorney, people must prepare living trusts while they still have the capacity to do so. First of all, your father must want to make a trust. If he does, his lawyer may determine his ability to make a trust agreement. Sometimes, this is done by having him examined by a family physician or perhaps a gerontologist. His lawyer will know what standard of capacity must be proven. If your father does not have that capacity, he cannot make and sign a living trust.

Q. May I decide that I want to change, or revoke, a living-trust arrangement?

A. It depends on whether the trust is revocable or irrevocable. If your trust is revocable and you still have capacity, then you always may change or

---

ⓘ TAX IMPLICATIONS

Living trusts may have significant tax consequences, and may or may not reduce the amount of your estate that is subject to the probate process after your death. In addition, trusts may have an effect on your eligibility for Medicaid coverage of your nursing-home care. Trusts are very complicated; considerable caution is required in making them, and the assistance of a lawyer is highly recommended.

even revoke it completely. An irrevocable trust cannot be changed or revoked.

Q. How may I ensure that my trustee will manage my affairs properly after I become incapacitated?

A. Your trust instrument should contain specific instructions. You should include a precise statement of what the trustee should do on your behalf, and specify the trustee's particular duties, responsibilities, and limitations.

Q. My wife and I hold most of our assets in common. May I still draft a living trust to protect my share of the estate?

A. Yes, but take care to ensure that the trust does not violate the rights or interests of your wife in her portion of the estate. You may do this through careful drafting of the document and sound financial planning before incapacity. You and your wife may need separate counseling and planning advice, as your interests may conflict with each other. Remember that you must transfer money or property into the trust to make it effective.

Q. It sounds as though a living trust is a very complex type of financial planning tool. Who can help me decide if one is right for me?

A. It is best to consult with a lawyer or a trust officer familiar with living trusts to determine if one is right for you. Do not rely solely on mail-order or do-it-yourself trust kits, as they may contain information that is misleading or inappropriate for your circumstances or your state's law. There is more information on living trusts in chapter 18, "Estate Planning."

Joint Ownership

Q. I have most of my property and bank accounts held jointly with my spouse and an adult child. Isn't this good enough to ensure management of my property if I become incapacitated?

A. No. Joint ownership, or joint tenancy with right of survivorship, is a common and simple form of ownership for property such as your home, cars, securities, and bank accounts. The **right of survivorship** means that when one joint owner dies, the surviving owner or owners own 100 percent of the property. It is a convenient way to allow another person access to property or money you have in a bank account or to deposit or write checks on your behalf.

However, joint ownership is not a substitute for other planning tools because it has serious disadvantages. For example, an untrustworthy joint owner may withdraw all the money in a bank account and leave you with nothing. It is possible to challenge a co-owner's improper use of your money, but it may be difficult. In some states, creditors of a co-owner may be able to reach your account, even though that person is only listed on your account to help you manage your money. In addition, being listed as a co-owner of a bank account could affect the co-owner's eligibility for public benefit programs such as Medicaid. Fi-

---

⚠ LIVING-TRUST SCAMS

Although living trusts certainly can be an effective estate-planning tool, marketing living trusts has become a common consumer scam. Official-sounding companies promote living trusts as a surefire way to save thousands of dollars in lawyers' fees, taxes, and probate costs, and to protect privacy and avoid court delays. These scams use misrepresentations, scare tactics, and high-pressure techniques to persuade elders to purchase prepackaged living trusts at inflated prices. Watch out for tactics like fake affiliation claims (for example, that the product is endorsed by the AARP), exaggerated benefits, package deals, time limits, and other high-pressure sales tactics.

nally, transfer of a home, a car, or securities normally requires the signature of all owners. The loss of capacity of one owner may prevent a needed sale or transfer of the property.

Q. I'm concerned about the disadvantages of joint bank accounts. Is there another way that I can give someone access to my bank account without giving that person ownership of my money?

A. Some states have laws allowing persons to create what is referred to as an **agency bank account** or **convenience account.** This works very much like a durable power of attorney. You name an agent on your bank account, who then has the authority to make deposits or withdrawals and manage your account. The authority remains effective if you become incapacitated or disabled, unless you indicate otherwise. The agent has no right of ownership in the money in the account before or after your death, unless you indicate that the agent is to receive the money when you die. This may be a useful tool for you if you do not want to give someone authority over other aspects of your financial affairs through a durable power of attorney. It also may be useful as a supplement to your durable power of attorney, because some banks are reluctant to accept a durable power of attorney and prefer their own forms and procedures. Your banker or lawyer should be able to tell you whether your state's law allows agency bank accounts and how one might benefit you.

Representative Payees

Q. I have no income other than my Social Security check. Would a living trust or a power of attorney help me manage my money?

A. A living trust is far too costly and complicated for this kind of situation. A durable power of attorney definitely would be helpful. However, if the primary need is to take care of the Social Security check, a representative payee may be the simplest way to help you take care of your daily expenses and manage your small income.

Q. What is a representative payee?

A. A **representative payee** is a person or an organization appointed by a government agency, such as the Social Security Administration (SSA) or the Department of Veteran Affairs (VA), to receive and manage public benefits on behalf of someone who is incapable of doing so. The payee actually receives your government benefits on your behalf and is responsible for managing those benefits and making sure that they are spent for your welfare.

Q. What types of income may a representative payee manage?

A. He or she may only manage the income paid by government programs (usually federal programs such as Social Security, veterans benefits, black-lung benefits, and supplemental security income programs). The representative payee has *no* authority over any other income or property that you might receive. If you have additional income from other sources, you may need other assistance (such as help from an agent under your durable power of attorney or from a money management program, discussed on page 641) in addition to the help of a representative payee.

Q. How is a representative payee set up?

A. You, or someone on your behalf, must ask the Social Security Administration (or other program) to appoint a representative payee. Generally, you must have some sort of disability that prevents you from managing your own financial affairs, and you probably will need medical records of your disability. The government agency that provides the benefits must decide that you need help managing them. Your disability may be physical or mental. Although the decision is made by the agency and not by a court of law, you have the right to contest the appointment of a representative payee if you disagree, including the right to a hearing and all the appeals rights that apply to any claim before the agency.

Q. How can I be sure a representative will manage my money properly?

A. Supervising representative payees can be a problem. In principle, the payee must provide a detailed accounting to the agency paying the benefits. An annual report must be filed with Social Security. However, some exceptions exist. For example, if you live in a few types of mental health institutions, an annual accounting is not required, but the Social Security Administration will audit the institution once every three years. Under some benefits programs, such as the VA, reporting requirements vary with the size of the benefit. There is not much you may do to protect yourself ahead of time in such circumstances, except to plan for incapacity through other methods that allow someone else of your choice to manage your income for you.

Q. If I regain my ability to control my own finances, may I dismiss a representative payee?

A. Yes. First you need to file a form with the Social Security Administration asking to take care of your own financial affairs. You must then notify the government agency of your wish to dismiss the representative payee, and the agency must determine that you have regained the capacity to manage your own benefits.

Money Management Services

Q. I do not have a durable power of attorney or other legal tool for managing my property, but I have heard of some organizations offering "money management" services. What are these?

A. Money management programs, also known as **daily money management** or **voluntary money** **management**, represent a broad group of services designed to help older people or people with disabilities who need assistance managing their financial affairs. These services might include check depositing, check writing, checkbook balancing, bill paying, insurance claim preparation and filing, tax preparation and counseling, investment counseling, and public benefit applications and counseling.

Q. Who provides money management services?

A. An individual or an organization may provide this assistance. An organization may provide services on a for-profit or not-for-profit basis. Services may be provided for free, on a sliding fee scale basis (where you pay according to your income), or for a flat rate.

Q. How do money management programs help me keep control of my life?

A. A money management program may be able to help you by providing the financial management assistance you need in the way you want it. It may also help you avoid the need for guardianship. Money management services work on a voluntary basis, so you must be able to ask for help or accept an offer of help. Money management services may be particularly useful if you have no family or friends who are able or who you trust to act as your agent or trustee.

⚠ MONEY MANAGEMENT

If you receive or are considering money management services, you should make sure that your service provider has a system of cash controls to prevent or at least lessen the risk of embezzlement of client funds. The service provider also should be bonded and insured to protect clients from theft or loss of funds.

Guardianship

Q. What exactly is a guardian?

A. A guardian is someone who is appointed by a court to make personal and/or financial decisions on behalf of another person. **Guardian** is a general term for a court-appointed surrogate (substitute) decision maker. Your state may use other terms, such as **conservator, committee,** or **curator.** Some terms may apply only if the decision maker has authority over financial and property matters; other terms may apply if the decision maker has authority over personal decisions such as living arrangements and health care. A person who has a guardian may be called a **ward,** an **incapacitated person,** or some other term.

Q. When is the appointment of a guardian appropriate?

A. People need a guardian when

1. they can no longer manage their affairs because of serious incapacity;

2. no voluntary arrangements for decision making and management have been set up ahead of time (or if they have been set up, they are not working well); and

3. serious harm will come to the individual if no legally authorized decision maker is appointed.

Q. Are there any disadvantages to the appointment of a guardian?

A. Yes. Although a guardianship may be necessary to protect the welfare of an incapacitated person, it also may result in the loss of individual rights. The person under a guardianship may lose several civil rights: the right to marry, the right to vote, the right to hold a driver's license, the right to make a will, the right to enter into a contract, and other rights. Because of its serious consequences, guardianship should be considered the last resort for helping someone who is experiencing incapacity.

In addition, the court proceedings themselves can be costly, time-consuming, and emotionally trying for a family. Moreover, a guardian has less flexibility in management of the estate than a trustee or an agent under advance-planning legal tools such as durable powers of attorney or living trusts. Guardians must operate within strict fiduciary limitations and normally must file annual accountings with the court. On the positive side, the fiduciary rules and court accountings ensure at least some oversight and accountability of the guardian.

Q. Who appoints a guardian?

A. Procedures vary among the states, but generally a court appoints a guardian after hearing evidence that a person is incapable of making decisions and deciding that the person needs a surrogate decision maker.

In most states, the law requires some form of due process rights. These rights are intended to protect a person from inappropriately being declared incapacitated. The rights include the right to be notified of the date and place of the hearing, the right to be present at the hearing, and the right to be represented by a lawyer.

Q. My elderly mother is often confused. I think she ought to have a guardian to look after her interests. What do I do?

A. First, you may want to contact your local area agency on aging to see if there are any programs or services that might help your mother manage and make it unnecessary to obtain a guardian. It

---

ⓘ **GUARDIANSHIP**

A guardianship is a serious step and should relate to a serious inability to make or understand the consequences of decisions. It should not depend on stereotypical notions of old age, mental illness, or disability. A person has a right to make foolish or risky decisions. These decisions by themselves do not mean that the person has a decision-making incapacity.

also will help to have her examined by a doctor or a psychologist experienced in geriatric evaluation. A geriatric evaluation typically will involve evaluation by more than one specialist from different disciplines, such as medicine, nursing, and social work. Often, a person's decision making may be impaired because of physical or other causes that can be corrected.

If the evaluation supports the need for a guardianship, check with a lawyer to learn the specifics of your state's guardianship law and procedures, as they vary substantially from state to state. The appointment of a guardian normally requires the filing of a petition with the court, notice to your mother and other interested parties, and a court hearing. You probably will need a lawyer to help you through it.

The court also may appoint an investigator, or "visitor," to interview your mother and make a report, or a lawyer to represent your mother. At the hearing, a judge will review the petition, the investigator's or lawyer's report, and medical reports.

The judge may ask the person filing the petition why the other person needs a guardian. The judge also may ask the allegedly incapacitated person some questions. The hearings are usually fairly informal. If there is disagreement, the judge may set the case for a formal hearing with witness testimony, cross-examination, and argument by counsel.

Q. What if someone thinks I need a guardian, and I do not want one?

A. Every state gives the allegedly incapacitated person a chance to fight the petition for guardianship. If you do not think you need a guardian, you must let the court know that. Usually, you do this by appearing in court on the day of the hearing or asking someone to represent you at the hearing.

It is best to get your own lawyer to represent you at the hearing. If you cannot afford one, many states require that the court appoint one at the state's expense. Some free legal services programs for older persons will help you fight a guardianship. If you cannot get to court or hire a

lawyer, you may write the court about your objection to the guardianship.

Q. This sounds very expensive. Who pays for a guardianship?

A. It can be expensive. There are court charges and lawyer's fees and fees for the doctor or other persons who examine the alleged incapacitated person to assess his or her capacity. If the court appoints a guardian, the estate usually pays the guardian's fees. Older people who are either seeking guardianship over a family member or challenging a guardianship may be able to get free legal help through legal services programs or through lawyers who volunteer their services pro bono (free of charge).

Q. If I need a guardian, may I specify whom I want and do not want to play this role?

A. Yes. The court will give due weight to your preference, and in some states must follow your

---

ⓘ WHO MAY BE A GUARDIAN?

Laws vary from one state to another. In most states, the courts may appoint almost anyone as guardian if the person meets legal requirements. Often, the court appoints the person filing the petition. Most courts like to appoint a relative who knows the person and is most likely to act in his or her best interests. However, the court may appoint a friend or a lawyer, especially if no family members are available. The courts also may appoint co-guardians, either with shared responsibilities or with responsibilities split between them. If there are no friends or family willing or able to serve as guardian, many states permit public or private agencies to act as the guardian and to charge fees for that service if the estate of the incapacitated person is unable to pay.

preference unless there is good cause not to do so. You should nominate a guardian as part of your general planning for incapacity. Because sometimes even the best plans for incapacity fail (for example, if your agent under your durable power of attorney dies after you become incapacitated), it is a good idea to name in your planning documents one or two people whom you want as your guardian if that becomes necessary.

Q. May the court remove a guardian?

A. Yes, a guardian may be removed if the incapacitated person can prove that he or she has regained the capacity to make decisions. But it can be hard to have a guardian removed. Therefore, if someone's incapacity may be temporary, consider whether some other arrangement (such as money management or a representative payee) will meet the person's need for help and make it unnecessary to get a guardianship.

A court also may remove a guardian who is not properly carrying out his or her responsibilities. Usually, a new guardian will replace the person who is removed.

Q. My elderly aunt needs some help with her affairs, but she is not totally incapable. Might a guardianship meet her needs?

A. In most states, if a person has partial capacity, a guardian may be given only partial power over his or her affairs. This is generally called a **limited guardianship.** In your aunt's case, the court's guardianship order would identify the specific matters over which the guardian has authority. Your aunt would retain legal authority over all other areas of her life.

In all states, the courts try to ensure that a guardianship is the **least restrictive alternative.** This means that a guardianship restricts the ward as little as possible, letting the ward do whatever the disability allows.

Suppose your aunt can no longer manage her large estate, but she can handle her daily finances. A guardianship should let her keep control over everyday expenses. Or, let's say your

aunt needs placement in a nursing home by the guardian. If she can say what type of nursing home she wants to live in, the guardian should honor those wishes.

Even when a limited guardianship is not feasible, the guardian should try to involve the ward in making decisions whenever possible and should make decisions that are consistent with the lifelong values of the ward.

Health-Care Decision-Making Issues

Q. What is my right to control decisions about my health care?

A. With few exceptions, our system of law recognizes the right of capable individuals to control decisions about what happens to their bodies. This includes the right to refuse any suggested medical treatment. We normally exercise this right by talking to our doctors and other health-care providers. You have a right to:

- know all the relevant facts about your medical condition;
- know the pros and cons of different treatment options;
- talk to other doctors and get their opinions, too;
- say yes to treatment or care that you want, and no to treatment or care that you do not want; and
- have your pain and symptoms managed effectively, so that you can function in reasonable comfort.

Your doctor is the expert in medicine, but you are the expert in defining and applying your personal values and preferences.

Q. What happens to my right to make medical decisions if I am too sick to decide?

A. In an emergency, the law presumes consent. In all other instances, someone else must make decisions for you. The best way to ensure that decisions are made the way you would want, and by the person you want, is to do an advance directive for health care before you become incapacitated.

Q. What is an advance directive for health care?

A. An **advance directive** is generally a written statement, which you complete in advance of serious illness, about how you want medical decisions made. The two most common forms of advance directive are a **living will** and a **durable power of attorney for health care**, although in many states you may combine these into a single advance-directive document.

An advance directive allows you to state your choices for health care or to name someone to make those choices for you, if you become unable to make decisions about your medical treatment. In short, an advance directive enables you to have some control over your future medical care.

Q. What is a living will?

A. A living will is simply a written instruction spelling out any treatments you want or don't want in the event you are unable to speak for yourself and you are terminally ill or permanently unconscious. A living will simply says, "Whoever is deciding, please follow these instructions." It is called a living will because it takes effect while you are still alive. It is also called a **medical directive** or **declaration**.

Q. What is a durable power of attorney for health care?

A. A durable power of attorney for health care (sometimes called a **health-care proxy**) is a document that appoints someone of your choice to be your authorized agent (or attorney in fact or **proxy**) for purposes of health-care decisions. You can give your agent as much or as little authority as you wish to make some or all health-care decisions for you. And in most states, you can include the same kind of instructions that you would put in a living will.

Q. Which is better, a living will or a durable power of attorney for health care?

A. The most efficient approach is to combine the living will and the durable power of attorney for health care in one document. In most states, you can do this. However, some states have less-flexible rules for these advance directives. In these states, having both may be the preferred approach.

On its own, a living will is a very limited document because, under most state statutes, living wills apply only to terminal illness or permanent unconsciousness. They address only life-sustaining medical treatments and not other treatment decisions, and they provide fairly general instructions that may be difficult to interpret in complicated medical situations.

The durable power of attorney for health care is a more comprehensive and flexible document. It may cover any health-care decision and is not limited to terminal illness or permanent coma. More important, it authorizes someone of your choice to weigh all the facts at the time a decision needs to be made and to speak for you legally, according to any guidelines you provide.

Q. What happens if I do not have an advance directive?

A. If you have not planned ahead by executing an advance directive, many states have family consent (or health surrogate) statutes that authorize someone else, typically family members in the order of kinship, to make some or all health-care decisions for you. Even in the absence of such statutes, most doctors and health facilities routinely rely on the consent of family members, as long as they are close family members and no controversial decisions need to be made.

However, without an advance directive, decisions may not be made the way you would want them, or by the person you would want to make them. Making an advance directive also benefits your family members, because it spares them the agony of having to guess what you would really want.

If no close family or other surrogate is available to make decisions for you, a court-appointed guardian may be necessary. This is an option of last resort.

Q. *How do I make an advance directive?*

A. Requirements differ from state to state. Many states provide suggested forms, and in a few states, required language for advance directives. Most states have specific witnessing or notary requirements. Follow these requirements closely. Commonly, two witnesses are required; and often, several categories of persons are disqualified from serving as witnesses, such as relatives, heirs, or health-care providers.

Q. *What should my advance directive say?*

A. No one can tell you exactly what to say in your advance directive. However, the most important task to accomplish is to name someone you trust to act as your agent for health-care decisions. If there is no one whom you fully trust to act as your agent, then it is best not to name an agent, and instead only include instructions about what is most important to you if you face a serious and eventually fatal illness.

Also consider addressing these points:

1. Alternate proxies. Whenever possible, name one or more alternate or successor agents in case your primary agent is unavailable.

2. Life-sustaining treatments. Are there any specific types of treatment you want or don't want in any circumstances? Your personal or family medical history may make certain conditions or treatments more likely.

3. Artificial nutrition and hydration. Some states will presume that you want nutrition and hydration in all circumstances unless you instruct otherwise.

4. Organ donation. In many states, you can include instructions about donating organs in your advance directive.

Q. *Can I change or terminate my advance directive?*

A. Yes, you always have the right to change or revoke your advance directive while you have the mental capacity to do so. Normally, you can revoke it orally or in writing in any way that indicates your intent to revoke. Your intent should be communicated to your agent, your family, and your doctor.

If you want to change the document, it is best to execute a new document. The same formalities of signing and witnessing are required for changes.

Q. *Whom should I select as my agent or proxy for health decisions?*

A. The choice of agent is the most important decision you may make in doing an advance direc-

---

⚠ TELLING YOUR DOCTOR IS NOT SUFFICIENT

Telling your doctor and others what you want does provide important evidence of your wishes if you later become incapacitated, especially if your doctor writes your wishes down in your medical record. However, written advance directives are more likely to carry weight and be followed.

ⓘ DISCUSSING YOUR OPTIONS

The most important point to remember about forms is that they are supposed to aid, and not take the place of, discussion and dialogue. Therefore, a form ought to be a starting point, not an end point, for making your wishes known. There is no ideal form. Any form you use should be personalized to reflect your values and preferences. Before doing an advance directive, talk with your doctor, family members, and advisers. This will help you to understand the medical possibilities you may face and clarify your values and choices.

tive. Your agent will have great power over your health and personal care if you become incapacitated. Name a person whom you trust fully. If no such person is available, it may be best not to name a health-care agent.

Find out who can and cannot be your agent under state law. Some states prohibit health-care providers or health-care facility employees from acting as your agent. Speak to the person you wish to appoint beforehand to explain your intentions and to obtain his or her agreement. Preferably, do not name co-agents, because it opens up the possibility of disagreement among agents. Instead, name alternate or successor agents, in case the primary agent is unavailable. If there is anyone whom you absolutely want to keep out of playing any role in your health-care decisions, you may be able to disqualify that person expressly in your advance directive.

Q. What do I do with my advance directive after completing one?

A. Make sure someone close to you knows where it is located. If you have named an agent, give your agent a copy of the original. Also give your physician a copy and ask that it be made part of your permanent medical record. You may also want to make a small card for your purse or wallet that states that you have an advance directive and provides the name, phone number, and address of your agent or a person who can provide a copy of it.

Q. What if my doctor or hospital refuses to follow my advance directive?

A. First, find out ahead of time your doctor's views about advance directives and your specific wishes. If you disagree, you may wish to find a new doctor ahead of time.

Under federal law, most hospitals, nursing homes, and home health agencies must inform you of their policies about advance directives at the time of admission. Most will respect advance directives, but some may have restrictive policies. However, no facility can require you to have, or not have, an advance directive as a requirement of admission.

If you are in a condition to which your advance directive applies and your providers will not honor your directive, state law spells out their obligations. Usually, the provider must make a reasonable effort to transfer the patient to another provider who will respect the advance directive.

Q. Is a lawyer needed to do an advance directive?

A. No, a lawyer is not necessary, but a lawyer experienced in doing advance directives is very helpful. A lawyer can draft a personalized document that reflects your particular wishes and ensures that all legal formalities are followed. A lawyer is especially helpful if potential family conflicts or special legal or medical concerns are present.

ⓘ OUT-OF-STATE DIRECTIVES

Many people want to know whether, if they make an advance directive in one state, it will be recognized in other states. In many states, the law expressly honors out-of-state directives. But, in some states, the law is unclear. Realistically, providers will normally try to follow your stated wishes, regardless of the form you use or where you executed it. However, if you spend a great deal of time in more than one state (for example, summers in Wisconsin, winters in Arizona), you may want to consider executing an advance directive for each state. Or, find out whether one document meets the formal requirements of each state. As a practical matter, you may want different health-care agents if the same agent is not easily available in each location.

Abuse and Exploitation

Q. What is elder abuse?

A. In its most general sense, **elder abuse** is an act or failure to act by a person required to act that results in harm to an older person. Definitions of elder abuse vary from state to state, but generally include

- physical abuse—use of physical force that may result in bodily injury, physical pain, or impairment;
- sexual abuse—nonconsensual sexual contact of any kind;
- emotional and psychological abuse—infliction of anguish, pain, or distress through verbal or nonverbal acts;
- neglect—the refusal or failure to fulfill any part of a person's obligation or duties to an older person;
- abandonment—the desertion of an elderly person by an individual who has physical custody of the elder or by a person who has assumed responsibility for providing care to the elder;
- self-neglect—behavior of an older person that threatens his or her health or safety; and
- financial exploitation—illegal or improper use of an older person's funds, property, or assets.

Every state has specific elder abuse laws. You can get details on laws and programs from your area or state agency on aging or your state adult protective services program.

Q. Is elder abuse just a problem for very frail old people who live in nursing homes?

A. Elder abuse is a real problem for many older people regardless of whether they live in their own home or in a nursing home. Some victims are very frail and are unable to seek help on their own. However, many elder abuse victims are physically or mentally capable of seeking help but cannot or do not do so for a variety of reasons, including fear that they will not be believed, love or concern for the person abusing them, fear that

they will lose their independence, or a belief that nothing can be done about the abuse.

Elder abuse can be a problem for both the rich and the poor. It affects older people of all races and ethnic groups, social classes, and economic levels.

Q. My neighbor is very old and sick. She depends on her daughter for shopping, cooking, and cleaning. However, her daughter often leaves the older woman without food and clean clothes. Is there anything I can do to help?

A. Yes, you may report this neglect to your local adult protective services program. This may be your state or local agency on aging or some other human services agency. You may even report abuse and neglect to the police. To find the adult protective services program serving your community, you can call your area agency on aging or contact Eldercare Locator at 800-677-1116. Adult protective services programs are responsible for investigating reports of suspected abuse, neglect, or exploitation. If the program determines that abuse is occurring, they can provide or arrange a variety of services to help the victim.

You should not worry about being sued for reporting suspected abuse. Almost all states protect people who make such reports as long as they act in good faith. You may even make an anonymous report.

Q. My son is using all my money to buy illegal drugs. He is also running up large charges on my credit cards. (His name is on my credit card accounts and my bank accounts.) Since he is a co-owner of my home, I am afraid he will mortgage it or possibly even sell it to get more money. What can I do?

A. Even if he has the legal right to reach your funds, you can protect yourself from this type of financial exploitation. Ask your bank to help you transfer funds to new accounts that your son may not access. Write all your credit card companies and ask them to remove your son's name from your accounts. Have them issue new credit cards to you.

Contact a lawyer to see what you must do to protect your home. A free legal services program for older or poor persons may be able to help you. Your local area agency on aging can help you find those resources.

Finally, local social services agencies may be able to help you and your son. Many agencies have experience in dealing with family difficulties of this sort. You do not have to allow your son's problems to threaten your own well-being and financial security.

Q. My son and daughter-in-law live with me in my home. They are living rent free and give me no money for household bills or food. I feel like they are taking advantage of me. Can someone help me?

A. Yes. The situation you describe is surprisingly common. Over 75 percent of all abusers are family members. You can seek help from the adult protective services program in your area. Your community may have other programs that help victims of elder abuse. In addition, a legal services program for older or poor people may be able to help you.

THE WORLD AT YOUR FINGERTIPS

- *The ABA's Commission on Law and Aging has a consumer tool kit for health-care advance planning available at www.abanet. org/aging.*
- *Information about advance directives for health care is available from most state area agencies on aging and from many state bar associations and medical societies.*
- *State-specific information and forms are also available from Partnership in Caring (formerly Partnership in Dying), an organization concerned with excellent end-of-life care, at www.partnershipforcaring.org.*

- *Americans for Better Care of the Dying, at www.abcd-caring.org, publishes "Handbook for Mortals," an excellent guide for dealing with serious and eventually fatal illness. Last Acts provides a wealth of similar information on its website, www. lastacts.org.*
- *Information on elder abuse, including telephone numbers for state ombudsmen and adult protective services offices, is available at the website of the National Center on Elder Abuse, www.elderabusecenter.org. You can also find a local adult protective services program by calling Eldercare Locator at 800-677-1116.*
- *Another good source of information on elder abuse is the website of the National Committee for the Prevention of Elder Abuse, www.preventelderabuse.org.*
- *If you are a victim of domestic violence, call the National Domestic Violence Hotline for assistance and information at 800-799-7233. See the discussion of domestic violence in chapter 3, "Family Law," for more helpful information.*

REMEMBER THIS

- *Advance planning for financial and health-care decision making is the most effective means of ensuring that your wishes will be followed if you become incapacitated.*
- *Methods for dealing with financial incapacity or difficulties in managing finances include a durable power of attorney, a living trust, joint ownership, representative payees for government benefits, and money management services.*
- *You can use health-care advance directives, such as a living will and a durable power of attorney for health care, to provide instructions about your medical care in the event you are incapacitated.*

ⓘ **DOMESTIC VIOLENCE**

Suppose your spouse/partner sometimes hits you or pushes you around. You are both over sixty-five. This may have been going on for a long time or it may be a new problem. Because of your age or limited resources, it is harder for you to run away from him or her. Is there anything you can do?

You do not have to live with abuse, no matter what your age. Domestic violence is against the law. It is no more legal for your spouse/partner to hit you than for a stranger to hit you. A domestic violence or adult protective services program may be able to help you. Additionally, more and more police departments and courts are sensitive to domestic violence and are able to help victims. If your spouse/partner abuses you, call the police or your local domestic violence or adult protective services program. These agencies may be able to help you find temporary emergency shelter in a domestic violence or elder shelter in your community. They may be able to provide other services to help you protect your safety.

If you do not want to leave your home, a domestic violence program can counsel you about safety planning. You may seek from the courts an order of protection that requires your spouse/partner to stay away from you. With such an order, you can have your spouse removed from the home, even though he or she may be the owner.

- *In the absence of advance planning, a petition for guardianship may be necessary in cases of serious incapacity.*
- *Elder abuse includes physical and sexual abuse, emotional and psychological abuse, neglect, abandonment, financial exploitation, and self-neglect.*

THE OLDER AMERICANS ACT AND SERVICES

So you've read this chapter and have received so much information that you don't know where to start. Well, a good starting point for help or more information is your local area agency on aging.

The Older Americans Act is the main federal law that provides funding for services to the elderly. This section covers general information on programs and services that are provided locally through area agencies on aging and the state unit on aging.

Q. What kinds of services does the Older Americans Act provide?

A. The act provides funding for a wide variety of services. These include education, social services, recreation, personal assistance, and counseling. It also makes available transportation, legal and financial assistance, career and retirement counseling, advocacy, long-term care ombudsman services, services for the disabled, crime prevention, elder abuse prevention, and volunteer services. In addition, your local area agency on aging can provide information and guide you to services in your community. These might include home helpers, money management agencies, or special discounts available to seniors. The specific services offered in each category vary depending on where you live.

Q. How can I find out about programs that might help me?

A. Start at your local or state agency on aging, or call Eldercare Locator at 800-677-1116. This toll-free service helps to identify community resources nationwide. Also, you could view the website of the Administration on Aging at www.aoa.dhhs.gov.

Your local area agency on aging can tell you about the programs in your community that provide services to seniors. Most AAAs have written materials that describe resources in the community. Some have brochures that identify common problems that the elderly might face, with resources and ways to solve the particular problem. The AAA may have additional resource materials published by community, state, and national organizations. The AAA in your community is a good starting point to answer many questions by the elderly.

Q. Could an area agency on aging help me find legal services I can afford?

A. Probably. Publicly funded legal services also are available through programs funded under the Older Americans Act. These programs have lawyers, paralegals, and advocates who specialize in the rights of older persons.

State and local bar associations also may have information about programs for older persons that provide referrals or legal services on a pro bono basis. **Pro bono** programs operate for the good of the public and do not charge lawyer's fees.

Q. Do I need to be poor to get any of these legal services?

A. Some bar-sponsored programs may be limited to people with low incomes. Services offered through the Older Americans Act do not have an income requirement. You can find out more by contacting your local agency on aging or bar association.

Q. Do older Americans have different legal problems than younger Americans?

A. To some extent. In general, older adults benefit from a wide range of legal services. One small but growing area of specialization among lawyers has become known as **elder law**. Elder law lawyers focus on the legal needs of older people

---

ⓘ YOUR AREA AGENCY ON AGING

One important product of the Older Americans Act is the nationwide network of **area agencies on aging (AAAs).** Today, every area of the country is served by either an AAA or a state unit on aging. These agencies help local communities develop services specifically for older residents. The AAAs channel funds from the Older Americans Act to local communities.

AAAs also offer information and referral services to older adults. A few provide services directly, but most only coordinate services and provide assistance to designated service agencies in the local communities.

AAAs provide funding and programming for local senior citizen centers, too. Programs include recreation, socialization, meals, and educational programs. Many service organizations offer programs at the senior centers as well as at other sites in the community. Additional funds are generally provided by local and state governments, as well as by such organizations as the United Way, private foundations, corporations, and individual donors.

You can feel confident about calling your AAA with almost any question about services in your neighborhood for older people. You can also go directly to a senior center near you and ask for help. If staff there cannot provide help, ask them to put you in touch with someone in the AAA who can.

and work with a variety of legal tools and techniques to meet these needs.

An elder law practitioner typically handles general estate-planning matters and counsels clients about planning for incapacity with alternative decision-making documents. The lawyer might assist the client in planning for possible long-term care needs, including nursing-home care, locating appropriate types of care, coordinating public benefits and private resources to finance the cost of care, and working to ensure the client's right to quality care. The National Academy of Elder Law Lawyers (NAELA) can provide more information about lawyers who specialize in elder law. For more information, please access www.naela.org.

Q. My insurance company won't pay a claim. Is there anything I can do short of suing?

A. Many insurance programs provide an opportunity to obtain additional information about the claim and may provide for impartial hearings. These reviews may be done in writing or in person. Check with the insurance commissioner's office in your state about how such disagreements might be resolved. Some state insurance commissioners have complaint hotlines. Make sure your personal insurance agent is aware of the problem. He or she wants to retain your business and may provide extra help.

For problems in specific fields, bankers, accountants, real estate brokers, and stockbrokers may be able to help. But don't rely entirely on these individuals. If they can't resolve your problems, see a lawyer. A lawyer can discuss possible actions other than lawsuits.

Q. My Aunt Minnie is in a nursing home. I fear they do not treat her well. They may even tie her in a chair part of the day. Her husband is in a board care home, and they won't let him visit Aunt Minnie. Her younger sister lives in her own home. She had an aide and a nurse to help her when she left the hospital, but they just stopped visiting her. How can I be certain that all three receive quality care?

A. You should call the local long-term care ombudsman, an advocate who works to ensure that older Americans receive appropriate quality care.

Q. I have an elderly neighbor who is finding it hard to manage on her own, especially with shopping and preparing meals. Are there services that could help her?

A. Yes. Under the Older Americans Act, several types of nutrition programs and chore services are available to aid older adults. These include home-delivered hot meals, as well as meals

---

▶ **LEGAL HELP FOR THE HOMEBOUND**

If you are homebound and want to speak to a lawyer, call your local agency on aging. Request their help in contacting a lawyer who may be able to come to your home. If you live in a nursing home or assisted-living facility, you should speak with the long-term care ombudsman.

Many special programs and services are designed to meet the needs and enrich the lives of older adults. Some are funded with tax dollars, especially under the Older Americans Act. Others have been developed through agencies or private enterprise.

served at a "congregate" dining site. There may be limitations placed on home-delivered services because of the great need and the limited amount of funding. The AAA or someone designated will do an assessment of need. The result of such an assessment may lead to the identification of more services that may be arranged for your neighbor.

Q. I would like to use some of the services described here, but I really can't afford to pay for helpers or home-delivered meals. How can I use these programs?

A. The Older Americans Act targets services to low-income and minority elderly, as well as to those who are frail or disabled. Many of the programs funded by the act are provided without charge, although donations may be requested. Other programs offered by, arranged for, or provided through area agencies on aging may have a small fee or use a sliding scale, in which the fee is assessed on the basis of your ability to pay. Some programs are reimbursed by other governmental programs such as Medicaid. Do not let financial concerns keep you from benefiting from the variety of programs available.

Q. My elderly mother has been diagnosed with Alzheimer's disease. I would like to have her live with me. Are there services available to help me provide for her needs in my own home?

A. Maybe. Although the Older Americans Act authorizes grants to be made to provide such services, they may or may not be available in your community. These may include in-home supportive services for victims of Alzheimer's disease or related conditions, and for the families of these victims.

The services and the extent of services vary from place to place. They might include counseling and training for family caregivers, a needs assessment and assistance in locating and securing services, and case management (a case manager acts as an adviser and broker). Services might

also include homemaker and home health aides, in-home respite service so family caregivers can get away for short periods, assistance in adapting a home to meet the needs of an impaired older person, and chore maintenance.

A second very important resource is the state or local Alzheimer's Association. The Alzheimer's Association's local chapters provide extensive information about resources for families of Alzheimer's victims in your specific community. Chapters also offer support from others whose loved ones are victims.

Q. I would like help in getting a job, since I feel able to continue working even though I have retired. Can I get help under the Older Americans Act?

A. Yes. Through the Community Service Employment for Older Americans program, you may be able to get help in finding a job or a training opportunity. These may be part-time positions, at minimum wage. In general, this program is designed for lower-income seniors, so income and resource eligibility requirements may apply.

Q. I'm retired and I'm looking for new experiences, but I don't really want to enroll in a school. Is there anything for me?

A. Many universities, local junior colleges, and museum education programs provide special programs, reduced fees, and auditing of classes. A call to the one closest to you can provide information about such programs. The Elderhostel program also meets the needs of people like you. Elderhostel is a not-for-profit agency offering educational programs for adults age sixty years and older. Through an international network of colleges and universities, Elderhostel is able to offer low-cost residential academic programs both in America and abroad. Courses offered have included "The Literary Heritage of Oxford," offered in Oxford, England; "Political Controversies, Judicial Politics and You"; and lectures on Greek island society, in conjunction with a cruise of the

Greek Isles. University faculty usually teach these courses, and they run from one to three weeks. Most of the time, participants are housed in dormitories. On special trips, other arrangements may be made. Students can expect to spend approximately three hours a day in class, with many field trips and opportunities for sightseeing.

THE WORLD AT YOUR FINGERTIPS

- *For most older people, the main resource for information is their area agency on aging (AAA). It can supply details and referrals on many topics. To find your local area agency on aging, call the Eldercare Locator at 800-677-1116 or visit the website of the federal Administration on Aging at www.aoa.gov.*
- *Many other associations promote the interests of older adults. The best known— and the largest—is the American Association of Retired Persons (AARP). You can join if you are over age fifty. AARP has regional and local groups nationwide, and both its website and its publications provide information and resources on virtually any topic of interest to older persons. Look in the telephone directory for the nearest group. Or contact the AARP at 601 E Street NW, Washington, DC 20049; the organization can also be reached by telephone at 800-424-3410, or at at its website, www.aarp.org.*
- *Other associations that promote the interests of older persons and provide information and education to senior citizens include the following:*
  - *National Council on the Aging, which can be contacted at 409 Third Street SW, Washington, DC 20024 (telephone: 800-424-9046; website: www.ncoa.org)*
  - *Older Women's League, at 666 11th Street NW, Suite 700, Washington, DC*

  20001(telephone:800-825-3695; website: www.owl-national.org)
  - *Alliance of Retired Americans (formerly National Council of Senior Citizens), at 888 Sixteenth Street NW, Washington, DC 20006 (toll-free telephone: 888-373-6497; website: www.retiredamericans.org)*
- *You can get more information about Alzheimer's disease at your local Alzheimer's Association. Local chapters can be found through the Alzheimer's Disease Education and Referral Center, P.O. Box 8250, Silver Spring, MD 20907 (telephone: 800-438-4380; website: www. alzheimers.org).*
- *For more information about studying and traveling, contact your local agency on aging or write to Elderhostel at 11 Avenue de Lafayette, Boston, MA 02111 (toll-free telephone: 877-426-8056; website: www. elderhostel.org).*
- *If you need help in finding a lawyer who specializes in elder law, the NAELA website includes a geographical directory of its members that specifies those who are Certified Elder Law Lawyers. In addition, NAELA can provide consumer information about what questions to ask a lawyer to make sure he or she can meet your legal needs. You can contact NAELA at 1604 N. Country Club, Tucson, AZ 85716 (telephone: 602-881-4005; website: www. naela.org).*
- *Your state or local agency on aging can refer you to publicly-funded legal programs. These programs, along with other possible sources of legal assistance, are listed on the website of the American Bar Association's Commission on Law and Aging, www.abanet.org/aging (click on "Law and Aging Resource Guide," and then select your state).*

REMEMBER THIS

- *The Older Americans Act funds many services for seniors; you can find out what is available in your locality through your area agency on aging.*
- *Though services vary depending on locale, you might find help in education, social services, recreation, personal assistance, and counseling in your community, as well as help in transportation, financial assistance, and career and retirement counseling.*
- *Through the Older Americans Act, state and local bar associations, and private attorneys, legal services targeted to older persons are often available.*

Health-Care Law

We are all consumers of medical care, whether our care is for yearly checkups or ongoing illnesses. In the past, many of us accepted our treatment without question. Now, enlightened consumers of health care are taking a more active role in assessing their treatment and their options. This has led to patients becoming informed as much as possible about their health concerns, and taking an active part in decisions about their health care. It has become even more important to be informed about your health-care options today, when the law is struggling to keep up with technological and scientific advances in medicine.

    Each section of this chapter is self-contained; however, before drawing any conclusions or inferences from any particular question, it is advisable to read the entire relevant section of the chapter, so as to be well informed with respect to the context of the information given, and be aware of any qualifications to it.

PATIENTS' RIGHTS

Trevor worked for a large insurance company, and had access to millions of medical files. He set up a date with Caroline, and decided to look her up on the computer database. He saw that she had received medication for a sexually transmitted disease two years prior, and cancelled the date.

Caroline awoke in the middle of the night to splitting pain in her head, and found herself unable to move. Her sister took her to the emergency room of the nearest hospital. The emergency room nurse told Caroline that the hospital was too busy with other patients and told her to go to another hospital about fifteen minutes away. Her sister drove Caroline to the other hospital. When they got there, Caroline was unconscious. The doctors examined her immediately and discovered that she'd had a stroke, causing brain damage and paralysis.

This section covers patients' rights, including confidentiality, emergency care, and informed consent.

Confidentiality and Privacy

Q. What is in my medical records?

A. Your medical file contains personal information, including, but not limited to, the following:

- Your name, address, and phone number
- Your age, sex, and marital status
- Names and ages of your children
- Your occupation and Social Security number
- Results of lab tests and physical examinations
- Whether you have a living will, health-care power of attorney, or health-care proxy
- Your family medical history, including risk factors (such as smoking, obesity, or high blood pressure), allergies, immunizations, and any medications prescribed

Q. Who has access to my medical information?

A. Any time you enter a hospital or other medical facility, you automatically agree to let anyone directly involved with your care see your medical record. This includes secretaries, nurses, interns, residents, doctors, nutritionists, pharmacists, and technicians. This probably doesn't come as a surprise—it makes sense for these people to have access to your records. But there are dozens of other people and organizations that may be able to access your medical information.

Insurance Companies

Insurance companies require you to release your records before they will issue a policy or make payment under an existing policy. Medical information gathered by one insurance company may be shared with others through the Medical Information Bureau.

Government Agencies

Government agencies may request your medical records to verify claims made through Medicare, Medicaid, Social Security Disability, and workers' compensation.

Medical Information Bureau

The Medical Information Bureau (MIB) is a central database of medical information. Approximately 15 million Americans and Canadians are on file in the MIB's computers. Insurance firms use the services of the MIB primarily to obtain information about life insurance and individual health insurance policy applicants. A decision on whether to insure you is not supposed to be based solely on the MIB report. (Visit the MIB website at www.mib.com.)

The MIB does not have a file on everyone. But if your medical information is on file, you will want to be sure it is correct. You can obtain a copy for $9 by writing to Medical Information Bureau, P.O. Box 105, Essex Station, Boston, MA 02112, or calling 617-426-3660.

Employers

Employers usually obtain medical information about their employees by asking employees to au-

⚠ **BE CAREFUL WHAT YOU REVEAL ONLINE**

A tremendous amount of health-related information is found on the Internet. Many Usenet newsgroups and chat rooms are available for individuals to share information on specific diseases and health conditions. Websites dispense a wide variety of information. There is no guarantee that information you disclose in any of these forums is confidential.

thorize disclosure of medical records. When employers pay medical insurance, they may require insurance companies to provide them with copies of employees' medical records.

Other Disclosures

Other disclosures of medical information occur when medical institutions such as hospitals or individual physicians are evaluated for quality of service. This evaluation is required for most hospitals to receive their licenses. Your identity generally is not disclosed when medical practices

are evaluated. Occasionally, your medical information is used for health research and is sometimes disclosed to public health agencies like the Centers for Disease Control. Specific names usually are not included with the information.

While providing access to your medical information is necessary to provide you with the best treatment possible, it can be a bit unsettling to realize just how many people get to see your records.

Q. Is there a difference between "confidentiality" and "privacy"?

A. Yes. In everyday language these terms might seem interchangeable, but from a legal standpoint, they have distinct definitions.

Confidentiality means that a doctor should not reveal your personal information to anyone except those people that are caring for you. Confidentiality refers to your expectation that what you tell your doctor will not be repeated to anyone not involved in your treatment. It is your decision as to what other uses may be made of the information. It should be up to you whether your information is released to pharmaceutical companies, other patients, or anyone else not involved in your care. This duty is rooted in the Hippocratic oath.

⚠ **RECORDS ARE OFTEN MISUSED**

According to one survey, one-third of human resources employees admitted to using medical or insurance records in deciding whom to hire, promote, or fire, despite the fact that the use of medical information in this way is illegal.

The wrong person can do a lot of damage with medical information. In one instance, a Maryland banker sat on the state health commission. He got his hands on a list of cancer patients and compared that list with the loan records at his bank. He then called due any loans to individuals whose names were on the list of cancer patients.

In another case, a company executive found out which employees were taking certain medications, and realized that one employee in particular was taking a drug to fight AIDS. The executive then told coworkers. The employee sued the company, but the company won the case. Would you want your employer to know that you are taking birth control pills? Heart medication? Drugs for a sexually transmitted disease? Probably not, but it's all in your file.

Most information in the health record is not from the doctor-patient relationship. Laws regulating **health informational privacy** give protection against unauthorized disclosure of personally identifiable information even if it was not disclosed in the context of a doctor-patient relationship.

Q. What is doctor-patient privilege?

A. The doctor-patient **privilege** means the doctor cannot disclose the patient's personal information during a legal proceeding without the patient's consent. Not every state grants patients this right, and the privilege is not absolute—it may be overridden by a court order.

Q. How does the law protect my privacy and confidentiality?

A. The most significant law relating to medical privacy and confidentiality is the Standards for Privacy of Individually Identifiable Health Information, also known as the **privacy rule.** Developed by the Department of Health and Human Services (HHS), and issued as part of the Health Insurance Portability and Accountability Act of 1996 (HIPAA), the rule gives you more control over how your personal health information is used and disclosed. The rule went into effect in 2003.

Q. Who has to comply with the privacy rule?

A. The rule applies to most health plans, doctors, hospitals, clinics, pharmacies, and nursing homes.

Q. How will I know what procedures my health-care providers will follow?

A. When you go to a doctor, a dentist, or a hospital, you probably will be presented with a form in the waiting room, and asked to sign it before treatment. The form concerns how the provider will use (and protect) information about you. The HIPAA privacy rule requires a covered health-care provider with direct treatment relationships with individuals to give you the notice no later than the date of first service delivery to you, and

to make a good-faith effort to obtain your written acknowledgment of receipt of the notice. There also will be a posted notice on the premises, in a clear and prominent location where patients are likely to see it, that includes the same information that is distributed directly to the individual.

Q. How does the privacy rule protect my medical privacy?

A. Under the rule, you have significant rights to help you understand and control how your health information is used, including the following:

Access to Medical Records

The rule gives you the right to see and obtain copies of your medical records and request corrections if you identify errors and mistakes. Doctors, hospitals, health plans, and other organizations covered by the rule generally should provide access to your records within thirty days, and may charge you for the cost of copying and sending the records.

Notice of Privacy Practices

Doctors, hospitals, and health plans must provide you with a notice containing information on how they may use your personal medical information.

Limits on Use of Personal Medical Information

The rule sets limits on how doctors, hospitals, health plans, and other organizations to which the rule applies may use individually identifiable health information. The rule does not restrict the ability of doctors, nurses, and other providers to share the information needed to treat you. However, your personal health information may not be used for purposes not related to health care.

In addition, you have to sign a specific authorization before a covered entity can release your medical information to a life insurer, a bank, a marketing firm, or another outside business for purposes not related to their health care.

Prohibition on Marketing

The rule sets new restrictions and limits on the use of your information for marketing purposes. Doctors, hospitals, health plans, and pharmacies must obtain your specific authorization before disclosing your health information for marketing purposes. However, the rule does allow communication with patients about treatment options and other health-related information, including disease-management programs.

Stronger State Laws

The federal privacy standards do not affect state laws that provide additional privacy protections for patients, like those covering mental health, HIV infection, and AIDS information. When a state law requires a certain disclosure—such as reporting an infectious disease outbreak to the public health authorities—the federal privacy regulations do not preempt the state law.

Confidential Communications

Under the privacy rule, you can request that your doctor or health plan take reasonable steps to ensure that their communications with you are confidential. For example, you could ask a doctor to call your office rather than home, and the doctor's office should comply with your request if it can be reasonably accommodated.

Q. What do hospitals, doctors, and health plans have to do to comply with the privacy rule?

A. The privacy rule requires hospitals, doctors, health plans, pharmacies, clinics, and nursing homes to establish policies and procedures to protect the confidentiality of protected health information about their patients. This includes having written privacy procedures in place, and educating employees about those procedures.

Q. Can doctors ever give my personal medical information to others without my permission?

A. In theory, you have the right to dictate which people can and cannot see your medical informa-

tion. In the real world, doctors, nurses, and other health-care workers have considerable discretion in releasing your personal information. Doctors may, for example, release your personal information in the circumstances set out below.

You Are Unconscious

If you are unconscious or unable to make decisions regarding your care, the doctor has the right to provide your family members with all the information necessary to make an informed decision on your behalf. Otherwise, doctors should use only very general terms, such as "stable," when describing your condition.

Many people have anticipated that at some point in the future they might not be able to make decisions and have written and signed a living will, a **health-care advance directive,** a durable power of attorney for health care, or a health-care proxy. Through any of these devices, you can appoint a **health-care agent** to make decisions for you. If you have such a document, then that person alone is entitled to information regarding your medical condition. The chapter on the Rights of Older Americans can provide you with more information on your options in this area.

Reporting Vital Statistics

Just as the law requires some information to be kept under wraps, it also requires doctors, nurses, and other health professionals to release information in certain circumstances. For instance, most states have laws requiring doctors to file birth and death certificates. Doctors are also usually required to report injuries caused by guns or sharp instruments, such as knives.

When There Is Abuse or Danger to Others

There is a duty to protect that is spelled out by law in many states. For instance, when child abuse is suspected, doctors, nurses, and other health professionals must report the abuse. The same is true for situations when a doctor or therapist decides that the patient is a danger to others.

When You Have a Communicable Disease

Many states require doctors to report cases of communicable diseases, including smallpox, tuberculosis, pneumonia, measles, chicken pox, mumps, syphilis, gonorrhea, AIDS, and HIV. AIDS and HIV present a special challenge to patient privacy and confidentiality. Some states use unique identifiers in their records rather than names.

In general, confidentiality is needed so that people will be comfortable being tested for AIDS or HIV. That need for confidentiality must be balanced with the desire to protect others from contracting the disease. While doctors in all states are required to report AIDS cases to state public health departments, states differ in how this information is used.

In Legal Proceedings

Any time you make your health or physical condition the focus of a lawsuit, such as a suit for workers' compensation, injuries from a car accident or medical malpractice, and in some child custody cases, your doctor can be brought into court to testify about your medical condition, even when privilege exists between the doctor and the patient. Of course, if your medical condition is not really an issue during the proceeding, privacy rights do prevail.

With Other Doctors

A doctor is allowed to discuss a patient with health-care professionals who are not involved in the patient's care, but only if the patient consents or the doctor doesn't reveal the patient's identity. In other circumstances, you have a right to maintain your privacy. For example, imagine that a doctor shows up to examine you—and is trailed by a group of medical students. You have the right to refuse to let the medical students watch your examination.

Q. Do I have a right to know what's in my child's medical record?

A. To a certain extent, you control what goes into your child's medical record, particularly when your child is very young. If you do not tell the pediatrician that your child received medical treatment from an ophthalmologist or a chiropractor, the pediatrician will not be aware of that treatment.

The situation is very different for older children, who might be able to keep information from you. What happens when your child becomes a teenager? Do you still get to see your child's medical information?

The federal privacy rule generally gives parents the right to access information about their minor child. However, the federal rules do not preempt state laws, so state laws have the final say in most states.

The law differs from state to state. The rules often hinge on what the state defines as the age of majority for health-care purposes—in a few states, it's fourteen; in others, it's eighteen—and the age of majority may vary in a state depending on the circumstances. In many states, such as Illinois, if your child becomes pregnant and asks for an abortion, you no longer may be given access to her medical records. In Montana, on the other hand, parents retain the right to access a child's medical records because her parents are considered to have the right to protect her from decisions she makes as a minor. Many states have particular statutes dealing with minors' records and treatment for sexually transmitted diseases. Some states resolve the issue by letting the doctor decide whether it would be in the child's best interest to let parents see the information.

Q. What can I do if I believe my rights to privacy have been violated?

A. If you think your private information has been disclosed, you may file a formal complaint regarding the privacy practices of a covered health plan or provider within 180 days of when you knew the act occurred. You can complain directly to the covered provider or health plan, or to the Office for Civil Rights (OCR), which is charged with investigating complaints and enforcing the privacy regulation. Information about filing complaints should be included in each covered entity's notice of privacy practices. You can find more information about filing a complaint at the OCR website at www.hhs.gov/ocr/hipaa or by calling the HIPAA toll-free number, 866-627-7748.

Q. What happens to the doctor if my information is released without my consent?

A. Almost half of the states can take disciplinary action against a doctor if it is discovered that the doctor released confidential information without the patient's consent. This may include revoking the doctor's medical license, though reprimand is the more likely remedy.

Emergency Care

Q. What is an emergency medical condition?

A. An **emergency medical condition** means the symptoms are so severe that any delay in medical treatment could reasonably be expected

---

▶ HOW TO PROTECT YOUR MEDICAL INFORMATION

- Tell your doctor that you are concerned about who has access to your medical information. Ask her what steps are taken to keep that information confidential. Don't let your concerns be brushed aside.

- Take your time and read every form you are asked to sign at the doctor's office or the hospital. If you want insurance to pay your claim, you will have to sign the release form allowing the doctor to send your information to the insurance company. On the other hand, you can also specify that the doctor can only release the specific information necessary to pay the claim— no more.

- For particularly private medical issues, pay for the visit, medication, or therapy yourself so that the information will not be sent to the insurance company for reimbursement. This may seem unfair after paying insurance premiums, but it is the best way to keep the information out of your insurance company's database.

- Ask your doctor for the clinic or hospital's policy on discussing patients among the medical staff. Notice whether the staff discusses the personal information of patients while at the nurses' station, in the elevator, or in the cafeteria. In one situation, while sitting in a hospital visiting room with her young daughter, a lawyer listened as four medical residents discussed in very unflattering terms the personal hygiene of a patient in the maternity ward. Report such breaches to your doctor and ask that the situation be corrected.

- Do not discuss your medical concerns while talking on a cellular or cordless phone. A simple baby monitor will allow your neighbors to hear your conversation. Think twice before e-mailing an Internet discussion group and providing information about your medical history. This information can be traced back to you, compiled by the discussion group host, and sold to marketing companies.

- If you believe medical staff members are not treating your medical information confidentially, discuss your concerns with your doctor. If you feel your doctor is violating your confidentiality or privacy, report the situation to a managing partner in the clinic or to the chief of staff—even doctors have bosses. You can also report the problem to your state's medical licensing board and the local medical professional association. Both numbers are in your phone book.

to seriously harm you. In the case of a pregnant woman, it also means any serious harm that could come to the unborn child. In fact, any woman in labor is considered to have an emergency medical condition.

Q. I'm not insured. If there's an emergency and I have to go to the hospital, do they have to treat me?

A. At one time, some hospitals engaged in "patient dumping," refusing to treat patients who were uninsured or poor, or otherwise considered undesirable. These patients were either turned away or transferred to other hospitals. The result was that patients did not receive immediate treatment. At its worst, it meant the patient died because of the delay.

To deal with this problem, Congress enacted an "antidumping" law. The Emergency Medical Treatment and Active Labor Act (EMTALA) requires hospitals to

- give an appropriate examination to you when you go to the emergency room;
- decide whether an emergency medical condition exists; and
- stabilize you.

Health-care facilities are required to report another health-care facility if it is suspected that the other facility is violating EMTALA. If a facility is found to violate EMTALA, that facility could be fined or even lose its participation in the Medicare and Medicaid programs. In addition, hospitals' own policies may limit dumping. Many not-for-profit hospitals are required to provide some level of charity care beyond EMTALA.

There are exceptions to the antidumping law: If a person is being brought to an emergency room by ambulance, the hospital may divert the ambulance to another facility if it is full or cannot handle the problem. In some instances, though, an unstable patient will need to be transferred to get specialist treatment at another hospital. To do this, the doctor must certify that the benefits of the treatment you will get at the next hospital outweigh the risks of the transfer.

EMTALA requires that the hospital provide treatment to stabilize patients, but it does not require the hospital to provide treatment after stabilization. EMTALA is a limited antidumping law. It is not a malpractice law.

Q. Which hospitals must comply with EMTALA?

A. EMTALA applies only to hospitals that have emergency rooms and that receive federal Medicare funds. This does not mean that you, as a patient, need to be on Medicare. It means that the hospital participates in the Medicare program. Nearly every hospital in the country with an emergency room participates in the Medicare program, which ensures that most patients will receive the care needed. Hospitals that do not participate in Medicare are not subject to EMTALA, but may be subject to state laws.

Q. What is an "appropriate medical examination" under EMTALA?

A. Courts around the country are struggling with this very issue. Unfortunately, there is no clear standard in the law as to what is an "appropriate medical examination." In general, the hospital must give you a medical screening within the hospital's capabilities, although this standard has yet to be tested in most courts.

Usually, the court will look at whether you received treatment that was somehow different from treatment received by other patients. For example, you walk into an emergency room with abdominal pains and no health insurance. After waiting four hours to see a doctor, you're given a five-minute examination, told it's probably the flu, and sent home.

To prove that you were not given an appropriate medical examination, you would have to show that other patients with abdominal pain—and health insurance—were given a more thorough examination. You do not have to prove that you were treated differently because of your race, sex, political beliefs, religion, or some other improper motive. It doesn't matter why the examination was inappropriate. It only matters that it was not appropriate.

Q. When is a patient stabilized?

A. A patient is stabilized when it is unlikely that the patient's condition will worsen significantly during, or because of, the transfer. A pregnant woman is not considered stabilized until she delivers the placenta.

Q. Is it ever a good idea for a hospital to transfer a patient?

A. The hospital may transfer the patient if:

- the patient requests the transfer in writing; or
- the doctor certifies that the benefits of transferring the patient outweigh the risks.

There are times when transferring a patient is simply the best possible course of treatment—for example, if the problem is unique or if another facility would handle the problem better. In one case, a new mother collapsed in the emergency room of a children's hospital where her newborn was being treated. The pediatric staff got the woman onto a bed and started an IV. The woman's life was in no immediate danger, so the doctors, all pediatricians, had the woman

---

⚠ WHY PATIENTS LOSE EMTALA CASES

Hospitals win most cases brought under EMTALA. The patient usually loses because he or she is unable to provide enough evidence that the medical examination given was not appropriate. In other cases, patients have lost because they could not prove they ever actually went to the emergency room, or because the transfer was proper, although the paperwork regarding the transfer was filled out incorrectly.

---

taken by ambulance to a hospital a block away where she could be seen by doctors who regularly treat adults. The woman agreed to the transfer. She received emergency care, and returned to the children's hospital to be with her child after doctors determined she was well enough to do so.

Q. How should a patient be transferred?

A. When the hospital transfers the patient,

- the transport, such as an ambulance, must have adequate equipment and personnel;
- the hospital to which the patient is being transferred must agree to accept the patient; and
- the first hospital must give all the patient's medical records to the second hospital.

In one case, a woman with high blood pressure was in labor when the hospital transferred her to a hospital three hours away. In the woman's condition, it was possible that a cesarean section would have needed to be performed during the transport. The ambulance had neither the equipment nor the staff to perform such an operation. A court found that the transportation was not adequate.

Q. Do I have a say in whether I get transferred?

A. As the patient, you may choose to refuse to agree to the transfer, or request the transfer yourself.

Q. Can I sue the hospital for malpractice if there is a problem with emergency care?

A. Yes. In an EMTALA claim, you must prove that the hospital is required to comply with EMTALA, that you went to the hospital seeking treatment, and that the hospital either did not properly screen you or that the hospital sent you away before stabilizing your condition. Unlike other medical malpractice claims, the majority of courts hold that EMTALA creates a private right of action against the hospital only. Therefore, money damages are usually not obtainable from the doctors.

EMTALA claims are different from medical malpractice claims against doctors, but most lawsuits contain claims on both these legal issues.

In addition to money payable to you, the hospital also may be fined as much as $50,000, payable to the government.

Informed Consent

Q. What is informed consent?

A. In a nutshell, informed consent means that a doctor cannot treat you until he or she explains the procedure to you and you agree to the treatment. Informed consent protects your freedom to make decisions about your body. It allows you—rather than your doctor—to decide whether to undergo a particular treatment, despite your doctor's expertise and medical training. With informed consent, the patient makes the decision about treatment—and is the one who has to live with the decision, whatever the outcome.

Q. I trust my doctor to make the best decision for me in medical matters that I don't understand. Why do we need informed consent?

A. Informed consent came about so patients could better share in decisions about their treatment. One of the earliest cases dealt with a woman who claimed that a doctor operated on her, without her consent, to remove a lump from her stomach. The woman sued her doctor and won. As the judge in that case put it:

"Every human being of adult years and sound mind has a right to determine what shall be done with his own body; and a surgeon who performs an operation without his patient's consent commits an assault, for which he is liable in damages."

Of course, a patient also has the right to waive the right to full disclosure. After all, there are some health-care consumers who simply do not want to know the risks associated with a medical procedure, and believe that ignorance is bliss.

Q. My doctor told me about a medical procedure in very technical language that I didn't understand. I consented, but I didn't really know what I was letting myself in for. Does this count as informed consent?

A. You are properly informed when the doctor explains to you all the facts necessary to make a knowledgeable decision regarding your medical care. This information should be given to you when you are calm, sober, and preferably not medicated. There are times, of course, when you will have to make a fast, nerve-racking decision about treatment for yourself or a family member. When time is of the essence, the doctor should give you as much information as possible in order to make a sound decision, but this will no doubt be less in-depth information than in other, non-life-threatening situations.

You have to actually understand the information the doctor gives you. If your alternatives are couched in medical jargon that you do not understand, you cannot legally consent to the treatment because, in effect, you have no idea what your doctor is talking about. To be informed, you need to be given the information in terms you can understand. Of course, if you don't understand the information the doctor gives you, then you need to tell the doctor so that he or she can try again—doctors can't read your mind, and you can't expect them to divine whether you've understood the information or not.

▶ **YOUR RIGHT TO CHOOSE**

Informed consent is not a guarantee of a particular outcome. It is a method of allowing you to make a rational and educated decision regarding medical treatment.

Q. What exactly does the doctor have to tell me?

A. In most cases on informed consent, the patient consented to the treatment, but argues that he or she did not have enough information about the treatment to make the consent effective.

There are several pieces of information a patient needs to make a choice about treatment:

- A description of the proposed treatment or procedure in terms the patient can understand. Even the brightest among us can get lost when wading through medical jargon.
- The benefits, risks, and side effects of the treatment.
- The risks of not treating the ailment.
- Any alternative treatments that are available, along with the risks of those alternative treatments.
- The rate of success for the treatment, as well as how success is defined.
- Information on whether the procedure is experimental.

ⓘ INFORMED CONSENT

You do not have to give informed consent for every medical procedure performed. Informed consent generally is reserved for when

- there is a risk of death or injury;
- diagnostic tests (such as angiograms) are going to be performed; or
- a surgical procedure is going to be performed.

Regular examinations or the taking of blood samples usually do not require informed consent, unless an HIV test is going to be performed. Informed consent applies to elective procedures, such as plastic surgery and vasectomies, as well.

- A description of the recuperation period, including a time frame and possible complications.
- Conflicts of interest. Patients need to know if the doctor has something to gain financially by referring the patient to a particular facility or by recommending a specific treatment.

This does not mean that the doctor has to tell you of every conceivable ache, pain, or minor side effect that may occur. It does mean that the doctor has to tell you about any facts that might cause a reasonable person to decide not to agree to the treatment. For example, a reasonable person might decide not to have surgery after she finds out it carries a 50 percent risk of paralysis. The doctor needs to tell her of this risk in order for her consent to be "informed."

In most states, a jury will consider four questions to determine whether a patient's consent was informed:

1. Did the patient understand enough of the information to give an effective consent?
2. Was the patient given the same information as other patients in the same situation?
3. If the patient had been given sufficient information, would he or she have consented to the treatment?
4. Was the patient warned about the complication that later arose?

The patient cannot bring a lawsuit if the patient was not injured, even if the patient did not give an informed consent. However, the patient still is entitled to file a complaint with the state licensing agency against the doctor for professional misconduct, regardless of whether an injury resulted. The doctor may then face some form of discipline from that agency.

Q. My doctor gave me some information and then asked me to sign a consent form. Is this the way consent usually is given?

A. Many doctors will ask you to sign a consent form, simply to keep evidence of the fact that you consented in the medical record for the doctor's and your protection. However, informed consent does not necessarily mean written consent. The whole purpose of informed consent is to give you enough information so that you can share in the decisions regarding your health care. Whether you need to sign an informed consent form should be secondary to your decision as to whether you want to agree to the treatment.

You are not required by law to sign any kind of consent form for most procedures. Keep in mind, though, that the doctor can then choose not to treat you. Some states have laws that require the execution of specific informed consent forms for some procedures, including HIV testing and sterilization.

Q. Do I have to agree to everything in a consent form?

A. No. You have the option to cross out any clauses in the consent form if you do not agree with or consent to those clauses. Just put an X through the clause and initial it. The doctor must explain the risks of putting those restrictions on the treatment, if any. The doctor may require that the restrictions be noted in your medical record. If the restrictions are so strict as to make the procedure unsound, the doctor can choose not to proceed with the treatment.

Q. When is informed consent not necessary?

A. There are times when it is simply not possible for a doctor to explain a medical treatment or

---

▶ WHAT SHOULD I ASK MY DOCTOR?

There are several questions you can ask your doctor in order to make sure your consent is informed:

- What is the problem?
- How serious is it?
- How accurate are the test results?
- When does treatment have to begin in order to be most effective?
- Can you describe the treatment?
- What are the risks involved?
- What are the odds it will be successful?
- What if it is not successful?
- What are the side effects?
- What are the risks in not treating it?
- What alternative treatments are available?
- Will medical students or residents be involved with my treatment?
- Will students or residents be practicing any procedures on me that are unrelated to my care?
- How many times have you performed the procedure?
- What is your success rate?
- What other facilities or practitioners perform this procedure?

procedure to you. There are also times when it is not necessary for a doctor to provide you with such information. For example, doctors are not required to obtain informed consent from you when it is an emergency situation and you are unable to give or withhold consent.

Q. Can I withdraw my consent if I change my mind?

A. You can withdraw your consent at any time, but this may affect your treatment. Obviously, it is best to change your mind before the doctor begins a surgical procedure. Changing your mind can put both you and your doctor at risk. Once you withdraw your consent, the doctor has to discuss with you the effects of not proceeding with the treatment.

In Wisconsin, a woman went into labor and was admitted to the hospital. She had planned on, and was prepared for, a vaginal delivery. During delivery, she changed her mind, and three times asked her doctor to perform a cesarean. The doctor continued to prepare for a vaginal delivery. When complications arose during delivery, the doctor delivered the baby by cesarean. The baby was paralyzed from the neck down.

The woman sued the doctor because he did not acknowledge that she withdrew her consent to a vaginal delivery. The doctor argued that once the vaginal delivery began, the patient could not withdraw her consent. The woman won the case. Because a cesarean delivery was a viable medical alternative to a vaginal delivery, the woman had the right to withdraw her consent to a vaginal delivery. When she withdrew her consent, the doctor was obligated to discuss with her the consequences of her withdrawal and her options at that point.

Although the woman won in Wisconsin, the law varies from state to state. In every state, though, you have the right to withdraw your consent. Your doctor should discuss with you the effect this will have on your treatment, but the ultimate decision is generally up to you.

Q. What if a patient can't speak English?

A. Informed consent is the right of all patients, including those who are physically disabled or tourists and immigrants who do not speak English. The law requires that doctors and facilities take steps to ensure that these people are fully informed as to their treatment options before the treatment begins. For example, deaf people have the right to have someone communicate with them using sign language. If the person does not speak English, an interpreter usually will be used to ensure that the patient understands the illness or injury and the treatment options. The interpreter that is most commonly used today is a phone service that provides interpretation in dozens of languages.

Q. Can I choose to refuse treatment?

A. After being informed of your diagnosis, as well as the treatment options and the risks involved, you can choose not to undergo treatment. You can refuse any treatment, including life-sustaining treatment, as long as you are an adult, unless perhaps you are mentally incompetent under state laws and have lost your ability to make informed decisions. Although you have the right to refuse treatment, the public health department has the right to isolate you if you have a contagious disease and are a danger to others.

ⓘ CATCHALL CONSENTS

Written informed consent forms vary from doctor to doctor, hospital to hospital. Some are so vague that they seem to cover every imaginable situation that might arise. With forms this vague, many courts have concluded that the patient did not consent at all.

THE WORLD AT YOUR FINGERTIPS

• *An excellent and detailed guide to the privacy rule can be found at the Health* and Human Resources website at www.hhs.gov/ocr/hipaa/guidelines/ guidanceallsections.pdf.

- The American College of Emergency Physicians offers a comprehensive site discussing all aspects of emergency care at www.acep.org.

- Want to know what doctors really think about informed consent? Take a look at www-hsc.usc.edu/~mbernste/index.html, scroll through the topics, and click on "informed consent."

REMEMBER THIS

- The federal privacy rule protects the privacy of your medical records. Additional protections are provided by the confidentiality of the doctor-patient relationship.

- Emergency room doctors are required to examine you, determine whether there is an emergency, and then—if there is an emergency—either stabilize you or transfer you to another hospital.

- An appropriate medical examination is one that a doctor would give to any patient presenting your symptoms, vital signs, and complaints, regardless of your race, gender, religion, insurance status, or income level.

- Informed consent means that your doctor must explain the treatment or procedure to you, along with all of the risks and alternatives. You must then agree to be treated before the doctor may proceed.

- Consent does not require a written form for most procedures. If you are given a form, you are not required to sign it, although the doctor can choose not to treat you.

HEALTH-CARE OPTIONS

Dale is a single mother, at work on the first day of her new part-time job. Her supervisor keeps bringing paperwork for her to sign. In one folder is the information on the company benefits. There are three health plans from which Dale can choose. Dale skims through the policy books for each plan, but they all look the same to her. The only difference that she can see is the price. Dale does not want to spend the rest of her day wading through pages of boring legal and medical jargon. She figures that all health plans are similar and it does not really matter which one she chooses. She fills out the forms for the least expensive health plan, makes sure that her daughter will be covered, and gives the forms to her supervisor. Six months later, Dale is laid off from the job. Will she still be covered for health insurance? For how long? How much will it cost her? Will her daughter still be covered? Does she have any options if she does not find another job?

This section looks at patients' options when it comes to paying for medical care and focuses on current issues relating to managed care.

Health Insurance and Managed Care Organizations

Q. *What is a health insurance policy?*

A. A traditional health insurance policy is like insurance for your house or your car—you pay a premium, and the insurance company promises to pay your health-care services. Generally, in addition to payment of a premium, you are also responsible for payment of deductibles and co-payments (a percentage of actual charges or a fixed amount per visit), which are predetermined in the policy at set amounts or rates. You are free to choose your health-care provider, which then applies to the insurance company for reimbursement.

While traditional fee-for-service health insurance policies are available, premiums for them have become very expensive.

Q. Are there alternatives to traditional health insurance?

A. Yes. In an effort to control health-care costs, new forms of health insurance and health service plans have developed that have resulted in lower premiums. The lower premiums generally are achieved through a reduction in choice of health-care providers, a reduction in the type and the amount of benefits available, stricter controls on the type and the amount of care given by providers, and/or negotiated reduction of compensation to health-care providers. There are several types of these organizations, which are called managed care organizations (MCOs).

Q. What is a preferred provider plan?

A. A **preferred provider plan** is a fairly flexible form of MCO, which gives you the opportunity to choose a health-care provider from a list of providers who are members of the sponsoring insurer's **preferred provider organization (PPO)**. If you choose to see a health-care provider who is not a member of the PPO, then you will receive a reduced level of reimbursement.

Q. What are health maintenance organizations (HMOs)?

A. Private health service plans that promise to provide care, not merely pay for it, are often referred to as **health maintenance organizations (HMOs)**. Some are "closed panel plans" and operate out of a central facility, with all the health-care providers employed by the HMO. When you go to the facility, you may see the doctor on duty, or your "assigned physician."

Other HMOs are more loosely affiliated models, sometimes called **individual practice associations**, in which the participating health-care providers operate from their own offices.

Q. What about employer-sponsored plans?

A. Many large private employers provide health coverage through their own sponsored self-funded and self-administered employee welfare benefit plans. These plans may look very much like preferred provider plans or an HMOs, but they are administered for the employer by an insurance company.

Q. Are health insurers and MCOs governed by state or federal law?

A. Each state makes its own laws as to what level of care health insurance and managed care must provide. Federal law limits the preexisting conditions that health-care insurers and plans may put into their policies.

The state laws are often similar to one another. More than half the states require health plans to pay for visits to the emergency room. Almost every state now requires that new mothers be allowed to stay in the hospital for at least forty-eight hours after giving birth.

However, if an employer-sponsored health plan is exempt under the Employee Retirement Income Security Act of 1974 (ERISA), as discussed in the sidebar "Do You Have Access to External Review?" on page 673, then state and federal laws do not apply to the mandated coverage.

Q. What are typical problems that arise in getting health-care benefits provided or paid?

A. Coverage and benefit disputes in health-care insurance and health-care plans that frequently arise include the following:

1. The insurer or plan contends that care was not **medically necessary,** which is often defined as care that is reasonably required according to accepted norms within the medical community.
2. The insurer or plan contends that the charges were not "usual, customary and reasonable" for the services rendered.
3. The insurer or plan contends that the treatment was "experimental" or "investigational,"

which generally means that the care has not been accepted in the medical community as normal treatment or has not been proven to be effective medically.

4. The insurer or plan contends that medical care was received outside a specified geographical service area and was not emergency care.

5. The insurer or plan contends, with respect to extended care especially, that the care constituted "custodial care" or "long-term rehabilitation," which usually are excluded from coverage. This issue often arises in the context of persons confined to skilled nursing facilities or persons requiring home health care.

6. Coverage in a replacement policy is substantially and impermissibly different (more limited) than that in a group policy it replaced.

7. There are substantial differences between descriptions or terms in the evidence of coverage (member handbook, disclosure form, or summary) and the insurance policy or health plan contract in the circumstance where the denial of coverage or benefit is based on the evidence of coverage, not the contract.

8. There is substantial ambiguity in a particular term, definition, benefit or coverage description, or exclusion or limitation, or an ambiguity created by an interplay between or among the different provisions.

9. The insurer or plan attempts to effect a reduction in or elimination of a benefit or coverage contrary to a provision in the policy or plan, or without adequate notice.

10. The insurer or plan seeks cancellation of the policy or plan alleging that an insured or member had a preexisting condition not revealed in the application.

Q. What can I do if I have a dispute of this kind with my health insurance company or plan?

A. If a health insurance company or plan denies your claim or refuses to provide a benefit or service, you have several options.

Seek Internal Review

Health insurance companies and plans are required to establish rules and procedures for handling complaints and grievances internally. Utilizing these procedures is an important first step in seeking resolution of a dispute. You can start an internal review with a phone call to a complaints hot line. You may need to follow it up with a complaints form or a written complaint.

Some sample letters that demonstrate how to seek review can be found at *www. healthcarerights.org/letters/lettersindex.html*. Check your policy to see how long a review is likely to take—it can be anything from one business day to thirty days. If your dispute concerns the medical necessity of services to be provided and waiting for a standard review would seriously jeopardize your health, you may be eligible for an expedited review, and the plan will evaluate your dispute sooner.

Seek External Review

External review allows your case to be reviewed by a third party independent of the health-care plan. Most states have external review procedures, which can be pursued once internal review has been exhausted. Your health-care plan or insurance company may automatically refer your dispute to external review if your internal review is unsuccessful; or you may need to request external review in writing within a certain time period after internal review.

Most states will not review all disputes, only those involving "medical necessity." That means that there must be a dispute between you and your health plan over whether a particular procedure, treatment, or pharmaceutical is essential for your health and recovery.

The external review procedures are different in each state, but are usually free or available for a small fee. You can find a useful summary of the procedures involved in each state at www.kff.org/consumerguide/states.html.

▶ **KEEP GOOD RECORDS FROM THE BEGINNING**

- Assemble a file containing all the paperwork you already have, such as bills or physician information. If you are denied care, ask for a record of the denial in writing.

- Keep a log of every telephone call you make to the plan or insurance company. Record the date and the name of the person you talk to, and take notes about your conversation.

- Make copies of every document you send to the health plan or insurance company for your file, and record the date on which you send any correspondence.

- If you send correspondence to any other parties—government agencies or accrediting organizations, for example—then send a copy to your health-care plan.

Complain to the Accrediting Organization

Most HMOs are accredited with nongovernmental groups such as the National Committee for Quality Assurance (www.ncqa.org), the American Accreditation HealthCare Commission/URAC (www.urac.org), and the Joint Commission on Accreditation of Health Care Organizations (www.jcaho.org). HMOs rely on their accreditation by these organizations in their marketing to employers and unions. Making a well-documented complaint to the relevant organization and sending a copy to your HMO might have results.

Make a Complaint About Your Doctor—and Seek a Second Opinion

If you think your doctor is withholding treatment, then talk to your doctor about it. You might want to seek a second opinion about whether treatment is necessary. And if you believe your doctor is withholding treatment for his or her own pecuniary gain, you can file a complaint with your state's medical board.

Appeal to the State Insurance Department

This is a good option if you are covered by an HMO. Since all plans have to be licensed by a state's insurance department, these departments truly do have the last word. They are especially useful if you feel there has been discrimination, unfair denial, or a vagary of the rules, disclosures,

or booklets. HMOs are likely to respond out of concern that their license might be revoked or suspended.

Q. Can I sue my managed care organization for malpractice?

A. A federal appeals court has ruled that MCOs and their medical directors can be sued for medical malpractice when they make a decision about the treatment of a patient that causes the patient harm. This applies to individual decisions, not to overall corporate policies. This means that consumers can sue an MCO for injuries resulting from the company's refusal to authorize medically necessary treatment.

Q. How does ERISA affect my malpractice suit?

A. ERISA bars people from bringing a claim against health plans that are offered by employers, which means that few people manage to bring malpractice cases against health plans. If you purchase your health plan on your own or through some other type of organization, ERISA does not apply.

Several states now have statutes that remove ERISA protection and explicitly allow individuals to bring suits against health plans. Courts increasingly are interpreting ERISA to allow such suits as well.

ⓘ DO YOU HAVE ACCESS TO EXTERNAL REVIEW?

There are some health plans that do not have access to external review. Under the Employee Retirement Income Security Act of 1974 (ERISA), there are some kinds of self-insured employer-paid plans that are exempted from the state's external review procedures. In fact, nearly 70 percent of the health-care insurance currently in place in the United States is subject to ERISA. As a practical matter, this means that people who have disputes with their plans are limited to the internal grievance procedures and cannot sue in court for such things as breach of contract, breach of the implied covenant of good faith and fair dealing (bad faith), infliction of emotional distress, and fraud. As noted earlier, it also means that the plan may not have to comply with mandated coverage laws.

Consult your employer's human resources department to determine if your plan is self-insured. If it is, then you probably cannot use your state's external review process.

Q. Can I sue my health plan to recover the cost of my treatment?

A. ERISA does not bar claims for economic loss based on the denial of benefits. In other words, you can sue your health plan to try to get it to cover your medical bills. Any amount you are awarded is limited to the amount of the medical services that are disputed and your lawyer's fees. If you have a bill for $2,900, that amount and the cost of your lawyer's fees is all you are allowed to recover from your health plan. To win coverage for medical bills, you will have to show that you complied with your health plan contract. If you go to the emergency room for a migraine at a time when your doctor is holding office hours, even though this is clearly not allowed under your policy, you may not be able to get coverage for those medical bills.

Q. What happens if I lose my job? Does my employer stop paying for my health plan straight away?

A. A federal law called COBRA, short for the Consolidated Omnibus Budget Reconciliation Act, gives employees some protection. It applies to almost all businesses that employ more than twenty people, and covers full-time and part-time employees. If you lose your job, or your hours are reduced, COBRA allows employees to purchase their health coverage from their former employers at the same price the employer paid for up to eighteen months.

COBRA also kicks in during specific crises and transition times like divorce or death, covering the employee's spouse and dependents for up to three years. COBRA also applies to ensure coverage of a child who loses dependent child status—for example, by turning nineteen—for up to three years.

Continuing your coverage under COBRA can be expensive because you're still paying your contribution, plus the contribution your employer made, plus up to 2 percent for administrative costs, but often the cost is much lower than the cost of buying individual coverage.

Medicare and Medicaid

Q. What is Medicare?

A. Medicare is an insurance program. Medical bills are paid from trust funds, which those covered have paid into. It primarily serves people over sixty-five, whatever their income. It also serves younger disabled people and dialysis patients. Patients pay part of the costs through deductibles for hospital and other costs. Small monthly premiums are required for nonhospital coverage. Medicare is a federal program. It is basically the same everywhere in the United States and is run by the Centers for Medicare and Medicaid Services (CMS), an agency of the federal government.

You can find detailed information on Medicare in chapter 16, "The Rights of Older Americans."

Q. What is Medicaid?

A. Medicaid is a medical assistance program that serves low-income people of every age. Unlike Medicare, which offers the same benefits to all enrollees regardless of income, Medicaid is managed by individual states, and the benefits and eligibility vary from state to state. Medical bills are paid from federal, state, and local tax funds.

Q. Who is eligible for Medicaid?

A. States have some discretion in determining which groups their Medicaid programs will cover and the financial criteria for Medicaid eligibility. Here are some examples of the mandatory Medicaid eligibility groups:

- Low income families with children.
- Most supplemental security income (SSI) recipients.
- Infants born to Medicaid-eligible pregnant women. Medicaid eligibility must continue throughout the first year of life so long as the infant remains in the mother's household and she remains eligible, or would be eligible if she were still pregnant.
- Children under age six and pregnant women whose family income is at or below 133 percent of the federal poverty level.

States also have the option to provide Medicaid coverage for other "categorically needy" groups. These optional groups share characteristics of the mandatory groups, but the eligibility criteria are defined somewhat more liberally. Examples of the optional groups that states may cover as categorically needy (and for which they will receive federal matching funds) under the Medicaid program are

- some low income children;
- certain aged, blind, or disabled adults who have incomes above those requiring mandatory coverage, but below the federal poverty level;
- institutionalized individuals with income and resources below specified limits;
- people who would be eligible if institutionalized but are receiving care under home- and community-based services waivers;
- recipients of state supplementary payments; and
- low-income, uninsured women screened and diagnosed through the Centers for Disease Control and Prevention's National Breast and Cervical Cancer Early Detection Program and determined to be in need of treatment for breast or cervical cancer.

Q. If I qualify for Medicaid, what sorts of services do I get?

A. Medicaid covers a broad spectrum of services. Certain benefits are mandated by federal law. They include

- inpatient and outpatient hospital services;
- doctors' and nurse practitioners' services;
- inpatient nursing-home care;
- home health-care services; and
- laboratory and X ray charges.

ⓘ MEDIGAP

Medigap is a supplemental insurance policy that many people buy to cover some of the costs not covered by Medicare. Chapter 16, "The Rights of Older Americans," covers Medigap in detail.

You also may be entitled to services from podiatrists, optometrists, and chiropractors; mental health services; personal care in your home; dental care; physical therapy and other rehabilitation; prescription medications; eyeglasses; transportation services; and more. In all cases, you may receive these services only from a Medicaid-participating provider.

Q. What does Medicaid cost me?

A. Medicaid does not require you to pay premiums or deductibles like Medicare. Providers may not charge you additional fees beyond the Medicaid reimbursement amount. However, states are permitted to impose a nominal deductible charge or other form of cost sharing for certain categories of services and prescription drugs. If you are receiving Medicaid, a participating provider may not deny you services because of your inability to pay the charge.

Q. How do I apply for Medicaid?

A. You should contact the state or local agency that handles the Medicaid program. Its name will vary from place to place. It may be called Social Services, Public Aid, Public Welfare, Human Services, or something similar. Chapter 16, "The Rights of Older Americans," contains more detailed information on how to apply for Medicaid.

State Children's Health Insurance Program

Q. What is the State Children's Health Insurance Program? Does my state have this program?

A. The State Children's Health Insurance Program (SCHIP) is designed primarily to help children in working families with incomes too high to qualify for Medicaid but too low to afford private family coverage. All states and the District of Columbia offer health coverage through SCHIP and Medicaid.

Q. Are my kids eligible for SCHIP?

A. Each state can set its own income eligibility level. Most states have set the maximum eligibility level at 200 percent of the federal poverty level. This level is adjusted every year, and varies depending on size of family. In 2003, if you had an income up to $36,800 a year and a family of four, your kids would have qualified.

Q. What benefits can I get under SCHIP?

A. Although benefits vary from state to state, children are generally eligible for the following services:

- Regular checkups
- Immunizations
- Eyeglasses
- Doctor visits
- Prescription drug coverage
- Hospital care

Q. How much do I have to pay?

A. Health insurance provided to children through these programs is free or low-cost. The costs are different depending on the state and your family's income, but when there are charges, they are minimal. In some states, you may need to pay a premium or make a co-payment for your children's health insurance.

THE WORLD AT YOUR FINGERTIPS

- **The Complete Idiot's Guide to Managed Health Care,** by Sophie M. Korczyk and Hazel A. Witte (New York: MacMillan, 1998), explains in easy-to-read form how to get the most care out of managed care.
- **Managed Care Made Easy,** by Vikram Khanna (Allentown, Pa.: People's Medical Society, 1997), is a consumer-focused book that gives advice on how to choose the right health plan for you, and how to get the most out of it.
- You can find more information on Medicare at www.medicare.gov. Chapter 16, "The Rights of Older Americans," also provides more detailed information.

- You can find more information about Medicaid at cms.hhs.gov/medicaid/consumer. asp.
- For a website that provides links to every state, where you can find more information about the Children's Health Insurance Program that applies to you, visit the Insure Kids Now website, sponsored by the Department of Health and Human Services at www.insurekidsnow.gov/states.htm.

REMEMBER THIS

- Managed care is a way of keeping health-care costs lower, and thus more accessible to you.
- If your health plan is through your employer, ERISA may prevent you from having access to external review procedures in your state.
- Be sure to read your health plan closely so that you know exactly what coverage you have for medical care.
- Medicare is an insurance program that primarily insures those over sixty-five.
- Medicaid is a medical assistance program that serves low-income earners of every age.
- Even if you're working, your child may be eligible for the Children's Health Insurance Program.

REGULATING HEALTH-CARE PROFESSIONALS

Glenn knows she is overweight and needs to lose about a hundred pounds. She feels desperate until she sees an advertisement in a newspaper about a medication that helps people lose weight. She calls the number at the bottom of the advertisement and makes an appointment with the weight loss clinic. When she goes to the clinic, she is seated in the doctor's office.

Glenn is a smart woman. She looks closely at the framed certificates on the wall until she finds the doctor's license. If the doctor is licensed, he must know what he is doing. Or does he?

Jackie thought she had a cold. It started in February with a cough. When it did not go away by March, Jackie went to see her doctor. The doctor prescribed an antibiotic and told Jackie that if her cold did not get better within the next two weeks to make another appointment. Jackie took the antibiotic off and on for a couple of weeks. Her cold did not clear up, but she did not make another appointment for several months. By that time her cough was worse. When she finally returned to the doctor's office, the doctor ordered a CT scan of Jackie's upper chest. The scan showed that Jackie had a tumor that turned out to be Hodgkin's disease. Jackie started chemotherapy the next week. Her prognosis is good, but it would be better if she had returned to the doctor sooner rather than later. Jackie is angry that the doctor did not tell her it could be something other than a cold. She wants to know if she can sue for malpractice. Can she?

Adequate regulation of the medical profession is crucial. Care that falls short of a high standard can result in injury or death, as illustrated in the hypothetical situations above. This section covers the licensing of health-care professionals and medical malpractice, and also explores the legal and ethical issues in experimental research on humans.

Licensing of Doctors, Nurses, and Hospitals

Q. Who licenses health-care professionals and facilities?

A. Each state government sets its own requirements for how doctors, nurses, hospitals, and other health-care professionals and facilities are licensed. The state does this to protect your health and safety.

Once a doctor is licensed to practice medicine, that doctor is licensed to practice any type of medicine. In theory, a dermatologist can deliver a baby, an obstetrician can perform liposuction, and a plastic surgeon can perform brain surgery. In reality, hospital regulations, fear of malpractice claims, and the threat of disciplinary actions discourage doctors from giving medical care outside their fields of expertise. Many hospitals insist that a doctor be certified in a particular specialty. Specialty boards certify physicians as having met certain published standards. Twenty-four specialty boards are recognized by the American Board of Medical Specialties (ABMS) and the American Medical Association (AMA). To become board certified, doctors must undergo more training, receive assessments from their supervisors, and complete written exams. In order to retain certification, specialists must periodically go through an additional process involving continuing education in the specialty, review of credentials, and further examination.

Q. Who needs a license?

A. That varies by state. In general, states will license chiropractors, dentists, doctors, surgeons, physical therapists, nurses, optometrists, psychologists, physician assistants, respiratory therapists, pharmacists, and clinical social workers. Some states may also decide to license hearing aid dispensers, eyeglass and contact lens dispensers, clinical laboratory technologists, and midwives. Many states also require homeopaths and naturopaths to be licensed.

Q. Why do doctors need a license?

A. The state legislators believe that by requiring a license for doctors, they can help ensure that you will receive quality medical care. A license means they can make sure that doctors graduated from a medical school that taught them what they need to know to treat you. These laws can prevent you from being cared for by a person who has a criminal history or a character defect. It means that if a doctor does not care for you in

medically acceptable ways, the doctor may be disciplined by license revocation or suspension.

A state may use the licensing standards as a way to promote public policy. When the California legislature determined that many doctors knew less about human sexuality than most nondoctors, the California Medical Licensing Board added training in human sexuality as a requirement for licensing.

On the other hand, not everyone favors licensing requirements. Some commentators argue that the licensing requirements discriminate against minorities or raise the price of your medical care. Others argue that licensing requirements were written more than a hundred years ago, and are irrelevant to today's world. They suggest that the requirements impose a stifling conformity on medicine, because all doctors attend strictly regulated medical schools that teach the same classes and do not encourage other ways of thinking about or treating patients.

Once a physician passes a licensing exam, he or she never has to pass another licensing exam or be tested in that state for the rest of his or her life.

▶ **TO FIND OUT IF A DOCTOR IS LICENSED**

To find out if your doctor is licensed, call the licensing board in your state. These are usually listed in the phone book under your state's name, followed by medical examination or licensing board. Or check out the website for the Association of State Medical Board Executive Directors at www.docboard.org/. This website will link you to your state's licensing board. Many of the states give you instructions on the Internet for lodging complaints against your doctor in addition to helping you to check on a license.

Q. What should I do if I find out my doctor is not licensed?

A. First of all, double-check the information—you don't want to make a false report. If you're certain, report that person to the medical board in your state. You should also report it to the attorney general's office in your state, as the practitioner may be operating fraudulently. The person practicing without a license may be subject to criminal penalties and will face trial. Depending on the situation, you may have a civil action against the person for battery, and you may be able to bring a lawsuit seeking monetary damages against the person.

Q. What about nurses?

A. In many states, nurses are not required to attend college to take the standardized test and receive a license. A diploma from a hospital-based nursing school is enough. Many nursing associations believe that a college degree is needed for nurses to be fully trained. Hospital-based nursing schools and nurses without college degrees disagree and oppose adding an educational requirement.

Q. When can a license be revoked?

A. It is difficult to get a doctor or nurse's license revoked. A professional license is considered "property" under the Constitution, so the person must be told the reason for the revocation and given a fair hearing. The most common ground for suspending a license is unprofessional conduct.

Q. Can I file a complaint with licensing authorities about a health-care professional?

A. Each state has a medical board and other boards in charge of licensing, investigating complaints, and disciplining doctors and other health-care professionals. You can look in the telephone book or do an online search, using a search such as the name of your state medical board. The medical board or other board will tell you how to get a complaint form to begin the process. Some boards put this form on their website and you can print it from there. Be sure to fill out the form completely and clearly. This form will ask you to sign a release allowing the board to look at your medical records. You are not required to sign this, but without looking at your records, the board may not be able to investigate your complaint fully. Some states require that your complaint form be notarized, which would require your name on the form.

Q. What happens then?

A. Usually, the board will examine the complaint form and decide whether the complaint should be investigated. In some situations, the board will not have the authority to investigate. For example, if you complain that your doctor kept you waiting too long for your examination, the board may decide that your complaint does not have merit and will inform you that it will not be investigated.

Q. How is my complaint investigated?

A. The medical board will notify your doctor of the complaint and ask him or her to respond. When the board receives your doctor's response, it will decide whether to continue the investigation. If an investigation is needed, the board will look at your medical records (and others as deemed necessary) and interview witnesses.

ⓘ MINIMUM REQUIREMENTS

For a health professional to be licensed, he or she must usually

- graduate from an approved program, such as a medical or nursing school;

- pass a standardized licensing examination; and

- undergo a review of his or her personal history.

ⓘ SOME BACKGROUND ON NURSING

The profession of nursing really got its start on bloody battlefields in the mid-nineteenth century. The heroic contributions of Florence Nightingale and other nurses in the Crimean War and Clara Barton and her colleagues in the American Civil War established the value of nursing.

The first nursing school was founded in 1873. The early nursing schools were based in hospitals and provided unpaid labor by student nurses to the hospitals. In the 1890s, many of the first nursing students, particularly those from well-to-do families, were now nurses and teaching the next nursing classes their profession. At the same time, there were women from the lower classes of society who did not attend nursing schools but nevertheless held themselves out as nurses. The teaching nurses began to press for licensing of nurses so that they could improve patient care. By 1923, forty-eight states required nurses to be licensed. To be licensed, the nurses had to attend a nursing school. Today, professional nursing associations continue to push for more education in order to be licensed.

Q. How long does the investigation take?

A. Anywhere from a few weeks to several years, depending on how complex the complaint is and how difficult the investigation. You can check on the status of your complaint by contacting the medical board.

Q. What happens after the investigation?

A. If the board finds that the complaint is unwarranted, it will dismiss the complaint. If it finds the complaint is justified, it may request that the complaint be investigated further. In some cases, the complaint will be dismissed, but the board will notify the doctor that certain methods or ac-

ⓘ COMPLAINTS

Most customers who file complaints with the state licensing board find the complaint process frustrating. Customers are generally kept in the dark about what is happening. They do not have the right in most cases to attend hearings or see investigational documents, while the doctor sees everything the patient has filed.

▶ TYPES OF COMPLAINTS INVESTIGATED

A medical board will investigate complaints about

- substandard medical care;
- illegal sale of drugs;
- professional misconduct;
- a criminal conviction;
- sexual misconduct;
- neglect or abandonment of a patient;
- alcohol or substance abuse;
- mental or emotional illness that impairs the doctor's judgment;
- discrimination;
- billing for services not provided;
- false advertising;
- fraud;
- failure to provide medical records;
- overcharging for medical records; and
- failure to supervise staff.

tions must be changed in the future. It may order your doctor to undertake more training or stop performing particular treatments. It may require that the doctor enter into treatment for substance or alcohol abuse. If the board finds that the doctor should be disciplined, there will be an administrative hearing, at which time the doctor may be disciplined in some way, including having his or her license revoked or suspended.

Q. Do I have to give my name when I complain?

A. Some medical boards will not investigate a complaint that is anonymous. It would be nearly impossible to investigate a complaint without access to the complaining patient's medical records. On the other hand, medical boards often will keep your name confidential if you so request. In other words, your doctor will not find out directly from investigators that it was you that complained, even though the medical board knows your name and sees your medical records. However, the doctor may be able to infer that it was you when your records are sought.

Q. What happens to my complaint after either it is dismissed or the doctor is disciplined?

A. These documents typically become part of the doctor's file kept by the medical board. In some states, the doctor's file is available to the public because it is considered a public record.

Q. Can I appeal if my complaint is dismissed?

A. No. There is no appeal process through the medical board. When the medical board dismisses a complaint, it may mean only that an investigation would not provide enough proof to discipline the doctor.

Q. If the board does not take action, do I have other options?

A. Yes. The dismissal of your complaint by a medical board does not affect your right to bring a legal action against your doctor, such as for medical malpractice, unless the statute of limitations has run out.

Q. Do medical institutions need to be licensed?

A. Just as doctors must be licensed and meet certain standards, so must hospitals, nursing homes, and most other types of health-care facilities. Unlike doctors though, health-care facilities (including hospitals and nursing homes) are regulated by a combination of state and federal laws, including Medicaid and Medicare. These regulations dictate the type of care that may be provided and how the professional staff may be selected and trained, and provide standards for the maintenance and sanitation of the buildings and equipment. In addition, health-care facilities may choose to meet the standards of private accreditation organizations to boost their public image or increase their competitive edge.

Q. What is "the unauthorized practice of medicine"?

A. Each state has laws that forbid anyone but licensed doctors from practicing medicine. The practice of medicine by unlicensed doctors is known as the **unauthorized practice of medicine.** How these laws define "medicine" varies from state to state, with most states using a broad definition. For example, the Pennsylvania Medical Practice Act defines medicine as "the art and science of which the objectives are the cure of diseases and the preservation of the health of man, including the practice of the healing art with or without drugs, except healing by spiritual means or prayer."

Usually, home remedies, the self-injection of insulin, tattooing, the sale of books that discuss healing, or the sale of vitamins or nutritional substances are not considered to be unauthorized practices of medicine, as long as those activities do not involve making a diagnosis of a patient.

However, prescribing vitamins to cure an illness is practicing medicine and someone would need a license to do that. The same is true of taking blood or urine samples for analysis in order to diagnose or treat an illness or injury.

The unauthorized practice of medicine occurs when an unlicensed person does something that is part of the legal definition of "medicine." This does not include simply offering general advice (as, for example, in a magazine article for the general public), or offering informal advice about a coworker's cold, but it does involve holding yourself out as a licensed doctor when in fact you do not have a license to practice medicine. For instance, if you diagnose a person as having cancer, but you are not a doctor, you engaged in the unauthorized practice of medicine and you may be prosecuted in a criminal court. If you prescribe a healing salve for a skin condition or give obstetrical examinations, but you are not a licensed health professional, you engaged in the unauthorized practice of medicine and you may be prosecuted in a criminal court.

Medical Malpractice

Q. What is medical malpractice?

A. Medical malpractice is negligence committed by a professional health-care provider—a doctor, a nurse, a dentist, a technician, a hospital, or a nursing facility—whose performance of duties departs from a standard of practice of those with similar training and experience, resulting in harm to a patient. Most medical malpractice actions are filed against doctors who have failed to use reasonable care to treat a patient. Though million-dollar verdicts make headlines, in fact the big jury awards you hear about are few and far between.

The goal of a medical malpractice lawsuit is to pay you back if a doctor injures you. Malpractice lawsuits are time consuming and costly for doctors, even if the doctor is insured or wins the case. The fear of malpractice is meant to keep doctors from making medical mistakes and from acting carelessly. In this way, the law can control the quality of health care. Malpractice puts the responsibility on doctors to act in a way that will not result in an injury to you. If doctors are forced to pay for the costs of their medical mistakes, they will be more careful to make sure that mistakes do not happen in the first place.

Note, though, that some observers think that fear of malpractice does not so much improve medical care as make doctors more defensive in how they treat you. The result may be more tests and other measures to establish a solid record of care—good for defense in a malpractice case, but a factor in making health care more time consuming and expensive.

Medical malpractice is discussed in more detail in chapter 14, "Personal Injury."

Q. How would a jury decide if my doctor committed malpractice?

A. A jury will compare your doctor's conduct with how other doctors would have acted if faced with the same or similar circumstances. The doctor is not compared to a person in the general population. Instead, the doctor is compared to other doctors with the same type of medical training and skills.

For example, if you are a thirty-year-old woman who runs marathons and you tell your doctor you have chest pains, the actions your general practitioner doctor takes will be compared with what other general practitioners would have done if a thirty-year-old female marathon runner came in complaining of chest pains.

If a jury finds that your doctor did not act with the same level of care that other doctors would have used in a similar situation, the jury will find that your doctor committed malpractice.

Q. So if I get a bad outcome from my treatment, can I sue for malpractice?

A. It is not automatically malpractice when your doctor gives you medical care and something bad happens. As long as your doctor uses reasonable care and skill in treating you, your doctor did not commit malpractice. Five doctors can examine and diagnose the same person and come up with five different opinions as to what medical care is needed. That does not mean that four of the doctors are wrong or incompetent. It means that there are many ways to treat that person. The key is that all the doctors acted according to acceptable medical standards and treated you as any reasonable doctor would have treated you.

If your doctor is negligent but you are not injured as a result of it, there is no malpractice. For there to be malpractice, the doctor has to be reckless or negligent, and that recklessness or negligence has to cause your injury.

Research on Humans

Q. Why do we need medical research on humans?

A. The advances in medicine that we today take for granted—dialysis, organ transplantation, the artificial heart, and prescription drug therapies—are only available because someone was the first patient to use the experimental treatment. Without experimentation and research on humans, medical technology could not improve.

At the same time, it's essential that the rights of human subjects to confidentiality and privacy be observed, that their informed consent be obtained before experimentation begins, and that the research protocols are reviewed carefully for scientific merit. Unfortunately, in the past, some of that experimentation was forced on patients who were either unable to say no or did not know that they were being used as research subjects.

It is also very important that financial arrangements be fully disclosed. Most medical institutions and clinics fail to tell you that they are getting paid just for recruiting you into the study. This amount can be substantial—a clinic might receive over $1,000 for recruiting just one participant.

Q. How is medical research regulated?

A. Congress enacted the National Research Act in 1974 to protect the public when taking part in medical research and experiments. The act does not mean that doctors cannot experiment on you. Rather, the National Research Act set up standards for research on humans that must be followed if the researchers want to receive federal funds for their programs. These standards require the following:

- That you give informed consent to take part in experimental treatment. This means that the doctors must tell you about the procedure and the risks, side effects, and benefits associated with it. They must also tell you about any alternative procedures available to you.
- That you volunteer to take part in the research. Your doctor cannot force you or pressure you into being part of an experiment.

Q. What is an Institutional Review Board?

A. The National Research Act required that **institutional review boards (IRBs)** be established at every program conducting research funded by the U.S. Department of Health and Human Services or carried out on products regulated by the Food and Drug Administration. Since the federal government is a major source of research funds, IRBs have been set up at virtually all medical schools, universities, and hospitals where research on humans is conducted.

The IRB reviews the research plans or experiments that are requested and either approves or denies the request. It reviews the plans to make certain that they provide subjects with adequate

---

▶ **PROVING MALPRACTICE**

What you need to prove in a medical malpractice case:

1. There was a doctor-patient relationship.

2. The medical care the doctor provided was not up to the standard of care that other doctors in the same or a similar situation would have provided.

3. You suffered an injury.

4. Your injury was the result of your doctor not giving you appropriate medical care.

opportunity to provide informed consent and do not expose them to unreasonable risks. After the research is approved, the IRB provides continuing oversight to ensure that protections remain in force.

Q. How does an IRB make its decision?

A. It is the job of the IRB to assess the "danger" and merit of the research. The IRB must make seven findings in order to approve a research program:

1. The risk to subjects must be minimized as much as possible.
2. The risk to subjects must be reasonable compared to the benefits.
3. The selection of the subjects must be unbiased.
4. Each potential subject must be given adequate information to determine whether he or she wishes to participate.
5. The informed consent must be documented.
6. The data must be adequately monitored.
7. Subjects' privacy must be protected and their personal data must be kept confidential.

Q. What does "informed consent" mean in this context?

A. While each state may require something a little different, the basic concept of informed consent to research remains the same: You must be given sufficient opportunity to decide whether to be part of the research. When the research is explained to you, the researchers must use language that you understand. If they do not, your consent is not informed because you do not have all the information necessary to make your decision.

Q. How do I give informed consent?

A. Your informed consent to be a research subject most likely will be in written form and include eight parts:

1. An explanation of the research, including how long you would be expected to partici-

pate, a description of the procedures to be done and which of the procedures are experimental.
2. A description of any risks or discomfort you might be expected to experience.
3. A description of any possible benefits to you or to others that may come out of the research. It is important to remember that any benefit of an experimental procedure or drug is highly speculative. The reason why the researcher is conducting the experiment is because the researcher does not know if it is beneficial, and wants to find out. You should be highly suspicious if the described benefit is any more than merely having an additional medical exam or two. Getting "free" medicine is not a benefit—that is what they are studying.
4. An explanation of any other procedures or treatments that are available to you for your particular medical condition.
5. A description of how your privacy will be protected.
6. If the research involves more than minimal risk to you, a description of any medical treatments that are available if you are injured. In this case, the researcher should tell you whether you would be entitled to financial assistance for your injury. The researcher is not required to pay you, only to tell you whether compensation will be available.
7. The names of persons to contact for answers about the research or your rights as a research subject.
8. A statement that your participation is voluntary and that you can withdraw as a research subject at any time.

Q. What about research on children and the elderly?

A. The goal is to allow researchers to study children and the elderly while at the same time protecting them from abuse and mistreatment. Neither a child nor an elderly person suffering from a mental illness such as Alzheimer's has the legal capacity to consent to being part of a research study. So how can researchers study people who cannot consent to being studied?

Researchers must get consent from the parents or guardians of the people they wish to study in order to proceed with the research. When the research is on children, the researcher must also get assent from the children who participate.

Q. What about research on fetuses?

A. One of the biggest controversies in human research is the use of fetuses (either still in the uterus or aborted) and embryos. Research is al-

lowed on fetuses within the uterus as long as the risk is minimized and the mother gives her consent. There has been an additional ethical standard, which is that the research must be of therapeutic benefit to the fetus. This norm has been challenged in recent protocols involving stem cells and fetal ovarian tissues.

Federal regulations and many state laws severely limit the research that may be done on aborted fetuses. For those who oppose abortion, the regulations do not limit the research enough. Others believe that the regulations should allow

---

ⓘ PROBLEMS WITH INFORMED CONSENT

Many persons battling illness wish to get into clinical trial programs, in the hope of benefiting from drugs or procedures not generally available. This predisposes many of them to trust their hopes and not their fears, and so they fail to give careful consideration to whether they really want to accept the risk of the experimental treatment. In addition, a presidential advisory committee reported in 1996 that as many as a third of research studies had problems with informed consent, including consent forms that are overly optimistic about the benefits of research, inadequately explain the impact of the treatment, and are difficult for laypeople to understand.

Some celebrated experiments gone wrong also have raised widespread public concern. For example, eighteen-year-old Jesse Gelsinger died four days after being injected with genes at the University of Pennsylvania in 1999. Gelsinger's father later testified before a Senate subcommittee, saying that they were not told that a monkey had died in a similar experiment and that another patient had serious side effects. The university later announced that its gene therapy institute no longer would perform research on humans, and announced a systemwide review of its policies and procedures regarding research on humans.

The federal government has become more active in monitoring research. Federal investigators greatly increased their number of site visits in the late 1990s. They suspended some programs because of lax safety oversight, including almost all government-funded research involving humans at Duke University Medical Center.

In addition, the inspector general of the Department of Health and Human Services issued several reports analyzing the institutional review board system and making recommendations for improvements.

What does all this mean to you if you're contemplating entering a research program? You are your own best defense—make sure you investigate any possible research study as carefully as you can. Contact an experienced health research lawyer and get some advice—make sure you understand how the information and results will be handled and whether they will be communicated to you. Ask questions until you are sure you fully understand the consent form and your concerns have been addressed.

more testing on aborted fetuses so that others might benefit from the research, which possibly would lead to fewer miscarriages, stillbirths, and severe birth defects. In general, research on aborted fetuses is allowed only when needed to develop important biomedical knowledge that cannot be obtained in any other possible way. In addition, the mother must consent to the research.

Q. Is research allowed on embryos?

A. Couples who undergo fertility treatment and do not want the embryos sometimes donate the embryos for research. Current federal law prohibits research on embryos, as well as the creation of embryos for the sole purpose of research. This type of research brings religious and political controversy, as well as legal controversy.

The issue of conducting research using tissue from embryos or fetuses took on heightened importance in 1998, when two groups of scientists announced that they had successfully isolated and cultured human pluripotent stem cells. Stem cells potentially can be used to

- generate cells and tissues for transplantation and therapy for conditions such as Parkinson's disease, spinal cord injury, stroke, burns, heart disease, diabetes, and arthritis; and
- improve scientists' understanding of the complex events that occur during normal human development, as well as the abnormal events that cause conditions such as birth defects and cancer.

President George Bush entered the debate on stem cells in 2001, when he made an address to the nation on stem cell research. He said:

"As a result of private research, more than sixty genetically diverse stem cell lines already exist. They were created from embryos that have already been destroyed, and they have the ability to regenerate themselves indefinitely, creating ongoing opportunities for research. I have concluded that we should allow federal funds to be used for research on these existing stem cell lines, where the life and death decision has already been made."

President Bush prohibited subsidies for research that involved the creation or destruction of additional embryos. Of course, research on embryonic stem cells continues in private labs in the United States and around the world. (Great Britain, for example, expressly allows stem cell research.) President Bush gave support and committed federal funding to research on umbilical cord, placenta, adult, and animal stem cells, and named a president's council to monitor stem cell research, to recommend appropriate guidelines and regulations, and to consider all of the medical and ethical ramifications of biomedical innovation.

📄 FETUSES AND EMBRYOS

There are a number of medical terms used to describe a fertilized egg as it develops into a fetus in the womb. At the moment of fertilization, it is called a **zygote.** It will divide and redivide repeatedly, at about twenty-hour intervals. It develops into a solid, shapeless mass of cells called a **morula.** Later it becomes a **blastocyst.** Two weeks after fertilization, when it is implanted into the wall of the womb, it is called an **embryo.**

In popular usage, however, which is consistent with the fact that donated embryos exist outside the womb, the term "embryo" is used to refer to any stage of development from zero to eight weeks after fertilization. The term **fetus** generally is used to describe the developing cells from nine weeks after fertilization until birth. "Fetus" is Latin for "offspring" or "young one."

In September 2002, Governor Gray Davis of California signed bill SB 253 into law. It is the first law in the United States that expressly permits stem cell research and allows for both the destruction and the donation of embryos. The law specifies fertility clinics as the only source for embryos to be used in research. Davis simultaneously signed a bill that permanently bans all human cloning in the state for reproductive purposes—that is, any effort to create a cloned individual.

THE WORLD AT YOUR FINGERTIPS

- *The American Medical Association offers the Doctor Finder online. This service provides information on more than 650,000 licensed doctors in the United States. Use this site to get background information on your doctor. The site, www.ama-assn.org/aps/amahg.htm, does not give information on disciplinary actions or malpractice suits.*
- *The American Board of Medical Specialties offers a physician locator and information service at www.certifieddoctor.org. Use this service to find out if your doctor is truly certified within one of the twenty-four specialty areas.*
- *Dr. Timothy McCall explains how to determine whether your doctor is providing you with the correct medical care in Examining Your Doctor: A Patient's Guide to Avoiding Harmful Medical Care (Secaucus, N.J.: Birch Lane Press, 1995).*
- *Harmful Intent, by Baine Kerr (New York: Scribner, 1999), is a legal thriller centered on a medical malpractice lawsuit. This is a fictional account, but the concepts are sound and the average reader may find it more interesting than many nonfiction books.*
- *Author Eileen Welsome won a Pulitzer Prize in 1994 for reporting on research*

undertaken in the 1940s, in which the U.S. government subjected unsuspecting men, women, and children to radiation, then secretly studied them to learn the long-term effects of radiation poisoning. The Plutonium Files (New York: Dial Press, 1999) expands on her articles.
- *Children of the Flames: Dr. Josef Mengele and the Untold Story of the Twins of Auschwitz, compiled by Lucette Matalon Lagnado and Sheila Cohn Dekel (New York: Penguin, 1992), is a chilling account of Auschwitz's "Angel of Death," who experimented on thousands of twins, told by the few survivors of Mengele's experiments.*

REMEMBER THIS

- *Every state requires that doctors, nurses, hospitals, and laboratories be licensed.*
- *A license ensures that your doctor, nurse, hospital, or laboratory meets the minimum standards for providing medical care.*
- *Just because your doctor made a mistake or you had a bad result from medical treatment does not mean that your doctor committed malpractice.*
- *Subjects of human research must be volunteers.*
- *You must be informed of the type of research being done and agree to be a part of it.*
- *You have the right to withdraw from the research at any time.*

SPECIFIC ISSUES IN HEALTH CARE

Jackie is fifteen years old and unmarried. She wants to marry someday and have a family— but not now. Jackie just found out she is three weeks pregnant. She is considering having an abortion. Does she have to tell her parents?

Does she need their permission for an abortion? What about her boyfriend? Can he stop her from having the abortion?

Karl is fifty-four years old, and suffers from advanced terminal colon cancer. Every day he watches as the strain of his disease takes its emotional and physical toll on his wife and children. Then there is the financial strain. He worries that with the mounting medical bills, there will be nothing left for his family after he is gone. Karl wants to control the end of his life. Karl asks his doctor to prescribe barbiturates so that he can decide when and where to die. Karl's doctor does not want to give him the medication. Does Karl have a right to die by having his doctor help him to commit suicide?

This section looks at some specific health-care issues including assisted reproductive technologies, abortion, organ donation, and euthanasia.

Assisted Reproductive Technologies

Q. What are assisted reproductive technologies?

A. Baby making used to involve some nontechnical procedures—would-be mothers and fathers having intercourse. Now a person who has a medical condition that impairs his or her ability to have a baby can use assisted reproductive technologies, a term which includes in vitro fertilization, gamete intrafallopian transfer (GIFT) and other technologies, to conceive children.

Q. When does the law come into play?

A. When the intended parents use their own **gametes** (egg and sperm) with assisted reproductive technology, the couple needs to make decisions about the creation, storage, use, and disposition of their embryos, and sign legal documents to that effect. However, the process is relatively clear of legal worries on the issue of the identity of the parents of the baby.

Courts generally have placed more weight on the intent of the parents to create a child, and on whether there is a genetic connection to the child. Courts consistently have held that a party should not be forced to be a genetic parent against his or her will. The bounds of the agreements among the parties who accept or relinquish their parenting responsibilities are appropriately left to legislatures, which have taken a range of approaches, from banning agreements to providing a legal framework for both the parties and judges to use in setting appropriate expectations for the arrangements.

Q. Does my insurance cover infertility treatments?

A. Few insurance plans directly cover treatment for infertility, although some policies are starting to cover IVF as the cost decreases and the success rates increase. Policies may also cover treatment for illnesses (such as endometriosis) that contribute to infertility. Some policies will cover infertility treatment if the couple has been trying to conceive for a year or more. Consumers are fighting to get more coverage for infertility treatment. Some states now mandate that insurance companies include infertility treatment in their plans.

Q. Who owns the embryos produced in the process of in vitro fertilization?

A. In Virginia, a couple asked their fertility clinic to give them their frozen embryos so that they could try a different doctor and clinic. The clinic refused. The couple sued the clinic and won. The court found the couple did have a quasi-property interest in their embryos. Not all courts are comfortable with declaring embryos as "property." Nevertheless, you have a good chance of getting your embryos when third parties try to interfere. Courts tend to provide parents with some form of property rights to their embryos, such as the rights to possess, use, or donate. Things become much more difficult when the fight is between you and your spouse.

Q. What happens to the eggs, sperm, or embryos you don't use?

A. Whether you succeed in having all the babies you desire or decide to stop fertility treatments, there sometimes will be embryos or sperm left over. (There may be eggs, too, though it is still experimental to freeze eggs.) You can keep this genetic material frozen for possible future use by you, donate to another person or couple for their use in creating a child, donate it for research, or have it destroyed. Regardless of your decision, the clinic should ask you—before you start treatments—what you want to do with your genetic material. This is an important step. Unless you decide what you want done with it, the clinic will be unsure how to treat this material. You must have your decision in writing. Avoid relying on the clinic's informed consent documents regarding how you want your tissue treated. Create a separate document.

A problem arises when a couple divorces and cannot agree on what to do with the remaining embryos. This kind of dispute raises complex emotional, legal, and ethical issues.

If there is no agreement, the court will have to balance the interests of the people fighting for control. A New York couple had five frozen embryos remaining when they divorced. The wife asked for sole control of the embryos. The husband wanted to donate the embryos to the clinic. When they began their fertility treatments, the couple had signed an agreement stating that they would donate the embryos to the clinic. The court ruled in 1998 that the agreement was valid and the embryos were to be donated.

Q. My first wife and I divorced, and I received control of the embryos in the settlement. My second wife and I want to use the embryos to have children. Can my ex-wife stop us?

A. Yes. Even when a husband and wife sign a clear agreement giving one partner control of the embryos, courts are reluctant to enforce the agreement because it forces one person to become a legal parent against his or her will. Therefore, as a matter of public policy, a court most likely would allow your ex-wife to step in and prevent you from using the embryos with your second wife because your first wife would be the child's or children's genetic mother.

Q. What is surrogacy?

A. In **traditional surrogacy,** a woman (the surrogate) undergoes intrauterine insemination with sperm from the man who wants to be the legal father. The baby has genetic material from the father and the surrogate. Once the baby is born, the father's wife may have to adopt it through stepparent adoption in states that don't have laws setting forth the rights of the intended parents. Because the surrogate has both a genetic and a

---

🗎 FERTILITY TECHNIQUES

In vitro fertilization (IVF): The woman usually is given medication to make her body produce more eggs during ovulation. A woman's egg is removed from her body and placed into a dish with culture medium with a man's sperm. If the sperm fertilizes the egg, an embryo results. An embryo or several embryos are then placed into the woman's uterus or frozen for later use. If the embryo attaches to the woman's uterus, pregnancy results. Transferring multiple embryos can result in multiple births.

Artificial insemination (often referred to as intrauterine insemination, or IUI, in the medical lexicon): Using a very thin catheter, sperm is placed in the woman's cervix or uterine cavity at the time mature eggs are released. The hope is that the sperm will fertilize at least one of the woman's eggs. Artificial insemination is a technology that is decades old, and still is used today.

gestational connection to the baby, like a traditional birth mother, her parental rights are protected under law.

In a **gestational carrier surrogacy,** an embryo is transferred to the woman who agrees to gestate the baby, the gestational carrier. The baby has no genetic material from the carrier. Here is where it gets confusing: The gametes can come from either of the intended parents (or both), or from an egg donor or a sperm donor, or both. It is important to create parenting presumptions in law so that the intended parents are the legal parents. Courts consistently have held that in gestational carrier arrangements the intended parents are the legal parents.

Q. Is surrogacy legal?

A. Whether a surrogacy agreement will stand up in court depends on the state in which you live. Both legislatures and courts are suspicious of any contract that involves the payment of fees in exchange for a baby. Some states will uphold the arrangement if there is a contract clearly outlining the responsibilities of the parties. Some states require the intended father's wife to adopt the baby as though she were the baby's stepparent.

Some states refuse to recognize any type of contract that transfers parenthood from a surrogate to the couple who contracted with her; others won't recognize contracts where the surrogate is paid.

Q. Can children be "conceived" after a parent dies?

A. Through the use of assisted reproductive technology, children can be born months—even years—after one or both of the parents die. If a couple freezes its embryos, the wife can have the embryos transferred after her husband's death. If both parents die, the person who "inherits" the embryos could have them transferred to a carrier, thus creating a child whose parents are deceased.

Q. Can children conceived after the death of a parent receive Social Security benefits?

A. Under the Social Security Act, survivor's benefits are disbursed in order to support children who were dependent on the wage earner at the time of his or her death. Children conceived after the parent's death are not dependent on the wage earner at the time of death. Whether those chil-

---

ⓘ DONOR SPERM AND PATERNITY RIGHTS

When **artificial insemination** is performed using anonymously donated sperm, the woman's husband is considered the legal father as long as

- he consented to the procedure in writing, and
- a doctor or other medical professional supervised the insemination.

On the other hand, if no doctor is involved, a donor may be granted paternity rights. Only forty-two states have laws regarding artificial insemination, and only thirty-five of those clarify parental rights in cases of artificial insemination. In California, a known donor donated his sperm to a lesbian couple. One of the women was inseminated with the man's sperm at home. There was no assistance from medical professionals, and the man was not present when the woman was inseminated. Later, the man decided he wanted paternity rights, including visitation. Because no medical professional was involved in the actual insemination of the mother, and because the donor was known, the father was granted paternity rights.

dren still should collect benefits is a question that is being struggled with right now. The act is broadly interpreted by the courts so as to grant benefits to qualified applicants whenever possible. Some commentators predict that as Social Security funds begin to dwindle, courts will become more conservative in deciding who qualifies for those benefits. For now, these children usually receive benefits.

Q. Do inheritance laws apply to children conceived after the death of a parent?

A. State inheritance laws generally require a child to be born within three hundred days of the person's death (in practical terms, this means conceived before the parent died) in order for the child to inherit from his or her parent's estate. This is because at the time these laws were written, the technology did not exist for a child to be conceived after one parent died. These laws permit the state to distribute the estate among the heirs without wondering who might come along down the road. It also protects the courts from having to investigate suspicious claims from people claiming to be heirs conceived after the parent died.

The state has to balance those concerns with the goal of keeping children off public assistance when they could be taken care of through the deceased parent's estate. It also does not want to punish children for the way in which they were conceived.

If you have stored gametes or embryos, then you (and the co-progenitor, if an embryo is stored) should have a specific provision in your will stating your intention regarding the disposition of your gametes or embryos and whether you intend for them to be your child under your estate.

Abortion

Q. How did abortion become legal?

A. Until the early 1970s, about two-thirds of the states banned abortion except when it was necessary to save a mother's life. The other states had similar laws, but allowed for a few other instances when women could seek an abortion, such as when the pregnancy was the result of incest or rape.

In 1973, in the landmark case of *Roe v. Wade*, the U.S. Supreme Court decided that women have a fundamental right to have an abortion. In that case, a single pregnant woman (who appeared under the pseudonym "Jane Roe") brought a lawsuit against the state of Texas. A Texas law made abortion illegal except in situations where the mother's life was at stake. The Court decided that the Constitution guarantees you a right to privacy from state interference, which includes whether you decide to have an abortion. The decision remains highly controversial to this day.

Before abortion became legal, an estimated 1.2 million women sought illegal abortions each year. Unlicensed persons who were not doctors performed many of these abortions. The conditions were often unsanitary and women were at high risk of infection, hemorrhage, disfiguration, and death. Whiskey sometimes was used as an anesthetic.

At the same time, the fact that such laws were in place no doubt limited the number of abortions performed.

ⓘ CARRIER AGREEMENTS

The most common terms (which continue to evolve) in a surrogacy agreement are

- that the intended parents want to be included in prenatal doctor visits;

- that the intended parents will be present in the delivery room;

- that the carrier will refrain from behaviors that are harmful to the fetus; and

- that the parties share medical information with each other.

In the words of the majority opinion of the Supreme Court in a case decided in 2000, "Millions of Americans believe that life begins at conception and consequently that an abortion is akin to causing the death of an innocent child; they recoil at the thought of a law that would permit it. Other millions fear that a law that forbids abortion could condemn many American women to lives that lack dignity, depriving them of equal liberty and leading those with least resources to undergo illegal abortions with the attendant risks of death and suffering. [These are] virtually irreconcilable points of view. . . . "

Q. Are there any limits on the right to an abortion?

A. The Court has put some limits on the right to an abortion. There is no absolute right to have an abortion at any time, in any place. A state can pass laws regulating abortion as long as certain boundaries are not crossed. The state cannot completely override a woman's right to terminate a pregnancy, but the state does have an interest in protecting the health of pregnant women and the potentiality of human life. A man's right to prevent an abortion—or to force his partner to have an abortion—is not protected because the pregnancy is not considered part of a man's "bodily integrity."

Until the end of the first trimester, only the pregnant woman and her doctor can decide whether a pregnancy should be terminated.

After the first trimester, the state can pass laws regulating abortion as long as the laws are reasonably related to the pregnant mother's health. Once the fetus becomes **viable,** meaning that it can live outside the womb, the state can regulate—and even outlaw—abortion unless it is necessary to save the mother's life. There is no definite point, however, when a fetus becomes viable.

The legal standard for abortion is largely the same today as it was in 1973, with one major difference. Today, a court will look at a state law to see if it places an **undue burden** on a woman's right to have an abortion. If it does not place an undue burden on her access to an abortion, then the law is upheld. Again, after a fetus becomes viable, the state can pass laws making it more difficult for a woman to obtain an abortion.

Q. What are partial-birth abortions?

A. The biggest debate today is over so-called **partial-birth abortions.** State laws usually de-

---

ⓘ WAITING PERIODS

Twelve states currently require a waiting period, usually twenty-four hours, before a woman can have an abortion. This waiting period requires women to make two visits to the clinic where the abortion will be performed. At the first visit, the woman will talk to the doctor or other medical professional about her choice to terminate the pregnancy. The doctor may be required to give specific information to the woman, the effect of which may be to discourage her from having the abortion. The woman then has to wait twenty-four hours before having the abortion, in order to think about whether she wants to terminate her pregnancy.

Such laws have been upheld as constitutional, although opponents of the waiting period argue that the woman already has had time to think over her decision between the time she finds out she is pregnant and the time she schedules the abortion. Because the waiting period requires two visits to the clinic, some argue that it can be difficult and even traumatic for women considering abortion, especially if there are antiabortion protesters outside the clinic.

fine a partial-birth abortion as any abortion in which the doctor "partially vaginally delivers a living fetus before killing the fetus and completing the delivery." These bans generally apply to non-viable as well as viable fetuses.

In almost every state that has passed a law banning partial-birth abortions, courts have found the laws to be unconstitutional. These laws often impose an undue burden on a woman's right to terminate a pregnancy and place the health of women in danger. Most fail to include adequate exceptions for abortions when the woman's life or health require terminating the pregnancy.

Bills have been introduced repeatedly in Congress to make partial-birth abortions illegal on a national level. At the time of this writing, none of the laws has passed.

Q. Can minors have abortions without their parents' consent?

ⓘ **THE ARGUMENT ON PARENTAL CONSENT**

Those in favor of parental consent laws say young women need the support of their families when making such significant decisions about abortions. Many believe that parental consent laws promote abstinence, arguing that if girls knew they couldn't have abortions without telling their parents, then they would not be so willing to have sex and risk pregnancy.

Those against parental consent laws point out that such laws may exacerbate already difficult situations in certain families, may increase the risk of harm to the adolescent by delaying access to appropriate medical care, may result in a later-term abortion, and may even increase instances of abuse against the women involved.

A. The rights of parents to raise their children as they see fit collides with a woman's right to privacy and abortion when she is under the age of eighteen. When it comes to women under eighteen years of age seeking abortions, state laws fall into three groups:

- Girls do not have to get permission or notify their parents of the abortion.
- Girls do not have to get their parents' permission, but they do have to notify their parents that they are planning on having an abortion.
- Girls have to get their parents' permission to have an abortion.

Q. What is a judicial bypass option?

A. All parental consent laws are required to be very limited in their range, and they must include what is called a **judicial bypass option.** A judicial bypass option allows a woman under eighteen to go to court for a judicial hearing when her parents refuse to consent to an abortion. This option allows minor women to request that a judge waive parental consent requirements, particularly when the minor is mature or when the judge finds that an abortion would be in the best interests of the minor.

This can be a traumatic experience for young women. Courtrooms are intimidating even to adults, much less minors. Hearings are scheduled during school hours. The woman must discuss her most personal concerns with the judge, a total stranger.

Organ Donation

Q. Who can be an organ donor?

A. Almost anyone may be an organ donor, depending on his or her medical condition and the circumstances surrounding his or her death. You need to be at least eighteen years old (with a few exceptions), but there is no maximum age. Some donors are over age seventy.

Q. What can be donated?

A. You can donate your entire body for anatomical study, or you can specify organs and tissues.

The most needed organs are kidneys, hearts, livers, lungs, and pancreases. Tissue donations include eyes, skin, heart valves, bone, and bone marrow. You can donate bone marrow and a kidney while you are still living.

Q. Can I sell an organ?

A. No. The National Organ Transplant Act (NOTA), a federal law, makes it illegal to buy or sell organs for profit. You can be sentenced to five years in prison or a $50,000 fine, or both. It is also illegal under the law of most states to sell organs for profit. If you donate your organs, though, you can be reimbursed for some of the costs involved. For example, if you donate one of your kidneys, it is most likely legal for you to accept payment for your lost wages and medical expenses. Pennsylvania offers a few hundred dollars to the families of deceased organ donors to cover funeral expenses. The amount of these payments must be reasonable. Anything outlandish would be considered profit, which is not legal.

Q. May a living child or a mentally incompetent person be an organ donor?

A. Sometimes, but only if there is some benefit to the child or the incompetent person. Legally, a child or mentally incompetent person is not able to consent to being an organ donor. The fear is that people needing organs will prey upon vulnerable people. There are rare situations when the guardians of children or incompetent persons will be allowed to let them be organ donors.

📄 ORGAN DONATION

Organ donation is known in legal circles as an **anatomical gift,** which includes organs, tissue, and even bones. For the purpose of this chapter, though, we will use the word "organ" as a general term to describe any part of the anatomy that can be donated.

Q. Should I be an organ donor?

A. Your decision on whether to become an organ donor will not be based on legal concepts, but on your culture, religion, and values. The law does affect how your family or doctors carry out your decision. Nearly all of the world's major religions consider organ donation a gift of life to others. You may wish to ask your spiritual adviser whether your religion endorses organ donation.

Survey after survey shows that the vast majority of Americans are in favor of organ donation. Yet very few of us donate our organs. It is a very personal decision, but consider this: At this time, there are more than sixty thousand people on the waiting list for organs with the **United Network for Organ Sharing** (**UNOS**), which is the national organ waiting registry. About one-third of the people that need lifesaving organs such as hearts or livers will die before an available organ is found. Now consider the possibility that one day you—or your spouse or child—could be on that list.

One concern for donors is whether donating their organs will affect how their bodies will appear at open-casket funerals. Removal of organs is a surgical procedure and rarely will interfere with funeral or burial arrangements. The law requires that hospitals and doctors treat the body with the utmost care when removing organs and tissue.

Q. Why did the hospital ask me if I was an organ donor when I was admitted for a minor procedure?

A. Federal law requires hospitals that participate in Medicare to ask you, when admitted, whether you are an organ donor. If you say yes, the hospital

---

ⓘ HOW IT WORKS

Once the organs are removed, the body is returned to the family so that funeral or burial arrangements may be made.

is required to get a copy of your donor card, driver's license, or advance directive indicating that you wish to donate your organs. If you say no, the hospital is required to tell you about your options for deciding whether to become an organ donor.

If you are near death and the hospital has no record of your decision to be an organ donor, the hospital is required to ask your next of kin to donate your organs. The purpose of these laws is to find out and document your wishes, as well as increase the number of organs available for transplantation. Your doctor will make every effort to save your life even if you are an organ donor.

Q. When are you dead?

A. Sounds like a silly question, doesn't it? Medical technology is advancing at breakneck speed, and "death" is being redefined. Death used to occur when your heart stopped beating. Then artificial life support was developed for people with severe brain injuries. Suddenly there was a new form of death—brain death. Doctors and hospitals were afraid to stop treatment on a brain-dead person because that person's heart was still beating with the help of artificial life support.

In a brain-dead patient, brain function has stopped, including that which controls breathing and heart activity. All circulatory and respiratory functions are maintained by artificial life support. In essence, being brain dead is the same as being "dead."

In 1980, death received a new definition. You are dead either when your circulatory and respiratory functions stop for good, or when your entire brain, including the brain stem, irreversibly stops functioning. Most states legally define death in this way. If you are an organ donor, circulatory and respiratory functions will be kept going by artificial life support if you are brain dead to preserve your organs until they can be harvested for transplantation.

Q. What is non-heart-beating donation?

A. **Non-heart-beating donation** (**NHBD**) comprises about 2 percent of all organ donations, but is expected to increase in the future. It occurs when the patient is not brain dead, but is on a ventilator and is in a vegetative state or considered "hopeless," and the family consents to having the ventilator withdrawn. When the ventilator is removed, doctors wait for the patient's heart and breathing to stop, declare cardiac death either immediately or after a waiting period of a few minutes, and then harvest the organs in an operating room.

If, as sometimes happens, the potential NHBD patient does not stop breathing when the ventilator is removed and continues to have a heartbeat, doctors usually wait an hour before canceling the harvest. Since the decision to withdraw treatment already has been made, if the patient continues breathing, he or she is returned to the hospital room to die without treatment being resumed.

There are serious ethical concerns about NHBD. Although supporters of NHBD insist that the withdrawal of ventilators is legally and ethically allowable because such patients are hopeless, these decisions are sometimes made because of potential quality-of-life concerns rather than the patient's ability to survive. Critics claim that the pressure to find and harvest suitable organs is robbing some severely injured peo-

---

ⓘ DONATING YOUR ORGANS

Every state has some form of a law called the Uniform Anatomical Gift Act (UAGA). This law allows you, if you are at least eighteen years old and of sound mind, to

- donate all or part of your body at your death;

- designate that you are donating your organs for transplantation into someone else or for medical research; and

- name a hospital, a doctor, a person, or an educational institution as the donee.

ple of a chance to recover. Issues arising in the assisted suicide debate are also relevant here, with disability advocates concerned that the increase in NHBD will place growing pressure on disabled people who are dependent on life support to "pull the plug" to enable them to donate organs.

Q. How can I be sure that my organs will, or will not, be donated?

A. It is not a good idea to include your wishes regarding organ donation in your will. Doctors will need to remove your organs or tissue under very specific and delicate timelines and procedures. By the time your will is read, the opportunity to donate your organs will have passed. Instead, include your wishes regarding donation of organs in your advance directive on health care and tell your family what you want them to do in that situation.

In most states, your doctor requires your family's consent, regardless of your wishes or whether you filled out an organ donor card. Even if you include your donation in your will and advance directive, it is customary for doctors to ask your family to agree to the donation. In some states, hospitals are required by law to abide by the deceased person's wishes regardless of the family's consent. In practice, though, hospitals and doctors are reluctant to go against the wishes of the family members in order to avoid malpractice lawsuits.

Q. What happens if I don't make a decision about organ donation?

A. If you did not indicate whether you want your organs donated, then your family will make that decision for you when you die. Your family will decide whether to donate all or part of your body. Usually, your doctor will seek a decision from your spouse first. If you do not have a spouse, the doctor will turn to your adult son or daughter. If you do not have children, the doctor will get a decision from your parent, your adult brother or sister, a grandparent, or your guardian.

Q. What should I do if I change my mind about being, or not being, an organ donor?

A. You can change your decision at any time. To revoke your decision to be an organ donor, write a statement to that effect and put it with your driver's license and your advance directive. You can also revoke your decision orally, but this is not as surefire as a written statement. In either case, tell your family and loved ones about your decision so that there is no confusion about your wishes.

Q. Who gets my organs?

A. In 1984, Congress enacted the National Organ Transplant Act (NOTA). As part of NOTA, **organ procurement organizations (OPOs)** were established. These organizations are divided into separate service areas. When you die, they coordinate the procurement of your organs with the transplantation process. This includes keeping a list of possible recipients and training hospital staff in getting the family's consent.

There is no cost to the organ donor for donating organs. The OPO assumes all the expenses associated with organ recovery. This does not include funeral and burial expenses, which are still the responsibility of the donor's family.

When your doctor declares you dead and your family consents to organ donation, the OPO staff is called into the hospital to organize the process. OPO makes the arrangements to harvest

---

ⓘ WITNESSES ARE USUALLY NOT NECESSARY

At one time, the law required that an organ donor card be signed in the presence of two witnesses. Today, the law does not require you to have witnesses, unless you do not intend to put your wishes in writing. In that case, if you want to be an organ donor, make your wishes clear in front of at least two people.

your organs. This involves removing your organs surgically, testing your tissue to check for disease and to determine its type, comparing your gift to the list of potential recipients, and transporting your organs to the transplant center.

Q. Who chooses the recipients?

A. The United Network for Organ Sharing (UNOS) keeps a national computer list of patients waiting for transplants. This list is used to match your organs with patients who might receive them through a transplant. Information about you, such as your blood type, is entered into the computer-match program. Possible recipients are listed according to the time they have been on the waiting list, their age, and their degree of compatibility with the characteristics of the donor's organs. Organs are offered to local patients first. If there is no patient locally that is a good match for the organ, the organ will be offered on a regional or a national level. When transplants first became an option, committees would receive personal information about patients such as their race, income, gender, family status, and job before making a decision. The UNOS computer-match program makes every effort to select patients regardless of their race, gender, religion, or other personal information.

Assisted Suicide

Q. Is it legal to commit suicide?

A. It is not against the law to commit, or to attempt to commit, suicide. The rationale is that suicide is usually prompted by a mental illness and people should not be criminally punished for being mentally disabled.

Q. Is it against the law to help someone else commit suicide?

A. It is against the law in most states to aid or assist someone else in committing suicide. For instance, in Illinois and Ohio, it is considered homicide to help someone else commit suicide. This is where **physician-assisted suicide** comes

in. Physician-assisted suicide is legal in only one state—Oregon. In 1997, Oregon enacted the Death with Dignity Act. This law allows—but does not require—doctors to prescribe medication to competent, terminally ill patients, knowing that the medication is going to be used by the patient to end his life. The law is highly controversial.

During Oregon's first year of legalized assisted suicide, a study of all the patients who choose physician-assisted suicide showed that they based their decisions to commit suicide on the loss of autonomy and control of bodily functions. They were less concerned with the fear of uncontrollable pain or putting a financial burden on their families. This may be in part due to the progress medicine has made in dealing with pain.

Q. Is there a constitutional right to physician-assisted suicide?

A. In 1997, three terminally ill patients, four doctors, and a nonprofit group that counsels patients considering physician-assisted suicide filed

---

📑 EUTHANASIA VERSUS ASSISTED SUICIDE

Euthanasia (Greek for "easy death") is the act of putting to death painlessly a person suffering from an incurable and painful disease or injury. It is sometimes called **mercy killing. Suicide** is the taking of one's own life.

Physician-assisted suicide is different from euthanasia. In a physician-assisted suicide, patients ask a doctor to prescribe a lethal substance and patients administer it by themselves. In euthanasia, the doctor administers the lethal substance to the patient. Physician-assisted suicide is currently legal in only one state—Oregon; euthanasia is illegal in all states.

suit in federal court, claiming that Washington State's ban on physician-assisted suicide is unconstitutional. They asserted that the "right" to receive assistance in committing suicide is a liberty protected by the Due Process Clause of the Fourteenth Amendment. They prevailed at the district court and appellate court levels, but ultimately lost in the U.S. Supreme Court.

The Court stated that Washington's ban on physician-assisted suicide did not infringe on a fundamental liberty under the Due Process Clause. Rather, an examination of American history, legal practices, and legal traditions shows that there are no exceptions to the assisted-suicide ban for those near death. To find such a right in the Fourteenth Amendment, the Court would have had to overturn centuries of legal practice and doctrine and go against the public policy of nearly every state in the country. Rather, the Court held, the ban was rationally related to legitimate government interests, such as prohibiting intentional killing and preserving human life, protecting the medical profession's integrity and ethics and maintaining physicians' role as their patients' healers, and preventing harm to those people who are the most vulnerable, including the poor, the elderly, disabled people, and the terminally ill.

In a companion case decided the same day, the Court also held that New York State's ban on assisted suicide did not violate the Equal Protection Clause of the Fourteenth Amendment. Physicians and gravely ill patients filed suit, claiming that New York violated the equal protection of the laws by permitting patients to hasten their deaths by refusing life support systems, but not permitting them to hasten their deaths by self-administered prescribed drugs. An appellate court agreed with them, but the Supreme Court held that the distinction between letting a patient die and making a patient die is important, logical, rational, and well established: "[T]he two acts are different, and New York may, therefore, consistent with the Constitution, treat them differently."

The Court's rulings leave states free to decide to enact laws allowing physicians to assist patients who wish to end their lives. The Court's rulings simply mean that the states are not required by the Constitution to do so.

THE WORLD AT YOUR FINGERTIPS

- *The Fertile Thoughts website contains helpful information about infertility, assisted reproductive technology, and adoption. It also has links to other useful sites. Visit www.fertilethoughts.com.*

- *The American Society for Reproductive Medicine is a nonprofit group that studies infertility issues. Here you can research state insurance laws to find out what level of coverage is required for infertility treatments and obtain patient education booklets. Visit www.asrm.org.*

- *The website for the Center for Advanced Reproductive Care (CARC), University of Iowa Hospitals and Clinics (UIHC), www.uihc.uiowa.edu/pubinfo/arc.htm, will tell you everything you ever wanted to know—and a few things you didn't—about the different forms of assisted reproductive technology available.*

- *To find out about the state laws regarding surrogacy, access www.surro.net/toc/articles.htm or www.surrogacy.com/legals/states.html.*

- **The Ethics of Abortion: Pro-Life Vs. Pro-Choice (Contemporary Issues),** *edited by Robert M. Baird and Stuart E. Rosenbaum (Amherst, N.Y.: Prometheus Books, 1993), offers essays from both sides of the debate, as well as excerpts from three Supreme Court decisions regarding abortion.*

- **The American Civil Liberties Union's** *website offers a comprehensive look at women's rights to reproductive choices.*

The ACLU's website address is www. aclu.org/issues/reproduct/hmrr.html.

- *I'm Glad You're Not Dead: A Liver Transplant Story (Galveston, Tex.: Journey Publishing, 1996) is Elizabeth Parr's account of her struggle with liver disease and the process she went through while waiting for a transplant. Parr, a former nun and*

teacher, puts the stressful process of organ transplantation into comforting perspective.

- *The Ethics of Organ Transplants: The Current Debate, edited by Arthur L. Kaplan and Daniel H. Coelho (Amherst, N.Y.: Prometheus Books, 1999) is a series of essays on the ethical, legal, political, and religious issues surrounding organ trans-*

ⓘ A DEBATE

The Argument in Favor of Physician-Assisted Suicide

Many patients are demanding more say in their treatment, including their care at the end of their lives. They want to make their own decisions about their progress. They want to keep their dignity. They are worried that doctors will "play God" and keep their bodies alive long past the time when they or their families wish to let them die. No one wants to be a living corpse, and people around the country are calling for more freedom in their medical choice.

People in favor of making physician-assisted suicide legal propose several ways of ensuring that physician-assisted suicide is not abused. One suggestion is that the patient must be suffering from severe pain or indignity and that the patient repeatedly requests assistance in committing suicide. Another proposal is to require the doctor to consult with another doctor about whether assisted suicide would be appropriate in that situation. There are also proposed requirements that the doctor must be convinced that the patient is seeking assisted suicide without any coercion or incentive from others, that the patient must be able to understand what he or she is requesting, and that all other alternatives, including palliative care and hospice, must be explored.

The Argument Against Physician-Assisted Suicide

If physician-assisted suicide becomes the norm for those with certain types of illnesses, such as cancer, a misdiagnosis could lead a person to kill him- or herself before finding out that the test results were incorrect or that his or her particular type of cancer is highly treatable.

Then there is the problem of knowing if you want to take your own life to avoid pain and suffering, or if your children and/or spouse are pressuring you to kill yourself so that you will not be a financial or emotional burden to your family. There is also the concern that severely disabled people might be more likely to seek physician-assisted suicide than other groups of patients. There is some fear that the legalization of assisted suicide would be the same as telling the disabled that their lives have no value. Some people fear that if we let the terminally ill kill themselves, somehow this will be expanded to euthanasia, the involuntary killing of the uneducated, the unemployed, and any other group considered undesirable by society. In fact, surveys show that many people, especially those belonging to minority groups, worry that they will be denied care and left to die against their wishes if physician-assisted suicide becomes an accepted practice.

These are some of the questions and arguments that must be addressed before physician-assisted suicide is made legal throughout the country.

plantation. Topics include the use of animal organs in humans and ways to increase the number of organs available for transplantation.

- In Euthanasia and Physician-Assisted Suicide: Killing or Caring? *(Mahwah, N.J.: Paulist Press, 1998)*, author Michael Manning provides historical background and the framework that surrounds the controversy over euthanasia and physician-assisted suicide.

- To follow legal developments regarding assisted suicide, visit the website for the Choices in Dying organization at www.choices.org.

- To find out more about organ donations, search on that phrase in your favorite search engine. Among the many good resources are a federal government site (www.organdonor.gov) and several sites maintained by private organizations (www.transweb.org and www.shareyourlife.org).

REMEMBER THIS

- *You have the right to control how your gametes or embryos are used.*

- *Before beginning infertility treatments, make sure you have a written agreement with the clinic as to how your eggs, sperm, or embryos will be taken care of once you end your treatments.*

- *States can pass laws regarding abortion as long as the laws do not place an undue burden on a woman's right to have an abortion.*

- *Husbands do not have the right to stop their wives from having abortions.*

- *To be an organ donor, you must be at least eighteen years old and of sound mind.*

- *Removal of organs is a surgical procedure and rarely will interfere with funeral or burial arrangements.*

- *Your doctor or hospital will ask your next of kin to give their permission to take your organs, even if you sign an organ donor card or name organ donation in your advance directive. If your next of kin refuses, the hospital probably will not remove your organs.*

- *Do not put your organ donation only in your will. A better plan is to put it in your advance directive and discuss your wishes with your family and doctor. By the time your will is located, it will be too late to donate your organs.*

- *It is not illegal to commit suicide.*

- *It is illegal in every state but Oregon for a doctor to assist a patient in committing suicide.*

- *States are free to enact laws allowing or prohibiting physician-assisted suicide*

Estate Planning

Estate planning is planning for death. We're all a little squeamish about death, especially when we're the ones involved. This discomfort can lead to the procrastination that might account for the fact that only about two out of every five Americans have a will.

The fact that most Americans don't have a will is ironic. We spend our lives working hard to earn enough money and property to make the lives of our children and spouses and other loved ones happier, wealthier, and more secure than our own. And yet most of us fail to plan our estates—the one thing that's essential to make sure that those we care about receive the fruits of our labor.

This chapter answers, in nonlegal terms, commonly asked questions about estate planning. Keep in mind that the rules governing estate planning, wills, probate, and trusts are determined by state law, which means that some of the principles discussed in this chapter may not apply in your state. Similarly, the costs of estate planning vary, depending on such factors as where you live, the nature of your estate, and your particular needs. As you begin the process of estate planning, you should consult one or more lawyers with experience in this area of the law. After a consultation, they can give you a good idea of the cost of ensuring that your estate is in order for today and tomorrow.

ESTATE-PLANNING BASICS

Adrian and Susan have two young children and parents in their seventies. They each wrote a will right after they got married, but did not update them when the kids were born or after they bought a house in Vermont. They are in good health and have simply been too busy to pay attention to their estate. How urgent is writing or updating a will?

This section covers the basics of estate planning, including the value of writing a will and the logistics of getting started to plan an estate.

Q. Why should I go to the trouble of planning my estate and writing a will?

A. Estate planning pays real dividends—in results achieved, in dollars saved, and, most important, in security and peace of mind. And it doesn't have to be expensive, traumatic, or even especially time consuming.

An **estate plan** is your blueprint for where you want your property to go after you die. Estate planning lets you do the following:

- Determine what happens to your property—who, what, when, and how. It enables you to coordinate gifts in your lifetime with bequests in your will or trust. You can apportion property among your family members, your friends, and charities that are important to you. If you don't have a will or a trust, state law will step in and determine how to dispose of your property, in ways that you might not intend.
- Determine who will be in charge of carrying out your wishes—your executor if you have a will, and your trustee if you have a trust.
- Save money on probate, taxes, and other expenses of settling an estate.
- Be in control of your own life. A living trust can provide a way to manage your property should you become disabled. A living will or a health-care advance directive can set up a

plan for your medical care, should you no longer be able to make decisions for yourself.

- Coordinate estate planning with other kinds of financial planning. For example, the new tax law has made significant changes in incentives to save for education, making this an ideal time to look into planning for the education of children and grandchildren, as well as other financial issues.
- Decide whether your business will be sold or stay in the family—and if it stays in the family, who will run it.

Q. Isn't a will all I need?

A. Not necessarily. While a will is usually the most important part of an estate plan, it's not the only part. These days, it's common for a person to have up to a dozen **will substitutes**—that is, various ways of distributing property regardless of whether the person has a formal will. Pensions, life insurance, gifts, joint ownership, and trusts are but a few of the ways you can transfer property at or before death quickly and inexpensively.

Q. How can an estate plan make things easier on my family after I die?

A. You want your beneficiaries to receive promptly the property you've left them as part of your estate plan. Options include

- gifts made before you die;

ⓘ **WHAT IS AN ESTATE?**

Your estate consists of all your property, including

- your home and other real estate,
- **tangible personal property** such as cars and furniture, and
- **intangible property** like insurance, bank accounts, stocks and bonds, and pension and Social Security benefits.

- insurance or pension benefits paid directly to them as the named beneficiaries;
- a living trust;
- using expedited probate for wills, which is available in many states, especially for smaller estates; and
- taking advantage of laws in certain states that provide partial payments to beneficiaries while the estate is in probate.

Estate planning can also minimize expenses by keeping the cost of transferring property to beneficiaries as low as possible. For example, choosing a competent executor for your estate and giving the executor the necessary authority to carry out your directives can save money and simplify the administration of your estate.

If you have minor children, an estate plan enables you to designate the best available person to care for them after your death. Through a will, you can nominate a **legal guardian** for your children and name an executor to handle the distribution of your estate to your designated beneficiaries.

Q. How can we ensure that the guardians we've named for our children have the resources to raise them well?

A. If you have an estate plan that involves a living trust, the trustee will take the role of the property guardian. The trust will contain instructions for the financial well-being of the children. Just as parents can draft a memorandum to the guardians of their children, they can also draft a memorandum to their trustee that goes beyond what has been stated in the trust.

A trust document can give the trustee authority to assist guardians of the children with the financial burdens associated with raising additional children. Such burdens may include the need to buy a bigger car or put an addition on a house.

Whether you have a will-based or trust-based plan, it is important that your documents enable your trustees/property guardians and personal guardians to act in the best interest of the children in ways that are consistent with the wishes, directions, and values of the parents.

Q. Can an estate plan help reduce taxes on my estate?

A. Yes. Every dollar your estate has to pay in estate taxes is a dollar that your beneficiaries won't receive. A good estate plan gives the maximum allowed by law to your beneficiaries and the minimum to the tax collector. This becomes especially important as your estate approaches the magic number of $1.5 million, the current level at which the federal estate tax becomes payable. This figure will rise by increments until the year 2009.

Q. Isn't an estate plan just for old people?

A. Emphatically not. One glance at the news demonstrates that far too many young and middle-aged people die suddenly or become mentally or physically incapacitated. An estate plan can be tailored to anticipate both of these contingencies.

Q. When should I plan my estate?

A. The time to plan for death or disability is when you're healthy. As a general rule, people make better decisions when they feel good and tend to make worse decisions when coping with mental or physical stress, strain, or illness. Moreover, a so-called deathbed will, or one made by someone whose mental competence is questionable, may invite a legal challenge.

It's also important not to procrastinate. Don't put off making your estate plan until your estate reaches a certain level or value. Even if you don't have as many assets now as you expect to have someday, it's easy to update the plan every few years as your assets increase and your life circumstances change. If you put in a few hours now learning the basics and setting up your plan, you'll know you're covered in case of an unexpected event.

Q. My spouse doesn't like to talk about finances or estate planning. What should I do?

A. You can't plan your estate if you don't know all the facts about your family's assets. Yet many people don't have basic information about their spouse's income—how much he or she earns, what benefits he or she is entitled to, what his or her assets and debts are, and where assets are invested.

You need to know this information when planning your estate. It's especially important to know who holds title to real estate and what is known as titled personal property—for example, automobiles, boats, and recreational vehicles. It is also important for you to know the beneficiaries of your spouse's insurance policies, pension plans, retirement accounts, and other similar assets.

Q. What can I do to minimize the costs of estate planning?

A. A lawyer or other professional often charges by the hour for the amount of work put into the estate plan. Ask about fees at your first consultation and inquire about how much your total estate plan might cost. If your legal adviser charges by the hour, the more time you invest in locating relevant documents and putting your wishes in writing, the less preparatory work your adviser will have to do. This should go a long way toward reducing the final cost of your estate plan.

ⓘ INFORMATION YOU NEED TO PLAN YOUR ESTATE

In planning your estate, it's helpful to have as much of the following information on hand as possible.

- The names, addresses, and birth dates of all people, whether or not related to you, that you expect to name in your will

- The name, address, and telephone number of the person (or people) you expect to name as the executor of your will

- If you have minor children, the names, addresses, and telephone numbers of possible guardians

- The amount and source of your principal income and other income, such as interest and dividends

- The amount, source, and beneficiaries, if any, of your retirement benefits, including IRAs, pensions, Keogh accounts, government benefits, and profit-sharing plans

- The amount, source, and beneficiaries, if any, of other financial assets such as bank accounts, annuities, and loans due you

- The amount of your debts, including mortgages, installment loans, and business debts, if any

- A list (with approximate values) of valuable property you own, including real estate, jewelry, furniture, collections, heirlooms, and other assets

- A list and description of jointly owned property and the names of co-owners

- Any documents that might affect your estate plan, including prenuptial agreements, marriage certificates, divorce decrees, recent tax returns, existing wills and trust documents, property deeds, and so on

- The location of any safe-deposit boxes and an inventory of the contents of each.

Working with a Lawyer

Q. Should I consult a lawyer as I plan my estate?

A. If your estate is relatively small and your objectives straightforward, you might plan your estate mostly on your own, with the help of the ABA's *Guide to Wills and Estates* and other resource materials, and use professional help largely for tasks like writing a will or a trust. However, a caveat is in order. "How-to" guides can assist you as you start the estate-planning process. But before finalizing anything, consult with an experienced estate lawyer to make sure that your property goes exactly where you want it to; that your family is protected fully; and that you are assured of proper care in the case of incapacity.

As a general rule, the larger your estate, the more important it is to consult a lawyer. You should most certainly use a lawyer if you own a business, if your estate nears or exceeds $1.5 million (making tax planning a factor under current federal law), or if you anticipate a challenge to the will from a disgruntled relative or anyone else. Under current law, the federal floor for taxability of estates goes up to $2 million in 2006, but that might change within the lifetime of this book.

Q. Why can't I just use a book, or one of those computerized "will kits" I've seen in bookstores and do it myself?

A. For some people—those with very small or otherwise uncomplicated estates (no real estate, for example), such alternatives might provide sufficient help. Make sure that a book or kit is up-to-date and thorough, especially since probate laws vary from state to state.

But these alternatives don't provide you with legal expertise to review your work. Do-it-yourself books and kits, some lawyers say, have caused more work for lawyers (and bills for clients) than they have avoided. Once you begin totaling up all your assets, you may be surprised to find that your estate is larger than you thought, meaning a simple will isn't enough. At the same time, family relationships are becoming more complicated. Today, a do-it-yourself will might not do the job.

What's more, most do-it-yourself alternatives can't tell you what strategies you might be able to take advantage of to save money or to make sure your wishes are accomplished. Estate planning for most people should consist of more than just a will: IRAs, insurance, living trusts, and other elements can be a money-saving part of the mix. The precise mix that's best for you is as unique as your circumstances.

And because they cannot give legal advice, many alternative estate providers often fail to inform you when there might be a better (and cheaper) way to accomplish your goals. For example, a recent *New York Times* story recounted a reporter's experience with one such service. He wanted to leave his father part of his estate, but require the father to bequeath anything left over when he died to the reporter's children. "The service would not—could not—tell me that such a proviso is not binding (something I have since confirmed with a lawyer, who pointed out other ways to accomplish my goal)," he wrote. "I might have died in the naïve belief that my children were protected."

Law firms have other advantages—witnesses available (wills must be signed in front of witnesses to be effective), codes of conduct that protect clients' confidentiality, and, most of all, lawyers who know the various alternatives the law affords.

Although many people will fit a standard form, many more have unique situations that can benefit from the custom-made advice tailored to their specific situation by a lawyer who's charged to represent their best interest. And since lawyers generally charge less for less-complicated estates, you may be able to gain the benefits and flexibility of real legal advice at little more than the cost of a computerized will kit.

Knowing that your will and estate plan will pass legal muster will help you sleep better at night—and that peace of mind is worth a few dollars more.

Q. If I use a lawyer, how much should I expect to pay?

A. Among other factors, it depends on the size and complexity of your estate, the average legal fees for estate planning in your area, and your lawyer's experience. You'll pay more if your estate exceeds $1.5 million and you are interested in minimizing federal estate taxes and state inheritance taxes.

A lawyer's help doesn't have to be exorbitant. Many lawyers will see you for an initial consultation at no charge. You'll be able to discuss fees based on the specifics of your financial situation and exactly how you wish to distribute your estate. Ask the lawyer to give you a price or range of prices for preparing a will or estate plan; it might be cheaper than you think. Often, lawyers have a written fee schedule for various kinds of wills. If yours doesn't, before you give the final go-ahead to draw up your will, ask the estimated cost (or at least a range of likely costs).

Q. How can I find a lawyer to help me plan my estate and write any necessary documents?

A. You can ask friends who have hired lawyers to draw up their wills. Or you can use any of the Internet resources listed in this chapter. Or you can see if you are or can be covered by a legal service plan.

By some estimates, over 100 million Americans are eligible for the benefits of **legal service plans.** These plans enable members to get legal services either free or at reduced cost. In many programs, simple wills are either free or cost far less than the going rate. More comprehensive estate planning and preparation of other documents are available from lawyers at a reduced hourly rate. About 80 percent of plans are available to members of certain organizations (like AARP, the military, or a union), or to employees of certain companies as a result of collective bargaining agreements or adoption of a plan by the employer. Plans also may be available to credit card holders and bank customers or through individual sales agents. Some of these plans have no fee at all to the participant; others may require payment of a monthly fee.

Legal clinics are another low-cost alternative. They can prepare your will for modest amounts because legal assistants do much of the work under a lawyer's guidance. That work often consists of adapting standard computerized forms to fit the needs of the client. If you have a small, simple estate, the cost may be modest, and you get professional advice and reassurance that your will meets the standards for validity in your

---

▶ JUST A CLICK AWAY

The American Bar Association website has information on lawyer referral that may help you get a referral to an estate-planning lawyer in your community at www.abanet.org/legalservices/public.html. The site also has information that will help you find a lawyer online, and will give you some tips on hiring a lawyer, sources of information for the public, and how to resolve problems with your lawyer. Chapter 1, "When and How to Use a Lawyer," also contains information on how to find a lawyer.

▶ FEEL COMFORTABLE WITH YOUR LAWYER

An essential: Be comfortable with the lawyer you choose! A good estate lawyer will have to ask questions about many private matters, and you need to feel free in discussing these personal considerations with him or her. If you don't feel comfortable, you should find another lawyer who's willing to explain the options to you and who'll help you do it right.

state. You may be able to find a law school clinic or other clinic by looking in the yellow pages.

Q. How will I work with my lawyer to plan my estate?

A. Don't just expect to pile some papers on your lawyer's desk and have a will or trust magically appear in a few weeks. Preparing these documents is seldom as simple as filling in blanks on a form. Most people will meet with their lawyer several times, with more extensive estates requiring more consultations.

At the first meeting, be prepared to tell your lawyer about some rather intimate details of your life—how much money you have; how many more children you plan to have; which relatives, friends, or other associates you want to get more or less of your estate. Bring as much information and as many relevant documents as you can to the meeting (see "Information You Need to Plan Your Estate" on page 703).

After talking with you, your lawyer will explain the options the law provides for accomplishing your estate-planning goals. Based on your direction, your lawyer can draft a will or trust or both, depending on your circumstances.

It's a good idea to ask your lawyer to send you a draft of the will or trust document for your review. After examining the draft, ask for any clarification you might need and provide any necessary changes. This information will assist your lawyer in preparing the finalized will or trust document that, upon signing, will become legally effective to distribute your estate.

You should review your estate plan periodically, so you'll want to stay in touch with your lawyer. Don't think of estate planning as a one-time retail transaction, but rather as an occasional process that works best when you have a continuing relationship with your professional advisers.

ⓘ FINDING A SPECIALIST IN YOUR STATE

In a number of states, lawyers are certified as specialists in estate-planning matters. This typically means that these lawyers have demonstrated particular competence in this area. Specialists have been recognized by an independent professional certifying organization as having an enhanced level of skill and expertise, as well as substantial involvement in an established legal specialty. These organizations require a lawyer to demonstrate special training, experience, and knowledge to ensure that the lawyer's recognition as a certified specialist is meaningful and reliable.

The ABA website provides links to all states; visit www.abanet.org/legalservices/specialization/state.html.

THE WORLD AT YOUR FINGERTIPS

- *The American Bar Association's Section of Real Property, Probate, and Trust Law offers useful information for the public on its website at www.abanet.org/rppt/public/home.html.*
- *Nolo Press has an excellent website for the public. Check out wills and estate planning in Nolo's law center and in its online legal encyclopedia at www.nolopress.com.*
- *FindLaw is another excellent site for the public, with plenty of information on wills and estates at consumer.pub.findlaw.com/wills.*
- *The Internet Law Library contains a long list of links to estate-planning articles at www.priweb.com/internetlawlib/112.htm.*
- *The National Association of Financial and Estate Planning contains good information, especially for those with large estates, at www.nafep.com.*

- *Legal service plans usually give you reduced-cost estate planning. To begin your search for a legal service plan that you might join, check the American Prepaid Legal Services Institute website at www.aplsi.org. Not all plans are listed. You will have to click on the links to the listed plans to find out if you can join them.*

- *Sites on the Web that enable you to find more information and sometimes the names of lawyers in your area include the Senior Law website, www.seniorlaw.com, and the National Network of Estate Planning Attorneys website, www.netplanning.com.*

- *The American College of Trust & Estate Counsel offers a membership listing of lawyers by state whose practices concentrate in estate planning. To obtain a listing for your state, write to ACTEC at 3415 S. Sepulveda Blvd., Suite 330, Los Angeles, CA 90034. You can phone the college at 310-398-1888, fax it at 310-572-7280, or visit its home page at www.actec.org.*

- *The National Association of Estate Planners & Councils can provide a listing of lawyers certified in estate planning through experience, education, and examination. Write the association at 270 South Bryn Mawr Ave., P. O. Box 46, Bryn Mawr, PA 19010-2196; the telephone number is 610-526-1389, and the fax number is 610-526-1224. The website can be accessed at www.naepc.org.*

- *The National Academy of Elder Law Attorneys (NAELA) publishes a directory of elder law lawyer members, including those certified in elder law by the National Elder Law Foundation. NAELA also provides consumer publications for older people and their families. You can write to NAELA at 1604 N. Country Club, Tucson, AZ 85716 (telephone: 520-881-4005; fax:*

520-325-7925). *The website is available at www.naela.com.*

- *The American Academy of Estate Planning Attorneys website, www.aaepa.com/consumers.aspx, and the National Association of Financial and Estate Planning website, www.nafep.com, may also be useful if you are trying to find an estate-planning lawyer.*

- *Your local area agency on aging should be able to inform you about the availability of free or reduced-fee legal assistance available to people over sixty in your community. Look in the yellow pages for your local government listings under "aging," or call Eldercare Locator at 1-800-677-1116 to find the agency on aging nearest you. You can also search the database of Eldercare Locator online through its website at www.eldercare.gov.*

- *State bar associations can provide information regarding lawyer discipline and complaint procedures should you have a serious complaint about your lawyer. You can find a list of disciplinary agencies at www.abanet.org/cpr/disciplinary.html.*

REMEMBER THIS

- *Estate planning is not just for the elderly—it's a wise precaution at any stage of life.*
- *Estate planning puts you in control by letting you determine exactly how you want your property distributed.*
- *You can save money in taxes and fees through intelligent and thorough estate planning.*
- *Estate planning can provide a way for you to plan for any possible incapacity, letting you determine how you will be cared for when you're too ill to make decisions for yourself.*

WILLS

Homer's a laid-back sort of guy. His heart's in the right place, but he doesn't want to go through all the formalities involved in writing a will. He tells his wife, Marge, that he wants to leave everything to her, and he even scrawls that message on the back of a bar napkin. Any chance that this informal "will" is going to do the trick?

This section details the steps of preparing a will, including working with a lawyer or estate planner, deciding what to include in a will, choosing your beneficiaries and executor, and making the will legal.

Q. Do I have to have a lawyer to write my will?

A. No. If your will meets the legal requirements established by the law of your state, it is valid, whether you wrote it with a lawyer's help or by yourself. However, a lawyer can help ensure that your will is more than just valid. Your lawyer can make sure that the will does what you really want it to do. It is for this reason that more than 85 percent of Americans who have wills worked with a lawyer.

Q. Do I have to write my will?

A. The best rule to follow in creating a will is to put it in writing. By executing a written will, you are ensuring that your intentions are clear and that you have a degree of certainty about the exact distribution of your estate upon your death.

As with all general rules, there are exceptions. Some states recognize oral wills or holographic wills—handwritten, unwitnessed wills—but only under extremely limited circumstances.

A few states have **statutory wills** that are created by state law and allow people to fill in the blanks on a standard form. However, these form wills are designed for simple estates and provide little flexibility. They will not be useful if you have a large estate or if your wishes are complicated.

Also keep this caveat in mind—make sure your state treats as valid these alternatives to the traditional, time-tested written will and then make certain that you follow all the steps the law requires.

Q. What happens if I die without a will?

A. If you die without a will, you die **intestate.** Your property still must be distributed, and will be done so according to your state's laws of **intestacy.** The probate court in your area will appoint someone (who may or may not be the person you would have wanted to comb through all your affairs) as the administrator of your estate. He or she will be responsible for distributing your property in accordance with the law of your state.

The probate court will supervise the administrator's work closely and may require the administrator to post bond to ensure that your estate will not be charged with the costs of any errors made by the administrator. Of course, all this involvement may be much more expensive than administering an estate under a will—and these costs come out of your estate before it is distributed. Some of your property may have to be sold

---

ⓘ THE VIDEO WILL

More and more people are preparing a "video will," which is a videocassette showing them reading the will aloud and, perhaps, explaining why certain gifts were made and others not made. The video recording might also show the execution of the will. Should a disgruntled relative decide to challenge the will, the video can provide compelling proof that the **testator**—that is, the person making the will—really intended to make a will, was mentally competent to do so, and observed the formalities of execution. You should consult a lawyer before making such a video.

to pay these costs, instead of going to family or friends.

Q. Who gets my property if I die without a will?

A. By not leaving a valid will or trust, or by not transferring your property in some other way before death, you've left it to the law of your state to write your "will" for you. In the absence of a will, the law of your state has made certain judgments about who should receive a decedent's property. Those judgments may or may not bear any relationship to the judgments you would have made if you had prepared a will or executed a trust.

As a general rule, state law gives your property to the people most closely related to you by blood, marriage, or adoption. As a result, your hard-earned money might end up with relatives who don't need it, while others, whether or not related to you, who might be in greater need or who are more deserving, are passed over. In the unlikely event that you have no relatives or in the event that your relatives cannot be located after diligent efforts, your property will go to the state—a big reason to have a will or a trust.

Q. Does a will cover all my property?

A. Probably not. It is easy to think that a will covers all of your property. But because property can be passed to others by gift, contract, joint tenancy, life insurance, or other methods, a will might best be viewed as just one of many ways of determining how and to whom your estate will be distributed at your death.

Many of the various methods of distributing your estate are discussed in this chapter. Be sure to keep in mind the kinds of property that a will may not cover and include them in your estate planning.

📄 KINDS OF WILLS

Here's a brief list of terms used in the law for various kinds of wills.

- **Simple will** A will that provides for the distribution of the entire estate to one or more people or entities, known as beneficiaries, so that no part of the estate remains undistributed.

- **Testamentary-trust will** A will that sets up one or more trusts into which designated portions of your estate are placed after you die.

- **Pourover will** A will that leaves your estate to a trust established before your death.

- **Holographic will** A will that is unwitnessed and in the handwriting of the will maker. About twenty states recognize the validity of such wills.

- **Oral will** (also called **noncupative will**). A will that is spoken, not written down. A few states permit these.

- **Joint will** Two wills—the wife's and the husband's—contained in one document.

- **Living will** Not really a will at all—since it has force while you are still alive and doesn't dispose of property. A living will often is executed at the same time you make your true will. It tells doctors and hospitals which treatments, such as life support, you want or do not want in the event you are terminally ill or, as a result of accident or illness, cannot be restored to consciousness. (A **power-of-appointment for health care** or a **durable power of attorney for health care** also can be used to address this concern. For more on such advance directives, see chapter 16, "The Rights of Older Americans.")

Q. Are there any special legal formalities required to make my will legally valid?

A. After you've drawn up your will, there remains one step: the formal legal procedure called **executing** the will. This requires witnesses to your signing of the will. In almost all states, the signature of at least two witnesses is required. In some states, a will is not deemed legally valid unless the witnesses appear in court and testify about witnessing the will. However, in a growing number of states, a will can be "self-proved"— that is, the will is accepted as valid and the witnesses will not be required to appear and testify if, at the time the will was executed, the witnesses' signatures were notarized and each witness submits an affidavit attesting to the fact that he or she witnessed the signing of the will.

Q. Does it matter who my witnesses are?

A. Yes. The witnesses should have no potential conflict of interest—that is, they should not be people who receive gifts under the will or who might benefit from your death. Thus, in some states, a will is invalid if witnessed by a beneficiary. In other states, a beneficiary can serve as a witness but, in doing so, might lose whatever property or interest is left to him or her in your will.

Q. In my will, can I leave my property to anyone I wish?

A. In general, you can pick the people you want your property to go to and leave it to them in whatever proportions you want, but there are a few exceptions. For example, a surviving husband or wife may have the right to take a fixed share of the estate regardless of the will. Some states limit how much you can leave to a charity if you have a surviving spouse or children, or if you die soon after making the provision.

Some people try to make their influence felt beyond the grave by attaching bizarre or excessive conditions to a gift made in the will. Most lawyers will advise you not to try this. Courts don't like such conditions, and you're inviting a will contest if you try to tie multiple, unreasonable conditions to a gift. For the most part, though, it's your call.

Q. Can I disinherit my spouse and children?

A. You usually can't disinherit your spouse. State laws generally entitle a surviving spouse to take a portion of the deceased spouse's estate— regardless of the deceased spouse's will or estate plan.

The situation with children is dramatically the opposite. Except for Louisiana, every state permits you to disinherit your children. However, to be effective, it's better if your intent to disinherit is express, which usually means it has to be stated in writing.

Q. What share will my spouse receive under state law?

A. If a husband or wife dies with a will that makes no provision for the surviving spouse, or conveys to that person less than a certain percentage of the deceased spouse's assets, the surviving spouse can take a statutorily defined **elective share of the estate.** This means he or she can choose to accept the amount allowed by law, usually one-third or one-half of the estate.

The surviving spouse doesn't have to take an elective share of the estate—it's his or her choice. If he or she doesn't exercise the choice, the will stands and the property is distributed as stated in the will.

Elective share provisions are troubling to many people entering into second marriages, particularly late in life, because the surviving spouse of only a few years would be eligible to take up to one-half of the deceased spouse's property, even if the deceased spouse wanted it to go to his or her own children. Recent revisions to the Uniform Probate Code provide a sliding scale for surviving spouses who take against the will. Under this approach, which a few states have adopted, the longer the marriage, the higher the elective share. If the marriage lasted only a few years, the percentage could be quite low, minimizing one source of worry for older couples.

The Executor

Q. Whom should I make the executor of my will?

A. There's no consensus about who makes the best executor. It all depends on your individual circumstances.

One approach is to appoint someone with no potential conflict of interest—that is, someone who doesn't stand to gain from the will. Under this approach, you can minimize the likelihood of a will contest from a disgruntled beneficiary who might be tempted to accuse the executor of taking undue advantage of his or her role to the

---

ⓘ THE ESSENTIALS OF A VALID WILL

To be valid, your will doesn't have to conform to a specific formula. However, there are certain elements that usually must be present.

1. *Legal age.* You must be of legal age to make a will. This is eighteen in most states, but may be several years older or younger in some places.

2. *Sound mind.* You must be of sound mind, which means that you should know you're executing a will, know the general nature and extent of your property, and know the objects of your bounty, that is, your spouse, descendants, and other relatives who ordinarily would be expected to share in your estate. The law presumes that a will maker was of sound mind, and the standard for proving otherwise is very high—much more than mere absentmindedness or forgetfulness.

3. *Intended to transfer property.* The will must have a substantive provision that disposes of property, and it must indicate your intent to make the document your final word on what happens to your property—that is, that you really intended it to *be* a will.

4. *Written.* Although oral wills, if witnessed, are permitted in limited circumstances in some states, wills usually must be written and witnessed.

5. *Properly signed.* You must voluntarily sign your will, unless illness or accident or illiteracy prevents it, in which case you can direct that your lawyer or one of the witnesses sign for you. This requires a lawyer's guidance, or at least knowledge of your state's law, since an invalid signature could void a will.

6. *Properly witnessed.* In almost all states, the signing of a formal will must be witnessed by at least two adults who understand what they are witnessing and are competent to testify in court. In most states, the witnesses have to be **disinterested** (i.e., not getting anything in your will). If they aren't, you run the risk of voiding certain provisions in the will, opening it to challenge, or invalidating the entire will.

7. *Properly executed.* Your will should contain a statement at the end attesting that it is your will, the date and place of signing, and the fact that you signed it before witnesses, who then also signed it in your presence—and watched each other signing it. Most states allow so-called **self-proving affidavits,** which eliminate the necessity of having the witnesses go to court to testify that they witnessed the signing. The affidavit is proof enough.

If your will doesn't meet these conditions, it might be disallowed by a court, and your estate then would be distributed according to a previous will or under your state's intestacy laws.

detriment of others named in the will. On the other hand, if you believe that there is little possibility of a will contest, you could choose a beneficiary as executor. Since an executor who is a beneficiary usually waives the executor's fee to which he or she is entitled, your estate will save money.

For most people whose assets amount to less than a million dollars, a good choice is your spouse or the person who will be the main beneficiary of your will. This person naturally will be interested in making sure the probate process goes efficiently and with minimal expense. For larger estates and those that involve running a business, it may be advisable to use the estate-planning department of your bank, your accountant, or your lawyer.

Q. Why are paid executors sometimes preferable?

A. There are sometimes reasons for choosing a paid executor—usually a lawyer—instead of your spouse. Your spouse may be incapacitated by grief, illness, or disability. Nonetheless, he or she as executor will be personally liable for unpaid estate taxes and fines for late filings, even if he or she has delegated such tasks to a lawyer. Furthermore, since the executor must gather all the estate assets, your spouse may be faced with the odious duty of retrieving money or property you lent to other family members or friends.

If you think your spouse may not be up to the job (considering that he or she may also be saddled with sole responsibility for any minor children), you might choose a lawyer or other professionals, even though it means paying a fee. Remember, this is a job that, primarily because of tax procedures, can take more than three years of involvement, though most estates take far less.

Q. What if the executor I choose can't serve when the time comes, or doesn't want to?

A. Whomever you choose as executor, be sure to provide in your will for a successor executor in case the first named executor dies or is unable or

---

ⓘ LEGAL PROTECTIONS FOR SURVIVING SPOUSES

Depending on the state, a surviving spouse may also have the protection of homestead laws, exempt property laws, and family allowance laws. Typically, these protections are in addition to whatever the spouse receives under the will, the elective share that the spouse can choose to take under the will, or the statutory share that he or she receives if there is no will.

Homestead laws protect certain property from the deceased spouse's creditors. Typically, they permit the surviving spouse to shelter a certain value of the family home and some personal property from creditors. In some states, the homestead exemption protects a statutorily specified sum of money from creditors, rather than the deceased's real or personal property. As a general rule, the protection is temporary, extending to the lifetime of the surviving spouse or until any minor children reach legal adulthood. However, in a few states, homestead laws permanently shelter specified property from creditors of the deceased.

Exempt property laws give the surviving spouse certain specified property, provide protection from creditors, and protect against disinheritance.

Family allowance laws make probate less of a burden on family members. Under these laws, the family is entitled to a certain amount of money from the estate while the estate is being probated, regardless of the claims of creditors.

unwilling to perform. Without a backup executor, the probate court will have to appoint someone, and that person may not be to your liking.

One final caution—don't name someone as your executor unless you have spoken to the person and he or she agrees. This will ensure that the person of your choice, not the court's, will administer your estate.

Q. Can I appoint more than one executor?

A. Yes, naming coexecutors is popular with small business owners who name a spouse or relative to oversee the personal side of matters and a second person with business expertise to oversee the management of the business.

Naming coexecutors may be a good idea if the main beneficiary lives in a different state and is unable to make the trips necessary to handle the many details involved in administering an estate. While this person could be a coexecutor, another coexecutor living in the state in which the estate is being administered could be named to handle the day-to-day administration. Finally, don't forget to name one or more successor executors so that if a coexecutor dies or declines the position, someone else of your choice will be available.

Q. Is there anyone whom I shouldn't appoint as executor?

A. As a general rule, the executor can't be a minor, a convicted felon, or a non-U.S. citizen. In addition, while all states allow an out-of-state resident to act as executor, some require that the nonresident executor be a primary beneficiary or a close relative. Some states require that a nonresident executor obtain a bond or engage a resident to act as the nonresident executor's representative. For these reasons, and because handling an estate can take months and require several court appearances, it's a good idea to pick at least one executor who is a legal resident of the state in which your estate will be administered.

Q. What is an "independent executor"?

A. About a dozen states permit the appointment of an **independent executor,** who, after apprais-

ing the estate's assets and filing an inventory of assets with the probate court, is free to administer the estate without intervention from the court. This saves time and money. However, a court could become involved in the event someone challenges the independent executor's administration of the estate.

The independent executor has the power to do just about anything necessary to administer the estate. He or she can sue and be sued; settle claims made by others against your estate; deny or pay claims made by others against your estate; pay debts, taxes, and administration expenses; run a business if it is part of the estate; and distribute the assets of your estate to your beneficiaries as spelled out in your will. In some states, the independent executor can sell your property without first securing a court order to do so.

Q. How much does an executor charge for his or her services?

A. If the executor is a beneficiary—for example, a family member—he or she may choose to forgo the statutory executor's fee, but you can expect any executor who is not a beneficiary, such as a bank or a lawyer, to charge a fee. Fees vary by state and usually are set as a percentage of the estate's value. For small and mid-sized estates—estates under $200,000, for example—expect a fee of 1 to 4 percent of the total estate. Probate courts and state laws usually regulate fees.

Setting Up a Will

Q. Isn't there a set formula for what goes into a will?

A. Not really. All of us have unique circumstances in our lives that resist easy, one-size-fits-all definitions. However, there are some clauses that are found in most wills. Here's a very quick rundown. The *ABA Guide to Wills and Estates* discusses these clauses at greater length and includes a sample annotated will.

- *Funeral expenses and payment of debts.* Your debts don't die with you; your estate is still liable for them, and your executor has the authority to pay them off if they are valid and binding. You can also forgive any debts someone owes you by saying so in this clause. As for funeral directions and anatomical donations, while you can put them in your will, be aware that the will might not be found or admitted to probate until after you're buried. It's best to put these in a separate document.

- *Gifts of personal property.* It's important to identify carefully all recipients of your largesse, including their addresses and relationships to you. There are too many cases of people leaving property to "my cousin John," not realizing that more than one person might fit that description.

Remember also that personal property can include intangible assets like insurance policies (for instance, if you own a policy on your spouse's life, that policy and the cash value of the premiums paid into it can be passed on through your will), bank accounts, certain employee benefits, and stock options.

Finally, if you have several people whom you want to share in a gift, be careful to specify what percentage of ownership each will have. If you don't, the court probably will presume that you intended the multiple beneficiaries to share equally.

You can save on taxes by using gifts wisely. This section of your will can be used to give gifts to institutions and charities as well as to people.

- *Executors.* By giving the executor authority to act efficiently, by saying that a surety bond will not be required and by directing that the involvement of the probate court be kept to a minimum, which is now possible in many states, you can save your family money. It helps to spell out certain powers the executor

---

ⓘ WHAT EXECUTORS DO

The law requires an executor because someone must be responsible for

- collecting the assets of the estate,
- protecting the estate property,
- preparing an inventory of the property,
- representing the estate in claims against others,
- paying valid claims against the estate (including taxes), and, finally,
- distributing the estate property to the beneficiaries.

These last two functions may require liquidating assets; that is, selling items like stocks, bonds, even furniture or a car to have enough cash to pay taxes, creditors, or beneficiaries.

The will can impose additional duties not required by law on the executor. These include planning postdeath tax strategies, choosing which specific property goes to which beneficiaries, and even investing funds.

Sounds like a lot of work, doesn't it? It can be, and some of it can be complicated. However, the executor doesn't necessarily have to shoulder the entire burden. He or she can pay a professional out of the estate assets to take care of most of these functions, especially those requiring legal or financial expertise, but that will reduce the amount that goes to the beneficiaries. Therefore, handling an estate is often a matter of balancing expertise, convenience, cost, and so on.

can have in dealing with your estate: to buy, lease, sell, and mortgage real estate; to borrow and lend money; and to exercise various tax options. If you run a business, be sure to give your executor specific power to continue the business—or enter into new business arrangements.

- *Gifts of real estate.* Most people prefer that their spouses receive the family home. If the home isn't held in joint tenancy, you should have instructions about what will happen to it in your will. If you die before you've paid off the mortgage on your house, your estate normally will have to pay it off. If you're afraid this will drain the estate too much, or if you want the recipient of the house to keep paying on the mortgage, you must specify that in your will. If you haven't paid off the family house, and you're afraid your survivors can't afford to, you may be able to buy mortgage-canceling insurance to pay it off.

- *Residuary clause.* This is one of the most crucial parts of a will, covering all assets not specifically disposed of by other parts of the will. You probably will accumulate assets after you write your will, and if you haven't specifically given an asset to someone, it won't pass through the will—unless you have a **residuary clause** that covers everything. (If your will omits a residuary clause, the assets not left specifically to anyone would pass on through the intestate succession laws; in technical terms, your estate would be **partially intestate,** with some portions passing as you specified in your will and some according to state law.) No matter how small your residuary estate seems at the time you write your will, you should almost always leave it to the person you most care about.

- *Trusts.* In a trust clause, you can set up a testamentary trust in your will, or have your will direct funds from your estate into a trust you had previously established (your will would then be a pourover will).

Q. How do I make gifts of personal property in a will?

A. A **tangible personal property memorandum** or direction (abbreviated as **TPPM**) is a separate handwritten document that is incorporated into the will by reference, is dated, and contains lists of tangible personal property (e.g., jewelry, art-

---

▶   **WHAT IF?**

In writing your will, you should always play the "what if?" game, and try to figure out where a gift would go if something unexpected happened—then account for that possibility in your will. What if one of your beneficiaries dies before you do? In that event, the gift you made to the dead person is said to **lapse** (be cancelled), and the gift goes back into your residuary estate, to be distributed to whomever you made the residuary beneficiary. (See discussion of residuary clause in the text.)

Most states, however, have **antilapse** statutes that provide that if a beneficiary related to you predeceases you, that beneficiary's descendants would receive the gift (particularly gifts of real and personal property). So if you left your shoe collection to your daughter Imelda, and she died before you did, in a state with an antilapse statute the footwear would go to Imelda's descendants. In a state without an antilapse statute, it would go to whomever you had named to receive your residuary estate. If Imelda were your best friend and not your daughter, the antilapse statute would not apply.

work, furniture) and the people you want the property to go to.

This means that the will says something like "This will incorporates the provisions of a separate Tangible Personal Property Memorandum . . . " Then the TPPM is regarded as part of the will. Many states recognize the validity of such a signed instrument. Some require it to be in existence at the time the will is signed and will not give effect to changes made after the will is signed. If you use a TPPM, it's important to remember to make provisions for what happens to any of the property listed if the person who is in line to receive it should die before you do—and you neglect to adjust the TPPM accordingly before your death. Often, the reference in the will specifies that the gifts are to go to the recipients still living.

In addition, the reference in the will often states that if no TPPM is found within sixty days of the will maker's death, that is conclusive evidence that it does not exist. This provision means that the estate can be settled in a timely manner, without waiting indefinitely for something that may never turn up.

Q. Where should I keep my will?

A. Keep it in a safe place, such as your lawyer's office, a fireproof safe at home, or a safe-deposit box. If you do keep your will in a safe-deposit box, make sure to provide that the executor can take possession of the will when you die. Also, keep in mind that some jurisdictions require a decedent's safe-deposit box to be sealed immediately after death until certain legal requirements have been satisfied.

Q. What other estate documents should I keep with the will?

A. You should also keep a record of other estate-planning documents with your will, such as trust documents, IRAs, insurance policies, income savings plans such as 401(k) plans, stocks and bonds, and retirement plans.

▶ **GENERAL OR SPECIFIC? IT DEPENDS**

In making gifts of specific property, you should be certain to identify the property carefully to avoid disputes about which items you meant. For example, specify "my grandmother's three-carat diamond engagement ring" or "the portrait of my grandfather." Such language is advisable when the item is valuable or a dispute about the property is expected.

Generally speaking, however, it is preferable to make gifts in broad categories of property. For example, a category can be used if the meaning is clear—"all my jewelry." Similarly, "all my tangible personal property" has a reasonably clear legal meaning. The reason for this is that this covers the possibility that you will dispose of some items and acquire others between the time you write the will and the time you die. Another example of this kind of general bequest would be to leave your son not "my 1986 Yugo" but "the car I own when I die." The same applies to stocks or bank accounts—the bank may be taken over by another bank, or the stock may be sold. Better to include a general description or leave a dollar amount or fractional share.

And if you're trying to leave your children equal values of different kinds of property that's liable to fluctuate in value (say a stock portfolio or real estate), you might add a clause to the will that specifies that if one asset turns out to be worth more than the other, the difference will be made up between the children.

THE WORLD AT YOUR FINGERTIPS

- *The AARP has a wide range of good information about wills and estates at www.aarp.org/estate_planning.*

- *"Who Gets Grandma's Yellow Pie Plate?" is an excellent website to visit to help you think about inheritance planning (www.yellowpieplate.umn.edu/07-lm.html). The site also tells you how to buy a workbook and video on the topic.*

- *Many state bar associations offer information on wills and related topics. This has the added advantage of being specific to your state. For example, the Tennessee Bar Association site, www.tba.org/LawBytes/ T15.html, offers a wide variety of information. Access www.abanet.org/barserv/ stlobar.html to find your state bar's contact information.*

- *Books providing basic information on what goes in a will include Everything Your Heirs Need to Know, by David Magee (Chicago: Dearborn Financial Publishing, 1995), and Last Wishes: A Handbook to Guide Your Survivors, by L. P. Knox and M. D. Knox (Berkeley, Calif.: Ulysses Press, 1995).*

REMEMBER THIS

- *Even though you may not have a lot of assets, or you plan to use a living trust or other means of transferring your property to others after you die, you still need a will.*

- *Most of the time, you can leave your property to whomever you want under whatever conditions you desire. However, the law does impose some limits on this freedom. Your lawyer can fill you in on them before you write your will.*

- *To be valid, a will generally has to meet a number of standards. It has to be made by*

someone of legal age and sound mind. It has to be intended to transfer property, written, and properly signed, witnessed, and executed.

- *Take care in the selection of your executor, since that person will be charged with carrying out the directions you give in the will. For most estates, you may want to consider making the primary beneficiary the executor.*

- *There is no set formula for what goes into a will. The key clauses typically cover the payment of debts, gifts of property, the naming of an executor, and the disposal of assets that you may acquire after the will is written. Also, your will should give directions for what will happen if one or more of your beneficiaries dies before you do.*

TRUSTS AND LIVING TRUSTS

Mary is a widow, without children or any close relatives. She is no longer able to live alone in her home or to handle her finances. In her younger days, Mary loved to hike, and wants most of her estate to support organizations that protect the environment. And she wants to leave some of her assets to her close friend Maggie, who has been helping her as she's become more disabled.

Mary's lawyer advises her to establish a living trust and transfer her property and other assets to its trustee. She will move into an assisted-living center. The trustee will sell the home and invest the proceeds, along with the other assets, to provide for Mary's support during her lifetime. After she dies, the living trust will direct Mary's estate to Greenpeace and the Sierra Club, and to her friend Maggie. If Mary changes her mind about who should receive her estate, Mary can make a simple amendment to the trust by a written letter or a memo signed by her and delivered to the trustee.

This section covers trusts and living trusts, their advantages, their requirements, and your options among different types of trusts.

Q. What is a trust?

A. A trust is a legal relationship in which one person or qualified trust company (**trustee**) holds property for the benefit of himself or herself or of another (**beneficiary**). The property can be any kind of real or personal property—money, real estate, stocks, bonds, collections, business interests, personal possessions, and automobiles.

A trust generally involves at least three people: the **grantor** (the person who creates the trust, also known as the **settlor** or the **donor**), the trustee (who holds and manages the property for the benefit of the grantor and others), and one or more beneficiaries (who are entitled to the benefits).

Think of a trust as an agreement between the grantor and the trustee. The grantor makes certain property available to the trustee, for certain purposes. The trustee (who often receives a fee) agrees to manage the property in the way the grantor wants.

Putting property in trust transfers it from your personal ownership to the trustee who holds the property for you. The trustee has **legal title** to the trust property. For most purposes, the law looks at these assets as if the trustee now owned them. For example, many (but not all) trusts have separate taxpayer identification numbers.

But trustees are not the full owners of the property. Trustees have a legal duty to use the property as provided in the trust agreement and as permitted by law. The beneficiaries retain what is known as **equitable title** or **beneficial title**, the right to benefit from the property as specified in the trust.

Q. When are trusts set up?

A. Many trusts are set up in wills—a **testamentary trust**—and take effect upon death. Others can be established while you are still alive (see below).

Living Trusts

Q. What is a living trust?

A. A **living trust** is simply a trust established while you are still alive. It can serve as a partial substitute for a will. Upon the death of the person creating the trust, its property is distributed as specified in the trust document to beneficiaries also specified in the document.

As in other kinds of trusts, there are potentially three parties to a living trust (creator, trustee, and beneficiary, though in many living trusts all three are the same person). If you set up a **revocable living trust** (see sidebar definition on next page) with yourself as trustee, you retain the rights of ownership you'd have if the assets were still in your name. You can buy anything and add it to the trust, sell anything out of the trust, and give trust property to whomever you wish.

Q. How do I know whether a living trust is right for me and my estate?

A. A trust is likely to help under the following conditions:

1. Your estate has substantial property or assets that are difficult or costly to dispose by a will.
2. You don't want the task of managing your property (say you rent out a number of condos). A living trust allows you to give those duties to your trustee while you receive the income, minus the trustee's fee, if any.
3. You want your estate administered by someone who doesn't live in your state. A living trust might be better than a will because the trustee probably won't have to meet the residency requirements some state laws impose upon executors.
4. You have property in another state. Many lawyers recommend setting up a living trust to hold the title to that property. This helps you avoid additional probate procedures in another state, called **ancillary probate** procedures, which can be complicated.

Q. *What exactly can a living trust do for me?*

A. A trust is an important estate-planning tool. The flexibility of trusts makes them useful for many different people with all kinds of needs. In addition, trusts can do a number of things wills can't do, such as

- manage assets efficiently if you should die while your beneficiaries are minors;
- protect your privacy (unlike a will, trusts are confidential);
- provide a way to care for you if you should become disabled;
- avoid probate;
- speed transfer of your assets to beneficiaries after your death; and
- provide more options than a simple will (living trusts give you wide flexibility in distributing your property).

⧉ REVOCABLE AND IRREVOCABLE TRUSTS

A trust can be **revocable**—that is, subject to change or termination; or **irrevocable**—that is, difficult to change or terminate. Most living trusts are revocable, but you have the option of making yours irrevocable.

A revocable trust gives the creator great flexibility but no tax advantages. An irrevocable trust is the other side of the coin—it has less flexibility but considerable tax benefits. For example, an irrevocable trust can minimize federal and state taxes. In addition, an irrevocable trust may protect trust property from the creditors of the trust creator. However, an irrevocable trust often doesn't avoid taxes entirely. Because it can be difficult to balance the costs and benefits of an irrevocable trust, it's wise to consult with an estate-planning lawyer before you proceed.

In addition, depending on how they're written and on state law, they can protect your assets by avoiding creditors and reducing taxes. However, this usually requires the trust to be irrevocable, unlike most living trusts. If you want to lower taxes and shelter assets from creditors, you'll have to take special steps to go beyond what living trusts generally do.

Q. *What can't a living trust do for me?*

A. A living trust is a very important estate-planning tool. But it can't do everything. Here's a summary of what it can't do.

1. It won't necessarily help you to avoid taxes. A revocable living trust doesn't save any income or estate taxes that couldn't also be saved by a properly prepared will. Trust property still is counted as part of your estate for the purposes of federal and state income and estate taxes. Your successor trustee still has to pay income taxes generated by trust property and owed at your death. (Your executor would have to pay such taxes out of your estate if the property was controlled by a will instead of a trust.) And if the estate is large enough to trigger federal or state estate or inheritance taxes, your trustee will be required to file the appropriate tax returns. These and other duties can make the cost of administering an estate distributed by a revocable living trust almost as high as traditional estate administration, at least in some states.

2. It won't make a will unnecessary. You still need a will to take care of assets not included in the trust. If you have minor children, you probably need a will to suggest or nominate a guardian for them. While only a court can appoint a guardian, courts strive to implement your wishes in this regard if you have stated them.

3. It won't affect nonprobate assets. Like a will, a living trust won't control the disposition of jointly owned property, life insurance, pension benefits or retirement plans payable to a beneficiary, or other nonprobate property.

4. It won't necessarily protect your assets from creditors. Creditors can attach the assets of a revocable living trust. In fact, since the assets you put in a living trust don't have to be probated, they could lose the protection of the statute of limitations, which means that your creditors have longer to get at them.

5. It won't necessarily protect your assets from disgruntled relatives. While it is harder to challenge a living trust than a will, a relative can still bring suit to challenge the trust on grounds of fraud, undue influence, or duress.

6. It won't entirely eliminate delays. A living trust might well lessen the time it takes to distribute your assets after you die, but it won't completely eliminate delays. Many state laws impose a waiting period for creditors to file claims against estates of people with living trusts. The trustee still has to collect any debts owed to your estate after you die, prepare tax returns, pay bills, and distribute assets, just as would the executor of a will. All this takes time.

Q. Why doesn't a revocable living trust save taxes?

A. When you put property in a revocable living trust, the trustee becomes its owner, which is why you must transfer title to the property from your own name to that of the trustee. But you retain the right to use and enjoy the property and, be-

cause you do, under the tax law the property in the trust belongs to you for tax purposes. Thus, if the trust receives income from the assets, you must report the income from the trust on your individual income tax return.

Q. How can a living trust help if I become disabled?

A. You can set up a living trust, name a reliable co- or successor trustee to manage your property contained in the trust should you become ill, and fund the trust adequately by transferring title of assets to the trustee (or give someone in whom you have confidence power of attorney to do so in the event of your incapacity). This avoids the delay and red tape of expensive, court-ordered guardianship. And, at the same time, the trustee can take over any duties you had of providing for other family members. (For more information, see chapter 16, "The Rights of Older Americans.")

Q. Once I put my property in a revocable living trust, can I still manage it or sell it?

A. Yes. In a revocable living trust, you can retain the right to manage the trust property. This right includes the right to sell any of the property you placed into the trust.

Q. Can't a living trust substitute for a will?

⚠ YOU MAY NOT BENEFIT FROM A LIVING TRUST IF . . .

1. Your state's probate system has simple and easy procedures for administering estates your size.

2. You're young and healthy and don't have a lot of money. A will can usually take care of the immediate needs of a young family. You can think about a trust when you have children and your assets have grown.

3. You are not rich, but you have enough assets that reregistering them all would cost more than it's worth. For example, you might own a number of parcels of property, none particularly valuable, but all of the property would require retitling if placed into a trust.

A. Not entirely. A living trust can be a very useful part of estate planning. However, it alone can't accomplish many of the most important goals of estate planning. For example, you may have to have a will to nominate a personal guardian for your children, even if you have a trust. And even with a living trust, you'll need a simple will to dispose of property that you didn't put into the trust.

Probate is also no longer the costly, time-consuming demon it used to be. So preparing at least a simple, auxiliary will is recommended for just about everyone.

Other Kinds of Trusts

Q. What other kinds of trusts are there?

A. As discussed above, living trusts enable you to put your assets in a trust while still alive. You can wear all the hats—donor, trustee, and beneficiary—or have someone else be trustee and have other beneficiaries.

There are many, many other kinds of trusts that serve the particular needs of their grantors. Here's a brief rundown of some of the most popular trusts. Your lawyer can help you decide if they're right for you and can help you set one up.

- **Support trusts** direct the trustee to spend only as much income and principal as may be needed for the education, health care, and general support of the beneficiary.
- **Discretionary trusts** permit the trustee to distribute income and principal among various beneficiaries as he or she sees fit.
- **Charitable trusts** support a charitable purpose. Often, these trusts will make an annual gift to a worthy cause of your choosing.
- **Dynasty trusts** (also sometimes called **wealth trusts**) can last for a number of generations, and sometimes can last forever. They can help those with great fortunes control the distribution of their wealth over a very long period.
- **Generation-skipping trusts** are tax-saving trusts that benefit several generations of your descendants.
- **Insurance trusts** are a device used to avoid or, at least, minimize federal and state estate taxes. Here, trust assets are used to buy a life insurance policy whose proceeds benefit the creator's beneficiaries.
- **Special needs trusts** are for people with disabilities who want to keep their government benefits. **Medicaid trusts** are a particular kind of special needs trust. They help you qualify for federal Medicaid benefits. This device is mostly used when family members are concerned with paying the costs of nursing-home care.

Q. I understand that if I create a trust, I no longer own the property—the trustee does. This is profoundly unsettling to me. How can I be sure that the property won't be misappropriated?

A. The trust instrument itself, together with hundreds of years of legal cases and the current law in your state, provide rules for how the trustee must act. In legal terms, this body of law spells out the trustee's duties with respect to the trust property. To assuage your doubts, you might ask your lawyer to explain the trustee's duties and your legal rights.

Q. Why do people use trusts?

A. The reasons vary. Parents, for example, might use a trust to manage their assets for the benefit of their minor children in the event the parents die before the children reach the age of legal adulthood. The trustee can decide how best to carry out the parents' wishes that the money be used for education, support, and health care.

A trust is a good idea for anyone who is unable to manage money and other assets prudently. For someone who is unable to manage his or her estate because of mental or physical incapacity, a trust is an effective way to avoid the expense and undesirable aspects of a court-appointed guardian.

Q. Should I consider setting up a trust?

A. It depends on the size of your estate and what you want to do with it. For example, if you are primarily interested in protecting yourself in the event you become unable to manage your estate, a living trust is a good option. If you want to provide for minor children, grandchildren, or a disabled relative, a trust might be appropriate. Before making a decision, consult an estate-planning lawyer.

Setting Up and Maintaining a Trust

Q. Who can advise me about setting up a living trust?

A. Your lawyer is the obvious choice, but not the only one. Most banks provide trust services—for example, establishing the trust and managing the trust assets. Of course, the bank's management charges can add up and could exceed the cost of probating your estate. In addition, the bank may insist on managing the trust, which means that you won't be in control. Be sure to weigh these factors before deciding to use a bank as your trustee.

For people with more assets or people who don't want the uncertainty and work of writing and funding their own trust, it's definitely wise to work with a lawyer. It's especially good to have a lawyer's assistance in determining which assets to put into the trust and which to dispose of through a will.

Q. I just received a call from someone claiming to sell living trusts. Should I buy one?

A. No. A number of dubious companies, playing on people's fears of probate and suspicions about lawyers, have taken to selling living-trust kits door-to-door, by mail, or through seminars. Often, they deliberately exaggerate the costs and difficulties of the probate process, even though probate procedures and fees in many states, especially for simple estates, are increasingly manageable and less costly. Authorities in several states have filed consumer fraud suits against these promoters for misrepresenting themselves and deceiving consumers.

Most lawyers and financial advisers urge you to avoid such pitches, whether they're made in unsolicited telephone calls, through the mail, or in seminars. The products seldom live up to their touts and often cost $2,500 or more—far above what you'd typically pay to get a good personalized trust prepared by a lawyer. Because living trusts should be crafted to fit your particular situation, it's next to impossible to find a prepackaged one that will suit your needs as well as one prepared by your lawyer.

Q. How do I choose a lawyer to help me set up a trust?

A. First, make sure the lawyer you select has expertise in trust and estate law in your state and is willing to work with you to tailor the trust to your particular needs; otherwise, the primary benefit of a trust—its flexibility—might be lost. A knowledgeable lawyer will provide you with the finan-

---

▤ TOTTEN TRUSTS

Totten trusts are not really trusts at all. They are joint bank accounts that pass to a named beneficiary immediately upon the owner's death.

▤ SPENDTHRIFT TRUSTS

Trusts are handy tools if you aren't certain that a beneficiary can handle the money he or she will receive. They can be written to prevent a beneficiary from squandering the money, typically by limiting the income the beneficiary is to receive and making it difficult or impossible for the beneficiary to get at the assets contained in the trust. A trust written with these protections and established for such a beneficiary is sometimes known as a **spendthrift trust**.

cial expertise necessary to ensure that the trust property is preserved and, where possible, is invested wisely to ensure that the assets placed in trust actually grow in value.

Second, because trusts have tax consequences and are scrutinized closely by the IRS, choose a lawyer who understands the interplay between various types of trusts and their tax obligations.

Q. What are requirements for setting up a living trust?

A. Requirements for setting up a living trust vary with each state. In general, you execute a docu-

---

⚠ POSSIBLE DOWNSIDES OF TRUSTS

There are several possible disadvantages to trusts.

- *Hassle.* Besides preparing the trust document itself, if the trust is a living trust you will have to transfer all of the assets specified in the trust document to the trustee. This can require executing deeds or bills of sale, submitting tax forms, retitling assets, and other registration procedures.

  You have to be sure to keep transactions involving your trust separate from those involving property owned in your name. After creating the trust, each time you buy, inherit, or otherwise acquire an asset that you don't want subject to probate, you have to remember to buy it in the name of the trustee or transfer it to the trustee after purchase.

- *Cost.* While a lawyer isn't required for setting up a trust, it's usually a good idea to work with one. Also, a trust generally costs more than a will to prepare. In addition, there may be an annual management fee, particularly if the trustee is a bank or a trust company. (However, if all of your property is in trust so that there is no estate to probate at your death, these higher initial costs may be offset by costs that would have gone to probate.)

  Depending on the state the property is located in, putting your home in a living trust might jeopardize a homestead exemption, might require a transfer fee, or might cause your property to be reassessed for property tax purposes. Moreover, a revocable living trust will not reduce estate taxes.

- *Maintenance.* In some states, a revocable living trust, unlike a will, is not automatically revoked or amended on divorce. If you don't amend the trust, your ex-spouse could end up being the beneficiary.

- *Conflicts.* Beneficiaries often prefer riskier, higher-income investments than trustees, who have a duty to preserve the original assets of the trust as well as the duty to invest the assets prudently. Conflict of this sort is especially likely to occur if the trust is designed for the benefit of more than one generation.

  Conflicts also might arise among different classes of beneficiaries. For example, your child may be the current beneficiary, with your grandchildren becoming beneficiaries after your child dies. In this situation, your child and grandchildren may have conflicting interests in the trust. As the creator of the trust, you can minimize any conflict by clearly stating in the trust document whose interests are paramount.

ment saying that you're creating a trust to hold property for your benefit and that of any other designated beneficiary. Some trust declarations list the major assets (home, investments) that you're putting into trust; others refer to another document (a **schedule**) in which you list the exact property that will be in the trust. In either case, you can add and subtract property whenever you want. You will have to change the ownership registration on all property put into the trust—deeds, brokerage accounts, stocks or bonds, bank accounts, and so on—from your own name to the name of the trustee (for example, "Brett Campbell, Trustee of the John A. Smith Trust"). If you make yourself the trustee, you will have to transfer the ownership registrations to yourself as trustee and remember to sign yourself in trust transactions as "John A. Smith, Trustee," instead of using only your name.

Q. How do I put money and other assets in a living trust?

A. Setting up the trust is actually the easy part. The harder part is putting something in it—what's called funding the trust. This includes not just depositing money in the trust account, but also transferring title of assets to the name of the trustee.

Living trusts can be funded now, while you're living, or after you are dead. If you want to fund it before you die (a **funded trust**), you transfer title of your assets to the trustee and make the trustee the owner of any newly acquired assets you want to go in the trust. Any assets in the trust will avoid probate.

Be sure to go through each of your assets with your lawyer to determine whether it's wise to transfer that asset to the trust.

Many people choose to fund their trusts through their will. To do this, you set up a revocable trust and a pourover will, which transfers the assets to the trustee upon your death. You can transfer some assets to the trustee before you die, but, generally, the will would specify that all estate property would pour over into the trust, including life insurance and other death benefits.

Obviously, you can't avoid probate this way. So who would use this approach? Maybe people who don't want to go through the hassle of funding a living trust while they're alive, but also don't want their after-death gifts to be a matter of public record. They could give their estate to a trust via their will, and specify named beneficiaries through the privacy of the trust.

Q. How do I transfer titles to the trust?

A. Take a copy of the trust agreement to your bank, stockbroker, mortgage and title insurance companies, and anyone else who controls title to your assets and then request a transfer of ownership from your name to that of the trustee. Make sure to keep a record of these transfers; it will make your successor trustee's job much easier.

Q. Are there any assets I should leave out of my trust?

A. The special tax treatment given to individual retirement accounts (IRAs) might encourage you to leave them in your name. The fees your state charges to transfer title of a mortgage or other property could make the cost of transfer prohibitive. You might want to hold off on transferring your home to the trust until the mortgage is paid off or one spouse dies. Some people worry about taking the family home out of the husband and wife's names in joint tenancy and putting it into a living trust in the name of one of the spouses. In such cases, a lawyer may suggest putting the living trust in both your names—for example, "The Stephen and Diana Hogg Trust," with both spouses as cotrustees, instead of just one name.

If the trust is in one name only and the other spouse is not a cotrustee or successor trustee, many lawyers recommend leaving some property—for example, a sizable bank account—outside the trust. If you use a bank account, it should be in the names of both spouses so that if one should die, the other will have access to the funds. A word of caution is in order, however. The law in some states will freeze such accounts for a specified period of time after the death of the cosignatory. Consult your lawyer to get the specifics.

Finally, keeping a few assets out of the living trust can help protect against creditors' claims down the line. When your estate contains some property and goes through probate, it triggers the running of the statute of limitations on claims against your entire estate. Creditors are put on notice that you have died and, once the statutory period expires, the estate is safe from most creditors' claims.

The important point: Be sure to go through each of your assets with your lawyer to determine whether it's wise to transfer that asset to the trust.

Q. Whom should I pick as trustee?

A. A trustee's duties can continue for generations and, in many cases, require expertise in collecting estate assets, investing money, paying bills, filing periodic accountings, and managing money for beneficiaries.

The biggest decision to make in designating a trustee is whether to use a family member, a professional trustee, or both. Many trust creators choose a family member as a trustee. A family member usually won't charge a fee and, generally, has a personal stake in the trust's success. If the family member is competent to handle the financial matters involved, has the time and interest to do so, and if you're not afraid of family conflicts, naming a family member as trustee may be a good move, particularly for a small or medium-sized estate.

A professional trustee such as a bank will charge a management fee. In some cases, it can be substantial. Professional trustees also have been criticized for being impersonal in their dealings with beneficiaries who require, or at least desire, more personal attention. On the other hand, a professional trustee is immortal, unlikely to take sides in family conflicts, and commands the kind of investment and money-management expertise that a lay trustee may not possess. Particularly if you have a large estate, give serious consideration to a professional trustee.

Q. Can I name more than one trustee?

A. Yes. Many trust creators name cotrustees. For example, when a married couple decides to establish a trust, the spouse creating the trust often names himself or herself as one cotrustee and the spouse as the second cotrustee. As a further protection, the creator will name a successor trustee who would manage the trust in the event that one or both of the cotrustees dies or resigns their trustee duties.

Q. How can I reduce the costs of a revocable living trust?

A. By doing some preparation, you can minimize the time the lawyer spends on setting up the trust and reduce your legal costs. As in making a will, ask your lawyer what documents are important. After collecting the necessary records, deeds, bank statements, and so on, make a list of your assets and where you want them to go when you die. If you take over the task of transferring assets, that will save the lawyer time—and you money.

Q. What happens to the property in the trust when I die?

A. When you die, your trustee distributes the property according to the terms of the trust.

Q. How does a trust end?

A. A trust often terminates when the principal is distributed to the beneficiaries, at the time stated in the trust agreement. For example, you might provide that a trust for the benefit of your children would end when the youngest child reaches a certain age. At that time, the trustee would distribute the assets to the beneficiaries according to your instructions. The law generally allows a "windup phase" to complete the administration of trust duties (e.g., filing tax returns) after the trust officially has terminated.

You can also give your trustees the discretion to distribute the trust assets and terminate the trust when they think it's a good idea, or place some restrictions on their ability to do so. For example, you could allow the trustees to terminate the trust at their discretion, provided that your daughter has completed her education.

Q. What about irrevocable trusts? How do they end?

A. Your trust should have a termination provision even if it is an irrevocable trust. Irrevocability means that you, the donor, can't change your mind about how you want the trust to terminate. It doesn't mean that you can't set up termination procedures in the first place.

If you have an irrevocable trust and don't have a termination provision, the trust can usually terminate only if all beneficiaries consent and no material purpose of the trust is defeated.

However, an irrevocable trust can also be terminated if there was fraud, duress, undue influence, or other problems when the trust was set up; if the operation of the trust becomes impracticable or illegal; or if the period of time specified in state law expires. We're obviously into technical territory here, so the basic rule is, don't set up an irrevocable trust unless you're prepared to live—and die—by its terms.

THE WORLD AT YOUR FINGERTIPS

- *There are many books about trusts, including* The Complete Book of Trusts, *by Mar-*

ⓘ SOME RESPONSIBILITIES OF THE SUCCESSOR TRUSTEE

If you have become the successor trustee because of the death of the original trustee,

- obtain a copy of the deceased trustee's death certificate as well a copy of the trust creator's death certificate if the creator has died;
- tell the trust creator's family that you are the successor trustee;
- make sure each trust beneficiary has a copy of the trust document;
- inform all financial institutions holding trust assets that you are the new trustee;
- collect and pay all taxes and other debts;
- monitor all income;
- make sure there is an accurate inventory of all trust property;
- ensure that the trust property has been or will be distributed to beneficiaries;
- prepare and file all appropriate tax returns; and
- prepare a final accounting and distribute the assets from the trust to all beneficiaries.

If you become a successor trustee because the creator of the trust, who was also the trustee, has become incapacitated,

- obtain a medical opinion confirming the creator-trustee's incapacity;
- inform the family of the trust creator that you are his or her successor trustee;
- provide each beneficiary with a copy of the trust document;
- inform all financial institutions holding trust property that you are the successor trustee;
- pay all taxes and debts; and
- monitor all income.

tin M. Shenkman (New York: John Wiley &
Sons, 1997).

- There are some useful books that focus on
the mechanics of setting up a living trust,
including The Living Trust Workbook, by
Robert A. Esperti, David K. Cahoone, and
Renno L. Peterson (New York: Penguin,
2001), and Loving Trust: The Right Way to
Provide for Yourself and Guarantee the
Future of Your Loved Ones, Robert A.
Esperti and Renno L. Peterson (New York:
Viking, 1994).

- State law governs trusts, so it's a good idea
to check out the law of your state. Bar
associations often have state-specific information for the public; access www.abanet.
org/barserv/stlobar.html to find contact
information about bars in your state. State
university extension services also often
have public information on trusts. An
example from Ohio is www.oardc.
ohio-state.edu (search on "estate planning"
for information on trusts and many other
estate-planning topics).

REMEMBER THIS

- Trusts come in many different forms—some
help with reducing estate taxes; others
fund the education of children and grandchildren or help provide for people with
disabilities or those who might have trouble managing their own affairs; still others
fund charities.
- Trusts can also provide protection from
your beneficiaries' creditors.
- If a trust is right for you, be sure it's
funded properly and complies with all
legal requirements in your state.
- A living trust can be a useful device—but it
doesn't work automatically and all by
itself. You have to make sure that it is
funded, which probably entails retitling

assets and adding newly acquired assets to
the trust. You also should name one or
more successor trustees, who can take over
from you in case of your incapacity or
upon your death.

- Be sure to coordinate your living trust with
the rest of your estate plan—your will and
the beneficiary designations of insurance
policies, pensions, IRAs and other means
of transferring property.

- A trust must be maintained after it's set
up—that is, by making sure the beneficiary
designations are up to date.

OTHER ESTATE-PLANNING ASSETS AND TOOLS

Jeff and Josie are newlyweds, each of whom has
grown children from a previous marriage. They
decide to buy a house together and take title to
the house in joint tenancy with right of survivorship, making them co-owners.

After unpacking the last boxes, the happy
couple decides to complete the remaking of
their lives and rewrite their wills. Both of them
want their assets to go to their own children
from their first marriages. So each writes a
basic will that leaves everything to his or her
own children. Josie's daughter, who is living in
a tiny apartment with her husband and kids,
will get Jeff and Josie's house when Josie dies;
Jeff's children, who have nice homes already,
will get the rest of the couple's assets. A few
years later, Josie dies, content because she believes she has provided for her daughter and
her family.

Josie will never know that her estate plan
failed to accomplish the one thing she wanted
most: giving her house to her daughter. She
didn't realize that the joint tenancy she and Jeff
created meant that ownership of the entire
house passed to Jeff at the moment of her death,
regardless of what her will said. She never
knew that Jeff was later beset by several costly

illnesses and had to sell the house. His children—not hers—received what was left when Jeff died two years later.

Unfortunately, this situation is familiar to many estate lawyers. Too many people don't understand that there's more to estate planning than writing a will. This section will tell you what else you might need to do.

Q. Isn't a will enough to cover my estate-planning needs?

A. A will is usually the most important document in planning your estate, but it doesn't cover everything. In the community property states (see the community property discussion on page 731), your will can only control half of most marital assets. Other benefits not controlled by a will (or a trust being used as a will substitute) include IRAs, insurance policies, income savings plans, retirement plans, property held in joint tenancy, and, in some jurisdictions, property held in a special form of joint tenancy for married couples called tenancy by the entirety.

A good estate plan must coordinate these benefits with your will. Use them well and you can give your beneficiaries money much more efficiently than a will can. Use them badly and you can negate your estate plan and frustrate your wishes.

Q. My wife and I own our house in joint tenancy. Can't I use joint tenancy to pass property without having to draw up a will?

A. Yes. Joint tenancy is a form of co-ownership. If you and your wife buy a house or a car in both your names and as joint tenants, each of you is considered a joint tenant and has co-ownership. When one of the co-owners dies, joint ownership usually gives the other co-owner instant access to the jointly held property.

Q. What's the difference between joint tenancy and tenancy in common?

A. In **joint tenancy**, you and your spouse, or other co-owner, own *all* of the property—for ex-

ample, a home. Joint tenancy means, among other things, that each owner must agree on such issues as whether to sell the home.

In **tenancy in common,** on the other hand, each owner owns a *share* of the property. In some states, a tenant in common may sell his or her share of the property without the consent of the other owners. Keep in mind, however, that few buyers are interested in purchasing what amounts to part of a home. In tenancy in common, different partners can own unequal shares of the property.

If you own an asset in joint tenancy with anyone and you die, ownership of that asset passes to the other joint tenant automatically. In a tenancy in common, your share passes as provided in your will or trust, with possible consequences of probate, estate taxes, and so on.

Q. Is there another way to give money to minor children besides a will or trust?

A. Yes. The most common way is through the Uniform Gift to Minors Act (UGMA) or the Uniform Transfers to Minors Act (UTMA), which are

---

ⓘ **PROPERTY THAT DOES NOT PASS VIA A WILL**

- Property held in joint tenancy
- Life insurance payable to a named beneficiary
- Property held in a trust
- Retirement plans payable to named beneficiaries, including IRAs, Keogh accounts, and pensions
- Bank accounts payable to named beneficiaries upon the death of the depositor
- Transfer-on-death stock accounts payable to a named beneficiary
- Some community property
- Income savings plans

straightforward enough that you may be able to make a gift without consulting a lawyer. These statutes allow you to open an account in a child's name and deposit money or property in it. If the child is over age thirteen, the income is taxed at his or her tax rate, which, almost certainly, will be lower than yours. For younger children, the gov-ernment taxes income from the account at your tax rate.

Q. Are there some tax-favored ways of providing for children's education?

A. Yes. **Coverdell Education Savings Accounts,** which used to be known as **Education**

⚠ TEN TIMES YOU DON'T WANT TO USE A JOINT TENANCY

1. When you don't want to lose control. By giving someone co-ownership, you give him or her co-control. If you make your son co-owner of the house, you can't sell or mortgage it unless he agrees.

2. When the co-owner's creditors might come after the money. If creditors come after your co-owner, they may be able to get part of the house or bank account held in joint tenancy.

3. When you can't be sure of your co-owner. You and your co-owner could have a falling out and he or she would have rights to the property held jointly.

4. When you're using co-ownership to substitute for a will. Often, parents with several children will put one child's name on an account, assuming he or she will divide the money equally among the other children. But this method provides no control over the money. The surviving joint tenant can do with it what he or she pleases.

5. When it might cause confusion after your death. Unplanned ownership of property often leads to unwanted results—especially for people unable to manage assets.

6. When it won't speed the transfer of assets. Some states automatically freeze jointly owned accounts upon the death of one of the owners until the tax authorities can examine it. As a result, the surviving partner can't count on getting to the money immediately.

7. When it compromises tax planning. Careful planning to minimize the taxes on an estate can be completely thwarted by an inadvertently created joint tenancy that passes property out-right to the surviving tenant.

8. When you're in a shaky marriage. Your individual property may become marital property once it's transferred into joint tenancy.

9. When one of the joint tenants could become incompetent. If this happens, part of the property may go into a conservatorship, making it cumbersome at best if the other joint tenant wants to sell some or all of the jointly held property.

10. When you don't want to transfer assets all at once. Joint tenancies deprive you of the flexibility of a will or a trust in which you can use gifts and asset shifts to minimize taxes or pay out money over time to beneficiaries, instead of giving it to them all at once.

If you have an estate below the federal estate tax level, it might be alright to use joint tenancy—but you should check with a lawyer. Most of the advantages of joint tenancy can be achieved using a revocable living trust.

IRAs, can now be used to cover expenses in elementary and secondary school, not just higher education. You can give as much as $2,000 in a single year for each beneficiary of one of these accounts. Money withdrawn for qualified expenses is exempt from federal taxes.

Prepaid tuition plans, offered by many states, permit you to make payments now toward the tuition of someone not yet enrolled in college. By paying for these tuition credits or certificates at today's tuition rate, you protect yourself against tuition increases in the future. (Tuition has been increasing far more than the inflation rate for many years.) **College savings plans,** offered by almost every state, enable you to save for tuition and other expenses and use them at a wide range of colleges, in-state or out-of-state.

A federal income tax deduction is not available for your contributions to either of these plans (though you might get a state deduction). However, Section 529 of the Federal Tax Code now gives you a lot of attractive, tax-saving options. **Section 529 plans** allow earnings on your contributions to accumulate tax free until they are withdrawn. This is a significant benefit for taxpayers, and especially for high-income taxpayers. Earnings withdrawn to pay tuition and other expenses are now free from federal tax for state-sponsored programs and for qualified plans established by a private education institution.

Hope Tax Credits and Lifelong Learning Credits allow you to claim credits of $1,500 a year in the first two years of your dependent's college years, and up to $1,000 in subsequent years. You can claim one of these credits in the same year that you take a tax-free distribution from a Coverdell account, as long as you meet certain conditions. Unlike the Coverdell accounts, these credits contain income caps so that some high-income individuals cannot claim them.

Q. Are these plans flexible?

A. The Section 529 plans allow you to maintain control over the accounts you set up. You can even change beneficiaries or have the plan balance refunded to you. Even accounts established under the UTMA and the UGMA can be reconverted to a restricted form of a 529 plan. This enables people to control the disposition of assets beyond the time that the beneficiary attains the age of majority. However, assets in 529 plans, unlike the UTMA and UGMA accounts, must be used for educational purposes and not for any other purpose. Also, you cannot change the beneficiary of these restricted plans, nor can you have assets refunded to you. State law will govern what can and cannot happen to an UGMA or an UTMA account. It is important to check with your lawyer before converting an UGMA or an UTMA to a Section 529 plan.

Q. How can I use life insurance in my estate plan?

A. Life insurance often is a very good estate-planning tool, because you pay relatively little up front, and your beneficiaries get much more when you die. When you name beneficiaries other than your estate, the money passes to them directly, without probate.

Life insurance often is used to pay the immediate costs of death (funeral or hospital expenses), set up a fund to support the deceased's family so they won't have to return to work immediately after the death, replace the deceased's lost income, pay for the deceased's children's education, and so on.

You can use life insurance to distribute assets among children from different marriages. And, if your estate is large enough, you can set up an irrevocable trust for your children that's funded with the life insurance policy. You pay the premiums, but the trust actually owns the policy. When you die, your children receive the benefits from the trust, while your spouse gets the rest of your estate.

Q. How do retirement benefits affect my estate plan?

A. Many of us are entitled to retirement benefits from an employer. Typically, a retirement plan will pay benefits to beneficiaries if you die before reaching retirement age. After retirement, you can usually pick an option that will continue payments to a beneficiary after your death. In most cases, the law requires that some portion of these retirement benefits be paid to your spouse. This right may be waived only with your spouse's properly witnessed, signed consent.

IRAs (individual retirement accounts) provide a ready means of cash when one spouse dies. If your spouse is named as the beneficiary, the proceeds immediately will become his or her property when you die. Like retirement benefits (and unlike assets inherited via a will), they will pass to the named beneficiary without having to go through probate. The rules governing IRAs have been changing recently; check with a lawyer to see how such plans can be best coordinated with your estate plan.

Q. Do prenuptial agreements play a role in estate planning?

A. Any couple in a situation where one partner has a lot more money or property than the other, or where one partner is substantially older than the other, should consider entering into a prenuptial agreement as part of their estate planning.

Older people with grown children from another marriage may want their property to go to their own children after they die, rather than to the new spouse and his or her children. A prenuptial agreement can accomplish this purpose. See chapter 3, "Family Law," for more information about prenuptial agreements.

Q. I live in a community property state. How does this affect my estate plan?

A. The laws of eight states—Arizona, California, Idaho, Louisiana, Nevada, New Mexico, Texas, and Washington—and Puerto Rico provide that most property acquired during the marriage by either spouse is held equally by husband and wife as community property—that is, as property belonging to both spouses. (Alaska and Wisconsin have some community property elements in their law but are not true community property states.) The major exceptions are property acquired dur-

ing the marriage by inheritance or gift. In a community property state, when one spouse dies, his or her half of the property passes either by will or operation of law; the other half of the property belongs to the surviving spouse.

If you live in a community property state, you can only dispose of your half of the community property via a will or a trust. If you and your spouse have the same estate-planning objectives, it's no problem. But if you don't, living in a community property state could make it more difficult to meet your estate-planning goals.

Q. I live in a separate property state but own property in a community property state. Which law applies?

A. If the property is real estate, state laws may treat it as community property for estate-planning purposes. Thus, if you live in Arkansas (a separate property state) but own land in Texas (a community property state), an Arkansas court probating your will would treat the Texas property just as Texas would—as community property. But not every state would extend the same courtesy.

This separate/community property division can get pretty complicated—and this is only one example of how state laws differ. If you own property in more than one state, consult an estate-planning lawyer who is conversant with the estate laws of each different state.

Q. Should I give some of my property away before I die?

A. Making gifts during your lifetime can be a good idea, especially if you have a large estate. They can help you avoid high estate and inheritance taxes. In some states, they might enable you to reduce an estate to one that is small enough to avoid formal probate procedures. Another advantage of giving property away before you die is that you get to see the recipient's appreciation of your generosity.

But watch out for a few pitfalls. These gifts will be subject to gift taxes if they're larger than the amount provided by law. Current law allows you to give up to $11,000 per person per year

($22,000, if a couple makes the gift) before the gift tax applies. You can make gifts to any number of people, whether related to you or not. You can also make gifts to trusts, but keep in mind that not all trust gifts qualify for this exclusion.

You need to put in your will a statement that any gifts you have made before you died are not to be considered advances. Without such a clear statement of intent, the probate courts in some states may subtract the amount of the gift from the amount you left in the will.

When Circumstances Change

Q. Once I've planned my estate, do I have to worry about it again?

A. Life does not stand still. Children and grandchildren are born. You or people in your family might get married or divorced. Your income may go up or down, and your beneficiaries' needs may change.

After you've crafted your initial estate plan, your circumstances are likely to change—you may have more children, acquire more assets, or have a falling out with your spouse, other relatives, or friends you've named as beneficiaries. Other major changes in your life or in your financial situation might include the purchase of a new house, divorce or remarriage, moving to another state, a big jump (or decline) in income, death of relatives, and so on. These and other life changes will occasion a change in your estate plan.

It's a good idea to review your will or trust document along with your inventory of assets and list of beneficiaries every three or four years to make sure your past decisions continue to meet your current needs. Think of estate planning not as a onetime transaction, but as a process that works best if periodically reviewed.

Q. How do I change my will after it has been executed?

A. You can change, add to, or even revoke your will any time before your death as long as you are physically and mentally competent to make the change. An amendment to a will is called a **codicil.**

You can't simply cross out old provisions in your will and scribble in new ones if you want the changes to be effective. You have to formally execute a codicil, using the same procedures that were used when you executed the will itself. The codicil should be dated and kept with the will. It's a good idea to check with your lawyer before signing a codicil or revoking your will.

Q. When and how should I revoke my will entirely?

A. Sometimes, when you have a major life change, such as a divorce or a remarriage, winning the lottery, having more children, or getting the last child out of the house, it's a good idea to rewrite your will from scratch rather than making a lot of small changes through codicils. You can do this by executing a formal statement of revocation and executing a new will that revokes the old one.

If you write a new will, be sure to include the date it's signed and executed and put in a sentence to the effect that the new will revokes all previous wills. Otherwise, a court might rule that the new will only revokes the old one where the two conflict.

Q. What happens if I fail to keep my will up to date?

A. Some life changes may be accommodated by the law, regardless of what your will says. For example, if you have a new child, and don't explicitly say you don't want him or her to inherit anything, the law generally will put that child in the same position as the children that you did provide for in your will. So if you split your estate evenly between two children and didn't provide for a child born after the will was made, the court could give each child a third of the estate.

If you don't include your new spouse in the will (or the spouse you've had for years, for that matter), he or she has the right to take a share of the estate. This typically varies from 33 to 50 percent, depending on state law. If the spouse does not elect to take the share, the property is distributed as specified in your will.

Q. What about property that I acquire after I write my will?

A. If you come into property that is not accounted for by the will, it becomes part of your **residuary estate.** If you have a residuary clause in your will, you can specify which person or institution should get everything not specifically identified in the will.

But even if you have a residuary clause, it's best to modify your will periodically to account for life changes or "after-acquired assets." If you don't, you run the risk of paying higher taxes, giving certain property to people you don't want to have it, or creating confusion (and possibly pro-

---

▶ DO I NEED TO UPDATE MY ESTATE PLAN? A CHECKLIST

Ask yourself if any of these changes have occurred in your life since you executed your will or trust.

- Have you married or been divorced?
- Have your children married or been divorced?
- Do your children or any other beneficiaries need protection from creditors?
- Have relatives or other beneficiaries or the executor died, or has your relationship with them changed substantially?
- Has the mental or physical condition of any of your relatives or other beneficiaries or your trustee or executor changed substantially?
- Have you had more children or grandchildren, or have children gone to college or moved out of, or into, your home?
- Have you moved to another state?
- Have you bought, sold, or mortgaged a business or real estate?
- Have you acquired major assets (car, home, bank account)?
- Have you inherited significant property?
- Have your business or financial circumstances changed significantly (estate size, stock portfolio value, pension, salary, ownership)?
- Has your state law (or have federal tax laws) changed in a way that might affect your tax and estate planning?
- Have you changed your ideas about what to do with any of your assets?
- Have you decided to do more (or less) charitable giving?
- Have you made gifts that should be taken into account, such as by reducing bequests that were to occur under the will?

When you do update your estate plan, you should also update your final instructions and will with the addresses and phone numbers of beneficiaries, trustees, executors, and others mentioned in estate-planning documents. It will make settling the estate much easier.

bate delays or even litigation) among your grieving relatives after you're gone.

Q. What other documents should I update?

A. Other estate-planning documents you should take care to keep up-to-date include IRAs, insurance policies, income savings plans such as 401(k) plans, government savings bonds (if payable to another person), and retirement plans. You should keep a record of these documents with your will and update them as needed when you update your will.

Q. What if I set up a revocable living trust, then change my mind about it?

A. You can modify a trust through a procedure called an **amendment.** You should amend your trust when you want to change or add beneficiaries, take assets from the trust, or change trustees. You amend a trust by adding a new page for every change, specifying the new additions. To avoid a legal challenge from a disgruntled non-beneficiary, you should not detach a page from the trust document, retype it to include the new information, and put it back in its original place.

Q. What do I have to do to add property to the trust?

A. You don't have to write a formal amendment to the trust to add property to it, because a properly drafted trust will contain language giving you the right to include property acquired after the trust is drafted. Just make sure the new property is titled as being owned by the trustee and list it on the schedule of assets in the trust. You do have to amend the trust if the newly acquired property is going to a different beneficiary than the one already named in the trust.

Q. I want to make some very sweeping changes to my trust. How do I do this?

A. You should revoke, not amend, your trust when making major changes. You revoke a trust by destroying all copies of it or writing "revoked" on each page and signing them. When you create a new trust to replace a revoked one, give the new trust a different name, usually one containing the date the new document was executed.

THE WORLD AT YOUR FINGERTIPS

- *If you want to find out more about pension rights and options, the administrator of your pension is a good place to start; check with your employer. For more general information about pensions, access the site of the Pension Rights Center, which has many excellent links: www. pensionrights.org.*

- *For more information about IRAs, check the AARP website (www.aarp.org/ confacts/grandparents/ira.html).*

- *For beneficiary designations in general, personal finance sites often have good information. Try the Forbes site at www.forbes.com/estate_planning; the American Express site at www. americanexpress.com/homepage/mt_ personal.shtml, and the Merrill Lynch site at www.askmerrill.com.*

- *AllLaw.com (www.alllaw.com) has some articles on changing estate plans, as do law firm sites such as the Kern DeWenter Viere site at www.kdv.com/ nonprofit-articles/effective.html, and the Kegler Brown Hill and Ritter site at www.keglerbrown.com/publications/estate/ index.shtml.*

REMEMBER THIS

- *A will isn't the only thing involved in estate planning. Talk to your lawyer about your retirement plans, your bank accounts, and any property you hold in joint tenancy.*

- *Changes in your life often necessitate a change in your estate plan, so it's important regularly to schedule a review and, if necessary, update of your plan.*

- *Make sure to revise your estate plan if you've experienced major life or financial changes since it was prepared or last updated.*

SOME SPECIAL CIRCUMSTANCES

Most people who plan an estate probably have some special requirements that have to be taken into account—property in a different state, stepchildren, a divorced spouse, no spouse at all, or someone they live with but haven't married. This section provides a quick look at some of the ways planning can help.

Q. I own a vacation house in a state other than the one where I have my primary residence. Which law applies to property in different states?

A. The laws of the state where your primary home is located determine what happens to your personal property—car, stocks, and cash.

The laws of the state in which any other real estate is located govern its distribution. If you do own homes or land in different states, it's a good idea to make sure that the provisions of your estate-planning documents comply with the laws of the appropriate states.

Q. My life partner and I aren't married. Are there any special estate-planning strategies about which we should be aware?

A. It's especially important to write a will or a trust if you're in an unmarried relationship, because a will or a trust lets you leave your property

---

▶ **ARE YOUR AFFAIRS IN ORDER?**

Here are some questions to ask yourself to see if you've really done everything you can to prepare for your death.

- Where are your bank accounts?
- Where is the deed to your home and other real estate records?
- Who is your lawyer? Your broker? Your executor? Your accountant?
- What credit cards do you have? What are their numbers?
- Where is your will? Who drew it up?
- What insurance do you have? Where is the documentation?
- What other funds will be paid to your family after your death?
- Do you have a retirement account such as an IRA, or a pension fund? Where are the relevant documents?
- Where is your safe-deposit box?
- Where are your other valuables stored?
- What stocks, securities, bonds, annuities, and the like do you own? Where are the relevant documents?
- Have you provided for the guardianship of your minor children?
- What funeral arrangements have you made? Where are they written down?

to anyone or any organization you wish. A will or a trust also lets you name an executor or trustee for your estate to supervise distribution of your assets. If you want your partner to inherit a good share of your property, naming your partner or someone sympathetic to the relationship as executor or trustee can help to ensure that your wishes are carried out.

Furthermore, if you want your partner to receive the proceeds from a life insurance policy, IRA, bank accounts, and so on, you need to name your partner as the beneficiary in each of those documents separately. The advantage of using beneficiary designations and other nonprobate arrangements (such as holding property in joint tenancy with your partner) is that the transfers will take place automatically on your death; no disgruntled relatives can hold up your desires as they can in a will contest.

Q. How do gay or unmarried couples keep control over funeral arrangements?

A. Funeral arrangements can be an especially sensitive subject for an unmarried couple. Since tradition and the law often give the deceased's blood or legal relatives—not an unmarried partner—the right to control funeral arrangements, many nonmarital partners have been infuriated to find out at the funeral that no mention was made of the relationship or of the fact that the deceased had a life partner.

To prevent this, you should put your funeral instructions into writing and name your partner as the person responsible for carrying out those instructions. You might mention these instructions in your will as well, although you should remember that sometimes a funeral is over before the will is read. Still, the mention of your wishes in a will and a signed statement of funeral instructions should go a long way toward convincing funeral directors of your partner's authority in the event of a dispute between the partner and other family members.

Q. I've heard about cohabitation agreements. Can they help?

A. Sometimes unmarried people create cohabitation agreements to cover the rights and responsibilities of each partner. These agreements cover such contingencies as each partner's disability and division of property in case the relationship ends. They often are coordinated with wills and trusts. You'll want a lawyer who's experienced in nonspousal domestic partnerships to help you write yours.

A word of caution is in order, however. In some states, cohabitation, regardless of the sex of the parties, may be thought to be against sound public policy. In these states, the courts might not enforce cohabitation agreements.

Q. My marriage is on the rocks. How does divorce affect my estate plan?

A. Depending on your state's law, a divorce may revoke your will in its entirety or those provisions of your will that favored your former spouse. Either way, be sure to revise your will or write a new one when you get divorced, changing the provisions that relate to your former spouse and his or her family. Be sure to modify other related documents such as living wills, survivorships, and insurance policies.

Trusts may need to be specifically amended, and names of trustees changed if they were members of your ex-spouse's family. Settlement negotiations at the time of the divorce should include all these issues. Retirement benefits subject to the Employee Retirement Income Security Act, or ERISA (see chapter 12, "Law and the Workplace," and chapter 16, "The Rights of Older Americans") especially need to be looked into. Since ERISA rules preempt state law, the designation of your now ex-spouse as beneficiary won't be revoked and will have to be changed.

Q. I'm divorced and considering remarrying. How will this affect my estate plan?

A. If you're one member of an older couple in which both you and your spouse have children from a previous marriage, you might want to arrange things so your own money goes to your own children and your spouse's money goes to his or her children.

The versatility of a revocable living trust makes it a useful instrument for allocating assets among different families. You can set up a separate trust for the children of different marriages, or even for each family member.

Some families are using **qualified terminable interest property trusts** to address the special concerns of stepfamilies. This type of trust allows you to do several things: (1) leave your property in trust for your spouse during your spouse's lifetime; (2) give the trust property to someone else after your spouse's death; and (3) reduce estate taxes. Talk to your lawyer about the details of such a trust.

Q. I'm single. Would an estate plan help if I become mentally or physically incapacitated?

A. Yes. During estate planning, many people also plan for possible mental or physical incapacity. This planning is especially important for a single person who may want to designate someone other than a relative to manage his or her property and affairs in the event of incapacity. A living will or a durable health-care power of attorney can enable you to pick someone to make decisions for you about medical treatment, including decisions about using or terminating life support systems.

You can select someone to direct your financial affairs in the event of your incapacity by executing a durable power of attorney for financial matters. This type of power of attorney gives a specific named individual access to your assets and the authority to manage those assets, to pay bills, and to take any other action needed to keep your financial house in order during your incapacity. See chapter 16, "The Rights of Older Americans," for more information on living wills and similar legal documents designed for the purpose of providing health care in the event of incapacity.

Q. How does estate planning work in conjunction with preserving eligibility for Medicaid, so that it can pay for long-term care?

A. If you're unable to pay for long-term care, Medicaid planning can help you meet the Medicaid financial eligibility requirements and slow the depletion of your estate or preserve some of it for your spouse or dependents. Medicaid planning uses legally permitted options under Medicaid to preserve assets and try to assure your survivor some financial security. Unfortunately, most of the self-help advice regarding Medicaid planning is fraught with danger. Even with competent advice tailored to your needs, Medicaid planning is not easy, so be sure to see your lawyer.

Q. I have a business. Should I account for it in my estate plan?

A. Yes. An estate plan can make sure your business is not thrown into chaos upon your death or incapacity. You can provide for an orderly succession and continuation of its affairs by spelling out in your plan what will happen to your interest.

Q. Can I help a favorite cause through my estate planning?

A. Yes. Your estate plan can help support religious, educational, and other charitable causes, either during your lifetime or upon your death, while at the same time taking advantage of tax laws designed to encourage private philanthropy.

THE WORLD AT YOUR FINGERTIPS

- *The site of Divorce magazine has many articles on the legal side of divorce at www.divorcemagazine.com. The Divorce Online website (www.divorceonline.com/) also contains useful information.*

- *The Cornell Legal Information Institute site includes basic legal information about divorce as well as a state-by-state listing of the law at www.law.cornell.edu/topics/ divorce.html.*

- *Many gay rights groups offer publications and other information about the legal rights and needs of people who are in nontraditional relationships. A good place to start is the Lambda Legal Foundation at www.lambdalegal.org.*

- **Prenups for Lovers,** *by Arlene G. Dubin (New York: Villard Books, 2001), discusses the need for cohabitation agreements.*
- *Search on "cohabitation agreements" on the Internet to find many sources of information. A particularly useful site is the Equality in Marriage Institute at www.equalityinmarriage.org.*

REMEMBER THIS

- *Revise your will and trust when you feel a marriage is irretrievably broken. Even if state law does this for you when a divorce is final, it probably doesn't help you at all in the months and years it takes to become legally divorced. Change it now.*
- *Many people remarry, creating patchwork families that can be ripe for conflict. A number of estate-planning devices can help you deal with potential problems.*
- *Although society is slowly recognizing nontraditional partnerships, the law in most places is still written under the assumption that people in committed relationships will be legally married to a person of the opposite sex. If your partner-*

▶ YOUR FINAL INSTRUCTIONS

Your final instructions should list the following:

- Funeral arrangements—information about any funeral plan you've bought or account you've set up to pay burial expenses, location of cemetery and burial plot, choice of funeral director and services, and so on

- Disposition of your body—directions specifying burial, cremation, or donation to science

- Provision for donating certain specified organs for transplants

- The name of any charity or cause to which you wish contributions sent in your name

- The location of your will and the identity and telephone number of the executor and your lawyer

- The location of any trust document and the identity of any cotrustee or successor trustee

- The location of your safe-deposit box, the key to it, and any important records not located in it such as birth certificates; marriage, divorce, and prenuptial documents; military discharge records and your service number; important business, insurance, and financial records; and pension and benefit agreements

- An inventory of assets, including documents of debts owed and loans outstanding, credit card information, post office box and key, information on any investments, household contents, bank accounts, list of expected death benefits, and so on

- Important information: names, addresses, and dates and places of birth for you and your spouse, family members and other heirs, and ex-spouses, if any; Social Security numbers for you and your spouse and dependent children, along with the location of Social Security cards; policy numbers and telephone numbers and addresses of insurance companies and agencies that control your death benefits (employer, union, Veterans Affairs office, etc.)

- Information you want in your obituary

ship doesn't fit this traditional pattern, it's crucial to work with your lawyer to craft an estate plan that protects you and your partner in a way that you both prefer.

DEATH AND TAXES

Ever since Caesar Augustus imposed an estate levy to pay for imperial Roman exploits, death and taxes have walked hand in bony hand. No one really likes paying taxes, but let's not forget that they pay for most of the things we value in modern society: defending the nation; providing health care, jobs, and housing; paving the roads; and so on.

Death taxes also have been a way of redistributing wealth. Franklin Roosevelt used the estate and gift tax system to do so during the Great Depression. It enabled the transfer of money from those with wealth to those who were unfortunate during those hard times. This section explains the basics of federal and state estate taxes.

Q. I'm not rich. Do I have to worry about federal estate taxes?

A. Your estate isn't liable for federal estate taxation unless it exceeds the **available exemption amount.** This magic number is the value of assets that each person may pass on to beneficiaries without paying federal estate tax. The **Economic Growth and Tax Relief Reconciliation Act of 2001 (EGTRRA)** provides for a gradual increase in the exemption. It is now $1.5 million and will rise to $2 million in 2006.

In addition, you can pass your entire estate, without any estate taxes, to your spouse. (This is called the **unlimited marital deduction.**) If you simply leave your estate to your spouse and don't create an appropriate trust to take advantage of your exemption (see the previous paragraph for exemption amounts in particular years), your spouse's estate will pay taxes on any amount over the exemption amount when he or she dies.

If your estate is likely to exceed the current threshold, however, good estate planning can sharply reduce the amount of money that goes to the government instead of to your beneficiaries.

Q. The law allows me to leave everything to my spouse tax free, right? How can we use that to our children's maximum advantage?

A. The best provision of federal estate tax law from the taxpayer's perspective is the **unified credit,** which gives each person a $1.5 million total exemption from estate taxation in 2004 and 2005 (the amount will go up in later years). But what do you do if your wealth exceeds that amount?

One of the most basic tax-planning devices is the unlimited marital deduction. It allows one spouse to pass his or her entire estate, regardless of size, to the other—and not pay federal estate taxes. No matter how large the estate, no taxes are due when it is passed to the spouse.

If you only cared about leaving your property to your spouse, that would end your tax worries. Most people, however, want to leave property to their families at the death of the second spouse— and this is where tax planning pays off.

To take full advantage of the unified credit and the unlimited marital deduction, married taxpayers with assets above the exemption amount probably will be advised to use a trust. Trusts are one of the main ways to minimize taxes upon death.

Using the marital deduction properly, usually in conjunction with a tax-saving trust, you should be able to transfer at least double the exemption amount free of estate taxes to your children or other beneficiaries no matter which spouse dies first or who accumulated the wealth.

Q. What about state death taxes?

A. Some states charge an additional estate tax similar to the tax imposed by the federal government; other states impose an inheritance tax. (**Inheritance taxes** are charged to beneficiaries; **estate taxes** are charged to the deceased person's estate.)

What is taxed and at what rate depends on state law, not only of the state in which you live but also of the state where the property is located. Unless your state has an inheritance tax, your beneficiaries don't pay tax when they receive money or other property from your estate. But they will have to pay income tax on any earnings after they invest the bequest. In addition, death itself may produce numerous tax consequences.

Q. I'm the owner of a business, and I understand that my estate would have to pay taxes on the value of the business if I don't do anything—but what can I do to lighten the tax load?

A. Congress is sympathetic to the plight of business owners and has created several breaks in the tax code for you. One of these allows your estate to pay the estate tax on the business over as long as fifteen years, while paying only a 2 percent interest rate on the deferred tax. Another allows your executor to reduce the value of the business by as much as $300,000 for estate tax purposes. Both of these tax breaks have complex requirements, and you should not assume that you will qualify automatically.

But you are not limited to these targeted tax-reduction methods. There are a number of other tested estate-planning techniques—such as annual gifting and placing your business in a family partnership—that can have the effect of reducing the value of the business in your estate. The successful implementation of these techniques will require the services of an experienced estate-planning lawyer.

Q. What if I receive a bequest and don't want it?

ⓘ SUBJECT TO INCOME TAX

Most of us won't have to pay estate taxes, but what about income taxes that result from a death? Although the standard bequests in a will pass to the beneficiaries free of income tax, some income is still subject to income tax when received by the estate or its beneficiaries, including

- wages, bonuses, and fringe benefits;
- deferred compensation;
- stock options;
- qualified retirement plans;
- some IRAs (other than Roth IRAs);
- medical savings accounts;
- insurance renewal commissions;
- professional fees;
- interest earned before death;
- dividends declared before death;
- crop shares;
- royalties;
- proceeds of a sale entered into before death; and
- alimony arrearages.

A. Because of taxes or other reasons, those named as beneficiaries in a will or a trust document may not want the property left to them. For example, if you go bankrupt and then your father dies, your creditors may be entitled to first shot at the property he left to you. You might want to give up this property so that it will go, for example, to your sister instead of to your creditors. Or you may receive property that is subject to liens and mortgages greater than its market value, so it is a burden you would rather not have.

Most states permit beneficiaries to **disclaim** (that is, refuse) an inheritance or benefit. The Internal Revenue Code describes how a beneficiary may disclaim an interest in an estate for estate tax purposes. See a knowledgeable tax lawyer if you intend to disclaim any gift.

THE WORLD AT YOUR FINGERTIPS

- *The IRS is a good source of information about estate tax: access www.irs.gov or get publications from a local office.*
- *Many estate-planning law firms maintain useful sites with information about taxes and avoidance strategies. One such firm is Lena Barnett and Associates at www.lenabarnett.com/articles.htm.*
- *There are many books for laypeople on estate taxes. See, in particular,* Protect Your Estate: Definitive Strategies for Estate and Wealth Planning from the Leading Experts, *by Robert Esperti and Renno L. Peterson (New York: McGraw-Hill, 1999), and* JK Lasser's New Rules for Estate Planning and Tax, *by Harold Apolinsky and Stuart Welch III (New York: John Wiley & Sons, 2001).*

REMEMBER THIS

- *Your estate isn't liable for federal estate taxation unless it exceeds the available exemption amount. This is currently $1.5 million, and will rise to $2 million in 2006.*

- *The new tax act presents new income tax issues at death. All estate plans, especially those of married individuals, must address these new issues.*
- *If you're married, when your estate gets over the $3 million mark in 2004 and 2005 ($4 million in 2006), trusts are the way to save as many taxes as possible.*
- *By using the marital exemption and "unified credit," you can shelter much of your money from taxation, but the laws and accounting in this realm are so complicated that you should certainly rely on the advice of a good tax lawyer.*

PROBATE

We all know about traffic court and criminal court and small-claims court. But they don't do TV shows about probate court. What is this institution that most of us can live without but not die without?

This section covers the basics of probate, the procedure that determines the validity of a will, and the probate process.

Q. What is probate?

A. Probate is the court-supervised legal procedure that determines the validity of a will. Probate affects some, but not all of your assets. Nonprobate assets include things like a life insurance policy paid directly to a beneficiary.

The term "probate" also is used in the larger sense of administering your estate. In this sense, probate means the process by which assets are gathered, applied to pay debts, taxes, and expenses of administration, and distributed to those designated as beneficiaries in the will. Though probate has become far less complex and costly in recent years, the law continues to require that a court have a role in the probate process, and a court will be at least minimally involved in the probating of all wills.

Q. Who is involved in the probate process?

A. The main players are the probate court and your personal representative. The probate court's involvement varies depending on what kind of probate procedure exists in your jurisdiction. There are various degrees of court supervision required in different areas.

If you have a will, the **personal representative** is called your executor—the person you appointed in your will to administer your estate. The executor named in the will is in charge of this process, and probate provides an orderly method for administration of the estate. If you don't have a will, the court will appoint someone to handle these tasks.

Q. I've heard that probate is expensive, time consuming, and bureaucratic. True?

A. Probate used to be all that and more. But times have changed and so has the probate process in most states. Today, it is seldom as costly and time consuming as in the past.

Q. How long does probate take? How does my family survive before my estate is freed up?

A. The average estate completes the probate process in six to nine months, depending on the state's probate laws. The reformed probate procedures in many states now make it possible for your survivors to obtain funds to live on while your estate is being probated, without waiting for the entire estate to clear probate.

Q. What are the advantages of probate?

A. Despite its sometimes cumbersome nature, probate does help assure that those—and only those—entitled to take part of your estate do so, even if it takes them a year to get their share. It reduces the time for creditors to present claims against the estate. While it's a public proceeding, how many of us are really worried about someone going through our estate records? Privacy, though highly touted by living trust salespeople, is usu-

ally the concern of celebrities and the ultrarich, not the rest of us.

Q. How much does probate cost?

A. The expenses of probate (which can include court and appraiser fees) depend on the state in which you live and the size of your estate. If there are complications—for example, an invalid will or a will contest—naturally the costs will go up.

Q. How can I avoid or limit probate?

A. In many states, it may well not be worth the trouble to avoid probate. But if your lawyer thinks probate is apt to be costly or time consuming for your estate, good estate planning can minimize expenses. Passing most of your property through a living trust or by joint tenancy or some other means that avoids probate leaves very little property to be distributed through your will. The smaller the size of the probate estate, the lower the costs, especially if it is small enough to qualify for expedited processing. Most states have adopted alternatives to formal probate procedures for wills that do not pass real estate or assets over a certain amount. These procedures can help save court fees, lawyer's fees, and executor fees.

Q. What if my estate doesn't qualify for such simplified probate?

ⓘ WHAT HAPPENS IN PROBATE?

- Your will is filed with the probate court and its validity is determined.

- All property, debts, and claims of the estate are inventoried and appraised.

- All valid claims of the estate are collected.

- The remainder of the estate is distributed to beneficiaries according to the will.

A. If your estate is relatively small or uncomplicated and your will is well drafted, your spouse or other executor may not need a lawyer to help with the probate process. If things get more complex, the need for a lawyer becomes greater. The more complex the probate process, the more hours the lawyer will have to put in—and the more it will cost.

Q. Should I plan my estate to try to avoid probate?

A. For some people—such as those who own considerable property in states other than the one in which they reside, or who need rapid administration of their assets, such as stock speculators or people who own businesses in volatile markets, those who live abroad, and some others—probate avoidance should be the primary goal of their estate plan. They might be well advised to put their property into a living trust. But for many other families, especially those of moderate means, it can actually be more trouble to avoid probate than to go through it.

Q. Can't I just avoid probate by not writing a will?

A. No. You can't avoid probate by not having a will. Even if you don't write a will (i.e., if you die intestate), you'll still have one—the one the state writes for you. The court will appoint a personal representative—the **administrator.** The adminis-

---

> ▶ **DO IT RIGHT**
>
> If you do intend to save money by avoiding probate, don't make the mistake so many people eager to avoid probate have made—using a one-size-fits-all-estates trust form from a book or a computer program that doesn't take into account all your estate-planning needs (such as providing for your family) and the peculiarities of your individual situation.

---

trator's job is essentially the same as the executor's; the only difference is that he or she is appointed by the court instead of being selected by you in your will. Probate will take place, but it will cost more and take more time because you didn't leave a will.

Q. Is a lawyer necessary for probate?

A. It depends largely on what state you live in and the size of your estate. Even though probate laws have become simpler in most states, the process can be complex and time consuming. As a result, it may be more expensive for a nonlawyer to negotiate than it is for an experienced estate lawyer.

Some states even prohibit executors from handling probate without a lawyer's assistance. On the other hand, some states have simplified probate procedures so much that it is often possible for a nonlawyer to probate a small estate.

There is good news if you're in one of the categories of people who can profit from probate-avoidance techniques like a living trust or other nonprobate transfers of property, such as joint tenancy or life insurance. Even though in these cases you still need a will to dispose of residual property (most of your assets will be distributed in other ways), the cost and time to probate such a simple will is minimal, even with a lawyer's assistance.

Q. What can my family do to reduce the costs of probating my estate?

A. For most estates, you can appoint a non-lawyer as executor (usually a family member) to do most of the work, such as gathering information and records. The executor files the required forms, calculates and pays the taxes, and distributes the estate assets. If the executor has any questions, he or she can consult an experienced estate lawyer. The lawyer may be needed only for court appearances.

Q. What does it mean when a will is contested?

A. Human nature being what it is, some people who don't receive what they consider a fair share from a dead relative's will may want to challenge, that is, **contest,** the will.

Chief among the grounds for a will contest is that the will was not executed properly; the testator lacked **testamentary capacity** (the ability to make a will—for example, he was senile when he left his estate to the named beneficiary); undue influence (the evil sister hypnotized her dying brother into leaving her the whole estate); fraud (the evil brother retyped a page of the will to give himself the Porsche collection); or mistake (you will your million-dollar summer home to "my cousin John" and it turns out you have three cousins named John).

Q. How can I plan to avoid a will contest?

A. There's an old saying that you never really know someone until a will is read. However, if your will conforms to legal requirements, a challenge is unlikely to be successful. It's also another reason to consult with an experienced estate-planning lawyer and to update your will periodically.

There are other concrete steps you can take to reduce the chances of a will contest. One is called a **no-contest clause,** which in some states allows you to disinherit a beneficiary who unsuc-

cessfully contests the will. Of course, be aware that any heir can always challenge a trust or a will by claiming that the person who executed the document did not have the legal capacity to do so or did so as a result of fraud or undue influence. But if you exercise care and obtain good legal advice, these challenges will be defeated and your intentions will be carried out.

THE WORLD AT YOUR FINGERTIPS

- *IRS Publication 559 has tax information for executors and survivors. You can access it online at www.irs.gov/pub/irs-pdf/p559. pdf.*

- *Insurance company websites often have useful information for executors and family members. For example, the USAA site covers the duties of an executor, the probate process, and suggestions for coping with grief; you can access it at www. usaaedfoundation.org/family/coping/cp04/ cp04.htm.*

ⓘ PROPERTY THAT AVOIDS PROBATE

- Property in a trust
- Property that is jointly held (but *not* community property)
- Death benefits from insurance policies, the government, and employers and other benefits controlled by a designation of beneficiary
- Gifts made before your death
- Individual retirement accounts
- Money in pay-on-death accounts

▶ FREEZE-PROOF SOME ASSETS

One potential probate-related problem worth worrying about is the freezing of assets that automatically occurs in some states when a person dies and his estate goes into probate. Even jointly held bank accounts are sometimes frozen until state tax authorities can assess their value. Some state laws allow the spouse to receive some or all of the funds within a few days of death, but some do not. Lesson: when planning your estate, find out your state's law, and make sure your survivors have some freeze-proof method of getting hold of money during whatever the period of delay is in your state.

- *Helpful books that take you through the process include* The Executor's Handbook, *by Theodore E. Hughes and David Klein (New York: Facts on File, 2001);* Probate and Settling an Estate: Step-by-Step, *by James John Jurinski (New York: Barron's, 1997); and* How to Administer an Estate: A Step-by-Step Guide for Families and Friends, *by Stephen G. Christianson (Franklin Lakes, N.J.: Career Press, 2001).*

REMEMBER THIS

- *For most people, probate isn't nearly the monster that it used to be, so think carefully and consult your lawyer before investing in schemes to avoid it.*
- *At the same time, you can take steps now to minimize the probate court's involvement in administering your estate, so that the process is as quick and painless as possible.*

Appendix

A

acceptance – Consent to the terms of an **offer**, creating a **contract**.

acquittal – A trial verdict that indicates that the defendant in a criminal case has not been found guilty of the crime charged, beyond a reasonable doubt. Note that "acquittal" and "not guilty" are not the same as "innocent," a term not found in criminal law. See **guilty** and **not guilty**.

action – A legal dispute brought to court for trial and settlement (see also **case, lawsuit**).

actual damages – See **compensatory damages**.

actus reus – A Latin term meaning "the criminal act." The actus reus is the wrongful act that is the physical component of a crime; the other component of a crime is the **mens rea,** or criminal intention.

addendum – See **rider.**

ademption – Failure of a gift because the willmaker, by the time of death, no longer owns the property that the willmaker attempted to bequeath in the will.

adhesion contract – A contract between two parties of unequal bargaining power. It is not negotiated and usually is embodied in a standardized form prepared by the dominant party. Also called a **contract of adhesion.**

adjudication – Giving or pronouncing a judgment or decree; also the judgment given.

administration – The process of collecting the estate's assets; paying its debts, taxes, expenses, and other obligations; and distributing the remainder as directed by the will.

administrator – A personal representative, appointed by a probate court, who administers the estate of someone who dies without a will or leaves a will naming an executor who dies before the willmaker or who refuses to serve.

admissible evidence – Evidence that can be legally and properly introduced in a trial.

advance directive – A document in which a person expresses his or her wishes regarding medical treatment in the event of incapacitation. The two most common forms of advance directive are a living will and a durable **power of attorney** for health care. In the latter, a person can appoint a health care agent to make decisions on his or her behalf.

adversary system – The system of trial practice in the U.S. and some other countries, which is based on the belief that truth can best be determined by giving opposing parties full opportunity to present and establish their evidence, and to test by cross-examination the evidence presented by their adversaries, under established rules of procedure before an impartial judge and/or jury. An adversary proceeding is contested because it has opposing parties (differs from **ex parte** proceeding).

affidavit – A written statement of fact given voluntarily and under oath. For example, in criminal cases, affidavits often are used by police officers seeking to convince courts to grant a **warrant** to make an arrest or a search. In civil cases, affidavits of witnesses often are used to support motions for **summary judgment.**

affirmative defense – Without denying the charge, the defendant raises extenuating or mitigating circumstances such as insanity, self-defense, or entrapment to avoid civil or criminal responsibility. The defendant must prove any affirmative defense he or she raises.

affirmed – In the practice of appellate courts, the word means that the decision or order at issue is declared valid and will stand as rendered in the lower court.

age of majority – The age at which a person is considered to be legally responsible for all of his or her actions and is granted by law the rights of an adult. In most states the age of majority is eighteen.

agent – A person authorized to act on behalf of and under the control of another person, called the **principal.** The agent is a **fiduciary.**

alimony – A court-ordered payment for the support of one's estranged spouse in the case of divorce or separation. Alimony also is known as **maintenance** or **spousal support.**

allegation – The statement in a **pleading** of what a party expects to prove. For example, an indictment contains allegations of crime against the defendant.

alternative dispute resolution (ADR) – Means of settling a dispute without a formal trial. **Mediation** and **arbitration** are forms of ADR.

amicus brief – A document filed by an **amicus curiae** in support of a party in a lawsuit.

amicus curiae – A Latin term meaning "friend of the court." A party who volunteers information on some aspect of a case or law to assist the court in its deliberation.

ancillary bill or suit – A cause of action growing out of and supported by another action or suit, such as a proceeding for the enforcement of a judgment.

answer – A **pleading** by which a defendant resists or otherwise responds to the plaintiff's **allegation** of facts.

antenuptial agreement – see **premarital agreement.**

appeal – A request by the losing party in a lawsuit for higher court review of a lower court decision.

appearance – The formal proceeding by which a defendant submits himself or herself to the jurisdiction of the court.

appellant – The party appealing a decision or judgment to a higher court. Sometimes called a **petitioner.**

appellate court – A court having jurisdiction to review a **trial court's** decisions on procedure and law.

appellee – The party against whom an **appeal** is filed. Sometimes called a **respondent.**

arbitration – Dispute settlement conducted outside the courts by a neutral third party. May or may not be binding.

arraignment – The proceeding in criminal cases where an accused individual is brought before a judge to hear the charges filed against him or her, and to file a plea of guilty, not guilty, or no contest. Also called an **initial appearance** or a **first appearance.**

arrest – The act of being taken into custody by legal authority.

assault – An attempt or threat by a person to inflict immediate offensive physical contact or bodily harm, which the person has the present ability to inflict. An assault need not result in actual touching, but the victim must have reasonable fear of harm or contact. An assault can be a **crime** or a **tort.** Often combined with **battery.**

assignment – The transfer of one's interest in a right or property to another person or entity.

assumption of the risk – A defense that may be raised in personal injury cases, alleging that the plaintiff agreed to face a known danger and accepted the risk that some harm might result.

at issue – The contested points in a lawsuit are said to be "at issue."

attorney-at-law – A lawyer licensed to provide legal advice and to prepare, manage and try cases.

attorney-in-fact – The **agent** named in a **power of attorney.**

automatic stay – Imposed when bankruptcy proceedings are filed. An automatic stay prevents creditors from attempting to collect from the debtor for debts incurred before the filing.

B

bail (also called **bail bond**) – Money or other security given to secure the release of a criminal defendant or witness from legal custody. The money or security can be forfeited if he or she subsequently should fail to appear before the court on the day and time appointed.

bailiff – A court attendant whose duties are to keep order in the courtroom and to have custody of the jury.

bankruptcy – Refers to statutes and judicial proceedings involving persons or businesses that cannot pay their debts and seek the assistance of the court in getting a fresh start. Under the protection of the bankruptcy court, debtors may **discharge** their debts (no longer be liable for them), in some cases by paying a portion of each debt, and in some cases, where the debtor has no assets, paying no portion of them.

battery – Intentionally or recklessly causing offensive physical contact or bodily harm that is not consented to by the victim. Battery can be a crime or a tort. It is the component of actual touching found in "assault and battery."

bench trial – A trial heard by a judge without a jury.

bench warrant – Order issued by a judge for the arrest of an individual.

beneficiary – Someone named to receive property or benefits in a will. In a trust, a person who is to receive benefits from the trust.

beneficiary designations – The persons one selects to receive benefits of a life insurance policy, retirement savings plan, pension, and the like. Normally, these forms of property do not pass through a will, but rather through the beneficiary designations of the policies and plans, and so they avoid **probate.**

bequeath – To give a gift to someone through a will.

bequest – A gift made in a will. Also called **legacy.**

best evidence – Primary evidence; the best evidence available. Evidence short of this is "secondary"; for example, an original letter is the "best evidence," a photocopy is "secondary evidence."

beyond a reasonable doubt – The standard in a criminal case requiring that the jury be satisfied to a moral certainty that every element of a crime has been proven by the prosecution. This **standard of proof** does not require that the state establish absolute certainty by eliminating all doubt, but it does require that the evidence be so conclusive that all reasonable doubts are removed from the mind of the ordinary person.

bind over – To hold a person for trial on bond (**bail**) or in jail. If the judicial official conducting a preliminary hearing finds **probable cause** to believe the accused committed a crime, he or she will "bind over" the accused, normally by setting bail for his or her appearance at trial.

binding instruction – An **instruction** in which a jury is told that if it finds certain conditions to be true, it must decide in favor of the plaintiff, or defendant, as the case might be.

breach of contract – A legally inexcusable failure to perform a contractual obligation.

brief – A written statement prepared by each side in a lawsuit to explain to the court its view of the facts in a case and the applicable law.

burden of proof – In the law of evidence, the duty of proving the facts in dispute in a lawsuit. The responsibility of proving a point—the burden of proof—is not the same as the standard of proof. Burden of proof deals with which side must establish a point or points; **standard of proof** indicates the degree to which the point must be proven.

burglary – Entry into, or remaining in, any residence, building or vehicle without consent, with the intent to commit a **felony** or **larceny** within.

C

calendar – The clerk of the court's list of cases with dates and times set for hearings, trials or arguments.

calling the docket – The public calling of the docket or list of cases, for the purpose of setting a time for trial or entering orders.

case – A legal dispute.

case law – Law based on published judicial decisions; similar to **common law.** Law made by the legislature is **statutory law.**

cause – A lawsuit, litigation or legal action.

cause of action – Facts giving rise to a lawsuit.

caveat emptor – Latin term meaning "let the buyer beware." This phrase expresses the 19th century rule of law that the purchaser buys at his own risk.

certiorari – Latin term meaning "to be informed of." A writ of certiorari is a request to a higher court to review a case. An order of certiorari is an order to a lower court to deliver the record of a case to an appellate court.

challenge – An objection, such as when a lawyer objects at a **voir dire** hearing to the seating of a particular person on a civil or criminal jury; may be **challenge for cause** or **peremptory challenge.**

challenge for cause – Objection to the seating of a particular juror for a stated reason (usually bias or prejudice for or against one of the parties in the case); the judge has discretion to deny the challenge (differs from **peremptory challenge**).

change of venue – Moving a trial to a new location, generally because pre-trial publicity has made it difficult to select an impartial jury.

charge – A description of an offense in an accusation or **indictment** made in order to bring the accused person to trial.

charge to the jury – The judge's **instructions** to the jury before it begins deliberations. The instructions deal with the law in the case and the jury's authority to determine the facts and to draw inferences from the facts in order to reach a verdict. Instructions often include the questions the jury must answer.

charitable trust – A trust set up to benefit one or more charities.

circuit courts – In the federal system, the courts of appeal beneath the U.S. Supreme Court. In several states, the name given to a tribunal, the territorial jurisdiction of which may comprise several counties or districts.

circumstantial evidence – Evidence that suggests something by implication. Circumstantial evidence is indirect, as opposed to eyewitness testimony, which is **direct evidence**. For example, fingerprints at the scene of the crime are circumstantial evidence; a witness to the crime can give direct evidence of what he or she saw.

citation – A citation is the charging document issued for the least serious criminal offenses, which commands the appearance of a party in a proceeding. A citation is also a reference to a source of legal authority, for example a case citation.

civil actions – Noncriminal cases in which one private individual or business sues another to protect, enforce, or redress private or civil rights. Also called **civil suit**.

civil union – a voluntary union that gives same-sex couples the same benefits and protections as heterosexual couples who enter into marriage.

claim – An assertion of a right to money or property made by the party that is suing.

clear and convincing evidence – A **standard of proof** requiring the truth of the facts asserted to be highly probable. It commonly is used in civil lawsuits and in regulatory agency cases. This standard requires more than a **preponderance of the evidence** but less than **beyond a reasonable doubt**.

clerk of the court – A court employee who is responsible for maintaining permanent records of all court proceedings and exhibits, and administering the oath to jurors and witnesses.

closing arguments – The summaries of the evidence presented to the jury at the end of a trial by the lawyers for each side.

codicil – An amendment to a will.

common law – Law arising from judicial decisions rather than laws passed by the legislature. Similar to **case law**.

common law action – A case in which the issues are determined by common law legal principles established by courts, as opposed to statutes.

community property – Community property is generally the property and income acquired during a marriage; see also **marital property**.

community property states – States that adhere to the doctrine that each spouse shares equally in the income earned and the property acquired during a marriage. In these states, it is more difficult for a spouse to hold property separately from the other spouse.

comparative negligence – A legal doctrine according to which the responsibility for damages incurred between the plaintiff and the defendant is allocated according to their relative negligence. Comparative negligence largely has replaced the doctrine of **contributory negligence**.

compensatory damages – money paid to an injured party to compensate for losses sustained as a direct result of the injury suffered. Also called **actual damages**.

complainant – The individual who initiates a lawsuit; synonymous with **plaintiff**.

complaint (civil) – Initial document filed by the plaintiff in a civil case stating the claims against the defendant.

complaint (criminal) – A formal accusation or charge against someone alleging that he or she has committed a criminal offense.

concurring opinion – An appellate court opinion by one or more judges that agrees with the majority opinion in the case; often agrees with the result reached by the majority but offers different reasoning.

condition – A condition is an event that must occur if a contract is to be performed. For example, in real estate contracts the sale is often conditional on the buyers obtaining financing, or selling their current home, or on an acceptable home-inspection report.

conditional release – A release from custody, without the payment of bail, which imposes regulations on the activities and associations of the defendant.

condominium – A condominium is a common-interest community in which the owner has exclusive title to his or her own unit, from the interior walls in, and ownership of an individual interest in the common elements of the condominium, such as hallways, exteriors, and any land surrounding the building. As in a **cooperative,** all unit owners must pay their shares of the assessment for operation, maintenance, and repair.

consent judgment – A **judgment** in which the provisions and terms of the judgment are agreed on by the parties and submitted to the court for its sanction and approval. This is often the result of bargaining between the parties and formalizes their **settlement** of the case.

conservator – One appointed by a court to manage the property and financial affairs of someone deemed incapable of doing so for himself or herself. Similar to a **guardian,** except that a guardian usually has duties beyond the financial, such as responsibility for minor children.

consequential damages – A form of **compensatory damages** ordered to be paid when the injury done resulted from the other side's wrong but was not a natural or necessary consequence. Also called **special damages.** Special damages must be specifically pleaded and proven.

consideration – Something of value, including a promise to do (or not to do) something, given in return for another's performance or promise to perform. Consideration is one of the requirements of a **contract,** and distinguishes a contract from a mere gift.

contempt of court – Any act calculated to embarrass, hinder, or obstruct a court. Contempts are of two kinds: direct and indirect. Direct contempts are those committed in the immediate presence of the court; indirect is the term mostly used with reference to the failure or refusal to obey a court order. The penalty for contempt of court may be a fine or imprisonment.

contingency clause – A clause that makes a contract dependent on some particular event or circumstance. For example, contracts for the sale of land often contain a contingency clause stating that if the buyer is unable to obtain satisfactory financing within a certain period, the buyer may be released from his or her obligation.

continuance – The postponement of a proceeding to a later date.

contract – An agreement between two or more parties made either orally or in writing that the law will enforce. To form a contract, the parties must be of the requisite age and mental capacity; there must be **consideration;** and the subject of the promise cannot be illegal.

contract of adhesion – See **adhesion contract.**

contributory negligence – Legal doctrine that says that a plaintiff cannot recover damages in a civil action for negligence if the plaintiff was also negligent. Most states have overcome the harshness of this rule by adopting a **comparative negligence** rule.

conviction – A trial verdict or judgment that a criminal defendant is guilty of a crime.

cooperative – A common-interest community in which cooperative buyers purchase shares of stock in a corporation that owns an entire building, and then enter into a lease to occupy a particular apartment. Stockholders don't actually own any real estate. Compare to **condominium.**

copyright – The right to literary property, giving authors, composers, and other creators the sole right to reproduce and distribute their work for a limited period of time. Copyright is a form of **intellectual property.**

corroborating evidence – Supplementary evidence that supports the evidence already given.

co-sign – See **surety.**

counsel – Legal advice; also a term used to refer to lawyers in a case.

counterclaim – A claim by a defendant in a civil case that the plaintiff has injured him or her.

court costs – The expenses in addition to legal fees of prosecuting or defending a lawsuit.

court of last resort – The final court that decides a case on appeal (for example, the Supreme Court of the United States or the supreme court of any state).

court reporter – A person who records, transcribes, or stenographically takes down testimony, motions, orders, and other proceedings during trials, hearings, and other court proceedings.

crime – Conduct that is prohibited by law and has a specific punishment (for example, incarceration or a fine).

criminal case – A case brought by the government against an individual accused of committing a crime.

cross-examination – The questioning of a witness by the other side's lawyers.

cyberlaw – A developing area of law relating to

computers, electronic commerce, **intellectual property** on the Internet, and the like.

D

D.A. – Abbreviation of **District Attorney.**

damages – Money awarded by a court to a person injured by the unlawful act or negligence of another person. Damages can be **compensatory, punitive, consequential,** and even **nominal.**

decision – The judgment reached or given by a court of law.

declaratory judgment – A judgment that declares the rights of the parties or expresses the opinion of the court on a question of law, without ordering anything to be done.

decree – A decision or order of the court. A final decree is one that disposes of the litigation; an interlocutory decree is a provisional or preliminary decree that is not final.

deed – A written document that is used to transfer ownership of **real property** from one person to another.

defamation – That which tends to injure a person's reputation. See **libel** and **slander.**

default – Failure to discharge a duty. For example, people default on a mortgage if they fail to repay their home loan, and default on a contract if they fail to perform it.

default judgment – Judgment against a defendant who does not file the proper response within the time allowed or fails to appear at the trial.

defendant – In a civil case, the person being sued. In a criminal case, the person accused of committing the crime.

deliberation – The process by which a jury reaches a verdict at the close of a trial.

delinquent acts – Acts committed by juvenile offenders that would constitute crimes if committed by an adult.

demur – In some state courts, to file a pleading (called a **demurrer**) admitting the truth of the facts in the complaint or answer, and contending they do not make out a cause of action.

de novo – Latin term for "anew." A "trial de novo" is the retrial of a case. A "de novo" standard of review permits an appellate court to substitute its judgment for that of a trial judge.

deposition – The testimony of a witness taken under oath in preparation for a trial. Such statements often are taken to examine potential witnesses and to obtain information.

descent and distribution statutes – See **intestacy laws.**

direct evidence – Proof of facts by witnesses who saw acts done or heard words spoken, as distinguished from **circumstantial,** or indirect, evidence.

direct examination – The first questioning of witnesses by the party on whose behalf they are called.

directed verdict – An instruction by the judge to the jury to return a specific verdict because one of the parties failed to meet its burden of proof.

disbar – To remove a lawyer's license to practice law as a result of the lawyer's unethical or illegal practices. Lawyers may also be censured or reprimanded (publicly or privately criticized), or suspended (have the license to practice law taken away for a certain time).

discharge – To release from an obligation; for example, when a bankruptcy is discharged a person is relieved from the liability to pay debts.

disclaim – To voluntarily give up a right or claim. For example, to refuse a gift under a will one disclaims it.

disclaimer – A denial of responsibility for a thing or act. Many contracts and warranties disclaim liability for some events, and will not cover you if, for example, your new car breaks down because you tried to fix it yourself instead of taking it to an approved dealer.

discovery – The pre-trial process by which each party ascertains evidence the other party will rely upon at trial.

dismissal – A court order terminating a case. May be voluntary (at the request of the parties) or involuntary.

dissent – An appellate court opinion setting forth the minority view and outlining the disagreement of one or more judges with the decision of the majority.

dissolution of marriage – See **divorce.**

district attorney – A state government lawyer who prosecutes criminal cases. Also referred to as a **prosecutor.**

district courts – U.S. district courts are federal trial courts. State district courts are also often trial courts of general jurisdiction.

diversion – The process of removing some minor criminal, traffic, or juvenile cases from the full judicial process, on the condition that the accused undergo some sort of rehabilitation or make **restitution** for damages. Diversion may take place before the trial or its equivalent, as when a juvenile accused of a crime may consent to probation without an admission of guilt. If the juvenile completes probation successfully (takes a course or makes amends for the crime), then the entire matter may be **expunged** (erased) from the record.

divorce – The dissolution of the legal bonds of marriage.

docket – A list of cases to be heard by the court.

domestic partnership – Partnership of homosexual couples, and unmarried heterosexual couples in some states, who are living together without being married. To become domestic partners, the couple must register their relationship at a government office and declare that they are in a "committed" relationship.

domicile – The place where a person has his or her true and permanent home. A person may have several residences, but only one domicile.

donor – The person who sets up a trust. Also known as its **grantor** or **settlor.**

double jeopardy – Putting a person on trial more than once for the same crime; forbidden by the Fifth Amendment to the U.S. Constitution.

due process – United States law in its regular course of administration through the courts. The constitutional guarantee of due process requires that everyone receive such constitutional protections as a fair trial, assistance of counsel, and the rights to remain silent, to a speedy and public trial, to an impartial jury, and to confront and secure witnesses.

duress – Refers to conduct that has the effect of compelling another person to do what he or she would not otherwise do. Being under duress is a recognized defense to any act, such as a crime, contractual breach, or tort, all of which must be voluntary to create liability or responsibility.

E

easement – The right of a person to make lawful use of the land of another in accordance with an express or implied agreement. For example, easements often give a person the right to cross another's land.

eminent domain – The right of the government to take property from a private owner for public use, without the owner's consent. The Fifth Amendment to the U.S. Constitution requires the government to compensate the owner of property taken by eminent domain, stating "nor shall private property be taken for public use, without just compensation." State constitutions contain similar provisions.

en banc – French term meaning "by the full court." All the judges of an appellate court sit together to hear oral arguments in a case of unusual significance and to decide the case.

enjoin – To require a person, through the issuance of an **injunction,** to perform or to abstain from some specific act.

equal protection of the law – Guarantee of the Fourteenth Amendment of the U.S. Constitution that all persons receive equal treatment under law.

equitable action – An action that may be brought to restrain the threatened infliction of wrongs or injuries, and to prevent threatened illegal action. An action seeking an **injunction** is an equitable action.

escheat – The process by which a deceased person's property goes to the state if no heir can be found.

escrow – Money or a written instrument such as a deed that, by agreement between two parties, is held by a neutral third party (held in escrow) until all conditions of the agreement are met.

estate – All that a person owns. An estate consists of **personal property** (car, household items, and other tangible items), **real property,** and **intangible property,** such as stock certificates and bank accounts owned in the individual name of a person.

estate planning – A process by which a person determines what will happen to his or her property after death.

estate tax – A tax imposed on the transfer of property at death, charged to the person's estate.

eviction – The physical expulsion of a tenant from property, by force or by legal process.

evidence – Any form of proof presented by a party for the purpose of supporting its factual allegations or arguments before the court.

exclusionary rule – A judge-made rule that prevents unconstitutionally obtained evidence from being used in court to build a case against a criminal defendant.

execute – To complete the legal requirements (such as signing before witnesses) that make a will or other document valid. Also, to execute a judgment or decree means to put the final judgment of the court into effect.

executor – A personal representative, named in a will, who administers an **estate.**

exemplary damages – See **punitive damages.**

exhibit – A document or other article introduced as evidence during a trial or hearing.

ex parte – Latin term meaning "for one party." An **ex parte proceeding** is one in which only one side is represented, without any notice to any other party (differs from **adversary proceeding**). For example, a request for a search warrant is an ex parte proceeding, since the person subject to the search is not notified of the proceeding and is not present during the hearing.

expert witness – a witness with special knowledge, skill, training, or experience on the subject on which he or she gives evidence. An expert witness is the only kind of witness whose opinion on that subject is admissible as evidence.

ex post facto – Latin term meaning "after the fact." The Constitution prohibits the enactment of ex post facto laws—laws that make acts done before the passing of the law, that were not criminal at the time they were committed, punishable as a crime.

expungement – The official and formal elimination of part of a record.

extradition – The process by which one jurisdiction (state or nation) surrenders to another jurisdiction a person accused or convicted of a crime in the other jurisdiction.

F

fee simple ownership – Ownership of real property free from any conditions, limitations or restrictions.

felony – A serious criminal offense generally punishable by imprisonment of one year or more.

fidelity bond – See **surety bond.**

fiduciary – A person with a duty to act primarily for the other's benefit, for example, a guardian, trustee, or executor. A fiduciary has a duty to act with loyalty and honesty and in the best interests of the beneficiary of the fiduciary relationship.

finding – A formal conclusion by a trial judge or jury regarding the facts of a case.

first appearance – See **arraignment.**

foreclosure – A legal action in which a lender takes ownership of the property used to secure the loan, because the owner failed to make the required payments.

fraud – Intentional deception designed to deprive another person of property or to injure him or her in some other way.

G

garnishment – A legal proceeding in which a debtor's money, in the possession of another (called the **garnishee**), is applied to the debts of the debtor. An example is when a creditor garnishes a debtor's wages.

grand jury – A group of citizens assembled in secret to hear or investigate allegations of criminal behavior. A grand jury has authority to conduct criminal investigations and to charge a person with a crime through an **indictment.**

grantor – The person who sets up a trust. Also called a **settlor** or **donor.**

guaranty – An agreement or promise to be responsible for another's debt in the event that the person defaults and does not make the required payments. A person who gives a guaranty is called a **guarantor. Surety** is sometimes used interchangeably with guarantor.

guardian – A person appointed by will or by law to assume responsibility for incompetent adults or minor children. If a parent dies, this usually will be the other parent. If both die, it probably will be a close relative.

guardianship – A legal right given to a person to be responsible for the food, housing, health care, and other necessities of a person deemed incapable of providing these necessities for himself or herself. Can also include financial affairs, and thus perform additionally as a **conservator.**

guilty – The verdict of a jury that believes that a defendant committed the crime with which he or she is charged, or some lesser crime. Defendants may also plead guilty or **nolo contendere** if they do not want to contest the charges.

H

habeas corpus – Latin for "you have the body." One of the oldest protections in English (and now American) law, it is a procedure for obtaining a judicial determination of the legality of a person's custody. Generally, a writ of habeas corpus forces law enforcement authorities to produce a prisoner they are holding and to legally justify his or her detention. A federal writ of habeas corpus is used to test the constitutionality of a state criminal conviction and imprisonment.

harmless error – An error committed by a trial court during a trial that the appellate court finds not serious enough to have affected the outcome of a trial and therefore not sufficiently harmful to justify reversing the lower court's judgment.

hearing – Any form of judicial, quasi-judicial or legislative proceeding at which issues are heard, or testimony taken.

hearing on the merits – A hearing before a court on the legal questions at issue, as opposed to procedural questions.

hearsay – Statements by a witness who did not see or hear the incident in question but heard about it from someone else. Hearsay is usually not admissible as evidence in court.

holographic will – A handwritten will.

hostile witness – A witness who is subject to cross-examination by the party who called him or her to testify, because he or she exhibited antagonism towards that party in direct examination.

hung jury – A jury that is unable to reach a verdict.

I

immunity – A grant that a court gives someone to protect him or her against prosecution, in return for providing criminal evidence against another person or party.

impaneling – the process for selecting jurors and swearing them in.

impeachment of witness – An attack on the **credibility** (believability) of a witness by the testimony of other witnesses or other evidence.

implied contract – A contract that is not explicitly written or stated, and is determined by deduction from known facts or from the circumstances or conduct of the parties.

inadmissible evidence – Evidence that cannot under the rules of evidence be admitted in court.

in camera – Latin for "in chambers" or "in private." A hearing or inspection of documents in camera takes place in the judge's office, outside of the presence of the jury and public.

indictment – The formal charge issued by a **grand jury** stating that there is enough evidence that the defendant committed the crime to justify having a trial; it is used primarily for **felonies.**

indigent – Meeting certain standards of poverty, thereby qualifying a criminal defendant for representation by a public defender.

inferior courts – Courts of limited jurisdiction.

in forma pauperis – Latin for "in the manner of a pauper." By claiming indigence or poverty, someone may receive permission from the court to sue in forma pauperis and proceed without paying court fees.

information – A formal accusation by a prosecutor that the defendant committed a crime. An information is an alternative to an **indictment** as a means of charging a criminal.

infraction – A violation of law not punishable by imprisonment. Minor traffic offenses generally are considered infractions.

inheritance tax – A state tax on property that an heir or beneficiary receives from a deceased person's estate. The heir or beneficiary pays this tax. In contrast, the deceased person's estate pays the **estate tax.**

initial appearance – See **arraignment.**

injunction – An order of the court prohibiting (or compelling) the performance of a specific act to prevent irreparable damage or injury.

instructions – See **charge to the jury.**

intangible assets – Nonphysical items such as stock certificates, bonds, bank accounts, and pension benefits that have value and must be taken into account in estate planning.

intellectual property – Property that derives from the work of the mind or intellect. Trade secrets, patents, copyrights, and trademarks are all forms of intellectual property.

intentional tort – A **tort** in which the wrongdoer had the intention to commit the tort. Some common intentional torts against a person include **assault, battery, defamation, false imprisonment** and **intentional infliction of emotional distress.** Intentional torts against property include **trespass to land, trespass to chattel** (personal property) and **conversion** (converting someone else's property into your own). Intentional torts may also be crimes.

interlocutory – Provisional; temporary; not final. Refers to orders and decrees of a court.

interrogatories – Written questions asked by one party of an opposing party, who must answer them in writing under oath; a **discovery** device in a lawsuit.

intervention – A proceeding in which a court permits a third person to become a party to a lawsuit already in progress.

inter vivos – Latin term meaning "between the living." An inter vivos gift is one made during the giver's life.

inter vivos trust – Another name for a **living trust.**

intestacy laws – State laws that provide for the distribution of estate property of a person who dies without a will. Also called **descent and distribution statutes.**

intestate – Dying without a will.

intestate succession – The process by which the property of a person who has died without a will passes on to others according to the state's intestacy laws.

irrevocable trust – A trust that, once set up, the grantor may not revoke.

issue – The disputed point in a disagreement between parties in a lawsuit.

J

joint tenancy – A form of legal co-ownership of property that gives the parties an equal right to enjoy the property, and a right of **survivorship.** At the death of one co-owner, the surviving co-owner or co-owners become sole owners of the property.

judgment – The decision of a court on the outcome of a dispute, which determines the rights of the parties to the lawsuit. See also **consent judgment, default judgment, summary judgment** and **judgment notwithstanding the verdict.**

judgment notwithstanding the verdict – A judge's decision to rule in a case contrary to the jury's verdict.

judgment proof – A judgment for money cannot be enforced against a debtor who is judgment proof, either because he or she has no property, or because the property is not within the jurisdiction where the judgment was obtained, or because the property is protected from execution of the judgment by statute.

judicial review – The review by a court of the official actions of other branches of government; the authority to declare **unconstitutional** the actions of other branches.

jurisdiction – The power, right or authority to apply the law. A court's authority to hear cases. Also, the territory from which a court is authorized to hear cases.

jury – A certain number of persons—usually selected from lists of registered voters or licensed drivers— sworn to decide on the facts in issue in a trial.

jury panel – Same as **venire.**

justiciable claim – A claim that is capable of being resolved in the courts.

juvenile court – A court specifically established to hear cases concerning minors.

L

larceny – Larceny or **theft** is the unlawful taking or attempted taking of property from the possession of another, without force and without deceit, with intent to permanently deprive the owner of the property.

lawsuit – An action brought in court, in which an individual seeks a legal remedy for an alleged wrong.

leading question – A question that instructs a witness how to answer or suggests which answer is desired. These questions usually are prohibited on direct examination, but can be asked to hostile witnesses or on cross-examination.

lease – An agreement by which an owner of property gives exclusive possession of the property to another person for a period of time, usually in exchange for rent. At the end of the lease the owner may take possession of the property again.

legacy – See **bequest.**

liable – Legally responsible.

libel – Published words or pictures that falsely and maliciously defame a person, that is, injure his or her reputation. Libel is published defamation; **slander** is spoken.

lien – A legal claim against another person's property as **security** for a debt. A lien does not convey ownership of the property, but gives the lienholder a right to have his or her debt satisfied out of the proceeds of the property if the debt is not otherwise paid.

liquidated damages – A sum of money specified in advance by a contract or agreement, which must be paid if terms are violated.

litigant – An individual bringing a lawsuit. Participants (**plaintiffs** and **defendants**) in lawsuits are called litigants.

litigation – A civil case or lawsuit.

living trust – A trust set up and in effect during the lifetime of the grantor. Also called **inter vivos trust.**

living will – See **advance directive.**

M

magistrate judges – Judicial officers who assist U.S. district judges in getting cases ready for trial. They may decide some criminal and civil trials when both parties agree to have the case heard by a magistrate judge instead of a judge.

maintenance – See **alimony.**

malpractice – Negligence, misconduct, lack of ordinary skill, or a breach of duty in the performance of a professional service, resulting in injury or loss.

mandate – A judicial command directing the proper officer to enforce a judgment, sentence, or decree.

manslaughter – The unlawful killing of another without premeditation. This can be voluntary and upon a sudden impulse—for example, a quarrel erupts into a fistfight in which one of the participants is killed. Or it can be involuntary—for example, during the commission of an unlawful act not ordinarily expected to result in great bodily harm, or during the commission of a lawful act without proper caution, such as driving an automobile at excessive speed resulting in a fatal collision.

marital property – See **community property.**

mediation – A form of alternative dispute resolution in which the parties bring their dispute to a neutral third party, who helps them agree on a settlement.

mens rea – Latin term meaning "guilty mind." Mens rea is the mental intention necessary to establish criminal responsibility; the physical component of a crime is the **actus reus.**

merits – Issues of legal substance at stake in a case, as opposed to procedural considerations.

Miranda warning – The warning police must give suspects regarding their constitutional right to remain silent and their right to a lawyer.

misdemeanor – A less serious criminal offense than a **felony,** usually punishable by a sentence of one year or less.

mistake – An act or omission arising from ignorance or misconception. A **mutual mistake** is one made by both parties to a contract, and a court may set the contract aside on the basis that there has been no mutual assent. A **unilateral mistake** is a mistake on the part of one party to a contract. A unilateral mistake is not usually grounds for setting aside the contract, unless one party stands to profit or benefit improperly from the mistake.

mistrial – An erroneous or invalid trial; a trial that cannot stand in law because of lack of jurisdiction, incorrect procedure with respect to jury selection, or disregard of some other fundamental requisite; an invalid trial because of the inability of a jury to reach a verdict.

mortgage – A loan secured by property. Usually the loan is for the purchase price of the property minus the down payment. If the borrower (called the **mortgagor**) defaults on the loan, then the lender (called the **mortgagee**) has the right to **foreclose** on the property to pay the debt.

motion – An application to a court or judge for a ruling or order. For example, a motion to suppress is an application to the court to exclude evidence that was obtained illegally; a **motion to dismiss** is a formal request for the court to dismiss a complaint because of insufficiency of evidence or because the law does not recognize the injury or harm claimed. A document containing such an application is also referred to as a motion.

multiplicity of actions – Several lawsuits against the same defendant seeking to litigate the same right.

municipal courts – In the judicial organization of some states, courts whose territorial authority is confined to a city or community.

murder – The unlawful killing of a human being with malice aforethought (deliberate intent to kill). Murder in the first degree is characterized by premeditation; murder in the second degree is characterized by a sudden and instantaneous intent to kill or to cause injury without caring whether the injury kills or not.

mutual mistake – See **mistake.**

N

negligence – Failure to exercise ordinary care; the basis for many **tort** (personal injury) lawsuits.

nolo contendere – Latin for "I do not wish to contend." Has the same effect as a plea of guilty as far as the criminal sentence is concerned, but may not be considered an admission of guilt for any other purpose.

nominal damages – A trivial sum of damages (e.g., $10) awarded in cases in which a party has been injured but no loss resulted from the injury or the injured party failed to prove that loss resulted from the injury. Often awarded in intentional tort cases.

nominal party – One who is joined as a party or defendant merely because the technical rules of pleading require his or her presence in the record.

not guilty – Pleaded by a defendant who intends to contest the charges; also, the verdict of a jury who finds that the prosecution has not proven the defendant's guilt beyond a reasonable doubt.

notice – A formal notification to the party being sued that a lawsuit has been initiated.

notice to produce – A notice in writing requiring the opposite party to yield a certain described paper or document in advance or at the trial.

nuisance – In **tort** law, the legal term for a person's unreasonable action that interferes with your enjoyment of your property. Anything from noxious gases to annoying wind chimes may constitute grounds for a nuisance suit.

nuncupative will – An oral (unwritten) will.

O

objection – The act of taking exception to some statement or procedure in trial. Used to call the court's attention to improper evidence or procedure.

objection overruled – A judge's rejection of an objection as invalid. The statement or procedure objected to will stand.

objection sustained – A judge's support or agreement with an objection. The statement or procedure objected to will have to be rephrased or changed.

of counsel – A phrase commonly applied to a lawyer employed to help prepare or manage a case, but who is not the principal attorney of record. Also, a senior member of a law firm who may be retired or semi-retired.

offer – An act of willingness to enter into a purchase agreement that justifies another person in understanding that his assent to that purchase agreement is invited and will establish a contract. The person who makes the offer is called the **offeror;** the person to whom the offer is made is called the **offeree.**

one day-one trial jury service – System used in many jurisdictions in which potential jurors serve either for the length of a trial if assigned to a jury or, if not, complete their service in one day.

opening statements – The outlines of the evidence that each side expects to prove, presented to the jury by the lawyers.

opinion – A trial court's written explanation of its decision, or the written decision of a majority of judges of an appellate court. At the appellate level, a dissenting opinion or **dissent** disagrees with the majority opinion because of the reasoning and/or principles of law on which the decision is based. A **concurring opinion** agrees with the decision of the court but offers further comment.

option – A contract that gives the holder a right or option to buy or sell specified property, such as stock or real estate, at a fixed price for a limited period of time. The option holder is called the **optionee.**

oral argument – An opportunity for lawyers to summarize their positions before the court and also to answer the judges' questions.

order – A command from the court directing or forbidding an action.

original jurisdiction – A court's authority to hear a case in the first instance (i.e., to be the first court to hear it).

overrule – To not allow an objection in a trial; also, to declare that a lower court decision was in error.

P

parole – The supervised, conditional release of a prisoner.

parties – The persons who are actively involved with the prosecution or defense of a legal proceeding. **Plaintiffs** and **defendants** are parties to **lawsuits; appellants** and **appellees** are parties in **appeals.** (They may also be known as **petitioners** and **respondents.**)

patent – The exclusive right granted to an inventor to make or sell his or her invention for a term of years. A patent grants monopoly rights.

peremptory challenge – A **motion** by a party to reject a juror for an unspecified race-neutral reason. May only be used a limited number of times. Differs from **challenge for cause.**

perjury – The criminal offense of making a false statement under oath.

personal injury – See **tort.**

personal property – Tangible physical property (such as cars, clothing, furniture, and jewelry) and **intangible personal property,** but not **real property**—that is, not land or rights in land.

personal recognizance – When a person is released from custody before trial on his or her promise to return for further proceedings. Also known as **release on own recognizance.**

petit jury – The twelve (or fewer) jurors selected to sit in the trial of a civil or criminal case. Compare to **grand jury.**

petitioner – See **appellant.**

plaintiff – A person who begins a civil lawsuit.

plea – The defendant's declaration of guilty or not guilty, in response to the criminal charges contained in the information or indictment.

plea bargain – The process by which an accused person agrees to plead guilty to some of the charges in return for the government's promise to drop some of the charges or recommend leniency in sentencing.

pleadings – Written statements of fact and law filed by the parties to a lawsuit. Comprised of complaints, answers and replies.

polling the jury – A practice whereby the jurors are asked individually whether they agreed, and still agree, to the verdict.

pourover will – A will that leaves some or all estate assets to a trust established before the willmaker's death.

power of attorney – A document in which one person, called the **principal,** authorizes another, called the **agent,** to act on his or her behalf.

precedent – A previously decided case that guides subsequent decisions.

prejudicial error – Synonymous with **reversible error;** an error that warrants the appellate court in reversing the judgment before it.

preliminary hearing – A criminal hearing held after the **first appearance,** at which a judge determines whether **probable cause** exists to believe the suspect committed the crime with which he or she is charged.

premarital agreement – A contract entered into by a man and woman before they marry. The agreement usually describes what each party's rights will be if they divorce or when one of them dies. Premarital agreements usually set out who is entitled to what property, and how much support, if any, will be paid in the event of divorce. Also known as **prenuptial agreements** or **antenuptial agreements.** If such an agreement is entered into after a marriage, it is a **postnuptial agreement.**

premises liability – Legal responsibility arising from injuries or losses occurring on one's property.

prenuptial agreement – See **premarital agreement.**

preponderance of evidence – The greater weight of evidence, or evidence that is more credible and convincing to the mind, but not necessarily offered by the greater number of witnesses. This is the common standard of proof in civil cases.

pre-sentence investigation – An inquiry conducted at the request of the court after a person has been found guilty of a criminal offense. Provides the court with extensive background information to determine an appropriate sentence.

presumption – An assumption of a fact that is not certainly known, which can be drawn from the known or proven existence of some other fact.

pre-trial conference – A meeting in which lawyers for both sides meet the judge in advance of the trial to seek to clarify or narrow the issues. At such conferences, the judge often urges the parties to settle the case without a trial.

prima facie case – Latin term meaning "on its face." A case supported by at least the minimum amount of evidence and free from obvious defects. A party is entitled to have a case heard by a jury if he or she has a prima facie case.

principal – In criminal law, one who commits an offense, or an accomplice who is present during the commission of the crime. In commercial law, the amount received in loan, or the amount upon which interest is charged. In the law of agency, one who has permitted or engaged another (the **agent**) to act for his or her benefit.

privilege – Arises in confidential relationships, and grants the parties in the relationship an exemption from the legal requirement to disclose information at trial. For example, attorney-client **privilege** means that lawyers cannot give evidence about legal advice they gave to their client. This privilege can be waived by the client but not by the lawyer. The doctor-patient **privilege** means that the doctor cannot disclose the patient's personal information during a legal proceeding without the patient's consent.

probable cause – Sufficient facts and circumstances to justify the belief that certain circumstances exist (for example, that a crime has been committed; that a person is guilty of an offense, that a particular search will uncover a weapon, that an item to be seized is in a particular place).

probate – The judicial process of determining whether a will is valid; also, the process of settling an estate (gathering assets, paying claims, distributing bequests, etc.) under the supervision of the **probate court.**

probate court – The court with authority to determine the validity of wills and supervise estate **administration.**

probate estate – Estate property that may be disposed of by a will.

probation – A sentencing alternative to imprisonment in which the court releases convicted defendants under supervision as long as certain conditions are observed.

pro bono publico – Latin term meaning "for the public good or welfare." When lawyers work for clients without pay, they are said to be working pro bono.

procedural law – Law regulating the procedure of the courts and the legal system, including pleadings and evidence. Compare to **substantive law.**

promissory note – A note containing a promise to pay a sum of money to a specified person or the bearer at a specified future time.

pro se – A Latin term meaning "on one's own behalf"; in courts, it refers to persons who present their own cases without lawyers.

prosecution – The act of pursuing a lawsuit or criminal trial; the prosecution in a criminal suit is the state.

prosecutor – A government lawyer who tries criminal cases. See **district attorney.**

protective order – See **restraining order.**

provision – See **term.**

public defender – A lawyer employed by the government to represent individuals accused of crimes who cannot afford to hire their own lawyers privately.

punitive damages – An order to pay money as a form of punishment or deterrence from future error that has caused legal injury; also known as **exemplary damages.**

Q

quash – To overthrow; to vacate; to annul or void a summons or indictment.

question of fact – A disputed contention of fact that is usually decided by a jury, and may not be re-considered in an appeal.

question of law – A disputed legal contention that depends on an examination of the law. Questions of law are decided by a judge, and may be re-examined in an appeal.

quiet title – A type of lawsuit that determines which claimant has the right to certain real property or portions of such property.

R

rape – See **sexual assault.**

real property – Land, buildings, and other improvements affixed to land, as opposed to **personal property.**

reasonable doubt – Uncertainty that might exist in the mind of a reasonable person applying reason to the evidence introduced. See **beyond a reasonable doubt.**

reasonable person – A hypothetical person used in the law as an objective standard. The reasonable person has an ordinary degree of care, foresight, intelligence and judgment. Negligence stems from careless or thoughtless conduct under the reasonable person standard or a failure to act when a reasonable person would have acted.

rebuttal – The introduction of contrary evidence; the showing that statements of witnesses as to what occurred are not true; the stage of a trial at which such evidence may be introduced.

record – A written account of all the acts, proceedings and testimony in a lawsuit.

redirect examination – Follows **cross-examination** and is exercised by the party who called and questioned the witness first. Redirect examination must only extend to those matters brought up in cross-examination, and is not another chance for **direct examination.**

release on own recognizance – See **personal recognizance.**

reliance – Confidence or dependence upon what is deemed sufficient authority (for example, a warranty that provides a written guarantee of the integrity of a product).

remand – To send a dispute back to the court where it was originally heard. This often occurs when an appellate court sends a case back to a lower court for further proceedings.

remedy – The means by which a right can be enforced or a wrong can be redressed; also the relief that a court may order. For example, a court may order specific performance as a remedy for a breach of contract.

removal, order of – An order by a court directing the transfer of a case to another court.

reply – A plaintiff's response to a plea, allegation, or counterclaim in the defendant's **answer.** The purpose of a reply is to respond to new matters raised in the answer.

repossess – To take back—as in a seizure or **foreclosure**—to satisfy the obligation to the seller, bank or finance company after the debtor defaults on his or her payments.

repudiation – An act or declaration by a party to a contract that he or she will not perform the contract.

rescission – The cancellation of a contract, which returns the parties to the position they would have been in if the contract had never been made.

respondeat superior – See **vicarious liability.**

respondent – See **appellee.**

rest – A party is said to "rest" or "rest its case" when it has presented all the evidence it intends to offer.

restatement – In the law of **trusts,** a new trust that replaces an existing trust; rather than modify an existing trust with many changes, it is often simpler to restate the trust—create a new trust.

restitution – The making good of an injury, often by payment of money. A criminal may have to pay restitution to the victim of a crime.

restraining order – An order intended to protect one individual from violence, abuse, harassment, or stalking by another, by prohibiting or restricting access or proximity to the protected party.

reverse – To set aside the decision of a lower court because of an error. A reversal is often accompanied by a **remand** to the lower court that heard the case.

reversible error – An error sufficiently prejudicial (harmful) to justify reversing the judgment of a lower court; compare to **harmless error.**

revocable trust – A trust that the grantor may change or revoke.

revoke – To cancel or nullify a legal document.

rider – A page or several pages containing an addition or change to the main body of a contract. Often it's simpler to put changes in a rider, which supersedes any contradictory parts of the main contract, than to try to incorporate the changes on the original form.

robbery – The unlawful taking or attempted taking of property that is in the immediate possession of another, by force or threat of force.

rule of court – An order made by a court having jurisdiction. Rules of court are either general or special: the former are the regulations by which the practice of the court is governed; the latter are special orders made in particular cases.

rules of evidence – Standards governing whether evidence in a civil or criminal case is **admissible.**

S

search warrant – See **warrant.**

security – Property that can be sold to pay a debt if the borrower cannot pay. For example, a mortgage is a secured debt, because if the borrower defaults on the mortgage, the lender can foreclose on the house to pay the debt.

self-proving will – A will whose validity does not have to be testified to in court by the witnesses to it, since the witnesses executed an affidavit reflecting proper execution of the will prior to the maker's death.

sentence – The punishment ordered by a court for a defendant convicted of a crime.

separate property – Property of a spouse that is not community or marital property.

separation of witnesses – An order of the court requiring all witnesses to remain outside the courtroom until each is called to testify, except the plaintiff or defendant.

sequester – To separate. Sometimes juries are sequestered from outside influences during their deliberations.

serve – To deliver a legal document, such as a complaint, summons or subpoena.

service – The delivery of a legal document, such as a complaint, summons or subpoena notifying a person of a lawsuit or other legal action taken against him or her. Service constitutes formal legal notice.

settlement – Agreement resolving a dispute between parties in a lawsuit without trial. Settlements often involve the payment of compensation by one party in satisfaction of the other party's claims.

settlor – The person who sets up a trust. Also called the **grantor** or **donor.**

sexual assault – Forced sexual conduct or penetration without the victim's consent or when the victim is underage. These crimes are often called **rape, sexual conduct,** or **sexual battery,** and may include special designations when the victim is a child.

sheriff – An officer of a county, often chosen by popular election, whose principal duties are to aid the courts. The sheriff serves processes, summons juries, executes judgments and holds judicial sales.

sidebar conference – Confidential discussion between judge and attorneys to resolve legal matters, which could be prejudicial if aired before the jury.

slander – False and defamatory spoken words tending to harm another's reputation, business, or means of livelihood. Slander is spoken defamation; **libel** is published.

small-claims court – A court that handles civil claims for small amounts of money. People often represent themselves rather than hire a lawyer. Also called **magistrate court, justice of the peace court,** or **pro se court.**

special damages – See **consequential damages.**

specific performance – Where damages would be inadequate compensation for the breach of a contract, the party who breached the contract will be compelled to perform what he or she originally agreed to do.

spendthrift trust – A trust set up for the benefit of someone who the grantor believes would be incapable of managing his or her own financial affairs.

spousal support – See **alimony.**

standard of proof – The degree to which a point in dispute between the parties must be proven. For example, in a civil case the **burden of proof** rests with the plaintiff, who must establish his or her case by such standards of proof as a **preponderance of evidence** or **clear and convincing evidence.** In a criminal case, the standard of proof is much higher—the prosecution must prove guilt **beyond a reasonable doubt.**

standing – The legal right to sue or enter a lawsuit on a particular matter. Only a person with something at stake has standing to bring a lawsuit.

stare decisis – Latin term meaning "to stand by that which was decided." When a court has once laid down a principle of law as applicable to a certain set of facts, it will adhere to that principle and apply it to future cases where the facts are substantially the same.

statute – Law enacted by legislatures or executive officers.

statute of limitations – A law that sets the time within which parties must take action to enforce their rights.

stay – A court order halting a judicial proceeding.

stipulation – An agreement by lawyers on opposite sides of a case as to any matter pertaining to the proceedings or trial, such as to admit certain facts at the trial. It is not binding unless agreed to by the parties.

strict liability – Liability that is imposed on a party who is not negligent or at fault. Strict liability is often imposed in the context of ultrahazardous activities. For example, a person who uses explosives may be strictly liable for any injuries caused to a bystander, even if the bystander was too close and the person using the explosives was not at fault.

strike – To remove improperly offered evidence from the court record.

subpoena – A document issued by the court to compel a witness to appear and give testimony or to procure documentary evidence in a proceeding.

subpoena duces tecum – Latin for "under penalty you shall bring with you." A process by which the court commands a witness to produce certain documents or records in a trial.

substantive law – Law dealing with rights, duties and liabilities, as distinguished from law that regulates procedure.

summary judgment – A court order that decides a case in favor of one side on the basis of affidavits or other evidence, before the trial commences. It is used when there is no dispute as to the facts of the case, and one party is entitled to judgment as a matter of law.

summons – Legal notice informing an individual of a lawsuit and the date and location of the court where the case will be heard.

support trust – A trust that instructs the trustee to spend only as much income and principal (the assets held in the trust) as needed for the beneficiary's support.

surety – See **guaranty**. Traditionally, a surety can be distinguished from a **guarantor** because the guarantor is liable only if the principal defaults on the contract. The surety is directly and immediately liable for another person's debt and other obligations. Also sometimes called a **co-sign**.

surety bond – A bond purchased at the expense of the estate to insure the executor's proper performance. Often called a **fidelity bond**.

survivorship – The right of a person who holds property with another as a joint tenant or tenant by the entirety to take the interest of the other person when he or she dies.

sustain – A court order allowing an objection or motion to prevail.

T

temporary restraining order (TRO) – Prohibits a person from an action that is likely to cause irreparable harm. This differs from an **injunction** in that it may be granted immediately, without notice to the opposing party, and without a hearing. It is intended to last only until a hearing can be held.

tenancy by the entirety – A form of ownership of property in which husband and wife own the property together. The survivor of the marriage is entitled to the whole property; a divorce usually ends the tenancy by the entirety and converts it into a **tenancy in common**.

tenancy in common – A form of ownership of property in which each tenant is entitled to equal use and possession of the property, but neither party has any right to the other's interest when one person dies.

term – A period of time, for example, a court term or a prison term; also, a clause or **provision** of a contract.

testamentary capacity – The legal ability to make a will.

testamentary trust – A trust set up by a will.

testator – A person who makes a will.

testatrix – A female testator.

testimony – Evidence given by a competent witness, under oath, as distinguished from evidence derived from writings and other sources.

theft – See **larceny**.

third-party claim – An action by the defendant that brings a third party into a lawsuit.

title – Legal ownership of property, usually real property or automobiles.

tort – A civil wrong or breach of a duty to another person, as outlined by law. A very common tort is negligent operation of a motor vehicle that results in an automobile collision and subsequent property damage and personal injury. A tort lawsuit is often called a **personal injury** case.

trademark – Any word or words; name; symbol or

picture; or device that a company or business uses to distinguish its goods from someone else's. The use of trademarks is protected by common law; trademarks can also be registered to provide the owner with greater protection. Trademarks are a kind of **intellectual property.**

trade name – A name under which people identify their business, and which gives them the right to conduct business under that name in advertising, applying for permits, billing customers, paying taxes and so on.

transcript – The official record of proceedings in a trial or hearing.

transitory – A lawsuit is "transitory" when it can be brought wherever the defendant may be found and served with a summons, and the jurisdiction has sufficient contact with one of the parties and the incident that gave rise to the suit. A lawsuit is **local** if it can only be brought in the county where the subject of the suit is located—for example, the property being foreclosed on.

traverse – In **pleading,** to traverse means to deny. When a defendant denies any material allegation of fact in the plaintiff's declaration, he or she is said to traverse it.

trial – The examination of fact and law before a court.

trial court – The court that first tries and determines issues of fact and law. Compare to **appellate court.**

trust – A legal device used to manage property—real or personal—established by one person (the **donor, grantor** or **settlor**) for the benefit of another (the **beneficiary**). A third person or the grantor manages the trust. This person is known as the **trustee.**

trust agreement or declaration – The legal document that sets up a trust.

trustee – The person or institution that manages the property put in trust.

U

unconscionable – Unreasonably unfair to one party. For example, one-sided contracts signed by a party with little bargaining power may be so unfair and commercially unreasonable as to be unconscionable, and a court may set the contract aside.

unconstitutional – Conflicting with some provision of a constitution. A statute that is found to be unconstitutional—that is, conflicting with the United States Constitution—is considered **void,** or as if it had never existed.

undue influence – Influence of another that destroys the freedom of a testator or donor and creates a ground for nullifying a will or invalidating a future gift. The exercise of undue influence is suggested by excessive insistence, superiority of will or mind, the relationship of the parties or pressure on the donor or testator by any other means to do what he is unable, practically, to refuse.

unilateral mistake – See **mistake.**

V

venire – Latin for "to come." A writ summoning persons to court to act as jurors. More popularly, the panel of citizens called for jury service from which a jury will be selected.

venue – The particular county, city or geographical area in which a court with jurisdiction may hear and determine a case.

verdict – Formal decision made by a jury, read before a court, and accepted by the judge.

vicarious liability – Liability that is imposed on one person for the actions of another, in situations where the law judges that one person should be responsible for the actions of another. One specific kind of vicarious liability is that of an employer for the actions of an employee (this is the doctrine of **respondeat superior,** a Latin term meaning "let the superior reply").

void – Of no force or legal effect. For example, if a contract is declared void, it is unenforceable between the parties.

voir dire – French for "to speak the truth." Voir dire is a process in which prospective jurors are questioned to determine whether they can perform their duties in an impartial manner.

W

waive – To voluntarily give up a right or a claim.

ward – A person who is under the control of a guardian or under the protection of the court because of incapacity (for example, because the person is a minor).

warrant – A court order authorizing a law enforcement officer to perform a specified act required for the administration of justice. For example, an **arrest warrant** authorizes a police officer to make an arrest; a **search warrant** authorizes police officers to make a search and seize evidence.

warranty – A written or oral statement by one party to a contract that a fact is or will be as it is expressly declared or promised to be.

weight of evidence – The balance or **preponderance of evidence;** the inclination of the greater amount of credible evidence, offered in a trial, to support one side of the issue rather than the other.

will – A legal declaration that disposes of a person's property when that person dies.

with prejudice – As applied to a judgment of dismissal, the term refers to the adjudication of a case on its merits, barring the right to bring or maintain another action on the same claim.

without prejudice – A dismissal "without prejudice" allows a new suit to be brought on the same cause of action.

witness – One who testifies under oath as to what she or he has seen, heard or otherwise observed.

writ – An order issued from a court requiring the performance of a specified act, or giving authority and commission to have it done.

ABOUT THE AUTHORS AND EDITORS

This book benefited from the advice and careful review of more than 150 ABA members and other experts from all over the country. Their ranks included judges, law professors, and practicing attorneys. All of them generously gave of their time to assure that this book is accurate, up-to-date, and complete. We list them in the "Acknowledgments" section that follows.

The various drafts of this book were the work of many writers and editors. The main editorial responsibility for the book rested with Charles White and Katie Fraser of the staff of the Division for Public Education of the American Bar Association.

Mr. White is Senior Editor for the Division, and has produced numerous books, booklets, and periodicals for the ABA, all designed to help the public understand the law. He is a graduate of Brown University and received an M.A. and Ph.D. from the University of Pennsylvania. Before coming to the ABA he taught at Northwestern University and several other colleges.

Ms. Fraser is an Editor in the Division. She received an honors degrees in Arts and Law from the Australian National University, where she served as an Editor on the Federal Law Review and was Editor-In-Chief of the college newspaper. Before coming to the ABA she clerked for Justice Hely in the Federal Court of Australia, and wrote freelance articles and reviews for various publications.

Various authors and editors were responsible for each chapter. "Authors" of chapters wrote the chapters in the previous edition and updated their work for this edition. "Editors" of chapters brought the chapters up-to-date but did not write the original versions.

Katie Fraser served as primary editor of five chapters: "When and How to Use a Lawyer," "How the Legal System Works," "Forming and Operating a Small Business," "Criminal Justice," and "Health Law." For the small business and health law chapters she revised and updated material from *The American Bar Association Legal Guide for Small Business* (2000) and the *American Bar Association Complete and Easy Guide to Health-Care Law* (2001). For the other chapters, she revised and updated material from previous editions of this book.

Mary Lou Boland, Chair, Victims Committee, ABA Criminal Justice Section, contributed the sidebar on victims' rights for the Criminal Justice chapter.

Jeff Atkinson, author of the family law chapter, is a resident of Wilmette, Illinois. He teaches at DePaul University College of Law, Chicago, and serves as a professor-reporter for the Illinois Judicial Conference, responsible for training Illinois judges in Family Law. Professor Atkinson is the author of *Modern Child Custody Practice* (2000). His books and articles on family law have been cited by the United States Supreme Court and the supreme courts of eleven states. He is a member of the Illinois Bar (admitted in 1977) and the Bar of the United States Supreme Court (admitted in 1982). Jeff Atkinson is a former chair of the American Bar Association Child Custody Committee and has served as a member of the ABA Family Law Section Council.

Madelynn Hausman, editor of the chapter on buying and selling a home, is a lawyer in private practice in Chicago, Illinois, where she specializes in real estate matters. She earned a B.A. from the University of Pennsylvania and a J.D. from the University of Minnesota, where she served as an editor on the law review. She has spoken to public groups and written for other bar association publications on real estate and related issues.

Jane Easter Bahls, author of the chapter on home ownership and the law, is a freelance writer living in Rock Island, Illinois, who covers business and legal topics for various publications. She earned her B.A. at Cornell College and an M.A. in Philosophy of Religion at Trinity Evangelical School. Since 1985, she has been writing for a wide variety of national and regional magazines, including *Entrepreneur, Student Lawyer* and various ABA publications.

Michael Pensack, author of the chapter on renting residential property, is a graduate of The College of Wooster in Ohio and the John Marshall Law School in Chicago. He is a licensed and practicing attorney in Illinois. He is also the Executive Director of the Illinois Tenants Union.

David Hudson, editor of the chapters on consumer credit, bankruptcy, and personal injury is an attorney and author based in Nashville, Tennessee. He teaches tort law classes at Southeastern Career College and writes regularly for several ABA publications. He earned an A.B. from Duke University and a J.D. from Vanderbilt University Law School.

Steve Lash, a lawyer in Montgomery County, Maryland, is editor of the chapter on consumer law and author of the chapter on contract law. He reports on legal affairs for a variety of publications. He is president of Cert.ainty Publishing, an e-mail news service that covers every appeal the Supreme Court grants, hears and decides. He earned a B.S. in Journalism from Northwestern University and a J.D. from American University.

Lisa Stansky, editor of the chapter on automobile law, is a lawyer who lives in New Orleans, where she works as a writer. She earned her J.D. at the Yale Law School and received her undergraduate degree from Brown University. Her work has appeared in *The National Law Journal*, the *American Bar Association Journal*, and other publications, and she is a contributing editor to *Student Lawyer* magazine, published by the American Bar Association.

Barbara J. Fick, author of the chapter on law in the workplace, is an associate professor of law at the University of Notre Dame Law School, specializing in the field of labor and employment law and dispute resolution. Her publications include articles on worker rights, international labor law, collective bargaining and employment discrimination. She has acted as a consultant for the AFL-CIO Solidarity Center, conducting training programs on international labor standards for trade unions in Central and Eastern Europe. She is a faculty fellow in the Joan B. Kroc Institute for International Peace Studies and the Higgins Labor Research Center.

The Center for Law and Aging of the American Bar Association is author of the chapter on Law for Older Americans. Charles P. Sabatino, primary author and editor of the chapter, is the Assistant Director of the Commission on Law and Aging and Adjunct Professor at Georgetown University Law Center. The Commission writing team included legal staff Stephanie Edelstein, Naomi Karp, Lori Stiegel, and Erica Wood.

Brett Campbell, author of the chapter on wills and estates, is a lawyer-journalist who received his law degree from the University of Texas Law School. After practicing law he turned to writing full time and has contributed to a number of newspapers and magazines in Texas and elsewhere. He now teaches journalism at the University of Oregon and edits the *Oregon Quarterly*.

ACKNOWLEDGEMENTS

This book would not have been possible without the assistance of more than 150 American Bar Association members and other experts from all over the country. Law professors, judges, and practicing attorneys—as well as staff members of the American Bar Association and other bar associations—reviewed the material in the various chapters, assuring that the information was accurate, up to date, and expressed clearly, in laypersons' terms.

These experts generously donated their time to this effort. Many of them serve on American Bar Association committees in their areas of expertise. Others serve as writers and editors of American Bar Association scholarly and professional publications. They represent some of the finest minds in the association, and we are deeply grateful for their generosity with their time and their willingness to read drafts repeatedly as part of the process of making them accurate, clear, and helpful.

The reviewers are listed for each chapter to which they contributed.

CHAPTER ONE: WHEN AND HOW TO USE A LAWYER

Arthur Garwin, Director of Publications and Conference Planning, Center for Professional Responsibility, American Bar Association, Chicago, Illinois;

William Hornsby, Staff Counsel, Division for Legal Services, American Bar Association, Chicago, Illinois;

Frances Johansen, Unauthorized Practice of Law Counsel, State Bar of Arizona, Phoenix, Arizona;

George Kuhlman, Associate Director and Ethics Counsel, Center for Professional Discipline, American Bar Association, Chicago, Illinois;

Marian P. McCulloch, Attorney, Allen Dell, P.A., Attorneys-at-Law, Tampa, Florida;

James Bernard McLindon, Chair, American Bar Association Standing Committee on Lawyer Referral and Information Service, and Attorney-at-Law, Northampton, Massachusetts;

Karma S. Rodgers, President, America Prepaid Legal Institute; Member, American Bar Association Task Force on Lawyers Center for Personal Legal Services; and Member, Butler Rodgers & Johnson LLC, Attorneys-at-Law, Milwaukee, Wisconsin;

Alec M. Schwartz, Associate Director, Division for Legal Services, American Bar Association, Chicago, Illinois;

Leopold Sher, Co-Chair, Standing Committee on Continuing Legal Education, American Bar Association Section of Real Property and Probate, and Attorney, Sher Garner Cahill et al., Attorneys-at-Law, New Orleans, Louisiana;

Sheree Swetin, Executive Director, San Diego County Bar Association, San Diego, California.

CHAPTER TWO: HOW THE LEGAL SYSTEM WORKS

Honorable Rebecca Albrecht, Past Chair, Lawyer's Conference of the Judicial Administration Division, American Bar Association, and Judge, Superior Court of Arizona, Maricopa County, Phoenix, Arizona;

Seth S. Andersen, Project Manager, Standing Committee on Judicial Independence, American Bar Association, Chicago, Illinois;

Honorable Louraine Arkfeld, Member, Coalition for Justice, American Bar Association, and Judge, Tempe Municipal Court, Tempe, Arizona;

Honorable Lorenzo Arredondo, Former Member, Standing Committee on Public Education, American Bar Association, and Circuit Court Judge, Lake Circuit Court, Crown Point, Indiana;

Honorable Thomas Barland, Reserve Judge, Eau Claire County, Wisconsin;

Honorable B. Michael Dann, Judge (ret.), Superior Court of Arizona, Maricopa County, Phoenix, Arizona, and Visiting Fellow, National Center for State Courts, Williamsburg, Virginia;

David Durfee, Executive Director of Legal Affairs, Administrative Office of the Courts, Maryland Judicial Center, Annapolis, Maryland;

Robert D. Evans, Director, Governmental Affairs Office, American Bar Association, Washington, D.C.;

Eileen Gallagher, Staff Director, ABA Standing Committee on Federal Judicial Improvements, American Bar Association, Chicago, Illinois;

Michael F. Garrahan, Trial Court Services, Special Programs Unit, Administrative Office of the Courts, State of New Jersey, Trenton, New Jersey;

Honorable Janice Gradwohl, Former Presiding Judge, County Court, Third Judicial District of Nebraska, and Adjunct Professor of Law, University of Nebraska College of Law, Lincoln, Nebraska;

Honorable Gary Lumpkin, Presiding Judge, Oklahoma Court of Criminal Appeals, Oklahoma City, Oklahoma;

Jack B. Middleton, Past Secretary, American Bar Association; Member, House of Delegates, American Bar Association; and President, McLane, Graf, Raulerson & Middleton PA, Attorneys-at-Law, Manchester, New Hampshire;

Honorable Gayle A. Nachtigal, Circuit Court Judge, Washington County Circuit Court, Hillsboro, Oregon;

Paula Nessel, Staff Director, Coalition for Justice, American Bar Association, Chicago, Illinois;

Honorable James A. Noe, Past Chair, American Bar Association National Conference of State Trial Judges; Past Chair, American Bar Association Judicial Division; Past Judiciary Member, ABA Board of Governors; and Judge (Ret.), King County Superior Court, Seattle, Washington;

Robert O'Neil, Director, Thomas Jefferson Center, Charlottesville, Virginia;

David A. Sellers, Assistant Director for Public Affairs, Administrative Office of the United States Courts, Washington, D.C.;

Honorable Norma L. Shapiro, Chair, Coordinating Council of the Justice Center, American Bar Association, and Judge, U.S. District Court, Philadelphia, Pennsylvania;

Honorable James Scott Sledge, Chair, American Bar Association Judicial Division, and United States Bankruptcy Judge, Northern District of Alabama, Anniston, Alabama;

Honorable Daniel E. Wathen, Former Chief Justice, Maine Supreme Judicial Court, now Of Counsel

to Pierce Atwood, Attorneys-at-Law, Portland, Maine.

CHAPTER THREE: FAMILY LAW

Willard DaSilva, Member, Council of the Section of Family Law, American Bar Association, and Partner, DaSilva, Hilowitz & McEvily LLP, Attorneys-at-Law, Garden City, New York;

Howard Davidson, Director, Center on Children and the Law, American Bar Association, Washington, D.C.;

Linda Elrod, Past Chair, Family Law Section, American Bar Association, and Professor of Law, Washburn University School of Law, Topeka, Kansas;

Diane Geraghty, Professor of Law, Loyola University Chicago School of Law, Chicago, Illinois;

Honorable Debra Lehrmann, Judge, 360th District Court, Fort Worth, Texas;

Ira Harold Lurvey, Past Chair, American Bar Association Family Law Section, and Partner, Lurvey & Shapiro, Attorneys-at-Law, Los Angeles, California;

Laura W. Morgan, Vice-Chair, Conference of State and Local Bar Family Law Leaders, American Bar Association Family Law Section, and Owner, Family Law Consulting, Charlottesville, Virginia;

Ronald W. Nelson, Member, Council of the American Bar Association Family Law Section, and Partner, Nelson & Booth, Attorneys-at-Law, Overland Park, Kansas;

Arnold Rutkin, Attorney-at-Law, Westport, Connecticut;

Carolyn J. Stevens, Chair, Family Law Committee, American Bar Association General Practice Section, and Attorney-at-Law, Lolo, Montana.

CHAPTERS FOUR AND FIVE: BUYING AND SELLING A HOME AND HOME OWNERSHIP

Gurdon Buck, Former Member, Council of the Real Property, Probate and Trust Law Section, American Bar Association, and Counsel, Robinson and Cole, Attorneys-at-Law, Hartford, Connecticut;

Sally H. Foote, Partner, Thompson and Foote, P.A., Attorneys-at-Law, Clearwater, Florida;

Richard M. Frome, Vice-Chair, Committee on Assigning and Subleasing, American Bar Association Section of Real Property, Probate, and Trust Law, and Attorney-at-Law, New York, New York;

David Haron, Principal, Frank, Stefani, Haron & Weiner, Attorneys-at-Law, Troy, Michigan;

Jonathan Hoyt, Past Chair, Purchase and Sale of Residential Real Estate Committee, American Bar Association, and Attorney-at-Law, Clinton, Connecticut;

Jack S. Levey, Past Vice-Chair, Title Insurance Committee, American Bar Association; Member, Commercial Leasing Group, American Bar Association; and Attorney-at-Law, Columbus, Ohio;

Ronald J. Maas, General Counsel, Century/Intercounty Title Agency, Inc., Pine Brook, New Jersey;

Frank A. Melchior, Vice-President & Senior Underwriting Counsel, New Jersey Title Insurance Company, Parsippany, New Jersey;

Ellen G. Pollack, Council Member-at-Large, General Practice, Solo and Small Firm Section, American Bar Association, and Attorney, Fentin & Goldman LLP, White Plains, New York;

Julius Zschau, Partner, Pennington, Moore, Wilkinson, Bell & Dunbar, P.A., Attorneys-at-Law, Tampa, Florida.

CHAPTER SIX: RENTING RESIDENTIAL PROPERTY

Allison Gould, Vice-Chair, Committee on Affordable Housing, American Bar Association Section of Real Property, Probate, and Trust Law, and Attorney in Atlanta, Georgia;

Myron Moskovitz, Professor of Law, Golden Gate University School of Law, San Francisco, California;

Tracie R. Porter, Vice-Chair, Public Education Committee, American Bar Association Section of Real Property, Probate, and Trust Law, and Attorney, Brown Udell & Pomerantz, Attorneys-at-Law, Chicago, Illinois;

Frederic White, Jr., Professor of Law, Cleveland Marshall College of Law, Cleveland State University, Cleveland, Ohio.

CHAPTER SEVEN: CONSUMER CREDIT

James C. Conboy, President and Chief Operating Officer, Citizens National Bank, Cheboygan, Michigan;

John L. Culhane, Jr., Former Member, Consumer Financial Services Committee, American Bar Association Business Law Section, and Partner,

Ballard Spahr et al., Attorneys-at-Law, Philadelphia, Pennsylvania;

Marianne B. Culhane, Professor of Law, Creighton University School of Law, Omaha, Nebraska;

Michael M. Greenfield, Walter D. Coles Professor of Law, Washington University School of Law, St. Louis, Missouri;

Thomas B. Hudson, Member, Consumer Financial Services Committee, American Bar Association Business Law Section, and Member, Hudson Cook LLP, Attorneys-at-Law, Linchicum, Maryland;

Robert W. Johnson, Former Director, Credit Research Center, Krannert Graduate School of Management, Purdue University, and Member, Consumer Credit Intelligence LLC, Greenwich, Connecticut.

CHAPTER EIGHT: CONSUMER BANKRUPTCY

Sara A. Austin, Attorney, Blakey, Yost, Bupp & Rausch LLP, Attorneys-at-Law, York, Pennsylvania;

Honorable Bernice Donald, Judge, U.S. District Court, Memphis, Tennessee;

David A. Greer, Vice-Chair, Consumer Bankruptcy Committee, American Bar Association Business Law Section, and Principal, Hofeimer Nusbaum, P.C., Attorneys-at-Law, Norfolk, Virginia;

John P. Hennigan, Jr., Professor of Law, St. John's University School of Law, Jamaica, New York;

Shayna Michele Steinfeld, Co-Chair, Bankruptcy Committee, American Bar Association Family Law Section, and Partner, Steinfeld & Steinfeld, P.C., Attorneys-at-Law, Atlanta, Georgia.

CHAPTER NINE: CONTRACTS AND CONSUMER LAW

Michael M. Greenfield, Walter D. Coles Professor of Law, Washington University School of Law, St. Louis, Missouri;

Robert M. Langer, Chair, Consumer Protection Committee, American Bar Association Antitrust Section, and Attorney, Wiggin & Dana LLP, Attorneys-at-Law, Hartford, Connecticut;

Frederick H. Miller, Professor of Law, University of Oklahoma Law Center, Norman, Oklahoma.

CHAPTER TEN: COMPUTER LAW

Jeffrey Allen, Vice-Chair, Committee on Communications and Technology, American Bar Association Senior Lawyers Division, and Partner, Graves & Allen, Attorneys-at-Law, Oakland, California;

Elizabeth W. Benet, Chair, Emerging Issues Committee, American Bar Association Tort and Insurance Practice Section, and Second Vice-President and New Product Development Specialist, GeneralCologne Re, Stamford, Connecticut;

Katherine Catlos, Partner, Lewis Brisbois Bisgaard & Smith, Attorneys-at-Law, San Francisco, California;

Debbie Chong, CEO, Virtual Boardwalk/Lenos, San Francisco, California;

William Sloan Coats, Division Chair, Computer Law Division, American Bar Association Section of Science and Technology Law, and Partner, Orrick Herrington & Sutcliffe, Attorneys-at-Law, Menlo Park, California;

Daniel A. Cotter, Member, E-Commerce Committee, American Bar Association Section of Tort and Insurance Practice, and Counsel, Unitrin, Inc., Chicago, Illinois;

Richard Field, Secretary, American Bar Association Section of Science and Technology Law, and Attorney-at-Law, Cliffside Park, New Jersey;

Ivan K. Fong, Vice-Chair, American Bar Association Section of Science and Technology Law, and Senior Counsel, E-Commerce & Information Technology, General Electric Company, Fairfield, Connecticut;

Rolland E. Grefe, Liaison from American Bar Association Senior Lawyers Section to the Standing Committee on Technology and Information Systems and Co-Founder, Grefe & Sidney PLC, Attorneys-at-Law, Des Moines, Iowa;

Shannon B. Hartsfield, Vice-Chair, Committee on eHealth and Privacy, American Bar Association Health Law Section, and Partner, Holland & Knight LLP, Attorneys-at-Law, Tallahassee, Florida;

Lester L. Hewitt, Partner, Akin Gump Strauss et al., Attorneys-at-Law, Houston, Texas;

Jonathan S. Jennings, Chair, Federal Trademark Legislation Committee, American Bar Association Section of Intellectual Property Law, and Attorney, Pattishall McAuliffe et al., Attorneys-at-Law, Chicago, Illinois;

Armando Lasa-Ferrer, Member, American Bar Association Board of Governors and Partner, Lasa Monroig & Veve, Attorneys-at-Law, Guaynabo, Puerto Rico;

William Joseph Luddy, Jr., Vice-Chair, Computer Law Division, American Bar Association Section of Science and Technology Law, and Clinical Professor, Lally School of Management & Technology, Rensselaer Polytechnic Institute, Hartford, Connecticut;

David W. Maher, Chair, Committee on Internet Governance, American Bar Association Section of Science and Technology Law, and Partner, Sonnenschein Nath & Rosenthal, Attorneys-at-Law, Chicago, Illinois;

Joseph I. Rosenbaum, Partner, Reed Smith LLP, Attorneys-at-Law, New York, New York;

Randy V. Sabett, Vice-Chair, Committee on Information Security, American Bar Association Section of Science and Technology Law, and Attorney, Cooley Godward LLP, Attorneys-at-Law, Reston, Virginia;

Ruven Schwartz, Vice-Chair, Electronic Commerce Division, American Bar Association Section of Science and Technology Law, and Business Systems Consultant, Wells Fargo Cryptography Services, Minneapolis, Minnesota;

Thomas J. Smedinghoff, Past Chair, American Bar Association Section of Science and Technology Law, and Partner, Baker & McKenzie, Attorneys-at-Law, Chicago, Illinois;

Sandra P. Thompson, Chair, Special Committee on Patents and the Internet, American Bar Association Section of Intellectual Property Law, and Attorney, Rutan & Tucker LLP, Attorneys-at-Law, Costa Mesa, California;

Jonathan B. Wilson, Chair, Internet Industry Committee, American Bar Association Section of Public Utility Law, and Assistant General Counsel, Interland, Inc., Atlanta, Georgia;

Stephen S. Wu, Co-Chair, Committee on Information Security, American Bar Association Section of Science and Technology Law, and President and CEO, InfoSec Law Group, PC, Los Altos, California.

CHAPTER 11: AUTOMOBILES

James J. Ahern, Partner, Ahern, Maloney & Moran LLC, Attorneys-at-Law, Chicago, Illinois.

CHAPTER 12: LAW AND THE WORKPLACE

Tom Allison, Partner, Allison, Slutsky & Kennedy, P.C., Attorneys-at-Law, Chicago, Illinois;

Alan Blanco, Attorney, Rothman Gordon, P.C., Attorneys-at-Law, Pittsburgh, Pennsylvania;

Donald W. Cohen, Arbitrator and Mediator, Glenview, Illinois;

Jay Grenig, Professor of Law, Marquette University Law School, Milwaukee, Wisconsin;

Peggy Hillman, Attorney, Macey Macey & Swanson, Attorneys-at-Law, Indianapolis, Indiana;

Kenneth D. Kleinman, Co-Chair (Management), Occupational Safety and Health Law Committee, American Bar Association Section of Employment and Labor Law, and Shareholder, Stevens & Lee, Attorneys-at-Law, Wayne, Pennsylvania;

Louis B. Kushner, Co-Chair (Union), Employment Rights and Responsibilities Committee, American Bar Association Section of Labor and Employment Law, and Attorney, Rothman Gordon, P.C., Attorneys-at-Law, Pittsburgh, Pennsylvania;

Adrienne Mazura, Partner, Piper, Marbury, Rudnick, et al., Attorneys-at-Law, Chicago, Illinois;

Susan Potter Norton, Co-Chair, Employment and Labor Relations Committee, American Bar Association Section of Litigation, and Partner, Allen Norton & Blue, P. A., Attorneys-at-Law, Coral Gables, Florida;

Steven F. Pockrass, Attorney, Ice Miller, Attorneys-at-Law, Indianapolis, Indiana;

Theodore St. Antoine, Degan Professor of Law, University of Michigan Law School, Ann Arbor, Michigan;

Darlene A. Vorachek, Co-Chair (Plaintiff), Employment Rights and Responsibilities Committee, American Bar Association Section of Labor and Employment Law, and Partner, Abrahamson Vorachek & Mikva, Attorneys-at-Law, Chicago, Illinois;

Paul Wyler, California Unemployment Insurance Appeals Board, Los Angeles, California.

CHAPTER 13: FORMING AND OPERATING A SMALL BUSINESS

Jay Grenig, Professor of Law, Marquette University Law School, Milwaukee, Wisconsin;

David Haron, Principal, Frank, Stefani, Haron & Weiner, Attorneys-at-Law, Troy, Michigan;

John P. Hennigan, Jr., Professor of Law, St. John's University School of Law, Jamaica, New York;

Jonathan Hoyt, Member, American Bar Association Business Law Section, and Attorney-at-Law, Clinton, Connecticut;

Cindy Moy, Attorney-at-Law, Golden Valley, Minnesota;

Gerald Niesar, Partner, Niesar & Diamond LLP, Attorneys-at-Law, San Francisco, California;

Tom Pitegoff, Attorney, Pitegoff Law Offices, White Plains, New York;

G. Lane Ware, Co-Chair, Pro-Bono Committee, Section of Business Law, American Bar Association, and Shareholder, Ruder, Ware & Michler LLSC, Attorneys-at-Law, Wausau, Wisconsin.

CHAPTER 14: PERSONAL INJURY

William Ryan Acomb, Vice-Chair, Self Insurers and Risk Managers Committee, and Immediate Past Chair and Current Website Coordinator, Automobile Law Committee, American Bar Association Section of Tort and Insurance Practice, and Member, Porteous Hainkel et al. LLP, Attorneys-at-Law, New Orleans, Louisiana;

Stanley Jerome Cohn, Attorney, Lugenbuhl Wheaton Peck et al., Attorneys-at-Law, New Orleans, Louisiana;

Peter Kochanski, Attorney-at-Law, Baltimore, Maryland;

William R. Levasseur, Attorney-at-Law, Baltimore, Maryland;

Stephen I. Richman, Partner, Richman & Smith LLP, Attorneys-at-Law, Washington, Pennsylvania;

Mark L. Sklan, Attorney, Law Office of Linda Libertucci, Orange, California;

Michelle Tilton, Revenue Officer, Tort and Insurance Practice Section, American Bar Association; Former Director and Special Projects Chair, Young Lawyers Division, American Bar Association; and Executive Vice-President, First Media Insurance Specialists, Inc., Kansas City, Missouri.

CHAPTER 15: CRIMINAL JUSTICE

Mary Lou Boland, Chair, Victims Committee, American Bar Association Criminal Justice Section, and Attorney, Cook County State's Attorney's Office, Chicago, Illinois;

Stephen J. Bronis, Co-Chair, Defense Function/Services Committee, American Bar Association Criminal Justice Section, and Partner, Zuckerman Spaeder LLP, Attorneys-at-Law, Miami, Florida;

Vincent A. Citro, Chair, Criminal and Juvenile Justice Committee, American Bar Association Young Lawyers Section, and Attorney, Lowndes Drosdick Doster et al., Attorneys-at-Law, Orlando, Florida;

Amie L. Clifford, Member, American Bar Association Standing Committee on Substance Abuse, and Assistant Director, National College of District Attorneys, University of South Carolina, Columbia, South Carolina;

Gerald T. Giaimo, Co-Coordinator, Special Projects, American Bar Association Young Lawyers Division, and Attorney, Tyler Cooper & Alcorn LLP, Attorneys-at-Law, New Haven, Connecticut;

Jolanta Juszkiewicz, Deputy Director, Pretrial Services Resource Center, Washington, D.C.;

Steven M. Kowal, Chair, Criminal Practice and Procedure Committee, American Bar Association Section of Antitrust Law, and Member, Bell, Boyd & Lloyd LLC, Attorneys-at-Law, Chicago, Illinois;

Laura Ariane Miller, Co-Chair, Criminal Litigation Committee, American Bar Association; Past Chair, Health Litigation Committee, American Bar Association; and Partner, Nixon Peabody LLP, Attorneys-at-Law, Washington, D.C.;

Wallace John Mlyniec, Associate Dean (Clinical Education and Public Service Programs), Lupo-Ricci Professor of Clinical Legal Studies, and Director, Juvenile Justice Clinic, Georgetown University Law Center, Washington D.C.;

Barry Pollack, Chair, Subcommittee on Federal Rules and Jury Instructions, American Bar Association Section of Litigation Criminal Litigation Committee, and Partner, Nixon Peabody LLP, Attorneys-at-Law, Washington, D.C.;

Alan Raphael, Associate Professor of Law, Loyola University Chicago School of Law, Chicago, Illinois;

Kathy Swedlow, Assistant Professor of Law and Deputy Director, Cooley Innocence Project, Thomas M. Cooley Law School, Lansing, Michigan;

Pauline Weaver, Member, Board of Governors, American Bar Association; Member, General Practice, Solo and Small Firm Council, American Bar Association; and Public Defender, Alameda County, California.

CHAPTER 16, THE RIGHTS OF OLDER AMERICANS

The Center for Law and Aging of the American Bar Association is a nationally recognized source of information on law for older Americans. Its mission is to strengthen and secure the legal rights, dignity, autonomy, quality of life, and quality of care of elders. It carries out this mission through research, policy development, technical assistance, advocacy, education, and training.

Five lawyers on the staff of the Center reviewed this chapter. In addition to the team leader Charles P. Sabatino, Assistant Director of the Commission on Law and Aging and Adjunct Professor at Georgetown University Law Center, they were:

Stephanie Edelstein, Associate Staff Director, who specializes in housing, economic security, and legal services delivery issues;

Naomi Karp, Associate Staff Director, who specializes in grandparent visitation, kinship care, health care, nursing homes, and dispute resolution;

Lori Stiegel, Associate Staff Director, who specializes in elder abuse, alternatives to guardianship, consumer fraud, and legal services delivery; and

Erica Wood, Associate Staff Director, who specializes in issues concerning guardianship, long-term care, dispute resolution, court access, and legal services delivery.

CHAPTER 17: HEALTH-CARE LAW

Lawrence Gostin, Professor of Law, Georgetown University; Professor of Public Health, the Johns Hopkins University; and Director, Center for Law & the Public's Health, Washington, D.C.;

Ami S. Jaeger, Chair, Subcommittee on Genetic Research, Committee on Regulation of Research, American Bar Association; Co-Chair, Assisted Reproductive Technology and Genetics Committee, American Bar Association; and Principal, BioLaw Group LLC, Santa Fe, New Mexico;

Timothy Jost, Robert L. Willett Family Professor,

Washington and Lee University School of Law, Lexington, Virginia;

Joan Polacheck, Partner, McDermott, Will & Emery, Attorneys-at-Law, Chicago, Illinois;

Salvatore J. Russo, Past Chair, Health Law Section, New York State Bar Association, and Executive Senior Counsel, New York City Health & Hospitals Corporation, New York, New York;

Bethany J. Spielman, Member, Planning Board, *Health Lawyer*, American Bar Association, and Associate Professor, Department of Medical Humanities, SIU School of Medicine, Springfield, Illinois.

CHAPTER 18: ESTATE PLANNING

Lena Barnett, Attorney-at-Law, Silver Spring, Maryland;

Michael G. Cumming, Member, Dykema Gossett PLLC, Attorneys-at-Law, Bloomfield Hills, Michigan;

Edgar T. Farmer, Of Counsel, Husch & Eppenberger, Attorneys-at-Law, St. Louis, Missouri;

Thomas M. Featherston, Council Member and Probate Editor of *Probate and Property Magazine*, American Bar Association Section of Real Property, Probate and Trust Law, and Mills Cox Professor of Law, Baylor Law School, Waco, Texas;

Susan N. Gary, Associate Articles Editor for Probate and Trust of *Probate and Property Magazine*, American Bar Association Section of Real Property, Probate and Trust Law, and Associate Professor of Law, School of Law, University of Oregon, Eugene, Oregon;

Rik Huhtanen, Attorney-at-Law, Eugene, Oregon;

John Laster, Co-Chair, Committee on Estate Planning for Individuals with Multi-State Property or Contacts, American Bar Association Section of Real Property, Probate and Trust Law, and Attorney-at-Law, Falls Church, Virginia;

Rebecca C. Morgan, Vice-Chair, Health Care Decisions Committee, American Bar Association Section of Real Property, Probate and Trust Law, and Boston Asset Management Distinguished Professor of Law and Director, Center for Excellence in Elder Law, Stetson University College of Law, Gulfport, Florida;

Harold Pskowski, Acquisitions Editor for Probate and Trust, Media/Book Products, American Bar Association Section of Real Property, Probate and Trust Law, and Attorney, BNA Tax Management, Washington, D.C.;

Douglas J. Rasmussen, Member, Clark Hill PLC, Attorneys-at-Law, Detroit, Michigan;

Pamela L. Rollins, Partner, Simpson Thacher & Bartlett, Attorneys-at-Law, New York, New York;

Charles P. Sabatino, Associate Director, American Bar Association Commission on Law and Aging, Washington, D.C.;

Michael D. Whitty, Co-Chair, Committee on Estate Planning and Administration for Business Owners, American Bar Association Section of Real Property, Probate and Trust Law, and Partner, Winston & Strawn, Attorneys-at-Law, Chicago, Illinois.